T0181809

Communications
in Computer and Information Science 628

Commenced Publication in 2007
Founding and Former Series Editors:
Alfredo Cuzzocrea, Dominik Ślęzak, and Xiaokang Yang

Editorial Board

More information about this series at http://www.springer.com/series/7899

Aynur Unal · Malaya Nayak
Durgesh Kumar Mishra · Dharm Singh
Amit Joshi (Eds.)

Smart Trends in Information Technology and Computer Communications

First International Conference, SmartCom 2016
Jaipur, India, August 6–7, 2016
Revised Selected Papers

 Springer

Editors
Aynur Unal
Stanford University
Stanford, CA
USA

Malaya Nayak
IT Buzz Limited
Dagenham
UK

Durgesh Kumar Mishra
Microsoft Innovation Centre
Sri Aurobindo Institute of Technology
Indore, Madhya Pradesh
India

Dharm Singh
Namibia University of Science
  and Technology
Windhoek
Namibia

Amit Joshi
Sabar Institute of Technology
Sabarkantha
India

ISSN 1865-0929   ISSN 1865-0937 (electronic)
Communications in Computer and Information Science
ISBN 978-981-10-3432-9   ISBN 978-981-10-3433-6 (eBook)
DOI 10.1007/978-981-10-3433-6

Library of Congress Control Number: 2016960315

Printed on acid-free paper

This Springer imprint is published by Springer Nature
The registered company is Springer Nature Singapore Pte Ltd.
The registered company address is: 152 Beach Road, #22-06/08 Gateway East, Singapore 189721, Singapore

Preface

The First International Conference on Smart Trends for Information Technology and Computer Communications (SmartCom 2016) targeted state-of-the-art as well as emerging topics pertaining to information, computer communications and effective strategies for their implementation in engineering and managerial applications.

The conference attracted a large number of high-quality submissions and stimulated cutting-edge research discussions among many academic pioneering researchers, scientists, industrial engineers, and students from all around the world. It provided a forum where researchers could propose new technologies, share their experiences, and discuss future solutions in design infrastructure for ICT. The common platform offered the opportunity for the attendees to present their innovative and constructive ideas and focus on issues at international.

The conference was held during August 6–7, 2016, at Hotel Four Points by Shareton, Jaipur, India, and organized by the Computer Society of India, Udaipur Chapter, and the Association of Computer Machinery, Udaipur Professional Chapter, in association with the Rajasthan Chamber of Commerce and Industry (RCCI) and the Global Research Foundation. The event was technically supported by the Regional Institute of Engineering and Technology, Jaipur, and Manipal University, Jaipur.

In all, 519 research submissions – by authors from eight countries (Algeria, Australia, Canada, France, India, Iran, Sri Lanka, and Turkey) in various advanced technology areas were received, and after a rigorous peer-review process with the help of Program Committee members and 56 external reviewers, 108 papers were accepted with an acceptance ratio of 0.19. The event also featured the keynote speakers Dr. Aynur Unal, Stanford University, USA, and Dr. Ajay Data, Founder and CEO, Data Infosys Limited.

To make this event possible, we received a lot support and help from many people and organizations. We would like to express our sincere thanks to the authors for their remarkable contributions, all the Technical Program Committee members for their time and expertise in reviewing the papers within a very tight schedule, and the publisher Springer for their professional help. This is the first conference of the SmartCom series for which proceedings are published as a CCIS volume by Springer. We greatly appreciate our two distinguished scholars for accepting our invitation to deliver keynote speeches to the conference and the 11 technical session chairs for analyzing the work presented by the researchers. Last but not least, we are grateful for the local support from the local chairs and their hard work for the conference. This conference will be hosted at different location every year.

November 2016

Aynur Unal
Malaya Nayak
Durgesh Kumar Mishra
Dharm Singh
Amit Joshi

Organization

SMARTCOM 2016 was organized and hosted by the Computer Society of India, Udaipur Chapter, and the Association of Computing Machinery, Udaipur Professional Chapter in Jaipur, India.

General Chairs

Dharm Singh   Namibia University of Science and Technology, Namibia

Amit Kaul   UK

Program Chairs

Malaya Kumar Nayak   IT and Research Group, London, UK

Kalpdrum Passi   Chair, Dept of Computer Science, Laurentian University, Canada

Program Secretary

Mihir Chauhan   Member ACM

Technical Program Committee

Rashid Ansari	University of Illunios, USA
Harshal Arolkar	CSI Ahmedabad Chapter, India
Subhadip Basu	The University of Iowa, USA
Shalini Batra	Thapar University, Patiala, Punjab, India
R.K. Bayal	Rajasthan Technical University, Kota, India
Russell Beale	University of Birmingham, UK
Shajulin Benedict	St. Xaviers Catholic College of Engineering Chunkankadai, Tamil Nadu, India
Kristin P. Bennett	Rensselaer Polytechnic Institute, USA
Abhir Bhalerao	University of Warwick, UK
Rajendra Kumar Bharti	Kumaon Engg College, Dwarahat, Uttarakhand, India
Murali Bhaskaran	Dhirajlal Gandhi College of Technology, Salem, Tamil Nadu, India
Komal Bhatia	YMCA University, Faridabad, Haryana, India
Chintan Bhatt	Changa University, Gujarat, India
Norman L. Biggs	London School of Economics, UK
Liu Bing	University of Illinois, Chicago, USA
S.R. Biradar	SDM College of Engineering and Technology, Dharwad, Karnataka, India
Qin Bo	Universitat Rovira i Virgili, Tarragona, Spain

Dan Boneh	Stanford University, USA
Marcos Roberto da Silva Borges	Federal University of Rio de Janeiro, Brazil
Fatima Boumahdi	Ouled Yaich Blida, Algeria
Nikolaos G. Bourbakis	Dayton, Ohio, USA
Narimene Boustia	Boufarik Algeria
Mokrane Bouzghoub	Laboratoire PRiSM, Versailles, France
Alan Conrad Bovik	University of Texas at Austin, USA
Janez Brank	Institut Jožef Stefan, Slovenia
Torsten Braun	IAM, Bern, Switzerland
Jean Michel Bruel	IUT de Blagnac, France
Lionel Brunie	Institut National des Sciences Appliquées de Lyon, France
Dongbo Bu	Institute of Computing Technology, Chinese Academy of Science, Beijing, China
David Bull	London, UK
Alister Burr	University of York, York, UK
Luca Cagliero	University of Turin, Italy
Yves Caron	France
Berrut Catherine	LIG laboratory of Grenoble, Grenoble University, France
K.P. Chan	University of Hong Kong, SAR China
Zhou Chao	The Civil Aviation Flight University of China, Chengdu, China
Somayeh Mamizadeh Chatghayeh	Foundation Cooperation Tehran, Iran
Sandeep Chatterjee	Source Trace Systems, California, USA
A.K. Chaturvedi	IIT Kanpur, India
Ricardo M. Checchi	University of Massachusetts, USA
Cailian Chen	Shanghai Jiao Tong University, Shanghai, China
Yawen Chen	University of Otago, Dunedin, New Zealand
Yixing Chen	Shanghai Jiao Tong University, Shanghai, China
Zhidao Chen	Chuangyuan M&E Co. Ltd, Changchun, China
Janson Cheng	University of Birmingham, UK
Yang Chenghai	Weslaco, Texas, USA
Ngai-Man Cheung	University of Technology and Design, Singapore
Jitender Kumar Chhabra	NIT, Kurukshetra, Haryana, India
Ajay Choudhary	IIT Roorkee, India
Pradeep Chouksey	TIT College, Bhopal, MP, India
Alexander Christea	University of Warwick, London, UK
C.J. Chung	Lawrence Technological University, USA
Chin-Wan Chung	Korea
J. Andrew Clark	Computer Science University of York, UK
Jonathan Clark	STRIDe Laboratory Mechanical Engineering, Tallahassee, USA
Thomas Cormen	Dartmouth College, Hanover, Germany

Dennis D. Cox	Rice University, Texas, USA
Chhaya Dalela	JSSATE, Noida, Uttar Pradesh, India
Jayanti Dansana	KIIT University, Bhubaneswar, Odisha, India
Soura Dasgupta	SRM University, Chennai, India
	Iowa City, USA
Gholamhossein Dastghaibyfard	Shiraz University, Shiraz, Iran
David Delahaye	Saint-Martin, France
Andrew G. Dempster	The University of New South Wales, Australia
Alan Dennis	Kelley School of Business, Indiana University, USA
Jitender Singh Deogun	University of Nebraska - Lincoln, USA
Bharat Singh Deora	JRNRV University, India
Apurva A. Desai	Veer Narmad South Gujarat University, Surat, India
V. Susheela Devi	Indian Institute of Science, Bangalore, India
Bikash Kumar Dey	IIT Bombay, Powai, Maharashtra, India
Vijay Pal Dhaka	Jaipur National University, Jaipur, Rajasthan, India
K. Bhattachary Dhruba	Tezpur University, Assam, India
S.A.D. Dias	University of Moratuwa, Sri Lanka
David Diez	Leganés, Spain
Zhang Dinghai	Gansu Agricultural University, Lanzhou, China
Ali Djebbari	Sidi Bel Abbes, Algeria
Mohammad Doja	Jamia Millia Islamia, New Delhi, India
P.D.D. Dominic	Universiti Teknologi Petronas, Malaysia
Nitika Vats Doohan	Indore, India
David Douglas	Walton College of Business, University of Arkansas, USA
Kholaddi Kheir Eddine	University of Constantine, Algeria
Martin Everett	University of Manchester, UK
Sagayaraj Francis	Pondicherry Engineering College, Puducherry, India
Savita Gandhi	Gujarat University, Ahmedabad, India
K. Ganesh	Mckinsey Knowledge Center India Private Limited
	Mckinsey & Company, Gurgaon, Haryana, India
Shuhong Gao	Clemson University, USA
Sanjam Garg	University of California, Los Angeles, USA
Faiez Gargouri	Sfax University Tunisia, Tunisia
A. Garrett	Jacksonville State University, USA
Leszek Antoni Gasieniec	University of Liverpool, UK
Ning Ge	Tsinghua University, Beijing, China
Garani Georgia	University of North London, UK
Hazhir Ghasemnezhad	Shiraz University of Technology, Iran
Andrea Goldsmith	Stanford University, USA
Saeed Golmohammadi	University of Tabriz, Iran
K. Gong	Chongqing Jiaotong University, China
Crina Gosnan	Babes-Bolyai University, Cluj-Napoca, Romania
Mohamed Gouda	The University of Texas, Austin, USA
Vinit Grewal	Guru Nanak Dev University, Jalandhar, India

N.M. van Straalen	VU University Amsterdam, The Netherlands
S.N. Tazi	Govt. Engineering College, Ajmer, Rajasthan, India
Chirag S. Thaker	GEC, Bhavnagar, Gujarat, India
Feng Tian	Virginia Polytechnic Institute and State University, USA
Haibo Tian	Guangzhou University, Guangdong, China
XiuYing Tian	Yangtze Delta Region Institute of Tsinghua University, Jiaxing, China
Meenakshi Tripathi	MNIT, Jaipur, India
Aynur Unal	Standford University, USA
Bartel Van de Walle	University Tilburg, The Netherlands
Brent Waters	University of Texas, Austin, USA
Philip Yang	Pricewaterhouse Coopers, Beijing, China
Xiaoyi Yu	Institute of Automation, Chinese Academy of Sciences, Beijing, China
Gengshen Zhong	Jinan, Shandong, China

Reviewers

Rashid Ansari	University of Illunios, USA
Harshal Arolkar	Immd. Past Chairman, CSI Ahmedabad Chapter, India
Subhadip Basu	The University of Iowa, Iowa City, USA
Shalini Batra	Thapar University, Patiala, Punjab, India
R.K. Bayal	Rajasthan Technical University, Kota, Rajasthan, India
Russell Beale	University of Birmingham, UK
Shajulin Benedict	HPCCLoud Research Laboratory, St. Xaviers Catholic College of Engineering Chunkankadai, Tamil Nadu, India
Rajendra Kumar Bharti	Kumaon Engg College, Dwarahat, Uttarakhand, India
Murali Bhaskaran	Dhirajlal Gandhi College of Technology, Salem, Tamil Nadu, India
Komal Bhatia	YMCA University, Faridabad, Haryana, India
Chintan Bhatt	Changa University, Gujarat, India
S.R. Biradar	SDM College of Engineering and Technology, Karnataka, India
Dan Boneh	Stanford University, California, USA
Jean Michel Bruel	IUT de Blagnac, France
A.K. Chaturvedi	IIT Kanpur, India
Mihir Chauhan	Member ACM
Ricardo M. Checchi	University of Massachusetts, USA
Ngai-Man Cheung	University of Technology and Design, Singapore
Jitender Kumar Chhabra	NIT, Kurukshetra, Haryana, India
Ajay Choudhary	IIT Roorkee, India
Pradeep Chouksey	TIT College, Bhopal, MP, India
Alexander Christea	University of Warwick, London UK
J. Andrew Clark	University of York, UK

Chhaya Dalela	JSSATE, Noida, Uttar Pradesh, India
Jayanti Dansana	KIIT University, Bhubaneswar, Odisha, India
Soura Dasgupta	Department of TCE, SRM University, Chennai, India
Bharat Singh Deora	JRNRV University, India
Apurva A. Desai	Veer Narmad South Gujarat University, Surat, India
V. Susheela Devi	Indian Institute of Science, Bangalore, India
Bikash Kumar Dey	IIT Bombay, Powai, Maharashtra, India
Vijay Pal Dhaka	Jaipur National University, Jaipur, Rajasthan, India
K. Bhattachary Dhruba	Tezpur University, Assam, India
Mohammad Doja	Jamia Millia Islamia, New Delhi, India
Nitika Vats Doohan	Indore, India
Sagayaraj Francis	Pondicherry Engineering College, Puducherry, India
Savita Gandhi	Gujarat University, Ahmedabad, India
K. Ganesh	Mckinsey Knowledge Center India Private Limited Mckinsey & Company, Haryana, India
Vinit Grewal	Guru Nanak Dev University, Jalandhar, India
P.S. Grover	University of Delhi, India
Babita Gupta	College of Business California State University, USA
S. Hemalatha	CSE PSNA College of Engineering and Technology, Dindigul, India
Anitha Hemanth	Tamil Nadu, India
Hazra Imran	Jamia Hamdard, New Delhi, India
Anil K. Jain	Michigan State University, East Lansing, USA
S. Janakiraman	Pondicherry University, Puducherry, India
Bhavesh Joshi	Advent College, Udaipur, India
Shashidhar Ram Joshi	Institute of Engineering, Pulchowk, Nepal
A.P. Kabilan	Vivekanadha College of Engineering and Technology, Tiruchengode, India
Amit Kaul	UK
V. Kavitha	Anna University, Chennai, India
Ahmad Al-Khasawneh	The Hashemite University, Jordan
Yun-Bae Kim	SungKyunKwan University, South Korea
Paras Kothari	Samarth Group of Institutions, Gujarat, India
Rama Krishna	National Institute of Technical Teachers Training and Research, Chandigarh, India
R. Krishnamoorthy	Anna University, Chennai, BIT Campus, Trichy, India
Ernest Chulantha Kulasekere	University of Moratuwa, Sri Lanka
Amioy Kumar	IIT Delhi, India
Jagadeesh Kumar	Sri Krishna College of Technology, Coimbatore, India
Manish Kumar	IIIT, Jhalwa, Allahabad, India
S. Britto Ramesh Kumar	St. Joseph College, Trichirappalli, India
Sushil Kumar	Jawaharlal Nehru University, New Delhi, India
T. Arun Kumar	Vellore, Tamil Nadu, India
Jeril Kuriakose	Manipal University, Jaipur, India
Zhiling Lan	Illinois Institute of Technology, Chicago, USA

K.G. Langendoen	Delft University of Technology, The Netherlands
Michele Lanza	REVEAL Research Group, University of Lugano, Switzerland
Ting-Peng Liang	National Chengchi University Taipei, Taiwan
S. Maheswaran	Kongu Engineering College, India
Manju Mandot	CSI Udaipur Chapter, India
S. Mishra	M-SIG-WNs, CSI, KEC Dwarahat, Uttarakhand, India
Malaya Kumar Nayak	IT and Research Group, London, UK
D.A. Parikh	Head, CE, LDCE, Ahmedabad, India
Kalpdrum Passi	Laurentian University, Canada
Nisarg Pathak	SSC, CSI, Gujarat, India
Hoang Pham	Rutgers University, Piscataway, USA
Abrar A. Qureshi	University of Virginia, USA
Abdul Rajak A.R.	Birla Institute of Technology and Sciences, Abu Dhabi
Mustafizur Rahman	Endeavour Research Fellow, Australia
Louis M. Rose	University of New York, USA
K.C. Roy	Kautaliya, Jaipur, India
Sanjay M. Shah	GEC, Gandhinagar, India
Mukesh Shrimali	Pacific University, Udaipur, India
Dharm Singh	Namibia University of Science and Technology, Namibia
Prasun Sinha	Ohio State University Columbus, USA
Nedia Smairi	CNAM Laboratory, France
Hayden Kwok-Hay So	University of Hong Kong, Hong Kong, SAR China
N.M. van Straalen	VU University Amsterdam, Amsterdam, The Netherlands
S.N. Tazi	Govt. Engineering College, Ajmer, Rajasthan, India
Chirag S. Thaker	GEC, Bhavnagar, Gujarat, India
Meenakshi Tripathi	MNIT, Jaipur, India
Aynur Unal	Standford University, USA
Brent Waters	University of Texas, Austin, USA
Gengshen Zhong	Jinan, Shandong, China

Contents

Compartmentalization of New Released and Old Wheat Cultivars (*Triticum Durum* & *Triticum Aestivum*) of Gujarat Region of India by Employing Computer Vision

Mayur P. Raj[1,3(✉)], P.R. Swaminarayan[2,3], and Jatinderkumar Saini[4]

[1] College of Agricultural Information Technology,
Anand Agricultural University, Anand, Gujarat, India
rajmayur2005@gmail.com
[2] Parul Institute of Computer Application, Parul University, Baroda, Gujarat, India
swaminarayan.priya@yahoo.com
[3] Rai University, Ahmedabad, India
swaminarayan.priya@yahoo.com
[4] Narmada College of Computer Application, Bharuch, Gujarat, India
saini_expert@yahoo.com

Abstract. Machine learning methods majorly comprise of image processing and soft computing methods and are mainly responsible for automation. Wheat production is influenced by assorted varying factors. Sorting or grading of agricultural products influenced by computer varies product wise and even product variety wise which itself changes region wise. Grading for new varieties released by the agricultural scientists is the major concern as new varieties are produced by crossing existing varieties. For these varieties, proven optimized machine learning algorithms may give an adverse result. This paper introduces machine learning algorithm capable of classifying major 5 wheat cultivars cultivated in Gujarat region of India. Experimental data consist of 11 traits comprising of shape, color and morphological characteristics. After applying feature selection algorithm, 5 traits were considered and Levenberg-Marquardt back propagation was employed to classify above wheat cultivars which ensued to more than 90% overall accuracy.

Keywords: Artificial neural network (ANN) · Classification · Digital image analysis · Morphological feature · New released wheat cultivar

1 Introduction

The human body gets valuable nutrient from Wheat. India is the second largest producer of wheat and for the marketing year 2014–15 post forecasts for wheat production was 96 MMT [1]. Modern crop production insists quality of seed as one of the most important factors responsible for successful agricultural production. Seed quality is checked by healthiness, genetic & physical purity, and should also have a good physiological condition in accordance with the standards. Grading is also beneficial for getting better returns. Multiple factors affect Wheat sales and its price. Some of them are variety,

© Springer Nature Singapore Pte Ltd. 2016
A. Unal et al. (Eds.): SmartCom 2016, CCIS 628, pp. 1–10, 2016.
DOI: 10.1007/978-981-10-3433-6_1

wholesomeness, appearance, color, a presence of foreign matter, an admixture of inferior variety, moisture, harmful contaminants, etc. In order to promote sale and command more price grading is necessary. Thus computer assisted speedy and precise wheat sorting is essential for better production as well as sale.

Since inception of computer, computer vision techniques, precisely image processing and machine learning algorithms have been investigated for identifying agricultural products especially cereal grains [2–5], bifurcation of standard wheat seed from impurities like weed and other foreign entities [6, 7], broken grains or damaged grains i.e. bad grains [8]; Traits of wheat varies variety wise as well as region wise, so several researchers have successfully classified Canadian wheat seeds [9], Iranian rain-fed wheat varieties [10], Indian wheat cultivars [11], four spring wheat varieties from Xinjiang [12]. Literature review reveals that as traits of wheat cultivars differ (region/ variety wise), optimized classification algorithms of existing wheat cultivars will not give same results.

Soft computing components like Artificial Neural network (ANN), Bayesian network, fuzzy logic etc. resemble biological process and have forced researchers to take its benefit in logical systems. ANN is known as one of the most effective paradigms for classification or pattern recognitions. ANN has high sensitivity towards features set. In ANN, algorithm and type of network play a major role in its performance.

In India, grading of foundation or certified seeds of wheat is done manually by seed inspector according to standards published on seednet.gov.in. Precise grading requires a person to be fit mentally, physically and knowledge wise also. Hence, the notion of the current research was to formulate an optimized machine learning algorithm for wheat cultivars of Gujarat region of India. For this, the first step of optimization was traits selection of wheat. Class rank based Information Gain method was used for bifurcating highly dominant traits from a set of morphological, shape and color features. For training ANN, Levenberg–Marquardt algorithm was used. The proposed approach can be used to formulate an automated solution in order to ensure utilization & preservation of expert knowledge and eliminating a tedious and time-consuming process of grading wheat seeds.

2   Data Generation (Materials and Methods)

2.1   Grain Samples

Wheat grains of (*Triticum - Durum*) GDW 1255, (*Triticum - Aestivum*) GW 273, GW 322, GW 496 & LOK 1 cultivated in Gujarat region of India were collected. Wheat grains were first of all sorted precisely by an expert from samples bags. Broken, immature, and shrunken kernels were removed. Traits of these wheat cultivars are listed in below Table 1. It reveals, a proficient level of expertise is required in grading these wheat cultivars manually.

Table 1. Feature or traits of five wheat cultivar.

	Wheat Cultivars				
	GW 273	GW 322	GW 496	LOK 1	GDW 1522
Color	Amber	Amber	Amber	Amber	Amber
Texture	Hard	Semi Hard	Semi Hard	Hard	Hard
Shape	Ovate	Ovate	Ovate	Oblong	Elongated Oblong
Size	Bold	Bold	Bold	Bold	Short
Brush Hair Length	Prominent	Prominent	Prominent	Medium	Prominent

2.2 Image Acquisition

In order to design an optimize classification algorithm and trim pre-processing, necessary measures should be taken during image capturing. Hewlett–Packard Ink Advantage 3540 flatbed scanner was used to capture color images of cultivars at 24-bit depth and resolution of 300 dpi. To get high contrast, black cloth was applied on cover or flap of the scanner, this also resulted in an elimination of shadow effect of grains. To scale resolution of all images to the same level, a 5' × 5' square was created in the A4 page and grains were arranged in it. Grains were arranged uniformly to avoid connectedness or overlapping of grain's images, which reduce the processing time required to resolve it. Also, a set of 100 grains were arranged in equal rows and columns to avoid direction based image segmentation processing.

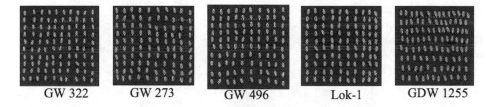

    GW 322   GW 273   GW 496   Lok-1   GDW 1255

Fig. 1. Scan image of 5 wheat cultivars

2.3 Image Pre-processing or Image Segmentation

Image pre-processing is a prelude to image analysis. For acute features extraction, images are refined in the pre-processing stage. Scanned images were pre-processed and analyzed using MATLAB script. During the pre-processing phase, to eliminate external

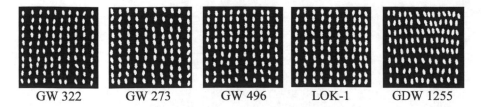

    GW 322   GW 273   GW 496   LOK-1   GDW 1255

Fig. 2. Effect of image segmentation

noise, initially, images were converted to gray-scale. The binary image was obtained from gray-scale based on the global threshold of an image. Global threshold lies between 0 and 1 which minimize the interclass variance of a different color (black and white) pixels. Next, all unwanted noisy spots or objects of up to 50-pixel area were eradicated. At end dilation or smoothing of edges was carried out.

2.4   Feature Extraction

After adequate segmentation, it becomes easy to extract features from an image. Extraction of classifying dominant features is of utmost importance in designing optimized machine learning algorithm. From traits extracted and from variety released note depicted in Table 1, it reveals that classification or machine learning algorithm needs to be a perfect combination of feature extraction, selection and ANN algorithms. It was discovered from past research [6, 7, 11, 13–15] that combination of features from different category can be very effective in the classification of wheat cultivars. A set of features from different categories viz. morphological, shape & color were extracted for each wheat grain.

Morphological Features. This feature type comprises of visual and shape features, here for this research we have considered following morphological features for training ANN and classification.

Area → Number of the pixel in the scanned image of individual wheat grain. It allows differentiating each cultivar on a size basis.

Major axis length and minor axis length will allow determining grain size in terms of maximum length and breadth in wheat grain image. Following figure shows how major and minor axis of individual wheat grain is calculated (Fig. 3).

Fig. 3. Major and minor axis

MajorAxisLength → The length of the longest diameter of the individual wheat grain (in pixels).

$$\text{Major axis} = a + b \tag{1}$$

MinorAxisLength → The length of the shortest diameter of the individual wheat grain (in pixels).

$$\text{Minor axis} = \sqrt{(a+b)^2 - f^2} \tag{2}$$

Perimeter → Number that specifies the boundary of the wheat grain.

Solidity → This trait specifies the ratio of the pixels in the convex hull/area (A smallest convex polygon that can contain wheat grain) that are also in the region.

$$\text{Solidity } = Area - Convex\ Area \tag{3}$$

Equivalent Diameter → To determine equivalent circular area.

$$\text{Equidial } = \sqrt{(4 \times Area) - \pi)} \tag{4}$$

Aspect ratio → Denotes ratio of longest diameter of the individual wheat grain to shortest diameter.

$$\text{Aspect ratio } = MajorAxisLength - MinorAxisLength \tag{5}$$

Shape Features. Data of axis and area was used to derive below shape factor details as follow:

$$\text{Shape factor 1 } = MajorAxisLength - Area \tag{6}$$

Color Features. Traits from Table 1 reveal that color of all selected wheat cultivars is Amber. RGB refers to a true color image and here in this case all wheat cultivars have same true color. The intensity of color will remain same for most of the pixels, so HSV color model was chosen. HSV color model describes a color as it is perceived by human eyes. HSV color model can also support visual texture feature extraction which focuses on local spatial changes of intensity in an image.

Morphological features viz. area, perimeter, major axis length, equidial, minor axis length, solidity and aspect ratio were extracted. Based on these features one shape factor was derived. For extracting hue, saturation and value color features, RGB image was converted to HSV.

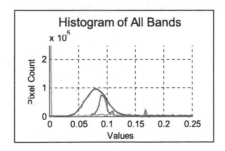

Fig. 4. Line graph depicting concentration of H, S & V values.

Figure 4 elucidate that from H, S & V, V (Value) is prominent classification factor for a certain range of values and the second factor which can be considered is H (Hue). S (Saturation) should be neglected.

For each H, S & V band minimum and maximum threshold were determined and applied on that band to derive binary images. Combined mask was applied to obtain an image to cross check correctness of mask of H, S and V layer. Then red parts of the image are masked off by masking all three mask images (H, S &V) leaving behind a yellow masked object. Wheat grain portion was identified from this combined mask image. At last mean value of H, S & V was derived from each wheat grain.

2.5 Feature Selection

During feature selection, distinguishing prominent traits are identified from the list of features extracted for optimized and precise machine learning classification algorithm of wheat cultivars. Feature reduction comprises of removal of redundant and noisy features which may ultimately compromise machine learning classification algorithm. Class ranked based Information gain feature selection algorithm was used for selecting best features from 11 extracted features.

Information gain algorithm assesses the importance of traits by evaluating the information gain with respect to the class. Here "H" is Entropy.

$$\text{InfoGain(Class, Attribute)} = H(\text{Class}) - H(\text{Class} \mid \text{Attribute}) \tag{7}$$

Information gain algorithm allows to binarize numeric attributes and missing values can be either distributed evenly with respect to frequency or can be treated as a separate value. It supports binary and nominal class. Attributes can be nominal, numeric, unary, date, and binary or even empty nominal attribute and missing value.

2.6 Artificial Neural Network

A neural network consists of 'n' processing elements or artificial neurons to which local memory is allocated and possess a small amount of information. It operates parallelly and creates a distributed processing structure interconnected via signal channels called synaptic(s) or connections [16].

A single hidden layer had limited power and so a multilayer Perceptron (MLP – one or more layers as Hidden, one layer each for input and output) learning algorithm was first invented by Werbos (published in his Ph. D thesis) in 1973, then later on it was reinvented independently by Le Cun 1985 and Parker 1985, most popularly known as Back Propagation Algorithm [17].

Merits of Levenberg–Marquardt algorithm are capability to solve the problem of minimizing a small and medium size nonlinear function, speedy and stable convergence compelled for training neural network. Thus, it was employed to train ANN.

Designed a neural network-based machine learning classification algorithm and it was stored for future application. After this, 40 grains of each cultivar were taken and same machine learning algorithm was simulated on it to test the efficiency of image segmentation, feature extraction and neural network algorithm.

3 Results

Fundamental digital image processing (DIP) steps for classification i.e. image acquisition, pre-processing, segmentation, feature extraction, feature selection and classification are widely accepted. These steps can be precisely defined for grading of grain seeds as show in Fig. 5.

Classification of five wheat cultivars of Gujarat region of India was carried in two stages. In the first stage, manual sorting of healthy seed from wrinkled or damaged seeds was carried out. During the second stage, 100 grains of each cultivar were scan using HP Ink Advantage 3540 scanner. This algorithm was executed on a computer with 2.3 GHz Intel i3 processor and 2 GB RAM.

There was no deformation and loss of information during detection or image segmentation, information such as germ shape, cheeks, crease etc. were clearly visible in the image (Figs. 1 and 2).

From this normalized images, 11 features: 7-morphological (area, perimeter, major axis length, minor axis length, solidity, equidial, aspect ratio), 1-shape (Major axis/Area) and 3-color (H, S & V) for each grain were extracted using MATLAB and stored in excel file. Feature reduction is necessary in order to remove redundant features which simply increases processing time and compromises algorithm's efficiency.

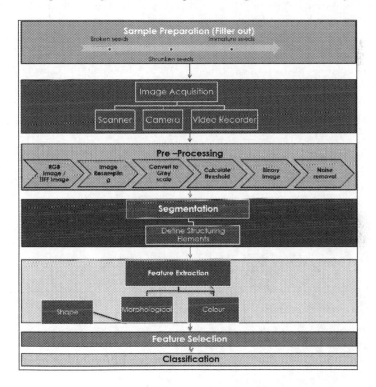

Fig. 5. DIP steps for grading seeds.

Ranker based Information Gain attribute evaluation algorithm was used for feature selection. Table 2 shows output ranks of prominent first 5 features. The notion was to considering at least 2 category features and then if required consider one more category, so features having rank greater than 0.89 were considered for machine learning algorithm. Thus first five features i.e. features having rank greater than 0.89 consists of 1-color and 4 morphological features (Table 2).

Levenberg-Marquardt back propagation artificial neural network was used for designing neural network classification machine learning algorithm. Training data, a set

Table 2. Rank of first five prominent features

Sr. #	Attribute Name	Rank
1	Area	2.0471
2	Equidial	2.0471
3	Solidity	1.5188
4	Major	1.1993
5	V	0.8912

of features of 500-wheat grains (100 grains × 5 wheat cultivars) was randomly bifurcated into three bins. First bin of 70% i.e. of 350-grain data (70 grains of each wheat cultivar) of 5 features was used for training neural network in a supervised manner. A second and third bin of 15% each i.e. of 75-grain data was used for validation and testing purpose.

Classification done using hidden layer size of 10 neurons was found optimal. Target data set was input from excel file. The performance of neural network was evaluated on the basis of mean squared error performance function. Confusion matrix (Fig. 6) generated at the end revealed the overall accuracy of 96.6%. Classification accuracy for GW 322 was 96% (total 98 grains were classified as GW 322 out of which 2 were GW 273 grains), GW 273 was 95% (total 103 grains were classified as GW 273 out of which 4 were of GW 322 and 4 of GW 496), GW 496 was 96% (total 99 grains were classified as GW 496 out of which 3 were of GW 273), LOK-1 was 98% (total 100 grains were classified as LOK-1 out of which 2 were of GDW 1255) and GDW 1255 was also 98% (total 100 grains were classified as GDW 1255 out of which 2 were of LOK-1). Receiver Operating Characteristic (ROC) in Fig. 7 depicts accuracy of NN.

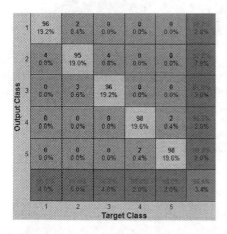 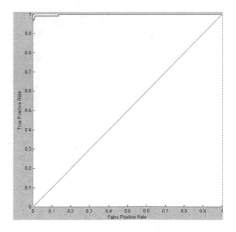

Fig. 6. Confusion matrix generated after training ANN   **Fig. 7.** ROC graph generated after training ANN

This machine learning algorithm was simulated on a data set of 40 grain of each cultivar. The overall accuracy obtained was 91% as per confusion matrix (Figs. 8 and 9).

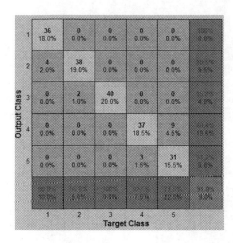
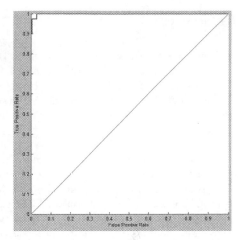

Fig. 8. Confusion Matrix of simulated ANN on 40 grains of each cultivar.

Fig. 9. ROC graph generated for simulation for 40 grains of each cultivar.

4 Discussion and Conclusion

In this study 11 features (1-shape, 3-color & 7-morphological) were extracted. After applying Rank based Information Gain attribute evaluation feature selection algorithm 5 traits (4-Morphological and 1 –color) were selected. Levenberg-Marquardt back propagation NN algorithm with 10 neurons was employed to classify wheat cultivars of Gujarat region of India which ensued to overall more than 90.0% accuracy.

Machine learning algorithm based on the combination of Digital Image Processing and Artificial Neural Network can be used for grading major 5 wheat cultivars (*Triticum Durum*: GDW 1255 (released in 2013 by ICAR) &*Triticum – Aestivum*: GW 273, GW 322, GW 496 & LOK 1) cultivated in Gujarat region of India.

The design of optimized Machine learning algorithm depends on a combination of set of algorithms pertaining to feature selection, ANN training algorithm and ANN architecture.

Grading for old and new released varieties (new varieties are produced by crossing existing varieties) is possible using existing machine learning algorithms but in some cases, it may require a sort of amendment.

A proper combination of a type of features (morphological, color, texture, shape etc.) can play an important role in the efficiency of machine learning algorithm. From a set of features extracted only, few will have a significant effect on classification algorithm. Thus, proper feature selection algorithm will eliminate redundant features and increase an efficiency of machine learning algorithm.

References

1. Singh, S.K.: GAIN Report No.: IN4005, USDA Foreign Agricultural Services, 14 Feb 2014. http://gain.fas.usda.gov/Recent%20GAIN%20Publications/Grain%20and%20Feed %20Annual_New%20Delhi_India_2-14-2014.pdf. Accessed 26 Sept 2015
2. Sapirstein, H., Neuman, M., Wright, E., Shwedyk, E., Bushuk, W.: An instrumental system for cereal grain classification using digital image analysis. J. Cereal Sci. **6**(1), 3–14 (1987). Elsevier
3. Sidnal, N., Patil, U.V., Patil, P.: Grading and quality testing of food grains using neural network. IJRET Int. J. Res. Eng. Technol. **2**(11), 545–549 (2013)
4. Visen, N., Paliwal, J., Jayas, D., White, N.: Image analysis of bulk grain samples using neural networks. Can. Biosyst. Eng. **46**(7), 11–15 (2004)
5. Ebrahimi, E., Mollazade, K., Babaei, S.: Toward an automatic wheat purity measuring device: A machine vision-based neural networks-assisted imperialist competitive algorithm approach. Measurement **55**, 196–205 (2014). Elsevier
6. Zayas, I., Pomeranz, Y., Lai, F.S.: Discrimination of wheat and nonwheat components in grain samples by image analysis. Cereal Chem. **66**(3), 233–237 (1989)
7. Han, X.-Z., Wang, K.-J., Yuan, Y., Chen, C., Liang, L.: Research on grading detection of the wheat seeds. Sci. World J. 2014, 6 Pages (2014)
8. Visen, N., Jayas, D., Paliwal, J., White, N.: Comparison of two neural network architectures for classification of singulated cereal grains. Can. Biosyst. Eng. **46**, 37–314 (2004)
9. Khoshroo, A., Arefi, A., Masoumiasl, A., Jowkar, G.-H.: Classification of wheat cultivars using image processing and artificial neural networks. Agric. Commun. **2**(1), 17–22 (2014)
10. Dubey, B., Bhagwat, S., Shouche, S., Sainis, J.: Potential of artificial neural networks in varietal identification using morphometry of wheat grains. Biosyst. Eng. **95**(1), 61–67 (2006). Science Direct
11. Bi, K., Jiang, P., Tang, C., Huang, F., Wang, C.: The design of wheat variety bp classifier based on wheat ear feature. Chin. Agric. Sci. Bull. **6**, 465–467 (2011)
12. Pazoki, A., Pazoki, Z.: Classification system for rain fed wheat grain cultivars using artificial neural network. Afr. J. Biotechnol. **10**(41), 8031–8038 (2011)
13. Pazoki, A., Pazoki, Z., Sorkhilalehloo, B.: Rain fed barley seed cultivars identification using neural network and different neurons number. World Appl. Sci. J. **22**(5), 755–762 (2013)
14. Shouche, S., Rastogi, R., Bhagwat, S., Sainis, J.K.: Shape analysis of grains of Indian wheat varieties. Comput. Electron. Agric. **33**, 55–76 (2001). Elsevier
15. Hecht-Nielsen, R.: Neurocomputing. Addison-Wesley, Boston (1990)
16. Nordbotten, S.: Data Mining with Neural Networks. Svein Nordbotten & Associates, Bergen (2006)

Real Time Sign Language Processing System

Dibyabiva Seth[(✉)], Anindita Ghosh, Ariruna Dasgupta,
and Asoke Nath

Department of Computer Science,
St. Xavier's College (Autonomous), Kolkata, India
meetdseth@gmail.com, anindita127@gmail.com,
dasguptaariruna@gmail.com, asokejoyl@gmail.com

Abstract. A communication gap has always existed between Sign Languages and other Natural Languages. This paper aims to build a real-time autonomous system that can help bridge this communication gap. The present system captures the gestures using a webcam and recognizes the gesture being shown, mapping it to the corresponding English Letter, Numeric Digit and Special Characters. The authors have proposed American Sign Language with some minor modifications. The present form of ASL can be used to recognize all alphabets (A–Z), all numerals (0–9), Backspace, Blank Space. Some Special Characters have been included as well. The present system is built to recognize the finger-spelling component of the American Sign Language (ASL), and can be extended to recognize other sign languages as well.

Keywords: Sign language · American sign language · Finger spelling · Perceptrons

1 Introduction

Sign language is used across the world to help bridge the communication gap for the hearing or speech impaired. The American Sign Language (ASL) is a fully developed natural language and is one of the world's many sign languages. It is neither a simplified language, nor a derivative of the English Language [1]. The largest influence on the development of sign language in America was Thomas Hopkins Gallaudet, a congregational minister. Together with Laurent Clerc, a graduate of the school for the deaf in Paris, Gallaudet transformed the old French Sign language into a sign language that American students would understand better. This system of sign language had a system of grammar and signs to represent every word and is known as the Old Signed English. Later they modified it to a language which was free of all grammar and shortened the sentences down to key phrases. This language later became known as the ASL. The fingerspelling component of ASL [2] has been shown in Fig. 1.

The aim of this paper is to design a practically useful real time processing system for the ASL based on the following broad objectives. The system should:

- be able to recognize the finger spelling gestures of the ASL,
- be able to show the corresponding numerical digits or letters of the English alphabet and some Special characters on the output device,

© Springer Nature Singapore Pte Ltd. 2016
A. Unal et al. (Eds.): SmartCom 2016, CCIS 628, pp. 11–18, 2016.
DOI: 10.1007/978-981-10-3433-6_2

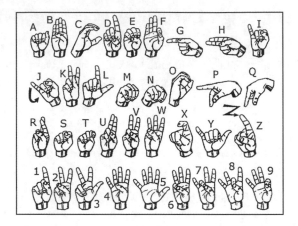

Fig. 1. The ASL fingerspelling gestures

- be able to show the corresponding sign language from a text file,
- be simple and easy to use,
- make use of already existing hardware components which are readily available,
- not use expensive hardware components,
- run on existing software environments.

1.1   Literature Review

Nachamai [3] has used the SIFT algorithm to recognize the English alphabets. Nachamai's method is space, size, illumination and rotation invariant. Pugeault and Bowden [4], on the other hand, have made use of a Microsoft Kinect device along with OpenNI+NITE framework for the acquisition, detection and tracking of the hand movements.

Vogler and Metaxas [5] have designed a framework to recognize isolated and continuous ASL sentences from three dimensional data. They have used Hidden Markov Models (HMMs) to recognize the hand movements. They have tested the framework on a vocabulary consisting of 53 signs.

In this paper, perceptrons have been used to identify the gestures of the ASL. A perceptron is a machine learning algorithm used primarily as a binary classifier. The system has been implemented to identify the 26 gestures of the letters and 9 gestures of the numeric digits of the English alphabet, along with the gestures for space and backspace. Perceptrons converge very fast, making them preferable for use in real-time.

The authors of [6] have implemented a Hand Gesture Recognition Library in MATLAB. They have used red LEDS mounted on a glove to track the hand movements. In this project, the red LEDs have been mounted near the webcam to better illuminate the hand, freeing the hand from the glove.

2   The Real Time Sign Language Processing System

The problem can be mainly divided into three modules, as follows:

- **Image Processing Module** – This module deals with the extraction of the hand gesture of the sign (foreground object) from the rest of the image (background). The extracted image is then scaled appropriately to predefined dimensions and sent to the Gesture Recognition Module.
- **Training Module** – This module forms the core of the Gesture Recognition Module. The purpose of this module is to train the program with a set of images of all the hand gestures used in a specific sign language. It needs to be executed only when one or more gestures need to be changed.
- **Gesture Recognition Module** – This module deals with the recognition of the hand gesture extracted by the Image Processing Module. It is pre-trained by the Training Module. If a sign is identified, it is mapped to the corresponding letter and displayed.
- **Gesture Mapping Module** – This module deals with conversion of a string of characters taken from a file or given by the user to sign language and speech.

Two sets of data need to be maintained.

- **Image Dataset** – This is the set of all the pre-clicked images of the gestures of a sign language. The original ASL signs [7] have been shown in Fig. 1, whereas the modified finger-spelling signs have been shown in Fig. 2. These images are used by the Training Module. The images are organized into folders, indexed as per the rule given below. There are multiple images of a single gesture. This is done to accommodate variations in the orientation of the gestures. The index (starting from 1) for a particular letter is named its "gesture index". For the English alphabets, the indexes are 1 through 26 accordingly, for space and backspace, the indexes are 27 and 28 respectively, for the digits 0 through 9, the indexes are 29 through 38 respectively and for the special characters the indexes 39 to 47 have been assigned. For instance, a path like "3/5.bmp" points to the 5th image of the gesture for letter 'C'; the index is calculated as: index of 'C' = (ASCII value of 'C') − (ASCII value of 'A') + 1 = 3.
- **Perceptrons** – The trained perceptrons are stored in simple text files, indexed following the same indexing procedure as above.

2.1   Algorithms

- **Image Processing Module** – The input is taken via the webcam. To make the extraction process easier, the webcam is surrounded by four red LEDs. The color ranges are then appropriately adjusted so that only the foreground object is detected.

Fig. 2. Modified ASL

Algorithm Image_Processing_Module

Step 1.   Capture an image via webcam.

Step 2.   Scan through all the pixels of the image. If a pixel lies within the pre-defined pixel value range, make it white. Else make that pixel black.

Step 3.   Check the area of all the white connected regions in the image.

Step 4.   Keep the white region with the largest area, and remove the other white regions in the image.

Step 5.   If the area of the largest white region is less than a predefined AREA_THRESHOLD, then remove that white region also and stop. Else, keep that white region and it is the extracted gesture shown by the user. Send this extracted gesture as an input to the Gesture Recognition Module.

End

- **Training Module** – This module uses the set of pre-clicked images of the different gestures to train the program. The output of this module is the set of perceptrons. There is a separate perceptron for each letter of the English Alphabet (one vs rest classification model).

Algorithm Training_Module:

For each perceptron, do (recall that perceptrons are indexed according to the letters, starting from 1)

   a.   For each gesture, do (n is the number of pixels in an image, same for all images here)

   i.   Convert the monochrome (0-1) image of the gesture to a vector
$$A = [a_1, a_2, ..., a_n]^T,$$
   where the superscript T stands for transpose.

   ii.   Denote the perceptron trained so far by the vector
$$W = [w_1, w_2, ..., w_n]^T.$$
   [W is initialized to $0_{n \times 1}$ in our case.]

   iii.   Compute
$$obtained\_result = A^T W = \sum_{i=1}^{n} a_i w_i$$

   iv.   If perceptron index = gesture index, then
$actual\_result = 1$.
   Else $actual\_result = 0$.

   v.   Compute $N = \|A\|_1$. Note that elements of A are either 0 or 1, so $\|A\|_1$ simply gives the number of 1's (white pixels) in A.

   vi.   Update W according to the relation
$W = W + A * ((actual\_result - obtained\_result)/N)$.

   b.   If perceptron satisfies the predefined MATCH_CRITERIA, then continue.
   Else repeat from (a).

End

- **Gesture Recognition Module** – This module tests the extracted gesture and tests it with all the perceptrons. If a match is found, then the corresponding letter is displayed.

  Algorithm Gesture_Recognition_Module
  Step 1. Repeat until all perceptrons have been tested
       a.   Convert the monochrome (0-1) image of the gesture to a vector
  $$A = [a_1, a_2, ..., a_n]^T.$$
       b.   Denote the current perceptron by the vector
  $$W = [w_1, w_2, ..., w_n]^T.$$
       c.   Compute
  $$obtained\_result = A^T W = \sum_{i=1}^{n} a_i w_i$$
       d.   If obtained_result > MATCH_THRESHOLD, then a match has been found and it is mapped to the corresponding letter and the search is stopped.
          Else continue.
  Step 2. If no match has been found, then the gesture is not a valid gesture and no output is provided.
  End

3 Results and Discussions

A typical result of the image processing module is given in Fig. 3. It can be seen that the foreground object (hand gesture) has been successfully extracted from the background.

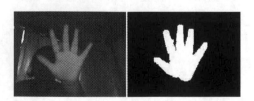

Fig. 3. Foreground Object Extraction

To obtain the system accuracy, each character has been tested 50 times and the accuracy is calculated by the rule.

$$accuracy = \frac{Total\ no.\ of\ correct\ outputs}{Total\ no.\ of\ tries}$$

Figure 4 shows the accuracy of the algorithm where each gesture is shown 50 times consecutively and the number of times the correct output obtained is recorded. The calculated overall accuracy is approximately 91.2%.

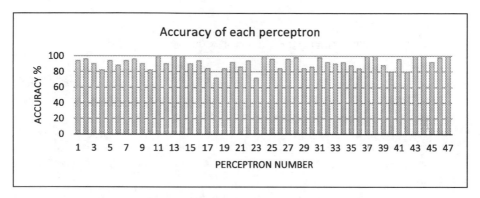

Fig. 4. Bar graph showing number of correct outputs.

The real-time working of the "Sign Language Interface" and the "Text to Sign Converter" have been shown in Figs. 5 and 6 respectively. The word "How" was tested and the results were recorded.

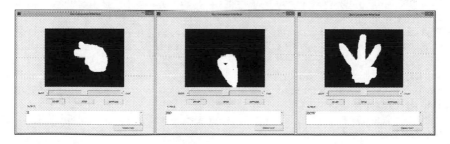

Fig. 5. Sign Language Interface showing the word 'HOW'.

4 Limitations

- This system is limited to the finger spelling method, which is not the most practical method for communication for deaf people. It would generally take too much time to finger spell a few sentences. So mainly this should be used to express proper nouns or short sentences conveying the meaning properly.

Fig. 6. Text to Sign Converter showing the word 'HOW'.

- Similar hand orientations are hard to distinguish. For instance, M and N have similar gestures, which make it difficult to distinguish between them. To overcome this difficulty, some modifications were made to these gestures.
- There are certain gestures which involve hand movements, as shown for J and Z. This system deals with image processing and hence there is no provision for video capturing to show these hand movements. Hence, such gestures have been modified accordingly.

References

1. History of ASL, http://iml.jou.ufl.edu/projects/fall05/rosen/history.html
2. Finger Spelling Alphabet, http://www.fingerspellingalphabet.com
3. Nachamai, M.: Alphabet recognition of american sign language: a hand gesture recognition approach using sift algorithm. Int. J. Artif. Intell. Appl. (IJAIA) **4**(1), 105–115 (2013)
4. Pugeault, N., Bowden, R.: Spelling it out: real-time ASL fingerspelling recognition. In: Computer Vision Workshops (ICCV Workshops), 2011 IEEE International Conference on 2011 Nov 6, pp. 1114–1119. IEEE (2011)
5. Vogler, C., Metaxas, D.: ASL recognition based on a coupling between HMMs and 3D motion analysis. In: Sixth International Conference on Computer Vision, pp. 363–369. IEEE, January 1998
6. Paul, J.F., Seth, D., Paul, C., Dastidar, J.G.: Hand gesture recognition library. Int. J. Sci. Appl. Inf. Technol. **3**(2), 44–50 (2014)
7. ASL University: Fingerspelling. http://www.lifeprint.com/asl101/fingerspelling
8. MathWorks: text-to-speech. http://in.mathworks.com/matlabcentral/fileexchange/18091-text-to-speech

EEE-AODV in MANET

Nishi Yadav$^{(\boxtimes)}$ and Nitika Srivastava

Computer Science and Engineering Department,
Institute of Technology, Guru Ghasidas University, Bilaspur, Chattisgarh, India
nishidv@gmail.com

Abstract. Mobile Ad hoc network is a collection of mobile nodes. It has the property to change according to changing topology due to the lack of centralized control. The nodes act as a sender and receiver both and communicate with each other through various protocols. We have analyzed the energy factor of existing AODV protocol and have done improvement in it by modifying MAC layer of nodes. We have made the nodes to sleep after the predefined interval which leads to reduction in energy consumption and thus enhances the lifetime of mobile nodes.

Keywords: EEE-AODV (Enhanced Energy Efficient-Ad Hoc On demand Distance Vector) · MAC · Energy · MANET

1 Introduction

MANET is a group of independent mobile nodes which have the capability to do communication with each other via radio waves shown in Fig. 1. Thus there is no centralized control. Every node act as a client, server and router. The other nodes in the network helps source to find the path to destination. MANET's are mainly useful at the places where the communication cannot be done easily or through the wired networks [11]. This is one of the main advantage of using MANET. Due to the lack of centralised control, topology of the network is undefined. Therefore we need such routing protocol that can work even in the changing topology. There are many predefined routing protocols available. MANET provides less security as compared to wired networks due to moving nodes. Power consumption becomes considerable due to changing topology. There is limited bandwidth available. The area or zone within which a node can send the data is limited [15].

MANET protocols are of different types like table driven and on demand. In table driven, each node maintains a routing table for the whole network. A periodic update is done so that any change in the topology can be forwarded to all the nodes in the network. This is basically done through flooding technique that is the each node sends the copy of its routing table to all the nodes in the topology [11]. Thus if any node wants to send the data, runs an appropriate path finding algorithm. Some already present algorithms like link state and distance vector are not suitable for wireless networks due to the changing topology in ad hoc networks. While in On demand routing protocol, routes are found only when they are needed. When sender wants to send the data then route

© Springer Nature Singapore Pte Ltd. 2016
A. Unal et al. (Eds.): SmartCom 2016, CCIS 628, pp. 19–26, 2016.
DOI: 10.1007/978-981-10-3433-6_3

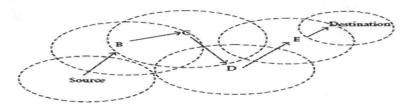

Fig. 1. Mobile Ad Hoc network

discovery is done. Due to this large control message is send to discover the route. Example of such type of algorithm is AODV. This algorithm is better than proactive algorithms due to less overhead to maintain routing information while it lacks behind proactive due to the large control message traffic [15].

1.1   Introduction to AODV

AODV protocol is one of the reactive protocol, the route is determined only when source wants to send message to destination. It has combined property of DSR and DSDV. The property of sequence number is acquired from DSDV. To find a new route to destination, source broadcast RREQ message as shown in Fig. 2. Route is determined if either RREQ reaches destination or one of the intermediate node [2]. The destination on receiving the packet sends RREP message to the source. The unicasting is done in this case. Each intermediate node cache the information. AODV has the property of link break detection. If any node does not get the control packet from its neighbors the link is said to be broken. A RRER packet is flooded to notify all nodes about the broken link and again path discovery is done to find the alternate path.

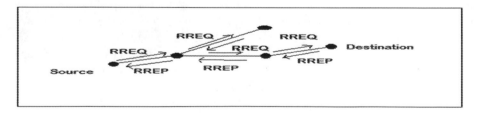

Fig. 2.   Route discovery in AODV

1.2   Introduction to MAC Layer of NS 2.35

MAC layer is responsible to transfer packet from upper layer to lower layer and vice versa. In ns2.35, MAC802.11 class is defined to perform the operation. As node receives the packet, recv () function calls send () function to transfer the packet to upper layer or lower layer. MAC 802.11 have many other functions to handle the incoming and outgoing packets. It also implement back off time and retransmission of packets. MAC classes are shown in Fig. 3.

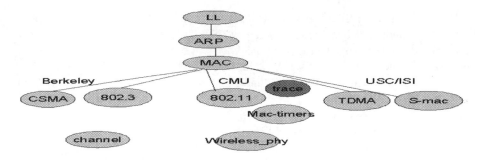

Fig. 3. Classes in MAC

2 Literature Review

V. Ramesh, Dr. P. Subbaiah, N. Koteswar Rao, and M. Janardhana Raju [1], found packet delivery ratio of AODV to be independent of sources while it suffers from end-to-end delay. In high mobility condition, DSDV shows low packet delivery fraction. The conclusion have been drawn that AODV is best suited when communication has to be done using UDP protocol.

Singh Annapurna, Mishra Shailendra [2] has done detail analysis of the MANET protocol's performance. They have done the analysis on AODV, DSR and TORA based on some important matrices such as traffic sent and received, time taken in route discovery and number of hops per route, load and throughput is calculated. Authors have shown the result that the performance of AODV and DSR are better than TORA and AODV performs better than other protocols in all respects.

V.K. Taksande, K.D Kulat [3], studied three protocols DSR, AODV and DSDV and simulated them using CBR traffic. Packet delivery ratio, average end to end delay and routing overhead under changing number of nodes has been considered as parameter. Authors have found that DSR outperforms other protocols in terms of end to end delay and dropped packets. While AODV outperforms in average end to end delay.

Ajay Kumar, Ashwani Kumar Singla [4] have studied the three MANET protocol namely DSDV, AODV and DSR and evaluated the performance based on TCP traffic pattern. They found that DSDV outperforms other two in terms of traffic pattern of TCP. They have also concluded that performance of these three protocols gets affected more when there is change in pause time rather than change in number of connections.

Nishi Yadav, P.M. Khilar [5], simulated the protocol in MATLAB. The experiments were conducted for the network of varying sizes of 8, 16, 32, 64,128 nodes. Authors have taken Diagnostic Latency, Message Complexity, and Hop Count Ratio as parameters and found dependency of diagnostic latency on number of messages exchanged, transmission and propagation delay and also found it to be directly proportional to the number of messages exchanged in the network to make diagnosis achievable. A hierarchically adaptive distributed fault diagnosis algorithm using clustering technique has also been proposed by them for diagnosing crash and value faulty nodes in Mobile Ad hoc Network (MANET) based on Hi-ADSD.

B.N. Jagdale, PragatiPatil, P. Lahane, D. Javale [6], found AODV to be better than DSDV due to more bandwidth consumption by DSDV while is not the case with AODV protocol. DSDV performs well in small network while AODV performs well in large network. And the throughput of DSDV is lee than AODV.

Ammar Odeh, Eman Abdelfattah, MuneerAlshowkan [7], studied the two MANET reactive routing protocol namely AODV and DSR. DSR has shown better performance in terms of packet size less than 700 byte.

K. Prabu, A. Subramani [8], have simulated the AODV, DSR and TORA protocols on the basis of parameters such as high mobility high traffic and low mobility and low traffic. In case of low mobility low traffic author have found DSR and AODV to have low routing overhead average end to end delay and high Packet delivery ratio and in case of high mobility high traffic, average routing overhead, end to end delay and packet delivery fraction, and AODV to have very high routing overhead.

V. Rajeshkumar, P. Sivakumar [9], showed the performance of three routing protocol of MANET namely DSDV, AODV and DSR. They found that AODV has best performance in network having large number of nodes, while DSR performance is better when the number of nodes is very less. Also they found that average end-to-end delay of DSDV is minimized and does not increase with the nodes.

Kumar Prateek, Nimish Arvind, Satish Kumar Alaria [10], evaluated the performance of the three routing protocol namely DSDV, AODV and DSR and found that reactive protocol performs well in high mobility scenario than proactive. The final result of this paper is DSR has performed well compared to all other protocol in terms of Delivery ratio while AODV performed well in terms of average delay.

Nabil Nissar, Najib Naja, Abdellah Jamali [11], have studied and compared DSDV, DSR, AODV, OLSR protocols taking number of nodes as 30 and found the results that no protocol outperforms other in terms of all parameter. DSDV gives best end to end delay while DSR and AODV give better throughput and packet delivery fraction.

Nidhi Singh, Ajay Kumar, Chandra Prakesh Sahu [12],in their paper have taken AODV, OLSR and ZRP for simulation. CBR traffic has been considered under Two Ray ground model. Simulation has been done by varying number of nodes and pause time. Authors have found average throughput of AODV as best.

Ashraf Abu-Ein, Jihad Nader [13], proposed a new protocol PH-AODV. It is modified version of AODV in which combination of power coefficient and the hop count parameter have been taken to improve the performance of AODV. The new protocol is better than AODV with respect to end-to-end delay, throughput and number of drop packets.

Charles E Perkins, Pravin Bhagwat [14], have explained the internal working of DSDV protocol.

Nitika Srivastava, Priya Dubey and Nishi Yadav [15], have simulated AODV, DSDV, DSR protocol on various parameters and have found that AODV gives highest throughput, DSDV consumes least energy and overall performance of DSR is better than the other two.

3   Proposed Work

Improvements have been done at MAC layer. This modification have resulted in improvement in energy consumption of AODV algorithm. As every node have MAC layer, nodes are made to sleep for some time. These results in less power consumption. As the nodes are going to sleep they are sending packet after some duration and thus saving the energy of the nodes.

MAC layer of a node is basically responsible for transferring data from upper layer to the physical layer of that node and vice versa. In ns2 the functionality of MAC layer is deployed using MAC802.11 shown in Fig. 3. We have added sleep and wakeup function of wireless-phy inside recv () function which is already defined inside MAC/MAC802-11.cc. As the node gets the packet, recv () function is called. The recv () function calls send () function which sends the packet to upper layer or to the lower layer as required. The inclusion of sleep and wakeup method inside the recv () function will make some nodes to sleep and change them to wakeup state after sometime. The nodes oscillate between sleep and wakeup state. The simulation environments have been shown in Table 1. The flow chart has been shown in Fig. 4.

Table 1. Simulation Environment

Simulator	NS 2.35
Protocols	AODV
No of Nodes	15,20,25
Speed	70 m/s
Pause time	2
Topology	Random
Simulation time	500 s
Traffic type	CBR
Propagation model	Two ray ground
Max packet in queue	50
Initial Energy	800.4 J
Packet Size	1000 Bytes
Time Interval	0.005 s

3.1   Basic Functions of General MAC Class

- sendRTS(intdst)
- recv (packet, handler)
- send(packet, handler)
- SendUp
- SendDown
- Handler* callback_
- Resume()
- Discard
- RetransmitDATA()

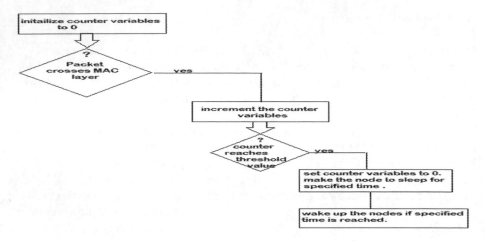

Fig. 4. Flow chart of algorithm

- RetransmitRTS()
- sendACK(intdst)
- sendDATA(Packet*)
- sendCTS(intdst, double rts_duration)

3.2   Algorithm

1. Keep a counter of total number of packets send by a node.
2. If a node has crossed the threshold number packets to be sent/received, Or if it has not crossed the threshold number of nodes that it should have crossed at particular interval.
3. Then make the node to sleep.
4. Wakeup the node after specified time.

4   Results

Changes in the MAC layer have resulted in less energy consumption by nodes as shown in Fig. 5. This is due to node going into the sleep state after crossing the threshold level.

In sleep state nodes neither transfer nor generate the packets. Thus transmission and receiving energy loss is saved at the cost of throughput. This has somewhat also decreased the routing overhead of AODV. Running some tcl files on new protocol have resulted in less routing overhead.

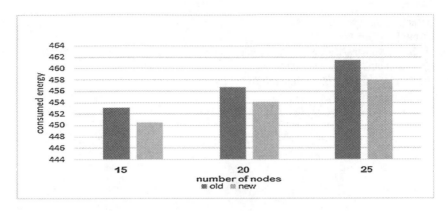

Fig. 5. Result of energy consumption EEE-AODV and AODV

5   Conclusion

After analyzing the existing result we have concluded that the routing protocol AODV is more energy efficient by improvement in MAC layer of nodes in MANET. In future, works can be on MAC layer and other layers to indirectly improve the performance of the other protocol too.

References

1. Ramesh, V., Subbaiah, P., Rao, N.K., Raju, M.J.: Performance Comparison and Analysis of DSDV and AODV for MANET. Int. J. Comput. Sci. Eng. **2**, 183–188 (2010)
2. Annapurna, S., Mishra, S.: Performance analysis of reactive routing protocols in mobile ad hoc networks. Int. J. Comput. Sci. Netw. Secur. **10**, 141–145 (2010)
3. Taksande, V.K., Kulat, K.D.: Performance comparison of DSDV, DSR, AODV protocol with IEEE 802. In: 11 MAC for Chain Topology for Mobile Ad-hoc Network using NS-2. IJCA Special Issue on 2nd National Conference: Computing, Communication and Sensor Network, CCSN, 26–31 (2011)
4. Kumar, A., Singla, A.K.: Performance evaluation of MANET routing protocols on the basis of TCP traffic pattern. Int. J. Inf. Technol. Convergence Serv. **1**, 41–48 (2011)
5. Yadav, N., Khilar, P.M.: Cluster based distributed diagnosis in MANET. Int. J. Comput. Inf. Technol. **1**, 2277-0764 (2012)
6. Jagdale, B.N., Patil, P., Lahane, P., Javale, D.: Analysis and comparison of distance vector, DSDV and AODV protocol of MANET. Int. J. Distrib. Parallel Syst. **3**, 121–131 (2012)
7. Odeh, A., Fattah, E.A., Alshowkan, M.: Performance evaluation of AODV and DSR routing protocols in MNAET networks. Int. J. Distrib. Parallel Syst. **3**, 13–22 (2012)
8. Prabu, K., Subramani, A.: Int. J. Adv. Res. Comput. Sci. Softw. Eng. **2**, 388–392 (2012)
9. Rajeshkumar, V., Sivakumar, P.: Comparative study of AODV, DSDV and DSR routing protocols in MANET using network simulator-2. Int. J. Adv. Res. Comput. Commun. Eng. **2**, 4564–4569 (2013)
10. Prateek, K., Arvind, N., Alaria, S.K.: MANET-evaluation of DSDV, AODV and DSR routing protocol. Int. J. Innovat. Eng. Technol. **2**, 99–104 (2013). 2319-1058

11. Nissar, N., Naja, N., Jamali, A.: A review and a new approach to reduce routing overhead in MANETs. Wirel. Netw. **21**, 1119–1139 (2014)
12. Singh, N., Kumar, A., Sahu, C.P.: Simulation based performance analysis of AODV OLSR and ZRP routing protocols in MANET. Int. J. Emerg. Sci. Eng. **3**, 2319–6378 (2014)
13. Abu-Ein, A., Nader, J.: An enhanced AODV routing protocol for MANETs. Int. J. Comput. Sci. Issues **11**, 872–877 (2014)
14. Perkins, C.E., Bhagwat, P.: Highly Dynamic Destination Sequenced Distance Vector Routing DSDV for Mobile Computers (1994)
15. Srivastava, N., Dubey, P., Yadav, N.: A comparative exploration and analysis of AODV, DSDV and DSR for MANET. Int. J. Comput. Sci. Mob. Comput. **5**, 42–53 (2016)

Nano Scale Dual Material Gate Silicon on Nothing Junctionless MOSFET for Improving Short Channel Effect and Analog Performance

S.C. Wagaj[1,2(✉)] and Y.V. Chavan[1,2]

[1] Department of Electronics and Telecommunication, JSPM's RSCOE, Tathawade, Pune, India
[2] Savitribai Phule Pune University, Pune, India
scwagaj@yahoo.com, chavan.yashwant@gmail.com

Abstract. Silicon-on-insulator (SOI) suffers with various drawbacks so Silicon-on-nothing (SON) has been the researchers recent target. The result shows that surface potential and electric field is maximum compare to Single Material Gate as well as Dual Material Gate SOI junctionless Transistor (DMG SOI JLT). Various targeted features comprise such as maximum on-state current, improved transconductance Gm, Gm/I_{DS} and reduced drain induced barrier lowering. In this paper is the work on the parametric effect of two layer gate stack (DGS) (High dielectric/Sio_2) on the Dual Material Gate (DMG) for SON Junctionless Transistor. The results obtained by the simulation for 40 nm channel length with work function as 4.77 and 4.1 eV with doping concentration (0.4×10^{18} cm^{-3}).

Keywords: Dual Material Gate (DMG) · Junctionless · Silicon on insulator · Silicon on nothing · Single material gate · Double layer gate stack

1 Introduction

According to Moor's law semiconductor technology shrinks and number of transistor double every two years. However, when the channel length gets shortened it reduces control of the gate over the channel area due to depletion width of source and drain mix with each other. Therefore, in nanoscale MOSFET short channel effect is big problem. The Silicon-On-Nothing (SON) MOSFETs best candidate for bulk MOS devices, fully depleted (FD) silicon-on-nothing MOSFETs are considered as one of the best candidates for control short channel effect [1]. As in deep-sub micrometer SON circuit simulation and modeling is very important in Ultra large scale implementation. The microelectronics industries required the fabrication of miniaturized components; as a result transistors are nowadays reaching to the nano-scale in size. At present challenges in front of new researchers are of to bring up new device design and manufacturing steps. The fabrication of S/D junctions in nano-scale devices is technological very difficult. The

---

Y.V. Chavan—Sr IEEE-Member

© Springer Nature Singapore Pte Ltd. 2016
A. Unal et al. (Eds.): SmartCom 2016, CCIS 628, pp. 27–38, 2016.
DOI: 10.1007/978-981-10-3433-6_4

junctionless transistor has now become popular technology as per as the parameters targeted in this paper, which may be compensated somewhere else by the device so the trade off need to be made based on application [3–5]. In Dual Material Gate MOSFET device, the perpendicular field is control by two different work function M1 and M2 [8, 14]. The dual material gate SON-MOSFET is best candidate to enhance the capability of current flow and to decrease the short channel effect problem for scaling of CMOS technology [1]. Combining the advantages of junctionless transistor and DMG structure [13] with SON we proposed Dual Material Gate (DMG) design increase the electron velocity due to step potential and enhance the electric field in the channel of the SON-JLMOSFETs for digital and analog applications [7, 12]. A novel SON junctionless MOSFET structure with Dual Material Gate [Double-layers (high dielectric/sio$_2$) two layer gate (DGS) design] has been simulated [2].

Device simulated is discuss in Sect. 2, and gives the influence of the two layer gate stack on SON junctionless transistors in Sect. 3, with DMG and without DMG SOI Junctionless Transistor. The channel potential, electric field, transconductance and output conductance are compared in Sect. 4.

2   Device Structures and Simulation Setup

Device is simulated using Visual-TCAD tool: COGENDA. For performance assessment of the Dual Material Gate silicon on nothing junctionless transistor (DMG SON JLT) with Dual Material Gate Stack (DGS) and Dual Material Gate Silicon-on-insulator (DMG SOI JLT) and Single Material Gate Silicon-on-insulator (SMG SOI JLT) the physical parameters such as doping density, channel thickness and work function kept constant. Figure 1 shows that the n type device DMG SON JLT. An n channel DMG SON JLT has homogeneous (N$^+$) doping uniformly through source, drain and channel region and p type and n type polysilicon is work as gate material. A DMG SON JLT has two different work function gate material, M$_1$ and M$_2$ respectively. For DMG SOI JLT device, W$_{M1}$ and W$_{M2}$ are set to be 5.0 eV and 4.1 eV respectively. Total gate oxide layer t$_{ox}$ of 4 nm is separated upper oxide layer High-k 3 nm and lower oxide layer sio$_2$ 1 nm

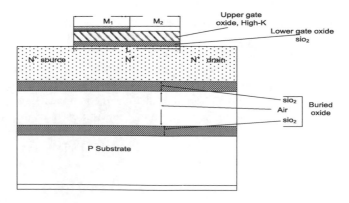

Fig. 1. A novel N-type DMG SON JLT with DGS

gate oxide material. The buried oxide stacks (BOS) thickness as 10 nm, where Sio_2 layer thickness is 2 nm. The middle layer (6 nm) is of air as a high dielectric material compare to sio_2 is useful for short channel effect problem (Table 1).

Table 1. Device parameters of different JLTs

Parameters	SMG SOI JLT	DMG SOI JLT	DMG SON JLT
L (nm)	40	40	40
$L_{M1}:L_{M2}$ (nm)	–	20:20	20:20
$W_{M1}:W_{M2}$ (eV)	4.1	4.77:4.1	5.0:4.1
N_D (cm^{-3})	0.4e18	0.4e18	0.4e18
T_{OX} (nm)	1 (sio_2)	1 (sio_2)	1 sio_2 3 High (k)
T_{si} (nm)	10	10	10
Buried oxide (nm)	300	300	2 sio_2 4 Air

In this TCAD simulation basic drift diffusion, impact ionization, band-to-band tunneling model incorporate with mobility model.

3 Results and Discussions

DMG SON JLT's characteristics are observed and compared result with DMG SOI JLT and SMG SOI JLT. The physical model accounting for Lombardi mobility model, Drift diffusion model, band gap narrowing, impact ionization, SRH recombination & generation and velocity saturation have been incorporate in simulation.

3.1 Electrical Characteristic of the DMG SON JLT

Figure 2 shows the plot of potential distributions along the channel direction. The potential distribution of DMG changes as a step potential due to workfunction W_{M1} and W_{M2}, whereas SMG SOI JLT potential distribution along the channel changes monotonically.

The change is due to the different gate workfunction [7, 8]. It is also observed that in the DMG SON JLT's channel potential is maximum compare to DMG SOI JLT and SMG SOI JLT, which indicate that the channel resistance increases in the DMG SON JLT is minimum than that of DMG and SMG SOI JLT [9]. DMG SON JLT potential maximum compare to DMG and SMG SOI JLT [19].

In the Fig. 3 it is seen that to enhance the electric field in the channel of DMG SON JLT. SMG SOI JLT, there is maximum electric field at the drain side. DMG SON JLT maximum electric field near source side as compare to DMG and SMG SOI JLT meaning that the current driving capability of DMG SON JLT is maximum compare to DMG and SMG SOI JLT. At drain side lower electric field in DMG SON JLT and DMG SOI JLT compared with SMG SOI JLT and its indicates that the short channel effect and hot electron effect suppresses more effectively [16]. The electron velocity in the channel increases due to high work function at source side gate [19].

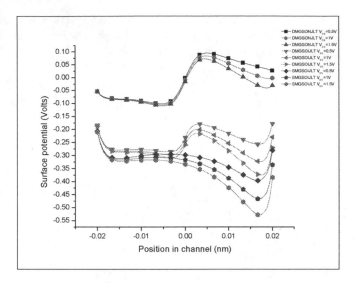

Fig. 2. Potential variation of SMG SOI JLT, DMG SOI JLT and DMG SON JLT along the channel with V_{DS} = 0.5, 1, 1.5 V, L = 40 nm. Tsi = 10 nm.

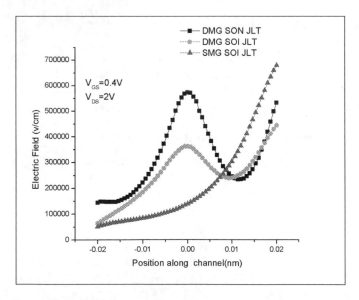

Fig. 3. In the SMG, DMG SOI JLT and DMG SON JLT electric field through the channel at V_{GS} = 0.4 and V_{DS} = 2 V. t_{si} = 10 nm and t_{ox} = 1 nm

In the channel high peak electric field of DMG SON JLT compare to small peak electric field of DMG SOI JLT and SMG SOI JLT, its indicate that channel resistance of DMG SON JLT is smaller than DMG and SMG SOI JLT. Figure 4 shows that drain current versus drain voltage for the device at V_{GS} = 1 V. DMG SON JLT breakdown voltage is 2.6 V and DMG SOI JLT's breakdown voltage is 2.65 V. The minimum breakdown voltage in DMG SON JLT compare to DMG SOI JLT [10].

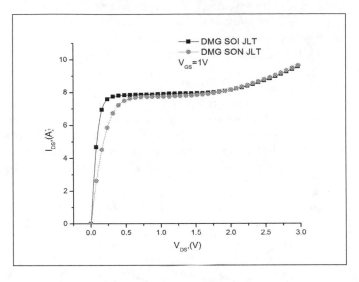

Fig. 4. Drain voltage v/s drain current

Figure 5 shows that off state current vary channel length. When channel length 10 nm DMG SON JLT off current is very small but channel length increases off state current decreases.

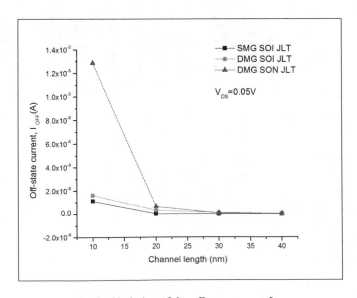

Fig. 5. Variation of the off state current I_{OFF}.

DMG SOI JLT off state current is 3×10^{-12} A and DMG SON JLT off state current is 1×10^{-8} A when channel length 40 nm. I_{off} deceases with channel length due to the enhanced potential barrier for the carriers moving caused by increasing channel length, it has been observed that off state current decreases when recombination (SRH) rate is high i.e. when diffusion length is smaller than channel length of MOSFET then off state current is lower [13, 18]. Leakage current reduces due to high-k dielectric is an alternate of sio_2 [2].

The I_D versus V_{GS} characteristics at $V_{DS} = 50$ mV of DMG SON JLT is shown in Fig. 6. We see the measured characteristics of the DMG SON JLT with well behaved transition from off to on state. The transfer curve shows on/off current ration beyond 10^3 at $V_{DS} = 0.05$ V at channel length 30 nm and 40 nm. High-k/sio_2 gate stack and junctionless both improve the on current I_{ON} (drain current I_{DS} at $V_{GS} = 1$ V and $V_{DS} = 0.05$ V) and decreased off state current I_{OFF} (drain current I_{DS} at $V_{GS} = 0$ V and $V_{DS} = 0.05$ V).

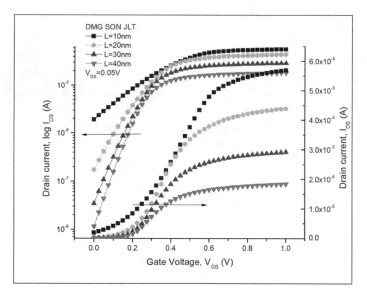

Fig. 6. Drain current I_{ds} versus gate voltage V_{gs} at a drain voltage of 50 mV and log scale for DMG SON JLT Channel length 10, 20, 30, 40 nm.

Figure 7 shows the device DMG SOI JLT with different channel length as a reduced off state leakage current. As the channel length increases the slope of the I_D-V_{GS} increases. This shows that a reduction in parasitic resistance [15] from the region below the channel. When channel length decreases then on state current decreases of DMG SOI JLT. In DMG SOI JLT on/off ratio decrease compare to DMG SON JLT when channel length below 30 nm. In DMG SON JLT channel length reduces then on state current increases. Hence, when channel length reduces better on/off current ratio compare to DMG SOI JLT.

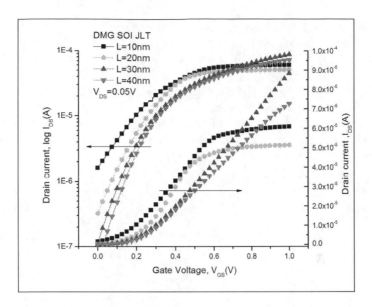

Fig. 7. Drain current I_{ds} versus input voltage gate voltage V_{GS} at V_{DS} of 50 mV and log scale for DMG SOI JLT Channel length 10, 20, 30, 40 nm.

Figure 8 shows the result for DIBL physical gate length versus threshold voltage for DMG SON JLT, DMG SOI JLT and SMG SOI JLT. Definition of DIBL is decrease in threshold voltage when drain voltage is increased from 0.05 V to 1.0 V [DIBL = V_{th} (V_{DS} = 0.05 V)-V_{th}(V_{DS} = 1 V)]. DMG SON JLT has a better performance compare to DMG and SMG SOI JLT when channel length reduces. A DIBL = 40 mV/V is achieved

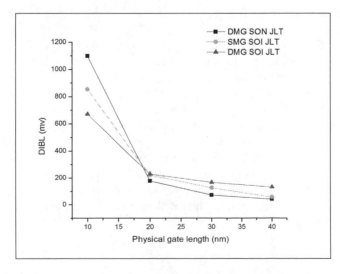

Fig. 8. DIBL at V_{DS} = 50 mV in DMG SON JLT, DMG SOI JLT and SMG SOI JLT devices with Tsi = 10 nm

at LG = 40 nm for DMG SON JLT and DIBL = 57 mV/V for DMG SOI JLT. A DIBL = 177 mV/V is achieved at L_G = 20 nm for DMG SON JLT and DIBL = 222 mV/V for DMG SOI JLT [19]. A DIBL = 73 mV/V is achieved at LG = 30 nm for DMG SON JLT and DIBL = 127 mV/V for DMG SOI JLT. A DIBL = 1098 mV/V is achieved at LG = 10 nm for DMG SON JLT and DIBL = 854 mV/V for DMG SOI JLT [19–21].

The DIBL value is evaluated as the changes in threshold voltage at V_{DS} = 50 mV and threshold voltage at V_{DS} = 1 V. It has been observed that DIBL has increases with the channel length decreases. Figure 9 shows that variation of DIBL versus physical channel length.

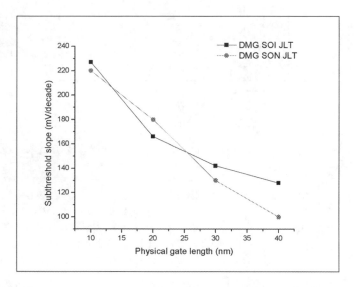

Fig. 9. Variation in sub threshold with physical channel length, channel length = 40 nm.

The sub threshold slope represents the gate voltage which could cause one decade change in drain current when off to on state changing capability of a device [11].

Figure 9 shows that Sub-threshold slope is lowest when channel length increase. When channel length is minimum sub threshold (10 nm) slope decreases in Dual Material Gate SON JLT MOSFET compare to DMG SOI JLT MOSFET. The Sub-threshold slope is inversely proportional to channel length of DMG SON JLT. Specifically, Gate length varying from L_G = 40 nm down to L_G = 10 nm are used in order to describe the low SCEs with steep Sub-threshold slope of JL devices.

Figure 10 shows that on state current of DMG SON JLT is an increase when channel length decreases. DMG SOI JLT on current maximum compare to other junctionless Transistor at V_{DS} = 0.05 V. On state current almost equal of all junctionless transistor when channel length 10 nm.

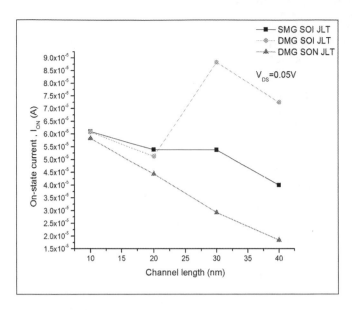

Fig. 10. Variation of I_{ON} versus channel length

Figure 11 shows that slower degradation of transconductance with V_{GS} is observed in SMG SOI JLT because other junctionless transistor decrease in mobility with gate voltage is much less [6]. In figure the transconductance values of G_m of the DMG SON JLT, DMG SOI JLT and SMG SOI JLT. The maximum value of transconductance at $V_{DS} = 0.05$ V are 0.2 mS, 0.14 mS, and 0.1 mS respectively.

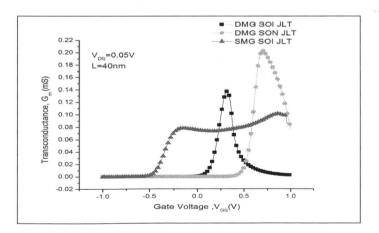

Fig. 11. Variation of transconductance G_m

Figure 12 shows that gain performance and convert dc power into ac frequency of DMG SON JLT & DMG, SMG SOI JLT. In sub threshold region DMG SON JLT has the highest value of G_m/I_D followed by DMG SOI JLT and SMG SOI JLT.

Transconductance (G_m) to drain current ratio (G_m/I_D) of DMG SON JLT = 37.8 V^{-1}, DMG SOI JLT = 26 V^{-1} and SMG SOI JLT = 3 V^{-1} at V_{GS} = 0.01 V [1, 17].

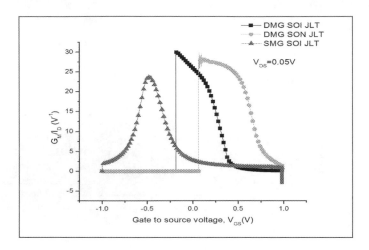

Fig. 12. G_m/I_D versus gate to source voltage V_{GS} at V_{DS} = 0.05 V

Figure 13 shows that the reduced output conductance in SON JLT device as shown improved intrinsic gain over another junctionless transistor. Intrinsic voltage gain also depend on G_m and gd ($A_V = G_m/gd$) [17]. Output conductance decreases means intrinsic gain increase.

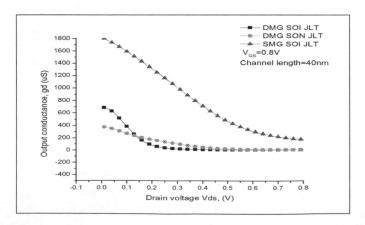

Fig. 13. Variation of output conductance gd versus drain voltage at channel length 40 nm.

4   Conclusion

A performance of DMG SON JLT with Double layer gate stack (DGS), DMG SOI JLT and SMG SOI JLT was performed using TCAD 2-D simulation. DMG SON JLT with

DGS shows excellent improvement such as suppression of DIBL, transconductance and channel potential enhancement and off state current reduces. DMG SON JLT with DGS configuration further increases G_m/I_D and output conductance. Hence, the DMG SON JLT with DGS has substantial benefits in low voltage and analog application.

References

1. Kasturi, P., Saxena, M., Gupta, M.: Dual-material double-layer gate stack SON MOSFET: a novel architecture for enhanced analog performance-Part II: impact of gate-dielectric material engineering. IEEE Trans. Electron Devices 55(1), 382–387 (2008)
2. Simoen, E., Mercha, A.: Low-frequency noise behavior of sio_2-Hfo_2 dual-layer gate dielectric nMOSFETs with different interfacial oxide thickness. IEEE Trans. Electron Devices 51(5) (2004)
3. Lee, C.-W., Afzalian, A., Akhavan, N.D., Yan, R., Ferain, I., Colinge, J.-P.: Junction less multigate field-effect transistor. Appl. Phys. Lett. 94(5), 053511-1–053511-2 (2009)
4. Lee, C.-W., Nazarov, A.N., Ferain, I., Akhavan, N.D., Yan, R., Razavi, P., et al.: Low sub threshold slope in junction less multigate transistor. Appl. Phys. Lett. 96(10), 1021061–1021063 (2010)
5. Lee, C.-W., Ferain, I., Afzalian, A., Yan, R., Akhavan, N.D., Razavi, P., et al.: Performance estimation of junction less multigate transistors. Solid State Electron. 54(2), 97–103 (2010)
6. Doria, R.T., Pavanello, M.A., Trevisoli, R.D., de-Souza, M., Lee, C.-W., Ferain, I., et al.: Junction less multiple-gate transistors for analog applications. IEEE Trans. Electron Devices 58(8), 2511–2519 (2011)
7. Long, W., Ou, H., Kuo, J.-M., Chin, K.K.: Dual material gate (DMG) field effect transistor. IEEE Trans. Electron Devices 46(5), 865–870 (1999)
8. Colinge, J.P., Lee, C.-W., Ferain, I., Yan, R.: Reduced electric field in junction less transistors. Appl. Phys. Lett. 96, 073510 (2010)
9. Colinge, J.-P., Lee, C.-W., Afzalian, A., Akhavan, N.D., Yan, R., Ferain, I., et al.: Nanowire transistors without junctions. Nat. Nanotechnol. 5(3), 225–229 (2010)
10. Lee, S.M., Yu, C.G., Jeong, S.M.: Drain breakdown voltage: a comparison between junctionless and inversion mode p-channel MOSFETs. Microelectron. Reliab. 52, 1945–1948 (2012)
11. Razavi, P., Orouji, A.A.: Dual material gate oxide stack symmetric double gate MOSFET: improving short channel effects of nanoscale double gate MOSFET. In: Proceedings of 11th International Biennial BEC, pp. 83–86, October 2008
12. Kumar, M.J., Chaudhry, A.: Two-dimensional analytical modeling of fully depleted DMG SOI MOSFET and evidence for diminished SCEs. IEEE Trans. Electron Devices 51(4), 569–574 (2004)
13. Gundapaneni, S., Ganguli, S., Kottantharayil, A.: Bulk planner junctionless transistor (BPJLT): an attractive device alternative for scaling. IEEE Electron Device Lett. 32(3), 261–263 (2011)
14. Shee, S., Bhattacharyya, G., Sarkar, S.K.: Quantum analytical modeling for device parameters and I-V characteristics of nano-scale dual-material double-gate silicon-on-nothing MOSFET. IEEE Trans. Electron Devices 61(8), 2697–2704 (2014)
15. Lou, H., Zhang, L., Zhu, Y.: A junction less nanowire transistor with a dual material gate. IEEE Trans. Electron Devices 59(7), 1829–1836 (2012)
16. Wang, P., Zhuang, Y., Li, C.: Subthreshold behavior models for nanoscale junction less double-gate MOSFETs with dual-material gate stack. Jpn. J. Appl. Phys. 53, 084201 (2014)

17. Baruah, R.K., Paily, R.: A dual-material gate junction less transistor with high-k spacer for enhanced analog performance. IEEE Trans. Electron Devices **61**(1), 123–128 (2014)
18. Gundapaneni, S., Bajaj, M., Pandey, R.: Effect of band-to-band tunneling on junctionless transistors. IEEE Trans. Electron Devices **59**(4), 1023–1029 (2012)
19. Wagaj, S.C., Chavan, Y.V.: Effect of process parameters variation on dual material gate SOI junctionless transistor. IOSR J. Electron. Commun. Eng. (IOSR-JECE), 93–99. e-ISSN: 2278-2834, p-ISSN:2278-8735, NCIEST-2015
20. Chavan, Y.V., Mishra, D.K.: Modeling of the photo-detectors for computer vision system. Int. J. Opt. **39**(4), 149–156 (2010). Springer Publication
21. Chavan, Y.V., Mishra, D.K.: Improved CMOS digital pixel sensor. In: Presented at the National Conference on Wireless Communication and Networking organized by L&T, Powai, 9–10 December 2008

Designing of Photonic Crystal Ring Resonator Based ADF Filter for ITU-T G.694.2 CWDM Systems

Neha Singh[1(✉)] and Krishna Chandra Roy[2]

[1] Career Point University, Kota, India
nehasinghsinsinwar@gmail.com
[2] Kautilya Institute of Technology and Engineering, Jaipur, India
dr.kcroy@gmail.com

Abstract. In this paper two dimensional photonic crystal ring resonator based add/drop filter is proposed. The layout of the proposed filter includes bus waveguide and drop waveguide which is coupled with the quasi-square resonator. The filter has a square lattice with rods suspended in air type structure. The add/drop filter has 1500 nm add (off resonance) wavelength and 1567 nm drop (on resonance) wavelength with drop efficiency 95%. This type of filter is mainly used in CWDM system. The size of the filter is very compact $11.1*10 \, \mu m^2$. The designed filter has quality factor of 3134. The layout of filter is designed using a layout designer tool. OptiFDTD software is used for the designing and simulation of filter.

Keywords: Photonic crystals (Phc) · One dimension (1D) · Two dimension (2D) · Three dimension (3D) · Photonic crystal ring resonator (PCRR) · Linear waveguide · Photonic · Add and drop filter (ADFs) · Coarse wavelength division multiplexing (CWDM) · Plane wave expansion method (PWE) · finite difference time domain method (FDTD)

1 Introduction

Photonic Crystal (PC) is a natural periodic material in which periodicity is due to the periodically arranged dielectric substrate. Depending upon the periodicity of photonic crystal, it is further classified into three categories 1D, 2D and 3D. One of the an important characteristic of crystal is photonic band gap. Inside the photonic crystal, light is traveled by using band gap characteristics. Band gap of a crystal is the region inside the spectrum which does not allow the propagation of photons. But by changing or making some defects into the crystal, this inhibited range of frequency is converted into the propagating band. The width of band-gap depends upon the difference between the two dielectric materials of the crystal. The property of photonic crystal provides manipulation, confinement as well as controlling of light and therefore it is used for the designing of various compact and ultra compact devices. Optical filters, demultiplexers, sensors and multiplexers are the most commonly used optical devices in the field of integrated optical circuits [1].

© Springer Nature Singapore Pte Ltd. 2016
A. Unal et al. (Eds.): SmartCom 2016, CCIS 628, pp. 39–46, 2016.
DOI: 10.1007/978-981-10-3433-6_5

One of the photonic crystal based optical filtering device is add/drop filter. It receives prime considerations in the field of optical filtering because this filter is also act as a de-multiplexer to reject a single channel or multiple channels. The function of ADF filter is to drop or select the desired wavelength from CWDM system. In Fig. 1 optical communication network is shown, in which different wavelengths are sent from head end to different places for respective applications and these wavelengths are dropped to the particular substations by using of add/drop filter [2].

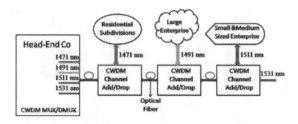

Fig. 1. Optical networks [2].

In the past various conventional ADFs have been designed such as fiber grating based filter, filter based on fabry perot liquid crystal, acoustic optic filters, and thin film filters etc. But the main limitation of these filters was their size so the integration of conventional ADF filters on the photonic crystal based integrated circuits (PICs) was not possible as the size of filter was very large [2].

In earlier stages, resonators were created by producing some defects into the single rod/hole (point defect) or multiple rod/holes (line defect) which generates micro cavity modes or waveguide modes respectively as defects break the periodicity of photonic crystal structures. Thus quantum bundles can be localized into the defected region [3]. Another important resonator is photonic crystal based ring resonator. This type of reso-nator is used in add/drop filter. In very first Kim et al. [4], has demonstrated the approach of PCRR in the field of photonic crystal, where they presented a laser which was based on 2D photonic crystals. Later in the literature, various works which were based on PCRRs was presented.

The ring resonator type structure provides good scalability in size, adaptability in structure designing as compared to the previously designed point defect cavities and line defect cavities. In recent years, various 2D photonic crystal based add/drop filter with ring resonator have been designed [5]. In 2007, Z. Qiang et al. [6] has proposed two dimensional square lattices with dielectric rods in air type structure based optical add/drop filter. In which they computed the normalize spectrum for single ring and dual ring resonator by using the finite difference time domain techniques. The 100% drop effi-ciency is achieved by introducing scattering rods. In 2008, M. Djavid et al. [7] gives a broadband Add/Drop filter which was based on L- shaped bend PCRR. M.R. Rakshani et al. [8] developed channel drop filter which was based on 2D triangular lattice with rods in air type structure. In 2016, Rahima Bendjelloul et al. [9] designed a T-shaped filter which was also based on photonic crystal ring resonator.

The proposed filter is based on quasi square ring resonator which is used for the application of ITU-T G.694.2 eight channel CWDM system to select (add) and drop a channel at a resonant wavelength (1567 nm). The proposed wavelength is suitable for accessing of metro optical network. The rest of the paper includes designing of PCRR add/drop filter, simulation results and conclusion.

2 Layout Design of ADF Filter

Proposed filter is designed by using 2D photonic crystal as a material. The filter layout designing steps are as follows:

2.1 Material Selection

For the designing of filter photonic crystal is used. A periodic dielectric material which shows periodicity in one, two and three dimensions is called photonic crystal. The dielectric material is an insulating material which does not allow the flow of electric current but it allows the propagation of EM wave. This filter has silicon rods in air type structure. Refractive index of silicon material is 3.59 and air has refractive index of 1.

2.2 Lattice Selection

Lattice or vector of lattice is the 'set of discrete points in a space which repeat in periodic manner'. On the basis of lattice vector the structure of crystal is further classified in two categories 'hexagonal' and 'square' lattice structure. The proposed filter lattice structure is square which easily allow light signal to propagate into the structure.

2.3 Lattice Unit Cell

The lattice unit cell is defined as "Any region in space which when translated maps out the entire function of the crystal". The filter structure has $r/a = 0.183$. The filter has radius $r = 0.099$ μm and lattice parameter 540 nm.

2.4 Defects

As photonic crystal is periodic crystal, whose band gap characteristics blocks the photon propagation into the crystal. To allow the propagation of light inside the structure periodicity of crystal is disturbed or some defect is introduced into the structure. For this, two linear waveguide and one resonator is introduced into the crystal structure. The shape of resonator is quasi square. For minimization of scattering inside the filter structure, scattering rods are introduced. The input wave is generated by the optical source which operates on the wavelengths of 1500 nm and 1567 nm. The optical detectors detect the filter output at ports B, C and D. Figures 2 and 3 represents the layouts of add/drop.

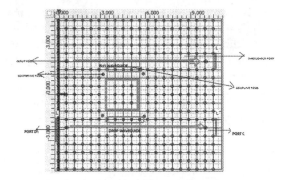

Fig. 2. 2D-PC based ADF layout.

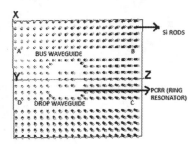

Fig. 3. 2D-PC based ADF layout.

3   Simulation Results

The complete simulation work of filter is performed using optiFDTD software. The transverse electric polarization mode is propagated into the structure as filter has rods in air type structure. In TE polarized wave the electric field is normal to the axis of rods. The theoretical concept of add/drop filter is also proved by simulation.

3.1   Band Gap (Width)

The photonic crystal band gap is the forbidden range of frequency which inhibits the traveling of photons into the crystal. To allow the flow of photons into the crystal, some defects are introduced into the crystal structure [10]. By using PWE band solver tool, band gap (PBG) of filter structure is calculated. The proposed filter has transverse band gap between 1252.60 to 1887.40 nm.

3.2   Field Distribution

The field distribution of ADF filter is simulated at on resonance wavelength and off-resonance wavelength. Figures 4 and 5 shows the 2D distributive field of a filter at

1500 nm off-resonance wavelength (add wavelength) and at 1567 nm on-resonance wavelength (drop wavelength) respectively.

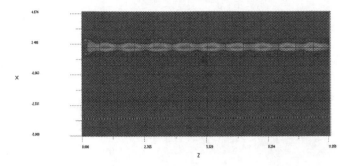

Fig. 4. 2D electric field distribution at 1500 nm.

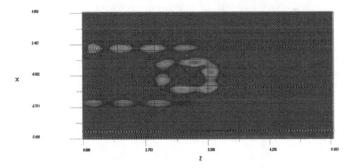

Fig. 5. 2D electric field distribution at 1567 nm.

The 3D distributive field of filter at off resonance wavelength $\lambda = 1500$ nm and on resonance wavelength at 1567 nm is shown in Figs. 6 and 7 respectively.

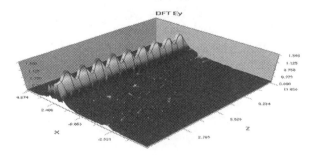

Fig. 6. 3D Electric field distribution of filter at 1500 nm.

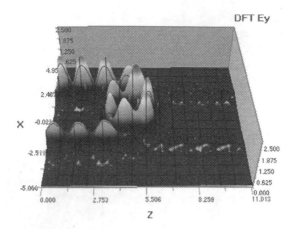

Fig. 7. 3D electric field distribution of filter at 1567 nm.

Figure 8 represents the transmission spectrum of add/drop filter. When no coupling is applied by the ring resonator i.e. at off resonance wavelength 1500 nm. At this wavelength the is negligible coupling exists between both the waveguide or resonance wavelength of resonator is off. The filter has resonant wavelength of 1.500 μm with the transmitted power 90.11%.

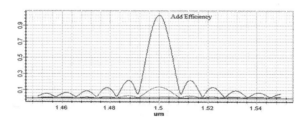

Fig. 8. Transmission spectra of filter at 1500 nm.

Figure 9 shows the transmission spectrum of filter at resonant wavelength. In this condition, the filter is tuned at resonance wavelength or resonator provide coupling between bus and drop waveguide. The on resonance wavelength (drop wavelength) of filter is 1567 nm and 95% is the drop efficiency of filter.

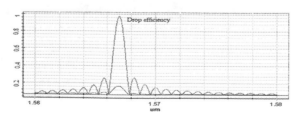

Fig. 9. Transmission spectra of the filter at 1567 nm.

4 Analysis of Filter

The analysis of filter is performed by using the simulation results of filter at different wavelengths. The filter is analyzed by calculating performance parameters. The performance parameters of filter are quality factor, coupling ratio, throughput power ratio etc. These are also calculated and listed below:

4.1 Quality Factor (Q)

The overall quality of the filter is calculated by this parameter. The ratio of resonance frequency (ω) to the full width at half maximum response ($\Delta\omega$) is called quality factor [11]. The symbol of this parameter is 'Q'.

$$Q = \omega / \Delta\omega$$

The designed filter has high q-factor for 1567 nm is 3134.

4.2 Coupling Ratio

It is the ratio of coupled power to the total power [12]. Its Mathematical expression is as follows:

$$\text{Coupling Ratio} = \frac{P_{Coupled}}{P_{Coupled} + P_{through\,put}}$$

The designed filter has coupling ratio at 1500 nm wavelength is 1.16 and at 1567 nm wavelength is 0.06.

4.3 Throughput Power Ratio

It is the ratio of throughput power to the total power [12]. The Mathematical expression is as follows:

$$\text{Throughput Power Ratio} = \frac{P_{throughput}}{P_{Coupled} + P_{through\,put}}$$

Throughput Power Ratio in dB is:

$$\text{Throughput Power Ratio} = 10\log \frac{P_{throughput}}{P_{Coupled} + P_{through\,put}}$$

The throughput power ratio of designed add/drop filter for off resonance wavelength and on resonance wavelength is 0.87, 0.93 respectively. The complete analysis of filter shows that the add/drop filter select the wavelength of 1500 nm and drop the wavelength of 1567 nm. This range of wavelength is mainly used in coarse wavelength division multiplexing system of optical metropolitan area network.

5   Conclusions

The designed optical add/drop filter is based on square shaped lattice with dielectric rods in air type structure of 2D photonic crystal. It is used for the filtration of wavelengths. The layout of filter is designed by introducing two line defects which are coupled with the resonator. The distance between two rods is a = 0.54 μm and the r/a is 0.183. The size of filter is very compact i.e. 11.1 × 10 μm². It is analyzed that at off resonance wavelength of the filter 1500 nm with transmission efficiency or add efficiency is 90.11% and in the presence of resonance (at on resonance wavelength), the 1567 nm wavelength and drop efficiency is 95%. Filter has very high quality factor of 3134 with coupling ratio 1.16 (for off resonance wavelength) and 0.06 (for on resonance wavelength) respectively.

References

1. Joannopoulos, J.D.: Photonic Crystals Molding the Flow of Light, 2nd edn. Princeton University of Press, Princeton (2008)
2. Robinson, S., Nakkeeran, R.: Add-drop filter for ITU-T G.694.2 CWDM systems. In: IEEE Conference (2011)
3. Park, D., Sangin, K., Ikmo, P., Hanjo, L.: Higher order optical resonant filter based on coupled defect resonator in photonic crystal. J. Lightwave Technol. 23(5), 1923–1928 (2005)
4. Kim, H.S., Han, Y.R., Hong, G.P., Guk, H.K., Yong, S.C., Yong, H.L., Jeong, S.K.: Two-dimensional photonic crystal hexagonal waveguide ring laser. J. Appl. Phys. Lett. 81(14), 2499–2501 (2002)
5. Juan, J.V.O., Masatoshi, T., Kenichi, K.: Photonic add-drop filter based on integrated photonic crystal structures. IEEE J. Quant. Electron. 16(1), 332–337 (2010)
6. Qiang, Z., Zhou, W.: Optical add-drop filters based on photonic crystal ring resonators. J. Opt. Express 15, 1823–1831 (2007)
7. Monifi, F., Djavid, M., Ghaffari, A., Abrishamian, M.S.: A new broadband photonic crystal add-drop filter. J. Appl. Sci. 8, 2178–2182 (2008)
8. Mohammad, R.R., Mohammd, A.M.B.: New design of channel drop filter by triangular photonic crystal. J. Electr. Comput. Eng. 3, 73–77 (2013)
9. Bendjelloul, R., Bouchemat, T., Bouchemat, M., Benmerkhi, A.: New design of T-shaped channel drop filter based on photonic crystal ring resonator. J. Nanosci. Nanotechnol. 6, 13–17 (2016)
10. Yasuhide, T.: Photonic crystal waveguide based on 2-D photonic crystal with absolute photonic band gap. In: IEEE Photonics Technology Letters, vol. 18, no. 22, 15 November 2014
11. Upadhyay, S., Kalyani, V.L., Charan, C.P.: Designing and optimization of nano ring resonator based photonic pressure sensor. Int. Conf. ICT Sustain. Dev. 408, 269–278 (2016)
12. Djavid, M., Monifi, F., Ghaffari, A., Abrishamian, M.S.: A new broadband l-shaped bend based on photonic crystal ring resonators. In: Progress in Electromagnetic Research Symposium, 24–28 March 2008

Object Localization Analysis Using BLE: Survey

Hrushikesh Zadgaonkar[✉] and Manoj Chandak

Department of Computer Science and Engineering,
Ramdeobaba College of Engineering and Management, Nagpur, 440013, Maharashtra, India
hzadgaonkar@gmail.com, chandakmb@gmail.com

Abstract. The paper provides wide range survey of techniques, methodologies and systems for Object localization in indoor environment space using BLE (Bluetooth Low Energy) technology. It also presents study to track moving smart objects and provides their comparison based on factors such as privacy, accuracy, and location type. One important problem in object localization using Bluetooth is to identify the position of BLE tags and produce accurate location results using certain algorithms. In this survey, theft prominent research directions are categorized, analyzed and discussed.

Keywords: Object localization · Bluetooth · Indoor localization · Tracking · RSSI

1 Introduction

Bluetooth Low Energy (BLE, called as Bluetooth Smart) is a technology focuses on to provide applications in the unit of beacons, healthcare, fitness, security and home automation industries etc.

For this survey, we would consider case to find location of BLE tag using Object Localization. Most of the new mobile devices launched in the market consist of GPS chip. We know that GPS (Global Positioning System) works in open space and not useful in indoor environment because a variety of object/wall barriers and interference sources make it difficult for the device to pinpoint device/object location accurately. To overcome such limitation and provide solutions for device location inside, researchers have been working over the past years to provide the optimal solution. Though, no standard procedure has been identified for indoor positioning, but the research has provided multiple alternatives in this domain [4].

The object localization has drawn great attention recently in the field of Indoor Positioning. The main goal of the research in this space is to enhance accuracy of object location. The terminology referred for calculation of the location of smart objects in indoor space is called as Location of things. With location accuracy on one side, factors like super easy deployment, configuration, complexity, cost, fall back mechanism and the ability to get the desired accuracy in certain areas are of utmost importance.

In this survey, we focus on with BLE technology which is used to transmit data over shorter distances. BLE also has very low energy consumption and plus less cost. As

© Springer Nature Singapore Pte Ltd. 2016
A. Unal et al. (Eds.): SmartCom 2016, CCIS 628, pp. 47–53, 2016.
DOI: 10.1007/978-981-10-3433-6_6

transmitters, there are many BLE tags (chips) available in the market by various vendors [9].

To find a location of object is not a recent problem. Over the past several years, researchers have tried lot of ways to find a generic process for location of the object. In current scenario, there are lots of approaches using different technologies to solve this issue. However, some of them are identical for certain contexts. One of the old and very common approaches is to track the smart objects and their motion in a video sequence using a camera. The vision-based techniques are not ideal for mobility due to lot of reasons. At first, the target object might not be visible due to physical barriers but it may be very close to the people. Secondly, the techniques used require expensive computation which is not recommended for a mobile device [7].

The paper is organized into the following sections: motivation, technical approaches, techniques used for object localization, methodologies, applications, conclusion and references.

2   Motivation

There are several reasons behind Bluetooth to be ideal for indoor environment system over other technologies:

2.1   Bluetooth Characteristics Suit Indoor Environment

- Form factor
- Battery
- Direct signal strength measurement
- Price
- Robust
- RSSI directly proportional to signal strength i.e. distance of tag from receiving device
- Technology available on most of the devices

2.2   Indoor Localization System Is Challenging

- GPS does not work in indoor space
- Infrastructure would be required
- To gain reliable location indoor with sufficient reliability

2.3   Indoor Localization Enables Location-Aware Services

- To track objects with the BLE chips
- To track mobile device in indoor space

2.4 Existing Solutions Require Changes on Mobile

- Dedicated hardware for phase measurement
- Calibration required for RSSI value measurements

2.5 Bluetooth Indoor Localization System with Approximate 1 m Accuracy

- Localization for any Bluetooth enabled device
- Localization for any BLE tag in smaller space

3 Advances in Technology

The companies likes Google and Apple have introduced BLE into their smart devices which have brought a revolution in indoor localization and navigation systems. Apple launched iBeacon with iOS7 to locate the beacons/objects inside malls, buildings and Google introduced Eddystone recently to fight against iBeacon. A setup is required for any beacon to make it available for all iPhone users to navigate with. It uses very little energy and provides considerable signal strength. It is lightweight and portable also.

Also, BLE support introduced in Android as well but it was not as advanced as far as Apple Technology. In the recent versions of Android, Google has introduced native stable APIs for BLE enabled devices. Google has brought Eddystone to give a strong competition to Apple iBeacon.

4 Object Localization Techniques

The core for most of the localization techniques depends on the run time measurement of various factors such as distance, angle or distance difference. These factors can be used to combine results to find the actual location of smart object in indoor environment.

There are three core techniques for location calculation and estimation. They are as follows:

1. Proximity method helps to find the target object location w.r.t location of the known objects. Broadcast node sends a signal to the object and the node location or identification of the symbolic cell provides the target location
2. Triangulation method determines the location of the point by measuring angles from it to known end nodes at either end of the fixed baseline. It uses trigonometry, geometry and does not depend on directly measuring distances to the point
3. Trilateration method determines the location of the point by measuring the distance with the help of geometrical figures like circle, rectangle and spheres [2]

The In-door tracking systems differ in parameters such as scope, precision and accuracy. They also vary based on the location type like symbolic, geometric and cost. The desired location is declared as accurate if it is relatively same as target object location.

The way to track moving indoor elements can be done either in 2D, 3D space or using different levels like floor, open area etc. GPS and cellular systems are mostly used to find location in open space, maybe whole earth whereas indoor localization systems determine location of the target object in terms of cell identifiers, buildings, room no etc. It is logical to say that there is an infrastructure which is not available in the open area but can be brought into indoor space [8].

5   Methodologies

Now-a-days, the research for indoor localization discusses BLE technology as it is present in all the mobile devices in the market. Thus, there is no additional cost, effort associated with it. The goal of the system is to provide a mobile solution to help everyone find their important belongings without spending much money on costly infrastructure [6].

The second most important part is that the environment setup should be easy for any person without any knowledge. Thirdly, the technology should be available to all users owning a smart device. The indoor positioning systems using BLE consists of the BLE tags which are attached to any objects which need to be tracked inside room, building [5] (Fig. 1).

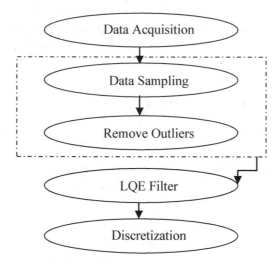

Fig. 1. Data Filter Process. This shows a figure consisting of different steps to purify data for object localization techniques for finding accurate location.

This process would focus on the core components required to find the location of the smart object in indoor space. They are as follows:

5.1 RSSI Data Collection

The BLE tags broadcast data to the receivers. The data is in terms of RSSI value. This raw is received by receiver on mobile device and used to estimate distance between the tag and mobile [1].

5.2 Data Sampling

The Bluetooth signal RSSI value is not quite stable at this stage to be only measurement factor for location estimation. The data received from tags provides various measurements of RSSI signals for the exact distance between emitter and the receiver device. Therefore, to reduce the noise and attenuate the extreme thresholds present in the measurements, sampling of the group of measurements is done to calculate distance.

5.3 Remove Outliers

Since the signal values are not very stable because of interferences, the outliers should be eliminated from the final results. These are removed with the help of Chebyshev Outlier Detection algorithm. The distinct values inside the boundary are finalized and then mean value is calculated.

5.4 LQE Filter

Various filter techniques such as the Kalman filter [3] used to estimate the mean value in a better way, which is to provide stable signal.

5.5 Discretization

The last step of the process is to find approx. distance from a predefined set.

An efficient way to handle BLE based tags (attached to objects) using smartphone based mobile application is proposed. There are different tags of same vendor attached to objects. The application discovers the BLE tags and establishes a connection with them. Once the successful connection has been established, it then receives different RSSI values from tags using GATT based profile. Please note that there is one-to-many relationship between application and BLE tags.

6 Applications

The proposed research would be great help in many use cases (applications) like quickly and intuitively locate objects with unprecedented precision at home, office, buildings and any other indoor places. The proposed system can also be used in the outdoor environment only when the objects with tags are placed in the Bluetooth range (small area) but outdoor localization is mostly dominated by GPS as there is no trouble of LOC.

BLE has many use cases which result in applications like finding lost car keys (attached with BLE tag) or find lost wallet inside room etc. This can also be used in navigation inside big buildings, malls etc. as a visitor navigation guide.

To provide advertisements to the consumers inside mall, BLE beacons can be widely used. Once the consumer comes near shop inside a mall, he/she will receive notifications about new offers.

7   Conclusions

Most of the critical elements in Indoor positioning based on BLE technology have been surveyed based on categories in positioning methods. The main aim was to evaluate Bluetooth technology for sustainability and applicability for indoor localization.

The approach can be considered to provide an accuracy of a few meters with the help of high precision. This is quite helpful for navigation and tracking of people and their belongings. With the help of RF properties, the response time has been tremendous. The simplicity in deployment is achieved using low cost Bluetooth chips, with keeping in mind that chips run for years on batteries. With the pros, there were couple of cons were also observed in the process of evaluation which would play a major role in the deployment of the system. The correlation between RSSI parameter and distance is not suitable due to noise issues. This problem can be minimized by characteristic based approaches.

RSSI sensitivity results in low robustness because of the changes in the environment. The RSSI signal values are not sufficient to calculate the distance between BLE tag and mobile device. This is because there are different interferences present in the environment like Wi-Fi, other radio signals which obstruct the RSSI signal and create noise Study concludes that BLE smart provides huge bonus for indoor localization in terms of cost and deployment complexity. Also, the response time is faster with help of flexible infrastructure, and support as well as efficient power consumption makes it way better.

BLE is an alternative to technologies which are generally used for navigation, such as Wi-Fi or GPS. It has huge opportunities with the help of several use cases to develop applications. The key players in Telecom and Media domain are rapidly involving the usage of BLE, and it won't take much time before 100% support is available for all smart devices. Once this happens, object localization and navigation will be one of the exciting use cases of BLE.

References

1. Pei, L., et al.: Using inquiry-based bluetooth RSSI probability distributions for indoor positioning. J. Glob. Positioning Syst. **9**(2), 122–130 (2010)
2. Subhan, F., Hasbullah, H., Rozyyev, A., Bakhsh, S.T.: Indoor positioning in bluetooth networks using fingerprinting and lateration approach. In: International Conference on Information Science and Applications, April 2011
3. Kalman, R.E.: A new approach to linear filtering and prediction problems. Trans. ASME J. Basic Eng. **82**, 35–45 (1960)

4. Schwarz, D., Schwarz, M., Stuckler, J., Behnke, S.: Cosero, find my keys! object localization and retrieval using bluetooth low energy tags. In: Robocop International Symposium, July 2014
5. Ionescu, G., Martınez de la Osa, C., Deriaz, M.: Improving Distance Estimation in Object Localisation with Bluetooth Low Energy, Institute of Services Science (2014)
6. Stojanović, D.H., Stojanović, N.M.: Indoor localization and tracking: methods, technologies and research challenges. Autom. Control Robot. **13**(1), 57–72 (2014)
7. Kim, E.: DeepBLE - Localized navigation using Low Energy Bluetooth, Department of CIS - Senior Design 2013–2014
8. Liu, H., Darabi, H., Banerjee, P., Liu, J.: Survey of wireless indoor positioning techniques and systems. IEEE Trans. Syst. Man Cybern. Part C Appl. Rev. **37**(6), 1067–1080 (2007)
9. Hansen, R., Wind, R., Jensen, C.S., Thomsen, B.: Algorithmic strategies for adapting to environmental changes in 802.11 location fingerprinting. In: Proceedings of International Conference on Indoor Positioning and Indoor Navigation, Zurich, Switzerland, pp. 1–10 (2010)

An Improved Image Compression Technique Using Huffman Coding and FFT

Rachit Patel$^{(\boxtimes)}$, Sapna Katiyar, and Khushboo Arora

ABES-Institute of Technology, Ghaziabad, U.P., India
rachit0508lgece@gmail.com,
arora.khushil9@gmail.com,
sapna_katiyar@yahoo.com

Abstract. Huffman coding and Fourier Transform technique are the basic technique used in image compression. Fourier transform is very powerful technique compared to Huffman coding because Fourier transform has ability to use in multiorders. The purpose of this paper is to compressed digital images using Huffman coding and Fast Fourier Transform and compare the results of both techniques. In calculation of parameters Matlab tool required. These techniques are compared with respect to various parameters such as mean square error (MSE), Peak signal to noise ratio (PSNR), Compression ratio (CR) and Bits per pixel (BPP) for the various input image of different size and it involves the new method of splitting or dividing an input image into equal rows & columns and at final stage sum of all individual compressed images.

Keywords: Image compression · Matlab · Huffman coding · Fast Fourier Transform (FFT) · PSNR · MSE · CR · BPP

1 Introduction

Compression of images is a very useful application for saving the storage data. Main motive of compression is to diminish superfluity of the image data in order to make storage or transit of data more efficient. Compression basically means diminish or removing the unwanted information or data in the image which only lead to the enhancement of memory space requirement without affecting quality of image [1]. The only way to say that, particular image compression technique is better by calculating the time taken to complete the processing i.e. compression speed which will depend upon the speed of the processor. Image compression is used in minimization of bits from images [2]. Aim of compression is to minimize redundant bits from image so that it can be store on low space or share with high efficiency. There are two type of image compression. First one lossy and second one is lossless. Lossless compression is applied for artificial images like technical drawings, icons or comics. In lossy compression low bit rate uses. Lossless compression [1] method may be used for image scans made for archival purposes. Lossy methods are useful in case of natural images like photos in applications. Fourier Transform can also use for compression. Block diagram of compression process can be shown in Fig. 1 [3]. Quantization is the process reduction in noise which makes the digital images have superior noise performance.

© Springer Nature Singapore Pte Ltd. 2016
A. Unal et al. (Eds.): SmartCom 2016, CCIS 628, pp. 54–61, 2016.
DOI: 10.1007/978-981-10-3433-6_7

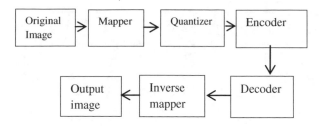

Fig. 1. Image compression process

2 Huffman Coding Algorithm

Huffman coding is a method for data compression and it is independent of data type. Image compression technique basically divided into two parts i.e. lossy technique and lossless technique [2]. Coding process begins by collecting all the probabilities for particular symbols in descending order [4]. The process starts from bottom and make a tree. At every leaf of tree, symbols are present. The process follows in steps. In each step, two probabilities are comparing and smallest one is selected. Selected probability is added to top of the tree. Selected probability deleted from the list. The process goes on until all the probabilities have been selected. In this paper the Huffman technique will be accomplished or applied after breaking the image into small parts (rows and columns) and apply this technique to each part [3].

3 Fast Fourier Transform

Fourier Transform is mathematical tool that use to convert one domain signal into other domain. Fourier Transform convert time domain signals in to frequency domain signals and Inverse Fourier Transform converts frequency domain signals to time domain signals [5]. FFT is an advance version of Discrete Fourier Transform (DFT) [5, 6]. It performs similar function in a better way within less time [7, 8]. DFT is highly recommended in frequency study because its convert a complex discrete time signal into simple discrete time frequency signal [7]. We can easily analyse the discrete nature of FFT with the help of Matlab or in real-time. With the help of FFT, N-point DFT is easily calculated with complexity of $O(N \log N)$ [9].

$$P^{(N)}Q = P_0^{\left(\frac{N}{2}\right)}(Q) + e^{-\frac{j2\pi k}{N}} P_1^{\frac{N}{2}}(Q)$$

where $P_0^{\left(\frac{N}{2}\right)}(Q)$ is $\left(\frac{N}{2}\right)$ point DFT for even and $P_1^{\frac{N}{2}}(Q)$ is point $\left(\frac{N}{2}\right)$ DFT of odd-numbered samples of $p(n)$. FFT is only applicable for the integer, means the value of N should be integer [8, 9] (Fig. 2).

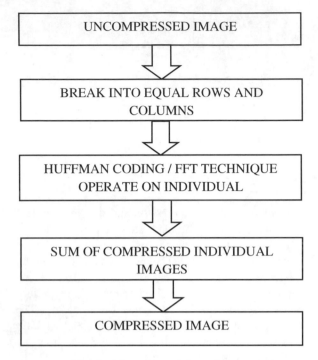

Fig. 2. Flow chart of the technique used

4 Image Quality Parameters

There are four major important parameters measure between uncompressed image and compressed image, these are following-

A. **Compression Ratio (CR)**

It is basically defined as ratio of size of uncompressed image and compressed image [1]. It is given as-

$$\text{Compression Ratio} = \frac{Size \text{ of uncompressed image}}{Size \text{ of compressed image}} = \frac{D1}{D2}$$

B. **Mean Square Error (MSE)**

It is defined as squared difference between an uncompressed and compressed image. It is given as-

$$\text{MSE} = \frac{1}{RC} \sum_{a=0}^{R-1} \sum_{b=0}^{C-1} [h'(a, b) - h(a, b)]^2$$

Where R is row and C is column $h'(a, b)$ the function of is compressed image and $h(a, b)$ is function of uncompressed image.

C. Peak Signal to Noise Ratio (PSNR)

PSNR means how much noise contains an output signal. It is mathematically expressed in logarithmic form. There exist a direct relationship between image size and PSNR.

$$PSNR = 10\log_{10}\left[\frac{R \times C}{MSE^2}\right] dB$$

D. Bits per Pixel (BPP)

It is given as-

$$BPP = \frac{\text{bits in compressed image}}{\text{pixel in the image}}$$

5 Mathematical Analysis

The complete M × M digital image can be given in the following compact matrix form where t(r, s) is the digital image, each of this matrix arrays is called an image pixel.

$$t(r, s) = \begin{bmatrix} k_{0,0} & k_{0,1} & \cdots & k_{0,M-1} \\ k_{1,0} & k_{1,1} & \cdots & k_{1,M-1} \\ \vdots & \vdots & & \vdots \\ k_{M-1,0} & k_{M-1,1} & \cdots & k_{M-1,M-1} \end{bmatrix}$$

this digital image $t(r, s)$ is break into a set of non-overlapping four sub images [1], i.e. two row and two column this can be represented as –

$$t(r, s) = \begin{bmatrix} t_1(r, s) & t_2(r, s) \\ t_3(r, s) & t_4(r, s) \end{bmatrix}$$

$$t(r, s) = t_1(r, s) + t_2(r, s) + t_3(r, s) + t_4(r, s)$$

these $t_1(r, s)$, $t_2(r, s)$, $t_3(r, s)$, $t_4(r, s)$ are the sub-matrix of original image after applying Huffman coding/FFT technique on these sub-matrix they gives $t'_1(r, s), t'_2(r, s), t'_3(r, s),$ $t'_4(r, s)$ respectively. The compressed image can be obtain by adding these $t'_1(r, s),$ $t'_2(r, s), t'_3(r, s), t'_4(r, s)$ matrixes.

6 Results Analysis

In this paper the author calculate different image quality parameters i.e. CR, PSNR, MSE and BPP in order to make a conceptual difference between Huffman and FFT and determine which will provide better result by analysing the above listed parameters. These parameters are calculated for 256×256, 512×512 of three images and the results are shows in the tables to the corresponding image.

A. **Original Images**
See Fig. 3

Fig. 3. Original image

B. **Compressed Images**

The compressed image can be obtain by adding these $t'_1(r,s), t'_2(r,s), t'_3(r,s)$, $h'_4(x,y)$ matrixes, it can be given as

$$t'(r,s) = t'_1(r,s) + t'_2(r,s) + t'_3(r,s) + t'_4(r,s)$$

By Huffman Coding
See Figs. 4 and 5

Fig. 4. Output image of 256×256

Fig. 5. Output image of 512×512

By FFT
See Figs. 6, 7, 8 and Tables 1, 2

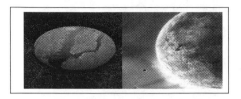

Fig. 6. Output image of 256 × 256

Fig. 7. Output image of 512 × 512

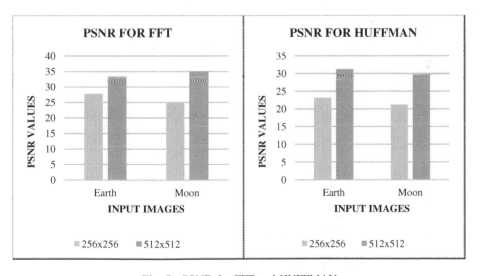

Fig. 8. PSNR for FFT and HUFFMAN

Table 1. Parameters

For earth image			For moon image	
Algorithm	Huffman		Huffman	
Resolution	256×256	512×512	256×256	512×512
CR	6.98	9.02	7.78	8.59
PSNR	23.09	31.22	21.19	29.48
MSE	18.34	14.17	20.34	17.32
BPP	2.44	1.98	2.35	2

Table 2. Parameters

For earth image			For moon image	
Algorithm	FFT		FFT	
Resolution	256×256	512×512	256×256	512×512
CR	8.75	9.53	9	9.07
PSNR	27.84	35.07	25.124	33.35
MSE	18.70	14.44	22.2052	17.45
BPP	2	1.62	2	1.75

7 Conclusion

Although the new method of splitting an image into different rows and columns will not only provide better results in image compression but also helpful for security purpose of the image transmission. Analysing the various image parameters as described in the tabular format after performing on the Matlab, it has been concluded that both compression technique will give good result, but FFT technique will provide better result than Huffman technique as seen from the image quality parameters tables. Hence it is clear that FFT technique for compression is much better than Huffman technique for image compression.

References

1. Gonzalea, R.C., Woods, R.E.: Digital Image Processing, 2nd edn. Prentice Hall, Upper Saddle River (2004)
2. Jain, A. k.: Image data compression: a review. In: Proceedings of IEEE, vol. 69, pp. 349–389 (1981)
3. Patel, R.: A fast and improved image compression technique using Huffman coding. In: IEEE WiSPNET 2016, Chennai
4. Chen, C.C.: On the selection of image compression algorithms. In: Pattern Recognition, Brisbane, Australia, August 1998
5. Sahnoun, K., Benabadji, N.: On-board satellite image compression using the Fourier transform and Huffman coding. In: WCCIT, pp. 1–5, June 2013

6. Kaushik, C.S.H., Elamaran, V.: A tutorial review on discrete Fourier transform with data compression application. In: ICGCCEE, pp. 1–6, March 2014
7. Zayed, A.I.: On the relationship between the Fourier and fractional Fourier transforms. IEEE Signal Process. Lett. **3**, 310–311 (1996)
8. Yusong, Y., Guangda, S., Chunmei, W., Qingyum, S.: Invertible integer FFT applied on lossless image compression. IEEE Robot. Intell. Syst. Signal Process. **2**, 1219–1223 (2003)
9. Van loan, C.: Transform computational framework for fast Fourier. In: SIAM (1992)

Comparison and Analysis of Cuckoo Search and Firefly Algorithm for Image Enhancement

Sapna Katiyar[✉], Rachit Patel, and Khushboo Arora

ABES-Institute of Technology, Ghaziabad, UP, India
sapna_katiyar@yahoo.com, rachit05081gece@gmail.com,
arora.khushi19@gmail.com

Abstract. Image enhancement is the process of highlighting some characteristics and carrying out certain features in original image for any problem oriented applications. Two domains in which image enhancement can be done is either in spatial domain and frequency domain with good SNR and keeping original colors of image intact. Metaheuristic approach provides a very effective search and optimization approach which gives good results in comparison to traditional approaches. In this paper author improve number of pixels, so that more details of image can be visualized easily and accurately. Two Metaheuristic algorithms, cuckoo search and firefly algorithms are applied here to find out optimal solution which gives peak performance. Experimental results of both the algorithms are tabulated and compared, which shows that firefly algorithm gives better performance as compared to cuckoo search algorithm in terms of robustness, fitness function and convergence rate. Some hybridization of metaheuristic algorithms can also be applied to improve performance.

Keywords: Image enhancement · Image processing · Metaheuristic · Fitness function · Peak signal to noise ratio (PSNR) · Firefly algorithm (FA) · Cuckoo search (CS)

1 Introduction

Main purpose of image enhancement to increase subjective quality parameters of image. This process is very simple and used to recover the image which is more appropriate than original one and gives better information about image for any explicit application. Its applications are in various areas like medical imaging, remote sensing, satellite image processing, airborne imaging, fingerprint matching, IRIS matching, digital camera applications etc. [1].

For every different type of image, optimizing the parameters and approach is a very meticulous job therefore image enhancement becomes a complex optimization problem. This paper describes the various metaheuristic algorithms. Every optimization algorithms have its own characteristics and limitations. Its objective is to take up the advantages of respective search algorithm while avoiding and ignoring limitations.

© Springer Nature Singapore Pte Ltd. 2016
A. Unal et al. (Eds.): SmartCom 2016, CCIS 628, pp. 62–68, 2016.
DOI: 10.1007/978-981-10-3433-6_8

In literature, various metaheuristic algorithms have been proposed like Genetic Algorithms, Differential Evolution, Ant Colony Optimization Algorithm, Cuckoo Search, Honey Bee Algorithm, Particle Swarm Optimization etc. these algorithms are capable to obtain low error rate with high computation time [2]. Here a comparison between traditional technique and metaheuristic technique for image enhancement is done.

2 Techniques Used for Image Enhancement

The process of image enhancement is heuristic in nature and basically there are two major categories of image enhancement:

- Frequency domain: It actually works with Fourier transform of an image.
- Spatial domain: It is a procedure, which works directly on pixels of an image.

For an image, frequency domain based techniques can be directly applied on an image via Fourier Transform, Discrete Wavelet Transform (DWT), and Discrete Cosine Transform (DCT). Its advantage is less computation complexity, easy to manipulate the frequency component of an image etc. [3, 4]. The main drawback is that, it can not enhance all parts of image all together. Here new image is obtained by the convolution of an image through linear position invariant operator, and is given by:

$$n(x, y) = h(x, y) * m(x, y) \tag{1}$$

Where,
$m(x, y)$: Input image
$n(x, y)$: New image
$h(x, y)$: Linear position invariant operator

The main advantage of spatial domain based technique is- it is very simple in nature and can be easily applied to a number of real time applications. Its limitation is that generally it enhances the whole image in uniform manner which is actually not desirable in many cases. The process of spatial domain is written as [4, 5]:

$$n(u, v) = T[m(u, v)] \tag{2}$$

Here,
$m(u, v)$: Input Image
$n(u, v)$: Processed Image
T: An operator on m, which is defined for some neighborhood of (u, v)

There are various type of image enhancement techniques used in spatial domain, few of them are: histogram equalization, grey scale manipulation, contrast stretching, image negative, compression of dynamic range, improving quality parameters using logical and arithmetic operations [6].

Image Quality Metrics. Always it is required to quantify the features of any image; therefore metrics are used to compute the image quality. It is divided into two categories:

- Objective fidelity criteria: they provide equations which are used to quantify errors and characterize quality of image.
- Subjective fidelity criteria: they are not based on any metrics.

  MSE- Difference between estimator and estimated value.

$$MSE = \frac{1}{mn} \sum_{i=0}^{m-1} \sum_{j=0}^{n-1} \left[I(i,j) - (k(i,j)) \right]^2 \tag{3}$$

  PSNR- Ratio of possible power (max.) of a signal to power of corrupting noise.

  SNR- Ratio of power of a significant signal to power of surroundings noise or unwanted signal.

$$SNR = \frac{P_{signal}}{P_{noise}} \tag{4}$$

Where,
P: average power.
It is necessary that both signal and noise power must be calculated at the same points in any system. It is also required that it should be within the same system bandwidth.

3   Cuckoo Search

Yang and De, in the year 2009 have given thought of CS. Similar to other metaheuristic techniques, this one also kind of population based optimization approach. Cuckoo species have a tendency of putting their eggs in nest to other swarm birds. Cuckoos have a special characteristic, known as Egg Laying Space, is used by research scholars in many daily life applications. These birds either destroy the eggs or they leave their nest within specified space [7, 8].

The procedure of CS is a three step:

- For a particular time a cuckoo lays 1 egg and haphazardly dump its egg into any other chosen nest.
- For consequently generation, finest nest having best quality of eggs will take over.
- When total number of present host nest is fixed then egg laid by a cuckoo is exposed by host birth with likelihood.

```
Start
Objective Function, M(U),U= (U₁, U₂,........Uₐ)ᵀ
Create Initial Population of k host nest Uᵢ(i = 1, 2,
3,.......,k)
While (t<maximum generation) or (stop criterion)
Randomly select a cuckoo
Calculate its fitness value
Randomly select a value of nest among k (let us say, j)
If (Fᵢ>F ⱼ)
Then replace the selected value of j by new solution
End
Poorer nest will be discarded and new one will built
Update the best solution
Rank the resultant solutions and obtaining current best
value
End while
Post processing of results and then visualization
Stop
```

Pseudo code of applied CS

4   Firefly Algorithm (FA)

Xin-She Yang in year 2010 given idea about FA for encouraging metaheuristic algorithm. FA is actually based on the characteristics of firefly. Firefly is a category of insect which is produced by the process of bioluminescence. They are capable for producing short and rhythmic flashes. Firefly moves because of the light intensity, and this behavior is used to solve worldwide optimization problem. FA gives better performance as compared to other metaheuristic algorithms due to of its automatic subdivision and the capability of dealing with multimodality. Generally Firefly algorithm follows three rules [9]:

- Since these are unisex, so they will be attracted towards others irrespective of their sex.
- Basically a flashing firefly is fascinated toward other firefly if other is brighter but if both fireflies have same brightness then other will move haphazardly. Attractiveness varies according to light intensity.
- Using background of function, brightness can be determined.

Variation of light intensity with distance is defined by following formula:

$$I(r) = I_0 e^{-\gamma r^2} \tag{5}$$

Where,
I- Intensity of intensity
I_0- Original intensity of light
γ- Absorption coefficient of light
r- Distance of one firefly from other firefly
β represents attractiveness. And given by

$$\beta = \beta_0 e^{-\gamma r^2} \tag{6}$$

Where,

β_0- Attractiveness known at distance r = 0

Distance between any two fireflies is calculated by helping Cartesian distance:

$$r_{ij} = \left| x_i - x_j \right| = \sqrt{\sum_{k=1}^{d} (x_{i,k} - x_{j,k})^2} \tag{7}$$

If brightness of j is greater than i, then i will be attracted toward firefly j. This type of movement is defined be the following expression:

$$\Delta x_i = \beta^{0e^{-\gamma r^2_{ij}}\left(x_j^t - x_i^t\right)^2} + \alpha\varepsilon_i, \quad x_i^{t+1} + \Delta x_i \tag{8}$$

In above equation, the first term explains attraction, γ is the limiting factor (either value approaching to zero or it is too large). If γ is very small and approaches to zero ($\gamma \to 0$), then the attractiveness and brightness will be constant, $\beta = \beta_0$ but if γ s too large the attractiveness decreases and firefly moves randomly.

```
Start
    Objective Function: M(U), U= (U₁, U₂,........Ud) ;
Create an initial population of fireflies Uᵢ(i = 1, 2, 3... k)
Originate I and γ
While (t < maximum generation)
for i =  1:k
for j = 1:k
If (Iⱼ ˃ I ᵢ)

then I move towards j;
    Calculate the new value and update I;
End
Grade fireflies and determine best value;
End while
Post-processing of results and then visualization;
Stop
    Post-processing of results and then visualization;
Stop
            Pseudo code of applied FA
```

5   Results and Discussion

The results of image enhancement using cuckoo search algorithm and firefly algorithms have been presented for two images of bird and leaf. Here the objective is to increase the overall intensity of edge of image, therefore maximizing the number of pixels in edge. The mentioned algorithms are compared in terms of computation time to run algorithm, fitness value, computational time for image enhancement, SNR and PSNR. Figure 1 shows the original image as well as images obtained after applying cuckoo search and firefly algorithm.

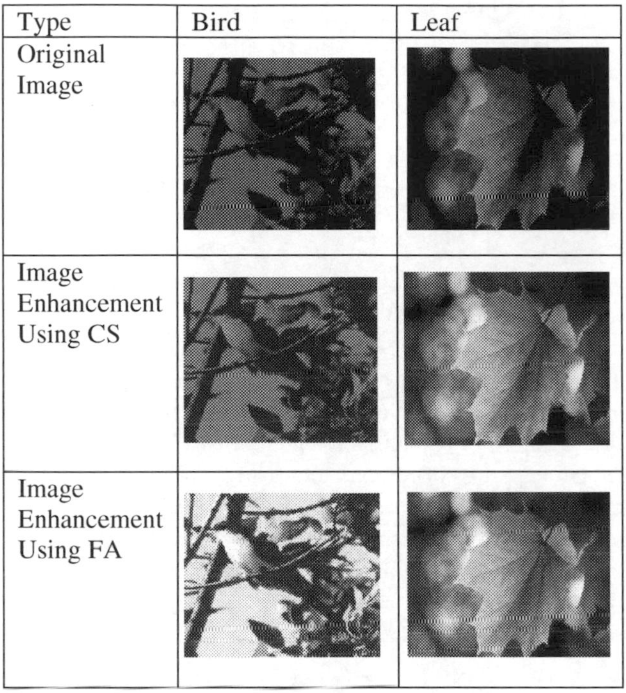

Fig. 1. Original image and enhanced images using CS and FA

After comparing all results author observed here, performance of Firefly Algorithm (FA) is much better in comparison Cuckoo Search (CS) because in case results obtained using Firefly algorithm, brightness and contrast level is appearing more visible with good PSNR. Image having higher number of pixels is viewed as more detailed content. Table 1 shows the various parameters obtained from both metaheuristic techniques and Table 2 shows the data obtained from both algorithms.

Table 1. Comparison of various parameters

Image	Fitness value		No. of edges detected		
	CS	FA	Original	CS	FA
Bird	102.320	121.911	2961	3099	3301
Leaf	119.712	126.048	1978	2203	2290

Table 2. Comparison of PSNR Value

Image	CS	FA
Bird	15.764	18.138
Leaf	16.387	18.751

Both the algorithms have been executed for 100 runs of times and below mentioned the values obtained for the simulation time for CS and FA:

CS: 169.78 s

FA: 150.49 s

Therefore after comparing all the data, it can be stated that FA gives better performance because it takes less simulation time as compared to CS.

6   Conclusion and Future Work

Author worked on performance of metaheuristic techniques like cuckoo search and firefly algorithms has been tabulated and compared for image enhancement. Two types of images have been taken for comparison and analysis. Result shows that firefly algorithms give much better results in comparison to cuckoo search; various parameters are evaluated and mentioned in table.

This approach can be extended to hybrid algorithms, which may consist of more than two search methodologies. Fine tuning of various parameters can also be done in terms of reducing maximum number of iterations. In future, optimization can also be accomplished with help of hyper heuristic.

REFERENCES

1. Hong, J.H., Cho, S.B., Cho, U.K.: A novel evolutionary approach to image enhancement filter design: method and applications. IEEE Trans. Syst. Man Cybern. **39**(6), 1446–1457 (2009)
2. Blum, C., Aguilera, M.J.B., Roli, A., Sampels, M. (eds.): Hybrid Metaheuristics: An Emerging Approach to Optimization. Studies in Computational Intelligence, vol. 114. Springer, Heidelberg (2008)
3. Yang, Q.: An adaptive image contrast enhancement based on differential evolution. In: 3rd International Congress on Image and Signal Processing, CISP (2010)
4. Agaian, S.S., Blair, S., Panetta, K.A.: Transform coefficient histogram-based image enhancement algorithms using contrast entropy. IEEE Trans. Image Process. **16**(3), 741–758 (2007)
5. Yang, F., Wu, J.: An improved image contrast enhancement in multiple peak image based on histogram equalization. In: IEEE ICCDA, vol. 1, pp. 346–349 (2010)
6. Rajavel, P.: Image dependent brightness preserving histogram equalization. IEEE Trans. Consum. Electron. **56**, 756–763 (2010)
7. Yang, X.S., Deb, S.: Cuckoo search via levy flights. In: IEEE (2009). ISBN 978-1-4244-5612-3
8. Rajabioun, R.: Cuckoo optimization algorithm. Appl. Soft Comput. **11**, 5508–5518 (2011)
9. Fister Jr., I., Yang, X.S., Fister, I., Brest, J.: Memetic firefly algorithm for combinatorial optimisation. In: Bio Inspired Optimisation Methods and Their Applications (BIOMA 2012), 24–25 May 2012, Bohinj, Slovenia, pp. 75–86 (2012)

An Exploration of Miscellaneous Palm Print Recognition Modalities

Mayank Mod[1]([✉]), Amit Mishra[1], Kusha Bhatt[2], Sonal Shah[2], Shivali Shah[2], and Urvashi Sanadhya[3]

[1] Shri Balaji College of Engineering and Technology, Jaipur, India
mayankmod@gmail.com, amitkumar.97@gmail.com
[2] Smarth College of Engineering and Technology, Himmatnagar, India
kusha.bhatt@gmail.com, shahsonal@gmail.com,
shah111990@gmail.com
[3] Dev Bhoomi Group of Institutes, Una, Himachal Pradesh, India
urvashi.udr@gmail.com

Abstract. Biometric recognition is a way of recognizing people on the basis of their behavioral and physiological characteristics. Palm print recognition is a very popular biometric recognition method because of its stable line features, need of low cost capturing device, low resolution imaging and user friendliness. Palm print recognition has been area of interest for many researchers since last many years due to the unique and stable characteristics present in a Palm. Researchers have suggested various preprocessing, feature extraction and matching techniques for recognition of a Palm print. This paper discusses various stages of Palm print recognition and research work performed in field of Palm Print recognition.

Keywords: Palm print · Principal component analysis · Gabor filter · K nearest neighbor

1 Introduction

Palm print recognition is a very useful method among biometric recognition techniques. A Palm print is a unique biometric feature which is believed to remain unchanged over most of the span of a human's life. Palm of a person has a number of features such as ridges and creases, principal lines, minutiae, delta points and geometric features and these features make a palm print unique. Various principal lines are made by flexing the hand and wrist. Palm print recognition is a low resolution, cost effective and non-intrusive recognition technique. It is mainly used in applications where access control is required. Palm print recognition techniques can be categorized in two ways. In the former approach images with lower resolution are used to extract texture, wrinkle and principal lines. In the latter approach which makes use of high resolution images, apart from wrinkles and principal lines, more detailed attributes such as singular points, minutiae and ridges are also extracted.

A palm print incorporates all the below mentioned properties which makes it a unique biometric feature with respect to an individual:

© Springer Nature Singapore Pte Ltd. 2016
A. Unal et al. (Eds.): SmartCom 2016, CCIS 628, pp. 69–76, 2016.
DOI: 10.1007/978-981-10-3433-6_9

- *Universality* : it demands that the every person must possess the characteristic
- *Uniqueness* : it indicates the capacity to differentiate a person from others
- *Permanence* : it measures the ability of a biometric to remain unchanged over time and retain its original form
- *Measurability* : it measures the ease of obtaining the biometric for recognition
- *Performance* : it measures the sturdiness, speed and accuracy of the technique used
- *User Acceptability* : majority of people must be interested in providing the characteristic
- *Circumvention* : ease with which the system can be compromised

Biometric systems which involve recognition by examining iris are costly and complex than Palm print recognition systems. Voice and face recognition techniques are easier to obtain but are not so reliable. Palm print recognition techniques however, are balanced as far as performance and cost issues are concerned (Fig. 1).

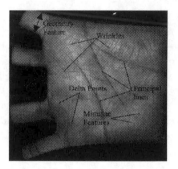

Fig. 1. Features of a Palm

1.1 Related Background Work

Some papers are reviewed for Palm print recognition and after reviewing them, aimed methodology is proposed:

KieYih et al. presented an easy and efficient approach according to which an image of a hand is captured through a camera which doesn't have any kind of lighting arrangement or pegs to secure its position. The image obtained is resized and enhanced and key points of hand and palm region are identified. Various feature extraction techniques such as SobelCode, Wavelet Transform energy and Discrete Cosine Transform energy [1] are used for extraction of feature vectors after the resizing of image is performed. Once the extraction of vectors is completed, a comparison is made by measuring the similarity and making use of back propagation neural network.

Khalifa et al. in this paper presents a palm print recognition system whose uniqueness lies in the manner in which extraction of features is performed in the system. Use of Gabor filter is done to analyze the texture of the palm print and double discrete wavelet transform and concurrence matrix techniques [2] for other feature extraction task. A vector machine is used as a classifier that compares the training and test images.

Puranik et al. proposes a palm print system which is not dependent on the camera type or its resolution. This system does not need the user to make any physical contact with the device used to capture the image of the palm. A camera with typically less resolution can be used to capture the image of the palm from a distance. After the image is acquired an efficient technique is used for palm print recognition. Use of PCA is made to convert a set of correlated variables into a bunch of non correlated variables which are called principal components [3].

Raut et al. presents a salient approach which suggests a method which makes use of image processing morphological [4] operation in image processing. In an image obtained from an image acquisition device various statistical attributes are computed and analyzed which can aid in recognition of a person. It explains biometric recognition of individual by making use of palm print image's statistical properties.

Kallibaddi et al. in this paper presents a way to enhance the performance of hand-geometry based identification system by incorporating palm print features. Palm print features and geometric properties of a hand are taken simultaneously from an image of a hand. Fourteen different hand-geometry distances are extricated from the hand image. Texture information from palm print is obtained using Symmelt-8 wavelet transform. Both palm print and hand geometry features are combined at feature level. Euclidean distance classifier [5] is used to perform the identification of a user.

Shashikala et al. suggests that the identification of a person can be done in an effective manner using palm print. It suggests palm print recognition whose basis is DCT, DWT and QPCA [6]. Contrast of a palm print image is improved through histogram equalization. LL, HH, HL and LH bands are generated by applying DWT on histogram equalized image. DCT coefficients are obtained by converting LL band using DCT. Feature enhancement is performed by application of QPCA on DCT coefficients. The database and palm print being tested are correlated by making use of Euclidean Distance (ED).

Kumar et al. propose a technique for palm print recognition in relation to biometric identification of an individual. The inner portion of a person's palm consists of a complicated random pattern of curves and lines. Such a random pattern can act as a unique feature of a person if some mathematical model can be created to express and compare it. In this paper the obtained palm print images are used to perform a mapping into Eigenspace [7] so that durable signature is obtained through various camera snaps of a palm which inculcates lighting and toner discrepancy. In order to perform identification, a signature is expressed by dimension features vector to minimize computing overhead. High recognition accuracies are obtained which indicates reliability of the feature.

Gayatri et al. suggests that Palm print verification is of great importance in e-commerce and security applications and serves as a fine tool for recognition of an individual. Due to its high user acceptance and reliability Palm print recognition has achieved high impact in comparison to the other biometric modalities. This paper proposes a palm print recognition method which makes use of a Gabor wavelet to extricate many features which are available on a palm print, by performing a feature level fusion and classification [8] using nearest neighbor approach. The features are obtained using wavelet entropy which consists of contrast, homogeneity, energy, and correlation. Nearest neighbor classifier is used to perform Palm print matching.

JinyuGuo et al. in his paper suggests a unique way of palmprint recognition obtained by a unique image from an individual. Firstly, a palm print image is converted to many small images, than most of the features vectors are obtained by five methods. They are Gabor transform, Fourier transform, DCT transform, statistics feature and local binary pattern (LBP) [9]. Features vector of a palm print is obtained by combining the features vector of all the sub-images. Lastly in the classification step a nearest neighbor classifier is used. For testing effectivity of this technique, an intense experimental investigation is performed using PolyUpalmprint database.

Seshikala et al. suggests that features extraction of a palm image acquired is done by making use of multi scale wavelet edge detection and a comparison of Sobel and Canny method is done with proposed algorithm. Poly-udatabase [10] is used in the experiment and performance of proposed algorithm is found to be better than the conventional method.

Malik et al. in this paper proposes an authentication system based on palm prints which improves the accurateness in order to promote it like a real time recognition system. Canny edge, Sobel Code operator and Phase Congruency techniques are implemented on the acquired images to obtain desired features. Palm prints feature vector is used to store the extracted Palm print features. The resulting feature vectors are compared using sliding window with Hamming Distance similarity measurement method [11]. Minimum Maximum Threshold Range (MMTR) technique is also described in this paper that aids in improving system precision by minimizing False Acceptance Rate.

Dai et al. presented a paper which suggests a recognition technique for palm prints with high-resolution. The main aspects of the proposed algorithm are: (1) Use of various features, namely orientation, minutiae, density and principal lines for palm print recognition to enhance the performance of the conventional algorithm. (2) Design and development of adaptive and quality based field estimation algorithm, which behaves better than the already existing algorithm in areas of regions with large number of creases. (3) Use of a novel fusion technique for identification application which behaves better than conventional methods, e.g. Neyman-Pearsonrule [12], weighted sum rule or SVMs. Besides, this paper elaborates the discriminative power of different feature combinations and suggests that density is useful for palm print recognition.

Han et al. Spatial relations and statistical texture information of local image regions are combined in the proposed method and discriminative texture features are represented by making use of a spatial enhanced histogram [13] generated for every image block.

A graph matching technique which utilizes structuring information of the image is used for similarity measurement.

Imtiaz et al. presents a multi-resolution feature extraction algorithm which makes use of spatial variations in the acquired image. Image is converted to small spatial modules and a recognition technique is evolved, which extricates histogram dependent wavelet features [14] from every module available locally. Due to this, feature dimensional characteristics are minimized drastically. Due to adjustment in the illumination characteristic and improved quality of extracted features is obtained.

Wang et al. presented this paper which enhances the Local Binary Pattern weighted Histogram technique and matches it with Dual-Tree Complex Wavelet Transform to suggest a DT-CWT based LBPWH [15] technique for palm print recognition and representation.

Sang et al. proposed that in order to introduce flexibility and improvement in accuracy of a touch-less palm- print recognition a sturdy palm print recognition system is proposed which is dependent on colored palm-print images. Use of skin-color thresholding and hand valley detection is proposed for extraction of the palm print. Palm print feature extraction is performed by the use of local binary pattern [16]. Finally, classification is performed using chi square statistic.

2   Proposed Palm Print Recognition System

A Palm print recognition system consists of following stages depicted in Fig. 2.

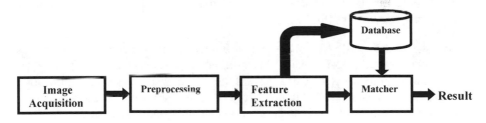

Fig. 2. Stages of a Palm print recognition system

Palm print Acquisition. Offline and online methods for Palm print image acquisition are present. In offline method Palm is painted with ink and pressed on paper and then that image is scanned. In online method various devices like cameras and scanners can be used to capture Palm prints. In the proposed system online method is used for Palm print image acquisition. Any image using a digital camera or scanner can be used (Fig. 3).

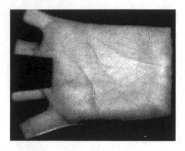 

Fig. 3. (a) Image of a Palm captured by a scanner (b) Scanner device

Preprocessing. Preprocessing is performed on the images acquired to reduce distortion, alignment and segmentation of the center. Various algorithms used for Preprocessing generally establish a coordinate system between fingers. Preprocessing basically comprises of following steps:

- Binarize the acquired image
- Boundary checking
- Key points identification
- Coordination system establishment
- Central part extraction

First and second steps are mostly common in majority of prevalent preprocessing algorithms. However in third step key points can be identified by either tangent based or bisector based approach. In the proposed system resizing of image is performed using the inbuilt resize function in MATLAB. After that RGB image is converted to gray scale image. After that in order to enhance contrast histogram equalization is carried out for adjusting image intensities (Fig. 4).

Feature Extraction. After preprocessing feature extraction phase appears. In this phase features of palm like principal lines, minutiae, texture, density map, singular points, orientation field etc. are extracted. All these features aid in either identification or verification of an individual. All the extracted features are stored in a database.

In the proposed system two dimensional Gabor filter and double density wavelet transform technique is used for extraction of texture feature information at different orientations and frequencies. Principal Component Analysis algorithm is used for dimensional reduction on Gabor palms.

Matching. After feature extraction matching phase appears. In the proposed system, the image acquired in the testing phase is matched against the image saved in the database. The system can perform either identification or verification. To perform identification many to one matching is done in which the matching of an input image is performed with all the templates present in the database, whereas to perform verification one to one matching is done in which matching of an input image is done with only those templates which a user claims to be his/her own. K Nearest Neighbor algorithm will be used for similarity measure.

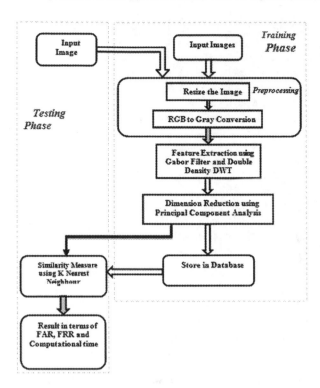

Fig. 4. Training and testing process for proposed Palm-print recognition

3   Conclusion

In this paper, we have discussed various Palm print Recognition techniques. The algorithms mentioned in this paper have their own advantages and disadvantages. After having an overview of available techniques a new system is proposed which involves the use of Gabor filter and K Nearest Neighbor algorithm. Implementation of the proposed system and analysis of the results obtained may be taken as the future scope of the paper. An improvement in performance in terms of False Acceptance Rate, False Rejection Rate, Equal Error Rate and Computation time is expected after implementation of the proposed technique.

References

1. Yih, E.W.K., Sainarayanan, G., Chekima, A.: Palm print based biometric system: a comparative study on discrete cosine transform energy, wavelet transform energy and SobelCode methods. Int. J. Biomed. Soft Comput. Human Sci. **14**(1), 11–19 (2009)
2. Khalifa, A.B., Rzouga, L., BenAmara, N.E.: Wavelet, gabor filters and co-occurrence matrix for palm print verification. Int. J. Image, Graph. Sig. Proc. (IJIGSP), **5**(8), June 2013. ISSN: 2074-9082

3. Puranik, A., Patil, R., Patil, V., Rane, M.: Touch less, camera based palm print recognition. Int. J. Appl. Res. Stud. (IJARS), **2**(4), April 2013. ISSN: 2278-9480
4. Raut, S.D., Humbe, V.T.: Biometric palm prints feature matching for person identification. Int. J. Mod. Educ. Comput. Sci. (IJMECS), **4**(11), December 2012. ISSN: 2075-0161
5. Kallibaddi, J.I., Hatture, S.M., Inamdar, S.R.: Hand image analysis for personal authentication. In: XI Biennial Conference of the International Biometric Society (Indian Region) on Computational Statistics and Bio-Sciences, March 2012
6. Shashikala, K.P., Raja, K.B.: Palm print identification based on DWT, DCT and QPCA. Int. J. Eng. Adv. Technol. (IJEAT), **1**(5), June 2012. ISSN: 2249 – 8958
7. Kumar, A., Parekh, R.: Palm print recognition in eigen-space. Int. J. Comput. Sci. Eng. (IJCSE) **4**(05), 788–794 (2012). ISSN : 0975-3397
8. Gayathri, R., Ramamoorthy, P.: Multifeature palm print recognition using feature level fusion. Int. J. Eng. Res. Appl. (IJERA) **2**(2), 1048–1054 (2012). ISSN: 2248-9622
9. Guo, J., Liu, Y., Yuan, W.: Palm print recognition using local information from a single image per person. J. Comput. Inf. Syst. **8**(8), 3199–3206 (2012). ISSN: 1553-9105
10. Seshikala, G., Kulkarni, U., Giriprasad, M.N.: Palm print feature extraction using multi scale wavelet edge detection method. Int. J. Adv. Res. Electr. Electron. Instrum. Eng., Issue 1, July 2012. ISSN: 2278 – 8875
11. Malik, J., Sainarayanan, G., Dahiya, R.: Personal authentication using palm print with sobel code, canny edge and phase congruency feature extraction method. ICTACT J. Image Video Process. **02**(03), February 2012. ISSN: 0976-9102
12. Dai, J., Zhou, J.: Multifeature-based high-resolution palm print recognition. IEEE Trans. Pattern Anal. Mach. Intell. **33**(5), 945–957 (2011). IEEE Biometrics Compendium, ISSN: 0162-8828
13. Han, Y., Tan, T., Sun, Z.: Palm print recognition based on directional features and graph matching. In: Advances in Biometrics Lecture Notes in Computer Science, vol. 4642, pp. 1164–1173. Springer (2007)
14. Imtiaz, H., Fattah, S.A.: A wavelet-based feature selection scheme for palm-print recognition. Int. J. Mod. Eng. Res. (IJMER) **1**(2), 278–287 (2011). ISSN: 2249-6645
15. Wang, Y., Ruan, Q.: Dual-Tree complex wavelet transform based local binary pattern weighted histogram method for palm print recognition. Comput. Inf. **28**, 299–318 (2009)
16. Sang, H., Ma, Y., Huang, J.: Robust palm print recognition base on touch-less color palm print images acquired. J. Sig. Inf. Process. 134–139 (2013)

Plugin for Instantaneous Web Page Rejuvenation and Translation

Shashi Pal Singh[1(✉)], Ajai Kumar[1], Hemant Darbari[1], and Nikita Maheshwari[2]

[1] AAI, Center for Development of Advanced Computing, Pune, India
shashipalsingh@gmail.com, {ajai,Darbari}@cdac.in
[2] Banasthali Vidyapith, Banasthali, India
nikita.mundra143@gmail.com

Abstract. This paper outlines the Plugin for various browsers for instant rejuvenation and translation of web pages into Indian languages. The websites with Hindi content are less than 0.1% of the total websites, similarly less than .01% for other Indian languages. While English content are more than 55% [13]. It is high time for realization to provide the information to the local uses into their local languages so, that they can take the advantage of various resource available on websites which would result in enhancement in communication and knowledge. The Plugin tool can be plugged in various browsers. On single clicks, the whole page gets translated and rebuild into the original format without losing any information and graphics, which makes it easy, convenient, and readable for the users. The methodologies used in our system are Extraction, Rebuilding and Translation Memory. Further, we will discuss the workflow among the processes and then concluded with experimental results that are obtained with this tool.

Keywords: Extraction · English to Hindi · Plugin · Rebuilding · Translation · Translation memory (TM)

1 Introduction

Translation is in existence since human wants to communicate with each other in their own language. At initial stage, the translator was a human being itself who knew both source and target language. After sometime, people start thinking to handle this problem with the help of computer based translators. Although, it was not as much efficient as a human being but work is still in progress to do so. The approaches like Statistical Machine Translation (SMT), Rule Based, Example Based, Dictionary Based etc. have been introduced for translation but each has its own advantages and disadvantages. Here, we are going to introduce a good and efficient approach for translation which is Translation Memory (TM). Translation Memory has evolved as an important area in the translation industry. It is widely used among translators but not much of the work has been done for Indian languages in comparison to other foreign languages. So, the main focus is to translate the English text into its corresponding Hindi text or Indian Languages.

© Springer Nature Singapore Pte Ltd. 2016
A. Unal et al. (Eds.): SmartCom 2016, CCIS 628, pp. 77–87, 2016.
DOI: 10.1007/978-981-10-3433-6_10

There are many translators that exist on web which can translate a web page. For example- Systran, Prompt, GTS Website Translator, Lucy KWIK Translator, Word lingo, Bing, and Google etc. But each translator has one or the other problem in it.

It is important to note, while translating a webpage, that the text content is not only the thing which is needed to be translated into target language. A webpage contains a lot more to be maintained like graphic, images, videos and other dynamic activities. If a translated page will look like same as it was originally then it will be more comfortable to read from the perspective of user. So, our concern is not only the translation but also the correct rebuilding of the webpage.

The complete process of extraction, rebuilding and translation is initiated by the extension. There is no specific reason to choose a particular web browser. The extension can be developed for any web browser. In this paper, we will discuss about web browser based extension, Extraction process, Rebuilding and Translation of the webpages. Further, the process flow among all these modules will be discussed.

2 Literature Review

2.1 Extension Plugin

The Extension is a Plugin, which is placed near the address bar and looks like a button. This extension can be made for any web browser for example- Chrome, Mozilla Firefox, Internet explorer, Safari etc. When this plugin button is clicked, the complete web page will be translated. There are some files which are related to make web browser extension plugin. Some of them are optional and some of them are compulsory. The files related to it are explained below [3, 4].

2.2 Manifest.json

The Manifest.json file is a very important file for making browser extension. This file tells web browser the important information about the extension like, the name of your extension, what kind of permission is needed, the icon image of the extension and the other files related to it etc. Every extension has a JSON-formatted manifest file. The name should be manifest.json otherwise it would not be recognized. There are many fields in this file. All these fields are not compulsory to be mentioned. It totally depends on the type of extension or on the application demand which you are developing.

2.3 Permission Block

Permission helps to limit the damage and protect by malware. Each permission can be either one of the list of known string example- http://www.google.com [3] or can be a match pattern example- "http://*/*", "https://*/*" that gives access to one or most hosts. For giving permission to each and every host you can mention "<all_urls >" in place of any known string or pattern. There are many field of permission. Some of them are given below-

```
"permissions": [
"tabs", "<all_urls>","http://*/*","https://*/*","background","notifications","downloads","history","location","active_tabs" ],
```

2.4   Browser Action Block

There are two types of actions when we make a browser extension –

1. Page Action
2. Browser Action

Page Action is not preferred when you want to make your extension to work for each and every page that your browser visits. For this browser action will be used. For Example- The RSS icon in the following screenshot represents a page action that allow you to subscribe the RSS feed for the current page [3, 4] (Fig. 1).

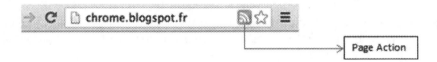

Fig. 1. Page action

In the following figure, the T-shaped icon, right of the address bar, is the icon for a browser action (Fig. 2).

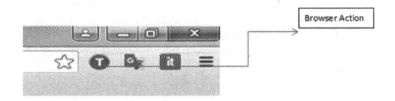

Fig. 2. Browser action

```
{  "name": " ",
   ...
"browser_action": {
"default_icon": {              // optional
},
     "default_title": " ",    // optional; shown in tooltip
     "default_popup": " "     // optional
   },     ...   }
```

2.5   Content Script

The content script [3, 4] is a JavaScript file that runs in the context of webpages. This means that the content script can interact with web pages that are currently open in the browser. JQuery is not necessarily required, but it makes the things easier.

```
"content_scripts": [ {
   "matches": [ "<all_urls>"   ],
   "js": [" "," "],
   "css": [" "]   }   ]
```

The 'matches' field tells Browser to inject Content.js file in every page open in the browser. If you want to inject this script to only some pages, we can use match patterns like-

["https://mail.google.com/*"] and [http://*/*] will match any http URL, but no other scheme like https sites.

A content script can access the current page, and is limited in the APIs it can access. For example, it can't listen the clicks on the browser action. So, a different type of script is needed to add to our extension that is 'background script', which has access to every Browser API but cannot access the current page.

So, the URL of the current page can be pull by content script, but this URL is needed to hand over, to the background script, to do something useful with it. In order to communicate, 'message passing' is done between background.js and content.js, which allows scripts to send and listen for messages. In this way content scripts and background scripts interact with each other.

2.6 Background Script

As we mentioned about the background script [3, 4] above in content script block, it is clear that it is an important part of extension and manifest file. The Browser API functions can only be used by background.js to listen the click on the browser action, so we'll have to add some more message passing since background.js can open the tab on browser, but can't grab the URL given in address bar. So for this, message passing is done between content.js and background.js. The Content.js file will grab the URL and pass it to Background.js for the further process.

```
{   "name": "My extension",
   ...
"background": {
   "scripts": [" "]
   "page": " "
}, ...}}
```

2.7 Translation Memory

Translation memory (TM) systems were available in the market in late 1990's commercially but the researches in this field have been in continuation since 1970's. There is a database that consists of existing translations which can be reused as a suggestion when translation is done.

Translation Memory (TM) technology belongs to CAT systems. It is used to providing a good precision translation. Basically, it is a database application that keeps record of previously translated units and reuse the existing if it is being repeated in future translations instead of translating the sentence from the scratch. It was believed that for translating monotonous type of texts, the translation memory could be better utilized. But other features incorporated make it useful for non-monotonous texts also.

"A multilingual text archive containing (segmented, aligned, parsed and classified) multilingual texts, allowing storage and retrieval of aligned multilingual text segments against various search conditions."

There are some benefits of Translation Memory which are-Consistency, Speed, Portability, Cost, Content Management. There are some limitations as well-Error can be propagated if misused and a memory is only as good as the maintenance it gets.

2.8   Jsoup Parser

Jsoup [10] is a Java HTML parser. It is a library for working with real-world HTML. It gives us a very convenient API which can extract and manipulate the data, using the best of DOM, CSS, and jQuery-like methods. Jsoup implements HTML5 specification, and parses HTML to the same DOM as modern browsers do.

2.9   Webpage Extraction

The source code of the web page can be downloaded via different-different methods. First method is via URL library of java and second method is via Parser. Here, we are taking Jsoup parser for parsing the HTML but we can't use it for downloading the source code of the webpage because of the drawback of Jsoup. Jsoup can't download the complete source code of the webpage. Sometimes, it leaves some tags or attributes of the tags at the time of downloading.

3   Proposed System

3.1   Brief Overview

The interface of our tool is an extension and a web browser. When, the user, who wants to translate the webpage, clicks on the extension button, and the source code of the webpage will be extracted. Each and Every tag that is present in the source code is parsed with the help of parser. The path of all the files (where these files are actually stored) present on that webpage is checked and modified according to the actual location of the file on the website's server. After that the complete webpage is traversed tag by tag and the text content present on the webpage is fetched from it. Then, these text strings are sent to the TM System for translation. Translation Memory is basically a database also called as TM base or Translation Memory database. TM base contains a bilingual pair of source and target language. Here the source language is English and Target Language is Hindi. There is also a concept of Term Base which is maintained to provide the translation of non-translatable English words (Fig. 3).

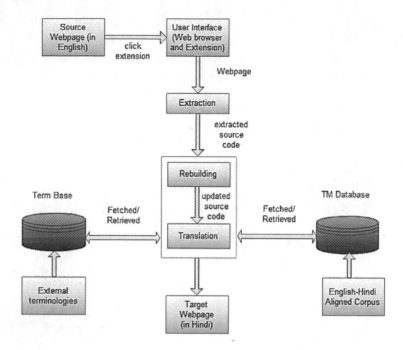

Fig. 3. System architecture

3.2 Extension

A web browser extension is a button near by the address bar of the web browser. It can be inside the address bar or outside the address bar depending on its action i.e. page action or browser action respectively. Page action is used for a particular webpage and browser action is used for many pages simultaneously open in the web browser. Here, we are opting 'browser action' to make this extension working for every webpage simultaneously open in web browser.

There are three basic files which are needed to develop an extension. These files are-Manifest.json, Background.js, and Content.js. Background.js file is needed because the click on the extension can only be listened by this file as it allows the web browser API's for example, chrome.* API in case of using Chrome browser while content.js can pull the URL of the webpage.

3.3 Extraction

When the user clicks on the extension button, the source code of the webpage is extracted by connecting with the URL of that webpage. There are some website which runs on https protocol which mandates that the communication can only be done via information provided in the certificate of that website then we need to download that certificate and import that certificate in the trustore, Default trustore java uses can be found in \Java\jdk1.6.0_29\jre\lib\security\cacerts, then if we retry to connect to the URL connection would be accepted.

3.4   Rebuilding

After the extraction phase, the source code of the webpage is parsed with the help of parser. Here, we are taking Jsoup parser (Version 1.8.3) [13] because Jsoup is better than other parser in web scraping. It can parse and clean the Html code like other parser but it can update the Html code as well.

The tags, which contains the path of any file (images, script, stylesheet, audio, video etc.), can be image tag, script tag, source tag, link tag, object tag, input tag, td tag, body tag, table tag, embed tag, meta tag, iframe tag, frame tag etc. These tags are required to be parsed. The path of the file, given in the source code, is updated, according to the absolute path of that file on the website's server, on which it actually exists. Further, the script tag, iframe tag and frame tag may contain the files which can itself have images, videos or any of the tag that are mentioned above. These are also needed to be handled in the same way as depicted above. The webpage can also contain some background images, imported CSS or scripting code which can contain images and other files. The parser can't parse these patterns. So, we need to make separate regular expression for each condition to detect these files and update their path. The path of the files is required to be updated because the tool is running on our server and the files are not present on our server.

Algorithm for Rebuilding:-

Input: - Click on the extension and **Output**: - Updated source code
Steps: -

1. Click on the extension.
2. Source code of the webpage will be downloaded.
3. Parse all the tags which have path of any file (ex- Images, scripts, stylesheets, video, audio).
4. Extract the source path of that file mentioned in one of the Tag's attribute.
5. Check whether we need to change the path or not.
6. If yes, then check the correct location of the file exist on the server, change the path according to that and put it back to the same position from where it was retrieved.
7. Make the regular expression for those Patterns which can't be parsed with the parser.
8. If the pattern exists then go to step 3 to 6.

The rebuilding of the webpage is a very important phase in webpage translation. It helps to maintain the webpage as it was before translation. A webpage may contain images, audio, video, stylesheets which gives it proper look and other dynamic activities. A user will feel comfortable in reading the webpage when it is in proper and managed format. So, only text based translation is not only the thing to be focused. Rebuilding of the webpage has to be focused too.

3.5   Translation

The complete source code of the web page is parsed on the basis of its opening and closing tags and the string between these tags are fetched and sent to the TM System to check its corresponding Hindi translation.

Algorithm for getting the text of the webpage-
   Input: - Updated source code and **Output**: - Source Language String for translation.
   Steps: -

1. Parse the source code on the basis of opening and closing tag.
2. Check whether the text exists between the last closing tag and next opening tag.
3. If yes, check whether the last tag was script tag or style tag.
4. If it was script tag or style tag then don't send that text string for translation.
5. Else send it for translation.

Algorithm for translation-
   Input: - Source Language String and **Output**: - Translated String in Target Language
   Steps: -

1. The text string is preprocessed. In which the text filtering and segmentation is done.
2. In segmentation process, if any delimiter is present in the string, which is sent for the translation, then split the string, on the basis of delimiters like ".", "?", "-", ":", ";", "!",
3. The hash code of each string is generated.
4. The generated hash code is matched with hash code stored in TM database.
5. If matched, return its corresponding Hindi
6. Otherwise, if number of tokens in the segment is <=7 then compute 2-grams, else if number of tokens in the segment is > 7 <=10 then compute 3-grams, else compute 4-grams. Each N-gram obtained is treated as a search token to fetch TM segments which contains that N-gram token so as to get useful results only by fetching hardly 100 to 1000 segments and reduce searching time [6].
7. Now that source segment that contains 50% unique tokens of query segment is only considered for matching thus reducing search space.
8. Now among them, names (using Named Entity Recognition), gender cases and other placeables like numbers, dates etc. are handled [8].
9. If considering B1 as the N-gram of the query segment and B2 as the N-gram of the TM source segment, apply Levenshtein algorithm.
10. If the value returned by the algorithm is either 0 or 1 then consider that N-gram in score computation else discard it. Increases the M (a variable) by 1 for each N-gram added.

Mathematically, the Levenshtein distance [11] between two strings a (Source string), b (Target String) is given by $Lev_{a, b} (i, j)$, which is the distance between the first "i" characters of "a" and the first "j" characters of "b".
   If $(a_i != b_j)$ then Cost function = 1
   If $(a_i == b_j)$ then Cost Function = 0
   If min $(i, j) = 0$,

$$\mathrm{Lev}_{a,\,b}(i,\,j) = \max(i,\,j) \tag{1}$$

Otherwise,

$$\mathrm{Lev}_{a,\,b}(i,\,j) = \min\{\mathrm{Lev}_{a,\,b}(i-1,\,j)+1,\ \mathrm{Lev}_{a,\,b}(i,\,j-1)+1,\ \mathrm{Lev}_{a,\,b}(i-1,\,j-1)+\mathrm{cost}\} \tag{2}$$

The advantage of Translation Memory is that it gives faster translation results comparative to other approaches. So the time taken in webpage translation is comparatively less and user doesn't need to wait more.

4 Result

There are so many tools for webpage translation like- Systran, Prompt, GTS Website Translator, Lucy KWIK Translator, Word lingo, Bing, and Google etc. But each translator has one or the other problem in it. Some can't translate in Indian Languages, some others cannot translate web pages based on https:// protocol and some don't rebuild the webpage correctly etc. So, this extension tool is made to overcome with some of these problems.

Total 155 webpages were tested by this extension tool. The result is only based on "How good rebuilding of a webpage can be done by this tool" The results are not calculated on the basis of quality of the translation. The webpages based on framework such as Joomla, WordPress etc. was taken. The webpages, either developed in HTML or HTML5 format, are considered too and it can also translate the https:// protocol based web page etc.

The following graph will show the results of this tool -

Testing is done using this tool and the results are obtained manually with human intervene for checking the result of rebuilding. Five parameters are decided to rank the rebuilding of the webpage. These parameters are- Excellent, Very Good, Average, Below Average and Poor. The webpage is put under the 'Excellent' category if there is no fault in the rebuilding of the webpage. If there are one or two images/video/audio missing then it is put in 'Very Good' category. If, more than two image/video/audio are missing or the content is not properly managed then it is put under 'Average' category. If almost nothing is present on the webpage after rebuilding or if the output is coming totally haphazard then it is put under 'Below Average' category and if the tool is unable

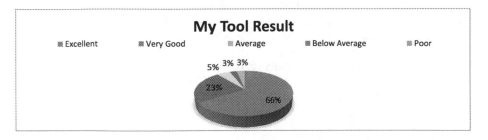

Fig. 4. TM translator tool result

to rebuild the webpage or giving nothing after rebuilding then it is put in 'Poor' category (Fig. 4).

On comparing the processing speed of other translation tools and this tool, we will see that this tool is little slow than other translation tools and sometimes, it also takes time to load the webpage which have heavy graphics.

5   Conclusion and Future Scope

Not much work has been done in the area of rebuilding and translation of a webpage for Indian Languages. So, we have developed an extension for performing this task which will extract the source code of the webpage, rebuild it and translate it. Jsoup parser is helping to parse the tags present in the source code and the advantage of using this parser has already been discussed. Total 155 webpages are tested by this extension tool and other translators. The final results of our tool are comparatively better. 66% of webpages are in 'Excellent' category when they are rebuilt with this tool, 23% are in 'Very Good' category, 5% are in 'Average' category, 2% are in 'Below Average' category and 2% are in 'Poor' category.

In Future, the enhancement can be done by finding out other different tags with their various attributes. And if they are necessary for helping in good rebuilding of webpage then they must be handled in the rebuilding process. The other thing which can be improved is the processing speed of rebuilding process which is slow in comparison of other translator. Also, the functionality of this tool can be extended to perform translation in other languages as well.

References

1. Srivastava, N., Singh, P., Chauhan, S., Singh, S.P., Kumar, A., Darbari, H.: Hindi-English translation memory systems. Int. J. Emerg. Trends Technol. Comput. Sci. (IJETTCS) (2014). AAI, Center for development of Advanced Computing, Pune, India
2. Joshi, N., Mathur, I.: Design of English-Hindi Translation Memory for Efficient Translation, Department of Computer Science, Banasthali Vidyapith University (2012)
3. https://developer.chrome.com/extensions/getstarted.html tutorial by Google Chrome. Accessed 23 Jan 2015
4. Berke-Williams, G.: A developer in San Francisco. https://robots.thoughtbot.com/how-to-make-a-chrome-extension. Accessed 23 Jan 2015
5. Somers*, H., Diaz**, G.F.: (UMIST, Manchester)* (Universidad de Sevilla)**, Translation Memory vs. Example-based MT – What's the difference? (2004)
6. Wołkowicz, J., Kulka, Z., Warsaw, V.K.: n-Gram-Based Approach to Composer Recognition, University of Technology Institute of Radioelectronic Nowowiejska 15/19, 00-665 Warszawa, Poland Dalhousie University Faculty of Computer Science, Canada (2008)
7. McTait*, K., Olohan**, M., Trujillo*, A.: A Building Blocks Approach to Translation Memory Centre for Computational Linguistics*, Centre for Translation Studies** Department of Language Engineering UMIST Manchester M60 1QD (1999)
8. Saha, S.K., Ghosh, P., Sarkar, S., Mitra.P.: Named Entity Recognition in Hindi using Maximum Entropy and Transliteration, Indian Institute of Technology, Kharagpur (2008)

9. Arthern, P.J.: Machine Translation and Computerized Terminology Systems a Translator's Viewpoint, Head of English Translation Division, Council of the European Communities, Brussels (1979)
10. http://jsoup.org/ tutorial by jsoup HTML parser © 2009 – 2015 Jonathan Hedley. Accessed 15 Feb 2016
11. Haldar, R., Mukhopadhyay, D.: Levenshtein Distance Technique in Dictionary Lookup Methods: An Improved Approach, Web Intelligence & Distributed Computing Research Lab Green Tower, C-9/1, Golf Green, Calcutta 700095, India (2011)
12. EAGLES Evaluation of Natural Language Processing System, Initial Survey on the Availability of Translation Memory Tools. Featurization: Design and function of translation memory. www.issco.unige.ch/research.projects/ewg95/node152.html
13. https://en.wikipedia.org/wiki/Languages_used_on_the_Internet. Accessed 23 Jan 2015
14. https://github.com/jhy/jsoup/. Accessed 23 Jan 2015

"Part of Speech Tagging – A Corpus Based Approach"

S. Rashmi[(✉)] and M. Hanumanthappa

Department of Computer Science and Applications,
Bangalore University, Bangalore 560056, India
{rashmi.karthik123, hanu6572}@bub.ernet.in

Abstract. POS tagging, an ideal way to augment a corpus is an imperative abstraction for text mining. However with an increase in the amount of linguistic errors and distinctive fashion of language ambiguities, the data filtered by POS tagging is noisier. In this paper, probabilistic tagging and tagging based on Markov models are combined to estimate the association probabilities. Based on this combined approach, error estimation model is defined. Comparison study is made on different corpus available in NLTK such as Crubadan, Brown and INSPEC. The results obtained by the proposed methodologies show a drastic increase in the accuracy rate of about 98% when compared to the existing algorithms which shows an average of 96% accurate. The performance measure is plotted to calculate the error ratio across the maximum-likelihood estimation.

Keywords: Part-of-Speech tagging (POS Tagging) · Hidden Markov Model (HMM) · Error estimation · Natural language processing

1 Introduction

Tagging defines an association. POS tagging tags Part-Of-Speech labels for a token in any language structure. POS is immensely used in text mining and it is an unsupervised/supervised classification. If a tagger is supervised then it counts the number of labeled set of data whose efficiency relies on the existence of the tagging dictionary. On the other hand unsupervised tagging seems to be a reasonable solution because they use un-annotated language models. The efficiency of any POS tagger depends on series of criterion as mentioned below

- Syntactic/Grammatical structure of the sentence should be correct. If there are any syntactical mistakes in a given sentence this could accelerate a chaos in an absolutely efficient POS tagger.
- When supervised model is used, the differences in working fashion, font styles, or the embodied texts between the input data and labeled/training data substantially drops the robustness of the system.
- Ambiguities in certain tenses in English language. For example, should the words such as 'have', 'be', 'book' and 'keep' be treated as verbs or their base/own forms?

A. Unal et al. (Eds.): SmartCom 2016, CCIS 628, pp. 88–96, 2016.
DOI: 10.1007/978-981-10-3433-6_11

- If a probabilistic measure is used for tagging then how much should be the support threshold? How to determine the base dependency of a tagger for a probable architecture?

To domicile the above issues, we propose a probabilistic tagging model which is data-rich and it overcomes the data scarcity encountered in unlabelled data sets. Intuitively the model proposed establishes a tag-engagement for each word of the operational data against the trained dataset. In the next step Markov models are used to visit the node probability of the hidden tags. A rigid performance evaluation is interfered to study the transitions among the labeling and the encoding of the tag-determiners [POS of Standard English].

2 Literature Review

Recent works in the field of NLP have reached a new horizon. There are multiple text processing system that shows an outrageous improvement in terms of accuracy and efficiency. Various researchers have proposed elementary methods to address the problem of POS tagging. Penn Treebank for English corpora was majorly used for the study of POS annotations. Depajan Das et al. [1] work on annotated corpus by building a dictionary. The word alignment exhibited in this work makes use of parallel data for label propagation. The scarcity of standard language corpora and the language challenges of defining a manual-tag construction are studied by Griffins et al. [2].

In the recent study made by Yoong Keok Lee et al. [3] an unsupervised POS tagging is constructed. The regular distributions of language projections is enforced for this study however the method falls costly and not suitable for many systems in a diverse range of applications. In [4], authors have shown a elegant way to enrich the corpus by showing labeling across ach word then assigning the tagged labels for a new word. The tagging schemes shown here make fair grammatical distinctions and hence as a result a large data set is formed. This is found helpful for inherit category of applications. Authors Leon et al. [5] has proposed a tagger using bootstrap constraints for unlabeled data. This is integrated with the probabilities of the existing-label tokens. An accuracy of 88.7% for tagging is achieved. The work also imposes the tagging issues related to a twitter text. Hand-annotated tagging is shown by the authors Clark and Ritter [6].

Reasonably, the classifier model designed with combinational machine learning models seems to provide greater results that transcend the ability of a human to tag the corpus. With this in mind, we have worked on uncertainties viewed in the existing literature. To overcome the problems associated with annotation, we decided to do the automatic tagging using Markov models and in scenarios where the tagging is not possible using the above said model, probabilistic measures are used. Subsequently the performance is enhanced due to the amalgamation of appending new features in tag-rule table. In our work we have shown how POS can be considered as a classification problem. Two lists are created; one says the available tags and the second talks about the POS tags taken as training set. A "HMM-POS [Hidden Markov Model – POS]" is an algorithm proposed in our work. This tags the POS for various lexicon units.

3 Our Approach – An Overview of the Methodologies

POS tagging can be achieved when it is viewed as a classification problem. Training set and positive tags are the two major considerations for this. However the problem of POS tagging is quite not simple and there are three prime elements for this deliberation.

The performance of a POS tagger is influenced by evaluation paradigm and an assessment criterion. The effectiveness of a tagger is relied upon the tagset. Tagset includes the tagging rules which can be projected as a statistical measure. In order to define a tagset either raw or annotated corpora is required. The granularity of the tagset is the main prerequisite as the higher granularity increases the accuracy of the tagger also increases. Perhaps this will chop off some areas and takes to count only the major consideration. In Fig. 1, the POS tagging model is shown. The figure shows the creation of tags and tags rules with the help of the statistical models such as entropy structure, randomization over conditional field, Hidden Markov model. These models are mainly used for POS tagging, Word Sense Disambiguation (WSD) and other areas of research interest under NLP.

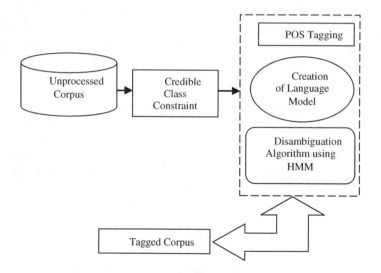

Fig. 1. A POS, our approach

3.1 Hidden Markov Model Based Tagging Approach

Hidden Markov Model (HMM) us a statistical language model that helps to define a time data. It is a process of converting an unobserved/unknown state into an known state. In POS tagging problem, the most appropriate and probable tag/label is selected for an input sentence by observing the previously marked labels in the chosen corpus. The tag sequence is chosen to maximize the probability as shown in equation [1].

$P(W_n|T).P(T|T_n) - -[1]$. The Current word W_n is allotted the tag (T) by observing the tag (T) as with the previous 'n' tags.

Taggers are usually developed using some of the types or approaches described below:

Tag with Stochastic Model: This evaluates the maximum likelihood of the observed tagset. HMM follows the below structure

$$present\_state(DET - N) > present\_state(DET - DET)$$

Tagging using Association Rules: Here the maximum likelihood of the tagset is determined using the predefined the association rules as shown below

$$if <any\_pattern>$$
$$then <Some\_pattern>$$

The prime approaches to be adopted while defining the tagging are, (1) HMM based tagging where all the prevalent information is used and to manoeuvre for deriving the assumption. Calculate the accuracy to study the integrity of this assumption. This approach is called bold approach. (2) Tagging based on constraint grammar. Here tagging assumption/hypothesis is not made as in (1) however the impossible/irrelevant tags are removed. This is called as cautious approach. (3) Tagging deployed on adaptation. A hypothesis is made and later can be changed if need arises. This kind of approach is also called as whimsical approach. In this section an algorithm based on HMM structure used for tagging is described. In this approach we choose the most likely tag for a given sentence where a POS can be derived. The criterion for searching a particular tag is given below.

$$P(n^{th}\_word - bit|tag).P(tag|tags\_of(n - 1)\_word\_sequence)$$

The tag sequence that maximizes the above condition is chosen as the most likely tag out of all the possible tags.

3.2   Hidden Markov Model Based Tagging Algorithm

The algorithm (Fig. 2) described in this section explains how tagging is done using HMM structure. The below algorithm is explained by considering two examples (Ex.1 and Ex.2) as stated below

I/PRP have/VBP to/TO book/VB a/DT flight/NN today/NN ——————Ex.1

The/DT book/NN series/NNS of/N Spider/NN man/NN are/VBP really/RB good/JJ————Ex.2

- Consider all the words in the above sentences (Ex.1 and Ex.2) are tagged. Let us consider the word 'book' is not tagged. Perform the step3 from the above algorithm.

to/TO book/? For Ex.1

The/DT book/? For Ex.2

- Possible tags for the word 'book' are NN and VB

step1:Input_the_word_sequence_which_
consists_of_unpragmatic_observations

step2:Assign_the_tags_for_the_known_
word_sequence

step3:for_a_bigram_transition_select_the
_the_tag-(t_a)for_word-(W_a)
Note:Only_when_known_observation_is
_encountered.
Observe_the_tag-t_{a-1}and_compare_with_(W_a)
i.e.,t_a=argmax$_b$P(t_b|t_{a-1},W_a)---(1)

step4:Now_in_HMM,make_an_hypothesis
i.e.,t_a=argmax$_b$P(t_b|t_{b-1})P(W_a|t_a)---(2)
where_P(t_b|t_{b-1})indicates_present_tag_sequence
P(W_a|t_a)indicates_the_maximum_likelihood_pair
repeat_step3_to_step4_for_all_word_sequence

step5:Pragmatic/tagged_observations_are_
deduced_for_all_wordpair_in_the_sentence

Fig. 2. HMM based POS tagging algorithm

- Apply (2) of step4 from the algorithm.

  We choose the maximum likelihood of the tag which is seen as described here.
  $P(NN|TO)P(book|NN)\_or\_P(VB|TO)$
  $P(NN|TO)P(book|NN)\_or\_P(book|VB)$

Phase 1: $P(NN|TO)$ and $P(VB|TO) --(a)$ - In this phase we scan the corpus to find the above probabilities as shown in (a). In reality the probability of 'to' preceding verb is more (example: to race, to fly, to eat…). However these are the sentences which the word 'to' precede a noun as well (example: run to temple, come to house, go to school…). Therefore calculate the likelihood ratio in the corpus. In our experiments we have considered three major available in NLTK. Those are Crubadan, Brown and INSPEC. The probability ratio of (a) is studied in each of these corpus and results obtained are tabulated in the Table 1.

Phase 2: $P(book|NN)$ and $P(book|VB) --(b)$

Table 1. Occurrences of TO as NN & VB in three corpuses

	$P(NN|TO)$	$P(VB|TO)$
BROWN	0.024	0.36
CRUBADAN	0.061	0.13
INSPEC	0.072	0.45

Table 2. Occurrences of BOOK as NN & VB in three corpuses

	$P(book|NN)$	$P(book|VB)$
BROWN	0.00043	0.00004
CRUBADAN	0.00037	0.13
INSPEC	0.072	0.45

As observed in Phase 1 the likelihood of 'to' being VB is more and hence Phase 1 talks about the maximum probability of the word 'to'. In this phase we estimate the maximum likelihood probability of book as NN or VB. Tests were conducted on the same three corpus. The results of this test are shown in Table 2. From Table 2 it is observed that the word 'book' has the maximum probability of being NN rather that VB as in all the three corpuses this is evident. Finally we combine the probabilities of Phases 1 and 2 by considering the highest probable factor. This evaluation is shown in the Table 3.

As shown in Table 3 the probability of the word 'book' being VB is more than NN.

Table 3. The probability of the word 'book'

	$P(VB|TO)P(BOOK|VB)$	$P(NN|TO)P(BOOK|NN)$
BROWN	0.00043	0.00004
CRUBADAN	0.00037	0.13
INSPEC	0.072	0.45

Therefore in the final stage the tag VB is assigned as POS for 'book'. Phases 1 and 2 explains how POS is done for a single word however for the multiple word sequence, the same paradigm is used but has to be elaborated using Bayesian theorem. This is portrayed in Phase 3.

Phase 3: In this phase all the word pair in a given sentence is tagged to their tag sequence based on the likeliness parameter. In order to do so, Bayesian theorem with chain rule is applied. Consider a set word sequence pair $W_1, W_2 \ldots W_N$ and a tag-set sequence $T_1, T_2 \ldots T_N$. Consider the tag-rule to be of the form γ. According to the Bayes' rule, we have,

$$T \in \gamma$$
$$\hat{T} = \arg\max\_P(T|W)$$
$$\hat{T} = \arg\max_{T\in\gamma} \frac{P(T)P(W|T)}{P(W)}$$
$$\hat{T} = \arg\max_{T\in\gamma} P(T)P(W|T)$$

According to the chain rule,

$$P(X,Y) = P(X|Y)P(Y) = P(Y|X)P(X)$$
$$P(X,Y,Z) = P(Y,Z|X)P(X) = P(Z|X,Y)$$
$$P(Y|X)P(X)$$
$$P(W,X,Y,Z) = P(W)P(X|W)P(Y|X,Y)$$
$$P(Z|X,Y,Z...)$$

$$P(T)P(W|T) = \prod_{i=1}^{n} \underbrace{P(W_i|W_iT_i,....W_{-i}T_{-i}T_i)}_{\textbf{Present Tag}}\underbrace{P(T_i|W_iT_i....W_{-i}T_{-i}T_i)}_{\textbf{Tag History}}$$

-- (A)

$$P(T)P(W|T) - P(W_i)P(W_2|W_1)P(W_3|W_2W_1)....$$

Trigram approximation can be deduced by using following condition,

$$P(T)P(W|T) - P(W_i)P(W_2|W_1)P(W_3|W_2W_1)....$$
$$P(W_i|W_1T_1.....T_{i-1}T_i) = P(W_i|T_i)$$

(a)

With trigram approximation (a), the trigram assumption can be made based on the recent two probable states in addition to the present. This is indicated in the (b)

$$P(T_i|W_1T_1.....T_{i-1}) = P(T_i|T_{i-2}T_{i-1})$$

(b)

By considering (a) and (b) for (A), we get,

$$P(T)P(W|T) = [P(T_1)P(T_2|T_1) \prod_{i=3}^{n} P(T_i|T_{i-2}T_{i-1}) \prod_{i=1}^{n} P(W_i|T_i)]$$

4 Results and Discussions

In order to evaluate our result the interface using Natural Language Tool Kit (NLTK) was developed. The tool kit provides all the linguistic features to implement the required the algorithm. The result was evaluated on the three corpuses namely CRU-BADAN, INSPEC, & BROWN. An accurate means of calculating the efficiency is by Recall and Precision. However each word is associated with utmost one tag for any given instance, calculating the F-measure score will not make good sense. Perhaps one can calculate the recall and precision for individual tag, for e.g. Recall and Precision for NN variations. For every tag encountered in the training data-set – The tagging associated with each word in the chosen corpus, three catalogues are maintained. These are True Positive (TP), False Positive (FP) and False Negative (FN). If the tag of trained dataset and test dataset match then increment the value of TP by 1. If there is no match between them we increment FN for the actual/original tag and also FP for those tags that our proposed algorithm mistakenly chose. With the obtained values, Recall and Precision can be calculated. The size of the corpus in terms of word ratio is approximately 10,000 words. We have Recall, which defines the likelihood of identifying the positive samples. This can be viewed as the proportion of every positive test samples which is modeled correctly. Recall is computed using the formula (i)

$$Recall = \frac{TP}{TP + FN} \qquad (i)$$

The precision talks about the hypothesis and assumptions. This is defined as being proportionate for every positive prediction that made on the test sample. Prediction can be calculated using the formula (ii)

$$Precision = \frac{TP}{TP + Fp} \qquad (ii)$$

Finally we arrive at F-measure. This defines the mean of recall and precision approximated by eq. (i) & (ii). F-measure is given by,

$$F - Measure = \frac{1}{\alpha \frac{1}{P} + (1 - \alpha)\frac{1}{R}} \qquad (iii)$$

The component α is called balance co-efficient. The value of α is considered as 0.5. This value can be changes conventionally. With the proposed algorithm, we arrive at the following values of Recall, Precision and F-measure that was obtained applying (i), (ii) & (iii) as indicated in the Table 4.

Table 4. Calculation of F-Measure with the values of Recall and Precision

Recall	0.98
Precision	0.97
F-Measure	**0.98**

5 Conclusions

POS tagger, a very important criterion for language analysis is often found in many variations but performance is a major issue with these taggers. With the advent of many POS tagging the accuracy has become a major challenge. Hence in this work, a novel POS tagger is defined adopting the features of HMM. To prove the accuracy of our system, three corpuses have been chosen. We showed how efficient can be increased. The results show that the recommended approach is about 98% efficient. The drawback of this system is the data processing time. This is directly proportional to the size of the input. Since the corpuses chosen for our experiments are huge, time of about 20 s was incurred to arrive at the output. Further extensions to this are comprised of defining the complex tags to increase of the speed of the tagger. In addition to this, one can define a morphological analyzer for multiple natural languages. POS tagging rule can be prepared beforehand. This helps the speed and also the accuracy.

References

1. Das, D.: Unsupervised part-of-speech tagging with bilingual graph-based projections. In: The 49th Annual Meeting of the Association for Computational Linguistics, Portland, Oregon, USA, pp. 600–609, June 2011
2. Goldwater, S.: A fully Bayesian approach to unsupervised part-of-speech tagging. In: Association for Computational Linguistics, vol. 45, p. 744 (2007)
3. Lee, Y.K.: Simple type-level unsupervised POS tagging. In: Association for Computational Linguistics Conference on Empirical Methods in Natural Language Processing, Cambridge, MA, pp. 853–861, October 2010
4. de Gruyter, W.: Corpus Linguistics: An International Handbook, vol. 1, ISBN 978-3-11-021142-9
5. Derczynski, L.: Twitter part-of-speech tagging for all: overcoming sparse and noisy data. In: Recent Advances in Natural Language Processing, Hissar, Bulgaria, pp. 198–206, pp. 7–13, September 2013
6. Ritter, A.: Named entity recognition in tweets: an experimental study. In: Association for Computational Linguistics Conference on Empirical Methods in Natural Language Processing, pp. 1524–1534 (2011)

Issues and Requirements for Successful Integration of Semantic Knowledge in Web Usage Mining for Effective Personalization

Sanjay Kumar Dwivedi and Bhupesh Rawat[✉]

Department of Computer Science, Babasaheb Bhimrao Ambedkar University, Lucknow, India
skd200@yahoo.com, bhr222@gmail.com

Abstract. Recommendation systems have been successfully used by e-commerce and other similar sites for recommendation of relevant items to the user. However majority of these systems are based on web usage mining which does not consider the semantic knowledge underlying a website in the recommendation process and based solely on usage data. Hence researchers realized the importance of semantic knowledge and began to use it as part of usage data which is primarily used by personalization systems to enhance the quality of items being recommended. However several issues emerged during the process of integration. For effective personalization these issues need to be addressed. We discuss this aspect of integration process and also suggest some of the ways to resolve these issues and also discuss few methods of representing domain knowledge under different situations.

Keywords: Semantic knowledge · Web usage mining · Personalization · RDF

1 Introduction

Recommender Systems is software which is used to suggest the most relevant items to user from large database. Data mining plays a crucial role in their development.

Web mining is the application of data mining on web logs, web content and web structures in order to find interesting patterns. Here we consider only the web usage mining as it is directly concerned to our topic.

Web usage mining involves discovering user access patterns from log file. One of the applications of this is in an e-commerce where we may find a rule of the form X -> Y, which indicates that if a user has bought an item X then he is likely to buy item Y. The web usage mining is being used extensively in educational data mining such as recommending the best combination of courses to learners, offering ads, links and other resources.

The web usage mining has few drawbacks as the recommendation is purely usage based and hence the new items added to the site recently cannot be recommended. Collaborative filtering approach is commonly used to deal with this problem [1, 12]. This is called keyword-based approach. However, the problem with this approach is that it is not able to capture more complex relationship that may exist among objects. Hence the semantic knowledge can help in recommending more complex objects, and this

© Springer Nature Singapore Pte Ltd. 2016
A. Unal et al. (Eds.): SmartCom 2016, CCIS 628, pp. 97–103, 2016.
DOI: 10.1007/978-981-10-3433-6_12

semantic knowledge needs to be combined at different stages of the web usage mining process.

Here we first provide an overview of semantic web mining and presents its architecture and then discuss different ways of representing domain knowledge and finally describe issues and requirements essential for semantic web usage mining.

2   Semantic Web Mining

Semantic web mining is the combination of two fast-developing research areas semantic web and web mining.

We describe in Fig. 1 different layers of semantic web architecture. The bottom layer consists of Unicode and URI which add incremental value to the layer above it. While Unicode is an encoding character set that allows all user languages to read and write on the web by using a standardized form, Uniform resource identifier (URI) refers to the identification of information representation constructs in an unambiguous way. Moreover, URI makes it easy to aggregate all data that points to a given source.

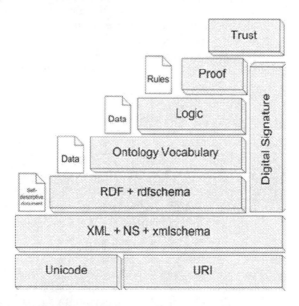

Fig. 1. The layers of semantic web architecture

Moving up to the hierarchy we have XML, which is an acronym for the extensible markup language. It is used to store and transport data but not displaying it. It allows users to define their own tags and document structure.

The next layer in the hierarchy comprises of RDF and RDFS which are the acronym for resource description framework and resource description framework schema respectively. They are primarily used to represent classes and properties of a domain in the form of generalization/specialization. Moreover, they are also used to provide metadata to its upper layers.

Ontology is analogous to database schema. It can be described as a formal specification of knowledge from some domain.

The outcome provided by agent is verified by the proof layer. The rules layer helps us derive new conclusions and how to implement them as well.

The top layer is trust which provides us a mechanism to establish trust and confidence between information source and information user.

3   Semantic Knowledge

Semantic information is useful in intelligent information integration by providing a technical means to share and exchange knowledge and/or information between humans and/or machines [4–6]. Ontology is considered to be the backbone of semantic knowledge.

Ontology is defined as formal specification of a conceptualization and it involves classes, objects, properties, relationships and axioms [3, 7, 13]. RDF or OWL is the formal languages to express ontology with the facility of inference support. The method of obtaining ontologies depends on the size of the website, i.e. if the site is small with static web pages then a manual or semi-manual method will be sufficient. However, if the site is large and dynamic then one of the possible ways is to obtain database schema for extracting ontology.

3.1   Requirements for Semantic Web Usage Mining

Here we discuss the essential requirements for the integration of semantic web usage mining process. One of the issues to deal with is how to represent domain knowledge.

3.1.1   Representation of Domain Knowledge
3.1.1.1   As Content Features

Several sources of domain knowledge exist which can be used in the mining and personalization, like website's textual data. The semantic of a site partially depends on the content features which are associated with items. This feature involves keywords, phrase, category name etc. Content preprocessing extracts relevant features from text and meta-data and then features are assigned different weights which show the relative importance of features, while in case of meta-data weights are derived automatically.

Machine learning algorithms can also be used to further preprocessing of content features. For instance, content feature's classification with concept hierarchy may be used to limit the discovered patterns to those having page views about a particular subject.

The content features are integrated in case of heavily textual site. However, finding complex relationships is still an issue with this approach which usually emerges when we move down semantically deeper.

3.1.1.2   As Structured Data

In web usage mining, they [2] focus on the semantics underlying a web transaction or a user profile which is usually composed of a group of pageview names and query strings. Though these features do not possess the semantics, therefore a mapping is required to associate features with their corresponding objects.

Many websites generate web pages using querying operational database from which semantic information can be obtained easily. Machine learning techniques are more appropriate when structured data is not available. Moreover, in order to perform further preprocessing the acquired knowledge should be easily understandable. So we must have a standard language to represent extracted knowledge.

DAML+OIL are an ontology language combining the Web standards from XML and RDF, with the reasoning capabilities from description logic SHIP (DL) [8]. The relational model and probabilistic model can be integrated to improve web personalization. Several personalization approaches have used relational markov model.

In [14], they utilized the syntax and semantics of another ontology representation framework, SHOQ (D), to represent domain ontologies. The following section discusses how to map usage level and domain level instances:

3.1.1.3   Building "Mappings" Between Usage-Level and Domain-Level Instances

This phase assigns usage level patterns like URL or pageview name to the instances in the knowledge base. For example instead of describing a user's navigational path as: "$u_1, u_2, \ldots, u_n$" (where u_i is a uniform resource locator), we need to depict it with the instances containing in the knowledge base, like: "movie (name = The Hangover), movie (name = Ghostbusters), movie (name = Austin Powers)". Moreover, concept hierarchy which we need to build before mapping process may help us to infer user's interest in the comedy category.

3.1.1.4   Using Content and Structural Characteristics

Another way to create the mapping between usage data and domain instances is to use classification algorithms. Literature has shown that they [9] are able to extract content and structural features from web pages. Another solution to create the semantic mapping is anchor text which is a part of hyperlinks. In order to do that, we must have complete navigation path which would be used to get anchor text for each URL.

3.1.1.5   Using Query Strings

A well-designed site has a semantic mapping between query parameters and objects. For example; on the following link if background database is available we can obtain the content of item 3456789 in the category 3456. Here book-name, price and author of the item can be obtained. For instance, a query string from a hypothetical online bookstore is given below:

http://www.abc.com/app.cgi?action=viewitem&item=3456789&category=3456.

3.1.1.6 Levels of Abstraction

Abstraction provides flexibility in extracting semantic knowledge at different level in different phases of semantic web usage mining. For example, if we focus on higher level concepts in concept hierarchy certain patterns would emerge which we would not have got otherwise. Domain knowledge having attributes and relations needs to manage a lot of data than the web usage mining. So, it is necessary to remove irrelevant attributes or relations. In [10] a multiple-level association rule mining algorithm is proposed that utilizes concept hierarchies.

4 Integration of Semantic Information in Different Phases of Web Usage Mining

The semantic information can be further exploited at various stages in the web usage mining process as explained below:

4.1 Preprocessing Phase

The main task in this phase is to make the data suitable for later phases of data mining such as pattern discovery phase. In [11] they have shown that applying appropriate data preprocessing techniques on usage data we could improve the effectiveness of Web personalization. This phase involves mapping the concept level mappings from the page view-level data to concepts. This results in the kind of data to which data mining algorithm can be applied. Particularly a transaction vector t can be transformed into a vector $t' = (w^t_{a1}, w^t_{a2}, w^t_{a3}, \ldots \ldots w^t_{an},)$ where each a_i represents a semantic object which is a part of a pageview and contained in the transaction and w_{ai} represents the weight of the object in a transaction.

4.2 Pattern Discovery Phase

In order to successfully integrate domain knowledge in this phase, we need to extend basic data mining algorithm to address relational data to concept hierarchies. For example, the clustering of a single relation consists of the computation of distance among transaction vectors. In such cases, simple vector-based operations of clustering are used. However, pattern discovery in integrated semantic web usage mining data mining algorithm such as clustering has to perform more computation. For instance even, if two user transactions may not have common page views, they may still be similar based on the similarity of items in both of the transactions. One of the challenges in this phase is to develop scalable and efficient algorithms to measure similarity.

4.3 Post-processing Phase

Usage patterns obtained from preprocessing phase can be further enhanced using domain knowledge. For that we first carry out different tasks such as preprocessing, and pattern discovery on the usage data which is further refined with semantic knowledge to better interpret the discovered patterns using concept heirarchy.

5   Aggregation Methods for Complex Objects

Patterns obtained using data mining need aggregation methods to represent them. For instance clustering in the web transaction yields a group of similar sessions. The centroid of the transaction represents all the transactions in a session. On the other hand for the semantic transaction, aggregation needs to be done for each attribute of the object in the cluster. For example Clustering results in similar objects and to understand them semantically better aggregation is required.

6   Conclusion

This paper emphasized the importance of domain knowledge in the web usage mining process in order to improve the quality of personalization which may not have been possible without semantic knowledge. We first described the semantic web and different layers of its architecture. Then we discussed different ways of representing domain knowledge such as content features or structured data and also justified which method is suitable for a given application in a given situation. Moreover, it is also worth discussing how the mapping between usage level and domain level instances is performed. We also discussed how the knowledge base can be enriched further by using query string. Different levels of abstraction were discussed which are required in order to provide flexibility in mining and recommendation phase. Then various issues regarding integrating semantic knowledge in different stages of the web usage mining process such as preprocessing phase, knowledge discovery phase, and recommendation generation phase were also discussed. In the integration process, the main challenge is to successfully integrate ontological information at each stage of web usage mining process. Finally, we discussed the most important issues and requirement which could lead to more intelligent personalization system in the future.

References

1. Claypool, M., Gokhale, A., Miranda, T., Murnikov, P., Netes, D., Sartin, M.: Combining content-base and collaborative filters in an online newspaper. In: ACM SIGIR Workshop on Recommender Systems: Algorithms and Evaluation, California (1999)
2. Dai, H., Mobasher, B.: Integrating semantic knowledge with web usage mining for personalization. School of Computer Science, Telecommunication, and Information Systems (2007)

3. Burkhardt, H., Smith, B.: Handbook of Metaphysics and Ontology, pp. 640–647. Philosophia Verlag, Munich (1991)
4. Wiederhold, G.: Intelligent integration of information. In: SIGMOD, pp. 434–437 (1993)
5. Abecker, A., Bernardi, A., Sintek, M.: Proactive knowledge delivery for enterprise knowledge management. In: 11th Conference on Software Engineering, Germany, pp. 17–19 (1999)
6. Schnurr, H.P., Staab, S.: A proactive inferencing agent for desk support. In: AAAI Symposium on Bringing Knowledge to Business Processes, Technical report, Germany (2000)
7. Zouaq, A., Nikambou, R.: A survey of domain ontology engineering: methods and tools. In: Nkambou, R., Bourdeau, J., Mizoguchi, R. (eds.) Advances in Intelligent Tutoring Systems. SCI, vol. 308, pp. 103–119. Springer, Heidelberg (2010). doi:10.1007/978-3-642-14363-2_6
8. Horrocks, I., Sattler, U.: Ontology reasoning in the SHOQ(D) description logic. In: 17th International Joint Conference on Artificial Intelligence, Seattle (2001)
9. Craven, M., DiPasquo, D., Freitag, D., McCallum, A., Mitchell, T., Nigam, K., Slattery, S.: Learning to construct knowledge base from the world wide web. Artif. Intell. **118**, 69–113 (2000)
10. Han, J., Fu, Y.: Discovery of multiple-level association rules from large databases. In: Very Large Data Bases, Switzerland, pp. 420–431 (1995)
11. Mobasher, B., Dai, H., Luo, T., Nakagawa, M.: Discovery and evaluation of aggregate usage profiles for web personalization. Data Min. Knowl. Discov. **6**, 61–82 (2002). Kluwer Academic Publishers
12. Resnick, P., Iacovou, N., Suchack, M., Bergstrom, P., Riedl, J.T.: Grouplense: an open architecture for collaborative filtering of netnews. In: Proceeding of the ACM Conference on Computer Supported Cooperative Work, pp. 175–186 (1994)
13. Gruber, T.R.: A translation approach to portable ontologies. J. Knowl. Acquisition **5**(2), 199–220 (1993)
14. Dai, H., Mobasher, B.: Using ontologies to discover domain level web usage profiles. In: Proceedings of the 2nd Semantic Web Mining Workshop at ECML/PKDD, Helsinki, Finland (2002)

Secure Serviceability of Software: Durability Perspective

Rajeev Kumar[1(✉)], Suhel Ahmad Khan[2], and Raees Ahmad Khan[1]

[1] Department of Information Technology,
Babasaheb Bhimrao Ambedkar Central University, Lucknow 226025, UP, India
rs0414@gmail.com, khanraees@yahoo.com
[2] Department of Computer Application, Integral University,
Lucknow 226026, UP, India
ahmadsuhel28@gmail.com

Abstract. Due to complexity of software design, software services are becoming essential with privacy and security. Service-Oriented Designing (SOD) pattern is one of the reputable patterns used for developing secure, reliable and flexible software. Consequently, the use of SOD to develop the durable security of software is increasing. Security measurement has considerable importance in the context of SOD since it determines how the requirements for secure service should be achieved for duration. In this paper, the relationship between durability and secure software of service-oriented design is proposed. The paper begins with intending a set of durability concepts to measure the security and concludes with the relationship between service-oriented design properties and durability of secure software.

Keywords: Software serviceability · Software durability · Software security · Service-oriented design

CCS Concepts: Software Engineering

1 Introduction

The use of computers for different types of applications is expanding rapidly e.g. for business purpose, educational purpose, commercial purpose etc. It was a period when software as an industry came into power. Over the decades, the software industry has looking forward, exposing financiers to new and tremendous opportunities to serve this expanding market. The last decade has seen an enormous change in both, enterprise and customer software businesses and its opportunities.

Today, the demand for a type of systems is increasing which are long time investments [1]. This can be seen in the gradual change in focus from a product-centered business to a service with constant maintenance for duration. Key contributor to this change is the internet that has not only increased demand for durable services but also allowed the appearance of durable security models. These changes eventually led to the birth of the durability of software.

© Springer Nature Singapore Pte Ltd. 2016
A. Unal et al. (Eds.): SmartCom 2016, CCIS 628, pp. 104–110, 2016.
DOI: 10.1007/978-981-10-3433-6_13

Generally, associated with secure software, Software as a Service (SaaS) is perceived as way of the cost effectiveness for businesses to obtain the equal profits of gain without the associated complexity and high initial cost [1, 2]. Designing a system with durable security is a concerned issue in today's era. Industry is focusing on service oriented designing hence it's a concern to apply durable security on service oriented designs.

Service-oriented design is one of the recognized designs for the software. To develop different types of secure software, positively, it has been applied in development. Design of software serviceability can be defined as an implementation of well defined functionality, which would be also self-contained. These are provided by service providers and used by service consumers. The services of software are designed with interface and operate on discovered mode.

After introducing the basic concepts, rest of the paper is organized in following way; second part describes the background and definition of software security and software serviceability with respect to durability. The third part focuses on the assessment of software security in the context of durability. Next part discusses impaction of service-oriented designing on durability whereas a section fifth describes the conclusion.

2 Definition and Background

A usage of durability makes it easy to estimate the running time of secure software. Performing an accurate calculation of security's operation time is a very labor-intensive process. Therefore, it will not make an accurate measurement; just a quantity of a certain order of magnitude. Durability may be considered as the period within which maximum number of primitive operations that software security may execute. Experts usually want to know how the performance time depends on a particular aspect of the software security [1, 2]. Durability effects design attributes and as well as other security attributes. Thus, there is a vast scope for obtaining durability of security in the field of software engineering by a large number of attributes depicted.

Secure services have to be identified as soon as possible in the development life cycle so to introduce treatments directly as part of the software design. Assessment of likelihood and severity of secure software services is a major problem that minimizes the duration of software and its security. In the software development community, many models are being estimated to find the secure software with long time services and finally assessing the probability of the occurrence of security failure [4].

Secure serviceability of software is a noteworthy problem in the area of software engineering and has a strong impact in the context of service-oriented design. There are three methods to measure the security of software design, these are; objective approach, subjective approach and hybrid approach. The objective approach focuses on measuring the structural properties of software security like autonomy, discoverability, coupling, cohesion, and abstraction [1]. In contrast, the second approach measures the subjective design data and evaluating the security attributes of services design by measuring security indicators that represent the security attributes and gives value to the current design to help the developers to make a decision about the alternative durable security attributes. In addition, the third approach combines first and second approaches.

The relationship between software durability with secure services and effect of risks on several attributes of the software has been discussed to get rid of security and services failure. This understanding helps a lot in the evaluation of design choices. Most of the critical aspects of secure and durable software are integrity, availability, and confidentiality which are related to unpredictability of services [5]. There are no more approaches to deal with uncertainty or unpredictability, mainly in the area of security, serviceability and durability. However, what is still missing is a clear understanding of the behavior of unpredictable software services that very often has produced mistreatments in the service oriented design.

This work clarifies about different nature of uncertainties and the manner in which they influence properties of security and durability and the relationship between security durability with serviceability can be used by any analyst to identify and mitigate risks of software services and evaluate their impact on the software according to their nature. Since serviceability and durability are an aggregation of different security, the assessment must be conducted on different dimensions which belong to durability.

3   Assessment of Software Security Durability

Nowadays, the software industry is facing tough business as well as operational challenges for the assessment and creation. There is a continuous pressure to reduce the cost of production and improve financial performance. At the same time, when the resources get older, their performance effected by high availability and consumption. There is a need to continuously focus on some factors with CIA such as reliability, usability, and durability to improve security in future and ensuring high-level asset integrity in the security based business environment [6]. Efficiency and effectiveness impaction of these issues are preventing the organizations from realizing the maximum value from their services improvement initiative for secure software.

It is believed and found by experienced persons that modification in development process may help in resolving these issues. The design stage takes the security with services requirements recognized in the appropriate requirements document as its initial input. For each and every development, a set of design elements are formed as a result of interviews, prototype efforts, or workshops.

Software design elements describe the desired features in details so that software engineers may improve and deliver the predictable services of software with minimal additional input design. There are following key principles that are common to improve services as well as durability for successful business process transformation:

- Establish a trustworthy design that connects the services value to assure the secure software to transform the program involving multiple complex securities.
- To address secure program that delivers well-defined business outcomes and enhances serviceability. This will help in gaining simplicity and get assurance in the early durable program of software.

- Identify relationships with existing secure programs to optimize durable program of software. Giving importance to such programs by including the availability, flexibility, reliability enhancement, a lot of cost and time can be saved by realizing the importance of economies of scale.

From the above discussion about durability and services, it is clear that durability is an essential attribute but hard to achieve while designing security of software. The objective of this short communication article is to discuss about enhancing the features of design using durable security for improving the serviceability as well as the quality of software. In previous works, it has already been identified that durability is a significant security factor and it influences security directly or indirectly [5, 6]. Therefore, a Fig. 1 is proposed for achieving durability while designing security for improving the services of software. A conceptual framework has been developed for uncertainty which can be used to improve qualities such as security with estimating technique for enhancing durability. The methodology described by flow chart helps developers to confine durable security in terms of other attributes of software serviceability.

The growing environment in the early 21st century creates new challenges for all, including software services design [7, 8]. It will contribute to important independent adaptation in the area of software development. Methods of design and coding are

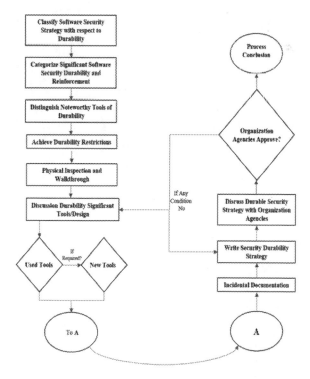

Fig. 1. A framework for durable software methodology with respect to security

Table 1. Relationships of between durability and service-oriented design properties

Durability principles/service-oriented design properties	Coupling	Abstraction	Reusability	Autonomy	Composability	Statelessness	Discoverability	Cohesion	Granularity	Complexity	Design Size	References
Software effectiveness evaluation	✓		✓		✓		✓		✓		✓	[1, 3]
User satisfaction						✓						[2, 4]
Robustness				✓	✓					✓	✓	[5]
Operational controls	✓		✓	✓		✓	✓		✓			[1, 3]
Time-efficiency			✓	✓		✓			✓	✓		[2, 4]
Auditability		✓				✓		✓				[1, 3]
Physiological acceptability	✓		✓	✓			✓		✓		✓	[1, 3]
Business continuity	✓		✓		✓							[5]
Accessibility				✓	✓	✓	✓			✓	✓	[1, 3]
Extensibility			✓				✓		✓			[5]
Flexibility	✓		✓	✓		✓			✓	✓		[1, 3]
Detectability			✓	✓		✓		✓				[2, 4]
Scalability		✓					✓					[1, 3]
Traceability	✓			✓		✓	✓		✓	✓	✓	[5]

being used that are essentially insecure [9, 10]. There are no services to take care of points where security can be broken. If it is concerned than it's also necessary to manage these secure services to ensure good security.

4   Impact of Durable Security on Service Oriented Design Properties

Security development models have been used to detect and describe security failure and risks in the context of software security. Security failures of software are caused by unpredictable events. While security risks are detected and reduced, software can be used for the prolonged use by increasing its security. There are so many approaches for estimation of security. Durability is an integrative concept which encompasses to the security attributes, while dependability for correct service, human trust for continuity service and trustworthiness for consistent service.

Durability has fifteen sub-characteristics as psychological acceptability, user satisfaction, business continuity, etc., which affect the security either directly or indirectly. There are relationship between service-oriented and durability attributes which are shown in Table 1. Service-oriented concepts are being used in designing of software security with concepts like coupling, cohesion, inheritance, encapsulation, and abstraction, etc., widely used in the field of security engineering. A software security consists of a set of interacting tools, while security failure originally executed security risks within the state of components. The above characteristics of durability may be highlighted to a greater or lesser extent depending on the reliability, safety, confidentiality etc. of the application.

5   Conclusion

Based on the actual engineering situations, the many attributes of design categories, which possibly cause accidents in the software development process, are identified with their relation to durability in this work. This paper addresses the problem of capturing stakeholders' requirements and achievement of service-oriented factors in a flexible environment. Developers able to pinpoint the essential SOD factors which ensures the successful implementation of secure software durability. This will enable developers to concentrate on the most important service-oriented factors and achieve high satisfaction among stakeholders with a constant maintenance for duration.

Acknowledgment. This work is sponsored by UGC-MRP, New Delhi, India under F. No. 43-391/2014 (SR).

References

1. Kelty, C., Erickson, S.: The Durability of Software, pp. 1–13. Meson Press, Germany (2015)
2. Nathan, E.: When good software goes bad: the surprising durability of an ephemeral technology. In: MICE (Mistakes, Ignorance, Contingency, and Error) Conference, Munich, pp. 1–16 (2014)
3. Abdulgader, A., Elhag, M., Mohamad, R.: Service-oriented design measurement and theoretical validation. J. Teknologi (Sci. Eng.) **77**(9), 1–14 (2015)
4. Avizienis, A., Laprie, J.C., Randell, B., Landwehr, C.: Basic concepts and taxonomy of dependable and secure computing. IEEE Trans. Dependable Secure Comput. **1**(1), 11–13 (2004)
5. Erl, T.: Service-oriented Architecture: Concepts, Technology, and Design. Prentice Hall PTR, Upper Saddle River (2005)
6. Khan, R.A.: From threat to security indexing: a causal chain. Comput. Fraud Secur. **2009**, 9–12 (2009)
7. Kumar, R., Khan, S.A., Khan, R.A.: Revisiting software security: durability perspective. Int. J. Hybrid Inf. Technol. (SERSC) **8**(2), 311–322 (2015)
8. Kumar, R., Khan, S.A., Khan, R.A.: Durable security in software development: needs and importance. CSI Commun. **10**, 34–36 (2015)
9. Nyfjord, J.: Towards Integrating Agile Development and Risk Management. Universitetsservice US-AB, Kista (2008)
10. Aziz, M.: Service based meta-model for the development of distributed embedded real-time systems. Real Time Syst. **49**(5), 563–579 (2013)

Image Fusion Based on the Modified Curvelet Transform

Malani Hareeta[1(✉)], Kumar Mahendra[2], and Paliwal Anurag[1]

[1] Department of Electronics and Communication Engineering,
Geetanjali Institute of Technical Studies, Udaipur, India
hmalani03@gmail.com, paliwal_rajasthan@yahoo.com
[2] Department of Electronics and Communication Engineering, UCE, RTU, Kota, India
miresearchlab@gmail.com

Abstract. A fuzzy type image fusion method using various image compression techniques is described in this paper. This method shows fusion of fuzzy images and can be used for fusion of multi model image. It is concluded that fusion with advanced single levels offers better fusion quality. The future algorithm Curvelet transform is very straight forward, effortless to execute and can be extended its use in existent time applications. This method provides a comparative study between proposed & literature techniques and validation of the projected algorithm as Peak Signal to Noise Ratio (PSNR), Root Mean Square Error (RMSE).

Keywords: Fuzzy type image · Curve-let transform · PSNR · RMSE

1 Introduction

Multi sensor data fusion plays a imperative role in defence in addition to civillian applications as it involves diversity of sensors offered and those working in diverse spectral bands. A further extensive tool in signal and image processing is multi-scale disintegration. In Biomedical Science it is required to increase the information content of an image and multiple registered images are combined together to get image fusion but it is an ongoing research part. Various image fusion algorithms such as multi-resolution [1, 2], multi scale [3] and statistical signal processing [4–6] based methods are presented and estimated. The progress in the domain of sensing technologies multi-sensor techniques have become a realism in a various fields such as machine vision, medical imaging, remote sensing and the military applications for which they were elaborated.

Image fusion presents an effectual means of reducing the growing amount of information even at the similar time extracting every valuable information from the source images. These techniques offers an increase in total amount of data accessible. Apart from sinking the quality of data, image fusion aims to craft new images so as to get more apposite for the function of human/machine perception, and for additional image- processing tasks like medical imaging and remote sensing also in applications like segmentation, target detection or object exposure. Multi-sensor data frequently offers corresponding information, so image fusion imparts an effectual method for analysis of data and to enable comparison. For e.g. Visible-band and infrared pictures may be fused to aid pilots landing aircraft in deprived visibility [3, 5, 7]. Finally, the functioning of the image fusion scheme is calculated as

© Springer Nature Singapore Pte Ltd. 2016
A. Unal et al. (Eds.): SmartCom 2016, CCIS 628, pp. 111–118, 2016.
DOI: 10.1007/978-981-10-3433-6_14

tradeoffs between true image and fused image. In preceding techniques when apply fuzzy type images, the performance standard is deprived. As a result this paper proposed a novel Curvelet transform techniques which provide fused image with superior quality. The paper remainder is prearranged as follows: Sect. 2 illustrates Proposed Curvelet transform image compression techniques. Section 4 describes different Fusion Performance evaluation criterion. Section 5 describes Results and comparatively study of techniques. Section 6 presents conclusion.

2   Proposed Modified Curve-Let Transform Image Compression Technique

Curvelet transform is effective at spotting image movement along curves. The discrete type uses Unequally spaced Fast Fourier transform algorithm [USFFT]. The fast discrete curvelet transform is easier, rapid and less disused [11–14, 21]. This principle make use of a decimated rectangular grid tilted along the key path of every curvelet.

To smoothly localize the fourier transform close to the sheared wedges obeying the parabolic scaling we use the windows $U_{j,l}$. Digital implementation is done by using 2 parameters of the CLT they are number of angles at the coarsest level and number of resolution. Since the region of significance is 16×16 pixels, the highest possible resolution extraction is 2 levels of resolutions (Fig. 1).

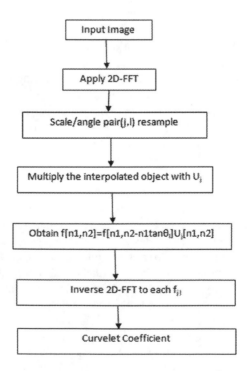

Fig. 1. Cuvelet transform (CLT) algorithm

3   Proposed Image Fusion System

Consider image 1 as fuzzy type image 1 and image 2 as fuzzy type image 2 and image compression and feature extracted by cuvelet transform technique and apply Image fusion algorithm as averaging method for fused image and compare actual/true image with fused image and calculate PSNR and RMSE to check effectiveness of proposed system [15–20] (Fig. 2).

Pseudo code:
```
Im1 = curvelet (image1)
Im1' = Icurvelet (De1)
Id1 = Im1-Im1'
Im2 = curvelet (image2)
Im2' = Icurvelet (De2)
Id2 = Im2-Im2'
Id = abs(Id1)-(Idf) >=0;
Imf = Idf + Imf
Imf = Icurvelet (Idfm)
```
This pseudo code shows the implementation Process [15–20].

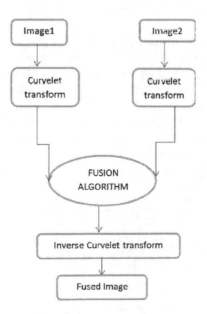

Fig. 2. Proposed image fusion system

4   Fusion Performance Estimation Parameter

In image fusion algorithms the performance parameters can be evaluated as following parameters [3, 5, 8, 9]:

(A) Root Mean Square Error. Root mean square error (RMSE) is the measure of the corresponding pixels in the true image It and the fused image If. When the true and fused images are identical error generated will be nearly zero and it will enhance when the dissimilarity between images raise.

$$RMSE = \sqrt{\frac{1}{MN} \sum_{x=1}^{M} \sum_{y=1}^{N} \left(I_r(x,y) - I_f(x,y)\right)^2}$$

(B) Peak Signal to Noise Ratio [PSNR]. It gives enhanced value when the fused and true images are identical and superior value entails superior fusion.

$$PSNR = 20\log_{10}\left(\frac{L^2}{\frac{1}{MN} \sum_{x=1}^{M} \sum_{y=1}^{N} \left(I_r(x,y) - I_f(x,y)\right)^2}\right)$$

Here, L indicates the number of gray levels.

5   Results and Comparative Study

True Fuzzy type image img1.jpg of size 420×342 is revealed in Fig. 3. The 2 images to be fused are produced from the Fuzzy type true image using fuzzy type method as revealed in Figs. 4 and 5. The fused image is nearly analogous to true image and the error image is approximately zero. Table 1 reveals the fusion quality evaluation metrics. The table shows proposed hybrid techniques where metrics demonstrated in dark font are superior amongst others. We got almost similar performance by using fusion with 6 level pyramids or some higher values. Figure 6 and 7 shows the comparative study of RMSE and PSNR performance parameters. By applying projected algorithm results are improved as error values are reduced which enhances PSNR values.

Fig. 3. Reference fuzzy type image

Fig. 4. Fuzzy type image 1

Fig. 5. Fuzzy type image 2

Table 1. Proposed hybrid technique

	Pyramid levels			
	Techniques	1	3	5	7
RMSE	DCTPT	10.0311	**9.3924**	9.4921	12.7680
	FFTPT	7.9812	**7.8937**	7.9885	8.0075
	SPIHT	**6.4560**			
	Proposed	**5.1039**			
PSNR	DCTPT	38.1513	**38.4370**	38.3912	37.1036
	FFTPT	39.1441	**39.1920**	39.1402	39.1298
	SPIHT	**40.0651**			
	Proposed	**41.0858**			

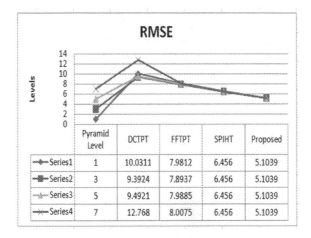

Fig. 6. Comparative study for RMSE

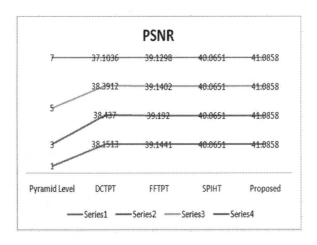

Fig. 7. Comparative study for PSNR

6   Conclusion

An innovative image fusion technique using CLT has been proposed and its performance is evaluated. We realized better fusion quality by enhancing the fusion levels till 6. This method can be efficiently used for fusion of fuzzy type images with multi spectral images also. The projected algorithm is easier and efficient to implement for real time applications. This paper also provides a comparative study between proposed & literature techniques and validation of the projected algorithm as Peak Signal to Noise Ratio (PSNR) and Root Mean Square Error (RMSE) in Table 1.

References

1. Toet, A.: A morphological pyramid image decomposition. Pattern Recogn. Lett. **9**(4), 255–261 (1989)
2. Naidu, V.P.S., Raol, J.R.: Pixel-level image fusion using wavelets and principal component analysis – a comparative analysis. Def. Sci. J. **58**(3), 338–352 (2008)
3. Naidu, V.P.S.: Discrete cosine transform-based image fusion. Def. Sci. J. **60**(1), 48–54 (2010). Special Issue on Mobile Intelligent Autonomous System
4. Kumar, M., et al.: Digital image watermarking using fractional fourier transform via image compression. In: IEEE International Conference on Computational Intelligence and Computing Research, IEEE ICCIC-2013, 26–28 December 2013 (2013)
5. Naidu, V.P.S.: A novel image fusion technique using DCT based laplacian pyramid. Int. J. Invent. Eng. Sci. (IJIES) **1**(2), 2319–9598 (2013)
6. Blum, R.S.: Robust image fusion using a statistical signal processing approach. Image Fusion **6**, 119–128 (2005)
7. Li, S., Kwok, J.T., Wang, Y.: Combination of images with diverse focuses using the spatial frequency. Inf. Fusion **2**(3), 167–176 (2001)
8. Naidu, V.P.S., Rao, J.R.: Pixel-level image fusion using wavelets and principal component analysis. Def. Sci. J. **58**(3), 338–352 (2008)
9. Seetha, M., MuraliKrishna, I.V., Deekshatulu, B.L.: Data fusion performance analysis based on conventional and wavelet transform techniques. In: IEEE Proceedings on Geoscience and Remote Sensing Symposium, vol. 4, pp. 2842–2845 (2005)
10. Yang, X.H., Huang, F.Z., Liu, G.: Urban remote image fusion using fuzzy rule. In: IEEE Proccedings of the Eighth International Conference on Machine Learning and Cybernetics, pp. 101–109 (2009)
11. Kumar, M., et al.: Fuzzy type image fusion using SPIHT image compression technique. Int. J. Eng. Res. Appl. (IJERA) (Accepted). (Impact factor: 1.69)
12. Kumar, M., et al.: Digital image watermarking using fractional fourier transform with different attacks. Int. J. Sci. Eng. Technol. **3**(8), 1008–1011 (2014). (ISSN:2277-1581)
13. Kumar, M.: Face recognition using som neural network with different facial feature extraction techniques. Int. J. Comput. Appl. (IJCA) **76**(3), 7–11 (2013). (Impact factor: 0.821)
14. Prabha, S., Sasikala, M.: Texture classification using curvelet transform. Int. J. Adv. Res. Technol. **2**(4), 451 (2013)
15. Kumar, M.: Matlab based high speed face recognition system using SOM neural networks. Int. J. Eng. Res. Appl. **34**, 785–790 (2013). (Impact factor: 1.69)
16. Kumar, M., et al.: Digital image watermarking using fractional fourier transform via image compression. In: IEEE International Conference on Computational Intelligence and Computing Research, IEEE ICCIC 2013, pp. 26–28, December 2013. (Published in IEEExplore)
17. Kakerda, R.K., et al.: Fuzzy type Image fusion using hybrid DCT-FFT based Laplacian pyramid transform. In: 4th IEEE International Conference on Communication and Signal Processing (ICCSP 2015), 02–04 April 2015, Melmaruvathur, TN, IND (2015). (Published in IEEExplore)
18. Kumar, M., et al.: Comparative study of different classifiers based speaker recognition system using modified MFCC for noisy environment. In: International Conference Green Computing and Internet of Things, ICGCIoT 2015, 08–10 October 2015, Delhi, IND (2015). (Published in IEEExplore)

19. Kumar, M., et al.: Robust digital image watermarking using DCT based pyramid transform via image compression. In: 4th IEEE International Conference on Communication and Signal Processing, ICCSP 2015, 02–04 April 2015, Melmaruvathur, TN, IND (2015). (Published in IEEExplore)
20. Kumar, M., et al.: Face recognition using SOM neural network with DDCT facial feature extraction techniques. In: 4th IEEE International Conference on Communication and Signal Processing, ICCSP 2015, 02–04 April 2015, Melmaruvathur, TN, IND (2015). (Published in IEEExplore)
21. Jain, R., et al.: Digital image watermarking using Hybrid DWT - FFT technique with different attacks. In: 4th IEEE International Conference on Communication and Signal Processing, ICCSP 2015, 02–04 April 2015, Melmaruvathur, TN, IND (2015). (Published in IEEExplore)

Performance Impact of Changing ICT Environment: A Case Study of Indian Hospitality and Tourism Sector

M.P. Sharma[✉] and Neha Sharma

Amity School of Hospitality, Amity University, Sector-125, Noida, 201303, UP, India
{mpsharma,nsharma11}@amity.edu

Abstract. Purpose: Like every industry, ICT applications have great impact on the Hospitality & Tourism industry. From social media to smart phones and automatic check-ins, Information and Communication Technology effects even the smallest areas of the industry. The utilization of Information and Communication Technology are evolving very rapidly and Hospitality and Tourism Industry have to acclimatize quickly to keep ahead in the competitive market.

The uptake of recent technological advances has been slow in the Industry. Unless this can be improved in the next number of months and years, many Hospitality and Tourism related companies risk falling even further behind when the new wave of technological advances comes along. Businesses that fail to adapt to the changing technological environment, inevitably, end up failing and shutting down. Technology in the Hospitality and Tourism industry has advanced a lot in recent years and will continue to advance at an incredible pace for the foreseeable future. Recently the Tourism industry has been slow to respond to change but luckily many Tourism related companies have seen the error of their ways and are beginning to adapt to these new technologies such as apps and smartphones. Providing the industry can catch up before a new wave of technology comes along, it should then be in a position to get ahead of the game and be proactive rather than waiting for every other industry to pass it out. Although it is seen as a difficult industry in which to innovate, there are now and will always be ways to adapt new and emerging technologies to the Hospitality and Tourism sector.

Keywords: ICT · Automatic check-ins · Social media · Inevitably · Incredible

1 Introduction

Like every industry, ICT applications have great impact on the Hospitality & Tourism industry. From social media to smart phones and automatic check-ins, Information and Communication Technology effects even the smallest areas of the industry. The utilization of Information and Communication Technology are evolving very rapidly and Hospitality and Tourism Industry have to acclimatize quickly to keep ahead in the competitive market.

With the growth of Facebook and Twitter, many companies have found it an ideal way to promote and sell their products and services. As it stands, it is difficult for travel

© Springer Nature Singapore Pte Ltd. 2016
A. Unal et al. (Eds.): SmartCom 2016, CCIS 628, pp. 119–127, 2016.
DOI: 10.1007/978-981-10-3433-6_15

related companies to utilise the likes of Facebook to its full potential. Unlike other, more physical technological advances, social media sites such as Facebook and Twitter cannot yet keep up to date with live changes in flight prices and schedules etc.

1.1 Current ICT Applications in the Tourism and Hospitality Industry

Smartphone apps are the new wave of technological advances, allowing users to download direct to their handheld device, anything they desire. These apps vary from simple gaming apps to photo modifying apps and, of course, include travel apps. Technology now allows us to check ourselves online before a flight and make changes to our bookings from our mobile. Many of us will be familiar with this process from booking flights with Ryanair. With Ryanair they actually require you to check-in online rather than at the airport. There are also apps available to download from different airlines which allow to book, check-in and modify bookings from smartphone. When it comes to other areas of Tourism, such as guided tours for example, technology has begun to strengthen its hold. It is now possible to download a guided tour of a museum from the museums website, or app if they have it. These tours sync in to your location within the museum and give you options on what to hear about. This is a step above the old Audio tours which were available and removes the need for a personal guide, although many people still prefer to have a person leading them so tour guides are not obselete yet. The same applications are also now available for entire cities and countries! Smartphone users can download guided tours from different companies or tourism bodies. Often tour operators will provide them with a link to their own guided tour app. These apps can vary from city tours to area guides to entire country guides.

1.2 The Effect of ICT Applications on the Tourism and Hospitality Industry

New advances in technology not only create opportunities but challenges also. The industry is now becoming much more active round the clock online and on social networks. Almost all major hotels, restaurants and travel agents have an active Facebook and Twitter page. The latter however have been slower in the uptake; this is mostly due to the fact that social network sites are, as yet, incapable of displaying live, up-to-date prices in relation to flights etc. But travel agents are still using these sites to promote themselves and build a good relationship with the public. Companies in the hospitality and tourism industry now interact with potential customers much more often, outside the usual 9 to 5 h and without seeing them face-to-face [10].

One of the main advantages of the new consumer technology, i.e. social media, is the ability of companies to see exactly where their audience is coming from, what interests them and the best way to market to them about their new products or services. Social media can also be used as a tool to give the consumer a positive feeling towards a destination before they even set foot there. Through the sharing of pictures, positive updates and videos, reviews, consumers can get a view of their potential destination.

1.3   The Changing ICT Environment

The uptake of recent technological advances has been slow in the Industry. Unless this can be improved in the next number of months and years, many Tourism related companies risk falling even further behind when the new wave of technological advances comes along. Businesses that fail to adapt to the changing technological environment, inevitably, end up failing and shutting down very rapidly. The reasons behind why a business are many, from stubborn management to lack of knowledge, but the end result is always the same. The business ends up falling behind, and unless drastic change is implemented, shuts down before long. The company has often been criticised for its "old-fashioned" and "backward thinking" way of conducting business on social networking platforms. With many stating that it has become more profit-driven than customer-driven. E – Today's hospitality and tourism market especially commercial activity and control on financial activity are heavily affected by recent Information and Communication Development.

1.4   E-Commerce

Electronic commerce is the buying and selling of goods and services, or the transmitting of funds or data, over an electronic network, which can be divided into the:(a) B2C; (b) B2B; (c) B2G; (d) C2C; (e) Business research; (f) B2C Communication.

Information and Communication Technology give tools for direct communication with customers [8].

In current situation the overall structure including Global distribution system, Internet distribution system, Central reservation system, Destination marketing organization and company moves towards an Internet-based value system (Fig. 1).

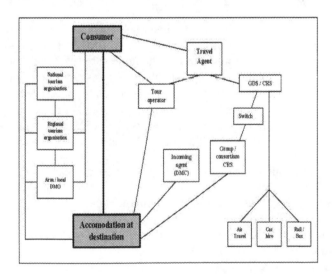

Fig. 1. Traditional value system

Direct interaction with customer and guest has increased in current trends of doing business in hospitality and tourism industry. There are many new intermediaries specializing in selling tourism products and services. Hospitality and tourism professionals have the challenge of finding the right channel to the right customer segment. Also in today's market scenario Information and Communication Technology has made customer relationship more visible and efficient in the Hospitality & Tourism Industry. ICT enables industry now able to interact with their customer and continuously to improve their products and services to meet customer expectations and satisfaction (Fig. 2).

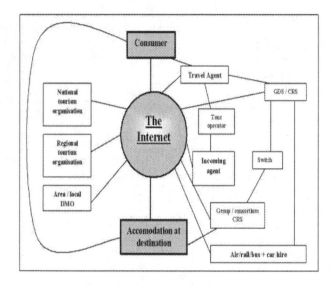

Fig. 2. Internet based value system

(a) Business to business communication: The huge variety of distribution channels is a challenge in the hospitality & tourism Industry. Success in hospitality and tourism demands rapid and efficient communication with all stake holders without a single mistake. The quantity of information analyzed and by tourism professionals are huge and also customers expect fast responses and real time confirmations. All these demand tourism professionals to be familiar with latest ICT tools.

(b) Changes in hospitality and tourism yield management: *Selling the right product to the right customer at the right time and for the right price* sounds relatively simple but is not easy to achieve. It is very difficult to find the right time, the right price and the right customers we should target especially in the hospitality and tourism industry? Yield Management or Revenue Management is about predictions and decisions to get the most revenue from that business. Management decisions are based on analysis of immense information about booking pace, competitors' rates, guest history, customer feedback and others [5].

2   Methodology

To achieve the objectives, the research has been focused on present scenario of international trends and role of Information and Communication Technology in the hospitality & tourism industry. To identify the gaps and to analyze the opinion of the industry professionals, a five point scale questionnaire has been developed.84 Hoteliers, Travel agents and Tourism organizations responded across India and the responses have been recorded online and offline using a questionnaire (Fig. 3).

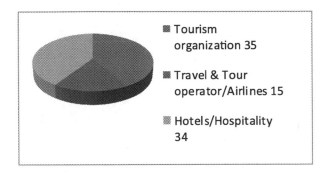

Fig. 3. Number of respondents

Among 84 respondents: 42% from tourism organizations. 18% from the Airlines Industry, Travel & Tour Operator & 41% from hospitality and hotel industry.

3   Scope of Research

The study has been conducted in tourism organizations, travel agents, hotels, restaurants, resorts, hospitality industry & professional across India. Data Analysis and Representation: The clarification and explanation on each statement responded from the sample are addressed below.

1. Improved technology with updated with latest Property Management System & Web Site will increase your business

Explanation regarding Fig. 4: 88% respondents are completely agree that the modernize website with lots of information has vital role in improvement the business potentiality. Only 12% of the respondents disagree with this statement.

2. Online reservation system contributed a great extent in hospitality & tourism industry

Explanation regarding Fig. 5: 84% agree that online reservation system is essential for selling the products and services in hospitality and tourism industry while 16% respondents disagree with this statement.

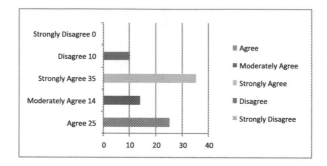

Fig. 4. Feedback based on latest computer technology & PMS.

3. Social media playing a vital role in promoting & marketing online for hospitality & tourism industry

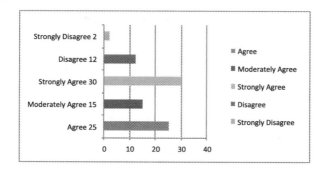

Fig. 5. Feedback based on - online reservation system.

Explanation regarding Fig. 6: 85% agree that social media is an important and constructive tool for online promotion and marketing, while only 15% of the respondents disagree.

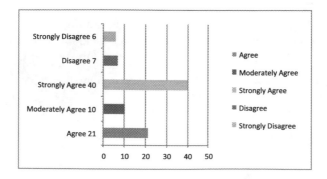

Fig. 6. Feedback based on role of social media.

4. Do you think that effectiveness of ICT is in Hospitality & Tourism industry in which 'a single website offers all products and services directly to their customer'?

Explanation regarding Fig. 7: 95% agree that websites may reduce the involvement of mediator in providing hospitality and tourism services to its customer. Yet, 5% of the respondents disagree the statement, which is somehow significant.

5. Do you think target customer will readily accept & absorb ICT trends?

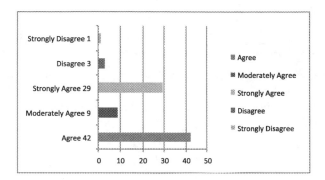

Fig. 7. Feedback based on importance of ICT in Hospitality & Tourism.

Explanation on Fig. 8: 96% readily agrees in accepting the ICT practices. While only 4% of the respondents disagree with this opinion.

6. Net banking is a very useful & perfect system for your hospitality and tourism financial operations in today's competitive scenario

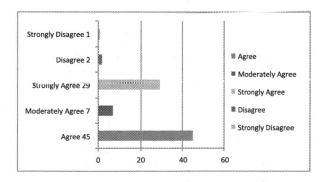

Fig. 8. Feedback based on effect of ICT on tourist.

Explanation regarding Fig. 9: 98% agrees that the net banking plays an important and crucial role in hospitality and tourism industry's commercial activity, while only 2% disagree with this opinion.

7. Mobile communications is going to be the next high demand service that facilitates hospitality & tourism services

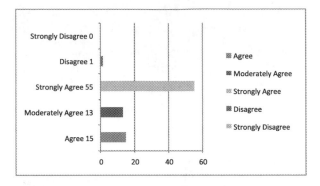

Fig. 9. Feedback based on Net banking & its importance in Hospitality and Tourism.

Clarifications regarding Fig. 10: 88% respondents agree while only 12% disagree with this opinion that the role of mobile trading is very high especially in hospitality industry.

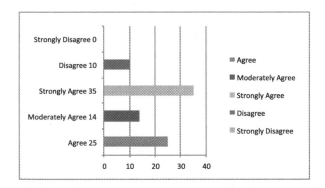

Fig. 10. Feedback based on importance of mobile communication.

4   Conclusion

Technology in the Tourism industry has advanced a lot in recent years and will continue to advance at an incredible pace for the forseeable future. Recently the Tourism industry has been slow to respond to change but luckily many Tourism related companies have seen the error of their ways and are beginning to adapt to these new technologies such as apps and smartphones. Providing the industry can catch up before a new wave of technology comes along, it should then be in a position to get ahead of the game and be proactive rather than waiting for every other industry to pass it out.

Although it is seen as a difficult industry in which to innovate, there are now and will always be ways to adapt new and emerging technologies to the Tourism sector. Smartphone apps are the most recent example of a new technology which has been adapted to suit the industry. All-in-all, the Hospitality and Tourism industry is playing catch up at the moment, particularly when it comes to the use of social media. However, it is catching up rapidly and, hopefully, will soon be in a position to be one of the more innovative industries. With ever increasing passenger numbers, more education in the area, and a highly motivated and passionate workforce, the future of Tourism and its use of technology looks as bright as ever.

References

1. Logan, K.: Adapt or die, the enduring rule of innovation, 23 January 2012, from Fast Company. http://www.fastcompany.com/1810048/adapt-or-die-enduring-rule-innovation. Accessed 29 Apr 2013
2. Moore, G.: Moore's law (1970), from Mooreslaw.org. http://www.mooreslaw.org/. Accessed 29 Apr 2013
3. Siliconerepublic.com: Connected Tourism, 11 August 2011, from siliconerepublic.com. http://www.siliconrepublic.com/new-media/item/23077-connected-tourism. Accessed 04 Apr 2012
4. Walker, J.R.: Introduction to Hospitality Management (2005)
5. Morrison, A.M.: Hospitality & Travel Marketing (2009)
6. Logan, K.: Adapt or die, the enduring rule of innovation, 23 January 2012, from Fast Company: http://www.fastcompany.com/1810048/adapt-or-die-enduring-rule-innovation. Accessed 29 Apr 2013
7. Moore, G.: Moore's law (1970), from Mooreslaw.org. http://www.mooreslaw.org/. Accessed 29 Apr 2013
8. Siliconerepublic.com: Connected Tourism 11 August 2011, from siliconerepublic.com: http://www.siliconrepublic.com/new-media/item/23077-connected-tourism. Accessed 04 Apr 2012
9. Walker, J.R.: Introduction to Hospitality Management (2005)
10. Morrison, A.M.: Hospitality & Travel Marketing (2009)

Comparison of Various Routing and Compression Algorithms: A Comparative Study of Various Algorithms in Wireless Networking

Shiv Preet[1], Ashish Kr. Luhach[1(✉)], and Ravindra Luhach[2]

[1] Lovely Professional University, Phagwara, Punjab, India
ashishluhach@acm.org
[2] Banasthali University, Banasthali, Rajasthan, India

Abstract. Wireless networking is on the verge of boom these days. Many multinational companies are trading in spectrum to provide data and voice services over wireless and mobile space. This research paper is a comparison of various network optimization as well as compression technologies for wireless network and mobile network. Asynchronous Transfer Mode (ATM), Genetic Algorithms (GA) is compared. It is reviewed that how it can bring efficiency in the current wireless as well as mobile networking. This research paper also reviews loseless and lossy compression and its efficacy in wireless networking scenario. This research paper provides reader a fair and honest view of current compression and speed optimization technologies, so that reader could get an insight of wireless network scenario in the prevailing conditions.

Keywords: Compression · Decompression · Genetic Algorithm · Network topology · Routing algorithms

1 Introduction

Wireless networking is growing by leap and bounds. Daily new mobile towers are being installed on different locations in India to facilitate mobile network coverage and make seamless connectivity options. Public Wi-Fi is being installed in different cities in different locations to cater to the need of data consumption of mobile internet users [2]. As the speed is growing so is the data consumption needed by the user. Users now like to watch YouTube video in at least 360p in mobiles and on the laptop they watch it in full HD (1080p). There are new services have been started like video conferencing of the go, music streaming etc. There is new private IPTV (Internet Protocol Television) Player which is ready to provide HD (High Definition) TV. They only need high speed data transfer, so that user could get good viewing experience while using their service. This makes it necessary that more data should be sent in smaller packet and that too on the best routing path available on the current network.

All these requirements made it mandatory that network must have reliable and high speed for data transfer. There are many techniques which are developed to make wireless networking streamlined. Some of these techniques are used for compressing the data

© Springer Nature Singapore Pte Ltd. 2016
A. Unal et al. (Eds.): SmartCom 2016, CCIS 628, pp. 128–134, 2016.
DOI: 10.1007/978-981-10-3433-6_16

while other technique involves routing algorithm [3]. This paper will try to discuss few of such technologies in details and it will also discuss its efficacy in current scenario.

1.1 Dynamic Source Routing (DSR)

Dynamic source routing is a routing mechanism in which routes are defined dynamically. Basically modus operandi of Dynamic Source routing is of route discovery and route maintenance. Route discovery is used to find out new paths for optimum data transfer while route maintenance maintains existing route paths [4]. It deletes the obsolete path and trim down existing path to make them best fit for a particular data transfer.

Algorithm
- Source node S wants to send some packet to destination node D.
- Source node initializes route discovery by route request mechanism.
- Each route request has address of source as well as destination and a unique random request id.
- Intermediate nodes append its own identifier while forwarding route request.
- In the end Source node has a set of possible routes to destination D.
  N = {y|y is in possible routes for destination d}
- Source node chooses best route for sending packets to Destination node.

DSR helps in making decision about best path available for data transfer over a wireless network. Its main limitation is that it drains battery juice of hand-held devices on a faster rate. It also consumes more processing power so in case of small devices it can have effect on overall performance of the device.

1.2 Location Aided Routing (LAR)

Location Aided Routing is another routing technique. In Location Aided Routing initially it sends data packet to all possible routes, then best route is identified and all packets are sent via that route. There is one alteration in which destination space is limited by IP Address or ports [5]. It helps in reducing the destination space. Initially all data packet is sent to all the directions available. Then route path is calculated on the basis of time taken in receiving the acknowledgment and rank is provided accordingly. Once route with shortest possible time is obtained, all other routes are discarded. Location Aided Routing helps in making data routing algorithm simple as it always choose best available route. Location Aided Routing has main limitations that it congest network for a while. Secondly as it does not maintain lists like DSR, as it is unable to ascertain if any new route is available with less cost after it has determined best route for its data transfer.

1.3 Genetic Algorithm (A)

Genetic algorithms are heuristic techniques which are used to find either perfect or approximate best solution for a problem. Mobile ad hoc network use this technology for determining approximate best route for transferring packets of data from source node to destination node.

Algorithm
- Genetic Algorithm create route table for all possible pairs of the nodes available.
- These Routes creates configuration strings or Meta data of those available routes.
- From the available routes best available route for data transfer is determined.
- Checking criteria can be fast response or less cell delay or multiple parameters as per the given criteria.
- Best Fit route is chosen which is given by the evaluation result.
- This process is repeated until best fit route is not find or until average fitness is not approximately equals to the maximum fitness provides by this model [6].

Genetic algorithm has advantages in terms of procuring optimum results for the given structure of solution and its parameters. It does not depend on complex formulas of mathematics or upon multi-disciplinary complex technologies [7]. One of the problems with Genetic algorithm is that it cannot be trusted completely to find a global optimum solution. Response time of Genetic algorithm is another factor which vary considerably between shortest route and longest route optimum solution. Its applicability in real life application is doubtful if the application is complex as well as of prime importance.

1.4   Asynchronous Transfer Mode (ATM)

Asynchronous transfer mode is a type of data transfer in which data is sent asynchronously without waiting for the acknowledgment from the recipient or sender side [9]. In such a case it increase speed manifolds and also it helps in seamless data transfer experience [10]. In ATM data is divided in small cell called packets. These small packets sent asynchronously towards destination [11].

ATM Structure.   ATM Cell structure consists of 5 byte header and 48 bytes of payload. First 8 bits are virtual path identifier Virtual channel identifier takes 16 bit. Both VPI and VCI define destination address of Cell. Payload type is of 3 bits and defines type of payload it carries in that cell. There is cell loss priority of 1 bit and header error control of 8 bit.

Algorithm
- Initial data packets are transferred to ATM Adaptation layer. Adaptation layer describes that how ip address, TCP ports etc. are configures in to ATM cells.
- ATM Layer makes connection between source and destination node for data transport and creates and release virtual circuits which are used for data transfer.
- Finally physical layer defines physical medium, electric voltage etc.

ATM has its own share of pie in the network. It can support legacy and old system. It can have multitude of services processed through a single channel. It can be used with simple yet efficient algorithms to support complex network transfer operations. ATM is not free from its pitfalls either. It is a generic solutions and for any kind of application a more optimized solution can be find by other means instead of ATM. ATM create small sized packets of same file size so ultimately it spend same amount of data transfer instead of reducing it [8] (Table 1).

Table 1. Comparison between various routing algorithms.

	DSR	LAR	GA	ATM
Algorithm	Routes are defined dynamically	Data is sent to all routes and then best route is chosen	It creates a route table for all nodes available in network	It does not wait for acknowledgment for former packet
Application	Suitable for Ad-hoc network	Suitable when need to calculate best possible route for transmission	Suitable when optimum route is required	Suitable for legacy systems

2   Compression

Compression is another technique which can be used to deliver more data at same speed. Compression can be of two kinds. One is Lossy compression in which part of data cannot be recovered while decompressing. User data gram protocol use Lossy compression [12]. Lossless compression is that technique in which no part of data is lost [13].

2.1   Huffman Coding for Data Compression

Huffman coding for data compression is a lossless technique [14]. First of all frequency of each character is measured and lowest frequency pairs are summed up together. It eventually makes a binary tree structure in which letters are on the leaf nodes. When decompressed, same data file is created as it was before compression.

Algorithm.   Huffman Coding Algorithm is based on set of number and its frequency of use. For example S is a set of elements for all the values and T is a set of elements describing frequency of use of each value. In Mathematical notation we can define it:

S = {x|x is an element of values used}

T = {y|y is an element of frequency of each value in S: $1 \leq y \leq N$}

Steps:
- Sort the list by frequency (Table 2).

Table 2. Sorted frequency list

Frequency	Value
3	1
4	2
5	3
6	4
7	5

- Create a parent node by merging first two elements of lowest frequency

```
        7:*
       /  \
      3    4
```

- Arrange new list again in sorted order (Table 3).

Table 3. New list in sorted order on frequency

Frequency	Value
5	3
6	4
7	5
7	*

- Next element 5 and 6 will be merged together.

```
        11:*
       /  \
      5    6
```

- Repeat last step until one final value is arrived. In this case it will be 25.

It can be infer from above algorithm that as number of frequencies increased, it also increase computation steps. Average compression performance of this algorithm is $O(N)^2$. Huffman coding can provide compression ratio up-to 80% which can help in achieving highly compressed data [15]. Huffman Coding has high Transfer time though. Its compression levels are low as compare to lossy compression techniques.

2.2 Joint Photographer Expert Group

Joint Photographer expert group or jpeg is a Lossy compression technique. This technique is used to compress high resolution images into small size. Though this algorithm produce a good quality image, it is possible that some of the data may be omitted while decompressing image [16].

Algorithm. Basic steps for Joint photographer expert group technique are as follows.

- First of all an image is divided in to blocks of 8 × 8 Size. If blocks are not exact multiple of 8 × 8 matrix then zero padding is added to make it into 8 × 8 blocks.
- Color of block is selected on the basis of value which is in the block.
- Discrete cosine transform is taken for each block for masking.
- While decompressing inverse of discreet cosine transform is taken to produce image [17].

This compression technique is faster as compared to lossless compression techniques. Its average compression performance comes out to be O(N). It also helps to achieve compression level of up-to 94% for image files. But there is a catch. Decompressing such images might lose some of the quality from the original images (Table 4).

Table 4. Comparison between various Huffman Coding and Joint Photographer expert group

	Huffman coding	Joint photographer expert group
Type	Loseless	Lossy
Speed	Slower than Lossy techniques	Faster than loseless techniques
Application	Where no data loss is permitted	Where some data loss is permitted
Complexity	$O(N)^2$	$O(N)$
Compression Ratio	Upto 94% (approx.)	Upto 80% (approx.)

This paper has compared many compression as well as routing algorithms. Each individual algorithm has its own pros and cons. Some of algorithm can act as catalyst in some of the networking environment but they cannot be used in all of these conditions. There is a need to use more than one algorithm to achieve better results as well as efficiency in network transfer [18, 19].

3 Proposed Methodology

Comparison of Compression as well as routing methodology has given an important insight that is there is a possibility of inculcating a modified algorithm on the basis of existing algorithm. This paper proposed a modified algorithm in which first data is compressed so that more data could be sent to receiving node in same packet size. Once this is done then on the receiving side compressed packet will be decompressed again. It will help in improving transfer capacity which in turn will increase data transfer rate as a whole. This technology can be useful where network speed is slow or where network is congested.

4 Conclusion

This paper compared different routing technologies as well as compression techniques. It highlights strengths of various technologies under different network situations. Proposed system can act as a clout to existing technologies in enhancing network efficiency and its efficacy. It might act as a catalyst in providing a seamless data transfer experience to users even under congested network conditions. In future this technique might be further optimized to achieve greater results.

References

1. Feng, Y., Ren, J., Jiang, J.: Object-based 2D-to-3D video conversion for effective stereoscopic content generation in 3D-TV applications. IEEE Trans. Broadcast. **57**, 50–57 (2011)
2. Bankoski, J., Wilkins, P., Xu, Y.: Technical overview of vp8, an open source video codec for the web, vol. 5, pp. 200–2012. IEEE (2011)
3. Ahmad, I., Zhang, Y.-Q.: Video transcoding: an overview of various techniques and research issues. IEEE Trans. Multimedia **7**, 450–467 (2005)

4. Arsha, M.D.: Automatic 2D-to-3D image and video conversion by learning examples and dual edge-confined in painting. Int. J. Adv. Res. Comput. Sci. Softw. Eng. **4**, 467–474 (2014)
5. Dass, R.: Video compression techniques. Int. J. Sci. Technol. Res. **1**, 67–75 (2012)
6. Ponlatha, S., Sabeenian, R.S.: Comparison of video compression standards. Int. J. Comput. Electr. Eng. **5**, 243–253 (2013)
7. Patil, S., Charles, P.: Review on 2D to 3D image and video conversion methods. Int. J. Comput. Appl. **14**, 890–898 (2015)
8. Limbachiya, A.M.: 2D to 3D video conversion. Int. J. Adv. Res. Comput. Sci. Softw. Eng. **5**, 78–84 (2015)
9. Wang, L.-C.: An industrial-strength audio search algorithm, vol. 6, pp. 65–70. IEEE (2004)
10. Pradhan, K.: Robust audio steganography technique using aes algorithm and MD5 hash. Int. J. Adv. Res. Comput. Sci. Softw. Eng. **4**, 68–74 (2012)
11. Tamimi, A.A., Abdalla, A.M.: An audio shuffle-encryption algorithm. WCECS **1**, 45–67 (2014)
12. Damodaram, A., et al.: Efficient method of audio stagnanography by modified LSB algorithm and strong encryption key. J. Theor. Appl. Inf. Technol. **5**, 67–78 (2005)
13. Iancu, D.A., et al.: A new local search algorithm for binary optimization dimitris bertsimas operation. J. Comput. **25**, 208–221 (2013)
14. Pushpa, S., et al.: Insertion and deletion on binary search tree using modified insert delete pair: an empirical study. Int. J. Comput. Sci. Netw. Secur. **7**, 269–280 (2013)
15. Kumari, A., et al.: Linear search versus binary search: a statistical comparison for binomial inputs. Int. J. Comput. Sci. Eng. Appl. **2**, 29–37 (2012)
16. Bryant, R.E., et al.: Graph-based algorithms for boolean function manipulation. Int. J. Comput. Sci. Eng. Appl. **4**, 34–45 (2013)
17. Keshet, J., et al.: Online passive-aggressive algorithms koby crammer. J. Mach. Learn. Res. **7**, 35–67 (2006)
18. Luhach, A.K., Dwivedi, S.K., Jha, C.K.: Implementing the logical security framework for e-commerce based on service-oriented architecture. In: Satapathy, S.C., Joshi, A., Modi, N., Pathak, N. (eds.) Proceedings of International Conference on ICT for Sustainable Development. AISC, vol. 409, pp. 1–13. Springer, Singapore (2016). doi:10.1007/978-981-10-0135-2_1
19. Luhach, A.K., Dwivedi, S.K., Jha, C.K.: Applying SOA to an E-commerce system and designing a logical security framework for small and medium sized E-commerce based on SOA. In: 2014 IEEE International Conference on Computational Intelligence and Computing Research (ICCIC), pp. 1–6. IEEE (2014)

Research and Analysis of Open Security Issues in Communication for Wireless Sensor Network

Ravindra Luhach[1], Chandra K. Jha[1], and Ashish Kr. Luhach[2(✉)]

[1] Banasthali University, Banasthali, Rajasthan, India
[2] Lovely Professional University, Phagwara, Punjab, India
ashishluhach@acm.org

Abstract. Sensors are resource constrained and computing devices used in wireless networks. These networks are comprised of large numbers sensors deployed randomly over an area. The wireless sensor network (WSN) has a direct impact on human welfare as their application can be extended to military surveillance, environmental monitoring and to healthcare also. Security breaches might lead to grave consequences, so it is important to protect wireless sensor networks against such threats. The specific characteristics of wireless sensor networks make them vulnerable to attacks on their communication channels and their hardware. This research work discusses the open security issues in WSN. Section 2 focuses on the problem statement and later, existing security mechanisms are discussed. This research paper also present an discussion on the Cryptographic mechanisms, which can be employed to protect against some of the possible attacks such as eavesdropping and the injection of messages by the attacker is prevented by authentication.

Keywords: Security issues · Eavesdropping · Encryption · Sensor network

1 Introduction

Wireless sensor networks are comprised of small size devices which are cheaper in cost and having limited resources, have the power to communicate with other devices and interact with their environment, either by silently sensing few parameters (generally named as in "passive mode"), or by triggering actuators ("active mode"). The major factor which limits the capability of these devices is the limited energy supply. The computational capabilities of these devices are comparable to those, which are used in embedded systems. The reason which makes these devices "comparable" is the underlying common hardware designs.

Sensor nodes make the use of wireless medium for communication in order to exchange data with other nodes. Initially, Wireless Sensor Networks were designed and deployed for military applications, for example, in order to track militants in inaccessible terrain; sensor nodes are deployed to keep track of the movement of militants or opponents. Due to the small size of sensor nodes and lesser cost, large number of sensor nodes need to be deployed in the area, where the aim is establish a network. But nowadays, Wireless Sensor Network is not only limited to Military Applications, but also applicable

© Springer Nature Singapore Pte Ltd. 2016
A. Unal et al. (Eds.): SmartCom 2016, CCIS 628, pp. 135–142, 2016.
DOI: 10.1007/978-981-10-3433-6_17

in many civilian applications, health applications, environmental applications and other engineering fields [1].

In numerous applications, security is the major issue of sensor networks. In the healthcare domain, handling of sensitive data of patients is one of the major concern. Without adequate security, the acceptance of sensor networks is likely to be limited [2]. So, it is important to identify the risks and vulnerabilities in deploying a sensor network in a sensitive environment, and how these risks can be managed and handled.

Sensor networks are vulnerable to external attacks as they are openly accessible by outer world. This allows intruders to sniff messages, or alter the messages, when in transit. Jamming the radio signals or replaying the snooped messages is the common types of attacks which occur in wireless sensor networks. Insider attacks are possible in any network if the attacker manages to deploy fake sensor nodes as the legitimate nodes in the sensor network area or takes control over the existing nodes, present in the network. Insider attacks are difficult to detect, because it bypasses the firewall and intrusion detection system and allows the intruder to gain access to cryptographic key information which is stored on sensor nodes [3]. Extraction of this type of information is difficult to intercept through an outside attack. Having complete access over a part of the network also allows the adversary to forge messages and sensor data, and which directly affects the operation of entire network.

2 Problem Statement

The main goal of a sensor network is the transmission of data between sensor nodes, while maintaining secrecy and privacy of data. Presence of multiple sensor nodes in a sensor network and due to the limited transmission range of a sensor node, messages have to traverse multiple intermediate nodes before reaching the destination, which in turn affects the transmission power of each intermediate hop and propagation time. Secure data transmission requires either a security association between the pair of sender- receiver sensor nodes, or the collaboration of the intermediate nodes. In the lifetime of a sensor node, it only communicates with very less number of nodes present in the sensor network due to its less transmission range [13].

It is not feasible to provide secure end-to-end data transmission in large sensor networks. For each pair of sender- receiver sensor nodes, a secret key is required and need to be stored somewhere for authentication. This is not an efficient way, since huge amount of memory is required for storing keys [13]. An alternative to this approach is to dynamically establish end-to-end connections, whenever it is required. However, performing a key agreement over multiple sensor nodes is an expensive operation.

In consideration to above mentioned drawbacks, "collaborative approaches" seem to be more suitable for wireless sensor networks. In such approaches, nodes rely on less number of sensor nodes, sometimes referred as "friendly nodes", and share a secret key with these "friendly nodes". They establish new security relationships with nearby nodes 'on the fly' by dynamically joining the network. Basically key agreements are limited to k-hop communications, by keeping the small value of factor 'k'. In order to transfer the messages over multiple sensor nodes, "friendly" nodes will help each other to forward the messages and to ensure that no malicious node will be in position to tamper the data [13].

In comparison to end-to-end security schemes, the collaborative approaches offer less security guarantees. End-to-end schemes are said to be *computationally* secure, i.e. no existing computing resources are sufficient to break the scheme. On the other hand, collaborative approaches provide either *threshold* or *probabilistic* security. It is therefore important to quantify the security properties of a wireless sensor network.

3   Security Requirements for WSN

There are numbers of security vulnerability issues which need to be addressed which are identified during Message Transmission through various layers such as Link layer, Routing layer etc. These vulnerabilities can become serious security threats if not handled after anticipation of attacks. Hence, it becomes a necessity to frame such requirements to avoid the development of such risks or potential threats. In the following section, we give an overview of sensor network security issues.

3.1   Message Transmission

When a message is sent from one node to another, it should not be susceptible to manipulation or eavesdropping by an attacker. This can be achieved by encrypting and authenticating messages in transit on Link layer. The necessary keys can be agreed upon when the wireless link is established. However, at this stage the above procedure is vulnerable against man-in-the-middle attacks. To avoid this attack, some kind of entity authentication is required [4]. This problem is prevalent in almost all wireless networks. For this, Sensor nodes need to ensure that other communicating nodes are legitimate participants in the network. It does not necessarily require the verification of another node's ID, but merely its membership in the group of legitimate nodes. It should be ensured through a light-weight process, preferably without the help of a base station acting as a trusted third party.

Link-level security is only effective against outsider attacks. A message that is transmitted over multiple hops is easily compromised if its path includes a malicious node. Therefore, a mechanism to set up end-to-end secure connections is desirable. However, this requires a means to establish a shared key between the endpoints of a connection, which turns out to be a challenging task in sensor networks [5].

3.2   Routing

Multi-hop routing is a fundamental service in large-scale sensor networks. There are protocols that are specifically designed to address the needs of sensor network applications. Usually, they do not rely on up-to-date routing tables, which would be too complex to maintain. Rather, they forward a message based on features of the message itself, or they set up paths on demand. A routing protocol ensures that messages reach their target. Attacks on the network layer, where routing functionality is located, aim at diverting or suppressing messages. This can lead to unauthorized data disclosure, missing critical events, energy exhaustion, or event triggering at undesired locations. A secure routing protocol must be resilient against such attacks.

3.3 Access Control

Access control plays an important role in ensuring the confidentiality and integrity of sensor network data as well as for the safe operation of a sensor networks. Thus, an effective access control mechanism is required. Preferably Access control must be implemented in a distributed manner in order to allow arbitrary entry points into the network. This avoids the use of a centralized entity which acts as a single entry point constituting of a single point of failure and a performance bottleneck.

Many sensor network applications deal with sensitive or commercially valuable data. Queries are propagated through the network by triggering the nodes to activate their sensors and transmit data. Actuators are triggered by the control commands. All these actions are significant with respect to the commercial operation of a sensor network and its interaction with its environment. Illegitimate use may have harmful consequences. Therefore, access to a sensor network should be restricted to authorized parties only.

3.4 Data Aggregation

One of the main tasks of sensor networks is data aggregation i.e. the combination of data gathered by various sensors into a single value that is meaningful within the application context and represents the monitored state to the maximum accuracy. This process needs to ensure robustness against random errors as well as security against malicious nodes that report deliberately false sensor data.

It is generally not feasible to detect whether the data reported by the sensor nodes is correct or not. Most of the existing approaches for securing the process of data aggregation aim at minimizing the errors generated by few malicious nodes. Moreover, the data reported by aggregating nodes might be rejected if the underlying raw data is inconsistent with the aggregated value. This verification can be performed by sampling a small portion of the raw data.

3.5 Location Verification

It is of due importance to know the details of the location correctly apart from what type of data is gathered in most of the sensor network applications. When the location is reported incorrectly, responsive actions may be misguided. This not only wastes resources but also leaves the location where the phenomenon actually occurred unattended. A malicious report with a falsified location can thus inflict heavy damage. A solution to this problem is the verification of the location of the reporting node. If the reporting node has to convince other nodes that it is indeed located at the reported location, it is much less likely that a falsely reported location is being accepted.

3.6 Intrusion Detection

Intrusion detection systems (IDS) have emerged as major security tools in Internet networking domain. Their purpose is to detect patterns in system behavior that indicate malicious activities by both outsiders and insiders. The impact of an attack can be drastically reduced if it is detected during the earliest stage. In sensor networks, Intrusion can occur at two levels. One case could be that the sensor nodes are completely taken under the control of the adversary. In second case the adversary could disrupt the sensor network's operation through external means. The latter type of attacks can easily be detected and defended. If the adversary manages to take control of sensor nodes, he gains access to sensitive information stored on these nodes such as cryptographic keys and is able to participate in the network's operation. If the compromised nodes do not show aberrant behavior, they may go undetected. The adversary can then use them for eavesdropping or subverting the network by injecting false messages in such a way that these actions will not be apparent to the legitimate nodes.

Host-based intrusion detection is directly not applicable in sensor networks. It must be assumed that once the adversary has gained control of a sensor node, he completely controls all the processes running on that node. This will allow him to disable any intrusion monitoring process. The reason is that an embedded computing platform such as a sensor node, does not provides the required level of memory protection and process separation which is available on a high-end platform with the appropriate operating system and hardware support.

3.7 Intrusion Tolerance

One bottleneck with intrusion detection is that the adversary might be able to adapt the behavior of compromised nodes in such a way that their aberrant behavior is not classified as such. Thus, these nodes operate seemingly normal and are able to influence the overall operation of the network. In order to introduce some level of intrusion tolerance, it is advisable not to rely on the reports from a single node but instead require some agreement by a number of nodes before a report is accepted and further processed.

3.8 Availability

Several factors are responsible which can reduce the lifetime of a sensor network. For example, naturally occurring phenomena, such as extreme temperature variations leading to exhaust of the batteries. An attacker could force the sensor nodes to frequently retransmit the messages by selectively inducing errors. Over the time, this leads to failure of the nodes and eventually in the inoperability of the overall network. Such disturbances could not easily be identified as malicious interferences and therefore no effective countermeasures exist. An attentive observer may notice a higher failure rate than expected, but still the cause may remain obscure.

Jamming and physical destruction of nodes are some of the simple forms of denial-of service attacks which can be compensated if they appear on a small scale i.e. if only a small area is affected. In some situations, the effects of a denial-of-service attack can be mitigated if nodes are able to extend their sleep cycle when they notice an attack has occurred so that they can conserve as much power as possible. This would make the sensor network inoperable during an attack, but at least can continue its operation once the attack has got ceased. But if an exhaustion attack gets successfully executed on a large scale affecting larger areas then there is no possibility to recover other than by deploying new nodes after destruction.

4 Existing Approaches to Wireless Sensor Network Security

The emergence of wireless sensor networks as an object of academic research as well as practical engineering has initiated the development of such networks towards a tool that can be applied in many environmental, industrial, and social environments. This development has triggered an interest in the security of such networks, as they are vulnerable due to characteristics such as deployment in open environments, wireless communication, and the absence of close administrative surveillance. Frequent node failures, changing topologies, and resource restrictions make the design of algorithms and protocols challenging including security mechanisms. Usually, techniques used in traditional computer networks are not directly applicable [11, 12]. This section discusses approaches to security that has been especially developed for wireless sensor networks.

4.1 Key Distribution and Agreement

Public-key cryptography is considered somewhat expensive for resource constrained sensor nodes, since the involved operations are time- and energy consuming. On a typical contemporary sensor node hardware platform, RSA private-key operations consume 10 s and more, and cryptographic operations based on elliptic curves in the order of seconds. On Energy-wise scale, a single key exchange based on RSA is reported to consume almost same energy as the encryption with AES approximately around 77 kb data [6]. The debatable consideration is whether these resource requirements make the use of public-key cryptography feasible or infeasible in sensor networks and will practically depend on the used hardware platform, the frequency of public-key operations, and the available energy resources. The availability of public-key operations may even be dangerous to the sensor network. It has been noted that the possibility for a node to create signatures could be exploited by an attacker for draining the batteries of sensor nodes [7].

In order to be prepared for the cases where resource availability is sufficient for public-key cryptography, alternatives should be designed. The most important use of public-key cryptography is for handshake, i.e. the exchange of the secret key. This key, which is shared only by the two parties involved in the handshake, can be used for encrypting and authenticating the messages. Therefore, techniques for establishing secret keys without using public keys cryptography are desirable [8] (Table 1).

Table 1. Sensor layers and their attacks and Defenses

Layer	Attacks	Defenses
Physical	Jamming of bits	Spread spectrum
		Low duty cycle
	Tampering	Region mapping
		Hiding
Link	Collision	Error correcting code
	Exhaustion	Rate limitation
Network and Routing	Homing	Encryption
	Misdirection	Authorization
	Black holes	Redundancy
Transport	Flooding	Client puzzles

4.2 Secure Communication

Key agreement as described in the previous section is a prerequisite for general secure node-to-node communication, either on the link level between neighboring nodes, or between remote nodes that are separated by multiple hops. For more constrained communication patterns, more economical techniques are conceivable. One of the most light-weight protocols is μTESLA. It is intended to be used in base station-centric networks, where the most prevalent communication patterns are point-to-point between a base station and a node (e.g. for queries and reporting sensor readings), and broadcasts from the base station to all nodes (e.g. for queries or reprogramming the entire network). It only assumes that every node shares a unique key with the base station. Using this key, the broadcast authentication mechanism can be bootstrapped [9, 10].

4.3 Secure Routing

Cryptographic keys being established through techniques discussed in the previous subsection helps to ensure secure communication with respect to the confidentiality and the authenticity of messages. It needs to be ensured that messages indeed arrive at their destinations without being misrouted or dropped. *Ariadne* is a route discovery protocol that is able to find routes from a source to a destination in a multi-hop network and pass them back to the sender [14]. It is secure in the sense that the hosts authenticate themselves and each host certifies the previous piece of the path from the source to itself. All host identities are linked through a hash chain. A basic assumption is an end-to-end secure link between the source and the destination. The most important attacks against sensor networks on the routing layer are identified. They comprise of Bogus routing information, Selective forwarding, Sinkholes, Wormholes, *HELLO* floods, Sybil attack and Acknowledgement spoofing.

5   Conclusion

This research paper focused on the open security issues in wireless sensor network. This research work also indentified the important threats in the same. In order to protect Wireless Sensor Network from these threats and to deal with the security issues a range of mechanisms are required which cover all components associated with the system. This includes the hardware design of the sensor platform, all protocol layers of the wireless communication, the platform's runtime environment, and the application software. In this work, we have focused on providing the foundation for secure communications in a WSN.

References

1. Akyildiz, I.F., Su, W., Sankarasubramaniam, Y., Cayirci, E.: Wireless sensor networks: a survey. Comput. Netw. **38**(4), 393–422 (2002)
2. Anderson, R.: Security Engineering. Wiley, New York (2001)
3. Anderson, R., Chan, H., Perrig, A.: Key infection: Smart trust for smart dust. In: 2004 Proceedings of the 12th IEEE International Conference on Network Protocols, ICNP 2004, 5 October 2004, pp. 206–215. IEEE (2004)
4. Arkin, B., Stender, S., McGraw, G.: Software penetration testing. IEEE Secur. Priv. **1**(1), 84–87 (2005)
5. Avancha, S., Undercoffer, J., Joshi, A., Pinkston, J.: Secure sensor networks for perimeter protection. Comput. Netw. **43**(4), 421–435 (2003)
6. Becher, A., Benenson, Z., Dornseif, M.: Tampering with Motes: Real-World Physical Attacks on Wireless Sensor Networks. Springer, Heidelberg (2006)
7. Benenson, Z., Gärtner, F.C., Kesdogan, D.: An algorithmic framework for robust access control in wireless sensor networks. In: 2005 Proceedings of the Second European Workshop on Wireless Sensor Networks, pp. 158–165. IEEE, January 2005
8. EO, B., Zitterbart, M.: Towards acceptable public-key encryption in sensor networks. In: IWUC 2005, pp. 88–93, May 2005
9. Burmester, M., Van Le, T.: Secure multipath communication in mobile ad hoc networks. In: 2004 Proceedings of the International Conference on Information Technology: Coding and Computing, ITCC 2004, 5 April, vol. 2, pp. 405–409. IEEE (2004)
10. Chan, H., Gligor, V.D., Perrig, A., Muralidharan, G.: On the distribution and revocation of cryptographic keys in sensor networks. IEEE Trans. Dependable Secure Comput. **2**(3), 233–247 (2005)
11. Luhach, A.K., Luhach, R.: Research and implementation of security framework for small and medium sized e-commerce based on SOA. J. Theor. Appl. Inf. Technol. **82**(3), 395 (2015)
12. Luhach, A.K., Dwivedi, S.K., Jha, C.K.: Implementing the logical security framework for E-commerce based on service-oriented architecture. In: Proceedings of International Conference on ICT for Sustainable Development, pp. 1–13. Springer, Singapore (2016)
13. Walters, J.P., Liang, Z., Shi, S., Chaudhary, V.: Wireless sensor network security: a survey. Secur. Distrib. Grid, Mob. Pervasive Comput. **1**, 367 (2007)
14. Luhach, A.K., Jha, C.K., Dwivedi, S.K.: Designing a logical security framework for E-commerce system based on service oriented architecture. Int. J. Soft Comput. **5**(2), 1–10 (2014)

Empirical Analysis of Image Segmentation Techniques

Neeraj Shrivastava[1,2(✉)] and Jyoti Bharti[1]

[1] Department of Computer Science and Engineering, MANIT, Bhopal, India
neeraj0209@gmail.com, jyoti2202@gmail.com
[2] Department of Computer Science and Engineering,
IES IPS Academy, Indore, India

Abstract. The paper delves into a relative examination of various Image Segmentation Techniques and also evaluated the performance of Thresholding and Region Growing Image Segmentation methods based on Jaccard Similarity Coefficient (JSC), Dice Similarity Coefficient (DSC) and execution time.

Keywords: Image segmentation · Jaccard similarity coefficient · Dice similarity coefficient · Region · Edge

1 Introduction

Image segmentation is very basic problem in image analysis process. It is the first step in any of the image analysis process, although there have been several image segmentation algorithms were proposed such as thresholding, region growing, edge based segmentation etc. The level of segmentation is decided on the amount of problem being solved i.e. The Segmentation process is stopped when the substances of interest of a particular application is isolated [1, 4].

Image Segmentation Techniques broadly categorize into Similarity Based and Discontinuity Based Image Segmentation. In Similarity Based Approach, it is tried to assemble pixels which are alike on some homogeneous criteria. In Discontinuity Based Approach, the separation or splitting of an image is performed based on some changes in intensity level or gray level of an Image [4]. Figure 1 results various Segmentation Techniques in hierarchical form.

In Thresholding, it is aimed to separate whole Image into two parts foreground and background images depended on the some threshold value [3, 6]. In Region Growing, we explicitly decide the number of seed points and endeavor to include neighbor pixel in the nearest seed point according to some homogeneity criteria [6, 8, 10]. In Split and Merge we first divide the complete Image into number of Sub-Images and strive to merge these Sub-Images into one following some specific criteria [3, 8, 16].

In Fast Scanning, we don't need any seed point in prior rather we start from left to right top most pixel and scan the complete Image starting from top to bottom, left to right manner following some homogeneity criteria [16]. DP clustering removes the disadvantage of K-Means, clustering in which there must be giving no. of clusters in

A. Unal et al. (Eds.): SmartCom 2016, CCIS 628, pp. 143–150, 2016.
DOI: 10.1007/978-981-10-3433-6_18

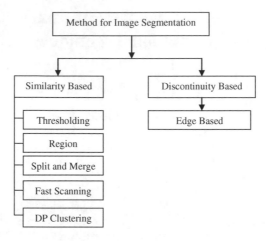

Fig. 1. Image segmentation techniques

advance [2]. Edge based detection detects edge in the image. Here edge is nothing but the boundary between two segments [4, 5, 10].

2   Image Segmentation Methods

2.1   Thresholding

Thresholding is one of the most widely used approaches for Image Segmentation. The gray level of pixels of foreground Image is different from the gray level of pixels of background Image. If the pixel values are less than some threshold value than these pixels are put are in one cluster and other pixels put in another cluster [18].

$$f(x, y) = 1 \text{ if } g(x, y) > t$$
$$f(x, y) = 0 \text{ otherwise}$$

(1)

Where t is the threshold value, (x, y) are the coordinate of the pixel value, g(x, y) represent the gray level of the image pixel [3, 6].

The value of threshold t can be computed as follows:

1. Calculate mean value of image pixels as t (start with mean value).
2. Divide the complete Image into two region R_1 and R_2 using t (one which is greater than t and another which is less t).
3. Calculate the new threshold using $(t = (\mu_1 + \mu_2)/2)$, where μ_1 and μ_2 are the intensity value of R_1 and R_2 respectively.

Repeat 2–3 until μ_1 and μ_2 do not change in successive iteration [5].

2.2   Region Growing:

In Region Growing, there some essential seed point through which algorithm start grows with certain threshold criteria. In these seed point is the start point. The algorithm steps are as follows:

1. Choose seed points as $P_1, P_2 \ldots P_n$ and then clustered image as $C_1, C_2 \ldots C_n$.
2. If difference of pixels value of P_i and its neighbor is less, then neighbor pixel could be classified into C_i, where i = 1, 2, ... n.
3. Otherwise P_i will be set as new seed point.
4. Repeat step 2–3 until all pixels in image must be lie in one the cluster.

Advantage: Connected component guaranteed and give good results with less noisy.

Disadvantage: If seed points are selected different by different users then the cluster/segments are different. So seed selection crucial task and also there is some necessary threshold criteria selection method must be present [6, 11–15].

2.3   Split and Merge

In this, first we split the entire image into different components following some criteria. Quad tree is a data structure which is generally applied for splitting followed by merging these sub images which are similar in some sense.

Advantage: Connected regions are guaranteed.

Disadvantage: Sometimes it will lead to blocky segmentation in later stage [3, 8, 16].

2.4   Fast Scanning

There are no given seed points initially so it removes the problem of Region Growing Segmentation as it requires initially seed points. In initially we convert the Image into its pixel value matrix and in these matrix left most top value is the seed point and then we scan whole matrix from left to right, top to bottom manner and if neighbor pixel value is less than some predefined threshold value then it belongs to same region otherwise it becomes new seed point and these process is repeated until all pixels belongs to one of the region.

Advantage: The speed is very quick and the outcome of Segmentation will be perfect with good connectivity.

Disadvantage: It will lead to gradient problem and it is very responsive to noise [16].

2.5   Image Segmentation Using DP (Density Peaks) Clustering

In the traditional K-Means clustering we have to decide no. of clusters already. In segmentation it is hard to determine no. of cluster in advance. In this, they cluster the

Fig. 2. (a) Original Image (b) Segmented Image using DP clustering based segmentation

region based on DP Clustering. DP clustering could cluster data by Fast Search and Find of density peaks and it is assumed that cluster centers are often surrounded by points that have lower density and have a relatively large distance from these points with higher density (Fig. 2). The following algorithm steps are:

1. Convert the image into three color channel.
2. Compute the density ρ and distance δ by using Eqs. 2 and 3 respectively:

$$\rho = \sum x(d_{ij} - d_c) \tag{2}$$

$$\delta_i = \begin{cases} \text{Min}_j\,(d_{ij})/\rho_j > \rho_i \\ \text{Max}\,(d_{ij})/\rho_j \text{ is the highest density} \end{cases} \tag{3}$$

Where ρ_i is the no. of data points within a distance d_c. d_{ij} is the Euclidean Distance between point i and point j, d_c is a cutoff distance.

3. Choose the data points with high density (ρ) and large distance (δ) as cluster centers.
4. Mark x_i with the same label of point x_j if satisfying the following conditions:
   a. $\rho_j > \rho_i$ and $d_{ij} = \text{min}_{l \neq i}\,(d_{il})$.

Advantage: There is no necessity of explicit seed points.

Disadvantage: There must be some criteria for selection of d_c (cutoff distance) [2].

2.6 Edge Based Detection

Edge is nothing but a boundary between two regions having distinct intensity/gray levels [1]. Edge Based Segmentation aims to extract information from the image and ascertain the area with strong intensity and displays present of an edge [8]. The most familiar gradient operators for Edge Detection are Robert, Prewitt and sobel operator [4, 5, 10].

The Image gradient is to find Edge strength and direction at location (x, y) of image [3, 10].

$$\nabla f \equiv \text{grad}(f) \equiv \begin{bmatrix} g_x \\ g_y \end{bmatrix} = \begin{bmatrix} \frac{\partial f}{\partial x} \\ \frac{\partial f}{\partial y} \end{bmatrix} \tag{4}$$

The magnitude (length) of vector, denoted as M(x, y):

$$M(x, y) = mag(\Delta f) = \sqrt{g_x^2 + g_y^2} \tag{5}$$

The direction of the gradient vector is given by the angle [1, 8]:

$$\alpha(x, y) = \tan^{-1}\left[\frac{g_y}{g_x}\right] \tag{6}$$

3   Performance Metrics

The performance of segmentation method can be evaluated using many of the parameter like JSC (Jaccard Similarity Coefficient), DSC (Dice Similarity Coefficient) and execution Time [3, 4].

The Jaccard Similarity Cocfficient is used to measure the degree of the correspondence between two segmentation and can be evaluated as follows:

$$JSC(A, B) = (A \cap B)/(A \cup B) \tag{7}$$

Larger the value of JSC indicates better image segmentation [3, 6, 7].

Dice Similarity Coefficient is just like the Jaccard Coefficient which measures the overlapping of two sets.

$$DSC(A, B) = 2(A \cap B)/|A| \cup |B| \tag{8}$$

Where A, B are two compared images [3, 6, 7].

4   Experimental Results and Discussion

In order to compare Thresholding and Region Growing Segmentation algorithm, we discuss here experimental results. A computer system with an Intel Core 2 Duo E4700 CPU 2.6 GHz Processor. All of the segmentation techniques were simulated using MATLAB R2014a. Performance comparison of different metrics was on 104 images.

Figure 3 describe an example of Thresholding Segmentation of three images using different threshold value.

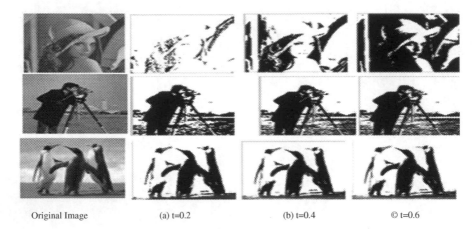

Original Image   (a) t=0.2   (b) t=0.4   © t=0.6

Fig. 3. Thresholding image segmentation

Figure 4 shows the result of Seeded Region Growing Segmentation at different threshold values. Table 1 shows the performance metrics for Thresholding and Region Growing Segmentation Techniques. It shows the mean value of the parameters (Fig. 5).

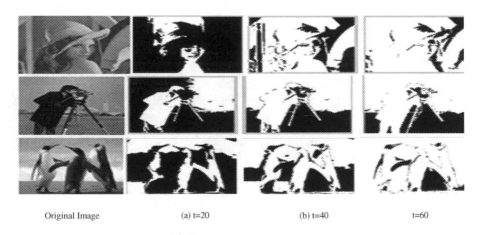

Original Image   (a) t=20   (b) t=40   t=60

Fig. 4. Seeded region growing

Table 1. Correlation study of various segmentation techniques

Metrics	Thresholding	Region growing
JSC	0.66	0.60
DSC	0.79	0.74
Time (second)	3.97	7.37

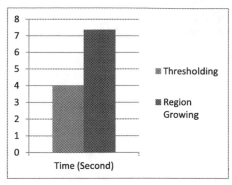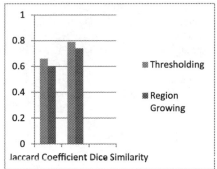

Fig. 5. Comparition graph for thresholding and region growing based on time (second), Jaccard coefficient, dice similarity index.

5 Conclusion

In this paper, we discuss various image segmentation algorithm used and we implement Thresholding and Region Growing Segmentation and compare various performance parameters. We observed that thresholding method gives better value for JSC, DSC and Time (Seconds) as 0.66, 0.79 and 3.971. Since its accuracy still depends on the value of threshold "t". Thus Region Growing Segmentation methods showed 0.60, 0.74 and 7.37 as JSC, DSC and Time (seconds), since it is usual, and the lightening affects the appearance.

Different segmentation algorithm imparts different performance. Since level of Segmentation is rely upon application requirement so we choose Segmentation methods based on application.

References

1. Zaitoun, N.M., Aqel, M.J.: Survey on image segmentation techiniques. Procedia Comput. Sci. **65**, 797–806 (2015). Elsevier
2. Chen, Z., Qi, Z., Meng, F., Cui, L., Shi, Y.: Image segmentation via improving clustering algorithms with density and distance. Procedia Comput. Sci. **55**, 1015–1022 (2015)
3. Haj-Hasan, H., Chaddad, A., Tanougast, C., Harkouss, Y.: Comparison of segmentation techniques for histopathological images. In: Fifth International Conference on Digital Information and Communication Technology and it's Application (DICTAP), Beirut, Lebanon, pp. 80–85. IEEE (2015). ISBN: 978-1-4799-4129-2
4. Gandhi, N.J., Shah, V.J., Kshirsagar, R.: Mean shift technique for image segmentation and modified canny edge detection algorithm for circle detection. In: International Conference on Communication and Signal Processing, 3-5 April 2014, India. IEEE (2014). ISSN: 978-1-4799-3358-7

5. Sivakumar, V., Murugesh, V.: A brief study of image segmentation using thresholding technique on a noisy image. In: International Conference on Information Communication and Embedded Systems (ICICES), 27-28 February 2014, pp. 1–6, Chennai, Tamil Nadu, India. IEEE (2014). ISBN: 978-1-4799-3835-3

6. Saranya, R., Daniel, J., Abudhahir, A., Chermakani, N.: Comparison of segmentation techniques for detection of defects in non-destructive testing images. In: International Conference on Electronics and Communication Systems (ICECS), Coimbatore, India, 13-14 Feb 2014. IEEE (2014). ISBN: 978-1-4799-2321-2

7. Kalavathi, P.: An image spatial alignment method for computing region overlapping measures. Int. J. Emerg. Trends Technol. Comput. Sci. (IJETTCS) $3(5)$, 251–255 (2014). ISSN: 2278-6856

8. Umaa Mageswari, S., Sridevi, M., Mala, C.: An experimental study and analysis of different image segmentation techniques. Procedia Eng. 64, 36–45 (2013). International Conference on Design and Manufacturing (IConDM2013). Elsevier

9. Polak, M.: An evaluation metric for image segmentation of multiple objects. Image Vis. Comput. 27, 1223–1227 (2009). Elsevier

10. Fan, J., Zeng, G., Body, M., Hacid, M.S.: Seeded region growing: an extensive and comparative study. Pattern Recognit. Lett. 26, 1139–1156 (2005)

11. Choong, M.Y., Kow, W.Y., Chin, Y.K., Angeline, L., Teo, K.T.K.: Image segmentation via normalised cuts and clustering algorithm. In: IEEE International Conference on Control System, Computing and Engineering, 23-25 November 2012, Penang, Malaysia, pp. 430–435 (2012)

12. Afifi, A., Ghoniemy, S., Zanaty, E.A., EI-Zoghdy, S.F.: New region growing based on thresholding technique applied to MRI data. Int. J. Comput. Netw. Inf. Secur. 7, 61–67 (2015). doi:10.5815/IJCNIS.2015.07.08, MECS http://www.mecs-press.org/. Accessed June 2015

13. Juan Shan, H.D. Cheng, Y.W.: A novel automatic seed point selection algorithm for breast ultrasound images. In: 19th IEEE International Conference on Pattern Recognition (ICPR), pp. 1–4 (2008). doi:10.1109/ICPR.2008.4761336, ISSN:1051-4651

14. Sanchez, J., Lzquierdo, E.M., Hidalgo, A.A.: Improving parameters selection of a seeded region growing method for multiband image segmentation. IEEE Lat. Am. Trans. $13(3)$, 843–849 (2015). doi:10.1109/TLA.2015.7069113, ISSN:1548-0992

15. Malek, A.A., Rahman, W.E., Yasiran, S.S., Jumaat, A.K., Jalil, U.M.A.: Seed point selection for seed-based region growing in segmenting microcalcifications. In: IEEE International Conference on Statics in Science, Business, and Engineering (ICSSBE), 6396580, pp. 1–5 (2012). doi:10.11.09/ICSSBE, Print ISBN: 978-1-4673-1581-4

16. Malek, A.A., Rahman, W.E., Ibrahim, A., Mahmud, R.: Region and boundary segmentation of micro calcifications using seed-based region growing and mathematical morphology. Procedia Soc. Behav. Sci. 8, 634–639 (2010). International Conference on Mathematics Education Research 2010 (ICMER 2010)

Adaptive Bi-Histogram Equalization Using Threshold (ABHET)

Subhasmita Sahoo, Jagyanseni Panda, and Mihir Narayan Mohanty[✉]

Department of ECE, S 'O' A University, Bhubaneswar, Odisha, India
subhasmita67@gmail.com, jagyansenipanda@soauniversity.ac.in,
mihir.n.mohanty@gmail.com

Abstract. Contrast enhancement and brightness preservation of the image are two important issues of image enhancement in research field now-a-days. The objective is to enhance the image uniformly over different parts of the image. General Histogram Equalization doesn't control degree of enhancement of the image. To overcome this drawback, another variant of Histogram Equalization method namely Adaptive Bi-histogram Equalization using Threshold (ABHET) is being proposed. The proposed method undergoes three steps, such as: Histogram segmentation using threshold, Clipping of histogram using mean value of occupied intensity and histogram equalization of each sub-images. Finally all the sub-images are combined into one complete image. Simulation results show that ABHET outperforms other existing HE-based methods and different image quality measures such as: Peak signal to noise ratio (PSNR), Absolute Mean Brightness Error (AMBE) and Structural Similarity Index (SSIM) are being used to test the robustness of the proposed method in terms of enhancement of contrast and preservation of brightness.

Keywords: Contrast enhancement · Histogram equalization · AIEBHE · AIEBHE-AHE · AHE-AIEBHE · AQHEMT · ABHET

1 Introduction

The objective of image enhancement is to improve the visual appearance of the image or to provide better enhanced image for further processing. It is difficult to capture good quality picture in darkness or in low light. Also in darkness small details of the object can not be perceived. In order to get better quality image different enhancement techniques are being used.

Histogram equalization (HE) is a very popular method of contrast enhancement technique among different contrast enhancement techniques exist. Hence HE improves the overall contrast of the image and preserves mean brightness [1, 2]. HE has different applications such as medical imaging system (X-ray), texture synthesis and video enhancement etc. But traditional HE is not suitable for consumer electronics systems [2]. This causes over enhancement, noise amplification, saturation effect etc. These are some of the biggest demerits of traditional HE.

© Springer Nature Singapore Pte Ltd. 2016
A. Unal et al. (Eds.): SmartCom 2016, CCIS 628, pp. 151–158, 2016.
DOI: 10.1007/978-981-10-3433-6_19

2 Related Literature

For the enhancement of image, many methods can be involved for different purpose such as, boundary detection is to enhance the boundary of the image. This has been approached by many authors [4]. Some of the equalization based methods used for such purpose are also given in this section. In [2], Kim proposed a technique namely Brightness Preserving Bi- HE (BBHE) for preserving brightness and enhancement of contrast. This technique sub-divide the gray image utilizing input gray image mean brightness value finally equalizes sub-histograms individually. In [5] Wan et al. used Dualistic Sub-image HE (DSIHE) that separates the histogram using median value thus containing approximately equal number of pixel. In [6] Chen and Ramli proposed a method named Minimum Mean Brightness Error Bi-histogram Equalization (MMBEBHE) that preserves the mean brightness optimally. MMBEBHE iteratively calculate AMBE and bisect the histogram into two sub- histogram. They have also used a Recursive Mean Separate HE (RMSHE) [7] which is another version of BBHE. A similar technique is proposed by Sim et al. [8] named as Recursive Sub-image HE (RSIHE), where subdivision is based on occupied median intensity. But no significant enhancement result is found for iteration to find the optimal value. In [9], Kim and Chung has used Recursively Separated and Weighted HE (RSWHE), which divides the histogram iteratively and modifies the histogram by means of a weighting process. In [10], Ooi and Isa have introduced adaptive contrast enhancement techniques for preserving brightness.

This paper is organized as follows: Sect. 3 describes the contrast enhancement techniques, Sect. 4 provides experimental results and Sect. 5 concludes the paper.

3 Enhancement Methods

There are different types of contrast enhancement techniques applied by many authors as described in literature. But in this work, authors tried on histogram based approach and compared among the proposed techniques. Though it is a common technique, still its variants work different way and made it attractive. Some of them are discussed in this section.

3.1 Adaptive Image Enhancement Based on Bi-Histogram Equalization with a Clipping Limit (AIEBHE)

This method based on Bi-Histogram Equalization [11]. This method divides the input histogram into two sub-histograms using median value of the occupied intensity. Then histogram is clipped so that it can control the degree of enhancement. The algorithm is as follows:

3.1.1 Algorithm for AIEBHE
(1) Find the histogram $H(k)$ of the gray image $I(x, y)$.
(2) Sub-divide the original gray image by utilizing median value of occupied intensity.

(3) Clipping of these two sub-histograms Th_{clip} is calculated using the smallest value among three values such as histogram bins, median and mean value of occupied intensity.

(4) Both the sub-histograms are equalized and integrated to get a single image.

3.2 Adaptive Histogram Equalization Followed by Adaptive Image Enhancement Based on Bi-Histogram Equalization with a Clipping Limit (AIEBHE- AHE)

In this method [10–12] of contrast enhancement two different techniques of contrast enhancement are used for better improvement of the quality of the image. This method consists of two methods namely by Adaptive Image Enhancement based on Bi-Histogram Equalization with a clipping limit (AIEBHE) [11] and Adaptive Histogram Equalization(AHE) [11, 12]. The implementation is done using following algorithm.

3.2.1 Algorithm for AIEBHE-AHE

(1) Find the histogram $H(k)$ of the gray image $I(x, y)$.
(2) Sub-divide the image using median value of occupied intensity.
(3) Clipping of the two sub-histograms Th_{clip} are done using mean.
(4) Both the sub-histograms are equalized integrated to get a single image.
(5) And the output image of the AIEBHE acts as the input image for AHE.
(6) AHE is applicable on small regions or tiles in the input image.

3.3 Adaptive Image Enhancement Based on Bi-Histogram Equalization with a Clipping Limit Followed by Adaptive Histogram Equalization (AHE- AIEBHE)

In this method [10–12] of contrast enhancement two different techniques of contrast enhancement are used for better improvement of the quality of the image. This method consists of two methods namely by Adaptive Image Enhancement based on Bi-Histogram Equalization with a clipping limit (AIEBHE) [11] and Adaptive Histogram Equalization (AHE) [11, 12]. The implementation is explained below,

3.3.1 Algorithm for AHE-AIEBHE

(1) Find the histogram $H(k)$ of the gray image $I(x, y)$.
(2) AHE is applicable on small regions or tiles in the input image.
(3) The tile contrast enhanced is done.
(4) Apply the output image of the AHE as the input image for AIEBHE.
(5) Sub-division of the original gray image by utilizing median value.
(6) Clipping of the two sub-histograms Th_{clip} are done using mean.
(7) Both the sub-histograms are equalized and integrated to get a single image.

3.4   Adaptive Quadrant Histogram Equalization Using Multi-Threshold (AQHEMT)

This technique divides the input histogram into four sub-histograms using multiple threshold. Firstly, Otsu's technique [13] is applied to find a particular threshold value which act as the separating point between two sub-images. Further division of these two sub-histograms into four sub-histograms is done using intensities set to 0.25 of the threshold level in the lower histogram region and 0.75 of the threshold level is being added to the threshold level in the upper histogram region in order to get the separating point. Then histogram is clipped so that it can control the over enhancement leading to natural enhancement. The algorithm is,

3.4.1   Algorithm for AQHEMT

(1) Find the histogram $H(k)$ of the gray image $I(x, y)$.
(2) Division of the image into two sub-images is done exactly at the middle point either in X-axis or Y-axis.
(3) Find the difference of the histogram of the two sub-images.
(4) Then apply Otsu's technique to find a particular threshold value which act as the separating point between two sub-images.
(5) Division of these two sub-histograms into four sub-histograms is done using intensities set to 0.25 of the threshold level in the lower histogram region and 0.75 of the threshold level is being added to the threshold level in the upper histogram region to get the separating point.
(6) Clipping of histogram Th_{clip} is done using mean.
(7) Both the sub-histograms are equalized and integrated to create a single image.

3.5   Adaptive Bi-histogram Equalization Using Threshold (ABHET)

This method based on bi-HE. The input histogram is sub-divided using Otsu's threshold [13]. Then histogram is clipped so that it can control the over enhancement leading to natural enhancement. These clipped sub-histograms are equalized and integration of all the sub-images is done to combine these two sub-images. Thus the algorithm consists of three steps such as: (1) Histogram segmentation using threshold, (2) Clipping of histogram and (3) histogram equalization of sub-images.

3.5.1   Segmentation of Histogram Using Threshold

For histogram segmentation sub-divide the image into two images exactly at the middle point either in X-axis or Y-axis. Difference of the histogram of the two sub-images is found out. Then apply Otsu's technique [13] to achieve a particular threshold value which act as the separating point between two sub-images. If TH is the threshold point then the two sub- histograms ranges from [0, TH−1] and [TH, L−1] respectively where L is total number of intensity value. Thus the histogram is sub-divided into total two numbers of sub-histograms namely lower and upper sub- histogram. This process preserves mean brightness of the original image.

3.5.2 Clipping of Histogram

Concept behind this clipping process is to limit the degree of over enhancement which is a major problem in traditional HE method. Thus this process results in the natural appearance of the image. It is calculated by average of the number of occupied intensities. Histogram bins higher than clipping threshold are replaced by that threshold and the remaining lower histogram bins less than the clipping threshold remain as it is.

$$Th_{clip} = mean[H(k)] \tag{1}$$

$$H_{clip}(k) = Th_{clip} \text{ for } h(k) \geq T_{clip} \tag{2}$$

$H(k)$ and $H_{clip}(k)$ are the original and clipped histograms respectively.

3.5.3 Histogram Equalization of Sub-images

Histogram of the input image is sub divided into two sub-images R_L and R_U. It ranges from intensity levels 0 to TH−1 and TH to L−1 respectively. The individual histograms are equalized by using the transfer function. Finally integration of both the sub images is done to get a complete image which can be used for further analysis.

3.5.4 Algorithm for ABHET

(1) Find the histogram $H(k)$ of the input image $I(x, y)$.
(2) Sub-divide the original image into two images exactly at the middle point.
(3) Find the difference of the histogram of the two sub-images.
(4) Then apply Otsu's technique to find a particular threshold which act as the separating point between two sub-images.
(5) Clipped histogram Th_{clip} and clipped histogram $H_{clip}(k)$ are calculated.
(6) Both the sub-histograms are equalized integrated to get a single image.

4   Results and Discussion

In this work, the performance of six different methods of contrast enhancement techniques i.e. HE, AIEBHE, AIEBHE-AHE, AHE-AIEBHE, AQHEMT and ABHET are being analyzed. Generally, to reduce noise component in the original image different contrast enhancement techniques utilizes median or mean based histogram segmentation as a pre-processing step to improve the results of later processing. But, in this paper the proposed methods i.e. AQHEMT and ABHET utilizes Otsu's technique to segment the histogram which reduces noise components.

To analyze and compare the robustness of these six methods of contrast enhancement two images namely Butterfly and Cerebrum images are taken to test the accuracy of the proposed methods. Due to shortage of space the experimental values of Butterfly, Cerebrum and Lena images are only shown in the table. We have used three different image quality measures for analysis, such as: PSNR, AMBE and SSIM. From Fig. 1 through Fig. 2, it is clearly observed that the ABHET increases the contrast of the original image with natural appearance without intensity saturation and noise amplification and controls the degree of enhancement. Simultaneously, PSNR and AMBE is calculated to test the robustness of the proposed method. PSNR is the peak signal to noise ratio and found out to test the quality of any image. If the PSNR value is high then the image is of good quality.

$$PSNR = 10\log_{10}\left[\frac{(L-1)^2}{\frac{1}{n}\sum_b |U(a,b)-V(a,b)|^2}\right] \tag{3}$$

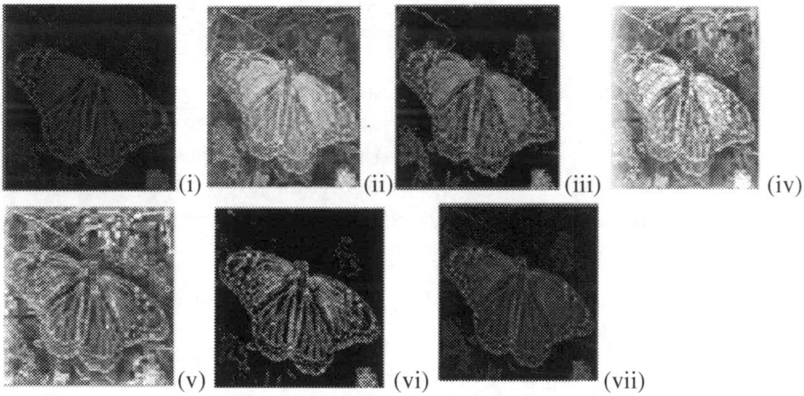

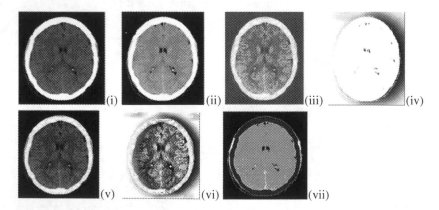

Fig. 1. Simulation result of 'Butterfly image' (i) Original image, (ii) HE, (iii) AIEBHE, (iv) AIEBHE-AHE, (v) AHE-AIEBHE, (vi) AQHEMT, (vii) ABHET.

Fig. 2. Simulation result of 'Cerebrum image' (i) Original gray image, (ii) HE, (iii) AIEBHE, (iv) AIEBHE-AHE, (v) AHE-AIEBHE, (vi) AQHEMT, (vii) ABHET

Here, PSNR value of ABHET is higher in comparison to other methods. Thus it is a good technique in terms of image quality. Absolute Mean Brightness Error (AMBE) is nothing but the absolute difference between the brightness value of the input image and the output image. If AMBE value is of low value then the brightness error is less and image gives natural look.

Structural similarity index (SSIM) describes how less information details are lost while enhancing the image SSIM is higher means it preserves the information details of the output.

$$SSIM(a, b) = \frac{(2A_m B_m + z1)(2S_{ab} + z2)}{(A_m^2 + B_m^2 + z1)(S_a^2 + S_b^2 + z2)} \qquad (4)$$

Where, A_m and B_m are the mean values of the input and enhanced image respectively. S_a^2 and S_b^2 are the variances and S_{ab} is the co-variance. SSIM of ABHET is of high value, i.e. the enhanced image is having least information loss.

Results of the comparison are summarized in Tables 1, 2 and 3. From these results it is clearly observed that in comparison to other methods, ABHET produces better image quality.

Table 1. Peak signal to noise ratio (PSNR)

Images	HE	AIEBHE	AIEBHE-AHE	AHE-AIEBHE	AQHEMT	ABHET
Butterfly	6.34	20.31	3.90	6.98	20.63	22.95
Cerebrum	11.27	10.73	3.68	6.43	20.86	25.73
Lena	16.04	6.76	4.89	10.35	25.87	16.58

Table 2. Absolute mean brightness error (AMBE)

Images	HE	AIEBHE	AIEBHE-AHE	AHE-AIEBHE	AQHEMT	ABHET
Butterfly	109.6	12.16	147.68	96.56	1.54e + 3	12.92
Cerebrum	62.09	45.87	146.52	66.14	2.31e + 3	6.90
Lena	85.97	23.65	181.50	65.35	2.74e + 3	5.66

Table 3. Structural similarity index (SSIM)

Images	HE	AIEBHE	AIEBHE-AHE	AHE-AIEBHE	AQHEMT	ABHET
Butterfly	1.01e + 1	9.09e + 8	1.24e + 1	7.1344e + 1	7.06e + 1	1.35e + 1
Cerebrum	1.03e + 1	5.09e + 1	6.47e + 1	9.8507e + 1	2.39e + 1	2.24e + 1
Lena	2.35e + 1	4.00e + 1	6.72e + 1	2.1928e + 1	1.24e + 1	1.48e + 1

5   Conclusion

In this paper, six different contrast enhancement techniques has been proposed and compared to test the accuracy, quality and effectiveness. And simulation result clearly shows that ABHET method not only preserves the brightness of the image but also controls rate of enhancement or over enhancement. In this method clipping of histogram provides control on degree of enhancement. Thus ABHET produces naturally enhanced image in comparison to other methods of contrast enhancement.

References

1. Gonzalez, R.C., Woods, R.E.: Digital Image Processing, 3rd edn. Prentice-Hall, Englewood Cliffs (2009)
2. Kim, Y.T.: Contrast enhancement using brightness preserving bi-histogram equalization. IEEE Trans. Consum. Electron. **43**, 1–8 (1997)
3. Mohanty, M., Mishra, A., Routray, A.: A non-rigid motion estimation algorithm for yawn detection in human drivers. Int. J. Comput. Vis. Robot. **1**(1), 89–109 (2009). Inder Science pub, SCOPUS, EI Comp., SNIP-1.108
4. Behera, S., Mohanty, M.N., Patnaik, S.: A comparative analysis on edge detection of colloid cyst: a medical image aproach. In: Patnaik, S., Yang, Y-M. (eds.) Soft Computing Techniques in Vision. SCI, 395. Springer, Heidelberg (2012)
5. Wan, Y., Chen, Q., Zhang, B.M.: Image enhancement based on equal area dualistic sub-image histogram equalization method. IEEE Trans. Consum. Electron. **45**, 68–75 (1999)
6. Chen, S.D., Ramli, A.R.: Minimum mean brightness error bi-histogram equalization in Contrast enhancement. IEEE Trans. Consum. Electron. **45**, 1310–1319 (2003)
7. Chen, S.D., Ramli, A.R.: Contrast enhancement using recursive mean-separate histogram equalization for scalable brightness preservation. IEEE Trans. Consum. Electron. **49**, 1301–1309 (2003)
8. Sim, K.S., Tso, C.P., Tan, Y.Y.: Recursive sub-image histogram equalization applied to gray scale image. Pattern Recogn. Lett. **28**, 1209–1221 (2007)
9. Kim, M., Chung, M.G.: Recursively separated and weighted histogram equalization for brightness preservation and Contrast enhancement. IEEE Trans. Consum. Electron. **54**, 1389–1397 (2008)
10. Ooi, C.H., Isa, N.A.M.: Adaptive contrast enhancement methods with brightness preserving. IEEE Trans. Consum. Electron. **54**, 2543–2551 (2010)
11. Tang, J.R., Isa, N.A.M.: Adaptive image enhancement based on bi-histogram equalization with a clipping limit. Comput. Electr. Eng. **40**, 86–103 (2014)
12. Anand, S., Gayathri, S.: Mammogram image enhancement by two-stage adaptive histogram equalizations. Optik **126**, 3150–3152 (2015)
13. Yang, X., Shen, X., Long, J., Chen, H.: An improved median based otsu image thresholding algorithm. AASRI Procedia **3**, 468–473 (2012)
14. Sahoo, S., Panda, J., Mohanty, M.N.: Performance analysis of HE methods for low contrast images. Procedia Comput. Sci. **92**, 72–77 (2016)
15. Senthilkumaran, N., Vaithegi, S.: Image segmentation by using thresholding techniques for medical images. Comput. Sci. Eng. Int. J. (CSEIJ) 6(1), February 2016

Sentiment Analysis at Document Level

Salima Behdenna[✉], Fatiha Barigou, and Ghalem Belalem

Department of Computer Science, Faculty of Sciences, University of Oran 1 Ahmed Ben Bella,
El M'Naouer, PB 1524 31000 Oran, Algeria
behdennasalima@gmail.com, fatbarigou@gmail.com,
ghalem1dz@gmail.com

Abstract. Sentiment analysis becomes a very active research area in the text mining field. It aims to extract people's opinions, sentiments, and subjectivity from the texts. Sentiment analysis can be performed at three levels: at document level, at sentence level and at aspect level. An important part of research effort focuses on document level sentiment classification, including works on opinion classification of reviews. This survey paper tackles a comprehensive overview of the last update of sentiment analysis at document level. The main target of this survey is to give nearly full image of sentiment analysis techniques at this level. In addition, some future research issues are also presented.

Keywords: Opinion mining · Sentiment analysis · Opinion · Review · Document · Machine learning

1 Introduction

Now days many applications and platforms on the web allow us to deposit views, to share the opinions and sentiments on a variety of topics. Because of the importance of this information in several areas (political, commercial or individual), it would be interesting to treat opinions automatically. The term "sentiment analysis" is used to refer to the automatic processing of opinions, sentiments and subjectivity in texts. This field is known as the opinion mining [16] or sentiment analysis [7].

Sentiment analysis is an extremely active field of research in natural language processing, which allows extracting the opinions from a set of documents. Sentiment analysis can be investigated at different levels [7]:

- Document level analysis: the task at this level is to determine the overall opinion of the document. Sentiment analysis at document level assumes that each document expresses opinions on a single entity.
- Sentence level analysis: the task at this level is to determine if each sentence has expressed an opinion. This level distinguishes the objective sentences expressing factual information and subjective sentences expressing opinions. In this case, treatments are twofold; firstly identify if the sentence has expressed or not an opinion, then assess the polarity of opinion. But the main difficulty comes from the fact that objective sentences can be carrying opinion.

© Springer Nature Singapore Pte Ltd. 2016
A. Unal et al. (Eds.): SmartCom 2016, CCIS 628, pp. 159–168, 2016.
DOI: 10.1007/978-981-10-3433-6_20

- Aspect level analysis: this level performs a finer analysis and requires the use of natural language processing. In this level, opinion is characterized by a polarity and a target of opinion. In this case, treatments are twofold: first identify the entity and aspects of the entity in question, and then assess the opinion on each aspect.

Sentiment analysis has many applications ranging from identifying consumer sentiment towards products [7] (this information can give companies valuable information as to the satisfaction or dissatisfaction of their consumers and it is also immensely valuable for consumers in their decisions to purchase a particular product) to voters' reaction to political adverts. Other application areas in which sentiment analysis can be very useful are: Business Intelligence, Recommendation systems, etc.

The rest of this paper is arranged as follows: Sect. 2 provides background information and related work of document level sentiment classification. Then a comparative study between different works is presented in Sect. 3. Last section concludes our study and discusses some future directions for research.

2 Related Work

The field of opinion mining is vast and knows a spectacular growth because of the commercial challenges. A relatively exhaustive state of art was drawn up in 2008 by Pang and Lee [16] they focused on the applications and challenges in sentiment analysis. They mentioned the techniques used to solve each problem in sentiment analysis.

In his book, Bing Liu [7] presents a synthesis of works in the sentiment analysis. It updates state of the art of Pang and Lee (2008) and distinguishes three levels of analysis: document, sentence and aspect level.

Existing approaches for sentiment analysis are categorized into three main classes' machine learning approaches, lexicon based approaches and hybrid approaches [1].

2.1 Machine Learning Approaches

Those approaches require labeling a corpus in advance (positive, negative or neutral) [28]. The main features used are: words, bigram, tri-gram, part of speech and polarity. Several supervised-based techniques are used, but two of them appear to provide the best results. These are the SVM and NB classifiers [9, 21, 25].

Pak and Paroubek [13] developed a new sub-graph-based representation extracted from syntactic dependency trees. They represent a text as a collection of sub-graphs, where the nodes are words (or word classes) and arcs the syntactic dependencies between them. Such representation avoids the loss of information associated with the use of "bag of words" models, the latter being based only on collections of n-grams of words. Thus, approaches based on n-grams cannot correctly identify the complex sentiment expressions. The authors use the Incremental Parser (XIP) to construct the dependency tree. They tested the model on a set of French reviews of video games, developed as part of the DOXA project [32] on opinion mining. Thus, they were able to show that SVM classifier using features built from sub graphs, extracted from dependency trees, gives better results than traditional systems based on unigram.

In [17], the authors propose the use of neural network to learn an effective model of sentiment classification. They compared their work with an SVM model using the multi-thematic Amazon corpus. The experiment results show identical performance.

In [30], the objective of the work is the classification of Chinese mobile reviews with SVM and NB classifiers; these reviews are much shorter on average than those of the PC. The scoring used in this work is iTunes' score. ITunes has a score of 1 to 5 points, the reviews with 1 or 2 points are marked as negative, reviews with 4 and 5 points are marked as positive and those with 3 points are marked as neutral. The results show that the NB classifier is the better.

Vinodhini and Chandrasekaran [26] evaluated the PCA (Principle Component Analysis) effect with two methods of sentiment classification: SVM and NB. The experiments are performed on product reviews. The performances are improved using the PCA as a method of features reduction.

Several works exist for sentiment analysis at document level treating movie reviews. Pang [14], is the first who experiments this approach with machine learning. The proposed method which proved to be good in text categorization, did not achieve good performance for the sentiment classification. He also demonstrated that the binary representation is more significant than the frequency representation.

The authors in [28] used Classification by minimizing the error (CME) to attribute a score of opinion to each sentence. They then used the SVM classifier to attribute a score to each document based on the values of some features (this features are defined based on subjectivity and the relevancy in all the sentences). So blogs are classified according to their final score based on the relevancy score multiplied by the score of opinion.

The first freely available corpus Arab (OCA) for sentiment analysis is proposed by Rushdi Saleh et al. [19]. The OCA corpus consist of 500 movie reviews collected from different Arabic web pages, 250 of them considered as positive and the rest as negative opinions. In addition, various experiments were conducted on this corpus using NB and SVM classifiers.

Govindarajan [6] proposed a hybrid method of classification based on the coupling of NB and genetic algorithm (GA). In this method, first the two basic classifiers NB and GA are built to assign a score of opinion, and then the classification of a new review is done by combining the predictions of two basic classifiers, by a majority vote. The author used a set of 2000 movie reviews (they have been extracted from the corpus of Bo Pang). The hybrid method is compared with the two base classifiers NB and GA. The results showed that the hybrid method has improved the performance.

Nguyen et al. [10] proposed a new type of feature named "rating-based feature". The rating-based feature is based on the fact that scores (in which users use to categorize entities in reviews) could provide useful information to improve the performance of opinion classification. For a review with no associated score, the authors use a regression model to predict the score. They combine rating-based feature with unigram, bigram, and tri-gram.

In [23], the authors propose a model for sentiment classification. First, various schemes of pre-processing are applied to the data set. Secondly, the behavior of the NB and SVM classifiers is studied in combination of different schemes of feature selection.

The results of classification show clearly that linear SVM give more precision than NB classifier.

In [5], the authors propose a method for sentiment analysis in Arabic Tweets with the presence of dialectical words. These words were replaced to their corresponding words of the Modern Standard Arabic (MSA) by the use of dialect lexicon. Both NB and SVM classifiers were used to determine the polarity of tweets. Two versions of the same data set are used. The first version consists of tweets containing dialectical words and the second version consists of tweets containing translated words. The results show that the replacement of dialectical words improves the accuracy of classifiers (3%).

2.2   Lexicon Based Approaches

Lexicon based approaches exploit a sentiment lexicon which is either built independently of any corpus (built from existing dictionaries), or generated from the corpus (words containing opinion are extracted directly from the corpus). The objective of these lexicons is to index the most words carrying possible opinion. If a document contains many subjective words, then it is considered as a document containing opinions [8, 11].

Turney presents a simple algorithm for sentiment classification of reviews [24]. The review is classified by the average of the semantic orientation (SO) of the sentences. A sentence has a positive SO when it has good associations and a negative SO when it has bad associations. The SO is calculated as the Point wise Mutual Information (PMI) between the given sentence and "excellent", and also between the given sentence "poor". Finally, the review is classified according to the average of the semantic orientation of the sentences that contains.

To overcome the problem of domain dependency in the sentiment analysis, Rothfels and Tibshirani [18] propose an approach for treating movie reviews using the automatic selection of items with positive or negative opinions. They choose two seed reference sets, one positive and one negative to calculate the semantic orientation (SO). SO is calculated as the PMI between the given sentence and the seed reference set.

Baloglu and Aktas [2] proposed a lexicon-based approach. This approach is divided into three phases. Phase 1: crawling phase; the data are collected from blogs on the Web. Phase 2: analysis phase, in which the data are analyzed to extract useful information (predefined keywords) and uses SentiWordNet to determine the sentiment score of each keyword and finally the review is classified based on the average of these scores. Phase 3: visualization, which information is displayed.

A sentiment analysis system named Document based Sentiment Orientation System is proposed in [20]. It uses a lexicon based approach which determines the SO of reviews and Word Net to identify synonyms and antonyms of opinion word list. Negation is also handled in this system. This approach provides a summary of the total number of positive and negative documents.

2.3 Hybrid Approaches

Hybrid approaches combine the strengths of machine learning and lexicon-based approaches by taking into account the linguistic processing of lexicon-based approaches before starting the learning process as in machine learning approaches.

Ohana and Tierney [12] assess the use of SentiWordNet. Firstly, the vocabulary has been employed to calculate the score of terms found in a document and determine the sentiment direction. Then this method was improved by the construction of a relevant feature by using SentiWordNet as a source and applying the SVM classifier. The results indicate SentiWordNet could be utilized as a source.

In [29], the authors proposed an ensemble learning method based behavior-knowledge space BKS, which four basic classifiers are used; single weighted sum of opinion words (SWS), weighted sum of opinion words (WSC), SVM and k-nearest neighbors (KNN). The results show the effectiveness of the proposed method, and show that this method is much higher than the basic classifiers.

Different ways to combine the analysis of discourse RST (Rhetorical Structure Theory) with the sentiment analysis are proposed in [3]: (i) a recurrent neural network on the structure of the RST and (ii) a reweighting discourse units. They show that the reweighting discourse units can lead to substantial improvements for the sentiment analysis based-lexicon, and show that the recurrent neural network using RST structure offers significant improvements over the basic classification methods.

3 Comparative Study

We use the following components to make a comparative study;

- Approach used
- Technique used
- Data source used
- Feature construction used
- Quantitative Evaluation

As we have seen in the surveyed works, three main classes of approaches used for sentiment analysis are: machine learning approach, lexicon based approach, and hybrid approach. Table 1 grouped the surveyed works into these categories.

Table 1. Comparative study by approach

Approach	Ref
Machine learning	[5, 6, 10, 13, 14, 17, 19, 23, 26, 28, 30]
Lexicon based	[2, 18, 20, 24]
Hybrid	[3, 12, 29]

From Table 1, the supervised approach is the dominant one compared to the other approaches.

Sentiment classification techniques are usually distinguished based on approach been used. Several machine learning algorithms are used as a technique for document classification. Prominent methods are: NB, Maximum Entropy, KNN, and SVM. The lexicon based methods are divided into dictionary-based and corpus-based. The surveyed works used different techniques. We have collected the various techniques used, Table 2 presents the results.

Table 2. Comparative study by technique

Technique used	Ref
SVM	[10, 13]
SVM & NB	[5, 19, 23, 26, 30]
SVM & NB & Maximum Entropy	[14]
SVM & CME	[28]
SVM & RNA	[17]
SVM & GA	[6]
Dictionary based	[2, 20, 24]
Corpus based	[18]
Dictionary based & SVM	[12]
Dictionary based & SVM & KNN	[29]
RNA	[3]

From Table 2, the most used methods seem to be based on SVM and NB, for the supervised approach. For unsupervised approach, dictionary-based approaches are the most frequent across the majority of works.

Several data sources used at the document level in the sentiment classification studies, but the most used at the document level is the reviews. Table 3 below presents data sources used in the different surveyed works.

Table 3. Comparative study by data sources

Data sources	Ref
Reviews of video games	[13]
Amazon reviews	[17]
Mobile reviews of We Chat	[30]
Product reviews	[26]
Movie reviews	[3, 6, 10, 12, 14, 18, 20, 23]
Blogs	[2, 28]
Corpus OCA	[19]
Opinions review	[24]
Hotel reviews	[29]
Tweets	[5]

From Table 3, the movie reviews are widely used in the field of sentiment classification at document level.

The goal of feature construction is to select good features for sentiment classification. Many features are used for sentiment analysis: unigram, bigram, n-gram, POS and opinion words. Table 4 presents the feature construction used in the surveyed works.

Table 4. Comparative study by feature construction

Feature construction	Ref
Sub graphs extracted from syntactic dependency trees	[13]
POS	[17]
n-gram	[30]
unigram	[26]
unigram, bigram, POS	[14]
unigram, bigram, trigram	[19]
bigram	[6]
rating-based feature, unigram, bigram, trigram	[10]
TF-IDF, unigram, bigram, trigram	[23]
POS, semantic orientation, PMI	[24]
4-gram, semantic orientation, PMI	[18]
POS, opinion words	[20]
POS	[12]
reweighting discourse units	[3]

From Table 4, the features most used are: Unigram, bigram, POS, semantic orientation and PMI.

The performance of different works used for opinion mining is evaluated by calculating various metrics like accuracy. Accuracy is calculated by using the following equation.

$$\text{Accuracy} = \frac{TN + TP}{TN + TP + FP + FN} \tag{1}$$

With

- TP: True Positive.
- TN: True Negative.
- FP: False Positive.
- FN: False Negative.

The following figure (Fig. 1) Summarize the accuracy of works using movie review data set [31].

From the figure (Fig. 1), we find that work [6], which used a hybrid method of classification based on the coupling of NB and GA, gave the best results in terms of accuracy. Even for work [10], which used a new type of feature named "rating-based feature".

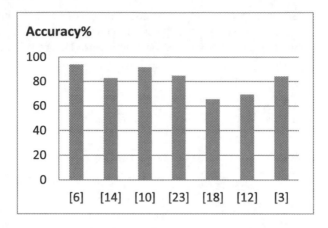

Fig. 1. Sentiment analysis for movie review dataset

4   Conclusion and Future Work

The number of documents expressing opinions is constantly increasing on the World Wide Web. Document Level Sentiment Classification provides an overall opinion of the document on a single entity. In this article, we have presented an overview of related work of sentiment analysis at document level, mainly the approach of machine learning is considered as dominance at this level. The main classifiers used are SVM and NB. The more text representation used is "bag of words" representation, but supervised approaches using n-grams features cannot properly modeled the negation, and cannot correctly identify the complex sentiment expressions due to the loss of information incurred when representing texts with bag of words models. Most of the work uses movie review data for classification. The classification of the documents is not always relevant:

- In many applications, the user needs to know what aspects of entities are liked and disliked by consumers, but this level of classification can not extract them.
- Comparing entities is not easily applicable at document level like forum discussion, blogs and new articles.
- Different emotions on the different aspects of an entity cannot be extracted separately.

It is therefore necessary to move at sentence level, i.e., to classify opinion expressed in each sentence. However, there is no difference between document level and sentence level sentiment classification.

In the future work, more efforts would be done to improve the performance measures, for this purpose, there is a need for finer-grained analysis at the aspect level. Furthermore, the languages that have been studied mostly are English. Presently, there are very few researches conducted on sentiment classification of other languages like Arabic. We intend to propose a new approach for aspect based sentiment analysis of Arabic texts.

References

1. Anitha, N., Anitha, B., Pradeepa, S.: Sentiment classification approaches – a review. Int. J. Innovations Eng. Technol. (IJIET) 3(1) (2013)
2. Baloglu, A., Aktas, M.S.: An automated framework for mining reviews from blogosphere. Int. J. Adv. Internet Technol. 3(3&4), 234–244 (2010)
3. Bhatia, P., Ji, Y., Eisenstein, J.: Better document-level sentiment analysis from RST Discourse Parsing. In: Empirical Methods in Natural Language Processing, pp. 2212–2218. EMNLP, Lisbon (2015)
4. Chen, Y.F., Miao, D.Q., Li, W., Zhang, Z.F.: Semantic orientation computing based on concepts. J. CAAI Trans. Intell. Syst. 6(6), 489–494 (2011)
5. Duwairi, R.M.: Sentiment analysis for dialectical Arabic. In: 6th ICICS International Conference on Information and Communication Systems, pp. 166–170 (2015)
6. Govindarajan, M.: Sentiment analysis of movie reviews using hybrid method of Naive Bayes and Genetic Algorithm. Int. J. Adv. Comput. Res. 3(4), 139–146 (2013)
7. Liu, B.: Sentiment Analysis and Opinion Mining. Morgan & Claypool Publishers, New York (2012)
8. Mishne, G., Multiple Ranking Strategies for Opinion Retrieval in Blogs. In: Online Proceedings of TREC (2006)
9. Nilesh, M.S., Deshpande, S., Thakre, V.: Survey of techniques for opinion mining. (IJCA) Int. J. Comput. Appl. (0975–8887) 57(13) (2012)
10. Nguyen, D.Q., Nguyen, D.Q., Vu, T., Pham, S.B.: Sentiment classification on polarity reviews: an empirical study using rating-based features. In: 5th Workshop on Computational Approaches to Subjectivity, Sentiment and Social Media Analysis, pp. 128–135, Maryland (2014)
11. Oard, D.W., Elsayed, T., Wang, J., Wu, Y., Zhang P., Abels, E.G., Lin, J.J., Soergel, D.: TREC 2006 at Maryland: Blog, Enterprise, Legal and QA Tracks. TREC (2006)
12. Ohana, B., Tierney, B.: Sentiment classification of reviews using SentiWordNet. In: 9th IT&T Conference, pp. 22–23 (2009)
13. Pak, A., Paroubek, P.: Classification en polarité de sentiments avec une représentation textuelle à base de sous-graphes d'arbres de dépendances. TALN (2011)
14. Pang, B., Lee, L., Vaithyanathan, S.: Thumbs up? Sentiment classification using machine learning techniques. In: Empirical Methods in Natural Language Processing, pp. 79–86. EMNLP (2002)
15. Pang, B., Lee, L.: A Sentimental education: sentiment analysis using subjectivity summarization based on minimum cuts. In: 42th Annual Meeting of the Associatoin for Computational Linguistics ACL, pp. 271–278 (2004)
16. Pang, B., Lee, L.: Opinion mining and sentiment analysis. Found. Trends Inf. Retrieval 2, 1–135 (2008)
17. Rafrafi, A., Guigue, V., Gallinari, P.: Réseau de neurones profond et SVM pour la classification des sentiments. In: COnférence en Recherche d'Information et Applications CORIA, pp. 121–133 (2011)
18. Rothfels, J., Tibshirani, J.: Unsupervised sentiment classification of English movie reviews using automatic selection of positive and negative sentiment items. CS224N-Final Project (2010)
19. Rushdi-Saleh, M., Martín-Valdivia, M.T., Ureña-López, L.A., Perea-Ortega, J.M.: OCA: opinion corpus for Arabic. J. ASIS&T 62, 2045–2054 (2011)
20. Sharma, R., Nigam, S., Jain, R.: Opinion mining of movie reviews at document level. IJIT, 3 (2014)

21. Sindhu, C., ChandraKala, S.: A survey on opinion mining and sentiment polarity classification. IJETAE, **3** (2013)
22. Socher, R., Perelygin, A., Wu, J.Y., Chuang, J., Manning, C.D., Ng, A.N., Potts, C.: Recursive deep models for semantic compositionality over a sentiment tree bank. In: Empirical Methods for Natural Language Processing. EMNLP (2013)
23. Tripathi, G., Naganna, S.: Feature selection and classification approach for sentiment analysis. MLAIJ, p. 2201 (2015)
24. Turney, P.D.: Thumbs up or thumbs down? Semantic orientation applied to unsupervised classification of reviews. In: 40th annual meeting of the Association for Computational Linguistics, pp. 417–424. ACL, Philadelphia (2002)
25. Vinodhini, G., Chandrasekaran, R.M.: Sentiment analysis and opinion mining: a survey. IJARCSSE **2277**, 282–292 (2012)
26. Vinodhini, G., Chandrasekaran, R.M.: Effect of feature reduction in sentiment analysis of online reviews. IJARCET (2013). ISSN 2278–1323
27. Wang, S., Manning, C.D.: Baselines and bigrams: simple, good sentiment and topic classification. In: 50th Annual Meeting of the Association for Computational Linguistics, pp. 90–94. ACL (2012)
28. Zhang, Q., Wang, B., Wu, L., Huang, X.: FDU at TREC 2007: opinion retrieval of blog track. In: Voorhees, E.M., Buckland, L.P. (eds), TREC 2007, vol. Special Publication, 500–274 (2007)
29. Zhang, Z., Miao, D., Wei, Z., Wang, L.: Document-level sentiment classification based on behavior-knowledge space method. In: Zhou, S., Zhang, S., Karypis, G. (eds.) ADMA 2012. LNCS (LNAI), vol. 7713, pp. 330–339. Springer, Berlin, Heidelberg (2012). doi: 10.1007/978-3-642-35527-1_28
30. Zhang, L., Hua, K., Wang, H., Qian, G., Zhang, L.: Sentiment analysis on reviews of mobile users. In: 11th International Conference on Mobile Systems and Pervasive Computing, Procedia Computer Science, vol. 34, pp. 458–465 (2014)
31. http://www.cs.cornell.edu/people/pabo/movie-review-data/
32. https://www.projet-doxa.fr/index.php

An Approach to Sentiment Analysis on Unstructured Data in Big Data Environment

Dilipkumar A. Borikar[(⊠)] and Manoj B. Chandak

Department of Computer Science and Engineering,
Shri Ramdeobaba College of Engineering and Management, Nagpur, India
{borikarda,chandakmb}@rknec.edu

Abstract. An enormous growth of the WWW has been instrumental in spreading social networks. Due to many-fold increase in internet users taking to online reviews and opinions, the communication, sharing and collaboration through social networks have gained importance. The rapid growth in web-based activities has led to generation of huge amount of unstructured data which accounts for over 80% of the information. Exploiting big data alternatives in storing, processing, archiving and analyzing this data becomes increasingly necessary.

In this paper we propose a generalized approach to analyzing sentiments in big-data environment. The proposed model would serve to incorporate different supervised and un-supervised approaches to extraction, classification and scoring of opinions and sentiment words.

Keywords: Sentiment analysis · Opinion mining · Big data · Social web · Polarity · Unstructured data · Subjectivity

1   Introduction

With the advancements in internet technologies, WWW and Web 2.0, there has been an exponential rise in generation of data. This enormous data available from varied sources acquired in the form of text, video, audio, multimedia, pictures, blogs, tweets, etc. has to be processed to yield useful information. The availability of multi-channeled inputs at micro-blogging sites, product websites, online review systems, etc., has enabled customers (users) to rely on the online reviews and opinion before making a commitment or even before deciding on the alternatives. Majority of these data are textual data and is unstructured. This demands efficient processing in presence of various problems associated with extraction and interpretation.

To extract essential, application-specific information for analysis from the voluminous and highly unstructured data has always been a challenging act. The text data has to be processed appropriately using Natural Language Processing techniques to identify the subjective content. The subjective text is further processed to ascertain the sentiment it conveys. Use of informal language, infrequent short forms and occasional abbreviations, summarized and shortened text, ambiguous statements with misleading context, and other factors contributes to major challenges in sentiment analysis over social web.

© Springer Nature Singapore Pte Ltd. 2016
A. Unal et al. (Eds.): SmartCom 2016, CCIS 628, pp. 169–176, 2016.
DOI: 10.1007/978-981-10-3433-6_21

The technological advances allow firms to generate, store and process data that are structured, semi-structured, and unstructured. Structured data stored in spreadsheets, relational databases and flat-file databases constitute roughly about 5% of all existing data. Unstructured data comprising of text, audio, video and images lacks structural organization necessary for analysis. Semi-structured data can be efficiently represented and stored using XML documents that contain user-defined tags and enables machine readability [1].

People reveal their personal view-point, inclination or preference when they interact with others, exchange information over some topic or item of interest, or deliberate over certain issues. People exhibit emotions through opinions indicating their personality. It has been observed that emotions and polarities are mutually influenced by each other and facilitates conditioning opinion intensities and emotional strengths [2].

The impact of globalization has necessitated multi-national and ecommerce companies to examine the unstructured and semi-structured data at increasingly faster rates for predicting the future trends. Besides understanding the buying behavior of the customer, it is necessary for companies to establish a collaborative network with them to promote products, inform strategies and invite suggestions through comments and reviews. According to IDC, the data volume is doubling every two years. While it accounted for about 25% of all information stored in 2000, in 2007 it rose to 94%. This is expected to grow 44 times to touch 35 Zettabytes by 2020 [3].

Today more people are making their opinions available to strangers via the Internet. The user's inclination towards online advices and recommendations demands special attention to dealing effectively with user sentiments. The interest shown by user in online opinions about products and services, and the potential influence such opinions exercise, has been a non-trivial issue for vendors to pay attention to [4].

Sentiment analysis reveals the viewpoint or opinion of the actor regarding a topic of interest and may facilitate computation of contextual polarity of the text ensemble. The opinions may constitute the individual judgments or evaluations, emotional orientation of an actor (or an affect) or an intended emotional communication. The aspect is investigated for analyzing the polarity. The sentiment acquired might undergo different stages of pre-processing and data cleansing.

This paper is an attempt to formulating an approach to sentiment analysis in a big-data environment. It aims at providing the sentence-level sentiment classification and analyses for big data applications. Section 1 introduces the domain of text analytics and unstructured data acquired through varied sources. Section 2 reviews the research contributions in the field of opinion mining and sentiment analysis. Section 3 throws light on the specific objects and challenges in the proposed domain of work. Section 4 introduces our approach to sentiment analysis on social data. Section 5 concludes the paper with prospective directions in attaining the stated objectives.

2   Literature Review

The research in the domain of opinion mining and sentiment analysis has gained momentum in the last decade. The contributing factors since 2001 include [4]:

- Development of machine learning methods in natural language processing and information retrieval;
- Availability of datasets for machine learning algorithms for training and testing.
- The spread of WWW and development of review-aggregation web-sites allowing benchmarking and comparison; and,
- Awareness about the academic and research avenues and opportunities for designing and developing commercial and intelligence applications.

The research in sentiment and subjectivity classification was treated as a text classification problem. Sentiment classification task is to ascertain whether an opinionated document (e.g., product reviews) or a sentence conveys a sentiment, positive or negative. Subjectivity classification differentiates among the subjective and the objective sentences in an opinionated text [5]. There has been contrasting views among researchers on analyzing large quantity of text at individual level or aggregate level. A cluster-based approach to document classification using N-grams has been proposed in [13] at word level. In identifying bipolar person names in a set of topic documents an unsupervised approach involving PCA, weighted correlation coefficient and off-topic block elimination techniques is used [12].

Sentiment classification is the task of classifying a given piece of natural language text (i.e., a short remark, blog post, or complete product review) according to the opinions expressed in it. Sentiment classification can be a binary classification in which focuses on detecting whether the given product review is positive or negative. When the opinions are expressed using finite scale of integers between one (very negative) to five (very positive), it refers to ordinal classification. The more accepted approach is to assign a certain number of "stars" to a product review based on textual content and orientation [9]. For binary classification was done using the normalized cross entropy, referred to as Kullback-Leibler Divergence (KLD). KLD has been found efficient in quantifying and predicting how the test items are distributed across the classes [9]. Due to complexities and issues influencing classification, the task of opinion classification has always been more difficult compared to traditional text mining methods involving topic-based document categorization.

Paltoglou et al. [10] have argued that although there has been substantial awareness about opportunities in sentiment analysis research and the scope of developing potential applications, the major work has been centered on the writer's sentiment. It is opined that sentiment analysis can be significantly enhanced by decoding the impact of text messages on users, thereby unveiling some of the consequences of typical Internet multiuser interactions.

Big Data Analytics provides companies a tremendous opportunity to leverage their data for better business insight through analytics. Big Data may encompass highly unstructured and complex information organized in varied formats and originating from web sites, emails, social media and networking sites, videos, presentations, blogs, etc. It is stated that for the practical application of highly unstructured information – the big data, everyone seems to revert to social media sentiment analysis.

Future trends in big data incorporate predictive analytics and brand management. To survive competition businesses should identify patterns in customer buying behaviors and to perceive consumer product feedback early. Predicative analytics identifies symptoms and clues in pushing an innovation. Brand management tracks trends between brands in similar sectors, or completely unrelated markets, knowing intentions and feelings of target customers and designing a winning marketing strategy [11].

3   Subjectivity and Sentiment Analysis

Subjectivity is defined as actor's perception of an event or an aspect influenced by individual opinions and beliefs and disregarding external stimuli. It strives to identify the private states – opinions, sentiments, beliefs, trust, sentiments, speculations or rumors, evaluation, etc. in the natural language. Sentiment classification extends subjectivity classification (which labels target text as subjective or objective) by introducing levels of granularity and allows labeling of text as positive, negative or neutral. For many NLP applications, this forms an initial major filtering phase in generating feasible data [6]. Wilson has distinguished between different types of subjectivity, which are called attitude types [7]. Wilson identifies the following attitude types:

1. Sentiments: It includes the positive and negative emotions, evaluations, and stances. The sentiment focus is on the entity under consideration.
2. Agreement: It refers to the private states exhibited by a person. The person may or may not agree, concede, consent, or give assent to something under consideration. The sentiment focus is on the attitude that is agreed to or otherwise.
3. Arguing: It refers to a private state wherein a person argues or expresses a belief or disbelief about something to be true or otherwise in his/her view of the world.
4. Intention: It includes aims, goals, plans, and other explicit expressions. It refers to a mental state representation a commitment to take certain action in future.
5. Speculation: It is a state which a person is speculating about tautology of an event or possible occurrence of something.
6. Other attitude: All other private states not contained in the attitudes above can be categorized under other attitudes.

The methods for extracting and annotating subjective terms include: the machine learning approaches which study conjunction relations between adjectives, grouping adjectives based on annotated seed words, extracting nouns using pattern-bootstrapping algorithms, ranking of subjective adjectives using Web-based mutual information, etc. [8]. Use of suffixes often changes the word meaning of an attitude word. This can be encoded within actual words of sentences lexically and morphologically. Most lexicon-based systems for analysis of sentiment on sentence or document levels face the difficulty of assigning sentiment scores to words that are not available in their databases [8].

Issues in Sentiment Analysis.   Sentiment classification process comprises of activities, namely

1. Object Identification: It focuses on identifying the target entity on which the opinion is expressed.
2. Feature Extraction and Synonym Grouping: It finds nouns and noun phrases with a better recall and a lower precision.

3. Opinion-Orientation Determination: This activity deals with finding whether a sentence contains an opinion on a feature under consideration. If it does, then to indicate whether it is positive or negative.
4. Integration: The opinion can be represented as a quintuple. The process of matching the five pieces of information in a quintuple and integrate it is a complex task. In situations when a sentence does not explicitly mention the some intended pieces of information the task become harder.

To deal with problems in activity (4) above, it becomes imperative to apply natural language processing techniques in the opinion mining context. This may involve incorporating parsing, word sense disambiguation, and co-reference resolution.

Challenges in Sentiment Analysis. The key challenges for sentiment analysis include:

1. Named Entity Recognition – In normal text many-a-times the meaning conveyed by the nouns is ambiguous. It becomes difficult to ascertain the intended target of the actor when different aspects are referred in the text. It is important to know what the actor is actually talking about. For example, 300 Spartans is a group of Greeks and also a movie, but the context would determine exactness of the entity.
2. Anaphora Resolution – Another problem faced in sentiment classification is to resolve the context implied by a pronoun, or a noun phrase. For example, "We attended a dance show and had lunch in hotel; it was lovely." The meaning conveyed by "it" in the sentence is not clear and needs further processing to resolve the same.
3. Parsing – This is a common step in text extraction to identify the subject and object of the sentence. But to determine to which subject the verb and/or adjective actually refer in the sentence is a crucial task.
4. Sarcasm – In the target text ironical word phrases may be present. These words may convey meaning opposite to what has been said and may be intended to insult or mock the target user. Such sarcastic words must be identified.
5. Level of analysis – sentiment classification at document level, sentence level or word level and comparative sentiment analysis.
6. Social Data (Twitter, Facebook, YouTube) – The data generated on the social web has its own language comprising of abbreviations, short forms and emoticons. The text tends to be short in size with ungrammatical utterances.

4   Our Approach

We propose a generalized approach to sentiment classification and analysis on the topic-based data acquired from Twitter, Facebook and other micro-blogging sites. Our approach in Fig. 1 highlights the inclusion of big data analytics for effective and efficient storage and retrieval of unstructured aspect data and also visualization over the specialized big data applications involving opinion mining and affect analysis.

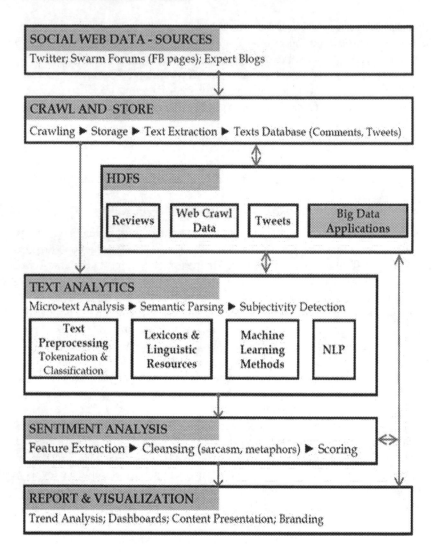

Fig. 1. An Approach to sentiment analysis

The opinion placed by the users comes from diversified sources such as social media, product review, blogs, Wikipedia, etc. This information is enormous and unstructured as well. Although it does convey high-volume of decision critical data but if processed in larger volume may provide sensible information for business. Big Data Analytics serves to provide a viable storage and access solution.

The process to classifying the document text as conveying positive or negative sentiment involves typical phases – extraction, pre-processing, scoring, feature-based sentiment evaluation, and visualization. Sentiment classifications play an important role in sentiment evaluation and affect analysis. Data mining techniques have found significance in determining the sentence opinion and also in calculation of overall score for the document. An alternative approach to deriving polarized aspects from the documents may include processes like - micro-blogging text analysis, semantic parsing, subjectivity detection and, aspect extraction and polarity detection.

Our proposed method would acquire the content for feature-based analysis from the social web through micro-blogging sites – Twitter, the swarm forums – Facebook and the expert blogs and other discussion forums. The crawled content from the web undergoes text extraction which results in a network of distilled comments and tweets to be populated into the texts database. It is a known fact that the stream data from web is largely unstructured. Hence a big data solution to archiving and retrieving the crawled and distilled data adds to the advantage of the approach. The Hadoop file system would store the extracted aspects (tweets and comments) for further processing and analysis.

The next major step involves text analytics incorporating natural language processing approaches to detecting subjectivity of the text. This can be ascertained at levels such as word-level, sentence-level, document-level and concept-level. The first stage in text analytics is essentially the pre-processing of the input text. Pre-processing is followed by semantic parsing which involves use of linguistic resources. The NLP-based classification techniques both supervised, un-supervised and semi-supervised provides the means for detection sentiment subjectivity of the aspect. These approaches include machine learning approaches, lexicon-based approaches and/or combination of these. Syntactic features include n-grams, word-n-grams, part-of-speech tags, etc. The linguistic features include synonyms, glosses, synsets, etc.

Manual approaches are more precise and do not necessitates defining rules, but require more time to set up the word lexicon. The dictionary-based, semi-automated approaches comprising of the positive-negative word dictionary augmented with synonyms and antonyms tends to be faster but with lower precision. The corpus-based approaches provide moderate precision and can be automated fully. Corpus-based approach starts with a seed set of positive-negative words and expands it using grammar bindings.

In the sentiment analysis, the tasks involve extracting aspects and cleansing them to deal suitably with sarcasm, metaphors and negation. This is followed by applying appropriate algorithms to process the opinionated text and evaluate their sentiment score. The final phase is reporting of the outcomes and visualization of the processing results. All the above stages are integrated with the Hadoop file system to leverage the power of big-data analytics.

5   Conclusion

With the proliferation of Web 2.0, there has been enormous increase in the generation of unstructured data every day. This data coming from varied sources has to be stored efficiently and retrieved timely for analysis. The processing of this highly complex multi-dimensional data necessitates use of big data analytics. Also the evaluation and extraction opinions expressed and sentiments conveyed through the social web have become essential. In this paper we have proposed an approach to sentiment analysis in big data environment.

References

1. Gandomi, A., Haider, M.: Beyond the hype: big data concepts, methods, and analytics. Int. J. Inf. Manage. **35**, 137–144 (2015). Elsevier
2. Bravo-Marquez, F., Mendoza, M., Poblete, B.: Meta-level sentiment models for big social data analysis. Knowledge-Based Systems (2014)
3. Mukherjee, D., Krishnamurthy, K.: Maximizing the returns of big data. Cognizanti – Fact-based Insights, vol. 5, issue 1 (2012)
4. Pang, B., Lee, L.: Opinion mining and sentiment analysis. Found. Trends Inf. Retrieval **2**(1–2), 1–135 (2008)
5. Liu, B.: Sentiment analysis: a multi-faceted problem. IEEE Intell. Syst. **25**(3), 76–80 (2010)
6. Banea, C., Mihalcea, R., Wiebe, J.: Multilingual sentiment and subjectivity analysis. Multilingual Natural Language Processing (2011)
7. Somasundaran, S.: Discourse-level relations for opinion analysis. PhD Dissertation Report, University of Pittsburgh (2010)
8. Neviarouskaya, A., Prendinger, H., Ishizuka, M.: SentiFul: a lexicon for sentiment analysis. IEEE Trans. Affect. Comput. **2**(1), 22–36 (2011)
9. Chen, H.: Trends and Controversies – AI and opinion mining part-2. In: IEEE Intelligent Systems (2010)
10. Paltoglou, G., Theunis, M., Kappas, A., Thelwall, M.: Predicting emotional responses to long informal text. IEEE Trans. Affect. Comput. **4**(1), 267–279 (2013)
11. Scagliarini, L.: Big Data, Unstructured Information Analysis is More Than Sentiment – a blog. Expert System – Semantic Intelligence
12. Chen, C., Chen, Z., Wu, C.: An unsupervised approach for person name bipolarization using principal component analysis. IEEE Trans. Knowl. Data Eng. **24**(11), 1963–1976 (2012)
13. Khabia, A., Chandak, M.: A cluster based approach with n-grams at word level for document classification. Int. J. Comput. Appl. **117**(23), 38–42 (2015)

Lung Cancer Diagnosis by Hybrid Support Vector Machine

Abhinav Trivedi$^{(\boxtimes)}$ and Pragya Shukla

Computer Engineering, IET, DAVV, Indore, India
abhinavtrivedi17@gmail.com,
pragyashukla_iet@yahoo.co.in

Abstract. A machine learning based classification technique to diagnose lung CT scan images as cancerous or noncancerous is proposed in this paper. Lung cancer is regarded as one of the major fatal disease among the population throughout the world. Early diagnosis of lung cancer can be an important factor which can decrease the death rate among people. In large medical organizations manual inspection of CT scan, MRI images etc. puts a lot of workload on doctors and radiologist. An effective diagnosis technique can really reduce their efforts. CT (Computerized Tomography) scan images are used in medical field to analyze various parts of body. Grey scale CT scan images are used here as dataset, image preprocessing and feature of images are used. SVM classifiers are used for diagnosis. The main objective of this paper is to improve accuracy rate for lung cancer diagnosis by designing a hybrid SVM.

Keywords: CT Scan · SVM · ROI · Thresholding · PCA

1 Introduction

In field of medical image diagnosis Computer science and Information Technology can prove to be very helpful and handy. Generally medical images are obtained with the help of X-rays, MRI, CT scan. Computed tomography (CT) of the body uses special x-ray technology to detect a various diseases. CT scanning of a patient is painless, efficient and accurate method. Lung cancer can develops due to various reasons like smoking, pollution etc. It is basically inappropriate growth of body cell which takes a form of a tumor. Radiologists examine the CT scans visually and analyses it. Analyzing large number of CT scan by a Radiologist may reduce efficiency and increases the chance of human error. Therefore there is a need of automated diagnosis system for medical image diagnosis and classification.

Many approaches and methods were developed by researchers for the purpose of computer aided diagnosis of lung related problems. Depending on the type of lung problem, each of the lung pathologies may follow a particular methodology in order to characterise the particular disease. Since the focus of this paper is on lung cancer detection, one way of lung cancer detection is to identify the lung nodules which are circular masses of tissue in lungs and are generally regarded as early signs of cancer and try to diagnose whether they are benign or malignant. Also by measuring the characteristics of these masses, one can predict their possibility of being malign.

© Springer Nature Singapore Pte Ltd. 2016
A. Unal et al. (Eds.): SmartCom 2016, CCIS 628, pp. 177–187, 2016.
DOI: 10.1007/978-981-10-3433-6_22

The diagnosis of lung CT scan images include following steps: CT scan images and data collection, Image preprocessing on CT scan images, desired feature extraction, Feature reduction, Training and Testing of a desired classifier, Result analysis and development of a hybrid SVM.

Data images may not be always suitable for direct use in feature extraction. Image processing is very important as it converts the image into appropriate form for feature extraction and it is also necessary to remove unwanted part of image. After the removal of unwanted details ROI (Region of interest) is clearly visible in image this is generally done by image segmentation.

Features of any image are quantitative measures of that image. Generally Images are not given as input to classifiers, their respective features acts as input to classifiers. After image preprocessing Features are extracted from images. Features can be entropy of image, contrast of image, area of particular section of image etc. When the input data to an methodology is too large to be processed efficiently and it is regarded as unnecessary to process all feature as input into the classifier then the input data will be converted into a compact representation of features [1]. Excessive features selected from image can enhance the computation cost in the phase of machine based classification thus to reduce features to a set of minimum important features PCA (Principal Component Analysis) algorithm is used [3].

After Feature reduction by PCA reduced features are given as input to classifiers for diagnosis. There can be various kinds of classifiers that can be used for this purpose like SVM (Support Vector Machines), PNN (Probabilistic Neural Network), ANN (Artificial Neural Network), K-Nearest Neighbour (KNN) etc.

ANNs, PNNs, as well as KNN capable tools which can be used for many kinds of classification but they all have some limitations. Accuracy of k-nearest neighbour classification is very much reduced when there is a presence of noisy or unrelated features, especially when the number of attributes is large and PNN requires more space as compared to other classifiers [1]. ANN is generally a better approach for classification but with the presence of hidden layers its computation cost increases. Among all the above classifiers discussed above SVM proved to be more accurate with less computation cost [10]. SVM is not generally well known as the ANN. However, it is also applied to some medical tools. A system for cancer diagnosis used the DNA micro-array data as a classification data set. Diagnosis error obtained by above discussed system was smaller than in systems which uses other known methods. Reduction of the error achieved 36% [11]. SVM is a supervised machine learning based classifier which is generally used as for binary classification In this proposed methodology three types of SVMs are used to diagnose the Lung CT images then results of two SVMs with maximum accuracy are integrated mathematically to analyse combined accuracy among the results. After getting combined accuracy kernel equations of those two SVMs are linearly combined to generate a hybrid SVM with improved accuracy. Basically this hybrid SVM gives best results when compared to the performance of other three types of SVMS individually. SVMs which are used in proposed methodology are Radial basis function SVM, Linear SVM and Polynomial SVM, all the above discussed SVMs differ in their kernel functions. Result integration algorithm for integration of results of two most accurate SVMs is also discussed in this paper which is based on mathematical data analysis. Hybrid SVM is developed by linearly combining the kernel equations of RBF and Polynomial SVM.

2 Methodology

Methodology to diagnose or classify CT images of lungs as cancerous and non-cancerous is shown in Fig. 1. This includes Database of Lung CT images with actual diagnosis report about each image. Then image preprocessing, feature extraction, feature reduction, training of all three SVMs. Here completes the Training part. In Testing part all steps till feature reduction are repeated on different Image dataset, then reduced features are applied as input to all three SVMs one by one and result of each SVM are analyzed. Results from two SVMs having more accuracy as compared to one SVM are integrated to generate optimized accuracy results.

2.1 CT Scan Images

Computed tomography uses a beam of X-rays and high processing machine to get images of bones and soft-tissues. It let a doctor to viusalize the size, shape, and position of structures that are deep inside the body.

2.2 Image Preprocessing

Image preprocessing of CT image is necessary since there are various objects in lung CT images which are of no use. Image database consist of grayscale image so first step of image processing is to convert grayscale images into binary images. Binary image every pixel value is either 0 or 1 means it is either black or white it is called bi-level or two level image while in gray scale image can have any value between 0 to 256.

2.2.1 Thresholding

After conversion of image from grayscale to binary next step is to find the ROI (Region Of Interest) i.e. nodules in lung an discard the remaining portion. It is also known as segmentation of image and it is done by image thresholding. For image segmentation firstly very small objects of CT image which have no possibility of being a nodule are removed then very large connected objects in images are removed which are large lung tissues and ROI is segmented from image (Fig. 2).

2.3 Feature Extraction

After the image preprocessing the segmented region of image is subjected to feature extraction. Features provide more quantitive and detailed understanding of image. 4 grayscale features, 5 geometric features and 4 texture features are taken from each image hence total 14 features are taken from each image.

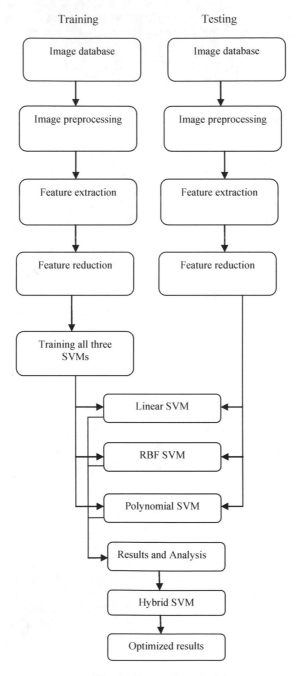

Fig. 1. Proposed methodology

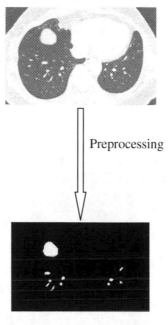

Fig. 2. Preprocessing

(a) **Texture Features:** These are the features calculated with the help of GLCM (Grey Level Co-occurrence Matrix).
  (1) *Entropy:* Measure of randomness which can be used to characterize the texture of the image.
  (2) *Contrast:* Measures the local variations in the GLCM. It calculates intensity contrast between a pixel and its neighbour pixel for the whole image. Contrast is 0 for a constant image.
  (3) *Energy:* It is the sum of squared elements in the GLCM. It is also known as uniformity.
  (4) *Homogeneity:* It measures the closeness among distribution of elements in the GLCM to the GLCM diagonal.
  (5) *Correlation:* Measures the joint probability occurrence of the specified pixel pairs.
(b) **Geometric Features:** These are the physical dimensional features which are defined as follows
  (1) *Area:* The area is the summation of areas of pixel in the image that are marked as 1 in case of binary image.
  (2) *Convex area:* It is a scalar value that gives the number of pixels in convex image of the Region of Interest which is a binary image with all pixels within the hull filled in.
  (3) *Perimeter:* The perimeter [length] is the total pixels in the boundary of the object. Perimeter P is calculated as the sum of the distances between every consecutive boundary points.

(4) *Eccentricity:* The eccentricity is the ratio of the distance between the foci of the ellipse and length of its major axis. Its value is between 0 and 1.

(5) *Solidity:* It is the proportion of the pixels in the convex hull.

(c) **Gray Scale features:** Gray scale features which are used in this paper are standard deviation, variance, kurtosis and skewness.

(1) *Skewness:* Skewness is a measure of the asymmetry of the data around the sample mean.

(2) *Kurtosis:* It is a measure of how outlier-prone a distribution is.

(3) *Variance:* Variance is the way in which pixel value is spread.

(4) *Standard deviation:* It is a measure of how much that gray levels differ from mean.

2.4   Feature Reduction

Processing too many features in a classifier can really enhance the computation cost and complexity of the problem. In this paper PCA is used to reduce features of images. PCA shows the variance by each feature with respect to images. Features showing a considerable variance are fed as input to classifiers and rest of the features are neglected. By this technique number of features in feature set is reduced without decreasing efficiency of system rather it decreases system complexity. In this paper we have reduced to 2 features only from 14 features because they are together contributing more than 70% in total variance.

2.5   Classification by SVM

SVM was initially introduced by Vapnik. SVM [9] is a binary classifier which uses supervised learning technique. SVM basically creates an appropriate and optimal hyperplane among the dataset and that hyperplane divides the whole dataset in two classes. Hyperplane must separate the data points with maximum possible margin and data points nearest to hyperplane are known as support vectors. The space in which hyperplane or line is created for data classification may not be necessarily two dimensional or three dimensional it can be multidimensional depending upon the number of features.

SVMs can be broadly classified into two categories:

(a) Linear SVM: It is the most simplest form of SVM. It is used when training dataset is linearly separable. Graphically it uses a line or hyperplane which classify the dataset. Its linear function is given below:

$$F(x) = w^t x + b \tag{1}$$

This is the generalized equation of hyperplane which separates the data points, here w is weight vector, b is threshold and x, are the data points (Fig. 3).

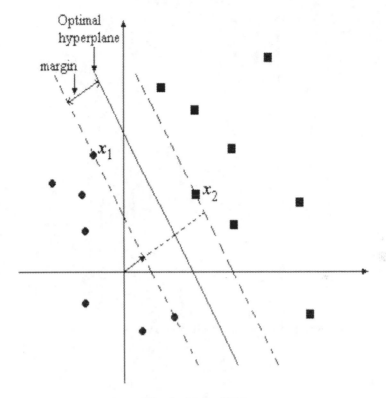

Fig. 3. Linear SVM

(b) Non linear SVM: When the training dataset is linearly non separable the non linear SVMs are used for classification. These SVMs uses non linear kernel function to classify dataset into two classes in a high dimensional feature space. In two dimensional feature space non linear SVMs generates a polynomial or quadratic curve to spate datasets into two classes, Curve separates the datasets in a feature space. Non linear SVM classifier can be mathematically defined as

$$F(x) = w^t \emptyset(x) + b \tag{2}$$

On the basis of kernel function SVM can be of many types. Other than Linear SVM in this paper two Non linear SVMs are used for classification (Fig. 4).

(1) *Polynomials:*

$$K(x, y) = (1 + <x, y>)^d \tag{3}$$

(2) *Radial basis function:*

$$K(x, y) = \exp\left(- <(x - y), (x - y) > /(2\sigma^2)\right) \tag{4}$$

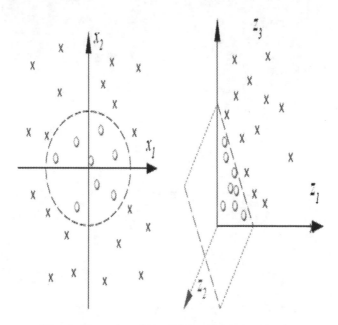

Fig. 4. Examples of Non Linear SVM classification

2.6   Performance Measures

All diagnosis results may have some error and on some point will either unable to identify correct results. So for proper understanding of their performance it is better to generalize performance measures as follows

- True Positive (T1): Cancerous lung CT image correctly diagnosed as Cancerous.
- True Negative (T2): Non cancerous lung CT image correctly diagnosed as Non cancerous.
- False Positive (F1): Non cancerous lung CT image incorrectly diagnosed as Cancerous.
- False Negative (F2): Cancerous lung CT image incorrectly diagnosed as Non cancerous.

$$(1)\ Sensitivity = \text{T1}/(\text{T1} + \text{F2}) * 100\%$$
$$(2)\ Specificity = \text{T2}/(\text{T2} + \text{F1}) * 100\%$$
$$(3)\ Accuracy = (\text{T1} + \text{T2})/\text{T1} + \text{T2} + \text{F1} + \text{F2} * 100\%$$

2.7   Result and Analysis

As it is clear from the results shown in Table 1, that most accurate among all SVMs is SVM with RBF kernel. Sensitivity is also maximum in case of RBF kernel however Specificity is maximum with Polynomial kernel.

Table 1. Results

Sr. no.	Kernel function	Sensitivity	Specificity	Accuracy
1	RBF	72.73%	72.73%	72.73%
2	Linear	63.64%	72.73%	68.18%
3	Polynomial	54.55%	81.82%	68.18%

2.7.1   Result Integration

If we consider accuracy as a primary parameter most accurate results are given by RBF kernel SVM. Results of any two SVMs can be integrated to generate new results which are more close to correct results so new results can be equivalent to a hybrid SVM with more accuracy. The motive behind integration of results is that there may be some data elements which are classified correctly by one SVM and incorrectly by another and vice versa may also be true so by integrating results one can enhance the overall accuracy. Steps for integration of results from two SVMs in this paper are as follows

- Two results SVM1 & SVM2 and one empty array A.
- Mark the correct result elements from SVM1.
- Mark the incorrect result elements from SVM1.
- Mark the correct result elements from SVM2.
- Mark the correct result elements from SVM2.
- Label the elements which are commonly incorrect in both SVM1 & SVM2 as Incorrect and store them in A.
- Label the elements which are correct in SVM1 and SVM2 both as correct and store them in A.
- Label the elements which are either correct in SVM1 or SVM2 as correct and store them in A.
- A is the final array of integrated result of SVM1 & SVM2.

After successful mathematical integration of results from two SVMs performance measures are calculated from new results and accuracy is improved by 4.54%.

2.8   Hybrid SVM

As it is clear from result integration approach that combination of RBF and polynomial SVM provides better accuracy than using any of them separately, therefore a hybrid SVM is proposed in which kernel equations of RBF and polynomial SVM are linearly combined to generate a SVM with new kernel.

$$K(x,y) = (1 + <x,y>)^d + \exp(-<(x-y),(x-y)>/(2\sigma^2)) \qquad (5)$$

Experimental results of hybrid SVM and other SVMs is shown in table below (Table 2)

Table 2. New results

Sr. no.	Kernel function	Sensitivity	Specificity	Accuracy
1	RBF	72.73%	72.73%	72.73%
2	Linear	63.64%	72.73%	68.18%
3	Polynomial	54.55%	81.82%	68.18%
4	Hybrid	72.73%	81.82%	77.27%

As from above result it is clear when two SVMs with different kernel equations are integrated to generate a hybrid SVM it gives better result than individual SVM. With this hybrid SVM not only accuracy is improved but sensitivity and specificity is also improved.

3 Conclusion

In this work of research three variations of SVMs are used to classify lung CT images as cancerous and non cancerous. Results of all three SVMs are compared and result of two most accurate SVMs are integrated to generate new optimized results. Then those two SVMs are integrated with the help of their kernel equations to generate a hybrid SVM. In this paper a hybrid SVM with integrated kernel equations of RBF and Polynomial SVM gives 4.54% more accurate results, so for the future work to improve accuracy different mathematical combinations of different SVM kernels can be analyzed to generate new improved SVM kernels.

References

1. Nandpuru, H.B., Salankar, S.S., Bora, V.R.: MRI brain cancer classification using support vector machine. In: IEEE Students' Conference on Electrical, Electronics and Computer Science (2014)
2. Taher, F., Werghi, N., Al-Ahmad, H.: Bayesian classification and artificial neural network methods for lung cancer early diagnosis. IEEE (2012)
3. Zhang, Y., Wu, L.: An MR brain images classifier via principal component analysis and kernel support vector machine. Progress Electromagnet. Res. **130**(369), 388 (2012)
4. Sudha, V., Jayashree, P.: Lung nodule detection in CT images using thresholding and morphological operations. Int. J. Emerg. Sci. Eng. (IJESE) **1**(2) (2012). ISSN 2319–6378
5. Song, D., Zhukov, T.A., Markov, O., Qian, W., Tockman, M.S.: Prognosis of stage i lung cancer patients through quantitative analysis of centrosomal features. IEEE (2012)

6. Othman, M.F.B., Abdullah, N.B., Kamal, N.F.B.: MRI brain classification using support vector machine. IEEE (2011)
7. Qiao, Z., Zhou, L., Huang, J.: Sparse: linear discriminant analysis with application to high dimension low sample size data. IAENG Int. J. Appl. Math. **39**, 48–60 (2009)
8. Jia, T., Zhao, D.Z., Yang, J.Z., Wang, X.: Automated detection of pulmonary nodules in HRCT images. IEEE (2007)
9. Kumar, K., Bhattacharya, S.: Artificial neural network vs linear discriminant analysis in credit ratings forecast: a comparative study of prediction performances. Rev. Account. Finance **5** (2006)
10. Godbole, S.: Inter-class relationships in text classification, Ph.D. Thesis, IIT, Bombay, India (2006)
11. Huang, Ming, Kecman, Vojislav: Gene extraction for cancer diagnosis by support vector machines. Artif. Intell. Med. **35**, 185–194 (2005)

Fuzzy-PID Based Liquid Level Control for Coupled Tank (MIMO) Interacting System

Hafiz Shaikh[✉] and Neelima Kulkarni

Electrical Engineering Department, Modern College of Engineering, Pune, Maharashtra, India
hafizshaikh815@gmail.com, nrkmcoe@gmail.com

Abstract. Multiple input multiple output (MIMO) control system conflicts with single input single output (SISO) control system in many ways because of various parameters. Two tank coupled interacting is one such system which has two inputs and two outputs and the control strategy used for it is not like SISO. Electrical control of the system mainly deals with control of supply to the pump which is the actual source of water to both the tanks. PID controller is generally used for controlling the liquid level. Basic PID controller has some demerits related with overshoot in the response and steady state error. This responses experimented on actual hardware are shown. Intelligent controller like fuzzy logic controller (FLC) when combined with PID can give better responses. These responses are validated and shown in this paper which is formulated in the form of simulation.

Keywords: MIMO theory · Coupled tank system · Fuzzy system · Proportional-Integral-Derivative (PID) controller · Self-tuning Fuzzy-PID controller

1 Introduction

Multiple input multiple output (MIMO) systems are those in which two or more outputs are controlled by two or more manipulated variables. Because there is an interaction between other control loops of MIMO processes, therefore the method used for SISO system cannot be used for control of MIMO system. This paper focus on how the response of the PID controller can be improved by changing its coefficients using fuzzy logic controller. The very basic logic behind this is by giving error signal (difference between set value and manipulated variable) and rate of change in error as the inputs to the fuzzy and the output from the fuzzy will be the PID parameters, this output signal then combines with the classical PID controller to give overall controlled signal. This controlled signal is then given to the coupled tank interacting system. The merits of both fuzzy logic controller and PID can be achieved by this controller.

2 Coupled Tank (MIMO) Interaction Theory

While designing multi-variable control strategy the process must be parameterized using first order plus time delay transfer function.

© Springer Nature Singapore Pte Ltd. 2016
A. Unal et al. (Eds.): SmartCom 2016, CCIS 628, pp. 188–195, 2016.
DOI: 10.1007/978-981-10-3433-6_23

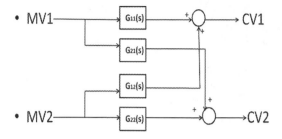

MV1 and MV2 are the process manipulated variables. CV1 and CV2 are the controlled variables of the process. In order to find the controlled variable which is nothing but the water level in the tank, process transfer function needs to be calculated. G11 and G22 are the process transfer function related with the inputs and output not interacting with each other. G21 and G12 are the process transfer functions which are responsible for the interaction of the coupled tanks.

The actual hardware based Multi Input Multi Output (MIMO) coupled tank interacting system is shown in Fig. 1. All the experimentation and results obtained in this paper are related with this hardware.

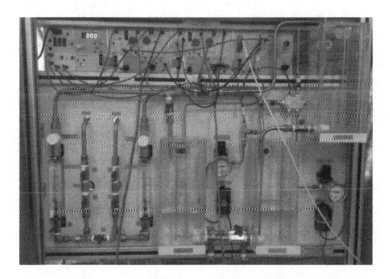

Fig. 1. Actual Hardware (PCT-3T) of coupled tank system

2.1 Two Tank Interacting System

Coupled tank system is shown in Fig. 2 having constant cross–sectional area A1 and A2 for two tanks. The density of the liquid is assumed to be constant. "m1" and "m2" are the two inputs to the two different tanks. These two tanks are coupled to one another and act as interacting system because of the discharge valve R1 connected in between them.

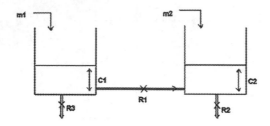

Fig. 2. Coupled tanks having two inputs and two outputs with an interacting valve (R1) connected at the bottom.

2.2   Coupled Tank Equation

Water inflows the coupled tank from the top and leaves through its outlet at the bottom. According to equation [1] shown which belongs to mass-balance equation, the first order equation for the tank can be written as

$$A\frac{dh}{dx} = q_i - q_0 + q_{mn} \tag{1}$$

Where +ve sign indicates flow into the tank, q_i = flow of water entering into the tank. q_0 = flow of water going out of the tank. q_{mn} = flow rate from connected tank from tank m to n if any (not applicable for single tank). h = liquid level in the tank. A = Area of cross section of the tank. For two Coupled tank interacting system the tank equation based on the mass balance theory can be given as

$$A1\frac{dC1}{dt} = m1 - \frac{(C1 - C2)}{R1} - \frac{C1}{R3} \tag{2}$$

$$A2\frac{dC2}{dt} = \frac{(C1 - C2)}{R1} + m2 - \frac{C2}{R2} \tag{3}$$

Where, for PCT – 3T system
A1 = A2 = 0.0169 m2.
R1 = R2 = R3 = Discharge Coefficient (sec/m2) = 4.2 mm/LPH = 15552 s/m2.
Substituting the parameters in Eqs. 2 and 3 we get,

$$\frac{dC1}{dt} = 59.1715m1 - 0.0076095C1 + 0.0038047C2 \tag{4}$$

$$\frac{dC2}{dt} = 59.1715m2 + 0.0038047C1 - 0.0076095C1 \tag{5}$$

The above equations are now in state space form, and in matrix form they can be written as follow,

$$\frac{dC}{dt} = AC + BM \tag{6}$$

Where,

$$A = \begin{bmatrix} -0.0076095 & 0.0038047 \\ 0.0038047 & -0.0076095 \end{bmatrix} \tag{7}$$

$$B = \begin{bmatrix} 59.1715 & 0 \\ 0 & 59.1715 \end{bmatrix} \tag{8}$$

$$C = \begin{bmatrix} C1 \\ C2 \end{bmatrix} \tag{9}$$

$$M = \begin{bmatrix} m1 \\ m2 \end{bmatrix} \tag{10}$$

Laplace transform can be used to find out the transfer function of the above matrix equations, which is given below,

$$Gp = (SI - A)^{-1} * B \tag{11}$$

$$\begin{bmatrix} S + 0.0076095 & -0.0038047 \\ -0.0038047 & S + 0.0076095 \end{bmatrix} = (SI - A) \tag{12}$$

After calculating (SI−A)−1*B we can obtain the Gp11, Gp12, Gp21 and Gp22. The transfer functions for Coupled tank interacting system are found out to be

G11	$\dfrac{S + 0.0076095}{S^2 + 0.015219S + 0.000434287}$
G12	$\dfrac{0.0038047}{S^2 + 0.015219S + 0.000434287}$
G21	$\dfrac{0.0038047}{S^2 + 0.015219S + 0.000434287}$
G22	$\dfrac{S + 0.0076095}{S^2 + 0.015219S + 0.000434287}$

3   Fuzzy-PID Controller

3.1   Self-tuning Fuzzy PID Controller

There are two inputs and three outputs given to the Fuzzy controller. Inputs to the fuzzy logic controller are error between set level and actual level and the other is the rate of change in error.

Three parameters of PID that is Proportional gain (Kp), Integral gain (Ki) and Derivative (Kd) when varied with the help of fuzzy logic controller it is termed as Auto tuning fuzzy based PID controller.

Error (set point – Manipulated value) and rate of change in error is calculated and fed to the controller as shown in Fig. 3. These are used as the input variables to the fuzzy controller, and the output (defuzzified) variables are the parameters of PID control, those are ΔKp, ΔKi and ΔKd. Here, e denotes the error in liquid level; ec denotes rate of change in error in process.

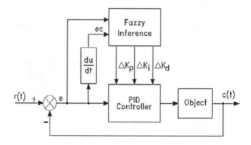

Fig. 3.   Auto tuning fuzzy based PID controller

4   Formulation of Auto Tuning Fuzzy Logic Based PID Controller

Two Mamdani types of fuzzy controllers should be used separately to control the manipulated are the actual level coming out from the each tank so that the controlled signal is passed to each process tanks separately (Fig. 4).

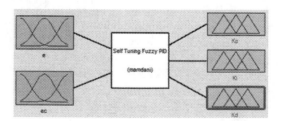

Fig. 4.   Fuzzy inference block

The parameters of PID controller Kp, Ki and Kd are given in the range of *Kpmin* to *Kpmax*, *Kimin* to *Kimax*, *Kdmin* to *Kdmax*. Based on the rule base, probability of error in the system and simulation results of PID the ranges of PID parameters are decided.

The ranges of these fuzzy inputs are between −0.1 to 0.1 for error and −0.025 to 0.025 for rate of change in error (Table 1). According to the above triangular functions for output, when set value is equal to manipulated value the fuzzy output should be near 0.5 (Fig. 5).

Table 1. Nomenclature of Linguistic membership functions

Input membership		Output membership	
NB	Negative big	S	Small
NS	Negative small	MS	Medium small
ZE	Zero	M	Medium
PS	Positive small	MB	Medium big
PB	Positive big	B	Big

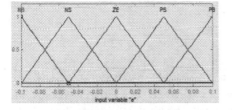 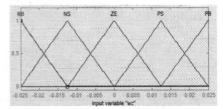

Fig. 5. **(A)** Membership functions of e(t). **(B)** Triangular Membership functions for ec

The ranges of outputs go from 0 to 1 that is positive signal is given to PID (Fig. 6). The practical experiments performed on the process can give a brief idea about the crisp values and rules can be according defined as

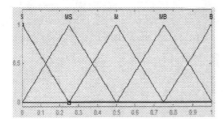

$De\e$	NB	NS	ZE	PS	PB
NB	S	S	MS	MS	M
NS	S	MS	MS	M	MB
ZE	MS	MS	M	MB	MB
PS	MS	M	MB	MB	B
PB	M	MB	MB	B	B

Fig. 6. **(A)** Triangular Membership functions for K'_p, K'_i and K'_d **(B)** Formulation of Rules for Fuzzy Inference System

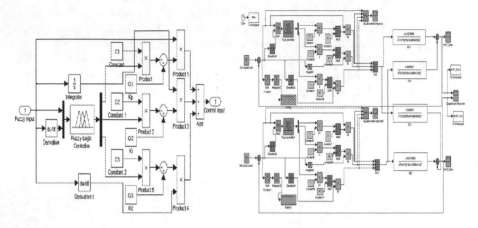

Fig. 7. **(A)** Formulation of Fuzzy PID simulation **(B)** Simulation of Fuzzy-PID controller for coupled tank interacting level control.

5   Simulation Responses and Discussion

Auto tuning fuzzy PID controller simulation is as shown in Fig. 7(A). The Simulink model of the overall system (closed loop system) consisting of process transfer function of coupled tank interacting system is shown in Fig. 7(B).

Fuzzy logic controller sends control signals to the PID changing the gain parameters. For the set point of 10 cm the simulated output response for the two tanks using fuzzy-PID controller is shown in the Fig. 8(A). It can be seen here that the response of both the tanks for same set point based on fuzzy-PID is achieved successfully and has less settling time.

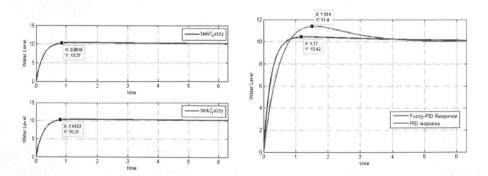

Fig. 8. **(A)** Output response of two tanks using Fuzzy-PID controller for set level of 10 cm **(B)** Simulation response comparing PID and Fuzzy-PID of the Liquid level for set value of 10 cm

The output response for the coupled tank interacting system using Fuzzy-PID controller has no oscillations and there is almost no overshoot (Table 2).

Table 2. Controller's performance comparison

Controller type	Integral square error for set point of 10 cm
PID	20.02
Fuzzy-PID	10.87

The settling time for tank to reach 50% set value is 350 s (175 samples*2) to reach 125 mm of water level in tank (red coloured response) (Fig. 9).

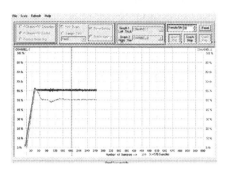

Fig. 9. Actual Hardware response (set value of 50% for Tank 1 and 60% set point for Tank 2) (Color figure online)

6   Conclusion

In this paper we have designed and implemented PID controller and Auto-tuning fuzzy-PID controller to control (MIMO) coupled tank interacting system The result shows significant improvement in maintaining performance over the widely used PID design method in terms of oscillations produced and overshoot. It has excellent dynamic and steady performance rather than PID and fuzzy controllers. The MIMO interacting system responses indicate that the water level in both the tanks can be controlled perfectly by the courtesy of the new Auto-tuning fuzzy-PID controller.

References

1. Marlin, T.E.: Process Control: Designing Processes and Control Systems for Dynamic Performance, 2nd edn. McGraw-Hill, Boston (2000)
2. Wayne Bequette, B.: Process Control – Modeling, Design and Simulation. PHI publication (2003)
3. Pornpatkul, C., Suksri, T.: Decentralized fuzzy logic controller for TITO coupled-tank process. In: ICROS-SICE International Joint Conference 2009, PR0002/09/0000-2862 ¥400 © 2009 SICE, Japan (2009)
4. Krivic, S., Hujdur, M., Mrzic, A., Konjicija, S.: Design and Implementation of Fuzzy Controller on Embedded Computer for Water Level Control. In: MIPRO 2012, 21-25 May 2012, Opatija, Croatia (2012)
5. Taneva, A., Muskinja, N., Petrov, M., Tovomik, B.: FPID controller: real time application. In: Second IEEE International Conference on Intelligent Systems, June 2004

Multi Chromatic Balls with Relaxed Criterion to Detect Larger Communities in Social Networks

Priyanka Sharma[(⊠)] and Manoj Singh

Gurukul Institute of Engineering and Technology, Kota, India
erpriyanka.sh@gmail.com

Abstract. Several unconventional clustering problems have been defined recently with some preliminary solutions. This paper discusses one such approach useful for community detection in social networks. Multi Chromatic Correlation Clustering deals with identifying groups of data objects based on the category of relation among the objects. The problem was originally defined and a solution proposed by Bonchi et al. This paper discusses their work, drawbacks and proposes a modification to overcome them. The focus is to be able to identify larger groups from seemingly sparsely connected social networks.

Keywords: Correlation clustering · Chromatic correlation clustering · Community detection · Clustering social networks · Edge-labeled graphs

1 Introduction

Easy access to internet and increasing awareness of people about its uses has led to rise of many social networking sites, customer oriented online shops, interaction and showcasing portals, collaborative entertainment sites etc. Some such popular sites are Facebook, Twitter, Amazon, eBay, YouTube etc. Besides serving the purpose for which these internet applications have been designed, these are also doing one important task constantly-task of generating huge amounts of 'people' data in the form of their profiles of general information, interests, opinions, inclinations etc. From a Business Analyst's point of view this data is a highly potential resource if desired information can be extracted. Moreover, the data is publicly available!!

So the only challenge is how to derive information from this data. Conventional clustering methods are not of much help here. In 2015, Bonchi et al. [1, 2] suggested a set of 5 algorithms each dealing with some version of Correlation Clustering Problem. The solutions are able to identify some prominent patterns (rather groups of data objects) within data networks.

Correlation Clustering is a clustering setting where the relation among data objects is categorical. Here clustering is done based on how are data objects related to each other and is not concerned with the properties of the objects themselves. It is very closely connected to the use of edge labeled graphs in clustering. The first work in the direction of Correlation Clustering was done by Bansal et al. [3] who defined the Correlation Clustering problem in its binary version. The Balls algorithm was then

© Springer Nature Singapore Pte Ltd. 2016
A. Unal et al. (Eds.): SmartCom 2016, CCIS 628, pp. 196–203, 2016.
DOI: 10.1007/978-981-10-3433-6_24

proposed by Ailon et al. [4] with minimum approximation factor achieved 2. Other noteworthy works are those of Giotis and Guruswami [5] for fixed number of clusters, Ailon and Liberty [6] for minimizing the disagreements between the generated clusters and the ground truth clusters and Ailon et al. [7] for the problem of Bipartite Correlation Clustering. Bonchi et al. [8] have also worked on extending the problem of Correlation Clustering to allow overlapping clusters.

This paper focuses on Multi Chromatic Correlation Clustering with a view to applying it for community detection in social networks. Such application requires robustness, scalability, time-efficiency and ability to detect large communities. The proposed algorithm is a modification of MultiChromaticBalls (MCB) algorithm described in [2].

The problem of Multi chromatic Correlation Clustering and its existing solution are discussed in Sect. 2. Proposed algorithm and the results for synthetic data, real life data of YouTube and runtime results are presented in Sects. 3 and 4.

2 Background

2.1 Multi-chromatic Clustering Problem

The Multi-Chromatic Correlation Clustering can be defined as in [1, 2]:

Let $G = (V; E; L; l_0; \ell)$ be an edge-labeled graph, where V represents a set of vertices, $E \subseteq V_2$ represents a set of edges, L represents a set of labels, $l_0 \notin l$ represents a special label, and $\ell : V_2 \rightarrow 2^L \cup \{l_0\}$ denotes a labeling function to assigns a set of labels to each unordered pair of vertices in V such that $\ell(x; y) = l_0$ provided the condition $(x; y) \notin E$ is true. Let also $d_\ell : 2^L \cup \{l_0\} \times 2^L \cup \{l_0\} \rightarrow R^+$ be a distance function between sets of labels. A clustering $\mathcal{C} : V \rightarrow \mathbb{N}$ and a cluster labeling function $c\ell : C[V] \rightarrow 2^L$ is desired such that the following cost is minimized

$$Cost(G, \mathcal{C}, c\ell) = \sum_{\substack{(x,y) \in V_2 \\ C(x) = C(y)}} d_\ell(\ell(x,y), c\ell(\mathcal{C}(x))) + \sum_{\substack{(x,y) \in V_2 \\ C(x) \neq C(y)}} d_\ell(\ell(x,y), \{l_0\})$$

(1)

Here d_ℓ is a distance measure that measures by how much the label sets $L_1 \subseteq L, L_2 \subseteq L$ differ from each other and is defined through the Hamming distance as

$$d_\ell(L_1, L_2) = |L_1 \setminus L_2| + |L_2 \setminus L_1|$$

(2)

The value is in the range $[0..|L| + 1]$.

2.2 Bonchi et al.'s Solution

The method proposed by Bonchi et al., namely Multi Chromatic Balls can be briefly outlined as (for details reader may refer [2]):

1. Pick a pivot edge uniformly randomly from available edges.
2. Find similar edges adjacent to the pivot edge, such that pivot edge is a part of a triangle of edges with labels at 0 Hamming distance.
3. Mark all the discovered triangles as one cluster called ball.
4. Remove the edges and vertices of the ball from the graph.
5. Repeat the process and vertices of the ball from graph.
6. Repeat the process for reduced graph until all edges have been removed.
7. Remaining points in the graph are marked as singleton clusters.

The drawback of the above approach is that formation of a triangle of identical labels with pivot edge is not a trivial problem to solve in the first place. Secondly, the strict rule of finding only labels with Hamming distance 0 may result in very small clusters, mostly of 2 points per cluster in the output. This is not at all a desirable characteristic from a practical application point of view.

3 Proposed Solution

The major change that we propose is with the focus that the probability of discovering a larger ball should increase. This involves relaxing the strict constraint of picking identical labeled triangles. Instead of treating similarity/dissimilarity of labels in terms of Hamming distance, it is viewed in light of set theory.

3.1 Data Model

A data object is a set of attributes and relationships exist among the data objects. Multi Chromatic Correlation Clustering is independent of the attributes of objects and is concerned only with the relationships of objects. The relationships are efficiently expressed through edge-labeled graphs where vertices show data points and labeled edges represent the relationships between them. Each category of relationship is represented through a different color, and the reason behind naming of "Chromatic

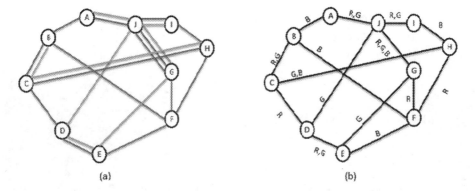

Fig. 1. (a) Example of multi chromatic edge labeled graph, (b) Example graph of (a) represented as per adopted data model (Color figure online)

Correlation Clustering". Figure 1(a) shows an example edge labeled graph with 10 vertices and 3 labels. Colors on edges joining the vertices denote the category of relationship that exists between objects.

To have an easier array representation, concept of parallel edges needs to be converted to a single edge with multiple labels. Instead of referring these as multiple labels, it is still called a 'label'. The definition of a label has now changed from a single value to a set of values.

3.2   Proposed Algorithm

The proposed Multi Chromatic Balls with Relaxed Criterion (MCBRC) algorithm is formally given in Fig. 2. An edge labeled graph G is input to the algorithm which actually consists of a set of vertices V, a set of edges E, set of edge labels L, a special label l_0 to indicate non-existent edge and a labeling function ℓ which maps a pair of vertices into a set of labels or an empty label. 2^L is the power set of L excluding the empty subset. Instead of empty subset ϕ, the special symbol l_0 is used. Output of the algorithm is a clustering function C which maps each vertex to a cluster number and a cluster labeling function cl which maps the cluster numbers to a set of labels.

Algorithm 1. Multi Chromatic Balls with Relaxed Criterion
Input: Edge-Labeled graph $G = (V, E, L, l_0, \ell)$, where $\ell: V_2 \rightarrow 2^L \cup \{l_0\}$
Output: Clustering $C: V \rightarrow \mathbb{N}$; cluster labeling function $cl: C[V] \rightarrow 2^L$
Step 1: $i \leftarrow 1$
Step 2: while $E \neq \emptyset$ do
Step 3:   pick an edge $(x, y) \in E$ uniformly at random
Step 4: $C \leftarrow \{x, y\} \cup \{z \in V \mid \ell(x,z) \subseteq \ell(x,y)$ and $\ell(y,z) \subseteq \ell(x,y)\}$
Step 5: $C(x) \leftarrow i$ for all $x \in C$
Step 6: $cl(i) = \ell(x,y)$
Step 7: $V \leftarrow V \backslash C, E \leftarrow E \backslash \{(x,y) \in E \mid x \in C\}$ (remove C from G)
Step 8: $i \leftarrow i + 1$
Step 9: End while
Step 10: for all $x \in V$ do
Step 11: $C(x) \leftarrow i$
Step 12: $cl(i) \leftarrow a\ label\ set\ from\ 2^L$
Step 13: $i \leftarrow i + 1$
Step 14: end for

Fig. 2. Proposed algorithm

A counter variable i is used to keep track of current cluster number. It is incremented by 1 each time a new cluster is formed. The algorithm proceeds majorly in iterative fashion until all the edges have been removed from the graph. The process per iteration is to select a pivot edge uniformly randomly from the existing edges of the graph (Step 3). Once a pivot edge (x, y) has been picked, any third vertex z in the graph is to be included in the same cluster as x and y if the following condition is satisfied – "The label of edge (x, z) and edge (y, z) should be a subset of label of edge (x, y)".

This is a relaxed criterion to discover a triangle as compared to that of MCB. All such z vertices are included in current set C which already contains x and y. When the set C of current iteration is complete, only then the algorithm proceeds to Step 5. Now, the clustering function is applied to assign a cluster number to all the vertices of current set C. This number is equal to the current value of i. The cluster labeling function assigns the label of pivot edge to the cluster number i in step 6. In Step 7, all the components of the current cluster are removed from the graph. After this, i is incremented and the process repeats until there is some edge in the graph. Once all the edges have been removed, there could be some vertices which have not been included in any cluster. All these isolated points are marked as singleton clusters in Steps 10 to 14.

The major change proposed here as compared to MCB is the criterion to discover a triangle to be included in the cluster ball. The criterion now depends on subset-superset relations of labels of the edges instead of the Hamming distance. Since, the cluster will have a label same as that of pivot edge of that cluster, all the edges in the cluster should have labels which are either same as the cluster label or a subset of it.

4   Experimental Analysis

The experiments are conducted on MATLAB Computing Environment which is a simple yet powerful platform for matrix manipulations, data and function plotting and algorithm implementation. Testing of the proposal is done on synthetic as well as real life dataset. All experiments are run for 10 times and an average of the results is noted.

4.1   Results on Synthetic Data

The synthetic data is generated through synthetic data generation algorithm listed in Fig. 3. The inputs of this algorithm decide the size of the output graph.

Algorithm 2. Synthetic MultiGraph
Input: Number of vertices n, number of labels h and density of edges in graph p
Output: A 2-dimensional array G
Step 1: For $i = 1$ *to* n, repeat steps 2 to 7
Step 2: For $j = 1 + 1$ *to* n, repeat steps 3 to 6.
Step 3: Generate a random number r
Step 4: if $(r < p)$
Step 5: Assign a value to G_{ij} uniformly randomly from $\{1,2,...,2^h - 1\}$
Step 6: $G_{ji} \leftarrow G_{ij}$
Step 7: $G_{i,i} \leftarrow 0$

Fig. 3. Algorithm for synthetic data generation

The testing of the proposal is done by first varying the parameter n from 10 to 50 keeping the parameters h and p fixed at 3 and 0.5. Table 1 lists the experimental results for both MCB and the proposed MCBRC. Though the number of output clusters does not increase much, there is a significant increase in the size of largest cluster observed. Since the number of data objects is increasing, more clusters will be obtained as the output. With increasing number of nodes, the edges in the graph also increase. As a result the size of output clusters increases. Effect of increasing the number of vertices is not much evident over number of isolated points.

Table 1. Results for varying number of data points

Data points	Total output clusters		Isolated points		Size of largest cluster		Cost	
	MCB	MCBRC	MCB	MCBRC	MCB	MCBRC	MCB	MCBRC
10	4	4	2	1	3	3	33	28
20	5	3	2	1	6	8	170	176
30	6	6	0	1	10	15	391	385
40	7	5	4	0	9	17	681	768
50	7	6	2	1	18	19	1134	1129

The value of h is varied from 3 to 6 with n and p fixed at 100 and 0.5. The results of this set of experiments over MCB and MCBRC are in Table 2. The increase in number of output clusters is more evident when h is varied, rather when n was varied for both the algorithms. A great decrease in the largest cluster size is also observed in both the tables. When labels in graph increase, the points belonging in the same cluster will decrease thereby decreasing the largest cluster size. This also means that there will be a larger number of clusters with smaller sizes. Cost depends on the difference of labels. Therefore, with increasing number of labels, the cost contributed through intra-cluster edges increases.

Table 2. Results for varying number of labels

Labels	Total output clusters		Isolated points		Size of largest cluster		Cost	
	MCB	MCBRC	MCB	MCBRC	MCB	MCBRC	MCB	MCBRC
3	8	4	2	0	20	49	4591	4723
4	16	9	2	1	15	35	5442	5703
5	27	7	0	1	10	25	6549	7305
6	33	12	2	1	8	18	7304	8055

In last set of experiments parameter p is varied from 0.4 to 0.8 keeping n and h fixed at 100 and 4. The results are listed in Table 3. The number of output clusters is not affected by p in MCB. But for the proposed algorithm a drop in the number of output clusters is observed. It can be attributed to more number of edges available to form larger clusters, and reducing the total number of clusters. This explanation is supported by the significant increase in the size of largest cluster for the proposed algorithm as the density of graph is increased. With increase in density, both the intra-cluster and inter-cluster edges increase thereby increasing the cost of clustering.

Table 3. Results for varying density

Density	Total output clusters		Isolated points		Size of largest cluster		Cost	
	MCB	MCBRC	MCB	MCBRC	MCB	MCBRC	MCB	MCBRC
0.4	13	9	2	0	12	19	4453	4919
0.5	15	10	0	1	14	26	5621	6070
0.6	15	8	0	2	14	34	6554	6766
0.7	15	5	2	1	14	51	7314	7788
0.8	14	4	2	1	18	69	8502	9213

It can therefore be concluded that whereas the MCB algorithm is dependent only on the number of vertices of the graph or the data points and does not consider all the characteristics of the graph, the proposed MCBRC algorithm performs better with respect to all the characteristics of the graph.

Runtime: To observe the utility of the proposed algorithm in real life applications, the behavior in terms of runtime needs to be analyzed against the size of dataset. The time complexity of MCBRC is $O(n^2 hp)$, theoretically. Practically the relation can be verified through experiments. When varying n from 10 to 50, runtime value was in the range of 0.0024 s to 0.0072 s. While a growth of $O(n^2)$ was expected, the results show a linear growth of runtime thereby showing more efficiency and robustness. In the case of varying labels, there is an almost constant runtime observed, around 0.0158 s, indicating that runtime of proposed algorithm is independent of the number of labels. With varying density, runtime is observed to be nearly constant, around 0.0160 s. The reason for this is as density increases, the edges in the graph increase and therefore overall number of iterations to be performed increases. Yet, the increase in the runtime is not very high, rather constant. This might be because as the iterations proceed, the number of edges in the graph to be processed decrease. Since very large clusters have been identified in earlier iterations, very few edges would actually be left later in the graph.

4.2 Results on Real Data

For the purpose of community detection, YouTube dataset has been picked. The YouTube dataset compiled by Tang et al. [9] is an edge-labeled network graph having five kinds of associations among users, videos and channels in the popular YouTube site. There are in total 15088 vertices, 19923067 edges and 5 labels in the network. The results on YouTube dataset for both MCB and MCBRC algorithms are listed in Table 4.

Table 4. Results on YouTube dataset

Algorithm	Total output clusters	Isolated points	Size of largest cluster	Runtime (in seconds)
MCB	32	1068	4398	10094.46
MCBRC	32	1040	5254	3855.02

The proposed MCBRC is able to discover a larger community. Lesser isolated points indicate that MCBRC can associate more users together. Moreover, MCBRC has three times lesser runtime than MCB.

5 Conclusion

The problem of Multi Chromatic Correlation Clustering in context of community detection in social networks has been addressed in this paper. Such real life applications demand that clustering technique used should be able to detect presence of community as large as possible from given point of view of study. A solution namely, Multi Chromatic Balls, have been suggested by Bonchi et al. in 2015. We present a modification to it by relaxing some criteria for cluster decision. This gives a clustering algorithm which is able to identify larger groups in data network. Moreover, the proposed algorithm is more scalable, robust, time-efficient and works through consideration of all the characteristics of data. The results on both synthetic and real life data of YouTube prove that the proposal is more suitable than MCB for practical applications, especially community detection.

As a future work, the algorithm can be extended to overlapping clusters. The cost objective function in Chromatic Correlation Clustering is based on Hamming distance, and can be modified according to set theory.

References

1. Bonchi, F., Gionis, A., Gullo, F., Ukkonen, A.: Chromatic correlation clustering. In: Proceedings of the 18th ACM SIGKDD International Conference on Knowledge Discovery and Data Mining (KDD 2012), pp. 1321–1329 (2012)
2. Bonchi, F., Gionis, A., Gullo, F., Tsourakakis, C.E., Ukkonen, A.: Chromatic correlation clustering. ACM Trans. Knowl. Discov Data (TKDD) **9**(4), 34 (2015)
3. Bansal, N., Blum, A., Chawla, S.: Correlation clustering. Mach. Learn. **56**, 89–113 (2004)
4. Ailon, N., Charikar, M., Newman, A.: Aggregating inconsistent information: ranking and clustering. J. ACM (JACM) **55**, 23:1–23:27 (2008)
5. Giotis, I., Guruswami, V.: Correlation clustering with a mixed number of clusters. In: Proceedings of ACM-SIAM Symposium on Discrete Algorithms (SODA), pp. 1167–1176 (2006)
6. Ailon, N., Liberty, E.: Correlation clustering revisited: the true cost of error minimization problems. In: Proceedings of International Colloquium on Automata, Languages and Programming (ICALP), pp. 24–36 (2009)
7. Ailon, N., Avigdor-Elgrabli, N., Liberty, E., van Zuylen, A.: Improved approximation algorithms for bipartite correlation clustering. SIAM J. Comput. **41**(5), 1110–1121 (2012)
8. Bonchi, F., Gionis, A., Ukkonen, A.: Overlapping correlation clustering. Knowl. Inf. Syst. (KAIS) **35**(1), 1–32 (2013)
9. Tang, L., Wang, X., Liu, H.: Uncovering groups via heterogeneous interaction analysis. In: Proceedings of IEEE International Conference on Data Mining (ICDM), pp. 503–512 (2009)

Image Segmentation and Object Recognition Using Machine Learning

Ashima Sood[1(✉)] and Sahil Sharma[2]

[1] Punjabi University Regional Centre, Mohali, India
soodashima91@gmail.com
[2] Thapar University, Patiala, India
sahil.sharma@thapar.edu

Abstract. The digital image processing is a fast pace growing field which requires pre-processing of the images before their actual usage and experimentation. Image Segmentation and Object Recognition is one of the phase which requires the prior information about the object to give the extracted attributes as output of the images. Here, in the present research work we have already some outdoor segmented images which have been identified as to which category of classification they belong. This work has been accelerated with the help of machine learning that is a novel technique to identify the objects with outstanding accuracy. The machine learning algorithms have aided in this process of identifying the objects like sky, brick, cement, grass etc. This collaboration of image segmentation with machine learning has proved to be accessible in large datasets where after segmentation images can classify themselves into a category provided it has attributes of the images.

Keywords: Image segmentation · Object recognition · Machine learning · Classification · Ensemble learning

1 Introduction

The immeasurable growth in the digital images has given created a new trend of technology in the area of digital image processing and image segmentation is one of the indispensable step in the field of images, videos and other computer applications which has been introduced in the next section. There has been many image segmentation techniques evolved so far which has resulted in many improvements and advancements in this field. These segmented images need to identified so that the work of relating the images and recognizing them is made easier. This comes under the area of object recognition which means finding the images with the help of various methods used so far like binary pattern matching, gradients, edges, Haar wavelets and other feature based techniques. The current work deals with object recognition of already segmented images using machine learning models where images are identified on the basis of attributes like intensity mean, region pixel count, saturation mean, hue mean and many more. On the basis of these attributes a class distribution of randomly selected 7 outdoor images has been done and the objective is to perform practical experimentation to show how accurately the machine learning models

© Springer Nature Singapore Pte Ltd. 2016
A. Unal et al. (Eds.): SmartCom 2016, CCIS 628, pp. 204–210, 2016.
DOI: 10.1007/978-981-10-3433-6_25

can identify these images with the help of the attributes given in the dataset. This work requires the detail study of image segmentation and object recognition area where we can understand how the images have been pre segmented with the help of the various key features given. The variety of algorithms in machine learning give a vast scope improvement in this field. The models are further subjected to ensemble learning which gives diversification of models as models give better results together with more data points. It is like polling in the parliament where different views can give the better decision patterns rather than one taking the decision as a whole. There are different approaches of ensemble learning such as bagging, boosting, voting based techniques, combination rules, AdaBoost, decision templates, hierarchical mixture of experts and stack generalization [1]. In the present work average of accuracies of models has been taken for the ensemble learning approach. This has proved the consistency of models as the accuracies of respective models chosen best fit for ensemble learning has shown the as better results as it was with the individual models. This technique has been clearly shown in further section in the methodology and results section.

The remainder section follows, Sect. 2 which gives the introduction of image segmentation; Sect. 3 gives the basic idea of object recognition. The Sect. 4 has discussed the related work which has been done previously in this field. The Sect. 5 covers the methodology part in which the subsections secondary dataset, feature reduction, setting target value, machine learning, K-Fold validation and ensemble learning is discussed. At last the work has been concluded with the future scope of the work.

2   Image Segmentation

Image segmentation is breaking down the image into segments in order to obtain area of interest and also differentiating these segments from the background. In this, the objects of the image are separated according to the property of those objects. Image Segmentation is a pre-processing technique used in digital image processing. It is the method in which an image is segregated in different regions of concern based on properties such as texture, intensity, or colour [2]. The extraction of object and replacing it with the some other background is very common method of segmentation and very often used in movie industry. The process of segmentation depends on the extent of problem to be solved, therefore the segmentation process is stopped once the area of interest have been isolated [3]. With the improvement in image processing field the colour image segmentation techniques are more into concern which can be consider as the extension of gray scale segmentation process. But many gray image methods of segmentation are not directly applied to colour image.

Image segmentation is done by using various algorithms and these algorithms are broadly classified on the basis of two basic approaches of intensity values:

Discontinuity: In this segmentation is done on the abrupt changes in an image like edges.
Similarity: This category of partitioning is done on the regions of image which define a specific set of predefined properties.

3   Object Recognition

The object recognition is closely related to segmentation process. They are mutually dependent on each other. Object recognition is used to extract objects from the image in the real world. We have been given the set of objects and the main task is to set labels to these objects in an image. This task of labeling the object is done with the help of various features like color, size, shape, pixel intensity etc. The dataset used contains the objects which have been recognized based on the different features and the study of this concept comes under this area of how features are detected and possibilities are made about the rightly identified object from the image. There is a systematic approach of objet recognition which involves various parameters which are discussed in Fig. 1 below.

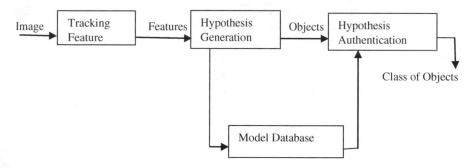

Fig. 1.   Object recognition process

In the above system of block diagram various constituents play their specific roles for recognizing the object. The features are attributes of the objects which help in describing the object for example color, shape, boundary, size of the object. Tracking feature is like feature detector which identify the features of the object which further helps in forming the hypothesis. The hypothesis generation phase gives the likelihood to the objects and thus reduces the search space for the system [4]. After this, the model database in which different models of object recognition are present eliminates the objects which are of less likelihood and refines the hypothesis for the verification of the same. At the end after verification of hypothesis using models, the distribution class of objects is formed which is the result of object recognition from the scene of real world.

4   Related Work

The previous work done in image segmentation has used many techniques and algorithms with its diverse applications and explanation with examples. The concerned area is of different image segmentation methods based on the technology of histogram and segmentation on neighborhood [5]. The color images somehow use the enhance technique of gray scale images, however the collaboration of region based algorithm and watershed algorithm has been used for color image segmentation. This combined method of color image segmentation has reduced the time complexity of seed growing method unlike traditional methods [6]. Likewise many other techniques of image segmentation has been discussed so far like Edge-based image segmentation using neutral networks machine learning which is implemented in MATLAB and C++ with the help of optimal border selection [4]. The image segmentation and object recognition work jointly on the images where selecting and recognizing the images require generative models. These models require features or attributes which are like active parameters to make hypothesis of the objects obtained. In case of missing values like region, area and features a well-known tool has been used known as EM algorithm. This Expectation-Minimization algorithm is used to generate the maximum likelihood of parameters for the probabilistic models. This maximum likelihood is used to figure out the features and obtain the candidate objects out of it [7]. Previously, for pattern recognition, machine learning techniques has been used. The detection of images related to building material is to be done. The approach used in this work is mainly of two steps i.e. feature extraction and classification. After the task of detection feature set, the vectors of features are encapsulated and fed into the classifier for classification of objects and detection task is performed. This has been done with the help of machine learning algorithms which has been termed as classifiers namely Radial Basis Function, Support Vector Machines and Multilayer Perceptron. After using these classifiers, the best performing model has been chosen [8]. This has been the novel approach of how the machine learning algorithms can accurately perform object recognition. Different machine learning algorithms have proved to be successful in various research fields and are able to perform well in different scenarios [9–13].

5 Methodology

The proposed method in this work is the result of various machine learning models which have been implemented on the segmented images for object recognition. The class distribution of objects is done in prior in the dataset on the basis of some features. These features can be reduced to make the dataset with instances and attributes more appropriate which is helpful in large dataset i.e. removing the redundancy from the data. Once the feature reduction is done, the classification of objects is done to make it relevant for machine learning algorithms. The practical implementation is supported by R environment. Once the implantation is done the accuracies of the respective models is generated. The consistency check is made on these accuracies to make the work more authenticated and validated. At the end, ensemble learning is done to take the average result of the output obtained.

5.1 Secondary Dataset

The dataset collected is of secondary type involving the data of image segmentation. It includes the instances of seven outdoor images which are drawn randomly. These images are already hand segmented so that classification of images can be done. In total there are 2310 instances and 19 attributes giving the vast features of the images obtained. The classes of objects are distributed as 1 = brick face, 2 = sky, 3 = foliage, 4 = cement, 5 = window, 6 = path, 7 = grass [14]. The dataset is of classification type. The attributes of this dataset represent the features of the images collectively like vedge-mean, hedge-sd, value-mean, saturation-mean, hue-mean, exblue-mean, exgreen-mean, exred-mean, rawred-mean, rawblue mean, rawgreen-mean and many other which has been used as attributes in the dataset.

5.2 Feature Engineering

In the process of feature engineering we opted for reducing the number of features using Pearson Correlation technique. So, the original 19 features has been reduced to 14 features for improving the time complexity for building the machine learning models. The 19 features also contain one numeric constant feature which does not affect the overall performance of the output so that feature can be ignored. Table 1 below shows the accuracy comparisons when models were built with 18 features and 14 features respectively.

Table 1. Feature engineering

S. No.	Model name	18 features accuracy	14 features accuracy
1.	CART	87.52381	89.14286
2.	Random Forest	95.76190	94.80952
3.	Gaussian SVM	86.76190	86.47619
4.	Linear Model	91.76190	91.47619

5.3 Training and Testing

After the feature engineering phase, it was clear that the models can be trained and tested just using 14 features selected using Pearson Correlation method. Thus machine learning models were tested for their performances. Total of 13 models were trained to do the correct classification based on the training and testing data set. Table 2 shows the accuracy, confusion matrix error and the time taken to build each model.

Table 2. Results of training and testing

S. No.	Model name	Method, Package	Accuracy	Confusion matrix error	Time taken (s)
1.	CART	rpart, rpart	89.14286	10.85	0.04
2.	Conditional Inference Tree	cpart, party	53.00000	47.00	0.05
3.	Random Forest	rf, randomForest	94.80952	5.19	0.33
4.	Conditional Inference Random Forest	cforest, party	90.38095	9.61	2.54
5.	Gaussian SVM	rbfdot, kernlab	86.47619	13.52	0.43
6.	Generalized Linear Model	lm, glm	91.47619	8.52	1.60
7.	Polynomial SVM	polydot, kernlab	91.00000	9.00	0.42
8.	Linear SVM	vanilladot, kernlab	91.00000	9.00	0.39
9.	Hyperbolic Tangent SVM	tanhdot, kernlab	42.09524	57.90	0.43
10.	Laplacian SVM	laplacedot, kernlab	86.61905	13.38	0.48
11.	Bessel SVM	besseldot, kernlab	85.71429	14.28	0.61
12.	ANOVA RBF SVM	anovadot, kernlab	93.04762	6.95	0.79
13.	Spline SVM	splinedot, kernlab	88.90476	11.09	1.46

5.4   Ensemble Learning

Ensemble learning means mixing up the results of multiple machine learning models to get more reliable outputs. This in a way gives versatility to the prediction modelling. Hence, top 3 models namely Random Forest, ANOVA RBF SVM and Generalized Linear Model from the training and testing table based on their accuracy were selected for the ensemble modelling using average method. The accuracy obtained by using average ensemble method is 93.11111 which is neither maximum nor minimum making performance more reliable.

5.5   Cross Validation

This phase has its own importance for checking the consistency of performances given by selected machine learning models. A 5-fold cross validation has been applied using the three top models mentioned in previous section along with the consistency of ensemble model. Figure 2 below shows the accuracy of 5 folded cross validation in the form of histogram.

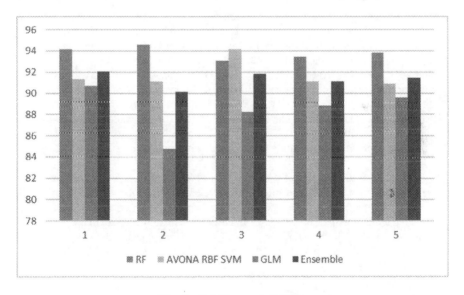

Fig. 2. 5-fold cross validation

6   Conclusion and Future Scope

The result of implementation shows that for the object recognition in the discussed problem can be best solved with the ensemble model of Random Forest, ANOVA RBF SVM and Generalized Linear Model, giving the accuracy of 93.11111% as discussed in Sect. 5. This work can be extended on large datasets with millions of images of real world with features being extracted. Many other machine learning models can also be explored and built according to the type of datasets of related problems.

References

1. Polikar, R.: Ensemble based systems in decision making. IEEE Circuits Syst. Mag. **6**(3), 21–45 (2006). Third Quarter
2. Bali, A., Shailendra, N.S.: A review on the strategies and techniques of image segmentation. In: 2015 Fifth International Conference on Advanced Computing & Communication Technologies (ACCT). IEEE (2015)
3. Rother, C., Kolmogorov, V., Blake, A.: Grabcut: interactive foreground extraction using iterated graph cuts. ACM Trans. Graph. (TOG) **23**(3), 309–314 (2004). ACM
4. Brejl, M., Sonka, M.: Edge-based image segmentation: machine learning from examples. In: International Joint Conference on World Congress on Computational Intelligence on Neural Networks Proceedings, vol. 2. IEEE (1998)
5. Yan-Li, A.: Introduction to digital image pre-processing and segmentation. In: Seventh International Conference on Measuring Technology and Mechatronics Automation (ICMTMA). IEEE (2015)
6. Tang, J.: A color image segmentation algorithm based on region growing. In: 2nd International Conference on Computer Engineering and Technology (ICCET), vol. 6. IEEE (2010)
7. Ramadevi, Y., Kalyani, B., Sridevi, T.: Synergy between object recognition and image segmentation. Int. J. Comput. Sci. Eng. **2**, 2767–2772 (2010)
8. Rashidi, A., Sigari, M.H., Maghiar, M., Citrin, D.: An analogy between various machine-learning techniques for detecting construction materials in digital images. KSCE J. Civ. Eng. **20**, 1178–1188 (2015). Springer
9. Alpaydin, E.: Introduction to Machine Learning. The MIT Press, Cambridge, Massachusetts London, England (2010)
10. Liaw, A., Wiener, M.: Classification and regression by randomForest. R News. **2**(3), 18–22 (2002)
11. Burges, J.C.: A tutorial on support vector machines for pattern recognition. Bell laboratories. Lucent technologies. Data Min. Knowl. Discov. **2**, 121–167 (1998)
12. An, T.K., Kim, M.H.: A new diverse adaboost classifier. In: International Conference on Artificial Intelligence and Computational Intelligence, pp. 359–363 (2010)
13. Wu, X., Kumar, V.: The Top Ten Algorithms in Data Mining. Data Mining and Knowledge Discovery Series. Chapman & Hall/CRC, Minneapolis, Minnesota, USA (2009)
14. https://goo.gl/mTetx0

Proposed Algorithms to the State Explosion Problem

Lamia Allal[1]([✉]), Ghalem Belalem[1], Philippe Dhaussy[2], and Ciprian Teodorov[2]

[1] Faculty of Exact and Applied Sciences, Department of Computer Science,
University of Oran 1 Ahmed Ben Bella, Oran, Algeria
allal.lamia@gmail.com, ghalem1dz@gmail.com
[2] Lab-STICC UMR CNRS 6285 ENSTA Bretagne, Brest, France
{philippe.dhaussy,ciprian.teodorov}@ensta-bretagne.fr

Abstract. Model checking is a very powerful formal verification technique. Formal verification of complex systems is a major challenge in many areas of human society. The verification of properties of these systems is recognized as a difficult problem and faces a number of practical and theoretical problems. The main limitation of the formal verification is known as the state explosion problem. In this paper, we discuss about two contributions to this problem for the improvement of performance in time and memory space.

Keywords: Model checking · State explosion problem · Parallel exploration · Reachability graph

1 Introduction

Real time systems are often complex and critical, and require rigorous development to assert their functional and temporal correction. The technique called model checking is in this context, a very important tool for formal and automatic verification of a large class of systems. When the graph modeling the system is about reasonable size (it can be managed by the main memory), model checking methods are very effective in exploring this graph and detection of possible mistakes. However, most real software systems, have very large graphs size in a number of states. A state or a configuration, represents the behavior of a system at a moment. Indeed, the state space, represents all possible behaviors of a system. These important developments in graphs size known as the state explosion problem, is the main obstacle to the automatic verification by model checking. In this article, we cite two proposed solutions to this problem [2,3]. The first approach [2], is based on the concept of states compression in order to improve performances in memory space. The second solution [3], is based on a parallel exploration of state space, by distributing the state graph on several threads which allows a gain in execution time.

Outline of the paper: the article is divided into 3 sections, the second section presents some works which offer solutions to the state explosion problem. Section 3 presents two solutions to the state explosion problem.

© Springer Nature Singapore Pte Ltd. 2016
A. Unal et al. (Eds.): SmartCom 2016, CCIS 628, pp. 211–217, 2016.
DOI: 10.1007/978-981-10-3433-6_26

2　Related Work

Several studies have been performed to fight the state explosion problem [4,9,11]. In this section, we present some solutions to this problem.

The approach proposed in [10], is based on a sequential algorithm. States are stored in their compressed form. The initial state is stored in an explicit way, the other states are stored in a compressed form. To verify if any generated state was explored, all states are decompressed which represents the disadvantage of this solution because the execution time can increase quickly.

Visser [13] proposed an approach based on the storage of states in an OBDD structure (Object Binary Decision Diagram) during the on the fly model checking. This structure is an acyclic tree representing boolean functions. For each state, an OBDD tree is generated. This will store the explored states. The author has conducted a series of experiments using the SPIN model checker and this using hash tables and the OBDD structures. The authors conducted the state space exploration using SPIN [6,7], they added many functions used on OBDD tree, to the SPIN tool in a straight forward fashion, to obtain an experimental implementation for an on the fly model checker that uses an OBDD trees, to store explored states. The model on which the experiments were performed is n counters that increment from 0 to 9 and then return to 0.

In the approach presented in [12], authors have presented a solution to this problem. The proposed algorithm is as follows: take a non-visited state, calculate its successors and check if they have been visited or not. For this, authors used a shared memory architecture. The state space is shared by processors. The algorithm presented by the author is based on a bloom filter (probabilistic data structure) to indicate whether a state has been visited or not and on local data structures. The bloom filter was used because it is fast in time execution and compact memory. The algorithm is divided into three phases, exploration, collision and termination. During the first phase (exploration), the Bloom filter is used. This phase allows to treat all states. During this step, the states treated by a processor are stored in two AVL tree structures (Adelson-Velskii and Landis) [1] which are binary trees. When checking states (old or new), the bloom filter can make a positive result while the state has not been seen yet. This is called a "false positive", which represents the drawback of this solution. A collision occurs when a state is assumed to have been processed (information given by the bloom filter) while it has not yet been.

3　Proposed Solutions to the State Space Explosion

Model checking is a technique that consists in exploring the states of a model in order to verify some properties. Fig. 1 shows a part of the exploration of a model consisting of 5 counters incremented until a precise value (fixed at the experiments). All states are explored.

In this section, we present two proposed solutions to fight the state explosion problem.

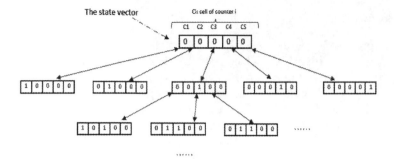

Fig. 1. A part of reachability graph of 5 counters incremented up to 5 and decremented down to 0

3.1   Solution 1

In [2], we proposed a distributed solution (state space compression) to the problem posed by storing states in compressed form in a hash table. Whenever a state is generated, a check is applied on it to check if it is new or not, to avoid duplication of states. The check is performed within the hash table without decompression of states. If the state is new, it will be stored. The exploration process is performed to generate from each state, all its next states (successors). The latter are stored in a stack to be visited in turn. The exploration step ends when all states have been observed (when the stack is empty). The proposed algorithm is executed in a distributed manner using a cluster of machines. Each node will process a part of the state space.

This method is divided in several steps, each one is represented by an algorithm. The first step is the generation of states that is executed by visiting each state of the model. The second step represents the storage of visited states to achieve treatment of these states later, the latter is not studied in this article. A state is stored when it is new. The last step is the verification of termination which represents the end of the exploration of the model. It is triggered when the stack containing states is empty. The proposed algorithm in [2] is presented as:

```
program Distributed state space exploration
   begin
     State-generation();
     while(termination-not-detected)
         if(visited-state)
             State-popped();
             Termination-verification();
         else
             State-storage();
             Successors-generation();
         endif
     endwhile
end.
```

214   L. Allal et al.

3.2 Solution 2

In [3], we proposed a parallel algorithm to the state explosion problem to have a
gain in execution time. We realized a comparison between our algorithm and a
proposed algorithm in [8] for a parallel exploration in SPIN. The aim of the proposed approach is to explore a model in parallel starting from the initial state.
For each state successor (from the initial state), a thread will be created to treat
the generated state and all the states explored later. Each thread manages a
queue containing states to be explored in parallel. In this solution, both data
structures have been used, a set S containing visited states and a queue Q containing the states to be explored. This approach is based on using the framework
Executor [5], where each thread performs a function returning all visited states
(Fig. 2).

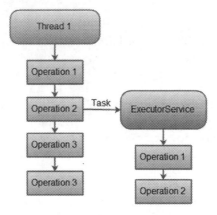

Fig. 2. Main components of the Frawework Executor

The proposed algorithm is as follows [3]:

```
program Parallel Exploration Algorithm
   begin
      S := S_{0};
      Q := S_{0};
      X := Q.dequeue();
   for(allNextStates)do
   begin
      Tasks.add(work);
      Executor.submit(Tasks);
   end {for};
   while (!Q.isEmpty()) do
   begin
      X := Q.dequeue();
      Successors := X.getSuccessors();
```

```
    for (State K : Successors)
    begin
      if (!S.Contains(K)) then
        S.add(K);
        Q.add(K);

      end {if}
    end {while}
  end.
```

The exploration starts with the generation of the initial state, this state is stored in the set S. Subsequently, all its successors are generated and stored in the queue Q. All states from this queue are visited, one following the other until the queue Q is empty, which indicates the end of the exploration. Each thread, executes a part of the state space at the same time, allowing to improve performance in execution time. Each thread manages its queue Q. The set S containing visited states is shared between threads.

Experiments. We realized two types of experiments, in the first one, we made a comparison between the proposed approach and a parallel algorithm proposed for the SPIN model checker [8]. In this experiment, we wanted to prove that our approach showed better results in execution time. In the second experiment, we realized a comparison between the proposed approach and a sequential approach. Fig. 3 detailed the first experiment. The example used, is composed of five counters by varying the maximum counter value. This value varies from 2 to 20. The execution consists on the construction of the state space of a model composed of 5 counters and to apply both parallel algorithms. In the second experiment (Fig. 4), we explored a model consisting of six counters which increment up to 20. We proved that our algorithm showed better results than SPIN algorithm. From this experiment, we created a regression line from the generated points to predict the future execution time, it helps to have a knowledge on the behavior of each algorithm for a high number of configurations (states). We also studied the complexity of each parallel algorithm (proposed approach and the approach of SPIN). We have shown that our algorithm contained fewer instructions and thus leads to greater complexity.

4 Conclusion

Model checking is a very powerful formal verification technique, it is used to check whether a system satisfies its specification. However, this method suffers from a major drawback, the state space explosion, which limits the size of verifiable systems. In this article, we presented two solutions already proposed to address the problem of combinatorial explosion. The first approach is based on states compression before storage. In the second solution, for each successor state (from the initial state), a thread is generated, thereby reducing the execution time.

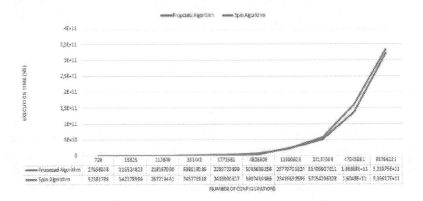

Fig. 3. Execution time by varying the number of configurations

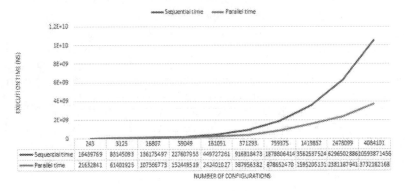

Fig. 4. Execution time by varying the number of configurations

We present two types of experiments in order to compare our approach to the parallel solution in SPIN model checker [8]. We proved that our solution was better in performance. As future work, we are currently achieve a distribution of our approach [3] on a distributed environment for better results.

References

1. Adelson-Velskii, G., Landis, E.M.: An algorithm for the organization of information. In: Proceedings of the USSR Academy of Sciences, vol. 45, pp. 1259–1263 (1962)

2. Allal, L., Belalem, G., Dhaussy, P.: Towards distributed solution to the state explosion problem. In: Satapathy, S.C., Mandal, J.K., Udgata, S.K., Bhateja, V. (eds.) Information Systems Design and Intelligent Applications. AISC, vol. 433, pp. 541–550. Springer, New Delhi (2016). doi:10.1007/978-81-322-2755-7_56

3. Allal, L., Belalem, G., Dhaussy, P., Teodorov, C.: Sequential and parallel algorithms for the state space exploration. Cybern. Inf. Technol. **16**(1), 3–18 (2016)

4. Clarke, E.M., Grumberg, O., Jha, S., Yuan, L., Veith, H.: Progress on the state explosion problem in model checking. In: Informatics - 10 Years Back. 10 Years Ahead., pp. 176–194 (2001)

5. Daugherty, J.: Java concurrency framework (2011)

6. Dhaussy, P., Roger, J.C., Boniol, F.: Reducing state explosion with context modeling for model-checking. In: Proceedings of the 13th International Symposium on High Assurance Systems Engineering, pp. 130–137 (2011)

7. Holzmann, G.J.: The model checker spin. IEEE Trans. Soft. Eng. **23**(5), 279–295 (1997)

8. Holzmann, G.J.: Parallelizing the spin model checker. In: Proceedings of the 19th International Conference on Model Checking Software, pp. 155–171 (2012)

9. Kalyon, G., Massart, T., Meuter, C., Begin, L.: Testing distributed systems through symbolic model checking. In: Proceedings of the 27th IFIP WG 6.1 International Conference on Formal Techniques for Networked and Distributed Systems, pp. 263–279 (2007)

10. Mukherjee, A., Tari, Z., Bertok, P.: Memory efficient state-space analysis in software model-checking. In: Proceedings of the Thirty-Third Australasian Conference on Computer Science, vol. 102, pp. 23–32 (2010)

11. Pelánek, R.: Fighting state space explosion: review and evaluation. In: Cofer, D., Fantechi, A. (eds.) FMICS 2008. LNCS, vol. 5596, pp. 37–52. Springer Berlin Heidelberg, Berlin, Heidelberg (2009). doi:10.1007/978-3-642-03240-0_7

12. Saad, R.T., Zilio, S.D., Berthomieu, B.: A general lock free algorithm for parallel state space construction. In: Proceedings of the 9th International Workshop on Parallel and Distributed Methods in Verification, pp. 8–16 (2010)

13. Visser, W.: Memory efficient state storage in spin. In: Proceedings of the 2nd SPIN Workshop, pp. 21–35 (1996)

Predicting Software Maintainability Using Object Oriented Dynamic Complexity Measures

Anjana Gosain and Ganga Sharma[✉]

University School of Information and Communication Technology,
Guru Gobind Singh Indraprastha University, Sec-16C, Dwarka 110078,
New Delhi, India
anjana_gosain@hotmail.com, ganga.negi@gmail.com

Abstract. Dynamic measures are the class of software measures which are obtained when the software is executing and hence can give accurate information regarding the run-time quality of software. For this reason, many dynamic measures have been proposed in recent past, however, little or no empirical evidence exists about the usefulness of these measures for software quality prediction. The objective of this paper is to empirically validate an OO dynamic complexity measure from authors' previous work [19] to assess its ability for predicting maintainability as external software quality attribute. A controlled experiment is carried out in this regard and correlation and linear regression have been performed on the experimental data. The results of the experiment suggest that OO dynamic complexity measures can serve as a useful indicator of maintainability.

Keywords: Dynamic measures · Software complexity · Software quality · Maintainability · Controlled experiment

1 Introduction

Maintainability of software is an important external quality attribute which is concerned with how well the software accommodates a change in requirements of the user or real world [1]. One of the main reasons for high maintenance of software is its complexity: the more complex a software, the more will it require maintenance [2]. Figure 1 demonstrates the relationship between complexity and external quality factors like maintainability etc. [3]. As can be inferred from Fig. 1, reducing complexity can have the effect of producing more maintainable software.

The use of OO paradigm has become widespread these days. This is because OO paradigm uses the notion of classes and objects, and classes are expected to be high-quality units that are easy to maintain [4]. Also, the use of hierarchical decompositions and abstractions in OO approach helps developers produce a less complex software [5]. However, these claimed benefits of OO paradigm have not paid off. And therefore maintaining software has still remained a time/effort consuming activity and a costly affair [6]. In order to control and manage maintenance time/effort related costs, there is an increasing need for predicting software maintainability. Researchers argue that v if

© Springer Nature Singapore Pte Ltd. 2016
A. Unal et al. (Eds.): SmartCom 2016, CCIS 628, pp. 218–230, 2016.
DOI: 10.1007/978-981-10-3433-6_27

accurate prediction of software maintainability can be made, it can help in effective decision making in areas like resource and staff allocation, comparing productivity and costs etc. [7].

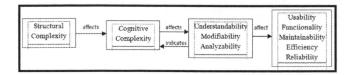

Fig. 1. Structural complexity, cognitive complexity and their relationship with external quality attributes [3]

One of the important approaches to control software maintenance is the usage of software metrics [8]. Many studies have been conducted in the past to examine the link between OO metrics and maintainability [4, 7–16]. All these studies have used static metrics that quantify the static aspects of the structural complexity of OO code at class level. However, OO code is inherently dynamic due to the presence of concepts of polymorphism, late binding etc. Therefore, it is of utmost importance that the quality of OO system be measured using run-time aspects. To achieve this, a class of software metrics has emerged in recent years, called dynamic metrics, which are collected while the software is under execution [17]. Various dynamic metrics have been proposed in the past few years for OO software [17, 18], however, little or no evidence exists about the effectiveness of these metrics for prediction of software maintainability.

In this paper, we use a dynamic system complexity measure from authors' previous work [19] to find its usefulness for predicting maintainability of OO software. The measure is calculated at system level by taking into account the dynamic complexity of all its classes. A dynamic class complexity measure, in turn, is obtained from the dynamic complexity of its objects. The object level dynamic complexity measure is calculated as a function of the complexities arising due to the following three factors:

(i)   methods invoked by the object at run-time, i.e., static complexity of the methods being invoked.
(ii) the way in which methods are being invoked, i.e., run-time object-method invo-cation relationship. Three types of run-time object-method invocation relation-ships are identified in authors' work [19]: direct method invocations, transitive method invocations, and coupling method invocations.
(iii) the number of times a method is invoked, i.e., frequency of method invocation by an object.

An experimental study is set up using 12 sample Java programs. A controlled experi-ment is then carried out and statistical techniques consisting of correlation and linear regression are conducted to correlate the proposed dynamic complexity measures with maintainability of OO software as external quality attribute. The results show that a significant positive correlation exists between the proposed dynamic complexity meas-ures and maintainability of OO software and therefore can serve as useful indicators of maintainability.

This paper is organized as follows: Sect. 2 reviews the literature work, Sect. 3 briefly describes the authors' previous work [19] on dynamic complexity measurement for object-level, class-level and system level dynamic complexity measures while Sect. 4 elaborates the empirical set-up and the controlled experiment. Section 5 discusses the results of the study, Sect. 6 gives an overview of validity threats of the experimental results and in the end, Sect. 7 concludes the paper.

2   Literature Overview

Maintainability is defined as *"the ease with which a software system or component can be modified to correct faults, improve performance or other attributes, or adapt to a changed environment"* in the IEEE Standard Glossary of Software Engineering [20]. A systematic review of maintainability prediction studies [21] indicates that researchers in the field of software engineering have used different facets/aspects of maintainability in their respective studies such as *"time required to make changes"* [22], *"time to understand, develop, and implement modification"* [23], *"the number of revised lines of code"* [12], *"the number of revisions in which the class was involved during the maintenance history"* [11] etc.

There have been empirical evidences on the link between OO static software measures and maintainability [4, 7–16]. However; no such claim can be made about OO dynamic measures. Several past review studies [18, 24] have indicated that very few authors have conducted empirical validation of their proposed dynamic measures. Yacoub *et al.* [25] proposed dynamic complexity measure for OO designs and used it to formulate architecture level reliability risk assessment methodology [26]. Arisholm et al. [27] proposed dynamic *import* and *export* coupling measures at different granularities and tried to find the relationship between these measures and change-proneness. For this, they presented a case study of an open source software *Velocity*, to analyze the changes (lines of code added and deleted) across its four sub-releases. The authors found that most of their dynamic export coupling measures serve as indicators of change-proneness. The work of Gupta and Chhabra [28] proposes dynamic cohesion measures and tries to find the effectiveness of these measures in predicting change-proneness of classes. The study suggested that their proposed dynamic cohesion measures can serve as better indicators of change-proneness in comparison to the existing cohesion measures.

3   Measuring Dynamic Complexity

In their previous work [19], the authors' proposed that object level dynamic complexity is a function of the complexities arising due to the following three factors:

- methods invoked by the object at run-time, i.e., static complexity of the methods being invoked.
- the way in which methods are being invoked, i.e., run-time object-method invocation relationship. Three types of run-time object-method invocation relationships are

identified in this paper: direct method invocations, transitive method invocations, and coupling method invocations. A direct invocation is characterized when an object invokes a method of its class directly whereas a transitive invocation is characterized when an object invokes a method of its class which in turn invokes other methods of its class. A coupling invocation, on the other hand, results when an object invokes a method of its class which in turn invokes other methods of other classes. These three run-time relations contribute towards measuring the dynamic complexity of an object.

- the number of times a method is invoked, i.e., frequency of method invocation by an object.

The dynamic complexity of a class (system) is then obtained by aggregating the dynamic complexity of all its objects (classes).

The measure, $DOCPX_x(o)$, i.e. dynamic object complexity, of an object o under scenario x is defined as

$$DOCPX_x(o) = \frac{w_1 * DC\_D_x(o) + w_2 * DC\_T_x(o) + w_3 * DC\_C_x(o)}{w_1 + w_2 + w_3} \qquad (1)$$

where

$DC\_D_x(o)$, $DC\_T_x(o)$ and $DC\_C_x(o)$ are the dynamic complexity of object o due to direct, transitive and coupling method invocation respectively while w_i are the cognitive weights [29] assigned to the three types of dynamic complexity relations (i.e. dynamic, transitive and coupling) in terms of their importance towards measuring dynamic complexity. Given the cognitive weights for direct, transitive and coupling invocations as w1, w2 and w3 respectively, one can infer that w3 > w2 > w1. These weights can be assigned values depending upon the opinions of experienced analysts and software engineering experts [29].

The values $DC\_D_x(o)$, $DC\_T_x(o)$ and $DC\_C_x(o)$ are measured in similar fashion. We illustrate here how $DC\_D_x(o)$ is calculated. If no methods are invoked directly then $DC\_D_x(o)$ value is 0. Otherwise, $DC\_D_x(o)$ is the summation of the product of frequency of a method invoked directly and its static complexity. The dynamic complexity of object o in entire application scope is then defined as the average of dynamic complexity values for object o under all execution scenarios i.e.,

$$DOCPX(o) = \frac{\sum_{j=1}^{|x|} DOCPX_x(o)}{|X|} \qquad (2)$$

The measure, DCCPX, called dynamic class complexity, is defined as follows

$$DCCPX(C) = \sum_{i=1}^{k} DOCPX(o_i) \qquad (3)$$

where k is the number of objects created by class C. The measure, DSCPX, called dynamic system complexity, is defined as follows

$$DSCPX(S) = \sum_{i=1}^{n} DCCPX(C_i) \tag{4}$$

where n is the number of application classes in OO system S.

Now, consider an example in Fig. 2. Here, *obja1* has one direct invocation for methodA(), two direct invocation for methodAA() and two transitive invocation for methodA(), object *obja2* has one direct invocation for methodAA() and one transitive invocation for methodA(); while *objb* has one direct invocation for methodB() and one coupling invocation for methodA(). Considering the $w1 = 1$, $w2 = 2$ and $w3 = 3$, and the static complexities of all methods as unity, we get:

$$DOCPX(obja1) = (1 * 3 + 2 * 2 + 0)/(1 + 2 + 3) = 7/6$$
$$DOCPX(obja2) = (1 * 1 + 2 * 1 + 0)/(1 + 2 + 3) = 1/3$$
$$DOCPX(objb) = (1 * 1 + 0 + 3 * 1)/(1 + 2 + 3) = 2/3$$

$$Hence \; DCCPX(A) = 7/6 + 1/3 = 9/6 = 3/2$$
$$DCCPX(B) = 2/3$$
$$DSCPX(S) = 3/2 + 2/3 = 13/6 = 2.16$$

Fig. 2.   Sample Java code

4   Empirical Validation

Empirical validation of a measure tries to establish its practical utility by correlating it to some external quality attribute [30, 31]. It involves performing controlled experiments, case studies etc. to gather empirical data and then statistically analyzing this data to prove the practical utility of the metrics [32]. In this paper, we have performed a controlled experiment to correlate the dynamic complexity measure DSCPX with maintainability of OO software.

4.1 Empirical Set-up

We have used 12 sample Java programs randomly selected from various sources like [33] and web for our experimental study. The authors developed a dynamic analyzer tracer code in their previous work [19] using AspectJ [34], an aspect oriented programming (AOP) [35] extension for Java, to facilitate the collection of dynamic complexity metric data for these sample programs. AOP [35] is a way of modularizing cross-cutting concerns such as tracing, logging etc. that may be scattered throughout an application. Researchers [28] have suggested AOP as an efficient technique for dynamic metric data collection.

Table 1 provides summary of sample Java programs and lists the lines of code(LOC) and NC (number of classes) along with the values of the dynamic complexity measure DSCPX for the sample Java programs.

Table 1. DSCPX values for the sample programs

Program	LOC	NC	DSCPX
P1	84	4	3.44
P2	488	8	10.86
P3	92	1	2.76
P4	110	1	2.00
P5	215	3	4.96
P6	214	4	5.12
P7	301	3	6.98
P8	240	3	7.02
P9	71	1	1.05
P10	187	2	3.98
P11	426	4	7.88
P12	582	8	10.95

4.1.1 Experimental Goal

The main goal of our experiment is to find how the dynamic complexity measures are related with maintainability of OO software. As suggested in Wohlin et al. [32], we use GQM [36] approach to define this goal as follows:

Analyse	dynamic complexity measures
For the purpose of	evaluating
With respect to	relationship with maintainability of OO software
From the point of view of	researchers
In the context of	final year postgraduate computer science students

4.1.2 Planning

Context Selection: This experiment addressed the problem whether dynamic complexity measures can be used as indicators of maintainability of OO software.

Selection of subjects: The experiment was carried out with final year postgraduate computer science students of USICT, GGSIPU, New Delhi as subjects. There were a total of 28 subjects whose CGPA averaged 7.6. These subjects participated voluntarily and had adequate knowledge of concepts of OOP, Java and Software Engineering. Being post graduate students, some of them had industrial experience also. Students were chosen as subjects for convenience. Many empirical studies in the field of metric validation have chosen students as subjects [8, 37]. Researchers have suggested that students are acceptable as subjects [38] and that there is no difference in students and professionals under some conditions [39]. Also, it has been suggested to do pilot investigations in academic environment before going to an industrial set-up [36].

Selection of variables: We have taken OO dynamic complexity as independent variable and OO software maintainability as dependant variable.

Instrumentation: The independent variable (OO dynamic complexity) was measured using the measure DSCPX (defined in Sect. 3).

The dependent variable (maintainability) was operationalized as "the time/effort expended in understanding the software artefact and then incorporating a new/changed requirement". This approach has been used by many researchers in the field of maintainability prediction [8, 37, 40]. We call it as maintainability time (maint-time for short) and have measured it in terms of person-hours as has been done in various other studies [40].

Experimental Design: Twelve groups (2–3 students) were formed and were given one sample Java program each. Formation of subject groups as well as assignment of a program to a group was done randomly. Randomization helps in curbing bias in the experiment [41].

Hypothesis Formulation: The hypothesis to be tested is stated as under:

Null Hypothesis H_0: There does not exist statistically significant correlation between dynamic complexity measure DSCPX (independent variable) and maintainability of OO software (dependent variable).
Alternate Hypothesis H_1: There exists statistically significant correlation between dynamic complexity measure DSCPX (independent variable) and maintainability of OO software (dependent variable).

4.1.3   Operation
Preparation: Before performing the experiment, the subjects attended to a training session in which the subjects were given instructions on how to perform the experimental task, e.g. how to behave during experimental task, how to report maint-time values etc. However, full care was given so that the subjects never came to know about the intended study aspects and were never told about the hypothesis under test.

The subjects were provided with a document for their experimental task containing source code of the sample Java program under study, a brief description (two or three line) of what the program was all about, and one new requirement that had to be incorporated into its functionality. For example, the Employee program (P7) required the a new functionality to be added-computing the tax from salary of the regular employee.

Execution: The experiment was done as a subject assignment. All the subjects were provided the material described in the previous paragraph. The subjects took the tasks home and did the tasks without any supervision. The subjects were asked to incorporate the new functionality and accordingly report the time spent by them in carrying out the task.

Table 2 depicts the DSCPX values along with the collected maint-time values.

Table 2. Average Maint-Time (in person-hours)

Program	DSCPX	Maint-Time (in person hours)
P1	3.44	1.25
P2	10.86	5.18
P3	2.76	2.10
P4	2.00	1.75
P5	4.96	4.88
P6	5.12	2.75
P7	6.98	4.45
P8	7.02	3.25
P9	1.05	.95
P10	3.98	2.25
P11	7.88	3.56
P12	10.95	4.20

4.2 Data Analysis

We have performed correlation and linear regression analysis on the data. For correlation analysis, we have used both non-parametric and parametric tests in order to avoid assumptions about distribution of data (as the data set is very small). These tests include Kendall's Tau'b statistic, Spearman's rho and Pearson's product moment coefficient. The level of significance $\alpha = 0.01$ was used. Linear regression was performed to depict the causal relationships between DSCPX and maint-time. Regression analysis identifies whether independent variable is the cause of variation in dependent variable and is the most basic and commonly used predictive analysis.

5 Results

Table 3 presents the coefficients of correlation of Pearson, Kendall's Tau'b and Spearman's rho correlation analysis. As can be inferred, all the three coefficients depict significant positive correlation between DSCPX and maint-time. Therefore, null hypothesis H_0 is rejected and alternate hypothesis H_1 is accepted.

Table 3. Summary of correlation coefficients

Correlation	Coefficient value	Significance
Pearson	0.823	0.001
Kendall's Tau'b	0.667	0.003
Spearman	0.811	0.001

Table 4 presents the regression coefficients. We see that the unstandardized coefficient value is .363. This means that one unit increase in independent variable (i.e., DSCPX) causes the predicted value of dependent variable (i.e., maint-time time) to change by .363 person-hours (or approx. 21 person-minutes).

Table 4. Regression coefficients

Model	Unstandardized coefficients		Standardized coefficients	t	Sig
	B	Std error	Beta		
(Constant)	1.018	.506		2.010	0.072
DSCPX	0.363	.079	.823	4.583	0.001

Table 5 presents regression model summary. In general, this table is used to obtain information about the regression line's ability to explain the total variation in the dependent variable. The adjusted R^2 gives an unbiased estimate of the population R^2 and accounts for the variance in the dependent variable due to independent variable. In our case, adjusted R^2 value is 0.645. It means that the independent variable (DSCPX) is able to explain 64.5% variance in dependent variable (maint-time) which is quite high for a single variable prediction model. Standard error gives an estimate of how close the predicted values of the dependent variable are to the observed values. In our case, its value is .85077. It means that the observed values fall within. ±1.7% approx. of the fitted regression line, giving a 98% (approx.) prediction interval.

Table 5. Regression model summary

Model	R	R^2	R^2 adjusted	Std error
1	0.823	0.677	0.645	.85077

6   Threats to Validity

Researchers [32] identify four types of validity threats in an experimental study: construct, internal, external and conclusion validity. The following sub-sections provide a brief overview of these threats, and the methods that we used to mitigate them.

6.1   Construct Validity

It describes the degree to which a variable (dependent or independent) is accurately measured by the measurement instruments used in the study. The construct validity of the independent variable DSCPX has been established in authors' previous work [19] by performing theoretical validation using Briand et al. framework [42]. A dynamic analyzer tracer code was used to collect the metric values. However, one problem associated with such tracer code is to decide when the trace should be stopped so that the collected dynamic complexity values represent the complete application [28]. Therefore, it may be argued that the dynamic complexity values obtained in this study depend on the authors' understanding of the source code of the sample Java programs under study. The dependent variable i.e., maint-time, is recorded as the time spent by the subjects in performing the experimental task. This approach has been used in experimental studies like [8, 37, 40] etc. to measure maintainability, so we consider this variable also constructively valid.

6.2 Internal Validity

It describes the degree to which a study can establish the cause-effect relationship between the independent variables and the dependent variable by controlling for any extraneous factors. We took a lot of measures to curb some of these extraneous factors. First of all, we used randomization wherever necessary to minimize any kind of bias. Although the subjects participated voluntarily, we also encouraged them by convincing that the effort they put in would help them in long run in growing as good software professionals. This boosted their enthusiasm and morale. Dividing the subjects into groups and assigning single experimental task to each group also helped in minimizing fatigue effect. Further, the subjects had never participated in a similar experimental task, therefore we can claim that the persistent effect was also not present.

Although clear instructions were given to the subjects how to behave during the task, plagiarism and influence among subjects could still be an issue. This is because the task was carried out without any supervision. The subjects might have discussed amongst them the type of problem they were solving. Finally, the effect of any confounding variable (like size) have not been taken into account in the current study. We plan to address this issue as a separate study in future.

6.3 External Validity

It refers to the extent to which results of an experimental study can be generalized about the population under study or other research settings. The two important issues concerning external validity of the current study can be (i) material and tasks used, and (ii) subjects. Regarding material and tasks used, for our data set, the sample programs were chosen randomly. However, care was given so that the chosen sample programs represent wide variety of domains. Still, it can be argued that our conclusions may be biased because of the representative data set. Also, due to the difficulty of obtaining professional subjects, the experiments were conducted using post graduate students. However, using students as subjects is not a big issue as researchers like [39] argue that *"students are next generation of software professionals and therefore are close to the population of interest"*.

6.4 Conclusion Validity

It is defined as the degree to which conclusions drawn in the experimental study are statistically valid. The major factor affecting the conclusion validity of this study that we could identify is the size of the sample data (12 programs). We are currently working on collecting bigger data set, to conduct a replication study.

7 Conclusion

In this paper, we have empirically validated the system level OO dynamic complexity measure DSCPX from authors' previous work to determine its usefulness for predicting maintainability of OO software. An experimental study consisting of 12 sample Java programs and 28 subjects was set-up. Further, statistical techniques like correlation and linear regression were performed on the data obtained from the experimental study. The results of correlation analysis suggest a significant positive correlation between DSCPX and maintenance time. Moreover, the regression analysis results indicate that DSCPX can serve as a useful indicator of maintainability as external quality attribute.

References

1. Deligiannis, I., Shepperd, M., Roumeliotis, M., Stamelos, I.: An empirical investigation of an object-oriented design heuristic for maintainability. J. Syst. Softw. **65**, 127–139 (2003)
2. Banker, R.D., Datar, S., Zweig, D.: Software complexity and maintainability. In: Proceedings of the Tenth International Conference on Information Systems, pp. 247–255 (1989)
3. Briand, L.C., Wüst, J., Ikonomovski, S.V., Lounis H.: Investigating quality factors in object-oriented designs: an industrial case study. In: ICSE, pp. 345–354 (1999)
4. Al Dallal, J.: Object-oriented class maintainability prediction using internal quality attributes. Inf. Softw. Technol. **55**(11), 2028–2048 (2013)
5. Booch, G.: Object-Oriented Design with Applications. The Benjamin/Cummings Publishing Company, Redwood City (1991). ISBN 0-8053-0091-0
6. Ahn, Y., Suh, J., Kim, S., Kim, H.: The software maintenance project effort estimation model based on function points. J. Softw. Maintenance Evol. Res. Pract. **15**, 71–85 (2003)
7. Elish, M., Elish, K.: Application of treenet in predicting object-oriented software maintainability: a comparative study. In: 13th European Conference on Software Maintenance and Reengineering (CSMR 2009), pp. 69–78 (2009)
8. Bandi, R.K., Vaishnavi, V.K., Turk, D.E.: Predicting maintenance performance using object-oriented design complexity metrics. IEEE Trans. Softw. Eng. **29**(1), 77–87 (2003)
9. Aggarwal, K., Singh, Y., Kaur, A., Malhotra, R.: Application of artificial neural network for predicting maintainability using object-oriented metrics. In: Proceedings of World Academy of Science, Engineering and Technology, vol. 15, pp. 285–289 (2006)
10. Briand, L.C., Morasca, S., Basili, V.R.: Measuring and assessing maintainability at the end of high level design. In: IEEE Conference on Software Maintenance, Montreal, Canada, pp. 88–97 (1993)
11. Dagpinar, M., Jahnke, J.H.: Predicting maintainability with object-oriented metrics – an empirical comparison. In: Proceedings of the 10th Working Conference on Reverse Engineering (2003)
12. Li, W., Henry, S.M.: Object-oriented metrics that predict maintainability. J. Syst. Softw. **23**(2), 111–122 (1993)

13. Sheldon, F., Jerath, K., Chung, H.: Metrics for maintainability of class inheritance hierarchies. J. Softw. Maintenance Evol. Res. Pract. **14**, 1–14 (2002)
14. Li-jin, W., Xin-xin, H., Zheng-yuan, N., Wen-hua, K.: Predicting object-oriented software maintainability using projection pursuit regression. In: 1st International Conference on Information Science and Engineering (ICISE), pp. 3827–3830 (2009)
15. Lee, Y., Chang, K.: Reusability and maintainability metrics for object-oriented software. In: Proceedings of the 38th Annual on Southeast Regional Conference, USA (2000)
16. Cartwright, M., Shepperd, M.: An empirical investigation of an object-oriented software system. IEEE Trans. Softw. Eng. **26**, 786–796 (2000)
17. Chhabra, J.K., Gupta, V.: A survey of dynamic software metrics. J. Comput. Sci. Technol. **25**(5), 1016–1029 (2010)
18. Gosain, A., Sharma, G.: Dynamic software metrics for object oriented software: a review. In: Mandal, J.K., Satapathy, S.C., Sanyal, M.K., Sarkar, P.P., Mukhopadhyay, A. (eds.) Information Systems Design and Intelligent Applications. AISC, vol. 340, pp. 579–589. Springer, India (2015). doi:10.1007/978-81-322-2247-7_59
19. Gosain, A., Sharma, G.: Object oriented dynamic complexity measures for software understandability. Communicated to Innovations in Systems and Software Engineering
20. Mamone, S.: The IEEE standard for software maintenance. SIGSOFT SE Notes **19**(1), 75–76 (1994)
21. Riaz, M., Mendes, E., Tempero, E.: A systematic review of software maintainability prediction and metrics. In: Proceedings of 3rd International Symposium on Empirical Software Engineering and Measurement, pp. 367–377. IEEE Computer Society (2009)
22. Gibson, V.R., Senn, J.A.: System structure and software maintenance performance. Commun. ACM **32**(3), 347–358 (1989)
23. Rising, L.S.: Information hiding metrics for modular programming languages. Ph.D. Dissertation, Arizona State University (1992)
24. Tahir, A., MacDonell, S.G.: A systematic mapping study on dynamic metrics and software quality. In: Proceedings of 28th IEEE International Conference on Software Maintenance (ICSM), pp. 326–335. IEEE (2012)
25. Yacoub, S.M., Ammar, H.H., Robinson, T.: Dynamic metrics for object oriented designs. In: Proceedings of Sixth International Software Metrics Symposium, pp. 50–61. IEEE (1999)
26. Yacoub, S., Ammar, H., Robinson, T.: A methodology for architectural-level risk assessment using dynamic metrics. In: Proceedings of 11th International Symposium on Software Reliability Engineering, pp. 210–221 (2000)
27. Arisholm, E., Briand, L.C., Foyen, A.: Dynamic coupling measurement for object-oriented software. IEEE Trans. Softw. Eng. **30**(8), 491–506 (2004)
28. Gupta, V., Chhabra, J.K.: Dynamic cohesion measures for object-oriented software. J. Syst. Archit. **57**(4), 452–462 (2011)
29. Wang, Y., Shao, J.: Measurement of the cognitive functional complexity of software. In: Proceedings of the IEEE International Conference on Cognitive Informatics, ICCI 2003, pp. 67–71 (2003)
30. Briand, L.C., El Emam, K., Morasca, S.: Theoretical and empirical validation of software product measures. International Software Engineering Research Network, Technical report ISERN-95-03 (1995)
31. El-Emam, K.: A methodology for validating software product metrics. NRC/ERB-1076, National Research Council of Canada, Ottawa, Ontario, Canada (2000)
32. Wohlin, C., Runeson, P., Höst, M., Ohlsson, M.C., Regnell, B., Wesslen, A.: Experimentation in Software Engineering. KluwerAcademic Publishers, Norwell (2000)

33. Schildt, H.: Java™: The Complete Reference, 7th edn. McGraw Hill Companies Inc., New York (2007)
34. Kiczales, G., Hilsdale, E., Hugunin, J., Kersten, M., Palm, J., Griswold, W.G.: An overview of AspectJ. In: Knudsen, J.L. (ed.) ECOOP 2001. LNCS, vol. 2072, pp. 327–354. Springer, Heidelberg (2001). doi:10.1007/3-540-45337-7_18
35. Kiczales, G., Lamping, J., Mendhekar, A., Maeda, C., Lopes, C., Loingtier, J.-M., Irwin, J.: Aspect-oriented programming. In: Akşit, M., Matsuoka, S. (eds.) ECOOP 1997. LNCS, vol. 1241, pp. 220–242. Springer, Heidelberg (1997). doi:10.1007/BFb0053381
36. Basili, V.R., Weiss, D.M.: A methodology for collecting valid software engineering data. IEEE Trans. Softw. Eng. **10**(6), 728–738 (1984)
37. Genero, M., Piattini, M., Calero, C.: An empirical study to validate metrics for class diagrams. In: Proceedings of International Database Engineering and Applications Symposium (IDEAS 2002), Edmonton, Canada, pp. 1–10 (2002)
38. Carver, J., Jaccheri, L., Morasca, S., Schull, F.: Issues in using students as subjects in empirical studies in software engineering education. In: Proceedings of the 9th International Software Metrics Symposium (METRICS 2003), Washington DC, pp. 239–250. IEEE Computer Society (2003)
39. Kitchenhem, B., Pfleeger, S., Pickard, L.M., Jones, P.W., Hoaglin, D.C., El Emmam, K., Rosenberg, J.: Preliminary guidelines for empirical research in software engineering. IEEE Trans. Softw. Eng. **28**(8), 721–734 (2002)
40. Chhabra, J.K., Aggarwal, K.K., Singh, Y.: Code and data spatial complexity: two important software understandability measures. Inf. Softw. Technol. **45**(8), 539–546 (2003)
41. Shadish, W.R., Cook, T.D., Campbell, D.T.: Experimental and quasi-experimental designs for generalized causal inference. Cengage Learning (2002). ISBN-13: 9780395615560/ ISBN-10: 0395615569
42. Briand, L.C., Morasca, S., Basili, V.R.: Property-based software engineering measurement. IEEE Trans. Softw. Eng. **22**(1), 68–86 (1996)

Security Enhancement of Blowfish Block Cipher

Rajan Patel[1,2(✉)] and Pariza Kamboj[3]

[1] Faculty of Technology, RK University, Rajkot 360020, Gujarat, India
rajan_g_patel@yahoo.com
[2] Sankalchand Patel College of Engineering, Visnagar 384351, Gujarat, India
[3] Sarvajanik College of Engineering and Technology, Surat 395001, Gujarat, India
parizak@gmail.com

Abstract. Cryptography is the first line of defense to protect the data from intruder. Symmetric cryptography and asymmetric cryptography are two cryptographic based algorithms that serve the security goals: confidentiality, availability, authentication and integrity. Asymmetric algorithms are known as public key cryptography that uses two keys: one public key for encryption and second private for decryption while symmetric algorithms are known as private key cryptography that uses the single private key for encryption and decryption. Symmetric algorithms are less costly compare to asymmetric algorithms. Normally asymmetric algorithms are used to distribute the secret sharing key of symmetric algorithm and symmetric algorithms are used for data encryption. Wide range of symmetric algorithms exists like Blowfish, DES, 3DES, AES, Twofish, RC2, RC5, CAST-128, and IDEA. Among these symmetric algorithms, AES and Blowfish give better throughput compare to other symmetric ciphers. In this article, we proposed the scheme to enhance the Blowfish block cipher security. In proposed scheme, total numbers of Blowfish rounds are altered by skipping few Blowfish rounds using round key. As a result, proposed scheme increase additional Blowfish cipher security against brute-force attack apart from minimum to maximum size of Blowfish key. In addition to that the proposed scheme also decreases encryption and decryption execution time of Blowfish cipher.

Keywords: Blowfish · Security · Round function · Round key · Block cipher · S-Box

1 Introduction

Cryptography is the techniques in which the message is converted into coded form so that the other party cannot understand the meaning until they have official access. It is the first line of defense to protect the data from intruder. The process of converting from original plain text to coded form is called encryption and the reverse process is called decryption. Symmetric cryptography and asymmetric cryptography are two cryptographic based algorithms that serve the security goals: confidentiality, availability, authentication and integrity. Symmetric algorithms are less costly compare to asymmetric algorithms. Asymmetric algorithms are public key cryptography that uses two

© Springer Nature Singapore Pte Ltd. 2016
A. Unal et al. (Eds.): SmartCom 2016, CCIS 628, pp. 231–238, 2016.
DOI: 10.1007/978-981-10-3433-6_28

keys: one public key for encryption and second private key for decryption while symmetric algorithms are known as private key cryptography that uses the single private key for encryption and decryption. Normally asymmetric algorithms are used to distribute the secret sharing key of symmetric algorithm and symmetric algorithms are used for data encryption. Wide range of symmetric block ciphers [1] are exists like Blowfish, DES, 3DES, Twofish, RC2, RC5, CAST-128, IDEA, AES etc. Among these symmetric algorithms, AES, DES, 3DES, Blowfish are popular symmetric block ciphers [2, 3]. AES and Blowfish give better throughput compare to other symmetric ciphers [2, 4]. In this article, we proposed the scheme to enhance the security of Blowfish by varying the number of Blowfish rounds and skipping the few Blowfish round instead of regular sixteen Blowfish rounds.

The paper is organized as follow: first section describes brief about cryptographic security. Second section discusses the background of Blowfish block cipher. Third section describes the contributed proposed scheme. Forth section provides the results discussion and last section is concluded with remarks.

2 Background

The Blowfish is efficient on hardware, free, compact, fast, simple and secure. It is suitable and efficient for hardware implementation and no license is required [5]. It is compact algorithm that can run in less than 5 K of memory [6]. It can perform fast encryption on large 32 bit micro processor. It is simple because it required only XORing, modulo addition and table lookup with 32 bits length word. It is key length varying block cipher: 32 bits to 448 bits. It is suitable for applications in which the key does not often change [7]. Till date it is not patented and it is royalty free.

Blowfish was designed by Bruce Schneier in 1993 [7, 8]. It is the one of the modern symmetric block cipher. It is the key varying block cipher. It takes minimum 32 bits key length to maximum 448 bits key length with fixed number of 16 rounds. It has 64 bits fixed block size. It is fast and free alternative to other symmetric cryptographic algorithms. It includes S-box and P-array tables. It is purely based on feistel cipher structure [9]. It uses sixteen Blowfish round function F which is simplification of the principles of DES (Data Encryption Cipher). Hence Blowfish provides the same security as DES with greater speed of operation. Blowfish Sub-key and S-Box generation and data encryption/decryption are two main parts of Blowfish block cipher. For Sub-key generation, it uses the Blowfish encryption algorithm.

2.1 Sub-key and S-Box Entry Generation

Blowfish uses large number of sub-keys: 32 bits of P-array from P1 to P18 and 32 bits of four S-boxes from S1 to S4 with 256 entries each. These P-arrays and S-boxes are generated using Blowfish encryption algorithm. The steps of key generation are illustrated in Fig. 1.

```
Step1. Initialize 18 P-array and four S-boxes.
Step2. P1 XOR first 32 bits of the key, P2 XOR with
       second 32-bits of the key, and so on for all
       bits of the key.
Step3. Encrypt the all zero string using Blowfish
       algorithm with the sub-key generated in
       step 1 and step 2.
Step4. Replace P1=32bits and P2=32bits using the
       output of step 3.
Step5. Encrypt the 64bits output of step 3 using the
       Blowfish algorithm using the modified sub-keys
       P1 and P2.
Step6. Replace P3=32bits and P4=32bits with the
       output of step 5.
Step7. Continue the process above step 5 and step 6
       for replacing all 18 entries of the P array,
       and after then for all four S-boxes.
```

Fig. 1. Sub key and s-box generation

2.2 Data Encryption

Divide 64 bits of block into two 32 bits of left (L) and right (R) block. L performs XORing with round sub Pi arrays (32 bits), where $1 \leq i \leq 16$. Give L as an input to round function F. In round function F, 32 bits of L divided into 8 bits of four group for four S-boxes i.e. F = ((S1 perform modulo addition with S2) then XORing with S3) then modulo addition with S4). Now R performs XORing with output of round function F. Swap L and R. Repeat this process for sixteen times. Finally the two sub parry P17 and P18 perform the XORing with L and R. At last merge L and R that is 64 bits cipher text. For decryption, same as encryption only reverses the sub-keys P arrays i.e. P18 to P1. The complete steps for data encryption using Blowfish cipher are illustrated in Fig. 2. Figure 3 shows the feistel structure (block diagram) of Blowfish with 32 bits modulo addition and XORing operation, 32 bits Sub-keys P-arrays: P_1–P_{18}, 4 S-Boxes and sixteen Blowfish rounds.

```
Step1. Divide 64bits of block plaintext into two
       32bits halves:L=32bits and R=32bits
Step2. L = L XOR Pi, where i= 1 to 16
Step3. F (L) = (((S1 modulo addition S2) XORing S3)
       modulo addition S4)
Step4. R = F (L) XORing R
Step5. Swap L and R
Step6. Repeat Step 2 to 5 sixteen times
Step7. R = R XORing P17 and L = L XORing P18
Step8. 64bit cipher text= Recombine L and R
```

Fig. 2. Blowfish encryption

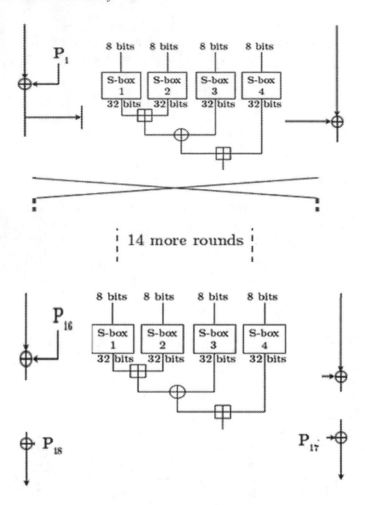

Fig. 3. Blowfish feistel structure

3 Our Contribution

We tried to randomize the Blowfish rounds [10] using round key to enhance the Blowfish security. The round key is use to vary number of Blowfish rounds with skipping the few Blowfish round based binary status of round key. Bruce schneier mentioned that Blowfish block cipher is unbreakable upto five Blowfish rounds [8, 11]. Hence, we consider the alteration of the number of Blowfish rounds instead of regular sixteen Blowfish rounds using round key that will enhance the Blowfish security.

We keep the functionality as it is for Blowfish key generation/expansion operation. Only modify the number of rounds during the data encryption. Suppose the sender have the eight bit RK (Random Key) is 0X65 $(01000001)_2$ from the Blowfish key. Concatenate this RK with invert of 8 bits of RK. The final round key is {RK ‖ (RK)'} i.e. RK = $_{MSB}(0100000110111110)_{LSB}$, LSB to MSB indicates the Blowfish round's binary value as shown in Fig. 4 that is either binary value 0 (Skip round) or 1 (perform round). Binary zero means no Blowfish round operation and binary one means perform Blowfish round operation. According to Table 1, Blowfish round numbers 2, 8, 9, 11, 12, 13, 14 and 15 are performed while Blowfish round numbers 1, 3, 4, 5, 6, 7, 10 and 16 are skipped for Blowfish round operation. The Fig. 4 shows the steps of modified Blowfish algorithm in which skipping the Blowfish round function operation if the ith bit of RK is zero at particular round number, otherwise perform Blowfish round function if the ith bit of RK is one at particular round number. The rest of steps are same as original Blowfish block cipher.

```
Step1. Divide
       Divide 64bits of block plaintext into two
       32bits      halves: L=32bits and
       R=32bits
Step2. Ex-oring
       L = L XOR Pi, where i= 1 to 16
Step3. Round Function Operation
       If Round[i] == 1 Then Perform F(L) = (((S1
       modulo    addition S2) XORing S3) modulo
       addition S4)
       Else F(L)=L
Step4. Ex-oring
       R = F (L) XORing R
Step5. Swapping
       Swap L and R
Step6. Looping
       Repeat Step 2 to 5 sixteen times
Step7. Ex-oring with last two P-array
       R = R XORing P17 and L = L XORing P18
Step8. Recombining
       64bit cipher text= Recombine L and R
```

Fig. 4. Modified Blowfish

Table 1. Blowfish round (BR)

BR 1	BR 2	BR 3	BR 4	BR 5	BR 6	BR 7	BR 8	BR 9	BR 10	BR 11	BR 12	BR 13	BR 14	BR 15	BR 16
0	1	0	0	0	0	0	1	1	0	1	1	1	1	1	0

4   Results Discussion

The single 64 bits block encryption executing time of Blowfish block cipher is 555 μs with 1 GB Pentium Dual 2.20 GHz CPU, 1 GB RAM and 32 bit Operating System configuration parameters. Figure 5 represents that as number of rounds increase, the encryption time is also increase. However the encryption operation time can reduce by

Encryption Time (µs)

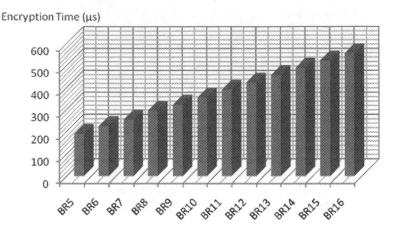

Fig. 5. Minimum to maximum Blowfish round execution

decreasing the total number of Blowfish rounds operation instead of regular sixteen Blowfish rounds. The important aspect is the modification of Blowfish rounds for security enhancement.

According to Kerckhoffs' principle in cryptography, the cryptosystem should be secure even if everything about the cryptosystem, except the key, is public knowledge [12]. If the attacker knows the used Blowfish key size and try to apply brute force search attack on cryptosystem then also the attacker will be fail to decrypt the cipher text because of varying and skipping the Blowfish rounds using round key. An attacker does not have any idea about round key. Furthermore Blowfish provides strong avalanche effect [13] which is the one of the main property of cryptosystem. That's why change in single round number or total number of rounds, the cryptosystem will provide wrong text or destroyed text.

Encryption operation with less than 16 rounds (Due to the modification of Blowfish rounds using round key) and decryption operation with 16 Blowfish rounds (Because Blowfish uses 16 rounds). As shown in Fig. 6(a), if attacker try to decrypt cipher text using Blowfish block cipher with regular 16 Blowfish rounds operation then the attacker will be only receive the completely destroy text even though the attacker have Blowfish key. Because of an attacker do not have any idea about modification of Blowfish round using round key.

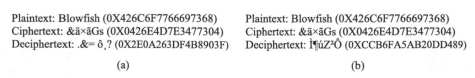

Plaintext: Blowfish (0X426C6F7766697368)
Ciphertext: &ä×ãGs (0X0426E4D7E3477304)
Deciphertext: .&= ô,? (0X2E0A263DF4B8903F)

Plaintext: Blowfish (0X426C6F7766697368)
Ciphertext: &ä×ãGs (0X0426E4D7E3477304)
Deciphertext: Ì¶úZ²Ô (0XCCB6FA5AB20DD489)

(a)   (b)

Fig. 6. Encryption/Decryption using Blowfish round (a) with unequal number of Blowfish round (b) with equal numbers and different position of Blowfish round

Encryption operation with equal number of Blowfish round and decryption operation with equal number of Blowfish rounds with different position of rounds. As shown in

Fig. 6(b), during the encryption, Blowfish round numbers R2, R8, R9, R11, R12, R13, R14 and R15 are used while during decryption, equal total numbers of Blowfish rounds that is eight (R2, R8, R9, R11, R12, R13, R14 and R16) are used but different position of round (R16 round performed during decryption while R15 round performed during encryption). It means change in round number the whole plain text destroyed even though the attacker knows the key. Because of an attacker do not have any idea about how to skip the Blowfish rounds using round key.

5 Conclusion

Cryptography is the first line of defense to protect the data from intruder. Symmetric algorithms are less costly compare to asymmetric algorithms. Hence, symmetric cryptographic algorithms are preferable for data encryption. Wide range of symmetric algorithms exists. Among them AES and Blowfish symmetric ciphers give better throughput. The proposed scheme enhances the security level of Blowfish block cipher by varying the total number of Blowfish rounds and skipping the few Blowfish round using round key. The results show that giving little change in Blowfish rounds, the proposed scheme enhances the Blowfish security. The proposed scheme improves little performance of Blowfish by performing less number of the round operations.

References

1. Indal, P., Singh, B.: Analyzing the security performance tradeoff in block ciphers. In: IEEE International Conference on Computing, Communication & Automation (ICCCA), pp. 326–331. IEEE Press, Noida (2015)
2. Patil, P., Narayankar, P., Narayan, D.G., Meena, S. M.: A comprehensive evaluation of cryptographic algorithms: DES, 3DES, AES, RSA and Blowfish. In: 1st International Conference on Information Security & Privacy, Procedia Computer Science, vol. 78, pp. 617–624. Science Direct (2016)
3. Poonia, V., Yadav, N.S.: Analysis of modified Blowfish algorithm in different cases with various parameters. In: IEEE International Conference on Advanced Computing and Communication Systems, pp. 1–5. IEEE Press, Coimbatore (2015)
4. Ramesh, A., Suruliandi, A.: Performance analysis of encryption algorithms for information security. In: IEEE International Conference on Circuits, Power and Computing Technologies (ICCPCT), pp. 840–844. IEEE Press, Nagercoil, March 2013
5. Mousa, A.: Data encryption performance based on Blowfish. In: IEEE 47th International Symposium ELMAR, pp. 131–134. IEEE Press, Zadar (2005)
6. Ali, N.B.Z., Noras, J.M.: Optimal datapath design for a cryptographic processor: the Blowfish algorithm. Malays. J. Comput. Sci. **14**(1), 16–27 (2001)
7. Schneier, B.: Description of a new variable-length key, 64-bit block cipher (Blowfish). In: Anderson, R. (ed.) FSE 1993. LNCS, vol. 809, pp. 191–204. Springer, Heidelberg (1994). doi:10.1007/3-540-58108-1_24
8. Blowfish Block Cipher. https://www.schneier.com/academic/blowfish/
9. Kumar, S.S., Shanmugam, A.: Modified F-function for Feistel network in Blowfish algorithm. Int. J. Eng. Innovative Technol. **4**(4), 229–232 (2014)

10. Patel, P., Patel, R., Patel, N.: Integrated ECC and Blowfish for smartphone security. In: 1st International Conference on Information Security & Privacy, Procedia Computer Science, vol. 78, pp. 210–216. Science Direct (2016)
11. Meyers, R.K., Desoky, A.H.: An implementation of the Blowfish cryptosystem. In: IEEE International Symposium on Signal Processing and Information Technology, pp. 346–351. IEEE Press, Sarajevo (2008)
12. Kerckhoffs's Principle. https://en.wikipedia.org/wiki/Kerckhoffs's_principle
13. Alabaichi, A., Ahmad, F., Mahmod, R.: Security analysis of Blowfish algorithm. In: IEEE 2nd International Conference on Informatics and Applications (ICIA), pp. 12–18. IEEE Press, Lodz (2013)

Comparative Analytical Study for News Text Classification Techniques Applied for Stock Market Price Extrapolation

Hiral R. Patel[1(✉)] and Satyen Parikh[2]

[1] Department of Computer Science, Ganpat University, Ganpat Vidyanagar, Mehsana 384012, Gujarat, India
hrp02@ganpatuniversity.ac.in
[2] Faculty of Computer Applications, Ganpat University, Ganpat Vidyanagar, Mehsana 384012, Gujarat, India
satyen.parikh@ganpatuniversity.ac.in

Abstract. The current technological growth is tremendous so people are too much attached with technology. The most popular investing money portfolio is stock market and it's too dynamic in nature so the risk is also high to loss the money. Now days lots of research ongoing to predict the price. This study considers news impact as semantic analysis and as a technical view stock prices and index is measured. The text mining is one of the latest technologies to perform textual based analysis. There are many techniques available to perform auto news classification which is one most important phase in this research work. This paper focus on comparative study about different available techniques for semantic analysis by measuring different parameters like the accuracy, the data set used. This paper concludes with best news classification approach for stock price prediction.

Keywords: Chi-square · Classification · Noun phrase · Stop word removing · Text mining

1 Introduction

The Stock market price movements are too dynamic in nature. This paper shows that short term stock price movement prediction using financial news impact calculation. This paper shows that short-term stock price movements can be predicted using financial news articles. Given a stock price time series, for each time interval classify the price movement as "up," "down," or (approximately) "unchanged" relative to the volatility of the stock and the change in a relevant index. Each article in a training set of news articles is then labelled Negative, Positive or Neutral according to the contextual semantic analysis of published news and movement of the associated stock in a time interval surrounding publication of the article. For this purpose this paper shows the implementation of automated news classification using the text mining techniques which convert unstructured information into machine readable form. The first phase for this is Bag of Words model which compile the text as unordered words. Text mining basically focuses on to search most relevant feature of given text. This model approached by

© Springer Nature Singapore Pte Ltd. 2016
A. Unal et al. (Eds.): SmartCom 2016, CCIS 628, pp. 239–243, 2016.
DOI: 10.1007/978-981-10-3433-6_29

creating bag of words dictionary and occurrences of some used words. The extended approach is TF-IDM which known as information retrieval measure. The initial step for this model is to explore complex and effective word combinations that capable of capturing semantic of news. The next step is to classify the news as positive or negative affection basis by picking discriminant features. This can be based on stock market response based on news. This paper shows the features of capturing news and its impact on stock. For this objective this study focus on stock related to crude production and marketing with the news related to crude sector. It also collects the crude index for that short time period prediction. So this paper mainly focuses on news classification and its impact on stock market.

2   Related Work

In this section, the existing model used for news classification is discussed and also comparative analysis is given in terms of the data set, model, machine learning classification technique and accuracy used for information retrieval to fulfil the objective [1].

✓ The data set in terms of news articles used in the work and the method of fetching electrical form of news.
✓ The model means the approach used to generate machine readable information from news.
✓ The machine learning classification technique means the technique used to make news auto classification.
✓ The accuracy comparative studies for identifying best optimised modelling approach for this prediction.

Table 1 shows the comparative study [1, 9].

Table 1. Applied technique comparison

Published year	Data set	Modelling approach for feature processing	Machine learning approach	Accuracy
Mittermayr 2004 [3]	Financial News +Daily Stock Price	Bag of Words +TF-IDF with fix terms limit	SVM	50%
Groth et al. 2009 [2]	Ad-hoc Announcement +Daily Stock Price	Bag of Words +Chi Square based feature selection	SVM	56.5%
Li 2010 [4]	Corporate Findings+Daily Stock Price	Bag of Words +Predefined Dictionary	Naïve Bayes	NA
Schumaker et al. 2012 [1]	Financial News +Stock Price [Intraday]	Noun Phrases [Min Occurrence Per Doc]	SVM	59%

This study focus on news auto classification based on different modelling combined approach.

3   Research Complexity

The proposed approach also be required to care with following complexity otherwise the model goes down [1, 3, 9].

✓ Accuracy for Complex Terms Frequency: The Bag of words approach hardly catches up complex text but less capability to deal with combined similar complex patterns.
✓ Impact of Selection method in terms of accuracy: The over fitting problem occurs with some model which effect the model accuracy negatively [1, 3, 4].

4   Proposed Approach

Our proposed model based on dataset fetched from selective news article and classifies the news using combined approach of Bag of Words, Noun Phrase and TF-IDF. The text mining is used for to convert textual information in to machine readable approach. This paper collects the news from pre-selected financial news. This model based on text mining. The Bag of Words approach is basically process of to maintain tokenization which represents tokens of documents also implies stop word removal and stemming. It also defines the importance of tokens. Noun phrases are also applied for to remove unused words and noun from the text. Another approach is Term Frequency - Inverse of the Document Frequency. It introduces in two phases first is TF which focus on term occurrences in the document an another is IDF which focus on document collection does it appear. This methodology also have component to calculate weight by following equation. [1]

$$idf = \log\left(\frac{N}{df}\right)$$

5   Auto News Classification Methodology

The main goal of this study to perform comparative analysis for news classification an conclude with best approach to improve the accuracy. This is the heart of paper which includes the steps for proposed auto news classification.

5.1   Pre-processing

Pre-processing is simple but always requires for performing any analytical steps. The accuracy is also depends on the data which are provide for the research. In this step the news collection sources, web sites link and most authorised feeds are observe and collected. For this the automatic news fetching model is developed which store the detailed news in model data base in well format.

5.2 Stop Word Removing Method

Most of applications remove the words used most often in document, but here the stop word removing approach removes the unused and non-completed words, prepositions, verbs and articles. Then the most frequently words occurrence calculation is performed and considers the average happening of particular words are stored in database with average calculation.

5.3 Semantic Approach

The semantic analysis is used to identify the textual information and match up with related objective work. In this paper semantic analysis is used to identify the news impact to predict the stock price prediction. The auto news classification for this study use semantic analysis with classifying news in three predefined classes that is Positive affection news, negative affection and neutral. To classify the news auto updated dictionary is maintained which have numerous words an updated impact is stored. This is used as knowledge base for classification. According to the news and its impact dynamic rules are generated to classify the each news effect.

5.4 Weight Assignment

The TF-IDF approach mostly depends on weight assignment and weight assignment always play measure role for improving accuracy and reduce the dimensionality space. In this study the weight assignment is require to assign the impact of frequently occurred words in document it means simply assign the importance value to each term and more important term has higher weight. The general idea is to assign the weight by calculating log average occurrence of terms with the current news.

$$W(x) = \text{Log} \sum_{n=1}^{\infty} \left(\frac{\sum Tn}{n} \right)$$

5.5 Result and Conclusion

The experimental study gives very fruitful results in terms of auto news classification. As per the existing work discussed previously achieve the 55% accuracy. This fusion approach achieve improve accuracy by more than 70%. As an example this paper provides the news collection of one month related to crude sector and perform automated classification and get the 72% accuracy. To recapitulate, the method also improved by defining more effective weight assignment strategy.

References

1. Hagenau, M., Liebmann, M., Neumann, D.: Auto-mated news reading: stock price prediction based on financial news using context-capturing features. Decis. Support Syst. (2013). doi: 10.1016/j.dss.2013.02.006
2. Schumaker, R.P., Chen, H.: Textual analysis of stock market prediction using breaking financial news: the AZFin text system. ACM Trans. Inf. Syst. **27**(2), 1–19 (2009)
3. Groth, S.S., Muntermann, J.: Supporting investment management processes with machine learning techniques. In: Hansen, H.R., Karagiannis, D., Fill, H.-G. (eds.) Proceedings of the 9 Internationale Tagung Wirtschaftsinformatik, Österreichische Computer Gesellschaft, Wien, Austria (2009)
4. Mittermayr, M. A.: Forecasting intraday stock price trends with text mining techniques. In: Proceedings of the 37th Annual Hawaii International Conference on System Sciences (2004)
5. Li, F.: The information content of forward-looking statements in corporate filings - A Naïve Bayesian machine learning approach. J. Account. Res. **48**(5), 49–102 (2010)
6. Ramya, M., Alwin Pinakas, J.: Different type of feature selection for text classification. Intl. J. Comput. Trends Technol. (IJCTT) **10**(2), 102–107 (2014)
7. Ikonomakis, M., Kotsiantis, S., Tampakas, V.: Text classification using machine learning techniques. WSEAS Trans. Comput. 4(8), 966–974 (2005)
8. Lee, K., Timmons, R.: Predicting the Stock Market with News Articles: CS224N Final Project-2014
9. GyőzőGidófalvi: Using news articles to predict stock price movements. Thesis submitted (2010)

Goal Oriented Approaches in Data Warehouse Requirements Engineering: A Review

Anjana Gosain and Rakhi Bhati[✉]

University School of Information and Communication Technology,
Guru Gobind Singh Indraprastha University, Delhi, India
anjana_gosain@hotmail.com, rakhibhati11@gmail.com

Abstract. Requirements engineering (RE) is an important phase for data ware-house development. Earlier, DW development did not emphasize on RE phase. In recent past, several authors have suggested to give prime importance to this phase. Various approaches have been proposed for Data Warehouse Require-ments Engineering which may be categorised as goal-driven, user-driven, mixed-driven etc. In this paper, we provide a detailed and updated review of goal oriented requirements engineering approaches proposed till date. It also provides a deep insight into goal oriented approaches through comparative analysis, which can be fruitful for enhancing the research in this field.

Keywords: Data warehouse · Requirements engineering · Early requirements engineering · Late requirements engineering · Goal-oriented

1 Introduction

Data warehouse is a collection of an enterprise's current and historical information. It makes the information available for analysis and strategic decision making [9]. In the domain of decision making process, two different approaches namely data-driven and requirements-driven have been used for data warehouse development [1]. In data-driven approaches, data warehouse is developed by gathering data from operational systems. In requirements driven approaches, the information needs are identified to be fulfilled by data warehouses [2].

Different studies have indicated that requirements engineering is an important phase for data warehouse development. A number of approaches [1, 2, 5, 10–12, 18] have been proposed to carry out the requirements engineering phase in a systematic way namely goal-driven, user-driven and mixed-driven. In goal-driven, data models are developed based only on business goals. User-driven approaches derive the data model directly from user requirements and in mixed-driven approaches; a combination of any of the said approaches is used to form a data model.

In requirements engineering domain, most of the proposed approaches are goal-driven approaches [3]. In this paper, we focus on goal-driven approaches for data ware-house requirements engineering (DWRE).

The paper reviews the Goal-Oriented Requirements Engineering (GORE) approaches in the field of DWRE. The remainder of the paper is divided into subsections

© Springer Nature Singapore Pte Ltd. 2016
A. Unal et al. (Eds.): SmartCom 2016, CCIS 628, pp. 244–253, 2016.
DOI: 10.1007/978-981-10-3433-6_30

that are as follows: In Sect. 2 we discuss about GORE for data warehouse development. Section 3 discuss the review method in which review questions are formulated to boost the research. Then, in observations and discussion section, which is Sect. 4, the answers to the review questions stated above are provided. Finally, the last section sums up the whole review process and provides an effective conclusion.

2 Goal Oriented Requirements Engineering

The process of identifying the needs of involved stakeholders and supporting those needs by modelling and documenting them in a form that is analyzable is known as requirements engineering [3]. In last few years, relation of requirements engineering to organization context has attracted much interest from the data warehouse community. In order to support RE for data warehouse systems, a dedicated approach is required. A systematic approach of data warehouse requirements engineering will help to maintain the quality of a data warehouse [20]. An approach of requirements analysis that will focus on goals and strategies of the organization for efficient decision-making is called Goal-oriented Requirements Engineering Approach [4]. GORE addresses the problems associated with the business goals, plans, processes and systems to be developed in order to achieve organizational objectives [6]. The modelling of goals is done at various levels of abstraction, ranging from strategic concerns at high level to technical concerns at low-level. Hence a structured mechanism is required for the identification of goals [3].

According to Guo et al. [5], a set of goals are obtained by analyzing the business, by interviewing the top and middle management through GORE approaches. Later these goals are converged in order to get quantifiable Key Performance Indicators (KPIs). Then these KPIs are used to form logical data models.

According to Kavakli [6], the initial stage foreseen requirements are quite different from the ones that belong to later stages. And this leads to different ways of conceiving goals. Different authors have proposed different ways to elicit goals for requirements engineering process of a data warehouse, which we will discuss in Sect. 4.

3 Review Method

This review study presents a thorough study of goal oriented approaches for data warehouse proposed till now. To conduct the review, a determined and dedicated approach was used [23]. This approach consists of various steps in order to conduct the successful review based on the guidelines of Kitchenham [23]. The first step to conduct the review is to formulate the review questions. Then various databases are searched to get the relevant articles capable of answering those questions. Various observations are made after analyzing the articles on the basis of different parameters. These observations are represented in tabular form or graphically represented using bar graphs to increase the level of understanding.

3.1   Formulating Review Questions

This review article collects the updated information about GORE approaches for the development of data warehouses in order to provide the answers to the review questions framed below:-

RQ1. Assessing how the selected articles bring advantage to the research.

RQ2. Analyzing each GORE approach on the basis of five different parameters like early requirements engineering, late requirements engineering, functional requirements, non-functional requirements and automation tool support.

RQ3. Determining the summarized effects of these approaches with respect to the publication trends.

3.2   Study Selection

This step helps in deciding which papers to include in the review process. Only the papers which are in coherence with the proposed review questions are included. Initially, we spotted about 73 articles on goal oriented requirements engineering approaches. But these articles were a mix of GORE approaches for software engineering and data warehouse. Therefore, the articles were filtered by reading their abstract and conclusion. After this step, we were left only with the articles related to Data Warehouse Requirements Engineering. Finally, 14 articles were selected as only they can provide a better answer to the proposed review questions.

4   Observations and Discussion

The review work is followed by the study of many articles related to the GORE approaches for data warehouse requirements engineering which lead to various observations. These observations are represented in tabular form or graphically represented

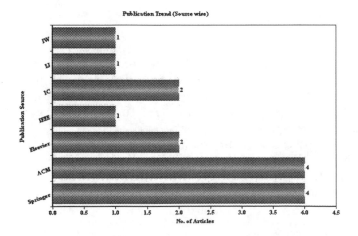

Fig. 1. Publication Trend of articles according to source.

using bar-graphs (see Figs. 1 and 2). The results of these observations contribute in answering the research questions stated above in Sect. 3.

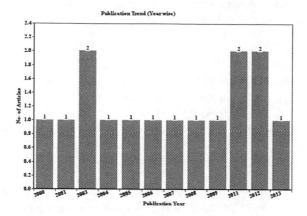

Fig. 2. Publication Trend of articles according to year of publication.

RQ1. The selected articles are beneficial to the research as each of them is giving a new angle to GORE process for data warehouse development. These articles provide the new methodology, concept, approach or framework to achieve the same. Here we discuss different goal-oriented approaches proposed by different authors for data warehouse requirements engineering. The role of the selected articles to strengthen the further research in this field is discussed below. Hence the review question 1 is answered.

Boehnlein et al. (2000). In this paper [7], authors have developed a SOM (Semantic Object Model) based goal-oriented approach for modelling the requirements of a data warehouse. It begins with the determination of two types of goals-one represents the services and products to be provided whereas the other defines the extent to which the goal is to be achieved. Here the data warehouse structures are derived from business-process models. It is based on the nominal information requirements as a whole.

Bonifati et al. (2001). In this [8], authors have proposed a three step method to keep up with the data mart design. The steps are: (1) A top-down analysis to obtain the requirements of users. It is attained through a goal-oriented method based on goal/question/metric (GQM) criterion. (2) A bottom-up approach in which the candidate data marts are extracted from conceptual data model. (3) This step compares several ideal data marts to get a collection of data marts that are in accordance with the underlying information system and satisfy the user requirements to the maximum.

Silva-Paim and Castro (2003). In this paper [13], authors have proposed DWARF (Data Warehouse Requirements Definition) approach which consists of four phases for clearly defining and managing the requirements of Data Warehouse. The more detailed view of target application is portrayed by each phase of DWARF approach, with the intention of analyzing requirements to form requirement baselines. Authors have used various techniques for functional requirements elicitation like interview, workshop, prototyping, scenarios etc. and for non-functional requirements they have used NFR framework. Requirements conformance to achieve robustness and requirements validation is done through review sessions. Finally many of requirements are carried out by traceability matrices.

Prakash and Gosain (2003). In this paper [1], authors have proposed a model named GDI (Goal decisional information), which has two associations, one is the goal-decision association that captures the decisions to be taken for goal achievement and other is decision-information association that depicts the information required for decision making process. In this model, two types of relationships are represented along with goal and decision hierarchy, one is *satisfied by* that exists between goals and decisions and other is required *for* that exists between decisions and information.

Prakash et al. (2004). In this paper [14], a requirements elicitation process is presented to arrive at the GDI model. This process consists of two steps. The first step goal-decision coupling and second step decision-information coupling. Here authors deal with the second step of this process. Each decision is represented by an informational scenario and that is a sequence of pairs of form <Query, Response>. The necessary information is requested by a query to take a decision and the response given by the query is the information itself.

Giorgini et al. (2005, 2008). In this [15, 16], an approach called GRAnD, goal-oriented requirement analysis for data warehouse design based on Tropos methodology is proposed. This approach adapts two different perspectives for requirement analysis: organizational modelling, whose focus is on stakeholders whereas decisional modelling centred on decision makers. The analysis of decision maker's goals is directly related to an explicit given goal model of organization. Authors implemented the proposed methodology through CASE tool.

Gam and Salinesi (2006). This paper [17] proposes a method named CADWA (Collaborative Agents in Distributed Web Application). It transfers the focus from where information to how information should be structured and when they are needed. The communication gap between stakeholders and developers is bridged through this approach by considering the requirements from decision makers and technical specification from the existing data marts in addition to operational data models. This working principle of requirements gathering is implemented by goal oriented approach.

Mazon et al. (2007). In this paper [2], a GORE approach is proposed for modelling organization goals that are supported by data warehouse and relating them to information requirements. They classified the goals as strategic, decision and information goals and the various kind of goals are incorporated using i* modelling framework. A Model Driven Architecture (MDA) framework is derived by integrating the stated approach. A Computation Independent Model is defined in this framework which deals with goals and informational requirements. Then a corresponding Platform Independent Model is derived from CIM through QVT (query/view/transformation) which is used to specify multi-dimensional properties at computational level and also a Platform Specific Model customized to a particular database technology.

Kumar et al. (2009). In this paper [18], authors have proposed an AGDI model in which the various users of an organization are represented by introducing the aspect of agent. In previous GDI model, stakeholders were assumed as the only decision makers of any organization but here they can be stakeholders, system analysts, decision makers, information providers, etc. Here, early requirements have been modelled by organization modelling and goal modelling activities.

Kumar et al. (2011). In this paper [19], authors have proposed a quality perspective to the requirements model for a Data Warehouse. The introduction of the soft goals is done in the existing AGDI model in order to enhance the quality of requirements model for a data warehouse. The two perspectives are defined for a soft goal: decisional and quality. In former perspective, a soft goal is refined into a goal whose achievement criteria is well defined and thus called as decisional goal, whereas in later the goals are linked with various constraints like timing constraint, budgetary constraint etc. as defined by the agent.

Nasiri et al. (2011). In this paper [3] a GORE based method for data warehouse systems is proposed. This method is developed by using a methodology which is based on Method Engineering Approach. It includes (1) the adoption of components from existing GORE based methods, (2) selection of appropriate components based on best coverage of abstracting the decision-making process and (3) proposal of guidelines to mention the necessary activities for abstracting the decision making process. Hence this paper focuses on early phase of system development where requirements are abstracted and different decision alternatives are constructed unlike other proposed methods.

Di Tria et al. (2012). In this paper [21], Hybrid methodology is defined which incorporates the merits of Dimensional Fact Model and formalization of user requirements represented by UML schemas obtained from i* framework. A framework is proposed for conceptual design of data warehouses. This framework begins with the analysis of goals defined by decision makers. These goals are used to produce a schema which represents information requirements. Then, information requirements are used to discover facts and dimensions.

Prakash and Bhardwaj (2012). In this paper [20], authors have proposed two important steps of data warehouse requirements engineering. The first step is known as an early info step where information is captured for decision making process and the second step called late info step where this information is used to structure the facts and dimensions. Here the emphasis is on early information step in which the targets are defined as key pair of form <A, I> where A defines the aspect of an organization and I represents a set of indicators. Aspect defines the quality that should be maintained in an organization and indicators represent the measures to indicate the desired performance level of aspects.

Cravero et al. (2013). This paper [22], suggests an approach that considers the business perspective to the data warehouse design by focusing on the analysis of business strategies, mapping of the strategies of a firm with the goals of a data warehouse, modelling of goal-oriented information requirements and derivation of multidimensional data warehouse model. A Business strategy is considered in this approach using goals, strategies, requirements analysis scheme, a business motivation model (BMM) for mapping goals of DW and strategy of a firm, modelling the objectives by using i* and then the multidimensional model of the DW is derived by using unified modelling language (UML) profile.

RQ2. In this section we answer the review question 2 by analyzing the different GORE approaches discussed in previous section on the basis of different parameters. The comparative analysis (as shown in Table 1) of different goal-oriented approaches is being done to ease the task of selecting the GORE approach as there is no consensus on which goal-oriented approach is best. The comparison is done on the basis of five parameters that are described in the following subsections:

Table 1. Comparison of various Goal-Oriented Approaches on the basis of information elicitation, type of requirements taken into account and tool support.

Aspects of comparison	Early Req. Engg. phase	Late Req. Engg. phase	Non-functional Req.	Functional Req.	Automation support	P.Source	P.Year
Boehnlein et al.	Yes	Yes	Yes	No	No	Springer	2000
Bonifati et al.	Yes	Yes	Yes	No	No	ACM	2001
Silva-Paim and Castro	Yes	Yes	Yes	Yes	Yes	IEEE	2003
Prakash and Gosain	Yes	No	Yes	No	Yes	IC	2003
Prakash et al.	Yes	No	Yes	No	Yes	Springer	2004
Giorgini et al.	Yes	Yes	Yes	No	Yes	ACM, Elsevier	2005, 2008
Gam and Salinesi	Yes	Yes	Yes	No	No	IC	2006
Mazon et al.	Yes	Yes	Yes	No	Yes	Springer	2007
Kumar et al.	Yes	No	Yes	No	Yes	ACM	2009
Kumar et al.	Yes	No	Yes	Yes	No	ACM	2011
Nasiri et al.	Yes	Yes	Yes	No	No	IW	2011
Di-Tria et al.	Yes	Yes	Yes	No	Yes	Elsevier	2012
Prakash and Bhardwaj	Yes	No	Yes	No	Yes	Springer	2012
Cravero et al.	Yes	Yes	Yes	No	No	IJ	2013

[P.Source- Publication Source, P.Year Publication Year, ACM- Association for Computing Machinery IW- International Workshop, IC- International Conference, IJ- International Journal]

1. **Early Requirements Engineering Phase**
   In this phase, identification of facts is done and then associates them to goals of different actors and information relevant to decisions is discovered.
2. **Late Requirements Engineering Phase**
   In this phase, facts are mapped to their respective dimensions and then a set of measures identified and linked with facts. Basically information is structured as facts and dimensions.

3. **Functional Requirements**

   Functional requirements define the functionalities that a system should exhibit. They define specific behaviour and functions and 'what a system is supposed to do'. Here we analyze whether a particular GORE approach deals with functional requirements.

4. **Non-functional Requirements**

   Non-functional requirements specify the parameters or criteria that can be used to judge the operation of a system like cost, time, performance, reliability, quality etc. They define 'how a system is supposed to be'.

   Again we analyze if non-functional requirements are taken in account for a particular GORE approach.

5. **Automation Support**

   This aspect also plays a prime role while selecting an appropriate approach. It will tell us whether there is any tool support available for the techniques proposed in the various papers.

RQ3. The articles studied provide a constructive work to the researchers for the analysis of various proposed GORE approaches. The summarized effects of these approaches are shown with respect to the publication trends. Publication trends are classified as publication according to source or year in which they are published. These trends are depicted in Figs. 1 and 2 respectively.

It can be inferred from the Fig. 1 that most of the articles included in this study are of Springer or ACM. Figure 2 depicts that the advent of goal-oriented approaches is done in year 2000. And also no paper is published on GORE approach in the year 2002 and 2010. This graphical representation helps in showing the analysis of articles in consolidated manner.

5   Conclusion

We have studied different goal-oriented approaches proposed by different authors for data warehouse development. In this paper an overview of data warehouse GORE approaches is provided. This review will help to select an appropriate approach for a given data warehouse project. We have analyzed the fourteen goal-oriented approaches to data warehouse requirements engineering on the basis of five different parameters namely early requirements engineering, late requirements engineering, functional requirements, non-functional requirements and automation tool support. And from the analysis, it can be concluded that various researchers have put huge attention towards GORE approach for DWRE. But still there is need to work on the inclusion of non-functional requirements in the GORE approach.

References

1. Prakash, N., Gosain, A.: Requirements driven data warehouse development. In: CAiSE Short Paper Proceedings (2003)

2. Mazón, J., Pardillo, J., Trujillo, J.: A model-driven goal-oriented requirement engineering approach for data warehouses. In: Advances in Conceptual Modeling – Foundations and Applications, pp. 255–264 (2007)
3. Nasiri, A., Zimanyi, E., Wrembel, R.: Requirements engineering for data warehouses. In: EDA, pp. 49–64 (2011)
4. Yu, E., Mylopoulos, J.: Why goal oriented requirements engineering. In: Proceedings of 4th International Workshop on Requirements Engineering for Software Quality, Foundations of Software Quality-REFSQ, p. 1522 (1998)
5. Guo, Y., Tang, S., Tong, Y., Yang, D.: Triple-driven data modeling methodology. In: DOLAP'06 ACM in Proceedings of National Workshop on Data Warehousing: A Case Study (2006)
6. Kavakli, E.: Goal oriented requirements engineering: A unifying framework. Requirements Eng. **6**(4), 237–251 (2002)
7. Boehnlein, M., Ulbrich-vom Ende, A.: Business process oriented development of data warehouse structures. In: Data Warehousing 2000, pp. 3–21. Heidelberg, Physica (2000). Methoden, Anwendungen, Strategien
8. Bonifati, A., Cattaneo, F., Ceri, S., Fuggetta, A., Paraboschi, F.: Designing data marts for data warehouses. ACM Trans. Softw. Eng. Methodol. **10**(4), 452–483 (2001)
9. Inmon, W.: Building the Data Warehouse, 2nd edn. (1996)
10. List, B., Schiefer, J., Tjoa, A.: Process-Oriented Requirement Analysis Supporting the Data Warehouse Design Process A Use Case Driven Approach. LNCS, pp. 593–603 (2000)
11. Winter, R., Strautch, B.: Demand-Driven Information Requirements Analysis in Data Warehousing. Journal Of Data Warehousing (2003)
12. Frendi, M., Salinesi, C.: Requirements engineering for data warehousing. CAiSE'03 Klagenfurt/Velden, Austria.(2003)
13. Silva Paim, F., de Castro, J.: DWARF: An Approach for Requirement Definition and Management of Data Warehouse Systems. 11th IEEE International Req. Engg Conference: 75–84.(2003)
14. Prakash, N., Singh, Y., Gosain, A.: Informational scenarios for data warehouse requirements elicitation. In: Atzeni, P., Chu, W., Lu, H., Zhou, S., Ling, T.-W. (eds.) ER 2004. LNCS, vol. 3288, pp. 205–216. Springer Berlin Heidelberg, Berlin, Heidelberg (2004). doi: 10.1007/978-3-540-30464-7_17
15. Giorgini, P., Rizzi, S., Garzetti, M.: Goal-oriented requirements analysis for data warehouse design. In: 8th International Workshop on Dolap'05. ACM (2005)
16. Giorgini, P., Rizzi, S., Garzetti, M.: Grand: a goal-oriented approach to requirement analysis in data warehouses. Decis. Support Syst. **45**(1), 4–21 (2008)
17. Gam, I., Salinesi, C.: A requirement driven approach for designing data warehouse. In: REFSQ'06 Requirement Engineering for Software Quality (2006)
18. Kumar, M., Gosain, A., Singh, Y.: Agent oriented requirements engineering for a data warehouse. SIGSOFT Softw. Eng. Notes **34**(5), 1–4 (2009)
19. Kumar, M., Gosain, A., Singh, Y.: Quality-oriented requirements engineering for a data warehouse. SIGSOFT Softw. Eng. Notes **36**(5),1–4 (2011)
20. Prakash, N., Bhardwaj, H.: Early information requirements engineering for target driven data warehouse development. In: Sandkuhl, K., Seigerroth, U., Stirna, J. (eds.) PoEM 2012. LNBIP, vol. 134, pp. 188–202. Springer Berlin Heidelberg, Berlin, Heidelberg (2012). doi: 10.1007/978-3-642-34549-4_14
21. Di-Tria, F., Lefons, E., Tangorra, F.: Hybrid Methodology for data warehouse conceptual design by UML schemas. Inf. Softw. Technol. **54**, 360–379 (2012)

22. Cravero, A., Mazon, J.-N., Trujillo, J.: A business-oriented approach to data warehouse development. Ingeniera e Investigation **33**(1), 59–65 (2013)
23. Kitchenham, B.: Procedures for undertaking Systematic Reviews, Joint Technical Report, Computer Science Department, Keele University (TR/SE-0401) and National ICT Australia Ltd (040011T), July 2004

Indexing of Information Systems Using Intuitionistic Rough Fuzzy Groups with Intuitionistic Fuzzy Decision Attributes

B. Krishnaveni[1]([⊠]), S. Chandrika[1], and G. Ganesan[2]

[1] Department of Humanities and Basic Sciences, Aditya Engineering College,
Surampalem, Andhra Pradesh, India
krishnavenibadam@yahoo.co.in,
surapureddy.chandrika9@gmail.com
[2] Department of Mathematics, Adikavi Nannaya University,
Rajahmundry, Andhra Pradesh, India
prof.ganesan@yahoo.com

Abstract. A naïve approach in rough computing under fuzziness and intuitionistic fuzziness through thresholds was given by G. Ganesan in 2005. Later in 2013, B. Krishnaveni and G. Ganesan had derived a procedure of characterizing information systems using intuitionistic fuzzy decision attributes through intuitionistic rough fuzzy groups. Using this, G. Ganesan and B. Krishnaveni in 2014 introduced the indexing procedure in characterization obtained using fuzzy decision attributes. In present paper, let us apply this procedure under intuitionistic fuzzy decision attributes.

Keywords: Intuitionistic rough fuzzy groups · Information system · Indexing algorithm

1 Introduction

The concept of Rough Sets [9] was given by Z. Pawlak, which gives the approximations of a given input with respect to the available knowledge. On the other hand, fuzzy concepts introduced by Zadeh, gives the generalization of a classical set. Due to enormous applications, both the concepts were hybridized and emerged two new concepts namely fuzzy roughness and rough fuzziness [2].

A group structure namely intuitionistic rough fuzzy group [6] was introduced by G. Ganesan et al., in 2005. In that work, the closed intuitionistic fuzzy matrices were defined for the elements of the given finite quotient group using intuitionistic rough fuzzy approximations. Besides, G. Ganesan also gave the importance and procedure of introducing a threshold in rough fuzzy approximation. In 2008, G. Ganesan et al., [5] introduced an indexing algorithm in an information systems with fuzzy decision attributes. In 2013, B. Krishnaveni and G. Ganesan introduced a naïve algebraic procedure [8] of characterizing information system with intuitionistic fuzzy decision attributes. The above characterization was done using indexing algorithm using fuzzy decision attributes [7] in 2014 by G. Ganesan and B. Krishnaveni. In this paper, we

© Springer Nature Singapore Pte Ltd. 2016
A. Unal et al. (Eds.): SmartCom 2016, CCIS 628, pp. 254–263, 2016.
DOI: 10.1007/978-981-10-3433-6_31

introduced a group structure in information system using intuitionistic fuzzy decision attributes through indexing algorithm.

The paper comprises of five sections. In Sect. 2, we dealt the basics of intuitionistic rough fuzzy sets and information systems. In Sect. 3 we discussed about the analysis of intuitionistic fuzzy sets using a threshold and intuitionistic rough fuzzy groups. Section 4 gives the characterization of information system of information system using intuitionistic fuzzy decision attributes through indexing algorithm. The Sect. 5 concludes with few remarks.

2 Intuitionistic Rough Fuzzy Sets and Information Systems

2.1 Intuitionistic Rough Fuzziness

Consider a finite universe of discourse $U = \{a_1, a_2,..., a_n\}$ and $\mathbf{W} = \{W_1, W_2,..., W_n\}$ be a partition of U. For any intuitionistic fuzzy subset A of U, define as in [6]

$$\mu_{\underline{A}}(W_i) = \inf\{\mu_A(a_j) : a_j \in W_i\} \tag{1}$$

$$\gamma_{\underline{A}}(W_i) = \sup\{\gamma_A(a_j) : a_j \in W_i\} \tag{2}$$

$$\mu_{\overline{A}}(W_i) = \sup\{\mu_A(a_j) : a_j \in W_i\} \tag{3}$$

$$\gamma_{\overline{A}}(W_i) = \inf\{\gamma_A(a_j) : a_j \in W_i\} \tag{4}$$

Then the approximations are given as follows:

$$\underline{A} = [(\mu_{\underline{A}}(W_1), \gamma_{\underline{A}}(W_1)), \ldots, (\mu_{\underline{A}}(W_t), \gamma_{\underline{A}}(W_t))]$$

$\overline{A} = [(\mu_{\overline{A}}(W_1), \gamma_{\overline{A}}(W_1)), \ldots, (\mu_{\overline{A}}(W_t), \gamma_{\overline{A}}(W_t))]$ termed as lower and upper approximations respectively.

The matrix $\begin{bmatrix} \mu_{\underline{A}}(W_i) & \gamma_{\underline{A}}(W_i) \\ \mu_{\overline{A}}(W_i) & \gamma_{\overline{A}}(W_i) \end{bmatrix}$ is termed as Intuitionistic fuzzy matrix for each W_i.

2.2 Information Systems

Let D = (U, P, K, T), be any decision table with U as the set of all records, P as primitive features, and the subsets K and T as conditional and decision features. Define IND(W) = {(x, y) ∈ UxU : a(x) = a(y) for all a in W} where W is a subset of P. Hence U/IND(W) or U/W denotes the partition made by IND(W) with respect to W. Now, define $\underline{W}X = \cup\{Y \in U/P : Y \subseteq X\}$ and $\overline{W}X = \cup\{Y \in U/P : Y \cap X \neq \Phi\}$ which gives the lower and upper approximation respectively for the indiscernibility relation IND(W).

The condition and decision classes are given by U/IND(K) and U/IND(T) respectively and $POS_K(T) = \bigcup_{X \in U/T} \underline{K}X$ called Positive region of T. The element k ∈ K is called indispensable if $POS_{K-\{k\}}(T) \neq POS_K(T)$, otherwise dispensable. If D' = (U, P, R, T) is independent and $POS_R(T) = POS_K(T)$ then the features R in K is called a reduct or minimal feature. CORE(K) [5] representing features indispensable in K. That is, CORE(K) = $\cap$RED(K) where RED(K) denotes reducts of K.

3   Intuitionistic Rough Fuzzy Groups

Suppose D be a set which is called IRF Domain such that,

(a) $D \subset (0, 1)$
(b) Remove the values $\mu_A(x), \mu_A^C(x), \gamma_A(x)$ and $\gamma_A^C(x)$ such that $\mu_A(x) + \gamma_A(x) \leq 1, \forall$ x∈U from D, if they exist from intuitionistic fuzzy set A.
(c) Include the eliminated values of (b) in D such that A should not go in further calculation

Suppose that U is any universe of discourse, A is an intuitionistic fuzzy set. Then (α, β)-cut of A, denoted as $A[\alpha, \beta]$ is the crisp set which is given by $A[\alpha, \beta] = \{x \in U: \mu_A(x) \geq \alpha \; \gamma_A(x) \leq \beta\}$.

Now, for any partition Let $\Psi = \{B_1, B_2,..., B_t\}$ on U, given set A, the approximations with respect to α, β can be defined as $A_{\alpha,\beta} = \underline{(A[\alpha, \beta])}$, $A^{\alpha,\beta} = \overline{(A[\alpha, \beta])}$.

Now, we describe the group structure on Intuitionistic Rough Fuzziness as described in [6].

3.1   Intuitionistic Rough Fuzzy Groups

Consider $\Omega = \left\{ \overrightarrow{0}, \overrightarrow{1}, ..., \overrightarrow{n-1} \right\}$ any congruence class for a positive integer n. Define addition(modulo n) $\overrightarrow{p} +_n \overrightarrow{q} = \text{Rem}(p+q,n)$ for any $\overrightarrow{p}$ and $\overrightarrow{q}$ such that Rem (p + q,n) gives the remainder acquired by dividing p + q by n. Let F be any Intuitionistic fuzzy subset [8] of Z. Therefore every element of Ω can be associated with respect to F. Hence we can express Ω as a set of intuitionistic fuzzy matrices

$$\left(\begin{pmatrix} \overrightarrow{0}_{b,i} & \overrightarrow{0}_{nb,i} \\ \overrightarrow{0}_{b,u} & \overrightarrow{0}_{nb,u} \end{pmatrix}, ..., \begin{pmatrix} \overline{(n-1)}_{b,i} & \overline{(n-1)}_{nb,i} \\ \overline{(n-1)}_{b,u} & \overline{(n-1)}_{nb,u} \end{pmatrix} \right) \text{ with respect to F.}$$

To find the closed intuitionistic fuzzy matrices as in [8] we proceed as follows:

Consider $\begin{pmatrix} \overrightarrow{k}_{b,i} & \overrightarrow{k}_{nb,i} \\ \overrightarrow{k}_{b,u} & \overrightarrow{k}_{nb,u} \end{pmatrix}$ be any intuitionistic fuzzy matrix of $\overline{k}$ under F, define

$$\overrightarrow{k}_{b,l}^{(s+1)} = \overset{\max}{\overrightarrow{p}_{b,l}^{(s)} +_n \overrightarrow{q}_{b,l}^{(s)}} = \overrightarrow{k}_{b,l}^{(s)} \min(\overrightarrow{p}_{b,l}^{(s)}, \overrightarrow{q}_{b,l}^{(s)}) \qquad (5)$$

$$\overrightarrow{k}_{nb,l}^{(s+1)} = \underset{\overrightarrow{p}_{nb,l}^{(s)} + {}_n\overrightarrow{q}_{nb,l}^{(s)}}{\min} = \overrightarrow{k}_{nb,l}^{(s)} \ \max(\overrightarrow{p}_{nb,l}^{(s)}, \overrightarrow{q}_{nb,l}^{(s)}) \tag{6}$$

$$\overrightarrow{k}_{b,u}^{(s+1)} = \underset{\overrightarrow{p}_{b,u}^{(s)} + {}_n\overrightarrow{q}_{b,u}^{(s)}}{\max} = \overrightarrow{k}_{b,u}^{(s)} \ \min(\overrightarrow{p}_{b,u}^{(s)}, \overrightarrow{q}_{b,u}^{(s)}) \tag{7}$$

$$\overrightarrow{k}_{nb,u}^{(s+1)} = \underset{\overrightarrow{p}_{nb,u}^{(s)} + {}_n\overrightarrow{q}_{nb,u}^{(s)}}{\min} = \overrightarrow{k}_{nb,u}^{(s)} \ \max(\overrightarrow{p}_{nb,u}^{(s)}, \overrightarrow{q}_{nb,u}^{(s)}) \tag{8}$$

The closed intuitionistic fuzzy matrices can be found by iteration process. Hence Ω is closed with respect addition modulo n and the group of closed intuitionistic fuzzy matrices is called *intuitionistic rough fuzzy group on Ω*.

Next the generalization approach in a finite group is given as in [6].

3.2   Algorithm

Consider a congruence group of Z under addition modulo k and an epimorphism f:G→Ω. Then

1. begin
2. Input ((G, *), Ω, f, F)
3. Compute the quotient group L = G/K
4. By the axiom of choice, denote each element of L by any of it member. For example, if a $\in$ K_x for some x $\in$ G, then denote K_x by [a].
5. Compute closed intuitionistic rough fuzzy matrix for each element of Ω using the intuitionistic fuzzy subset F of Z.
6. Associate the closed intuitionistic rough fuzzy matrix with the preimage of each element of Ω in G/K.
7. The group L associated with the intuitionistic fuzzy matrices is called the intuitionistic rough fuzzy group, denoted by (G, *, Ω, f, F).
8. return

Now, in the next section, we imbibe all these in the information systems through indexing algorithm.

4   Indexing of Intuitionistic Rough Fuzzy Groups

Let us consider the information system under intuitionistic fuzzy decision attributes. Now let us make a characterization of this system as follows:

4.1   Algorithm

(a) Find the reducts by using the threshold which is chosen From D. Let it be A_1, A_2, ..., A_k.
(b) Group the records of the information system for each reduct A_j.
(c) Find the intuitionistic fuzzy matrices for each of the cluster obtained by using Intuitionistic Rough Fuzzy Approximations.
(d) Let the number of clusters acquired using A_j be n_j then consider a group Z_{nj} of integers Congruence modulo n_j.
(e) Here note that there are n_j! ways to define bijections between the clusters and the group Z_{nj}.
(f) For each bijection, we get a Intuitionistic Rough Fuzzy Group of Clusters of the records of the Information System.

Take any decision table given by

	A	B	C	D	(μ_I, γ_I)
t_1	2	0	3	2	(0.7, 0.1)
t_2	2	0	3	0	(0.8, 0.1)
t_3	2	3	0	0	(0.3, 0.5)
t_4	2	3	3	2	(0.4, 0.5)
t_5	3	2	0	0	(0.9, 0.1)
t_6	3	2	2	0	(0.2, 0.7)
t_7	3	2	3	2	(0.6, 0.3)

where A, B, C, D are conditional attributes, I represents Intuitionistic fuzzy decision attribute.

Choose $\alpha = 0.5$, then the given information becomes as

	A	B	C	D	$I[\alpha]$
t_1	2	0	3	2	1
t_2	2	0	3	0	1
t_3	2	3	0	0	0
t_4	2	3	3	2	0
t_5	3	2	0	0	1
t_6	3	2	2	0	0
t_7	3	2	3	2	1

For the above system the reducts are {B, C} and {B, D}.

Now, for illustration take the reduct {B, C}. By using {B, C}, we get the indiscernibility classes as {{t_1, t_2},{t_3},{t_4},{t_5},{t_6}, {t_7}}. Hence the intuitionistic fuzzy matrices by using Intuitionistic Rough Fuzzy approximations which is given by

$$\{t_1, t_2\} \leftarrow \begin{pmatrix} 0.7 & 0.1 \\ 0.8 & 0.1 \end{pmatrix}$$

$$\{t_3\} \leftarrow \begin{pmatrix} 0.3 & 0.5 \\ 0.3 & 0.5 \end{pmatrix}$$

$$\{t_4\} \leftarrow \begin{pmatrix} 0.4 & 0.5 \\ 0.4 & 0.5 \end{pmatrix}$$

$$\{t_5\} \leftarrow \begin{pmatrix} 0.9 & 0.1 \\ 0.9 & 0.1 \end{pmatrix}$$

$$\{t_6\} \leftarrow \begin{pmatrix} 0.2 & 0.7 \\ 0.2 & 0.7 \end{pmatrix}$$

$$\{t_7\} \leftarrow \begin{pmatrix} 0.6 & 0.3 \\ 0.6 & 0.3 \end{pmatrix}$$

Now, consider $\Omega = \left\{ \overrightarrow{0}, \overrightarrow{1}, \ldots, \overrightarrow{5} \right\}$, the congruence group of Z under addition modulo 6. Here, it is possible to find 6! ways of defining bijections in between the indiscernibility classes and Ω. However, for illustration, we consider the following bijection.

$$\{t_1, t_2\} \leftarrow \overline{1}$$
$$\{t_3\} \leftarrow \overline{4}$$
$$\{t_4\} \leftarrow \overline{5}$$
$$\{t_5\} \leftarrow \overline{2}$$
$$\{t_6\} \leftarrow \overline{3}$$
$$\{t_7\} \leftarrow \overline{0}$$

Therefore, the intuitionistic fuzzy matrices associated with the elements of Ω are given by

$$\overline{0} \leftarrow \begin{pmatrix} 0.6 & 0.3 \\ 0.6 & 0.3 \end{pmatrix}$$

$$\overline{1} \leftarrow \begin{pmatrix} 0.7 & 0.1 \\ 0.8 & 0.1 \end{pmatrix}$$

$$\overline{2} \leftarrow \begin{pmatrix} 0.9 & 0.1 \\ 0.9 & 0.1 \end{pmatrix}$$

$$\overline{3} \leftarrow \begin{pmatrix} 0.2 & 0.7 \\ 0.2 & 0.7 \end{pmatrix}$$

$$\overline{4} \leftarrow \begin{pmatrix} 0.3 & 0.5 \\ 0.3 & 0.5 \end{pmatrix}$$

$$\overline{5} \leftarrow \begin{pmatrix} 0.4 & 0.5 \\ 0.4 & 0.5 \end{pmatrix}$$

In this case, set of two closed intuitionistic fuzzy matrices are obtained which are given as

$$\bar{0} \leftarrow \begin{pmatrix} 0.7 & 0.1 \\ 0.8 & 0.1 \end{pmatrix} \quad \bar{0} \leftarrow \begin{pmatrix} 0.7 & 0.1 \\ 0.8 & 0.1 \end{pmatrix}$$

$$\bar{1} \leftarrow \begin{pmatrix} 0.7 & 0.1 \\ 0.8 & 0.1 \end{pmatrix} \quad \bar{1} \leftarrow \begin{pmatrix} 0.7 & 0.1 \\ 0.8 & 0.1 \end{pmatrix}$$

$$\bar{2} \leftarrow \begin{pmatrix} 0.7 & 0.1 \\ 0.8 & 0.1 \end{pmatrix} \quad \bar{2} \leftarrow \begin{pmatrix} 0.9 & 0.1 \\ 0.9 & 0.1 \end{pmatrix}$$

$$\bar{3} \leftarrow \begin{pmatrix} 0.7 & 0.1 \\ 0.8 & 0.1 \end{pmatrix} \quad \bar{3} \leftarrow \begin{pmatrix} 0.7 & 0.1 \\ 0.8 & 0.1 \end{pmatrix}$$

$$\bar{4} \leftarrow \begin{pmatrix} 0.9 & 0.1 \\ 0.9 & 0.1 \end{pmatrix} \quad \bar{4} \leftarrow \begin{pmatrix} 0.7 & 0.1 \\ 0.8 & 0.1 \end{pmatrix}$$

$$\bar{5} \leftarrow \begin{pmatrix} 0.7 & 0.5 \\ 0.8 & 0.5 \end{pmatrix} \quad \bar{5} \leftarrow \begin{pmatrix} 0.7 & 0.5 \\ 0.8 & 0.5 \end{pmatrix}$$

Hence, for $\alpha = 0.5$ characterization with respect to the reduct $\{B, C\}$ is given by

$$\{t_1, t_2\} \leftarrow \bar{1} \leftarrow \begin{pmatrix} 0.7 & 0.1 \\ 0.8 & 0.1 \end{pmatrix} \leftarrow \begin{pmatrix} 0.7 & 0.1 \\ 0.8 & 0.1 \end{pmatrix}$$

$$\{t_3\} \leftarrow \bar{4} \leftarrow \begin{pmatrix} 0.3 & 0.5 \\ 0.3 & 0.5 \end{pmatrix} \leftarrow \begin{pmatrix} 0.9 & 0.1 \\ 0.9 & 0.1 \end{pmatrix}$$

$$\{t_4\} \leftarrow \bar{5} \leftarrow \begin{pmatrix} 0.4 & 0.5 \\ 0.4 & 0.5 \end{pmatrix} \leftarrow \begin{pmatrix} 0.7 & 0.5 \\ 0.8 & 0.5 \end{pmatrix}$$

$$\{t_5\} \leftarrow \bar{2} \leftarrow \begin{pmatrix} 0.9 & 0.1 \\ 0.9 & 0.1 \end{pmatrix} \leftarrow \begin{pmatrix} 0.7 & 0.1 \\ 0.8 & 0.1 \end{pmatrix}$$

$$\{t_6\} \leftarrow \bar{3} \leftarrow \begin{pmatrix} 0.2 & 0.7 \\ 0.2 & 0.7 \end{pmatrix} \leftarrow \begin{pmatrix} 0.7 & 0.1 \\ 0.8 & 0.1 \end{pmatrix}$$

$$\{t_7\} \leftarrow \bar{0} \leftarrow \begin{pmatrix} 0.6 & 0.3 \\ 0.6 & 0.3 \end{pmatrix} \leftarrow \begin{pmatrix} 0.7 & 0.1 \\ 0.8 & 0.1 \end{pmatrix}$$

and

$$\{t_1, t_2\} \leftarrow \bar{1} \leftarrow \begin{pmatrix} 0.7 & 0.1 \\ 0.8 & 0.1 \end{pmatrix} \leftarrow \begin{pmatrix} 0.7 & 0.1 \\ 0.8 & 0.1 \end{pmatrix}$$

$$\{t_3\} \leftarrow \bar{4} \leftarrow \begin{pmatrix} 0.3 & 0.5 \\ 0.3 & 0.5 \end{pmatrix} \leftarrow \begin{pmatrix} 0.7 & 0.1 \\ 0.8 & 0.1 \end{pmatrix}$$

$$\{t_4\} \leftarrow \bar{5} \leftarrow \begin{pmatrix} 0.4 & 0.5 \\ 0.4 & 0.5 \end{pmatrix} \leftarrow \begin{pmatrix} 0.7 & 0.5 \\ 0.8 & 0.5 \end{pmatrix}$$

$$\{t_5\} \leftarrow \bar{2} \leftarrow \begin{pmatrix} 0.9 & 0.1 \\ 0.9 & 0.1 \end{pmatrix} \leftarrow \begin{pmatrix} 0.9 & 0.1 \\ 0.9 & 0.1 \end{pmatrix}$$

$$\{t_6\} \leftarrow \bar{3} \leftarrow \begin{pmatrix} 0.2 & 0.7 \\ 0.2 & 0.7 \end{pmatrix} \leftarrow \begin{pmatrix} 0.7 & 0.1 \\ 0.8 & 0.1 \end{pmatrix}$$

$$\{t_7\} \leftarrow \bar{0} \leftarrow \begin{pmatrix} 0.6 & 0.3 \\ 0.6 & 0.3 \end{pmatrix} \leftarrow \begin{pmatrix} 0.7 & 0.1 \\ 0.8 & 0.1 \end{pmatrix}$$

4.2   Indexing Algorithm

Algorithm index $(t, A, \alpha, \beta])$

//Algorithm to obtain index of t an element of universe of discourse
//Algorithm returns the index

1. Let t_index denotes an integer make at first to 0
2. If $\mu_A(t) = 1$, $\gamma_A(l) = 0$
    begin
           t_index=K
           goto 6
    end
3. If, $\mu_A(t) = 0$, $\gamma_A(l) = 1$
    begin
           t_index=-K
           goto 6
    end
4. compute $A_{\alpha,\beta}$ and $A^{\alpha,\beta}$
5. If $t \in A_{\alpha,\beta}$
    while $(t \in A_{\alpha,\beta})$
      begin
            α=sqrt(α) //square root of α
            β= sqr(β) //square of β
            t_index=t_index+K+1
            Find A_{α}
      end
      else
            if $t \notin A^{\alpha,\beta}$
            while $(t \notin A^{\alpha,\beta})$
              begin
                  α=sqr(α) //square of α
                  β= sqrt(β) //square root of β
                  t_index=t_index-1-K
                  compute $A^{\alpha,\beta}$
              end
              else
              B=A; γ =α,β=η
              compute $B^{\gamma,\eta}$
              while $(t \notin A_{\alpha,\beta}$ and $t \in B^{\gamma,\eta})$
                begin
                   α=sqr(α) // square of α, β=sqrt(β) // square root of β
                   γ =sqrt(γ) // square root of γ, η=sqr(η) // square of η
                   compute $A_{\alpha,\beta}$, $B^{\gamma,\eta}$
                   t_index=t_index+1
                end
              if $t \in A_{\alpha,\beta}$ then t_index= -t_index
      end
6. return t_index

The indices are called intuitionistic rough indices

4.3   Indexing Procedure

Now take the information system characterization with $\alpha = 0.5$ as below:

$$\{t_1, t_2\} \leftarrow \begin{pmatrix} 0.7 & 0.1 \\ 0.8 & 0.1 \end{pmatrix}$$

$$\{t_3\} \leftarrow \begin{pmatrix} 0.9 & 0.1 \\ 0.9 & 0.1 \end{pmatrix}$$

$$\{t_4\} \leftarrow \begin{pmatrix} 0.7 & 0.5 \\ 0.8 & 0.5 \end{pmatrix}$$

$$\{t_5\} \leftarrow \begin{pmatrix} 0.7 & 0.1 \\ 0.8 & 0.1 \end{pmatrix}$$

$$\{t_6\} \leftarrow \begin{pmatrix} 0.7 & 0.1 \\ 0.8 & 0.1 \end{pmatrix}$$

$$\{t_7\} \leftarrow \begin{pmatrix} 0.7 & 0.1 \\ 0.8 & 0.1 \end{pmatrix}$$

Here, $K = \{\{t_1, t_2\}, \{t_3\}, \{t_4\}, \{t_5\}, \{t_6\}, \{t_7\}\}$ for the reduct $(B, C\}$ and $\mu_E = ((0.7, 0.1), (0.8, 0.1), (0.3, 0.5), (0.4, 0.5), (0.9, 0.1), (0.2, 0.7), (0.6, 0.3))$. Therefore, $I[\alpha] = \{t_1, t_2, t_5, t_7\}$. Hence, we get indices [5] on the characterization of information system [8] by using the indexing algorithm which is given by

$$\{t_1, t_2\} \leftarrow (K+1, -K-1)$$
$$\{t_3\} \leftarrow (-1-K, K+1)$$
$$\{t_4\} \leftarrow (-1-K, K+1)$$
$$\{t_5\} \leftarrow (K+1, -K-1)$$
$$\{t_6\} \leftarrow (-K-2, K+2)$$
$$\{t_7\} \leftarrow (K+1, -K-1)$$

5   Conclusion

This paper gives the implementation of algebraic structure in information system using intuitionistic fuzzy decision attributes through indexing procedure

References

1. Atanassov, K.: Intuitionistic fuzzy sets. Fuzzy Sets Syst. **20**, 87–96 (1986)
2. Dubois, D., Prade, H.: Rough fuzzy sets and fuzzy rough sets. Int. J. Gen Syst. **17**, 191–209 (1989)
3. Ganesan, G.: Rough fuzzy group induced by epimorphisms. Intl. J. Comput. Math. Sci. Appl. **2**(2), 151–154 (2008)
4. Ganesan, G., Raghavendra Rao, C.: Rough set: analysis of fuzzy sets using thresholds. In: Computational Mathematics, pp. 81–87. Narosa Publishers, India (2005)
5. Ganesan, G., Latha, D., Raghavendra Rao, C.: Rough indexing in information system with fuzziness in decision attributes. Intl. J. Fuzzy Math. **16**(4) (2008)
6. Ganesan, G.: Intuitionistic rough fuzzy groups. Intl. J. Comput. Math. Sci. Appl. **4**(3–4), 339–344 (2010)
7. Ganesan, G., Krishnaveni, B.: Indexing information systems with fuzzy decision attributes-an approach through rough fuzzy groups. Intl. J. Adv. Trends Comput. Sci. Eng. **3**(6), 107–114 (2014)
8. Krishnaveni, B., Syamala, V., Ganesan, G.: Naïve intuitionistic rough fuzzy characterization of information systems with intuitionistic fuzzy decision attributes, ISST J. Math. Comput. Syst. **4**(1), 13–20 (2013)
9. Pawlak, Z.: Rough sets. Intl. J. Comput. Inf. Sci. **11**, 341–356 (1982)
10. Pawlak, Z.: Rough Sets-Theoretical Aspects and Reasoning about Data. Kluwer Academic Publications, Dordrecht (1991)

Cluster Based Hierarchical Addressing for Dynamic Source Routing

Samidha Shirke, Vitrag Shah$^{(\boxtimes)}$, Tejas Ruikar, and Jibi Abraham

Department of Computer Engineering and Information Technology,
College of Engineering, Pune (COEP), Shivajinagar 411005, Pune, India
{shirkesp12.it,shahvn12.it,ruikarts12.it,ja.comp}@coep.ac.in

Abstract. A Wireless Ad-Hoc Network (WANET) is a group of wireless mobile nodes which are self creating, self organizing and self administering. In such networks, selection of routing protocols is an important concern as it affects the performance of ad-hoc networks in terms of average end-to-end delay, reduced packet processing etc. This paper proposes a Cluster Based Logical Hierarchical Addressing scheme for Dynamic Source Routing protocol (CBHDSR) which enhances DSR. This scheme reduces the flooding of RREQ packets in the network by searching a direct path based on the addressing scheme which results in the reduced congestion.

Keywords: WANETs · Hierarchical addressing · Clustering

1 Introduction

Ad-hoc networks [1,2] are wireless networks that have no fixed infrastructure. Such kind of networks are created dynamically and they provide special challenges beyond those in standard data network. Because ad-hoc networks do not rely on existing infrastructure and are self organizing, they can be rapidly deployed to provide robust communication in variety of hostile environments. The structure of wireless ad-hoc network was initially designed to be a flat type, which means that the ad–hoc network is assumed to be homogeneous. Based on the flat structure, the routing work can be simply done by flooding.

In Ad-hoc network [3], the packets may need to traverse through multiple nodes before they reach the destination node. Each individual packet contains the identity of the sender's node as well as the destination node. Thus, the unique identity of each individual node is important for proper functioning of the network.

Various Addressing schemes have been discussed below which aim at providing unique identity to the nodes in the ad-hoc network for reducing flooding and end-to-end delay. This paper proposes a new addressing scheme which uses Dynamic Source Routing protocol with Clustering.

Dynamic Source Routing protocol (DSR) [4] is a reactive MANET routing protocol designed specifically for use in multi-hop wireless ad-hoc networks of

© Springer Nature Singapore Pte Ltd. 2016
A. Unal et al. (Eds.): SmartCom 2016, CCIS 628, pp. 264–275, 2016.
DOI: 10.1007/978-981-10-3433-6_32

mobile nodes. The network can be entirely self-configuring and organising and without using any the central infrastructure. DSR uses the source routing in which the complete path from source to the destination is stored in the header of each data packet. Route Delivery and Route maintenance are two major functions of DSR and as the names suggest they help in delivering the packets and maintaining the routes.

The key characteristic of DSR is flooding [1]. In order to make connection from one node to another, entire network is flooded with Route Request (RREQ) packets. This motivated us as it seems unnecessary to flood the entire network which might cause high bandwidth utilization and higher battery usage. The need to eliminate unnecessary flooding of RREQ packets as well as searching the member tables which is used to store cluster information, made us come up with Cluster Based Logical Hierarchical Addressing in DSR (CBHADSR).

The rest of this paper is organized as follows. Section 2 gives a brief overview of the related work. Section 3 introduces the proposed system in detail. Section 4 describes the performance analysis. Section 5 shows the simulation results. Finally, Sect. 6 concludes the paper.

2 Related Work

The aim of this section is to give information about Logical Hierarchical Addressing and Clustering Schemes within literature.

2.1 Logical Hierarchical Addressing (LHA)

The main idea of LHA protocol [10] for MANETs is to logically divide the IPv4 address space (32 bits) into three parts: MANET ID (16 bits), Extended MANET ID (6 bits) and HOST ID (10 bits). Any node in the network can act as an address agent (AA) and is capable of assigning one of the available addresses to the node requesting address. Here, hierarchy table is maintained at each node which has information about the addresses and parameters of its predecessor and successors. MAC address is used for address generation (NetworkID).

2.2 Clustering

In Clustering [5] the entire network is divided into smaller entities. These self-manageable entities are called as clusters. [6] Cluster Head (CH), Cluster Member (CM) or ordinary node (ON) and Gateway Node (GN) comprises of every cluster. ONs send the packets to their CH. These CHs then distributes the packets inside the cluster or forwards them to a GN. Clustering can reduce the transmission overhead during flooding on a large scale. In order to reduce the flooding of RREQ packets in reactive protocols like AODV, DSR etc. passive clustering can be implemented with them.

Ad Hoc OnDemand Distance Vector (AODV) with Passive Clustering.
Ad Hoc OnDemand Distance Vector (AODV) routing with passive clustering [2]
reduces the routing overhead and improve performance. By monitoring the MAC
traffic, the passive clustering algorithm will form a cluster infrastructure which
can effectively control RREQ flooding.

1. Each node periodically sends out HELLO messages every 1.5 s. The broadcast
   of HELLO message is cancelled if there is a data packet sent by the node in
   last period. Every transmission which includes data packets, RREQ, RREP
   and RERR will result into the timer scheduled earlier for HELLO messages
   being cancelled. HELLO messages are used for two reasons i.e. to detect link
   breaks and to prevent partial/stale cluster formation.
2. RREQ is forwarded only by Clusterhead, Gateway node and all nodes during initialization. These reduces RREQ broadcast as compared to standard
   AODV protocol, since ordinary do not participate in routing.

3   Proposed System

In DSR, in order to make connection from one node to another entire network
is flooded with requests. This motivated us as it seems unnecessary to flood the
entire network which might cause traffic congestions. In this section we present
our approach to reduce flooding of packets during Route discovery process. The
proposed system uses addressing scheme to efficiently reach destination node
avoiding excessive flooding. It is divided into mainly two parts: Address Assigning Protocol and Routing Protocol.

3.1   Address Assigning Protocol

In ad-hoc networks IPv4 addressing scheme is used where every node in network
is assigned 32 bit unique address. In order to facilitate effective route discovery,
idea of logically dividing IPv4 address space into Cluster Head address (24 bits)
and Node Member address (8 bits) is proposed here. This addressing scheme
allows the network to be partitioned into maximum 2^{24} clusters with each having maximum of 256 nodes. Nodes which are close to each other form clusters and
each clusters elects one node from the cluster as cluster-head. Along with management of intra and inter cluster communication, the cluster-head also does the
task of electing new cluster-head when required. There are three types of members in a cluster, namely, a cluster head, gateways nodes and ordinary nodes. As
the ordinary nodes do not forward any packets, the flooding is reduced as compared to standard DSR. Using a hierarchical addressing scheme our proposed
idea further reduces the flooding.

Cluster Address. Cluster address will be the same for every node belonging to
the same cluster which will consist of significant 24 bits of complete 32 bit address
of a node. Whether the destination of RREQ packet is a member of particular

```
if (requester is a non-cluster head)
{
        if(Table for cluster members shows available
        addresses)
                assign IP address
        else
                node cannot join current cluster
        /*
        Here the cluster address is same as the cluster head.
        We only need to check which nodeaddress ranging from
        0 - 255 is available for a non-cluster head
        */
}
else if(requester is a cluster head)
{
        /*
        Cluster address is divided into set of 4 bits.
        A data structure is maintained with to keep track of
        which cluster addresses from 0 - 15 are assigned and
        which are available. It will be an one dimensional
        array with row number representing cluster address
        and its value representing its availability
        E.g. int IPCH [16];
        Suppose IPCH [3] = 0. Then it means that cluster
        address 3 is not assigned and is available.
        */

        if((cluster head address table show available cluster
          address) && (not all the sets of 4 bits from cluster
          address are used))
        {
                Replace the set of bits after the one the
                ones that are already occupied with the
                count shown by the row number of cluster
                head address table.
        }
        else
        {
                Current cluster cannot assign address to the
                requester cluster head.
        }
}
```

Fig. 1. Address assignment

cluster can be easily determined by checking the significant 24 bits of destination address. If this address is same as the cluster address of the cluster head then the packet is meant for node inside this cluster. This eliminates the need for a cluster head to check its member table to search whether the destination address node is a part of its cluster or not.

Node Address. Node address consist of the least significant 8 bits of complete address. Each node in a particular cluster will have different node address making it unique in a network. Hierarchical addressing is used for addressing of nodes. In this system, cluster head can act as address agent and assign address to requester node. Each node can have only one predecessor i.e. address agent node assigning address and each cluster head has k successor nodes i.e. requester node. In our case only cluster heads are address agents. At the end of addressing, a tree like structure is formed where the addresses of child clusters are derived from their parent clusters and then addresses of node in a cluster are derived from their cluster head address.

Figure 2 gives us an example the addressing of clusters (Cluster Address) in a Network using Fig. 1 for addressing. The spheres represent clusters in a network and their addresses are given in both IPv4 format and hex format. The IPv4 format gives complete address of one of the nodes in cluster while the one in hex gives cluster address part of complete address.

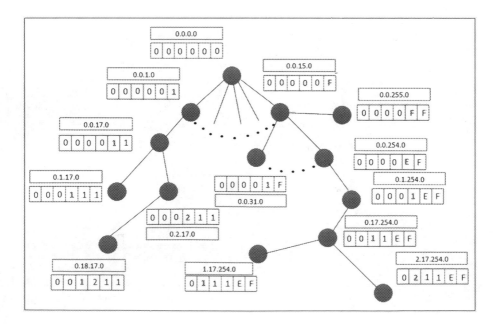

Fig. 2. Addressing of cluster heads

Working Scenarios

New Node enters the network. Addressing of the new node (successor) joining the network depends upon the cluster of which it becomes part of. The predecessor of the new node would always be a cluster head. The address of the new node would depend on the predecessor it joins. The new node joining the network can be an ordinary node or a CH or a gateway node. Address of new node depends on the type of node it becomes. For e.g., If a new node is an ordinary node and the address of the predecessor is 0.0.0.0 then new node joining would have address as 0.0.0.1. And if a new node is a CH and the address of the predecessor is 0.0.0.0 then new node joining would have address 0.0.1.0.

Node moves from one cluster to another. Due to mobility of the node, it may happen that node may leave the cluster and may form part of another cluster in the network. The cluster from which node exits will maintain IP addresses of the node left and assign it to the any new node joining the same. The cluster head maintains the table of cluster members so whenever new node joins the cluster, new address can be assigned to incoming node after checking availability of address in table.

Two independent network move closer to each other. When two independent networks form a single network, i.e. any node from each of the independent network form a link, our proposed addressing protocol would run again to form tree-like structure in the network.

Cluster head moves or exits from the network. When CH moves or exits the network, another member from the cluster would become CH using Lowest Id protocol. The address of moving CH would be assigned to the newly formed CH.

3.2   Routing Protocol

The base protocol to be used is Dynamic Source Routing (DSR). DSR is reactive routing protocol which does not rely on periodic table-update messages which are necessary in the table-driven approach. Routes are established in route construction phase of DSR by flooding Route Request (RREQ) packets in the network. Once the destination node received RREQ packet. It sends a Route Reply packet (RREP) to the source node which contains the route by which RREQ packet reached destination node.

Using clustering along with DSR, the network is divided into clusters. Information is exchanged to maintain the clusters and their neighbouring cluster information. Clustering is used divide the network and hierarchical addressing is used to create a tree like structure in the network. If the source node and destination node share as immediate predecessor or if source node is predecessor of destination node, then the destination node finding is the most easiest. The presence of a node in cluster can be easily determined by its cluster address part of complete address. If by comparing cluster addresses, it is found that the node cannot be present in the current cluster or any of its successor clusters then the forwarding of IP packets is contained at that node. This reduces unnecessary flooding of RREQ in network. Also there is no need to check member table for the purpose of determining whether a particular node belongs to the current cluster or not. However when destination node is not a successor of source node or if the destination node cannot be reached through immediate predecessor of destination node the packet processing cannot take place entirely by method described above. Here the RREQ packet needs to travel towards the common predecessor of source and destination. This upward movement cannot be transpired by simply comparing the destination and current node address. Here the node checks whether it is a predecessor of source node and forwards the packet only if its turns out that condition is true. It indicates that the packet needs to travel towards the root node in the hierarchy in order to find the common predecessor cluster of the source cluster and destination node cluster. The way it works is by treating 00000000 as intermediate destination address till it finds common predecessor cluster of source and destination node. On reaching common predecessor, normal working of comparing cluster addresses of current and destination address in order to find destination node takes place. Figure 4 gives an example of working scenario of Route Discovery. It represents a network formed by using clustering with DSR and gives us an example of working scenario of Route Discovery process in the proposed CBHADSR scheme. The spheres represent clusters formed and they are addressed using addressing scheme described earlier. Here source node is 0.1.17.0 which is part of cluster with cluster address 0.1.17 and destination address is 0.1.35.0 which is part of cluster with cluster address 0.1.35. The arrows represent the RREQ packet traveling from source to destination using algorithm in Fig. 3. The solid arrows mean that the packet is forwarded to current cluster's neighboring node while the dashed arrows represent discarding of RREQ in current cluster. Consider the following working scenarios:

Source Node is Part of Root Cluster or is a Predecessor of Destination Node. Consider source node having an IP address 0.0.0.0 and destination node with IP address 0.49.18.0 referring Fig. 4. For this situation, using algorithm in Fig. 3, we can find that the source node is predecessor of destination node though not an immediate one. So after comparing destination cluster address with source cluster address we know that it is a child of source node. Hence the source node will forward the packet to its child nodes. Clusters with cluster address 0.0.34.X, 0.0.10.X, 0.33.18.X and 0.17.18.X will not forward packets to their children as they have different cluster address as compared to destination cluster address. This process of forwarding and comparing cluster address will continue until destination address is reached.

Source Address :
0.0.2.0 [00000000 00000000 00000001 00000000]

Destination Address :
0.49.18.0 [00000000 01001001 00010010 00000000]

```
if(tvs_allowedtoforwardpacket(Node_Addr,Destination_Addr))
{        /* Broadcast the RREQ packet. Here source and
         destination part of same subtree */
}
else
{        if(tvs_allowedtoforwardpacket(Node_Addr,Source_Addr))
         {       /*
                 Broadcasts the RREQ packet. Here source and
                 destination are part of different subtrees.
                 */
         }
         else
         {       //Discard the message
         }
}
int  tvs_allowedtoforwardpacket(Addr_1,Addr_2)
{        /*
         Compares Addr_1 and Addr_2 address finds whether the
         Addr_1 can forward the packet or not
         */
}
```

Fig. 3. Packet processing

Node Address (Can forward the packet) :
0.0.18.0 [00000000 00000000 **00010010** 00000000]

Node Address (Cannot forward the packet) :
0.0.34.0 [00000000 00000000 **00100010** 00000000]

The cluster address of destination is compared to that of the current node cluster address until all zero section of 4 bits is encountered. The number of occupied sections tell us about the level of the cluster in hierarchy. Figure 4 depicts pictorially above example. The number 1 besides the arrow denotes the packets from example of this scenario. The dashed arrow means that the packet is discarded at the current node while the solid means that they are forwarded by the current node.

Source and Destination Do Not Have Same the Immediate Predecessor. Consider source node having an IP address 0.18.17.0 and destination node with IP address 0.49.18.0 referring Fig. 4. For this situation, using algorithm in Fig. 3, we can find that source and destination node do not have same immediate predecessor. Hence the source node will forward the packet upwards until it reaches a node common to source and destination node. In this scenario node with IP address 0.0.0.0 will be the common predecessor.

Source Address :
0.18.17.0 [00000000 00010010 00010001 00000000]

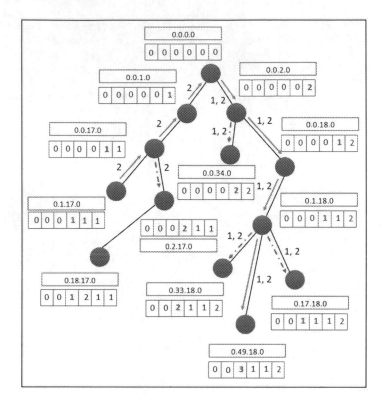

Fig. 4. Route discovery process

Destination Address :
0.49.18.0 [00000000 01001001 00010010 00000000]

Node Address (Can forward the packet) :
0.0.17.0 [00000000 00000000 **00010001** 00000000]

Node Address (Cannot forward the packet) :
0.1.17.0 [00000000 00000001 **00010001** 00000000]
The upward movement of packet is performed by comparing cluster address of
source node with the cluster address of current node. The node can broadcast
the packet if is predecessor to source node. The number 2 besides the arrow in
Fig. 4 denotes the packets from example of this scenario. Once common node is
found, packet can be forwarded to destination node using steps defined in above
scenario.

4   Performance Analysis

The proposed system will be effective as follows. In original DSR, while making a connection from one node to another, flooding takes place. Every node broadcasts a RREQ packet.

That is if there are N nodes in a network then N−1 nodes will broadcast the RREQ packets. Where as in the proposed algorithm, the nodes on the path broadcast the packet. If there are H nodes in the path then

$$H - 1 \tag{1}$$

nodes will broadcast the packet. Therefore, the proposed algorithm broadcasts

$$N - 1 - (H - 1) \quad i.e. \quad N - H \tag{2}$$

less packets than the original DSR.

The Best Case Analysis. As the addressing is done by dividing the address space, the algorithm will work best, for a given number of nodes, if the depth of the tree is minimal. That is if every Cluster Head has maximum possible adjacent cluster head/Neighbor cluster heads. This way addresses are saved for more nodes and network can be expanded efficiently. In short, for a dense network the algorithm will be more useful.

The Worst Case Analysis. A vice-a-versa to the best case, if the clusters appear in a linear structure, i.e., if every cluster head is connected to only one successor, the address space will be used up fast and the algorithm will work as standard DSR..

5   Results

Below is the comparison of proposed algorithm with original DSR algorithm. Figure 5 shows the efficiency achieved in terms of RREQ Flooded in the network. The proposed algorithm was simulated using stationary nodes (20, 30 and 50) and simulations results show reduction in RREQ flooding. QualNet allows us to simulate entire Ad-hoc Network Environment. It also allows us to set various parameters for each node like mobility, routing protocol etc.

We implemented Cluster Based Hierarchical Addressing for Dynamic Source Routing without node mobility and assigned our addresses manually. Only cluster heads were considered in simulation. In each scenario every node acted as cluster head. Various parameters such as animation speed, statistics generation etc. can be controlled before execution of scenario. The node mobility was not considered during the simulation (Fig. 6 and Table 1).

Table 1. Comparison of RREQ forwarded in CBHADSR and ordinary DSR

Number of nodes	Total number of RREQ packets forwarded using CBHADSR	Total number of RREQ using DSR	Percentage deduction
20	17	82	79.26
30	11	121	90.90
50	17	204	91.66

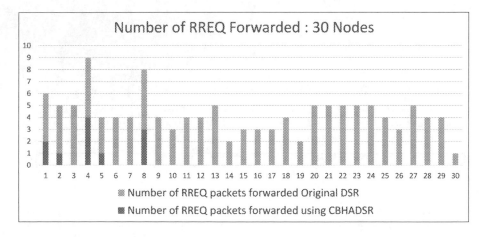

Fig. 5. RREQ flooding in DSR and CBHADSR: 30 nodes

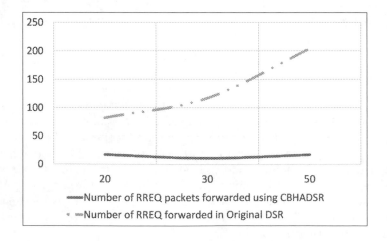

Fig. 6. RREQ flooding in DSR and CBHADSR comparison

6 Conclusion

In this paper, Cluster based Hierarchical Addressing for Dynamic Source Routing i.e. CBHDSR is proposed for ad hoc networks. Comparing the proposed protocol with DSR protocol, it is found that CBHDSR performs better than DSR in terms of flooding and congestion as it reduces the route requests packets remarkably. Even in the worst case the CBHDSR will be equivalent to the original DSR. As the flooding is decreased it can result into better battery lives of the nodes in the network.

By introducing Hierarchical address in DSR the number of unnecessary flooding was reduced by 79% in ad hoc networks (stationary nodes) in scenario of 20 nodes. Even though the above results are recorded with zero node mobility, node mobility won't majorly affect the results as number of floods to keep node addresses will be far less than original DSR.

References

1. Bhatt, U.R., Nema, N., Upadhyay, R.: Enhanced dsr: an efficient routing protocol for manet, pp. 215–219 (2014)
2. Rani, P., Kumar, C., Kumar, G.: Efficient-dynamic source routing (e-dsr)
3. Munjal, A., Singh, Y.N.: Review of stateful address auto configuration protocols. Ad Hoc Netw. 3(C), 257–268 (2015)
4. DSR. https://tools.ietf.org/html/draft-ietf-manet-dsr-10
5. Lala, A., Kolici, V., Mirjeta, A., Spaho, E.: Clustering algorithms in MANETs: a review. In: Ninth International Conference on Complex, Intelligent, and Software Intensive Syaytems (CISIS), pp. 330–335 (2015)
6. Harous, S., Bentaleb, A., Boubetra, A.: Survey of clustering schemes in mobile ad hoc networks. Commun. Netw. 5(02), 8–14 (2013)
7. Kwon, T.J., Gerla, M., Pei, G.: On demand routing in large ad hoc wireless networks with passive clustering. In: Proceedings of Wireless Communications and Networking Conference (WCNC), vol. 1, pp. 100–105 (2000)
8. Prakash, R., Nesargi, S.: Manetconf: configuration of hosts in a mobile ad hoc network. In: Proceedings of the Twenty-First Annual Joint Conference of the IEEE Computer and Communications Societies, vol. 2, pp. 1059–1068 (2000)
9. Mutka, M.W., Zhou, H., Ni, L.M.: Prophet address allocation for large scale manet, vol.3, pp. 423–434
10. Mitschele-Thiel, A., Yousef, A., Al-Mahdi, H.: Lha: logical hierarchical addressing protocol for mobile ad-hoc networks. In: Proceedings of the 2nd ACM Workshop on Performance Monitoring and Measurement of Heterogeneous Wireless and Wired Networks

Design of an Area Efficient and Low Power MAC Unit

Vinod Kapse[1(✉)], Aashmi Jain[1(✉)], and Manisha Pattanaik[2]

[1] Department of Electronics and Communication Engineering,
Gyan Ganga Institute of Technology and Sciences, Jabalpur, India
vinodkapse@ggits.org, aashmijain17@gmail.com
[2] Department of Information and Communication Technology, ABV-Indian
Institute of Information Technology and Management, Gwalior, India
manishapattanaik@iiitm.ac.in

Abstract. A design of an area efficient and low power 16 bit Multiply and Accumulate (MAC) unit is implemented in this paper. MAC unit performs various Digital Signal Processing applications generally contain number of repetitive methods having multiplications and additions. The MAC unit is designed by Modified Wallace Multiplier (MWM) using compressor with Carry Increment Adder and Carry Select Adder as final adder separately. The proposed design is implemented in Verilog Hardware Description Language (HDL) using Xilinx 14.5 Virtex7 and synthesis is done in Synopsys Design Compiler using Designware logic standard cell area library of 90 nm and 45 nm technology.

Keywords: Modified Wallace Multiplier · Compressor · Carry Increment Adder · Carry Select Adder · Multiply and accumulator

1 Introduction

In the modern world, devices are made use of RISC processor and Digital Signal Processing (DSP). In DSP, one of the most intricate operation is the multiply accumulate operation [1, 2]. For high performance MAC unit is the basic element in applications like in convolution, inner products, and filters. DSP uses non linear functions such as Discrete Cosine Transform (DCT) and Discrete Wavelet Transform (DWT). As MAC unit runs independent of the CPU, can process data separately.

The basic concern of MAC design is to achieve increase in its speed. As speed and output rate are always the main concerns of DSP systems [3, 4]. MAC unit performs many DSP applications involving multiplications and/or additions. The rate of the processor mainly depends on the speed of the MAC unit hence complexity of MAC unit design and power consumption is the major concern for real time processing applications.

MAC operation is the basic operation used in digital design of DSP applications, multimedia processing, image processing and other applications which require repetitive multiplications and additions such as Fast Fourier Transform (FFT), Finite Impulse Response (FIR). To improve the speed, MAC unit depends on the two main sub-units. The first is the multiplication process and the other one is to accumulate.

© Springer Nature Singapore Pte Ltd. 2016
A. Unal et al. (Eds.): SmartCom 2016, CCIS 628, pp. 276–284, 2016.
DOI: 10.1007/978-981-10-3433-6_33

The basic function of proposed 16 bit MAC unit is to multiply the multiplier and multiplicand and add the required product with the result stored in an accumulator.

The paper is alienated into six sections. In the first section discuss about the introduction of the MAC unit. Second section describes the basic function of MAC unit. Section third deals with the operations of MWM without using 4:2 compressor, MWM using 4:2 compressor and Reduced Area Multiplier (RAM). Carry Increment Adder (CIAD) and Carry Select Adder (CSIA), discuss in the fourth section. The obtained results of 8 bit and 16 bit MAC unit and conclusions are made in fifth and sixth sections.

2 Operation of MAC Unit

MAC unit consists of three sub blocks – multiplier, adder and accumulator. Multiplier involves number of partial products. Adder is use to add up the results of partial product generate in multiplier and then final save into an accumulator. The inputs of MAC unit are taken from the location of memory and sends to the building block of multiplier. The input obtained from memory location is of n bit, after multiplication the obtained output is of 2n bit. The 2n bit output acts as the input of the adder where the addition operation will be carry out. The generated output of an adder is of $2n + 1$ bit (sum + carry). Output of an adder is then forward to an accumulator as Parallel in Parallel out (PIPO) which is taken as the final output of MAC or fed back as one of an input of adder. Figure 1 shows the basic structure of 16 bit MAC unit. The basic purpose of MAC unit describe by the following equation.

$$z \leftarrow z + (x \times y) \tag{1}$$

Where, x and y represent the n bit of multiplier and multiplicand each and addend z is of $2n + 1$ bit. As the processor performance has improved, the requirement of high

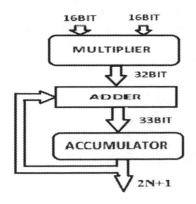

Fig. 1. Basic architecture of 16 bit MAC unit.

speed and optimum power consumptions of arithmetic blocks also increased. The hardware unit performs such an operation called as a MAC unit.

$$Z = \sum J_i K_i \tag{2}$$

3 Architecture of Multiplier

The basic function of the multiplier is to multiply the two values and generate an output which is their product only. Multiplication has two operations, the partial product generation and their accumulation. Therefore, there are two ways to speed up the multiplication, reduce the partial product and pace up the accumulation. The second, a smaller number of partial products also reduce the complexity of multiplication results decrease the requirement to accumulate the partial products.

To design a fast multiplication process should follow the three steps:-

- To produce the partial products.
- To reduce the partial products by reduction schemes.
- Carry propagation adder for final stage addition.

3.1 Modified Wallace Multiplier Without Using Compressor

Modified Wallace reduction method of partial product matrix in a multiplier [1], as the partial product (N × N bits) generated simply by multiplying the multiplicand with the multiplier then shift the left half bits upward to figure an upturned pyramid to generate the next phase of reduction. In next phase the adjacent rows are grouped into three rows such that each set of three rows are further reduce to two rows using half adder for two rows and full adder for three rows and passing a single bit as same as to the further stage. This method of reduction is continued to every stage until two rows remain left. The left over two rows are summed by carry propagation adder.

Figure 2 shows 8 bit MWM without using 4:2 compressor have total number of four stages to reduce the partial product matrix of multiplication.

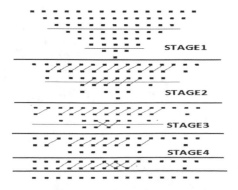

Fig. 2. 8 bit Modified Wallace Multiplier without using compressor.

3.2 Proposed Modified Wallace Multiplier Using 4:2 Compressor

In the proposed MWM using 4:2 compressor first generate the partial products by just multiply the multiplicand with the multiplier. In the next step an invert pyramid figure is designed by aligning the bits taking from last row and continues with the last bit of every row up to the last bit of first row. The process of above alignment is continue till the upend pyramid shape of reduction stage will occur. The pyramidal shape is design to deal the maximum number of bits at a same time in each row. Figure 3 shows the pyramidal shape of 8 bit partial product.

An 8 bit MWM using 4:2 compressor have only two stages of partial product reduction. In this reduction scheme the adjacent rows are grouped in such a way that the three rows are convert into two rows using full adder (3, 2 counter) and four rows are reduce to two rows using 4:2 compressor and passing a single bit and two rows as same as to the next stage. The process of reduction is continue until the group of two rows are left then using carry propagation adder to sum up the final two rows and generate the final multiplier product output.

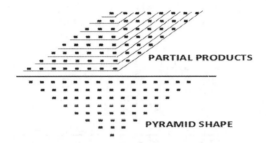

Fig. 3. Pyramid shape of 8 bit partial products.

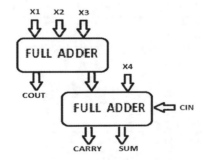

Fig. 4. Basic architecture of 4:2 compressor.

In this way numbers of rows of partial product matrix are quickly convert into two rows and numbers of stages get decrease. MWM using 4:2 compressor have only two stages to reduce the partial products which make design faster and have less power consumption. Figure 4 shows the 4:2 compressor include five number of inputs (four input bits + Cin) and three number of outputs (sum + carry + Cout) using two stages of full adders connected serially.

Different designs of compressors discussed [3] but above described basic compressor only give the correct output for every four combination of input bits. The basic 4:2 compressor have no incorrect error rate (output) for any combinations of input bits where error rate equals to the ratio of the number of the incorrect output over the total number of outputs. Figure 5 shows the 8 bit MWM using basic 4:2 compressor have two stages to reduce the partial products matrix.

3.3 Reduced Area Multiplier

Reduced Area Multiplier (RAM) [7] is one of the method has been discussed for high speed parallel multiplication of two binary bits and to reduce the partial products such that whose sum equals to the product of two binary numbers. Carry propagation adder is used to sum the resulting two binary numbers.

The reduction scheme requires less components and fewer complexities compare to Wallace and Dadda multiplier. Figure 6 shows the 8 bit RAM include three stages of reduction matrix. The reduction technique uses only (3, 2) counter and (2, 2) counter.

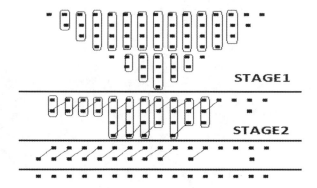

Fig. 5. A 8 bit Modified Wallace Multiplier using 4:2 compressor.

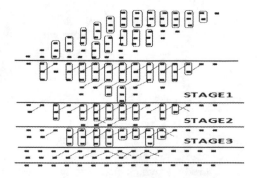

Fig. 6. A 8bit Reduced area multiplier.

In this approach the partial products are not change into pyramidal shape but directly reduced using counters. RAM has total three number of reduction stages for partial product matrix. The RAM has advantage in area as well as speed compare to MWM without using compressor.

4 Adder Topology

Arithmetic unit is an indispensable block for any digital system, microcontroller and DSP application or in any data processing unit. Additions become an important operation and a hardware unit used to implement such an operation called Adders.

4.1 Carry Increment Adder

Carry Increment Adder (CIAD) comprises of Ripple carry adder (RCA) with carry increment circuit. CIAD is an area efficient adder as the carry out increment to the increment block. The increment circuit consists of number of half adders arranged in a sequential manner [2]. The addition operation of CIAD is performed by simply dividing all the bits into four groups and each group performs 4 bit Ripple carry addition have sequential full adder structure.

The first RCA adds the desired bits and generate the separate sum and carry. The carry out of first RCA sends to the Cin of conditional incremental block and the first four bits of sum of first RCA is directly taken from RCA output. The second RCA performs the same as the first RCA. Figure 7 shows the 16 bit Carry Increment adder. The conditional incremental block performs the carry increment operation and generates the second RCA sum bits and so on.

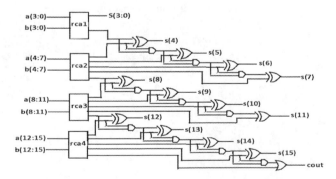

Fig. 7. A 16 bit Carry Increment adder.

4.2 Carry Select Adder

Carry Select Adder (CSIA) is designed by share out the Common Boolean Logic term in summation generation. CSIA architecture has independent production of sum and carry i.e. Carry in = 0 and Carry in = 1 are executed parallel. Depending upon Cin, the exterior multiplexer selects the carry to be propagated to next stage [5]. Further based on the input carry, obtained the sum bit. Hence, the delay will also reduce. Figure 8 shows the 16 bit CSIA is shared by the combinational logic term contain an XOR gate and an inverter to produce every sum bit and OR, AND gates for carry output, MUX is used to select the desired output according to the Cin.

5 Performance Evaluation of MAC Units and Simulation Results

The complete design of MAC unit is developed using Verilog-HDL. For design synthesis purpose Xilinx ISE 14.5 tool is used. Simulation is done on Xilinx Integrated simulation environment and evaluated on Synopsys Design compiler in 90 nm and 45 nm technology. The MAC unit operates at a frequency of 740.741 MHz. Tables 1 and 2 shows the comparative analysis of area and power in 90 nm and 45 nm.

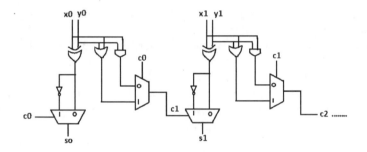

Fig. 8. A 16 bit Carry Select adder.

Table 1. Cell area and power analysis of 8 bit MAC unit

MAC Unit		Technology	Total area (μm^2)	Total power
MWM w/o compressor	CIAD	90 nm	12986.41	293 µW
		45 nm	2437.06	0.249 mW
	CSIA	90 nm	13718.04	290 µW
		45 nm	2571.23	0.257 mW
MWM with compressor	CIAD	90 nm	11450.48	282 µW
		45 nm	2097.67	0.23 mW
	CSIA	90 nm	12124.68	278 µW
		45 nm	2231.85	0.237 mW
Reduced Area Multiplier	CIAD	90 nm	11325.22	291 µW
		45 nm	2116.02	0.226 mW
	CSIA	90 nm	11999.42	284 µW
		45 nm	2250.19	0.233 mW

Table 2. Cell area and power analysis of 16 bit MAC unit

MAC Unit		Technology	Total area (μm^2)	Total power
MWM w/o compressor	CIAD	90 nm	48295.84	1045 μW
		45 nm	8878.16	0.869 mW
	CSIA	90 nm	49482.13	1021 μW
		45 nm	9112.13	0.878 mW
MWM with compressor	CIAD	90 nm	42005.99	994 μW
		45 nm	7482.9	0.793 mW
	CSIA	90 nm	43192.28	980 μW
		45 nm	7716.88	0.804 mW
Reduced Area multiplier	CIAD	90 nm	41443	1027 μW
		45 nm	7583	0.771 mW
	CSIA	90 nm	42630	1028 μW
		45 nm	7817	0.786 mW

A 16 bit MAC unit is designed using different multipliers and adders. For comparative study the multipliers used are

- MWM without using compressor
- MWM using compressor
- Reduced area multiplier

The different adders used in the study are

- Carry Increment adder
- Carry Select adder

6 Conclusion

A high performance of 16 bit MAC unit is implemented in this paper. From the design analysis of proposed MAC unit with MWM using 4:2 compressor and RAM have better performance, area efficient with low power compare to MAC unit includes MWM without using compressor. The cell area analysis of proposed MAC unit with MWM using compressor and RAM provide an improvement of 13.02% and 14.18% compare to MAC without using compressor in 90 nm and 15.72% and 14.5% in 45 nm with CIAD respectively.

Similarly, the cell area analyses of proposed MAC unit include CSIA with MWM using compressor and RAM give an improvement of 12.7% and 13.8% compare to MAC without compressor in 90 nm and 15.3% and 14.2% in 45 nm. Hence, MAC unit enhance the performance using compressor in a multiplier.

Acknowledgment. The authors acknowledge the support of labs and tool resources used in Indian Institute of Information Technology and Management, Gwalior.

References

1. Waters, R.S., Swartzlander, E.E.: A reduced complexity Wallace multiplier reduction. IEEE Trans. Comput. **59**, 1134–1137 (2010)
2. Vijayan, R.U.V., Mohanapriya, M., Paul, S.: Area, delay and power comparison of adder topologies. Int. J. VLSI Commun. Syst. (VLSICS) **3**, 153–168 (2012)
3. Chang, C.H., Gu, J.: Ultra low-voltage low-power CMOS 4-2 and 5-2 compressors for fast arithmetic circuits. IEEE Trans. Circ. Syst. **51**, 1985–1997 (2004)
4. Ramkumar, B., Kittur, H.: Low-power and area-efficient carry select adder. IEEE Trans. Very Large Scale Integr. (VLSI) Syst. **20**, 371–375 (2012)
5. Wey, I.C., Ho, C.C., Lin, Y.S., Peng, C.C.: An area-efficient carry select adder design by sharing the common logic term. In: Proceedings of the International MultiConference of Engineers and Computer Scientists (IMECS), vol. 2, March 2012
6. Jagadeesh, P., Ravi, S., Mallikarjun, K.H.: Design of high performance 64 bit MAC unit. In: International Conference on Circuits Power and Computing Technologies (ICCPCT), pp. 782–786, March 2013
7. Bickerstaff, K., Schulte, M., Swartzlander, E.: Reduced area multipliers. In: Proceedings of the International Conference on Application Specific Array Processors, pp. 478–489, October 1993

An Approach for Efficient Machine Translation Using Translation Memory

Sunita Rawat[1]([✉]), M.B. Chandak[2], and Nekita Chauhan[1]

[1] Information Technology, GHRCE, Nagpur, India
ssunitarawatt@gmail.com, nekita.chauhan@raisoni.net
[2] Computer Science and Engineering, RCOEM, Nagpur, India
chandakmb@gmail.com

Abstract. Since 1980s, Translation Memory (TM) have been accessible. It becomes an important language technology to assist the translation. It is a database that saves "segments", which may be sentences, paragraphs or sentence-kind elements. Tree Adjoining Grammar (TAG) is planned to use along with Machine Translation System (MTS). To make efficient machine translation and to reduce the response time of online machine translation, we come up with the use of a TM. The combined architecture of machine translation with translation memory is indicated. To make the translator's task faster, more efficient and easier, translator tools were designed. Translation tools were designed with the objective to minimize monotonous translation work.

Keywords: Machine Translation (MT) · Tree Adjoining Grammar (TAG) · Translation Memory (TM)

1 Introduction

The Overall requirement for translation is growing strongly without an abundant growth in the several translation experts. Translation Memory is a categorized, organized, segmented and parsed corpus of already-translated examples, utilized to reduce the overload on the industries. It acts as a reference model to help the existing experts in new translations. It provides excellent coherent translation when the likeness in texts is more such as updated manuals. TM is not only solution for human translation professionals but also it can be a solution for a complicated online translation system to fulfill the industry requirements.

Currently, hybrid methods of TM are used in most of the applications, in which TM is combined with MTS for better performance. To increase the performance of Example-Based Machine Translation and Statistical Machine Translation, many methods so far used TM [2–5]. For finding the better match these systems uses fuzzy matching algorithm [6]. Already translated texts are not completely utilized as this method also has dependency on sequencing of lexicon. To get rid of the language dependency of Translation Memory and to adequately make use of the already translated text; we come up with a MTS integrated with language independent Translation Memory approach,

© Springer Nature Singapore Pte Ltd. 2016
A. Unal et al. (Eds.): SmartCom 2016, CCIS 628, pp. 285–291, 2016.
DOI: 10.1007/978-981-10-3433-6_34

formed on the Tree Adjoining Grammar aka (TAG). As Tree Adjoining Grammar uses sentence structure, it is not depend on input sentence lexicon [1].

Near about all TM tools prior to indexing the text do the process of segmentation and alignment. whereas, few tools uses different approach, known as the full-text method. Rather than segmenting the texts in the prior, they keep it as full bitexts. Compared to the conventional approach this method has two important benefits: (a) Creation of very big Translation Memory database in less time which includes previously translated text (b) the confinement of context for any likeness found and recommend to the user.

2   Corpora

Here, we discussed distinct datasets of parallel corpora accessible for English <->
Hindi. In 2010, Bojar discussed about three datasets use as the language pair [17, 18].
Out of that one corpus accessible from the CIIL/EMILLE corpus made by a partnership between Central Institute of Indian Languages, India and Lancaster University, by the EMILLE plan. The parallel corpora contains English text with its Hindi translation. The corpus consists of texts from various domains like health, education, etc. A part of this parallel corpus was approved and distributed as module of the ACL (2005) dispensed work on word-alignment [19]. DARPA-TIDES is the second corpus that available for English <-> Hindi.

Excluding above mentioned datasets, attempt to make substantial multilingual parallel corpora for English, Hindi and various Indian languages is also a part of both the projects: Indian Languages Corpora Initiative also known as ILCI and English to Indian languages MT also known as EILMT. Mentioned projects have targeted on gathering resources for health and tourism domains [21]. An attempt to make these resources promotes fast creation of substantial parallel corpora.

3   Machine Translation for English→Hindi

Although techniques for Statistical Machine Translation have enhanced greedily in the last few years, task focussed on applying SMT approaches for Indian languages has started currently. In last few years there has been a rise in making general-purpose Statistical Machine Translation systems for interpreting from English to any other Indian languages [13–16]. English to Hindi MT not only suffering due to deficiency of substantial training corpora, but also deal with a number of problems due to unlikeness in both the languages.

In [16] author discussed techniques to manage the morphological complications of languages used in India, while translating among themselves. In [15] author designed a context based technique for English to Hindi translation. Also, he developed a dependency-based static machine translation for English to any other Indian language.

In case of Transfer-based machine translation, the task of translation is done in three parts – first is to analyse the source sentence, a second step is transfer component and last step is generation module to form translations in the resultant language. In first phase, by using a syntactic parser along with other modules like word-sense disambiguation, sentence in the source language is analyzed. In second step, translation of the source text is done by the transfer component by using bilingual dictionary. İt also perform syntactic transformations to represent ordering of the word to the target language. In last step, the generation module generates exact word in the resultant language.

By applying transfer based techniques, Anusaaraka was built, that was one of the earliest effort to develop machine translation systems for English to any other Indian languages. Two things that system uses are: one is multiple state-of-the art parsers which is used in the source sentence analization. And second is components to recognize multi-word expressions. Parallaly the EILMT project results into manufacturing of both example-based translation system and another is Shakti, a transfer-based system.

Both transfer-based system and statistical system uses various pipelines setup to analyze texts available in Hindi and English. The differences in these pipelines creates problem in duplicating experiments and exactly correlating the outputs from various systems.

4   Translation Memory Tools - An Overview

The task of TM is to "memorise" or to remember the translations created by a human translator. Commonly used TMs contains database that saves segment pairs which includes input text pairs with its translation. By applying certain predefined rules the tools analyze a segment. While translation process TM tool use to look up each input segment in that TM. In case, exact match is available, system will give translated part of that matched segment as an advice for reuse to the translator. In case exact match is not available, system try to find somewhat similar segments. As the input string not matches fully but some percentage, so it is known as fuzzy matches. Along with input if translator gets any fuzzy match then they have to decide how much they can reuse for the given translation. Generally, translator can also fix the margin of "fuzziness". Therefor use of a TM can improve consistency and it also saves the time. Specially it works very well for the translation of monotonous documents such as manuals, technical documentation, etc.

5   Different Models Using Translation Memory

Essentially all TM tools were manufactured with the same purpose in mind: the text that has been translated already before need not have to be translated another time from zero or beginning. It should be available in reference material or in the database. Translator takes the decision whether to reuse the available translation or to modify it. Various technologies are used to get this done [20]. Few of the available tools use the concept of referencing the files of an old project. This model takes already translated files as the source for opinions of new translations. Reference model outperforms for projects or manuals having too much updates containing very few changes (Fig. 1).

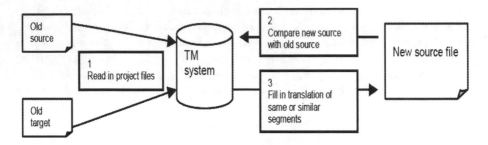

Fig. 1. Reference model

All the translations made by the translator stores in the database, that is not depend on context and is very helpful if same kind of segment comes in different document. TM that uses mostly can work with any language available on user sysem (Fig. 2).

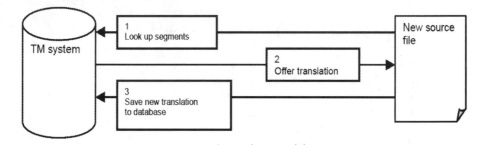

Fig. 2. Database model

6   Translating by Using Translation Memory Tools

The text which we want to translate it includes headings, index entries, list items, sentences, etc., known as "segments". TM has some rules, by using which it remember, beginning and ending of a segment. While translating, TM reads one by one segment, finds if any already translated or related text present in the database and if it is available, along with segment it will offer to the translator. After this translator takes the decision, whether to reuse the already translated text or modify it to form new translation and save it to database [20]. Therefore, translator use to make segment pairs that may be available for future reference. This is very helpful while processing very big batch of files.

7   Exchange of Data Between Translation Memory

In some cases, translators were not able to access data from one TM to another for using it again. Tools developers tried to solve this problem by including export functionalities for few proprietary patterns of other developers. However, it was not possible for every tool to support all import and export facility of remaining other tools. Recently, the tool developers decided to use one common pattern for representing the data. Because of using standard formats it becomes very simple to exchange translation memory data between two systems but still results are not ever totally acceptable. This standard format is known as Translation Memory Exchange format, also denoted by TMX. In this format, data available in translation memory (TM) is represented in XML.

8 Machine Translation Using Translation Memory

Proposed Machine Translation System is a domain precise online multi-user Machine Translation application. It consists of different mutually connected modules like pre-processor module, pre-parser module, Tree Adjoining Grammar based parser and generator module, semantic analyzer module and last one is synthesizer module as shown in Figs. 3 and 4.

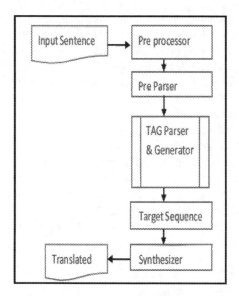

Fig. 3. Architecture of MTS

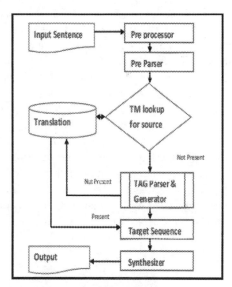

Fig. 4. Architecture of MTS with TM

The task of Pre-processing module is to break down the text into paragraphs, and then paragraph will get divide into sentences and atlast a sentence will get break into words. Depending on Named-Entity Recognition rule primary chunking of lexicons can be accomplish in this module [7]. In pre-parsing, it use to categorize the words depending on lexical class thus also known as Part-of-Speech (POS) tagger. In next module the POS output of source sentence is syntactically and semantically gets compile by the TAG parser and finally transforms it into derivation tree. Compiled output of the parser comes to the TAG generator and TAG generator translates it into required language. The task assigned to TAG parsing and generation includes considerable calculation complexity like selection of tree, its alternative and addition of one tree on another [1]. Therefore, for parsing it requires very large memory and processing time. Finally, the task of synthesizer module is to perform more smoothening of the resultant output for fluency.

In Machine Translation System each sentence has to go through all the given modules which takes too much time. Whereas, expectation from online translation engine is, it should give output as fast as possible, to accomplish this we will do data parallelization as well as task parallelization [8, 9]. To distribute multiple sentences among all nodes, we will use a load balancing technique [10]. As we will use task parallelism, at the architectural level we need to form multithreading between different modules. We will accomplish a great enhancement in execution time by parallelising the system [8]. As machine translation is a time consuming and complicated task [11, 12], we need to keep finding different techniques to accomplish more speedup.

9   Conclusion

In this paper, we introduced about the distinct datasets of parallel corpora accessible for English <−> Hindi. A conventional Translation Memory is used to help the translator, and it saves the already translated human translator's text to use it further. To speed up the manual translation different translation tools are developed along with translation memory technology. Manual interference is needed in these type of tools for post editing the similar text from the translation memory which slows down the process of translation. To overcome this problem, translation memory combined with machine translation system to achieve efficiency and accuracy in translation process.

We are also planning to combine translation memory with fully automated machine translation system which is based on TAG to get rid of the problem of dependency on language in the reusability of a translation memory. The complete translation memory depends on arrangement of input sentence. Correlation of input sentence with the previously translated sentence enhances consistency as well as saves time. Already available translations can be used as it is if it matches or can be edited to make relevant translations.

References

1. Joshi, A.K., Levy, L.S., Takahashi, M.: Tree adjunct grammars. J. Comput. Syst. Sci. **10**(1), 136–163 (1975)
2. Biçici, E., Dymetman, M.: Dynamic translation memory: using statistical machine translation to improve translation memory fuzzy matches. In: Gelbukh, A. (ed.) CICLing 2008. LNCS, vol. 4919, pp. 454–465. Springer, Heidelberg (2008). doi:10.1007/978-3-540-78135-6_39
3. Zhechev, V., Genabith, J.V.: Seeding statistical machine translation with TM output through tree-based structural alignment. In: SSST-4 4th Workshop on Syntax and Structure in Statistical Translation, Beijing, China, pp. 43–51, 28 August 2010
4. Wang, K., Zong, C., Su, K.: Integrating translation memory into phrase-based machine translation during decoding. In: The 51st Annual Meeting of the Association for Computational Linguistics (ACL 2013), Sofia, Bulgaria, 4–9 August 2013
5. Simard, M., Isabelle, P.: Phrase-based machine translation in a computer assisted translation environment. In: The Twelfth Machine Translation Summit (MT Summit XII), pp. 120–127 (2009)
6. Fuzzy Match Algorithm. http://en.wikipedia.org/wiki/Fuzzy_string_searching

7. Nadeau, D., Sekine, S.: A survey of named entity recognition and classification. Lingvisticae Investigationes **30**(1), 3–26 (2007)
8. Tomar, A., Bodhankar, J., Kurariya, P., Anarase, P., Jain, P., Lele, A., Darbari, H., Bhavsar, V.C.: Parallel implementation of machine translation using MPJ express. In: Proceedings of the National Conference on Parallel Computing Technologies (PARCOMPTECH), Bangalore, India, pp. 223–233. Center for Development of Advanced Computing (CDAC), 21–23 February 2013
9. Tomar, A., Bodhankar, J., Kurariya, P., Anarase, P., Jain, P., Lele, A., Darbari, H., Bhavsar, V.C.: High performance natural language processing services in the GARUDA grid. In: Proceedings of the National Conference on Parallel Computing Technologies (PARCOMPTECH), Bangalore, India, pp. 249–261. Center for Development of Advanced Computing (CDAC), 21–23 February 2013
10. Bannon, C., Faruqui, M.N., Battacharjee, G.P.: Dynamic load balancing algorithm in a distributed system. North-Holland Microprocess. Microprogram. **29**(5), 273–285 (1990/1991)
11. Zadrozny, W.: Natural language processing: structure and complexity. In: Proceedings of the SEKE 1996, 8th International Conference on Software Engineering and Knowledge Engineering, Lake Tahoe, pp. 595–602 (1996)
12. Rogers, J.: A Unified Notion of Derived and Derivation Structures in TAG. University of Central Florida, Gainesville (1997)
13. Ramanathan, A., Hegde, J., Shah, R.M., Bhattacharyya, P., Sasikumar, M.: Simple syntactic and morphological processing can help English-Hindi statistical machine translation. In: Proceedings of the Third International Joint Conference on Natural Language Processing, vol. I, Hyderabad, India, pp. 513–520. Asian Federation of Natural Language Processing (AFNLP), January 2008
14. Venkatapathy, S.: Machine translation for English to Hindi. In: Proceedings of the International Conference on Natural Language Processing (2008)
15. Venkatapathy, S., Bangalore, S.: Discriminative machine translation using global lexical selection. ACM Trans. Asian Lang. Inf. Process. **8**, 8 (2009)
16. Ramanathan, A., Choudhary, H., Ghosh, A., Bhattacharyya, P.: Case markers and morphology: addressing the crux of the fluency problem in English-Hindi SMT. In: Proceedings of the Joint Conference of the 47th Annual Meeting of the ACL and the 4th International Joint in Proceedings on Natural Language Processing of the AFNLP, vol. 2, Suntec, Singapore, pp. 800–808, August 2009
17. Bojar, O., Stranák, P., Zeman, D.: Data issues in English-to-Hindi machine translation. In: Proceedings of the Seventh Conference on International Language Resources and Evaluation (LREC 2010), Valletta, Malta. European Language Resources Association (ELRA), May 2010
18. Bojar, O., Diatka, V., Rychlý, P., Stranák, P., Tamchyna, A., Zeman, D.: Hindi-English and Hindi-only Corpus for machine translation. In: Proceedings of the Ninth International Language Resources and Evaluation Conference (LREC 2014), Reykjavik, Iceland. ELRA, European Language Resources Association, May 2014
19. Mihalcea, R., Pedersen, T.: An evaluation exercise for word alignment. In: Proceedings of the HLTNAACL 2003 Workshop on Building and Using Parallel Texts: Data Driven Machine Translation and Beyond, pp. 1–10 (2003)
20. Zerfass, A.: Evaluating Translation Memory Systems, Freelance Translation Tools Consultant. Holzemer Str. 38, 53343 Wachtberg Germany
21. Yeka, J.R., Kolachina, P., Sharma, D.M.: Benchmarking of English-Hindi parallel corpora. In: The 9th Edition of the Language Resources and Evaluation Conference (LREC-2014) (2014)

Human Activity Recognition Using Ensemble Modelling

Amandeep Kaur$^{(\boxtimes)}$ and Sahil Sharma

Department of Computer Science and Engineering,
Thapar University, Patiala, India
deepaman5177@yahoo.in,
sahil.sharma@thapar.edu

Abstract. In pervasive computing, human basic activity recognition has become one of the major challenges as recognizing every day basic activities and then classification of diverse activities using various devices has become arduous task. With the help of various machine learning models and data mining tools prediction has been applied. The dataset has total 10299 labelled activity instances with 561 features, to get the results more optimize we have successfully reduced features to 35 and the results were brilliant. Various machine learning models have been evaluated on the dataset for prediction of human basic activities. Results show that the large features and the reduced features were almost maintained in the terms of accuracy. The best models have been investigated for ensemble learning to get sustainable results on the basis of accuracy to classify the set of common activities carried on whole day. Encouraging results have been obtained with ensemble model. Cross validation has been performed to check the consistency of the ensemble model and accuracy more than 85% has been obtained. Finally, various human activities have been classified using ensemble model with good results.

Keywords: Classification · Ensemble learning · Feature reduction · Human activity recognition · Machine learning

1 Introduction

Human basic activity recognition is one of the challenging task in area of research as tracking the whole day activity and then classifying it is a very tedious task. The classification of the basic activities has a wide range of applications in healthcare, security and human survey system [1]. The secondary data set has been examined. Human basic activity has been considered because classifying the basic activities is the multiclass prediction. The prediction has been evaluated on the group of 6 locomotive activities classified as walking, walking down, walking up, sitting, standing and laying. To compact the size of features, GINI index and Pearson correlation have been applied on the features. The features with more importance have been filtered out in excel. The main target is to classify the activity using compact feature. For training and testing, various machine learning models and data mining tools have been applied on the secondary data set. All work has been performed in the R environment using supervised

© Springer Nature Singapore Pte Ltd. 2016
A. Unal et al. (Eds.): SmartCom 2016, CCIS 628, pp. 292–298, 2016.
DOI: 10.1007/978-981-10-3433-6_35

machine learning where various parameters have been used for mapping the accurate prediction [2]. Models have been built and prediction of the models has been evaluated.

To perform ensemble learning on the models top three models with highest accuracy have been selected and combined. The results were marvelous as the models were very consistent on the data set with compact features when applied on ensemble model. K-fold validation has been used to evaluate the consistency of the selected models.

The paper is structured as: Related work and background is depicted in Sect. 2. The description of the data set is presented in Sect. 3. The implementation section further contains sub section such as technical details about the Feature Reduction, Model Building and Predicting, Model Evaluation, Ensemble Learning and Cross validation is presented in Sect. 4 and the Conclusion of this research paper is described in Sect. 5.

2 Background and Related Work

The aim of the Activity-Based Computing [3] is to capture the user's state. There is growing demand of recognizing the human activity in various sectors especially in healthcare and security domain. Model used for recognition, svm has been considered one of the best model for classification. A number of naturalistic dataset has been collected but does not quantify the accuracy. Various smart phone based online human activity recognition using machine learning techniques have been predicted [4]. Also, the recent work has been done using auto encoders with wearable sensors [11].

Data mining and machine learning models [5] play an important role in data analysis. Different data mining algorithms have been used such as classification and regression tree-cart, which is a greedy algorithm which picks the splits from the data [6], conditional inference tree-ctree, svm-support vector machine [13], neural network, partial least square, generalized linear model, random forest [7], decision tree, multivariate adaptive regression spline all have been referred for contrasting the parameters and the methods have been implemented in R. Work in this paper has 35 numeric and 1 nominal attributes with the class being numeric. The class is further classified as multiclass. The implementation has been done in R and the detailed analysis of the work has been presented in the Sect. 4.

3 Dataset Description

Secondary dataset has been used for analyzing and the experiment was carried out by the group of 30 volunteers, within the age group between 19 to 48 years. The dataset of human activity recognition is publicly available [8]. To obtain user related set of 6 daily activities information, wrist-mounted smartphone has been used. The obtained dataset has been randomly partitioned to 70% for training and 30% for testing Total 561 features have been recognized from the dataset of 7352 as training set [15]. After supervised learning, testing has been applied on 2948 dataset. Further the classes of the dataset is multiclass that is the class contains many classes such as walking, walking down, walking up, sitting, standing and laying which distinguish group of activity which have been performed by the humans and the main goal is to achieve accuracy of activity detected on the basis of the features captured. To find the most promising model, the models have been applied to the training set and then afterwards applied to the testing dataset. The model itself detects the class to which the data belongs to. For best and consistent results ensemble learning has been applied on the selected models with randomly generated dataset.

4   Implementation

The implementation part begins with feature reduction as secondary dataset has been considered and preprocessing has been applied to it. Further sub sections elaborate the implementation section in detail. Figure 1 below depicts the work flow.

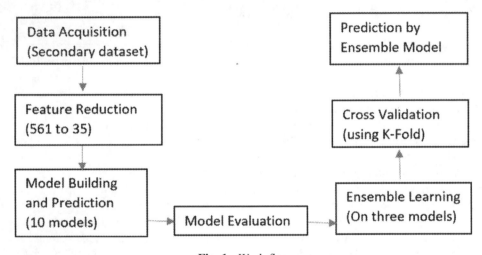

Fig. 1. Work flow

4.1   Feature Reduction

The dataset contains total 561 features for every instance. Each feature has its own importance. Pearson correlation and GINI Index has been used for feature reduction. Which has been applied on the dataset. The dataset retrieved has been made more compact as the number of attributes further reduced to 35. Considering the compact dataset, features such as mean value, standard deviation, entropy measure have proved important and useful. Data cleansing has been applied on dataset using excel [14].

In our work, we have successfully pruned the features from 561 to 35 which show expected results and these features have been used for learning and testing. The dataset with 561 features and reduced features have been implemented on various models. The machine randomly selected the features and prediction has been made. The dataset with more descriptive and important features resulted better than the one which has irrelevant features or more features [9]. The compact dataset has been preferred, as the performance of the models was not degraded with feature extraction. Table 1 shows the different features and the accuracy obtained when executed on different models.

Table 1. Evaluating different features on different models

Features/model	Ctree (%)	Decision tree (%)	Random forest (%)	SVM (%)
561	83.8819	81.4387	92.8401	95.2154
210	84.7641	83.3389	91.6864	94.4689
44	82.8639	80.0475	89.5486	91.3471
35	82.2531	80.8279	88.6664	91.8221

4.2 Model Building and Predictions

After the successful examination of the less important features various models have been applied to the dataset and results has been obtained. Classes to which the instance belongs to have been predicted. The machine has randomly selected the data and the models have been applied on the training data and learning has been done by the model from the dataset and then testing has been performed on another dataset. In this paper, we have applied total 10 models to evaluate our results. Models building, after feature selection has been successfully accomplished and predictions have been done by the models.

4.3 Model Evaluation and Analysis

All these models have been evaluated on the basis of various evaluating parameters. Various models have been executed and evaluated on the basis of accuracy of prediction and total time taken. Since, the problem is of multiclass we have evaluated confusion matrix error.

Table 2 shows evaluation results obtained from 10 models with 5 columns in the table. Column 1 represents model name which illustrates the name of model used for the model building. Column 2 represents Methods and packages have been used to build the model as these are the essential elements for building the models. Column 3 presents accuracy which represents the percentage of the test data that have been classified into correct class by the model and the model with higher accuracy has been considered better than the model with less accuracy. Next column depicts confusion matrix error which is specifically the problem of statistical classification, a confusion matrix [10]. The confusion matrix has been evaluated by the total percentage subtracting the accuracy percentage and the percentage of total error which does not match when matrix between the actual and predicted has been made. Last column represents total time taken in seconds which is total time taken for learning, model building and predictions using the model built and compared with the various model. Quicker models have been considered better. In Table 2 we analyzed that the model support vector machine with highest accuracy and the model yielding lowest accuracy was partial least square. Also we found that the partial least square takes longest amount of time followed by the generalized linear model with 10.25 and 8.56. The quickest model among all was decision tree. Hence considering accuracy and time trade off we considered top three models to finally conclude the top three models, support vector machine with accuracy 91.82% and total time taken 1.89 s, random forest with accuracy 88.66% and total time taken 1.68 s and the third model conditional inference tree 82.25% and total time taken 1.42 s.

Table 2. Model evaluation results

Model name	Method, Packages	Accuracy (%)	Confusion matrix error	Time taken (s)
CART	rpart, rpart	80.4886	19.5114	1.56
Conditional Inference Tree	ctree, party	82.2531	17.7469	1.42
Generalized linear Model	glm, caret	77.3328	22.6672	8.8
Earth	earth, earth	61.7577	38.2423	2.82
Multivariate Adaptive Regression Spline	earth, earth	77.3328	22.6672	5.11
Neural Network	nnet, nnet	80.9636	19.0364	8.56
Partial Least Squares	kernelpls, pls	37.2921	62.7079	10.25
Decision Tree	rpart, rpart	80.8279	19.1721	1.36
Random Forest	rf, randomForest	88.6664	11.3336	1.68
Support Vector Machine	ksvm, kernlab	91.8221	8.1779	1.89

4.4   Ensemble Learning

In order to get consistent results ensemble learning [12] has been applied on the models with best result among the various models and further work has been done it in the next section. As shown in the Table 3 the top models with decreasing order accuracy. The models were combined to get reliable results. Each model with its own prediction has been compared with the actual value as a base model. In ensemble model, average of combined models has been evaluated. The results from the ensemble model was consistent too as their accuracy has been evaluated. To verify the results, K-fold cross validation has been applied to the ensemble model which is represented in the next sub section.

Table 3. Ensemble models with their accuracies

Model name	Accuracy (%)
Svm	91.8221
Random Forest	88.6664
Ctree	82.2531

4.5   Cross Validation

K-fold validation has been used for cross validation where the model has been executed for 10 times to check the consistency of the ensemble model and the accuracy of the model has been calculated each time. The ensemble model is consistent and the scatter plot has been used to draw the consistency of the ensemble model and the selected top three base models. Model is said to be consistent if it gives the almost same accuracy each times it runs. The ensemble model after cross validated found the most consistent model. Table 4 shows the accuracy calculated at each run with the ensemble model as well as the individually executed models that is the top three models. Basically comparisons have been performed to check the consistency of the models. All the models have been executed in the R environment. Figure 2 shows scatter of top three models including the ensemble model with respect to their consistency.

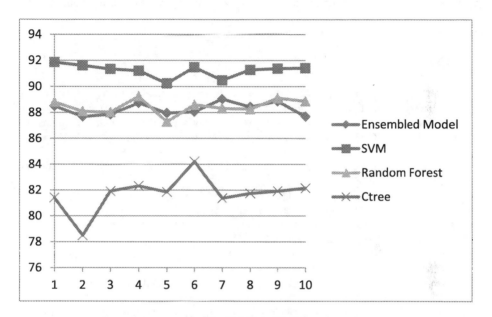

Fig. 2. K-fold validation

Table 4. Comparison of models in cross validation

Runs	Ensemble model	SVM	Random forest	Ctree
1	88.4967	91.866	88.8096	81.40482
2	87.6823	91.6186	88.0856	78.4866
3	87.8520	91.3457	88.02172	81.91381
4	88.7343	91.2114	89.2433	82.321
5	87.9538	90.2379	87.2861	81.84595
6	88.0556	91.4829	88.5985	84.22124
7	89.0397	90.4828	88.3271	81.37089
8	88.4289	91.2848	88.25925	81.74415
9	88.8700	91.3810	89.10757	81.91381
10	87.6823	91.415	88.87004	82.15134

5 Conclusion

In this paper we have proposed ensemble model for human activity recognition in order to improve consistency of the models. Predictions have been done by the model to know the human activity. K-fold validation has been used to verify the consistency. The experiment results confirm that the ensemble model-combination of models has proved more consistent model than other models. The results achieved in this research show that it is possible that human activity recognition can be applied on real-time applications and can be experimented to anticipate future people requirements.

References

1. Bayat, A., Pomplun, M., Tran, D.A.: A study on human activity recognition using accelerometer data from smartphones. Procedia Comput. Sci. **34**, 450–457 (2014). Elsevier
2. Caruana, R., Mizil, A.N.: An empirical comparison of supervised learning algorithms. In: Proceedings of the 23rd International Conference on Machine Learning, pp. 161–168. ACM (2006)
3. Davies, N., Siewiorek, D.P., Sukthankar, R.: Activity-based computing. Pervasive Comput. **7**, 20–21 (2008). IEEE
4. Kose, M., Incel, O.D., Ersoy, C.: Online human activity recognition on smart phones. In: 2nd International Workshop on Mobile Sensing, pp. 11–12. ACM (2012)
5. Settles, B.: Active learning literature survey. Computer Sciences Technical report 1648. University of Wisconsin-Madison (1995)
6. Breiman, L., Friedman, J., Olshen, R.A., Stone, C.J.: Classification and Regression Trees. CRC Press, New York (1984)
7. Liaw, A., Wiener, M.: Classification and regression by randomForest. R News. **2**, 18–22 (2002)
8. Anguita, D., Ghio, A., Oneto, L., Parra, X., Reyes-Ortiz, J.L.: A public domain dataset for human activity recognition using smartphones. In: European Symposium on Artificial Neural Networks, Computational Intelligence and Machine Learning (2013)
9. Williams, G.: Data Mining with Rattle and R: The Art of Excavating Data for Knowledge Discovery. Springer, Heidelberg (2011)
10. Salmon, B.P., Kleynhas, W., Schwegmann, C.P., Oliver, J.C.: Proper comparison among methods using a confusion matrix. In: International Geoscience and Remote Sensing Symposium (IGARSS), pp. 3057–3060. IEEE (2015)
11. Wang, L.: Recognition of Human Activities Using Continuous Auto Encoders with Wearable Sensors, vol. 16. Multidisciplinary Digital Publishing Institute Sensors (2016)
12. Alpaydin, E.: Introduction to Machine Learning. The MIT Press, Cambridge (2010)
13. Maroco, J., Silva, D., Rodrigues, A., Guerreiro, M., Santana, I., Mendon, A.: Data mining methods in the prediction of Dementia. A real-data comparison of the accuracy, sensitivity and specificity of linear discriminant analysis, logistic regression, neural networks, support vector machines, classification trees and random forests. BMC Research Notes (2011)
14. Tang, H.: A simple approach to data mining in excel. In: 4th International Conference Wireless Communications, Network and Mobile Computing, pp. 1–4 (2008)
15. http://goo.gl/YrCJax

Performance Evaluation of Word Count Program Using C#, Java and Hadoop

Ravinder Yadav[✉], Aravind Kilaru[✉], Devesh Kumar Srivastava,
and Priyanka Dahiya

Manipal University Jaipur, Jaipur, Rajasthan, India
ravinder.yadav@gmail.com, kilaru.arvind@gmail.com,
devesh988@yahoo.com

Abstract. Trends and technologies are changing very rapidly with time. In advent of 20th century, the scope of internet was limited and so forth the expectations of the users were also limited. Now a days; internet is in the reach of every one and therefore the way of use and expectations have changed a lot. Huge amount of data is being created every day. Social media has become very powerful. The volume of data is increasing exponentially every year. So it has become difficult to process huge amount of data to extract useful information. A new concept has been proposed to resolve the issue named as Big-Data. To use the concept of Big-Data, Apache has proposed a framework named as Hadoop. In this paper, a comparative study has been performed on Big-Data and serial Processing by using a simple word count example and found that the result obtained using Map Reduce (Hadoop) are encouraging as compared to traditional processing.

Keywords: Big Data · Map Reduce · Hadoop · Traditional processing · HDFS · Hive · C#

1 Introduction

The term 'big' refers to something very large in nature & Data refers to raw information. The question is how big can be the data. In the recent present scenario technology is changing very rapidly and new trends of life styles are emerging continuously. In this present scenario world seems to be in the pocket; in a small electronic gadget. Every source of information is only a few second away from the user. But the important issue is how this information comes to the end user? Where is it stored? How it is organized? What volume of data is coming on internet every day? my leading organizations have come up with following surveys [1, 2, 4, 6].

a. New York Stock Exchange generate s 1 TB data per day
b. Google processes 700 PB/month.
c. Facebook host 10 billion photos taking 1 PB of storage.
d. 12 + TB of tweets data every day.
e. 25 + TB of log data on Facebook everyday.

© Springer Nature Singapore Pte Ltd. 2016
A. Unal et al. (Eds.): SmartCom 2016, CCIS 628, pp. 299–307, 2016.
DOI: 10.1007/978-981-10-3433-6_36

f. In march 2007 as per John F. Gantz, David Reinsel and other researchers at IDC have forecasted that 161 Exabyte's of new data will be generated in 2006 and it will be doubling in every 18 months and will reach 988 exabytes by 2010, but the real scenario was very different form the proposed; 1227 exabytes of new data has been produced by 2009, and it will be reach of 2838 exabytes of data by 2010.

g. As per Bret Swanson and George Gilder. U.S IP traffic could reach one zettabyte by 2015 and the U.S. Internet-2015 will be at least 50 times larger than it was in 2006.

Technology: maximizing the computation power and algorithmic accuracy to gather, analyze, link, and compare large data sets (Fig. 1).

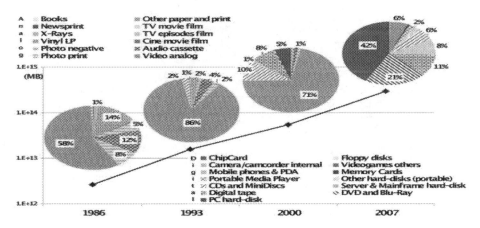

Fig. 1. Changing trends in storage devices [5]

- Analysis: drawing on large data sets to identify patterns in order to make economic, social, technical, and legal claims [6].
- "Mythology: the widespread belief that large data sets offer a higher form of intelligence and knowledge that can generate insights that were previously impossible, with the aura of truth, objectivity, and accuracy" [6].

2 Big-Data, Hadoop Framework

Hadoop: - The technology, Analysis, Methodology for big data were together implemented by Hadoop framework given by apache as shown in Fig. 2. Hadoop works on the concept of distributed file system (HDFS). A large file is broken in to small files, by default having 64 MB size on Hadoop 1.x and 128 MB on Hadoop 2.x size. It is stored on different system grouped to form Hadoop cluster, to integrate the file from small chunks of data is again a big issue. This problem is resolved by using Name Node. Name Node is a machine in cluster which acts as a controller and keeps track of all the segments of data. In this architecture, Data protection is a very serious issue. If Name Node fails, it can lose the capability to reintegrate the data file. To avoid this situation, Hadoop keep s redundant copies of Name Node, called Secondary Name Node. If the Name node fails at any time, same can be recovered with the help of Secondary Name Node. There is another major issue of data content management. If any of the machine holding small size file fails; Hadoop Name Node can't integrate our file back. To resolve this issue HDFS system always keep 3 redundant copies of the file. If information is lost from one place due to machine failure or connection failure then it is replaced by the redundant copy. In case of failure, redundant copy of the failed machine is again created to maintain the data integrity.

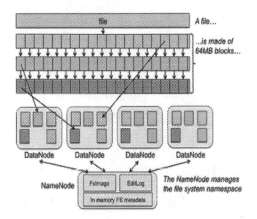

Fig. 2. Hadoop architecture [7]

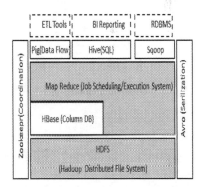

Fig. 3. Hadoop eco system [7]

Hadoop Eco system as shown in Fig. 3, consists of various technology/frameworks which directly or indirectly interact with HDFS.

The major part of the hadoop ecosystem are enlisted below [3, 8, 9]

a. HDFS: A distributed filesystem that runs on large clusters of commodity machines.
b. MapReduce: A distributed data processing model and execution environment that runs on large clusters of commodity machines.
c. Pig: A data flow language and execution environment for exploring very large datasets.
d. Hive: A distributed data warehouse. Query language based on SQL (and which is translated by the runtime engine to Map Reduce jobs) for querying the data.
e. HBase: A distributed, column-oriented database.
f. ZooKeeper: A distributed, highly available coordination service.
g. Sqoop: A tool for efficiently moving data between relational databases and HDFS.

3 Execution Time of Algorithm Between MapReduce and Traditional Programing Language

The traditional programing language are common in use. Microsoft C#, java technologies are among those few of them which have been chosen to simulate/calculate the execution time. As a sample 8 to 10 different data set has been taken into consideration. The data set starts from 265 MB and a multiple of 265. In this paper; the frequency of the word s has been counted from the sample data set.

Algorithm 1: The following algorithm has been implemented in C# and JAVA.

Step-0:   Start

Step-1:   List all the files at a specified path

Step-2:   Read one line from the file

Step-3:   Split the line into words

Step-4:   If key = word exists then increment the counter in HashMap
          Else add the new key and initialize the counter by 1

Step-5:   Repeat the steps from 2 to 4 until the end of file

Step-6:   Repeat the steps from 2 to 5 until for all the files at the specified path

Step-7:   Write the output at specified path

Step-8:   Exit

The above said algorithm read s every line of the file and split that in to token. Each token is then compared with the existing HashMap database. If key exist, then its values are incremented by one other wise key is added to HashMap and values is initialized by one. The same process is repeated for each file at the specified path and file results are written on the out path.

Algorithm 2: The following algorithm has been implemented in JAVA on Hadoop Platform.

Algorithm 2-I: Write DriverClass

Step -1:   Start

Step -2:   Create a new Job and set the name of the job

Step -3:   Set the input and output Data Types for mapper and Reducers class

Step -4:   Set the input and Output Path

Step -5:   Run JobConfiguration

Step -6:   Exit

Algorithm 2-II: Write Mapper Class

Step -1:   Start

Step -2:   Initiate to over-ride the Map Function

Step -3:   Read one line at a time

Step -4:   Tokenize the line in to words

Step -5:   Assuming every occurrence of the word as first occurrence; Write the word to HDFS and its count as 1

Step -6:   Repeat step 5 for words

Step -7:   Exit

Algorithm 2-III: Write Reducer Class

Step -1:   Start

Step -2:   Initiate to over-ride the Map Function

Step -3:   Read one line at a time

Step -4:   Tokenize the line in to words

Step -5:   Assuming every occurrence of the word as first occurrence; Write the word to HDFS and its count as 1

Step -6:   Repeat step 5 for words

Step -7:   Exit

As discussed earlier, Hadoop use Map-Reduce technique therefor e the algorithm is divided into three sections i.e. 2-I, 2-II, 2-III. The Algorithm 2-I is meant for the admin or configuration purpose. It is almost common for every program. The Sect. 2-II is reading the data at specified path and mapping that in to the specified format. In this particular program; it is dividing the entire data into word s and writing that onto HDFS assuming that every time its occurrence is the first occurrence. The Sect. 2-III describe the reduce s function. It finds the key and count its occurrence and finally it writes to HDFS as output.

As algorithm has been implemented in different platform i.e. C#, Java, Hadoop it generates different time pattern for the dataset. Figure 4 Show the time pattern for C# program performance. Similarly Figs. 5, 6, 7 and 8 shows the Java Program, comparison between C# and Java program, Hadoop program, comparison between C#, Java, Hadoop respectively.

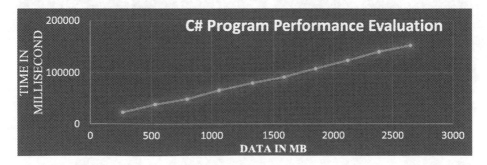

Fig. 4. C# program performance

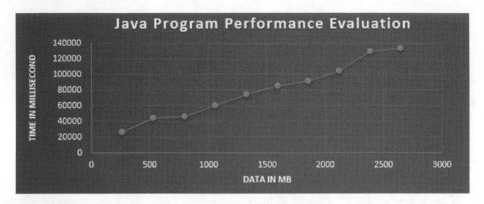

Fig. 5. Java program performance

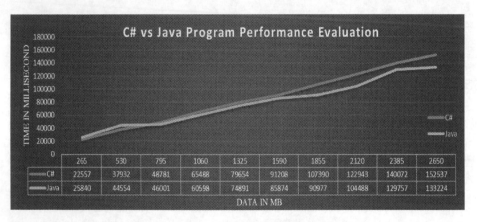

Fig. 6. C# vs. Java program performance

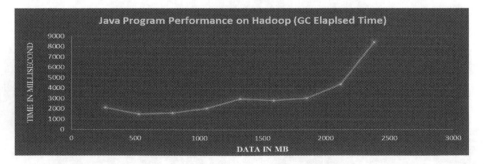

Fig. 7. Java Hadoop program performance

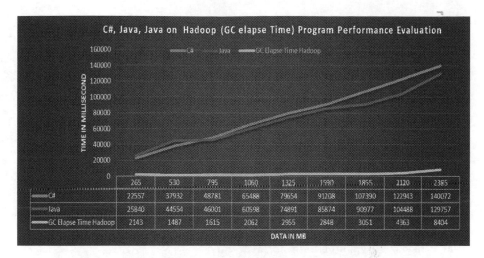

Fig. 8. C#, Java, Hadoop program performance

4 Conclusion and Future Work

In this paper a comparative study between traditional processing and Big Data processing has been performed. As a traditional processing language/environment C# and Java has been opted on windows 7 and Linux, whereas on Big Data Java is chosen as a programing language and Apache Hadoop 2.6.0 is chosen for Map Reduce program execution environment.

Hadoop execution environment contains a cluster of 10 slaves with 1 master node. Secondary Name Node is configured on the master node itself. The entire Hadoop cluster is configured on virtual environment having 4 GB RAM for each node including Name Node. The C# program is executed on virtual machine having operating system windows 7 with 4 GB of RAM. The Java program execution is carried out on Ubuntu virtual machine with 4 GB of RAM. The common data set chosen for the experimenting the results. The data set size starts from 265 MB to a multiple of 265 from 1 to 10. By the execution of the same algorithm as specified in above section following results are obtained.

1. C# Program Performance Evaluation:
   a. When the program is executed in C#; its execution starts very quickly with a data set of 265 MB.
   b. As the data set size increases its shows the almost linear behavior. The execution time increases with the increase in the data set size. The behavior of program execution is shown in Fig. 4.
2. Java Program Performance Evaluation:
   a. When the program is executed in Java; its execution starts quickly with a data set of 265 MB.
   b. As the data set increases; time of execution increases. As the behavior shown in Fig. 5; it shows following behavior.

      i. As the data set size is increasing from 265 MB to 530 MB; time of execution is more inclined.

     ii. From data set size 530 MB to 795 MB, it is almost horizontal. The time of execution increases very less as compare to 265 MB to 530 MB.

    iii. The data set size increasing from 795 MB to 1855 MB shows linear inclination of time behavior.

    iv. With the increasing data set size from 1855 to 2120; the behavior is more vertical than the earlier one and after that it shows a less inclination.

3. A comparison of C# and Java Program Performance Evaluation:
   a. As shown in Fig. 6; C# is faster in starting the execution of program than JAVA.
   b. With the increase in the data set size java show better behavior than C#.
   b. Java takes less time of execution than C#.
   c. As the data set size grow more and more; java shows more and more better performance as compared to C#.

4. Java Hadoop Program Performance Evaluation:
   a. Initially Hadoop environment takes more time to start the program execution as shown in Fig. 7.
   b. With the data set size of 530 MB it shows a decrease in time of execution. c. From data set size 530 MB to 1325 MB; it shows linear inclination.
   c. From data set size 1325 MB to 1855 MB, it shows the same time of execution.
   d. Almost no change in the time of execution
   e. The data size greater than 1855 show a rapid inclination of time graph.

5. C#, Java and Hadoop Program Performance Evaluation:
   a. As shown in Fig. 8. C# program execution is faster than Java, but Hadoop GC Elapse time is much lesser than C# as well.
   b. Java shows better performance as compare to C# with the increase in the data set size, but always Hadoop time is lesser than both the technology.
   c. From the above behavior; one can conclude that for the large Data Set, Hadoop execution environment is better than the traditional one.

In this paper; a comparison between C#, Java and Java on Hadoop environment is carried out. The performance is evaluated and observed that Hadoop environment is faster for large data sets. In future the same behavior can be studied with various load on system and network. A comparison study can be done with other big data technology and traditional technology to conclude the fastest among them.

References

1. Introduction to Hadoop, Map Reduce and HDFS for Big Data applications, June 2014. http://www.snia.org/sites/default/education/tutorials/2013/fall/BigData/SergeBazhievsky_Introduction_to_Hadoop_MapReduce_v2.pdf
2. Edvancer Eduventures. http://www.edvancer.in/the-big-data-evolution-is-here/
3. A very short history of Big Data, June 2014. http://www.forbes.com/sites/gilpress/2013/05/a-very-short-history-of-big-data/

4. A very short history of Big Data, May 2014. http://www.forbes.com/sites/gilpress/2013/05/a-very-short-history-of-big-data/2/
5. The world's technological capacity to store, communicate, and compute information, June 2014. http://www.sciencemag.org/content/332/6025/60.full
6. Critical questions for big data, May 2014. http://www.tandfonline.com/doi/pdf/10.1080/X.2012.678878
7. Introduction to the Hadoop software ecosystem, May 2014. http://www.revelytix.com/?q=content/hadoop-ecosystem#hdfs
8. Srivastav, D.K.: Big challenges in Big Data research. CiiT Int. J. Data Mining Knowl. Eng. **6** (7), 282–286 (2014)
9. Kadel, L.B., Soni, D.K., Yadav, R.: Noun phrase detection and its challenges in large-scale natural language data processing. CiiT Int. J. **7**(5), 139–143 (2015)

Bio-cryptographical Key Generation Using Euclidean Algorithm for Smart Meter Communication

Vijayanand Radhakrishnan[✉], Devaraj Durairaj, Kannapiran Balasubramanian, and Kartheeban Kamatchi

Kalasalingam University, Srivilliputtur, Tamilnadu, India
rkvijayanand@gmail.com, deva230@yahoo.com,
kannapiran79@gmail.com, kartheeban_ku@yahoo.com

Abstract. Smart meter is an essential component of smart grid that measures and transmits power consumption details of customer to control center for billing and monitoring purpose. The open nature of two way communication network used in smart meter is susceptible to cyber attacks. Hence the cybersecurity gets high priority in smart meter applications. Key management system is an essential requirement of cyber security. Implementing it to dynamic, large scale smart meters by existing methods is more complex and also it is not possible to authenticate the key derived from genuine user. The emerging bio-cryptography provides solution to these problems by generating keys from user biometrics in smart meters. In this paper, an efficient key management system is proposed in which keys are derived from a bio-cryptography technique using fingerprint biometrics with Euclidean distance algorithm. The proposed technique is simulated in Matlab and its performance is evaluated. Simulation results demonstrate that the proposed technique is well suitable for data security in smart meter applications.

Keywords: KMS using fingerprint biometrics · AMI security · Data security · Key generation using euclidean algorithm · Bio-cryptography

1 Introduction

Smart meters are advanced energy meters that transmit power usage information automatically to control server for disturbance free power distribution. The smart meter data is highly sensitive and direct communication with end user might cause multiple attack possibilities [1]. So there is a need for advanced security mechanism for data generated by smart meters. In [2], the communication networks suitable for smart grid are reviewed and the authors have suggested wireless mesh network for the local area data collection from smart meters.

Cryptography is an important data security providing technique where Key management plays an important role. The implementation of existing key management system (KMS) to smart meter is a complex task and also verification of authentication keys increase the burden of smart meter [3]. Bio-Cryptography is an emerging technology that inherits the advantages of biometrics and cryptography provides efficient key

© Springer Nature Singapore Pte Ltd. 2016
A. Unal et al. (Eds.): SmartCom 2016, CCIS 628, pp. 308–314, 2016.
DOI: 10.1007/978-981-10-3433-6_37

management system. Key generation using fingerprint biometric is a recent technique in which keys are generated by extracting fingerprint features mostly by rotating images at certain degree [4] and creating sub-templates from original templates [5]. Nowadays it is possible to catch the fingerprint of user without their knowledge. So the keys generated from the existing methods are cracked easily through reverse engineering. Thus the advanced technique is essential in key generation to make the fingerprint biometric unpredictable by the intruder.

The recent studies have shown that bio-cryptography might be suitable for smart grid because of providing high security and privacy compared to conventional cryptography [6]. An efficient key generation technique based on fingerprint biometrics with chaff points using Euclidean Distance algorithm for smart meters is proposed in this research work. The inclusion of different chaff points to each meter resists against fingerprint template theft attack whereas the unique nature of fingerprint biometric helps to reduce the inclusion of number of chaff points. In this work, an AMI communication network is simulated in Matlab and the performance of the proposed technique is analyzed.

2 Proposed Key Generation Scheme

In this work, we propose the Fingerprint based Key Generation using Euclidean distance algorithm (FKGE) for secure key generation in smart meters. The proposed FKGE protocol includes:

2.1 Smart Meter Registration

Each smart meter is featured with a unique ID (M_{ID}) during manufacturing. The registration of smart meter starts with the collection of user biometrics i.e., fingerprint. The fingerprint impression collected from the user needs to be clear. After getting the impression, thinning of images would be done for removal of noise in fingerprint biometric. The collected fingerprint biometric with the inclusion of random chaff points is manually loaded into smart meter and control server by authorized official that are unknown to others. The confidentiality and uniqueness of chaff points increase the complexity of the biometric features used in key generation and the attackers may not be able to identify the keys even if the fingerprint template is known to the attackers. The same fingerprint impression loaded in meter and control server instead of getting separate impression also provides solution to variability problem in the fingerprint information. The initial communication of smart meter with control server is authenticated with user ID (U_{ID}) through the match between loaded fingerprints available in smart meter and control server. The control server periodically sends the secret key through which the smart meter generates its keys for encryption. The smart meter considered in this work is a two and half minute basis meter i.e., the meter send the power usage information atleast 24 times per hour.

2.2 Feature Extraction

Fingerprint template is used in this work by representing the features as point co-ordinates (x, y). In this work, the bifurcation feature of user fingerprint is used to generate random keys. Bifurcation in fingerprint is defined as the point where the ridge divides into two ridges. Each fingerprint has different bifurcation points and is found throughout the fingerprint. In some cases, minutiae i.e., ridge endings are used with bifurcation points to increase the randomness of generated keys.

2.3 FKGE Protocol for Key Generation

After the feature extraction is completed, the smart meter utilizes the proposed FKGE technique with unique fingerprint biometrics for secure key generation. The smart meter could encrypt the data with keys generated by FKGE protocol. According to the meter consideration, atleast 24 data need to be transmitted per hour. For each day 576 data is required. The key generation starts from the secret key received from control server in a secured way as in [7]. The first step of key generation is X-OR secret key (K) with smart meter U_{ID} marked as the starting key K_1.

$$K_1 = X - OR\ (K, U_{ID}) \qquad (1)$$

From the starting key, the initial keys K_2 are randomly generated. From the initial key, the smart meter further generates the keys used for encryption. Let us consider that the control server send the starting key atleast once in an hour. From the starting key, initial keys are generated once in an hour. The initial keys are generated by the method proposed in [8] where the secret key list L has numbers arranged in ascending order with K_1 as starting key. The randomness in keys are achieved by placing the list L in table T of size Sk × ID where,

$$Sk = (Tk)/ID \qquad (2)$$

$$Row = i\ \%\ Sk \qquad (3)$$

$$Column = i\ \%\ ID \qquad (4)$$

Where, Tk is total number of keys required, i is the number in L used to generate secret key. The initial keys are the numbers in T which is accessed by column order fashion. Each secret key is generated from the initial key of size n. Let the bifurcation points of fingerprint template be arranged in ascending order in bifurcation point list (BPL). Let us consider the total number of bifurcation points extracted is considered as num. The random keys are generated by calculating the distance between n bifurcation points of fingerprint template. Let us take the intermediate points as n = 4. Then the intermediate points are selected by the method proposed in [9] using,

$$K_3(1) = K_2 \times U_{ID} + (K_2 + 1) \times U_{ID}^2 \qquad (5)$$

$$K_4(1) = K_3(1)\ \%\ num \qquad (6)$$

$$K_3(2) = K_4(1) \times U_{ID} + \left(K_4(1) + 1\right) \times U_{ID}^2 \qquad (7)$$

$$K_4(2) = K_3(2) \% \, num \qquad (8)$$

$$K_3(3) = K_4(2) \times U_{ID} + \left(K_4(2) + 1\right) \times U_{ID}^2 \qquad (9)$$

$$K_4(3) = K_3(3) \% \, num \qquad (10)$$

$$K_3(4) = K_4(3) \times U_{ID} + \left(K_4(3) + 1\right) \times U_{ID}^2 \qquad (11)$$

$$K_4(4) = K_3(4) \% \, num \qquad (12)$$

The above $K_4(i)$ contains starting point $K_4(1)$, two intermediate points $K_4(2)$ and $K_4(3)$ and ending point $K_4(4)$. The points represent the position in BPL. The position contains the co-ordinates (x,y) of corresponding bifurcation points. The distance calculated between starting and ending point through intermediate points using Euclidean distance shown below is the random key used for data encryption.

$$K_s = ceil\left(\sqrt{\left(\left(y_2 - y_1\right)^2 + \left(x_2 - x_1\right)^2 \right)} \right) \qquad (13)$$

Similarly all the keys are generated from initial keys. The FKGE securely generates the key and the randomness in keys ensures the level of security. The operations used in the FKGE protocol are simple and so the keys are generated rapidly.

3   Simulation Setting

The performance of FKGE protocol is evaluated by simulating a sample AMI communication system, shown in Fig. 1. The communication between meters is made with Wi-Fi LAN network and is arranged in wireless mesh topology fashion. To make the communication network resemble real time operation; the meters are made communicated through channel file that have the properties of channel like data loss, added Gaussian noise, etc. The path during communication is randomly selected by meters using IF condition.

In this paper, Smart meters are modeled as Matlab file (m-file) where readings are given manually. Each meter is represented in separate file with encryption algorithm, unique ID and fingerprint biometric. The fingerprint image used in the proposed method is a grayscale image of John Doe [10]. During encryption, the FKGE file is method. The fingerprint is received as argument during the function calling of FKGE file during encryption. The first step of encryption is key generation and the second step is encrypting the data with the generated key. Different methods are available to generate keys from fingerprint biometric by analyzing its feature.

In this work, the bifurcation feature of fingerprint is used to generate random keys. The fingerprint biometric is represented in two dimensional x and y axis with the size

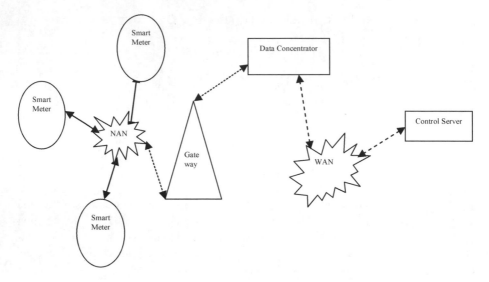

Fig. 1. Simulation model of smart meter communication

of 600×600. The position of bifurcation points are filtered from the fingerprint image using 'nlfilter' function of Matlab. The nlfilter is a sliding neighborhood function that is used to found the major features of fingerprint i.e., minutiae points. The function accepts an M-by-N matrix as input and sliding through each pixel of the image and returns a scalar. The size of the sliding block is taken as [3, 3] and it could found 75 bifurcation points in the given image. Each bifurcation point is represented as x and y values. The co-ordinates of bifurcation points are used to calculate the distance using Euclidean distance algorithm. The outputs of distance algorithm are floating point value which is further rounded by ceil function to generate secret key.

Each smart meter generates its secret key by calling the FKGE function during encryption. The proposed technique is suitable for small group of meters in neighborhood area network (NAN) communication and the last node in the group acts as collector that collects and transmits every meter's data to control center through wide area network communication that is included in the simulation as separate file. The proposed technique provides an efficient key management system for smart meters and the level of security is evaluated.

4   Performance Analysis

Smart grid is a resource limited time constrained system in which the data are received and processed without any latency. The performance of proposed scheme is analyzed on the basis of time cost of maximum computation. The proposed scheme is implemented in 10–50 Mb/s speed which is the minimum requirement of any processing system and considering it as smart meter and its operation rate is analyzed.

The operations used in the proposed scheme are simple and consumes only limited time. The key generation time of proposed FKGP protocol is compared with the existing

Yu et al. scheme [11] is shown in Fig. 2. The result shows that the proposed scheme is little bit faster for single key generation but for the consideration of large number of keys the proposed scheme is much faster than Yu et al. scheme. According to the communication requirement of smart grid, the allowable latency for AMI systems data transmission is 2–15 s [12]. The proposed scheme generates key in microseconds that ensures it does not affect the data transmission of AMI.

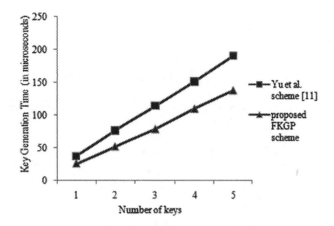

Fig. 2. Time cost comparison of key generation time

Another issue to be addressed in the application of bio-cryptography in smart meter is the inclusion of biometric image in smart meter because it has very low memory. Third party compression softwares provide solution to the storage problem of biometric images. They compress the image with the size of less than 10 kb without compromising the image quality. Many of the semi conductor manufactures like MAXIM, IDT, etc. can provide the chip with 128 kb flash memory support to place the compressed biometric image to smart meter. Thus based on the performance analysis, the proposed key generation method is most suitable for secure AMI key generation.

5   Conclusion

The various cyber threats in smart meter communication cause heavy financial loss and disturbance to power distribution. In this paper, various security issues in smart meter communication and the importance of protecting smart meters from various cyber attacks are analyzed. Based on the security requirements of smart meter data transmission, a secure and efficient key management system using bio-cryptography has been proposed. In this proposed key management system, keys are randomly generated by calculating the distance between bifurcation points of user fingerprint. The distance calculated using Euclidean distance algorithm is used as key. Each key uses different bifurcation points and is selected by random techniques. The randomness in keys ensures that keys are secure and the adversary could not be able to predict. The keys are used to encrypt the power usage data measured by smart meter. The simulation results of proposed key generation approach using Matlab and the performance analysis ensures that the proposed technique is well suitable for secure key generation in smart meter communication.

Acknowledgments. The authors would like to thank the Management of Kalasalingam University for supporting the research through Kalasalingam University Research Fellowship scheme.

References

1. Kosut, O., Jia, L., Thomas, R.J., Tong, L.: Malicious data attacks on the smart grid. IEEE Trans. Smart Grid. **2**(4), 645–658 (2011)
2. Ancillotti, E., Bruno, R., Conti, M.: The role of communication systems in smart grids: architectures, technical solutions and research challenges. J. Comp. Comm. **36**(17), 1665–1697 (2013)
3. Liu, J., Xiao, Y., Li, S., Liang, W., Chen, C.L.P.: Cyber security and privacy issues in smart grids. IEEE Commun. Sur. Tut. **14**(4), 981–997 (2012)
4. Zhang, P., Hu, J., Li, C., Bennamoun, M.: A pitfall in fingerprint bio-cryptography key generation. J. Comp. Secur. **30**(5), 311–319 (2011)
5. Habib, A., Ateeq, I.S., Hameed, K.: Biometric security system based on fingerprint recognition. Int. J. Sci. Eng. Technol. **2**(9), 892–894 (2013)
6. Hu, J., Pota, H.R., Guo, S.: Taxonamy of attacks for agent-based smart grids. IEEE Trans. Parallel Distrib. Syst. **25**(7), 1886–1895 (2014)
7. Kartheeban, K., Venkatesulu, M.: EAB – Euclidean Algorithm Based key computation protocol for secure group communication in dynamic grid environment. Int. J. Grid Distrib. Comput. **3**(4), 45–55 (2010)
8. Singh, S., Agarwal, G.: Use of Chinese remainder theorem to generate random numbers for cryptography. Int. J. Appl. Eng. Res. **1**(1), 168–174 (2010)
9. Nath, A., Ghosh, S., Mallik, S.A.: Symmetric key cryptography using random key generator. Int. Conf. Secur. Manag. **2**, 239–244 (2010)
10. Standard reference fingerprint template. http://in.mathworks.com/matlabcentral/fileexchange/48295-matlab-biometric-fingerprint-recognition-code
11. Yu, K., Arifuzzaman, M., Wen, Z., Zhang, D., Sato, T.: A key management scheme for secure communications of information centric advanced metering infrastructure in smart grid. IEEE Trans. Instrum. Measur. **64**(8), 2072–2085 (2015)
12. Kounev, V., Tipper, D.: Advanced metering and demand response communication performance in Zigbee based HANs. In: IEEE Conference Computer Communications Workshops, pp. 31–36 (2013)

WiMAX Based Scanning Schemes in Vehicular Ad-Hoc Network: A Survey

Prasanna Roy, Sadip Midya, and Koushik Majumder[✉]

Department of Computer Science and Engineering, West Bengal University of Technology,
Kolkata, India
prasanna.roy.durgapur@gmail.com, sadip20@gmail.com,
koushik@ieee.org

Abstract. Vehicular Ad-Hoc Network (VANET) has gained the interest of the researchers in the current decade. VANET can be implemented to improve safety of vehicles on road and offer greater comfort to the drivers and passengers in traffic. Due to high mobility of vehicles frequent handoffs are required in VANET. These frequent handoffs must be carried out in an efficient manner with reduced handoff latency. To reduce the handoff latency during a switch, the scanning time to search for the new access point must be reduced significantly. Various schemes have been proposed which perform a pre-scanning in order to reduce handoff delay. This paper presents a survey of such pre-scanning schemes and tries to explore new areas of enhancements which will result in decrease of handoff latency. A qualitative comparison of these schemes is also carried out which leads to newer areas of research, where significant improvement can be beneficial.

Keywords: Pre-scanning · VANET · Access points · WiMAX · QoS

1 Introduction

Internet has shifted from the wired to the wireless paradigm in a far greater way than expected. People now have the ability to access the Internet from anywhere and anytime with the help of the different web-based devices. This has become possible because the available bandwidth has increased and various enhancements in the field of wireless networking have taken place. One such field where wireless networking has been vastly applied is VANET. There has been a notable effort from both the academia and manufacturers to integrate wireless networking with Intelligent Transportation System (ITS) to provide assistance to drivers and ensure safety on road [1]. Apart from this other web based services related to information and entertainments are also provided. However, there is a significant difference between the nodes in a VANET and the nodes in a traditional wireless network. The vehicles, that are the prime components of a VANET, move about at a high speed. This results in frequent handoffs which is a very serious challenge. Thus, this challenge needs special attention. Connections may break and as a result packets may be lost during the handover process [2, 3].

If the roads are busy, the network traffic also increases in VANET. One of the easy ways to solve the problem of congestion is by installing more APs (Access Point). This

© Springer Nature Singapore Pte Ltd. 2016
A. Unal et al. (Eds.): SmartCom 2016, CCIS 628, pp. 315–322, 2016.
DOI: 10.1007/978-981-10-3433-6_38

will distribute the traffic flow in the network. Generally in most of the handoff schemes, the AP is chosen based on its signal strength [4]. This may lead to imbalance in load distribution in the network. Depending on the relative position of the APs and the Mobile Nodes (MN) the signal strength of one AP may be more compared to another AP to a MN. Thus, it is impractical to predict the flow of traffic in the network considering the AP's signal strength only. Many other schemes are present which evaluate more than just the signal strength of Access Point while choosing or scanning the target AP. A literature review of such scanning scheme is presented in this paper. A comparative analysis is done among them with the aim of discovering their limitations and identifying the areas where enhancements can be done in order to develop an efficient scanning algorithm.

The paper is arranged as follows. Section 2 gives a review of the existing scanning schemes in VANET. Conclusion and future scope is given in Sect. 3.

2   Review of Some Existing Schemes of Scanning in VANET

2.1   Reducing Scanning Latency in WiMAX VANET

In order to reduce the delay in scanning during the handoff process a new protocol was proposed in [5]. The direction and velocity of the concerned vehicle is used by the Current Road Side Unit (RSU) to forecast when the vehicle will start scanning. This helps a lot in reducing the scanning delay (Fig. 1).

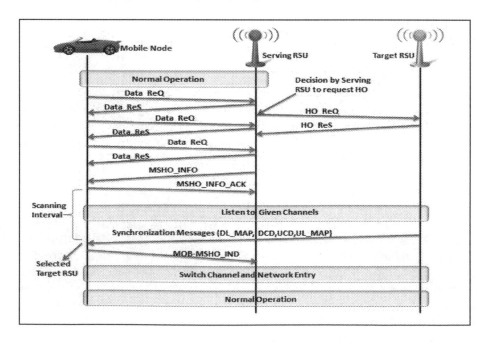

Fig. 1. Timing diagram for reducing scanning delays in WiMAX VANET

While the vehicle is still associated to the Current Road Side Unit, it takes part in the pre-selection and preauthorization of the target Road Side Unit. To notify the selected RSU about the incoming vehicle a backbone server is used. The arrival time and the ID of the vehicle are sent to the target RSU. On the other hand, the information about the dedicated channel and time that has been estimated for scanning is sent to the vehicle (Mobile Station). The scanning process is initialized using this.

This solution proposes that the RSU which is presently serving the vehicle helps in selecting the target RSU on the basis of the movement of the vehicle. It has been assumed that all the RSUs in the region taken into consideration are tightly associated with a backbone server. The RSU stores all the information about the vehicle. This information is obtained during data communication. As soon as a vehicle reaches the coverage area of a RSU, and it gets associated, the table of the RSU containing information about the vehicles in its coverage area is updated. The attributes of the table are moving direction, vehicle arrival time and vehicle speed.

2.2 Adaptive Channel Scanning

The Adaptive Channel Scanning (ACS) algorithm [6] is used to determine the frequency and duration during which the channel will be scanned. This helps in discovering the base stations in the neighborhood. Handovers in different IEEE 802.16 networks can also be carried out easily. The algorithm provides support for requirements that ensure QoS. It also ensures a scenario where more than one device can scan the channel simultaneously.

This scheme focuses on the way of determining the frequency and duration of channel scanning. It is assumed that it is not possible to avoid the channel scanning procedure. According to this algorithm multiple MNs are allocated scanning intervals. The QoS requirements of the applications supported by them are also maintained. The ACS algorithm aims to reduce the adverse effects on the application traffic which is caused due to scanning. The algorithm can be broken down into two major components which are estimating the time that the MN requires for scanning a group of BSs which are in the neighborhood, and interleaving the intervals between scanning of channels and transmission of data.

The time required for scanning the channel is dependent on the association latencies and synchronization. According to IEEE 802.16e the MN has to receive the frame allocation information and uplink and downlink channel descriptors to get synchronized with the BS that has been targeted. The average synchronization latency is estimated to take up two frame cycles. The downlink channel descriptors and the uplink channel descriptors take up one frame cycle, while the downlink map and the uplink map messages take up another frame cycle. However, the association level is considered to determine association latency. Each BS has the capability of estimating its own time required for scanning the channel. A few extensions might be required to estimate the corresponding time required for scanning the channel for BSs in the neighborhood. The BS which is presently serving calculates the duration of scanning the channel, the time gap between two successive scans and the total number of scanning intervals that can be provided in the stipulated time. The QoS requirement of the active mobile application and the bandwidth available is used by the algorithm to consider the maximum tolerable jitter and latencies. It then interleaves scanning operations between the periods of data transmission to reduce the scanning time for channels. It uses the scanning period, which is taken as the minimum value for jitter and latency for each MS in the network. Using the minimum scanning period, the algorithm calculates number of scanning intervals and interval between two scanning operations which is used by the algorithm to carry out adaptive scanning (Fig. 2).

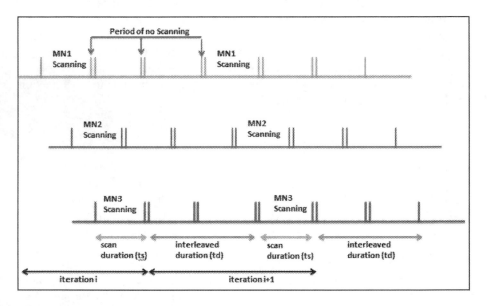

Fig. 2.   Illustration of channel scanning intervals for three MNs

2.3   A Pre-scanning Scheme for Vehicular Ad-Hoc Networks

The Quality Scan scheme [7] reduces handover delay and maintains a balanced load among the co-located APs. A pre-positioned AP Controller (APC) is used to collect every nodes loading state. This helps in forecasting the traffic in the network in the next instant. The MN carries out passive scanning to receive various parameters. After analyzing these parameters the MN chooses the best AP that can offer the best QoS.

The states of numerous APs in a region are considered by this scheme. The prime parameters are busy or usage level of the APs and their signal strength. In order to enhance the quality of the network environment, groups are created with the local APs. The network traffic is then distributed when necessary with the help of these groups. The AP controller is integrated with the Transportation Information System (TIS) which gathers information about regional traffic and velocity of the MN. APC collects information about the APs at regular time intervals. By carrying out calculation on the gathered information the network flow in the future can be predicted.

The calculation result about the APs is provided by the APC. Beacon frames are used by the APs to send information about the neighbor APs to the MNs. The MNs can then perform passive scanning to obtain information about the neighboring APs. This helps the MN in determining the AP with which it will carry out the next handoff and at the same time keep the load balanced. In this manner the operation of active scanning can be avoided at the time of handoff thus preventing disruption in data communication caused by active scanning.

Each AP sends information status about its queue state, channel, location etc., at regular intervals to the APC. The loading state of the corresponding APs in future is then calculated by the APC on the basis of the information it receives. This calculation result is then attached to the beacon frames that the APs send out on periodic basis. This information also contains the queue states and busy level of the APs along with the detailed information of the neighbor APs. The APC transmits appropriate information along with the list of neighbors to the APs situated at various locations (Fig. 3).

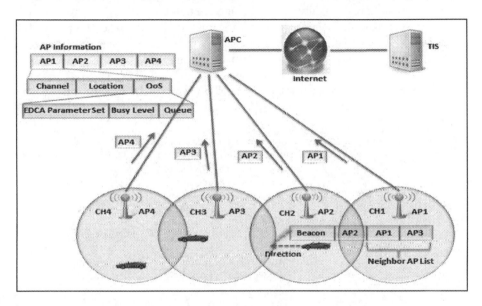

Fig. 3. Architecture of pre-scanning in cooperative VANET

2.4   Fast Scanning in WiMAX Network

This paper [8] addresses MN scanning from two perspectives. Firstly, MN must find a downlink frequency which is available while arriving to a network. Secondly, when the BS is performing the handoff it must start scanning the target BS.

Here scanning is carried out in two major steps. In the first step, the past successful scanning frequencies are recorded. Using this, the MN chooses the frequencies that will be used for scanning in the future. In the second step, the use of the MOB_NBR-ADV message is improved. The currently serving BS sends the message to the MN to inform it about the BSs in the neighborhood. Thus, the MN is able to get a list containing the handovers history among the BSs. The MN uses this information to decide which neighbor BS is likely to become the next target BS to carry out the handoff. Thus MOB-NBR-ADV message provides the list of neighbors and the associated parameters to the MN. The scanning operation is improved as the MN knows in advance which BS has the highest probability of becoming the handover target.

According to [8], the MN utilizes its handover history and the information acquired from the neighbor advertisement (MOB_NBR-ADV) message to scan the new BS. The MOB_NBR-ADV message is broadcasted by the current BS of MN. It is assumed here that the MN gets the list of all the BSs which are in the neighborhood. The frequency of each neighbor is also advertised along with this list in the MOB_NBR-ADV message. After the BS provides the information to the MN, the MN starts guessing the target BS to carry out the handover. The MN must attempt to obtain some particular parameters in order to determine the most suitable BS at which it can carry out handover. These parameters are not obtained during the scanning operation in IEEE 802.16E. The MN is left with the task of deciding the neighbor to which it is going to communicate. The MN has to continue scanning the neighboring BSs in the given order supplied in the MOB_NBR-ADV message if no other information is supplied.

Table 1. Overview of advantages and disadvantages of mentioned schemes

S. No.	Scheme	Advantages	Disadvantages
1	Reducing scanning latency in WiMAX VANET [5]	Anticipation of vehicle movement beforehand reduces handoff latency. As next RSU is pre-selected before handoff, vehicle gets continuous service. Uniformity in network due to presence of backbone server	Assumes that vehicles move with uniform speed. The network will fail due to failure of backbone server
2	Adaptive channel scanning [6]	Reduction in disruptive effects on application traffic when MN starts scanning. Scanning intervals allocated to multiple MNs. QoS of application running currently is not degraded	Bandwidth must be accurately measured for this algorithm which needs to be done carefully
3	A pre-scanning scheme for vehicular Ad-hoc networks [7]	AP is selected in a way that traffic flow in network is distributed. Transmission quality is enhanced. Load information of neighboring APs is also considered in decision making	Doesn't consider the scenario where the vehicle moves in both directions
4	Fast scanning in WiMAX network [8]	Scanning operation time is reduced. No requirement of additional network support. Limited computational and memory resources requirement by MN. Number of frequencies checked is reduced	Load condition on the target AP is not considered in the selection procedure. If more and more vehicles are handed off to a particular AP, It will result in network overhead and may cause a system failure

3 Conclusion and Future Scope

From the above discussed schemes it is evident that the handoff latency can be reduced by improving the scanning procedure significantly (Table 1). In [5] scanning latency is reduced as the vehicle movement is anticipated beforehand. However here the algorithm assumes that the vehicle moves in uniform speed and also, it just evaluates two parameters for pre scanning which are velocity and distance, which is not enough for efficient scanning. This can be overcome by the scheme introduced in [7] where many more parameters like queue state or load state, channel and location of the neighbor APs are also evaluated. Also in [5], the scanning latency has been notably reduced with the assistance of the backbone server. However, the failure of the backbone server might lead to performance degradation. Dependency of the whole network on the backbone server can be lessened by creating RSU clusters. The scheme also assumes that the vehicles are moving with a constant velocity. Thus, it is necessary to address the scenario when vehicles are moving with varying speed. In [6], the performance of the algorithm depends on the accurate measurement of the bandwidth which needs to be done carefully. In [7] the bidirectional traffic is not considered which leads to a performance restriction. This can be overcome by incorporating the scheme in [8] where probability of frequency of handoff is taken into consideration. By using this most likely neighboring AP is selected as the Target AP. Also in [8] the load on the neighboring base stations is not evaluated before handoff which may lead to increase in network overhead. This can be overcome by adding another parameter to consider the current load status of the neighboring AP as shown in [7].

The various scanning strategies proposed so far reduces the handoff latency by pre-scanning the probable neighboring BSs with which the MN might get attached in the near future. The Scanning process needs to evaluate a good number of parameters instead of a handful, to reduce the scanning latency. Also, the scanning techniques can be improved by including some nature inspired algorithms which give an optimal solution from a given search space. The best suited scanning frequency for a particular vehicle must be selected out of many in order to deliver better QoS to the users. Thus working on scanning latency opens up a fresh field of research where suggested improvements can be made.

Acknowledgment. The Authors are grateful to the West Bengal University of Technology TEQIP II program.

References

1. Chiu, K.L., Hwang, R.H., Chen, Y.S.: A cross layer fast handover scheme in VANET. In: 2009 IEEE International Conference on Communications, pp. 1–5. IEEE, June 2009
2. Pack, S., Choi, J., Kwon, T., Choi, Y.: Fast-handoff support in IEEE 802.11 wireless networks. IEEE Commun. Surv. Tutorials **9**(1), 2–12 (2007)
3. Mishra, A., Shin, M., Arbaugh, W.: An empirical analysis of the IEEE 802.11 MAC layer handoff process. ACM SIGCOMM Comput. Commun. Rev. **33**(2), 93–102 (2003)

4. Hartenstein, H., Laberteaux, L.P.: A tutorial survey on vehicular ad hoc networks. IEEE Commun. Mag. **46**(6), 164–171 (2008)
5. Ahmed, S.H., Bouk, S.H., Kim, D.: Reducing scanning latency in WiMAX enabled VANETs. In: Proceedings of the 2014 Conference on Research in Adaptive and Convergent Systems, pp. 161–165. ACM, October 2014
6. Rouil, R., Golmie, N.: Adaptive channel scanning for IEEE 802.16e. In: Proceedings of 25th Annual Military Communications Conference (MILCOM 2006), Washington, DC, pp. 23–25, October 2006
7. Wu, T.Y., Lee, W.T., Liu, F.H., Chan, H.L., Lin, T.H.: An efficient pre-scanning scheme for handoff in cooperative vehicular networks. In: 2011 IEEE 22nd International Symposium on Personal, Indoor and Mobile Radio Communications, pp. 583–587. IEEE, September 2011
8. Boone, P., Barbeau, M., Kranakis, E.: Strategies for fast scanning, ranging and handovers in WiMAX/802.16. Int. J. Commun. Netw. Distrib. Syst. **1**(4–6), 414–432 (2008)

Software Testing and Information Theory

Meenu Dave and Rashmi Agrawal$^{(\boxtimes)}$

Computer Science Department, Jagan Nath University, Jaipur 302022, India
guptarashmi1979@gmail.com

Abstract. An adequacy criterion in software testing are the rules or guidelines for quantitative analysis of any test cases and sets the target to be achieved as to stop the testing process or test data generation. Search based test data generation is the application of the Evolutionary Algorithms to achieve an optimized test suit which is tested against the fitness function to check its distance from the target. The Entropy of Information Theory can be defined and the measure of "uncertainty". The paper is the study of the relation between the entropy, Information Gain and the uncertainty regarding the random generation of test data.

Keywords: Information theory · Entropy · Fitness function · Evolutionary Algorithms · Adequacy criteria

1 Introduction

The quality of any product developed (software) is dependents on the quality of test cases. Manual test case generation is effective but expensive, time consuming and laborious task. The advancements in software, there is a rise in complexity, reuse of components and dependencies, making test case generation a more challenging and provides scope for testers and researchers to design new techniques and tools. Automatic test case generation is a proven and well established technique as it is both economic and time saving. The test cases are generated automatically through random generation of variables. The test case generations may have other aspects other than just generating a test suit:

1. Generate a test suit which is minimal in size, having scope to add more in future for new versions.
2. Test suit size is kept minimal to meet the time and space restrictions.
3. The tester may wish to have a test suit which has high probability of error/fault detection rate with the given limits.
4. Tester tries to generate a suit which achieves the maximum adequacy criteria for good coverage of SUT to increase the confidence in software in the earlier stages.

Software testing is an approach to resolve the uncertainty, and to gain knowledge of a software system by running it against some test cases [1].

A. Unal et al. (Eds.): SmartCom 2016, CCIS 628, pp. 323–330, 2016.
DOI: 10.1007/978-981-10-3433-6_39

The software testing has both the probability and uncertainty involved with it as the probability of pass/fail can be measured by bringing down the randomness of the numbers generated for test cases. Entropy is a well established mathematical theory to measure the uncertainty or information. Information theory, Entropy can be used as coverage criteria for it is syntactic independent [1]. The existing coverage criteria like branch coverage or block coverage are highly effective in generating good cases but software developed for domains which are directly related to life, are safety- critical (banks) or real time (aeronautics, aerodynamics) additional criteria or analysis is mandate that the complement the existing ones. The test cases which have high probability of error detection have the high probability of testing software effectively. The diagnostic analysis of the test cases helps to bring down the randomness and generate test cases with more Information Gain. The probability and uncertainty regarding the test data can be brought down to generate effective test cases.

The aim of the paper is to review the literature for the probabilistic analysis of the software under test for test case generation. The background of the adequacy criteria is discussed in Sect. 2. The concepts of Information theory Entropy are covered in Sect. 3 with the review of previous related work in Sect. 4. Section 5 is the methodology where the experimental setup and analysis are elaborated and finally Sect. 6 is the conclusion and scope for future work.

2   Background

Initially some random numbers are used to generate the test cases which are run the Software Under Test (SUT). The output is analyzed to understand the process and measured for some adequacy criteria.

Adequacy criteria: The Software testing can be classified into two main broad categories: (a) Black Box or Specification Testing: The tester is has no knowledge about the internal details of the program. The interface based criteria algorithms [2] also comes under this as the tester has only the type and range of inputs as the specifications to be covered. (b) White box or Structure testing is the process where the SUT source code is analyses is done and a test data adequacy criteria is decided based upon the structure of the program. The most common representation of the structure and its execution is Control Flow Graph.

Definition of CFG: A program with n statements and m predicates (control/decision statements) can be represented as a CFG. The CFG is a directed graph with a combination of nodes and edges which represents the execution paths which may be traveled explicitly during execution. A CFG has imaginary start node and an exit node. The nodes that are decisions have two outgoing edges labeled T/F. Update nodes have single outgoing edges. The goal/objective of any control-flow-graph based adequacy criteria is to cover maximum number of branches (decisions/predicate statements) or statements. Multiple decision/control coverage and path coverage are advance coverage criteria. The aim is to generate test suit which gives 100% coverage.

Test Suit: A test suit (T) is a set or a collection of test cases (t), where $T = t_1....t_n$, which are executed with the SUT to check if it meets specified requirements, or behavior or generates output.

Test Case: A test case has a collection of values for variables as input and the expected output. If the output generated with the given input is same, the test case is said to pass, else fail.

Testing adequacy criteria has two main notions; (a) it is the metric to measure the quality of the test cases against some defined conditions; (b) the stopping criteria when the tester can say that test suit generated is sufficient enough to meet the requirements [2]. Test data adequacy criteria: A rule that determines whether a test is adequate or efficient with reference to the given criteria [2].

Test case selection criteria: A rule where a set of guidelines or specifications are set in for test case generation algorithms [2]. Statement coverage, branch coverage and path coverage the most common structure based frequently used both in industry tools and research.

Statement coverage: The percentage/number of statements executed is the indication of statement adequacy of a test suit after executing it against the SUT.

Branch coverage: The number/percentage of control statements executed by a set of test cases for a SUT is the branch adequacy. Path coverage: The requirement for this adequacy is the coverage of all the paths of a SUT during the test case execution from the entry to exit of program.

3 Information Theory

Entropy: The entropy of a random variable is a measure of the uncertainty of the variable, the amount of information required on average to describe the random variable [3]. The Shannon Entropy $H(X)$ can be defined as: Let X, be a random discrete variable with finite discrete probability distribution $P = (p_1, p_2, p_3...p_n)$.

The uncertainty related to the variable with probability density function $Pr(X = x)$, is called the entropy. **The entropy is defined as the measure of impurity**. The $p_i = 0$ *for* $i = 1...n$ and $\sum_{(i=1)}^{x} log_2[p_i = 1]$, $H(x) = -\sum_x p(x)log_2 p(x)$ as defined by [3,4].

Entropy can be useful diagnosis prioritization strategy to calculate the Information gain where (a) there is minimal or no knowledge about the internal structure or the semantics of the SUT, just specifications regarding inputs and outputs (b) coverage criteria are different for the any two test cases to be compared [5]. The work compares the entropy before testing H(T), i.e. the maximum entropy with the entropy after testing. The Information gain is given by $G(t) = H(T) - H(T|after\ testing\ t)$ [5]. The uncertainty (or entropy) related to the behavior of a software can be brought down with testing. The test cases selected based on the information-optimal strategy are the ones which have most of the information gain or the one which is the fastest to cool down the system [5].

326   M. Dave and R. Agrawal

4   Related Work

Entropy based test data generation has not been studied and researched much. We searched journal, conference proceedings and references of the published work for "test data generation", "search based test data generation", "test data generation + ", "information theory and test data generation". We found that a lot of work has been done and still going on in test data generation area encompassing the various software development stages, adequacy criteria, machine learning, heuristic algorithms and hybrid techniques. This motivated us to work in the test data generation with entropy as the research area. The work by Campos [6] suggests entropy as the fitness function for a search based test generation. Based on entropy candidates for fault location are ranked according to probability diagnostic report generated based on entropy as a strategy for optimization. A drastic reduction of 91% was noted in the candidate numbers to be inspected for fault localization with reduction of 49% in uncertainty in the original test suit. The paper is the study of Search Based Software Testing for the generation of optimized test cases with improved diagnosis [6]. The paper presents a novel approach of trace classification based on their entropies.

Table 1. The diagnostic matrix

	Test cases						
Source Code	t1	t2	t3	t4	t5	t6	t7
{ Print("empty"); }	*	*	*	*	*	*	*
if (a >b) {		*			*		*
if (a >c) {		*					*
max = a;							
min = b;							
} else {							
max = c;					*		
min = b;}}							
else {	*		*	*		*	
if (b > c) {			*			*	
max = b;							
if (a > c) {			*				
min = c;}							
} else {	*			*			
min = a;							
max = c;}							
return true;}							
Entropy	0.530	0.530	0.5	0.530	0.53064	0.530	0.530
Information Gain	0.966						

An algorithm is designed for trace ranking by calculating the distance between traces through entropy based fingerprints. The trace classification can have following applications, (1) defect classification and mapping (2) test case prioritization (3) analysis of the software execution paths [7]. The paper is a study of Information gain based online test case prioritization for detection of faults. The proposed approach shows a reduction of 53% in cost of QA, when applied to Siemens programs and compared to other existing techniques. The work shows a diagnostic prioritization, where the reduction of the cost of diagnosis is related with decrease in entropy and increase in the information gain [8].

5   Experimental Setup and Analysis

The source code was instrumented and traces were inserted at block level and predicate level. A set of seven test cases were run through the SUT and a diagnostic matrix was created, Table 1. Entropy for each test case is calculated along with the branches covered for each true outcome. The Entropy H(ti) for test case t1 $= 3/8 \log (3/8)$, where each true outcome $= 1$. The density matrix [6]

Table 2. Diagnostic matrix after adding t8 to the suit

	Test cases							
Source Code	t1	t2	t3	t4	t5	t6	t7	t8
{ Print("empty"); }	*	*	*	*	*	*	*	*
if (a > b) {		*			*		*	
if (a > c) {		*					*	
max = a;								
min = b;								
} else {								
max = c;					*			
min = b;}}								
else {	*		*	*		*		*
if (b > c) {		*				*		*
max = b;								
if (a > c) {		*						*
min = c;}								
} else {	*			*				
min = a;								
max = c;}								
return true;}								
Entropy	0.530	0.530	0.5	0.530	0.530	0.530	0.530	0.5
Information Gain	0.9666							

is generated where the total number of branches covered by test case is divided by the total number of test cases. The average of the probability p is given by X P(ti)/n where P(ti) is the probability of each test case and n is the total number of test cases. In the given table the p = .39 or 39%. The Information gain is the decrease in the entropy [3]. We have calculated the information gain as per [6]. $IG(p) = -p.[log]_2(p) - (1-p).[log]_2(1-p)$. The density function can be a guide to add new test cases to the test suit. If the addition of the new test cases brings the p closer to .5, then it should be included into the test suit. The ranking of the test cases can be done based on their probability and then with p as heuristic, new can be added. The diagnostic analysis show the path covered by each test case, in our case the branches covered along with the entropy of each test case and finally information gain. Test case t8 was added to the test suit, the decrease in entropy shows increase in information gain of the test suit. The results are shown in Table 2. The p changes to 0.40625 and Information gain changes to 0.974489 (Figs. 1, 2 and 3).

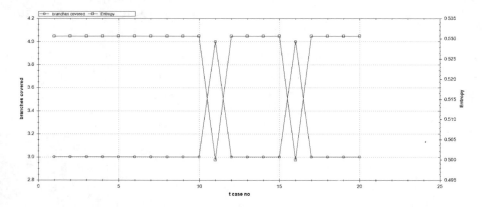

Fig. 1. Entropy and branch adequacy criteria

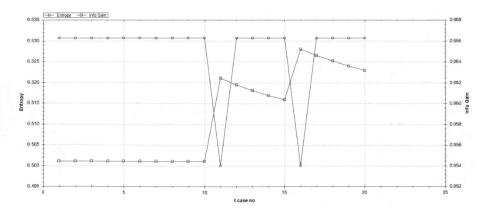

Fig. 2. Entropy and information gain

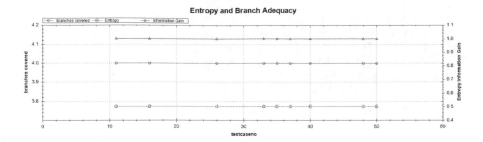

Fig. 3. Entropy, branch adequacy and information gain

6   Conclusion and Future Work

Any population generated for optimization, needs to be evaluated for its standard/suitability through fitness function. The most common adequacy criteria for test cases are statement, block, path or branch coverage. This paper is a study of new diagnostic analysis, entropy, for the generation of test suit. The main advantage of the diagnostic evaluation over branch coverage is that it allows the analysis to narrow down from branch level to variable/predicate level for better coverage. We observed that the decrease in entropy can results in information gain. The concept has been applied to java class. It was observed that selection and ranking of test cases based on entropy gives test cases with improved information gain. The trends show that after with increase of test data to the suit, there is an overall increase in Information Gain for the test suit with local maxima. The future work is to apply the technique to larger programs. An investigation needs to be done to check the effectiveness of the test suit against other search based test data generations techniques. The above technique can be applied to various areas like test case prioritization, regression testing, fault localization, static code analysis, unreached or traversed paths of control flow graph, code prioritization and security.

References

1. Yang, L., et al.: Entropy and software systems: towards an information-theoretic foundation of software testing. In: Proceedings of the FSE/SDP Workshop on Future of Software Engineering Research. ACM (2010)
2. Zhu, H., Hall, P.A.V., May, J.H.R.: Software unit test coverage and adequacy. ACM Comput. Surv. (CSUR) **29**(4), 366–427 (1997)
3. Cover, T.M., Thomas, J.A.: Information theory and statistics. In: Elements of Information Theory. Wiley, New York (1991)
4. Shannon, C.E.: A mathematical theory of communication. ACM SIGMOBILE Mob. Comput. Commun. Rev. **5**(1), 3–55 (2001)
5. Yang, L., Dang, Z., Fischer, T.R.: Information gain of black-box testing. Formal Aspects Comput. **23**(4), 513–539 (2011)

6. Campos, J., et al.: Entropy-based test generation for improved fault localization. In: 2013 IEEE/ACM 28th International Conference on Automated Software Engineering (ASE). IEEE (2013)
7. Miranskyy, A.V., et al.: Using entropy measures for comparison of software traces. Inf. Sci. **203**, 59–72 (2012)
8. Gonzalez-Sanchez, A., et al.: Prioritizing tests for software fault diagnosis. Softw. Pract. Experience **41**(10), 1105–1129 (2011)

Efficient Way for Tracking Electricity Consumption with Meter Pulse Reader (MPR) Algorithm

Preeti Arora$^{(\boxtimes)}$, Mritunjaya Sharma, Himanshu Jindal, and Arpit Mittal

Bhagwan Parshuram Institute of Technology, New Delhi, India
erpreetiarora07@gmail.com, mritunjay.sharma2@gmail.com,
himanshujindal1994@gmail.com, arpitmittal555@gmail.com

Abstract. Electricity bill generation and meter reading is a very complex process in today scenario. The existing method of billing process uses manual work of taking reading of the meter, updating details of meter and sending bill to the customer. Till now, this is being implemented by using OCR but it does not allow user to track the consumption each second. We are developing a method on IoT platform which is more efficient and can be used for keeping track of electricity consumption. User can get the reading on android any time. Our electricity distributor will no longer need to take reading manually. The data will be directly transferred to them which will be used to create electricity bills. For multiple meters in single household, combined result can be viewed. Also, Client is able to view the graphical usage for a particular duration.

Keywords: IoT · Sensors · OCR · Home automation

1 Introduction

The Internet of Things [1, 4] (IoT) is a system of inter-connected computing devices, electronic and mechanical machines, physical objects, devices that are distinguished by unique identifiers and the capability to share and transfer data over a network without human intervention. Using this technology, data can be automatically sensed from objects and transferred to the desired location for further processing. We can use sensors for this purpose. "Things" in the term "Internet of Things" may refer to any object like speakers, alarm clocks, electronic components etc. We create a network of these things to share data synchronously.

This IoT can be effectively used in Home Automation [2–4]. Home Automation the usage and controlling of home based appliances from remote location automatically. Some of the home automation devices are standalone parts and cannot communicate, for example programmable light switches, on the other hand others follow the concepts of the internet of things and are connected to network for remote controlling and data sharing. At present scenario, an employee from electricity distributor company comes and note down the readings which is forwarded to the company for drafting electricity bills monthly. This process is very complex and can be made efficient.

© Springer Nature Singapore Pte Ltd. 2016
A. Unal et al. (Eds.): SmartCom 2016, CCIS 628, pp. 331–339, 2016.
DOI: 10.1007/978-981-10-3433-6_40

The remaining parts of this paper are organized as Sect. 2 comprises of literature review. Section 3 comprises of the proposed process. Section 4 gives the implementation and results. Section 5 contains the conclusion. Section 6 defines the future scope of the work done.

2   Literature Review

Till now, the work done in this field is mostly based on OCR i.e. Optical Character Recognition [5]. In the paper [6], the author explains that the image of the reading is clicked from which reading is fetched. After this an email is sent to user about the bill amount which is then paid by the user using their web application. If user is facing any issue, complaint can be registered on their website.

A similar work is done in other forms. In a paper [7], the author followed a similar process. The image of meter reading is then send for further processing and the data is saved on server which is used for preparing bills.

But there are many problems with this method. First, of all processing an image is time consuming. So, it reduces efficiency. This makes the method of OCR not fit for continuous tracking. In our proposed algorithm, we are not processing any image. We are directly fetching the reading. Second, OCR is more error prone. There are high chances of occurring error in processing an image while in our method there are very less chances of error because no interception of data from an image is performed here. A careful checking is required to implement OCR. Also it is not worth doing for small amounts of text. It takes more cost and time than our proposed method.

3   Proposed Work

In this paper, a way which reduces human efforts to get the reading from house hold electricity meters, has been presented. Also, it provides the user with the facility of getting information of his current electricity usage anytime and anywhere he/she wants. For this purpose Internet of Things concept has been used. In the MPR Algorithm, the readings from electricity meters would be taken. This can be done by analyzing the speed of the LED embedded in electricity meters the phase and thus the consumption reading can be tracked, which is then used for further processing. After all processing and calculation on readings, these readings can be shared with electricity distributor-company. The company will construct electricity bills using this. Also this reading can be transferred to customer using any android/IOS/web application that is used by the user. This will help the user to reduce electricity wastage. At present, it is very tedious and complex process of fetching the reading from electricity meters and sends them to the electricity distributor company. For this purpose, an employee is used to note down the reading manually for each house meter. This reading is then used to construct electricity bills of each customer which are send to them for further payments. In this era of technology, this work is very tedious and can be made effective n simple which consumes lesser manpower and more technology. Also, the user or customer is only allowed to get monthly reading of his/her usage. He can never be aware of his current statistics of electricity consumption.

There are lots of problems in this existing process. First of all it is very time consuming. All this work takes a lot of precious time. This process needs a proper synchronization off various units. This is totally manual process and consumes a lot of manpower. All this creates a huge burden on employees. It is more error prone. Doing this process manually can cause a large number of errors.

Using the Framework below with MPR algorithm, multiple meters in a house, can be linked to single customer account and integrated data can be shown if the user wants. All these meters along with application server, customer account and internet connection will create a network to share data and thus implements IoT. Since complete process is depending upon reading of pulse from the blinking of LED embedded in meter, hence we name this method as meter pulse reader.

3.1 Block Diagram

The block diagram of the Meter Pulse Reader (MPR) and involved units is explained in Fig. 1.

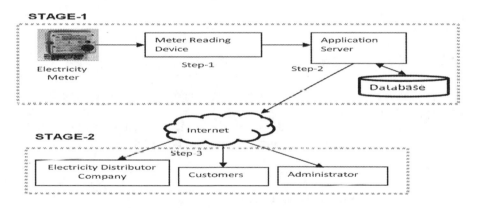

Fig. 1. Block diagram of MPR

The MPR algorithm with Framework consists of two stages.

Stage 1 defines the process of fetching of pulse count directly by sensing the pulse indicator LED from meter. Stage 1 has two steps. Step **1** is the sensor app taking pulse count from the meter. Step **2** is to upload that reading to server. This is saved in database.

Stage 2 defines the process of calculating the electricity consumption from this reading and sending them to user and electricity distributor company. This data is used by customers for keeping track and by electricity distributor companies to prepare bills. This is defined as Step **3** in our procedure. All this is managed by an Administrator.

3.2   Proposed Algorithm

S = Sum of visible bits on frame, **P** = Boolean stating if frame has pulse or not, ἡ = Threshold value for the sum of visible bits when pulse is on frame, ¶ = Standard pulse count for 1 kWh (3200 in India), **T** = time taken between previous pulse and current pulse.

Algorithm:
1. Scan the image of the meter pulse indicator frame by frame
2. Initialize P as "false" and for each frame calculate S.
3. If (P="true")
   a. Set P as "false"
4. If (P="false" and S > ἡ)
   a. Calculate T
   b. *Power Consumption* $= \frac{1000*1000*360}{\P*T}$
5. Append 1 to current pulse_count .
6. If (pulse count = 3200)
   a. Add 1 to Meter reading and set pulse_count=0.
7. Repeat step 2-6 for next frame.

---

4   Implementation and Results

For implementing the MPR algorithm Framework, Android platform (Version 2.0) have been used. The implementation has been done in three major phases. First is our Pulse Identifier Sensor phase. Second is the Transfer of Data between Serve and Client via Server. Third is Client-Side Application. A comparison between MPR and OCR is also performed.

4.1   Step-1 (Reading the Pulse and Data)

This is the most important phase of the framework as the basis of our implementation lie solely on the accuracy of the sensors to read the Meter Reading accurately. For the initial implementation, an Android Device was used with a Camera to detect the pulses on the meter. The Camera of the Android Device is placed in front of the Meter where the Meter Pulse is blinking depicting the rate at which the electricity is being consumed. These pulses form the base of our Meter Reading which should be accurate enough to detect real time variations in environment and gather the information accordingly. To increase the accuracy of the detection the meter should be covered from all sided. A Threshold value is also set automatically by the Device which notices the change of brightness around the pulsing LED hence increasing the accuracy of our sensor app. As depicted in Fig. 3, the pulse is being read and a constant rate at which the electricity is being used is also depicted. The rate depicted is shown that is the power consumption at that time of hour at which the reading is being seen as this feature was not available in existing systems (Fig. 2).

```
if (!state && (sum > threshold)) {
    pulseCount++;
    //··········algo to compute power at real time··········
    {
        long currTime = System.currentTimeMillis();
        if (prevTime > 0) {
            intervals[intervalsIdx] = currTime - prevTime;
            intervalsIdx = (intervalsIdx + 1) % (intervals.length);

            double avg = 0.0;
            double samples = 0.0;
            for (int i = 0; i < intervals.length; i++) {
                if (intervals[i] > 0) {
                    avg += intervals[i];
                    samples += 1.0;
                }
            }
            if (samples > 0) {
                int f = 1000 * 3600 / intervalsPerKwh;
                mStatusBar.setText(String.format("%.0f W", 1000.0*f*(samples / avg)));
            }
        }
        prevTime = currTime;
        state = true;
    }
}
if (pulseCount==3200)
{meterReading++;
    pulseCount=0;
}
```

Fig. 2. Code for MPR sensor app

After the pulse is detected, the pulse counter is incremented as can be seen in the Fig. 3. After 3200 pulse count, 1 kWh of energy is consumed and the reading counter is incremented.

Fig. 3. MPR output

4.2   Step-2 (Sensor-Server-Client)

The outputs of the Step-1, the Meter reading of the user, was sent to server where the Database consisted of the User Information and the daily readings. These readings will be coded in a Jason Script and the Jason String will be sent to the Client Application (Figs. 4 and 5).

←T→			id	day	month	year	slot1	slot2	slot3	slot4	total
Edit	Copy	Delete	1	1	March	2016	10112	10114	10116	10119	10123
Edit	Copy	Delete	2	2	March	2016	10123	10125	10127	10130	10134

Fig. 4. Application server database

←T→			id	ca_no	name	email	password	address	contact
Edit	Copy	Delete	1	123456789	Arpit Mittal	arpitmittal007@gmail.com	12345678	A-161, Sector-8, Rohini, New Delhi-89	27578912
Edit	Copy	Delete	2	234567890	Himanshu Jindal	himanshu23@gmail.com	11111111	H-89, Punjabi Bagh, New Delhi	24658912
Edit	Copy	Delete	3	345678901	Keshav Goel	keshav11@yahoo.com	23456789	E-121, Shalimar Bagh, New Delhi	28456578
Edit	Copy	Delete	4	456789012	Mritunjay	mritunjay34@hotmail.com	22222222	A-65/56, Karol Bagh, New Delhi-110005	25724566

Fig. 5. User account database

4.3 Step-3 (Client Side Application)

An android application was designed for the Client side as a GUI for the users where the input from the server was taken after the user login in and check for the consumption of their daily electricity usage. Users can monitor and analyze their Meter from a far distant with just over access of internet. They can get a statistical representation of their daily usage. A section showing the proper Cost calculation was also shown giving users an estimate about the time of day the electricity is mostly used. An integrated usage plan can also be given integrating all the meters of a household (Figs. 6 and 7).

```
public class Usage extends Fragment {
    static MeterData dm = new MeterData();
    TextView reading,cost;
    @Override
    public View onCreateView(LayoutInflater inflater, ViewGroup container,
                             Bundle savedInstanceState) {
        View rootView = inflater.inflate(R.layout.usage, container, false);

        reading=(TextView) rootView.findViewById(R.id.reading);
        cost=(TextView) rootView.findViewById(R.id.cost);


        reading.setText(Integer.toString(dm.currentReading));
        int readDiff=dm.currentReading-dm.lastMonthReading;
        String readingdiff = Integer.toString(readDiff);
        cost.setText(readingdiff);

        GraphView graph = (GraphView) rootView.findViewById(R.id.graph);
        LineGraphSeries<DataPoint> series = new LineGraphSeries<>(new DataPoint[] {
                new DataPoint(1, dm.reading1),
                new DataPoint(2, dm.reading2),
                new DataPoint(3, dm.reading3),
                new DataPoint(4, dm.reading4),
        });
        graph.addSeries(series);

        return rootView;
    }
```

Fig. 6. Code for Client side

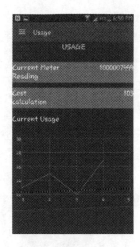

Fig. 7. Client side GUI

4.4 Comparison Between OCR and MPR

In Table 1, for any 5 random instances of meter reading time taken to fetch and save the reading server is calculated for both the methods. After this, a comparison is performed.

T_{OCR} = Time taken by OCR to scan and read the Meter Reading

T_{MPR} = Time taken by MPR (Meter Pulse Reader) to read one pulse and add it to current reading

Average Time to scan one image using OCR (based on reading taken) = 84.2 ms

Average Time to scan one pulse for Meter Reading using MPR (based on reading taken) = 8 ms

Table 1. Time taken by OCR and MPR

Reading No.	1	2	3	4	5
Meter reading	5155	5902	7896	15714	16756
T_{OCR} (ms)	79	90	96	89	67
T_{MPR} (ms)	5	7	4	15	9

Therefore the MPR method reduces the time overhead of scanning the Meter Reading to 9.5% as to the previous existing method. Based on above data a graphical analysis is performed in Fig. 8.

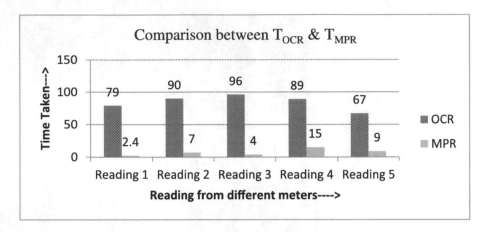

Fig. 8. Graphical analysis for T_{OCR} and T_{MPR}

In Table 2, both the methods (Meter Reading By OCR and MPR) are compared based on various factors.

Table 2. Difference between both method (by OCR and MPR)

Comparison factor	By OCR	By MPR
Time or efficiency	More due to image processing	Lesser as compared to OCR
Error prone	More error prone	Less error prone
Cost	More than MPR	Lesser
Fit for small amount of text	No	Yes

In OCR, the image is needed to be saved to the sensor memory to process it for scanning and reading the meter reading. Therefore the Approximate memory taken by OCR to store and process the image is 2.0 MB. In MPR, the image is not needed to be saved as we sense the pulse that is being detected at the frame level. Therefore the Approximate memory taken by MPR to store the pulse reading after scanning reduce to just storing and scanning the variables needed to store the pulse data.

5   Conclusion

IoT is a platform in which a network of various things is created for easy transfer and manipulation of data. This method MPR can be implemented for practical use easily. Not only android it can be implemented on any of the platform depending upon the ease of customer. Since OCR is time consuming, we conclude that it is unable to provide continuous tracking. Our proposed method MPR is more efficient and helps the user to track his usage any particular time. The user can minimize electricity usage and thus prevent wastage of natural resources. Thus in terms of efficiency and other stated problems Meter Pulse Reader can be implemented for practical use. MPR system allows user to view his usage in any form for any particular period. Also use of technology reduces human efforts and makes works simpler than before. User can see his current usage from a remote location also. These preventions methods are highly in need at this point of time for balancing our natural resources which are in rapid extinction.

6 Future Scope

In future, this work can be continued and extended allow the user to control his home electricity appliances from android application also. Along with tracking consumption, user will be able to control consumption even from any remote location. Not only for electricity usage, this process can be devised for other resources like water usage or LPG gas usage etc. These processes will support technology, makes our life smarter and helps in conserving our natural resources.

References

1. Gubbia, J., Buyyab, R., Marusica, S., Palaniswamia, M.: Internet of Things (IoT): a vision architectural elements and future directions. Future Gener. Comput. Syst. **29**, 1645–1660 (2013). Elsevier
2. Palaniappan, S., Hariharan, N., Kesh, N.T., Vidhyalakshmi, S., Angel Deborah, S.: Home automation systems – a study. Int. J. Comput. Appl. **116**, 11–18 (2015)
3. Ramlee, R.A., Leong, M.H., Singh, R.S.S., Ismail, M.M., Othman, M.A., Sulaiman, H.A., Misran, M.H., Meor Said, M.A.: Bluetooth remote home automation system using Android application 1R. Int. J. Eng. Sci. **2**, 149–153 (2013)
4. Vinaysagar, K.N., Kusuma, S.M.: Home automation using Internet of Things. Int. Res. J. Eng. Technol. **2**, 1965–1970 (2015)
5. Bhatia, N.: Optical character recognition techniques: a review. Int. J. Adv. Res. Comput. Sci. Softw. Eng. **4**, 1219–1223 (2014)
6. Dayama, R., Chatla, A., Shaikh, H., Kulkarni, M.: Android based meter reading using OCR. Int. J. Comput. Sci. Mob. Comput. **3**, 536–539 (2014)
7. Kotwal, J., Pawar, S., Pansare, S., Khopade, M., Mahalunkar, P.: Android app for meter reading. Int. J. Eng. Comput. Sci. **4**, 9853–9857 (2015)

Circularly Polarized Cross Bisect Koch Fractal Dual Band MSA for ISM Band Applications

Kishor B. Biradar$^{(\boxtimes)}$ and Mansi S. Subhedar

Department of Electronics and Telecommunication,
Pillai HOC College of Engineering & Technology, Tal. Khalapur,
Dist. Raigad, Rasayani 410206, Maharashtra, India
kbiradar@mes.ac.in, mansi_subhedar@rediffmail.com

Abstract. A new single layer simple probe feed asymmetrical koch fractal dual band microstrip patch antenna (MSA) is proposed for ISM band (2.4 and 5 GHz) applications. To achieve circular polarization (CP) and dual band resonance, koch fractal curves are embedded on sides of square patch. The radiating cross bisected antenna resonates at ISM band. Without increasing structural complexity, improvement in bandwidth is achieved. Proposed design fulfils requirements of IEEE 802.11a/b/g standards. The measured 3-dB axial ratio bandwidth is 3.48% (2.4–2.485 GHz) and 12.31% (5.15–5.825 GHz) and 2-dB VSWR bandwidth is 6.1% (2.35–2.5 GHz) and 15.55% (5.10–5.96 GHz) respectively at center frequency of 2.45 GHz and 5.5 GHz. Experimental results show perfect match between simulated and measured bandwidths.

Keywords: Circular polarization · Dual band · Koch fractal · Microstrip patch antenna

1 Introduction

Due to precipitate development in portable systems, microstrip antenna attracts more attention. The most commonly used polarization technique in present wireless communication systems is circular polarization as it does not depend on orientation of transmitting and receiving antenna. For the handheld and portable wireless devices, circular polarized microstrip antennas are more flexible and insensitive to multipath effects. With the advancements in WLAN protocols, miniature and multiband antennas are more required. Nowadays, IEEE 802.11a/b/g WLAN standards are popularly used. IEEE 802.11b/g standard covers 2.4 GHz ISM band i.e. from 2.4 to 2.485 GHz and IEEE 802.11a covers 5 GHz ISM band i.e. from 5.15 to 5.825 GHz and U-NII band. For device miniaturization, flexibility and feasibility, antennas must resonate in both operation bands.

Excitation of two orthogonal modes of same amplitude and 90^0 phase difference on radiating patch, results in circular polarization (CP). These two orthogonal modes are obtained by properly adjusting physical dimensions of antenna

© Springer Nature Singapore Pte Ltd. 2016
A. Unal et al. (Eds.): SmartCom 2016, CCIS 628, pp. 340–345, 2016.
DOI: 10.1007/978-981-10-3433-6_41

with single feed or with dual feeds [1,7]. The single feed based circular polarized microstrip patch antennas (CPMA) are appressed when compared with dual feed based CPMA [4]. As compared to single feed, dual feed uses large area of ground plane for power divider circuit, but comparatively it provides a greater CP bandwidth [12]. Proximity feed based antenna structure for circular patch antenna having cross shaped slot and probe feed of triangular antenna can be contemplated for radiation of CP and reduction in size [6,9]. By introducing asymmetry in radiating patch and feedline by embedded pentagonal slot, a CP dual band antenna is designed [11]. Also at edges embedding slits of T-shape and Y-shape at corners gives dual band CP [14]. A simple, single probe feed asymmetrical fractal at boundary of MSA is presented for triband circular polarization operation [8]. Chen et al. demonstrates a slot antenna with dual band inherited with two linear and narrow slots one for 5.2 GHz and another for 2.4 GHz bands [10]. A small size equilateral triangular dual-band slot antenna for 2.4 and 5 GHz is designed in [13], but it covers only a part of 2.4/5 GHz bands. To gain dual-frequency operation a cross shaped slot in coplanar waveguide (CPW), feeding a planar monopole antenna is described in [5]. A dual broadband antenna for 2.4 and 5 GHz in which the rectangular strips are infixed along centreline of rectangular-slot antenna is described in [2]. But, antenna design proposed in [2,5] are very large in size and are not suitable to integrate with other circuit.

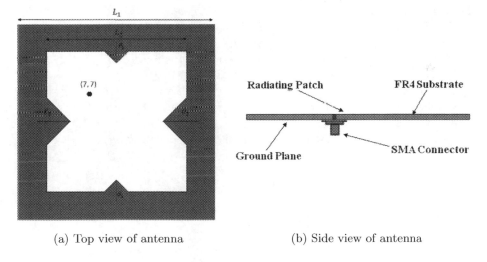

(a) Top view of antenna   (b) Side view of antenna

Fig. 1. Proposed antenna structure

This paper proposes an asymmetrical Koch fractal dual band microstrip patch antenna with a single layer and simple probe feed technique. To achieve CP, koch fractal curves are introduced on radiating patch along the edges. The remaining article is organised as follows. The proposed antenna design and geometry is portrayed in Sect. 2. Section 3 illustrates measured and simulated results.

Table 1. Description of dual band CP antenna parameters

Parameters of Antenna	Dimensions
Length of ground plane (L_1)	80 mm
Length of radiating patch (L_2)	36 mm
Koch along Y axis θ_1	45^0
Koch along X axis θ_2	45^0
Feed point location	(7, 7)

Section 4 concludes the findings in paper. Method of Moment (MoM) software i.e. Integral Equation Three Dimensional (IE3D) is employed to carry out simulations of proposed work.

2   Design and Geometrical View of Antenna

Figure 1 exhibits geometrical view of proposed antenna. It can be seen from Fig. 1a that quadrangle shaped ground plane of antenna has size L_1, at basal side of antenna. The side view of antenna is shown in Fig. 1b. The square cross bisect radiating patch of length L_2 consists of asymmetrical koch fractal at the edges at an angle of θ_1 and θ_2 along Y and X axis respectively as demonstrated in Fig. 1a. This antenna is simulated and fabricated using FR4 substrate ($\epsilon_r = 4.4$, $\tan\delta = 0.02$ and $h = 1.6$ mm) where, ϵ_r is dielectric constant, $\tan\delta$ is loss tangent and h is thickness. The diagonal feed location (7, 7) is in second quadrant. This parameters are given in Table 1.

Geometry of antenna comprised of square patch and four triangular shaped slots embedded on edges of patch. There are two scenarios to obtain CP radiation from patch (a) if $\theta_1 \neq \theta_2$, depth must be equal. (b) $\theta_1 = \theta_2$ depth must be unequal [8]. Due to this geometry, current distribution length on radiating patch

Table 2. Comparison with existing structures

Reference	Operating frequency			
	2.4 GHz		5.5 GHz	
	VSWR bandwidth	AR bandwidth	VSWR bandwidth	AR bandwidth
[7]	1.8%	0.6%	1.6%	0.5%
[8]	8.7%	3.2%	5%	3%
[3]	3.5%	2.6%	3.2%	2.0%
[14]	3.2%	1.7%	2.8%	1.05%
Proposed structure	6.1%	3.48%	15.55%	12.31%

is different in basic TM_{01} and TM_{10} modes and CP is generated. Table 2 shows comparative analysis of proposed work the exiting antenna designs. Proposed design offers wider VSWR and AR bandwidth at both 2.4 GHz and 5.5 GHz

3   Simulated and Measured Results

Fabricated low cost dual band CP antenna is used as a prototype to verify simulation results. Figure 2 shows physical model of proposed antenna and antenna testing. Figure 3 shows that measured VSWR bandwidth below 2dB is 6.1% (2.35–2.5 GHz) and 15.55% (5.10–5.96 GHz). Axial ratio below 3dB is 3.48% (2.4–2.485 GHz) and 12.31% (5.15 5.825 GHz) as reflected in Fig. 4. Figure 5 shows plot of radiation pattern at center frequency of 2.45 GHz and 5.5 GHz. A close agreement between measured and simulated results is observed in Fig. 6.

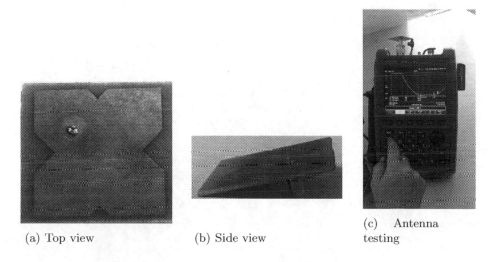

(a) Top view   (b) Side view   (c)   Antenna testing

Fig. 2. Physical module of proposed dual band CP antenna.

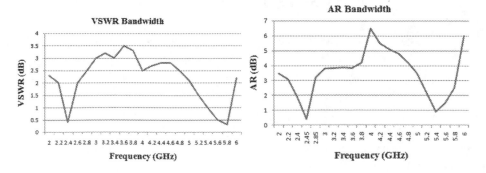

Fig. 3. Simulated VSWR bandwidth   **Fig. 4.** Simulated AR bandwidth

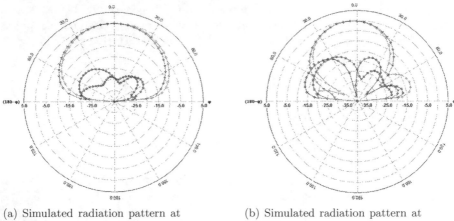

(a) Simulated radiation pattern at 2.4 GHz.

(b) Simulated radiation pattern at 5.5 GHz.

Fig. 5. Radiation pattern of proposed antenna at 2.4 GHz and 5.5 GHz

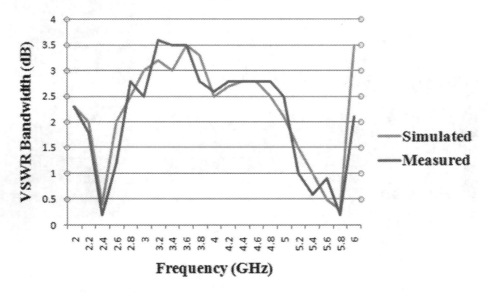

Fig. 6. Comparison between measured and simulated result.

4   Conclusion

A new single layer asymmetrical koch fractal dual band microstrip patch antenna for ISM band i.e. 2.4 and 5 GHz is presented in this paper. Proposed simple probe feed antenna is simple to fabricate compared to other feeding techniques. Fractal geometry helps to obtain circular polarization. From simulated and measured results, it can be seen that WLAN band (2.4 GHz–2.485 GHz and 5.15 GHz–5.825 GHz) can be effectively covered with proposed design.

References

1. Gautam, A.K., Benjwal, P., Kanaujia, B.K.: A compact square microstrip antenna for circular polarization. Microw. Opt. Technol. **54**(4), 897–900 (2011)
2. Hsiao, H.M., Wu, J.-W., Wang, Y.-D.: Novel dual-broadband rectangular-slot antenna for 2.4/5-GHz wireless communication. Microw. Opt. Technol. Lett. **46**, 197–201 (2005)
3. Wu, J., Yin, Y., Wang, Z., Lian, R.: Dual-band circularly polarized antenna with differential feeding. Prog. Electromagn. Res. C **49**, 11–17 (2014)
4. Wang, K.L.: Compact and Broadband Microstrip Antenna. Wiley, New York (2002)
5. Liu, C.W.: Broadband dual-frequency cross-shaped slot cpw-fed monopole antenna for wlan operation. Microw. Opt. Technol. Lett. **46**, 353–355 (2005)
6. Liu, Q., Shen, J., Liu, H., Wu, Y., Su, M., Liu, Y.: Low-cost compact circularly polarized directional antenna for universal uhf rfid handheld reader applications. IEEE Antennas Wirel. Propag. Lett. **14**, 1326–1329 (2015)
7. Nasimuddin, Chen, Z.N., Qing, X.: Asymmetric-circular shaped slotted microstrip antennas for circular polarization and rfid applications. IEEE Trans. Antennas Propag. **58**(12), 3821–3828 (2010)
8. Reddy, V.V., Sarma, N.V.S.N.: Triband circularly polarized koch fractal boundary microstrip antenna. IEEE Antennas Wirel. Propag. Lett. **13**, 1057–1060 (2014)
9. Row, J.S., Ai, C.Y.: Compact design of single-feed circularly polarised microstrip antenna. Electron. Lett. **40**(18), 1093–1094 (2004)
10. Su, C.M., Chen, H.T., Chang, F.S., Wong, K.L.: Dual-band slot antenna for 2.4/5.2 GHz wlan operation. Microw. Opt. Technol. Lett. **35**, 306–308 (2002)
11. Sung, Y.: Dual-band circularly polarized pentagonal slot antenna. IEEE Antennas Wirel. Propag. Lett. **10**, 259–261 (2011)
12. Targonski, S.D., Pozar, D.M.: Design of wideband circularly polarized aperture-coupled microstrip antennas. IEEE Trans. Antennas Propag. **41**(2), 214–220 (1993)
13. Wu, J.W.: 2.4/5-GHz dual-band triangular slot antenna with compact operation. Microw. Opt. Technol. Lett. **45**, 81–84 (2005)
14. Yang, K.P., Wong, K.L.: Dual-band circularly-polarized square microstrip antenna. IEEE Trans. Antennas Propag. **49**(3), 377–382 (2001)

Extraction Based Text Summarization Methods on User's Review Data: A Comparative Study

Pradeepika Verma[(✉)] and Hari Om

Indian School of Mines, Dhanbad 826004, India
pradeepikav.verma093@gmail.com, hariom4india@gmail.com

Abstract. This paper provides a comparative analysis of various graph based extraction methods for automatic text summarizations using ROUGE on review dataset. We consider five techniques that include TextRank, LexRank, LSA, Luhn, and Edmundson. These methods concentrate on predicting the semantics of an entity. The experimental results on summarizing the users' opinions show that the LexRank method gives the best performance among all. Generated summaries are understandable and convey informative opinions.

Keywords: Summarization · User review data · Graph based algorithm · Recall · Precision · F-Measure

1 Introduction

Text summarization is an exercise of transfiguring a text in a meaningful form. Though text summarization helps to capture a quick view of a large document, yet it is a challenging task to summarize a text automatically like human generated summary by some computational system. Extractive and abstractive are two types of automatic text summarization. Extractive summarization extracts the most relevant sentences, whereas abstractive summarization rephrases the extracted sentences.

Here we discuss a comparative performance of various extractive text summarization methods [5] on an opinion based dataset with the help of the ROUGE (Recall- Oriented Understudy of Gisting Evaluation) evaluation system. We present the analysis of five different techniques: TextRank, LexRank, LSA, Luhn, and Edmundson. TextRank [11] is a graph based technique for text processing that relies on ranking of sentences for extraction. LexRank [2] is also a graph based approach that quantify likeness between two sentences using the TF-IDF vector and cosine similarity function. It relies on similarity between sentences, their centrality and overall importance of each sentences. LSA (Latent Semantic Analysis) [13] is an approach that emphasizes on finding the connection between terms and their associated documents by using the singular value decomposition (SVD) algorithm. Luhn [10] describes a simple technique that relies on term density measure that is the dispersion of a word within a document. Edmundson [1] has proposed a technique which uses four basic features

© Springer Nature Singapore Pte Ltd. 2016
A. Unal et al. (Eds.): SmartCom 2016, CCIS 628, pp. 346–354, 2016.
DOI: 10.1007/978-981-10-3433-6_42

(word frequency, positional importance, cue words and title words of the document) to produce summary.

We also carry out performance evaluation of these techniques using the ROUGE evaluation system [9]. It includes ROUGE-N, ROUGE-L, ROUGE-W, ROUGE-S and ROUGE-SU methods of evaluation to which we consider two best methods ROUGE-N and ROUGE-SU for experimental analysis.

The remaining paper consists of followings. We present literature survey of related papers Sect. 2. Section 3, briefly mentions the salient features of the summarization techniques adopted in this work. Section 4 discusses about data and tools used. We describe our experimental results in Sect. 5 and at last Sect. 6 concludes the paper.

2   Related Works

Several papers have discussed different extractive text summarization techniques and different automatic evaluation methods of summaries. Ferreira et al. [3] have evaluated 15 algorithms for sentence scoring on three datasets:News, Blogs and Article context. Lin [7] discussed about the effectiveness of performance measurement method used in the DUC (Document Understanding Conference). They introduced ROUGE to conduct a comprehensive evaluations of the automatic measures on DUC data of 3 years. They also presented consequences of using single/multiple model summaries on the strength of the results. Ganesan et al. [4] introduce an abstractive summarization framework called *Opinosis* and conclude that the Opiniosis summaries are better than the extractive summaries. Jin et al. [6] discussed on various issues on extractive text summarization like ranking/sentence scoring issue and sentence selection issue. They also compared three classes of learning-to-rank algorithm as ranking issues and scrutinized several strategies for selection problem.

3   Approaches

We attempt to study the working and performance of different extractive summarization methods on customer feedback data that include TextRank, LexRank, Latent semantic analysis, Luhn, and Edmundson.

3.1   TextRank

TextRank [11] is based on graph based ranking that is used for text processing. It consist of two stages: in first stage, it explores the likeness between two sentences in the document and in second phase it computes overall importance of the sentences. Consider a digraph $G = (V, E)$ where V and E denote set of nodes and directed edges, respectively. Here a node denotes a sentence and an edge denotes the link between two sentences. The computation of word overlap between two sentences finds the similarity between them that is given as below:

$$sim(S_x, S_y) = \frac{|W_k|W_k \in S_x \& W_k \in S_y|}{log(|S_x|) + log(|S_y|)}$$

where S_x and S_y denote the words in x and y sentences, respectively. The numerator part denotes no. of k-words that are similar in both the sentences and the denominator part denotes the sum of the length of each sentence. With this graph, page ranking algorithm is used to compute overall significance of each node in a graph. Consider a vertex V_x, denote $In(V_x)$ and $Out(V_x)$ as a collection of nodes that are its predecessors and successors, respectively. When one node links to other, it is seen as fling a vote to its successor and the high votes refer to high significance of node. The score of node V_x in the PageRank (page ranking algorithm) is given as follows:

$$SR(V_x) = (1 - d) + d * \sum_{x \in In(V_x)} \frac{1}{|Out(V_y)|} SR(V_y)$$

Here, d: a damping factor lies in $[0,1]$. Based on cut-off level, the summary length is chosen in terms of no. of sentences(n). The top-n sentences in decreasing order of scores are considered as output summary.

3.2   LexRank

LexRank [2] is also a graph based approach. This algorithm is also based on similarity between sentences, their centrality, and overall importance of each sentences. A graph is created by considering each sentence in the document as a node. The edges between two sentences are developed by formulating semantic similarity. It computes the similarity between two sentences on the basis of TF-IDF vector associated with each sentence and cosine similarity function. The TF denotes term frequency and IDF denotes importance of that term over document.

Cosine-similarity between x and y TF-IDF vectors is given by:

$$cosine - similarity(x, y) =$$

$$\frac{\sum_{w \in (x,y)} tf_{w,x} tf_{w,y} (idf_{w,x} idf_{w,y})}{\sqrt{\sum_{i=1, x_i \in x}^{n} (tf_{x_i,x} idf_{x_i})^2} \sqrt{\sum_{i=1, y_i \in y}^{n} (tf_{y_i,y} idf_{y_i})^2}}$$

here $tf_{w,s}$ is number of occurrences of word w in sentence S. By using eigen vector, it determines the centrality of each sentence to obtain the most significant ones. It also uses the PageRank algorithm for centrality measurement.

3.3   Latent Semantic Analysis (LSA)

The LSA [13], an approach of natural language processing, finds the connection between terms and their associated documents by using Singular value decomposition (SVD). In LSA, the words approximately similar in meaning appear in similar form of text. It create a matrix whose column denotes the unique term of the document and row denotes the paragraphs or sentences of document. Then SVD is concerning for decomposing the matrix into three form Right singular vector, left singular vector and singular diagonal vector. It helps in decomposing the rows of a matrix while maintaining the resemblance in column. The SVD function of an $m \times n$ matrix A can be defined as follows:

$$SVD(A) = U\sigma V^T$$

here $U = [u_{ij}]$ and $V = [v_{ij}]$ denote left singular and right singular vectors, respectively; σ is a diagonal matrix with non-negative real numbers. The similarity of words are evaluated by using cosine similarity function. The values that are close to 1 denote very similar words, whereas the values close to 0 denote very dissimilar words.

3.4 Luhn

Luhn [10] discusses a method that uses the term frequency to weight sentences which are then extracted to form an abstract. First, it filters terms in the document using stop-words list. Then terms are normalized on the basis of aggregating similar terms together. Frequencies of each terms are noted and sentences are ranked using the resulting set of significant terms and term density measure.

3.5 Edmundson

Edmundson [1] is a weight based method for text summarization. This technique extracts the sentences by computing weight of each sentence in a document based on some features like keywords, stigma words, cue words, title words, and location of sentences. Ranking these features also depends on type of document (like in a scientific document, sentences residing in abstract and conclusion consist of more important words than other). The sentences are extracted in decreasing order of their score based on cut-off level to create summary of the document. Significance of a sentence is calculated by weight function as given below:

$$W(s) = wK(s) + xS(s) + yT(s) + zL(s)$$

where $W(s)$ represents total weight of a sentence and $K(s)$, $S(s)$, $T(s)$, $L(s)$ represent weights of keywords, stigma words/cue words, title words, location of sentences, respectively, and w,x,y,z are constants.

4 Data and Tools Used

Here we discuss the data and data tools used in experiment.

4.1 Data

We have used the Opinosis Dataset[1]. This dataset contains review or opinion part on a given topic. Example of topics are *accuracy garmin nuvi* 255*W*, *battery life amazon kindle*, etc. It contains 51 topics, each consisting about 100 sentences. The opinions are obtained from various forums like Trip advisor, flipkart, Edmunds and Amazon.

4.2 Tools Used

We use SUMY for text summarization and ROUGE for evaluating these summaries.

SUMY[2], an automated text summarizer, is a command line utility for sentence extraction from HTML pages or plain text. It also comprises an evaluation framework for text summarizers. Implemented summarization methods are TextRank, LexRank, LSA, Luhn, Edmundson, SumBasic, and KL-Sum. Here we do text summarization for top five methods on Opinosis dataset.

ROUGE [8], a popular text summarization evaluation tool, includes several metrics for analyzing the similarity between two summaries. Here we have used two metrics for evaluation that are ROUGE-N and ROUGE-SU. ROUGE-N is a process of measuring n-gram recall, precision, and F-score between a system/candidate summary and a set of gold/model summaries. The recall in ROUGE-N is computed by [8]:

$$Recall_{ROUGE-N} = \frac{\sum_{A \in ModelSummary} \sum_{gm_n \in A} C_{match}(gm_n)}{\sum_{A \in ModelSummary} \sum_{gm_n \in A} C(gm_n)}$$

Here A, n, gm_n, $C_{match}(gm_n)$, and $C(gm_n)$ stand for sentence, length of $n - gram$, $n - gram$, maximum no. of n-grams counted in candidate summary & the reference summaries, and number of $n - gram$ counted in model summary, respectively.

The precision is computed as follows [9]:

$$Precision_{ROUGE-N} = \frac{\sum_{A \in SystemSummary} \sum_{gm_n \in A} C_{match}(gm_n)}{\sum_{A \in SystemSummary} \sum_{gm_n \in A} C(gm_n)}$$

Here A, n, gm_n, $C_{match}(gm_n)$, and $C(gm_n)$ stand for sentence, length of $n - gram$, $n - gram$, maximum no. of n-grams counted in a candidate summary & a set of gold/model summaries, and number of $n - gram$ counted in system summary, respectively.

---

[1] https://archive.ics.uci.edu/ml/datasets/Opinosis.
[2] https://github.com/miso-belica/sumy.

F-Score is defined as the harmonic mean of precision $Precision_{ROUGE-N}$ and recall $Recall_{ROUGE-N}$.

$$F - Score_{ROUGE-N} = 2\left(\frac{Precision_{ROUGE-N} \times Recall_{ROUGE-N}}{Precision_{ROUGE-N} + Recall_{ROUGE-N}}\right)$$

Skip-bigram is the pairing of two words in a sentence. It allows gaps of any length for pairing. The measurement of skip-bigram co-occurrence statistics represents the overlapping of skip-bigram between a system summary and a set of model summary. Let A and B be model/gold summary of length a and a system summary of length b, respectively. Then we can calculate recall, precision, and F-score as follows:

$$Recall_{skip} = \frac{Skip\_bigram(A, B)}{C(a, 2)}$$

$$Precision_{skip} = \frac{Skip\_bigram(A, B)}{C(b, 2)}$$

$$F_{skip2} = \frac{(1 + \beta^2)Recall_{skip}Precision_{skip}}{Recall_{skip} + \beta^2 Precision_{skip}}$$

here $Skip\_bigram(A, B)$ refers to number of skip-bigram matches between A and B, β controls the respective significance of $Precision_{skip}$ and $Recall_{skip}$, and C is a combination function.

The ROUGE-SU is an extended version of the ROUGE-S that can be obtained from ROUGE-S by counting the unigrams of their sentences in system summary and model summary both.

5   Experimental Results

Here we discuss text summarization and performance evaluation of the approaches discussed above in Sect. 3.

5.1   Text Summarization

The experimental data contains 51 different topics related to the user's review. Here, we have done summarization using SUMY for each topic. These topics are summarized using five summarization methods: TextRank, LexRank, LSA, Luhn, and Edmundson. All these methods extract different sentences from the same document according to their features. Here, the SUMY extracts two most relevant sentences and produces a summary of length 2 for every topic.

5.2   Performance Evaluation

The SUMY generates the summary is in a plain text. So we have converted it into respective HTML file for evaluation. We also have 5 human generated summary as gold summary or model summary for each topic in plain text. So we have converted it into HTML file for comparing with their system summary. We have evaluated the performance of 5 different methods of summarization. First, we have created an XML file to pair the model summary with their respective system summary. In each pairing, there is one system summary and five model summaries. The system summary is compared with each of their respective model summaries and the score of the best matched summary is evaluated. We have done evaluation on the basis of Unigram, bigram, and skip bigram co-occurrence statistics methods using the ROUGE. An n-gram of length 1 is referred to as unigram and of length 2 as bigram.

The performance results of our experiment for various methods of summarization with various evaluation methods have been shown in Table 1. The last baseline score that we have taken from [4] has been measured using the MEAD [12], which is a text summarization and evaluation system.

Comparative Analysis. Table 1 contains the recall, precision, and F-score of methods of text summarization. As evident from this table, the recall score of the baseline summarizer is the best. It is because the length of the extracted summary sentences in the MEAD is larger than that of other methods. So, number of words in extracted summary is greater. Precision score of the LexRank summary is highest because the no. of relevant words in extracted summary are more than any other summarizer and hence the LexRank method gives the highest F-score followed by the Edmundson and TextRank methods. We have shown graphical representation of results in Fig. 1.

Table 1. Performance Results

Performance parameters	Evaluation methods	Text summarization methods					
		TextRank	LexRank	LSA	Luhn	Edmundson	Baseline
Recall	ROUGE-1	0.40471	0.32025	0.41058	0.36850	0.33495	0.4932
	ROUGE-2	0.08169	0.07495	0.07692	0.07087	0.06976	0.1058
	ROUGE-SU	0.16617	0.11466	0.17089	0.13894	0.12324	0.2316
Precision	ROUGE-1	0.12855	0.20144	0.08782	0.11330	0.14409	0.0916
	ROUGE-2	0.02394	0.04737	0.01464	0.01829	0.02898	0.0184
	ROUGE-SU	0.02625	0.05852	0.00940	0.01620	0.02985	0.2316
F-Score	ROUGE-1	0.17791	0.23214	0.14189	0.16743	0.18698	0.1515
	ROUGE-2	0.03350	0.05365	0.02414	0.02793	0.03755	0.0308
	ROUGE-SU	0.03210	0.06143	0.01733	0.02693	0.03876	0.0102

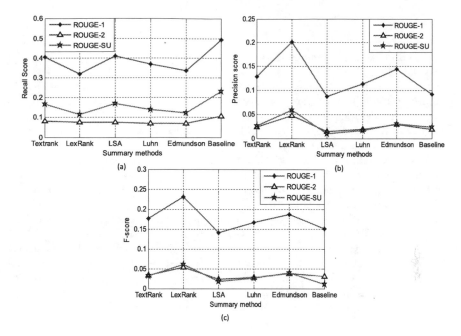

Fig. 1. Graphical representation of Results

Graphical Analysis. Here we observe that the ROUGE-1 gives the highest score (Approximately 122% higher than others) in respect to all explained methods and parameters. It is due to the fact that if there is a matching term in ROUGE-2, then it will also be in ROUGE-1; however, the reverse needs not be true. So, the ROUGE-1 will always give higher score. The score of the ROUGE-SU is also slightly higher than that of the ROUGE-2, but lower than that of the ROUGE-1. This is because it takes into account the forward pairing terms as well as reverse pair terms that are not considered in the ROUGE-2.

6   Conclusion

In this paper, we have discussed important extractive summarization methods that are based on graph. The experiential results on a set of a review document show that LexRank performs better than others. So LexRank summaries are more concise and communicate essential information. Here, we have presented a comparison on single dataset of the user's review. The result can vary on other dataset; so it can not be concluded that the LexRank will always give the best results. We have taken the system summary of length 2 that can also effect the outcomes. In future, We will do exhaustive studies on multiple datasets like news, blogs, articles, etc.

References

1. Edmundson, H.P.: New methods in automatic extracting. J. ACM (JACM) **16**(2), 264–285 (1969)
2. Erkan, G., Radev, D.R.: Lexrank: graph-based lexical centrality as salience in text summarization. J. Artif. Intell. Res. **22**, 457–479 (2004)
3. Ferreira, R., de Souza Cabral, L., Lins, R.D., e Silva, G.P., Freitas, F., Cavalcanti, G.D., Lima, R., Simske, S.J., Favaro, L.: Assessing sentence scoring techniques for extractive text summarization. Expert Syst. Appl. **40**(14), 5755–5764 (2013)
4. Ganesan, K., Zhai, C., Han, J.: Opinosis: a graph-based approach to abstractive summarization of highly redundant opinions. In: Proceedings of the 23rd International Conference on Computational Linguistics, pp. 340–348. Association for Computational Linguistics (2010)
5. Gupta, V., Lehal, G.S.: A survey of text summarization extractive techniques. J. Emerg. Technol. Web Intell. **2**(3), 258–268 (2010)
6. Jin, F., Huang, M., Zhu, X.: A comparative study on ranking and selection strategies for multi-document summarization. In: Proceedings of the 23rd International Conference on Computational Linguistics: Posters, pp. 525–533. Association for Computational Linguistics (2010)
7. Lin, C.Y.: Looking for a few good metrics: automatic summarization evaluation-how many samples are enough. In: Proceedings of the NTCIR Workshop, vol. 4 (2004)
8. Lin, C.Y.: Rouge: a package for automatic evaluation of summaries. In: Text Summarization Branches Out: Proceedings of the ACL-04 Workshop, vol. 8 (2004)
9. Lin, C.Y., Hovy, E.: Automatic evaluation of summaries using n-gram co-occurrence statistics. In: Proceedings of the 2003 Conference of the North American Chapter of the Association for Computational Linguistics on Human Language Technology, vol. 1, pp. 71–78. Association for Computational Linguistics (2003)
10. Luhn, H.P.: The automatic creation of literature abstracts. IBM J. Res. Dev. **2**(2), 159–165 (1958)
11. Mihalcea, R., Tarau, P.: Textrank: Bringing order into texts. Association for Computational Linguistics (2004)
12. Radev, D., Allison, T., Blair-Goldensohn, S., Blitzer, J., Celebi, A., Dimitrov, S., Drabek, E., Hakim, A., Lam, W., Liu, D., et al.: MEAD-a platform for multidocument multilingual text summarization (2004)
13. Steinberger, J., Jezek, K.: Using latent semantic analysis in text summarization and summary evaluation. In: Proceedings of the ISIM'04, pp. 93–100 (2004)

A New PCA Based Hybrid Color Image Watermarking Using Cycle Spinning - Sharp Frequency Localized Contourlet Transform for Copyright Protection

K. Kishore Kumar[(⊠)] and Movva Pavani

Faculty of Science and Technology,
Department of ECE, IFHE, Hyderabad, India
{kkishore,pavanimovva}@ifheindia.org

Abstract. Hybrid watermarking techniques are gaining importance in the field of image watermarking as they meet criterions like Imperceptibility and Robustness. A novel approach for the hybrid color image watermarking using Cycle Spinning based Sharp Frequency Localized Contourlet Transform (CS-SFLCT) and Principal Component Analysis is proposed. Contourlet Transform (CT) is applied to decompose the images into various sub bands for all the color spaces of both the host and water mark images. For inclusion operation principal components of middle band(X bands) are considered and CS-SFLCT is chosen for watermarking. CS-SFLCT provides better frequency localization resulting in a very good PSNR and Principal Component's helps in fruitful extraction of watermark from the host image. This hybrid technique has shown better correlation between input watermark and extracted one and shown very high very high robustness under various intentional and non intentional attacks.

Keywords: Color image watermarking · Contourlet transform (CT) · Principal component analysis (PCA) · Cycle spinning · Frequency localization

1 Introduction

With the enormous increase of multimedia content over the web enabling us to access, distribute and manipulate digital data. Digital watermarking [1] had become a good answer for safeguarding the multimedia content by preventing its unauthorized duplication. It is the process of embedding/hiding an undetectable data into the given data. The invisible data is termed as watermark/metadata and the given data is called cover work.

Spatial and Transform domain methods are the two types of watermarking methods. Spatial methods [2, 3] are simple but they are not strong against various intentional or unintentional attacks. In transform domain methods [3–6], watermark is scattered over the image irregularly so that the attacker find difficulty to get the information of existence of watermark. These methods are more robust and complex compared to their counterpart. D. Kundur et al. [2] proposed a new scheme of embedding gray scale logos into wavelet transformed images by using the multi-resolution fusion based watermarking.

© Springer Nature Singapore Pte Ltd. 2016
A. Unal et al. (Eds.): SmartCom 2016, CCIS 628, pp. 355–364, 2016.
DOI: 10.1007/978-981-10-3433-6_43

Dawei et al. [5] proposed a new scheme of using chaotic logistic map for applying locally wavelet transform. Bandelets [10] was introduced to address the proper representations for sharp image transitions and smoothness along the contours [11] since a two dimensional wavelet is not able to address them. Martin Vetterli [11] proposed Contourlet to capture intrinsic geometrical structure. Yue Lu [8] proposed a contourlet variant called sharp frequency localization contourlet transform (SFLCT). In this paper, cycle spinning [13] was used to compensate the translation variance property of SFLCT in image watermarking context. Experimental results show that the proposed scheme had shown better results in terms of PSNR and visual effect when compared with the variants of contourlet transforms.

2 Contourlet Transform and Its Variants

The original contourlet [11] is a combination of Laplacian pyramid (LP) and the directional filter banks (DFB). Point discontinuities are captured by Laplacian pyramid first and these point discontinuities are linked into linear structure by DFB. In the frequency domain, a two dimensional image is decomposed iteratively into low pass & high pass sub bands by the laplacian pyramid and these high pass sub bands are divided into directional sub bands by DFB as shown in Fig. 1.

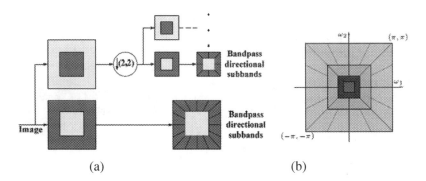

(a)   (b)

Fig. 1. (a) Block diagram of Contourlet Transform (CT) (b) Frequency Partitioning obtained with CT

Aliasing effect is resulted due to the combination of LP and DFB. Yue Lu [8] proposed the structure of sharp frequency localization contourlet (SFLCT) which is sharply localized in the frequency domain improving the watermarking performance. The down samplers and up samplers in the DFB's of SFLCT make them shift invariant which produces artifacts around the edges. Cycle spinning [14] is employed to compensate for the translation variance to provide the effective representation of texture information of the input image in extracted images and output watermarked image (Fig. 2).

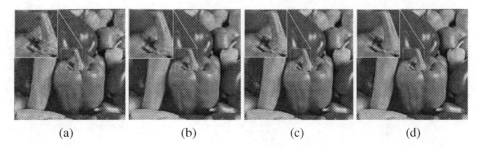

| (a) | (b) | (c) | (d) |

Fig. 2. (a) - (d) are the images processed by CT, CS-CT, SFLCT, CS-SFLCT and their inverses respectively

3 Principal Component Analysis

Principal component analysis (PCA) [14] is an effective way to suppress redundant information which acts as additional payload in the Meta data (the information to be embedded).

4 Proposed Algorithm

In this paper, a hybrid method [17] for color image watermarking is proposed using CS-SFLCT and PCA which gives better representation of curves without introducing redundant artifacts. Contourlet Transform (CT) is used to decompose the images into various sub bands for all the color spaces of both the host and water mark images. For inclusion operation principal components of middle band(X bands) are considered and CS-SFLCT is chosen for watermarking. This hybrid technique has shown better correlation between input watermark and extracted one.

4.1 Watermark Embedding Algorithm

Block diagram of the proposed watermark embedding [17] is shown in Fig. 3. Following are the steps of watermark embedding algorithm:

Step I: CS-SFLCT is applied to R, G, and B planes of true color host image to decay into sub bands.

Step II: PCA is applied to mid frequency sub band of each color space of host image.

Step III: Apply CS-SFLCT to the R, G, and B planes of color watermark to decompose into sub bands.

Step IV: Apply PCA to mid frequency sub band of each color space of watermark image.

Step V: Principal components obtained in steps 2 and 4 are processed by the following procedure.

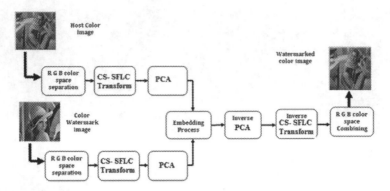

Fig. 3. Block diagram of watermark embedding process

$$\text{max} = \text{maximum } (\text{PCA\_MSB\_HI});$$
$$\text{min} = \text{minimum } (\text{PCA\_MSB\_HI});$$
$$\text{Range} = (\text{max} - \text{min})/\text{Count};$$
$$\text{temp} = (\text{PCA\_MSB\_HI}[i,j] - \text{min})/\text{Range};$$
$$\text{alp} = 0.001 + (\text{temp} - 1) * 0.005;$$
$$\text{PCA\_MSB\_Wmkd}[i,j] = \text{PCA\_MSB\_HI}[i,j] + \text{alp} * \text{PCA\_MSB\_WI}[i,j];$$

Where PCA_MSB_HI: Principal components of Middle Sub band of Host Color Image.

PCA_MSB_WI: Principal Components of Middle Sub band of watermark Image at one of the three color spaces.

PCA_MSB_Wmkd: Resulted Principal Components of Watermarked image.

alp is the watermarking coefficient varies from 0.001 to 0.25 (takes a total of 50 values).

Step VI: Apply inverse PCA of transformed original image with modified PCA values obtained in step V.

Step VII: Apply inverse CS-SFLCT to the coefficients obtained in step VI to obtain the Watermarked image and repeat for R, G, and B color spaces.

Step VIII: The watermarked image obtained will converted to unsigned integer 8 representations from double to be checked for invisibility using PSNR.

4.2   Watermark Extraction Algorithm

Block diagram of the proposed watermark extraction [17] is shown in Fig. 4. Following are the steps of watermark extraction algorithm:

Step I: R, G, B planes of true color host image and watermarked images are applied to CS-SFLCT to decompose into sub bands.

Step II: Apply PCA to mid frequency sub band of each color space of transformed watermarked image and host image.

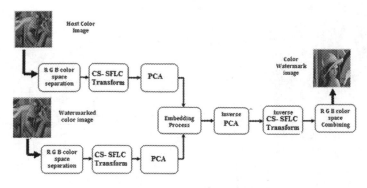

Fig. 4. Block diagram of watermark extraction process

Step III: Principal components obtained from step II are processed by the following procedure.

max = maximum(PCA_MSB_Wmkd);

min = minimum(PCA_MSB_Wmkd);

Range = (max − min)/Count;

temp = (PCA_MSB_Wmkd[i, j] − min)/Range;

alp = 0.001 + (temp − 1) * 0.005;

PCA_MSB_Extd[i, j] = (PCA_MSB_Wmkd[i, j] − PCA_MSB_HI[i, j])/alp;

Where PCA_MSB_Extd: principal components of Extracted image.

alp is the watermarking Coefficient varies from 0.001 to 0.25 (takes a total of 50 values).

Step IV: An authentication key is required which will be used as the Covariance matrix and other sub bands of Watermark image. They are used to apply inverse PCA and Inverse *CS-SFLCT* to get back the watermark image by doing same for R, G and B color spaces.

Step V: Extracted image obtained will converted to unsigned integer 8 representation from double to be check for Robustness by comparing with original watermark image using Normalized Correlation Coefficient.

5 Intervisibility and Robustness Measures

Watermarked and Host image should bear a resemblance to each other with respect to HVS. Mean Square Error (MSE) and Peak Signal to Noise Ratio (PSNR) provide the degree of variations. The more the PSNR, better the invisibility.

$$MSE = \sum_{q=1}^{M} \sum_{p=1}^{N} [I(p,q) - I'(p,q)]^2$$

$$PSNR = 20 \times Log_{10}\left(\frac{255}{\sqrt{MSE}}\right)$$

Robustness is also one of the quality measures of watermarking system with respect to intentional, unintentional attacks and channel actions. The quality of equivalence can be measured by Bit Error Rate and Normalized Correlation Coefficient.

$$NCC = \frac{\sum_{x=1}^{m} \sum_{y=1}^{n} \left(A_{mn} - \overline{A}\right)\left(B_{mn} - \overline{B}\right)}{\sqrt{\left[\sum_{x=1}^{m} \sum_{y=1}^{n} \left(A_{mn} - \overline{A}\right)^2\right]\left[\sum_{x=1}^{m} \sum_{y=1}^{n} \left(B_{mn} - \overline{B}\right)^2\right]}}$$

and

$$BER = No.of.ErrorBits/Total.No.of.Bits$$

Robust of the algorithm is checked by performing Low Pass & Median Filtering, Gaussian Noise, Histogram Equalization, Scaling, Gamma Correction, Cropping, Row or Column removal, Salt & Pepper noise, Rotation, Wiener Filtering, Blurring, Dilation, Color Space Conversions, Shearing etc attacks on the watermarked Image.

6 Experimental Results

In the experiments, color images barbara.pgm and lena.pgm of sizes 256 X 256 are used as host and watermarked images. The experiment is repeated for different values of alpha (the watermarking coefficient). The good invisibility is observed at alpha 0.001 to 0.25. Under ideal channel conditions without any attacks, the observed PSNR of 63.72 dB and NCC of 0.9999, BER=0.0002. The NCC less than 1 because the PCA is not completely reversible technique. Experiment is repeated for different intentional and unintentional attacks for testing the proposed watermark algorithm's robustness (Tables 1 and 2).

Table 1. PSNR, NCC, BER of extracted & watermarked Image under different attacks

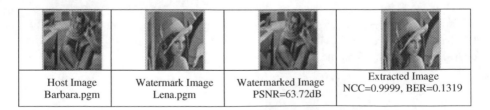

| Host Image
Barbara.pgm | Watermark Image
Lena.pgm | Watermarked Image
PSNR=63.72dB | Extracted Image
NCC=0.9999, BER=0.1319 |

Table 2. Performance Measures of Proposed Method

Salt and Pepper Noise PSNR=53.6935,NCC=0.9858 BER=0.3586	JPEG Compression PSNR=42.9998,NCC= 0.9861 BER= 0.3105	Gaussian Blur PSNR= 26.8958,NCC = 0.9899 BER = 0.2952
JPEG 2000 Compression PSNR=53.5443, NCC=0.9995, BER = 0.1658	Low Pass Filtering PSNR= 51.0915, NCC= 0.9893 BER = 0.2966	Dilation PSNR=35.3595,NCC = 0.9851, BER= 0.6405
Rotation PSNR=40.2362, NCC = 0.9868, BER = 0.3055	Histogram Equalization PSNR= 26.8958, NCC = 0.9807 , BER = 0.3512	Shearing Attack PSNR=25.856, NCC = 0.9893 BER = 0.2969
Median Filtering PSNR= 36.9651, NCC= 0.9852 BER= 0.3298	Contrast Adjustment PSNR= 38.8907, NCC= 0.9998 BER= 0.1058	Color to Gray scale conversion PSNR= 25.0829, NCC = 0.9441 BER = 0.3775
Wiener Filtering PSNR=48.3950, NCC=0.9989 BER = 0.2158	Gamma Correction PSNR=56.2008, NCC = 0.9996 BER = 0.0728	Row Column removal PSNR= 35.5668, NCC = 0.9977 BER = 0.1931
Gaussian Noise PSNR=38.4451, NCC = 0.7266 BER = 0.5851	Sharpening PSNR=40.6818, NCC = 0.8448 BER = 0.5177	Row column copying PSNR=38.9696, NCC = 0.9895 BER= 0.3208
Rescaling (150%) PSNR=48.9696, NCC = 0.9861 BER = 0.6408	Automatic cropping (85%) PSNR= 28.9606, NCC= 0.9936 BER= 0.2852	Speckle Noise PSNR=38.5177,NCC= 0.7031 BER= 0.5683

Figures 5 and 6 shows that with the increase in the percentage of cropping & angle of rotation the Normalized Correlation Coefficient (NCC) is almost less than Unity and Bit Error Rate (BER) are within the permissible limits. Figures 7 and 8 indicate that

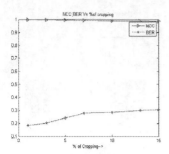

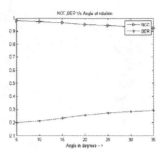

Fig. 5. NCC,BER Vs % of cropping

Fig. 6. NCC, BER Vs Angle of Rotation

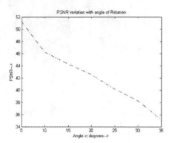

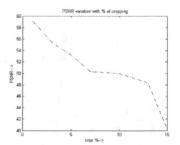

Fig. 7. PSNR Variation with the Angle of Rotation

Fig. 8. PSNR variation with % of Cropping

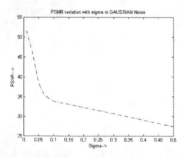

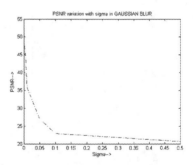

Fig. 9. PSNR variation with sigma in Gaussian Noise

Fig. 10. PSNR variation with sigma in Gaussian Blur

with the increase in the angle of rotation and percentage of Cropping, PSNR value decreases. Figures 9 and 10 indicate the PSNR value decreases with increase in the Gaussian Noise and Blur (Table 3).

Table 3. Comparison of NCC for different algorithms under various attacks

S.No	Attacks Tested	Normalized Correlation Coefficient(NCC)		
		CS-SFLCT + PCA	NSCT + SVD	CT + SVD
1	JPEG 2000	0.9995	0.9995	0.9996
2	JPEG Compression	0.9861	0.9985	0.9996
3	Salt & Pepper Noise	0.9858	0.6948	0.6823
4	Low Pass Filtering	0.9893	0.9729	0.9839
5	Automatic Cropping	0.9936	0.9538	0.9658
6	Histogram Equation	0.9807	0.9808	0.9733
7	Rotation	0.9868	0.9958	0.9750
8	Median Filtering	0.9852	0.9484	0.9680
9	Contrast Adjustment	0.9998	0.9985	0.9991
10	Weiner Filter	0.9989	0.9982	0.9989
11	Gamma Correction	0.9996	0.9989	0.9995
12	Gaussian Noise	0.7266	0.8399	0.7538
13	Sharpening	0.8448	0.8379	0.8212
14	Gaussian Blurring	0.9899	0.9719	0.9841
15	Shearing	0.9893	0.9744	0.9857
16	Dilatations	0.9851	0.9443	0.9678
17	Color to Grayscale	0.9441	0.8163	0.8693
18	Row & Colum Removal	0.9977	0.9977	0.9972
19	Row Colum Copying	0.9895	0.9902	0.9820
20	Scaling (150%)	0.9861	0.9187	0.9417

7 Conclusion

In this paper, hybrid approach watermarking [17] technique using CS-SFLCT and PCA is proposed for copyright protection which gives better representation of curves without introducing redundant artifacts. Our proposed hybrid method is showing better performance when compared with CT and SVD [15], NSCT and SVD [16], in both invisibility and robustness. Since our approach being non blind requires host image and some partial information of watermark also at the receiving end. Knowledge of security key still further improves the authentication. The proposed method preserves and maintains high perceptual quality of the watermarked image providing an exceptional robustness to various kinds of attacks.

References

1. Cox, I.J., Miller, M.L., Bloom, J.A.: Digital watermarking. Morgan Kaufmann, San Francisco (2001)
2. Kundur, D., Hatzinakos, D.: Towards robust logo watermarking using multiresolution image fusion. IEEE Trans. Multimedia **6**, 185–197 (2004)

3. Bors, A.G., Pitas, I.: Image watermarking using DCT domain constraints. In: Proceedings of IEEE International Conference on Image Processing, vol. 3, pp. 231–234 (1996)
4. Schyndle, R.G.V., Tirkel, A.Z., Osbrone, C.F.: A Digital watermark. In: Proceedings of IEEE International Conference on Image Processing, vol. 2, pp. 86–90 (1994)
5. Dawei, Z., Guanrong, C., Wenbo, L.: A chaos based robust wavelet domain watermarking algorithm. Chaos, Solitons Fractals 22, 47–54 (2004)
6. Reddy, A.A., Chatterjii, B.N.: A new wavelet based logo-watermarking scheme. Pattern Recogn. Lett. 26, 1019–1027 (2005)
7. Majer Ali, U., Vinoth Kumar, E.: Digital watermarking using DWT and SVD. NCACSA 2012, IJCA (2012)
8. Lu, Y., Do, M.N.: A new contourlet transform with sharp frequency localization. In: Proceedings of 2006 IEEE International Conference on Image Processing, pp. 1629–1632. IEEE, Atlanta (2006)
9. Ohnishi, J., Matsui, K.: Embedding a seal in to a picture under orthogonal wavelet transform. In: Proceedings of IEEE International Conference on Multimedia and Computing System, pp. 514–521. IEEE, Hiroshima (1996)
10. Pennec, E., Mallat, S.: Sparse geometric image representation with bandelets. IEEE Trans. Image Process. 14(4), 423–438 (2005)
11. Do, M.N., Vetterli, M.: The contourlet transform: an efficient directional multiresolution image representation. IEEE Trans. Image Process. 14(12), 2091–2106 (2005)
12. Coifman, R.R., Donoho, D.L.: Translation invariant de-noising. In: Antoniadis, A., Oppenheim, G. (eds.) Wavelets and Statistics, pp. 125–150. Springer-Verlag, New York (1995)
13. Eslami, R., Radha, H.: The contourlet transform for image denoising using cycle spinning. In: Proceedings of Asilomar Conference on Signals, Systems & Computers, pp. 1982–1986 (2003)
14. Jolliffe, I.T.: Principal Component Analysis, 2nd edn. Springer-Verlag, New York (2002). ISBN 978-0-387-95442-4
15. Venkata Narasimhulu, C., Satya Prasad, K.: A hybrid watermarking scheme using contourlet Transform and Singular value decomposition. IJCSNS: Int. J. Comput. Sci. Netw. Secur. 10 (9), 12–17 (2010)
16. Venkata-Narasimhulu, C., Satya-Prasad, K.: A robust watermarking technique based on nonsubsampled contourlet transform and SVD. Int. J. Comput. Appl. 16(8), 0975–8887 (2011)
17. Kumar, K.K., Pavani, M., Babu, S.V.: Color image watermarking using cycle spinning based sharp frequency localized contourlet transform and principal component analysis. Int. J. Image Process. (IJIP) 6(5), 363–372 (2012)

Securing Internet of Things in 5G Using Audio Steganography

Tanya Singh[1(✉)], Seema Verma[2], and Vidushi Parashar[1]

[1] Amity Institute of Information Technology, Amity University Uttar Pradesh, Noida, India
tsingh2@amity.edu, parashar.vidushi00@gmail.com
[2] Department of Electronics, Banasthali Vidyapeeth, Vanasthali, Rajasthan, India
seemaverma3@yahoo.com

Abstract. The data usage pattern is changing rapidly in many real life applications and these applications have converged in Smart Phones. 5th generation wireless networks will envision a widespread use of Internet of Things (IoT). With the growing demands for communication between Internet of Things using 5G networks, securing devices will emerge as a big challenge. There will be hidden exchange of data between the devices for which security can be achieved with audio steganography. The aim of the paper is to formulate the model supports the methodology and infrastructure desired to implement the security for IoT in 5G networks. Audio steganography is an invisible communication used for hidden exchange of the data. Internet of things applications varies from ubiquitous computing to machine to machine communications with most applications will be on Voice over IP and will require securing of data from eavesdroppers and attackers. So, the focus of this research paper is on how can we secure internet of things using audio steganography in 5G Platform.

Keywords: 5G · Internet of things (IoT) · Challenges of 5G · Audio steganography

1 Introduction

The 5th generation technology has emerged with new frequency bands above 6 GHz and below 6 GHz with varied demands for different applications ranging from transfer of data in Gb/S per recurrence channel when actually the spectrum is struggling to send Mb/S; voice calls, Industry Automation, UHD screens, work and Play in the cloud, Augmented Reality, Unmanned Vehicles [1, 3]. It utilizes a new radio interface using Multiple-Input Multiple-Output (MIMO) and Orthogonal Frequency Division Multiplexing. The choice of low-range wireless networks for 5G communications will be a huge success for thickly populated urban regions, though numerous base stations could be sent to propound super-quick speeds in a little area. The fifth generation model is all IP based which is used for non-wired and network interoperability. The All IP Network (AIPN) gives a common platform which gives access to all the radio technologies. Packet Switching is being used in AIPN with enhanced performance and price [3].

In 5 G, the architecture consists of a user terminal and many number of Radio Access Technologies depending on varied use of applications. The IP based molecule

© Springer Nature Singapore Pte Ltd. 2016
A. Unal et al. (Eds.): SmartCom 2016, CCIS 628, pp. 365–372, 2016.
DOI: 10.1007/978-981-10-3433-6_44

applications will be implemented using 5G communications, for example: Mobile - Health Care centers, Banking, Government and many more are open using Cloud Computing Resources. Cloud Computing allows the consumers to practice applications without connecting them on their devices. They can access their private data from any computer having internet access of 5G [2]. Following are the features of 5G which has been built upon by the consensus IMT 2020 vision [2, 3].

- *Improved battery life time-* 5G ensures the increased battery life which will increase in the performance of the device.
- *Higher system capacity-* This deals with the storage capacity of a device which will help us in managing larger amount of data.
- *Delay the interface to 1 ms-* Interface help us running a device better. 5G would be an important factor for delaying of the interfaces to at-least 1 ms.
- *Flexible systems-* The systems will be flexible for the users to access as per the convenience.
- *High assurance on security-* Securing the data is one of the most important features which we can avail using 5G.
- *Affordable technology-* 5G will be affordable for users providing the best facilities out of the previous technologies.

Table 1. Comparison of 2G, 3G, 4G, 5G networks

Generation	2G	3G	4G	5G
Deployment	1980–1989	1990–2002	2000–2010	2017–2022
Data bandwidth	14–64 Kbps	2 Mbps	200 Mbps	1 Gbps
Standards	TDMA/ CDMA/GPS/ GPRS	WCDMA	Single Unified Standard	Single Unified Standard
Technology	Digital Cellular	Broadband with CDMA, IP technology	Unified IP and Seamless Communications	IPv6 and Seamless Communications including Broadband and WWWW.
Services	Digital Voice, SMS, Higher Capacity Packetized	Integrated High Quality Audio and Video	Dynamic Information Access, Wearable Devices	Body Area Networks
Multiplexing	TDMA/CDMA	CDMA	WCDMA	OFDM/MIMO
Switching	Circuit and Packet	Packet	Packet	Optimized Packet
Core-network	PSTN	Packet Network	Internet	Internet
Hand-off	Horizontal	Horizontal	Horizontal and Vertical	Horizontal and Vertical

There will be several use-cases applications such as smart shirt, smart city, smart e-health, unmanned vehicle network, direct device to device communications, machine to machine communications that would be requiring ultra-secure and reliable communication. The literature is also very few in this area as this field is completely use-case product driven. The comparative study of the various generations has been done for understanding the benefits of the application in future [7, 8]. The techniques applicable for 2G are Global System Mobile (GSM)/Time Division Multiplexing Access(TDMA)/ Personal Digital Cellular(PDC), the techniques applicable for 2.5G networks are CDMAone/IS 96 B/Global Packet Radio Service (GPRS). The techniques applicable for 3G are CDMA 2000 1x/CDMA 2000 1x EV/Wideband Code Division Multiple Access (WCDMA)/Multi-Mode/Multi- Band/Multi- network.4G network uses the technology Long Term Evolution (LTE). 5G network will use the technology that is mix of all the technologies (Table 1).

2   Internet of Things (IoT)

Internet of Things, IoT, is a network that consists of physical objects that can be devices, vehicles, appliances, buildings, which are basically electronics, software, network connections and this helps in exchanging the data. Internet of Things is an environment using internet where almost each and every object is capable of sending and receiving data via internet connection, thus making the objects intelligent and operable even when the controller is not physically present near the object. The report Detection and actuation on an IoT platform will drive the complete system. IoT will help digitizing all day to day activities, delay free transportation. Applications will also be customized, for example -in cities, there may not be any need for traffic signal lights. Buildings will not only be secure from threats but also take care for one's comfort, energy saving, security, wellbeing and health aspects [6, 7]. As per the study report of 5G recommendations [4], the arrangements of prerequisites such as longer battery life, completely peer to peer connected devices, higher data rates upto Gbps, may require re-architecting key 4G cell system for sufficiating the needs of the interest as per the use. The accompanying illustration use case includes Machine Type Communication (MTC) 10, smart homes, smart buildings, industry automation, and augmented reality. As there will be invisible communication between the various interfaces at the same time, any security technique and the encryption techniques implemented will only reduce the speed of the communication as well interfere with the performance of the system [5, 9].

2.1   Security Perspective of 5G

The 2G and 3G have many security loopholes. Security functions were introduced to some extent because of the shortcomings observed in previous systems and also because of the appeared threats. Firstly, encryption of radio interface was introduced. In early systems, simple radio receivers were used enabling eavesdropping while making a conversation using mobile systems. It was considered strong enough for estimated life-time of GSM (Second Generation). Later, the risk of deception like, connecting calls charged to other subscribers- emerged as a big issue which led to the invention of tamper-resistant SIM cards which added strong authentication and a strong binding to robust charging. Finally, the privacy of the user for which a mechanism was introduced that assigned a temporary identifier and this made it hard to locate the users.

Further improvements were made for the security including mutual authentication to diminish threats and making the network strong. The advent of 4G LTE required returning the subscriber's encrypted data down to base station. This resulted as a major and important security measures. Rather, there is no claim by the players that all the previous generations of mobile networks give completely zero configuration security from the subscriber's point. With the emergence of Machine to Machine communications and IoT, there is a need for ultra –secure and reliable communications and the challenge is 5G requires to give much more throughput.

This paper aims at providing how that additional security with high speed and reliability can be achieved using the technique called audio steganography to secure message exchanges between "Internet of Things" in 5G networks.

3   Audio Steganography

There is always an issue of securing short and long distance communication reliably without compromising the confidentiality of the data. Despite of available various methods of encryption, the drawback of every encryption is the mathematics behind it. The code can be easily decoded. The complex algorithms only buy the security administrator the time. The important technique to solve the problem is steganography. Steganography is a strong tool that provides the defense when the technique is combining with encryption [10–12]. Audio steganography defines hiding of information in a host audio signal in an undetectable way. Hidden data from the audio signal is retrieved using a key which should be same as employed on both the sides during hiding the data. Both the Time Domain and Frequency Domain can be used to perform audio steganography. The audio manager can be embedded in WAV, AU, MP3 files [13].

Various components sway on the nature of sound steganographic procedure. The significance and the effect of all components rely on upon the transmission environment and the application. Most imperative properties of sound steganography are heartiness to clamor and to flag control, covering limit of installed message and security. In sound steganography framework, mysterious information is implanted in computerized sound article. The paired succession of a spread sound item is significantly adjusted by including mystery information in it. The advanced sound record designs utilized by as a part of sound steganography strategy are AU, WAV and MP3 sound documents. The adjusted sound record ought not to be made distinguished to the human ear. Numerous malicious attacks are against image and video steganography calculations (e.g., spatial scaling and geometrical contortions) can't be actualized against audio steganography plans.

3.1   Methodology of Audio Steganography

The methodology of Audio Steganography is with the use of Least Significant Bit Insertion (LSBI). The signal during audio steganography is sent to the destination in the form of music files which forms a *"Stego Signal"*. The embedding is solved by LSB Replacement (Least Significant Bit) is done where total no of key are to be same on both source and destination.

Following is the algorithm that is used for the implementation of the technique. The encoder will read the message audio signal and also read the sound record that is played on the drive. Once the reading is done, the key is entered, and the music document utilizing LSB coding is done. Finally the steganographed signal is written on the drive.

At the decoder side, the decoder will once receiving the signal, read the steganographed audio sign and will find the embedded key. The next information is the required information as can be seen in the Fig. 1.

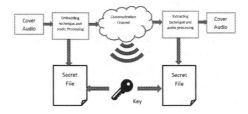

Fig. 1. Audio steganography

The Fig. 2 shows the step by step method used for encoding and decoding the signal.

Encoding-
- Read the given message audio signal.
- Read sound record put away on the drive.
- Enter the key.
- Inert the sign as music document utilizing LSB coding.
- Write stego signal on the drive.

Decoding-
- Read the given stego audio sign.
- Find the key embedded.
- Next information is the required information.

Fig. 2. Algorithm for audio steganography

4 Discussion

Vigor, security and concealing limit are the three noteworthy execution criteria that spin around the existing steganography techniques. To arrange and assess the above-talked about techniques considering these criteria, the transmission environment and the application being used are considered. Undercover correspondence for illustration requires abnormal state of heartiness because of the section of information by one of the current coders that can intensely influence the trustworthiness of the transmitted information. The encoder procedure diminishes the measure of information in the sound sign by taking out repetitive or pointless information. Opposing the encoder/decoder procedures is difficult to fulfill and when satisfied it is normally done at the expense of the concealing limit. Consequently, we decide to study the conduct of the checked on steganography techniques as for their event in the coders. The security part of every strategy is assessed by an outsider exertion expense to recover the implanted information. Three unmistakable installing gatherings are utilized when planning information as a part of sound steganograhic framework which we clarify next [14].

1. <u>Pre-Encoder Embedding</u>- The pre-encoder strategies apply to time and recurrence areas where information inserting happens before the encoding process. A larger part of the strategies having a place with pre-encoder installing class does not ensure the uprightness of the concealed information over the system.
2. <u>Post-Encoder Embedding</u>- In this methodology, information are implanted in the bitstream coming across because of the encoding procedure and extricated before navigating the decoder side. Since the bitstream is more sensitive to alterations than the first sound flag, the concealing limit ought to be kept little to maintain a strategic distance from inserted information detectable quality. Moreover, transcoding can adjust inserted information qualities and accordingly could modify the uprightness of the steganographic framework.
3. <u>In-Encoder Embedding</u>- This methodology depends on information installing operation inside the code book of the codecs. The transmitted data is covered up in the code book parameter after a re-quantization operation. Hence, every sound sign parameter has a twofold essentialness: installed information worth and sound code book parameter.

5 Proposed Model of 5G

In the below given diagram, the Radio Users are managed and the data is driven for the usability with a good performance and management of the devices. The

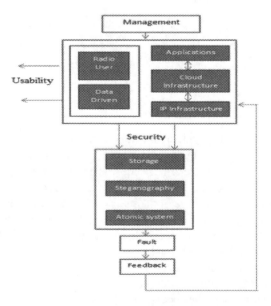

Fig. 3. Model for the deployment

applications are interconnected with the cloud infrastructure implementing the features of cloud technology and IP infrastructure. These together give the security measures to the users for helping the users to secure the data. It also provides high capacity to store large amount of data. In security, the Steganography which defines an invisible communication is of great help. If there occurs any fault in the system, then the feedback is given to the device which then returns back to the management tab and then reties the procedure again (Fig. 3).

This model defines how the 5G technology will work. Usage of Audio steganography will not only enhance the features but also increase the performance in speed. The key that can be an audio will provide protection to the high storage capacity of the database. Audio steganography adds a point in the security perspective of 5G providing encrypted data with great security.

5.1 Graphical Analysis of Securing Data Interoperability in IOT Using 5G

The devices that are explained in Sect. 5 is interoperable. The word "Interoperability" means devices will exchange information with the method that is agreed between the two parties. They mutually exchange information to update the same in the real time. Every time a hidden message is exchanged between the two devices, it is encrypted using audio steganography (Fig. 4).

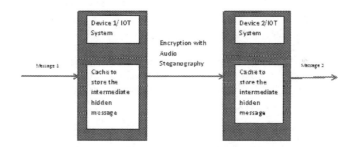

Fig. 4. Securing data interoperability between the devices

6   Conclusions and Future Scope

Looking at the major challenges that are envisioned for the new use cases and applications requires trust, privacy, reliability and confidentiality of the data. 5G is not exactly an innovation but realization of applications that has integrated various techniques through different radio interface. The priority is to appetize the users with very high data rate, extended battery life, reduced end to end latency. The challenge is to secure the hidden exchange of the data. This paper has proposed hiding the data using the audio steganography. The model has integrated the cloud infrastructure in the model along with the Internet of Things. Audio steganography algorithm has been proposed to secure the network. The implementation of the technique has also been shown. The advantage of this audio steganography encoding is its simplicity. A high level of security of data is maintained when a valuable data is to be transmitted. This method can be used for providing an audio password to protect the database.

References

1. Pirinen, P.: A brief overview of 5G research activities. In: 1st International Conference on 5G for Ubiquitous Connectivity (5GU), pp. 17–22. IEEE (2014)
2. Tudzarov, A., Janevski, T.: Functional architecture for 5G mobile networks. Int. J. Adv. Sci. Technol. **32**, 65–78 (2011)
3. Mousa, A.M.: Prospective of fifth generation mobile communications. Int. J. Next Gener. Netw. (IJNGN) **4**(3), 1–30 (2012)
4. Jeffrey, G., Stefano, B., Wan, C., Stephen, H., Angel, L., Anthony, C.K.S., Charlie, Z.: What will 5G be. In: IEEE JSAC Special Isuue on 5G Wireless Communication System (2014)
5. Singh, S., Singh, P.: Key concepts and network architecture for 5G mobile technology. Int. J. Sci. Res. Eng. Technol. (IJSRET) **1**(5), 165–170 (2012)
6. Chen, Y.P., Yang, Y.H.: A new 4G architecture providing multimode terminals always best connected services. IEEE Wirel. Commun. (2007)
7. Xichun, L., Gani, A., Omar, Z.: The future of mobile wireless communication networks. In: International Conference on Communication Software and Network (2009)
8. Farooq, M., Ishtiaq, A.M., Usman, MAl: Future generations of mobile communication networks. Acad. Contemp. Res. J. **VII**(I), 15–21 (2013). ISSN: 2305-865
9. Rappaport, T.S.: Wireless Communications Principle and Practice, 2nd edn, Chap. 2. Pearson Education (Singapore) Pte. Ltd
10. El-Emam. N.N.: Hiding a large amount of data with high security using steganography algorithm. Computer Science (2007)
11. Morkel, T., Eloff, J.H.P., Oliver, M.S.: An overview of audio steganography. In: Proceedings of the ISSA. Steganography Protection against removal (Document marking) (2005)
12. Yahya, A., Ahmad, B., Osamah, M.A.: Protection against detection (Information hiding). Qershi International Journal of Computer Science (2005)
13. Johnson, N.F., Jajodia, S.: Exploring steganography: seeing the unseen. IEEE Computer Journal (1998)
14. Jamil, T.: Steganography: The art of hiding information in plain sight. IEEE Potentials (1999)

Mutation Testing and Test Data Generation Approaches: A Review

Meenu Dave and Rashmi Agrawal$^{(\boxtimes)}$

Computer Science Department, Jagan Nath University, Jaipur 302022, India
guptarashmi1979@gmail.com

Abstract. Software advancement has increased the complexities many fold and to meet the quality standards, a lot of research is being done in designing new testing methodologies and tools. Mutation testing is a proven effective technique but the high cost attached with it averts it from establishing it as an industrial tool. The review is an extension of the previous work where a review was done on search based test data generation and mutation testing. The objective is to study the remaining techniques/approaches and summaries the discussion of both the reviews. The application of mutation testing with various techniques at various phases of software development along with various languages/tools show that it is a versatile, adaptable and efficient, which is motivating the researchers to explore the new areas.

Keywords: Mutation testing · Evolutionary algorithms · Constraint based · Mutation analysis · Test data generation

1 Introduction

Software testing is the process of identification and removal of bugs and validating against the requirements and specifications. The advancement in hardware and software technologies have added to the complexities to the software products which require advance testing methods, tools and technologies. To meet this requirement researchers are working various methodologies and techniques to cope with advancements and deliver quality products. The most common method of testing is manual testing which is both laborious and time consuming. The alternate is automation of testing which can handle the complexities of modern software and look for options which are beyond the human thinking. The use of standardized technology and tools can help developers to standardize their product.

The objective of our review is to study the test data generation combined with mutation testing. A lot of research has been done in the area of mutation testing but the high cost of mutant generation is the main obstacle in establishing it as industrial tool. The review of the literature can guide the new students, researcher, professional and intended users to get knowledge about the various techniques and approaches that have been applied. In our previous work we have encompassed the search based test data generation with mutation testing [1] and this paper is the extension.

© Springer Nature Singapore Pte Ltd. 2016
A. Unal et al. (Eds.): SmartCom 2016, CCIS 628, pp. 373–382, 2016.
DOI: 10.1007/978-981-10-3433-6_45

The testing process usually has some test data which are given as input to the software and the behavior or the outcome is analyzed. The quality of test data which test highly affects the quality of testing. *How to test the quality of test data?* Mutation testing can help in accessing the test data through mutation analysis. The source code of the Software Under Test (SUT) is altered with one syntactic change at a time and multiple copies are generated called *mutants*. A set of test cases is first run with SUT and an oracle is generated. Then this set is run with each mutant. Outputs of the mutants are compared with the oracle and if they differ the mutant is said to be *killed* else it is *alive*. Sometimes there are some mutants that are never caught, they are called *equivalent mutants*. There are multiple mutants to a single program and hence multiple test cases are required to kill these mutants. The test cases are assessed by how many mutants they can kill, this is called *mutation analysis*.

The aim of this review is to study the literature (a) study the already proven techniques, proofs and frameworks; (b) the various issues or problems related to the mutation testing combines with test data generation, (c) classification (d) look for areas, or problems which can be the research question for future work.

The quality of testing is directly affected by the generation and selection of efficient test data. The manual generation of test data can generate good test cases, but laborious [2], and expensive. Automation of test case generation can be seen as a possible solution. A lot of research has been done and going on in the field of automatic test case generation and lot of tools, techniques and algorithms are available, both commercial and open source. This paper is the review of the automation tools, techniques for test data generation which are mutation analysis adequate. The paper is organized as Sect. 2 is the background, Sect. 3 is the elaboration of the review, Sect. 4 is the discussion and Sect. 5 concludes the paper.

2 Background

2.1 Mutation Analysis

Mutation testing was first suggested out by De Millo, is a fault based unit testing which is effective in generating good test data set through mutation analysis [3–5]. For mutation testing, many faulty copies of software under test, called mutants are created, with one syntactic change per mutant [4–9]. Test cases are run with these mutants and if the output is incorrect, then the mutant is said to fail or be killed, else it is said to be alive. Live mutants reveal that either the test data is not capable or there is no such data (equivalent) [8]. The mutants that cannot be killed by any test case, and which always give output as the original program, are equivalent mutants [7]. For other live mutants, the test sets are incapable to kill them, but they are killable [7]. The mutation score = no of mutants killed/ total non equivalent mutants. The ultimate aim of any test set in testing is to look for bugs and mutation score can help to prioritize, or reduce or select test data as optimization which can further decrease the time and resources consumed. The mutation score can be a heuristic for test data generation by searching for test data suit which is capable of mutants and generate a reduced test set.

2.2   Mutation Variants

Mutation testing as proposed by DeMillo et al. [3, 10] is "strong" mutation. There are strong, weak and firm mutations, depending upon the mutation location and program behavior at run time. Injecting faults artificially in a program creates mutant. Many mutants can be created from the same program by injecting different faults for each mutant. The classical aim of any mutation testing is to "kill" these mutants. The test cases are first run with the original program and outputs are stored, it is run with the mutants and collecting the results. The outputs are compared and if they differ, the mutant is said to be "killed". Strong mutations have been termed as external observation by Mathur [9]. The results are compared in the form of global variables or files during execution or at termination (external). The 'weak mutations' was proposed by Howden [8] to overcome the high costs of computation related with strong mutation.

The comparisons are at the same place where the alteration was made. As describes as internal observations by Mathur [9], at the intermediate stage of the execution, the internal variables are checked if the mutant has been killed. The "First Order Mutants" [3] are the traditional ones, where one alteration at a time is made to the SUT and mutants are generated. The "High order mutants" [3] are the ones in which multiple changes have been injected into source code. As stated by DeMillo [10], the Coupling effect: "test data that distinguishes all programs differing from a correct one by only simple errors is so sensitive that it also implicitly distinguishes more complex errors." According to Mathur [9], first order mutation can be used to obtain high level of program correctness. That is the complex errors are coupled to simple errors can be uncovered if the tester attempts systematic search of simple errors [10].

According to the definition of the necessity condition [11], "Given a program R, by altering a statement S of R a mutant is generated M, For M to be killed by T test case, it is necessary that the state of M immediately following some execution of S be different from the state of R at the same point". The test case generation approaches has been further classified as dynamic and static by Papadakis [2]. Further he has put symbolic execution into static type and other approaches like search based optimization, random testing and dynamic symbolic as dynamic.

2.3   Mutation Process

The main parts of the mutation analysis for white box testing are Software Under Test (SUT), Source code Parser and Instrumenter, Test Data generator, Mutant repository, Test Oracle, Mutant Generator, Mutant Analyzer, Test Case Optimizer. The SUT is first executed with some pre generated test cases or new data are generated and test oracle is generated. Then the SUT is parsed and instrumented and mutants are generated. The generated mutants are executed against the test oracle and the output is sent to the Mutant Analyzer which will check for equivalent mutants, no of mutants killed and generate mutant score or check if there is some error in original code. The mutation score acts as heuristic for test optimizer and a reduced test set is generated (Fig. 1).

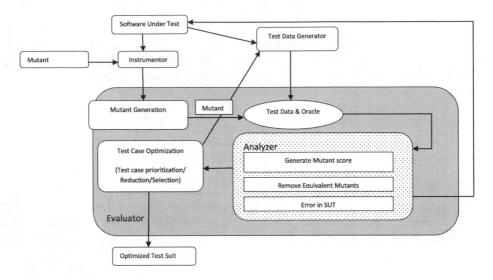

Fig. 1. Mutation testing

3   Related Work

Work by Souza, Francisco Carlos M. [7] states that mutation testing for generating test data is a major challenge; it consists of identifying a set of test data that kills maximum number of mutants. The study identified 10 different techniques for test data generation and classified them into four main categories: (1) search based techniques -comprises techniques that use heuristics (2) code coverage based techniques-analysis of the data flow and control flow (3) restriction based techniques-resolution of restriction systems and (4) hybrid techniques -combine one or more techniques [7]. This paper is a study of the previous work done in test case generation techniques and approaches with mutation testing.

3.1   Heuristic Test Data Generation

In our previous work we have discussed the search based techniques or meta-heuristic techniques with mutation testing. We found more than 25 papers being published under this category and most of them have been published in recent decade. This shows that there is a rise in this direction as the results are good and the scope is huge to explore more techniques. This can guide the new researchers to experiment new heuristic techniques and design new tools.

3.2   Hybrid Approaches

Dynamic Symbolic Execution (DSE): Work by Zang [12] in this paper proposed a general approach with Dynamic Symbolic Execution (DSE) to automate the generation of test inputs to kill mutants by implanting in a tool called PexMutator. The results shows that the proposed approach is more "efficient" and "effective" then the existing techniques and can be applied to the real-world problems. The work by Papadakis [2] proposes an automated framework for test generation which is mutation based with dynamic symbolic execution and mutant schema.

Random Testing: Work by Patrick [13] proposed a combination of meta-heuristic optimization, random testing, mutation analysis, and static analysis [14]. This paper is the first to apply mutation analysis with random test data generation, as earlier it was thought to be inefficient to meet the testing goals. Patrick [15] in his work developed mutation based random testing technique with efficient input sub-domains for test data generation.

3.3 Dynamic Domain Reduction Approach

The application of Dynamic Domain Reduction technique for automated test case generation is proposed in work by Offutt [16].

3.4 Specification Based Approach

Okun, Vadim [17], in his work in 2004 successfully applied specification-based mutation to test programs and it gave good program-based coverage. Programs with large intermediate states could be tested for black-box testing with fault visibility. Nilsson et al., Robert, Jeff Offut [18] studied the mutation based testing of timeliness. In this testing the mutation operators are generated by mutant generator, are applied to the specifications and the resultant mutant is sent to an execution order analyzer to check the effect on the timeliness failure. The paper by Aichernig [19] presents a method for testing pre- and post-condition specifications by fault-based test case generation, by mutating the pre- and post-conditions. The work by Wimmel [20] generated test sequences using mutations of the system specifications and targeting scenarios that increased the confidence in the system with relevance to security requirements. Shan [21] proposed an approach which generates test cases, from a few seed test cases, through data mutation.

3.5 Constraint Based Approach

DeMillo et al. [22] introduced the concepts of Constraint Based Testing for test case generation. The program symbol representing mathematical constraints are the base to reveal the faults. Results show that using these constraints, test cases which is very near to mutation adequacy can be generated automatically with low cost. The work by Baudry [23] is the study to check the contracts efficiency only on mutants that are killed by at least one test case, using the behavioral difference oracle (deep-equals on object programs). Liu, et al., [24] proposed an approach to kill many mutants at the same time based on the concept of reachability condition. The mutants that are present at the same location present at the same location can be killed with the same reachability condition, and hence reducing test generation and execution time.

3.6 Coverage Criteria Based Approaches

An empirical study was conducted by Smith [25] to compare the emerging technologies like mutation testing with coverage analysis. The study indicates that the 74% of the mutation operators under study were useful in generating new test. The work by Papadakis [5] is a study of application of the weak mutation testing along with path based selection approach to kill mutants for test case generation. The paper by Papadakis [26] proposes the strategy with the aims to reduce the cost of test generation and mutation testing by using path selection.

3.7 Other Approaches

Brillou [27] proposed a methodology for automated test case generation for Simulink models. The framework has fault models for test coverage and goals which are directly related to the requirement specifications, both functional and non-functional. The Simulink program is tested with fault and mutation based testing where the test suits are created in terms of detection of injected faults [27]. Fraser [28] presented μTEST, which generates unit tests for object-oriented classes based on mutation score, automatically. Fraser [29] worked on pre-conditions and post –conditions to generate a parameterized unit tests. By mutating post-conditions and inputs, a set of relevant oracles, post conditions and pre-conditions are figured to simplify test cases. The paper [30] proposes the use of fuzzy logic to equivalent mutant detection for efficient testing.

3.8 Recent Publication

In recently published work by Souza, et al. [31], test data was generated automatically for strong mutation which showed better results than random testing. The aim was to kill the strong mutants and generate a quality test suit for structural testing. Mutation testing was applied to the feature testing in Software Product Lines to generate test data that can find the faults in a given feature model by killing mutant in work by Matnei Filho, Rui Angelo, and Silvia Regina Vergilio [32]. The application of Genetic Algorithms and Simulated Annealing was applied to generated test data for Simulink and analysis the test data by mutation score Le Thi My Hanh, Khuat Thanh, and Nguyen Thanh Binh Tung [33] (Figs. 2 and 3).

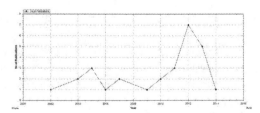

Fig. 2. Publications for search base test data generation

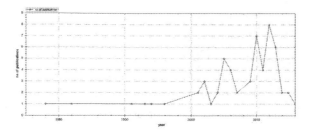

Fig. 3. Publications for test data generation and mutation testing

4   Discussion

There has been a rise in the publication of research papers. From year 2000 every year some publications are there, showing that even though the number of publications are different but they are continuous, which is an indication that mutation testing is a promising area for test data generation. The concept of mutation testing has been applied to all major phases of software development like white box testing, specification based testing, feature testing, contracts, pre-condition post-condition testing, which shows versatility in the application of the mutation testing. For structural testing also many papers have worked upon. The analysis of the position of mutant and its infection which can be seen as a major classification in the mutation testing showing the depth and accuracy in the research work done.

Mutation testing has been adopted with approaches like path oriented testing, dynamic symbolic execution, random testing, predicate/ branch adequacy testing, data flow testing, which establishes it a supporting technique to the major existing techniques. The major problems discussed in most of the papers regarding mutation testing are the cost of mutant generation, equivalent mutants and time. Simultaneously majority of them establish mutation testing as an effective technique and the expenses are one time which can give good results in long run. From all the techniques/ approaches, majority of recent work is done in heuristic search where the mutation score is adopted as the fitness evaluator or to assess the quality of the test data generated along with other adequacy criteria giving mutation score adequacy criteria for test set. Research has been done in the direction of mutation testing and Simulink/Matlab showing the suppleness of the technique. Most of the research papers are a joint effort of many researchers and we can infer that the work is laborious and need high skills and knowledge. Cost of strong mutation testing is high and this is the reason that most of the research is done as weak mutation testing.

There is no publication regarding the research work on any live industrial work. Most of the work is done on small programs and nothing has been said about is scalability to large systems.

Mutation testing test data generation Classification: Here the author would like to display own views about the classification which are based on the review of the available research papers.

(a) Classification based on languages
(b) Classification based on mutant variants
(c) Classification based on phases of software development where the mutation testing has been applied.

Much more information can be deduced from the survey and many more trends can be drawn, which might help the intended users to get a better knowledge of the particular area/ topic or phenomenon.

5 Future Work and Conclusion

The survey has studied the established proof and framework done in the field of mutation testing and test data generation. The main areas which can be looked upon for future work are the (1) identification of equivalent mutant in the early stage (2) reduce the cost of mutant generation (3) scalability for large programs (4) application to live projects (5) code prioritization (6) mutation clustering for reduced test data generation (7) high order mutant generation for nested predicates (8) predicate analysis.

The review is a survey of the literature encompassing the test data generation with mutation testing. The work has been organised into two papers. In our previous work we covered the search based test data generation and in this paper we discuss the remaining techniques. The discussion and the future work can guide the intended users to look for areas for future research. Mutation testing is an established technique which can be a heuristic to generate optimized test data. The various issues which need to be resolved are the equivalent mutants, time and cost along with the space and execution complexities (large programs).

References

1. Dave, M., Agrawal, R.: Search based techniques and mutation analysis in automatic test case generation: a survey. In: 2015 IEEE International Advance Computing Conference (IACC). IEEE (2015)
2. Papadakis, M., Malevris, N.: Automatic mutation test case generation via dynamic symbolic execution, Software reliability engineering (ISSRE). In: 2010 IEEE 21st International Symposium on IEEE (2010)
3. Offutt, A.J.: A practical system for mutation testing: help for the common programmer. In: Proceedings of the International Test Conference 1994. IEEE (1994)
4. Papadakis, M., Malevris, N.: Mutation bases test case generation via a path selection strategy. Information and Software Technology (2012)
5. Jia, Y., Harman, M.: An analysis and survey of the development of mutation testing. IEEE Trans. Softw. Eng. (2011)
6. Mateo, P., Reales, M.P.U., Offutt, J.: Mutation at system and functional levels. In: 2010 Third International Conference on IEEE Software Testing, Verification, and Validation Workshops (ICSTW) (2010)
7. Souza, F.C.M., et al.: Test Data Generation Techniques for Mutation Testing: A Systematic Mapping

8. Howden, W.E.: Weak mutation testing and completeness of test sets. IEEE Trans. Softw. Eng. 4 (1982)
9. Mathur, A.P.: Foundations of Software Testing, 2/e. Pearson Education India (2008)
10. De Millo, R.A., Lipton, R.J., Sayward, F.G.: Hints on test data selection: help for the practising programmer. Computer **11**(4), 34–41 (1978)
11. DeMillo, R.A., Jefferson, A.: Offutt., Constraint-based automatic test data generation. IEEE Trans. Softw. Eng. **17**(9), 900–910 (1991)
12. Zhang, L., et al.: Test generation via dynamic symbolic execution for mutation testing. In: 2010 IEEE International Conference on Software Maintenance (ICSM). IEEE (2010)
13. Patrick, M.T.: Mutation-Optimised Subdomains for Test Data Generation and Program Analysis. Diss. University of York (2013)
14. Papadakis, M., Malevris, N.: Searching and generating test inputs for mutation testing. SpringerPlus **2**, 121 (2013)
15. Bybro, M., Arnborg, S.: A mutation testing tool for java programs. Master's thesis, Stockholm University, Stockholm, Sweden (2003)
16. Offutt, A.J., Untch, R.H.: Mutation 2000: uniting the orthogonal. In: Eric-Wong, W. (ed.) Mutation testing for the new century. Springer, New York (2001)
17. Okun, V.: Specification mutation for test generation and analysis. Diss. University of Maryland Baltimore County (2004)
18. Nilsson, R., Offutt, J., Mellin, J.: Test case generation for mutation-based testing of timeliness. Electronic Notes in Theoretical Computer Science (2006)
19. Aichernig, B.K., Salas, P.A.P.: Test case generation by OCL mutation and constraint solving. In: Fifth International Conference on Quality Software (QSIC 2005). IEEE (2005)
20. Wimmel, G., Jürjens, J.: Specification-based test generation for security-critical systems using mutations. In: George, C., Miao, H. (eds.) ICFEM 2002. LNCS, vol. 2495, pp. 471–482. Springer Berlin Heidelberg, Berlin, Heidelberg (2002). doi:10.1007/3-540-36103-0_48
21. Shan, L., Zhu, H.: Testing software modelling tools using data mutation. In: Proceedings of the 2006 International Workshop on Automation of Software Test. ACM (2006)
22. De Millo, R.A., Jefferson Offutt, A.: Experimental results from an automatic test case generator. ACM Trans. Softw. Eng. Methodol. (TOSEM) **2**(2), 109–127 (1993)
23. Le Traon, Y., Baudry, B., Jézéquel, J.-M.: Design by contract to improve software vigilance. IEEE Trans. Softw. Eng. **32**(8), 22 (2006)
24. Liu, M.-H., et al.: An approach to test data generation for killing multiple mutants. In: 22nd IEEE International Conference on Software Maintenance, ICSM 2006. IEEE (2006)
25. Smith, B.H., Williams, L.: On guiding the augmentation of an automated test suite via mutation analysis. Empirical Softw. Eng. **14**(3), 341–369 (2009)
26. Papadakis, M., Malevris, N.: An effective path selection strategy for mutation testing. In: Software Engineering Conference, APSEC 2009, Asia-Pacific. IEEE (2009)
27. Brillout, A., He, N., Mazzucchi, M., Kroening, D., Purandare, M., Rümmer, P., Weissenbacher, G.: Mutation-based test case generation for Simulink models. In: Boer, F.S., Bonsangue, M.M., Hallerstede, S., Leuschel, M. (eds.) FMCO 2009. LNCS, vol. 6286, pp. 208–227. Springer Berlin Heidelberg, Berlin, Heidelberg (2010). doi: 10.1007/978-3-642-17071-3_11
28. Fraser, G., Zeller, A.: Mutation-driven generation of unit tests and oracles. IEEE Trans. Softw. Eng. **38**(2), 278–292 (2012)
29. Fraser, G., Zeller, A.: Generating parameterized unit tests. In: Proceedings of the 2011 International Symposium on Software Testing and Analysis. ACM (2011)
30. Jhamb, M., Singhal, A.: An Efficient Approach for Equivalent Mutants Detection using Fuzzy Logic

31. Souza, F.C.M., et al.: Strong mutation-based test data generation using hill climbing. In: Proceedings of the 9th International Workshop on Search-Based Software Testing. ACM (2016)
32. Filho, M., Angelo, R., Vergilio, S.R.: A mutation and multi-objective test data generation approach for feature testing of software product lines. In: 2015 29th Brazilian Symposium on Software Engineering (SBES). IEEE (2015)
33. Hanh, L.T.M., Thanh, K., Tung, N.T.B.: Mutation-based test data generation for simulink models using genetic algorithm and simulated annealing. Int. J. Comput. Inf. Technol. **3**(04), 763–771 (2014)

Keystroke Dynamics: Authenticating Users by Typing Pattern

Abhimanyu[(✉)] and Tripti Rathee

Maharaja Surajmal Institute of Technology, Janakpuri, New Delhi, India
abhimanyutehlan@gmail.com

Abstract. With exponentially increasing users and crucial information accumulation over the internet, it has become a necessity to introduce a system which is powerful in terms of providing protection, and effective in cost required in authentication process. Biometrics is the only thing that cannot be stolen or copied as every human being has their own unique features that cannot be imitated by any intruder. The only disadvantage of biometrics authentication process, the need of additional devices is removed in the proposed system. This method can make the computer uniquely identify a user by typing behavior and defeat intruders. As accurate as any other biometric security technique, keystroke biometrics is cost effective because it does not require any additional hardware. In this paper a new system is introduced having keystrokes biometric added with password hardening techniques as an effective authentication method to defeat intrusion attempts.

Keywords: Authentication · Keystroke biometrics · Typing pattern · Soft biometrics

1 Introduction

The internet which was once used as a source of information only is now a place where you can shop and pay using your cards, you can do business, and you can also promote your work and what not. We depend so much on computers and Internet to store and process sensitive data, and it has become extremely necessary to secure them from intruders [1–5]. With internet playing such an important and inseparable role in our life, concerning about security over the internet becomes the most crucial issue.

Authentication is a process in which the credentials we provide to prove our identity to the system are compared with those already filled in the database. If all the factors matches well, your identity is proved and you can access all the information you want from your account. In case you fail to prove that you are the same user you have claimed to be, access is denies for any type of resource. But things are not as simple as that. With exponentially increasing internet enabled devices, and the uploading of highly sensitive information over the network, it is mandatory nowadays to provide a reliable machine authentication.

For an unbreakable authentication system we need to choose a credential that cannot be stolen, or copied. Most widely deployed and simple way of authentication is username

© Springer Nature Singapore Pte Ltd. 2016
A. Unal et al. (Eds.): SmartCom 2016, CCIS 628, pp. 383–389, 2016.
DOI: 10.1007/978-981-10-3433-6_46

and password pair. Password or Personal Identification Number (PIN) is a knowledge based method entrusting on something you know. This is not only the most popular way to authenticate user, but the most vulnerable as well because users tend to choose passwords that they can memorize easily. Passwords that consist of common words, phrases, or terms associated with a particular user are considered weak because of the relative ease with which an intruder can guess them or find them via brute force and dictionary attacks [6]. On the other hand if we talk about those complex and obscure passwords which are hard to be guessed or cracked are too difficult to remember.

Another way of authentication is a token based method that counts on something you have, like a smartcard and one time password (OTP). But unfortunately this method does not have a mechanism to deal with man in the middle attack or spoofing effectively because we can only verify that the user has right information but we are clueless the user is a genuine user or an intruder. Taking hardware token into consideration, carrying token all the times is inconvenient for users.

There are two key factors around which the concept of authentication or computer security revolves. The first one is that the authorized user should gain access to the system, which is well addressed by a simple password but cannot be always fulfilled by the onerous type of password which is the only option to make the second key component happen. The second one is to prevent the unauthorized user from accessing the resources. Both of these are equally crucial in providing computer security. And hence although we use the password matching technique often, it is not at all a reliable way to ensure secure access.

A more secure and stable way to prove your identity is biometrics. Biometrics is the science of identifying individuals by a particular physiological characteristic, such as voice, fingerprint, face, iris etc. or behavioral characteristic such as signature, keystroke dynamics [7]. All these biological characteristics are unique and unalterable unless they are modified by physical harm [8]. Fingerprints are arguably the most popular biometric currently in use [9, 10]. Fingerprints are the most commonly used attributes in this field as the probability of two person having same finger prints is infinitely small. We can also use other biological traits like voice, retina etc. But the disadvantage associated with biometric authentication is cost required to build such a system of authentication and the additional equipments needed to be deployed. All the high level of security provided by biometrics is something everybody cannot afford.

There is a need of a security system that not only ensures the denial of services to intruder, but also should enable easy and guaranteed access of those who are the genuine users. Besides this, it should be feasible to be employed with the existing resources of computer and should not demand any high cost set up. We developed a system based on simple behavioral feature that inherits uniqueness but does not require any additional equipment to authenticate users. Typing rhythm is the tool which is based on timing information related to the activity of the keys (time when the keys are pressed and released). Our Authentication system uses set of parameters based on key press interval timings that correspond to the typing pattern of user and then identifies him as genuine user or intruder. The developed system measures typing characteristics that are believed to be unique to an individual's physiology and behavior, and thus difficult to duplicate [6]. This paper presents a system for authentication built over keystroke biometrics and also has a touch of a few password- hardening techniques. This makes it an effective complementary authentication system that does not use any additional equipment and provides secure access combined with username password pair.

2   Keystroke Biometrics

Keystroke biometrics is based on the dynamics of every individual stroking a key. Keystroke recognition is the process of analyzing human typing patterns in order to identify individual computer users [11]. The system can exactly identify a particular user after evaluating the identity against certain recorded parameters like the rhythm the user follows while typing, the total time for which the user presses certain key etc. Numerous studies have demonstrated the uniqueness of keystroke patterns for each individual [7, 8]. As early as 1975, scientists have noted that keystroke patterns have characteristics that are unique to individual typists [12]. With keystroke dynamics you can record and match the users' behavioral features that are as unique as hand signatures. The way a user type one key and the time it takes between subsequent keystrokes can determine whether the user is the same user he is claiming to be or someone else is trying to forge his identity.

The system designed requires a user to register with a username and password. Along with the username and password the user will have to enter a string of alphabets, a part of which is fixed and the rest is customized according to the user. The typing analysis will be done while the user types this string. After registration, when the user wants to login into his account, he will have to provide correct username and password and type the text again. It is not important to enter the correct string; even if the string entered contains some typing errors the user can get access to his/her account provided all the other typing credentials are matched.

False acceptance rate (FAR) is defined as the rate at which an intruder is granted access. On the other hand, false rejection rate (FRR) is the rate at which a genuine user is denied access to his account. While designing the system, focus is on minimizing the rate of false acceptance as false acceptance is often dangerous than false rejection, which is the case when some user authorized to get access is denied to use the resource due to some reasons. In the case of false rejection, the user is allowed to retype the string a limited number of times.

3   Parameters

Typing behavior of the user is observed on the basis of following parameters. The system designed records the following parameters based on which it later authenticates the user.

3.1   Total Time

This is the simplest one to measure and test. Total time, in context with keystroke analysis refers to the time the user takes to type the entire string. It is subject to variations and hence a tolerance value of −30% to +20% is taken. In case the total time varies beyond tolerance values, access is denied to the user.

3.2   Time Taken in Typing the Username

User tend to type his username more frequently than anybody else and takes less time in typing the username relative to time he takes in typing rest of the string. This is the idea behind the second parameter used in analyzing user's typing pattern. This parameter is considered to be matched if the observed time is within tolerance limit of 20% of the recorded value in both negative and positive dimensions.

3.3   Key Press Time (Dwell Time)

This is the most powerful parameter that governs the success of the keystroke biometrics. Dwell time refers to the time for which a particular user keeps his/her finger on the key. This time in milliseconds is not noticeable by humans, but is really significant for the system. It is the parameter that is not at all possible to copy because before copying you need to find a way to note it. And if at all you manage to note the time which is practically impossible as it is in fraction of a second, it is not possible to perform the action within the same time limits. This is the factor behind the success of keystroke biometrics. It is compared with tolerances of −15% and +25%.

3.4   Average Space Key Press Time

Space key press time is the time for which the user keeps the space key pressed i.e. the time elapsed between the press and release of the space key. It measures the pressure used by the user in pressing the keys and hence is unique to the user. It is of the order of centiseconds (of the order 10^{-2}) and is compared with the tolerance values of −30% and +25%.

3.5   Average Key Press Interval Time (Flight Time)

It is also known as flight time. Specifically, a key press interval is defined as the elapsed time between two consecutive key presses or two consecutive key releases [5]. For someone typing very fast this is very small and for those who take time this time is considerable. This parameter is measured with tolerances of −25% and +25%. Again this is not possible to take note on how many milliseconds gap was there between the pressings of two keys.

All these parameters are recorded in the database of the system and are matched at the time of login after relaxing the limits according to the tolerance values. If the entire parameters match with the values registered, then the user is given access to the system, otherwise asked to enter the details again. Even when one of the parameters lies out of range, the user is granted access. To make the authentication process even stronger one can remove this relaxation and make it a compulsion that all parameters match in order to get access.

4   Password Hardening

Keystroke biometrics is strong enough to prevent any type of intrusion, but to make it even more secure, the system is introduced with password hardening techniques. Some signals are stored inside the database of the system and a different signal is assigned to every user at the time of registration. For instance, one user is told to stop typing once beep sound is announced by the system, and for some other user beep sound would make no difference. At the same time the third user will be instructed to start typing the sentence only after it beeps two times. If any intruder tries to imitate the behavior, he/she would not be able to decode this secret key at all. This is like a seal on the lock if we see the keystroke biometrics as a lock.

5   Experimental Results

By using tightly controlled experiments, the parameters are analyzed that are recorded while registration and authentication of the users by the system. We have collected data for 10 users during their registration and during authentication for 25 times. All the users were made to type on standard QWERTY keyboards with no numerical values in the string (Figs 1 and 2).

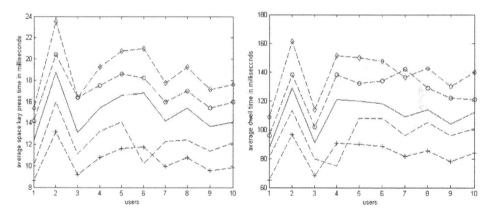

Fig. 1. Average flight time of users   **Fig. 2.** Average dwell time of users

The graphs shows the minimum value of each parameter for each user in all the entries during registration & authentication in plain dotted line, the maximum value by dotted line marked with "o" symbol and the value of parameter recorded at the time of registration in regular simple line. The dotted line marked by diamonds and the dotted line marked with " +" symbol denote the range of parameters with the tolerance values (Figs. 3, 4 and 5).

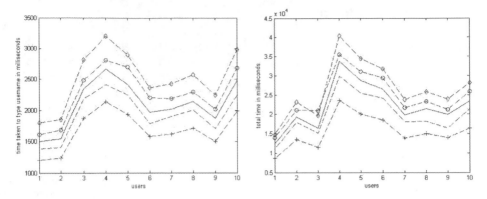

Fig. 3. Time taken to type username   **Fig. 4.** Total time of different users

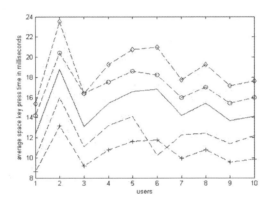

Fig. 5. Average space key press time of users

6   Conclusion

Keystroke biometrics addresses the needs of current security demand most appropriately, and is applicable to all domains with highly sensitive information to less personal details. For instance, applications involving financial transactions are among the most likely to be targeted by attackers, and other less profitable application are less prone to hacking, but keystroke biometrics can act as a barrier between intruder and any type of application. The intent behind designing this system was to make it impossible for the intruder to have access by any mean, and accomplishing this too with the basic input output devices of a computer system. With extremely low False Acceptance Rates (FAR) of 1.3%, it is a complimentary authentication method which when used in conjunction with username password is better than any other authentication process in terms of accuracy and cost.

References

1. Keystroke Dynamics - Benchmark Data Set. http://www.cs.cmu.edu/~keystroke/
2. Karnan, M., Akilab, M., Krishnarajc, N.: Biometric personal authentication using keystroke dynamics: a review. Appl. Soft. Comput. **11**, 1565–1573 (2011)
3. Gaines, R.S., Lisowski, W., Press, S.J., et al.: Authentication by keystroke timing: Some preliminary results. Rand Corp, Santa Monica CA (1980)
4. Young, J.R., Hammon, R.W.: Method and apparatus for verifying an individual's identity. U. S. Patent No. 4, 805, 222. U.S. Patent and Trademark Office, Washington, DC (1989)
5. Monrose, F., Rubin, A.D.: Keystroke dynamics as a biometric for authentication, future gener. Comput. Syst. **16**, 351–359 (2000)
6. Peacock, A., Ke, X., Wilkerson, M.: Typing pattern: a key to user identification. MIT. IEEE Secur. Priv. **2**, 40–47 (2004)
7. Hu, J., Gingrich, D., Sentosa, A.: A k-nearest neighbor approach for user authentication through biometric keystroke dynamics. In: IEEE Conference on Communications, pp. 1556–1560 (2008)
8. Giroux, S., Wachowiak-Smolikova, R., Wachowiak, M.P.: Keystroke-based authentication by key press intervals as a complementary behavioral biometric. In: IEEE International Conference on Systems, Man, and Cybernetics, San Antonio, TX, USA (2009)
9. Germain, R.S., Califano, A., Colville, S.: Fingerprint matching using transformation parameter clustering. IEEE Comput. Sci. Eng. **4**, 42–49 (1997)
10. Wang, Y., Hu, J., Philip, D.: A fingerprint orientation model based on 2D Fourier Expansion (FOMFE) and its application to singular-point detection and fingerprint Indexing. Special Issue on Biometrics: Progress and Directions. IEEE Transactions on Pattern Analysis and Machine Intelligence, 573–585 (2007)
11. Hosseinzadeh, D., Krishnan, S.: Gaussian mixture modeling of keystroke patterns for biometric applications. IEEE Trans. Syst. Man Cybernetics—Part C: Appl. Rev. 38 (2008)
12. Spillane, R.: Keyboard apparatus for personal identification. IBM Tech. Discl. Bull. **17**, 3346 (1975)

ABC and TLBO Technique for Evaluating Data Rate in Wireless Network

Sharada Ohatkar and Yogitha Gunjkar[✉]

Department of Electronics and Telecommunication, MKSSS's CCOEW,
Savitribai Phule Pune University, Pune, India
sharada.ok@gmail.com, yogithagunjkar10@gmail.com

Abstract. Cellular concept is major breakthrough in solving spectral congestion but it faces spectrum availability crisis due to increase in requirement of data rate. In order to satisfy the growing traffic demand and to optimize channel allocation, cognitive cellular network (CCN) is taken into consideration. CCN consists of primary (cellular) and secondary (cognitive) users where secondary users try to accommodate in primary band without causing interference to them. Artificial Bee Colony (ABC) and Teaching Learning Based Optimization (TLBO) algorithms are the population based optimization techniques, taken into account to analyze and improvise the network capacity. In this paper, these techniques are studied and used to find SINR in terms of data rate in Mbps with the help of fitness function. The obtained results of ABC and TLBO are compared with reported work of Particle Swarm Optimization (PSO). The proposed techniques are found to be better than PSO.

Keywords: Artificial Bee Colony (ABC) · Teaching Learning Based Optimization (TLBO) · Optimization (Opt) · Primary (Pr) · Secondary (Se)

1 Introduction

Cellular network is a communication network distributed over land areas [1, 2]. Enormous number of users domicile in it over a massive geographic area within restrained frequency spectrum [1]. As the quantity of cellular users is increasing rapidly every year, the cellular network faces spectrum availability crisis [3, 4]. There is a need of improvement in network to meet the necessity of enlarging traffic. Current and future wireless architecture are inevitable responses to fundamental constraints of wireless operation. Spectrum has become more crowded, devices are becoming increasingly plentiful and applications are more demanding of content [4, 5].

The improvements in wireless capacity must derive from fundamental changes in architecture of wireless system. Cognitive radio provides one of the few opportunities to make fundamental and enabling changes to architecture and operation of wireless system [4]. The users with cognitive network desirous of opportunistic use of spectrum are referred to as secondary users (unlicensed). The incumbent (licensed) users occupying the spectrum are referred to as Pr users. Se users communicate with other Se users without interfering the active primary users [8].

© Springer Nature Singapore Pte Ltd. 2016
A. Unal et al. (Eds.): SmartCom 2016, CCIS 628, pp. 390–399, 2016.
DOI: 10.1007/978-981-10-3433-6_47

Cog technology is a progressive spectrum access scheduled so as to get maximum benefit of the resources of frequency band [1]. Cognitive network consists of WiFi hotspots (femto cells) to be accommodated into macro cell (cellular devices) network area [7]. Femto cells are small, low power base stations and operators have less control over them. Cognitive network can acknowledge the interference issues by dispensing femto base stations with the proficiency to sense the environment, interpret the signal from macro base station and allocate spectrum resources intellectually.

The different optimization techniques like Particle swarm optimization (PSO), Ant colony optimization (ACO), ABC, TLBO can be considered for opportunistic to licensed bands without interference to the actual residing users. ABC is one of the effectual optimization technique used to solve many engineering problems [10]. It is heuristic method based on intelligent food exploration behavior of honey bees. TLBO is a novel evolutionary algorithm inspired by relationship between students and teachers. In this paper, ABC and TLBO techniques are studied and ABC technique is used to evaluate the fitness.

1.1   ABC

In ABC algorithm, colony of unnatural bees consist of employed bees (Ebe), onlooker bees (Obe) and scouts (Sc). The Ebe search for food position (solutions) and Obe choose the best of it with probability depending on employed bees. Sc bees are those Ebe whose food source is abandoned [8, 10].

1.2   TLBO

TLBO technique is a population established method and it is based mainly on consequence of influential teacher on output of learning students in the set of group [8]. For TLBO, population is taken into account as a group of learners. This method comprises of distinctive design variables where learners result is corresponding to "*fitness*".

2   Problem Formulation

Cognitive radio network proposes a crucial technology to well maintain and upgrade wireless networks. It is a novel approach for improvising the usage of the spectrum band and it also protects from harmful interference [5, 6].

As spectrum fragment wireless network is distributed, the two type of users present in network are primary and secondary users. The licensed users have precedence to access the spectrum as they are license-possessor of band whereas unlicensed users may access the spectrum later without interfering Pr users [9]. In cognitive cellular network approach, Pr and Se users can peacefully coexist in the one system so as to share the spectrum and improve efficacy of the licensed spectrum. Since we consider cellular LTE, the bandwidth of primary channel is taken into account as 20 MHz [6].

The SINR (in dB) is a dimension to articulate the amount of interference perceived by receiving device on a current link. SINR for secondary links is given by [6]:

$$SINR_j = \frac{\frac{P}{lds(j)^n}}{\sum_{k \in \Phi} \frac{P}{dss(k,j)^n} + \frac{P}{dps(i,j)^n}}, \quad 1 \le j \le Sl. \tag{1}$$

where P is transmission power, lds(j) is link distance of Se device pair, dss(k, j) is distance from Se transmitter to receiver, Φ is set of Se users. Similarly, SINR for primary links is given by [6]:

$$SINR_i = \frac{\frac{P}{ldp(i)^n}}{\sum_{k \in \Phi} \frac{P}{dps(k,i)^n}}, \quad 1 \le i \le Pl. \tag{2}$$

where P is transmission power, ldp(j) is link distance of Pr device pair, dps(k, i) is distance from Se transmitter to Pr receiver, Φ is set of Pr users.

3 ABC and TLBO Algorithms Used for Optimization

ABC and TLBO algorithms are developed progressive optimization methods.

3.1 ABC Algorithm

ABC process is a speculative advanced approach established on swarm intelligence, used for optimizing multiform functions. The swarm of bees comprises of different bees where Ebe go to pursue food and Obe make decision based on food source(Fsc). In this design, the site of food source can be exhibited as accessible solution of optimization issue and nectar quanity of food resembles the quality (fitness) of the affiliated solution [10]. The main steps for every iteration of ABC process are [10]:

(1) Initialize
(2) REPEAT

- Set the Ebe on Fsc in the memory.
- Set the Obe on Fsc in the memory.
- Set the scouts to search region for new food.

(3) UNTIL (requirements are met)

Set out Ebe for memorizing the food source. The following step indicates selfish choosing procedure for Ebe phase [10].

$$V_{ij} = x_{ij} + r_{ij}(X_{ij} - X_{kj}) \qquad (3)$$

Set out Obe for selection of best food source position. The Obe choose the best Fsc by calculating probability eventually depending on fitness [10].

$$p_i = \frac{F_i}{\sum\limits_{n=1}^{N} F_n} \qquad (4)$$

where Fi is fitness of solution i evaluated by its employed bee.

Set out Sc for random search. The scouts are abandoned Ebe. They go in search of food in random manner [10].

Algorithm 1. Ebe phase

1. Initialize
2. for k= 1 to PN do
3.   for j= 1 to D do
4. $V_{ij} = x_{ij} + r_{ij}(X_{ij} - X_{kj})$
          $k \in 1,2 \ldots\ldots PN$, r
          $=(0,1)$ and $k \neq i$
5.   end for
6. Calculate f(x)
7. end for

Algorithm 3. Sc phase

1. for i=1....PN do
2.   if (Sc (i) = lim) then
3. $V_{ij} = x_{ij} + r_{ij}(X_{ij} - X_{kj})$
4.   generate Vij
5.   end if
6. end for

Algorithm 2. Obe phase

1. for i = 1....PN do
2.   r (i,j) = (0,1)
3.   tot_1 = 0
4.   j = 0
5.   while (tol_1 < r (i,j) do
6.   tot_1 = tot_1 + p_i
7.   j= j+1
8.   for k = 1....D do
9. $V_{ij} = x_{ij} + r_{ij}(X_{ij} - X_{kj})$
          $k \in 1,2 \ldots\ldots PN$
10. end for
11. Calculate f(Xi)
12. If f(Xi) < f(Xj) then
13.   Xj = xn
14. end if
15. end for

3.2 TLBO Algorithm

TLBO form is built on eventuality of impact of a teacher on the outcome of students in a class. Similar to other nature motivated methods, TLBO considers a population based scenario that contemplates probable outcomes that advances to the universal solution [8]. For all optimization methods, the population size contains divergent valuables. Here, various valuables can be taken equivalent to various subjects offered to learners and learner's outcome is in turn equivalent to "fitness" as in different optimization techniques [8].

The working of TLBO process is partitioned into two segments. First part comprises of *"Teacher Phase"* referring to students learning from teacher and *"Learning phase"* refers to gaining knowledge by interaction between the learners.

Main steps for this method are as follows:

(1) INITIALIZE parameters
(2) Generate random population
(3) Obtain objective function
(4) REPEAT

- Update solutions obtained by Teacher teaching the students.
- Upgrade solutions of learner phase if new outcome contains better result than existing one.
- Identify the duplicate solution and alter it.

(5) UNTIL (ternination criteria is met)

Algorithm 4. Teacher period

1. for i= 1 : allSubject do
2. GPA[i]
    =calculateGradePointAverage(P,PS)
3. $X_{new,j} = X_{old,j} + r_i (M_{new} - T_F M_i)$
    $i \neq j$ and r = [0,1]
4. Determine $f(X_i)$
5. end for

Algorithm 5. Learner Period

1. for i= 1: PS do
2. choose another learner X_j,
    $i \neq j$
3. if $f(X_i) < f(X_j)$
4. $X_{new,i} = X_{old,i} + r_i (X_i-X_j)$
5. else
6. end if
7. end for

4 Simulation Results

The Cognitive cellular network is considered here to accommodate the primary and secondary users in system. The users are disbursed over region of 5000 X 5000. The primary users are macro cells having more coverage area compared to secondary users. The initial location of Pr and Se users is demonstrated in Fig. 1.

The final location of Pr and Se users using ABC algorithm is shown in Fig. 2. The final location of Pr and Se users using TLBO algorithm is shown in Fig. 3. The Se users accommodate themselves in the network in such a manner so as without interfering the active Pr users.

Ebe in ABC help to find the best fitness solution for the network using greedy selection procedure. Scouts are the left out Ebe. Obe choose the best quality of solution by finding out the probability. Table 1 shows the ABC parameters and Table 2 shows results obtained for ABC technique. Similarly Table 3 shows results obtained by TLBO method.

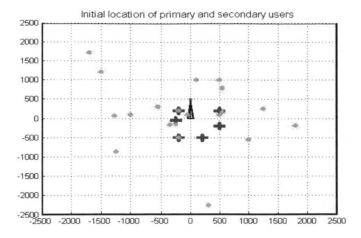

Fig. 1. Initial location of Pr and Se users

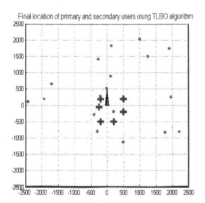

Fig. 3. Final location of Pr and Se
Users using TLBO algorithm

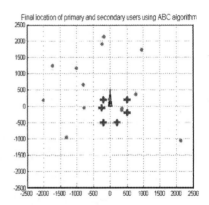

Fig. 2. Final location of Pr and Se
users using ABC algorithm

Table 1. ABC and TLBO parameters

S.No	Parameters for ABC	Values
1.	Colony size	40
2.	Maximum Cycle Number	100
3.	Primary users	6
4.	Secondary users	20
5.	Cycles	100
6.	Bandwidth	20 MHz

Table 2. Results for ABC

S.No	Results for ABC	Values
1.	Colony size	40
2.	Cycles	100
3.	SINR Threshold value	10
4.	Highest fitness value (data rate) in Mbps	1243.87
5.	Time taken by ABC	53 secs

Table 3. Results for TLBO

S.No	Results for TLBO	Values
1.	Colony size	40
2.	Cycles	100
3.	SINR Threshold value	8
4.	Highest fitness value (data rate) in Mbps	1756.009
5.	Time taken by TLBO	75 secs

Particle Swarm Optimization is a technique based on swarm intelligence that is inspired by flocking and schooling of birds and fishes. The author of [7] has worked on PSO for same scenario. The figures below show comparison of ABC and TLBO with published results of PSO (Figs. 4, 5, 6 and 7).

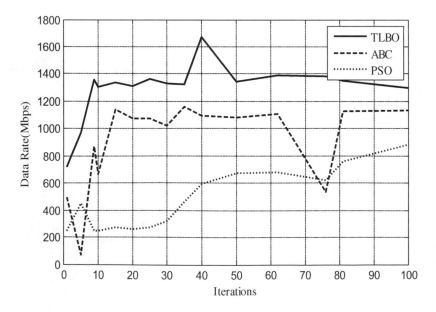

Fig. 4. Comparison of PSO, ABC and TLBO for SINR threshold alpha = 4

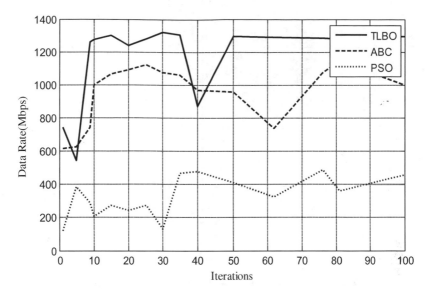

Fig. 5. Comparison of PSO, ABC and TLBO for SINR threshold alpha = 6

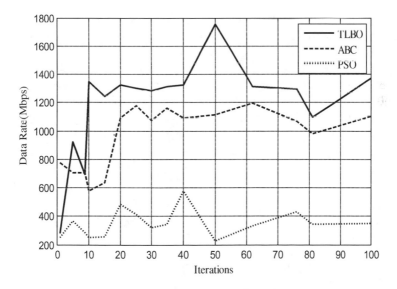

Fig. 6. Comparison of PSO, ABC and TLBO for SINR threshold alpha = 8

From the comparison and the results it is seen that our obtained results are better compared to PSO.

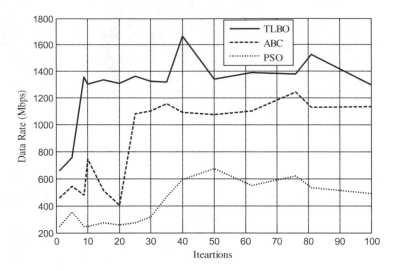

Fig. 7. Comparison of PSO, ABC and TLBO for SINR threshold alpha = 10

5 Conclusion

Cognitive Cellular Network acknowledges the interference issues in the cellular network and helps in assignment of unlicensed users in the spectrum in a form such that frequency band doesn't get effected. ABC and TLBO techniques are implemented to achieve minimum interference between the primary and secondary users. These algorithms are used to find the best fitness of system in turn determining the values of SINR and data rate. Comparison of ABC, TLBO and PSO shows that ABC and TLBO give better result than PSO in form of data rate.

References

1. Rappaport, T.S.: Wireless Communications. Prentice-Hall, Upper Saddle River (2002)
2. Lee, W.C.Y.: Mobile Cellular Telecommunications: Analog and Digital Systems. McGraw Hill, New York (1989)
3. Ohatkar, S.N., Bormane, D.S.: Hybrid channel allocation in cellular network based on genetic algorithm and particle swarm optimisation methods. IET Commun. **10**(13), 1571–1578 (2016). doi:10.1049/iet-com.2015.0757
4. Marshall, P.: Scalability, Density, and Decision Making in Cognitive Wireless Networks. Cambridge (2013)
5. Vargas, A.M., Andrade, A.G.: Particle swarm optimization applied to a spectrum sharing problem. Int. J. Electron. Commun. **66**, 969–978 (2012)
6. Vargas, A.M., Andrade, A.G.: Deployment analysis and optimization of heterogeneous networks under the spectrum underlay strategy. EURASIP J. Wirel. Commun. Netw. **55**,1–15 (2015)

7. Ohatkar, S.N., Bormane, D.S., Kirwai, N: Optimization of channel assignment for cognitive cellular networks. In: IEEE Conference on Advances in Signal Processing (CASP), Pune, India, pp. 391–396 (2016)
8. Savsani, P., Jhala, R.L., Savsani, V.J.: Optimized trajectory planning of a robotic arm using TLBO and ABC optimization techniques. In: IEEE International System Conference (SysCon), pp 381–386. Orlando (2013)
9. Gardellin, V., Das, S.K., Lenzini, L.: Self-coexistence in cellular cognitive radio networks based on the IEEE 802.22 Standard. IEEE Wirel. Commun. **20**, 52–59 (2013)
10. Karaboga, D., Akay, B.: A comparative study of Artificial Bee Colony (ABC) algorithm. Appl. Math. Comput. **214**, 108–132 (2009)

An Optimal Design of Fractal Antenna Using Modified Sierpinski Carpet Geometry for Wireless Applications

Narinder Sharma[1(✉)] and Vipul Sharma[2]

[1] ECE Department, Amritsar College of Engineering and Technology, Amritsar, Punjab, India
narinder.acet@gmail.com
[2] ECE Department, Gurukul Kangri Vishwavidyalaya, Haridwar, Uttrakhand, India
vipul.s.sharma@gmail.com

Abstract. The paper explains an optimal design of fractal antenna using modified Sierpinski Carpet geometry for wireless applications. The proposed antenna is designed on substrate (FR4 glass epoxy) by considering the thickness of 1.6 mm and $\varepsilon_r = 4.4$. The resonant frequency taken for proposed antenna is 2 GHz. It is observed that on increasing the antenna iterations the gain also increases with it. The (HFSS V13) High Frequency Structure Simulator is used for designing and simulation of proposed antenna. The performance parameters of antenna like Voltage Standing Wave Ratio (VSWR), Return loss and gain for different iterations are also observed and explained in this paper.

Keywords: VSWR · HFSS · Return loss · Sierpinski carpet antenna

1 Introduction

The fractal geometries have been widely used in the wireless communication systems because of their wideband and multiband characteristics [1]. It was first developed by N. Cohen in 1995 [3]. Fractal geometries are designed by using two distinctive properties like space filling and self-similarity [2, 4]. Space filling is used to minimize the size of antenna and self-similarity describes the multiband and wideband nature of an antenna [6]. To overcome the drawbacks caused by printed and microstrip patch antenna like low bandwidth and low gain [5], the fractal antennas are used in the various wireless devices. Because they provide high gain, high bandwidth and also exhibits multiband and wideband characteristics [8, 9].

The fractal antenna is also capable to receive and transmit the signal over the wide range of frequencies [1]. A discontinuity in the geometry of fractal antenna increases the directivity and radiation properties of the antenna. Fractal geometries of antenna allow it to operate on different resonant frequencies [7]. The main advantages of fractal antennas are its less cost, compact size, easy to fabricate, portability because of light weight etc.

© Springer Nature Singapore Pte Ltd. 2016
A. Unal et al. (Eds.): SmartCom 2016, CCIS 628, pp. 400–407, 2016.
DOI: 10.1007/978-981-10-3433-6_48

2   Antenna Design and Configuration

The antenna is designed on substrate (FR4 glass epoxy) by considering the thickness of 1.6 mm, $\varepsilon_r = 4.4$ with resonant frequency of 2 GHz. The dimensions of the substrate like length = 60 mm and width = 60 mm are taken for designing the antenna. The length and width of patch are computed by taking the Eqs. (1)–(4). The calculated dimensions of antenna are given in Table 1. The 0th iteration, 1st iteration and 2nd iteration of designed antenna is depicted in Figs. 1, 2 and 3 respectively.

Table 1. Dimensions (Parametric values) of antenna

S. No.	Dimensions	Value (in mm)
1.	Substrate Length	60
2.	Substrate Width	60
3.	Ground Plane Length	60
4.	Ground Plane Width	60
5.	Patch Length	35
6.	Patch Width	45
7.	Length of Feed-line	19.78
8.	Width of Feed-line	2

Fig. 1. 0th iteration of antenna

Width of patch is found by considering equation as:

$$w = \frac{C}{2fo\sqrt{\frac{\in r + 1}{2}}} \tag{1}$$

Whereas, ε_{reff} is calculated by taking equation as:

$$\in reff = \frac{\in r + 1}{2} + \frac{\in r - 1}{2}\left[1 + 12\frac{h}{w}\right]^{\frac{1}{2}} \tag{2}$$

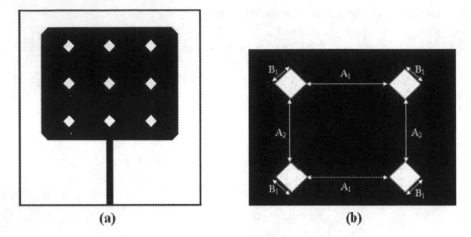

Fig. 2. (a) 1st iteration of antenna and (b) Slots dimensions for 1st iteration of antenna

ΔL (Increase in length) is occurred because of fringing effect and calculated as:

$$\Delta L = 0.412h \frac{(\in reff + 0.3)}{(\in reff - 0.258)} \frac{\left(\dfrac{w}{h} + 0.264\right)}{\left(\dfrac{w}{h} + 0.8\right)} \tag{3}$$

L(Actual length of patch) is calculated by the following equation:

$$L = \frac{c}{2fo\sqrt{\in reff}} - 2\Delta L \tag{4}$$

The above stated dimensions in the Table 1 are considered for designing the rectangular patch. In the 0th iteration, all the four corners of rectangular patch are being cut in equal size of 2.82 mm, as shown in Fig. 1.

The 1st iteration is being derived by considering the dimensions of 0th iteration, and also assumed as base geometry. The design of 1st iteration is depicted in Fig. 2(a). The dimensions of slots and distance among the various slots are indicated in Table 2 and Fig. 2(b) respectively.

Table 2. Dimensions of slots for 1st iteration of antenna

S. No.	Dimensions	Value (in mm)
1.	A_1	9.76
2.	A_2	7.76
3.	B_1	2.75

The 2nd iteration of antenna is designed by taking the dimensions of 1st iteration as a base geometry. The design of 2nd iteration (Final geometry of proposed design) of antenna is depicted in Fig. 3(a). The dimensions of the slots used to design the 2nd iteration of proposed antenna to make it a sierpinski carpet fractal antenna as shown in Fig. 3(b) and its dimensions are given in Table 3.

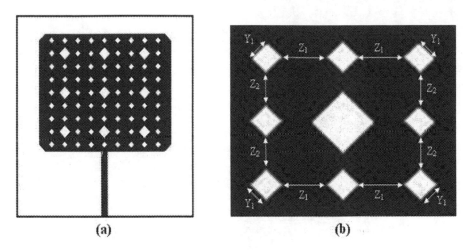

(a)   (b)

Fig. 3. (a) 2nd iteration of antenna (Final geometry of proposed design) and (b) Slots dimensions for 2nd iteration of antenna

Table 3. Dimensions of slots for 2nd iteration of antenna

S. No.	Dimensions	Value (in mm)
1.	Z_1	2.55
2.	Z_2	1.89
3.	Y_1	1.41

3   Results and Discussions

Simulated return loss versus frequency curves of 0th, 1st, and 2nd iteration of proposed antenna are discussed in Figs. 4, 5 and 6 respectively. The proposed antenna resonates on five distinct frequencies for all the three iterations. The value of the return losses for all the iterations at different frequencies is less than -10 dB which is the acceptable range for the practical use of antenna. The values of return loss for all the iterations with respect to frequency are given in Table 4.

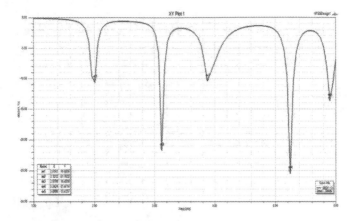

Fig. 4. 0th iteration - Return loss of proposed antenna

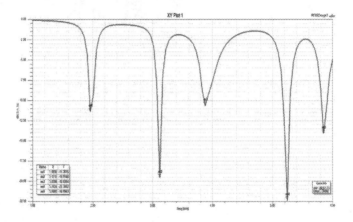

Fig. 5. 1st iteration - Return loss of proposed antenna

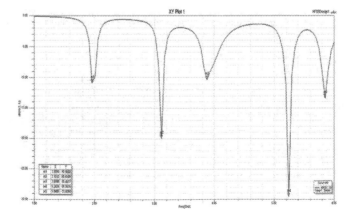

Fig. 6. 2nd iteration - Return loss of proposed antenna

Table 4. Values of return loss and VSWR for 0th iteration, 1st iteration and 2nd iteration of antenna

Iteration	Frequency (in GHz)	Return loss (in dB)	VSWR
0th iteration	2.01	−10.68	1.82
	3.12	−21.74	1.17
	3.87	−10.49	1.85
	5.24	−25.47	1.11
	5.89	−13.65	1.52
1st iteration	1.95	−11.38	1.80
	3.12	−19.55	1.24
	3.87	−10.65	1.80
	5.24	−22.34	1.14
	5.84	−14.09	1.82
2nd iteration	1.95	−10.96	1.78
	3.12	−20.01	1.22
	3.87	−10.40	1.86
	5.24	−29.55	1.06
	5.84	−13.42	1.54

Voltage Standing Wave Ratio (VSWR) describes the impedance matching of the antenna. It is the measure of impedance (Z) mismatch between the antenna and feed line. For practical use of antenna, it is necessary that value of VSWR should always be less than or equal to 2. The VSWR V/s frequency curves for 0th iteration, 1st iteration and 2nd iteration are shown in Figs. 7, 8 and 9 respectively, and the values of VSWR for all the iterations are shown in Table 4.

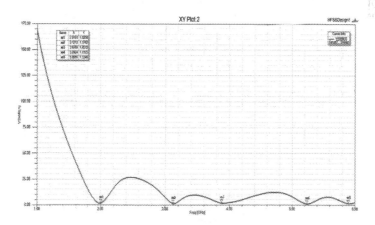

Fig. 7. 0th iteration −VSWR of proposed antenna

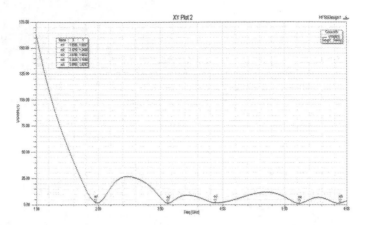

Fig. 8. 1ˢᵗ iteration -VSWR of proposed antenna

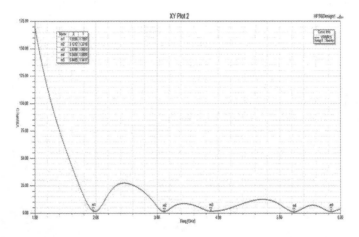

Fig. 9. 2ⁿᵈ iteration - VSWR of proposed antenna

Gain is the most important parameter of antenna it shows the efficiency and the directional capabilities of antenna. Basically the gain above 3 dB is required for the antenna to work efficiently. The 3-D gain plot at resonant frequency of 2 GHz for

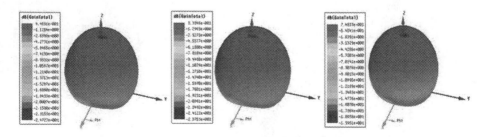

Fig. 10. 3D gain plots for 0ᵗʰ, 1ˢᵗ and 2ⁿᵈ iteration of antenna

0th iteration, 1st iteration and 2nd iteration of antenna is depicted in Fig. 10. The value of gain for 0th iteration, 1st iteration and 2nd iteration is 4.46 dB, 3.33 dB and 7.48 dB respectively.

4 Conclusion

An optimal design of fractal antenna using modified Sierpinski carpet geometry for wireless application has been presented in this paper. The designed antenna resonates at five different frequencies and the return loss is less than -10 dB for all the frequencies. The gain of antenna at resonant frequency is increases on increasing the iteration number and shows the gain above 3 dB which is the acceptable value of the antenna gain. The advantage of the designed antenna is to enhance the gain up to 7.48 dB.

References

1. Wanjari, P., Meshram, V.P., Sangara, V., Chintawar, I.: Design and fabrication of wideband fractal antenna for commercial applications. In: Conference on Machine Intelligence and Research Advancement, ICMIRA, pp. 150–154 (2013)
2. Sivia, J.S., Bhatia, S.S.: Design of fractal based rectangular patch antenna for multiband applications. In: IEEE Advance Computing Conference (IACC), pp. 712–715 (2015)
3. Jeemon, B.K., Shambavi, K., Alex, Z.C.: Design and analysis of a multi-fractal antenna for UWB application. In: IEEE Conference on Emerging Trends in Computing, Communication and Nanotechnology, ICECCN (2013)
4. Sahu, B.L., Chattoraj, N., Pal, S.: A novel CPW fed sierpinski carpet fractal UWB slot antenna. IEEE (2013)
5. Singh, M., Sharma, N.: A design of star shaped fractal antenna for wireless applications. J. Comput. Appl. (IJCA) **134**(4), 41–43 (2016)
6. Anitha, V.R., Sindhu, M.Y.: Simulation of a novel design fractal tree antenna for multiband applications with re-configurability. IEEE (2013)
7. Lincy, B.H., Srinivasan, A., Rajalakshmi, B.: Wideband fractal microstrip antenna for wireless application. In: Proceedings of Conference on Information and Communication Technologies (ICT 2013). IEEE (2013)
8. Jilani, S.F., Rahman, H.U., Iqbal, M.N.: Novel star-shaped fractal design of rectangular patch antenna for improved gain and bandwidth. IEEE (2013)
9. Bharti, G., Bhatia, S., Sivia, J.S.: Analysis and design of triple band compact microstrip patch antenna with fractal elements for wireless applications. Procedia Comput. Sci. In: Conference on Computational, Modeling and Security (CMS-2016), vol. 85, pp. 380–385. Elsevier (2016)

Real-Time Traffic Monitoring with Portable AMR Sensor System

Surabhi P. Jinturkar$^{(\boxtimes)}$ and Sushant J. Pawar

Sandip Institute of Technology and Research Center, Nasik, India
jinturkarsurabhi@gmail.com, sushant.pawar@sitrc.org

Abstract. Performances of current vehicle supervision techniques are require being improved using portable sensing scheme. In this paper the technique used is advance projected system for parameter measurements of vehicles using AMR sensors. Objective of the projected system is to develop an automated and improvised system where there are 3 AMR sensors that give height of vehicle and speed estimation and number of vehicle passing near range of sensors scheme. Thus, speed, classification and total count of vehicle these parameters are expected correctly.

The anisotropic magnetic sensor scheme rooted alongside the road-way and tested the traffic measurements. Calculation of Td (time-delay) and distance among two sensors estimate the speed of vehicle. This system is suitable for reliable count of number of vehicles. Height of vehicle is calculated for the categorization in low and high level vehicle. This system is simple and utilize in real time measurements. The system gives the average speed of total low/high vehicle pass from the track of sensor scheme. The result gives improved presentation for constraint measurements.

Keywords: Portable roadside sensors · Parameter measurement · Anisotropic sensors · Real time measurement · AMR sensors

1 Introduction

For vehicle counting, estimation of vehicle speed and high-low level classification a novel sensor system is designed. This is system is adjacent to a road. Currently there numerous vehicle surveillance technologies with video-camera, infrared sensor, image sensor, loop sensor, etc. Because of limited exposure with huge costs of execution and maintaining their performance is not sufficient. They have some defects like huge costs for setting and maintaining the line-of-sight, bad environment and weather conditions, low exactness, cannot work continuously in day and night, *etc.*

Over the years by using inductive loop signatures, the vehicle categorization information on a network-wide level [7], is focused. Improvements in traffic modeling, simulation, vehicle re-identification algorithms, roadway design, roadway maintenance, traffic safety, emissions management of vehicles and also computerized toll collection improved by vehicle classification information. The assemblage of a vehicle sorting database is also an important resource for study purpose in the areas of transportation controlling and planning.

© Springer Nature Singapore Pte Ltd. 2016
A. Unal et al. (Eds.): SmartCom 2016, CCIS 628, pp. 408–417, 2016.
DOI: 10.1007/978-981-10-3433-6_49

Most popular work was done with the surveillance video cameras. For real time measurements of parameter of vehicle this system is proposed each track on roadways. In [4] camera vision based system which detects in unfavorable change in atmospheric conditions. Such systems deteriorates under bad conditions of weathers, mostly like during snow fall and both during day/night time. Video-based Vehicle recognition and Classification system can covered the live video or images. First the users must know virtual loop locations, pixel-representation and a shadow sample to compose the system after that apply system for traffic data collection. Then backdrop image is evoked from video input is regularly updated to acclimate to the atmospheric variations. After collecting data it observes the implicit circle for detection. A outline of each detected vehicle is removed. Finally, sorting is done considering the pixel length and the long vehicle are sorted according to threshold value such as LV/SV. The proposed work uses a low cost apparatus to collect instantaneous data for each lane on roadways.

Portable sensor system provides better results than previous one. The estimation of speed is done using 2 (magnetic) mesmeric sensors placed horizontally apart by considering the cross-correlation in between the signals and sensors. The speed assessment process is established using GPS. In [1] paper researcher study the experimental results obtained at the MnROAD (Minnesota Road Research Facility) for vehicle speed estimation. Nearby to the lane, sensors were deployed. Laptop inside the vehicle says the data i.e. captured from the test vehicle containing GPS18 LVC. A different data collection system is used to acquire the sensor data. The tolerance between the GPS measurement system and the sensor system, speed is calculated using the variation in the recognition time. Proposed results show a 2.5% error in speed estimation along the range 5 to 27 m/s. The limitations are only in the classification rate is poor. But there is no traffic disturbance due to sensor system installation.

The automated portable system is embedded for the accurate design of pavements with clear results in quality and cost. The new system uses the sensors that are fixed aside to the road which are able to count the speed, number of vehicle passed and sorting according to their respective type. All the parameters are studied simultaneously for traffic organization. The track nearby to the sensors is useful for the traffic constraint calculations. The sensor is having magneto-resistance property. It is useful to consider a each and every situations because of the resistance of material is depends on a magnetic field with different mechanism. This is directly depends on the magnetic field and indirectly depends on the magnetization. Vehicles are classified into respective types such as cars, LCV's which generally are measured according to the size or length, number of axles etc.

A classification of vehicle magnetic height is lying on the feature extraction and it can be can vary from 40% to 100%. It is not 100%. With the assist of multiple spatially separated magnetic sensors [6], the vehicle classification and speed estimation is observed. Many researchers study in this area. Simulation and experimental results illustrate that this system enhances classification of vehicle with better performance with solid robustness.

This paper ordered with the study of our conceptualization is presented; next session is with experimental results and discussion, and finally conclusion.

2 Proposed System

2.1 Projected System

The main aim of a project developing an automated system in which 2 sets of amr sensors gives height of vehicle and the third set will be placed at a predefined distance. Thus, we get the speed and other all parameters of the vehicle. The controlling device system of the whole system is PIC Microcontroller.

The two important sections in this proposed system sensor section which having of three AMR sensors, LCD, zigbee interfaced to the PIC microcontroller and Monitoring section include Zigbee, USB to TLL, and Interfacing to PC. Microprocessors are general purpose processors. Generally microcontrollers takes a data as inputs and interface manipulates data with other devices and controls the data in order to give accurate results.

Signals recorded from sensors are embedded nearby road, which are much uniform than other sensors on the road. This performance makes the exposure much consistent. Particularly, the signals which are measured around z-axis posses similar patterns for a large quantity of vehicles. Hence, outputs along z-axis of sensor 3 are used to detect and count number of vehicles going nearby lanes (Fig. 1).

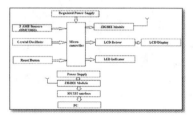

Fig. 1. Block diagram of system

In order to count speed of each vehicle, 2 horizontally spaced sensors are used. In order to measure speed along 2 magnetic sensors generally depends on the recognition time of 2 sensors. If the time of recognition of vehicle for sensors "a" & "b" are ta_ON, ta_OFF, tb_ON, and tb_OFF, speed of vehicle is obtained by the following formula:

$$v = \frac{d_{a-b}}{\left(\left(t_{b,}ON - t_{b,}ON\right) + \left(t_{b,}OFF - t_{b,}OFF\right)\right)/2} \tag{1}$$

Where, d_(a − b) is the distance inbetween the sensors a & b.

Vehicle categorization having various applications including traffic control, road safeguarding and organizing, emissions evaluation, roadway design, multimode traffic model development, design of traffic signal, & development of toll systems as noted in paper [1]. Benefits of these sensors for vehicle sorting and detection. They are mainly adoptable to atmospheric changes, less expensive, and much easy to build. This system is potable, hence placed along the road, and system provides the better results of categorization without disturbing the traffic.

3 Outline of Different Sensor Systems

Vehicle sensors with detection scheme are sorted into intrusive and non-intrusive sensors. The sensors are embedded in opening on the road plane by burrowed under road plane and/or fixed the sensors on the road or above the road are intrusive sensors. Today's technologies are embedded next to the roadways with sensors. For example, loops, pneumatic road tubes, Active infrared sensors, magnetometers, magneto resistive sensors, piezoelectric cables and weight-in-motion. Due to deviation of sensors in the market with cost & scale of implementation, system design, environmental conditions are the factors would have to be taken while choosing which kind of sensor.

During installation and also maintenance on/in the road causes trouble to the drivers. Non-intrusive sensors conclude the microwave radar, passive acoustic array sensors passive infrared sensors, RFID, ultrasonic and video image processing, etc. These classes of sensors overcome the disadvantages of intrusive sensor system of installation problem.

The different types of sensors used for vehicle detection and parameter measurements are discuss below:

3.1 Pneumatic Road Tube

Pneumatic road tube vehicle identify through air pressure created which closes the switch, create a signals when vehicle passed or stop over the tube. While it offers a low cost solution as well as quick installation and easy to maintain. Pneumatic road sensors are temperature sensitive. In addition, the tubes are prone to vandalism.

3.2 Inductive Loop Detector

Inductive loop detectors (ILDs) are a widespread technology by many transportation agencies for vehicle detection and measurement of traffic flow rates. Individual vehicle speed is not measured by single inductive loop.

3.3 Active Infrared Sensors

The sensor emitted the infrared energy and detecting the reflected energy. Multiple lane operations can be conducted by utilizing the active infrared sensors. An absolute measurement of vehicle position and class, many beams are transmitted from the sensor. The limitation is only its sensitivity towards environmental conditions which affects the operation of the sensor system.

3.4 Piezoelectric Sensors

Piezoelectric sensors are form by the material which converts kinetic energy to electrical energy when subjected to vibrations. Based on weight it will provide more accurate data of vehicle speed and class of vehicle. To use multiple detectors to tackle the location, this is the advantage of these sensors. And it also has high sensitive to temperature.

3.5   Magnetoresistive Sensor

Lenz and Edelstein encompasses the Magnetoresistive sensors as Anisotropic Magnetoresistance Sensors (AMR), Giant Magnetoresistance Sensors (GMR), Magnetic tunnel Junction sensors, Ballistic and Extraordinary Magnetoresistance that are simply energized by giving constant current. These sensors are small in size and light in weight which makes it versatile in placement. Other advantages are the low cost and wide range of temperature; it has been widely used for vehicle detection.

3.6   RFID

RFID having three units: transceiver, transponder, antenna and used for vehicle detection. The transceiver sends and read the information from transponder which contains coded data by antenna. For low cost installation and maintenance as well as high speed RFID is precise.

3.7   Magnetometer

Flux-gate magnetometer works by detecting magnetic anomaly in earth's magnetic field. These sensor system provides benefits of weather conditions like fog, snow rain etc. These sensors are more accurate and also not disturbed the traffic. The main disadvantages of using magnetometer are the small detection zones in some model which requires more than one unit are required for full lane detection and also proximity required for absolute detection.

3.8   Weight-in-Motion Sensors

WIM sensors recognized the weight of vehicle. Whatever data observed is useful for highway planner, designers and law enforcement agencies. There are mainly four methods are available – bending plate, piezoelectric, load cell and capacitance mat. Each sensor has its own benefits and also limitations. While bending plate WIM is more accurate and costly compared to piezoelectric sensor system, it is less accurate than load cell sensors and considered as cheaper.

3.9   Acoustic Sensors

Sensor system recognized vehicle through acoustic energy or audible sounds generated the vehicle by microphones installed for vehicle detection.

3.10 Ultrasonic Sensors

The sensors transmit the pulse waveforms between 25 to 50 kHz to the road by detecting transmitted energy which are reflected back the sensors. The reflected ultrasonic energies are analyzed to take data in roadside controller. It will do multiple lane detection with easy to install. Temperature change and extreme air turbulence affects the performance of sensor.

4 Sensing System Pattern and Signal Strength

AMR sensors have a silicon chip coated with Piezo-resistive nickel iron. Presence of automobile near range of sensors reason to change in magnetic field. Hence changes resistance of nickel iron layer. For developing the new as well as automated system, in this paper, HMC5883L 3-axis AMR sensors are used. The main advantages of these sensors are surface mount, multichip module for low-field magnetic sensing device and high resolution.

The comparison of magnetic field reading taken from sensors fixed on a road and embedded on a next to the road-side, gives the better results in a portable system. Figure 2 illustrates the magnetic field Analysis for vehicle from x, y & z 3–axis AMR Sensor Fixed on the center of road line. The x-axis represents the way of vehicle passed longitudinally, way of vehicle is perpendicular to the y-axis and z-axis is at right angles to the road plane & upward direction. Figure 3 illustrates the Magnetic Field Analysis for vehicle from AMR Sensor nearby to the Road with a height of 0.6 m approximately. From the above observation magnetic field analysis of the observed vehicles are 10 times much stronger when sensor system set on the road.

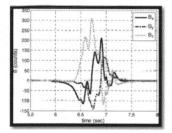
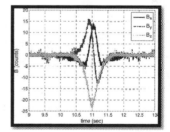

Fig. 2. Magnetic field analysis for vehicle from AMR sensor fixed on the Road [1].

Fig. 3. Magnetic field analysis for vehicle from AMR sensor nearby to the Road [1].

Figures 2 and 3 illustrates the comparison of two different pattern of sensors systems. With the sensors which are fixed on the road have lots of different ferromagnetic parts bottom of the vehicle will go by the sensors at near proximity & generate more fluctuations in the signal. Advanced amplification is done to acquire a better SNR.

Hence, to diminish the noise intensity, the signal was improved by setting 100 Hz cut-off frequency using instrumentation amplifiers.

Figure 4 represents the overview of the 3 AMR sensors sensing scheme embedded resting on side of the road. Sensors 1 and 3 are horizontally spaced from each other & give better results in speed calculation parameter. Vehicle sorting estimated with the help of all 3 sensors.

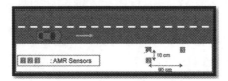

Fig. 4.   Sensor sensing Scheme for vehicle detection and parameter measurement

5   Results and Discussion

5.1   Simulation Results

Obtaining results have proven a better improvement in the vehicle counting & sorting which provides a better management of transport system. When all vehicles are passes through the sensors in its sensitivity direction we obtain the measurements of all parameters of the car. Figure 5 illustrates the simulation results of proposed system which shows the output on LCD. Total count of the vehicle pass through the region of sensor is detected and classification of vehicle is done like high/low level vehicle. Simulation result gives the reliable count and category of that vehicle correctly.

5.2   Hardware Setup

For achieving the above stated objectives, the algorithm is developed to obtain a desired number of vehicles for automated system. For experimentation, 10 vehicles are consider and gives the speed of each vehicle in kmph as sown in Table 1. Classification is done based on the height of vehicle in mainly two classes such as High Vehicle (HL) and Low Vehicle (LL). From the observation of experiment, 6 Low Level Vehicles are detected with 4 High Level Vehicles are detected. Vehicle speed is estimated individually using

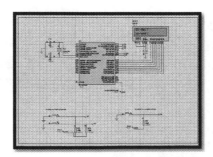

Fig. 5.   Simulation results of counting and classification

formula mention in above section. Representation of hardware setup and experimental results are shown in below Fig. 6 and Table 1.

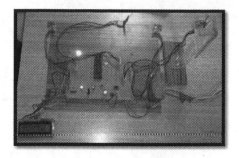

Fig. 6. Hardware setup

Table 1. Observations of experiment

Vehicle count	Speed estimation	Classification (HL\LL)
1	3.3 kmph	LL
2	1.3 kmph	HL
3	2.9 kmph	LL
4	2.7 kmph	LL
5	1.4 kmph	HL
6	2.5 kmph	LL
7	0.9 kmph	HL
8	2.1 kmph	LL
9	1.4 kmph	LL
10	1.5 kmph	HL

Figure 7 shows the speed estimation and sorting of vehicles using graphical representation. Proposed algorithm applied to acquire data from the experimentation. The statistics was acquired with all the sensors which are fixed at 2 various connections with recording indicator as of passing automobile. In graphical representation 1 and 0 shows the High and Low Level vehicle. Using this algorithm, classification is done correctly as shown in Fig. 7.

Table 2 illustrates the Average counting of vehicle with average speed of Low vehicle and average speed of high vehicle. These results give the better total average estimations. More-over, it can be studied that average speed of LL vehicles is 2.483 kmph & HL vehicles are 1.275 kmph.

Table 2. Distribution of average vehicle classification and speed of each class

Total No. of vehicles	No. of low level vehicle	No. of high level vehicle	Average speed of low level vehicle	Average speed of high level vehicle
10	6	4	2.483 kmph	1.275 kmph

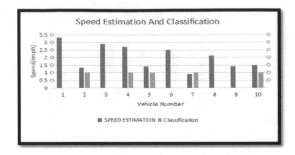

Fig. 7. Graphical representation of speed estimation and classification of vehicles

6 Conclusion

This paper has proposed the different methods to Vehicle detection and parameter measurements. From the above discussion, proposed sensors system is more suitable than others. This proposed system generally used for 3 parameters such as counting, speed measurement & sorting. Magnetic sensors are work properly in all weather conditions. So, this proposed system results will be significant supplement in management in traffic area and highways and automatic Tollbooth. The count and speed calculation are enabled obtained from the experiment of this system. The hardware components used to develop the interfacing features. This system are contributes the better working of the system.

This paper recommend a straightforward, nevertheless, influential & usual system used for actual time automobile sorting in two different classes. The approach is an invention with progression of previously developed techniques. This novel proposed algorithm boosted performance of vehicle observation by means of much more exact and highly robust is has been verified.

References

1. Taghvaeeyan, S., Rajamani, R.: Portable roadside sensors for vehicle counting, classification, and speed measuremen. IEEE Trans. Intell. Transp. Syst. **15**(1), 73–83 (2014)
2. Liu, J., Han, J., Lv, H., Li, B.: An ultrasonic sensor system based on a two-dimensional state method for highway vehicle violation detection applications. ISSN 1424-8220
3. Mishra, D.P., Asutkar, G.M.: Vehicle detection and classification using wireless sensor network. Int. J. Adv. Res. Electr., Electron. Instrum. Eng. **2**(10), (2013). (An ISO 3297: 2007 Certified Organization)
4. Zhang, G., Avery, R.P.: A video-based vehicle detection and classification system for real-time traffic data collection using uncalibrated video cameras. TRB 2007 Annual Meeting CD-ROM
5. Meshram, S.A., Malviya, A.V.: Traffic surveillance by counting and classification of vehicles from video using image processing. Int. J. Adv. Res. Comput. Sci. Manage. Stud. **1**(6), (2013)
6. Lavanya, A.S., Srivani, S.: Real time portable vehicle counting and speed measurement using Arm11 processor. Int. J. Mag. Eng., Technol., Manage. Res. **2**(8), (2015)
7. Sun, C.: An investigation in the use of inductive loop signatures for vehicle classification. Research reports, 3 January 2000. http://escholarship.org/uc/item/93j2v5d8

8. Zhang, W., Tan, G.-Z., Shi, H.-M., Lin, M.-W.: A distributed threshold algorithm for vehicle classification based on binary proximity sensors and intelligent neuron classifier. J. Inf. Sci. Eng. **26**, 769–783 (2010)
9. Gupte, S., Masoud, O., Martin, R.F.K., Papanikolopoulos, N.P.: Detection and classification of vehicles. IEEE Trans. Intell. Transp. Syst. **3**(1), (2002)
10. Cheung, S.Y., Coleri, S., Dundar, B., Ganesh, S., Tan, C.-W., Varaiya, P.: Traffic measurement and vehicle classification with a single magnetic sensor. Working papers, 9 January 2004. https://escholarship.org/uc/item/2gv111tv
11. Ki, Y.-K., Baik, D.-K.: Model for accurate speed measurement using double-loop detectors. IEEE Trans. Veh. Technol. **55**(4), 1094–1101 (2006)
12. Haoui, A., Kavaler, R., Varaiya, P.: Wireless magnetic sensors for traffic surveillance. Transp. Res. Part C: Emerg. Technol. **16**, 294–306 (2007)
13. Sun, X.: A set of new traffic-responsive rampmetering algorithms and microscopic simulation results. Transp. Res. Rec. J. Transp. Res. Board (2006)
14. He, Y., Du, Y., Sun, L.: Vehicle classification method based on single-point magnetic sensor. In: 8th International Conference on Traffic and Transportation Studies Changsha, China, 1–3 August 2012
15. Leduc, G.: Road traffic data: collection methods and applications. Working papers on Energy, Transport and Climate Change N.1
16. Huang, W.: Wireless vehicle detection node based on tunnelling magneto resistance sensor. Comput. Model. New Technol. **18**(11), 1132–1137 (2014)
17. Daponte, P., De Vito, L., Picariello, F., Rapuano, S.: Wireless sensor network for traffic safety
18. Pelegri-Sebastia, J., Alberola, J.: Vehicle detection and car speed monitoring system using GMR magnetic sensors (2002). http://www.researchgate.net/publication/4005354
19. Caruso, M.J., Withanawasam, L.S.: Vehicle detection and compass applications using AMR magnetic sensors. www.ssec.honeywell.com
20. www.ifh.uni-karlesruhe.de

Ambiguity Attacks on SVD Based Watermarking Technique

Neha Singh$^{(\boxtimes)}$ and Sandeep Joshi

Department of Computer Science Engineering,
Manipal University Jaipur, Jaipur, India
{neha.singh, sandeep.joshi}@jaipur.manipal.edu

Abstract. Fast growing internet coupled with advancements in image processing technology, has resulted in increased incidents of image deception. Digital image watermarking is widely used as a tool to establish ownership and restore the trust in digital images. The paper presents a study of solutions as proposed by Ali and Ahn in [1] to overcome the problem of false positive detection by SVD based technique, specifically the one proposed by Agarwal et al. in [2] The solutions are tested against re-watermarking as another class of ambiguity attacks.

Keywords: Digital image watermarking · Watermarking attacks · False positive problem · Ambiguity attack · Re-watermarking · False cover generation · Unauthorized watermark extraction

1 Introduction

Digital image watermarking is a technique where self-authenticating information is embedded in a digital image with the main concern of establishing ownership of the content. To achieve this goal, robust watermarking has been quickly developed. The digital image in which the information is hidden is called the cover image and the hidden information is generally known as the watermark, which can be a bit string representing copyright message, serial number, grayscale or colored image, plain text, etc. Any inconsistency in the embedded watermark at the time of recovery will confirm manipulation of the data and even locate the tampering. The watermark need not always be hidden but sometimes visible watermarks are used such as a company logo. The major components of an image watermarking system are listed in Table 1, with their inputs and outputs and purpose of each component.

It is desirable that the watermark and the method of hiding it in the cover image should be chosen such that the watermark is irremovable even under most of malicious or intended and non-malicious or unintended attacks [1].

A. Unal et al. (Eds.): SmartCom 2016, CCIS 628, pp. 418–425, 2016.
DOI: 10.1007/978-981-10-3433-6_50

Table 1. Digital watermarking functions.

Function	Inputs and output(s)	Purpose
WGn()	Inputs: message (M), cover (C), key (optional) Output: watermark (WM)	Needs to generate the watermark
		Many a times neglected when a logo or any other specific data is chosen as watermark
		Needs to generate cover dependent watermark for security and robustness requirements
WEm()	Inputs: watermark (WM), cover (C), key (optional) Output: watermarked image (C_WM)	Needs to identify where and how the watermark is embedded within the cover image
		It may be visible or invisible, reversible or irreversible and blind or non-blind
		Needs to ensure that the embedded watermark is able to sustain most of the intentional and unintentional attacks on the output watermarked image during its journey
WDe()	Inputs: watermarked image (C_WM), cover (C), watermark (WM), key(optional) Output: binary decision	Needs to identify if some information is hidden in the test image
		It generates a binary valued output as true or false
		It is mostly used in steganography where detection of the presence of hidden information defeats the complete purpose
		Not useful for image watermarking which requires to reconstruct the hidden information
WEx()	Inputs: watermarked image, cover, watermark, key (optional) Output: estimated watermark, estimated cover image	Needs to recover the watermark and/or the original cover if required

2 Ambiguity Attacks

The field of image watermarking is quite old now and a lot many techniques have been proposed in spatial domain and transform domain. Spatial domain did not attract the researchers due to ease of losing the watermark due to unintentional image processing. Many digital image watermarking techniques have been developed based on different image transforms for example, Discrete Wavelet Transform (DWT), Discrete Cosine Transform (DCT) and Singular Value Decomposition (SVD) etc. Image transforms have been explored individually as well as in combinations to achieve better robustness and imperceptibility. To ensure even better robustness and imperceptibility, the techniques now evolving not only use combinations of image transforms but optimization techniques [2, 3] also for optimized selection of location for embedding and strength of watermark. Yet another trend in image watermarking techniques developed over years is in reference to the choice of watermarks. The watermarks have evolved from being binary logo to randomly generated images to gray-scale and colored images to cover image dependent watermarks. However, all these types of watermarks are almost equally used today.

Amongst numerous image transforms, use of SVD is promising for imperceptible and robust watermarking of digital images because small variations in singular values does not affect the quality of image and singular values of an image have high stability so they are robust against various intentional and unintentional attacks. Some of the attacks generally analyzed are compression, histogram manipulation, image resizing, contrast manipulation, rotation, scaling and translation. The list of attacks to test the robustness of any watermarking technique is growing hand in hand with the development of techniques and availability of means for image manipulations. Since many of the watermarking techniques are non-blind, their failure stands a big chance against identifying the correct owner failing which the entire purpose of watermarking. It will be clear with the ambiguity attack possibilities modelled as four scenarios that follow Fig. 1:

Scenario 1-False Positive Detection: Suppose that the owner O embeds a legitimate watermark WM into the cover C such that WEm(C, WM) = C_WM. To claim the ownership of the cover data C, O performs the extraction such that WEx(C_WM,WM) = WM. However, the attacker A uses his fake watermark, WM' to be extracted with WEx(C_WM, WM') = WM'. Thus, both claim the ownership of the cover C though the attacker did not embed the watermark.

Scenario 2-Re-watermarking: Assume that the owner O uses WEm(C, WM) to obtain the watermarked image C_WM and the attacker A embeds the fake watermark WM' into the originally watermarked image C_WM to obtain a re-watermarked image C_WM'. The attacker A extracts his watermark from the image C_WM and tries to claim that C_WM was the original cover and not C.

Scenario 3-False Cover Generation: Assume that C is the original cover and WM is the legitimate watermark. The owner O generates the watermarked image C_WM = WEm(C, WM). An attacker computes a pattern WM', a counterfeit original C' and an embedding function WEm'() such that WEm'(C', WM') = C_WM. He claims C' and W' to be the original cover and watermark, thus creating an ownership dispute over C_WM.

Scenario 4-Unauthorized Watermark Extraction: Assume, an attacker copies a valid watermark from watermarked data C_WM (containing a valid watermark WM) and embeds it into another host data, X, producing X_WM. The attacker can do this without any knowledge of the original embedding algorithm or of the key used to embed the original watermark. The watermark detector will declare that both C_WM and X_WM contain the watermark W. This attack can lead to an ambiguous situation. For example, the attacker may claim that the original owner of the watermark has stolen his data, X, and use the copied watermark as proof.

SCENARIO 1: False Positive Detection

Authentic owner, O	: $WEm(C, WM) = C\_WM$
O extracts	: $WEx(C\_WM, WM) = WM$
Attacker, A extracts	: $WEx(C\_WM, WM') = WM'$

Ambiguity: Both watermarks were successfully extracted resulting in the ownership dispute over C.

SCENARIO 2: Re-watermarking

Authentic owner, O	: $WEm(C, WM) = C\_WM$
Attacker, A	: $WEm(C\_WM, WM') = C\_WM'$
O extracts	: $WEx(C\_WM, WM) = WM$
A extracts	: $WEx(C\_WM', WM') = WM'$

Ambiguity: A claims that C_WM was the original cover and not C and O claims vice versa, thus, ambiguity.

SCENARIO 3: False Cover Generation

Authentic owner, O	: $WEm(C, WM) = C\_WM$
Attacker, A	: $WEm'(C', WM') = C\_WM$
O claims	: C is original unwatermarked cover for C_WM
A claims	: C' is original unwatermarked cover for C_WM

Ambiguity: Which one, C or C' is the original cover.

SCENARIO 4: Unauthorized Watermark Extraction

Authentic owner, O	: $WEm(C, WM) = C\_WM$
Attacker, A	: $WEx(C\_WM) = WM$
	$WFm(X, WM) = X\_WM$

Watermark detector will declare that both C_WM and X_WM contain the watermark WM.

Ambiguity: A claims that O has stolen his data X and use the copied watermark as proof.

Fig. 1. Summary of ambiguity attack scenarios

The requirement of the original watermark or the cover during detection and/or extraction increases the probability of false positive detection. Moreover, the strength factor plays an important role when re-watermarking is to be countered. The strength factor is the measure of strength of the embedding watermark against the cover image. Larger strength factors result in perceptible embedding and smaller strength factors offer less robustness. Thus, to encounter re-watermarking attacks, described as scenario 2, the strength factor needs to be large enough so that when a watermark is embedded in an already watermarked image, the original watermark is not suppressed. Watermarking can be made resistant to false cover generation and unauthorized watermark extraction, the embedding method should be complex and use a private key, Also, robustness can be increased by using watermarks comparable in size to the cover image.

3 Experimental Results

The authors in [1] brought to light failure of the work presented in [2] against false positive detection and suggested to embed principal components of the watermark instead of its singular values. Another suggested solution is to embed the entire watermark in place of its singular values. A similar approach is used in [4] against false positive detection. The proposed solutions are now tested for re-watermarking attack too. The embedding and extraction schemes proposed by Agarwal et al. and Ali and Ahn are presented here.

Agarwal et al. scheme [2]
Embedding

1. Apply 3-level DWT to the cover image, C, using Haar filter.
2. Perform SVD on the 3rd level approximate sub-band, LL3 such that

$$[U\,S\,V] = SVD(LL_3) \tag{1}$$

3. Perform SVD on the watermark W such that

$$[U_w\,S_w\,V_w] = SVD(W) \tag{2}$$

4. Choose a strength factor δ to embed the Singular values of the watermark into the singular values of the LL3 sub-band such that

$$S' = S + \delta \times S_W \tag{3}$$

5. Reconstruct LL3 using the modified singular values such that

$$LL'_3 = U \times S' \times V^T \tag{4}$$

6. Apply 3-level inverse DWT to obtain the watermarked image Cw.

Extraction

1. Apply 3-level DWT on the possibly attacked watermarked image Cw* to obtain 3rd level approximate sub-band, LL3*.
2. Perform SVD on the 3rd level approximate sub-band, LL3* such that

$$[U^*S^*V^*] = SVD\left(LL_3^*\right) \tag{5}$$

3. Obtain the singular values of the approximate of the possibly distorted watermark using the singular values of the original cover, S, such that

$$S_w^* = (S^* - S)/\delta \tag{6}$$

4. Using the matrices Uw and Vw of the original watermark, reconstruct the possibly distorted watermark such that,

$$W^* = U_w \times S_w \times V_w^T \tag{7}$$

Ali and Ahn Principal Components Scheme [1]
Embedding:

1. Follow embedding steps 1 to 3 as for Agarwal et al. scheme.
2. Choose a strength factor δ to embed the Principal Components of the watermark into the singular values of the LL3 sub-band such that

$$S' = S + \delta \times PC_w \tag{8}$$

3. Follow embedding steps 5 to 6 as for Agarwal et al. scheme to obtain watermarked image.

Extraction:

1. Follow extraction step 1 as for Agarwal et al. scheme.
2. Obtain the principal components of the approximate of the possibly distorted watermark using the 3rd level approximate sub-band, LL3 of the original cover and its matrices U and V.

$$PC_W^* = \left(U^T \times \left(LL_3^* - LL_3\right) \times V\right)/\delta \tag{9}$$

3. reconstruct the possibly distorted watermark such that,

$$W^* = PC_W^* \times V_w^T \tag{10}$$

Ali and Ahn Complete Watermark Scheme [1]
Embedding:

1. Follow embedding steps 1 and 2 as for Agarwal et al. scheme.
2. Choose a strength factor δ to embed the complete watermark into the singular values of the LL3 sub-band such that

$$S' = S + \delta \times W \tag{11}$$

3. Follow embedding steps 5 to 6 as for Agarwal et al. scheme to obtain watermarked image.

Extraction:

1. Follow extraction step 1 as for Agarwal et al. scheme.
2. Obtain the possibly distorted watermark such that

$$W^* = \left(U^T \times \left(LL_3^* - LL_3\right) \times V\right)/\delta \tag{12}$$

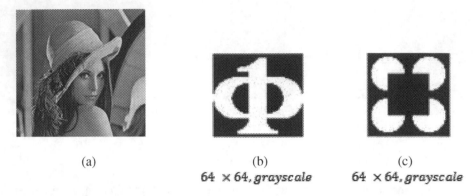

(a)   (b)   (c)
64 × 64, grayscale   64 × 64, grayscale

Fig. 2. (a) Cover image (b) Owner's watermark (c) Attacker's watermark

The three schemes are tested against false positive detection and re-watermarking attacks. The cover image, owner's watermark and attacker's watermark used in the experiment are shown in Fig. 2.

The success of each technique to identify the owner correctly is measured in terms of correlation with the attacker's watermark and the owner's watermark for the false positive and re-watermarking tests respectively. Table 2 shows the result of tests against false positive detection and re-watermarking for the originally proposed technique and suggested improvements.

Table 2. Result for Ambiguity test.

Scheme	Test for false positive		Test for re-watermarking	
	Recovered watermark	Correlation with attacker's watermark	Recovered watermark	Correlation with owner's watermark
Agarwal et. al.		0.9945		1.0000
Ali & Ahn Principal components		0.2348		0.7754
Ali & Ahn Complete watermark		0.0456		0.5163

It is clear that the scheme proposed by Agarwal et al. though failed for false positive test but was most robust against re-watermarking amongst the three schemes. Embedding principal components instead of singular values of the watermark proves to be successful to fail the false positive test. Additionally, it is able to recover the owner's watermark even after re-watermarking to some extent But, using the entire watermark though tackled the problem of false positive detection successfully but, it failed when the originally watermarked image was re-watermarked with similar or different watermark.

4 Conclusions

SVD based non-blind watermarking techniques suffer from failure against false positive detection since the watermark is extracted using the original cover and the watermark [1, 5]. To improve robustness against false positive detection, blind techniques need to be developed so as to eliminate the use of original cover and watermark during recovery. When principal components of the watermark are embedded, the technique proposed by Ali and Ahn is able to resist false watermark detection but when complete watermark is embedded, the original watermark is found. The reason is clear, that no watermark (neither owner's nor attacker's) is used during recovery. Thus, the Ali and Ahn schemes have scope to be improved for better robustness against ambiguity attacks. Also these techniques need to be tested for attacks other than ambiguity attacks.

References

1. Ali, M., Ahn, C.W.: Comments on optimized gray-scale image watermarking using DWT-SVD and firefly algorithm. Expert Syst. Appl. **42**, 2392–2394 (2015)
2. Agarwal, C., Mishra, A., Sharma, A., Bedi, P.: Optimized gray-scale image watermarking using DWT-SVD and firefly algorithm. Expert Syst. Appl. **41**(17), 7858–7867 (2014)
3. Tsai, H., Jhuanga, Y., Lai, Y.: An SVD-based image watermarking in wavelet domain using SVR and PSO. Appl. Soft Comput. **12**, 2442–2453 (2012)
4. Mohammad, A.A., Alhaj, A., Shaltaf, S.: An improved SVD-based watermarking scheme for protecting rightful ownership. Sig. Process. **88**, 2158–2180 (2008)
5. Guo, J.M., Prasetyo, H.: False-positive-free SVD-based image watermarking. J. Vis. Commun. Image R. **25**, 1149–1163 (2014)

Clustering Gait Data Using Different Machine Learning Techniques and Finding the Best Technique

Anubha Parashar[1(✉)] and Deepak Goyal[2(✉)]

[1] Manipal University Jaipur, Jaipur, India
anubhaparashar1025@gmail.com
[2] Vaish College of Engineering, Rohtak, India
deepakgoyal.vce@gmail.com

Abstract. Clustering is done in order to group the entities which are alike in one group so that grouping of more similar objects can be done. The objects placed in one group are known as clusters. In this paper we are using clustering in order to identify the human locomotion and categories the dataset making clusters. We are using two clustering techniques i.e. SOM and K-mean. So we first selected the feature and identify the principle feature then we cluster gait data and use different machine learning technique (K-mean and SOM) and performance comparison is shown. Experimental result on real time datasets propose method is better than previous method as far as humanoid locomotion classification is concerned.

Keywords: Clustering · Biometric identification · Feature selection · SOM · K-mean

1 Introduction

In order to authenticate humans we use various verification and validation technologies. To know whether a person is authenticated or not we need verification. To authenticate some person and to check his/her identity various authentications techniques are used. First is *knowledge*; in this technique a person must have particular knowledge about of his PIN, password, or any other secret code. Second is *Possession;* in this technique a person must know particular token or item like identity card, smart card. Third is *Biometric*; in this technique a person's body part is taken to identify unique identity of person like fingerprint, retina, iris, facial expression. But there are various disadvantages of above techniques [1–3]. A person may forget its password or PIN. A person may lose its identity card or smart card. Biometric authentication may not be always user friendly and is expensive too (Fig. 1).

In contrast with such authentication techniques GAIT based biometric method outperforms all above disadvantages.

© Springer Nature Singapore Pte Ltd. 2016
A. Unal et al. (Eds.): SmartCom 2016, CCIS 628, pp. 426–433, 2016.
DOI: 10.1007/978-981-10-3433-6_51

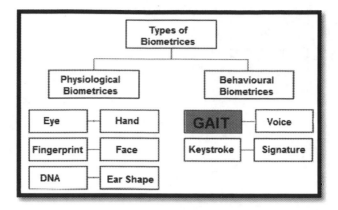

Fig. 1. Biometrics types

Gait means how a human move/walk and is very useful to identify person from a distance. It is very useful in detecting diseases and in surveillance system. In this paper we have taken four data sets namely croubh2, croubh3, croubh4, normal shown in Fig. 2.

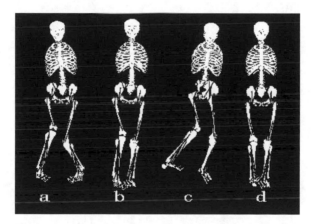

Fig. 2. Contrast enhanced images in gait sequences of Gait Database (Dataset - a (croubh2) b (croubh3) c (croubh4) d (normal)). Four samples from left to right show the gait of pathological walking (a, b, c) and normal walking (d).

2   Proposed System

Proposed system consists of eight phases [4]. They are collection of Data Preprocessing, Gait Cycle Detection, Feature Extraction, Feature Reduction (PCA) [5], Output Feature Vector, Clustering (K-Mean) (SOM), and output (Fig. 3).

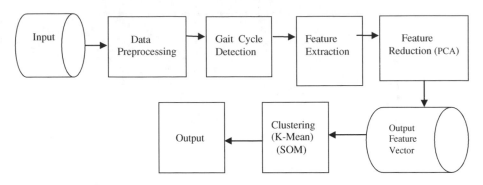

Fig. 3. Proposed system

3   Methodology

Firstly, we have collected data of different gait using HMDC [7], and then features were selected, then different combinations of features are made using K-mean and SOM clustering [6]. Then 10 fold cross-validation test also conducted to validate the statistical significance of the results.

3.1   Trajectory Smoothening

After smoothening, we detect and remove the self-co-articulated strokes. And as these strokes are not part of gesture therefore they need to be removed at this stage as they are just hand movements [9].

3.2   Feature Extraction

The features have been collected from [6].

3.3   Feature Selection

Here 16 features are extracted. The features are collected from different joints while locomotion [1]. In all the four datasets 16 features are extracted which is listed in Table 1.

Table 1. Crouch dataset description

Feature category	Feature name	Feature category	Feature name
F1	Pelvis_tx	F9	hip_rotation_r
F2	Pelvis_ty	F10	knee_angle_r
F3	Pelvis_tz	F11	ankle_angle_r
F4	Pelvis_tilt	F12	hip_flexion_l
F5	Pelvis_list	F13	hip_adduction_l
F6	Pelvis_rotation	F14	hip_rotation_l
F7	hip_flexion_r	F15	knee_angle_l
F8	hip_adduction_r	F16	ankle_angle_l

4   Clustering

Clustering is done using following machine learning techniques.

4.1   K-Mean

The k-mean algorithm is generally used for compact clustering. It is very much sensitive for outlier and noise. It is applicable only for numerical data. Results of K-Mean is shown in Table 2 and Overall clustering using different no of majority vote is shown in Fig. 4.

Table 2.   K-mean results

Exp. No.	Training accuracy (%)	Test accuracy (%)
1.	100	80

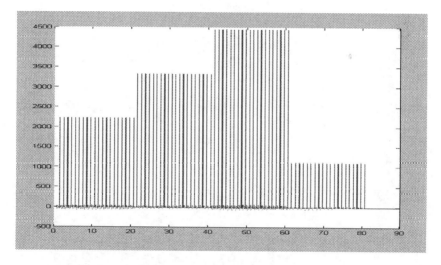

Fig. 4.   Overall clustering using different no of majority vote

4.2   Clustering Based on SOM

SOM is unsupervised learning method. SOM is used to map the training samples and thus is known as self-organising maps. Results of SOM classification is shown in Table 3.

Table 3.   SOM results

Exp. No.	Training accuracy (%)	Test accuracy (%)
1.	100	71

Figure 5 shows the number of SOM layer and inputs and outputs. Figure 6 shows SOM neighbouring distances. Figure 7 shows Biometrics types and Fig. 8 shows SOM weight planes.

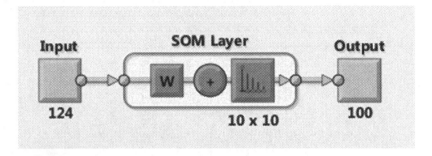

Fig. 5. SOM network architecture

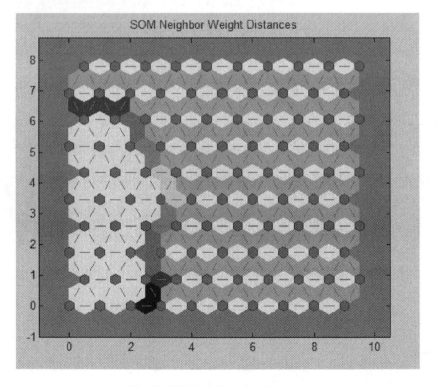

Fig. 6. SOM neighbouring distances

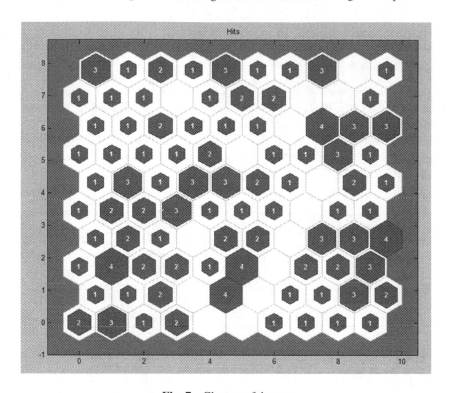

Fig. 7. Clusters of dataset

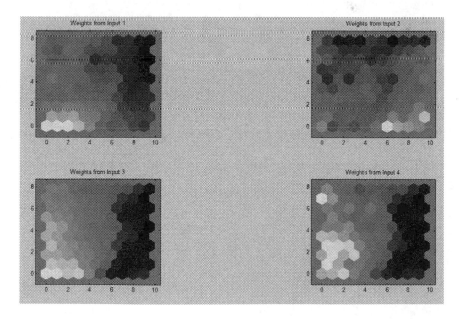

Fig. 8. SOM weight planes

5 Experimental Results and Discussions

5.1 Data Set Used

To evaluate the proposed method of gait activity recognition, we have used crouch datasets. There are four classes in the datasets. Each of them having three different data base therefore total number of datasets for all four classes are 12. There are total 16 features taken from the dataset [8]. The dimension of data is 16*300 for a particular data set, in which we choose one gait cycle for our experiment. So our dataset has 16*100 elements each. Hence total 16*4*3*100 elements.

5.2 Performance of the Classifiers

10-fold cross validation is used to determine the performance and validity of the model. Results of cross validation process are shown in Table 4.

Table 4. Comparison of success rate by different classifier using 5–fold cross validation

Classifier	Rate of success (%)
K-mean	80
SOM	71

5.3 Validation

Correlation coefficient	0.9955
Mean absolute error	8.2394
Root mean squared error	117.3938
Relative absolute error	0.741%
Root relative squared error	9.4381%
Total Number of Instances	203

It is noted that from all the other individual classifiers for various feature set performed the performance of the K-Mean is best. Therefore we get the highest overall accuracy of 90%.

5.4 Conclusion

The proposed system can be used for developing any gait based recognition system making human-computer interaction easier. From the set of all features we have taken a total of 16 features. To test the statistical significance of the 16 features ANOVA test was performed. The 16 significant features were then arranged in the descending order of the F-static value which was then fed to the IFS to select the optimal features. Total number of features or the optimal features was observed to be 7 and 8 for K-Mean and SOM respectively [10]. After this, 10-fold cross validation was used to provide overall accuracy of the system. Overall accuracy was observed to be 80, 71.1%, using the K-Mean and SOM respectively.

References

1. Thanasoontornerk, R., Pongmala, C., Suputtiada, A.: Tree induction for diagnosis on movement disorders using gait data. In: 2013 5th International Conference on Knowledge and Smart Technology (KST) (2013)
2. Katoh, K., Katoh, M.: Using FS in tuning a biped locomotion surrogate robot for walking training. In: 2011 4th International Conference on Biomedical Engineering (2011)
3. Yoneyama, M., Kurihara, Y., Watanabe, K.: Accelerometry-based gait analysis and its application to Parkinson's disease assessment—part 2. IEEE Trans. Neural Syst. Rehabil. Eng. 21(6), 999–1005 (2013)
4. Ogata, M., Karato, T., Tsuji, T., Kobayashi, H., Irie, K.: Development of active walker by using hart walker. In: SICE-ICASE International Joint Conference, 18–21 October 2006, Bexco, Busan Korea (2006)
5. Kobayashi, H., Karato, T., Tsuji, T.: Development of an active walker as a new orthosis. In: Proceedings of the 2007 IEEE International Conference on Mechatronics and Automation, 5–8 August 2007, Harbin, China (2007)
6. Lai, D.T.H., Khandoker, A., Begg, R.K., Palaniswami, M.: A hybrid support vector machine and autoregressive model for detecting gait disorders in the elderly. In: Proceedings of International Joint Conference on Neural Networks, Orlando, Florida, USA, 12–17 August 2007
7. Parashar, A., Goyal, S., Parashar, A., Sahjalan, B.: Push recovery for humanoid robot in dynamic environment and classifying the data using K-mean. In: ICTCS 2016 - CSI-Udaipur Chapter (2016)
8. Semwal, V.B., et al.: Biped model based on human gait pattern parameters for sagittal plane movement. In: 2013 International Conference on Control, Automation, Robotics and Embedded Systems (CARE). IEEE (2013)
9. Semwal, V.B., et al.: Biologically-inspired push recovery capable bipedal locomotion modeling through hybrid automata. Robot. Auton. Syst. 70, 181–190 (2015)
10. Parashar, A., Parashar, A., Goyal, S.: Classifying gait data using different machine learning techniques and finding the optimum technique of classification. In: International Conference on ICT for Sustainable Development

An Experimental Analysis on Removal of Salt and Pepper Noise from Digital Images

Nirvair Neeru$^{(\boxtimes)}$ and Lakhwinder Kaur

Computer Engineering Department,
Punjabi University, Patiala, India
nirvair_neeru@yahoo.com, mahal2k8@yahoo.com

Abstract. Images are normally degraded with noise. The main goal of the denoising technique is to eliminate the noise with minimum distortion. In this paper, work has been done to remove the salt & pepper noise from some of the standard images. The image denoising has been performed with median filter (MF), adaptive median filter (AMF), decision based unsymmetrical trimmed median filter (DBUTMF), modified decision based unsymmetric trimmed median filter (MDBUTMF) and decision based unsymmetric trimmed midpoint filter (DBUTMPF). The performance of each technique has been evaluated on the basis of four parameters namely, signal to noise ratio (SNR), Structure similarity index measure (SSIM), edge preservation index (EPI) and multiscale structure similarity index measure (MSSSIM).

Keywords: Filters · Image denoising · Salt & pepper noise · Noise detection

1 Introduction

There are many roles of digital images in various fields such as, signature verification, traffic monitoring, geographical information systems, remote sensing and medical sciences etc. Images are normally received in defective condition because of the poor scanning devises, poor quality of camera sensors and transmitting devices which degrades the quality of image by adding noise to them [5]. Image denoising is the process of recovering image without changing the basic information of the image. Noise removal is a fundamental step to improve the quality of images [2]. The process of noise removal is always done before using the images for different tasks [1]. It is very difficult to develop such a noise filtering technique which should be capable to preserve the important information of image by removing noise from it.

2 Salt and Pepper Noise

Salt & pepper noise stores the maximum or minimum values in the corrupted pixels [1]. It contains two types of pixels namely dark pixels and bright pixels [8]. The failure of memory cells, damaged camera sensor cells and bad transmission media are the main reason of salt & pepper noise.

© Springer Nature Singapore Pte Ltd. 2016
A. Unal et al. (Eds.): SmartCom 2016, CCIS 628, pp. 434–441, 2016.
DOI: 10.1007/978-981-10-3433-6_52

3 Image Denoising

A noise is a major element which is responsible for degradation of the quality of image and hence if any processes like image recognition, edge detection, segmentation etc. are to be applied on the image then the noise should be eliminated from it to have appropriate results. Sometimes the data in the original image gets deviated. This deviated data is referred to as noise. In image processing, removing noise from an image without blurring or destroying its fine details is the main challenge. Image denoising is used as an independent process or as a component in other process [3]. Noise removal task is not a simple because filter may alter the important information in the image [8]. A good noise reduction filter should always preserve the edges and other fine details in the image.

4 Image Denoising Techniques

4.1 Median Filter (MF)

MF is a commonly used to remove noise from images [11]. It replaces the pixel value with median of its neighboring pixels after sorting into numerical order [3]. The median is the centre value of sorted pixels. The main disadvantage of MF is that, while removing noise, it also removes corners, small lines and other fine details from the image. Also sorting process of pixel values is very slow [9].

4.2 Adaptive Median Filter (AMF)

The median filter has been improved to develop adaptive median filter. AMF removes the noise from image by preserving its important information [9]. AMF gives excellent performance at low noise density because when noise density is low then the count of corrupted pixels is small that are replaced by the median values [10].

4.3 Decision Based Unsymmetrical Trimmed Median Filter (DBUTMF)

DBUTMF includes the combination of decision based algorithm (DBA) and unsymmetrical trimmed median filter (UTMF). In the first step, DBUTMF finds the noisy pixels, and then all the pixels are arranged in sorted array. After removing all 0's and 255's, a median is calculated from rest of sorted array and is replaced with noisy pixel [10]. Figure 1 shows the step by step description of DBUTMF.

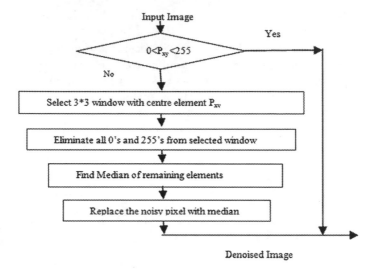

Fig. 1. Flow chart for DBUTMF

4.4 Modified Decision Based Unsymmetric Trimmed Median Filter (MDBUTMF)

MDBUTMF [13] is an improvement to the DBUTMF [10]. Here first of all it is checked that the pixel under consideration is noisy or not, if pixel is not noisy then it is not processed further and stored unaltered. If the pixel under consideration is a noisy

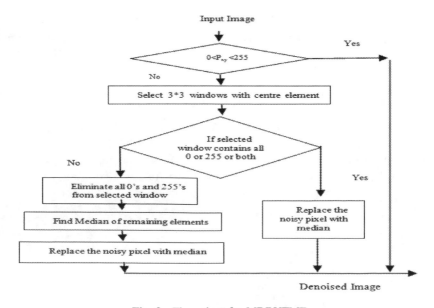

Fig. 2. Flow chart for MDBUTMF

pixel then it is further processed. In first case, if the entire pixels are noisy in selected window then mean value of all the pixels is calculated and replaced with noisy pixel. In second case, where all the pixels present in selected window are not noisy, all the noisy pixels are removed and then from the rest of pixels, a median is calculated and replaced with the noisy pixel [13] as shown in Fig. 2.

4.5 Decision Based Un-Symmetric Trimmed Midpoint Filter (DBUTMPF)

DBUTMPF [12] is an improvement to MDBUTMF [13]. Figure 3 shows its all processing steps. First of all it finds the noisy pixel as it has been discussed in above two filters. If it is not a noisy pixel then it is kept as it is. If the window under consideration contains some noisy pixels then all the noisy pixels are removed and the processing pixel is replaced with the midpoint of left over pixels [12].

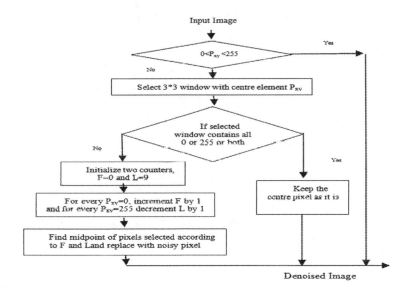

Fig. 3. Flow chart of DBUTMP

5 Image Quality Assessment Metrics

5.1 Signal to Noise Ratio (SNR)

SNR is calculated as following [14]:

$$SNR = \frac{P_{signal}}{P_{noise}} \qquad (1)$$

Where p is average power.

5.2 Edge Preservation Index (EPI)

EPI is used to calculate edge preservation property of denoising technique and calculated as following [7]:

$$EPI = \frac{\sum (\Delta I - \overline{\Delta I}) \sum (\Delta F - \overline{\Delta F})}{\sqrt{\sum (\Delta I - \overline{\Delta I})^2 \sum (\Delta F - \overline{\Delta F})^2}} \qquad (2)$$

5.3 Structure Similarity Index Measure (SSIM)

It is the improvement over traditional methods like Peek signal to noise ratio (PSNR), and Mean square error (MSE) etc. it is calculated as following [6]:

$$SSIM(x, y) = [l(x, y)]^{\alpha} . [c(x, y)]^{\beta} . [s(x, y)]^{\gamma} \qquad (3)$$

5.4 Multi Scale Structure Similarity Index Measure (MS-SSIM)

Multi-scale method is used to include details of image at various resolutions. The MS-SSIM is obtained as following [4]:

$$MSSSIM(x, y) = [l_m(x, y)]^{\alpha M} . \prod_{j=1}^{M} [c_j(x, y)]^{\beta j} [s_j(x, y)]^{\gamma j} \qquad (4)$$

6 Implementation and Result

All the experiments have been performed in Matlab environment. The noise reduction capability of MF, AMF, DBUTMF, MDBUTMF and DBUTMPF has been evaluated in terms of SNR, EPI, SSIM, and MSSSIM. The EPI shows that up to which extent the edges in the denoised image have been preserved. SSIM has been evaluated to check structural similarity between original image and denoised image. To incorporate the detail of image at different resolutions, the MS-SSIM has been calculated at level-5. The performance of all filters has been tested by adding salt & pepper noise at various noise densities. Table 1; demonstrate the results evaluated with Lena image (512 × 512). It has been observed that MDBUTMF is well capable to preserve edges in denoised image at low noise density. On the other hand DBUTMPF provides better EPI results at higher noise density. The SNR value shows that even DBUTMPF gives fine results at low and average noise densities but it is not suitable at high noise density. Figures 4, 5, 6 and 7; demonstrates performance comparison among different filters on the basis of SNR, EPI, SSIM and MS-SSIM respectively. Large SNR value means better image quality which is yielded by DBUTMPF at low noise density. The value of EPI reveals that performance of DBUTMPF and MDBUTMF is very near to each other. For the better image quality SSIM and MS-SSIM should be near to 1, hence it has been observed that DBUTMF, MDBUTMF and DBUTMPF are well capable to retain structure and fine details in the denoised image. The overall analysis shows that the DBUTMPF provides better results among all other filters.

Table 1. SNR, EPI, SSIM and MS-SSIM values

Filters	Noise density	Lena image (512 × 512)				
		MF	AMF	DBUTMF	MDUTMEDF	DBUTMPF
SNR	10	18.44	26.05	27.17	27.17	27.41
	30	9.40	21.20	22.34	22.45	22.83
	50	1.05	13.66	15.52	18.64	19.01
	70	−4.26	2.48	4.89	10.24	11.04
	90	−7.63	−5.68	−4.72	1.40	2.07
EPI	10	0.4987	0.8023	0.8313	0.8823	0.8840
	30	0.1118	0.6671	0.7100	0.7217	0.7101
	50	0.0360	0.2900	0.3194	0.4649	0.4670
	70	0.014	0.0536	0.0632	0.1384	0.1401
	90	0.0028	0.0063	0.0088	0.0308	0.0406
SSIM	10	0.9785	0.9807	0.9808	0.9918	0.9976
	30	0.7640	0.9762	0.9812	0.9814	0.9901
	50	0.2959	0.9081	0.9450	0.9667	0.9716
	70	0.0857	0.3979	0.5850	0.7628	0.8229
	90	0.0206	0.0514	0.1251	0.2455	0.4438
MS SSIM	10	0.9885	0.9886	0.9899	0.9901	0.9905
	30	0.8788	0.9729	0.9814	0.9825	0.9851
	50	0.5235	0.9510	0.9684	0.9716	0.9718
	70	0.2298	0.5920	0.7792	0.8793	0.9009
	90	0.0682	0.1358	0.3213	0.4507	0.6201

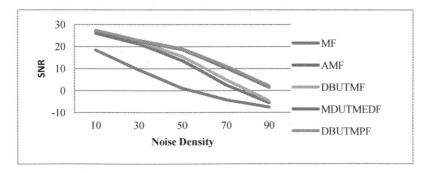

Fig. 4. SNR value of different techniques at various noise densities

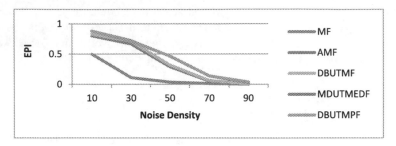

Fig. 5. EPI value of at different techniques at various noise densities

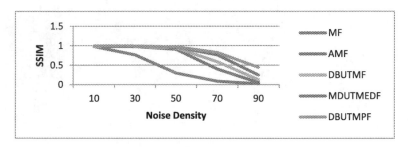

Fig. 6. SSIM value different techniques at various noise densities

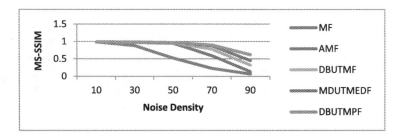

Fig. 7. MS-SSIM (Level-5) different techniques at various noise densities

7   Conclusions

This paper presents the experimental analysis of various filters for removing the salt & pepper noise present in digital images. The performance comparison of MF, AMF, DBUTMF, MDBUTMF and DBUTMPF has been performed in terms of quality assessment metrics SNR, EPI, SSIM, and MSSSIM. The study show that, among all the filters, which have been compared, the DBUTMPF is a suitable method because it efficiently removes the noise from image and also capable to preserve edges and useful structure of the image at low and average noise densities. Hence it shows its superiority among all other filter.

References

1. Annadurai, S., Shanmugalakshmi, R.: Fundamentals of Digital Image Processing. Pearson Education, Upper Saddle River (2007)
2. Jassam, K.I.: Removal of random noise from conventional digital X ray images. Int. Soc. Photogrammetry Remote Sens. **29**, 113–118 (1992). Part 5
3. Dangeti, S.: "Denoising Techniques - A Comparison", A Thesis Submitted to the Graduate Faculty of the Louisiana State University and Agricultural and Mechanical College (2003)
4. Wang, Z., Simoncelli, E.P., Bovik, A.C.: Multi-scale structural similarity for image quality assessment. In: Proceedings of the 37th IEEE Asilomar Conference on Signals, Systems and Computers, Pacific Grove, CA, 9–12 November 2003 (2003)
5. Motwani, M.C., Gadiya, M.C., Motwani, R.C.: Survey of image de-noising techniques. In: Proceedings of GSPx, Santa Clara, CA (2004)
6. Wang, Z., Bovik, A.C., Sheikh, H.R., Simoncelli, E.P.: Image quality assessment: from error visibility to structural similarity. IEEE Trans. Image Process. **13**(4), 600–612 (2004)
7. Gupta, S., Kaur, L., Chauhan, R.C., Saxena, S.C.: A versatile technique for visual enhancement of medical ultrasound image. J. Digital Sig. Process. **17**, 542–560 (2007). Elsevier
8. Yazdi, H.S., Homayouni, F.: Impulsive noise suppression of images using adaptive median filter. Int. J. Sig. Process. Image Process. Pattern Recogn. **3**(3) (2010)
9. Thivakaran, T.K., Chandrasekaran, R.M.: Nonlinear filter based image denoising using AMF approach. Int. J. Comput. Sci. Inf. Secur. **7**(2), 1–12 (2010)
10. Shekar, D., Srikanth, R.: Removal of high density salt & pepper noise in noisy images using decision based unsymmetric trimmed median filter. Int. J. Comput. Trends Technol. **2**(1), 25–32 (2011). ISSN: 2231-2803
11. Geoffrine Judith, M.C.: Study and analysis of impulse noise reduction filters. Sig. Image Process. Int. J. (SIPIJ) **2**(1), 82–92 (2011)
12. Vasanth, K., Senthilkumar, V.J.: A decision based unsymmetrical trimmed midpoint algorithm for the removal of high density salt and pepper noise. J. Theor. Appl. Inf. Technol. **42**(2), pp. 245–251, 31 August 2012
13. Bethina, C.: Removal of noise in images using modified decision based un-symmetric trimmed median filter with FPGA implementation, **1**(2), 01–08 (2012). ISSN: 2319-4200, ISBN No.: 2319–4197
14. Hymagayathri, M., Jaya Prakash, A., Madhusudhana Rao, T.V.: An efficient adaptive linear filtering algorithm for image restoration using inverse filter. Int. J. Adv. Res. Electr. Electron. Instrum. Eng. **3**(11), November 2014. ISSN (Print): 2320–3765

Literature Study on Multi-document Text Summarization Techniques

Chintan Shah[1(✉)] and Anjali Jivani[2(✉)]

[1] Shankersinh Vaghela Bapu Institute of Technology, Gandhinagar, India
`Chintan.shah84@gmail.com`
[2] The Maharaja Sayajjirao University, Baroda, India
`Anjali_jivani@yahoo.com`

Abstract. Text summarization is a method which generates a shorter and a preciseform of one or more text documents. Automatic text summarization plays an essential role in finding information from large text corpus or an internet. What had actually started as a single document Text Summarization has now evolved and developed into generating multi-document summarization. There are a number of approaches to multi-document summarization such as Graph, Cluster, Term-Frequency, Latent Semantic Analysis (LSA) based etc. In this paper we have started with introduction of multi-document summarization and then have further discussed comparison and analysis of various approaches which comes under the multi-document summarization. The paper also contains details about the benefits and problems in the existing methods. This would especially be helpful for researchers working in this field of text data mining. By using this data, researchers can build new or mixed based approaches for multidocument summarization.

Keywords: Text summarization · Cluster · Multi-document summarization · Graph · LSA · Term-Frequency based

1 Introduction

For retrieving information, People widely use internet such as Google, Yahoo, Bing and so on. Since amount of material on the internet is growing rapidly, for users it is not easy to find relevant and appropriate information as per the requirement. Once a user sends a query on a search engine for data or information then the response is most of the times thousands of documents and the user has to face the tedious task of finding the appropriate information from this sea of rejoinder. This problem is called as "Data Overloading" [1]. Automatic text summarization is the summary of source of text in shorter version, that retain the main feature of the content and help the user to quickly understand large volume of information. A number of authors have proposed techniques for automatic text summarization which can be broadly classified as: extractive summarization and abstractive summarization. In extractive summarization, it selects sentences that have the highest weightage in the retrieved document and put them together to generate a summary version of original document without changing or altering the main text, where as in abstractive summary, the original text gets converted into another semantic form with the help of linguistic methods to get a shorter summary of original document [2].

The primary goal of multiple-document summarization is to build summary which has maximum coverage, less redundant data and maximum cohesiveness between sentences [2]. In another words, main sentences are extracted from each document and then are re-arranged to get multi-documents summary. Multi-document summarization flow is shown in Fig. 1.

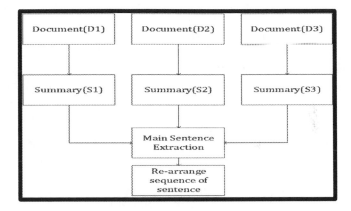

Fig. 1. Multi-document process flow

This survey paper covers various aspects which are given below

1. Several approaches of Graph, Cluster, Term Frequency, and Latent sematic analysis for multi-document summarization
2. Issues and problems shown by different researchers for improvement in this area
3. Evaluation criteria for comparing automatic summary and human summary

We have in Sect. 2 of this paper, described related work done on multi-document text summarization with help of Graph, Cluster, Term-Frequency and Latent semantic analysis methods. In the Sect. 3 we have shown analysis and comparison of all methods with scope of improvement, Sect. 4 contains the evaluation criteria and Sect. 5 contains conclusion.

2   Related Work

Research on multi-document summarization is the need of the present scenario with respect to Information Retrieval and Internet Surfing being the most popular applications. Many methods and approaches are available for information retrieval from various sources [3]. Many techniques have been developed till date on multiple-document summarization. In this paper, different methods are grouped into different categories as per their implementation criteria.

2.1 Graph Based Methods

Rada Mihalcea [4] **(2004).** Proposed Text Rank method on Graph based method which takes into consideration local vertex-specific information as well as full graph global statistics repeatedly for determining significance of vertex. Below steps are elaborate in summary generation:

a. To build a graph model, from the graph, identify vertices which describe given task as text units
b. Draw edges between text units on basis of common match and computerelationship for each edge
c. We may have weighted or un-weighted edges as well as directed or un-directed graphs
d. In the model, apply rank algorithm and repeat until convergence takes place
e. In this graph method, all vertices will be sorted on score of respectively vertex based on last mark of each vertex. And finally, scores will be used for selection purpose

Julin Zhang [5] **(2005)** projected Hub/Authority framework on basis of Graph theory. In that method, content feature is merged with surface feature i.e. location and length of sentence, cue phrase etc. For sentence selection purpose, it may extract significant sub-topic features under Hub/Authority framework. In this model, sentences are ranked and final summary will be generated on basis of score of each sentences under the hub and authority score.

Shanmugasudaran Hariharan [6] **(2009)**, projected two primary methods with differences, with or without omitting the nominated sentences. Where this paper concentrates on summarization of news articles with help of graph based methods. With help of adjacency matrix, representation can be one via similarity measures between sentences of documents which is the first step of this Graph based approach. In this approach, two techniques are discussed wherein primary one proposes cumulative sum and second one degree of centrality. With aid of these two methods, a method is proposed by the author for assessing adjacency matrix. Precision and recall have been used for calculating extractive summaries as metrics. This paper presents two metrics: Effectiveness 1 & Effectiveness 2 for evaluating human summaries against system summaries. With the help of discounting method for testing for single and multi-document summaries, after investigating the result, we come to know that the second method is better than the previous method but there are few scopes for improvement in this area.

Khushboo [7] **(2010)**, introduced methodology of Text Rank method by few variances. In said method, it uses shortest path algorithm for generating summaries. Sentences will be selected from path with help of shortest path algorithm, where each sentences may be similar to pervious sentences for generating summaries over choosing top ranking sentences such as Text rank. In first step for representing text, it will build graph model. Text units can be word, phrases, collocation, sentence or others, these will have considered as a Text units and it will be added as vertices for the graph. After completion of the step, score will be calculated with help of ranking algorithm (Graph Bases) such as HITS, Page Rank of each vertex. After finishing the above step, shortest path algorithm will be applied for generating summaries.

Shuzhi Sam ge [8] **(2010),** proposed hybrid approach for weighted graph model that include two concepts, sentences clustering & ranking for text summarization. In other words, method depends on cluster as well as Graph based approaches for generating summaries for text. There are few steps for this approach-

a. There are two ways first is Graph model for sentence ranking and second is cluster for merging same sentences
b. Clustering of sentences can be completed on basis on Singular non matrix factorization, so there are possibilities of using Latent Semantic Analysis, which has gained popularity nowadays for text summarization
c. In weighted graph model, it reflects discourse association between sentences in order to cluster and rank sentences in a document

Tu-Anh Nguyen-Hoang [9] **(2012),** proposed method which has three steps, during first step, for the data set, specific structure will be added to every document. Undirected weighted graph can be measured as a structure. For graph, title and sentences will play major role for construction of the graph. In the second phase, Weighted page rank which is Graph based ranking algorithm will be used for calculating score of each sentences of the document. Few sentences are extracted from the document for building summaries of documents for that ranks and scores are considered on the basis of relevant features of the document. In later stage, all different summaries will be merged into a single summary. Finally, MMR (Maximal Marginal Relevance) algorithm is used to form the final extractive summary.

2.2 Cluster Based Methods

Judith D. Schlesinger [10] **(2008)** has presented CLASSY for multi-document summarization. CLASSY(Clustering, Linguistics, and Statistics for Summarization) is a model of extractive automatic summarization which operates both on single and multi-document summarization. Topic or generic summaries can be produced by this model. It practices language method for trimming, statistical method for scoring and that is why it is known as CLASSY. This technique includes trimming rules to reduce the distance of sentences in the document and the identification of sentences on the basis of importance that are probable to be involved in the summary. The summary is generated for individually document and then summaries are re-arranged and then merged to form the final combined summary. CLASSY construction contains of five steps: to prepare document, to trim sentence (using stop word removal, stemming), to compute score of each sentence, redundancy removal and collection of sentence based on score.

Xiao-Chem Ma [11] **(2009)** has proposed summarization model, which has three parts: pre-processing, soft clustering and summary generation. The main and the most important portion of system is clustering. In the clustering algorithm, there are four stages: primary is to construct Vector Space Model (VSM), second one is preparing relationship matrix, where third is to set initial parameters and finally, build clusters recursively. For summary preparation, Maximal Marginal Relevance (MMR) has been usedso summary sentences will designate the core content of the multi-set of documents and deliver connection with the request which is a query.

Virendra Gupta [12] **(2012)** has introduced a clear approach for multi document summarization by linking simple summary of the document using the phrase clustering. For clustering, syntactic and semantic analytics both are used for similarity between sentences. Document, sentence reference index, location and concept similarity features, all have been used for generating single document summary. Summaries of single document for sentences are clustered and best sentences from each cluster are used to generating multi-document summary.

2.3   Term Frequency Based Methods

Salton [13] **(2005)** has proposed method of term frequency inverse document frequency model (TF-IDF), where the mark of a term in this document is the ratio between the amount of terms in this document to the frequency of the amount of documents that contain those terms. Importance of evaluating the expression is given by the principle TFI X IDFI, where TFI is the term frequency of 'I' in the document and IDFI is the inverted frequency in which that term 'I' occurs. Therefore, sentences can be scored for illustration with help computing relevance of terms in the sentence.

Jun'ichi Fukumoto [14] **(2004)** proposed a technique for multi-document summarization in which an easy strategy to build abstract with help of TF-IDF based extraction is used. Summaries for individual documents are generated and same summaries will be used for generating multi-document summary. The proposed system automatically categorizes a document into three different sub-sets with help of info of high frequency nouns and named object, the categories are one topic, multi-topic type and others. To summarize, the first sentences are take out from each document based on TF-IDF, the position of the sentence and weighing of a sentence. During the next step, needless parts of sentences are discarded. Then all sentences which are extracted are sorted in the original order in a document to generate summarized form of each single document. In the next stage, all extracted sentences are grouped in clusters and the repeated clauses are removed. The remaining clauses are sorted for generating the final summary.

2.4   Latent Sematic Analysis Methods

Shuchu Xiong [15] **(2014)** proposed a method based on LSA wherein sentence taking out summarizer evaluates a set of summary sentences based on its prediction similarity to that of the full sentences set on the top latent singular vector. There are few steps required to build summary with the help of Latent semantic analysis. First step is applying singular value decomposition (SVD) to document. Second is choosing sentence by its capacity of projection similarity. And finally, LSA-based forward sentence selection algorithm is applied to build summary. Here they have used centroid-based MEAD and MMR (Maximal Marginal Relevance) methods.

Josef Steinberger [16] (**2004**) shows that basic LSA has two main disadvantages, first is that it uses matching number of dimensions as is the number of sentences that we want in a summary. Second disadvantage is that large index value will not be chosen even when required for the summary. The author has proposed modification in the existing SVD-based summarization. In the proposed method, he recalculates SVD of a term by sentences matrix. For summary evaluation, this paper shows few techniques such as similarity of main topic, Term Significance, etc.

3   Analysis and Comparative Study of Various Methods

Author, Year	Description	Benefits	Problems	Scope of improvement
Grid Based Method				
Rada Mihalcea, 2004 [4]	With help of Text Rank it builds summary which chooses top most sentences	It considered Text Unit for local information	Calculation of vertex score is complex	Possible improvement in score calculation for summary generation
Julin Zhang, 2005 [5]	Hub/Authority framework is used, merge surface feature and content feature	Effective graph-ranking method used for text summary	Not easy to find sub-topics	Limited surface features are used, possible to add more to find sub-topics
Shanmugasudaran Hariharan, 2009 [6]	Two main techniques, cumulative sum & degree of centrality	Single & multi-documents summarization, both work	Precision and recall have been used for result, not any other standard formula	Extra method needs to be developed for better result
Khuhboo, 2010 [7]	Shortest path algorithm has been used for selection of top most sentences for summary	Compared to other methods, it generates better summary	It considers only shortest path for selection of sentences	It should add another feature along with shortest path algorithm
Shuzhi Sam ge, 2010 [8]	Find sentences from document through sentence ranking & clustering method for summarization	Work with hybrid approach	Weight balance parameter & sparseness degree may influence performance of system	Need to improve system performance

(*continued*)

(continued)

Author, Year	Description	Benefits	Problems	Scope of improvement
Tu-Anh Nguyen-Hoang, 2012 [9]	Preprocessing, graph construction & sentence ranking used for summary generation via MMR	It is unsupervised training method so need to train data	Information loss may be possible during graph building	Need to work for optimizing information loss
Cluster based Methods				
Judith D, 2008 [10]	CLASSY architecture has been used	Works for multi-lingual summarization method	Machine translation is difficult task	CLASSY should work for all languages
Xiao-Chem Ma, 2009 [11]	To build cluster and extract summary based on modified MMR	For sentence extraction MMR is used for result	Only considers query sentences	Possible improvement is readability of summary
Virendra, 2012 [12]	Merge single document summary with multi-document summary	Used syntactic & sematic similarity for sentence clustering	Single document summary is to be considered for final summary	Syntactic similarity are founded on work order which can be substituted with other structural comparison measures
Term Frequency Based Method				
Salton, 2005 [13]	Works with TF-IDF for summary	Easy and fast for generation of summary	No major drawbacks	Work with other features to remove duplication
Jun'ichi Fukumoto, 2004 [14]	Multi-document summarization to build abstract with help of single document summarization	Categorized into three – one topic, multi-topic and others	No major drawbacks	Result can be improved
Latent Semantic Analysis Methods				
ShuchuXiong, 2014 [16]	LSA based sentence pulling out summarizer which assesses a	Applied SVD and have used Centroid based MEAD and	Only LSA based algorithms used	Need to use another method to build better summarization

(continued)

⌐ (*continued*)

Author, Year	Description	Benefits	Problems	Scope of improvement
	set of summary sentences based on its prediction similarity to that of the full sentences set on the top latent singular vector	MMR (Maximal Marginal Relevance) to examination and experiment	for summary generation	
Josef Steinberger, 2004 [15]	Recalculates SVD of a term by sentences matrix	Presenting techniques similarity of main topic, Term Significance.	Not any standard method used for evaluation for summary generation	Need to work for solid method for evaluation summary generation

4 Evaluation Measures

Evaluation of summary is typically constructed on readability and content of information. Primary purpose of text summarization is to find non redundant text that have contained significant information from the original corpus. There is no fixed parameter for text summarization on which we can rely for evaluation. There are two approaches for evaluation of summarization i.e. intrinsic and extrinsic. Intrinsic method calculates the actual information of a summary, compares with human summary or with the full document source. In extrinsic methods evaluate the summary via task-based performance i.e. information retrieval-oriented tasks.

The Rouge toolkit can help us to check performance of the summary generated. Rouge is a software package which can be used to measure summary in period of number of word overlaps in machine generated summary and human reference summary [17]. In Rouge toolkit, as input, we can provide two types of summaries. Standard summary can be considered as location summary which we can compare our summary results and other that are generated via some methods. Rouge toolkit has five evaluation metrics i.e. ROUGE-N, ROUGE-L, ROUGE-W, ROUGE-S and ROUGE-SU based on word co-occurrence statistics [18].

There is another toolkit called MEAD which is a publicly open toolkit for multi-lingual summarization and evaluation. This toolkit implements several summarization algorithms i.e. position-based, centroid, TF-IDF, and query-based methods, etc. Methods for evaluating the quality of the summaries include co-selection (precision/recall, kappa, and relative utility) and content-based measures (cosine, word overlap, bigram overlap).

5 Conclusion

This literature survey paper contains various methods for multi-document text summarization. Several techniques have been explored for multi-document summarization such as Graph Based, Cluster Based, Term-Frequency Based and Latent Semantic Analysis (LSA) based. Researchers can focus only on specific approaches from existing techniques and make an improvement in those approaches to generate new or hybrid approach for building better summaries which take less effort. We have compared in this paper, Graph, Cluster, Term-Frequency and LSA. New approach or hybrid approach can be developed with help of natural language processing approach and linguistic approach, which can help us to generate better summary for multi-document.

References

1. Kan, M.-Y., Klavans, J.L.: Using librarian techniques in automatic text summarization for information retrieval. In: Proceedings of the 2nd ACMlIEEE-CS Joint Conference on Digital Libraries, pp. 36–45. ACM (2002)
2. Meena, Y.K., Jain, A., Gopalani, D.: Survey on graph and cluster based approaches in multi-document text summarization. In: Recent Advances and Innovations in Engineering (ICRAIE), Jaipur, pp. 1–5 (2014). doi:10.1109/ICRAIE.2014.6909126
3. Haque, M., Pervin, S., Begum, Z., et al.: Literature review of automatic multiple documents text summarization. Int. J. Innov. Appl. Stud. 3(1), 121–129 (2013)
4. Mihalcea, R., Tarau, P.: Textrank: bringing order into texts. In: Proceedings of EMNLP, vol. 4, Barcelona, Spain (2004)
5. Zhang, J., Sun, L., Zhou, Q.: A cue-based hub-authority approach for multi-document text summarization. In: Proceedings of 2005 IEEE International Conference on Natural Language Processing and Knowledge Engineering, IEEE NLP-KE 2005, pp. 642–645. IEEE (2005)
6. Hariharan, S., Srinivasan, R.: Studies on graph based approaches for single and multi-document summarizations. Int. Comput. Theory Eng 1, 1793–8201 (2009)
7. Thakkar, K.S., Dharaskar, R.V., Chandak, M.: Graph-based algorithms for text summarization. In: 3rd International Conference on Emerging Trends in Engineering and Technology (ICETET) 2010, pp. 516–519. IEEE (2010)
8. Ge, S.S., Zhang, Z., He, H.: Weighted graph model based sentence clustering and ranking for document summarization. In: 2011 4th International Conference on Interaction Sciences (ICIS), pp. 90–95. IEEE (2011)
9. Nguyen-Hoang, T.-A., Nguyen, K., Tran, Q.-V.: Tsgvi: a graphbased summarization system for vietnamese documents. J. Ambient Intell. Humanized Comput. 3(4), 305–313 (2012)
10. Schlesinger, J.D., O'Leary, D.P., Conroy, J.M.: Arabic/English multi-document summarization with CLASSY—the past and the future. In: Gelbukh, A. (ed.) CICLing 2008. LNCS, vol. 4919, pp. 568–581. Springer, Heidelberg (2008). doi:10.1007/978-3-540-78135-6_49
11. Ma, X.-C., Yu, G.-B., Ma, L.: Multi-document summarization using clustering algorithm. In: International Workshop on Intelligent Systems and Applications, ISA 2009, pp. 1–4. IEEE (2009)

12. Gupta, V.K., Siddiqui, T.J.: Multi-document summarization using sentence clustering. In: 4th International Conference on Intelligent Human Computer Interaction (IHCI), pp. 1–5. IEEE (2012)
13. Salton, G.: Automatic Text Processing: The Transformation, Analysis, and Retrieval of Information by Computer. Addison Wesley Publishing Company, USA (1989)
14. Fukumoto, J.I.: Multi-document summarization using document set type classification. In: Proceedings of NTCIR-2004, Tokyo, pp. 412–416 (2004)
15. Xiong, S., Luo, Y.: A new approach for multi-document summarization based on latent semantic analysis. In: 2014 Seventh International Symposium on Computational Intelligence and Design (ISCID), Hangzhou, pp. 177–180 (2014)
16. Steinberger, J., Jezek, K.: Using latent semantic analysis in text summarization and summary evaluation. In: Proceeding ISIM 2004, pp. 93–100 (2004)
17. Lioret, E., Palomar, M.: Text summarization in progress: a literature review. Artif. Intell. Rev. 37(I), 1–41 (2012)
18. Das,D., Martins, A.F.: A survey on automatic text summarization. In: Literature Survey for the Language and Statistics II course at CMU, vol. 4, pp. 192–195 (2007)

A Localization Based Resilience Enhancement in Ad Hoc and Wireless Sensor Networks

Amit Kumar[1(✉)], Vijay Kumar[1], and Kamal Kumar[2]

[1] Department of Computer Engineering, M.M. Engineering College, M.M. University,
Mullana, Ambala, Haryana, India
amitaussie@gmail.com, katiyarvk@mmumullana.org
[2] Center for Information Technology (CIT), UPES, Dehradun, Uttarakhand, India
kkumar@ddn.upes.ac.in

Abstract. Wireless Ad hoc networks represent a form of cooperative networking through peer to peer behavior with others nodes in the networks. Hop by hop communication is default way of communication. Most of the communications are localized and interaction among local nodes requires local security provisioning. In the absence of any centralized certification authority and absence of viable localization and synchronization hardware, schematic localization and periodic refreshing proved to be a feasible solution. Several solutions have exploited GPS based localization and periodic refreshing cycles to provide a viable security solution for wireless ad hoc networks. In this paper, we have proposed an accelerated hashing mechanism with schematic localization based on variable or multiple transmission range of few nodes. The solution has been simulated for evaluated for performance parameters like connectivity, storage overhead and computation.

Keywords: Cell · Uniform · Heterogeneous · Non-uniform

1 Introduction

Ad hoc and Wireless Sensor Networks are inexpensive infrastructure-less networks deployed on the fly and are useful in circumstances where infrastructure is unavailable. These networks offers reliable, accurate and flexible mode of operations. These networks find their applications in the field of data collection and surveillance and monitoring and other supervisory processes [1]. In the absence of any infrastructure these networks has to rely upon the hop-by-hop communications in hostile environments. The mere absence of any control on the memberships of the networks and easier physical level attacks including node replication, node capture and passive attacks, these networks require a security provisioning. Securing hop-by-hop communications gives better control over local attacks like replay and ensures confidentiality and integrity. Pair wise keying between neighbouring nodes for hop level communications requires location information of nodes which is unavailable in these networks due to random deployment and absence of control on topology.

Through this paper an extension of work proposed in [2–4] is proposed and idea is to exploit local relationship crafted out of broadcasts received from Anchor Nodes

© Springer Nature Singapore Pte Ltd. 2016
A. Unal et al. (Eds.): SmartCom 2016, CCIS 628, pp. 452–459, 2016.
DOI: 10.1007/978-981-10-3433-6_54

(ANs). The proposal is organized into 6 sections with Sects. 1 and 2 introducing the gaps and proposal. Section 3 presents the network model. Section 4 highlights the intricacies of the work with Sect. 5 presenting a Simulation Model. Finally, concluded in Sect. 6 with performance discussion as well.

2   Related Work

Authors in [5] authors studied threats on ad hoc network and explored new approaches to secure its communication. In [6] authors proposed a new key management protocol (MKMP) for addressing end-to-end data privacy and security issues. In [7] authors proposed media mixing algorithm to choose what type of and how information should be provided to each user. In [8] a group based key management scheme was proposed for use with DSR and AODV. Similar scheme was proposed in [9] to allow any two members of a group to establish session key for secure communication based on PKI. The decentralized approach was subsided the need for trusted third party. A composite trust based public key management scheme [10] was proposed for providing the security at high performance levels as well as counter the attacks. Scheme ensured high acceptability and low communication overheads. A novel trust based multipath routing scheme was proposed in [11] with an approach that nodes with trust were given fewer encrypted parts of messages and making it difficult for intruders to gain the access of information. A secure routing scheme based on the anonymity of route to source and destination was proposed in [12]. The routing process was improved by using authenticated key exchange procedure. REFRAHN (Resilience Evaluation Framework for Ad Hoc Routing protocols) was proposed in [13] for evaluation of impact of malicious and accidentals faults injected in ad hoc routing schemes. The resilience performance of protocol can be evaluated under various configuration parameters related to nodes. An IDS was proposed in [14] while using SecAODV over handheld devices. Hop-by-hop, efficient authentication protocol (HEAP) was implemented in [15] and was compared with likes of TESLA, LHAP and other schemes. A trust based security provisioning was proposed where source considers RREP from all its neighbours [16]. A group based key management scheme for security provisioning in MANETs was proposed [17] where group leader performed the function of key management. An Authenticated anonymous secure routing (AASR) was proposed in [18] to counter the attacks in ad hoc networks.

3   Network Modelling

The focus in this proposal is ad hoc and sensor networks with heterogeneous keying material and transmission ranges. On the basis of heterogeneity in quantity of keying material pre-distributed in each node and nodes are classified as either H-nodes or L-nodes. This paper considers the flat architecture. Nodes and Anchor Nodes are only elements in this network (Fig. 1).

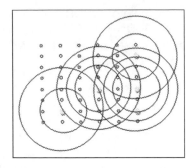

Fig. 1. Network architecture

Nodes: Normal node is a role that is performed by each node as a part of the data collection network. All the nodes are limited in terms of sizes, transmission range, and storage capacity and battery life. Nodes can thus store limited number of keys.

Anchor Nodes (ANs): ANs is a role bestowed over a node when it is selected for transmission of nonce, where nonce is special kind of value used for generation of security materials. The selection of ANs is based on the Eq. 1 and role is rotated such that a node will become AN next time only after each node has performed as AN after it. Network model considers a random deployment of nodes in unattended fields. Network considers multi-hop relays. Few nodes which are given less keys in non-uniform key distribution are called L-nodes which are more in quantity whereas H-nodes are given more keys in key pre-distribution phase (Fig. 2).

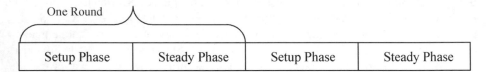

Fig. 2. Protocol operation

Anchor Selection Process: Each node generates a random number between 0 and 1 and if random number's value is smaller than threshold T(n), the node will be a new Anchor Node (AN); otherwise, it performs as normal member.

The value of T(n) is computed as follows:

$$T(n) = \begin{cases} \dfrac{p}{1 - p(r \bmod 1/p)} & \text{if } n \in G \\ 0 & \text{otherwise,} \end{cases} \tag{1}$$

Where p is the percentage of ANs desired out of total number of nodes. Variable r is the identifier value for current round, and G is the set of nodes that have not been anchored in the last $1/p$ rounds [19].

4   Keying Scheme

Network initialization proceeds through key establishment and followed by realizing secure GPSR [20]. Notations specific to this work are presented in Table 1. The phases of key management are discussed below.

Table 1. Notations

Notations	Meaning
n_2	Quantity of H-nodes
K	Size of Pool
N	Scale of Network
k_1	Key set of L-nodes
k_2	Key set of H-nodes
n_1	Quantity of L-nodes

4.1   Key Pre-distribution and Cell Wise Unique Key Pool Generation

Considering that network consists of N nodes, two classes as per keying material is to be pre-distributed. Considering that n_1 and n_2 represent the number of L-nodes and H-nodes. Each of the L-node is pre-distributed with k_1 keys and H-node with k_2 unique keys such that $k_1 \leq k_2$ with replacement. Keys are chosen from a large sized key pool with size K. Nodes which receive same nonce sets constitute a cell. The set of nonce in a cell can be used to construct group key K_G (Eq. 2). This association of nodes in a cell is due to their location in the field.

$$K_G = Hash(N_{ij}) \text{ Where } \{i, j | i = 1..m \& j = 1..n\} \tag{2}$$

Where m, n correspond to number of nodes acting as of AN and number of transmissions levels respectively. At any time the value of m can be computed using value of p such that $m = 100 * p$. N_{ij}'s are nonce broadcast from AN_i and transmitting at j^{th} power. K_G can be used for ensuring semantics of message but is useless when comes to eavesdropping, replay and Denial of Service attacks.

Member nodes of a cell exchange key ids among them. Nodes may conclude common pre-distributed keys with all the members of the cell. Nodes use hashing on common pre-distributed keys and group key to generate cell-wise key pool. This cell-wise key pool is set of localized keys (Eq. 3). Encryption using keys from this pool can be very useful in identifying the location of event. Besides that nodes maintain pre-distributed keys intact.

$$K_{G_i} = Hash(K_G, K_i) \tag{3}$$

Where K_i is one of common key among pre-distributed keys. Similarly other cell wise keys can be generated from other common pre-distributed keys.

Pair-wise Key Establishment: Pair-wise key establishment requires information on keys pre-distributed to each node. The Ids of keys are exchanged between neighbouring nodes. With this information, nodes may now proceed to establish one-hop and two-hop path with its one hop neighbours. As per network model considered, pair of nodes in question may belong to same cell or neighbouring cells. Such co-cell or neighbouring cell based interaction improves the chances of sharing few nonce received from ANs. Let the nodes identities are Id_i and id_j. Along with these, nodes may share some keys in pre-distributed set. Both these sets of common keys (one on the basis of cells and other from pre-distributed common keys) provide the keys to be used on one hope key paths. Nodes tend to obtain two-hop key paths with their neighbour. If nodes with identities Id_i and id_j do not share any keys in pre-distributed key sets, node Id_i may find a one-hop node with identity Id_k which shares some keys both with Id_i and Id_j. This results in two-hop keyed path $i - k - j$. This proposal considered all two-hop keyed paths and one-hop direct keyed path for improvement of resilience of link between Id_i and Id_j [1] with an improvisation through cell based membership. After all two-hop paths and direct one-hop path is identified, node Id_i constitutes enough shares of key to be shared among Id_i and Id_j. These shares are dispatched to Id_j through all paths such that each path carries one share in encrypted format by using common keys on the path. This increases the effort of intruder by many-folds to crack into all keyed paths and obtain shares. Let there be n two-hop keyed path and one direct one-hop keyed path, then the number of keys shared between i and j may be computed as follows:

$$K(I_i, I_j) = Keys(I_i, I_j) + \sum_1^n \min\big(Keys(I_i, I_k), Keys(I_k, I_j)\big) \tag{4}$$

$K(I_i, I_j)$ is measure of effort to invest to break into security proposed in this proposal. An enhancement in the form of keys from local memberships of same cell or co-located cells improves the number of keys shared on direct and two-hop keyed paths.

5   Simulation and Performance Discussion

Simulation modelling is used to establish that end to end resilience in routes is scripted by number of keys in the links on the paths. We have proposed a location based keying mechanism which may result in some of co-located nodes to share some keys for use in encryption/decryptions over links. Our approach is evaluated as against [3] by using GPSR [20] in simulation set-up and using routing paths form tree rooted at one node. The simulation model allows the evaluation of secure single source all destinations scenario (Fig. 3).

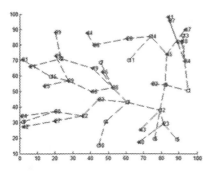

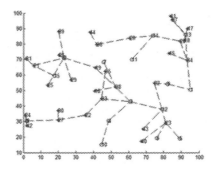

Fig. 3. Spanning tree in GPSR routed at source

Fig. 4. Path tree GPSR using UNIFORM key pre-distribution

The number of keys shared on a keyed path is considered as metric for simulation purposes. Simulation considers source as root of the rooted tree and all other nodes as destinations. Simulation study of GPSR is considered under uniform and non-uniform key distribution scheme and then effect of cell based membership is evaluated on uniform and non-uniform key pre-distributed schemes. The values of simulation parameters are as follows, $c = 2$, $k_1 = 45$, $k_2 = 90$, $N = 45$, $n_1 = 30$, $n_2 = 15$ and $K = 1000$. The deployment area is assumed to be 100×100 with transmission range = 20.

Node 1 is source node and remaining nodes are destination as in Fig. 4. Rooted tree exhibits the connectivity in GPSR under uniform (GPSR-UNIFORM), non-uniform (GPSR-NONUNIFORM) and Local effect GPSR under non-uniform (GPSR-LOC-NONUNIFORM) cases in Figs. 4, 5 and 6 respectively (Fig. 7). The routing length comparison is drawn in Fig. 8 under distinct keyed variants of GPSR.

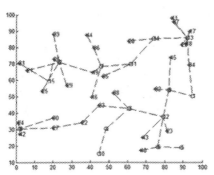

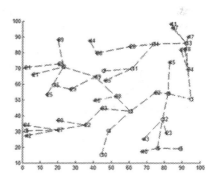

Fig. 5. Path tree GPSR using NON-UNIFORM key pre-distribution

Fig. 6. Routing Tree in GPSR under Local NON-UNIFORM key distribution

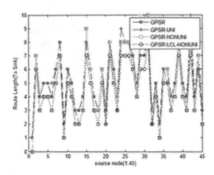 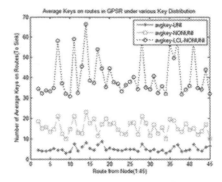

Fig. 7. Route lengths comparison in GPSR under all scenarios

Fig. 8. Comparison of average keys on routes in GPSR, GPSR-NONUNIFORM and GPSR-LCL-NONUNIFORM Key

Figure 8 describes the average number of keys on the path from any destination to source node. The difference in average number of keys on the paths explains the effect of uniform, non-uniform and local effect on non-uniform keying schemes. The performance difference in average keys establishes the superiority of non-uniform keying on uniform keying and further the effect of local cell based membership on non-uniform keying scheme. The extent of improvement ranges from 400% to 600% with respect to uniform keying and about 100% with respect to non-uniform keying scheme.

6   Performance Discussion and Conclusion

The objective of this proposal is to evaluate the impact of location based keying information on the average number of keys in the routes from destination nodes to source nodes. We qualitatively conclude but do not compute that resilience which is measured as the probability that at least one of the key in the link is not disclosed to the attacker. If we can increase the keys in the links we can increase the end-to-end resilience as proposed in [2, 3]. The sole difference between work in [3] and ours is mainly due to introduction of local connectivity which is result of our customized post-deployment keying scheme. The impact of localization without using location information is realized in this paper through simulation of secure GPSR under various configurations.

References

1. Akyildiz, I.F., Su, W., Sankarasubramaniam, Y., Cayirci, E.: Wireless sensor networks: a survey. IEEE Comput. Netw. **38**(4), 393–422 (2002)
2. Traynor, P., Kumar, R., Choi, H., Cao, G., Zhu, S., La Porta, T.: Efficient hybrid security mechanism for heterogeneous sensor networks. IEEE Trans. Mob. Comput. **6**(6), 663–677 (2007)
3. Gu, W., Dutta, N., Chellappan, S., Bai, X.: Providing end-to-end secure communications in wireless sensor networks. IEEE Trans. Netw. Serv. Manag. **8**(3), 205–218 (2011)

4. Kumar, K., Verma, A.K., Patel, R.B.: A location dependent connectivity guarantee key management scheme for heterogeneous wireless sensor networks. J. Adv. Inf. Technol. 3(3), 105–115 (2010)
5. Zhou, L., Haas, Z.J.: Securing ad hoc networks. IEEE Netw. 13(6), 24–30 (1999)
6. Ferng, H.W., Nurhakim, J., Horng, S.J.: Key management protocol with end-to-end data security and key revocation for a multi-BS wireless sensor network. Wireless Netw. 20(4), 625–637 (2014)
7. Khan, Z.S., Moharram, M.M., Alaraj, A., Azam, F.: A group based key sharing and management algorithm for vehicular ad hoc networks. Sci. World J. 2014, 1–8 (2014)
8. Cui, B., Wang, Z., Zhao, B., Liang, X., Ding, Y.: Enhanced key management protocols for wireless sensor networks. Mob. Inf. Syst. 2015, 1–10 (2015)
9. Chauhan, K.K., Tapaswi, S.: A secure key management system in group structured mobile Ad hoc Networks. In: Proceedings of the International Conference on IEEE Wireless Communications, Networking and Information Security (WCNIS), Beijing, China, pp. 307–311, 25–27 June 2010
10. Cho, J.H., Chen, R., Chan, K.S.: Trust threshold based public key management in mobile ad hoc networks. Ad Hoc Netw. 44, 58–75 (2016)
11. Narula, P., Dhurandher, S.K., Misra, S., Woungang, I.: Security in mobile ad-hoc networks using soft encryption and trust-based multi-path routing. Comput. Commun. 31(4), 760–769 (2008)
12. Lu, R., Cao, Z., Wang, L., Sun, C.: A secure anonymous routing protocol with authenticated key exchange for ad hoc networks. Comp. Stand. Inter. 29(5), 521–527 (2007)
13. Friginal, J., de Andrés, D., Ruiz, J.C., Martínez, M.: REFRAHN: a resilience evaluation framework for ad hoc routing protocols. Comput. Netw. 82, 114–134 (2015)
14. Patwardhan, A., Parker, J., Iorga, M., Joshi, A., Karygiannis, T., Yesha, Y.: Threshold-based intrusion detection in ad hoc networks and secure AODV. Ad Hoc Netw. 6(4), 578–599 (2008)
15. Akbani, R., Korkmaz, T., Raju, G.V.S.: HEAP: a packet authentication scheme for mobile ad hoc networks. Ad Hoc Netw. 6(7), 1134–1150 (2008)
16. Bhalaji, N., Shanmugam, A.: Dynamic Trust based method to mitigate grey hole attack in mobile adhoc networks. Procedia Eng. 30, 881–888 (2012)
17. Chauhan, K.K., Sanger, A.K.S.: Securing mobile Ad hoc networks: key management and routing, May 2012. arXiv preprint: arXiv:1205.2432
18. Liu, W., Yu, M.: AASR: authenticated anonymous secure routing for MANETs in adversarial environments. IEEE Trans. Veh. Technol. 63(9), 4585–4593 (2014)
19. Heinzelman, W.B., Chandrakasan, A.P., Balakrishnan, H.: An application-specific protocol architecture for wireless microsensor networks. IEEE Trans. Wireless Commun. 1(4), 660–670 (2000)
20. Karp, B., Kung, H.T.: GPSR: greedy perimeter stateless routing for wireless networks. In: Proceedings of the 6th Annual International Conference on Mobile Computing and Networking (MobiCom 2000), pp. 243–254. ACM, New York (2000)

Dynamic Routing Protocol for Virtual Cellular Networks

Farzad Kiani[1][(✉)] and Sayyad Alizadeh[2]

[1] Computer Engineering Department, Engineering and Natural Sciences Faculty,
Istanbul Sabahattin Zaim University, Istanbul, Turkey
Farzad.kiyani@gmail.com
[2] Computer Engineering Department, Engineering Faculty,
Karadeniz Technique University, Trabzon, Turkey
Alizadeh@ktu.edu.tr

Abstract. In this paper, a novel dynamic routing protocol is proposed so it is suitable for port addition, removal and link/port failures. The proposed protocol is favorable for virtual cellular networks and it does not suffer in the transmit power when it needs to rerouting phase. The transmit power of the proposed rerouting is compared with that of the complete power minimized one. The simulation results shows the transmit power and time and number of messages for route reconstruction in the paper protocol is efficient.

Keywords: Virtual cellular networks · Routing · Dynamic routing · Port addition

1 Introduction

A Virtual Cell Network (VCN) is consists of a number of VCs so they have a central port and one more distributed wireless ports. The central port plays network gateway role and another distributed ports are similar to slave nodes that deployed in VC randomly. The group of wireless ports altogether works as a virtual base station. Figure 1 shows an example of VCNs architecture. In the single hop communication method, the wireless ports have directly communication with central port, so, it cause to increasing power consumption and the packets lost. Therefore, a multi-hopping system is a good idea for solving this problem. In the VCNs, many wireless ports can be used in the signal relaying between central port and mobile terminals for data transmission. In these cases, the intermediate nodes are important issue and they must select correctly. For this reason, the routing protocols have high importance in the VCNs. Generally, almost routing protocols in the ad-hoc networks are usable in the VCNs. Especially; the multi-hop based routing algorithms [1, 2]. A suitable routing protocol must spend low power and reach to destination nodes at least hops numbers [3]. Based on the science of computer networks, data transmission has two models. One of them uplink, another is downlink [3].

In Chap. 2, the minimum transmit power algorithm was explained. Using this algorithm, the multi-hop routes in the wireless ports to the central port will determine and each wireless port will notify about the route construction. Because of the malfunction of some ports or some interference obstacles in a link between wireless ports, some link

A. Unal et al. (Eds.): SmartCom 2016, CCIS 628, pp. 460–467, 2016.
DOI: 10.1007/978-981-10-3433-6_55

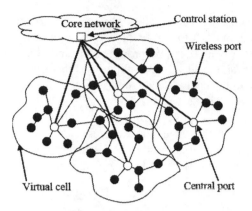

Fig. 1. Virtual cellular concept

or port failure may occur. Besides, continuously changes in the network structure and variable traffic distribution can be caused to ravages and disorder. For solving the problem, the network topology has to resistant against the changes and it must has the ability to add or remove wireless ports to get the adequate network topology.

In those cases of port addition/removal or link/port failures, rerouting is necessary to construct new routes from mobile terminal to the central port. In this chapter, a table-driven adaptive routing algorithm applied for port addition, port removal and link/port failure is proposed. Since the transmit power of the reconstructed route by this rerouting algorithm may not be perforce the minimum transmission power, the transmit power of the adaptive rerouting is compared with that of the complete power minimized one. The time and number of messages for route reconstruction are theoretically analyzed, and the transmit power efficiency is evaluated by computer simulation. Hybrid ARQ (HARQ) with Turbo codes was first proposed in [4]. Turbo encoder is usually followed by a puncture that punctures the encoded sequences to obtain higher rate codes. In [5] it is shown that Rate Compatible Punctured Turbo codes (RCPT) used in HARQ in a manner similar to Rate Compatible Punctured Convolution codes [6] can achieve enhanced throughput performance over an additive white Gaussian noise (AWGN) channel. Ji and Stark [7] compared the throughput of RCPT in hybrid ARQ scheme and normal ARQ schemes. In this paper, the performance of different HARQ schemes is compared and the effect of various system parameters is like to the frame length, the fading rate, the factor of spreading, the diversity antennas number [8] and the of transmissions and users numbers. In addition, propagation parameters like the fading rate and the power delay profile of the multipath channel (number of paths and profile shape) on the RCPT HARQ has been analyzed.

2 Dynamic Routing Protocol

For the complete power minimized rerouting algorithm, to decrease the interference power and increase the frequency efficiency, a routing algorithm that minimizes the total uplink transmit power while limiting the hops number was introduced in [9]. After a port addition or removal and port/link failure, the rerouting performs the same operation as the original routing. In order to reduce the number of messages for rerouting after a port addition and removal or failure, we propose an adaptive routing algorithm. After a port addition or removal, the adaptive rerouting uses the original routing information. It should be noted that the newly added wireless ports only work as end-ports and do not contribute in any other route as a relaying port.

Port addition: For the adaptive routing, Fig. 2 shows an example of the route construction process in a VCN with four wireless ports (K = 4) and the allowable maximum hops number being four (N = 4). Before a new port #3 addition, routes from each end-port toward the network central port are constructed. The route reconstruction algorithm is as follows:

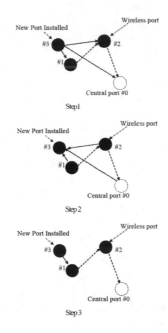

Fig. 2. Example of route construction and message flow for the adaptive rerouting

Step 1: The newly installed wireless port (#3) sends the Route REQuest (RREQ). Step 2: The wireless ports (#2, #1, #0) that received the RREQ, sends the Route REPly (RREP) including the information of its total transmit power until the central port. The step 3: The newly installed port receives the RREPs from the other wireless ports, computes its minimum transmission power and send the route discovery notification packet to its immediate previous port (#1).

Port Removal/Failure: For the complete power minimized rerouting algorithm, after a port removal or failure, the routing restarts again to construct the minimum transmission power routes between wireless ports and central port. Therefore, the time spent during the route reconstruction is expected to be as long as the route construction time. In order to reduce the route reconstruction time, a routing table is used to store not only the information in the RREQ of the previous port, but also the RREQ of a certain number of candidates of previous wireless ports. As the number of candidates becomes larger, the routing table in each wireless port becomes larger too. If the information of only one previous port is stored in the routing table, this port may be the failed or the removed port and the route reconstruction algorithm may fail. Therefore, to reduce the memory size in each wireless port, we assume that each wireless port only stores in its routing table the information of two different candidates of previous port.

Figure 3 shows an example of the route reconstruction process in a VCN with 7 wireless ports and N = 4. Route reconstruction algorithm is as follows:

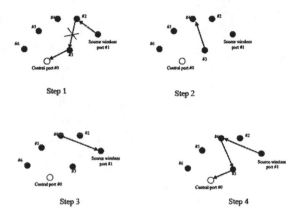

Fig. 3. Example of route reconstruction and message flow

Step 1: A port #2 is removed from the constructed route, and the port removal notification message is sent in VC. Step 2: The wireless port #3 receives the message, and sends a new route reconstruction message to its other previous port #4 including the removed wireless port ID #2. Step 3: Since the candidate port of previous port of port #4 for the minimum transmit power, route is the removed port #2. Port #4 relays the route reconstruction message to its other candidate port of previous port #1 for the second minimum transmit power route. Step 4: The source wireless port receives the route reconstruction message and sends the route discovery notification packet to the central port.

The RCPT encoder and decoder are illustrated in Fig. 1. The RCPT encoder consists of a turbo encoder followed by a puncture and a buffer. We can reach to family of RCPT codes by puncturing the coded bits of a rate 1/R turbo code.

Each output bit stream that it is reached by the turbo code is punctured with P period time. The puncturing patterns for R bit streams from the turbo encoder (R = 3 in this paper) are demonstrated by an matrix R × P, where the first row of the matrix expresses the puncturing pattern for the first bit stream (r = 0~R−1). The various sequences obtained after puncturing, are saved for possible re-transmissions in the buffer.

The RCPT decoder consists of a turbo decoder, a de-puncture, a buffer. The de-puncture combines the newly received sequence with the previously received sequences (stored in the buffer) to form a lower rate code and substitutes the unsent bits by a 0. The R sequences (corresponding to R bit streams at the transmitter side) are as input to the turbo decoder, which is an iterative decoder. The various ARQ schemes considered here are obtained from the rate 1/3 (= 1/R) turbo code by puncturing. They are shown in the Table 1. I and II types hybrid ARQ schemes are considered.

Table 1. Turbo encoder/decoder parameters

Encoder	Rate	Lowest rate 1/3
	Component encoder	(13,15) RSC
	Interleaver	S-random (S = K1/2)
Decoder	Component decoder	Log-MAP
	Number of iteration	8

3   System Model

In VCNs, the propagation channel is modeled by product of distance dependent path loss, log-normally distributed shadowing loss and multipath fading channel gain. We assume an L-path Rayleigh fading channel and an ideal rake combining. The transmit power $P_t(i)$ from port #i to port #j is reachable by:

$$P_t(i) = \frac{P_{req}}{d_{i,j}^{-\alpha} 10^{-\frac{\eta_{i,j}}{10}} \sum_{l=0}^{L-1} \left|\xi_{i,j}(l)\right|^2} \tag{1}$$

where, α is the lost routes exponent, P_{req} is the required received signal power, and $d_{i,j}$ is distance, $\eta_{i,j}$ and $\xi_{i,j}$ are shadowing loss (in dB). If power delay in multi-hopping channel and $\{\xi_{i,j}\}$ are independent complex Gaussian variables with zero-mean and $E\left[\left|\xi_{i,j}\right|^2\right] = 1/L$, $E[*]$ demonstrates the group average operation. If the receiver finds errors in the sequence that is decoded, a packet retransmission is wanted. This packet will be same to pervious packet and it uses the same puncturing matrix. In addition, the mistake packet is stored and combined with the retransmitted packet utilizing the time diversity (TD) effect [10] instead of discarding.

The normalized average power (P_{norm}) is related to the average total transmission power. For example, P_{norm} is reachable as followed formula with i = 0 (source wireless port) and j = n (central port). Therefore, the P_{norm} is reachable by:

$$P_{norm} = \frac{E[P_{total}]}{E[P_{single-hop}]} = \frac{E\left[\sum_{i=0}^{n-1}\left(\frac{P_{req}}{d_{i,i+1}^{-\alpha}10^{-\frac{\eta_{i,i+1}}{10}}\sum_{l=0}^{L-1}|\xi_{i,i+1}(l)|^2}\right)\right]}{E\left[\frac{P_{req}}{d_{0,n}^{-\alpha}10^{-\frac{\eta_{0,n}}{10}}\sum_{l=0}^{L-1}|\xi_{0,n}(l)|^2}\right]} = \frac{E\left[\sum_{i=0}^{n-1}\left(\frac{P_{req}}{d_{i,i+1}^{-\alpha}10^{-\frac{\eta_{i,i+1}}{10}}\sum_{l=0}^{L-1}|\xi_{i,i+1}(l)|^2}\right)\right]}{E\left[\frac{P_{req}}{d_{0,n}^{-\alpha}10^{-\frac{\eta_{0,n}}{10}}\sum_{l=0}^{L-1}|\xi_{0,n}(l)|^2}\right]} \tag{2}$$

4   Performance Simulations and Analysis

To evaluate the increase in the relay time after the route reconstruction, we measure the cumulative distribution of the hops number after a port addition and removal for both the adaptive and complete rerouting algorithms. Figure 4 shows the gathered propagation of the hops number after a port addition with N as a parameter for 3.5, 7 dB, and K = 50 for both the adaptive and complete rerouting. It is seen that the hops number for the adaptive algorithm is almost the same as that of the complete one. As a conclusion, the adaptive algorithm does not increase the hops number in the multi-hop route after a port addition. Figure 5 shows the gathered propagation of the hops number after a port removal with N as a parameter for 3.5, 7 dB, and K = 50 for both the adaptive and complete rerouting. It is seen that the hops number in the multi-hop routes increases by 5% for the adaptive routing compared to the complete one. It is seen that the number of hops increases for the adaptive rerouting.

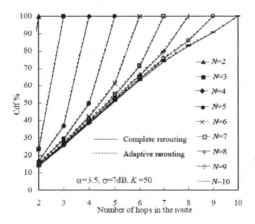

Fig. 4. Cdf of the number of hops in the route after a port addition with N as a parameter

Figure 6 shows the probability of having different reconstructed routes for both adaptive and complete rerouting with N as a parameter for 3.5, 7 dB, and K = 50 for port addition and removal cases. Apparently, the probability of having different reconstructed routes is much larger for port removal compared to the port addition, and it is around 23% for port removal and 7% for port addition when N = 10. This result explains the increased hops number for port removal of Fig. 5.

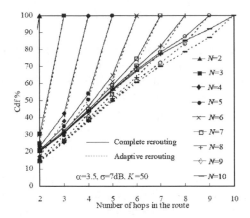

Fig. 5. Cdf of the number of hops in the route after a port removal with N as a parameter

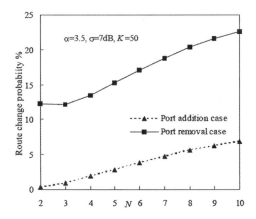

Fig. 6. Probability of having different reconstructed routes using adaptive and complete rerouting algorithms

5   Conclusion

In this paper, an adaptive rerouting algorithm is proposed for port addition and removal/ failure in a VCN and we compared it with the complete power minimized rerouting algorithm. For the complete routing, the route reconstruction operation restarts in any port addition or removal; therefore, the constructed routes are always the minimum transmit power routes. However, the routing time and messages number are in the same order as the original routing. On the other hand, in the adaptive routing, the information stored during the original routing are used in order to reduce the routing time and messages number. However, the constructed routes may not be perforce the minimum transmission power. The routing time and the maximum messages number were discussed. It was found that the adaptive routing reduces significantly the routing time and the maximum messages number for the port addition and the port removal. The overall transmission power for the complete and adaptive routing were evaluated by computer simulation for both port addition and removal cases. It was found that the total transmit power for the adaptive routing is almost the same as the complete one. It was shown that the hops number in the route after a port addition is the same using either the adaptive or the complete algorithms; however, after a port removal, the hops number in the route increases by 5% when using the adaptive routing.

References

1. Tao, J., Wu, Y.: An overview: peak-to-average power ratio reduction techniques for OFDM signals. IEEE Trans. Broadcast. **54**(2), 257–268 (2008)
2. Müller, S.H., Huber, J.B.: A novel peak power reduction scheme for OFDM. In: Proceedings of the IEEE PIMRC, Helsinki, Finland, pp. 1090–1094 (1997)
3. Lim, D.W.: A new SLM OFDM scheme with low complexity for PAPR reduction. IEEE Signal Process. Lett. **12**(2), 93–96 (2005)
4. Wang, C.L., Ku, S.J.: Novel conversion matrices for simplifying the IFFT computation of an SLM-Based PAPR reduction scheme for OFDM systems. IEEE Trans. Commun. **57**(7), 1903–1907 (2009)
5. Lu, G., Wu, P., Aronsson, D.: Peak-to-average power ratio reduction in OFDM using cyclically shifted phase sequences. IET Commun. **1**(6), 1146–1151 (2007)
6. Hill, G., Faulkner, M., Singh, J.: Cyclic shifting and time inversion of partial transmit sequences to reduce the peak-to-average power ratio in OFDM, pp. 1256–1259. Proc. IEEE PIMRC, London, UK (2000)
7. Sklar, B.: A primer on turbo code concepts. IEEE Commun. Mag. **35**(12), 94–101 (1997)
8. Adachi, F., Ito, S., Ohno, K.: Performance analysis of a time diversity ARQ in land mobile radio. IEEE Trans. Commun. **37**, 177–183 (1989)
9. Ji, T., Stark, W.E.: Turbo-coded ARQ schemes for DS-CDMA data networks over fading and shadowing channels: throughput, delay and energy efficiency. IEEE J. Sel. Areas Commun. **18**, 1355–1364 (2000)
10. Andoh, H., Sawahashi, M., Adachi, F.: Channel estimation filter using time-multiplexed pilot channel for coherent RAKE combining in DSCDMA mobile radio. IEICE Trans. Commun. **E81-B**, 1517–1526 (1998)

Innovative Approach Towards Cooperation Models for Multi-agent Reinforcement Learning (CMMARL)

Deepak A. Vidhate[1(✉)] and Parag Kulkarni[2]

[1] Department of Computer Engineering, College of Engineering,
Shivajinagar, Pune, Maharashtra, India
dvidhate@yahoo.com
[2] EKLaT Research Lab, Shivajinagar, Pune, Maharashtra, India
parag.india@gmail.com

Abstract. We propose an innovative approach towards Cooperation Models for Multi-agent Reinforcement Learning (CMMARL) using reinforcement learning methods. Communication methods for reinforcement learning depend on multiagent scheme is proposed & implemented. Different cooperation methods for cooperative reinforcement learning based on expertness measure of each agent proposed here i.e. group method, dynamic method, goal-oriented method and expert agent method. Implementation results have demonstrated that the suggested communication and cooperation methods are able to accelerate the aggregation of the agents that accomplish best action strategies. This approach is developed for dynamic products availability in a three retailer shops in the market. Retailers can cooperate with each other and can get benefit from cooperative information by their own policies that accurately represent their goals and interests. The retailers are the learning agents in the problem and apply reinforcement learning to learn cooperatively from the situation. By making considerable theory on the dealer's inventory strategy, refill period, and entry procedure of the customers, the problem turn out to be Markov decision process model thus facilitating to apply learning algorithms.

Keywords: Cooperation models · Multi-agent learning · Reinforcement learning

1 Introduction

Hundreds of shops across a region retailing thousands of products to millions of buyers are a good model of market chain. The sale point of each retailer confirms the information of each transfer i.e. date, buyer ID code, products purchased and their spent sum. This naturally yield huge amount of records every day. If accumulated records are analyzed and turned into information then it becomes useful so that we can utilize an illustration to build forecasts. We can only gather information and expect to take out the answers to questions from data [1].

It is considered that it presents a procedure to facilitate the demonstration the observed data. Even if it is not known the highlights of the procedure responsible for the creation of

© Springer Nature Singapore Pte Ltd. 2016
A. Unal et al. (Eds.): SmartCom 2016, CCIS 628, pp. 468–478, 2016.
DOI: 10.1007/978-981-10-3433-6_56

records – for instance, buyer behavior – it is known that it is not totally accidental. Public do not walk to markets and purchase items at casual. We may be unable to recognize the procedure totally, but still we can build a *useful and good approximation*. These temporary computations might not give details of everything, but may still be able to construct for some part of the data. There are many real world problems that engage more than one thing for maximization of results [2]. Retailers have always encountered the difficulty of sale the right goods that would produce the highest income for them. Finding the right products for a buyer or a service is a difficult task. In forthcoming time, retailers would suggest special package, simply customized for each purchaser, simply for the instant on the whole thing (correct item to the correct purchaser at the correct period) [3]. Different parameters need to be considered in this: variation in seasons, the dependency of items, special schemes, discount, market conditions. Retailers can cooperate with each other for yield maximization in different situations [3, 4].

We consider three retailer shops in the market. A scenario of four retailer shops in which shop A sales clothes, shop B sales jewelry, and shop C sales footwear. The internals of all retailers A, B, and C can be modeled to build a system to automate some features of the marketing process. The solution is to allow the various stores to create their own policies that accurately represent their goals and interests. The goal of each retailer is to maximize the profit by an increase in sale [4]. The paper presents some contributions as given below

– Three seller retail stores are considered in this paper. These stores sell a specific product and gives major concessions for customers buying multiple items.
– We propose an innovative approach towards Cooperation Models for Multi-agent Reinforcement Learning (CMMARL) using reinforcement learning methods. Communication methods for reinforcement learning build on multiagent scheme is proposed & implemented [4, 5].

The paper is ordered as given. Section 2, describes innovative approach towards Cooperation Models for Multiagent Reinforcement Learning (CMMARL). Section 3, illustrate the system kinetics of retail shops modeled by Markov decision procedure. Section 4 describes a simulation results all four methods with continuing price as the profit parameter. Section 5 describes concluding remark.

2 Cooperation Models for Multi-agent Reinforcement Learning (CMMARL)

The communication in multiagent reinforcement can construct an advanced set of performances gained from the agents' proceedings. Piece of the performance group (i.e. a universal action plan) is distributed among the agents through a *Limited Action Plan* (Q_i). Typically such limited strategies hold partial knowledge about the situation. These polices can be integrated to enhance the total of the incomplete reinforcements achieved using adequate communication model. The action strategies are produced by means of multiagent Q-learning algorithm by collecting the reinforcements and building the agents to move towards the best plan Q^*. When strategies $Q_1,...,Q_x$ are integrated, it is feasible to develop new plan that is *Universal Action Plan* ($UAP = \{UAP_1, ..., UAP_x\}$), in which U*AP_i* indicates the **excellent rewards** obtained by the agent i throughout the learning method [5].

Algorithm 1 describes the *share_plan* algorithm which distributes the agents' learning details. The plans are calculated by the Q-learning algorithm for each model. The excellent rewards are given toward *UAP* that forms a collection of the excellent accumulated reinforcements by the agents. These reinforcements will be again distributed by means of the additional agents [5, 6]. Cooperation is carried out by the transformation of limited reinforcements as *UAP* is predicted by means of the excellent rewards. A *value* function is used to find out the best policy among the early states and target state for a given strategy that estimates *UAP* with the best rewards. The value function is determined by the counting of stages the agent required to arrive at the target-state and the total of the obtained values in the policy among each start state and the target state. Figure 1 shows communication between the agents [5].

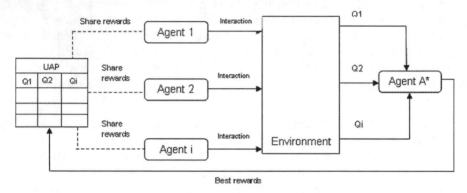

Fig. 1. Cooperation system

Figure 1 show ability of the agents to maintain with the information of all by the communication. The agent *i* make use of the Q-learning algorithm to produce and accumulate the reinforcements in Q_i. As soon as the agent *i* go from a start state to the target-state with the reduced rate, the agent would be capable to allocate these reinforcements (collective rewards as given in Algorithm 2) with new agents using a **communication method.** Agents can update their knowledge after accepted the reinforcement transferred of each incomplete policy Q_i, and interact into the environment using the *UAP*.

Algorithm 1 uses following definitions:

- o   set of states S = {s_1,............,s_m} and set of agents I = {i_1,..........., i_x};
- o   set of actions A = {$a1$, ...,an}
- o   Universal Action Plan UAP = {UAP_1,..........., UAP_x},
      where UAP_i stand for the incomplete plan of the agent i;
- o   reward function st(S)→ST and learning table Q_i : (S x A) → R
- o   coordination method set M = {group, dynamic, goal oriented, expert agent};
- o   function *cooperate:* (e x t x s x a x I) → {true, false} that describes the stop
      condition and coordination methods. e→episode   t→technique   s→ state
      a→ action i→ agent

Algorithm 1: Multi-agent Reinforcement Learning Algorithm

   Algorithm *share_plan* (I, technique)

   Table: Q_i, Q*, UAP;

   Environment: e

  1.   for each agent i ε I do
  2.   for each s ε S & a ε A do
  3. Q_i(s, a)← 0;
  4. UAP_i(s, a)← 0;
  5.   end
  6.   end
  7.   episode ← 0;
  8.   for each agent i ε I do
  9.   while not Q-Learning stop condition is arrived do
 10.   episode ← episode +1;
 11.   select s ε S, a ε A
 12.   renew:
 13.   renew Q(s, a) as
         Q(s, a)← Q(s, a) +α (r +γ Q(s', a') – Q(s, a))
 14.   *cooperate (episode, technique, s, a, i);*
 15.   end while
 16. end for
 17. for each agent i ε I do
 18. Q_i←UAP;
 19. end for
 20. return

Algorithm 1 can be explained like:

Lines 1-4: Initialization Q_i(s, a) and UAP_i(s, a)

Line 8: Communication by means of the agents *i* ε I;

Line 9-10: Agents cooperate till the target state is found;

Line 12: Renew rule which calculates the reinforcement value;

Line 14: The *cooperate* task choose a cooperation method. *episode, technique, s, a,* are the parameters, in which *episode* is existing iteration, coordination *technique* is {*group, dynamic, goal-oriented, expert_agent method*}, *s* and *a* are state and action selected correspondingly;

Lines 17-18: Q_i of agent *i* ε I is modified with UAP_i.

2.1 Expertness Based Rewards

More skilled agents find more reinforcements and penalties of the group. Whether the received signal is reward or punishment is depend on the agents expertise acquired by each agent through reward signal. As a result, if the group obtains a reward then expert agents will acquire extra reinforcements as compared to other agent. On the contrary, other agents get extra penalty as compared to expert agents when the team gets penalty. Skilled agents frequently perform superior than other agents. They get more opportunity to carry out right action as compared to other less skilled agents. Less expertise agents have incomplete information and they cannot perform as well as skilled agents. The possibility of faults occurrence by such team of agents is more than the skilled agents. Reinforcement distribution is carried out as per agents' expertise rank. Agents obtain reward indicator (reinforcement and penalty) as follows [6]:

$$r_i = R_x \frac{e_i}{\sum_{j=1}^{N} e_j} \tag{1}$$

2.2 Expertness Measure

Expertness measure considers both rewards and punishments as a sign of being experienced. It means that failures and successes, weighted by the value of reward and punishment signals, are both valuable for the agent. This is the sum of the absolute value of the reward signals [6, 7].

$$e_i = \sum_{t=1}^{now} |r_i(t)| \tag{2}$$

2.3 Cooperation Methods

Different cooperation methods for cooperative reinforcement learning based on expertness measure of each agent are proposed here [5–7]:

(i)   *Group method* – Expertness based rewards are distributed in a sequence of steps.
(ii) *Dynamic method* – Expertness based reinforcement are distributed
(iii) *Goal-oriented method* – distributing the total of expertness based rewards when the agent arrives at the target-state (S_{goal}).
(iv) *Expert Agent method* – Sharing the learning only between the expert agents learning. The cooperation communication methods algorithm is shown below.

Algorithm 2. Cooperation model

Fcooperate (episode, technique,s,a,i) /*cooperation between agents as four cases*/

   q : count of sequence

    1.   switch technique
    2.   Case "group":
    3.   if episode mod q = 0 then
    4.   get_Ereward(e_i, e_j, N, R);
    5.   get_Policy(Q_i, Q*,UAP_i);
    6.   end if
    7.   Case "dynamic":
    8.   get_Ereward (e_i, e_j, N, R);
    9.   r ← $\sum_{j=1}^{x} Qj(s,a)$;
    10. Q_i(s,a)← r;
    11.   get_Policy(Q_i, Q*,UAP_i);
    12.   Case "goal-oriented":
    13.   if S = S_{goal} then
    14.   get_Ereward (e_i, e_j, N, R);
    15.   r ← $\sum_{j=1}^{x} Qj(s,a)$;
    16. Q_i(s,a)← r;
    17.   get_Policy(Q_i,Q*,UAP_i);
    18.   end if
    19.   Case "expert agent":
    20.   get_ExpertAgent(e_a);
    21.   If e_i= e_a then
    22.   get_Ereward (e_i, e_j, N, R);
    23.   r ← $\sum_{j=1}^{x} Qj(s,a)$;
    24. Q_i(s,a)← r;
    25.   gct_Policy(Q_i, Q*,UAP_i);
    26.   end if
    27. end switch

Algorithm 3. get_Policy

Function get_Policy(Q_i, Q*,UAP_i)   /* find out universal agent policy */

    1. for each agent i ε I do
    2.   for each s ε S do
    3.   if value(Q_i, s) ≦ value(Q*,s) then
    4. UAP_i(s,a) ← Q_i(s,a);
    5.   end if
    6.   end for
    7. end for

Algorithm 4 uses following definitions:

R: total teams reward signals

e_i: expertise of ith agent

r_i: section of ith agent from reward signal

N: number of agents

Algorithm 4. get_Ereward

Function get_Ereward(e_i, e_j, N, R)   /* calculate the expertness based reward */

   1.   for each agent i ∈ I do

   2.   for each s ∈ S do

   3.   get_Expertness(e_i);

   4. $r_i = Rx \dfrac{e_i}{\sum_{j=1}^{N} e_j}$

   5.   end for

   6.   end for

   7.   return r_i

Algorithm 5. get_Expertness

Function get_Expertness(r_i)   /* calculate expertness of agent */

   1.   for each agent i ∈ I do

   2.   for each s ∈ S do

   3. $e_i = \sum_{t=1}^{now} |r_i(t)|$

   4.   end for

   5.   end for

   6.   return e_i

Algorithm 6. get_ExpertAgent

Function get_ExpertAgent(e_i) /*find out expert agent based on expertness value*/

   1.   for each agent i ∈ I do

   2.   for each s ∈ S do

   3.   get_expertness(ei);

   4.   If ei > ej then

   5.   ea← ei;

   6.   end for

   7.   end for

   8.   return ea;

Group Method: Agents gather Expertness based reinforcement acquired from its actions during the learning progression. At the last part of the sequence (step q), every agent throw out the cost of the Q_j to the *UAP*. If the reinforcement cost is appropriate, i.e. it enhances the efficiency of another agents for the given state (Algorithm 3 line 3) the agents will afterward contribute to these expertise base reinforcements (Algorithm 3 line 4). Agent will persist to utilize its reinforcement with the intention for congregating latest values [8].

Dynamic Method: The communication in the *dynamic method* is obtained as: every action carried out by the agent generates a reward value (positive or negative), that is the total of the collected expertness based reinforcements to all agents to the action *a* obtained in state *s* (Algorithm 2 line 7). Every agent cooperates to maximize the reinforcement value complying its own policy. The aim of this method is to gather superior expertness based reinforcements in the Q_i (Algorithm 1 line 19) [9].

Goal-Oriented Method: The coordination happens as agent arrives at its target-state (Algorithm 2 line 11). Agent cooperates through situation intended to congregate maximum number of expertness based rewards. It is essential for the reason that in the *Goal-oriented method* the agent distributes its reinforcement with a changeable count of occurrences. This coordination method utilizes as a quick collection of expertness based reinforcements collected by the agent during the communication. When the agent arrives at a target-state it throws out the cost of the obtained reinforcements in the situation to the *UAP* [10, 11].

Expert Agents Method: Sharing the learning only among the expert agents learning [11].

3   Model Design

We considered the case with wedding season. Beginning from deciding the venue, booking the caterers, decoration, invitation cards, photography, beautician, cosmetics, shopping of clothes, jewelry & other accessories for bride and groom. Such seasonable situations can be realistically implemented as follows: Customer who would go for clothing shop certainly will buy jewelry, footwear, and other accessories. Customer who selects the wedding venue would certainly opt for caterers and decorators. In such scenarios, retailers of different products can come together and jointly satisfy customer requirements and would achieve the benefit of an increase in the product sale. Figure 2 display this scenario.

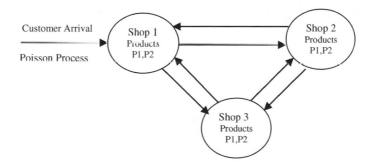

Fig. 2. A model of a retail store with three retailers

Following is the mathematical notation for the proposed methods.

- Buyers arrive as a Poisson process with rate λ at the market.
- The shopper display per unit product price *p* to the arriving customers.
- The shopper has finite stock ability I_{max} and uses a permanent reorder rule for refilling; This is traditional (*q, r*) plan of stock.

We define action set as the sale of the possible product. i.e. A = {Products P1, P2, P3 ... P10} and action a A. State of the system is a queue of the customer in the particular month for the given shop agent. So state is described by a vector X = {TID, Customer, Product Price, Month} = {TID, x1, x2, m} where

TID = Transaction ID.
x1 = {Y, M, O} → customer age vector i.e. young, middle and Old age customer
x2 = {H, M, L} → product price vector i.e. High, Medium, Low
m = {1, 2, 3, 4 ... 12} → month of product sale

The retailer instantaneously selects the products at casual time gap in order to increase the probable benefits. Under the above Markovian distributional assumptions, the dynamic product problem can be reduced to a Markov Decision Process. Retailers do not know the facts about the distributions of original model and about customers' behavior. These retailers find out about their mainly profitable products over time using Reinforcement Learning. A decision is required to be made concerning whether to accept or deny the customer request when the customer places a demand for a product. Action space, which is general to all the decision-making states is, A = {Product} i.e. select the products to sold by the retailer. Another retailer observes the action taken by the first retailer and be prepared to sell his product.

4   Result

Four cooperation models i.e. group, dynamic, goal oriented and expert agent methods are implemented. Result shows how a shop agent successfully uses reinforcement learning in selecting products dynamically in order to make best use of its profit matrix. In cooperative learning multiple agents use each other information and action set. Each one receives its Q table after learning cooperatively from each other using group, dynamic, goal oriented and expert agent methods. Agents learn cooperatively to

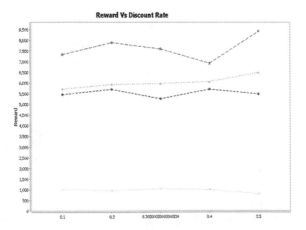

Fig. 3. Reward vs episode for four cooperation methods (Color figure online)

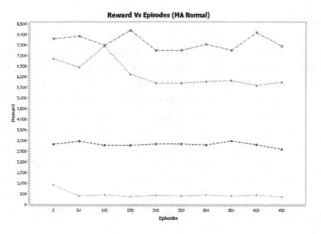

Fig. 4. Reward vs learning rate for four cooperation methods (Color figure online)

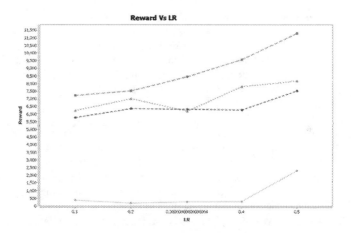

Fig. 5. Reward vs discount rate for four cooperation methods (Color figure online)

increase the sale of products so as to maximize the profit. Figures 3, 4 and 5 shows graphical representation of Rewards Vs Episodes and Rewards Vs Learning Rate and Rewards Vs Discount Rate for all four cooperation methods i.e. group, dynamic, goal oriented and expert agent methods through yellow color line, blue color line, green color line and red color line respectively.

Expert agent method and goal oriented method shown by red color line and green color line in the graph performs better than dynamic method and group method shown by blue color line and yellow color lines in all the situations.

5 Conclusion

Dynamic customer behavior is clearly understood using the new approach. Agents learn cooperatively with expertise to increase the sale of products so as to maximize the profit. By knowing the exchanging the Q function through four different methods i.e. group, dynamic, goal oriented and expert agent method, the shop agent calculate best probable product that gives maximum profit to it. The proposed models show how shop agents successfully use cooperation in establishing products dynamically in order to make best use of its profit matrix. Cooperation Models of Multi-agent Reinforcement Learning (CMMARL) shows that such methods can put in to a fast linking of agents that replace rewards. It also indicates that the cooperation methods introduce a healthy performance in high-dimensional, incomplete and complicated situation. It provides the help to replace of the most excellent reinforcement to accomplish a universal action plan.

References

1. Al-Khatib, A.M.: Cooperative machine learning method. World Comput. Sci. Inf. Technol. J. (WCSIT) **1**(9), 380–383 (2011). ISSN: 2221-0741
2. Araabi, B.N., Mastoureshgh, S., Ahmadabadi, M.N.: A study on expertise of agents and its effects on cooperative Q-learning. IEEE Trans. Evol. Comput. **14**, 23–57 (2010)
3. Raju, C.V.L., Narahari, Y., Ravikumar, K.: Learning dynamic prices in electronic retail markets with customer segmentation. Ann. Oper. Res. **143**, 59–75 (2006). doi:10.1007/s10479-006-7372-3
4. Hamid, R., Vengerov, B.D.: Learning, cooperation, and coordination in multi-agent systems. In: Proceedings of 9th IEEE International Conference on Fuzzy Systems (2000)
5. Enembreck, F., Borges, A.P., Ribeiro, R.: Interaction models for multiagent reinforcement learning. In: CIMCA 2008, IAWTIC 2008, and ISE 2008 (2008)
6. Tao, J.-Y., Li, D.-S.: Cooperative strategy learning in multi-agent environment with continuous state space. In: IEEE International Conference on Machine Learning and Cybernetics, pp. 2107–2111 (2006)
7. Gao, L.-M., Zeng, J., Wu, J., Li, M.: Cooperative reinforcement learning algorithm to distributed power system based on multi-agent. In: 2009 3rd International Conference on Power Electronics Systems and Applications (2009)
8. Panait, L., Luke, S.: Cooperative multi-agent learning: the state of the art. J. Auton. Agents Multi Agent Syst. **11**(3), 387–434 (2005)
9. Xu, L.-H., Xia, X.-H., Luo, Q.: The study of reinforcement learning for traffic self-adaptive control under multiagent markov game environment. Hindawi Publishing Corporation, Mathematical Problems in Engineering (2013)
10. Nagendra Prasad, M.V., Lesser, V.R.: Learning situation-specific coordination in cooperative multi-agent systems. Auton. Agents Multi Agent Syst. **2**(2), 173–207 (1999)
11. Kinney, M., Tsatsoulis, C.: Learning communication strategies in multiagent systems. J. Appl. Intell. **9**(1), 71–91 (1998)

Food Intake Detection System Through Autodietry Using Acoustic Sensors

Jyoti Patil and Prashant Salunke[✉]

Electronics and Telecommunication Department,
SITRC, University of Pune, Nashik, India
itmejyoti.patil@yahoo.com, prashant.salunkhe@sitrc.org

Abstract. Nutrition and obesity related diseases are now become dangerous to human health. Now a days people go on dieting and not taking proper care of their health and food intake calories. So to solve these problems a system is developed which is automatic dietary food intake detection system by using wearable sensors. It consists of embedded system and signal processing system in which food intake is sensed by high fidelity microphone and signal is pre-processed by embedded hardware part and through bluetooth it is sent to smart phone. Here we have used hidden markov models to recognize chewing and swallowing events to extract time and frequency domain features as well as volume and weight of food intake. Algorithm for decision is developed for types of food detection. For e.g. in diet control patient suffering from diabetes precisely monitor daily food intake. An application on smart phone is developed to show the results of food intake as well as give guidance for better eating habits.

Keywords: Food intake detection · Acoustic sensor · Decision tree · Embedded system

1 Introduction

To maintain healthy life is very important in our daily life, for that daily food intake should be proper and if any abnormalities takes places due to imbalance leads to diseases like obesity etc. [1]. If proper treatment is not taken then severe disorders may take place. A prime solution to resolve these problems is to measure and monitor daily nutrients and calorie balance [2]. Various methods are there to measure food intake but they are either not accurate and some are not properly existing.

For this we propose Automatic dietary for food intake recognition system in which food is recognize through a wearable sensor. The system is made of two blocks (i) Embedded system containing hardware block & (ii) Smartphone application. Hardware collects and processes food intake data. A wearable sensor is in necklace form which is wear around neck and picks up acoustic sound signals and non invasive manner. The data which is collected is send Via Bluetooth module to Smartphone.

Food type detection includes various steps. The sound signals are first collected together and then they are processed through by hidden markov models to detect chew and swallow events via fluid intake [3]. Through this events we extract the time and

© Springer Nature Singapore Pte Ltd. 2016
A. Unal et al. (Eds.): SmartCom 2016, CCIS 628, pp. 479–486, 2016.
DOI: 10.1007/978-981-10-3433-6_57

frequency domain and non linear features. A simple decision tree is developed to recognize the type of food intake. For this, experiments are conducted for 4 different types of food. The accuracy is calculated and identified based on chewing and swallowing events which is nearly 86.6%. To Identify liquid and solid food accuracy is 97.6% and 99.7%.

2   Overview

Various researches had been done till now in the field of food detection system. Meyer et al. prepared a method to study digestive behaviour of swallow and chew of any type of food. The main moto is to investigate various different types of food consumption and to produce weight and volume of food energy intake. The monitoring is done via sensor located below the ear strain.

Amft [4] presented a sensor which is used in ear in form of pad type to monitor and collect air feelings of food chew. He collected all the features from chew sounds and averaged using sliding windows. He recorded 375 chewing events for 4 different foods and 86.6% accuracy was obtained. But main problem with his system is, it requires various different microphones to collect audio or acoustic signals. Thus such type of system is not feasible for users.

Pabler and wolff [5] planned a one such model that is based on sound developed during food intake, the signals are then recorded by mini microphone in the outer part of ear canal. In this system hidden markov models are used for detection of chew and swallow results. Microphones used are not comfortable to wear. RFID tags are used and placed on food packets to detect and distinguish the content and amount of food taken by people. The amount of food ate is recorded by dining table but this sensor is still under development and few limitations are there. But here also some disadvantage found, i.e. it is having some restriction to only one location for keeping record of various foods. And system is more costly and extra efforts are required to place tags on the food.

Lester et al. [6] presented a method which consumes electrical PH and sensors to detect food intake. They prefer a various types of liquids which gathers PH, conductivity, and light spectrum to finger print. Unfortunately, none of the method came into existence and worked out properly due to some disadvantages and finally this food intake detection system become user friendly with the people.

3   Proposed System

There are two main units in auto dietary system, i.e. one is embedded system used for audio data gaining & pre-giving out. Second is food type detection which is done in smart phone using application apps developed in it and data is collected in data base.

3.1 Audio Sensors

A high fidelity & precise throat micro phones collect audio signals at the time of eating. The wearable sensor called microphone is placed over the neck. It converts vibrations from the skin to acoustic signals it connects only high quality signals for the purpose of automatic dietary system by reducing interference of noise. It is comfortable to wear. The throat microphone has frequency range of 20 Hz–20 kHz which is suitable for collecting chew & swallow sound (Fig. 1).

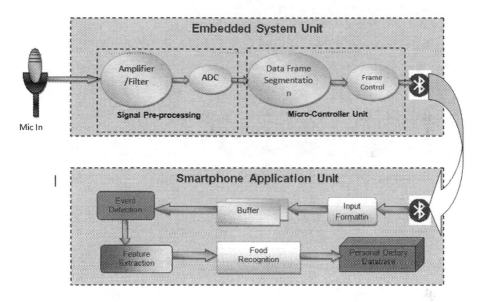

Fig. 1. System architecture of automatic food dietary

3.2 Hardware System

An embedded hardware system is actually developed for data working and it is transmitted when collected from throat microphone. When data is collected from throat micro phone it is amplified and filtered for high quality signals. Through analog to digital converter signals are converted into proper format [7]. These converted signals are send to micro controller through I2C. The sound signals are divided in to frames for further giving out. The micro controller frames raw signals from throat micro-phones which is MSP430 microcontroller [8]. The data frames are send to a Blue-tooth module & further send to smart phone. A lipo battery is introduced to energies the hardware system (Fig. 2).

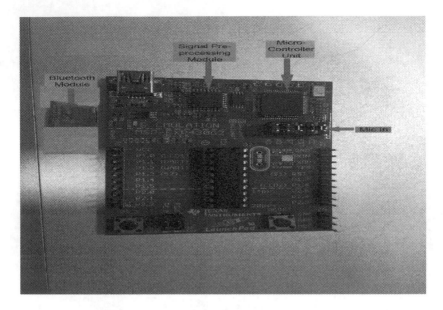

Fig. 2. Hardware board

3.3 Smartphone Application

In smart phone application, B4A (basic for android) software is used for creating activity layout in apps. Application on smart phone works with two roles. First is, it works on food type recognition & second, it performs as data manger & provides to interface to users when user begins to eat, system will recognize nature of food and store the data in data base. The user checks the records & gets suggestions on healthy eating habits by analyzing data (Figs. 3 and 4).

Fig. 3. Screenshots of the connection of Bluetooth devices for data transfer

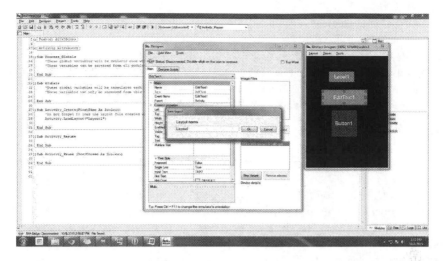

Fig. 4. Screen shots of developing activity layout in smart phone application

The suggestion includes alerts on chew hydration intake, excessive food, intervals between meals (Fig. 5).

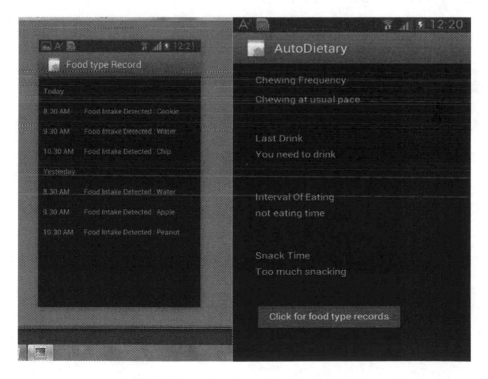

Fig. 5. Screenshots for results of food records

484 J. Patil and P. Salunke

4 Food Detection

In three steps food is identified. At first sound frames are collected during eating process which include chew and swallow trials. Secondly it includes hidden markov models which identify chew and swallow events from sound frames. In last step each trials are computed to pull out features and identify various food types [9–11]. Also, these values are evaluated with our simple decision tree to calculate the food type.

5 Sorting of Various Foods and Its Detection

Here in this technique two types of foods are analogous to chew and swallow events that can be achieved through calculated feature and time values based on previous learnings or informations. Here we have included simple decision tree to identify various foods which will also check the text classification as well as its behaviour activity [12] (Fig. 6). Here that simple tree used is a large piece of whole tree to recognize apple and milk. To determine these foods first we have extract it feature values i.e. (max peak is calculated) and division satisfies that is taken, again re process is started to get better feature values in the processing. When last step of node is reached, a final decision on the food type is returned (Tables 1, 2 and 3).

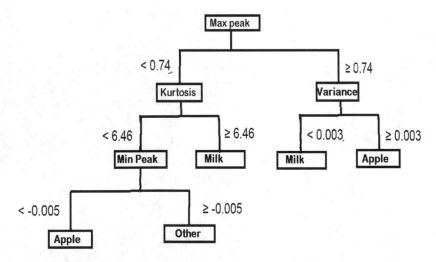

Fig. 6. Decision tree

Table 1. Time domain features

Features	Descriptions
High peak	Maximum value of a event
Low peak	Minimum value of a event
Mean	Average value of a event
Variance	The square of Std. variance
Std. variance	Measure of spreadness of event

Table 2. Frequency domain features

Features	Descriptions
Pmax	Maximum power
Pmean	Mean power of event
P250 * (i − 1) − 250 * i, (i = 1, 2,⋯ 10)	Power at 250 * (i − 1) − 250 * i Hz
Ei (i = 1, 2,⋯ 8)	Energy of 8 sub-bands after WPD

Table 3. Non-linear features

Features	Descriptions
DetrenFlu	Quantify fractal scaling properties
AppEn	Measure of regularity & complexity
FraDimen	Index of complexity how detail in a event changes with the scale
Hurst-E	Measure of the smoothness
CorDimen	Measure of fractal dimension

6 Conclusion and Future Scope

In this paper, we have presented the Automatic food dietary in comprehensive way for food intake detection. We prepared the embedded hardware and smart phone application to gather various foods which is sensed by signal data through a throat microphone placed on neck to record audio signals during eating. Here we have used hidden markov models to identify swallow and chew actions and then they are processed to draw the time and frequency domain or field features. We developed Smartphone apps which not only gives food detection results but also suggests for healthier eating habits and provides message to doctor whose phone number is stored in the application for particular patients which are not taking proper diet.

In the future we made proposal to improve automatic Food dietary in various ways first, we propose to add different techniques to the system such as volume & weight of food intake, second to minimize the size of device which is wearied on neck & embedded hardware unit so that user can worn like necklace pendent & put in to the chest pocket as well as it should work as a bio monitoring device.

References

1. World Health Organization: Obesity and overweight. What are overweight and obesity. Fact sheet, 311 (2006)
2. Sazonov, E.S., Schuckers, S.: The energetics of obesity: a review: monitoring energy intake and energy expenditure in humans. IEEE Eng. Med. Biol. Mag. **29**(1), 31–35 (2010)
3. Durasiwami, R., Beha, J., Han, D.K., Ko, H.: Hidden Markov model on a unit hypersphere space for gesture trajectory recognition. Pattern Recognit. Lett. **36**(15), 144–153 (2014)
4. Amft, O.: A wearable erapad sensor for chewing monitoring. IEEE Trans. Sensors **1**(4), 222–227 (2010)
5. Pabler, S., Wolff, M., et al.: Food intake monitoring: an acoustical approach to automated food intake activity detection and classification of consumed food. Physiol. Meas. **33**, 1073–1093 (2012)
6. Lester, J., Tan, D.S.: Food crushing sounds. An introductory study. In: Automatic Classification of Daily Fluid Intake, pp. 1–8 (2010)
7. Texas Instruments: Ti homepage: Tlv25431. http://www.ti.com/product/tlv2541. Accessed 24 Sep 2014
8. http://www.texasinstruments.com
9. Zhou, X., Zhuang, X., Liu, M., Tang, H., Hasegawa-Johnson, M., Huang, T.: HMM-based acoustic event detection with Adaboost feature selections. In: Stiefelhagen, R., Bowers, R., Fiscus, J. (eds.) CLEAR 2007 and RT 2007. LNCS, vol. 4625, pp. 345–353. Springer, Heidelberg (2007)
10. Zieger, C.: An HMM based system for acoustic event detection. In: Stiefelhagen, R., Bowers, R., Fiscus, J. (eds.) CLEAR/RT -2007. LNCS, vol. 4625, pp. 338–344. Springer Berlin Heidelberg, Berlin, Heidelberg (2008). doi:10.1007/978-3-540-68585-2_32
11. Temko, A., Malkin, R.: Acoustic event detection and classification in smart-room environments: evaluation of chil project systems. Cough **25** (2006)
12. Kumar, A.U.: Mining land cover information using multiplayer perception and decision tree from modis data. IEEE Eng. Med. Biol. Mag. **38** (2010)

Knowledge Discovery Through Social Media Posts Mining for Making Data Driven Decisions: A Survey

Sherin Mariam John[1(✉)] and Kamatchi Kartheeban[2]

[1] Thiagarajar School of Management, Madurai, India
sherin@tsm.ac.in
[2] Kalasalingam University, Krishnankoil, India
k.kartheeban@klu.ac.in

Abstract. Organizations have more data than they can use effectively. Organizational leaders are now aware of the need to employ analytics to exploit their growing data and use computational power to become smart and innovative. Senior management now a days demand that businesses should run on data driven decisions and expects data to be churned out into information very quickly. Data analysis is required for making real-time decisions. Better reporting and decision making enables the industry people to excel in the areas of sales, marketing, delivery and operations [11]. Companies are heavily investing in technologies that help them collect data, which are mostly unstructured and semi structured, analyze it in real time to understand consumer's sentiments and take appropriate actions. This paper is an overview emphasizing the need of data analytics in business.

Keywords: Data analysis · Sentiment analysis · Big data mining · Knowledge discovery

1 Introduction

The volume of data getting generated on the World Wide Web is very large and it is freely accessible to the public. Anyone online can express their views on any topic such as product reviews, movie reviews, current social issues and political issues. The Internet users can post any content on blogs, social media websites or on review sites. This provides an opportunity for mining the content on websites for knowledge and discovering useful tips for improving the product features or services delivered.

Analysis of data should yield results within a time frame. Action should be taken to utilize the information uncovered. Current computing power is not enough to scale up with the user generated content which is getting generated at an exponential rate.

The organization needs to identify the strategic data that will yield valuable logical perceptions. For example, what data is needed to discover the hidden patterns in stock market transaction? Choosing the right technology that best suits the organizational needs is a challenge [11].

© Springer Nature Singapore Pte Ltd. 2016
A. Unal et al. (Eds.): SmartCom 2016, CCIS 628, pp. 487–494, 2016.
DOI: 10.1007/978-981-10-3433-6_58

Various vendors like Amazon, Google, IBM, Microsoft etc. are providing the tools and technologies to handle the huge volume of user generated content in web, do real time analysis and predict future requirements with predictive analysis.

1.1   Web Data Mining

Three mining tasks are involved while evaluating a text from Internet. They are Sentiment Analysis and Classification, opinion mining based on product features and mining Comparative sentences and their relations [13].

Sentiment Analysis and Classification: Sentiment Analysis determines the viewpoint of a writer with respect to a product or service. Sentiment analysis comprises of recognizing the emotions of the writer and constructing a method to collect and classify opinions about a product. If a company fails in understanding the importance of doing sentiment analysis, it may lose customers to other companies which do so.

Opinion mining and Sentiment analysis are not exactly same but slightly different. Opinion mining concentrates on detecting the polarity of a sentence. The different polarities can be positive, negative or neutral in nature [1]. Detecting the polarity is one step in sentiment analysis.

An opinion mining system supports managers to search for opinions posted on anything. It can help marketing people evaluate the success of an advertisement campaign they have recently launched for a new product or decide which versions of a product or service are popular and identify which category of people like or dislike particular product features.

Sentiment analysis tools are creating a kind of customer intelligence which knocks out traditional market research. It facilitates an organization's business strategy development. The seller acquires a much stronger representation of public opinion than surveys. Customer service and marketing departments have expressed their great interests in social media analytics tools. The Research wing in organizations can identify new product-development opportunities.

The task of opinion mining can be treated as a text classification problem. It sorts a piece of review text as being positive, negative or neutral. The system takes as input a text containing review on a particular product and defines whether the review shows a positive or a negative sentiment of the writer. The classification is done at the document-level.

Opinion Mining Based on Product Features: The document level mining determines the overall sentiment of a review. Going further down we can find out what are the specific features of the product that customers liked or disliked. For this we need to mine at the sentence level. For each feature identified, we can determine whether the review is oriented more towards the positive side or negative side.

Consider the review statement, "The display screen of the mobile phone I recently purchased is not good". The feature specified here is about screen resolution and the sentiment is negative. Similarly we can do the analysis for each sentence in the review and come out with a summary report of the mining results [13].

Comparative Sentence and Relations: Some sentences compare the features of two brands of the same product. For example, the sentence "The picture taken from mobile phone x is more clear than mobile y", here we can mine which feature is being talked about and the apparent relationship between the two product features [13].

1.2 Information Retrieval Method in Web

The user who is in need of an information issues a query in the search engine, the user query is translated into a format that can be understood by the query execution engine. The document retrieval system uses an index for every document for quickly selecting the documents which contain the query words [13]. The relevance of a document with respect to the query words are calculated using a function. This value is used to rank the document (Fig. 1).

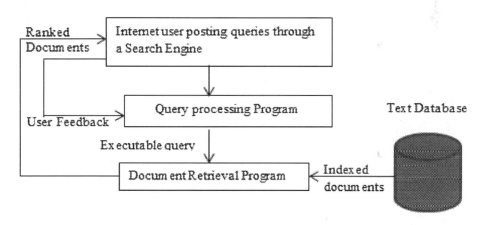

Fig. 1. Information retrieval method

The documents are then displayed to the user according to the rank position. The relevance feedback from users is used to improve the accuracy of retrieved documents with respect to the query words.

Relevance feedback is calculated with the help of user feedback. The user classifies the retrieved documents as either relevant or irrelevant documents [13]. The original query is now modified to include some words from the user identified relevant and irrelevant documents. Then the same process is repeated for retrieving the documents based on the modified query. A classification model can be built with the relevance feedback which is used for training and testing how to classify the documents. There is another kind of relevance feedback called pseudo relevance feedback where a computer algorithm plays the role of the user [13].

2   Related Work

Pooja Kherwa [5] in her paper explains about a sentimental analysis system which is web based. It takes the relevant features, analyzes and summarizes the state of mind of people corresponding to each feature, and categorizes them into a set of positive and negative terms. Their work uses the rules of natural language processing.

Lizhen Liu [8] demonstrated the plan, evolution and assessment of Fuzzy domain Sentiment Ontology tree to facilitate opinion mining. It includes extraction of product features, sentiment words and predicts the polarities of sentiments; gap identified is lack of social media monitoring tools to identify customer satisfaction levels.

Xing Fang and Justin Zhan [3] tackle the problem of sentiment polarity categorization with detailed process descriptions. Data used in this study are online product reviews collected from Amazon.com. Experiments for both sentence-level categorization and review-level categorization are performed.

R. Nitish and S. Sabarish [7], propose a model to store information as ontologies, takes data from tweets and blogs. Sentiment analysis done at the feature level on reviews to rate product features. Feature extraction is done using NLP tool. The major disadvantages are low volume of data and no automation in extracting tweets which will make ontology up to date with latest tweets.

Jeyapriya [4] in her paper discusses about extraction of frequent item set in customer product reviews and mining opinions whether it is positive or negative.

Xinzhi Wang [6] analyzes and predicts user's sentiment about specific information, introduced four laws for general constraints of human sentiments. They were able to predict sentimental leaders who lead pivotal role in leading public opinions.

3   Predicting the Future with Social Media

The popular social media website Twitter has a valuable collection of data where one can find value if they properly analyze. Twitter is also focusing on the same direction by acquiring companies that have access to Twitter's fire hose of data. It later packaged the data and sold it to companies who were interested in slicing and dicing it and discovering valuable insights for their business [12]. Analyzing Twitter data enabled capturing the varied opinions of the online community. It was different from the existing surveys. Twitter is one of the fastest and simplest way to communicate [2]. With Twitter, we can work with real data and real problems [12] (Fig. 2).

Understanding sentiments of people from News Analysis, Facebook status updates are also popular research areas. On Flipkart's Big Billion Day Crash, people used Facebook and Twitter to vent out their anger. Common complaints include offers presented in the newspaper not available on the web site, waiting long period to access the website and non-availability of many popular products [10].

The growth of Indian Tourism Sector is being influenced by social media interactions [9]. The analysis of sentiments on reviews posted by tourists is useful for marketing Indian Tourism and for people who are searching to visit places in India.

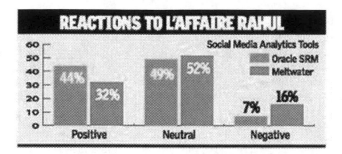

Fig. 2. The graph shows the sentiment analysis done by The Hindu Newspaper on a topic by mining social media websites like YouTube, Twitter, Facebook and blogs. (Source: http://www.thehindu.com/multimedia/dynamic/02940/Oracle-SRM_col__Or_2940066e.jpg)

IBM's Watson Analytics enables business professionals to pull Twitter data into any project. Watson analytics automates cleaning of data, predictive analysis and visual story telling. Watson Analytics can identify and explain hidden patterns and relationships. It can explain why things happen and what is likely to happen in the future [12] (Fig. 3).

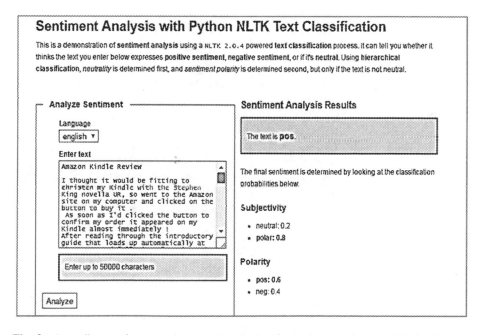

Fig. 3. An online sentiment analyzer tool analyzing the reviews on Amazon Kindle (Source: http://text-processing.com/demo/sentiment/)

4   Big Data Analytics

Most of the business executives do not understand how to leverage on the huge volume of data which we call as Big Data, getting generated every second around them. The advantages of Big Data analytics should be explained aligning with the business operations. A business problem can be identified and explained to them. Focusing only on the technical side is not advisable. Formulate the questions that must be answered to meet the business objectives. Then focus on discovery of knowledge. Identify technologies which best fit the problem and align with the business process. Building an infrastructure that is scalable is important [11].

Specialized skills are needed for the team that makes Big Data Analysis work in the company. The team should possess statistical skills, data mining knowledge, machine learning and experience with algorithms and coding. The most critical skill needed is the ability to transform the data in a way that can be easily understood by others [11].

The analytics team can be placed under the IT department of a company or work with the business functions for which they are trying to find answers. For example, in order to find the answer to the problem of churning out of customers, the analytics team can work with marketing department. The team should have experts from different areas since this is not only an IT job but also needs business knowledge. That means in addition to the technology skills, the team should have required business skills [11] (Table 1).

Table 1.   Some open source big data mining tools

Name	Description
RapidMiner	RapidMiner is a text mining open source software. The server version is known as RapidAnalytics
Hadoop	Open Source. Very popular and efective framework for distributed storage and distributed processing of very large data sets
Mahout	This is the product of Apache. It offers algorithms for clustering and classification. This runs on top of Hadoop. The advantage is scalablity
Orange	It gives access to about 100 widgets and data can be visualized for better understanding
Weka	Weka stands for "Waikato Environment for Knowledge Analysis," It offers a set of tools for data mining techniques

5   Open Issues

There are many known and unknown issues in Sentiment Analysis on Online Product Review. The quality of the data collected known as Veracity, is not guaranteed. Millions of people around the world are connected to the Internet every second. They can post their comments in social media websites about any topic. Finding out the authenticity of data being uploaded in the social media websites is a difficult task.

The problem of analyzing data which is not standardized is the next area of concern. People have different ways of expressing their feelings. Shorthand's and acronyms in online data is a major challenge in Natural Language Processing. The text may not be in English. They may use native language for communicating with their friends. The data is highly unstructured and also the volume of data is very huge (Big Data). We should apply proper filters during cleaning and pruning.

Another inability of sentiment analysis tools is recognizing sarcastic or colloquial language. The meaning of a word changes according to the context where that word has been used. The same word or sentence can give positive viewpoint in one domain and negative expression in another domain. So context based sentiment analysis is a challenge to the existing algorithms.

Talking about spam data, people will upload false data for two reasons. First reason is that to increase the ratings of their own products, they post positive reviews in different sites by logging in with different user names and second reason is to tarnish the image of their competitor's product by purposely giving negative comments.

6 Conclusion

After the public acceptance of Internet, communication between organizations or individuals has never been a bottleneck for business professionals. Internet has changed people's life style. Most of the Internet users, before purchasing an item go through reviews online for knowing the reaction of people using that product. Product designers always welcome feedback for the recently launched products for further improvement of their product features. Sentiment Analysis plays a vital role in analyzing the public sentiments towards a topic of discussion. It is an ongoing field of research in the field of text mining. This survey paper to some extent summarizes the recent research trends and directions of Sentiment Analysis.

References

1. Priyanka, S., Sivakumar, M.: Big data processing in sentiment and opinion mining. Int. J. Adv. Res. Comput. Sci. Softw. Eng. **5**(4), 1208–1216 (2015)
2. Mahalakshmi, R., Suseela, S.: Big-SoSA: social sentiment analysis and data visualization on big data. Int. J. Adv. Res. Comput. Sci. Softw. Eng. **4**(4), 304–3061 (2015)
3. Fang, X., Zhan, J.: Sentiment analysis using product review data. J. Big Data (2015). SpringerOpen Journal
4. Jeyapriya, A., Kanimozhi, C.S.: Extracting aspects and mining opinions in product reviews using supervised learning algorithm. In: 2015 2nd International Conference on Electronics and Communication Systems (ICECS), pp. 548–552. IEEE (2015)
5. Kherwa, P., Sachdeva, A.: An approach towards comprehensive sentimental data analysis and opinion mining. In: 2014 IEEE International Advance Computing Conference (IACC), pp. 606–612. IEEE Xplore (2014)
6. Wang, X., Luo, X.: Sentimental space based analysis of user personalized sentiments. In: 2013 Ninth International Conference on Semantics, Knowledge and Grids, pp. 151–156. IEEE (2013)

7. Nithish, R., Sabarish, S.: An ontology based sentiment analysis for mobile products using tweets. In: 2013 Fifth International Conference on Advanced Computing (ICoAC), pp. 342–347. IEEE (2013)

8. Liu, L., Nie, X.: Toward a fuzzy domain sentiment ontology tree for sentiment analysis. In: 2012 5th International Congress on Image and Signal Processing, pp. 1620–1624. IEEE (2012)

9. Senthil, V.: A study of social media applications in Indian tourism. In: 10th INDIACOM; 2016 3rd International Conference on Computing for Sustainable Global Development, pp. 115–120 (2016)

10. Khanna, P., Sampat, B.: Factors influencing online shopping during diwali festival 2014: case study of Flipkart and Amazon. J. Int. Technol. Inf. Manag. **24**(2), 65–86 (2015). Article 5

11. Ohlhorst, F.J.: Big Data Analytics: Turning Big Data into Big Money. Wiley and SAS Business Series. Wiley, Chichester (2012)

12. Zikopoulos, P., Eaton, C., Zikopoulos, P.: Understanding Big Data: Analytics for Enterprise Class Hadoop and Streaming Data. McGraw Hill, New York (2011)

13. Liu, B.: Web Data Mining: Exploring Hyperlinks, Contents, and Usage Data. Data-Centric Systems and Applications. Springer, Heidelberg (2009)

Energy Aware Routing Based on Multi-sensor Data Fusion for Wireless Sensor Networks

Soumitra Das[1(✉)], S. Barani[2], Sanjeev Wagh[3], and S.S. Sonavane[4]

[1] Department of CSE, Sathyabama University, Chennai, India
soumitra_das@yahoo.com
[2] Department of Electronics and Control Engineering,
Sathyabama University, Chennai, India
baraniselvaraj77@gmail.com
[3] Department of Computer Engineering, KJCOEMR, Pune, India
sjwagh1@gmail.com
[4] Department of E&TC, Dr. D.Y. Patil School of Engineering, Pune, India
sssonavane@gmail.com

Abstract. In this paper a multi-sensor data fusion approach for wireless sensor system based on Bayesian strategies and Ant Colony Optimization procedures have been recommended. In this methodology, every node is furnished with various sensors (i.e. temperature and humidity sensors). Usage of more than one sensor gives additional information about the environmental conditions. The data fusion based on the competitive type hierarchical processing has been considered for experimentation. In the data fusion, the data gathered by the sensors are set in the sensing fields and afterward the data fusion probabilities are registered. In our suggested approach, the gathered temperature and humidity information are prepared by multi-sensor data fusion strategies, which then helps in diminishing the energy utilization and also communication cost through accumulation of the repetitive information. The multiple information merging process is reliable and accurate in addition to being energy-efficient which our primary goal is. The proposed algorithms were simulated utilizing Matlab. The implementation of the proposed algorithms were conducted with and without multi-sensor data fusion and the outcomes demonstrate that the proposed algorithms could reduce the energy- consumption, rather save additional energy, thus enhance the entire lifetime of the system.

Keywords: Multi-sensor data fusion · Optimization techniques · Energy aware routing · ACO · WSN

1 Introduction

The general definition of Fusion is to combine two or more distinct things. The term sensor fusion is the process of merging sensory data derived from different sources in a way that the resulting information is better than would have been possible when these sources were used individually. In the hierarchical architecture as shown in Fig. 1 there are majorly two levels: the top level has a solitary, central fusion node and last level contains several local fusion nodes. Each of these neighbouring fusion nodes may get

© Springer Nature Singapore Pte Ltd. 2016
A. Unal et al. (Eds.): SmartCom 2016, CCIS 628, pp. 495–502, 2016.
DOI: 10.1007/978-981-10-3433-6_59

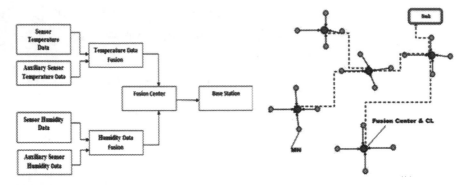

Fig. 1. Hierarchical architecture of Temperature and Humidity recognition system

Fig. 2. Hierarchical processing (competitive type)

inputs from a small cluster of sensors or an individual sensor [1]. Our emphasis is on fusion of data sensors, which collated numerical information from various sources, most likely measuring physically distinctive things. The aim was to make MSDF informational and educative compared to source data. The primary aim was to lengthen overall lifetime of the network using MSDF and enhanced Ant Colony Optimization. The remaining section talks about related work (Sect. 2), design and experimentation of the proposed system (Sect. 3), result and discussions (Sect. 4) followed by concluding remarks.

2 Related Works

Improvement of WSN lifetime is being researched by various groups of scientists. They have recommended and experimented multiple algorithms, conventions, methodologies and protocols like data aggregation, efficient scheduling and a few more to improve and prolong the network lifetime. The concept of data fusion in WSN is still evolving and researchers worldwide is developing effective algorithms based on this novel idea like cluster design and tree-based data fusion.

Xiajun Zhai et al. [2] proposed a calculation SWIPE, wherein two different types of information are handled distinctly in the fusion module. They discussed housekeeping and technical data and the way of handling or melding as per the need. A furry rationale based information combination calculation to gather the wellbeing status of a node was being proposed. In [3], Chen Hui-fang et al. reported about an algorithm based on the combination of the clusters and depicted adaptive design of data fusion. This prevented the cluster head node failure, which makes it less reliable. In [4], Kaihong Zhang et al. showed the importance of time-driven network data aggregation (combining sensor nodes scheduling and batch estimation). They demonstrated superiority of the network data and energy consumptions than LEACH and TEEN. In [5], Chair et al. proposed another fusion algorithm with use of the smallest amount of probability of error criterion for local decision-making. For applying this rule, it is essential to know the chances of detection and the probability of false alarm for each sensor. As per research work in [6–9], the use of data fusion technology can minimize the total energy consumption of the WSNs to a larger extent. A well-distributed clustering algorithm (called Energy-efficient Clustering) was proposed which efficiently determined the optimal cluster sizes as per the hop distance to the sink node, simultaneously maintaining equalization of a sensor node lifetime and reduced energy utilization [10]. In [11] a new QoS algorithm (for mobile ad hoc network), the proposed algorithm fused the concept of ACO and Optimized Link State Routing (OLSR) protocols to recognize multiple courses between the source and destination nodes. In view of the Dynamic Traffic Routing (DTR) problem for a traffic network as a directed flowchart is shown, this process considers the mathematical facet of the optimization. Networks have numerous edges and nodes, resulting in a substantial and computationally complex DTR optimization crisis. ACO was selected as the most favorable method to solve issues in [12, 13]. A new ACO algorithm was proposed to find the best allocation of traffic on the network as against standard ACO [12]. In [14], the author presented an ant colony–based routing algorithm and local search to determine optimal routes, which can be more effective in terms of path length, delay and sensor node energy.

3 Design and Experimentation of the Proposed System

The proposed framework is phased out into three stages.

3.1 Cluster Leader Selection and Cluster Development Approach

In clustering engineering, the sensors are assembled together to form a group according to the given conditions and one node is termed as CL. In the beginning, "N" number of sensor nodes arbitrarily gets positioned in the region of 500×500 M^2 field. The algorithm for cluster arrangement is summarized in Algorithm 1

3.1.1 Algorithm 1

1. Start
2. ClustorDevelopment (Integer NoR)
3. Integer A; //Area of Network
4. Integer Cn; //No. of Cluster to be developed
5. Integer Ac; //Area of Cluster
6. Integer NoN; //Number of nodes in total area of Network
7. Read(A); Read (Cn);
8. Ac = A/Cn; //Calculate the area of each cluster
9. For (k = 1 to NoN) do
10. Setup the energy and the location of each node.
11. For (c = 1 to NoR) do
12. CL = Highest energy node of the Clusters.
13. CL Broadcasts advertising messages to all the nodes of cluster area Ac
14. Cm sends acknowledge message to CL
15. CL calculates d(CLi, nodej);
16. CL and all Cm are synchronized for further communication.
17. End.

Time complexity of Algorithm 1 can be computed to $T(N) = O(NM)$ and Space complexity can be computed to $O(N^2)$, where N is numbers of nodes.

3.2   Data Fusion Approach

In our proposed system, MSDF fuses data from two sensors namely temperature and humidity sensors from multiple sensors by using bayesian strategies in order to provide better energy utilization. The bayesian strategies for data fusions techniques use probabilistic observations and procedures to consolidate this data. Every sensor detects the data event and passes it to the CL of the respective clusters. The CL node waits for more data from member nodes to ultimately send collated data further, which enhances performance and conserves energy. The CL is responsible to compare new and old datasets and do fusion, considering some earlier probabilities. To formulate the fusion equation let us consider two sensors as shown below termed as sensor 1 and sensor 2 respectively.

Sensor 1	Sensor 2
S_{nd1} = New data set	S_{nd2} = New data set
S_{od1} = Old data set	S_{od2} = Old data set
S_{cd1} = Current sensed data	S_{cd2} = Current sensed data

At the fusion mode, the probability of a particular data x (e.g. temperature/humidity) can be computed based on the latest set of data using bayes rules as

$$p(x|S_{nd1}, S_{nd2}) = p(x|S_{cd1}S_{cd2}S_{od1}S_{od2})$$

$$= \frac{p(S_{cd1}S_{cd2}|x, S_{od1}S_{od2})\boldsymbol{p}(x|S_{od1}S_{od2})}{\boldsymbol{p}(S_{cd1}S_{cd2}|S_{od1}S_{od2})}$$

As sensor measurements are independent of each other, we get

$$= \frac{p(S_{cd1}|x, S_{od1})p(S_{cd2}|x, S_{od2})p(x|S_{od1}S_{od2})}{p(S_{cd1}S_{cd2}|S_{od1}S_{od2})}$$

$$= \frac{p(x|S_{nd1},)\boldsymbol{p}(S_{cd1}|S_{od1})p(x|S_{nd2},)\boldsymbol{p}(S_{cd2}|S_{od2})p(x|S_{nd1}, S_{nd2})}{p(x|S_{nd1})\boldsymbol{p}(x|S_{nd2})\boldsymbol{p}(S_{cd1}S_{cd2}|S_{nd1}S_{nd2})}$$

At the fusion node

$$= \frac{\boldsymbol{p}(x|S_{nd1})\boldsymbol{p}(x|S_{nd2})\boldsymbol{p}(x|S_{od1}S_{od2})}{\boldsymbol{p}(x|S_{od1})\boldsymbol{p}(x|S_{od2})} \tag{3}$$

Equation (3) is the required fusion solution at fusion centre. Once the fusion of data is done, the fused data which are small in size are transmitted to the BS via multi-hop communication techniques as shown in Fig. 2. In this *competitive type* processing architecture, the CL plays a dual role, as Local Fusion Center (LFC) and a CL at the same time.

3.3 Data Dissemination Approach

The Data dissemination approach is based on ACO. The concept of Forward and Backward ants is used to find routes from source to the BS in order to route the fused data. In this strategy, node with the greatest energy and pheromone levels are chosen to assure a higher system lifetime. The cost matrix of nodes is calculated based on minimal distance and maximum energy is shown in Algorithm 2.

- $PH(i) = PH(i) + \alpha$, where α is constant. //backward ant travels through node n_i
- $R(i) = \{n_i, RE(i), PH(i)\}$ //Routing table R, maintained at each node
- Now Probability $p(i)$ of selecting n_i as next node for forward ant as well as data is

$$p(i) = \frac{PH(i) + RE(i)}{Max(PH) + Max(RE)}$$

Where

- $p(i)$ = probability of node n_i for forward ant to forward the data.
- $PH(i)$ = Pheromone value of node n_i
- $RE(i)$ = Remaining Energy of node n_i

Above probability is calculated periodically, giving equal priority to shortest distance and energy, leads to an energy efficient path. Figure 2 show the how the fused data is routed from source to BS, using multi-hop communication.

3.3.1 Algorithm 2

1. Start
2. CostMatrix = zeros([num_nodes num_nodes]);
3. for i = 1: num_nodes
4. x1 = node_x(i); y1 = node_y(i);
5. energy = node_energy(i);
6. for j = 1:num_nodes
7. x2 = node_x(j); y2 = node_y(j);
8. if(i == j) then CostMatrix(i,j) = 0;
9. continue;
10. distance = pdist([x1 y1;x2 y2]);
11. cost = distance /energy;
12. CostMatrix(i,j) = cost;
13. End

Time complexity of Algorithm 2 can be computed to $T(N) = O(N^2)$ and Space complexity can be computed to $O(N^2)$, where N is numbers of nodes.

4 Results and Discussions

The Proposed algorithm has been assessed through simulations in Matlab for better execution regarding balance network energy, network energy consumption per round and balance energy left in every node. Simulations parameters utilized for assessment are Network Area of 500×500 M^2, Number of node ranges from 1 to 500, Number of cluster will be 5, Initial energy of 100 J, Transmission energy 0.1 mJ, Receiving energy 0.05 mJ, Sleep energy 0.0001 mJ, Transition energy 0.05 mJ and Number of rounds are 500 and 1000.

The simulations were carried out with respect to MSDF and NMSDF for 500 and 1000 iterations (rounds) individual node residual energy, communication energy and network lifetime. Figures 3 and 4 demonstrates that the residual energy of every node

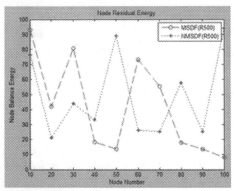

Fig. 3. Node residual energy for 500 iterations

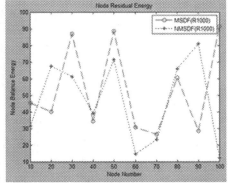

Fig. 4. Node residual energy for 1000 iterations

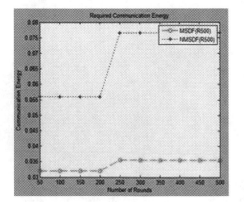

Fig. 5. Required Communication energy for 500 iterations

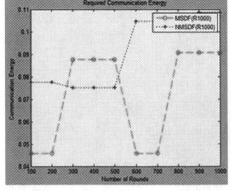

Fig. 6. Required Communication energy for 1000 iterations

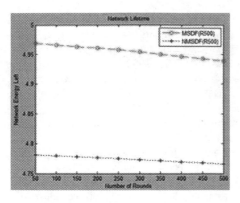

Fig. 7. Network lifetime for 500 iterations

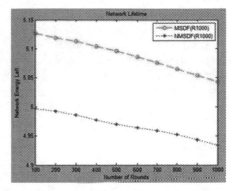

Fig. 8. Network lifetime for 1000 iterations

is significantly better when MSDF algorithm is utilized as a part of both cases for 500 and 1000 rounds when contrasted with NMSDF algorithm. Figures 5 and 6 demonstrates that the required communication energy is significantly less when contrasted with MSDF and NMSDF when the algorithms as tried for 500 and 1000 rounds. Figures 7 and 8 demonstrates that the system life has increased significantly. From the graphs it is evident that when MSDF algorithm is utilized it can lengthen the lifetime of the system as contrasted and NMSDF algorithm for 500 and 1000 rounds.

5 Conclusion

To conclude, we proposed a novel method of energy conservation by using data fusion technology for wireless sensor networks. This energy-aware routing was designed based on multi-sensor data fusion with the ability to merge the data at the central point along with the regional fusion centers. This technique is capable to provide optimum outcomes as per the probability of route selection based on pheromone and remaining energy based on ACO. The simulation results demonstrate better residual energy, need of reduced communication power and lastly, the prolongation of overall network lifetime with multi-sensor data fusion than NMSDF. Therefore, our proposed protocol is more energy efficient and conserves energy, which prolongs the network lifetime.

References

1. Zou, P., Liu, Y.: An Efficient data fusion approach for event detection in heterogeneous WSNs. Appl. Math Inf. Sci. **9**(1), 517–526 (2015)
2. Zhai, X., Jing, H., Vladimirova, T.: Multi-sensor data fusion in WSNs for planetary exploration. In: NASA/ESA Conference on Adaptive Hardware and Systems pp. 188–195. IEEE (2014)
3. Chen, H.F., Mineno, H., Mizuno, T.: Adaptive data aggregation scheme in clustred WSNs. Comput. Commun. **31**(25), 3579–3585 (2008)

4. Zhang, K., Li, C., Zhang, W.: Wireless sensor data fusion algorithm based on sensor scheduling and batch estimate. Int. J. Future Comput. Commun. **2**(4), 333–337 (2013)
5. Chair, I., Varshney, P.: Optimal data fusion of correlated local decisions in multiple sensor detection system. IEEE Transaction on AES **28**(3), 916–920 (1992)
6. Choi, W., Shah, P., Das, S.K.: A framework for energy-saving data gathering using two-phase clustering in WSNs. In: The First Annual International Conference on Mobile and Ubiquitous Systems: Networking and Services, pp. 203–212 (2004)
7. Chen, Y., Liestman, A.L., Liu, J.: A hierarchical energy-efficient framework for data aggregation in WSN. IEEE Trans. Veh. Technol. **55**, 789–796 (2006)
8. Mitchell, H.B.: Multi-sensor Data Fusion. Springer, Heidelberg (2007)
9. Mhatre, V., Rosenberg, C.: Design guidelines for WSNs: communication, clustering and aggregation. Ad Hoc Netw. **2**, 45–63 (2004)
10. Wei, D., Jin, Y., Vural, S., Moessner, K., Tafazolli, R.: An energy-efficient clustering solution for WSNs. IEEE Trans. Wirel. Commun. **10**(11), 3973–3983 (2011)
11. Roy, B., Banik, S., Dey, P., Sanyal, S., Chaki, N.: Ant colony based routing for mobile ad-hoc networks towards improved quality of services. J. Emerg. Trends Comput. Inf. Sci. **3**(1), 10–14 (2012)
12. Cong, Z., De Schutter, B., Babuska, R.: A new ant colony routing approach with a trade-off between system and user optimum. In: Intelligent Transportation Systems 14th International IEEE Conference, pp. 1369–1374 (2011)
13. Xing, L.N., Rohlfshagen, P., Chen, Y.W., Yao, X.: A hybrid ant colony optimization algorithm for the extended capacitated arc routing problem. IEEE Trans. Syst. Man Cybernet. **41**(4), 1110–1123 (2011)
14. Jafari, M., Khotanlou, H.: A routing algorithm based an ant colony, local search and fuzzy inference to improve energy consumption in WSNs. Int. J. Electr. Comput. Eng. **3**(5), 640–650 (2013)

A Compact Data Structure Based Technique
for Mining Frequent Closed Item Sets

Kamlesh Ahuja, Durgesh Kumar Mishra[✉], and Sarika Jain

Sri Aurobindo Institute of Technology, Indore, India
Ahujakamlesh24@gmail.com, drdurgeshmishra@gmail.com,
sarika.jain@sait.ac.in

Abstract. Frequent pattern mining is top chart research field for young researchers. It has a huge array of real world applications. Although many algorithms, tools, techniques are available for performing the task of frequent pattern mining. Apriori and fp growth are very popular frequent pattern mining techniques. This paper presents an updated methodology for frequent closed item set mining. The proposed model is based on the concept of data reduction. Useless data is eliminated from the transaction data base. The experimental results have shown that the proposed updated method is outperforming the existing methods.

Keywords: Data mining · Frequent pattern mining · Frequent closed item sets · Data mart · Data warehouse

1 Introduction

In many cases it is useful to use support thresholds are minimum as possible. But, unfortunately, the number of extracted patterns grows exponentially as we decrease. It thus happens that the collection of discovered patterns is so large to require an additional mining process that should filter the really interesting patterns. Various data bases scattered around the world are integrated in to a data ware house. It is huge data repository this new database functions as a type of data mart (Fig. 1).

The same holds with dense datasets, such as census data. These contain strongly correlated items and long frequent patterns. In fact, such datasets are hard to mine even with high minimum support threshold. The Apriori property [2] does not remove the extent of candidates: every subset of a candidate is likely to be frequent. In conclusion, the complexity of the mining task becomes rapidly intractable by using conventional algorithms. Closed item sets are a solution to the problems described above. These are obtained by partitioning the lattice of frequent item sets into equivalence classes according to the following property: two distinct item sets belong the same class if and only if they occur in the same set of item sets. Closed item sets are the collection of maximal item sets of these equivalence classes. When a dataset is dense, the number of closed item sets extracted is order of magnitudes smaller than the number of frequent ones. This leverages the problem of the analyst of analyzing a large collection of patterns. Also, they reduce the complexity of the problem, since only a reduced search space has to be visited. For example, the pattern found within the sales knowledge of a food market

© Springer Nature Singapore Pte Ltd. 2016
A. Unal et al. (Eds.): SmartCom 2016, CCIS 628, pp. 503–508, 2016.
DOI: 10.1007/978-981-10-3433-6_60

would indicate that if a client buys onions and potatoes along, he or she is probably going to additionally get hamburger meat. Such information are often used because the basis for decisions regarding marketing activities like, e.g. promotional evaluation or product placements. In addition to the above example from market basket analysis association rules are used these days in several application areas as well as web usage mining, bioinformatics and intrusion detection. As against sequence mining, association rule learning generally doesn't take into account the order of things either inside a transaction or across transactions (Fig. 2).

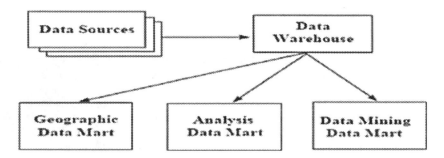

Fig. 1. Depicts that data warehouse and its relations with other streams

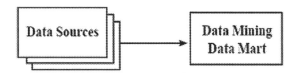

Fig. 2. Depicts that data warehouse and data mart

High performance data mining often tries to solve an expensive problem looking for an equivalent one that it is easier to solve. In fact, from closed item sets it is trivial to generate the whole gathering of frequent item sets along with their supports. In other words, frequent and closed frequent item sets are two different representations of the same knowledge. Moreover, recent FIM algorithms, use the concept of closed item sets to speed up their computation, and when possible they explicitly extract closed item sets and then generate frequent ones in a sort of post processing phase. The first of these kind of algorithms was Pascal [1, 7–9], and now any FIM algorithm uses a similar expedient. More importantly, association rules extracted from closed item sets have been proved to be more meaningful for analysts, because many duplicate items are discarded [2]. Suppose to have two frequent rules r1 : {diapers} -> {milk, beer} and r2 : {diapers} -> {milk} having the same support and confidence. In this case, the rules r1 is more informative since it includes r2: it tells something more about the implications of item diapers. Note that supp(diapers, milk) = supp(diapers, milk, beer), i.e. the two item sets occur in the same set of transactions and therefore they belong to the same equivalence class, but since r2 incudes r1 then {diapers, milk} is not closed. Thus, an algorithm based on closed item sets will not generate the redundant rule r2. Something more about the implications of item diapers. Note that supp(diapers, milk) = supp(diapers, milk, beer), i.e. the two item sets occur in the same set of transactions and therefore they belong to the same equivalence class, but since r2 incudes r1 then {diapers, milk} is not closed. Thus, an algorithm based on closed item sets will not generate the redundant rule r2. This is why many algorithms for mining closed frequent item sets have been proposed, and why the idea of closed item sets has been borrowed by other frequent pattern mining tasks: there are algorithm for the extraction of closed sequences [6], closed trees [3], closed graphs [5], etc. The idea of closed item sets come from the application of formal concept analysis (Fig. 3).

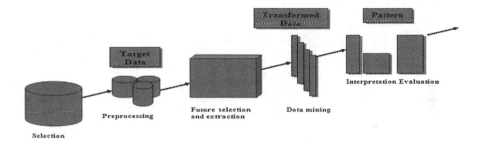

Fig. 3. Depicts that general concept of data mining

This was formalized in the early 80 s by Rudolf Wille [4] and years later it has found many application in data mining, information retrieval and artificial intelligence. Guo et al. [11] proposed a vertical variant of the a priori algorithm. In apriori, several scans of the data base are required. The author proposed a version of the improved a priori algorithm. In this version lesser scans of the data base are required.

2 Problem Definition

We are given a transaction data base D with user defined threshold. The problem is to find all the frequent closed patterns from d in such a way that they satisfies the minimum user defined threshold & also it uses less computational resources as compared to the existing technique.

3 Proposed Solution

Step 1: input:

  1. a transaction database.
  2. User defined Threshold.

Step 2: The transaction database scanned the whole database once and the count of each item is found.

Step 3: If count of any item of step 2 is less than user defined threshold then eliminate the infrequent item.

Step 4:   Now arrange the frequent items found in step 3 in decreasing order of their count. It will be used in construction of the compact tree (CF-Tree).
Step 5:   Construct CF tree by reading one transaction at a time.
Step 6:   Extract a sub tree ending in an item (Suppose X).
Step 7:   • Check that the item of step 5 is frequent or not.
           • If it is frequent then extract it as frequent item.
           • New item X is frequent so now find the other frequent items ending with X.
           • Continue this recursive procedure until no item found.
Step 8:   Arrange the frequent item sets in the decreasing order of their size.
Step 9:   For each frequent item sets having support more than the MST.

           • Find all the super sets(S) of the frequent item stets.
           • If any super set of the frequent item set is not having the same support as the frequent item set then add both in CFIS list.
           • Otherwise add only superset in the CFIS list.
Step 10:   Delete duplicate items from the CFIS list if any.
Step 11:   Return CFIS.

4   Comparison Between Existing and Proposed Algorithm

The existing method work on the basis of generate and test method. It means that the algorithm first generates all the candidates of size 1 and then performs the pruning according to the MST. Then it generates all the candidates of size 2 and then perform the pruning according to the MST. The same process is repeated for the subsequent size elements.

The proposed method generates all the candidates of size 1 and then performs the pruning according to the MST. After that it eliminates all the infrequent items of size 1 from the data set to generate a new compact data set. Then this compact data structure is used to generate the subsequent size elements. So it will save time n space.

As shown in Figs. 4 and 5 Comparison based on the existing and proposed algorithm. This experiment use a Traffic Accidents Data Set. This data set of traffic accidents is obtained from the National Institute of Statistics (NIS) for the region of Flanders (Belgium) for the period 19912000. The traffic accident data contain a rich source of information on the different circumstances in which the accidents have occurred.

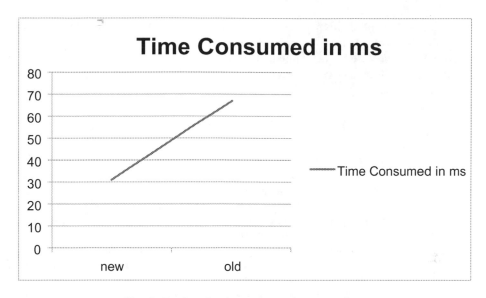

Fig. 4. Depicts the time consumption comparison

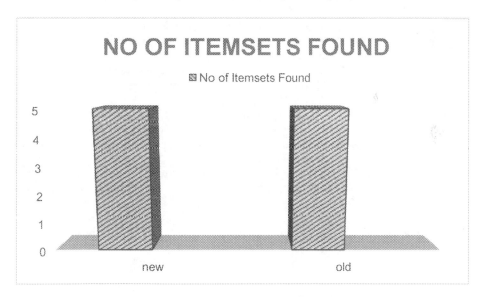

Fig. 5. Depicts the result comparison

5   Conclusion

The basic objective of frequent closed item set mining cum association rule mining is to find strong correlation among the items in the transaction data set. All the researchers are aware of the fact that they are required to deal with the voluminous data while performing mining on the data. So the goal is to device such algorithms which are time and memory efficient. In this paper, we presented a novel algorithm for mining frequent closed item sets from a data sets. Frequent closed mining of data mining is used for that purpose. Frequent closed item set mining is crucial for association rule mining. We have evaluated the performance of our proposed algorithm. It is fast.

References

1. Bastide, Y., Taouil, R., Pasquier, N., Stumme, G., Lakhal, L.: Mining frequent patterns with counting inference. SIGKDD Explor. Newsl. **2**(2), 66–75 (2000)
2. Chi, Y., Yang, Y., Xia, Y., Muntz, R.R.: CMTreeMiner: mining both closed and maximal frequent subtrees. In: Dai, H., Srikant, R., Zhang, C. (eds.) PAKDD 2004. LNCS (LNAI), vol. 3056, pp. 63–73. Springer, Heidelberg (2004). doi:10.1007/978-3-540-24775-3_9
3. Wille, R.: Restructuring lattice theory: an approach based on hierarchies of concepts. In: Rival, I. (ed.) Ordered Sets, pp. 445–470. Reidel., Dordrecht (1982)
4. Yan, X., Han, J.: Closegraph: mining closed frequent graph patterns. In: KDD 2003: Proceedings of the Ninth ACM SIGKDD International Conference on Knowledge Discovery and Data Mining, pp. 286–295, August 2003
5. Yan, X., Han, J., Afshar, R.: Clospan: mining closed sequential patterns in large datasets. In: SDM 2003: Proceedings of the Third SIAM International Conference on Data Mining, pp. 166–177, May 2003
6. Pasquier, N., Bastide, Y., Taouil, R., Lakhal, L.: Discovering frequent closed itemsets for association rules. In: ICDT 1999: Proceeding of the 7th International Conference on Database Theory, pp. 398–416, January 1999
7. Pei, J., Han, J., Mao, R.: Closet: an efficient algorithm for mining frequent closed itemsets. In: DMKD 2000: ACM SIGMOD Workshop on Research Issues in Data Mining and Knowledge Discovery, pp. 21–30, May 2000
8. Zaki, M.J., Hsiao, C.-J.: Charm: an efficient algorithm for closed itemset mining. In: SDM 2002: Proceedings of the Second SIAM International Conference on Data Mining, April 2002
9. Gouda, K., Zaki, M.J.: Genmax: an efficient algorithm for mining maximal frequent itemsets. Data Min. Knowl. Disc. **11**(3), 223–242 (2005)
10. Grahne, G., Zhu, J.: Efficiently using prefix-trees in mining frequent itemsets. In: FIMI 2003: Proceedings of the ICDM 2003 Workshop on Frequent Itemset Mining Implementations, November 2003
11. Guo, Y., Wang, Z.: A vertical format algorithm for mining frequent item sets. In: 2nd International Conference on Advanced Computer Control (ICACC), vol. 4, pp. 11–13 (2010)

Typical Effect of CoMP Under Imperfect CSI in LTE-A

Ankit Saxena[(⊠)] and Ravi Sindal

Institute of Engineering and Technology, Devi Ahiliya Vishwavidyalaya, Indore,
Madhya Pradesh, India
ankitsaxena_17@hotmail.com, rsindal@ietdavv.edu.in

Abstract. EUTRAN LTE–A have the capability for adaptive connectivity
between base stations (eNodeB or eNB) and its consistent remote radio head
(RRH)/relay node (RN). In this paper, we have described the effect of downlink
multipoint connectivity with interference. We analyze the performance of
Transmission Point under imperfect CSI with Coordinate Multi Point (CoMP)
connectivity. In the simulation results, we found Multi Point connectivity
enhances throughput with more reliable connectivity of UE with core nodes.
Apart from these we measure performance of direct path (UE-eNB) and alternate path (UE-RRH/RN-eNB), and found an improved radio signal in a relationship of throughput, Bit Error Rate (BER), and Block Error Rate (BLER).
Also observe throughput performance of the direct path is higher than alternate
path due to transmission inherent effect.

Keywords: Channel State Information (CSI) · LTE-A · EUTRAN · CoMP

1 Introduction

To satisfy the increase of the demand and services, a new technology such as UMTS,
LTE, and LTE-Advance were developing different schemes to enhance the user deliv-
erables in terms of network availability, throughput and delay. It is preferable to have
better radio quality radio signal with consistent connectivity between the User Equipment
(UE) and backhaul Core Server (eNB/PDN/SGW), for a high throughput and low latency.
Networks are formed through transmission point to transmission point connectivity.
A "Transmission Point (TP)" is defined as a point consisting a transmitter antenna with all
supporting units forming a single serving geographical area or cell, as shown in Fig. 1.
The One cell can be formed through more than one TP through a transmit antennas spread
in multiple geographical locations with RRH in a particular cell.

1.1 Related Literature

In LTE architecture, follow the conventional structure of the network where each UE can
connect to a single serving base station or eNB for a particular instant of time, even with
the available base station/relays or eNB in the cellular system while in LTE-A UE can be
connected to more than one transmitting point simultaneously. The authors in [1] have
described the transmission of two parallel flows through a multipoint connectivity for UE,

© Springer Nature Singapore Pte Ltd. 2016
A. Unal et al. (Eds.): SmartCom 2016, CCIS 628, pp. 509–517, 2016.
DOI: 10.1007/978-981-10-3433-6_61

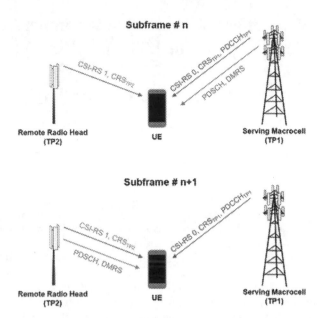

Fig. 1. CoMP Connectivity for PDSCH, and PDCCH channel with CSI-RS and CRS

allowing UEs to divide transmitted power over simultaneous links to the BS and the relay node. And model decision rule for UEs, that is based on allocating transmit power over these links, to make best use of their total throughput rate. The authors in [2] using system level simulations compare the performance of five different schedulers under uniform LTE (EUTRAN) network in terms of Key Performance Indicators (KPI's) for cell and UE. The authors in [3] have described a Signal-to-Noise-plus-Interference Ratio (SINR) for a different type of radio terrain, as per their results obtained in a rural environment the value of SINR quite better in comparison with an urban. And as per their result add-on relay nodes (RN) in LTE systems would provide a better solution to optimize the problems of path loss and SINR at the cell boundaries. The authors in [4] have analyses the LTE and HSPA + system, using the key performance metric of Reference Signal Received Power (RSRP), Reference Signal Received Quality (RSRQ), BLER, CQI, SINR, and spectral efficiency. And as per their results the uplink and downlink throughput performances affected by the path loss and follow a linear relationship between the SINR and CQI. The authors in [5] show a significant improvement of coordinated multi-point (CoMP) in comparison with non-coordinated multi-point (N-CoMP) link adaptation in LTE-A, with interference. In [6] authors give an analysis of cell re-selection and conclude that in EUTRAN selected cell have highest RSRP and selection delay varies with the mobility of UE.

1.2   Major Contribution

In our work, we have simulated a coordinate multipoint dynamic scheme using MATLAB where UEs have the capability to use parallel links with corresponding eNB and relays/RRH, and measure the performance of coordinated multi-point of UEs and TPs with a dominating link. For the measurement we use Signal to noise ratio (SNR), Channel Quality Indicator (CQI), Bit Error Rate (BER), Block Error Rate (BLER) and Throughput as Key Performance Indicators (KPI's). As per CoMP algorithm, based on the dominating link CQI report, the UE were selected corresponding transmitting point (TP or TP1 and TP2) to send data toward the eNB.

1.3   Outline

The paper is structured as follows. Section 2 discusses on link adaptation techniques using CoMP with a dynamic point selection scheme in radio link. System Model with the help of specific KPI are explained in Sect. 3. Simulation setup and the result of different link scenario based on radio link quality is examined in Sect. 4, and are followed by conclusions in Sect. 5.

2   Coordinated Multi Point Link Scheme (CoMP) Link Adaptation

Selection of the best radio links between direct radio link and alternate supporting link is of prime concern. And the performance of link adaptation technique becomes more complex when more than one TPs are available in wireless system. For the best performance a new approach of Dynamic Point Selection (DPS) is developed between eNB and relay node or RH [1] to reduce the interference or utilizing interference as a useful radio link. The CoMP Scheme takes advantage of low latency and high capacity backhaul in serving high throughput network. The DPS approach is used to manage the transport layer TP to maximize connectivity (for Physical Downlink shared Channel (PDSCH) transmission toward the UE).

In Dynamic Point Selection (DPS), UE data are available at multiple base stations within the coordinating set, but data are only transmitted from one TP at a time. TP point is changing dynamically sub frame-to-sub frame on the basis of CSI, to provide the best transmission for a UE with varying channel conditions. This scenario is most likely at a cell edge, where long term channel characteristics favor the serving base station, but short term characteristics may favor other cooperating base system. In our experimental model we have taken two cooperative transmission point called as TP1 (eNB) and TP2 (RRH/RN) with a capability of transmitting PDSCH toward the UE. Initially TP1 is serving toward UE in a EUTRAN cell. As per scheme network opt the PDSCH TP and the corresponding modulation and coding scheme are reported by the UE follow DPS approach as shown in Fig. 1. Here both the TPs are transmitting a CSI-RS and cell-specific reference signal (CRS). The serving cell transmits a downlink control information toward the UE through the Physical Downlink Control Channel (PDCCH). The PDSCH TP can be changed from sub frame-to-sub frame, select it as the best instantaneous channel conditions. As shown in the Fig. 2 the PDSCH TP changes its connectivity from TP1 (sub frame n) to TP2 (sub frame n + 1).

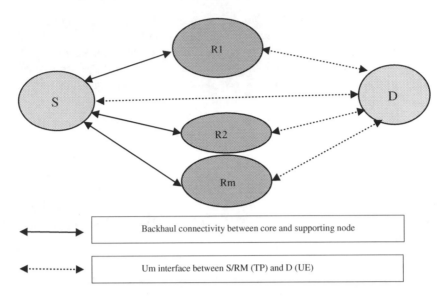

Fig. 2. Illustration of multipoint connectivity between core node and UE followed by direct and indirect through remote radio head/relay node.

3 System Model Using Key Performance Indicators (KPI)

To represent model we denote delay ($\emptyset$) for all S to D links. The delay varies with interface profile, fading effect and geographical location. We assume the identical distance between TP location, interface coupling loss, and geographical terrain. Apart from these $\emptyset 1, \emptyset 2, \emptyset 3$ or $\emptyset 4$ vary depending upon location of the UE, while selection of Hr_x $(where\, x =\; 1, 2, 3\; or\, m)$ depends upon the CSI (Δ) information (including SNR, throughput, BLER or BER with RI, PMI and CQI).

$$link\, 1:\;\; \text{S-R1-D}\quad \emptyset 1 = \Delta(H_{r1}\;\cup\; R_{1d}) \tag{1}$$

$$link\, 2:\;\; \text{S-D}\quad \emptyset 2 = \Delta(H_d) \tag{2}$$

$$link\, 3:\;\; \text{S-R2-D}\quad \emptyset 3 = \Delta(H_{r2}\;\cup\; R_{2d}) \tag{3}$$

$$link\, 4:\;\; \text{S-Rm-D}\quad \emptyset 4 = \Delta(\boldsymbol{H_{rm}}\;\cup\; \boldsymbol{R_{md}}) \tag{4}$$

We consider multiple point connections between source S to destination D and R relay nodes Rm, m = 1, 2 ...M as shown in Fig. 2. Here the function of relay nodes is to decode, amplify and forward signal between sources to destination. We assume relays only receive signals from corresponding link and no inter relay communication. There are two types of connectivity link, one is backhaul connectivity between source (eNB/TP) and relay (TP) {Hr1, Hr2, Hrm} and another one is front end Um {R1d, R2d, Rmd and Hd} interface connectivity between destination (UE) and TP. All mentioned links have their gain or coupling losses with delay, refer given equation. To avoid delay, we can prefer physical/fiber connectivity for back end communication.

CoMP with Dynamic Point Selection Algorithm

1. Check the power level of radio link ($\emptyset$) connected between TP with corresponding UE.
2. TP assigned radio resources via PDSCH toward the UE, as per CSI (Δ) report for corresponding TP serve and connect.
3. On each sub-frame, on the basis of the CSI report for a corresponding pair of TP and UE, a cluster or a group of TP, select the best channel for UE as per feedback receive toward corresponding channel.

TP were selected based on a combination of ($\emptyset$) and Δ, where

$\emptyset \in (\emptyset_1, \emptyset_2, \emptyset_3, \emptyset_4)$... Eqs. 1, 2, 3 and 4

$\Delta \in (\psi, \Omega, \varphi, \mu)$... as ψ_x is SNR, Ω_x is CQI, φ_x is BER, μ_x is BLER with corresponding link.

To generate a CSI report, a network is configured as per the CSI process. It consist of a CSI Reference Signal (CSI-RS) resource, a CSI interference Measurement resource (CSI-IM) and a reporting mechanism. All four CSI processes named as 0, 1, 2, and 3 as shown in Figs. 3 and 4 are followed. Each process for UE are reported with corresponding channel quality indicator (CQI) and a respective sub frame number as shown in Fig. 4. The major dominating CSI process is process 2 and 3, once allocated PDSCH is transmitting, and other associated PDSCH were interfering.

Process	TP1	TP2
0	Transmitting PDSCH	Muting
1	Muting	Transmitting PDSCH
2	Transmitting PDSCH	Interfering
3	Interfering	Transmitting PDSCH

Fig. 3. Multipoint process between both TP

4   Simulation and Result

In this section we describe the experimental setup and its results. We have created an LTE network with a single UE, connected to the base station via two corresponding TP link, First wireless link is directly connected through eNB (or TP1) and second through RRH/RN (or TP2). Here, both the TPs are configured to measure the reference signal and interference of corresponding radio links. For confirmation, the performance of the multipoint CoMP DPS is checked through KPI's such as throughput, BLER and BER. Here we configure TP1 as a macro cell (initial serving TP from eNB) and TP2 as a supporting alternate TP (from remote radio head). Table 1 describe all major parameters for eNB cell. The same parameters are used for TP2 or RRH. Our all scenarios are considered with respect to a different UE position between both TPs.

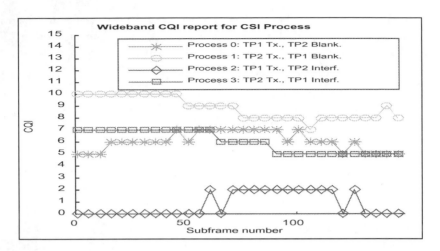

Fig. 4. Channel Quality Indicator (CQI) report for two different Transmitting Point (TP). All four process states named process as Process 0, Process 1, Process 2 and Process 3.

Table 1. eNB Cell Configuration parameters

eNB or TP1 Cell Parameter	
NDL RB	50
Cell Ref P	2
Duplex Mode	'FDD'
CFI	3
Cyclic Prefix	'Normal'
N Frame	0
N Cell ID	0
PDSCH	1 × 1 structure
CSI Ref P	[4, 2]
CSI RS Configuration	[0, 1]
CSI RS Period	1 × 2 cell
NCSIID	[10, 16]
Zero Power CSI RS Configuration	'0110000000000000'
Zero Power CSI RS Period	[5, 1]
Number of Sub frame	149

In referring table test with respect to different terrain are defined in terms of SNR value at TP. We performed both test and analyzed results with respect to different UE position. We set SNR for respective link between the UE and TP (TP1/TP2) and evaluate performance of the respective radio link. Throughput is calculated at 150 sub frame. Summarized four different scenarios as scenario 1 UE position near to TP2 (RRH) with SNR value '10 to 11 dB' and TP1 (eNB) with SNR value '7 to 8 dB' gives throughput rate 666 kps (max) 536 kbps (min) shown in Fig. 5 scenario 1, scenario 2 UE position near to TP2(RRH) at other terrain with SNR value '14 to 15 dB' and TP1

Table 2. Configuration of Fading Channel parameters

Delay Profile	'EPA'
N Rx Ants	2
Doppler Frequency (Hz)	5
MIMO Correlation	'Low'
Sampling Rate	15360000
Seed	[1 2]
Init Phase	'Random'
Model Type	'GMEDS'
N Terms	16
Normalize TX Antennas	'On'
Normalize Path Gains	'On'
Init Time	0.149

(eNB) with SNR value '9 to 10 dB' gives throughput rate 880 kbps(max) 747 kbps (min) shown in Fig. 5 scenario 2 (Table 2).

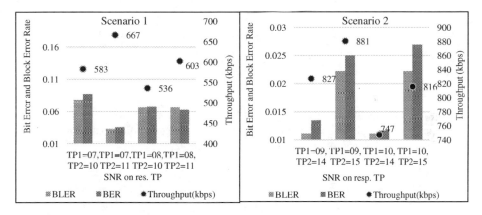

Fig. 5. Performance analysis with respect to scenario 1 and 2

Similarly scenario 3 UE position near to TP1 (eNB) with SNR value '10 to 11 dB' and TP1 (eNB) with SNR value '7 to 8 dB' gives throughput rate 323 kps(max) 290 kbps(min) shown in Fig. 6 scenario 3, and last scenario 4 UE position near to TP1 (eNB) with SNR value '14 to 15 dB' and TP1 (eNB) with SNR value '9 to 10 dB' gives throughput rate 325 kbps(max) 297 kbps(min) shown in Fig. 6 scenario 4.

Our consolidate results are in the Table 3 with respective KPIs. As it indicate CoMP performance in terms of throughput, that is for SNR difference of 3–4 dB between both TP1-eNB and TP2-RRH/RN offers high throughput while compared with the SNR difference of 5–6 dB between respective TP's. Here one more observation observes as when we select TP1 as eNB, the UE get higher throughput in comparison when we select TP1 as RRH/RN, but when TP1-RRH/RN calculated BER and BLER

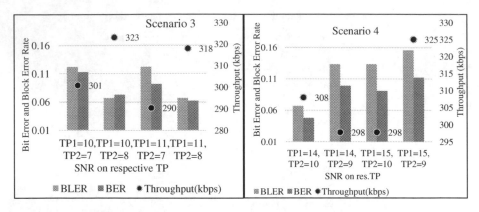

Fig. 6. Performance analysis with respect to scenario 3 and 4

Table 3. CoMP Down-Link performance summary report

Scenario	SNR (dB)		Through.(kbps) @150sub frame	BER	BLER
	TP1	TP2			
1	7 & 8	10 & 11	530–660	0.03–0.08	0.03–0.09
2	9 & 10	14 & 15	740–880	0.01–0.02	0.01–0.03
3	10 & 11	7 & 8	290–320	0.01–0.07	0.01–0.09
4	14 & 15	9 & 10	295–325	0.06–0.16	0.48–0.12

are comparative less than TP1-eNB. These is effect of back haul following path of $\emptyset 1, \emptyset 3$ and $\emptyset 4$ through RRH/RN but on U_m interface better radio quality in the relationship of low BLER and BER.

5   Conclusion

In this paper we have analyzed, a two-link EUTRAN cellular downlink network for the CoMP scheme where TPs are used to serve the UE control through link power mechanism. In our analysis, CoMP links with DPS offer best connectivity with TP under varying channel condition. The measured KPIs shows high throughput, low BER and BLER for direct and alternate links corresponding to TP. Apart from these we compare performance of direct and alternate link and found adding intermediate nodes such as an RRH/RN affect throughput toward to the UE but gives better signal quality in the relationship of BLER and BER.

References

1. Ahmad, S.A., DaSilva, L.A.: Power control and soft topology adaptations in multihop cellular networks with multi-point connectivity. IEEE Tans. Commun. **63**(3), 683–693 (2015)
2. Saxena, A., Sindal, R.: Performance analysis of MAC scheduler in LTE (EUTRAN) for "ASAR": resource allocation. In: Next Generation Mobile Applications, Services and Technologies (NGMAST 2016), Cardiff UK (2016)
3. Parik, J., Mishra, S.: Effect of ISD on pathloss and SINR in 4G systems. In: IEEE IMPACT-2013 (2013)
4. Elnashar, A., El-Saidny, M.A.: A Performance analysis of the LTE system based on field test results: looking at LTE in practice. IEEE Vehicular Technol. Mag. **8**(3), 81–92 (2013)
5. Saxena, A., Sindal, R.: Characterizing the effect of N-CoMP and CoMP with interference in LTE-A. In: International Conference on Computer Communication and Informatics ICCCI 2016, Coimbatore (2016)
6. Saxena, A., Sindal, R.: Analysis of cell reselection in evolved UMTS radio access network radio resource management. In: 2nd IEEE International Conference on Engineering and Technology, Coimbatore, TN, India, 17th–18th March 2016

Methods and Techniques of Intrusion Detection: A Review

Somya, Palak Bansal, and Tameem Ahmad[✉]

Department of Computer Engineering, Z. H. College of Engineering and Technology,
Aligarh Muslim University, Aligarh, India
somya1595@gmail.com, palakb1995@gmail.com, tameemahmad@gmail.com

Abstract. Malware is an abbreviated term meaning "malicious software". This software has a capability to gain access or infect a system without the knowledge of the owner. In this paper, we have tried to provide brief information about different types of malwares known till date such as virus, rabbits, botnet, adware etc. Apart from those we have mentioned the cure to it i.e. intrusion detection. We have described various techniques of intrusion detection such as signature based, anomaly based, behavior based etc. Methods for implementing these techniques include neural networks, data mining etc. A brief description of Intrusion detection system is also provided which is a software application used to monitor the network and system activities and also to detect malicious actions. The objective of this paper is to provide complete study about the types of malware, techniques and methods of intrusion detection, challenges and applications.

Keywords: Intrusion detection · Techniques and methods · Malware · Signature based IDS · Anomaly based IDS

1 Introduction

Malwares are a big threat to modern computer world. These are mischievous programs crafted to prohibit the normal operations, gain unauthorized access to data and resources of the system that may lead to privacy violation and other abusive behavior. Poor separation between code and data is the foremost cause of malware. Intrusion detection is a technique that attempts to discover the unauthorized access to a computer by analyzing the malicious activities and negatively identifying all the non-attacks. This paper will begin with an introduction describing various types of malware. Section 2 will discuss about Intrusion detection. Various Techniques will be explained in Sect. 3. Methods to employ the two most widely used techniques (i.e. signature based and anomaly based) are described in Sect. 4.

At the end, we have concluded the paper with its future scope discussion continued with references list.

1.1 Types of Malware

Virus. A computer virus is a kind of a special program that loads onto computer without the knowledge of the user. Computer viruses are man-made and can also replicate and

© Springer Nature Singapore Pte Ltd. 2016
A. Unal et al. (Eds.): SmartCom 2016, CCIS 628, pp. 518–529, 2016.
DOI: 10.1007/978-981-10-3433-6_62

therefore need some host for its propagation through some communication medium like email attachment or trade program [1]. It can easily corrupt a system, steal information or destroy the data (Fig. 1).

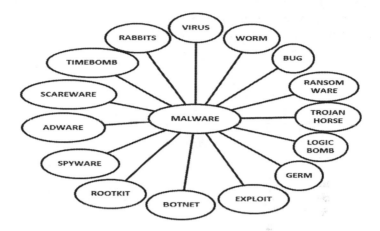

Fig. 1. Types of malware

Christmas tree, Melissa, CIH, Virus, Redlof, Autorun.abt, Peacomm, and NewHeur_PE is the most encountered examples.

Worms. Computer worms spread over computer networks by exploiting operating system vulnerabilities. It cause harm to their host networks by consuming bandwidth and overloading web servers. Furthermore, it can also contain payload to perform action on affected computers to steal or delete files or to create botnet. Worms have the ability to self-replicate and spread independently while viruses need human interference [14].

Blaster, Morris, Code red, Netsky, Stration, Sasser, Bagle, Skipi, no_virus are some of the examples.

Bugs. Bugs are nothing but human errors in the code or the program that compiles it. This flaw produces undesirable results. It can minutely affect programs behavior but when it persist for longer period, it can cause crashing or freezing.

JSONP is one of the most common bugs.

Ransomware. This malware holds a computer system captive while demanding a ransom. The malware limits user access to computer by displaying messages, encrypting files on hard disk or by form of denying the access on the system.

Examples are Reveton, CryptoLocker

Trojan Horse. It is a software program which trick users into downloading and installing malware. It could provide the access to the malicious party over the infected system and hence the attacker can easily bargain data, install more malwares, and modify files without the knowledge of legitimate user.

Some of the commonly encountered examples are Netbus, Nuker, Back Orifice, Limbo/NetHell, Pidief, ZeuS/PRG, Banker.bdn, PGPCoder, Torpig, and Gozi.

Logic Bomb. Logic Bomb are a group of line of code, kept associated with the program without knowledge, conditioned under some circumstance. As soon that condition met, it burst out with harmful effect. It does not replicate on other applications [13].

Examples are Jerusalem, SOBIG worm, Michelangelo.

Germs. Germs are considered as first generation virus which does not have a host program. It exists in its original form. When it infects files, it does not leave any mark of infection on that file leading to unawareness of the user. The problem continues in acquiring resources again and again to infect the unaffected file.

Examples are Germ was written for book sector.

Exploits. Exploits occur due to flaws which are exploited to create security hole to get into the system. Attackers execute a program to locate system's problem and used to make hidden paths to access confidential data.

White hat is an example.

Spyware. It's all about collecting information of the user or the organization without their knowledge that includes the spying the users' activity, keystrokes information collection, data harvesting in terms of account information and login credentials. These all are possible by putting in spyware program on someone's computer secretly and relay it to interested party.

Examples: Spyware Quake, Security toolbar, WhenUSave, PuritySCANVirtumonde.

Rootkits. It is malicious software program develop to control a computer without being detected by user. It is used to gain system administrator's access by compromising it. Because it continually hides its presence, typical security products are not effective in detecting rootkits [14].

Examples are Adore, Knark, LRK, AFX, SInAR, Rustock, and Mebroot.

Botnet. Bots are software program created to perform specific operation automatically. Bots can be used by botnets which is a collection of computers to be controlled by the third party for attacks. It is usually a zombie program [13].

Examples are LowSec, Rbot, Agobot, Slackbot, Mytob, SdBot, poebot, IRCBot, VanBot, MPack, and Storm.

Adware. It is advertising supported software. It includes the pop up ads on websites, free trial versions shown on an already infected system helping other malicious programs to get full access to the system including stealing information and tracking user activity [15].

Examples are DeskAd, AdBlaster.

Scareware. It usually comes from unreliable Internet sources like hacked websites, useful applications or exciting offers. When the user unknowingly downloads it, it produces vulnerable results leading to execution of malicious code and making system prone to attacks.

Smart Fortress, Android Defender are the most common examples.

Time Bomb. It is quite similar to logic bomb. As the name symbolize, there will be a particular time at which destructive effects will take place after the execution of the malware i.e. time is the parameter for its execution. Time bomb can be used by an internal user, who wishes to abolish the data of an organization due to some reason or his/her termination. Many incidents have occurred previously like an organization named Omega Engineering lost millions of dollars due to this malware [15].

Examples are The Christmas Day, Conficker.

Rabbits. Arabbit also known as "computer bacteria" is a computer program which lacks the logic bomb. It has a high rate of reproduction and replication in a shorter period of time. It slows down the computers and clog to the point of being nearly unusable. Cleaning a system is a long and complicated process in this case.

Fork Bombs, cmd.exe are few examples encountered.

2 Intrusion

An intrusion is an unauthorized attempt to break into a computer system. Such a break may force the system to move into an insecure state. It is a deliberate attempt made by the intruder to gain access of, manipulate or misuse valuable resources. If successful, it may result in rendering the resources as unreliable or unusable.

2.1 Intrusion Detection

The National Institute of Standards and technology classifies [4] Intrusion Detection as "The process of monitoring the events occurring in a computer system, or network and analyzing them for signs of intrusions, defined as attempts to compromise the confidentiality, Integrity, availability or to bypass the security mechanism of a computer or network" [5].

Intrusion detection is a type of security management system which is not only to identify an attack but also it includes the following [5]:

a. Monitoring the user and system activities
b. Analyzing system configurations and target vulnerabilities
c. Analysis of abnormal activity pattern
d. Accessing file integrity
e. Track of user policy violation
f. It provides the ability to recognize patterns typical of attacks by providing access to system and file integrity. If any target found vulnerable it would notify.

2.2 Intrusion Detection System

Intrusion Detection System is a security system that dynamically monitors and observes the target system for any misuse and handles the abnormal activity either by itself or by raising an alarm [2].

It can be configured to respond to predefined suspicious activities (e.g. when someone is trying to compromise the system's information through malicious activities) or it can even monitor the internet for latest attacks that could result into some future attack [10].

Primary criterions of measurement for IDS are as follows [3].

TRUE POSITIVE: legitimate attack (IDS gives alarm).
FALSE POSITIVE: no attack (IDS gives alarm).
FALSE NEGATIVE: legitimate attack (IDS gives no alarm).
TRUE NEGATIVE: no attack (IDS gives no alarm).

	T	F
T	TP	FN
F	FP	TN

Further IDS is classifies into three broad categories [8]:

Host Based IDS. This type of IDS collects information from an individual computer system.

It is the combination of signature based, rule based and heuristics based approach to detect intrusion. It monitors local host events, so can even detect attacks that a Network based IDS may miss. Events monitored include contents of operating systems, system and applications logs [9]. Its shortcoming is that it can easily be disabled by certain denial-of-service attacks.

E.g. Tripwire

Network Based IDS. This type of IDS collects information from the entire network. Sensors are placed that monitor all network traffic. Packets are collected and the captured data is then analyzed for predefined patterns and signatures to generate alerts [7]. There are 3 signatures that are very important [5]:

a. String signatures
b. Port signatures
c. Header signatures

This type of IDS does not actually impact the network performance, and are independent of the operating system. Its only when the networks are flooded, the packets are lost.

E.g. SNORT [11]

Vulnerability Assessment. This type is similar for scanning the attacks from the network and point out the drawbacks that are needed to be fixed. It is done on regular basis for the defensive works and ensures that the system or network is strengthened.

There are basically two models for the detection purpose: Anomaly detection and misuse detection which works simultaneously [16].

3   Techniques of Intrusion Detection System

3.1   Signature Based Intrusion Detection Technique

This is a primitive, simple and efficient technique of intrusion detection. This technique basically scans the malware program code and extracts its signature pattern [1]. Later it matches this signature pattern with the ones already fed in the database. During the extraction of signatures, all the system logs, executable files, records are taken into account. An alarm is raised immediately notifying the system user of the attack. The database is created by the antivirus developer, who analyses the new discovered malwares to find a specific pattern or a signature. Once the signature is extracted, it is then updated into the database. Since, detection rate and accuracy largely depends on the preexisting database, antiviruses need to be updated timely to provide better

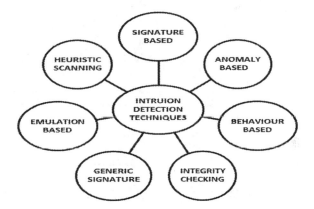

Fig. 2.   Techniques of intrusion detection

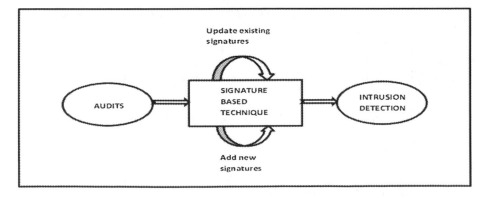

Fig. 3.   Signature based intrusion detection

protection against the new upcoming latest malwares. This is in fact one of its major disadvantage [12] (Figs. 2 and 3).

3.2 Anomaly Based Intrusion Detection Technique

This technique overcomes the limitations of the signature based technique. The process of detection is divided into two phases namely, training phase and detection phase. In the training phase the system is trained about the normality whereas in the detection phase it compares the real data with the established profile to flag deviations and raise alerts [6]. It considers heuristics and artificial intelligence type techniques to differentiate between normal and abnormal activities.

Its main advantage is that it can easily detect unknown viruses as they also produce a different, anomalous behavior.

The only disadvantage with this technique is that there are a very large number of false positive attacks (Fig. 4).

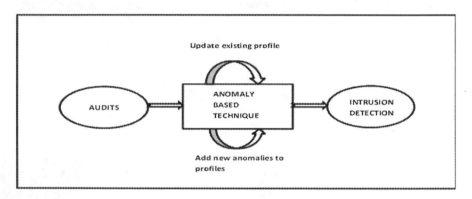

Fig. 4.   Anomaly based intrusion detection

3.3 Emulation Based Intrusion Detection Technique

It is a trial-and-error detection technique that creates a virtual environment, and malware is executed by emulating its instructions. The recorded behavior is then used to propose a remedy. It is the best technique for the detection of metamorphic, polymorphic and encrypted viruses. The only disadvantage with this type of virus is that it does not detect all those malwares that do not show their abnormal behavior during the emulation.

3.4 Generic Signature Scanning Intrusion Detection Technique

This technique is used to detect malwares that belong to the same family i.e. they differ very little in their signatures.

This technique overcomes disadvantage of Signature based technique as it scans using patterns and wildcards to detect the various variants of a family. Generally new malwares are evolved by incorporating minor changes in the pre-existing malware codes. That is that it cannot detect entirely different or new malwares and also they require a skilled researcher to extract variant patterns [1].

3.5 Integrity Checking Intrusion Detection Technique

It is simple to implement and gives efficient results. The first step includes computing and storing san uninfected file's hash value.

All other important files of the system like log files, boot files and executable files are scanned and their hash values calculated. This calculated hash value is compared with the ones already stored to detect intrusion. Integrity checker can also use other methods such as checksums or fingerprints of a file. The main disadvantage with this technique is that it may raise alerts even when minor changes are incorporated in any file.

3.6 Heuristic Scanning Based Intrusion Detection Technique

This is time consuming technique which requires extensive scanning of various boot record files, log files and executable files for code comparable to malicious code. Malicious program instruction include worm propagation routines, virus replication routine etc. Heuristic scanning can be of 2 types [1]:

Static Scanning: It includes direct scanning of a program to look for malicious code.
Dynamic Scanning: It includes emulation of the programs on emulators to detect for malware presence.

The main disadvantage of this technique is the generation of a lot of false positive alarms, and the chances of not detecting a known virus are also high in this case.

3.7 Behavior Based Intrusion Detection Technique

It is used for detection of viruses in terminals like PCs and mobile phones. This technique observes behavior of various malwares and fetches information like its source and destination, attachment size, type etc. Based on this behavior; it can flag a particular source as an intruder. It is capable of detecting known and unknown viruses with self-reference replication behavior. The only disadvantage is generation of false positives and false negatives [1].

4 Methods

4.1 Anomaly Based Intrusion Detection

Statistical Model. The parameters that are considered into account in the statistical methods are such as monitoring the CPU utilization by the user along with the user's session time and the Bandwidth (Fig. 5).

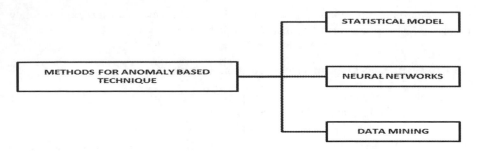

Fig. 5. Methods for anomaly based intrusion detection

These parameters are collected over time and are compared with the baseline criteria [7]. This technique works by looking for deviations from the ideal behavior and determining similarities of events with those which are typical of indicating an attack.

Neural Networks: This method takes into consideration typical characteristic of a system user and then establishing differences and variations from the user's established behavior.

It consists of three phases [9]

a. *Collection of training data*: This includes obtaining audits, log files for a user for a specified period..
b. *Training*: Neural networks are trained to identify users on the basis of these mapped audits.
c. *Performance*: The network is allowed to identify user according to its mapped audits. If the identified user and actual user differ then an anomaly is detected [3].

Data Mining: Data mining is the process of identifying valid, novel and useful patterns in data. The technique is the process of information extraction with an objective to trace the hidden facts in the repository [17]. The technique would verify this information and determine if it is an attack.

Data mining parameters include:

a. *Association*: Patterns are taken into consideration where there are dependencies and connection among them.
b. *Sequence analysis*: This parameter consider the patterns where one event takes to another event
c. *Classification*: looking for new patterns.
d. *Clustering:* finding facts not previously known.
e. *Forecasting*: discover patterns that can lead to sensible estimates.

4.2   Signature Based Intrusion Detection System

Signature Analysis: It is used as carving which is used as identifying the virus using predefined signatures and find the deleted files affected by the virus. It converts the semantic format statement of an attack into an appropriate audit trial format. Low detection rate for zero day attacks is one of its disadvantages (Fig. 6).

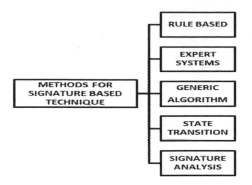

Fig. 6. Methods for signature based intrusion detection

State Transition Based: This model is collection of states, transitions and actions. An attack is described in a form of a transition that must be achieved by an intruder to compromise with a system [5]. It denotes various network states as states of a finite state machine. If a sequel state is identified from the network state of finite state machine, an intrusion is detected [3].

The graphic representation of intrusion is used for the successful completion.

Genetic Algorithms: It is a programming technique that mimics the biological evolutionary technique as a problem-solving strategy. The method possesses natural selection using a chromosome-like data structure and evolves that chromosome.. An evaluation function (also called "Fitness function") is used to compare the quality of each chromosome (survival for the fittest) with view of the desired goal [5].

It efficiently detects numerous types of network intrusion. This approach filters the traffic data using evolutionary theory, converges in less time and thus decreases the complexity.

Rule Based: Rule Based Approach observes deviations from the pre-defined rules; this information is provided to the expert system for detection of intrusion [7]. The demerit is that it could not able to detect the attacks that may occur over an extended period of time. The variations in an attack can affect the activity-rule comparison to a level that intrusion detection system fails to determine.

Expert Based. Previously, data audits and logs were manually analyzed. The disadvantage with this technique was extra time requirements and efforts for this analysis. The expert based System have been evolved to overcome this effort and mechanism have been developed with the creation of knowledge base [18] along with the set of rules, based on heuristics to trap the intrusion automatically without the human intervention.

5   Conclusion and Scope of Improvement

Security is an abstract concept, networks are prone to malware attacks. So, exposing the data or the resource, to an unauthorized person is risky. Proper steps must be taken care to prevent the network / system attacks and preserve the security and integrity. In this paper, a brief overview of different types of malwares, Intrusion detection techniques and methods is presented and it also highlights its advantages, disadvantages and applications.

For the sake of improvement in the existing intrusion detection systems we propose the idea of a modification in a form of approximate string matching which can increase the efficiency of present intrusion detection algorithms. According to this idea, we can compare the signature string and if at most four mismatches are detected, then this algorithm automatically puts some random values and detect the nearest possible match and then raises alarm. Along with alarm it can also update the database with the newly found malware. In case of Signature Based Intrusion Detection System, the new viruses are not detectable. So, with the help of the above proposed algorithm, this issue can be resolved to some extent. It can be considered more reliable and less resource consuming. Various malicious coders basically modify the signatures of existing malwares to develop new ones. We also know that this slight variation in signatures cannot be detected by signature based technique. The implementation of the proposed algorithm will reduce this failure rate as little changes in the signatures will still be detected.

References

1. Slade, R.: Guide to Computer Viruses: How to Avoid them, How to Get Rid of them, and How to Get Help. Springer, Heidelberg (2012)
2. Bashir, U., Chachoo, M.: Intrusion detection and prevention system: challenges and opportunities. In: International Conference on Computing for Sustainable Global Development (INDIAcom). IEEE (2014)
3. Asif, M.K., Khan, T.A., Taj, T.A., Naeem, U., Yakoob, S.: Network intrusion detection and its strategic importance. In: Business Engineering and Industrial Applications Colloquium (BEIAC) (2013)
4. Shah, B.: How to Choose Intrusion Detection Solution. SANS Institute Resources, 24 July 2001
5. Akbar, S., Rao, K.N., Chandulal, J.A.: Intrusion detection system methodologies based on data analysis. Int. J. Comput. Appl. 5(2), 14–18 (2010)
6. Nascimento, G., Correia, M.: Anomaly based Intrusion detection in software as service. In: 41st International Conference on Dependable Systems and Networks Workshops (DSN-W). IEEE (2011)
7. Mukherjee, B., Heberlein, L.T., Levitt, K.N.: Network intrusion detection. IEEE Netw. **8**(3), 26–41 (2002)
8. Sabahi, F., Movaghar, A.: Intrusion detection: a survey. In: 2008 Third International Conference on Systems and Networks Communications (2008)
9. Reddy, E.K.: Neural networks for intrusion detection and its applications. In: Proceedings of the World Congress on Engineering, vol II, London, UK (2013)
10. Kabiri, P., Ghorbani, A.A.: Research on intrusion detection and response: a survey. Int. J. Netw. Secur. **1**(2), 84–102 (2005)

11. Dharmapurikar, S., Lockwood, J.W.: Fast and scalable pattern matching for network intrusion detection systems. IEEE J. Sel. Areas Commun. **24**(10), 1781–1792 (2006)
12. Chou, T.-S.: Development of an intrusion detection and prevention course project using virtualization technology. Int. J. Educ. Develop. Using Inf. Commun. Technol. (IJEDICT) **7**(2), 46 (2011)
13. Hardikar, A.M.: Malware 101 – Viruses GSEC Gold Certification. SANS Institute (2008)
14. Szor, P.: The Art of Computer Virus and Defense. Addison Wesely Professional, Harlow (2005). ISBN 10: 0321304543, 13: 978-0321304544
15. Mathur, K., Hiranwal, S.: A survey on techniques in detection and analyzing malware executables. Int. J. Adv. Res. Comput. Sci. Softw. Eng. 3(4) (2013). ISSN: 2277 128X
16. Reddy, E.K.: Neural networks for intrusion detection and its applications. In: Proceedings of the World Congress on Engineering, vol. 2. no. 5 (2013)
17. Marakas, G.M.: Modern Data Warehousing, Mining, and Visualization: Core Concepts. Pearson Education, Upper Saddle River (2002). ISBN 0131014595
18. Ahmad, T., Ahmad, S., Jamshed, M.: A knowledge based Indian agriculture: With cloud ERP arrangement. In: 2015 International Conference on, Green Computing and Internet of Things (ICGCIoT), Noida, pp. 333–340 (2015). Doi:10.1109/ICGCIoT.2015.7380484

Signal Processing Based Raindrop Parameter Estimation

Pandharinath A. Ghonge[(✉)] and Kushal Tuckley

Ramrao Adik Institute of Technology, NERUL, Navi Mumbai 400706, India
ghongepa@yahoo.com

Abstract. This paper deals with Drop size distributions and number of drops and its volume in a frame. We are using video to frame conversion so that we can calculate the amount of rain water in a particular time. This system found to be more accurate and errors free like spreading, evaporation of drops induced errors are neglected as this system uses image processing tool to make analysis of data. It involves many operations which performed on raw data collected from high definition camera. System response time is also less.

Keywords: Raindrop count · Raindrop volume · Region bounding · Metric

1 Introduction

Rain is very important parameter on Earth and has much impact on life of living beings. Many techniques have been developed to measure the rain fall in particular terrestrial area, although Radar provides information accurately but limited by several errors. One of the main systems used for rain analysis are rain gauges but they have not so much accurate due to different losses incurred by them like Wind-induced errors, Evaporation and Wetting Losses. In this novel work, we used image processing techniques such as improved segmentation technique and morphological operations. We could determine the rain drop size distributions in the image. Then the volume of the drops is estimated assuming the spherical size of the rain drop. The input image set can be taken from 3D dataset. The complete operations is developed using Matlab tools.

2 Existing Methods

Measuring rain parameter is ancient process. In modern days Digital distrometer and rain gauges which are popular methods. But as inters of accuracy the gauges depends on many factors like wind, light, evaporation this losses led's will result into false readings. The evaporation types of losses are observed in storage type gauges where readings are taken after some days or in long duration. Other errors are device problem if device is not calibrated accurately all reading will be false.

© Springer Nature Singapore Pte Ltd. 2016
A. Unal et al. (Eds.): SmartCom 2016, CCIS 628, pp. 530–533, 2016.
DOI: 10.1007/978-981-10-3433-6_63

3   Methodology

This section explains the algorithm of IPRDPE system (Fig. 1).

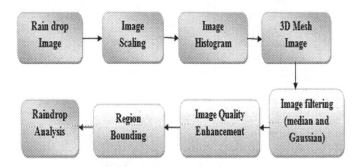

Fig. 1. Operational algorithm of IPRDPE system

This algorithm contain pre-processing, the selected image is scaled to [256 256] to make standard size. Histogram of resized image is to know the intensity variations in frames which can be used further processing. Gaussian and median filtering is applied to get image response becomes smooth. Median filter is used to reduce salt and pepper noise which is recognized by black and white spots on image can be inherently reduced by the use of median filter [1]. M-canny edge detection technique to trace the boundaries of raindrops, morphological operators used to extract the vital information, modified optimal segmentation helps to separate drop size distributions [2].

In this stage the Otsu thresholding method is used to enhance the quality of image in our context. Due to thresholding the image will be divided into two classes as background and foreground. Let we have two classes as C1 and C2 so e have to count the number of pixel that fall under each category for that we have to calculate probabilities of each class [3].

Probabilities of individual class can be calculated as,

$$P_1(k) = \sum\nolimits_{i=0}^{k} P_i \tag{1}$$

$$P_2(k) = \sum\nolimits_{i=k+1}^{L-1} P_i = 1 - P_1(k) \tag{2}$$

Mean intensity value for pixels under C_1, C_2

$$m_1(k) = \frac{1}{P_1(k)} \sum\nolimits_{i=0}^{k} iP_i \tag{3}$$

$$m_2(k) = \frac{1}{P_2(k)} \sum\nolimits_{i=k+1}^{L-1} iP_i \tag{4}$$

Average intensity is given by,

$$m_G = \sum_{i=0}^{L-1} iP_i \tag{5}$$

$$\sigma^2{}_B(k) = \frac{(m_G P_1(k) - m(k))^2}{P_1(k)(1 - P_1(k))} \tag{6}$$

Once k* is calculated image will be segmented as

$$g(x, y) = \begin{cases} 1 & if \ f(x, y) \geq k^* \\ 0 & if \ f(x, y) \leq k^* \end{cases} \tag{7}$$

K* is the threshold value which is the interclass variance.

Drop size are detected using different morphological operations such as Boundary Extraction and Hole felling techniques.

$$\beta(A) = A - (A \ominus B) \tag{8}$$

The rain drops can take either spherical or non spherical sizes. We are considering both objects. The objects are determined by using image morphological operations. The sphere object is determined by the formula and other objects are treated as non spherical [4].

4   Experimental Results

By implementing the algorithm of IPRDPE system. The background and drops are separated by thresholding and morphological operators helps to vies the drop size distributions as shown Fig. 2.

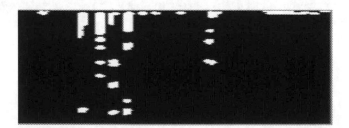

Fig. 2. Drop size distribution

To analyses the continues rain fall numbers f drops per frame can be calculated it helps to study rain fall rate in the particular time as shown Fig. 3. In this system mainly dealing with Raindrop counts, Drop size distributions associated with each frame.

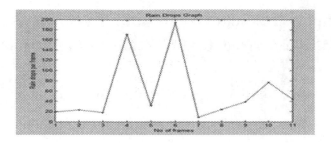

Fig. 3. No. of drop per frame

5 Conclusions

As we are counting raindrop and its volume before touching the ground surface our analysis is more accurate because errors like spreading of drops, evaporation, losses, wind induced errors are not affecting our calculations.

This system uses image processing tool to perform analysis it is cost effective and can be used in many applications like alertness to disaster managements in the city.

6 Future Scope

Since the performance of this project depends on selections of optimum threshold we will find possible method to select threshold values which will improve accuracy of system. 3D data and quality image sensing instruments of drops can improve experimental results.

References

1. Gupta, G.: Algorithm for image processing using improved median filter and comparison of mean, median and improved median filter. Int. J. Soft Comput. Eng. (IJSCE) **1**(5) (2011). ISSN: 2231–2307
2. Sawant, S., Ghonge, P.A.: Estimation of rain drop analysis using image processing. Int. J. Sci. Res. (IJSR) (2013)
3. Kumar, L.S., Lee, Y.H., Ong, J.T.: Truncated gamma drop size distribution models for rain attenuation in Singapore. IEEE Trans. Antennas Propag. **58**(4), 1325–1335 (2010)
4. Saylor, J.R., Sivasubramanian, N.A.: Edge detection methods applied to the analysis of spherical raindrop images. Appl. Opt. **46**, 5352–5367 (2007). Optical Society of America edition

Text Mining Methodology to Build Dependency Matrix from Unstructured Text to Perform Fault Diagnosis

Amruta Kulkarni[1(✉)], Jyoti Nighot[1], and Ashish Ramdasi[2]

[1] Kalyan Jadhav's College of Engineering and Management Research, Pune, India
amrutak0307@gmail.com, jyotinighot67@gmail.com
[2] Sinhgad Academy of Engineering, Pune, India
ramdasiap@gmail.com

Abstract. IEEE Standard 1232 provides the D-matrix for diagnosing quality in models. The framework give the ability to detect dependency in relation to symptoms and failure modes [1]. This paper describes an approach to construct D-matrix by mining unstructured repair verbatim text. At first d-matrix is constructed for different dataset, and then we can form a combined d-matrix from different dataset to identify common patterns in it. In this proposed method training is performed by using different classification methods on unstructured verbatim (Combined D-Matrix) collected from the medical domain.

Keywords: Text mining · Fault analysis · Fault diagnosis · Text processing · Unstructured repair verbatim

1 Introduction

Now a day's digital information is increasing at an incredible rate because of the internet [1]. Maintaining such unstructured data is recognized as one of the major problem in almost every organization. Even though this data will create some problem, it contains a large amount of expensive and valuable resources. Thus, effective management of electronic documents, especially management of complexity and specialization of knowledge expressed in those text documents, is vital to enterprise knowledge management [1]. One of such unstructured data is maintained in a database when the fault diagnosis process is performed on a system. One challenge that managers are facing is how to find a deep knowledge or required data from a collection of documents to solve a problem [1].

Data mining is gaining importance because digital data is growing so rapidly in recent years, and therefore a need is seen of getting knowledge and useful information [1, 8, 10, 11]. The goal of data mining is to derive useful information from a large set of data, finding specific required patterns across data sets [1, 10]. This paper proposes, a text mining method [1] for the purposes of getting the diagnostic information extracted from unstructured repair verbatim, which is then represented by a D - matrix. Recently, there has been lots of stress layed on the importance of ontologies and the corresponding efforts to manually develop them.

© Springer Nature Singapore Pte Ltd. 2016
A. Unal et al. (Eds.): SmartCom 2016, CCIS 628, pp. 534–540, 2016.
DOI: 10.1007/978-981-10-3433-6_64

Previously, different data mining techniques were presented to perform different knowledge tasks. D-matrix is one of the best diagnostic model provided by IEEE Standard [1, 2, 9]. The frameworks provides the facility to catch causal connections between symptoms and failure modes in a proper manner by constructing D-matrix [4, 9].

The process starts with fault diagnostics. Fault diagnosis is done by extracting the error codes present in the system. Using the error codes generated, the technicians follow certain diagnostics procedures to identify the nature of faults [9]. The data is then mined to find useful information and for developing D-matrix. These models are then used by the technicians [1, 10].

Paper is divided into following sections. The relevant literature survey is discussed in Sect. 2. The motivation for this work in giving in Sect. 3. The proposed work is provided in Sect. 4. Section 5, provides the result got and the evaluation of the approach by employing medical domain data. Section 6 provides the paper's conclusion.

2 Literature Survey

Ontology involves identification, definition and placing the concept definitions and their relationship. This paper [6] provides approach for extracting relevant ontology concepts from different text documents which the researcher then applied and validated in the domain of e-learning. This paper uses two evaluation measures precision and recall.

The D-matrix models are successfully utilized in the aerospace industry for identifying the causal dependencies among different parameters such as failure modes, symptoms etc. This is done by analyzing the structured service manual data [1].

In [3] researcher worked on developing D-matrices in various ways from different information layout and data sources in real world systems. The author then compares the various d-matrices and gives semantic problems raised during comparison.

The Steppard provides an assessment of the D-matrix's representation power. The paper also shows the limitations of using a d-matrix. The authors also states how to overcome those limitations and suggests algorithms and model types for which the D-matrix is appropriate [4]. The approach described in [4] gives solution at a great cost and has limit of not including all failure modes.

In [5] Deb and Pattipati present a multi-signal D-graph modeling methodology for cause-effect dependency modeling and develop diagnostic strategies for isolating faults in shortest possible time and provided a brief overview of the TEAMS software package. It also provides an algorithm to exploit the capabilities of this model to meet real world requirement.

In previous research d-matrix construction is by physically or using first principal. The D-matrices are constructed by using different types of data such as history information, engineering data, and sensory data [1–3, 5, 7] and yet no understanding is given for the inclusion of new or on time faults. While developing a d-matrix new faults should be considered, and d-matrix should give the homogeneous fault model.

3   Motivation

Fault diagnosis is critical process when performed on unstructured data. D-matrix generation from fault diagnosis on unstructured data makes it easier to identify faults and also shows the relationship between symptoms and fault. This is helpful to take action. This motivates the work in this paper. Implementing this using a different technique (in our case ANN, SVM and Naive Bayes) will give more accuracy.

4   Proposed System

Proposed Ontology-Based Comprehensive D-Matrix consists mainly three steps.

- Generating D-Matrix from unstructured repair verbatim
- Generate a combined D-Matrix
- Supply test verbatim on SVM, ANN and Naive Bayes machine learning algorithms.

In this system first a collection of repair verbatim is mined by using the [10] a. Document annotation b. Term extraction and c. Phrase merging. In these steps fault diagnoses ontology is applied to text. The d-matrix is created for each mined dataset [10]. Then a combined D-Matrix is generated by accepting only the common terms selected from D-matrices, ultimately generating single, generic D-Matrix.

The system will create D-Matrix for each dataset file of unstructured repair verbatim. [10] Here we are using a dataset containing diseases and its repair actions from a hospital domain. At first, the repair verbatim data is got by getting them from the OEM database which recorded during the fault diagnosis. In the first step, the terms, for example, part, symptom, and failure mode, repair actions which are appropriate to generate the D-Matrix are annotated from each repair verbatim by using the document annotation step. In this step, stop word are removed from the dataset and also lexical matching is performed to find a correct meaning of abbreviations.

Here, a boundary of sentence is identified by checking sentence separator [10]. Then identified terms are getting checked in repair verbatim. At last, Naïve Bayes, Support Vector Machine and Artificial Neural Network model are developed to perform training on unstructured repair verbatim. A comparison of both the technique will show the accuracy of fault diagnosis.

Algorithm:

Input: Hundreds of unstructured text repair verbatim for training and for testing single verbatim

Output: Combined D-Matrix and Fault Detection

Steps:

1. Accept verbatim field like medicine, mechanical etc.
2. Accept multiple verbatim files.
3. Perform document annotation: detect boundary of sentence by checking for full stop and other sentence separators.
4. Perform term extraction: search words like "parts", "symptoms", "fault/failure" and "action/repair".

5. Perform phrase merging: Search for association words with repair action. Fetch association word value from the database.
6. Store terms and association word into OEM database.
7. Generate D-Matrix for each verbatim file.
8. Combine same field D-Matrices into single D-Matrix. Perform union on D-Matrices.
9. Perform training using Support Vector Machine (SVM), Artificial Neural Network (ANN) and Naïve Bayes on hundreds of unstructured verbatim (Combined D-Matrix).
10. Supply test verbatim on SVM, ANN and Naïve Bayes machine learning algorithms.
11. Evaluate test results using SVM, ANN and Naïve Bayes. (Fault detection)
12. Compare SVM, ANN and Naïve Bayes on parameters such as accuracy, learning time and evaluation time (Fig. 1).

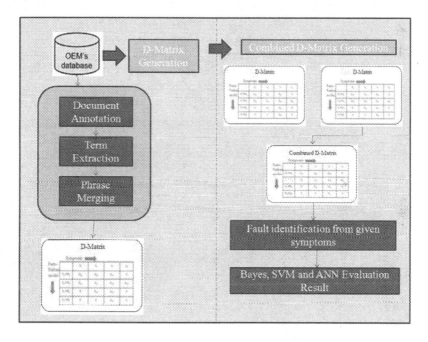

Fig. 1. System architecture (Source: [1], p. 69)

5   Results

Considered 500 repair verbatim from medical domains which are collected through the internet. The following criteria's have been used to evaluate the performance of our system- fault accuracy, execution time, and functions like probability distribution function and cumulative distribution function. Our method reduces the large number of unstructured dataset of repair verbatim into structured D-matrix. Figure 2 shows sample d-matrix which contains a repair verbatim related to brain diseases.

disorder.txt	unusual s...	child may h...	impairmen...	communic...	restricted r...	an insisten...	depresion	heightene...	flight of ide...	increased...	decreased...	hyperactivity	depressed...
brain body	0.5	0.5	0.5	0.5	0.5	0.5	0	0	0	0	0	0	0
brain body	0	0	0	0	0	0	0.2	0.2	0.2	0.2	0.2	0.2	0
brain body	0	0	0	0	0	0	0	0	0	0	0	0	0.2
brain body	0	0	0	0	0	0	0	0	0	0	0	0	0
brain body	0	0	0	0	0	0	0	0	0	0	0	0	0
brain body	0	0	0	0	0	0	0	0	0	0	0	0	0
brain body	0	0	0	0	0	0	0	0	0	0	0	0	0

Fig. 2. Sample D-matrix

In the existing system Naïve Bayes is used for training, and we are using two additional methods that are SVM and ANN [12, 13]. Use of SVM gives better result as compared to ANN and Naive Bayes. Figure 3 shows approximate SVM, ANN and Naive Bayes comparison in terms of fault detection accuracy. Here we also show the actual fault detection. Figure 4 shows the comparison result based on execution time. For this first we have calculated the time required for each method (SVM, ANN and Naive Bayes) by using system time and then compared the same timing with each other. It shows that SVM required less time for its operation.

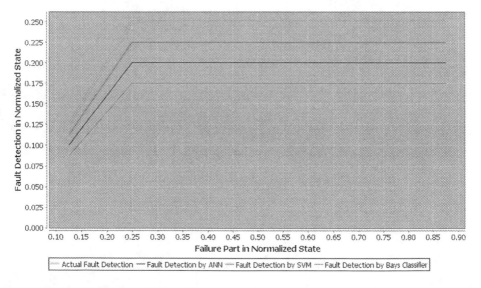

Fig. 3. Comparing SVM, ANN and Naïve Bayes parameter used is fault accuracy

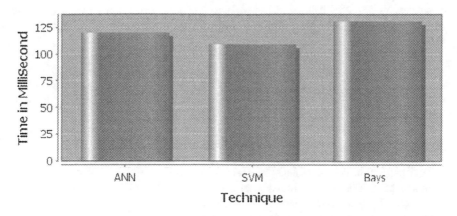

Fig. 4. Comparing SVM, ANN and Naïve Bayes fault detection techniques in terms of execution time

6 Conclusion

Generating D-Matrix automatically for fault diagnosis by using a text driven approach has more impact than manual construction of d-matrix. This framework will helps the service technician, or doctor in medical domain to detect the faults and take actions according to it. This will help to solve various problems such as removing ambiguity and to establish a better co - relation between the terms. Implementing this with different techniques gives better accuracy.

Acknowledgment. Amruta Kulkarni would like to thank to her guide Asst. Prof. Jyoti Nighot for her guidance and instructive comments on this paperwork. The authors would like to offer regards to all of those who supported in any respect during the completion of this paper.

References

1. Rajpathak, D.G., Singh, S.: An ontology-based text mining method to develop D-matrix from unstructured text. IEEE Trans. Syst. Man Cybern. Syst. **44**(7), 966–977 (2014)
2. Sheppard, J., Kaufman, M., Wilmering, T.: Model based standards for diagnostic and maintenance information integration. In: Proceedings of IEEE Autitestcon Conference, pp. 304–310 (2012)
3. Singh, S., Holland, S.W., Bandyopadhyay, P.: Trends in the development of system-level fault dependency matrices. In: Proceedings of IEEE Aerospace Conference, pp. 1–9 (2010)
4. Sheppard, J.W., Butcher, S.G.W.: A formal analysis of fault diagnosis with D-matrices. J. Electron. Test. Theory Appl. **23**, 309–322 (2007). Springer Science
5. Deb, S., Pattipati, S.K., Raghavan, V., Shakeri, M., Shrestha, R.: Multi-signal flow graphs: a novel approach for system testability analysis and fault diagnosis. IEEE Aerosp. Electron. Syst. **10**(5), 14–25 (1995)

6. Gaeta, M., Orciuoli, F., Paolozzi, S., Salerno, S.: Ontology extraction for knowledge reuse: the e-learning perspective. IEEE Trans. Syst. Man Cybern. Part A Syst. Hum. **41**(4), 798–809 (2011)
7. Strasser, S., Sheppard, J., Schuh, M., Angryk, R., Izurieta, C.: Graph based ontology-guided data mining for D-matrix model maturation. In: Proceedings of IEEE Aerospace Conference, pp. 1–12 (2011)
8. Zhong, N., Li, Y., Wu, S.-T.: Effective pattern discovery for text mining. IEEE Trans. Knowl. Data Eng. **24**(1), 30–44 (2012)
9. Thombare, T.R., Dole, L.: D-matrix: fault diagnosis framework. Int. J. Innovative Res. Comput. Commun. Eng. **3**(3) (2015)
10. Kulkarni, A., Nighot, J.: Text mining method to develop D-matrix for fault diagnosis. Int. J. Recent Innovation Trends Comput. Commun. **4**(3) (2016)
11. Dunham, M.H.: Data Mining: Introductory and Advanced Topics. Pearson Education
12. https://en.wikipedia.org/wiki/Support_vector_machine
13. https://en.wikipedia.org/wiki/Artificial_neural_network

A Comprehensive Survey on Intrusion Detection Systems in Wireless Sensor Network

Amol R. Dhakne[✉] and P.N. Chatur

Department of CSE, Government College of Engineering, Amravati, India
dhakne.amol5@gmail.com, prashant_chatur@rediffmail.com

Abstract. Wireless sensor network is of prime importance because of its applicability in various domains ranging from healthcare applications to military applications. Security of such networks is important as these carry confidential information. Security of Wireless Sensor Network is divided in three phases, prevention, detection and mitigation. In Prevention phase, care is taken so that attack should not occur. But most of the times it is not possible to prevent attacks, so it is very important to detect them as early as possible so that these will not harm a lot to wireless sensor network and that phase is called as intrusion detection. Once Intrusion has been detected we have to take actions to cure from it and it is called as mitigation. So, Intrusion detection is most important phase as far as security of wireless sensor network is concerned. This paper discusses about various detection methodologies such as Anomaly based, Misuse based and Specification based IDS, various decision making schemes for intrusion. Major focus of this paper is to understand various Intrusion Detection Systems that are proposed for wireless sensor network. These are discussed with different issues with advantages and disadvantages. Finally paper gives future directions for selection of Intrusion Detection System.

Keywords: Intrusion · Intrusion detection · Wireless sensor network (WSN) · Mobile ad hoc network (MANET) · Security

1 Introduction

Wireless Sensor Network is widely used in various fields of Science and Technology as they are capable to gather information about human beings and environment. Now days WSN is used for various applications including highway traffic, health care and military surveillance, also in earthquake prediction, water quality analysis, building safety, pollution, ocean and wildlife, manufacturing machinery performance, and so on [1]. So, Security of WSN is of utmost importance as we need to keep patient health records confidential so that it can be secured from third parties in healthcare application. Also in military applications we need to tackle security gap in the network. More Information on Security can be found in [2–4].

Security attacks in WSNs are mainly partitioned in two types: Active attacks and Passive attacks. Passive attacks are not visible or hidden and they can tap communication channel to gather data; or they can harm the networking elements that are working. Node

© Springer Nature Singapore Pte Ltd. 2016
A. Unal et al. (Eds.): SmartCom 2016, CCIS 628, pp. 541–549, 2016.
DOI: 10.1007/978-981-10-3433-6_65

malfunctioning, traffic analysis and eavesdropping are some examples of passive attack. Active attacks affect the operations in network. Networking services can degraded because of these attacks. Black hole, Sinkhole, wormhole attacks, jamming and Denial-of-Service (DoS) are some examples of active attack [3–5].

Securing WSN from these attacks works in 3 phases, Prevention step is aimed to prevent attack before it should happen and it is called as defense against attack. In Detection phase we need to know presence of attack and identify the nodes that are being harmful. If first phase fails then it is always important to find the attacks quickly so that it can harm less to network. Most of the time it is not possible to defend attack from happening so Detection phase is very important as far as security of WSNs is concerned. Mitigation (reacting to the attack) is last phase and is aimed to mitigate any attack after its proper detection and in this phase affected nodes are removed to secure the network.

Intrusions are any unauthorized (unwanted) behaviors in network. Intrusion detection is detection of any malicious activity in a network carried out by any network member. Intrusion detection systems provide following information to supportive system such as identification of intruder, time of intrusion, activity, type and layer where intrusion occurs. This information is useful in third line of defense as specific information is available to mitigate the attacks. Therefore, IDSs are of utmost importance for security of network.

WSNs are limited by various factors such as small memory size, limited battery etc. IDS that are applicable to traditional networks are not applicable to WSN [6]. So, developing effective IDS for WSNs is very important task which lead us to do some survey on existing IDSs in WSN.

2   Intrusion Detection System Methodologies

IDS are equivalent of burglar alarms that notify the presence of intrusion if any. IDSs are majorly categorized in three categories according to their functionality as follows:

2.1   Anomaly Based Detection

In this normal operations are recorded and deviation is from normal behavior is considered as anomaly. The drawback of this type is that normal operations need to be recorded and updated regularly. The benefit of this methodology is that it detects previously unencountered or unknown attacks. Anomaly based IDSs are divided into three types based on nature of processing such as Statistical based, Knowledge based and Machine learning based Intrusion detection methodologies [7, 8].

Statistical based IDSs work by analyzing network traffic and then it generates profile reflecting its operating nature. Reference profile is created when network is functioning in normal condition in absence of any attack. Then after, profiles are created periodically and network is monitored. By comparing profiles to reference profile, anomaly Score is generated. If deviation is above certain threshold, IDS will indicate existence of intrusion.

Knowledge based anomaly IDSs depends on pre information or knowledge of network parameters at normal conditions and at different attacks. These can be dependent on expert systems based on rules of classification for audit data, finite state machine or any data clustering and outlier detection techniques.

Machine learning based anomaly IDSs generate model of some analyzed pattern. These can be updated periodically, for improvement in performance of intrusion detection based on previous results. These can make use of different techniques such as fuzzy logic, Marrow models, Bayesian networks, neural networks or genetic algorithms.

2.2 Misuse Based Detection

This can be called as Rule based or Signature based detection as signatures of already known attacks are generated to detect future attacks. If suppose there are 3 wrong login attempts, we can consider it as intrusion and whenever next time such attempts/signatures are recorded it is considered as Intrusion. Benefit of this method is that it can detect known attacks very effectively and so these have low false positive rate. Drawback of this technique is that by these methods it is not possible to detect the new types of attacks. These can be considered similar to Anti-Virus systems as these detect mostly known attack patterns [9]. In rule based IDSs the behaviors that attempt to break the rules of networking are considered as anomalies. In [10], author presented some rules to detect network anomalies, such as Interval, Retransmission, Integrity, Delay rule.

2.3 Specification Based Detection

In this technique, specifications and limits about the correct execution of some program is already described. Operation of program with respect to described specifications is checked [11]. These kinds of methods are capable of detecting the previously unknown attacks. Also, these incur low false positive rate.

Major difference between Anomaly based and Misuse based detection method is that, first tries to detect effects of bad behavior and second tries to detect already known bad behaviors [9].

Specification based technique take advantage of both techniques to characterize illegal behavior. In this method, attacks are detected as deviations from specifications about execution of program similar to anomaly based approach. These have low false alarm rate as compared to anomaly based method as specifications are selected manually. Disadvantage of this technique is that cost and time associated with development of specifications and constraints is high relative to low false alarm rate [12].

3 Decision Making in IDS

There are two ways of making a decision about the intrusion in a system.

3.1 Collaborative Decision Making

In this method, decisions about events are taken by considering the collaboration and interaction among all (or some) network members. In this, event is decided as intrusion if majority of voting is against the normality of event.

3.2   Independent Decision Making

In this, each and every member of network (sensor node) takes decision about the events around them.

According to [8], decisions about particular event are divided in four categories such as False Negative, False Positive, True Negative and True Positive.

Some of the events such as limited transmission power, collisions, fading battery supply, and packet drop etc. lead to false positives due to wireless nature of communication for IDSs in WSNs [13].

- After alert from IDS about any intrusion IDS doesn't try to prevent because prevention part is left with IPS. After alert from IDS following actions should be taken.
- It should generate audit records.
- Network members, system administrator and base station should get notification of intrusion.
- Location of intrusion and its identity should be provided with notification of intrusion.
- If intrusion exists, in order to stop the intrusion, mitigation method should be induced. For example, there should be collaborative system where all network members are able to take corrective action. Especially, network members which are near to location of incident should start taking corrective actions.

4   IDS Proposed for WSNs

In this section, IDS proposed for WSNs are summarized. Applying traditional IDSs directly to WSN is difficult, so first in Sect. 4.1, limitations of WSN and challenges of WSN are presented. Section 4.2 presents the overview on major IDSs for WSNs.

4.1   Limitations and Research Challenges in WSNs

WSNs are lacking in infrastructure (i.e. gateways, routers, base stations, etc.) which makes designing algorithms and WSNs are limited by resources such as bandwidth, throughput, which need to be used wisely. Following are some of the major limitations and related challenges that need to be considered while designing IDSs for WSN.

- WSNs are lacking in Infrastructure to support the operations of communication, routing, encryption, traffic analysis etc.
- There is always chance of physical capture, tampering or hijacking of sensor node which can compromise network operation.
- Nodes which are compromised are prone to various attacks such as black hole, wormhole, sinkhole etc., which can halt the operation of network.
- Decisions need to be taken in collaborative fashion. There is lack of trusted authority in WSNs.
- There is possibility of eavesdropping as communication is wireless which can reveal important data to adversaries.

Whenever there is need to design IDS for WSN, above limitations and challenges should be considered.

4.2 Proposed Schemes

IDSs that are proposed for Wireless Sensor Network are as follows.

4.2.1 Clustering (Hierarchical) Based IDSs

In [14], author proposed hierarchical framework for intrusion detection and processing in WSN. For the experiments they gave the importance to one hop clustering and believed that IDS is helpful for securing industrial applications which is carried out through two lines of defense.

In [15], Method is used to detect intrusion in energy efficient way based on isolation table. They proposed IDS with two- level of clustering. According to the experiments they have conducted isolation table helps them to detect intrusions in efficient manner. The problem with this approach is that, each level need to monitor the other level and it should report abnormal behaviors to base station. But if higher level does not report intrusion to the base station then there can be problem to deal with intrusion. In this case, higher level nodes can just block the alert messages generated by lower level nodes.

In [16], IDS based on clustering approach focuses on security of CHs. In this approach, CH is monitored by members of cluster in time scheduled manner so that energy for cluster members will be saved. And at same time, cluster head monitors the cluster members by not taking help of them which also saves energy of cluster members. Even though this approach saves energy of cluster members, it has problem with its key management which is part of IDS that establishes pairwise keys among nodes. IDS make use of keys to authenticate the messages. In WSN new nodes need to be deployed with time, so key management approach is not that much appropriate for IDS.

In [17], hierarchical IDS model is considered where network is divided into different groups called cluster with cluster head for each. In this model centralized routing is used where packets are forwarded to CH first and then base station. Intruder detectors are placed at CH so that minimum number of detectors will be required. This work doesn't have any simulation result and it not clear whether this approach works as promised.

4.2.2 Distributed and Collaborative IDS

In [18], Distributed approach is proposed as solution to cooperative intrusion detection, where nodes are equipped with local detection mechanism and they are supposed to identify intrusion in distributed way. Detector modules get triggered when they identify any intrusion in neighborhood sensor node. In [10], Specification based intrusion detection algorithm is proposed, where decentralized approach is used in which intrusion detector were placed in entire network. Whatever information is collected and its processing is carried out in distributed fashion. Authors claim that their distributed approach is far better than centralized approach as intrusion detector at different places had different views of network being distributed throughout network.

4.2.3   Statistical Model Based Approach

In [19], authors presented algorithm which first identified the suspected nodes and then it start identifying intruder in list by making use of network flow graph. This algorithm helps to detect sinkhole attacks. Algorithm implemented the parametric technique of statistical approach based on chi-square test. According to author's observation, this approach is reasonable as far as communication and computational loads are concerned.

4.2.4   Game Theory Based Approaches

Maximum times these approaches are provided as solutions of security for wired networks. But, it is little bit difficult to implement it in Wireless sensor network as these are having some limitations of energy. Also performance of Wireless sensor network decreases as new node is added. In [20], non-co-operative approach was proposed for detecting misbehaving nodes in clustered sensor network. A non-co-operative game approach, which formulates attack defense game as non-co-operative two players non zero sum game, achieves Nash equilibrium whenever defense player finds and protects most vulnerable cluster.

In [21, 22], authors considered participants of game as attack and detection and strategies for both parties have been formulated. Non cooperative, non-zero game model approach has been considered as a normal strategy. Both of these approaches focus on finding out the weakest node in network and then strategy has been provided to defend that node. Drawback of these schemes is that only one of intrusion can be detected by leaving others not detected.

4.2.5   Anomaly Detection Based IDSs

In [23], authors have presented the survey article on anomaly based intrusion detection schemes. Authors have suggested considering energy consumption factor whenever one is going to design intrusion detection system so as to minimize energy consumption.

In [24], lightweight method has been proposed to detect the intrusion that is anomalous. In this approach, information from OSI layers of protocol stack such as routing tables, list of neighbors sleep/wake up schedules, strength of received signal, MAC layer transmission schedules has been considered as main idea to detect anomalous behavior. Multiple detectors have been placed to monitor different layers of OSI stack, so that detection rate will be increased. This approach considers only outsider attack by forgiving the outsider attack only.

4.3   Drawbacks of Existing IDS

(a) *Simulation*

No proper simulation has been proposed till now for anomaly based or misuse-based intrusion detection scheme. It is cumbersome to analyze IDS mechanism effectively as there is lack of real network.

(b) *Real world implementation*

As per today's knowledge, only some real world implementations of IDS schemes are available. In [13], author has shown some real world implementation of Cooperative intrusion detection scheme in wireless sensor network. Even though some simulations and some statistical analysis are available, these implementations are important to check applicability of IDS in real world.

(c) *Lightweight modules*

Sensor nodes in Wireless Sensor Networks are battery operated and these batteries are limited in power. So while designing any IDS one should consider energy factor so that IDS should consume less energy as much as possible.

(d) *Attack Specific*

Most existing IDS detect only one or two attacks by using different network and hardware considerations. It is hard to combine all methods in universal platform.

4.4 Issues Concerning the Proposed Schemes

Following issues are drawn in various proposed IDS in WSNs:

In Clustering based IDS, clustering algorithms may consume energy for formation of clusters. After creation of cluster, Cluster heads are elected and they can fail at some point so they need to be secured. If cluster head is not a powerful node then overhead of CH makes network to utilize resources very quickly.

In agent based IDS, network load and latency have been reduced, but they cause very high energy consumption of nodes. Communication in agents or in agent and coordinator can become reason for bottle neck or congestion in network.

Rule based IDSs need continuous updating of rules so as to deal with new attacks.

In game theory based IDSs, network security administrator can change the parameters to adjust the intrusion detection rate. Drawback of these IDSs is that, it is not-adaptive and it requires interference of people for stable operation.

4.5 Future Directions for Selecting the IDS for WSNs

Today, energy consumption is the biggest issue in wireless sensor network. WSN needs to sense surrounding phenomenon, process that information and then transmit the resultant data. For all these operations to be carried out WSN consumes a lot of energy. That's why, design of IDS should be such that it should consume least energy and should make WSN to utilize its energy for important operations. Hierarchical model of IDS is best suited as a solution of requirement of least consumption of energy. In this, network will be divided into different clusters and each cluster will have a CH. In this model, CH is responsible to do communication with Base Station (BS) and there is no need for all nodes to send data directly to BS, which ultimately reduces energy consumption and increases lifetime of WSN.

Apart from all these IDS that have been surveyed, we have to consider trust factor of sensor nodes to find out the malicious activities in WSN. To the best of our knowledge, there are no proper IDS that consider the trust factor to design IDS for WSN that consider the benefits of hierarchical approach. In future, this will be a good topic of research.

5 Conclusion

This paper gives introduction about various intrusion detection methodologies such as anomaly based, Misuse based, specification based intrusion detection methodologies. Also, this paper focuses on decision making methodologies that help to decide whether particular sensor node is malicious or not. Thirdly, the difference between MANET and WSN has been described with limitations of WSN and the IDSs proposed for WSN have been discussed with their important aspects. Finally, the drawbacks and issues concerning existing IDS have been discussed and future directions have been suggested in order to help researchers to select IDS.

References

1. Akyildiz, I.F., Su, W., Sankarasubramaniam, Y., Cayirci, E.: A survey on sensor networks. IEEE Commun. Mag. **40**(8), 102–114 (2002)
2. Zhou, Y., Fang, Y., Zhang, Y.: Securing wireless sensor networks: a survey. IEEE Commun. Surv. Tutorials **10**(3), 6–28 (2008)
3. Cayirci, E., Rong, C.: Security in Wireless Ad Hoc and Sensor Networks. Wiley, New York (2009)
4. Wang, Y., Attebury, G., Ramamurthy, B.: A survey of security issues in wireless sensor networks. IEEE Commun. Surv. Tutorials **8**(2), 2–23 (2006)
5. Padmavathi, G., Shanmugapriya, D.: A survey of attacks, security mechanisms and challenges in wireless sensor networks. Int. J. Comput. Sci. (IJCS) **4**(1), 1–9 (2009)
6. Butun, I., Sankar, R.: A brief survey of access control in wireless sensor networks. In: Proceedings of IEEE Consumer Communications and Networking Conference, Las Vegas, Nevada (2011)
7. Garcia-Teodoro, P., Diaz-Verdejo, J., Macia-Fernandez, G., Vazquez, E.: Anomaly-based network intrusion detection: techniques, systems and challenges. J. Comput. Secur. **28**(1–2), 18–28 (2009). Elsevier
8. Patcha, A., Park, J.M.: An overview of anomaly detection techniques: existing solutions and latest technological trends. J. Comput. Netw. **51**(12), 3448–3470 (2007). Elsevier
9. Sobh, T.S.: Wired and wireless intrusion detection system: classifications, good characteristics and state-of-the-art. J. Comput. Stand. Interfaces **6**, 670–694 (2006). Elsevier
10. da Silva, A.P., Martins, M., Rocha, B., Loureiro, A., Ruiz, L., Wong, H.C.: Decentralized intrusion detection in wireless sensor networks. In: Proceedings of 1st ACM International Workshop on Quality of Service and Security in Wireless and Mobile Networks (Q2SWinet 2005), pp. 16–23. ACM Press (2005)
11. Anantvalee, T., Wu, J.: A survey on intrusion detection in mobile ad hoc networks. In: Xiao, Y., Shen, X.S., Du, D.-Z. (eds.) Wireless Network Security, pp. 159–180. Springer, New York (2007)

12. Sun, B., Osborne, L., Xiao, Y., Guizani, S.: Intrusion detection techniques in mobile ad hoc and wireless sensor networks. IEEE Trans. Wirel. Commun. **14**(5), 63 (2007)
13. Michiardi, P., Molva, R.: Core: a collaborative reputation mechanism to enforce node cooperation in mobile ad hoc networks. In: Jerman-Blažič, B., Klobučar, T. (eds.) Advanced Communications and Multimedia Security. ITIFIP, vol. 100, pp. 107–121. Springer, Boston (2002). doi:10.1007/978-0-387-35612-9_9
14. Crossbow MICAz mote data sheet. http://bullseye.xbow.com:81/Products/Product_pdf_files/Wireless_pdf/MICAz_Datasheet.pdf
15. Chen, R.C., Hsieh, C.F., Huang, Y.F.: A new method for intrusion detection on hierarchical wireless sensor networks. In: Proceedings of ACM ICUIMC-09 (2009)
16. Su, C.C., Chang, K.M., Kuo, Y.H., Horng, M.F.: The new intrusion prevention and detection approaches for clustering-based sensor networks. In: Proceedings of IEEE Wireless communications and Networking Conference (2005)
17. Strikos, A.A.: A full approach for intrusion detection in wireless sensor networks. School of Information and Communication Technology (2007)
18. Krontiris, I., Benenson, Z., Giannetsos, T., Freiling, F.C., Dimitriou, T.: Cooperative intrusion detection in wireless sensor networks. In: Roedig, U., Sreenan, Cormac, J. (eds.) EWSN 2009. LNCS, vol. 5432, pp. 263–278. Springer, Heidelberg (2009). doi:10.1007/978-3-642-00224-3_17
19. Ngai, E., Liu, J., Lyu, M.: On the intruder detection for sinkhole attack in wireless sensor networks. In: ICC 2006, Istanbul, Turkey (2006)
20. Agah, A., Das, S.K., Basu, K., Asadi, M.: Intrusion detection in sensor networks: a non-cooperative game approach. In: 3rd IEEE International Symposium on Network Computing and Applications, pp. 343–346 (2004)
21. Agah, A., Das, S.K., Basu, K. Asadi, M.: Intrusion detection in sensor networks: a non-cooperative game approach. In: Proceedings of 3rd IEEE International Symposium on Network Computing and Applications (NCA 2004), pp. 343–346 (2004)
22. Agah, A., Das, S.K.: Preventing DoS attacks in wireless sensor networks: a repeated game theory approach. Int. J. Netw. Secur. **5**(2), 145–153 (2007)
23. Rajasegarar, S., Leckie, C., Palaniswami, M.: Anomaly detection in wireless sensor networks. IEEE Trans. Wirel. Commun. **15**(4), 34–40 (2008)
24. Bhuse, V., Gupta, A.: Anomaly intrusion detection in wireless sensor networks. J. High Speed Netw. **15**(1), 33–51 (2006)

Comparison of Support Vector Machine and Artificial Neural Network for Delineating Debris Covered Glacier

Rahul Nijhawan[1(✉)], Josodhir Das[1], and Raman Balasubramanian[2]

[1] Department of Earthquake Engineering, Indian Institute of Technology Roorkee,
Roorkee 247667, India
rahul.deq2014@iitr.ac.in, rahulnijhawan2010@gmail.com,
josoeqiitr@gmail.com
[2] Department of Computer Science and Engineering, Indian Institute of Technology Roorkee,
Roorkee 247667, India
balaiitr@gmail.com

Abstract. Glacier mapping accuracy plays very important role in studies like mass balance of glacier, water resource management and in understanding the health of the glacier. Several of the present glaciers are covered with debris of different thickness. So it becomes difficult to distinguish debris covered glacier from the adjacent valley rock, alone with the use of optical data because of the same reflectance in visible to near infrared region. In this paper we have trained Support vector machine (SVM) and Artificial neural network (ANN) on several parameters such as slope, surface curvature, thermal data and also on several texture parameter, such as variance, skewness, entropy, homogeneity, mean and dissimilarity. Then both the algorithms were applied on the part of the alaknanda basin. It was observed that both ANN and SVM produced good results, with accuracy of SVM slightly higher than that of ANN algorithm.

Keywords: Glacier · Debris · Artificial neural network · Support vector machine

1 Introduction

Change in the climatic conditions could be easily assessed by frequent monitoring of glacier in remote locations where it is very difficult to set up the climatic stations. Himalayan glaciers are retreating rapidly as in different parts of the world [1–3]. Glacier retreat results in more amount of debris covering the ice, which makes very difficult to map glacier with optical data because of same spectral reflectance with that of nearby rock materials.

One of the major way to distinguish the debris covered glacier from that of the surrounding rock is by means of surface temperature. As the ice present below the glacier will cause a low temperature to above present debris, compared to that of the neighboring rock. This we can easily measure with the help of the thermal information provided by the Landsat imagery, provided that the thickness of the debris do not exceed a given limit. It has been proven that the debris thickness should not exceed 0.5 m for the thermal data to identify the glacier present beneath [4]. Also non glacier area present in the shadow region have surface temperature same as that of the clean-ice region, while

© Springer Nature Singapore Pte Ltd. 2016
A. Unal et al. (Eds.): SmartCom 2016, CCIS 628, pp. 550–557, 2016.
DOI: 10.1007/978-981-10-3433-6_66

glacier covered with debris turns out to be more warmer, which makes things complicated in the shaded moraine complex to make distinction between the glacier and the non-glacier area.

A hierarchical model was constructed based on elevation, curvature, slope and aspect for identifying debris covered glaciers at Nanga Parbat (Pakistan) as discussed in [5]. This model works well but still contains some of the inaccuracies. This model works inefficiently at the glacier terminus and at the edges.

A semi-automated approach was manifested to delineate the debris covered glacier at Swiss Alps by using slope gradient and TM4/TM5 ratio image [6]. This approach was more improved by associating vegetation classification, change detection and analysis of neighborhood pixels. This approach when applied on the Himalayas did not produced optimal results. While on changing the gradient threshold in DEM to $12°$, many parts of the debris covered glaciers were identified. Further multi temporal data also turned out to be of no use to delineate the glacier termini, due to the stable nature of the glacier termini. Some of the debris covered areas were also covered with vegetation, so using NDVI (Normalized difference vegetation index) as threshold should be taken into consideration.

Another multi-dimensional approach was developed which made use of multispectral classification, filters and slope [7]. More acceptable results were obtained when the slope threshold value was changed to $12°$. Wherever bare rock was present, the methodology showed misclassification.

Further a method was developed for identifying debris covered glaciers by clustering surface curvature features [8]. This method was helpful in describing the surface characteristics but did not perfectly identified the debris covered glaciers.

2   Study Area

The study area covers Alaknanda river basin of Uttarakhand state in India constituting the higher Himalayan ranges as shown in Fig. 1.

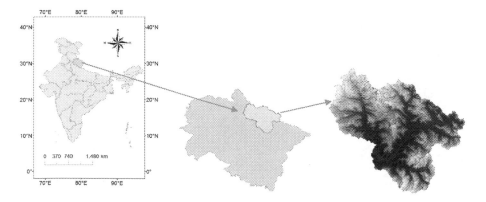

Fig. 1. Shows the location of the study region (Alaknanda basin, Uttarakhand). Landsat satellite image collected from the USGS website.

3 Methodology

3.1 Artificial Neural Network

In this section we would discuss how we will be using ANN for identifying the debris covered glacier in a section of alaknanda basin. Several of the terrain parameters were being used such as slope, aspect, surface curvature, elevation and surface temperature. Also texture parameters were being used such as entropy, skewness, homogeneity, variance, dissimilarity and mean. Table 1 shows the statistics for the obtained texture indices along with Fig. 2 representing the obtained images of the texture parameters. The chosen ANN was a totally connected feed forward multilayer perceptron which was being trained by a back propagation learning mechanism [9]. A perceptron basically contains an input layer, single or multiple hidden layers and a single output layer. The signal being given as input by the user moves forward in the network, layer by layer. The advantage of using ANN is that they provide the needful estimation function which basically inverts the relation between actual debris covered glacier and that obtained from multispectral image information [9–13].

Table 1. Mean statistics for the shown texture indices (Homogeneity, entropy and variance).

	Homogeneity	Entropy	Variance
Sand	0.42	1.77	1.85
Debris Cover	0.17	1.87	12.91
Clouds	1	0	0
Clean Ice	0.87	0.03	0.05

Training is the medium by which ANN adapts itself to the pattern or structure taken by the dataset. Data mining in such a way is very efficient and accurate compared to others such as geophysical modeling [10]. In case of ANN it is also possible to train it again on entirely different dataset. Like for the data which has been taken by completely different sensor. Also they are able to give arbitrarily complex functions and so is capable of inverting the interrelations of viewing geometry, geology, vegetation, morphology of snow and topography [14–16]. ANN serves in a better way as on investigating the trained ANN, it informs about the functional relations present between the debris and the data of satellite images, hence depicting the insight of the held processes. More advantages of using ANN are (a) more data adaptability, (b) data distribution has no prior assumption, (c) takes care of noise, (d) make use of prior knowledge (e) training is easy from satellite data or from other sources, and (f) fuzzy solutions are near to realistic decisions [10].

3.2 ANN Architecture

ANN architecture is very important step for any application of ANN. It is very essential to find out a simple structure which can resolve the problem. We tried many of ANN architectures, and found out the most suitable architecture was 40-18-12. It was done by hit and trial method. Here ANN contains 40, 18 and 12 neurons in the 3 hidden layers

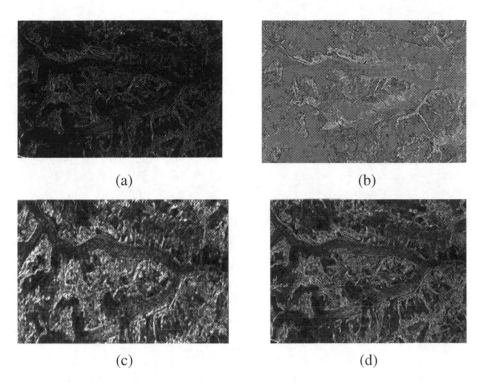

(a)

(b)

(c)

(d)

Fig. 2. Computation of texture parameters for delineating debris covered glaciers. (a) Variance, (b) Skewness, (c) Dissimilarity and (d) Mean euclidean distance

respectively. It was observed that this specific ANN structured allowed better data adaptability.

Here we have assigned a sigmoidal function to the first and the second layer of the ANN (transig) and the linear function (purelin) was assigned to the third layer of ANN. The training was done using Levenberg-Marquardt back propagation (LMBP) method [17]. ANN training also made use of some of the techniques such as Joint Approximate Diagonalization of Eigen matrix (JADE) [17], Self-adapting DE [18], Differential Evolution (DE) algorithm [19] and Efficient Population Utilization Strategy Particle Swarm Optimizer [20]. Also infact now a days EC Algorithms are very popularly being used but inspite of it LMBP performed better [21].

The LMBP technique is a method dependent on gradient which converge to a local minima. So the multi start approach was being used in order to optimize the chances for finding the minimum global error. In this approach we have repeated the training to around 120 times. The initial values were given randomly. Finally that ANN model was selected which outputs the most optimal value of correlation of determination (r^2). Initially random values were selected from the uniform distribution [−0.1, 0.1] [12]. Value of bias was assigned 1 [9].

There are several approaches which have been used to stop ANN overtraining such as weight update decay, Bayesian approach, early stopping [22]. Here we used early stopping with cross validation method. This technique halted the ANN when the value of error was small. We also validated the working of ANN model by applying it on 25% of the training dataset considering it as unseen dataset.

3.3 ANN Data Input

The input parameters given as training set were surface curvature, slope, aspect, surface temperature, elevation and also texture parameters such as entropy, variance, homogeneity, dissimilarity and mean. Also 7 spectral bands from the Landsat TM/ETM + images were inputted which basically gave the information of the snow, vegetation cover and also the thermal band was being included. The target dataset was a section of alaknanda basin.

The final selection of the inputs was done on the basis of hit and trial method. We have taken input several combinations. This was being governed by observing the value of correlation of determination (r^2), and that combination was selected in which the value r^2 was found to be highest.

4   Support Vector Machine

This algorithm is used for classification in remote sensing since many years. This algorithm is based on statistical learning which was originally developed by Vapnik [23]. Many of its pros include its statistical stability, effective in computation and robustness. When we solve any problem with very limited samples, above advantages serves uniquely to SVM in the field of classification and pattern recognition. Thus this particular algorithm has been widely used by researchers in mentioned fields. Particularly SVM is meant for binary classification, but researchers have been using it for multi-class classification in turn leading to its popularity.

Depending on the minimization of the structural risk, the generalization capacity of the SVM is improved by reducing the error of the training data set [24]. Dividing space vector of lower dimension is generally difficult, so we basically map them into a higher dimension region in turn using the kernel function to increase the separation. The most frequently used kernel functions include radial basis function (RBF) Eq. (1) and the sigmoid function Eq. (2).

RBF kernel function

$$K(x_i,\ x_j)\ =\ \exp(-\gamma \mid\mid x_i - x_j \mid\mid^2) \tag{1}$$

Sigmoid function

$$K(x_i, x_j) = \tanh(\gamma(x_i, x_j) + coef) \tag{2}$$

where, $x_i \in R^n$ represents the value of the sample, $x_j \in \{-1,1\}$ represents the value of the class, coef represents the bias coefficient and γ shows the width between the class one and class two.

In this study we have selected a total of 10,457 samples and 4,567 were used as the training samples and the remaining pixels as the testing samples. Here we performed the image classification by using different sets of kernel functions and parameters. Major parameters of the kernel function include its polynomial degree, its bias coefficient, kernel function width and the penalty factor. We performed various combinations till obtain with optimal results.

5   Results and Discussion

Above Fig. 3 shows the classification results obtained from the SVM and ANN. Quite promising results were obtained from both the classification algorithms. It was observed that ANN produced an overall accuracy and Kappa coefficient of 88.8% and 0.8045 respectively. While a slightly higher overall accuracy obtained from SVM algorithm was 92.81%, with Kappa coefficient of 0.8979 as shown in Table 2.

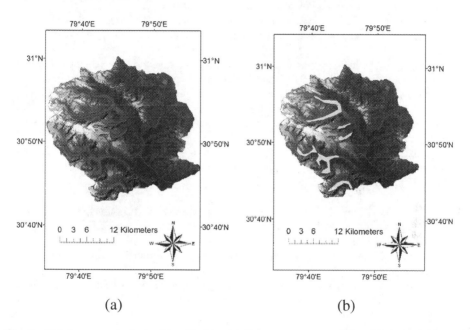

(a)   (b)

Fig. 3. Debris covered glacier identified by (a) Support vector machine, (b) Artificial neural network

Table 2. Classification accuracy of different classification algorithms

Classification Algorithm	Overall accuracy (%)	Kappa coefficient
SVM	92.81%	0.8979
ANN	88.8%	0.8045

References

1. Kadota, T., Seko, K. Aoki, T., Iwata, S., Yamaguchi, S.: Shrinkage of the Khumbu Glacier, east Nepal from 1978 to 1995, pp. 235–244. IAHS Publication (2000)
2. Ren, J., Jing, Z., Pu, J., Qin, X.: Glacier variations and climate change in the central Himalaya over the past few decades. Ann. Glaciol. **43**(1), 218–222 (2006)
3. An overview of glaciers, glacier retreat, and subsequent impacts in Nepal, India and China. WWWF Nepal Program (2005)
4. Ranzi, R., Grossi, G., Iacovelli, L., Taschner, S.: Use of multispectral ASTER images for mapping debris-covered glaciers within the GLIMS Project. In: 2004 Proceedings of the IEEE International Geoscience and Remote Sensing Symposium, IGARSS 2004, vol. 2, pp. 1144–1147. IEEE (2004)
5. Bishop, M.P., Bonk, R., Kamp Jr., U., Shroder Jr., J.F.: Terrain analysis and data modeling for alpine glacier mapping. Polar Geogr. **25**(3), 182–201 (2001)
6. Paul, F., Huggel, C., Kääb, A.: Combining satellite multispectral image data and a digital elevation model for mapping debris-covered glaciers. Remote Sens. Environ. **89**(4), 510–518 (2004)
7. Zollinger, S.: Ableitung von Parametern für die Identifikation und Beobachtung gefährlicher Gletscherseen in Nepal aus ASTER Satellitendaten (Doctoral dissertation) (2003)
8. Bolch, T., Kamp, U.: Glacier mapping in high mountains using DEMs, Landsat and ASTER data. Grazer Schriften der Geographie und Raumforschung **41**, 37–48 (2006)
9. Haykin, S.: Neural Networks: A Comprehensive Foundation, 2nd edn. ACM, Upper Saddle River (2004)
10. Benediktsson, J.A., Swain, P.H., Ersoy, O.K.: Neural network approaches versus statistical methods in classification of multisource remote sensing data. In: 1989 12th Canadian International Geoscience and Remote Sensing Symposium IGARSS 1989, vol. 2, pp. 489–492, July 1989
11. Carpenter, G.A., Gjaja, M.N., Gopal, S., Woodcock, C.E.: ART neural networks for remote sensing: vegetation classification from Landsat TM and terrain data. IEEE Trans. Geosci. Remote Sens. **35**(2), 308–325 (1997)
12. Kavzoglu, T., Mather, P.M.: The use of backpropagating artificial neural networks in land cover classification. Int. J. Remote Sens. **24**(23), 4907–4938 (2003)
13. Mas, J.F., Flores, J.J.: The application of artificial neural networks to the analysis of remotely sensed data. Int. J. Remote Sens. **29**(3), 617–663 (2008)
14. Hagan, M.T., Demuth, H.B., Beale, M.H., De Jesús, O.: Neural Network Design, vol. 20. PWS Publishing Company, Boston (1996)
15. Hertz, J., Krogh, A., Palmer, R.G.: Introduction to the theory of neural computation, vol. 1. Perseus Publishing, Cambridge (1991). Basic Books
16. Krasnopolsky, V.M., Schiller, H.: Some neural network applications in environmental sciences. Part I: forward and inverse problems in geophysical remote measurements. Neural Netw. **16**(3), 321–334 (2003)
17. Hagan, M.T., Menhaj, M.B.: Training feedforward networks with the Marquardt algorithm. IEEE Trans. Neural Netw. **5**(6), 989–993 (1994)
18. Qin, A.K., Huang, V.L., Suganthan, P.N.: Differential evolution algorithm with strategy adaptation for global numerical optimization. IEEE Trans. Evol. Comput. **13**(2), 398–417 (2009)
19. Storn, R., Price, K.: Differential evolution-a simple and efficient adaptive scheme for global optimization over continuous spaces, vol. 3. ICS, Berkeley (1995)

20. Hsieh, S.T., Sun, T.Y., Liu, C.C., Tsai, S.J.: Efficient population utilization strategy for particle swarm optimizer. IEEE Trans. Syst. Man Cybern. Part B: Cybern. **39**(2), 444–456 (2009)
21. Mandischer, M.: A comparison of evolution strategies and backpropagation for neural network training. Neurocomputing **42**(1), 87–117 (2002)
22. Bishop, C.M.: Neural Networks for Pattern Recognition. Oxford University Press, New York (1995)
23. Vapnik, V.: The Nature of Statistical Learning Theory. Springer, Heidelberg (2013)
24. Zhang, R., Ma, J.: State of the art on remotely sensed data classification based on support vector machines. Adv. Earth Sci. **24**(5), 555–562 (2009)

Concatenation of Multiple Features
for Face Recognition

Viswanath K. Reddy$^{(\boxtimes)}$ and Shruthi B. Gangal

Department of Electronics and Communication,
Faculty of Engineering and Technology,
M. S. Ramaiah University of Applied Sciences, Bangalore, India
viswanath.ec.et@msruas.ac.in,
shruthi.gangal@gmail.com

Abstract. Face recognition from surveillance camera is a challenging task due to variation in lighting conditions, motion blur and poses. Most of the face recognition algorithms perform well under controlled environments. In uncontrolled scenarios, face recognition algorithms are being developed to operate on information fused from multiple cameras. This approach increases the hardware and processing speed. In this paper effect of concatenating multiple features on the face recognition rate is being investigated. The developed algorithm is tested on the publicly available chokepoint dataset. Recognition rates achieved by concatenating multiple features are found to outperform the results of the methods using information from multiple cameras for face recognition. Further testing with various features need to be performed.

Keywords: Face recognition · Multiple feature · Support vector machine · Surveillance

1 Introduction

Surveillance is an important research area of computer vision because surveillance camera has been installed in both indoor and outdoor places for security purpose. Identifying a person is an important aspect in surveillance and can be done through various biometric techniques such as gait recognition, fingerprint recognition and facial recognition. Among many biometric techniques, Face recognition in smart CCTV is a particularly good example of a silent technology and is much flexible because it requires no participation of users like other biometric technique.

Face recognition is an important area of biometrics and most of the existing face recognition algorithms work well under controlled environment however, face recognition from surveillance cameras has become a challenging task due to limitations such as pose, illumination, noise and motion blur.

Typical face images of a person captured at different distances from a surveillance camera [1] are shown in Fig. 1. It is seen that captured image look different in terms of lighting condition and variation in poses and in such cases there is a variation in features for the same person. In this work, we investigate the effect of using multiple features in such unconstrained scenario.

© Springer Nature Singapore Pte Ltd. 2016
A. Unal et al. (Eds.): SmartCom 2016, CCIS 628, pp. 558–564, 2016.
DOI: 10.1007/978-981-10-3433-6_67

Fig. 1. Face image captured from surevillance camera [1]

2 Related Work

Face recognition for surveillance has gained a lot of attention of researchers. Illumination, resolution and pose variations are few of the challenges in developing robust face recognition algorithms. Significant amount of work is carried out to deal with various challenges in face recognition for surveillance application. Effect of variations in illumination was addressed by employing pre-processing techniques. Super resolution technique was employed to increase the quality of the surveillance images in terms of resolution [2]. PCA-DCT and GMM-SVM are combined together through score fusion combination using image acquisition distance [3]. A frontal face image is created from a set of face images from different cameras using a cylinder head model technique. Using these images, the images from different cameras are classified and these results are combined for better recognition rate [4]. Probabilistic method for face recognition using multiple cameras was introduced. Dynamic Bayesian Network classifier is used to incorporate information from different cameras and also it extracts the temporal information between the consecutive frames [5]. Unified Face Image was employed to produce frontal face image by fusing information from multiple cameras. To remove the variation due to lighting condition normalization technique was employed [6].

Face recognition algorithms are developed by fusing information from multiple cameras [4–6]. This increases hardware complexity and processing speed. In this work we investigate the effectiveness of face recognition method by concatenating multiple features of the face image obtained from a single camera.

3 Proposed Work

In this work, images in the indoor scenario are captured using single camera. Obtained images are subjected to face detection algorithm. Multiples features are extracted from the detected face region and then it is subjected to classification. Figure 2 gives the block diagram of proposed work and function of each block.

Face Detection. Face detection is carrried out using opencv Haar cascade face xml file. This is an implementation using viola jones algorithm along with the adaboost cascade classifier. Face region is cropped and resized to 96 × 96. The same size is used for both for training as well as testing of face images.

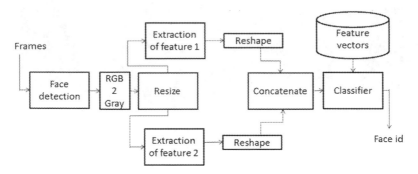

Fig. 2. Proposed block diagram

Feature Extraction. After face is detected from frame. Next step is to extract the feature from the face image. Here two feature extraction technique is combined to get a better representation of the face image so that it can be classified in a better way.

When face image of M × N is given to both feature extraction technique,

• Intensity is one of the basic representation of an image and it is used as one feature
  Example: Where X represent the original image

X=

25	60	55	96	42
22	30	40	45	56
35	95	69	65	45

• In LBP Each time 3*3 Neighborhood pixel is considered and Each pixel is labelled as 0 or 1 by considering center pixel as threshold. If surrounding neighbor pixel is greater than the center pixel it is labelled as 1 otherwise it is labelled as 0 and then binary string is considered in circular form and is converted into decimal [7]

$$Im = \sum\sum i(x,y)$$

Where Im represent the original image
If $i(x,y) >\ =$ center pixel then $i(x,y) = 1$
If $i(x,y) <$ center pixel then $i(x,y) = 0$
So $H = \sum\sum h(x,y)$
Where H gives the LBP values of an image
Example: When LBP is applied to X
First 3 × 3 pixel is considered, X (2, 2) is considered as threshold and Compared with the neighbors

Binary value will be = 11111100 equivalent decimal value is H(2, 2) = 252
Similarly H (2, 3) = 125 and H(2, 4) = 189

H=

So

0	0	0	0	0
0	252	125	189	0
0	0	0	0	0

- When intensity is used as feature vectors, it is reshaped to one dimensional.
  So Im will be of size 1 × MN
  Example: When X in example is reshaped to one dimensional

$$X = [25\,60\,55\,96\,42\,22\,30\,40\,45\,56\,35\,95\,69\,65\,45]$$

- Once LBP values are obtained it reshaped to one dimensional. So H will be of size 1 × MN
  Example: When H in example is reshaped to one dimensional

$$H = [0\,0\,0\,0\,0\,0\,252\,125\,252\,0\,0\,0\,0\,0\,0]$$

- Both H and 1 m is concatenated to represent the face image so feature vector of each face image will be of size 1 × 2 MN
  Example: concatenated feature will be

$$C = [0\,0\,0\,0\,0\,0\,252\,125\,252\,0\,0\,0\,0\,0\,0\,25\,60\,55\,96\,42\,22\,30\,40\,45\,56\,35\,95\,69\,65\,45]$$

After feature extraction, SVM classifier is used for classification purpose. Obtained concatenated features are used to train the SVM Linear classifier and faces are recognized.

4 Experimental Results

Dataset. Chokepoint dataset is used and it is designed for identification/verification of a person under real world indoor surveillance condition. Three Cameras are placed on each portal. Faces captured have variation in terms of illumination condition, pose, sharpness, as well as misalignment. The dataset has frame rate of 30 fps and the image resolution is 800 × 600 pixels. E and L represent the entering and leaving sequence [1].

The proposed work is tested for camera 1 and camera 2. Figure 3 shows the images from camera 1 entering sequence captured at different distances and this sequence is used for testing purpose. Figure 4 shows the data from camera 1 leaving sequence and this sequence is used for training purpose.

Result Evaluation. To evaluate the performance of face recognition algorithm. Formula used is as shown in Eq. (1). It gives the recognition rate of a face recognition algorithm. Where True positive (Tp) represents the Number of subjects that is correctly

Fig. 3. Camera 1 entering sequence [1]

Fig. 4. Camera 1 leaving sequence [1]

recognized and True Negative (Tn) represents the No of subjects that is wrongly recognized.

$$\text{Recognition Rate} = \text{Tp}/(\text{Tp} + \text{Tn}) \tag{1}$$

Results. First we examine the results of using single feature extraction technique along with SVM classifier for both camera 1 and camera 2. Tables 1 and 2 gives the recognition rate for camera 1 and camera 2 respectively.

In the proposed method, two feature namely intensity and LBP are used. Both the feature is concatenated. And the results of our proposed method are compared with the PCA, LBP, and intensity along with the SVM classifier.

Results are also compared with [7] where LBP and intensity are used as feature extraction along with DBN classifier. Results are also compared with [6]. Recognition rate of ES1 (enterance sequence 1) is compared with our method.

Table 3 shows the recognition rate of our method in comparison with other feature extraction technique and classifiers from camera 1 and camera 2.

From Table 3 for Camera 1 it can be seen that, performance of using multiple features along with SVM classifier gives a good recognition rate and has improved to 6% when compared to other feature extraction technique and classifier.

Table 1. Recognition Rate for SVM classifier using different feature extraction technique for camera 1

Feature-SVM classifier	Tp	Tn	Recognition rate %
PCA	594	724	45
LBP	561	757	42
Intensity	592	726	45

Table 2. Recognition Rate for SVM classifier using different feature extraction technique for camera 2

Feature-SVM classifier	Tp	Tn	Recognition rate %
PCA	187	764	19
LBP	262	689	27
Intensity	189	762	19

Table 3. Recognition Rate using different feature extraction techniques

Feature-classifier	Recognition rate %	
	Camera 1	Camera 2
PCA-SVM	45	19
LBP-SVM	42	27
Intensity-SVM	45	19
LBP-Intensity-DBN [5]	46	30
UFI-NN [6]	44	44
Proposed method	52	29

From Table 3 for Camera 2 it can be seen that performance of using multiple features along with SVM classifier gives a good recognition rate and has improved to 2% when compared to other feature extraction technique along with SVM classifier and recognition rate almost remains the same when compared with LBP- Intensity along with DBN classifier.

References

1. Wong, Y., Chen, S., Mau, S., Sanderson, C., Lovell, B.C.: Patch-based probabilistic image quality assessment for face selection and improved video-based face recognition. In: Computer Society Conference on Computer Vision and Pattern Recognition Workshops (CVPRW), pp. 74–81. IEEE Press (2011)
2. Xu, X., Liu, W., Li, L.: Low resolution face recognition in surveillance systems. J. Comput. Commun. **2**, 70–77 (2014)
3. Tome, P., Fierrez, J., Alonso-Fernandez, F., Ortega-Garcia, J.: Scenario-based score fusion for face recognition at a distance. In: Computer Society Conference on Computer Vision and Pattern Recognition Workshops (CVPRW), pp. 67–73. IEEE (2010)
4. Harguess, J., Hu, C., Aggarwal, J.K.: Fusing face recognition from multiple cameras. In: Workshop on Applications of Computer Vision (WACV), pp. 1–7. IEEE (2009)
5. An, L., Kafai, M., Bhanu, B.: Face recognition in multi-camera surveillance videos using dynamic Bayesian network. In: 6th International Conference on Distributed Smart Camera (ICDSC), pp. 1–6. IEEE (2012)
6. An, L., Bhanu, B., Yang, S.: Face recognition in multi-camera surveillance videos. In: 21st International Conference on Pattern Recognition (ICPR), pp. 2885–2888. IEEE (2012)
7. Ahonen, T., Hadid, A., Pietikäinen, M.: Face recognition with local binary pattern. In: European Conference on Computer Vision, pp. 469–481. Springer, Heidelberg (2004)

8. Banerjee, S., Samanta, S., Das, S.: Face recognition in surveillance conditions with bag-of-words, using unsupervised domain adaptation. In: Indian Conference on Computer Vision Graphics and Image Processing, p. 50. ACM (2014)
9. Faruqe, M.O., Hasan, M.A.M.: Face recognition using PCA and SVM. In: 3rd International Conference on Anti-Counterfeiting, Security, and Identification in Communication, pp. 97–101. IEEE Press (2009)
10. Granger, E., Gorodnichy, D.: Evaluation Methodology for Face Recognition Technology in Video Surveillance Applications. Border Technology Division, Division Report (2014)
11. Zhang, X., Gao, Y.: Face recognition across pose: a review. Pattern Recogn. **42**, 2876–2896 (2009)

Black Hole Attack Detection in MANET Using Mobile Trust Points with Clustering

Manjeet Singh[(✉)] and Prabhdeep Singh

Department of Computer Science and Engineering,
Guru Nanak Dev University, Amritsar, India
ms.bajwaa@gmail.com, prabhdeepsingh2991@gmail.com

Abstract. MANET is a set of mobile nodes in which communication occurs between them using wireless links. Infrastructure less, dynamical topology and Lack of central communication of nodes makes it vulnerable to various kinds of attacks. One of the major security problems is Black Hole attack in which node silently drops the packets in the network. In this paper, we propose a solution to mitigate this attack in MANET using mobile trust points with clustering. The proposed method uses some mobile trust points which monitor the activities of cluster heads to detect the attack and then generate alert in the network if any black hole node detected.

Keywords: MANET · Clustering · Black hole · Mobile trust points

1 Introduction

MANET (Mobile Ad hoc Networks) contains self organized mobile nodes without any infrastructure having dynamic topology. In MANET, Nodes can join and leave network anytime [1]. Nodes in the network can act as host or router. Nodes can route packet to help other nodes, thereby forming a network. Due to its simplicity and flexibility, MANETs are suitable for various applications such as emergency rescue operations, battlefield communication and vehicular communication. Lack of centralized management, dynamic topology and limited resources, make MANETs more vulnerable to various security issues than wired networks.

For routing in MANET various Protocols are used which control the way of packet transfer between source and destination [3]. Proactive, active and hybrid are three categories of protocol. In proactive, Routing tables are maintained for communication in the network. Continuously updating routing tables increases route availability but creates network overhead. Destination Sequenced Distance Vector (DSDV) is an example of Proactive Protocol [11]. Reactive protocol uses on demand route discovery process to calculate routes in the network which causes delays in the network. Dynamic Source Routing (DSR) and Ad hoc on demand Distance Vector (AODV) is an example of reactive protocol [10]. Hybrid protocol combines both reactive and proactive protocols to exploit efficient communication in the network. Zone Routing Protocol (ZRP) is an example of this routing protocol [12].

Passive and Active attacks are two categories of attacks in MANET. In Passive attacks, attacker gets the information from the network without doing any alteration [2]. Eaves

© Springer Nature Singapore Pte Ltd. 2016
A. Unal et al. (Eds.): SmartCom 2016, CCIS 628, pp. 565–572, 2016.
DOI: 10.1007/978-981-10-3433-6_68

dropping, traffic control and monitoring are examples of Passive attacks. Active attack disrupted normal functioning of network by altering or destroying data. Black hole and worm hole are active attacks. In this paper, we tackle black hole attacks in AODV routing protocol. In black hole attack, malicious node falsely claiming shortest path to destination by replying to every route request and then drops every packet coming to it [4].

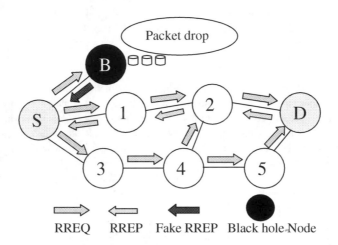

Fig. 1. Black hole attack

Figure 1 illustrates working of black hole attack in MANET. Black Hole node B falsely reply with Fake RREP claiming fresh route to the D (Destination Node) and node S (Source) starts sending data to node B. B (Black hole node) starts dropping all the packets.

The rest of the paper is organized as: Sect. 2 describes related work. Section 3 presents the proposed method and results are discussed in Sect. 4. Finally, conclusion and discussion is in Sect. 5.

2   Related Work

A number of works have been done to tackle black hole attacks in MANET. This section discusses some of these works.

In [5], network is divided into clusters and the trust value calculated between the nodes by their interaction behaviour. A secret key is distributed among various nodes by cluster heads to provide secure communication, only the nodes which know the key can decrypt the message. Another method is proposed by [6] in which TimerExpiredTable and CRRT (Collect Route Reply Table) are used. After the expired time all the entries in the CRRT table are checked. The RREP in which there is repeated next hop nodes are selected. It assumes that the path is correct. This Method is good only in those cases when more RREP packets arrive at source node to select a secure path. The limitation of this solution is that sometimes a secure and the shortest path gets eliminated at source.

Promiscuous mode is used to mitigate black hole and the alert of malicious node is generated in the solution discussed in [7]. In this method, after receiving RREP reply from an intermediate node, a node preceding the intermediate node switch on its promiscuous mode and sends a "hello" packet to the destination node using this node. If the destination receives the hello message from this node, then node and the route are safe to use. This method gives better results as database and extra memory is not required but have more average end-end delay than the normal AODV.

Secured and efficient protocol SAODV is implemented by [8]. In SAODV routing protocol destination is directly verified using the random numbers. SAODV can prevent black hole attack efficiently. But this protocol adds some burden to the network such as extra memory and calculations in route discovery phase. Another method detects the black hole in AODV and finds a safe route using wait and then checks the replies coming from the nodes [9]. The route is selected based on repliers of RREP. The activities of a node are noted by its neighbor nodes and send their opinion to the source node. After collecting all the opinions, a source node decides whether there is a Black hole node or not. The proposed method provides better performance but overhead is involved.

3 Proposed Method

In Proposed Method, network is divided into cluster form which contains mobile nodes, cluster heads and mobile Trust points.

3.1 Mobile Nodes

Nodes are free to move and can participate in communication with each other and cluster head.

3.2 Cluster Head

When the mobile node wants to communicate with any other node not within its range, it will send data packets using cluster head.

```
//Black Hole Detection at Cluster Head (CH) level
Prepare Black_hole_list

1. CH sends data to its member and waits for reply for
maximum time tm.
2. Within time tm members send reply data packet to their
CH   except black hole nodes.
3. CH checks the nodes from its table which has not send
data.
4. Add these nodes to the black_hole_list
```

//Black hole detection at Mobile Trust Point (MTP) level
Prepare Blackhole_list

1. MTP sends request to send black_hole_list to their cluster heads and wait for reply for maximum time tm.
2. Within time tm, CH sends black_hole_list except the clusters which are black hole.
3. MTP checks the Cluster head which has not send any list.
4. Add that CH to blackhole_list and elect any node in that cluster as CH.

Procedure for Black hole detection

3.3   Mobile Trust Points

These are used to check the activities of cluster head and do communication with cluster heads after some time to detect whether cluster heads are Black hole or not.

4   Simulation Results

The simulations are performed using ns-2. A flat plane of 1000×1000 m is used where nodes are placed. The Two Ray Ground model is used for radio propagation. Nodes mobilize at random speed which is 10 m/s. For Media Access Control protocol 802.11 is used. Each node has 250 m communication range. There are total 100 mobile nodes with 10 cluster heads and 10 mobile trust points. The number of malicious nodes is between 5, 10, 15 and 20 respectively.

Various parameters considered are packet delivery ratio (PDR), end to end delay, average throughput and detection rate. Detection rate is number of Black Bole node detected to total number of black hole nodes.

Figure 2 shows the comparison of packet delivery ratio and malicious nodes. Proposed method is showing better packet delivery ratio after detection of Black Hole attack. By calculating results of packet delivery ratio under 5, 10, 15, 20 Black Hole nodes, packet delivery ratio remains consistent even after increasing number of Black Hole nodes. It shows the consistency of proposed technique.

Next performance metrics is average end to end delay. Figure 3 showing significant delay occurs during communication under black hole in AODV. Under normal AODV delay is lesser and after applying the proposed method delay is almost similar to normal AODV. Results are clearly showing that proposed algorithm gives good result after detection of black hole attack.

Results in Fig. 4 are showing a good detection rate of black hole nodes. When detection rate calculated for 5 black hole nodes, all of them are detected using proposed method. Even after taking the number of black hole nodes as 10, 15 and 20, detection rate is almost 90%, which in itself shows how well this method is efficient to detect black hole nodes.

Average throughput is calculated for AODV, AODV under black hole attack and proposed method. There is decrease in network throughput in AODV under black hole

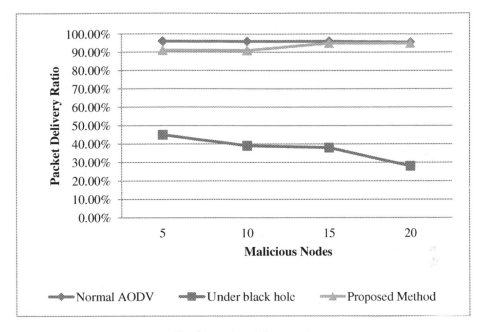

Fig. 2. Packet delivery ratio

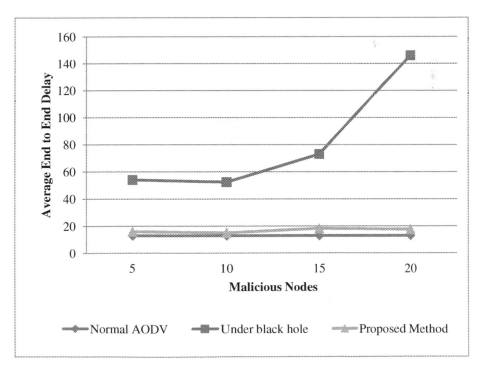

Fig. 3. Average end to end delay

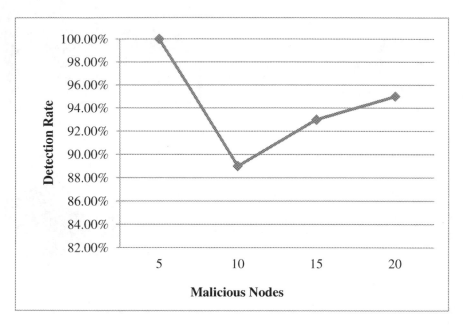

Fig. 4. Detection rate

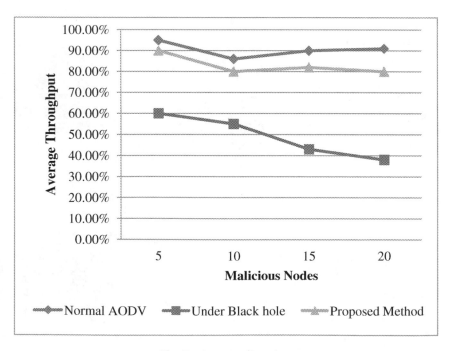

Fig. 5. Average throughput

attack but increases between 80 to 90%. So results in Fig. 5 are showing average throughput increases in proposed method.

5 Conclusion and Future Work

Clustering and Mobile Trust Points based technique has been proposed for detection of black hole attack. Overview of some previous work is listed for prevention and detection of black hole. The approach is to monitor the activities of cluster head and the normal nodes and maintain a list of black hole nodes. Results are showing effectiveness and consistency to detect black hole nodes. Performance is measured and the results are proving the proposed method as promising one. PDR (Packet delivery ratio) and the average throughput increases in proposed method after detection of black hole attack. Also, average end to end delay is very less as compare to AODV under black hole attack. Detection rate of black hole nodes is around 90% in this technique.

In future, this work can be extended to scale the network to find performance and accuracy of this technique. It can also be implemented for detection of other types of attacks. The technique is promising to give good results in other attacks too.

References

1. Ramanathan, R., Redi, J.: A brief overview of ad hoc networks: challenges and directions. IEEE Commun. Mag. **40**(5), 20–22 (2002)
2. Li, W, Joshi, A.: Security issues in mobile ad hoc networks-a survey. Department of Computer Science and Electrical Engineering, University of Maryland, Baltimore County (2008)
3. Hinds, A., Ngulube, M., Zhu, S., Al-Aqrabi, H.: A review of routing protocols for Mobile Ad-Hoc NETworks (MANET). Int. J. Inf. Educ. Technol. **3**(1), 1–5 (2013)
4. Jhaveri, R.H., Patel, S.J., Jinwala, D.C.: Dos attacks in mobile ad hoc networks: a survey. In: 2012 Second International Conference on Advanced Computing & Communication Technologies (ACCT), pp. 535–541. IEEE (2012)
5. Savner, J., Gupta, V.: Clustering of mobile ad hoc networks: an approach for black hole prevention. In: 2014 International Conference on Issues and Challenges in Intelligent Computing Techniques (ICICT), pp. 361–365. IEEE (2014)
6. Tamilselvan, L., Sankaranarayanan, V.: Prevention of blackhole attack in MANET. In: The 2nd International Conference on Wireless Broadband and Ultra Wideband Communications, AusWireless 2007, p. 21. IEEE (2007)
7. Singh, P.K., Sharma, G.: An efficient prevention of black hole problem in AODV routing protocol in MANET. In: 2012 IEEE 11th International Conference on Trust, Security and Privacy in Computing and Communications (TrustCom), pp. 902–906. IEEE (2012)
8. Lu, S., Li, L., Lam, K.-Y., Jia, L.: SAODV: a MANET routing protocol- that can withstand black hole attack. In: International Conference on Computational Intelligence and Security, CIS 2009, vol. 2, pp. 421–425. IEEE (2009)
9. Medadian, M., Mebadi, A., Shahri, E.: Combat with black hole attack in AODV routing protocol. In: 2009 IEEE 9th Malaysia International Conference on Communications (MICC), pp. 530–535. IEEE (2009)

10. Mbarushimana, C., Shahrabi, A.: Comparative study of reactive and proactive routing protocols performance in mobile ad hoc networks. In: 21st International Conference on Advanced Information Networking and Applications Workshops, AINAW 2007, vol. 2, pp. 679–684. IEEE (2007)
11. Tuteja, A., Gujral, R., Thalia, S.: Comparative performance analysis of DSDV, AODV and DSR routing protocols in MANET using NS2. In: 2010 International Conference on Advances in Computer Engineering (ACE), pp. 330–333. IEEE (2010)
12. Kaur, R., Rai, M.K.: A novel review on routing protocols in MANETs. Undergraduate Acad. Res. J. (UARJ) (2012)

Encrypted Audio Watermarking in Frequency Domain

Uma R. Nair[✉] and Gajanan K. Birajdar

Department of Electronics and Telecommunication, Pillai HOC College
of Engineering & Technology, Raigad, Rasayani 410206, Maharashtra, India
uma.nair20@gmail.com, gajanan123@gmail.com

Abstract. Watermarking methods have been utilized for safeguarding contents against unlawful replication. New immune watermark introduction and retrieval mechanism constituting FFT based approach along with chaotic encryption is presented here. Encrypting the procedure develops a secure environment for the scheme. The primary audio undergoes Fast Fourier Transformation. Introduction of encrypted secret contents is accomplished adopting Fibonacci numbers. Retrieval of mark is achieved by non-informed scheme. Error rate as well as SNR outcomes are the execution specifications computed for this method. Here robust quality in opposition to distinct processing actions like reverberation, echo and smoothness is administered. Also greater imperceptibility procured by this method demonstrates the proprietary rights of initial content.

Keywords: Encryption · Audio watermarking · Fast fourier transform · Information security

1 Introduction

With the upswing in technology massive conveyance of digital contents has been actualized. It has also induced unlawful distribution of digitalized contents. Watermarking can be utilized as an effective method against unwanted reproduction of data to impart content verification. Digital audio watermarking is the mechanism of inserting a mark in initial audio [2].

A watermarking strategy must full fill the four indispensable prerequisites like perceptual transparency, robust aspect, payload along with security. Audio watermarking mechanism comprises of mark insertion and removal. Introduction of the secret data into the initial signal is exercised by embedding process while, extraction process is employed to acquire back the secret data [3]. Marking mechanism is divided in two types (a) time based techniques (b) transform based techniques.

The article proposes watermark scheme utilizing Fourier based approach and encryption. Here chaotic scheme is employed for encrypting the secret image since it accomplishes greater encryption capability. Here first host is sub-divided in blocks. Later the chaotic encrypted mark is introduced adopting Fibonacci

© Springer Nature Singapore Pte Ltd. 2016
A. Unal et al. (Eds.): SmartCom 2016, CCIS 628, pp. 573–580, 2016.
DOI: 10.1007/978-981-10-3433-6_69

numbers into initial data. Chaotic scheme endeavours transmission of the mark securely. Fibonacci numbers on the other hand intensifies the imperceptibility of the scheme.

Remaining paper is put in order as enlisted: Sect. 2 contains survey of prior work. Section 3 puts forth the proposed system model. In Sect. 4 elaborates the chaotic scheme. In Sect. 5 experimental outcomes of scheme that is robust quality along with imperceptibility is considered. Section 6 winds up this article.

2   Literature Survey

Time based techniques performs insertion of mark without any transformation. In [15] GA scheme is demonstrated to overcome the inferior robust nature. Here data is introduced in deeper blocks and other contents are amended to reduce the faults. The prior echo schemes having inferior security outcomes are tackled in [10] by adopting pseudo noise distribution. Combination of pseudo noise distribution along with decipher action is suggested in it.

In transform domain the frequently adopted mechanisms are DWT, DCT as well as FFT. In [4] the initial information is disintegrated in lower and higher spectrum utilizing wavelet related approach. The mark is introduced employing maximized quantized index. Dependence between the successive aggregation of fragments is utilized in [12] for the watermark in DCT approach. Descriptive connection among the fragments is preserved in order to reveal the exact introduction of mark.

Employing FFT produces translation invariant characteristics for the mark. Two correlative insertion approaches are constructed utilizing the watermark mixture scheme as described in [9]. FFT related model is used to introduce correlative marks. Initial mark is introduced by affirmatively modulated method whereas the later one is introduced by anti-affirmatively modulated method. Variable byte geometric unvarying watermark method utilizing LCM is demonstrated in [6]. Scheme mentioned in [13] incorporates two condition which produces a superior quality mark. Acquisition of the intended spectrum being the initial one and adjusting the index extent being the other one. Data utilising FFT scheme is introduced by adjusting the index extent. The mark is introduced in coefficients through the above aspect employing a key produced capturing arrangement. A strategy to preserve the information by introducing a mark which can withstand distortions is considered in [8]. The mark insertion and retrieval is accomplished utilizing FFT transform based technique. The mark can be withdrawn employing hidden keys accompanying slight deformity. Mark method employing acoustic features along with fourier scheme is considered in [14]. Here mark is inserted in phase segments of contents following the transform. In [7] composition devoted watermark method to withstand TSM attacks is projected. Here the marks are introduced in the chosen stable greater energy locations. These locations intend to be unmodified for preserving greater audibility.

3   Proposed System

Sound perceiving characteristic of human ear diminishes while approaching higher spectrum so in the considered method secret information is introduced in higher spectrum. Two specifications (i) frequency band (ii) frame size are arranged prior to insertion procedure. Frame size influences the robust nature while frequency band influences imperceptibility as well as capacity. Here high frequency is adjusted as 16 kHz or lesser at the beginning. In addition, division of higher segments in frames of span, s = 7 is implemented.

3.1   Inserting Watermark

In the method put forward watermark employing fourier based scheme and chaotic encryption is accomplished. Figure 1 lays out the insertion procedure.

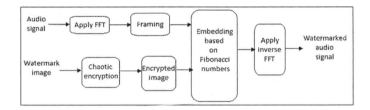

Fig. 1. Watermark insertion procedure of considered method

Steps of introducing the mark is observed as below.

1. Execute fourier transform to compute the FFT coefficients.
2. Separate fourier constituents in frames.
3. Encrypt the watermark image using chaotic encryption.
4. The y-th greatest Fibonacci number for FFT fragment is estimated which is less than FFT coefficients magnitude.
5. FFT marked fragments are acquired by (1) and (2).
   If encrypted mark bit is obtained as zero, then

$$A' = \left\{ \begin{array}{l} A_y, \text{ if } y \bmod 2 = 0; \\ A_{y+1}, \text{ if } y \bmod 2 = 1. \end{array} \right. \tag{1}$$

   here y stands for y-th Fibonacci number.
   If encrypted mark bit is obtained as one, then

$$A' = \left\{ \begin{array}{l} A_{y+1}, \text{ if } y \bmod 2 = 0; \\ A_y, \text{ if } y \bmod 2 = 1. \end{array} \right. \tag{2}$$

6. Marked data is achieved by inverse FFT.

3.2   Recovering Mark

Non informed approach of watermarking is applied, as initial information is not necessary throughout the retrieval procedure. Figure 2 lays out the retrieval procedure.

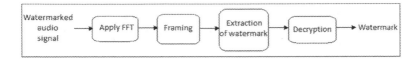

Fig. 2. Watermark retrieval procedure of considered method

Steps of retrieving the mark is observed as below.

1. Execute fourier transform to compute the FFT coefficients.
2. Separate fourier constituents in frames.
3. In the chosen frequency group for individual FFT element acquire nearest Fibonacci number with respect to magnitude of FFT coefficients.
4. Select lesser Fibonacci number as long as distance of FFT elements from two Fibonacci numbers is equal.
5. The retrieval of mark is estimated as:

$$C' = \begin{cases} 0, \text{ if } y \, mod \, 2 = 0; \\ 1, \text{ if } y \, mod \, 2 = 1. \end{cases} \tag{3}$$

where C' is mark bit recovered from every element.
6. Mark is secured depending on constituents tally that signify either zero or one is acquired following the acquisition of specification regarding the constituents. The identified bit is "0", considering the constituents tally designated as "0" is proportionate or above halved frame extent or else "1" is acquired. Execute the procedure for entire frames.
7. The mark is retrieved securely by decrypting the above obtained information.

4   Chaotic Encryption Technique

Chaotic Baker map is employed for accomplishing chaotic encryption for the mark. The permuted form of the square matrix of information is created by this map which jumbles a square matrix in its discrete format. The map in discretized format considered for J × J matrix is given by (4)

$$D(x, y) = [\frac{J}{w_i}(x - J_i) + y \, mod \, (\frac{J}{w_i}), \frac{w_i}{J}(y - y \, mod \, (\frac{J}{w_i})) + J_i] \tag{4}$$

Here D(x,y) are recent indices of information, $J_i = w_1 + w_2 + ... + w_i, J_i \leq x < J_i + w_i$ and $0 < y < J$. Chaotic encryption is employed since it accomplishes greater encryption capability. Book of the Abacas [5] was formulated by Leonard of Pisa who brought the string recognized as Fibonacci numbers that are 1, 1, 2, 3, 5, 8, 13, 21, 34, 55, 89. In accordance with [11] musical rhythm comprises Fibonacci sequence.

5   Experimental Outcomes

The album Rust by No, Really [1] is employed for examining the outcomes of the intended method. All elements employ 44.1 kHz accompanying 2 channels in addition to 16 bits for each element. Here 32×32 binary image is employed as mark. Outcome is determined by employing SNR, BER and payload.

Plot employing stop payment host is demonstrated in Fig. 3 and marked content is set out in Fig. 4. Initial mark is laid out in Fig. 5 while encrypted mark is demonstrated in Fig. 6. Extracted encrypted mark is laid out in Fig. 7 while decrypted mark is set out in Fig. 8

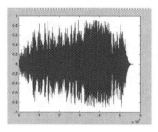

Fig. 3. Host information

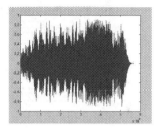

Fig. 4. Marked content

Fig. 5. Mark

Fig. 6. Encrypted mark

Fig. 7. Extracted encrypted mark

Fig. 8. Obtained decrypted mark

5.1   Robustness Test

Calculation of robust nature of audio signal is performed by Bit Error Rate as:

$$BER(E, E') = \frac{\sum_{y=0}^{Y-1} E(y) \oplus E'(y)}{Y} \tag{5}$$

where length of mark is indicated by Y, yth bit of introduced mark is indicated by $E(y)$ and yth bit of recovered mark is indicated by $E'(y)$. To assess robust feature of suggested mechanism, five separate activities outlined below were implemented.

1. Fusion with noise: Marked content is mixed AWGN.
2. Low-pass filtering: Low pass with termination 15 kHz.
3. Echo: Impairment factor denoting 50 percent with wait time of 100 ms.
4. Reverberation: Marked content with reverberate period 1 s along with extent of −24 dB.
5. Smoothness filtering: Evenly seep through marked content.

Table 1. BER Results for signal processing attacks

Attack name	Stop Payment	Rust	Do You Know
Echo	0.0077	0.0117	0.013
Noise addition	0.0075	0.012	0.012
Smoothness filtering	0.0069	0.010	0.0114
Reverberation	0.0065	0.0104	0.011
Lowpass filtering	0.0072	0.011	0.0114

Table 1 demonstrates that BER vary from 0.0065 to 0.013 during distinct activities for three files that is Stop Payment, Rust and Do You Know Where Your Children Are and hence suggests that mechanism contributes superior outcomes.

5.2   Imperceptibility Test and Payload

Here assessment of perceptual nature regarding audio signal is calculated utilizing SNR. It is computed as:

$$SNR = 10log_{10}\frac{\sum_{y=1}^{Y} E^2(y)}{\sum_{y=1}^{Y}[E(y) - E'(y)]^2} \tag{6}$$

where $E(y)$ is initial content and $E'(y)$ is marked content.

Perceptual transparency of watermark scheme becomes superior by incrementing SNR. The outcomes considering SNR of three files are laid out in Fig. 9. We accomplish that suggested mechanism contributes SNR up to 67.9 decibels from Fig. 9. Content payload specifies content insertion extent of mechanism. Figure 10 displays the content payload for the three audio files with the mechanism attaining payload of 3000 bps.

From the results of Table 2, it is achieved that proposed mechanism produces improved results compared to other mechanisms. Robust nature obtained here is higher along with greater imperceptibility than the other algorithms.

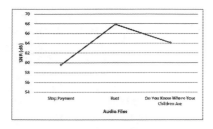 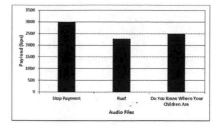

Fig. 9. SNR results   **Fig. 10.** Payload results

Table 2. Comparison of the proposed method with other schemes

Algorithm	SNR [dB]	BER
[6]	38.8	0.015
[13]	–	0.01
[8]	45.25	–
[14]	43.5	–
[7]	29.5	0.03
Proposed	67.9	0.0065

6   Conclusion

Highly imperceptible watermark inclusion scheme considering audio contents, that contributes robust feature with respect to processing activities is introduced. Greater encryption capability is accomplished utilizing chaotic encryption. Encrypting the procedure develops secure environment for the method. For mark insertion, FFT is exercised on host and later FFT elements are adjusted utilising Fibonacci numbers with encrypted watermark. Scheme utilized here imparts superior SNR and decreased BER along with high content payload. Here we apply non-informed scheme. Outcome of projected mechanism is calculated by employing BER, payload with SNR. By monitoring outcomes and contrasting with existing procedures, it is achieved that audio marking using FFT, chaotic encryption and Fibonacci numbers gives enhanced outcomes.

References

1. No really, rust. http://www.jamendo.com/en/album/7365. 17 July 2014
2. Boney, L., Tewfik, A.H., Hamdy, K.N.: Digital watermarks for audio signals. In: Proceedings of the Third IEEE International Conference on Multimedia Computing and Systems, pp. 473–480, June 1996
3. Cvejic, N., Seppanen, T.: Digital Audio Watermarking Techniques and Technologies: Applications and Benchmarks. IGI Global, Hershey (2007)

4. Hemis, M., Boudraa, B., Merazi-Meksen, T.: Intelligent audio watermarking algorithm using multi-objective particle swarm optimization. In: 4th International Conference on Electrical Engineering (ICEE), pp. 1–5, December 2015
5. Horadam, A.F.: A generalized fibonacci sequence. Am. Math. Mon. **68**(5), 455–459 (1961)
6. Kang, X., Yang, R., Huang, J.: Geometric invariant audio watermarking based on an LCM feature. IEEE Trans. Multimedia **13**(2), 181–190 (2011)
7. Li, W., Xue, X., Lu, P.: Localized audio watermarking technique robust against time-scale modification. IEEE Trans. Multimedia **8**(1), 60–69 (2006)
8. Loytynoja, M., Cvejic, N., Seppanen, T.: Audio protection with removable watermarking. In: 6th International Conference on Information, Communications Signal Processing, pp. 1–4, December 2007
9. Lu, C.S., Liao, H.Y.M., Chen, L.H.: Multipurpose audio watermarking. In: Proceedings of the 15th International Conference on Pattern Recognition, vol. 3, pp. 282–285 (2000)
10. Natgunanathan, I., Xiang, Y.: A novel pseudonoise sequence for time-spread echo based audio watermarking. In: Proceedings of the IEEE Global Telecommunications Conference (GLOBECOM), pp. 1–6, November 2009
11. Nickel, J.: Mathematics: Is God Silent?. Ross House Books, Vallecito (2001)
12. Roy, S., Sarkar, N., Chowdhury, A.K., Iqbal, S.M.A.: An efficient and blind audio watermarking technique in DCT domain. In: Proceedings of the 18th IEEE International Conference on Computer and Information Technology (ICCIT), vol. 1, pp. 362–367, December 2015
13. Seo, Y., Cho, S., Chong, U.: Audio watermarking alogrithm using subband energy. In: 7th International Forum on Strategic Technology (IFOST), pp. 1–4, September 2012
14. Wen, X., Ding, X., Li, J., Gao, L., Sun, H.: An audio watermarking algorithm based on fast fourier transform. In: Proceedings of the IEEE International Conference on Information Management, Innovation Management and Industrial Engineering, vol. 1, pp. 363–366, December 2009
15. Zamani, M., Manaf, A.B.A., Ahmad, R.B., Zeki, A.M., Magalingam, P.: A novel approach for audio watermarking. In: Proceedings of the Fifth IEEE International Conference on Information Assurance and Security (IAS), vol. 2, pp. 83–86, August 2009

Application of Maxcode Algorithm for the Enumeration of Kinematic Chains of 9 Links and 2 Degree of Freedom

Suwarna Torgal[(✉)]

Mechanical Engineering Department, Institution of Engineering and Technology,
Devi Ahilya Vishwavidyalaya, Indore, India
suwarnass@rediffmail.com, storgal@ietdavv.edu.in

Abstract. The enormous applications of kinematic chains (Mechanisms) has lead to more scope in the structural synthesis of the same. The interdisciplinary applications like in mechatronics, dental, medical (especially in human bone fractures), ergonomic design of machinery, physiotherapy machines, industrial robots, increased use of robots in every field, atomization in the industry etc. in almost every field the kinematic chain, being the basic element is necessary. Hence the more concentration is given to enumerate the feasible kinematic chains. The coding (Maxcode) methodology adopted for the enumeration of feasible, nonisomorphic, distinct kinematic chains has given an added advantage in the enumeration process by eliminating the infeasible, isomorphic chains during the process of enumeration. The present paper presents the methodology and the results of enumeration of nine link two degree of freedom kinematic chains.

Keywords: Kinematic chain · Assortments of links · Degree of freedom · Maxcode

1 Introduction

The selection of the best possible, feasible, nonisomorphic and distinct kinematic chain for specified number of links and degrees of freedom amongst all the enumerated chains is necessary at the conceptual stage of design of any type of mechanisms and/or for their applications. The research on kinematic chains enumeration started from long back. Some selected among them are: Freudenstein and Woo [1] defines the graph of a mechanism, with binary joints as a linear graph in which the vertices, representing mobile links were shown by small hollow circles while, the fixed link was represented by a vertex with a solid circle. A modification to the matrix notation was proposed by Mruthyunjaya and Raghavan, [2] with a view to permit derivation of all possible mechanisms from a kinematic chain and distinguishing the structurally distinct ones by, changing the concept of adjacency matrix. Rao and Raju [3], Rao [4] proposed the secondary Hamming Number Technique for the generation of planar kinematic chains. Similarly Hwang and Hwang [5], A.C Rao and Pratap B. Deshmukh [6] Mruthyunjaya [7–9], also synthesized the kinematic chains. The reason why designers have been

© Springer Nature Singapore Pte Ltd. 2016
A. Unal et al. (Eds.): SmartCom 2016, CCIS 628, pp. 581–589, 2016.
DOI: 10.1007/978-981-10-3433-6_70

trying through so many new methods rather than adopting a particular method is easy to visualize with an implied requirement of Decodability.

Read and Corneil [10] remark that a good solution to the coding problem provides a good solution to the isomorphism problem, though, the converse is not necessarily true. Ambekar and Agrawal [11] gave the concepts of maxcode and mincode as canonical number for the enumeration. So according to the authors [12] every kinematic chain of n-links, has n! different ways of labeling the links and hence, n! different binary numbers are possible for the same chain. This goes to suggest that a successful solution to the isomorphism problem can be obtained through coding. The algorithm was generated for the structural enumeration and identification of kinematic chains [13]. The algorithm has been proved. The present paper discusses on the enumeration of kinematic chains of 9-linked two degree of freedom by maxcode algorithm.

The advantage of the presented results is that the ready availability of kinematic chains in the dictionary form so that can be used as a basic element wherever needed. The coding method [13] give a unique, nonisomorphic distinct kinematic chain.

2   Philosophy of the Maxcode Algorithm

The characteristics of kinematic chains which are entirely determined by the pattern of interconnection among the links include the degree of freedom, the structurally distinct kinematic chains that are possible with a given number of links and given freedom. Hence, in this section the stress is given on the basic data like the degree of freedom (dof) of a kinematic chain, the effect of number of links on the degree of freedom of a kinematic chain and then minimum how many number of binary links are necessary to have a feasible kinematic chain is reviewed.

For the given number of links the possible Minimum number of Binary Links to be present in the mechanism is analyzed.

The link of highest degrees in the chains of given N and F.

For the given number of links and degrees of freedom the link assortment is made.

Then the enumeration using the coding technique is made rejecting the infeasible kinematic chains.

The methodology is applied for the 9 – link two degree of freedom kinematic chains.

2.1   To Establish Permutation of Kinematic Links

The basic requirements before using the algorithm has been explained in following sections.

2.1.1   Effect of Even/Odd Number of Links on Degree of Freedom (Dof)

According to the most popular mobility equation of Grubler, dof of a mechanism

$$F = 3(N - 1) - 2L \tag{1}$$

where
L   = number of simple turning pairs;
F   = Degrees of freedom(dof)
N   = Total number of mobile links

Thus, for '1' to be an integer:

a. If dof 'F' is odd (say, 1,3,5 ...), (N−1) should also be odd or N must be even.
b. If dof 'F' is even (say, 2,4,6 ...), (N−1) should also be even or N must be odd.

Summing up, for d.o.f. 'F' to be even, n must be odd and for 'F' to be odd, n must be even.

For the present problem the number of links are 9 (odd number) and degree of freedom (dof) is 2 (even).

2.1.2   Minimum Number of Binary Links in a Mechanism [14]

Let,

$n2$ = number of binary links
$n3$ = number of ternary links
$n4$ = number of quaternary links
.
.
nk = number of k − nary links

$$N = n_2 + n_3 + n_4 + n_5 + \ldots\ldots + n_k \qquad (2)$$

Since discussions are limited to simple jointed chains, each joint/pair consists of two elements. Thus, if 'e' is total number of elements in the mechanism, then e = 2L

By definition binary, ternary, quaternary (etc.) links consist respectively of 2,3,4 (etc.) elements. Hence, total number of elements are also given by

$$e = 2n_2 + 3n_3 + 4n_4 + 5n_5 + \ldots\ldots\ldots k\, n_k \qquad (3)$$

Hence,

$$2L = 2n_2 + 3n_3 + 4n_4 + 5n_5 + \ldots\ldots\ldots k\, n_k \qquad (4)$$

Substituting N and 2L from Eqs. (2) and (4) in Eq. (1), we have

$$F = 3[(n_2 + n_3 + n_4 + n_5 + \ldots\ldots + n_k) - 1] - [2n_2 + 3n_3 + 4n_4 + 5n_5 + \ldots\ldots\ldots k\, n_k] \qquad (5)$$

After simplification and rearrangement of Eq. (5),

$$n_2 = (F + 3) - [\, n_4 + 2\, n_5 + 3\, n_6\ldots\ldots \quad + (k - 3)\, n_k] \qquad (6)$$

Thus, number of binary links required in a mechanism, depend on number of links having elements > 3. Hence, minimum number of binary links can be deduced from Eq. (6) as:

$n_2 \geq 4$, for dof = 1; $n_2 \geq 5$, for dof = 2; $n_2 \geq 6$, for dof = 3; etc.

This proves that minimum number binary links for dof = 1 is 4, while for dof = 2 is 5.

2.2   Enumeration of Kinematic Chains

For given N and F, establish number of joints (hinges) using,

$$L = [\, 3N - (F+3)]/2 \tag{7}$$

The link of highest degrees in the chains of given N and F:

K = N/2 (when F is odd); K = (N + 1)/2 (when F is even)

Also from Eq. (6), we have

$$F = [n_2 - (\, n_4 + 2\, n_5 + 3\, n_6 \ldots \quad \ldots \quad + (k-3)\, n_k) - 3] \tag{8}$$

Equations (1), (2) and (4) can be used to list all combinations of n2, n3, n4, etc. which satisfy the conditions. The Table 1 shows the assortments of links for 9 linked two degree of freedom kinematic chains.

Table 1. Assortments of links

Number of links (N)	Degree of freedom (DF)	Number of binary links (N2/n_2)	Number of ternary links (N3/n_3)	Number of quaternary links (N4/n_4)	Number of pentagonal links (N5/n_5)	Link assortment number	Number of chains generated using proposed algorithm
(1)	(2)	(3)	(4)	(5)	0		(6)
9	2	7	0	2	0	9_2_7-0-2-0	3
9	2	7	1	0	1	9_2_7-1-0-1	2
9	2	6	2	1	0	9_2_6-2-1-0	16
9	2	5	4	0	0	9_2_5-4-0-0	19

From the above basic concept and using the algorithm [13], the enumeration of the 9 – link two degree of freedom kinematic chains has been done and explained in further sections

The input and output along with kinematic chains generated has been explained.

3 Input for the Assortment of Sl. No. 1 in Table 1: 9_2_7-0-2-0

Input is:

Number of links (n) = 9; degree of freedom (df) = 2;

N2 = 7; N3 = 0; N4 = 2; N5 = 0; N6 = 0

Output of the program: Shown in Table 2.

Total no. of valid chains enumerated = 3

Table 2. Output for the assortment of: 9_2_7-0-2-0

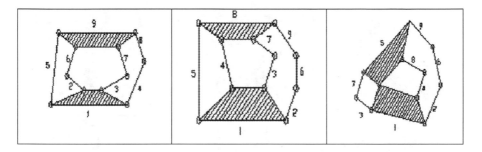

4 Input for the Assortment of Sl. No. 2 in Table 1: 9_2_7-1-0-1

Input is:

Number of links (n) = 9; degree of freedom (df) = 2

N2 = 7; n3 = 1; n4 = 0; n5 = 1; n6 = 0

Output of the program: shown in Table 3.

Total no. of valid chains enumerated = 2

Table 3. Output for the assortment of: 9_2_7-1-0-1

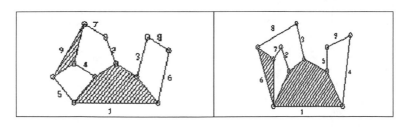

5   Input for the Assortment of Sl. No. 3 in Table 1: 9_2_6-2-1-0

INPUT IS:-

NUMBER OF LINKS (N) = 9; DEGREE OF FREEDOM (DF) = 2

N2 = 6; N3 = 2; N4 = 1; N5 = 0; N6 = 0

Output of the program: Shown in Table 4.

Total no. of valid chains enumerated = 16

Table 4.   Output for the assortment of: 9_2_6-2-1-0

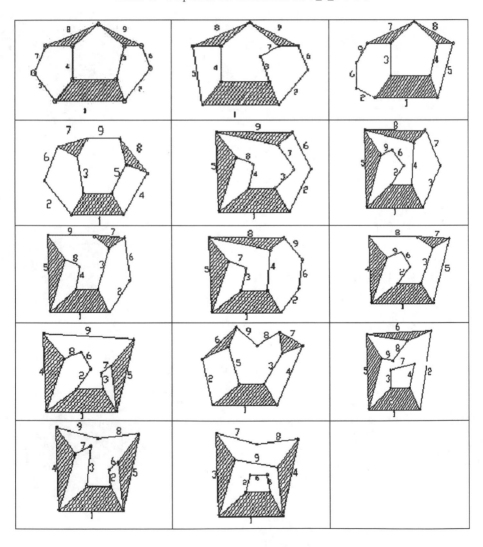

Table 5. Output for the assortment of: 9_2_6-2-1-0

6   Input for the Assortment of Sl. No. 4 in Table 1: 9_2_5-4-0-0

Input is:-

  Number of links (n) = 9; degree of freedom (df) = 2
  N2 = 5; n3 = 4; n4 = 0; n5 = 0; n6 = 0
  Output of the program: shown in Table 5.
  Total no. of valid chains enumerated = 19

  The Table 6 gives the program output as well as compares with results already established by the researchers for the number of chains generated for given combination of N and dof.

Table 6. Comparison of results

Sl. No	Number of links (N)	Deg. of freedom (dof)	Number of chains generatd using proposed algoritm [13]		Results reported by Hwang and Hwang [5]	Results reported by Rao A.C, and Deshmukh [6]	Results reported by Mruthy-unjaya [7–9]
1	9	2	3	40	40	40	40
			2				
			16				
			19				

7   Discussion

For the given combination of the binary, ternary and the quaternary links the number of chains generated are indicated in the Table 6 it is found that the number of distinct kinematic chains generated or enumerated for the 9 – link two degree of freedom are 40 in all. The results compare well with the established results obtained by the researchers [5–9]. The advantage of the application of the current method is that it uses coding algorithm which is the step towards digitalization of kinematic chains for the ease of storage and retrieval of the same and can be easily catalogued.

8   Conclusion

The paper illustrates the approach, based on Maxcode algorithm, to enumerate or generate the distinct kinematic chains for any selected assortment. The computer program therefore user interactive. The results in the output Tables (2, 3, 4 and 5) demonstrates an effective approach aiming at digital storage of generated chains for the ease of cataloguing.

References

1. Freudenstein, F., Woo, L.S.: Kinematic structure of mechanisms. In: Spillers, W.R. (ed.) North Holland/American Elsevier, New York, pp. 241–264 (1974)
2. Mruthunjaya, T.S., Raghavan, M.R.: Structural analysis of kinematic chains and mechanisms based on matrix representation. Trans. ASME J. Mech. Des. **101**(3), 488–494 (1979)
3. Rao, A.C., Raju, V.: Application of the hamming number technique to detect isomorphism among kinematic chains and inversions. Mech. Mach. Theory **26**(1), 55–75 (1991)
4. Rao, A.C.: Mechanism and Machine Theory, vol. 32(4), 489–499 (1994)
5. Hwang, W.-M., Hwang, Y.-W.: Computer aided structural synthesis of planar kinematic chains with simple joints. Mech. Mach. Theory **27**(2), 189–199 (1992)
6. Rao, A.C., Deshmukh, P.B.: Computer aided structural synthesis of planar kinematic chains obviating the test for isomorphism. Mech. Mach. Theory **36**, 489–506 (2001)
7. Mruthunjaya, T.S.: Structural synthesis by transformation of binary chains. Mech. Mach. Theory **14**, 221–231 (1979)
8. Mruthunjaya, T.S.: A computerized methodology for structural synthesis of kinematic chains: Part 1-formulation. Mech. Mach. Theory **19**(6), 487–495 (1984)
9. Mruthunjaya, T.S.: A computerized methodology for structural synthesis of kinematic chains: Part 2-Application to several fully or partially known cases. Mech. Mach. Theory **19**(6), 497–505 (1984)
10. Read, R.C., Corneil, D.G.: The graph isomorphism disease. J. Graph Theory **1**, 339–363 (1977)
11. Ambekar, A.G., Agrawal, V.P.: Canonical numbering of kinematic chains and isomorphism problem: maxcode. In: ASME, Design Engineering Technical Conference, pp. 5–8 (1986)
12. Ambekar, A.G., Agrawal, V.P.: Canonical numbering of kinematic chains and isomorphism problem: mincode. Mech. Mach. Theory **22**(5), 453–461 (1987)
13. Torgal, S.: Algorithm for the enumeration and identification of kinematic chains. In: Satapathy, S.C. (ed.) Proceedings of the International Conference on Data Engineering and Communication Technology. AISC, vol. 469, pp. 491–499. Springer, Heidelberg (2015). doi:10.1007/978-3-319-28868-0
14. Ambekar, A.G.: Mechanism and Machine Theory, PHI Learning, p. 43 (2000)

A Novel Model for NIDS with Evaluation of Pattern Classifiers and Facility of Rectification

Nikhil Gaikwad[(⊠)] and Sunil Sangve

Computer Department, ZCOER, Savitribai Phule Pune University, Pune, India
gaikwad.nikhil@gmail.com,
sunil.sangve@zealeducation.com

Abstract. As the Internet is expanding, the threat of intrusion is also increasing. Modern businesses which use Internet demand for strong computer and network security. Intrusion prevention is obviously the best choice from security viewpoint, but it has practical limitations as hackers develop new methods to breach security. Thus early detection of an intrusion is the sensible option and Network Intrusion Detection Systems (NIDS) carry out that task. In this paper, the authors propose extended empirical evaluation model specifically from NIDS perspective. The objective is to introduce multiple classifiers into the model along with feature selection method for improving performance of the classifiers. Additionally, the new model incorporates a feedback mechanism to ensure new prediction learn from rectifications of past records.

Keywords: Network intrusion detection · Pattern classifier · Feature selection

1 Introduction

The primary objective of Network Intrusion Detection Systems (NIDSs) is continuous examination of the network dataflow and identification of the malicious activity. When any doubtful activity is observed, it raises an alert to the (network or system) administrator. As mentioned by Biggio (2010) in [5], the main goal of NIDS is to differentiate between legitimate and intrusive network traffic. Intrusion detection has two approaches- (i) Misuse detection and (ii) Anomaly detection. In Misuse detection approach, the network traffic is compared with different kind of features of "known" attacks [14], whereas Anomaly detection approach, instead of looking for an exact match, looks for irregularity among other regular patterns. In this, a training set is created, and updated at regular time intervals to observe the changes in normal traffic during operation [14]. Though this approach resolves the limitation of Misuse detection, it could still fail if the hacker wisely constructs network packets which form wrong learning patterns for intrusion detection and sends over the network.

NIDS should be able to handle the massive volume of data, so the pattern classification techniques have been focused by researchers. As mentioned by Duda [3], the primary goal in pattern classification is to hypothesize the class of given models, process the identified data to eliminate noise, and for any identified pattern choose the

© Springer Nature Singapore Pte Ltd. 2016
A. Unal et al. (Eds.): SmartCom 2016, CCIS 628, pp. 590–599, 2016.
DOI: 10.1007/978-981-10-3433-6_71

model that fits the best. In simple words, it classifies the given set of patterns into a set of labels by analyzing the attributes (features) associated with the patterns.

Each packet entering the NIDS would be analyzed by the pattern classifier. A net-work packet contains number of attributes. However, not all attributes are much significant in deciding whether the packet is legitimate or malicious. So, if NIDS considers only important attributes which impact in deciding the category without adverse effect on result, then it would certainly reduce processing time. Feature Selection is the process of recognizing and eliminating the irrelevant and redundant features. Its advantages are [4] - (i) irrelevant features do not impact significantly on the accuracy of prediction, and (ii) redundant features do not improve of the result of prediction.

In this paper, the authors discuss on the study of classification model of attacks, classifier evaluation models, pattern classifiers for intrusion detection and feature selection methods in Sect. 2. Section 3 covers new systems implementation details, such as architecture, algorithms used. Then Sect. 4 presents test results observed so far. Finally it is ended with the conclusion in Sect. 5.

2   Related Work

This section covers study of previous research papers related to pattern classifiers and feature selection. The brief review of existing related work is discussed along with the key points taken up for this enhancement.

2.1   Empirical Performance Evaluation Model

The empirical performance evaluation model [1] was devised by Biggio et al. (2013) to resolve the limitations of classical model. The classical methods such as k-fold or bootstrapping [1] assume that the data distributed in training dataset will appear during the actual operation as well. In case of causative attacks [6], this could be useful, because the pattern during attack will generally be same as in the training dataset. But in case of other types of attack, it fails significantly. The pattern distribution during the attack is practically different than in training dataset.

To make the classifier ready before the occurrence of attack, the empirical per-formance evaluation model proposed an algorithm for forming the training set and testing set. As mentioned in [1], the empirical model has been tested for Indiscriminate Causative Integrity attack which permits at least one intrusion [6]. The empirical model used the testing strategy of increasing the number of malicious records injected into the training set and observed that the classifier performs correctly when number of malicious samples are less than or equal to legitimate samples.

However, it is a generalized model and only one kind of classifier (SVM) was tested for NIDS application.

2.2   Choosing a Pattern Classifier

Among many pattern classification techniques, the authors want to select a few, important ones which can be used in the new model. SVM pattern classifier was chosen as it was already referred in empirical evaluation model. Then the authors referred recent papers to understand the trend of selecting pattern classifiers by the re-searchers, specifically in network security domain. Observed that, k-NN and Naïve Bayes are majorly focused [8–10]. So they are selected. From implementation viewpoint, more details on SVM, k-NN and Naïve Bayes are obtained from [11, 12].

2.3   Choosing a Dataset

The Third International Knowledge Discovery and Data Mining Tools Competition were organized in association with The Fifth International Conference on Knowledge Discovery and Data Mining (KDD-99). The task for competition was to develop a network intrusion detector. It should possess prediction ability to categorize the connections into "good" (normal or legitimate) or "bad" (intrusions or attacks). The data set KDD-99 (also referred as KDDCup99) contains various intrusions which were simulated in military network environment [13]. KDD-99 is considered as a standard dataset for testing of classifiers for NIDS.

2.4   Feature Selection Methods

Feature selection is the process of selecting "interesting" features from the dataset [15]. The fast clustering-based feature selection algorithm (FAST) [2] is a latest technique devised by Song et al. (2013). This algorithm is based on MST (minimum spanning tree). As mentioned in [2, it is tested on 35 publicly available datasets and has shown encouraging results as compared to many other techniques viz. CFS, FCBF, Relief, Consist and FOCUS-SF.

As mentioned in [2], the Fast clusteringbAsed feature Selection algoriThm (FAST) is using MST (minimum spanning tree) concept. It works in three steps- (i) remove irrelevant features as they will not be used in further steps. (ii) construct MST from relevant features. (iii) cut down the MST to form a cluster of relevant features and then the most relevant (representative) features can be selected from each cluster. Thus, only a small number of important features are presented as output.

3   Implementation Details

The new system is an extension to the empirical model from NIDS perspective. It covers (i) use of multiple classifiers, (ii) introducing feature selection method, (iii) facility to compare classifiers result, and (iv) prediction and learning mechanism.

3.1   Architecture

Building blocks of new model are explained below-

- **Preprocessing**: The module accepts input data file (KDDCup99 10%) and applies basic preprocessing rules such as noise and duplicate removal. Then the training set generation algorithm [1] is executed to generate a dataset consisting n samples. Same algorithm is used for creation of testing dataset as well. To serve the practical purpose of the model, it provides save and load facility to the user.
- **Multiple Classifiers**: New model supports multiple pattern classifiers to be tested on tested on the given dataset. SVM, k-NN and Naïve Bayes are implemented here.
- **Feature Selection**: The FAST algorithm [2] is implemented to reduce the dimensionality of dataset. This reduced dataset is provided as input to multiple classifiers. KDDCup99, the input dataset, contains 41 features. However all 41 features need not be so important in deciding the category of packet. Also, whenever any network packet is to be examined, all 41 features will be checked against the trained dataset. In order to reduce the processing time, it is substantial to identify important features and carry out classification on that reduced dataset. But, at the same time, the accuracy of classifier should not be compromised.
- **Result Presentation**: The performance of multiple classifiers can be evaluated here when using full dataset as well as reduced dataset. Evaluation parameters are- Accuracy percentage and Time taken for processing. Accuracy means the percentage of records correctly classified. Processing time is difference between start-time and end-time of algorithm execution as captured in the logs and it is measured in milliseconds. The result is presented in tabular and graphical format Fig. 1.

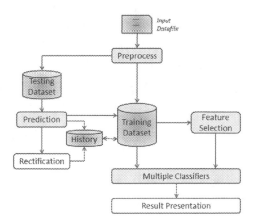

Fig. 1. Architecture of new model

$$\text{Accuracy } \% = (TP + TN) * 100 / (TP + TN\_FP + FN) \tag{1}$$

$$\text{Processing Time} = \text{Systime at end of operation} - \text{Systime at start of operation} \tag{2}$$

- **Learning module**: This module facilitates prediction of records classification. If new, unseen record is not found in training dataset, then it uses probability-based prediction [7] technique and predicts its class. In case, the obtained result is wrong, the administrator can rectify it and such history is explicitly maintained as supplementary to training dataset. The workflow is shown in Fig. 2.

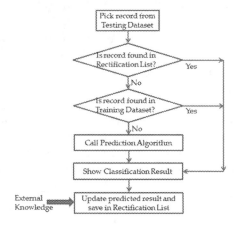

Fig. 2. Workflow of learning module

3.2 Mathematical Model

Since the proposed model comprised of interconnected module and each module consists of number of processes and has definite input and output, the mathematical model is represented in the form of set theory.

Let S is universal set of processes involved in the new system. S is represented as:
S = {P,F,C,L,R}

- *Preprocessing:* Let P is set of processes required for preprocessing activity.
  P = {Pr,Pn,Pd,Ptr} where,
  Pr is process for reading input file
  Pn and Pd are processes for removal of noise and duplicates respectively
  Ptr is process for generating training set
- *Feature Selection:* Let F is set of processes for feature selection implementation.
  F = {Pr,Fc,Fr} where,
  Fc is calculating Symmetric Uncertainty
  Fr is generating set of significant features

- *Classification:* Let C is set of classifiers, such as one-class SVM, k-NN and Naïve Bayes. Thus, C = {Csvm,Cknn,Cnb,Cr,Ca} where,
  Ca is process of calculating accuracy of classifier result Cr
- *Learning:* Let L is the set of processes required for prediction and learning module.
  L = {Pr,Lp,Lh} where,
  Lp is probability-based class prediction
  Lh saves rectified result for future use
- *Result:* Let R is the set of processes required for management of result generation which includes definition of metrics, data collection and graphical presentation.

4 Results and Discussion

4.1 Testing Approaches and Results

The testing approach mentioned in [1] is followed here. It suggests varying the number of legitimate and malicious samples in training dataset. All classifiers are processed for the given dataset. Additionally, the feature selection algorithm is executed and all classifiers are processed for the reduced dataset as well Table 1.

Table 1. Result of test cases for evaluation of different classifiers under different sizes of training set and with all/selected features

Classifier	Features	Accuracy	Time (in ms)	Malicious	Normal	Time (in s)
SVM	ALL	100	47832	2500	2500	47
SVM	SELECTED	99.98	31555	2500	2500	31
Naive Bayes	ALL	85.78	476	2500	2500	0
Naive Bayes	SELECTED	85.8	292	2500	2500	0
KNN	ALL	100	17377	2500	2500	17
KNN	SELECTED	100	8910	2500	2500	8
SVM	ALL	100	133959	2500	5000	133
SVM	SELECTED	99.98667	98017	2500	5000	98
Naive Bayes	ALL	89.80136	516	2500	5000	0
Naive Bayes	SELECTED	89.70804	297	2500	5000	0
KNN	ALL	100	37768	2500	5000	37
KNN	SELECTED	100	20015	2500	5000	20
SVM	ALL	100	194833	5000	5000	194
SVM	SELECTED	99.9	195789	5000	5000	195
Naive Bayes	ALL	92.26	782	5000	5000	0
Naive Bayes	SELECTED	91.56	433	5000	5000	0
KNN	ALL	100	75554	5000	5000	75
KNN	SELECTED	99.99	34682	5000	5000	34
SVM	ALL	100	577384	5000	10000	577
SVM	SELECTED	99.98667	579337	5000	10000	579

(*continued*)

Table 1. (*continued*)

Classifier	Features	Accuracy	Time (in ms)	Malicious	Normal	Time (in s)
Naive Bayes	ALL	94.42704	1405	5000	10000	1
Naive Bayes	SELECTED	94.46704	672	5000	10000	0
KNN	ALL	100	200585	5000	10000	200
KNN	SELECTED	100	94848	5000	10000	94
SVM	ALL	100	738498	10000	10000	738
SVM	SELECTED	99.65002	377944	10000	10000	377
Naive Bayes	ALL	95.71021	1401	10000	10000	1
Naive Bayes	SELECTED	95.47523	817	10000	10000	0
KNN	ALL	100	316543	10000	10000	316
KNN	SELECTED	100	140997	10000	10000	140
SVM	ALL	100	2020918	10000	20000	2020
SVM	SELECTED	99.71668	782516	10000	20000	782
Naive Bayes	ALL	97.05676	2161	10000	20000	2
Naive Bayes	SELECTED	97.1001	1316	10000	20000	1
KNN	ALL	100	663508	10000	20000	663
KNN	SELECTED	99.99667	358216	10000	20000	358
Naive Bayes	ALL	95.71261	2895	20000	20000	2
Naive Bayes	SELECTED	95.18012	1560	20000	20000	1
KNN	ALL	100	1453833	20000	20000	1453
KNN	SELECTED	99.9975	519548	20000	20000	519
Naive Bayes	ALL	95.66341	4351	20000	40000	4
Naive Bayes	SELECTED	95.60841	2620	20000	40000	2
Naive Bayes	ALL	96.25005	6091	40000	40000	6
Naive Bayes	SELECTED	96.2063	3627	40000	40000	3
Naive Bayes	ALL	96.14587	9235	40000	80000	9
Naive Bayes	SELECTED	96.11337	5409	40000	80000	5

Analysis of classifiers based on processing time: Graph shows the comparison of classifier according to their average processing time for each sample, across different size of training sets. As the size of training set increases, processing time of SVM is also increasing. As SVM took too much time (2020s i.e. 33 min) for 30000 records, SVM is not tested on further larger training sets. KNN performs moderately whereas Naive Bayes is indeed a winner here. Also observed that, though SVM took 33 min for 30000 records set, the system completed the task successfully; the code did not crash. This indicates the robustness of the system.

Analysis of classifiers based on accuracy: This graph shows the comparison of classifier according to their accuracy across different size of training sets. Starting from the training set of 5000 records, Naive Bayes classifier had low accuracy. However, it improves significantly when tested on larger size training sets. KNN performs moderately whereas SVM wins the race as it consistently gives almost 99% Figs. 3 and 4.

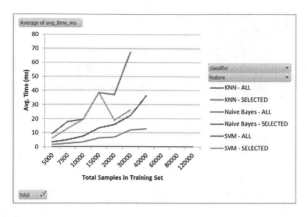

Fig. 3. Comparing average processing time of classifiers across different size of training sets

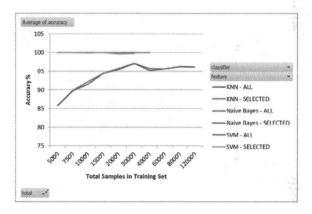

Fig. 4. Comparing accuracy of classifiers across different size of training sets

Analysis of average processing time of classifiers on machines with different RAM size: Additionally, the classifier processing time is recorded for a fix-sized training set of 10000 records (5000 normal and 5000 malicious samples), on two more machines. These three machines have identical configuration, except RAM size.

4.2 Comparative Analysis

The proposed model is an extension to empirical evaluation model and the authors have tried to cover few limitations in this enhancement. For comparative analysis, the key differences between two models are presented below Fig. 5 and Table 2:

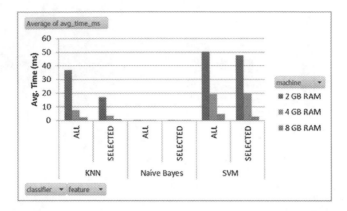

Fig. 5. Comparing processing time of classifiers on different machines

Table 2. Comparison between empirical model and proposed model

Empirical evaluation model	Extended empirical model (proposed)
This is a generalized framework	Presents NIDS-specific architecture
Contains only one classifier (SVM)	Presents modular approach to incorporate multiple classifiers
Result of SVM on different sizes of dataset are obtained	Results of multiple classifiers on different sizes of training dataset are obtained
Proposes incorporation of feature selection mechanism	Feature Selection algorithm is implemented and tested for different classifiers
Mechanism for accommodating new knowledge is not mentioned	Uses prediction algorithm with facility of rectification

5   Conclusion

Considering the reviewed literature, the authors proposed enhancement to the empirical model to mold it for NIDS. The steps for dataset construction and SVM are continued as mentioned in empirical model and also the SVM. The extension to the model has been done in 3 stages- (i) introducing feature selection method on the training dataset, (ii) incorporating multiple classifiers in the model, and (iii) introducing the prediction mechanism with facility to rectify a wrong prediction and corrected result can be used for future use. This is advantageous for practical use of the model.

The test results obtained so far show that SVM is consistent in achieving highest accuracy whereas Naïve Bayes is superior in processing time. K-NN performs moderately. Also, Feature selection improves the performance of classifier by reducing the processing time but impacts their accuracy.

Acknowledgements. The authors would like to thank the publishers and researchers for making their re-sources available. We thank the teachers for their guidance and suggestions. We are thankful to the college authority for providing necessary infrastructure and support.

References

1. Biggio, B., Fumera, G., Roli, F.: Security evaluation of pattern classifiers under attack. IEEE Trans. Knowl. Data Eng. **26**(4), 984–996 (2014)
2. Song, Q., Ni, J., Wang, G.: A fast clustering-based feature subset selection algorithm for high-dimensional data. IEEE Trans. Knowl. Data Eng. **25**(1), 1–14 (2013)
3. Duda, R.O., Hart, P.E., Stork, D.G.: Pattern Classification. Wiley-Interscience Publication, Hoboken (2000)
4. John, G.H., Kohavi, R., Pfleger, K.: Irrelevant features and the subset selection problem. In: Proceedings of the 11th International Conference on Machine Learning, pp. 121–129 (1994)
5. Biggio, B., Fumera, G., Roli, F.: Multiple classifier systems for robust classifier design in adversarial environments. Int. J. Mach. Learn. Cybern. **1**(1), 27–41 (2010)
6. Barreno, M., Nelson, B., Sears, R., Joseph, A.D., Tygar, J.D.: Can machine learning be secure? In: Proceedings of the ACM Symposium on Information, Computer and Communication Security (ASIACCS), March 2006
7. Thornton C.: Machine Learning Lecture 4: Naive Bayes Classifier. http://users.sussex.ac.uk/christ/crs/ml/lec02b.html
8. Safa, H., Hajj, W.E., Salem, F.K.A., Moutaweh, M.: Using K-nearest neighbor algorithm to reduce false negatives in P2P secure routing protocols. IEEE (2015)
9. Taruna, S., Hiranwal, S.: Enhanced Naive Bayes algorithm for intrusion detection in data mining. Int. J. Comput. Sci. Inf. Technol. **4**(6), 960–962 (2013)
10. Altwaijry, H., Algarny, S.: Bayesian based intrusion detection system. J. King Saud Univ. – Comput. Inf. Sci. **24**, 1–6 (2012). Elsevier
11. Han, J., Kamber, M.: Data Mining: Concepts and Techniques, 2nd edn. Elsevier, Amsterdam (2006)
12. Naive Bayes Classifier. https://en.wikipedia.org/wiki/Naive_Bayes_classifier
13. KDDCup99 dataset. http://kdd.ics.uci.edu/databases/kddcup99/kddcup99.html
14. Kang, D., Fuller, D., Honavar, V.: Learning classifiers for misuse and anomaly detection using a bag of system calls representation. In: Proceedings of the 2005 IEEE Workshop on Information Assurance and Security, United States Military Academy, NY, USA (2005)
15. Gaikwad N., Sangve, S.: Enhancement and evaluation of pattern classifiers in NIDS: a survey. Int. J. Comput. Sci. Inf. Technol. **6**(6), 5435–5438 (2015)

Research Confront in Software Defined Networking Environment: A Survey

Sankari Subbiah[1]([✉]) and Varalakshmi Perumal[2]

[1] Department of Information Technology, Sri Sai Ram Engineering College,
Chennai, Tamilnadu, India
sankari2705@gmail.com
[2] Department of Computer Technology, Anna University, Chennai, India
varanip@gmail.com

Abstract. The data centric networking resources are virtualized with the concept of Software Defined Networking (SDN). This is used to overcome the traditional networking issues such as traffic congestion, traffic delay, and to improve the network scalability. The networking topology is emulated in the mininet emulator. The customized traffic policy is implemented in the SDN controller. In this paper, mininet emulator and the OpenDaylight SDN controller are studied thoroughly in order to establish the SDN environment. The research challenges are discussed to set up the virtual network in the cloud based data center.

Keywords: Software defined networking · Data center · Network virtualization · SDN controller · Openflow

1 Introduction

The data plane and the control plane in SDN are separated via the Network Operating System (NOS), whereas in the traditional system both planes are present together in the networking devices. The function of the data plane is to forward the traffic from the source to destination using OpenFlow (OF) protocol and that of the control plane is to make an intelligent decisions when the traffic is generated. The networking resources such as switches, links, and ethernet interfaces are easily configured, managed and optimized via the plug-in implemented in the SDN controllers. The network virtualization concept in the controller is to create the virtual networks which consist of logical networking components. They are Open Source Virtual Switches (OVS), virtual link, virtual interfaces, virtual bridges, and Virtual Private Networks (VPNs). These resources are allocated and reused on-demand based on the network path capacity and provide flexibility when there is a traffic flow in the network [9, 10].

The different SDN controllers are NOX, POX, opendaylight, floodlight, and Ryu controller. Among these controllers, the opendaylight controller is studied thoroughly in this paper to establish the SDN environment. The Virtual Tenant Network (VTN) is used to improve the scalability of the network. Either the instance of the same controller or different types of controller are running in the same VTN or in the different VTN. Thus, the traffic is generated either within the VTN or across the VTN [11].

© Springer Nature Singapore Pte Ltd. 2016
A. Unal et al. (Eds.): SmartCom 2016, CCIS 628, pp. 600–608, 2016.
DOI: 10.1007/978-981-10-3433-6_72

In this paper our survey is organized as follows. The related works are discussed in Sect. 2. Section 3 explains the SDN environment having the different types of data centric network topology emulated in the mininet emulator over and above the SDN controllers. In Sect. 4, implementation of the SDN system and the results are discussed. Finally, the conclusion and the future scope are discussed in Sect. 5.

2 Literature Survey

Due to the development of large volume of data and the web based applications, data centers play a major role in accessing the computational, storage and networking resources. The traditional data centers are not suitable for this environment due to inflexibility, poor scalability of the network. These issues are solved by the data centeric network virtualization that is being discussed in [1]. In [2], the discussion centres round the technique that is demonstrated to map the Virtual Network (VN) in the SDN substrate in such a way that the traffic load is balanced among the switches and the delay between the controllers and the switches is minimized. The SDN controllers play a major role in optimizing the network performance.

The adaptability network environment results in the development of potential network functions. The research challenges such as scalability, security, networking performance, energy efficient and interoperability are discussed in [3]. In [4], the network virtualization introduces the concepts of flexibility, diversified networking, with security and manageability being ensured. The network virtualization concepts have led to the development of different categories of networks such as Virtual Local Area Networks (VLANs), Virtual Private Networks (VPNs), Programmable networks, and Overlay Networks. The main difference between the SDN and the traditional networking is discussed in [5]. The switch design and the control platforms that concentrate on resiliency, scalability, performance, security, and dependability are analysed.

In [6], the researchers concentrate on the network innovations by separating the data plane from the control plane and put their endeavour in the three components of SDN such as applications, control plane, and data plane. In [7], the servers are interrelated using DCell network structure. This structure establishes multiple paths to effect communication among the servers in it. The DCell Fault-tolerant Routing Protocol (DFR) is proposed in it to handle hardware, software and power failure in the network. The high bandwidth communication model is introduced using one-to-many and many-to-many communication models. The DCell network structure is suitable for the large volume and variety of data transfer in the MapReduce phase since it also supports the all-to-all communication model. In [8], Towards Really Energy-efficient Network Design (TREND) researchers put their effort in establishing the green networking. They collect the energy consumption values from the different devices and infrastructures and determine the total energy consumption of the networking components from these values. They optimize these values by finding out the minimal energy consumption of devices, technologies, algorithms, protocols and architecture to design the energy efficient network.

3   SDN Environment

Figure 1 shows the traditional networking environment which supports the hardware and distributed control plane. The SDN architecture shown in Fig. 2 supports the centralized control plane and makes use of the software to configure the network.

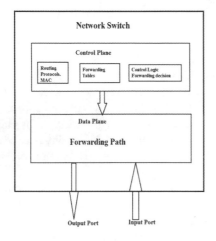

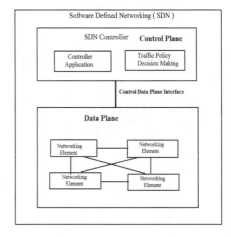

Fig. 1. Traditional Networking   **Fig. 2.** Software Defined Networking

The different data centric topologies are fat tree topology, BCube, and DCell topologies. These topologies support the features such as oversubscription, fault tolerance and cheapness when compared with the traditional topologies. Figure 3 shows the fat tree topology with k = 4 which consists of three layers, namely core, aggregation, and edge layer. There are four pods in this topology and each pod consists of $(k/2)^2$ hosts (i.e.) 4 hosts and the two layers such as edge and aggregate. The k/2 (i.e.) 2 port switches are present in each layer. The k/2 (i.e.) 2 hosts and k/2 (i.e.) 2 aggregate switches are connected to each edge switch. The k/2 (i.e.) 2 edge switches and k/2 (i.e.) 2 core switches are connected to each aggregate switch. The number of core switches are $(k/2)^2$ (i.e.) 4 core switches. Each core switch is connected to k pods (i.e.) 4. This

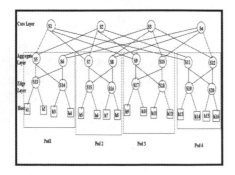

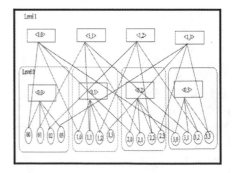

Fig. 3. Fat Tree Topology   **Fig. 4.** BCube Topology

topology supports $k^3/4$ hosts (i.e.) 16 hosts. If there is any failure of switch in the aggregation and the core layer, then the traffic flow takes an alternative path to route the packet without affecting connectivity in the network topology. The failure of switch in the edge layer may affect the less number of hosts.

The BCube topology is the server centric topology which is used for interconnecting data centres. The servers are represented by the circles and the switches are represented by the rectangles. The layer Level 0 consists of 'n' (i.e.) n = 4 servers in each switch and the 'n' (i.e.) n = 4 switches are present. The total number of hosts are 16 in the Level 0. The Level 0 switches are named as <0,0>, <0,1>, <0,2>, and <0,3> and the corresponding hosts are 00,01,02,03 in the switch <0,0>, 10,11,12,13 in the switch <1,0>, 20,21,22,23 in the switch <2,0> and 30,31,32,33 in the switch <3,0>. The Level 1 switches are the top layer of Level 0. Thus, the BCube topology is configured recursively. The $BCube_k$ (i.e.) for the Level k, where $k \geq 1$ is configured from n $BCube_{k-1}$ with n^k n-port switches, where 'n' is the number of servers and switches in each Level k. Figure 4 shows the two level (i.e.) Level 0 and Level 1 BCube topology. It shows the connectivity rule, i.e., the ith server in the jth $BCube_0$ connects to the jth port of the ith Level 1 switch. It supports the fault-tolerance since the multiple path exists for the traffic flow between any two servers.

The DCell topology is the recursive construction of server centric network architecture in which one server is connected to many other servers directly with the multiple Network Interface Cards (NICs). The basic topology is $DCell_0$ which contains 'n' number of hosts with an 'n' port switch. The network switch is used to connect each server within the $DCell_0$. The Level 1 topology is $DCell_1$ and is configured from the Level 0 and $DCell_1$ consists of n + 1 $DCell_0$ cells. In $DCell_1$, all servers in each of $DCell_0$ in a $DCell_1$ are connected to a server in another $DCell_0$. Similarly, the Level 2 contains k * n + 1 $DCell_1$. Thus the topology is configured recursively. The scalability and robustness is achieved in it even though the cross section bandwidth and network latency is one of the issues in this topology. Figure 5 shows the DCell topology.

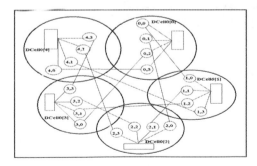 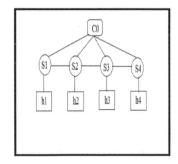

Fig. 5. DCell Topology   **Fig. 6.** Linear Topology

Thus, the different data centre topologies are discussed and these topologies are emulated using mininet emulator. The switches configured in the mininet, support the openflow which is suitable for customised flexible routing and software defined networking. The mininet is used to establish the network testbed for the openflow applications with the customised topologies [12]. The Service Abstraction Layer (SAL) in the controller makes use of the Java Interfaces, Maven, Open Service Gateway Initiative (OSGi) and karaf for the opendaylight application programming. The Apache maven simplifies the build process and creates the XML file known as the Project Object Model (POM). This file contains the dependency packages among the bundle list and mentions the start up bundle name when the bundle is loaded.

4   Experimental Set-Up and Results

The two 64-bit Ubuntu 14.04 LTS system was used to setup the SDN environment in this survey paper. Mininet emulator was installed in one machine and the Open daylight controller was installed in the second machine. The mininet command **sudo mn –topo linear, 4** was to emulate the linear topology with four switches and each switch was attached to the host as shown in Fig. 6. It shows that the four switches (s1, s2, s3, and s4) and the four hosts (h1, h2, h3, and h4) are attached with the corresponding switches. The switches are connected to the controller (c0). The switch s1 is connected to the host h1 via s1-etho interface.

The ip addresses of the networking components are configured in the emulated topology as given in Table 1.

Table 1. SDN Networking Components

S.No.	Component	IP address
1.	Host h1	10.0.0.1
2.	Host h2	10.0.0.2
3.	Switch s1	00:00:00:00:00:00:00:01
4.	Switch s2	00:00:00:00:00:00:00:02
5.	s1-eth1	1@OF|00:00:00:00:00:00:00:01
6.	s2-eth1	1@OF|00:00:00:00:00:00:00:02
7.	s3-eth3	3@OF|00:00:00:00:00:00:00:03
8.	s4-eth2	2@OF|00:00:00:00:00:00:00:04

The tree topology [13] was emulated with the mininet command **sudo mn –topo tree, depth=2, fanout=2** and the topology is shown in Fig. 7. The 'ping' command from the mininet prompt is given to test the connectivity between the two hosts which are attached either to the same switch or to the different switch as shown in Fig. 8. The link parameters such as bandwidth (bw) and delay are specified using the command **sudo mn –link tc, bw = 20, delay = 5 ms** from the command prompt. The customized network tree topology is written using python script and the topology is emulated using the command **$ sudo python sampletopo.py**. Alternatively, the custom topology is emulated using the command **sudo mn –custom simpletreetopo.py –topo mytopo**. Figure 9 demonstrates the emulation of customized tree topology along with the test connectivity between the hosts ('h1' to 'h4' and 'h2' to 'h3'). Thus the emulated topology consists of virtual switches, hosts attached to the virtual switches via the virtual ports and virtual link between the hosts and the switches.

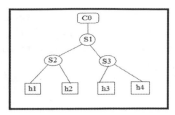

Fig. 7. Tree Topology

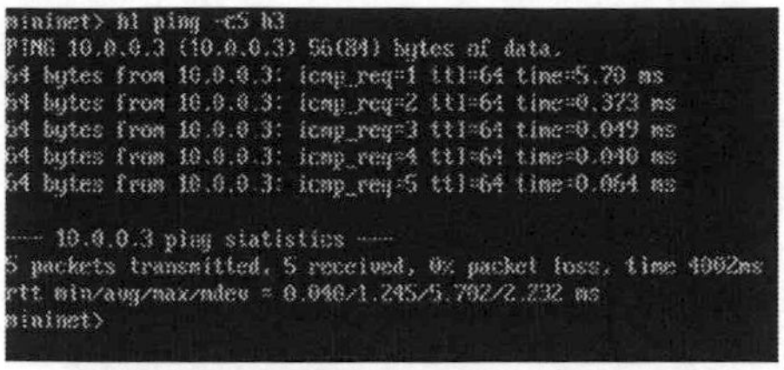

Fig. 8. Traffic generation between the hosts

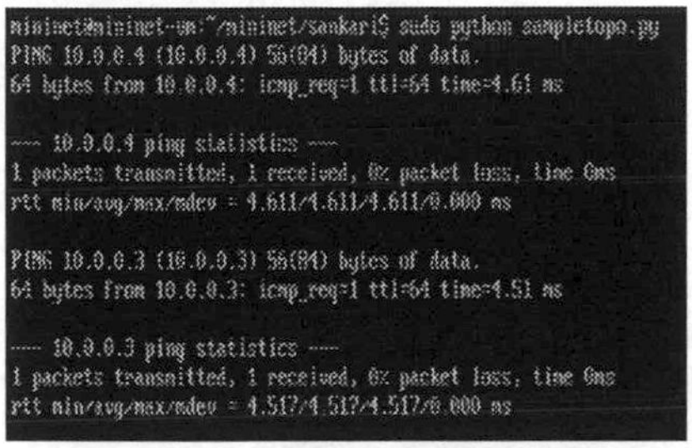

Fig. 9. Customized topology testing

Fig. 10. OSGi bundle List

The command to start the controller from the Ubuntu prompt is **$ sudo ./run.sh**. Once the controller is started, the OSGi prompt is displayed and it is listening to the port 6633. The web client is listening to the controller via port number 8080. The available bundle list in the OSGi is displayed in its prompt using the equinox 'ss' command which is shown in Fig. 10. It displays the bundle id, state (ACTIVE, RESOLVED and INSTALLED) and bundle name [18]. The traffic policy code is written using the Java language and it is implemented as one of the plugins in the OSGi environment. The 'maven' compiler is used to compile the java program in the opendaylight controller and create the jar file once the program is free from the error. Thus the created jar file is installed as plugin in the OSGi [14–16]. The steps to create the jar file using maven are as follows [17]:

(1) Create the directory 'helloworld' under the current directory using the command **mkdir/home/ubuntu/helloworld**

(2) The pom.xml file is created under the 'helloworld' directory. In this file, the group id is specified as 'org.opendaylight.controller', artifact id is as 'helloworld' and also mention the version of the new bundle as 0.1. The required exported and imported packages are also mentioned in it. This file is one of the supporting files to create new OSGi bundle with the bundle id and bundle name.

(3) The package 'org.opendaylight.controller.helloworld' has to be mentioned in the activator class. This class is needed to list the new OSGI component along with the existing bundle. The user defined policy is written in the 'helloworld' class in the controller application. The directory is organized for these two classes as **/home/ubuntu/helloworld/src/main/java/org/opendaylight/controller/helloworld**

(4) The pom.xml file is available under the directory **/home/ubuntu/helloworld** and is compiled using the maven command **mvn clean install** which is shown in Fig. 11.

(5) Now, the build is success and the 'helloworld-0.1.jar' file is successfully created in the directory **/home/ubuntu/helloworld/target**

(6) Then, **helloworld-0.1.jar** file is installed from the osgi prompt as:

osgi>install/home/ubuntu/helloworld/target/helloworld-0.1.jar

Figure 12 shows the output of the installed jar file details such as bundle id, bundle name, version and the needed exported and imported packages in the osgi prompt.

(7) The two functions are written as controller application and it is triggered during start and stop; the bundle stops by specifying the bundle id which is shown in Fig. 13.

(8) The installed bundle is removed from the osgi bundle list using the 'uninstall' command. Then, list the bundle using 'ss' command to verify the output.

(9) The 'exit' command is used to stop the controller in the osgi prompt.

Fig. 11. OSGI bundle creation using maven

Fig. 12. OSGi 'install' command   **Fig. 13.** OSGi 'start' and 'stop' commands

Thus, the controller application is written and compiled using maven compiler. Then, the newly created jar file is installed, started and stopped in the bundle. The emulated topology in the mininet is connected to the opendaylight controller as remote controller using the command **sudo mn –topo single,5 –controller remote, port=6633, ip="192.168.1.13"** which is shown in Fig. 14. The established five hosts are attached to a single switch which is connected to the opendaylight controller as remote controller with ip address as 192.168.1.13 and listening to the port 6633.

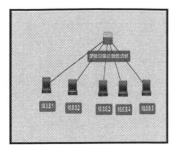 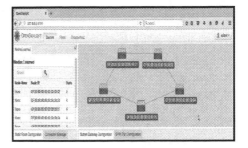

Fig. 14. Simple Topology   **Fig. 15.** Ring Topology

The customized ring topology is written in python script as shown in Fig. 15 and the topology is connected to the remote controller. The energy efficient traffic flow from the host 'h1' to the host 'h5' is shown in Fig. 16.

Fig. 16. Energy efficient optimal path selection

5 Conclusion and Future Work

The emerging next generation networking technology pioneers the perception of network virtualization in SDN. It brings in the adaptive network infrastructures and the virtual machines being configured dynamically in the ICT industry and supports the cloud based data center. The separation of the data plane and the control plane in SDN brings the agility in the network topology. The topology is emulated using mininet emulator and its commands are studied to establish the topology, generate the traffic and support the open flow using open virtual switch.

The python code was used to customize the network topology in the mininet. The SDN controller opendaylight was studied thoroughly to build the user defined bundle in the OSGI framework and the code was compiled using maven compiler. The traffic policy was implemented in the controller to trigger the event when there was a packet flow from the source to destination via the switches and the controller.

In future, the SDN provides the foundation for the enterprise network. Also, it provides further development of energy minimization in the campus networks and maximization of the bandwidth utilization in the Wide Area Networks. Thus, the network topology and its services are implemented, managed and controlled by the software.

References

1. Bari, M.F., et al.: Data center network virtualization: a survey. IEEE Commun. Surv. Tutorials **15**(2), 909–928 (2013)
2. Demirci, M., et al.: Design and analysis of techniques for mapping virtual networks to software-defined network substrates. Comput. Commun. **45**, 1–10 (2014). Elsevier
3. Sezer, S., et al.: Are we ready for SDN? Implementation challenges for software-defined networks. IEEE Commun. Mag. **51**(7), 36–43 (2013)
4. Kabir, Mosharaf, et al.: Network virtualization: state of the art and research challenges. IEEE Commun. Mag. **47**(7), 20–26 (2009)
5. Kreutz, D., et al.: Software-defined networking: a comprehensive survey. IEEE Proc. **103**(1), 14–76 (2015)
6. Farhady, H., et al.: Software-defined networking: a survey. Comput. Netw. **81**, 79–95 (2015). Elsevier
7. Guo, C., et al.: DCell: a scalable and fault-tolerant network structure for data centers. In: SIGCOMM'08, Conference Proceeding on Data Communication, Vol. 38, Issue 4, pp. 75–86 (2008)
8. Meo, M., et al.: Research challenges on energy-efficient networking design. Computer Commun. **50**, 187–195 (2014). Elsevier
9. Hu, F., et al.: A survey on software-defined network (SDN) and openflow: from concept to implementation. IEEE Commun. Surv. Tutorials **16**(4), 2181–2206 (2014)
10. Drutskoy, D., et al.: Scalable network virtualization in software-defined networks. IEEE Internet Comput. **17**(2), 20–27 (2013)
11. Assi, C., et al.: Towards scalable traffic management in cloud data centers. IEEE Trans. Commun. **62**(3), 1033–1045 (2014)
12. www.mininet.org
13. www.opendaylight.org
14. http://www.frank-durr.de
15. http://sdntutorials.com/hello-world-application-using-osgi-bundle/
16. https://isurues.wordpress.com/2009/01/01/useful-equinox-osgi-commands/
17. http://sdnhub.org/tutorials/opendaylight
18. https://isurues.wordpress.com/2009/01/01/useful-equinox-osgi-commands/

Hexagon Shaped Asymmetrical Fractal Boundary Microstrip Patch Antenna for Wireless Applications

Karmjeet Kaur[(⊠)] and Jagtar Singh

Yadawindra College of Engineering, Punjabi University, Talwandi Sabo,
Bathinda 151302, Punjab, India
iamkarm63l@gmail.com

Abstract. With advanced telecommunication systems, need for antennas with multiband features for wireless applications are increasing. The paper presents hexagon shaped microstrip antenna operating at 2.47 GHz with gain of 7.96 dB. The hexagon shaped antenna is converted to multiband antenna by enforcing fractal concept in the geometry of antenna. The iterations of the antenna are done in such a way that antenna size is reduced by 49% as compared to base geometry conventional antenna. The performance of antenna is evaluated using HFSS (High Frequency Structural Simulator); v13 software from Ansoft. Results show that improved performance parameters for instance gain, return loss, VSWR, bandwidth etc. are achieved with co-axial feed. The closing iteration is designed by FR4_Epoxy material having dimensions 27.5 (L) $\times$ 36.5 (W) $\times$ 3.2 (h) mm^3 with $\varepsilon r = 4.4$ appropriate for S-band applications.

Keywords: Fractal geometries · Microstrip patch antenna · High frequency structural simulator · Gain · VSWR · Wireless communication · Return loss

1 Introduction

In recent years designers are raising interest in antennas with reduced dimensions and wider bandwidths. This increased research in different directions, one of concept from which uses fractal shaped antenna [1]. Different fractal geometries has introduced for improving various antenna characteristics and performance parameters. These geometries are useful in antenna size reduction along with incorporating multiband characteristics [2]. A patch antenna comprises of lower ground plane, a thin patch above the substrate and a feed. Most of fractal geometries have characteristics features like fractional geometry, self-similarity, space filling etc. These features of fractal are utilized to achieve the following advantages: Multiband/Wideband antennas, miniaturization, better efficiency and improved gain. All these attributes of fractal antennas leads to its ever increasing demand in various wireless applications including both military and commercial applications. As per enlargements growing in various Wireless Local Area Network (WLAN) protocols the necessities for antennas working on frequency 2–5 GHz in S band is also growing. In recent days the extensive spread protocols of WLAN IEEE 802.11n, also make use of ISM band (2.1–2.5 GHz) [3].

© Springer Nature Singapore Pte Ltd. 2016
A. Unal et al. (Eds.): SmartCom 2016, CCIS 628, pp. 609–617, 2016.
DOI: 10.1007/978-981-10-3433-6_73

In this paper, designed antenna comprises of different iterations in which various hexagon slots are subtracted according to fractal concept (1/3rd concept). It exhibits multiband behavior, improved performance parameters for example acceptance value of return loss along with improved gain, bandwidth etc. despite of less complexity and compact size. The conventional antenna has a gain of 1.38 dB, return-loss of −15.05 dB and VSWR of 1.42 at 2.9 GHz frequency. Further by introducing fractal design concept gain has been improved by 7.96 dB, return losses by −11.56 dB and VSWR of 1.45 at the frequency of 2.1 GHz till the last iteration of the antenna. The antenna is planned for S-band (2.1–2.5 GHz) used for Bluetooth and wireless applications. Co-axial feed is used which helps in reduction of dispersion and lesser radiation leakage than microstrip transmission line [5]. This feed technique has another advantage that it could be positioned at desired location on patch to attain better impedance matching and to avoid unwanted radiations from feed [6].

2   Antenna Design and Configuration

2.1   Software Design

Steps for designing different iterations of proposed antenna are mentioned below:

Step1: Design of proposed fractal antenna starts with ground plane on lower side and patch above the dielectric substrate termed as base geometry as shown in Fig. 1(a). Dimensions of antenna are calculated using Eqs. (1 and 2) as given in [7–9].

Practical width of patch that points to better efficiencies given by

$$W = \frac{1}{2f_r\sqrt{\mu_0\varepsilon_0}} \sqrt{\frac{2}{\varepsilon_r + 1}} = \frac{v_0}{2f_r}\sqrt{\frac{2}{\varepsilon_r + 1}} \tag{1}$$

The actual length of patch is given by

$$L = \frac{1}{2f_r\sqrt{\varepsilon_{reff}}\sqrt{\mu_0\varepsilon_0}} - 2\Delta L \tag{2}$$

The designed antenna resonates at frequency 'f_r' 2.47 GHz, FR4_Epoxy with dielectric constant (ε_r) = 4.4 is used as substrate material and patch is placed 3.2 mm above from the ground plane. The substrate is planned using FR4_Epoxy due to various reasons such as it act as a primary insulating backbone upon which majority of rigid PCB are designed. FR_4 glass epoxy is versatile and popular high-pressure plastic laminate of decent plastic strength to weight ratios. FR_4 is compound material of glass cloth woven fiber with the epoxy resin that is self-extinguishing (flame-resistant) [10]. Various parametric specifications and dimensions calculated by equations for the base antenna geometry are shown in Table 1.

Step 2: During 1st Iteration various hexagon slots are subtracted from the patch. 1st Iteration of patch antenna contains four hexagon slots as shown in Fig. 1(b). Side of each hexagon is 6 mm. By using this technique 1st iteration of the fractal boundary antenna is designed. The co-axial or probe feed is the technique used for feeding the

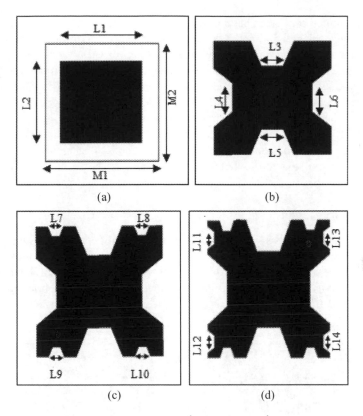

Fig. 1. (a) Base geometry (b) 1st Iteration (c) 2nd Iteration (d) 3rd Iteration of proposed antenna

Table 1. Various parametric specifications of antenna

S No	Parameters	Value
1	Substrate material used	FR4_Epoxy
2	Dielectric constant of the substrate (ε_r)	4.4
3	Thickness of dielectric substrate (h)	3.2 mm
4	Feed type	Coaxial Feed
5	Length of the substrate (M1)	27.5 mm
6	Width of the substrate (M2)	36.5 mm
7	Length of the patch (L1)	23.5 mm
8	Breadth of the patch (L2)	32.5 mm
9	L3 = L4 = L5 = L6	6 mm
10	L7 = L8 = L9 = L10	2 mm
11	L11 = L12 = L13 = L14	2 mm

antenna. The outer conductor having radius 1 mm of dielectric material 'vacuum' is linked to ground plane while inner conductor of radius 0.5 mm of dielectric material 'pec' extends to radiating patch through the substrate.

Step 3: The 2nd iteration of antenna is designed by cutting four more hexagon slots from the patch in the fractal geometry as shown in Fig. 1(c). The side of smaller hexagon is 2 mm which is one third of the side of larger hexagon. By using this technique 2nd iteration of proposed antenna is designed.

Step 4: To improve performance parameters of proposed antenna in terms of improving the bandwidth and decreasing antenna size, 4th iteration is introduced. Four more hexagon slots are subtracted from antenna as shown in Fig. 1(d).

2.2 Hardware Design

To validate the hypothesis of proposed antenna experimentally, it is fabricated in addition to testing. The antenna is designed firstly using software AutoCAD; v17. Further hardware is fabricated on FR4 epoxy with dielectric constant 4.4 and thickness 3.2 mm. For the feed SMA four hole female connector is used. The fabricated design of hexagon shaped fractal antenna for 1st and 3rd iteration is shown in Fig. 2.

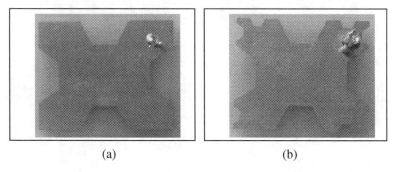

(a)   (b)

Fig. 2. Fabricated design of fractal antenna for (a) 1st Iteration (b) 3rd Iteration

3   Results and Discussions

Using software HFSS, performance parameters of antenna are analyzed. At frequency of 2.9 GHz base geometry has gain of 1.38 dB, return losses of −15.05 dB and VSWR of 1.42 whereas 1st iteration has gain of 6.89 dB, return losses of −10.45 dB and VSWR of 1.85 at 1.9 GHz. Further 2nd iteration has gain of 3.11 dB, return loss −14.99 dB and VSWR of 1.43 at 6.3 GHz. 3rd iteration has improved the gain up to 7.96 dB, return losses to −11.56 dB and VSWR of 1.45 at frequency of 2.1 GHz respectively. Hexagon slots are subtracted to achieve size reduction of 49% and improved bandwidth from 200 MHz to 300 MHz at resonating frequencies of 2.9 GHz and 2.1 GHz respectively. The bandwidth largely depends upon dimensions of the subtracted hexagon slots.

Table 2. Comparison of proposed antenna with some exiting antenna

Author	G(dB)	Patch size (mm²)	Substrate material	H(mm)	ε_r
Saleekaw [11]	3	33.54 × 33.54	FR4 dielectric	1.6	4.1
Kumar [2]	4.35	55 × 44	FR4	1.6	4.4
Karli [4]	6.34	28.2 × 36.7	Arlon AD320	1.58	3.2
Reddy [1]	6.8	36 × 36	RoggerRT/Duroid5880	3.2	2.2
Proposed	7.96	23.5 × 32.5	FR4_Epoxy	3.2	4.4

Comparison of the proposed antenna with some existing antenna in terms of Gain (G), Patch Size, Substrate material, Substrate Height (H) and Dielectric constant (ε_r) is shown in Table 2.

3.1   Return Losses

Return loss or scattering parameters graph is also known as S parameter graph used to measure transmission losses and reflection between the reflected and incident waves [10]. The comparison of return losses v/s frequency simulation results for base geometry, 1st, 2nd & 3rd iterations of projected antenna is shown in Fig. 3.

Figure 4 shows the comparison between simulated and measured return loss characteristics for 1st and 3rd iterations of hexagon shaped fractal boundary patch antenna. It shows that 1st iteration has good return loss from 2.7 GHz to 3 GHz with respect to −10 dB whereas 3rd iteration fractal antenna has better return loss from 2.1 GHz to 2.3 GHz. Also bandwidth up to 300 MHz has been analyzed by final iteration of the proposed antenna. Deviations of the results appearing between the simulated and measured results are due to tolerance levels during the fabrication process of the antenna.

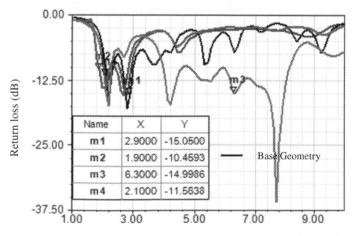

Fig. 3. Plot of return loss v/s frequency for base geometry, 1st, 2nd and 3rd iteration

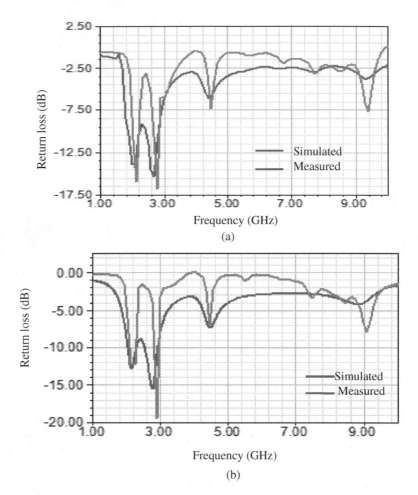

Fig. 4. Comparison between simulated and measured return loss characteristics for (a) 1st iteration (b) 3rd iteration

3.2   Radiation Pattern

Radiation Pattern or far-field pattern in the arena of antenna design refers to angular dependence of radio waves strength from the antenna or else supplementary source.

Two dimensional radiation patterns of proposed antenna for base geometry, 1st, 2nd and 3rd iteration in E and H plane at resonant frequency of 2.9 GHz, 1.9 GHz, 6.3 GHz and 2.1 GHz are shown in Fig. 5.

3.3   VSWR

Antenna Voltage Wave Standing Ratio (VSWR) is the belongings of antenna used to get impedance matching [12]. The VSWR of antenna is also less than 2 for all resonant

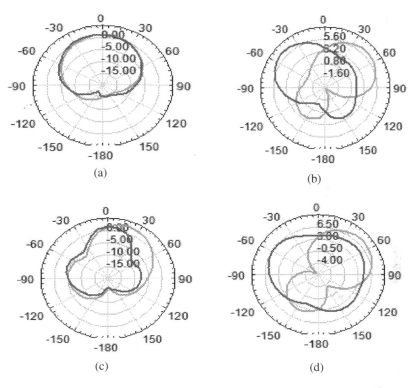

Fig. 5. Two dimensional radiation pattern of (a) base geometry at 2.9 GHz (b) 1st Iteration at 1.9 GHz (c) 2nd Iteration at 6.3 GHz (d) 3rd Iteration at 2.1 GHz

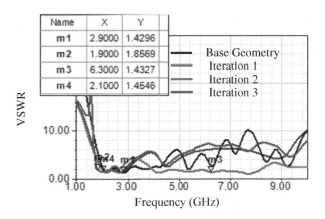

Fig. 6. Plot of VSWR v/s frequency

Table 3. Simulation results

Case	Resonant frequency (GHz)	Return loss (dB)	Gain (dB)	VSWR
Base geometry	2.8	−17.82	1.25	1.29
	2.9	−15.05	1.38	1.42
1st Iteration	1.9	−10.45	6.89	1.85
	2	−13.83	2.4	1.51
	2.6	−14.43	2.28	1.46
2nd Iteration	6.3	−14.99	3.11	1.43
	7.7	−35.8	1.83	1.63
3rd Iteration	2.1	−11.56	7.96	1.45
	2.2	−12.32	4.4	1.32
	2.6	−11.97	4.80	1.79

frequencies. Plot of VSWR v/s frequency for the iterations of the antenna is as shown in Fig. 6.

Table 3 shows the comparative results of proposed antenna for Base geometry, 1st iteration, 2nd iteration and 3rd iteration respectively.

4 Conclusion

The proposed asymmetrical fractal boundary hexagon shaped patch antenna with co-axial feed having compact size of 27.5 mm × 36.5 mm × 3.2 mm is designed for S-band applications. As the iterations order of antenna increases, size reduction occurs, resonant frequency decreases more to minor side as well as number of frequency bands also increases. Size of proposed antenna is reduced by 49% from base geometry by subtracting various hexagon slots from the patch. After calculation of results at resonant frequency of 2.1 GHz final iteration of proposed antenna has gain of 7.96 dB, return loss of −11.56 dB along with VSWR of 1.45 and bandwidth of 300 MHz. Therefore, final iteration of proposed antenna shows improved results in terms of return loss, gain, VSWR etc. Also the frequency swing towards lower side which makes the antenna efficient and useful and meets the need of S-band of ISM band and various wireless applications.

References

1. Reddy, V.V., Sarma, N.V.S.N.: Compact circularly polarized asymmetrical fractal boundary microstrip antenna for wireless applications. IEEE Antennas Wirel. Propag. **13**, 118–121 (2014)
2. Kumar, Y., Singh, S.: A quad-band hybrid fractal antenna for wireless applications. In: International Advance Computing Conference: IACC, pp. 730–733. IEEE (2015)

3. Cohen, N.: Fractal antenna applications in wireless telecommunications. In: Professional Program Proceedings of Electronics Industries Forum, pp. 43–49. IEEE, New England (1997)
4. Karli, R., Ammor, H.: Rectangular patch antenna for dual-band RFID and WLAN applications. Wirel. Pers. Commun. **83**(2), 995–1007 (2015). Springer, New York
5. Khan, O.M., Islam, Z.U., Islam, Q.U.: Novel miniaturized koch pentagonal fractal antenna for multiband wireless applications. Prog. Electromagn. Res. **141**, 693–710 (2003)
6. Chitra, R.J., Yoganathan, M., Nagarajan, V.: Co axial fed double L–Slot microstrip patch antenna array for WiMAX and WLAN application. In: International Conference on Communication and Signal Processing, pp. 1159–1164, 3–5 April 2013
7. Singh, I., Tripathi, V.: Microstrip patch antenna and its applications: a survey. Int. J. Comput. Technol. Appl. **2**(5), 1595–1599 (2011)
8. Pharwaha, A.P.S., Singh, J., Kamal, T.S.: Estimation of feed position of rectangular microstrip patch antenna. IE J. ET **91**, 20–25 (2010)
9. Singh, J., Singh, A.P., Kamal, T.S.: On the design of triangular microstrip antenna for wireless communication. IP Multimed. Commun. Spec. Issue IJCA **1**, 103–106 (2011). www.ijcaonline.org
10. Parsad, K.D.: Antenna and Wave Propagation. Satya Parkashan, New Delhi (2005)
11. Saleekaw, S., Mahatthanajatuphat, C., Akkaraekthalin, P.: A rhombic patch monopole antenna with modified minkowski fractal geometry for UTMS, WLAN, and mobile WiMAX application. Prog. Electromagn. Res. PIER **89**, 57–74 (2009)
12. Balanis, C.A.: Antenna Theory and Design, 3rd edn. McGraw Hill publishing company, New Delhi (2003)

Design and Implementation of Automation System Using Eye Blink Parameters

Shubhanshu Khandelwal[(✉)], Utkarsh Katara, and Manish Kumar Sharma

Computer Engineering, Poornima College of Engineering, Jaipur, India
shubhanshukhandelwal95@gmail.com, utkarshpce526@poornima.org,
kumar.manish.sharma786@gmail.com

Abstract. The purpose of automation should not be restricted to power conservation but it should also facilitate ease of control of devices with minimal intervention of human being [1]. In this paper we have proposed an alternative approach to allow the human to control the home appliances through their normal blink of human eyes with occurrences of reflected infrared light by the eyes pupil. In this paper an IR emitter and detector aligned at such a coordinates that the infrared light would be able to get reflected through the pupil. It is connected to Universal Board by wireless connection which is being used to control the supply of current to the appliances by a two way switch connection. An Infrared Emitter is mounted over the main device frame to pin point the particular device. The main eye device has a timer switch which turns OFF the device after few seconds for minimum exposure of IR on eye and push button to turn it ON.

Keywords: Home appliances · Eye blink · Smart automation system · Infrared detector panel · Timer switch

1 Introduction

Today we are working on various controlling system for technological development and nowadays automation is taking over the whole world. We all are in a race to finish our work in the least possible time and for this to happen we need an automation system to do our task with just a trigger or sometimes without a trigger. Not only for minimizing the time we need automation but for those disorder people we need the automation systems. Also at the time when we are busy doing main task we need small task to be done automatically specially at that time when the main task is too sensitive for ex- in aeronautical space where we are busy doing special task so we need other smaller task to be done automatically when needed. So while in this we can use any mechanism to do the whole system with just a trigger into the automation system from that body part which is not been used. Automation system using Eye Blink Parameter acts as automatic control of home appliances by blinking eyes. By using this system a person can easily operate home appliances without direct indulgence. It is designed to save the electricity and also beneficial for security purpose. This will be also very helpful to tetraplegia patients, also identified as quadriplegia, as paralysis affected by sickness or injury to a human that gives partial results or total loss of use of all their limbs. The major problem

© Springer Nature Singapore Pte Ltd. 2016
A. Unal et al. (Eds.): SmartCom 2016, CCIS 628, pp. 618–624, 2016.
DOI: 10.1007/978-981-10-3433-6_74

that Tetraplegic patients face is leading their own life without anyone else's help. This includes basic day to day operations like switching on an appliance [1]. Here in our proposed work we are using our eye as a measure to give the trigger to a system to do multiple tasks.

2 Related Work

Many researchers already developed various systems with precise devices which is use for very expensive, excessively sensitive and very costly purpose [2, 3] EEG or Statistical active appearance model technologies are been used. The different basic devices used in existing system [1] there is no test case and the patterns are too much tough to be implemented and also it is wired leading to more complexity. Here in our research work we are implementing a simpler approach with some more efficient and with simpler way to do the task with the testing the output at our side and the appliance side too. In the present scenario we also require Network Controlling devices and internet medium to control the long distance home appliances. The paper [1, 2] used same concept to control the home appliances easily but in this paper we use alternative approach to control the appliances.

3 General Architectural Diagram

In this automation System overall architecture divided into two basic blocks namely user block and appliance block. The user block is used to take input from the user whereas appliance block is placed at appliance side to change the state of the appliances with various small blocks consisting of many electronics components. Following is the block diagram representing the whole system.

3.1 User Block

The Fig. 1(a) user block, we are using Infrared signal as measure to give input to the system for defining the working of whole system. Generally IR Transmitter is also one type of LED uses to emit infrared rays similarly at receiving side the IR Receiver uses to receive the IR rays transmitted by IR transmitter and both IR transmitter and receiver should be placed within a line. When input is taken from the IR sensing circuit then the timer circuit get switched on, switching the 4 LEDs at a circular motion of blinking 1st LED then after a fix interval of time(1s) 2nd LED blinks and this process goes on till the IR sensing circuit is switched off by removing the input in it. According to this the output is given to the next phase Hold on Circuit for further processing and set data is transmitted through the next phase i.e. RF transmitter. The main component of Hold on Circuit is microcontroller which determines what will be send to the receiver through transmitter so that according the user input the selected output i.e. appliance is turned off/on. In this processor microcontroller is programmed to change the outputted data accordingly. There are many reasons of RF Transmission which is better than IR (infrared). Firstly, signals can travel longer distances through RF which can be making it proper applications of higher range. Secondly, however typically infrared ray operates in line-of-sight mode, so any obstruction is occur between transmitter & receiver the RF signals can travel easily.

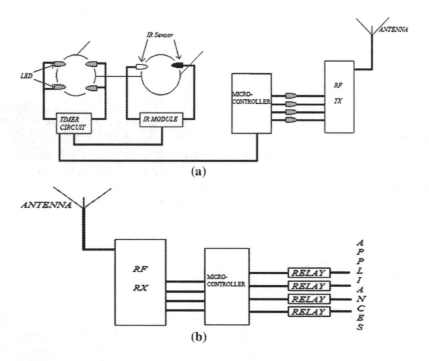

Fig. 1. (a): Block diagram of user block (b): Block diagram of appliances block

3.2 Appliances Block

In Fig. 1(b) Appliances block we are receiving the data from the user block through the RF Receiver; the data is been decoded in this phase and processed after signal is transmitted to the particular relay and finally the states of appliances will be flipped.

4 Circuit Diagram

In Fig. 2(a) and (b) show the Basic Circuit diagram of the system. The main components of Basic Circuit Diagram are as follows.

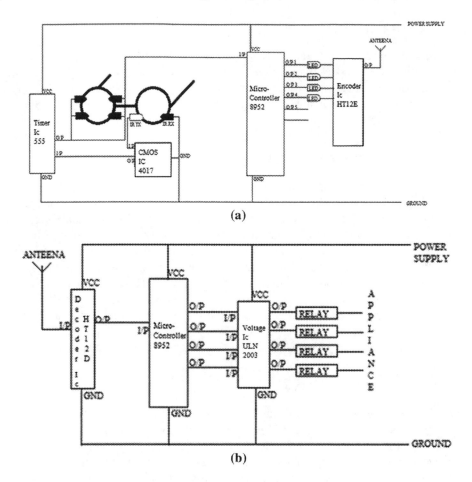

Fig. 2. (a): Basic circuit diagram of user block (b): Basic circuit diagram of appliances block

4.1   Eye Blink Sensor (IR Based)

Infrared sensor is a measure to give input signal to the system for defining the working of the whole system. An IR sensor consists of two parts: IR transmitter and IR receiver. IR Transmitter is also one type of LED uses to emit infrared rays similarly at receiving side the IR Receiver uses to receive the IR rays transmitted by IR transmitter and both IR transmitter and receiver should be placed within a line.

4.2   Microcontroller (8952)

The Microcontroller AT89C52 represents a circuit with combination of a Flash programmable and erasable read only memory (PEROM) with 8 KB and a Random Access Memory with 256 bytes. The AT89C52 takes maximum 1000 times to erased and programmed with 1000 Writes/Erase endurance.

4.3   Timer IC - NE555P

The Timer IC (NE555P) generates precise values of timing pulse. It is combination of 8 pin circuit and two modes of operations: astable and monostable. In astable mode at least two external resistors and capacitors require for controlling the frequency & duty cycle whereas in monostable mode time delay of the pulses can be controlled by single external resistor and capacitor.

4.4   Encoder and Decoder (HT-12E and HT-12D)

HT12E is an integrated circuit of various encoders and decoders of 2^{12} series use in various applications of remote control system. The HT12E has a transmission enable pin with low active and transmission of both programmed addresses/data are together with the header bits through a RF or an infrared transmission medium when we received a trigger signal on TE pin. It initiates a 4-word transmission cycle upon a transmission enable acknowledgement and the cycle repetition as long as TE is reserved low. The output of encoder is completes its final cycle then stops and TE returns to high.

We can convert the serial input into various parallel outputs using HT12D. It decodes the received data by an RF receiver and serial addresses into parallel data finally sends them to output data pins. The serial input data is compared with the local addresses constantly three times. Input data code and no error or unmatched codes are found.

4.5   Voltage IC (ULN2003APC)

The ULN2003 represents to a maximum voltage and array IC of maximum current Darlington with Darlington pairs of seven open collector and common emitters. The voltage IC **ULN2003** is related to family of ULN200X series of ICs and various versions is connecting to various logic families. The ULN2003 is using for logic devices of CMOS and 5 V TTL. When driving load with extensive range and used as relay drivers, line drivers and display drivers by these ICs. We can normally use ULN2003 while driving Stepper Motors.

4.6   Relay

The relay represents to electromagnetic device it is use to connect two circuits magnetically and separate them electrically. The relay also work as an interface between electronic circuit (operate in a low voltage) and electrical circuit (operate in a high voltage). Example, a relay can be switching from a 5 V DC battery circuit to a 230 V AC mains circuit. We can use two parts of relay switch: In input part: A magnetic field generating coil and applied a minor voltage (operating voltage) to this coil from an electronic circuit. In output part: The contactors are mechanically connect or disconnect. In a simple relay circuit we have three types of contactors: normally open (NO), normally closed (NC) and common (COM) the NC contactors is connected to COM contactors at the input state.

5 Working

In proposed System user block, we have used an Infrared, IR sensor which is placed in our spectacles at an angle such that the signal from the IR transmitter will be reflected back to the IR receiver from the pupil of our eye. When the illumination of eye with an infrared light, the pupil becomes white generally it gives improvement of half of the "red-eye effect" seen normally in pictures. Joined to the IR sensor we have used the IR module (monostable) to sense the signal from the IR sensor. Now when we close our left eye lid the signal get break from the IR sensor due to the non-reflective ability of our eye lid, the timer circuit (astable) gets switched on enabling the glow of LEDs placed on the other eye frame. The LEDs are of different color representing the different appliance also same colors LED are placed on the appliance for the simplicity of the representation of the LED to the appliance. The LEDs will glow one at a time and will glow again in a circular manner if the eye lid is being closed for a while. To choose an appliance we have to check for the color of the LED and chose the same LED and when the same color LED glows we have to open our eye lid to give a signal to the microcontroller. The microcontroller is placed in a Hold On circuit used to hold on to the signal and to process it and then to send the set data to the Radio Frequency, RF transmitter. We have also placed a LED segment with the Hold On circuit to confirm the signal by making the same color of the LED glow to give a confirmation to the user that the he is sending signal to switch the state of this particular appliance. We can use various other means to send the signal wireless like Bluetooth, Wi-Fi depending over the range of signal that how much is the distance of the appliance from the user. Even we can use mobile signals to send over a vast distance. Now after the transmitting the signal from the user block to appliances block. In appliance block we have used RF receiver according to our proposed work. The RF receiver is used to catch the signal from the user side. After receiving the signal, the signal is forwarded to microcontroller which is used as latch circuit. This latch circuit is used to choose the appliance and to send the data to the particular relay attached to the selected appliance. The microcontroller sends the same signal to the relay. The relay has a property to switch the state with the same input. So here the replay is used to switch the state (ON & OFF) of the appliance.

6 Results

Table 1 shows the working of the system with change in output state of chosen appliance. The timing of blinking of eye will decide the processing in microcontroller which in turn helps in choosing the appliance and further switching the state (ON & OFF) of appliance.

Table 1. Functional table of automation system

S. No	Appliance number	State	
		Previous state	Final state
1	Appliance 1	OFF	ON
		ON	OFF
2	Appliance 2	OFF	ON
		ON	OFF
3	Appliance 3	OFF	ON
		ON	OFF
4	Appliance 4	OFF	ON
		ON	OFF

7 Conclusion

In this research work when we are breaking the signal in the IR sensor then 4 LED glows after again make the signal in IR sensor then number of LED which glows is taken as input and thus is transmitted to the appliance block where respective appliance is switch ON if it is OFF, or it is switched OFF if it is ON.

References

1. Sourab, B.S., D'Souza, S.: Implementation of home automation using eye blink sensor. In: 2014 International Conference on Electronics, Communication and Computational Engineering (ICECCE), pp. 242–244. IEEE (2014)
2. Bacivarov, I., Ionita, M., Corcoran, P.: Statistical models of appearance for eye tracking and eye-blink detection and measurement. IEEE Trans. Consum. Electron. **54**(3), 1312–1320 (2008)
3. bin Abd Rani, M.S.: Detection of eye blinks from EEG signals for home lighting system activation. In: 2009 6th International Symposium on Mechatronics and its Applications (2009)
4. Banerjee, A., Pal, M., Tibarewala, D.N., Konar, A.: Electrooculogram based blink detection to limit the risk of eye dystonia. In: 2015 Eighth International Conference on Advances in Pattern Recognition (ICAPR), pp. 1–6. IEEE (2015)
5. Khowaja, S.A., Dahri, K., Kumbhar, M.A., Soomro, A.M.: Facial expression recognition using two-tier classification and its application to smart home automation system. In: 2015 International Conference on Emerging Technologies (ICET), pp. 1–6. IEEE (2015)

A Scalable Data Mining Model for Social Media Influencer Identification

Jyoti Sunil More[1,2(✉)] and Chelpa Lingam[3]

[1] Ramrao Adik Institute of Technology, Mumbai, India
[2] Department of Computer Engineering, Lokmanya Tilak College of Engineering
(Affiliated to University of Mumbai), Navi Mumbai, India
jyotis8582@gmail.com
[3] Department of Computer Engineering, Pillai's HOC College of Engineering
(Affiliated to University of Mumbai), Rasayani, India
chelpa.lingam@gmail.com

Abstract. Social network mining is a growing research area which combines together different fields such as machine learning, graph theory, parallel algorithms, data mining, optimization, etc., with the aim of dealing with issues like behavior analysis, finding interacting groups, finding influencers, information diffusion, etc. in a social network. This paper deals with one of these important issues i.e., Influencer Identification in social networks. This paper presents a data mining modelling approach for a twitter network, to find the most influential user among the given pair of users. This could be scaled over the entire network. We used a data mining model to score the test data and predict the influential user among the given pair of users. This approach of modeling can potentially be used for building many of the marketing and sales strategies wherein the influencer may be motivated for diffusing information or new ideas.

Keywords: Data mining · Influencers · Social network mining · Decision tree · Logistic regression

1   Introduction

Data mining is the process of studying data having different hidden behaviour, analyzing the patterns and deploying it to produce significant information. This information further can be used for carrying out predictive analytics and descriptive analytics. To construct a data mining model, we need to uncover the characteristics of dataset, create a model and deploy it [1].

Social network analysis [SNA] is the process of analyzing the behavior and interactions between different entities in the social networks. SNA has a great potential to evaluate the issues like, the likelihood of a particular community to grow, probability that the node gets influenced by other node, probability that a node acts as an influencer, etc. [1, 2].

The main aim of SNA is to explain the dependencies between the attributes of related nodes and predict the attributes like link probabilities, node behaviour, etc. in a given social network [1].

© Springer Nature Singapore Pte Ltd. 2016
A. Unal et al. (Eds.): SmartCom 2016, CCIS 628, pp. 625–631, 2016.
DOI: 10.1007/978-981-10-3433-6_75

In this context, social influence can be defined in terms of conformity or the act of manipulating attitudes and behaviors, or dominance on peer group. Three broad varieties of social influence have been identified by Herbert Kelmen [3] as: Compliance, Identification and Internalization. Social Media Influencer Marketing [4] is the strategy of identifying the influencing people and motivating them to form new customer pool for the owners. It is irrespective of the size of pool of the audience of the influencer. The influencer can reach to consumers more efficiently than the direct ability of the brand itself.

2   Related Work

Different measures have been developed to identify the influencers in social networks. There are various ways to measure influence, some of them include number of followers, outreach, degree centrality, etc. Some of the tools used for this are Klout score, Kred, topsy, peerindex, etc.

Duanbing Chen, L. Lu, M. Sheng Shang, Y Cheng Zhang, T. Zhou [5], to observe the pattern in which the influence gets propagated among the nodes, proposed a semi-local centrality measure. For this, they used Susceptible Infected Recovered (SIR) model. In this, different centrality measures were used to rank the nodes. They analyzed the same for several real networks and showed that their approach involving the degree centrality of the nodes was relatively efficient to determine the influential nodes than other network parameters. Christine Kiss and Martin Bichler [6], carried out comparison of different centrality measures with respect to their impact on message distribution i.e., diffusing information in social networks. They examined existing measures and also evaluated the outdegree and SenderRank as centrality measures for the message distribution in social networks. They found that the performance of SenderRank was relatively better than other parameters. Na Li and Denis Gillet [7] investigated the functioning measures of scholars and observed their influence. The experimentation was carried out by aggregating various network centrality metrics.

Zsolt Katona, Peter Pal Zubcsek and Miklos Sarvary [8], in their experiment, analyzed the social network data and attempted to identify the impact of the word of mouth in the network. Their main goal was to discover how the structure of local communication network affects the information diffusion process. Their findings showed that in case of strong communities, beyond the network size, the influence of word of mouth is more effective. Their proposed model has a potential to identify customer pool who in turn will act as influencers for the diffusion activity of the new product or service.

Patrali Chatterji [9] in her research emphasized the significance of recommendation and referral behavior to social media and incorporates the role of underlying covariates. E. Bakshy, J. Hofman, W. Mason, D. Watts [10] investigated two groups of users and found that the users who have a record of being influential in the past and the users who have large number of followers, generate the largest share of information that is passed in successive levels. They concluded that the information diffusion through the word of mouth directly gets affected by the number of potential influencers and hence they are the potential targets. Isabel Anger, Christian Kittl [11] proposed an approach which presented a quantitative method of determining twitter SNP. They proposed that there are two major aspects of Twitter: content and influence. They deliberately dropped an important factor i.e. number of followers and also proposed that the influence is largely affected by personal relations. Eytan Bakshy, Brian Karrer, Lada Adamic [12] developed a simple model, which exploited the information about the evolving structure of social network. This model gives a greater flexibility and shows the significance of network effects in the adoption of social network content. It is used to analyze the influence identification by exploiting the relationship and the information adoption rate among the nodes.

3   Problem Formulation

Given a social network interpreted as a directed graph, $G = (V, E)$ where, V represents set of social network nodes (users) and E represents the network edges. The objective is influence detection, i.e. finding the set of nodes which can be targeted to diffuse an idea across the network such that the spread will be maximum. This can be viewed as a scalable problem. Our contribution is to define and analyze a model using the data mining stages, for two users at a time. This analysis can be scaled to n nodes in the network.

We consider a dataset comprising of only two users and their influence status. This analysis can be further scaled to other users from the network and overall influencers could be possibly found out. The dataset [13], provided by Peerindex, comprises a standard, pair-wise data records, meant for preference learning task. Each record describes two individuals, A and B with few characteristics. For each person, 11 pre-computed, positive numeric features based on twitter activity (such as number of mentions received, number of followers, etc.) are provided [13].

The binary label in the dataset represents a human judgment mentioning which one of the two individuals is more influential. A label '1' means participant A is more influential than B. 0 means participant B is more influential than A. The objective is to train a machine learning model which predicts the human judgment on who among A and B is more influential, with high accuracy.

The data consisted of 11 various parameters like: followers, retweets mentioned, number of posts, etc.

Exploring the data generally involves basic analysis of a dataset. This can be achieved by observing variable summaries and visual plots. By exploring our data, we can observe few characteristics of the data i.e. its range, its numeric characteristics mean, its spread, its deviation etc. There are numerous inherent problems associated with the data that include missing values, outliers i.e. one exhibiting abnormal characteristic, erroneous data, and skews in the data distributions. This in turn will affect the choice of the most appropriate tools for preparing and transforming our data and for learning the patterns in the data.

The input training data is found to be skewed and is largely messed with outliers. The dataset is first normalized. The linear model is checked for skewness, and skedesticity and was found adequate to proceed. The data is further tested for the data showing abnormal characteristics i.e. outliers. The outliers are the data points which cause noise in the model and hence they should be detected and treated appropriately. A boxplot can be used for detecting the outliers as shown in Fig. 1. The outliers can be smoothened by substituting them with mean value. Correlation between all the variables is checked for collinearity and multicollinearity.

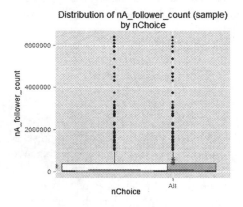

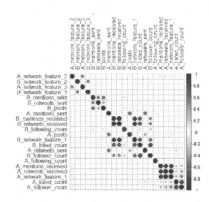

Fig. 1. The box plot showing the outliers   **Fig. 2.** Correlation matrix

Correlation in a given model can be either positive or negative. It represents the relationship mutually between two variables, and also cardinal i.e. one against all other variables. For Example, a strong correlation is observed between the parameters, A_retweets_received and A_mentions_received as shown in Fig. 2.

4 Model Building and Validation

This stage involves considering various data mining models depending on the characteristics of data. The predictive analytics phase may use mathematical models, graphical models, statistical models, etc. to draw inferences. This stage is considered as core of predictive data mining.

The entire dataset is distributed as 70/15/15 for training, validation and testing respectively. The model building involves two functions- Description and Prediction. For descriptive analytics, the techniques like clustering, summarization, linguistic summary, visualization etc. can be used. For predictive analytics any of the techniques like classification or regression can be used. Depending on the type of the data one of the suitable technique is chosen. In this context, the prediction is to be done by modeling the binary value- Choice of the most influential participant among the given pair of twitter users. The resulting probabilities are restricted to [0, 1] through the logistic distribution function [14]. The logistic regression predicts the event rate, i.e., probability of the event. Hence logistic regression technique is preferred for this case study. The general equation for logistic regression [14] is given as-

$$Log(p/(1-p)) = \beta 0 + \beta_1 X_1 + \beta_2 X_2 + \ldots\ldots + \beta_n X_n + e \qquad (1)$$

The log of odds function denotes the expected probability that the outcome is present, X_1 to X_n are independent variables and β_0 to β_n are the regression coefficients. Null Hypothesis is defined as: The data coefficients β are null. Our objective is to model and show that the β values are not null. After reviewing the statistical significance of the parameters using the Z score and P values, some of the insignificant parameters were dropped from the regression. The retained parameters were as follows-

A_listed_count, A_mentions_received, A_mentions_sent, A_network_feature_2, B_listed_count, B_mentions_received, B_mentions_sent, B_retweets_sent, B_network_feature_2, B_network_feature_3.

Using the outlier test it is confirmed that no studentized residuals remain in the data. The logistic regression model is shown in Fig. 3. Another modeling technique was used to predict the influential user i.e. Regression tree or classification tree.

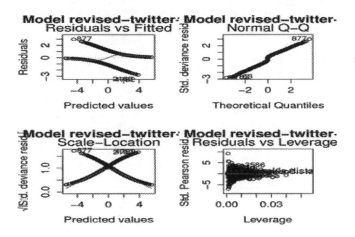

Fig. 3. Logistic regression model

5   Results and Interpretation

The variables actually used in the tree construction are- A_follower_count, A_network_feature_1, A_network_feature_2, B_follower_count, B_listed_count, B_network_feature_1, B_network_feature_3.

Error matrix for the Linear model on revised twitter data and the error matrix for the Decision Tree model on revised twitter data could be compared. The precision and recall parameters could be used to evaluate the models. The graphs when plotted are visualized and are shown in the following Figs. 4, 5, 6 and 7.

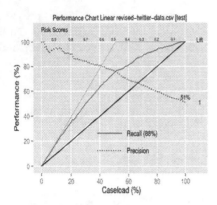

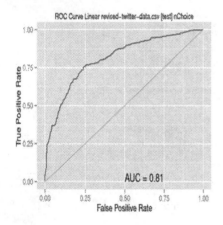
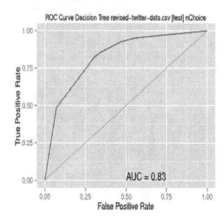

Fig. 4. The precision-recall for logistic regression model

Fig. 5. The precision-recall for decision tree model

Fig. 6. ROC chart for logistic regression model

Fig. 7. ROC chart for decision tree model

6   Deployment

This is the final stage of predictive analytics. In this, the elite models build from the training set and chosen parameters, are preserved and are applied to the test data in order to generate predictions of the expected results. It is sometimes termed as score.

The decision tree and Logistic regression models have above average accuracy (Figs. 4, 5, 6 and 7) and hence can be used to find the score of the test data. The test data is scored on their probabilities i.e. what is the probability that either A or B is influencer.

7   Conclusion and Future Scope

Social network mining is a growing, exciting area of research that has a great scope, with the contribution of many research fields. Understanding the user behavior in a social network has a potential to improve the marketing strategies by targeting precisely the influencers for information diffusion, or propagating ideas and thus optimizing the viral marketing techniques. From the point of view of mining and analysis of social networks, it is also necessary to develop efficient graphical models to exploit the structural properties of network and different statistical methods which are efficient and uniform. Different influence maximization approaches can be proposed. Optimizing the spread could be one of the goals. Considering large size of the social networks and redundant nature of sub graphs in a social network graph, the parallelism in the graphical structure could be exploited.

References

1. More, J.S., Lingam, C.: Reality mining based on social network analysis. In: Proceedings of IEEE International Conference on Communication Information and Computing Technology (ICCIT), pp. 1–6 (2015)
2. Huang, F., Cheng, N.X., Xiao, R.: An approach to mining social networks in chat room. J. Comput. Inf. Syst. **1**, 135–143 (2011)
3. Kelman, H.: Compliance, identification, and internalization: three processes of attitude change. J. Conflict Resolut. **2**, 51–60 (1958)
4. www.grouphigh.com
5. Chen, Duanbing, Lü, L., Shang, M.S., Zhang, Y.C., Zhou, T.: Identifying influential nodes in complex networks. Phys. A Stat. Mechan. Appl. **391**(4), 1777–1787 (2011)
6. Kiss, Christine, Bichler, Martin: Identification of influencers- measuring influence in customer networks. Decis. Support Syst. **46**, 233–253 (2008)
7. Li, N., Gillet, D.: Identifying influential scholars in academic social media platforms. In: ASONAM Proceedings IEEE/ACM International Conference on Advances in Social Network Analysis and Mining, pp. 608–614 (2013)
8. Katona, Z., Zubcsek, P.P., Sarvary, M.: Network effects and personal influences: the diffusion of an online social network. J. Mark. Res. **48**(3), 425–443 (2011)
9. Chatterjee, P.: Drivers of new product recommending and referrel behavior at social network sites. Int. J. Advertising **30**(1), 77–101 (2011)
10. Bakshy, E., Hofman, J.M., Mason, W.A., Watts, D.J: Everyone's an influencer: quantifying influence on twitter. In: WSDM Proceedings of Fourth ACM International Conference on Web Search and Data Mining, pp. 65–74 (2011)
11. Anger, I., Kittl, C.: Measuring influence on twitter. In: International Conference on Knowledge management and Knowledge Technologies. ACM (2011)
12. Bakshy, E., Karrer, B., Adamic, L.A.: Social influence and the diffusion of user-created content. In: Proceedings of the 10th ACM conference on Electronic commerce, pp. 325–334 (2009)
13. www.kaggle.com
14. James, G., Witten, D., Hastie, T., Tibshirani, R.: An Introduction to Statistical Learning, pp. 130–137. Springer, New York (2013)

Gain Enhancement of Microstrip Patch Antenna Array with AMC Structure Using Multilayer PCB Technology

Vaishali Ekke[(✉)] and Prasanna Zade

Department of Electronics and Telecommunication,
Yeshwantrao Chavan College of Engineering, Hingana Road, Nagpur, India
vaishali_dhede@rediffmail.com, zadepl@yahoo.com

Abstract. Placement of artificial magnetic conductor (AMC) structures at the inset feed line of the patch operating at 2.4 GHz is analyzed. Proposed design for four element patch array using AMC with multilayer PCB technology which gives improvement in return loss and gain. Analysis had done for low cost stack up material for multilayer purpose. FR4 epoxy finally used as stack up material which is low cost and ease to fabricate. In antenna array AMC structure at the feed line considerably reduce side lobe level and back lobe level and improves gain. Simulated results are validated experimentally.

Keywords: Antenna array · Artificial magnetic conductor · Gain · Multilayer PCB · Stack up structure

1 Introduction

Extensive growth of further generation WLAN applications requires patch antennas for its low profile, simple design and ease of fabrication on PCBs. Microstrip patch antennas are the better solution for compact and low-cost design [1]. To overcome the drawbacks or limitations of single element antennas multiple patches are connected in an array. Surface waves along the ground plane limit antenna gain and efficiency. It can be overcome by reducing the surface wave using AMC structures with or without vias. The designs using the AMC improves the gain of the patch antenna. Surface waves create ripples in the radiation pattern [2–5]. The development of surface waves causes a serious problem in the microstrip patch antenna array which reduces gain, efficiency, limits bandwidth, increases cross-polarization levels. Various approaches like designing probe-fed microstrip radiators [6], use of parasitic elements [2, 7] use of different substrates which lowers effective dielectric constant of the substrate or use of reduced surface wave antenna [3–5], photonic crystals are known as electromagnetic band gap (EBG) structures [8] which used significantly to improve antenna performance. Multilayer stack-up structure can be used to improve antenna performance [9]. Artificial magnetic conductor (AMC) structure [10], relative impedance surface (RIS) [11], uniplanar compact photonic band-gap structure [12] are used enhance antenna performance.

© Springer Nature Singapore Pte Ltd. 2016
A. Unal et al. (Eds.): SmartCom 2016, CCIS 628, pp. 632–639, 2016.
DOI: 10.1007/978-981-10-3433-6_76

AMC structure has in-phase reflection coefficient such as perfect magnetic conductor (PMC). The microstrip antenna with high impedance structure (HIS) or with AMC can give higher gain and larger bandwidth [13]. AMC structure when used as antenna ground plane, the periodic surfaces can enhance the radiation patterns, antenna gain and impedance bandwidth [13–16]. Improvement in return loss, gain, bandwidth is observed by implementing AMC along with inset feed in 4 × 1 microstrip patch antenna array and the concept of AMC along with feed line is analyzed and tested [17].

Based on this idea [17] AMC structure along with feed line with standard multilayer PCB prototype investigated and proved the improvement in the performance of antenna array is referred in proposed multilayer antenna.

2   Design of Proposed Antenna Array

Schematic of proposed technique of multilayer printed circuit board (PCB) technology is shown in Fig. 1.

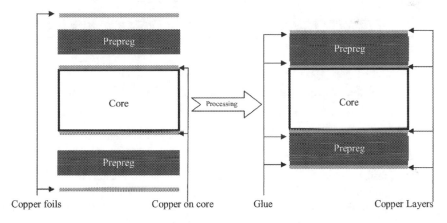

Fig. 1. Multilayer stack up structure.

Figure 1 consists of core (dielectric substrate) and two prepreg for PCB fabrication (uncured fiberglass epoxy resin) which is cost effective. Copper foil bonded with cured epoxy resin. To avoid mechanical stress, stack up arrangement is symmetric about centre of PCB.

Figure 1 shows multilayer PCB fabrication process. It consists of prepreg and laminate. Copper foil bonded on both sides of copper with epoxy resin (cured). Alternate layer of core and prepreg are mounted. Copper foils are bonded on both sides of prepreg which acts as surface foils. Glue of small thickness is used for bonding core and prepreg. There are insignificant losses due to glue where resonating frequency is low (<10 GHz).

Using this multilayer PCB fabrication technique, proposed antenna array with AMC is designed as shown in Figs. 2 and 3.

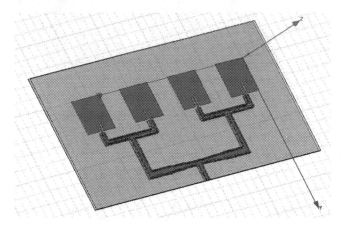

Fig. 2. Simulation model of the proposed designed antenna in HFSS.

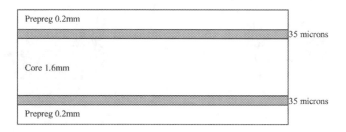

Fig. 3. Layers of the proposed designed antenna.

Before fabrication of the prototype, different materials are tested in the simulation model to obtain better radiation pattern. As antenna model is covered with different materials from the front and back side. Materials with different permittivity are selected also considering the other factors like cost of the material and durability also. Radiation pattern obtained using these materials is shown below. Simulated return loss plots and radiation patterns are given in Figs. 4 and 5. It shows no more increase in simulation parameters. But materials like glass, Rogers RT duroid are very expensive materials. To reduce the cost with the same performance it is concluded that epoxy resin is more cost effective and easy to fabricate.

Figure 2 shows simulation model, Fig. 3 shows layers and Fig. 6 shows prototype of array with AMC and proposed antenna array using multilayer stack up structure. It is resonate at a center frequency of 2.45 GHz. In proposed array, the height of FR4 epoxy is 1.6 mm top and bottom prepreg is 0.2 mm. Bonding glue of 35 microns. The performance of the fabricated antenna array is tested using Vector Network Analyzer (E5071C). Figures 7, 8 and 9 show the Simulated and measured results.

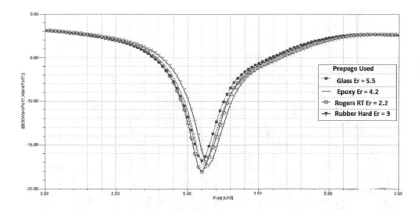

Fig. 4. Return loss using different materials as prepage

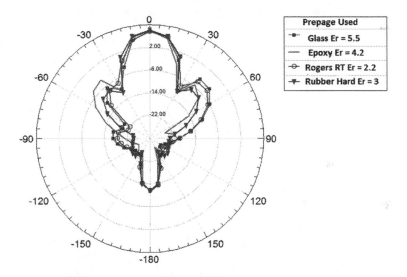

Fig. 5. Radiation patterns using different materials as prepage

Percentage bandwidth at 10 dB is 4.49% and 4.48% for simulated and measured antenna array respectively.

Addition of AMC improves the gain. Measured results of antenna with AMC along its feed line [17] and same with multilayer structure using PCB technology are given in Table 1. Cross polarization level reduced to −44.39 dB for proposed antenna. The difference between simulated and measured results was produced due to fabrication errors.

Fig. 6. Prototypes of array with AMC and proposed array antenna with stack up structure.

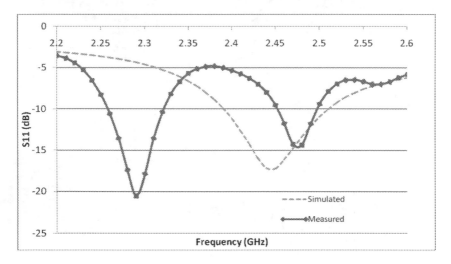

Fig. 7. Measured and simulated return loss for proposed antenna array

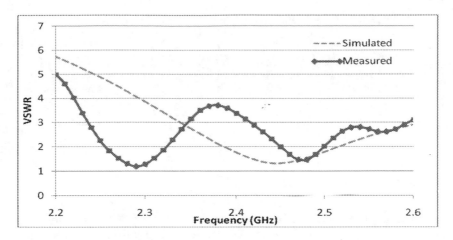

Fig. 8. Measured and simulated VSWR for proposed antenna array

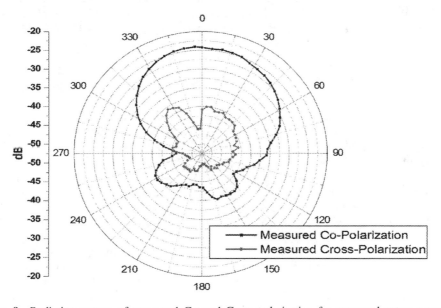

Fig. 9. Radiation pattern of measured Co and Cross polarization for proposed antenna array with stack up structure

Table 1. Comparison between different multilayer array antennas

	Frequency (GHz)	Size of array (mm^3)	No. of layers	No. of elements	Gain	Directivity (dB)
[6]	2.5	150 × 330 × 9.8	3	4	N.A.	12.
[7]	5.797	170 × 170 × 7.6	3	9	8.656	N.A.
[9]	2.4	200 × 125 × 45	3	4	10.4	N.A.
Proposed antenna	2.45	300 × 106 × 2	3	4	14.492	16.530

3 Conclusion

New AMC antenna array was developed with multilayer PCB technology. AMC structure with multilayer stack up reduces surface wave which improves gain and suppress cross polarization. Enhancement of antenna performance by multilayer stack up is economic with easy fabrication process. Developed antenna consists size of 300 mm × 106 mm × 2 mm with measured gain of 14.492 dB and impedance bandwidth 4.48% (from 2.26 GHz–2.32 GHz and 2.45 GHz–2.5 GHz).

References

1. Collin, R.E.: Field Theory of Guided Waves, 2nd edn. Wiley-IEEE Press, New York (1990)
2. Rojas, R.G., Lee, K.W.: Surface wave control using nonperiodic parasitic strips in printed antennas. In: IEE Proceedings - Microwaves, Antennas and Propagation, vol. 148, pp. 25–28 (2001)
3. Bhattacharayya, A.K.: Characteristics of space and surface-waves in a multilayered structure. IEEE Trans. Antennas Propag. **38**, 1231–1238 (1990)
4. Jakson, D.R., Williams, J.T., Bhattacharayya, A.K., Smith, R.L., Buchleit, J., Long, S.A.: Microstrip patch designs that do not excite surface waves. IEEE Trans. Antennas Propag. **41**, 1026–1037 (1993)
5. Khayat, M., Williams, J.T., Jakson, D.R., Long, S.A.: Mutual coupling between reduced surface-wave microstrip antennas. IEEE Trans. Antennas Propag. **48**, 1581–1593 (2000)
6. Nascimento, D.C., da S. Lacava, J.C.: Design of arrays of linearly polarized patch antennas on an FR4 substrate: design of a probe-fed electrically equivalent microstrip radiator. IEEE Antennas Propag. Mag. **57**(4), 12–22 (2015)
7. Abdullah, R., Ali, M.T., Ismail, N., Omar, S., Dzulkefli, S.N.: Multilayer parasitic microstrip antenna array for WiMAX application. In: Proceedings of 2012 IEEE Asia-Pacific Conference on Applied Electromagnetics (APACE), pp. 128–131. Publisher IEEE (2012)
8. Joannopoulos, J., Meade, R.D., Winn, J.N.: Photonic Crystals: Molding the Flow of Light, 2nd edn. Princeton University Press, Princeton (2008)
9. Caso, R., Serra, A.A., Rodriguez-Pino, M., Nepa, P., Manara, G.: A wideband slot-coupled stacked-patch array for wireless communications. IEEE Antennas Wirel. Propag. Lett. **9**, 986–989 (2010)

10. Cure, D., Weller, T.M., Miranda, F.A.: Study of a low-profile 2.4-GHz planar dipole antenna using a high-impedance surface with 1-D varactor tuning. IEEE Trans. Antennas Propag. **61** (2), 506–515 (2013)
11. Mosallaei, H., Sarabandi, K.: Antenna miniaturization and bandwidth enhancement using a reactive impedance substrate. IEEE Trans. Antennas Propag. **52**(9), 2403–2414 (2004)
12. Coccioli, R., Yang, F.R., Ma, K.P., Itoh, T.: Aperture-coupled patch antenna on UC-PBG substrate. IEEE Trans. Microw. Theory Tech. **47**(9), 2123–2130 (1999)
13. Foroozesh, A., Shafai, L.: Application of combined electric-and magnetic-conductor ground planes for antenna performance enhancement. Can. J. Electr. Comput. Eng. **33**(2), 87–98 (2008)
14. Yang, F., Rahmat-Samii, Y.: A low profile single dipole antenna radiating circularly polarized waves. IEEE Trans. Antennas Propag. **53**(9), 3083–3086 (2005)
15. Nakamura, T., Fukusako, T.: Broadband design of circularly polarized microstrip patch antenna using an artificial ground structure with rectangular unit cells. IEEE Trans. Antennas Propag. **59**(6), 2103–2110 (2011)
16. Nashaat, D., Elsadek, H.A., Abdallah, E.A., Iskander, M.F., Hennawy, H.M.E.: Ultrawide-bandwidth 2×2 microstrip patch array antenna using electromagnetic band-gap structure (EBG). IEEE Trans. Antennas Propag. **59**(5), 1528–1534 (2011)
17. Ekke, V., Zade, P.L.: Design and implementation of artificial magnetic structure along with feed line for microstrip patch antenna array. In: Proceedings of IEEE Global Conference Wireless Computing and Networking (GCWCN), pp. 51–55 (2014)

Fuzzy Logic Based Multi-input Criterion for Handover Decision in Wireless Heterogeneous Networks

Archa G. Mahira[✉] and Mansi S. Subhedar

Department of Electronics and Telecommunication,
Pillai HOC College of Engineering & Technology,
Khalapur Taluka, Raigad District, Rasayani 410206, Maharashtra, India
archageeson@gmail.com, mansi_subhedar@rediffmail.com

Abstract. Vertical handover is one of the most prominent challenges in heterogeneous networks (Hetnets) since most of the user devices come with mobility feature. In order to provide a seamless handover between various network topologies, several additional parameters other than signal strength must be taken in account to satisfy user preferences at an acceptable level. This paper proposes a fuzzy logic based multi-input criterion for handover decision in wireless heterogeneous networks that uses received signal strength indicator (RSSI), monetary cost, data rate and mobile station (MS) velocity as the input parameters. The simulation results show that proposed fuzzy logic based algorithm gives an improvement in reduction percentage of number of handover as compared to existing systems.

Keywords: Wireless heterogeneous networks · Self adaptive handover · Fuzzy logic

1 Introduction

For the past two decades, communication systems and portable devices have made a drastic change in our day to day life. This emerging demand of mobile devices need to have an incoherent connectivity in broadband networks and it is a major challenge for the network providers. This challenge is due to the increasing traffic of audio and video streams during any one of the ongoing application processes that includes handover of mobile devices between several base stations (BS) within a specified time duration. Since mobility feature of user devices comes in picture, a new critical operation handover exists in wireless heterogeneous networks during an on call process [8].

When MS travels from one BS to another, it may experience a horizontal or a vertical handover. Horizontal handover involves transfer of active connection between two different base stations within same wireless network where as vertical handover occurs between two different BSs of different wireless technologies [3]. The proposed handover decision algorithm is presented to reduce the number of

© Springer Nature Singapore Pte Ltd. 2016
A. Unal et al. (Eds.): SmartCom 2016, CCIS 628, pp. 640–646, 2016.
DOI: 10.1007/978-981-10-3433-6_77

handover in wireless heterogeneous networks. Simulation results show that when velocity of mobile station is increased, urgency of handover is more and when velocity is low and RSSI is high, number of handover occurred is very less compared to the different approaches described in [8].

The remainder of the paper is organised as follows: Sect. 2 reviews prior work. Section 3 discusses proposed fuzzy based algorithm. Simulation results are presented in Sect. 4. Section 5 concludes the paper.

2   Related Work

Nowadays, tremendous growth in the research area of mobile communication has been occurred. Hence, a number of research proposals have been found for the handover mechanism in the literature. Kustiawan et al. proposed a Kalman filtering and Fuzzy logic (FL) based approach to reduce the number of handover [8]. Simulation results show a reduction percentage of 88.88%. Another adaptive neuro-fuzzy based vertical handoff decision algorithm is developed for wireless heterogeneous networks [3]. Results show that it can provide an improvement in performance for both network and user. Calhan et al. discussed several adaptive fuzzy logic based vertical handoff decision making algorithms for wireless overlay networks which consist of UMTS, WiMAX, Wi-Fi, GPRS, GSM technologies [5]. According to the results obtained after comparison with classical MADM (Multiple Attribute Decision Making) method, the system is capable of deciding handover properly and selection of best access point. A FL-based handover method in LTE (Long Term Evolution) is proposed by utilizing input parameters like RSS, coverage area and data rate to improve the packet delivery ratio (PDR) [6]. The results showed a reduction of 33% in packet loss delivery after handover. A combination of genetic algorithm and fuzzy logic is employed to propose a new adaptive vertical handoff decision algorithm [4]. Results shows that the performance of the system significantly improved for user as well as network by reducing number of handover. Singhvora et al. implemented an adaptive neuro-fuzzy inference system to reduce the ping pong effect that inturn improves the performance of heterogeneous networks in [9]. A new adaptive fuzzy based handoff management algorithm is introduced for next generation wireless systems that uses mobile speed and handoff signalling delay information to improve the performance of HMIP (Hierarchical Mobile IP) handoff significantly in [7]. A combination of fuzzy logic and a PRE-MT (Pre-determined Motion Trend) based on motion trend and RSS is presented to mitigate the ping pong effect and thereby increasing system performance [10]. Another vertical handover algorithm, NG-VDA (Next Generation Vertical Handover Decision Algorithm), based on fuzzy logic to provide vertical handover between WLAN and LTE to the customer with reference to multiple parameters is proposed in [1]. Mubarak et al. proposed a handover mechanism based on fuzzy logic with multiple inputs and self adaptive handover parameters in [2]. Simulation results indicate that proposed FuzSAHO (Fuzzy logic based Self Adaptive Handover algorithm) managed to decrease ping pong effect and its delay.

3   Proposed System

Figure 1 exhibits framework of proposed handover algorithm. It consists of four input variables as RSSI, monetary cost, data rate, MS Velocity, fuzzifier, fuzzy inference engine with knowledge base, defuzzifier and output variable as handover decision.

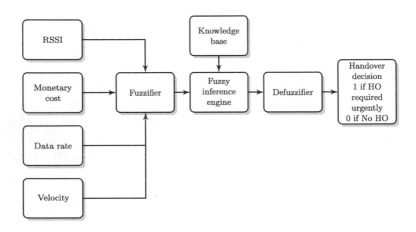

Fig. 1. Block diagram of proposed system

RSSI (Received Signal Strength Indicator) gives the information about availability of a network to access. Network bandwidth conditions are indicated with the help of data rate (DR). Velocity indicates movement of mobile terminal in network coverage area [1]. Monetary cost indicates cost of different services offered to the user. These input parameters are then converted to grades of membership functions from crisp values with the help of a fuzzifier. Mamdani based Fuzzy Inference engine is used to interpret these fuzzified input values based on several predefined rules. The membership functions used in fuzzy logic for these four input variables are shown in Fig. 2. Their linguistic variables are defined as Low (L), Medium (M), and High (H). Information rules are defined in terms of fuzzy IF-THEN rules. For example, *If RSSI is low and Monetary Cost is low and Data rate is low and MS Velocity is low then Handover factor is medium.* To fuzzify all the input and output parameters, both triangular and trapezoidal membership functions are used. Output values are again converted to a set of crisp values by defuzzifier and output parameter i.e. handover decision will determine the urgency of handover.

4   Experimental Results

Experiments are carried out in MATLAB R2012a environment. In proposed system, RSSI, monetary cost, data rate and MS velocity are the fuzzy input variables and handover decision is considered as output variable. It varies between

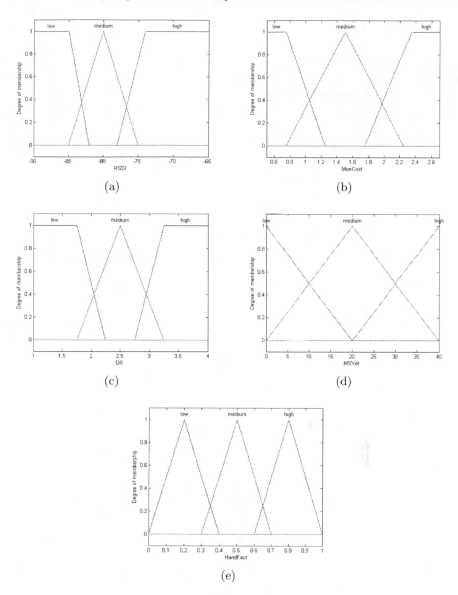

Fig. 2. Membership functions of (a) RSSI (b) Monetary cost (c) Datarate (d) MS velocity and (e) Handover decision factor

0 and 1 where 0 represents no handover and 1 represents urgently required handover. The handover decision factor is set to 0.65. The range of RSSI is between -90 dBm to -68 dBm and velocity ranges from 0–40 m/s. To fuzzify input and output parameters, both triangular and trapezoidal membership functions are

selected in the proposed system. It is found that they gives better performance for most of the real applications [3].

The knowledge base of the fuzzy system consists of several predefined rules and they are exploited by a series of IF-THEN rules which can be defined as a model of expected sequences of possible events. Since proposed algorithm utilizes four input parameters and one output parameter, knowledge base consists of 81 rules (3^4) which are generated by all the possible combinations of input and output parameters of the system. Based on these IF-THEN rules, it unfolds the meaning of input vector values and allots these values to its output vector i.e. whether the handover is urgently required or not. According to different input values i.e. RSSI, Monetary Cost, Data Rate and MS velocity, proposed fuzzy based algorithm provides a handover decision which is self-adaptive.

For this self adaptive fuzzy based multi input handover decision algorithm (FLMCHO), Figs. 3 and 4 show simulation results as per the predefined knowledge base. In Fig. 3a, it shows that when velocity is high, handover decision factor

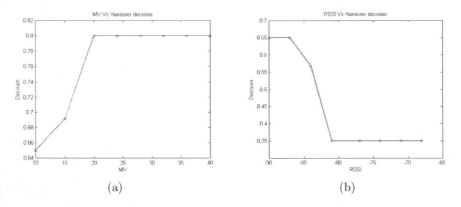

(a)   (b)

Fig. 3. Simulation results (a) MS velocity Vs handover decision (b) RSSI Vs handover decision

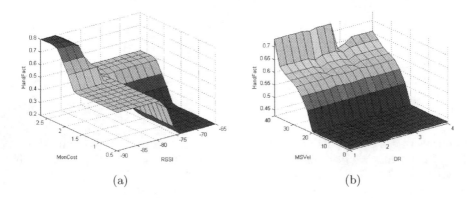

(a)   (b)

Fig. 4. Surface view for (a) RSSI, monetary cost Vs handover decision (b) MS velocity Vs handover decision

possess high value, i.e. handover is urgently required when velocity is more than 20 m/s. Similarly, when RSSI is low(less than −80 dBm), handover decision is high as shown in Fig. 3b. As per simulation results, our system is able to decide the urgency of handover whenever the signal strength is low and the velocity of the mobile station is high. Figure 4a and b shows surface plot of handover decision factor with respect to input variables. We compared handoff initiation scenarios with several existing schemes in literature. We have 4, 14, 27 and 36 number of hanoffs using combination of Kalman filter and fuzzy logic scheme [8], Mamdani fuzzy logic, Kalman filtered RSSI and traditional fixed RSS approaches. In Fig. 5, it shows that proposed algorithm i.e., FLMCHO reduces the number of handover to 3 as compared to the other approaches hence improves the reduction percentage is improved to 91.66%. The calculation of relative reduction is given as follows: $[(36 − 3)/36] * 100 = 91.66\%$.

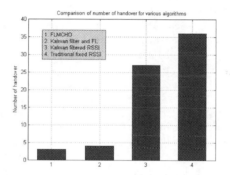

Fig. 5. Comparison of number of handover for various algorithms

5   Conclusion

Due to the impact of several input parameters, handover decision making phase is a crucial task to be performed during vertical handover process. In this paper, we proposed multi-input criterion fuzzy system to verify the urgency of handover. This is done effectively by employing multiple input parameters like RSSI, monetary cost, data rate, and MS velocity. The handover factor should not be either too low or too high to manage quality of services at an acceptable level. Hence, we determined good handover initiations by setting handover decision factor to 0.65. Simulation results show that proposed method effectively reduces number of handover. It improves reduction percentage by 91.66% and outperforms existing handover decision schemes.

References

1. Aziz, A., Rizvi, S., Saad, N.M.: Fuzzy logic based vertical handover algorithm between lte and wlan. In: 2010 International Conference on Intelligent and Advanced Systems (ICIAS), pp. 1–4, June 2010

2. Ben-Mubarak, M.A., Mohd. Ali, B., Noordin, N.K., Ismail, A., Ng, C.K.: Fuzzy logic based self-adaptive handover algorithm for mobile wimax. Wireless Pers. Commun. **71**(2), 1421–1442 (2013)
3. Calhan, A., Ceken, C.: An adaptive neuro-fuzzy based vertical handoff decision algorithm for wireless heterogeneous networks. In: 21st Annual IEEE International Symposium on Personal, Indoor and Mobile Radio Communications, pp. 2271–2276, September 2010
4. Çalhan, A., Çeken, C.: An optimum vertical handoff decision algorithm based on adaptive fuzzy logic and genetic algorithm. Wireless Pers. Commun. **64**(4), 647–664 (2012)
5. Calhan, A., Ceken, C.: Case study on handoff strategies for wireless overlay networks. Comput. Stand. Interfaces **35**(1), 170–178 (2013)
6. Datta, P., Kaushal, S.: Fuzzy logic-based handover in 3GPP LTE network. In: Mandal, D., Kar, R., Das, S., Panigrahi, B.K. (eds.) Intelligent Computing and Applications. AISC, vol. 343, pp. 213–222. Springer India, New Delhi (2015). doi:10.1007/978-81-322-2268-2_23
7. Israt, P., Chakma, N., Hashem, M.M.A.: A fuzzy logic-based adaptive handoff management protocol for next-generation wireless systems. In: 2008 11th International Conference on Computer and Information Technology, ICCIT 2008, pp. 288–293, December 2008
8. Kustiawan, I., Chi, K.H.: Handoff decision using a kalman filter and fuzzy logic in heterogeneous wireless networks. IEEE Commun. Lett. **19**(12), 2258–2261 (2015)
9. Singhrova, A., Prakash, N.: Adaptive vertical handoff decision algorithm for wireless heterogeneous networks. In: 2009 11th IEEE International Conference on High Performance Computing and Communications, HPCC 2009, pp. 476–481, June 2009
10. Tao, Y., Peng, R.: A fuzzy logic vertical handoff algorithm with motion trend decision. In: 2011 6th International Forum on Strategic Technology (IFOST), vol. 2, pp. 1280–1283, August 2011

Big-Data Approaches for Bioinformatics Workflows: A Comparative Assessment

Rickey T.P. Nunes[1(✉)] and Santosh L. Deshpande[2]

[1] VTU Research Resource Centre, Visvesvaraya Technological University,
Belagavi, India
rickeynunes@gmail.com
[2] Centre for Postgraduate Studies, Visvesvaraya Technological University,
Belagavi, India
sld@vtu.ac.in

Abstract. There is a big-data explosion in the field of bioinformatics, with the rapid growth in the size of biological data. In bioinformatics, workflows are used to integrate and analyze biological data. Orchestration and choreography are the two approaches used to execute bioinformatics workflows. However, big-data poses several challenges in these approaches. One of the challenges is how to handle the movement of big-data during workflow execution. With the advent of big-data, a number of modified orchestration and choreography approaches have also been developed to handle big-data. In this paper, we review and make a comparative assessment of the state-of-the-art approaches to execute big-data workflows. We examine the big-data handling in these approaches and finally recommend a solution that could be a way forward in executing big-data bioinformatics workflows.

Keywords: Big-data · Bioinformatics · Workflows · Orchestration · Choreography

1 Introduction

There is a big-data explosion in the field of bioinformatics, with the rapid growth in the size of biological data. Bioinformatics experiments typically involve analyzing data from one or more biological data sources using one or more analysis tools [1]. The biological data sources and the analysis tools are usually distributed and available as web services. Hence, workflows are used to integrate these distributed bioinformatics resources. Bioinformatics workflows are collection of analysis tool and data services combined in a certain way to represent a bioinformatics experiment. Each analysis tool or computation service in the workflow does some data analysis based on the input that it receives and produces some data based on the analysis for the next service. Bioinformatics workflows are executed based on data-flow. However, they can be executed based on control-flow or combining both data-flow and control-flow [2]. A data-flow describes the

© Springer Nature Singapore Pte Ltd. 2016
A. Unal et al. (Eds.): SmartCom 2016, CCIS 628, pp. 647–654, 2016.
DOI: 10.1007/978-981-10-3433-6_78

flow of specific dataset among the services of the workflow, whereas the control-flow describes the correct order of execution among the different services of the workflow.

In literature, there are two workflow execution approaches i.e. the orchestration and the choreography approach [3]. In the orchestration approach, the workflow is executed using a central coordinator called the orchestrator or workflow engine. The orchestrator controls the data-flows and the control-flows among the services of the workflow. On the other hand, in choreography approach, the workflow services interact with each other directly to execute the workflow. The services share the control among themselves. Each service of the workflow knows with whom to interact and when to carry out its operations. Both these approaches are used to execute bioinformatics workflows.

Bioinformatics workflows are inherently complex. Their execution requires monitoring, reporting of workflow execution progress, handling of failures and recording of provenance data. Bioinformatics workflows are also data-intensive. They produce and move large volumes of data during workflow execution [4]. The complexity of bioinformatics workflow increases with big-data in it. Big-data pose several challenges in bioinformatics workflow execution. One of the challenges is how to handle the movement of big-data in bioinformatics workflows. With the advent of big-data, a number of modified approaches based on orchestration and choreography approaches have also been developed to handle the big-data and improve the performance of workflow execution. In this paper, we review and make a comparative assessment of the state-of-the-art approaches to execute big-data bioinformatics workflows. We examine the big-data handling in these approaches and finally recommend a solution that could be a way forward in executing big-data bioinformatics workflows.

2 Classical Approaches: Orchestration and Choreography

In this section, we review the classical orchestration and the classical choreography approaches. In order to understand the execution of bioinformatics workflows using these approaches, let us consider a workflow in the Fig. 1(a) with two services s_1 and s_2. Let in be the input from the user to service s_1. Based on this input in, s_1 produces the data d that is passed on to service s_2. Service s_2 then produces the final output out which is passed to the user. The execution of the workflow using orchestration and choreography approaches is shown in the Figs. 1(b) and (c) respectively.

In the classical orchestration approach Fig. 1(b), the input in received from the user is sent to service s_1 by the orchestrator. Upon the receipt of the input in, the service s_1 produces the data d which it passes to the orchestrator. The orchestrator then passes the data d to the service s_2 which produces the final output out. The service s_2 passes this final output out to the orchestrator who forwards it to the user. In this approach all the data is routed among the services of the workflow through the central coordinator i.e. the orchestrator.

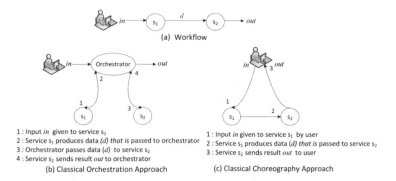

Fig. 1. (a) Workflow (b) Classical orchestration approach (c) Classical choreography approach

Using orchestration in bioinformatics workflow has several advantages; this includes controlled and monitored execution of workflow, collection of provenance data and handling of task failures during workflow execution. However the classical orchestration approach suffers from performance bottlenecks. This is due the fact that all the data is indirectly passed between the services of the workflow resulting in unnecessary data-flows, consuming more bandwidth and hence weakening the performance of the workflow execution. Another issue with this approach is the scalability [5]. The overall performance of the bioinformatics workflow reduces as the number of services and the volume of the data to be orchestrated in the workflow becomes larger. The services of the workflow are distributed but the decision and coordination logic are centrally located at one point, this also creates a single point of failure in this approach.

In the classical choreography approach Fig. 1(c), the input in is given to the first service of the workflow i.e. the service s_1 by the user. The service s_1 produces the data d. This data d is passed directly to service s_2 which produces the final output out which is transfered to the user. In a choreography approach the services of the workflow do not depend on the central coordinator. The approach achieves the composition by peer-to-peer communication between the services of the workflow [6].

The choreography approach facilitates the services of the workflow to transfer data directly between them without going through any central coordinator [7]. This direct data transfer between services consumes less bandwidth and thus provides performance benefits in bioinformatics workflow which are data-intensive. Further more the choreography approach is more scalable than orchestration approach [8]. However in this approach it is difficult to handle provenance of data, monitor and handle components failures. The choreography approach also suffers from implementation challenges i.e. the approach require complex design processes and execution infrastructure compared to orchestration approach. These difficulties make the orchestration as the preferred choice to execute bioinformatics workflows.

Table 1. Summary of orchestration and choreography approaches

Factors	Method	
	Orchestration	*Choreography*
Composition	Centralized	Decentralized
Data movement	Indirect/Centralized	Direct/Peer-to-Peer
Monitoring	Easy	Difficult
Provenance	Easy	Difficult
Failure-handling	Relatively easy	Difficult
Scalability	Not scalable	Scalable
Single point of failure	Possible	Not possible
Implementation	Simple and straight-forward	Complex

Table 1 summarises the orchestration and choreography approaches. As see from the Table 1, both the approaches have their share of advantages and disadvantages in executing bioinformatics workflows. In order to combine the benefits of both the approaches, several authors proposed modified orchestration and choreography approaches to handle big-data in workflow execution.

3   Modified Orchestration and Choreography Approaches

This section reviews the modified classical orchestration and choreography approaches. They are mostly based on decentralized and hybrid design. In a decentralized design both the control-flow and the data-flow are distributed. Whereas in a hybrid design the control-flow is centralized and the data-flow is distributed.

Binder et al. proposed a solution using *triggers* in [9]. A trigger is a lightweight infrastructure placed between the orchestrator and the services of the workflow. Each service is associated with a trigger, which invokes that service. Triggers act as data buffers and collect the required data for the services of the workflow before invoking the service. They forward the outputs to other triggers according to the routing information without involving the orchestrator for data transfers. The approach uses choreography to achieve decentralized control for workflow execution and overcomes the problem associated with the classical orchestration approach. Although the approach improves performance of the orchestrator, the data now moves between the triggers and the services, thereby increasing the traffic between them.

Barker et al. in [10] proposed a *proxy* based approach. This is a hybrid approach that combines the benefits of orchestration and the choreography approaches. A proxy is a lightweight piece of middleware placed between the orchestrator and the services of a workflow, controlled by orchestrator. The orchestrator sends a request to a proxy and the proxy then invokes the service on behalf of the orchestrator. The proxies buffer the intermediate data and pass it to the other proxies according to the data flow in the workflow. This allows the services of the workflow to pass that data among themselves without passing through the orchestrator. The proxies however pass references of the data passed between the services to the orchestrator. This allows the orchestrator to monitor the progress of workflow execution.

In [11], Fleuren et al. proposed a hybrid model that makes use of orchestrator and choreography approaches to execute workflow. The orchestrator is used to execute the main workflow and to integrate sub-workflows called *workflow skeletons* of the main workflows. While the choreography approach is used to execute the workflow skeletons. This approach also makes use of proxies, which are associated with each workflow skeletons to execute the workflow. Although proxies relieve the orchestrator from handling the intermediate data, the data now flows between proxies and services of the workflow increasing the data traffic between them.

Bahman Javadi et al. in [12] proposed decentralized orchestration approach based on *cloud* to execute workflows. The approach uses a cloud between the orchestrator and the services of the workflow to store and process data. Here the output data of the service invocation which is usually of large volumes are directly moved to the cloud bypassing the centralized orchestrator. In this way the orchestrator is relieved from sending the intermediate data and thus reducing the traffic between the services and the orchestrator. Since cloud provides high amount of storage and processing, this approach can handle much more data then the triggers and proxies approach. However, this approach directs all the data from the services to the cloud, thus increasing the traffic between services and the cloud.

Ward Jaradat et al. in [13] also proposed a cloud based workflow execution approach that makes use of *distributed orchestration*. This decentralized orchestration approach partitions the workflow into smaller sub-workflows and then transmits these sub-workflows to appropriate cloud location and then their execution happens in parallel. At each location an orchestrator is used to coordinate the sub-workflow execution. The distributed orchestrators transfer intermediate results between them to complete the workflow execution. Since the workflow is executed in parallel the performance of workflow execution improves. Although clouds provide advantages in execution of bioinformatics workflows in terms of large storage space and computing facilities, one of the big challenge faced on the cloud is handling the movement of the large data sets in and out of the cloud.

Wieland et al. in [14] proposed the concept of *pointers* to pass data by reference rather than by value from one service to another service of the workflow. The service that produces the data, transfers a reference of data to consuming service via the orchestrator. The consuming service then uses this reference to get the data from shared data storage. The orchestrator only has to handle the reference and not the data. Thus, this mechanism reduces the load on the orchestrator leading to faster workflow execution. However, the data moves between the service which increases the communication cost between the services especially when the data is too big to move.

Table 2. Overview of the modified approaches

Approach Name	Design	Interface	Environment	Single point of failure places	Data-flow Type	Between
Triggers [9]	Decentralized	Mediator	SOA	Orchestrator/ Triggers	Indirect	Triggers-and-Services
Proxy [10]	Hybrid	Mediator	SOA	Orchestrator/ Proxies	Indirect	Proxies-and-Services
Workflow Skeletons [11]	Hybrid	Mediator	SOA / Grid	Orchestrator/ Proxies	Indirect	Proxies-and-Services
Cloud [12]	Decentralized	Mediator	SOA / Cloud	Orchestrator	Indirect	Services-and-Cloud
Distributed Orchestration [13]	Decentralized Orchestration	Distributed Orchestrators	SOA / Cloud	Distributed Orchestrators	Indirect	Distributed Orchestrator-and-Services
Pointers/ Reference passing [14]	Decentralized	Mediator	SOA	Orchestrator	Indirect	Shared data storage-and-Services
Data Flow Delegated (DFD) [15]	Hybrid	Direct/ Peer-to-Peer	SOA	Orchestrator	Direct	Services
Pipelined Data Flow Delegated (PDFD) [16]	Hybrid	Direct/Peer-to-Peer	SOA	Orchestrator	Direct	Services

Subramanian et al. proposed a *Data-flow delegated (DFD)* approach in [15]. The data required in the workflow execution are dynamically assigned to the workflow services as per their requirements. This is achieved by enabling direct transport of data between participating services of the workflow controlled by the orchestrator. The orchestrator informs the services from where they will receive the input data and where they have to send the output data. The Data-Flow Delegated (DFD) approach relieves the orchestrator from handling the data but the services of the workflow move the data directly between them.

Although pipelined parallelism is used in workflow systems such as Kepler, Taverna and Triana, they carry the problem associated with the orchestration i.e., they require the orchestrator to transmit (and receive) all the input and output data of the component services. Subramanian et al. attempted to overcome this problem in [16]. The authors proposed an approach called *Pipelined data-flow delegation (PDFD)* for web services-based workflows. Pipelined data-flow delegation is orchestrator coordinated approach that allows partitioning of large datasets into independent subsets and that can be communicated in a pipelined manner without going through the centralized orchestrator. This approach improves workflow execution but is feasible only if data can be split into independent chunks and processed in batches.

4   Discussion and Conclusion

Table 2 gives an overview of the modified approaches reviewed in this paper. Most of the approaches are based on decentralized and hybrid design. The approaches handle big-data in a workflow by moving the data either directly between the services or indirectly using mediators and data references. Parallelism is also combined in some of the approaches to handle big-data and to speedup workflow execution.

The modified approaches are data-driven. They move data which is varying in size from one computing service to another computing service during the workflow execution. The orchestrator is used to control and monitor the workflow execution, while the computing services of the workflow handle the data-flow directly or indirectly between them. In other words the data coordination responsibility of the orchestrator is distributed to the workflow components. However, such distribution can optimize the workflow performance to some extent, but not extensively as the distribution of responsibilities does not help to overcome all the difficulties in handling big-data. With the size of biological data increasing and the workflows having to handle data in the range of terabytes to petabytes and more, moving data to computation in a workflow is not feasible solution. The size of the analysis tools associated with computing services are much smaller than the size of the data that flows in a workflow. To handle the big-data in a bioinformatics workflow, this paper suggests changing the paradigm of workflow execution by moving the computation to data. Moving computation means moving analysis tools from computation services to data services. We feel this will lead to more efficient handling of big-data in bioinformatics workflows and thereby mark a shift in big-data analysis.

References

1. Stevens, R.D., Tipney, H.J., Wroe, C.J., Oinn, T.M., Senger, M., Lord, P.W., Goble, C.A., Brass, A., Tassabehji, M.. Exploring Williams-Beuren syndrome using myGrid. Bioinformatics **20**(suppl 1), i303–i310 (2004)
2. Yang, X., Wang, L., Jie, W. (eds.): Guide to e-Science: Next Generation Scientific Research and Discovery. Springer, Heidelberg (2011)
3. Barker, A., van Hemert, J.: Scientific workflow: a survey and research directions. In: Wyrzykowski, R., Dongarra, J., Karczewski, K., Wasniewski, J. (eds.) PPAM 2007. LNCS, vol. 4967, pp. 746–753. Springer Berlin Heidelberg, Berlin, Heidelberg (2008). doi:10.1007/978-3-540-68111-3_78
4. Liu, J., Pacitti, E., Valduriez, P., Mattoso, M.: A survey of data-intensive scientific workflow management. J. Grid Comput. **13**(4), 457–493 (2015)
5. Barker, A., Besana, P., Robertson, D., Weissman, J.B.: The benefits of service choreography for data-intensive computing. In: Proceedings of the 7th International Workshop on Challenges of Large Applications in Distributed Environments, pp. 1–10. ACM, June 2009
6. Barker, A., Weissman, J.B., Van Hemert, J.: Eliminating the middleman: peer-to-peer dataflow. In: Proceedings of the 17th International Symposium on High Performance Distributed Computing, pp. 55–64. ACM, June 2008
7. Barker, A., Walton, C.D., Robertson, D.: Choreographing web services. IEEE Trans. Serv. Comput. **2**(2), 152–166 (2009)
8. Pedraza, G., Estublier, J.: Distributed orchestration versus choreography: The FOCAS approach. In: Wang, Q., Garousi, V., Madachy, R., Pfahl, D. (eds.) ICSP 2009. LNCS, vol. 5543, pp. 75–86. Springer, Heidelberg (2009). doi:10.1007/978-3-642-01680-6_9

9. Binder, W., Constantinescu, I., Faltings, B.: Service invocation triggers: a light-weight routing infrastructure for decentralised workflow orchestration. Int. J. High Perform. Comput. Networking **6**(1), 81–90 (2009)
10. Barker, A., Weissman, J.B., van Hemert, J.I.: The circulate architecture: avoiding workflow bottlenecks caused by centralised orchestration. Cluster Comput. **12**(2), 221–235 (2009)
11. Fleuren, T., Götze, J., Müller, P.: Workflow skeletons: increasing scalability of scientific workflows by combining orchestration and choreography. In: IEEE European Conference on Web Services (ECOWS), pp. 99–106, September 2011
12. Javadi, B., Tomko, M., Sinnott, R.O.: Decentralized orchestration of data-centric workflows in cloud environments. Future Gener. Comput. Syst. **29**(7), 1826–1837 (2013)
13. Jaradat, W., Dearle, A., Barker, A.: Workflow partitioning and deployment on the cloud using orchestra. In: Proceedings of the 2014 IEEE/ACM 7th International Conference on Utility and Cloud Computing, pp. 251–260. IEEE Computer Society, December 2014
14. Wieland, M., Görlach, K., Schumm, D., Leymann, F.: Towards reference passing in web service and workflow-based applications. In: IEEE International Enterprise Distributed Object Computing Conference, pp. 109–118. IEEE, September 2009
15. Subramanian, S., Sztromwasser, P., Petersen, K., Puntervoll, P.: Direct data transfer between SOAP web services in orchestration. In: Proceedings of the 14th International Conference on Information Integration and Web-based Applications and Services, pp. 91–100. ACM, December 2012
16. Subramanian, S., Sztromwasser, P., Puntervoll, P., Petersen, K.: Pipelined dataflow delegated orchestration for data-intensive eScience workflows. Int. J. Web Inf. Syst. **9**(3), 204–218 (2013)

Various Code Clone Detection Techniques and Tools: A Comprehensive Survey

Pratiksha Gautam[(✉)] and Hemraj Saini

Department of Computer Science and Engineering,
Jaypee University of Information Technology, Waknaghat, Solan 173234, India
pratikshamtech20@gmail.com, hemraj.saini@juit.ac.in

Abstract. In this paper, we have discussed several code replication detection methods and tools in different dimensions. This review has provided an extensive survey codec clone detection techniques and tools. Starting from clone perceptions, classification of clones and an overall assortment of selected techniques and tools is discussed. This paper covers the whole paradigm in clone detection and presents open research avenues in code clone detection.

Keywords: Software security · Code clone · Program dependency graph · Detection techniques

1 Introduction

Code segments usually occurs due to replication from one place and then rewrite them in to another section of code with or without variations/changes are software cloning and the copied code is called clone. Various researchers [1–5] have reported more than 20–59% code replication. The problem with such copied code is that an error detected in the original must be checked in every copy for the same bug. Moreover, the copied code expansions the effort to be done when augmenting the code [5, 8]. However, the code quality analysis (improved quality code), replication identification, virus recognition, facet mining, and bug exposure are the other software engineering tasks which require the mining of semantically or syntactically identical code segment to facilitate clone detection significant for software analysis [6]. Fortunately, there are a number of comparison and evaluation studies which are related to numerous clone detection techniques. Recently, Rattan et al. [7], has presented a methodical survey on clone detection while Roy et al. [8] has presented an qualitative comparison and evaluation of clone detection tools and techniques. Bellon et al. [9] has presented an extensive quantitative assessment of six clone detectors which is based on large C and Java programs for clone detection. Further, the potential studies have evaluated the clone detection approach in other context [10–15].

In this paper, we have provided a comprehensive review on presently accessible clone detection approaches and tools. We will start with the basic introduction of code clones after that classify and compare the techniques and tools in two different ways. Foremost, the classification of clone types and their techniques and subsequent categorization of clone detection tools. The remaining of the paper is structured as follows.

A. Unal et al. (Eds.): SmartCom 2016, CCIS 628, pp. 655–667, 2016.
DOI: 10.1007/978-981-10-3433-6_79

The Sect. 2 presents the taxonomy of code clones. The Sect. 3 related to various clone detection methods. The Sect. 4 explores the code clone detection tools. Research gaps are discussed in Sect. 5 and finally, Sect. 6 concludes the paper.

2 Classification of Code Clones

Figure 1 characterizes the taxonomy of code clones. It can be categorized on the basis of three aspects which are illustrated below. Clone classifications are used for expansion reengineering and detection methods. On the basis of clone classification, we have reiterated on the most prominent types of clone, which eventuates at the time of reengineering. In the following, code clones are assorted on basis of three facets such as: (1) similarities between two code segments, (2) clone instance position in program, and (3) refactoring opportunities with the replicated code.

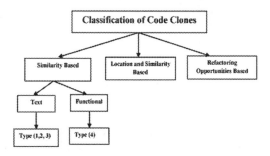

Fig. 1. Classification of code clones.

The similarity based clones are mainly of two types such as: (1) two code segment can be identical on the basis of similarity of their program content and (2) it can be similar in their functionalities without being textually identical. However, textual similarity based clones are of three types as type-1 (similar code segment without modification except for modification in whitespace and comments) type-2 (structurally/syntactically similar copied code, except for changes in names of function identifiers, variables, types), and type-3 (identical code fragment with or without further modifications; statements were changed, added or removed). The syntactic elements are to be measured in this taxonomy which has been altered by the programmer after replication. For instance, the methods which are same except the name or the methods which are identical for the types of parameters integrated in high-similarity code clones. The type-4 (similar computation but different structure) clone based on similar functionalities.

The similarity between two functions is of three types which are based on four points of comparisons such as name of the function, layout of the code, lexis in the functions and control flow of the functions has been given by Mayrand et al. [3]. A taxonomy for clone methods proposed by Balazinska et al. [16] with 18 different categories which considers each group of clone methods on the basis of differences existing between them. The categories specify the amount of contents of the method has been copied and also what type of syntax elements have been altered. At the first level, two categories based on general similarities such as identical and external changes.

The second instances, the token variations and method aspects based on three categories. The third point based on the significance of the particular token in method body and, moreover the fourth phase is based on token-sequence distinction in function body. The three distinct types of clones such as exact clones, parameterized clones, and clones which have other pervasive features illustrated by Bellon and Koschke [9, 17, 18] for accomplish a good assessment between different detection tools. The objective of this categorization is to analysis the detection and classification adequacy of different clone detection tools. A clone topology with one supplementary type (type-4) presented by Davey et al. [19] which is based on the Bellon and Koschke [9, 17, 18]. In addition to this, the authors [18] detected type-1 to type-3 clones and the detection of type-4 leaving it as future work. Kontogiannis [20] details four types of clones, which are based on functional scheme of replication such as exact clones, the clones which are similar except for analytically replaced with variable names as well as data types; the third is clones with further adaptations. The fourth is clones with statements have been added or deleted.

Further, classification is related to location and similarity of code clones. This categorization is based on place distinctions as well as physical expanse between clone instance positions. The refactoring opportunities or impediments based on the fact that the code segments which are located in the same file, same function or in files from different directories can be improved without affecting their external behavior by using refactoring. The clone instances in object oriented system are to be found at specific position in the class hierarchy. The rudimentary parsing technology is sufficient for extracting such type of assortments for a clone pair. The illustrations of such types of classifications provided by various authors are as follows. A hierarchical categorization of software clones which are consists of three partitions using two aspects such as locations and functionality given by Kapser and Godfrey [21]. The first classification of clones is based on their substantial position in the program text. Second, clones taxonomy is based on the type of realm in which they are located and third is function to function code clones. Monden et al. [22], has described how to simplify the relation between software quality and code by using module-based categorization of code clones and they have also provided taxonomy of modules.

Finally, the refactoring opportunities based classifications discussed the simplicity to extort the copied code from the refactoring perspective. The classifications of such kinds of differences are based on methods which have been defined outside of the copied code fragment and the uses of variables. The context analysis has been proposed by Balazinska et al. [16] to complete the difference analysis of code clones for computer-assisted refactoring. Fanta and Rajlich [23] proposed an approach of reengineering scenarios to eliminate clones, which is based on automated restructuring tools. The object-oriented systems (in SMALLTALK) investigated by Golomingi [24] and the author have also provided a clone relationship scenarios taxonomy based on the class hierarchy relationships of the methods which consists of duplicate code fragments. Basically, there are four types of clone and each type is classified as shown in Table 1 below.

Table 1. Summary of clone taxonomy.

Type 1	Type 2	Type 3	Type 4
Exact clone	Renamed clone	Near-miss clone	Structural clone
Structural clone	Parameterized clone	Gapped clone	Function clone
Function clone	Near-miss clone	Non-contiguous clone	Reordered clone
	Function clone	Reordered clone	Intertwined clone
		Structural clone	Semantic clone
		Function clone	

Table 1 characterizes four types of clones as well as their sub-types. The similarity based taxonomy such as text based (type-1 to 3) and function based (type-4). Type 1 clone has been categories as follows. (1) The exact clone (similar code except some variations in comments), Type 1, 3, 4 as (2) the structural (it is based on level of similarity), Type 1,2,3,4 as (3) function (subset of structural). Type 2 as (1) renamed (modification in copied code), (2) parameterized (renamed clone with renaming). Type 2, 3 as (3) near-miss (slight modifications in copied fragment but syntactic structure remains same). Type 3 as (1) gapped (add, delete, modify some portion between segment), (2) non-contiguous (Like near-miss, and gaps are allowed between code fragment). Type 3, 4 as (3) reordered (some statement have been reordered). Type 4 as (1) intertwined (making two segments in to one segment).

3   Code Clone-Detection Techniques

The clone detection techniques can be analyzed on the basis of code clone properties. There are variant code clone properties which are shown in Fig. 2.

Figure 2 depicts some clone properties such as normalization means apply a number of refinements as remove white space, comments etc. before actual comparison. The source representation, it is the result after the transformation. In the comparison phase the granularities are used for a particular technique. Comparison algorithms play a vital role in detection of dissimilar types of code clones. The complexity based on the types of comparison algorithms as well as types of transformations. The clone similarity means different kinds of clones can be identified by different techniques. The granularity can be fixed or free. The language independency property

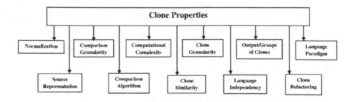

Fig. 2.   Various types of code clone properties.

verified language sustain of a detection tool. The output aspect indicates what kind of output will be occurred as clone pair or clone classes or both. Clone refactoring indicates restructuring existing code without changing its external behavior. The language paradigm implies programming paradigm which is targeted for the particular method of interest.

3.1 Classification of Code Clone Detection Techniques

There are following types of clone detection techniques.

(1) The text/string based approach: In this method, the source fragments are analyzed as subsequence of text. The two segments are compared textually with each other on the basis of different transformations like white space, newline and removing comments etc. to locate sequences of same strings. Several researchers have proposed numerous string/text based techniques for clone detection. The lexer as well as line-based string matching algorithm on tokens for the line of text used by Baker [27, 28] with the help of a tool named as Dup. It also used special parameter for identifying clones (which have different variables names). Although, it was not able to detect clone written in different style and it could not support exploration and navigation between the copied codes. Koshke et al. [18] has overwhelmed this problem by using tokens and non-parameterized suffixes. Although, authors were unable to detect the exact and parameterized clones as well as they could not make a distinction between them. Moreover, the clones (text based tool) which is proposed by Koshke et al. [18] does not check whether the identifiers had been renamed consistently. Karp-Rabin fingerprinting algorithm used by Johnson [25] for clone detection as well as to measures the fingerprints of a text for all length substring of the source code. The whole text is partitioned in to a set of substring because of each character in this technique is consists of at least one substring and then raw transformation [30] is applied for matching of those substrings. However, the limitation of this technique is that to keep 50 lines match resulting in to diminish large number of false positive. The island grammar technique used by Cordy et al. [29] for identifying syntactic constructs. Moreover, the author also provided the detection of near miss clones for HTML web pages. The constraints of this technique is that it was unable to normalize any code and it used smallest comparison. The string-based dynamic pattern matching algorithm which is language independent proposed by Ducasse et al. [2]. Further, this technique could not identify meaningful clone resolution in language-independent manner due to the cohesiveness of the code. The latent semantic indexing [31] based approach proposed by Marcuss [26]. This approach detect the clones by extremity its comparison domain within comments and the identifier in spite of compare whole source code. It cannot detect such types of clones which have same structure nevertheless the identifiers name is different. All of the detection approach which have been discussed above shows that it does not apply transformation on the source code, the recent approach which has been proposed by Ducasse et al. [2] has used several transformation on the raw source

code. Although the cost of text based approach is awfully less except the code having identifier changes, line split, amputation of parenthesis, type, etc. cannot be analyzed and identified whether it is a cloned code or not.

(2) The lexical/token-based approach: The token based approaches are also called lexical approach. In this technique, the whole source code is divided in to tokens by lexical analysis and then all the tokens are formed in to a set of token sequence. Finally, the sequence is scanned for identifying duplicated code. One of the foremost tool of token based approach named as CCFinder proposed by Kamiya et al. [32]. Foremost, the lexer partitions each line of text in to tokens and subsequently forms a single token sequence and moreover, the suffix tree matching algorithm is used to find similar sub-sequences of token sequence. Although, Dup is also a token-based approach tool in the sense that it is also used lexer for tokenization as well as for comparisons based on suffix tree matching algorithm proposed by Baker [27, 28]. CP-Miner [34, 35] has been introduced to overwhelm the problem of CCFinder and Dup, in which a frequent subsequence mining technique is used for clone detection rather than sequential analysis in CCFinder and Dup. A plug-in in visual studio based approach which detects clones in Java and C# and it was not able to handle defects from programmer side itself proposed by Juergens et al. [36]. However, the same approach for C ++ and C# was proposed by Kawaguchi et al. [37] and it could not overcome the problem as in [36].

(3) The syntactic/tree-based approach: In this approach, the program is represented in the form of abstract syntax tree (AST) rather than creating tokens for each statement and with the help of tree matching algorithm similar sub-tree is searched in the same tree. One of the initial AST-based tool named as CloneDR proposed by Baxter et al. [38]. It creates AST with the help of compiler generator and then compares its sub tree by using metrics which is based on hash functions. Although, it was not able to detect identical clones. To overcome this problem, the Bauhaus has provided a ccdiml [39] tool by avoiding the uses of hashing and similarity metrics. However, it was incompetent to verify the renamed identifiers. Yang [40] has presented one of the grammar based approach. It is used for finding the syntactic variations between the two versions of the same program by creating their parse tree and then apply dynamic programming technique for identifying similar sub tree. Wahler et al. [41] explored the approach to detect the exact and parameterized clone. This approach foremost convert the AST into XML and subsequently used frequent item set data mining technique [33] for extracting the clones. Evas and Fraser [42] provided a further abstraction of this approach by finding near miss clones as well as exact clones by using only AST leaves rather than whole AST. Even though, it could not detect much of the exact clones. A tool named Clone Tracker in Java was developed by Duala Ekoko et al. [43]. However, it was unable to identify post programming due to the numbers of false positives. A clone management tool in Java which has amplified the time for clone detection proposed by Nguyen [44]. However, aforementioned researches shows that gapped clones could not be find by the AST as well as it could not detect clones if the statements are reordered and does not follow the data flow. The limitations of AST can be easily overcome by the use of PDG-based technique.

(4) The semantic/PDG-based approach: The AST based problems was overwhelmed by the program dependency graph (PDG) [45–47]. The PDG approach used the data flow and control flow [50] for clone detection semantically and syntactically. PDG-DUP is one of the most prominent PDG-based clone detection approach proposed by Komondoor and Horwitz [45, 48]. It is based on program slicing technique for identifying PDG sub graph without changing its semantics behavior. Further, the same slicing based clone analysis approach accomplished by Gallagher and Lucas [49]. They compute program slices on all the variables of a code but could not find any analysis outcome. An iterative approach within PDG proposed by Krinke [46] for identifying maximal similar sub graph but it cannot be used on any type of system to find the clone. According to the several researchers who are using the PDG have concluded that PDG-based techniques can find non-contiguous clones but it cannot be applied to large systems and it will require more time for code clone detection.

(5) The syntactic/metric-based approach: In metric-based methods dissimilar metrics are assembled such as number of functions, number of lines etc. from code segments and then evaluates that metrics in spite of assessments of source code directly. Mayrand et al. [3] computed metrics from expression, layouts and control flow for each function elements of a program and then similar metrics returned as software clones. However, some metrics are not identified in that case they used intermediate representation language (IRL) for exemplifying each function of code. It detects function-based copy-paste instead of segment-based copy-paste which occurs recurrently. The feasible matches identified by an abstract pattern tool which is based on markov model provided by Kontogiannis et al. [4]. The authors used metrics for clone detection which is extorted from an AST of the code and then match detection is done by using dynamic programming. However, it was unable to identify copy-pasted code rather than it only measures similarity between the codes. Further, the identical approach used by Di Lucca et al. [51] for acquisition the similarity between the static HTML pages by evaluating their level of similarity, which is performed by computing the Levenshtein distance of the code [52]. eMetrics tool is used for detecting function clones and then detected clones are clustered according to refactoring opportunities by Calefato Lanuible [53, 54]. Moreover, the mined code is checked manually for finding that is a true positive or not yet it could not be executed on vast systems. So, the authors concluded that metric-based approach can identify simply clones from the code.

(6) The semantic/hybrid approach: There are numerous hybrid methods for code clone detection. The hybrid approach is a collection of several approaches and it can be classified on the basis of preceding techniques. The tree and token based-hybrid approach proposed by Koschke et al. [18] for finding type-I (exact) and type-II code clones. In this approach authors generate suffix tree for serialized AST nodes which is sequentialzed in preorder traversal and then by using suffix tree based algorithm comparisons is performed on the tokens of the AST nodes in place of AST nodes. The Microsoft's new phoenix framework [55], was also used for the detection of function level clones with the same approach. It can detect exact function clone as well as parameterized clone with identifier renaming not data type changes. The analogous approach proposed by Greenan [56] with the

sequence matching algorithm for the detection of method level clones. Jiang et al. [57] explored AST in Euclidean space for computing the vectors as well as group these vectors on the basis of similarity through the Locating Sesitive Hasing (LSH) [58]. A dynamic pattern matching as well as characterization based hybrid approach is provided by Balazinska [59] in which method of each bodies are computed with quality metrics and then evaluated identified clusters by using Patenaude's [60] metric-based approach. A dynamic change tracking and resolution in Java language based novel approach explored by DeWit [61]. Further, it was unable for data flow detection as well as data flows although, it detects the clones at the programmer's level. In addition to this, several other approaches for the clone detection in other context have been proposed in [10–15]. All these approaches mainly emphasized on the detection of type-1, type-2, and type-3 clones. However, aforementioned comprehensive survey has been presented graphically in Fig. 3.

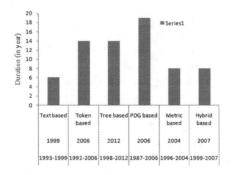

Fig. 3. Comprehensive survey of code clone detection techniques.

4   Comparisons of Clone Detection Tools

The software clone detection tools are multivariate and their abstraction entails a methodical scheme for recounting their property. In this section, we indexed the different clone detection tools presented in the literature in a tabular form as shown in Table 2. The Table 2 illustrates the assessments of various tools and techniques. In this table, the first column represents the author name, 2nd column refers to the tools name,

Table 2. Comparisions of Clone detection tools

Author	Tools	Techniques	Supported-language	Domain
Baker [1, 26]	Dup	Line/Text based	C, C++, Java	CD/Linux
Kamiya, et al. [24]	CCFinder	Transformation/Token comp. with suffix tree	C, C++, Java, COBOL etc.	CD/Windows/NT
Bellon [8]	Ccdiml (Bauhaus)	AST/Tree Matching	C, C++	CD/Linux
Krinke et al. [38]	Duplix	PDG, graph Matching	C?	CD

the 3rd column signifies the proposed technique, 4th column imply whether the tool supported languages and 5th column shows the domain of the tools.

5 Open Research Issues in Code Clone Detection

There is no code clone detection technique for the detection of non-trivial code clone, which is also ideal in terms of portability, scalability, precision and recall. Every tool has its own limitations, making it difficult to define which is realistic for clone detection. The type-1 as well as type-2 clone can be easily detected in comparison of type-3 and type-4. The PDG based-approach can only detect type-3 and type-4 clone but the shortcoming of this algorithm is that it produces many variants of the same clone, thereby taking longer time to process a program. Thus, it is essential for such type of technique and tool that may overcome the limitations of existing techniques for clone detection.

6 Conclusion

The code-clone detection is an emerging issue in the software ecosystem which degrades the software's comprehensibility as well as maintainability. Therefore, its analysis and detection is necessary for improving the quality, structure and design of the software system. In this paper, discussion in terms of attributes based clone categorization, classification of clone detection tools as well as approaches such as text based, token based, tree based, PDG based, metric based and hybrid technique on the basis of their property and sub-property. However, numerous algorithms have been developed based on aforementioned approaches, but sill now the detection of clone with accuracy and efficiency is a potential issue. There are various algorithms for clone detection in which some algorithms are less efficient when a large system is to be compared as well as some algorithms detects only a particular type of clone. This paper presents an extensive comparison of tools and techniques as well as research gaps in clone detection so that one can easily select an appropriate method according to the requirement and can analyze opportunities for hybridizing various techniques that may overcome the existing research gaps in clone detection algorithms.

Acknowledgments. The authors would like to thank Professor Ghanshyam Singh as well as anonymous reviewers for critical comments and suggestions to improve the quality of the manuscript.

References

1. Baker, B.S.: On finding duplication and near-duplication in large software systems. In: Proceedings of 2nd IEEE Working Conference on Reverse Engineering, Toronto, Ontario, Canada, pp. 86–95, July 1995
2. Ducasse, S., Rieger, M., Demeyer, S.: A Language independent approach for detecting duplicated code. In: Proceedings of 1st IEEE International Conference on Software Maintenance, Oxford, UK, ICSM 1999, pp. 109–118 (1999)
3. Mayrand, J., Leblanc, C., Merlo, E.: Experiment on the automatic detection of function clones in a software system using metrics. In: Proceedings of 1st IEEE International Conference on Software Maintenance, Monterey, CA, pp. 244–254 (1996)
4. Kontogiannis, K., Mori, R.D., Merlo, E., Galler, M., Bernstein, M.: Pattern matching for clone and concept detection. J. Autom. Softw. Eng. 3(1), 79–108 (1996)
5. Lague, B., Proulx, D., Mayrand, J., Merlo, E.J., Hudepohl, J.: Assessing the benefits of incorporating function clone detection in a development process. In: Proceedings of 1st IEEE International Conference on Software Maintenance, Washington, DC, USA, pp. 314–321 (1997)
6. Roy, C.K., Cordy, J.R.: A survey on software clone detection research. Technical report 541, Queen's University at Kingston (2007)
7. Rattan, D., Bhatia, R., Singh, M.: Software Clone detection: a systematic review. Inf. Softw. Technol. 55(7), 1165–1199 (2013)
8. Roy, C.K., Cordy, J.R., Koschke, R.: Comparison and evaluation of code clone detection techniques and tools: a qualitative approach. Sci. Comput. Program. 74(7), 470–495 (2009)
9. Bellon, S., Koschke, R., Antoniol, G., Krinke, J., Merlo, E.: Comparison and evaluation of clone detection tools. IEEE Trans. Softw. Eng. 33(9), 577–591 (2007)
10. Patil, R.V., Joshi, S., Shinde, S.V., Ajagekar, D.A., Bankar, S.D.: Code clone detection using decentralized architecture and code reduction. In: Proceedings of IEEE International Conference on Pervasive Computing, Pune, India (ICPC 2015), pp. 1–6, January 2015
11. Keivanloo, I., Zhang, F., Zou, Y.: Threshold-free code clone detection for a large-scale heterogeneous Java repository. In: Proceedings of 22nd IEEE International Conference on Software Analysis, Evolution and Reengineering, Montreal, QC (SANER 2015), pp. 201–210 (2015)
12. Chodarev, S., Pietrikova, E., Kollar, J.: Haskell clone detection using pattern comparing algorithm. In: Proceedings of 13th IEEE International Conference on Engineering of Modern Electric Systems (EMES 2015), Oradea, Romania, pp. 1–4 (2015)
13. Kamiya, T.: An execution-semantic and content-and-context-based code-clone detection and analysis. In: Proceedings of 9th International Workshop on Software Clones, Montreal, QC (IWSC 2015), pp. 1–7 (2015)
14. Singh, M., Sharma, V.: Detection of file level clone for high level cloning. In: Proceedings of 3rd Elsevier International Conference on Recent Trends in Computing (ICRTC 2015), India, pp. 915–922 (2015)
15. Basit, H.A., Jarzabek, S.: A data mining approach for detecting higher-level clones in software. IEEE Trans. Softw. Eng. 35(4), 497–514 (2009)
16. Balazinska, M., Merlo, E., Dagenais, M., Lague, B., Kontogiannis, K.: Measuring clone based reengineering opportunities. In: Proceedings of the 6th IEEE International Symposium on Software Metrics (METRICS 1999), USA, pp. 292–303, November 1999
17. Bellon, S:. Vergleich von techniken zur erkennung duplizierten quellcodes. Master's thesis no. 1998, University of f Stuttgart (Germany). Institute for Software Technology, September 2002

18. Koschke, R., Falke, R., Frenzel, P.: Clone detection using abstract syntax suffix trees. In: Proceedings of the 13th IEEE Working Conference on Reverse Engineering, Italy, pp. 253–262, October 2006
19. Davey, N., Barson, P., Field, S., Frank, R., Tansley, D.: The development of a software clone detector. J. Appl. Softw. Technol. 1(3/4), 219–236 (1995)
20. Kontogiannis, K.: Evaluation experiments on the detection of programming patterns using software metrics. In: Proceedings of the 4th IEEE Working Conference on Reverse Engineering, Netherlands, pp. 44–54, October 1997
21. Kapser, C., Godfrey, M.W.: Aiding comprehension of cloning through categorization. In: Proceedings of the 7th IEEE International Workshop on Principles of Software Evolution, Japan, pp. 85–94, September 2004
22. Monden, A., Nakae, D., Kamiya, T., Sato, S.I., Matsumoto, K.I.: Software quality analysis by code clones in industrial legacy software. In: Proceedings of 8th IEEE International Symposium on Software Metrics, Canada, pp. 87–94, June 2002
23. Fanta, R., Rajlich, V.: Removing clones from the code. J. Softw. Maintenance 11(4), 223–243 (1999)
24. Koni-N'sapu, G.G.: A scenario based approach for refactoring duplicated code in object oriented systems. Diploma thesis, University of Bern, Germany (2001)
25. Johnson, J.H.: Identifying redundancy in source code using fingerprints. In: Proceeding of the 1993 Conference of the Centre for Advanced Studies on Collaborative Research, Canada, pp. 171–183, October 1993
26. Marcus, A., Maletic, J.: Identification of high-level concept clones in source code. In: Proceedings of 16th IEEE International Conference on Automated Software Engineering (ASE 2001), pp. 107–114, November 2001
27. Baker, B.S.: A program for identifying duplicated code.de. In: Proceedings of Computing Science and Statistics, 24th Symposium on the Interface, pp. 49–57, March 1993
28. Baker, B.S.: Parameterized difference. In: Proceedings of the 10th ACM-SIAM Symposium on Discrete Algorithms (SODA 1999), Maryland, USA, pp. 854–855, January 1999
29. Cordy, J.R., Dean, T.R., Synytskyy, N.: Practical language-independent detection of near-miss. In: Proceedings of the 14th Conference of the Centre for Advanced Studies, Canada, pp. 1–12, October 2004
30. Cox, I.J., Linnartz, J.P.M.: Some general methods for tampering with watermarks. J. Sel. Area Commun. 16(4), 587–593 (1998)
31. Dumais, S.T.: Latent Semantic Indexing (LSI) and TREC-2. In: Proceedings of the 2nd Text Retrieval Conference (TREC 1994), Maryland, pp. 105–115, March 1994
32. Kamiya, T., Kusumoto, S., Inoue, K.: CCFinder: a multilinguistic token-based code clone detection system for large scale source code. IEEE Trans. Softw. Eng. 28(7), 54–67 (2002)
33. Baker, B.S.: Finding clones with dup: analysis of an experiment. IEEE Trans. Softw. Eng. 33(9), 608–621 (2007)
34. Li, Z., Lu, S., Myagmar, S., Zhou, Y.: CP-miner: a tool for finding copy-paste and related bugs in operating system code. In: Proceedings of the 6th Symposium on Operating System Design and Implementation (OSDI 2004), Berkeley, CA, USA, vol. 4, no. 19, pp. 289–302, December 2004
35. Li, Z., Lu, S., Myagmar, S., Zhou, Y.: CP-miner: finding copy-paste and related bugs in large-scale software code. IEEE Trans. Softw. Eng. 32(3), 176–192 (2006)
36. Juergens, E., Deissenboeck, F., Hummel, B.: Clone detective - a workbench for clone detection research. In: Proceedings of the 31st IEEE International Conference on Software Engineering, Vancouver, BC, pp. 603–606 (2009)

37. Kawaguchi, S., Yamashina, T., Uwano, H., Fushida, K., Kamei, Y., Nagura, M., Iida, H.: SHINOBI: a tool for automatic code clone detection in the idea. In: Proceedings of 16th IEEE Working Conference on Reverse Engineering (WCRE 2009), Lille, pp. 313–314 (2009)

38. Baxter, I.D., Yahin, A., Moura, L, Anna, M.S.: Clone detection using abstract syntax trees. In: Proceedings of the 14th IEEE International Conference on Software Maintenance (ICSM 1998), Maryland, pp. 368–377, November 1998

39. Raza, A., Vogel, G., Plödereder, E.: Bauhaus – a tool suite for program analysis and reverse engineering. In: Pinho, L.M., González Harbour, M. (eds.) Ada-Europe 2006. LNCS, vol. 4006, pp. 71–82. Springer, Heidelberg (2006). doi:10.1007/11767077_6

40. Yang, W.: Identifying syntactic differences between two programs. J. Softw. Prac. Exp. **21** (7), 739–775 (1991)

41. Wahler, V., Seipel, D., Fischer, G.: Clone detection in source code by frequent item set techniques. In: Proceedings of the 4th IEEE International Workshop on Source Code Analysis and Manipulation (SCAM 2004), USA, pp. 128–135, September 2004

42. Evans, W.S., Fraser, C.W., Ma, F.: Clone detection via structural abstraction. J. Softw. Qual. **17**(4), 309–330 (2009)

43. Duala-Ekoko, E., Robillard, M.P.: Clone tracker: tool support for code clone management. In: Proceedings of the 30th ACM International Conference on Software Engineering, Washington, DC, USA, pp. 843–846 (2008)

44. Nguyen, H.A., et al.: Clone management for evolving software. IEEE Trans. Softw. Eng. **38** (5), 1008–1026 (2012)

45. Komondoor, R., Horwitz, S.: Using slicing to identify duplication in source code. In: Cousot, P. (ed.) SAS 2001. LNCS, vol. 2126, pp. 40–56. Springer, Heidelberg (2001). doi:10.1007/3-540-47764-0_3

46. Krinke, J.: Identifying similar code with program dependence graphs. In: Proceedings of the 8th IEEE Working Conference on Reverse Engineering (WCRE 2001), Germany, pp. 301–309, October 2001

47. Liu, C., Chen, C., Han, J., Yu, P.S.: GPLAG: detection of software plagiarism by program dependence graph analysis. In: Proceedings of the 12th ACM International Conference on Knowledge Discovery and Data Mining (KDD 2006), Philadelphia, pp. 872–881, August 2006

48. Komondoor, R.V.: Automated duplicated-code detection and procedure extraction. Doctoral thesis, University of Wisconsin- Madison, USA (2003)

49. Gallagher, K., Layman, L.: Are decomposition slices clones? In: Proceedings of the 11th IEEE International Workshop on Program Comprehension (IWPC 2003), USA, pp. 251–256, May 2003

50. Ferrante, J., Ottenstein, K.J., Warren, J.D.: The program dependence graph and its use in optimization. ACM Trans. Program. Lang. Syst. **9**(3), 319–349 (1987)

51. Di Lucca, G.A., Di Penta, M., Fasolino, A.R., Granato, P.: Clone analysis in the web era: an approach to identify cloned web pages. In: Proceedings of the 7th IEEE Workshop on Empirical Studies of Software Maintenance, Italy, pp. 107–113, November 2001

52. Di Lucca, G.A., Di Penta, M., Fasolino, A.R., Granato, P.: An approach to identify duplicated web pages. In: Proceedings of the 26th International Conference on Computer Software and Applications, England, pp. 481–486, August 2002

53. Calefato, F., Lanubile, F., Mallardo, T.: Function clone detection in web applications: a semi automated approach. J. Web Eng. **3**(1), 3–21 (2004)

54. Lanubile, F., Mallardo, T.: Finding function clones in web applications 2003. In: Proceedings of 7th IEEE European Conference on Software Maintenance and Reengineering (CSMR 2003), Italy, pp. 379–386, March 2003

55. Tairas, R., Gray, J.: Phoenix-based clone detection using suffix trees. In: Proceedings of the 44th ACM Annual Southeast Regional Conference (ACM-SE 2006), Melbourne, pp. 679–684, March 2006
56. Greenan, K.: Method-level code clone detection on transformed abstract syntax trees using sequence matching algorithms. Student report, University of California, Santa Cruz, USA (2005)
57. Jiang, L., Misherghi, G., Su, Z., Glondu, S.: Scalable and accurate tree-based detection of code clones. In: Proceedings of the 29th IEEE International Conference on Software Engineering (ICSE 2007), USA, pp. 96–105, May 2007
58. Datar, M., Immorlica, N., Indyk, P., Mirrokni, V.S.: Locality-sensitive hashing scheme based on p-stable distributions. In: Proceedings of the 20th ACM Annual Symposium on Computational Geometry (SoGG 2004), New York, pp. 253–262, June 2004
59. Balazinska, M., Merlo, E., Dagenais, M., Lagüe, B., Kontogiannis, K.: Measuring clone based reengineering opportunities. In: Proceedings of the 6th IEEE International Software Metrics Symposium (METRICS 1999), Florida, USA, pp. 292–303, November 1999
60. Patenaude, J.F., Merlo, E., Dagenais, M., Lagüe, B.: Extending software quality assessment techniques to java systems. In: Proceedings of the 7th IEEE International Workshop on Program Comprehension (IWPC 1999), USA, pp. 49–56, May 1999
61. De Wit, M., Zaidman, A., Van Deursen, A.: Managing code clones using dynamic change tracking and resolution. In: Proceedings of IEEE International Conference on Software Maintenance (ICSM 2009), Edmonton, AB, pp. 169–178 (2009)

Enhancing the Security and Quality of Image Steganography Using a Novel Hybrid Technique

Vaidehi Verma and Trapti Ozha[(✉)]

Sushila Devi Bansal College of Enginering, Indore, India
Verma.Vaidehi@yahoo.com, Trapti_Ozha@yahoo.com

Abstract. Steganography is a technique of hiding the private messages inside the cover image. The main objective of steganography is to send information or message in hidden manner from source to destination in such a way that the intruder or attacker cannot crack the contents of the message and even would be unable to feel the presence of secret message. The proposed method introduced as a new hybrid security model based on steganography. AES algorithm with chaos function to encrypt secret message on first level has been used and RSA algorithm to encrypt secret message on second level have been used. LSB technique is used to hide encrypted message into cover medium. The proposed technique is tested on various images. The PSNR value is calculated for better picture quality of stego image.

Keywords: Steganography · Cryptography · AES · Chaos · RSA · PSNR · Encryption

1 Introduction

Steganography is composed of two characters. First word is 'stegano' that meaning is covered and second word is 'graphy' that meaning is writing. When secret information is hidden in coded language in an image, text or video file and then sent, such a technique is called Steganography [1]. To protect the images and text from hackers and online attackers, steganography provides secrecy to them. To hide the presence of any message in the image, steganography provides that secret communication. This is how it works: There is a cover object which covers the original message, a main image that is also the main message to be sent, a stego key which helps in hiding the message image into the cover image and finally the algorithm which has the required object. After all the stages are done, the final outcome is the stego image having the hidden message to be sent [2] (Fig. 1).

CHAOS theory teaches us that even very simple rules can lead to extremely complex and unpredictable behavior. AES algorithm with chaotic properties such as random and sensitive dependence on initial conditions, so it is used practically in secure communication. In AES, Chaos function applies on S-box. In implemented work is used a new S-box. The generated chaotic S box is sensitive to initial condition and noisy.

© Springer Nature Singapore Pte Ltd. 2016
A. Unal et al. (Eds.): SmartCom 2016, CCIS 628, pp. 668–673, 2016.
DOI: 10.1007/978-981-10-3433-6_80

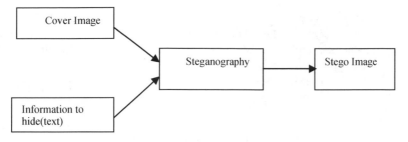

Fig. 1. Basic model of steganography

2 Literature Survey

Yang Rener, Zheng Zhiwei, Tao Shun, Ding Shilei [3] have presented DES algorithm for encryption along with LBS algorithm used for embed message into image in Steganography so that the hidden information is given a dual protection and the information is compressible and invisible to anyone else.

Mr. Madhusudhan Mishra, Mr. Gangadhar Tiwari, Mr. Arun Kumar Yada [4] the authors has used a new technique. The author has used RSA algorithm for encryption in steganography along with F5 algorithm. To hide the encrypted message in the lower image, the author has also used a two tier security layers- first using cryptography key and second using stego key.

Manu Devi, Nidhi Sharma [5] the proposed steganography system the author has used LBS steganography for image embedding. The author has calculated the PSNR for the better quality of the image and how it is calculated has also been mentioned. The higher the PSNR value, the better is the quality of the stego image. The main aim of the research was developing a new and enhanced technique of hiding the data. The main motive was to make the encrypted message totally unbreakable from the inside.

Phad Vitthal S., Bhosale Rajkumar S., Panhalkar Archana R. [6] has proposed a model gives two tier securities. Further they proposed method gives high quality stego images using symmetric key algorithm to encrypt secret message and then PVD with LSB substitution is used to hide encrypted message into cover image.

Rasul Enayatifar, Fariborz Mahmoudi, Khadije Mirzaei [7] Authors focuses on a new method used for image steganography. New method is based on chaotic signals. By using chaotic signal we can change little amount in input but the final result will be completely different. By doing so the integrity of input is saved as to decrypt this attacker have to use large numbers of key. Which is quite impossible and also authors have calculated PSNR value for stego image for the better quality of image.

3 Proposed Work

Sender Side Algorithm
Step1. Select the text message.
Step2. First important message is encrypted by using

- 1st level of encryption uses advance encrypted standard (AES) symmetric key encryption algorithm and chaos function. That encryption algorithm generates cipher text. This cipher text is plain text for the next level encryption.
- 2nd level of encryption uses RSA Asymmetric key encryption algorithm. That encryption algorithm generates cipher text.

Step3. Select the cover image.

Step4. Then encrypted message is hiding into cover image by using LSB substitution.

Step5. The resultant image is stego image (Fig. 2).

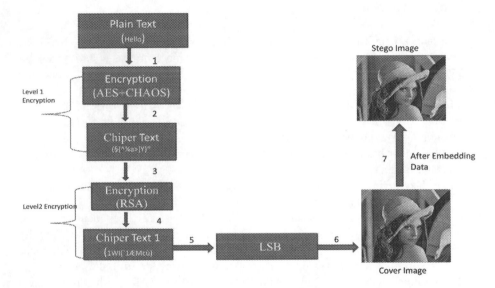

Fig. 2. Sender side encryption

Receiver Side Algorithm

Step1. Read the stego image.

- 1st level of decryption uses (RSA) Asymmetric key algorithm.
  This decryption algorithm generates plain text. This plain text is cipher text for next level decryption.
- 2nd level of decryption uses advance encrypted standard (AES) symmetric key encryption algorithm and chaos function. This decryption algorithm generates plain text.

Step2. Then extract the encrypt message using LSB substitution.

Step3. Decode message using decryption algorithm.

Step4. Get input data.

Step5. The Resultant image is cover image (Fig. 3).

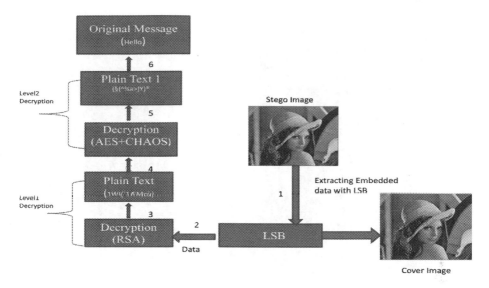

Fig. 3. Receiver side decryption

4 Experimental Results

The implementation of the proposed work is done in MATLAB. The PSNR is used as quality measure to prove the utility of the proposed work. Peak Signal to Noise Ratio (PSNR) is calculated to measure the stego image's quality [8]. For a better quality of image, the PSNR value should be larger due to less distortion. Larger values may increase the chances of an attack (Table 1).

$$PSNR = 10 \cdot \log_{10}\left(\frac{MAX_I^2}{MSE}\right)$$

$$= 20 \cdot \log_{10}\left(\frac{MAX_I}{\sqrt{MSE}}\right)$$

$$= 20 \cdot \log_{10}(MAX_I) - 10 \cdot \log_{10}(MSE)$$

Table 1. PSNR of stego image with different embedding capacity

Bits embedded in Lena image	PSNR value (in db) calculated by pervious paper [9]	PSNR value (in db) Calculated by implemented model
2037	41.00	69.976
4302	40.939	66.864
4998	40.931	66.134
7167	40.904	64.587
8365	40.879	63.739

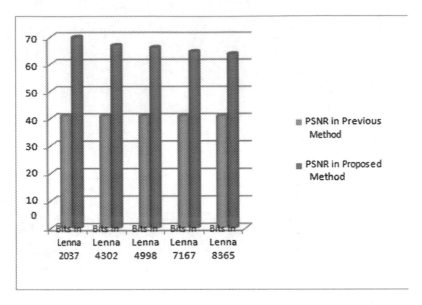

Fig. 4. Graph of PSNR (DB) comparison

5   Conclusion

Steganography is the technique of sending confidential information in embedded manner using the cover medium such as a audio, video, text, image etc. Although many methods exist to deliver secret messages from source to destination, there is a continuous need for a better method. It can also have adverse applications like activities performed by criminals and terrorists (Fig. 4).

In this thesis a critical review of the modern methods has been done. On the basis of the research gap, Proposed and implemented a novel hybrid model based on the fusion of Steganography and cryptography has been in the proposed model, in which two level security is provided. Advance encryption standard (AES) with chaos function and RSA algorithm is used to encrypt secret Message. LSB substitution method is used to hide encrypted secret message into cover image.

In our proposed method, provides dual level encryption to hide hidden information into cover image. It is very difficult to break the cipher text by the attackers. Our proposed method also provides better PSNR value where larger PSNR indicates that image has lower distortion

References

1. Manjunath, N., Hiremath, S.G.: Image and text steganography based on RSA and chaos cryptography. Algorithm Hash LSB Tech. IJEECS **3**(5) (2015) ISSN: 2347-2820
2. Ramaiya, M.K., Hemrajani, N., Saxena, A.K.: Security Improvisation in Image. Steganography using DES, IEEE (2012)
3. Yang, R., Zheng, Z., Tao, S., Ding, S.: Image: steganography combined with DES encryption pre-processing. In: IEEE 6th International Conference on Measuring Technology and Mechatronics Conference, pp. 323–326 (2014)
4. Mishra, M., Tiwari, G., Yadav, A.K.: Secret Communication using Public key Steganography. IEEE (2014)
5. Devi, M., Sharma, N.: Improved Detection of Least Significant Bit Steganography Algorithms in Color and Gray Scale Images, IEEE UIET panjab university Chandigarh (2014)
6. Vitthal, S., Bhosale Rajkumar, S., Panhalkar Archana, R.: A Novel Security Scheme for Secret Data using Cryptography and Steganography. IJCNIS (2012)
7. Enayatifar, R., Mahmoudi, F., Mirzaei, K.: Using the Chaotic Map in Image Steganography. In: IEEE Computer Society- International Conference on Information Technology and Management, pp. 491–495 (2009)
8. Dagar, S.: RGB based dual key image steganography (IEEE Electronic Library), pp. 316–320. IEEE (2013)
9. Alam, S., Kumar, V., Siddiqui, W.A., Ahmad, M.: Key dependent image steganography using edge detection. In: IEEE Fourth International Conference on Advanced Computing & Communication Technologies, pp. 85–88 (2014)
10. Akhtar, N., Johri, P., Khan, S.: Enhancing the security and quality of LSB based image steganography. In: IEEE 5th International Conference on Computational Intelligence and Communication Network, pp. 385–390 (2013)
11. Masud Karim, S.M., Rahman, S., Hossain, I.: A new approach for LSB based image steganography using secret key. IEEE ICCIT (2011)

Prediction of Environmental Changes in Dumpyard Sites: A Case Study of Pallikaranai Dumpyard, Chennai, Tamilnadu

T. Sree Sharmila and R. Swathika[✉]

Department of Information Technology, SSN College of Engineering,
Kalavakkam, Chennai 603110, India
{sreesharmilat,swathikar}@ssn.edu.in

Abstract. The rapid growth in population has led to the increase in the amount of solid waste disposed at dump yards. Every year, several tons of solid waste is being deposited into the Pallikaranai marshland, Chennai, India impacting the environment ominously and causing serious health issues. Using time series satellite images and gas sensors, the environmental changes over the years are determined and environmental changes in the near future are predicted. Satellite images of the area under study are obtained chronologically from CNES/Astrium and DigitalGlobe. The approximate area of the dump yard in each image is calculated by using Google Maps API. The variation in the area occupied by the dumpyard over the years is determined by using change detection technique. Gas sensors are used to measure the levels of various harmful gases such as methane compounds, Carbon Monoxide and Carbon Dioxide. Air Quality at the dump yard and a couple of locations near the dump yard also determined. Based on the results, the possible environmental changes in the near future are predicted.

Keywords: Dump yard · Time series satellite images · Prediction · Gas sensors · Air quality

1 Introduction

The proper disposal and handling of solid waste have always been and continue to be one of the major environmental concerns in mega cities such as Chennai. Commercial, residential, infrastructural and industrial development are necessary for the progress of the nation and in pursuit of development in the above fields combined with an ever growing population, deterioration and damage to the environment is seen as mere collateral damage necessary for development. The collection of numerous satellite images from the past and present make it possible to analyse the impact on the environment caused by human activities.

Since 1972, the population of Chennai and its suburbs has doubled. From 4,500,000 in 1972, the population is now about to leap the 10,000,000 mark and grow further, making Chennai a "Mega City", an elite category of cities with a population over 10

© Springer Nature Singapore Pte Ltd. 2016
A. Unal et al. (Eds.): SmartCom 2016, CCIS 628, pp. 674–682, 2016.
DOI: 10.1007/978-981-10-3433-6_81

million. With growth in population comes exponential growth in solid waste, further enlarging the burden on Chennai's largest dumpyard, the Pallikaranai Marshland/ Perungudi Dumpyard. Up until 1980, the Pallikaranai marshland occupied a ginormous area of 14,000 acres, consuming today's residential localities such as Velachery, Thoraipakkam, Perungudi and Pallikaranai itself. But, following years of waste disposal at the marshland, infrastructure projects, industrial and residential development, the dump yard expanded rapidly, reducing the marshland to a mere 1470 acres today. This Marshland is home to around 337 species of flora and fauna, many of which are endangered. The dumping of solid waste has a potential to pollute our environment through the air, land, and water at local and global levels to a greater extent and hence leads to a serious public health problem. The pollution caused by the relentless disposal of wastes in the marsh is destroying several endangered aquatic and estuarine species every year. In addition to the damage caused to flora and fauna, the dump yard pollution also causes several health issues to people living near the dump yard and to people travelling through. Hence proper disposal of solid waste, hazardous materials, and toxic emissions must be implemented to protect this valuable treasure and to protect the environment. In remote sensing applications, change-detection is the process of identifying the changes of specific features by analysing a pair of images acquired in the same geographical area at different times. It provides the spatial distribution of features and qualitative and quantitative information of features changes [1, 2].

This paper aims at studying the land use of dump yard site at Pallikaranai marshland, Chennai with a view to detecting the land consumption rate and the changes that have taken place so as to predict possible changes that might take place in the next few years using time series satellite images. Also, this work aims to predict air quality to see how pollutants are being dispersed through air to nearby localities.

2 Related Work

The Earth surface is being significantly altered in some manner and man's presence on the earth and his use of the land had a profound effect on the natural environment thus resulting in an observable pattern in the land use/land cover over time [3]. Through the ISCST3 model [4], the maximum concentration of the target pollutant in the air at the sensitive point could be obtained, and then the human health risk at the maximum concentration level of the target pollutant could be calculated by the health risk assessment model [5]. Toxic Persistent Organic Pollutants (POPs) and heavy metals are produced along with the emission of Green House Gases (GHGs) during incineration and open burning of Electronic-waste (E-waste) disposal. They modify the DNA and cause genetic defects to future generations [6]. Rapid urbanisation led to seasonal inundation of many of the habitation in the area and increased the population pressure in a small settlement area. In addition, the sitting of the Perungudi solid waste dump site in Pallikaranai marsh caused further degradation of water quality and implicated on public health [7].

A disposal site for urban trash, also called landfill, is a major environmental problem present worldwide on account of the health hazards they pose. An analysis of the air sample collected in dump yards area reveals 40–60% of methane & Carbon-di-oxide [9].

Landfill waste disposal adversely impacts the environment through the release of air pollutants and greenhouse gases to the atmosphere, and through the generation of leachate that may contaminate water sources [8].

Landfill gas is potentially hazardous as its major content is methane which affects the respiratory tract on inhalation. Hence, continuous monitoring and assessment of landfill gases become essential. Regulations insisting the close of Perungudi and Kodungaiyur dump yards have also necessitated the need for monitoring and analysing the air pollutants present in areas near the dump yard. The study of the dump yards has become important owing to the twin problems of health and safety.

3   Proposed Work

Our work involves collecting the satellite images of the study area, area calculation, applying change detection techniques for analysis, measurement of pollutant gas levels at various locations around the dump yard and estimating the impacts. The workflow is shown in Fig. 1.

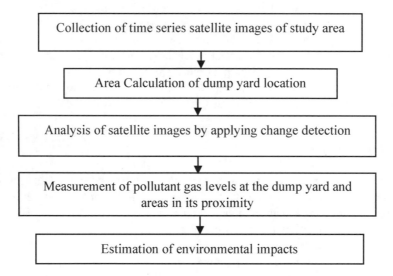

Fig. 1. Work flow

3.1   Study Area

The Pallikaranai marshland is situated adjacent to the Bay of Bengal, about 20 km south of the city centre, and has a geographical area of 80 km^2. This marshland is the only surviving wetland ecosystem of the city and is among the few and last remaining natural wetlands of South India. The Latitude and Longitude of the study area is given in Table 1.

Table 1. Area calculation

Date of image	Length (km)	Latitude & Longitude	Width (k)	Latitude & Longitude	Area (sqkms)	Perimeter (kms)
04/01/2016	0.91	Top:12^57'32.12"N 80^13'27.43"E Bottom:12^57'02.93"N 80^13'23.72"E	1.32	Left:12^57'20.51"N 80^13'10.96"E right:12^57'14.80"N80^13'53.84"E	0.77	5.14
24/08/2015	0.91	Top:12^57'32.12"N 80^13'27.43"E Bottom:12^57'02.93"N 80^13'23.72"E	1.32	Left:12^57'20.51"N 80^13'10.96"E Right:12^57'14.80"N 80^13'53.84"E	0.73	5.69
09/09/2014	0.77	Top:12^57'28.23"N 80^13'28.53"E Bottom:12^57'03.51"N 80^13'24.27"E	1.25	Left:12^57'19.04"N 80^13'14.05"E Right:12^57'14.86"N 80^13'55.26"E	0.70	5.50
12/04/2013	0.75	Top:12^57'29.93"N 80^13'25.94"E Bottom:12^57'05.39"N 80^13'27.15"E	1.16	Left:12^57'16.54"N 80^13'15.37"E Right:12^57'14.98"N 80^13'53.64"E	0.64	5.34
19/03/2012	0.75	Top:12^57'29.89"N 80^13'25.98"E Bottom:12^57'05.48"N 80^13'27.10"E	1.10	Left:12^57'17.25"N 80^13'15.00"E Right:12^57'14.88"N 80^13'51.53"E	0.62	5.61
4/05/2008	0.66	Top:12^57'28.20"N 80^13'19.01"E Bottom:12^57'07.06"N 80^13'22.98"E	1.07	Left:12^57'18.54"N80^13'06.10"E Right:12^57'14.30"N 80^13'41.35"E	0.60	5.48
27/08/2004	0.60	Top:12^57'27.93"N 80^13'24.56"E Bottom:12^57'08.54"N 80^13'24.58"E	1.07	Left:12^57'19.70"N 80^13'9.36"E Right:12^57'14.13"N 80^13'44.45"E	0.59	5.40
31/08/2001	0.43	Top:12^57'22.30"N 80^13'26.20"E Bottom:12^57'08.09"N 80^13'25.90"E	0.86	Left:12^57'20.61"N 80^13'09.96"E Right:12^57'14.13"N 80^13'37.86"E	0.56	5.32

3.2   Calculation of Dump Yard Area

The approximate area of the dump yard in each image is calculated by employing the polygon area calculation method of Google Maps API. By calculating the area, the amount by which the dumpyard has expanded annually is determined as follows:

```
Function CalculateArea
Input: Map points p1, p2
Output: area
begin
   p1 = coordinates[i];
   p2 = coordinates[i + 1];
   area+=(p2.Longitude-p1.Longitude)*(2+
   Math.Sin(ConvertToRadian(p1.Latitude))+Math.Sin
   (ConvertToRadian(p2.Latitude)));

end
```

$$(1)$$

3.3   Change Measurement

The difference in area occupied by the dump yard in the various time series satellite images is calculated using change detection method [3]. By converting the value of a pixel in terms of how much it translates to in the real world, the area calculations performed previously with Google Maps API can be verified. The below formula is used to calculate the pixel difference between the images.

$$\text{Image difference} = \frac{\sum \text{nonzeros}(X1 - X2)}{\text{Number of nonzeros samples}} \qquad (2)$$

Where X1, X2 are temporal images.

3.4   Measurement of Pollutant Gas Levels

The MQ4 methane gas sensor is used to measure the amount of methane and its compounds. The MQ7 gas sensor is used to measure the amount of CO (carbon monoxide). The MQ135 Air Quality sensor is highly sensitive to the presence of Benzene, Smoke (CO_2), Alcohol and Ammonia. Using these sensors, air quality is measured at the dump yard and areas in its proximity.

3.5   Prediction of Environmental Changes

From the data obtained from the satellite images, the amount by which the dumpyard expands annually, on an average is determined. With the help of this value, we can predict the amount by which the dumpyard will expand in the near future, assuming that no preventive measures/conservative efforts are applied.

4 Experiments and Results

The proposed system uses Arduino Uno R3 for data collection from sensors, MQ4, MQ7 and MQ135 gas sensors for detecting air pollutants. The satellite images for the area under study, it being the Pallikaranai dump yard are obtained chronologically for the years 2001, 2004, 2008, 2012, 2013, 2014, 2015 and 2016 from the satellites DigitalGlobe and CNS Astrium operated by NASA. The Fig. 2 shows the images obtained for the study area for the various years.

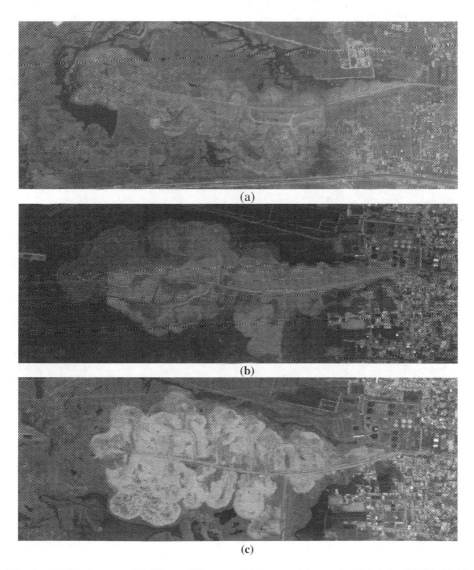

(a)

(b)

(c)

Fig. 2. Satellite images of Pallikaranai/Perungudi Dumpyard (year wise) (a) 4 April 2001 (b) 12 April 2013 (c) 24 August 2015

The area value of the dumpyard in each satellite image is calculated using the polygon area calculation method of Google Maps API described in the algorithm (1). This method takes Latitude and Longitude coordinates of the points on the polygon as input and performs the calculations described in the function definition specified above. Table 1 describes the parameters of area calculation.

The difference in the area occupied by the dump yard in the various time series satellite images is calculated. Table 2 shows the change measurement values (yearwise). The variation in the area of dump yard for the period 2001 to 2016 is shown in graph (Fig. 3). Clearly, the area of the dump yard has gradually increased over the years as evidenced by the graph. Using these values, it is discerned that the difference between the area of the dumpyard in 2016 (0.77 sq km) and the area in 2001 (0.56 sq km) is 0.21 sq km. When this is converted to acres is 51.89 acres. Hence on average, the dump yard has expanded by 3.7 acres over 14 years. Each image is compared with all other images (i.e. 2016 is compared with 2015, 2014, 2013, 2012, etc.) and the difference between the images in terms of pixels is calculated. The pixel difference between 2016 and 2001 is 34. The area of the entire region in view is calculated using the ComputePolygonArea(). This value is divided by the total amount of pixels in view which is 1280*720. Thus the value of one pixel is calculated as 1.6 acres. Therefore, the difference between the satellite images in 2001 and 2016 translates to 54.4 acres which are approximately equivalent to the difference in area calculated using Google API.

Table 2. Change measurement

Year (pel)	2016	2015	2014	2013	2012	2008	2004	2001
2016	–	25.10	22.77	46.40	33.35	51.80	28.40	31.68
2015	30.61	–	25.94	47.90	34.20	50.40	33.80	38.63
2014	41.95	35.00	–	64.17	38.18	56.37	36.31	40.66
2013	30.22	23.46	25.94	–	16.40	31.36	24.90	22.28
2012	39.27	31.66	23.70	40.13	–	45.43	31.20	34.20
2008	45.29	42.81	30.92	55.47	37.15	–	23.64	32.07
2004	36.60	34.12	23.29	48.54	31.40	43.32	–	23.03
2001	34.94	32.67	21.23	45.15	30.60	46.94	20.29	–

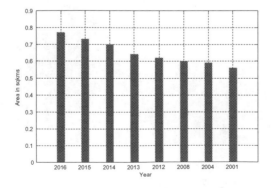

Fig. 3. Changes in area of the dumpyard

The composition of air pollutants is measured at three locations: at dumpyard, Thoraipakkam tollgate, Velachery. Table 3 shows the measured composition of air pollutants. Using MQ-4 gas sensor, the composition of methane measured at the dumpyard was 1023 ppm. This value was found to be above the threshold limit for methane (1000 ppm) as prescribed by the National institute for Occupational safety and Health (NIOSH). The value measured at Velachery, 358 ppm was found to be below the threshold limit for methane (1000 ppm) as prescribed by the NIOSH as it was further away from the dumpyard. Methane is considered an asphyxiant at extremely high concentrations and can displace oxygen in the blood.

Table 3. Composition of air pollutants

Gas sensor	Air pollutants	Composition of gas levels at the dump yard and areas in its proximity (measured in ppm)		
		At dumpyard	At thoraipakkam toll	At velachery
MQ-4	Methane (CH_4)	1023	1023	358
MQ-7	Carbon monoxide (CO)	440	393	411
MQ-135	Carbon dioxide (CO_2)	1023	567	158

Using MQ-7 sensor, the value measured, 440 ppm was found to be above the threshold limit for Carbon Monoxide (400 ppm) as prescribed by the NIOSH. This causes harmful effects include Headache and Nausea. The MQ135 gas sensor is highly sensitive to the presence of Benzene, Smoke (CO_2), Alcohol and Ammonia (NH_3). This Air quality sensor detects the presence of gases such as carbon di oxide and Ammonia. According to a recent survey conducted at the marshlands, the CO_2 values range from 500–600 ppm. This indicates the presence of a large amount of gases such as benzene and ammonia. CO_2 being a greenhouse gas could potentially have an impact on local climate. The average value of CO_2 at any particular point in the world is 400 ppm according to a survey conducted by UNESCO. The value measured at toll is 567 ppm, indicates that the amount of ammonia and benzene is lesser than at the dumpyard. The side effects of Ammonia gas exposure may damage the respiratory tract, decreased metabolic function and decreased oxygenation of tissues. People who are exposed to benzene for several hours could experience the following symptoms : drowsiness, dizziness and headaches. The NIOSH has prescribed 2.5 ppm as the threshold for benzene exposure.

According to the data, we have obtained, the dumpyard expands by 3.5 acres on an average annually between the October of 2001 and January of 2016 and by an even alarming rate of 9.2 acres since 2012. In simpler terms, 3.5 acres is larger than the size of 3 football grounds put together. If expansion continues at this alarming rate, most parts of what remains of the Pallikaranai marshland (roughly 1470 acres) would be consumed by the dumpyard before the end of the 21st Century. At this rate, another 50 acres of the marsh could be consumed by the dumpyard in the next 5 years. Based on the above analysis and the composition of gases measured, it is absolutely essential that the following preventive measures have to be taken to preserve the environment and protect the people : reduce/stop garbage disposal completely, impose material use restrictions, implement the Municipal Solid Waste Act, careful with the cures, Composting and reducing waste.

5 Conclusion

In this paper, time series satellite images were used to detect changes in the area at the Pallikaranai dumpyard over the past 15 years. The area was determined more accurately in terms of pixels and the area calculations. The amount by which the dumpyard would grow in the near future was predicted. The composition of harmful gases at the dumpyard was measured and their impact on the environment was determined. The Pallikaranai Marshland is a very diverse ecosystem providing asylum to numerous endangered species and must be protected at all costs. The suggested measures must be implemented to protect the people and the environment in the areas surrounding the dumpyard.

References

1. Coppin, P., Jonckheere, I., Nackaerts, K., Muys, B., Lambin, E.: Review article digital change detection methods in ecosystem monitoring: a review. Int. J. Remote Sens. **25**, 1565–1596 (2004)
2. Im, J., Jensen, J.R.: A change detection model based on neighbourhood correlation image analysis and decision tree classification. Remote Sens. Environ. **99**, 326–340 (2005)
3. Saidu, Y.M., Abdulrazaq, S., Hassan, S.A., Abubakar, A.B.: The dynamics of land use land cover change: using geospatial techniques to promote sustainable urban development in ilorin metropolis, Nigeria suleiman. Asian Rev. Environ. Earth Sci. **1**(1), 8–15 (2014). ISSN: 2313-8173
4. Zhi-Guo, W., Huai-Zhong, Y., Li, T.-Y., Wang, E.Y.: Spatial distribution simulation of vehicle exhaust pollution using ISCST3 dispersion model in Jinan. Res. Environ. Sci. **13**, 26–33 (2000)
5. Ji, W.-J., Wang, Q., Huang, Q.-F., Huang, Z.-C.: Health risk assessment of atmospheric environment in hazardous wastes landfill disposal. In: 4th International Conference on Bioinformatics and Biomedical Engineering (iCBBE). IEEE (2010)
6. Devika, S.: Environmental Impact of Improper Disposal of Electronic Waste. IEEE (2010)
7. Vaidhyanathan, L., Gowri, V.: Sanitation quality index and its relation with diarrheal prevalence in Pallikaranai, Southern Chennai, India. In: Global Humanitarian Technology Conference (GHTC), vol. 9, pp. 372–375. IEEE (2013)
8. Lai, K., Li, L., Mutti, S., Staring, R., Taylor, M., Umali, J., Pagsuyoin, S.: Evaluation of Waste Reduction and Diversion as Alternatives to Landfill Disposal. IEEE (2014)
9. Cynthia Sheba J., Dawn, S S.: A study on the importance of greenhouse gas emissions from Dumpyards/Landfills. Nat. J. Chembiosis, **4**(2) (2013)
10. https://en.wikipedia.org/wiki/Pallikaranai_wetland

Testing Resource Allocation for Fault Detection Process

Md. Nasar$^{(\boxtimes)}$ and Prashant Johri

School of Computing Science and Engineering, Galgotias University,
Greater Noida, India
nasar31786@gmail.com, johri.prashant@gmail.com

Abstract. Developing quality software is one of the most challenging tasks, for developing quality software we have to remove the entire bug from software before the software switch into operational phase. For this we have to allocate our testing and debugging resource based on the time so that we can finish off our work. For distributing the testing and debugging resource we are using software reliability growth model (SRGMs). Numerous SRGMs has been developed in past couple of decade for allocating the testing and debugging resource but mostly under static condition. In this article we developed a mathematical model for allocating the resource in dynamic environment. In this article we utilized Pontryagin maximum principle for illuminating the model. Finally one numerical illustration is explained for distributing the software testing resource for created module. Here Genetic Algorithm (GA) is used for allocating resource optimally.

Keywords: Software testing resource allocation · Software Reliability Growth Model (SRGMs) · Genetic algorithm

1 Introduction

Now a day's almost every field is getting computerized. Lot of complicated work is controlled by the software systems. In Software Reliability Engineering (SRE), Software reliability growth models (SRGMs) are the very good tools basically developed for estimating the software product reliability throughout testing and operational stage. For developing software which is reliable is one of the complex tasks faced by the software organizations. Thus for developing reliable software it would be time consuming and complex task. It is very difficult to identify whether or not the software is going to deliver is reliable. After delivery of the software its reliability is measured by client's comment and error report, but it is too late to measure because clients want the software's reliability before the delivery. Hence the company needs to maximize the detection of fault and fixing fault during software testing and debugging. For the period of software testing and debugging resources are consumed. The fault identification and deletion phase depends on the amount of resource spent and nature of software.

Lot of models (SRGMs) has been anticipated in previous ten years to minimize the entirety testing effort expenditure. Majority of the mathematical models have been produced based on the assumptions that the association between the total software

© Springer Nature Singapore Pte Ltd. 2016
A. Unal et al. (Eds.): SmartCom 2016, CCIS 628, pp. 683–690, 2016.
DOI: 10.1007/978-981-10-3433-6_82

testing effort expenditure and time of the testing follows Rayleigh and Exponential distribution [1–5]. In general, exponential curve will use if the resources of testing are consistently used as far the software testing time. From past few decade lots of models (SRGMs) have been developed however dominant part of models are produced in static condition. However in this paper our main goal is to analyze an optimal allocation of resource to optimize the testing and debugging for S-shaped model of fault detection model throughout the testing stage under dynamic condition.

This article is isolated into the accompanying areas. Segment second clarified the related work of this exploration, third depict the model advancement. In area fourth we portray cost enhancement displaying, in segment fifth we examines arrangement system, segment sixth a numerical illustration for disseminating testing exertion. In segment seventh, we finish up our paper with an exchange on discoveries and results.

2   Review of Related Work

Basically we have two types of fault detection model one is exponential and another is S-shaped. In exponential model when the fault is detected that time only fault is going to remove but in S-shaped models, models depend on the assumption that the early testing is not as productive as testing advancement, so there must be a time gap throughout which the fault detection rate increases. With the fast development in Information Technology all simple and confounded sort of works are controlled by the product. So complexity and size of the product is going high. Amid the testing stage, every one of the exercises of testing for diverse modules is competing for the limited accessible testing asset. In this way, a genuine trouble is the way to disseminate the aggregate existing testing-asset among accessible modules. Number of research is done in allocating the testing effort; few have also been incorporated in some SRGMs [1, 4, 7–12]. [7] Proposed that the software system must be developed as well as tested in separate steps sequentially. [13] Suggested that in software development, testing and debugging can be viewed as concurrent activities. [14] Examine a software development in which module will integrate when the total number of faults in the software system achieved a specified condition. [15] Analyzed the resource distribution difficulty to maximize the given number of removed faults in the software modules with reliability and budgetary constraint. [12] Author utilized dynamic programming way to deal with optimization problem in testing assets distributing in software, that software product having modular structure. [16] Explained about an optimization issue for distributing the existing software testing resource among the modules. [17] Given an ideal resource allotment plan to minimize the software expense amid the testing and operational stage under dynamic condition. Author utilized Genetic Algorithm (GA) method for ideal resource allocation.

Notations Used.

T: The time period for testing of application.
w: Consumed total resources throughout the Life Cycle of Software Development at any given time 't'.

$w_1(t)$:   Consumed total resources throughout the Life cycle of Software development for testing at any given time 't'.

$w_2(t)$:   Consumed total resources throughout the Life Cycle of Software Development to fix faults at any given time 't'.

$r(t)$:   Total number of fault removed till time 't'.

c_2:   Expense of software testing per unit testing effort.

'a':   preliminary total amount of faults available in the software.

'b':   Exposure rate at which residual faults cause failure.

'c':   Detection speed at which extra errors are recognized without Their creating any failure.

3   Model Development

We start our investigation by stating a general model with only some assumptions. We are concentrating our investigation of an organization that wants to manage its resources for software testing and debugging within a given time span.

As discussed, there exist number of successful S-shaped models in the software reliability literature but we are mainly concern here with the [18] due to its simplicity and capability to study the failure growth rate of software. The detail discussion on [18] is as follows:

The mathematical model is developed in view of the subsequent assumptions:

- It has been observed that during testing, the team can remove several faults in the software, without causing any failure; even though it will take some extra effort.
- Error, which is detached resulting to a failure, is identified as a leading error.

The software fault deletion amount per unit time can be given below as:

$$\frac{dr(t)}{dt} = b[a - r(t)] + c\left(\frac{r(t)}{a}\right)[a - r(t)] \tag{1}$$

Taking initial condition; at $t = 0$, $r(t) = 0$:

$$r(t) = a\left[\frac{1 - e^{-(b+c)t}}{1 + \left(\frac{c}{b}\right)e^{-(b+c)t}}\right] \tag{2}$$

During fault detection modeling we assume that that later testing is more effective then early testing, and the total number of faults identified will keep on increasing with time till it attains a maximum peak before it starts decreasing. [18] Proposed that detection of a fault during testing can detect some additional fault. Consistent with the idea of [18], we propose the differential equation for fault detection as:

$$x(t) = \frac{d}{dt}r(t) = w_1(t)\left[b(a - r(t)) + c\frac{r(t)}{a}(a - r(t))\right]; m(0) = 0 \tag{3}$$

4 Proposed Cost Optimization Model

Thus, the entire expenditure at some given point of time 't' throughout the software testing stage of Software development life cycle (SDLC) is consisting of:

- Software testing cost $c_2 w_1(t)$ and
- Software debugging cost $c_1(t)x(t)$

Now suppose the organization wants to minimize the total expenses during testing phase over the restricted time span T. Then the objective function for the organization for optimally allocating the resource is:

$$\min \int_0^T [c_1(t)x(t) + c_2 w_1(t)]$$

subject to

$$x(t) = \frac{dr(t)}{dt} = w_1(t)(a - r(t))\left(b + c\frac{r(t)}{a}\right) \tag{4}$$

where,

$$r(0) = 0 \quad and \quad w_1(t) + w_2(t) = w$$
$$(w_1(t); w_2(t)) \geq 0 \quad and \quad c_1(t) = c_1(r(t), w_2(t))$$

5 Solution Procedure

For solving the above optimization problem given by Eq. (4), we used the Pontryagin's maximum principle. Hamiltonian function is used for the dynamic environment given by the below Eq. (4) as:

$$H(r(t), \lambda(t), w_1(t), t) = -[c_1(t)x(t) + c_2 w_1(t)] + \lambda(t)x(t) \tag{5}$$

The necessary conditions for w_1^* to be an optimal control is:

(i) $H(r^*, w_1^*, \lambda, t) \geq H(r^*, w_1, \lambda, t)$

(ii)   All boundary conditions must be fulfilled. $\tag{6}$

The optimal control $w_1^*(t)$ will be given by the below essential condition

$$w_1^*(t) = \max_{w_1(t) \in \Omega} H(r^*(t), w_1(t), \lambda(t)) \tag{7}$$

Where, $\lambda(t)$ is the adjoint variable (shadow cost of $x(t)$). The adjoint variable satisfies the below differential equation.

$$\frac{d}{dt}\lambda(t) = \dot{\lambda}(t) = -\frac{\partial H}{\partial m} \tag{8}$$

The transversality condition for this case is:

$$\lambda(T) = 0 \tag{9}$$

We can infer $\lambda(t)$ as the minimal estimation of defect at time 't', the physical explanation of the Hamiltonian H can be given as follows: $\lambda(t)$ means the future expenditure incurred as one extra defect occurs in the software system (at time t). In short, H represents the instantaneous total cost of the firm at any point of time t.

The essential condition holds for an optimal solution as follows:

$$\frac{\partial H}{\partial w_1} = 0 \Rightarrow -(c_1(t) - \lambda(t))x_{w_1} - c_{1w_1}x(t) - c_2 = 0 \tag{10}$$

Solving Eq. (10), we have

$$\Rightarrow w_1^*(t) = \left(\frac{\lambda(t) - c_1(t)}{c_{1w_1(t)}}\right) - \left[\frac{c_2}{c_{1w_1(t)}(a - r(t))\left(b + c\frac{r(t)}{a}\right)}\right] \tag{11}$$

and

$$w_2^*(t) = w + \left[\frac{c_2}{c_{1w_1(t)}(a - r(t))\left(b + c\frac{r(t)}{a}\right)}\right] - \left(\frac{\lambda(t) - c_1(t)}{c_{1w_1(t)}}\right) \tag{12}$$

Now differentiating Eq. (10) with respect to 't', we can have

$$\dot{w}_1(t) = \frac{\dot{\lambda}x_{w_1} - x(xc_{1w_1m} + x_mc_{1w_1} + c_{1m}x_{w_1} + (c_1 - \lambda)x_{w_1m})}{(xc_{1w_1w_1} + 2c_{1w_1}x_{w_1} + (c_1 - \lambda)x_{w_1w_1})} \tag{13}$$

In this section we have assume that the aggregate expense per unit for collective fault removed at time 't' is constant.

i.e. $c_1(t) = c_1$ For constant error deletion function, the cost optimal control problem in below Eq. (4) as

$$\min \int_0^T [c_1 x(t) + c_2 w_1(t)] dt$$

subject to

$$x(t) = \frac{dm(t)}{dt} = x(m(t), w_1(t)) \tag{14}$$

where

$$m(0) = 0 \quad and \quad 0 < w_1(t) \le w$$

The above issue will be simplifying by Genetic Algorithm (GA). GA is an incredible optimization algorithm for determining complex sort of issues which is impractical to unravel by general techniques [6, 19]. There are five phase in genetic algorithm, Initial Population, Fitness Function, Selection, Crossover and Mutation.

Initial Population: it begins with randomly generated states. In my problem the initial population is generated from given total effort W.

Fitness/objective Function: The fitness or objective function produce the next generation of states. A good fitness function should return better state. The probability of being chosen for reproduction is based on your fitness score.

Selection: two pairs of chromosome are selected at random to reproduce they are selected based on their fitness function score.

Crossover: For each pair will be mate, a point of crossover is chosen at random from within the bit string. Offspring are generated by exchanges between the parents at the crossover point.

Mutation: mutation is a genetic operator and basically used to alter one or more gene value from the offspring produced by the crossover operator. We are using mutation for finding the good solution.

In Genetic Algorithm we set all the parameters. We used Eq. 4 for simulating this problem. Below parameters are used for allocating the resource. We used MATLAB and C++ for running the simulation.

Parameter	Value
Population size	20
Number of generations	85
Selection mode	Tournament
Crossover probability	0.9
Mutation probability	0.2

6 Numerical Problem

This section describes the results of the optimal policies for the proposed model. The main goal of this investigation is to get the result of number of fault removed based on time with different- different effort. The base values are as follows for allocating the resource based on time (Fig. 1):

$$a = 100 \quad b = 0.03 \quad c = 0.7 \quad w_1(0) = 0.6 \quad \lambda(0) = 40$$
$$x(0) = 2 \quad c_0 = 1000 \quad c_2 = 5000 \quad w = 1$$

After running the simulation we got the allocation of resource. In this experiment we used different value for effort for allocating the resource.

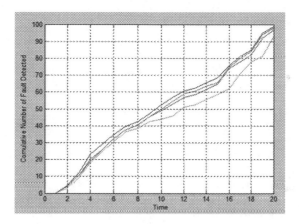

Fig. 1. Optimal allocation of resource vs. time

7 Conclusion

This paper addresses an alternate foundation for allocating the testing resource optimally. Here author used [18] model for developing the model for fault detection process. During this study we have allocated the defined testing resource for a given time frame. In this experiment we changed the effort value for seeing the behavior of the model. If we compare our result with any static model result in static model fault detection rate will be in increasing but in dynamic case some time it will increase or some time it will decrease. Because for identification of the fault it will not take constant effort. It means the tester or manager will allocated the resource to the specified personnel and work will finish on time. Pontryagin's Maximum principle is used for simplifying the mathematical model and Genetic Algorithm is used for allocating the resource optimally. For optimization purpose MATLAB and C++ is used.

References

1. Putnam, L.: A general empirical solution to the macro software sizing and estimating problem. IEEE Trans. Softw. Eng. SE **4**, 345–361 (1978)
2. Basili, V.R., Zelkowitz, M.V.: Analyzing medium scale software development. In: Proceedings of the 3rd International Conference on Software Engineering, pp. 116–123 (1979)
3. Kapur, P.K., Garg, R.B., Kumar, S.: Contributions to Hardware and Software Reliability. World Scientific, Singapore (1999)
4. Huang, C.-Y., Kuo, S.-Y., Chen, J.Y.: Analysis of a software reliability growth model with logistic testing effort function. In: Proceeding of 8th International Symposium on Software Reliability Engineering, pp. 378–388 (1997)
5. Yamada, S., Hishitani, J., Osaki, S.: Software reliability growth model with weibull testing effort: a model and application. IEEE Trans. Reliab. R **42**, 100–105 (1983)
6. Holland, J.H.: Adaptation in Natural and Artificial Systems. University of Michigan Press, Ann Arbor (1975)
7. Myers, G.J.: Software Reliability: Principles and Practices. Wiley, New York (1976)
8. Ichimori, T., Yamada, S., Nishiwaki, M.: Optimal allocation policies for testing-resource based on a software reliability growth model. In: Proceedings of the Australia–Japan Workshop on Stochastic Models in Engineering, Technology and Management, pp. 182–189 (1993)
9. Kapur, P.K., Bardhan, A.K.: Testing effort control through software reliability growth modelling. Int. J. Model. Simul. **22**, 90–96 (2002)
10. Kapur, P.K., Younes, S., Agarwal, S.: Generalized Erlange software reliability growth model. ASOR Bull. **14**, 5–11 (1995)
11. Kapur, P.K., Gupta, A., Shatnawi, O., Shatnawi, O.: Testing effort control using flexible software reliability growth model with change point. Int. J. Perform. Eng. **2**(3), 245–262 (2006)
12. Kapur, P.K., Bardhan, A.K., Yadavalli, V.S.S.: On allocation of resources during testing phase of a modular software. Int. J. Syst. Sci. **38**(6), 493–499 (2007)
13. Blackburn, J.D., Scudder, G.D., Van Wassenhove, L.N.: Concurrent software development. Comm. ACM. **43**(11), 200–214 (2000)
14. Chiang, I.R., Mookerjee, V.S.: A fault threshold policy to manage software development projects. Inform. Systems Res **15**(1), 3–19 (2004)
15. Yamada, S.: Optimal allocation policies for testing-resource based on a software reliability growth model. Math. Comput. Model. **22**(10–12), 295–301 (1995)
16. Kapur, P.K., Aggarwal, A.G., Kaur, G.: Optimal testing resource allocation for modular software considering cost, testing effort and reliability using genetic algorithm. Int. J. Reliab. Qual. Saf. Eng. **16**(6), 495–508 (2010)
17. Nasar, Md., Johri, P., Chanda, U.: Dynamic effort allocation problem using genetic algorithm approach. IJMECS **6**(6), 46–52 (2014)
18. Kapur, P.K., Garg, R.B.: A software reliability growth model for an error removal phenomenon. Softw. Eng. J. **7**, 291–294 (1992)
19. Goldberg, D.E.: Genetic Algorithms: in Search Optimization and Machines Learning. Addison-Wesley, New York (1989)

An Overview of Big Data Opportunity and Challenges

Pooja Pant[1] and Rajneesh Tanwar[2(✉)]

[1] Department of Computer Science, Amity University,
Noida, Uttar Pradesh, India
ashima81k@gmail.com
[2] Department of Information Technology, Amity University,
Noida, Uttar Pradesh, India
rajneeshtanwar15@gmail.com

Abstract. This decade has seen massive explosion of information and data, voluminous data bring about many challenges – data storage, data analysis, noise accumulation, data privacy, security and heterogeneity of data. With the emergence of this voluminous data also known as Big data, an explosion of data have been seen in all fields related to science and engineering. In current scenario this term often applies to data sets with extreme size (Exabyte's). In this article we present an overview of the need of big data, its applications and challenges.

Keywords: Big data · Big data opportunity · Big data applications · Big data challenges

1 Introduction

Evolution of voluminous data from major industries has been termed as big data. In 2001, Doug Laney defined the three V's of big data that are volume (billions of rows and columns), variety (existence of semi structured and unstructured data) and velocity (speed creation of new data). According to [1] these three characteristics should coexist to confirm that the source data is big data. But since then many authors have put forward new definition and characteristics of big data.

This paper presents various opportunity, applications and challenges in big data application.

2 Big Characteristics

In 2001 big data was mainly defined by its 3v's characterized. The 3V's included volume, velocity and variety. In 2013 Mark van Rijmenam proposed four more V's in order to get a better understanding of big data. Each of the Big Data characteristics consists of the data can be described with the following features. Big Data consists of the following V's attributes as shown in Fig. 1 which includes:

© Springer Nature Singapore Pte Ltd. 2016
A. Unal et al. (Eds.): SmartCom 2016, CCIS 628, pp. 691–697, 2016.
DOI: 10.1007/978-981-10-3433-6_83

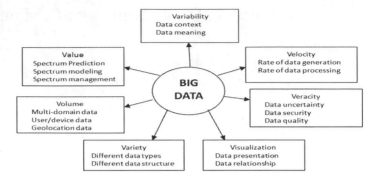

Fig. 1. 7V's of Big Data

A. Variety: the data stored and analyzed goes beyond structured data about 90% data is unstructured data. Today there are many types of data structured, semi structured, quasi structured and unstructured data, each of which require a different technique for analysis.

B. Velocity: it defines the rate at which data is generated, stored and analyzed. The rate at which in created is unmanageable. Every minute Twitter user sends about 277k tweets, Facebook processes 350 GB data and Google processed around 2 million queries.

C. Volume: it is the amount of data which determines whether the quality of data is enough to be called big data. big data doesn't refer to a specific quantity but any data which is in Terabytes or Exabyte is considered big data. More than 90 TB of data is generated or uploaded on facebook every day. More than 80% of data has been created over the past 2 years. It has been calculated that by 2020 the total data will be fifty times the total data in 2014.

D. Veracity: concerns with the uncertainty of with huge amount of data being processed with high speed of no use if the data stored was incorrect. The accuracy of the result or the analysis depends upon the accuracy and correctness of the stored data.

E. Value: the potential value of all the data is huge in every sector: organizations, societies and consumers. But data in itself is not valuable at all. The data is nothing if it's not turned into information and then knowledge. The value is how the different major sectors use their data to make itself information driven is totally based on how the sectors during the data analysis gives a proper insight for decision making.

F. Visualization: with numerous relationship and dependencies among hundreds of attributes the presentation of data becomes crucial. Visualization defines the representation of the finding in a way that it is readable and understandable.

G. Variability: in voluminous data the real meanings and interpretations of raw data depends on its context. In social media a word can mean different things. Words do not have a static meaning and vary by context. A word on its own cannot be considered as a signifier of a sentiment. In order to make use of data understand their real meaning organizations are building sophisticated programs which tries to capture the real meaning and context of the data.

Over the last decade there have been some researchers who added a few characteristics: complexity it becomes analyzes the complicated relationships among various variables, validation the scope of the fulfillment of the purpose, immutability the permanent nature of data and verification analysis complies with some specification.

3 Difference Between Small Data and Big Data

Small data is the information businesses collect directly from customers in a particular with a number of limitations small data paved a way for big data. The some difference between big data and small data are shown in Table 1.

Table 1. Difference between small data & big data

Characteristics	Small data	Big data
Data source	Traditional enterprise data	Data generated from outside of the enterprise from nontraditional data source
Data size	Gigabytes to terabytes	Terabytes to exabyte's
Data processing	Centralized	Distributed
Velocity	Near real time	Often real time
Variety	Structured Unstructured	Semi structure Unstructured Structured Quasi structured
Operation	Provides information of daily base event	Integrated with operational Processing
Value	Business intelligence, analysis and reporting	Complex, predictive advance business analysis
Access	Manual or Batch oriented analytics	Presents real time data.
Nature	Doesn't require immediate response	Requires immediate response

4 Big Data Opportunities

Today voluminous is generated in every major field and domain. The analysis of big data brings valuable insight. Researchers from every field have outlined the opportunities of big data. In this section we summarize the availability, benefits and opportunity of big data in various sectors: banking, health care, education and trading [2]. Table 2 shows the availability of data in these sectors.

Table 2. Data availability in various sectors

Sectors	Logs	Images	Audio	Video
Education				
Health Care				
Banking				
Trading				

	HIGH
	MEDIUM
	LOW

4.1 Banking Sector

Banking sector has the largest amount of data in the form of logs and videos. Large number of transaction are done on daily basis whose record has to be stored maintained, analysis of this data can provide valuable insight of this sector. The opportunity available by the applying big data techniques are mentioned hereafter:

1. Fraud detection and security: by gaining a conclusive view of the customers by identifying data, cluster information from normal activities using machine learning and big data technologies.
2. Customer segmentation: by grouping customers into different categories increases sales, promotion by collecting processing and analyzing data stored.
3. Risk management: meet new increasing demands for better management support by building a centralized-integrated risk management platform.
4. Personalized product offering: by observing customers buying habits and channeling the right customer buying a new product or service offering.

4.2 Education

Education sector contains large amount of data in the form of logs image and videos. The opportunity available by the applying big data techniques are mentioned hereafter

1. Personalized learning: by collecting incremental information, through various tests, assignments and activities. There can be a check on the progress of students and personalize their education.
2. Revolutionize the domain: By observing the study material i.e. Video, audio, eBooks student prefer for studying during the examinations, we can recognize the domain which enables students to understand their basic concepts and try reducing its cost and making it widely accessible.

4.3 Health Care

Health care sector have a large number of log files which are mainly patient history, treatment and rate of success. This sector will provide the maximum number of opportunities mentioned hereafter:

1. Resource management: big data analysis can enable us to monitor the real time quality service, observe the performance and recognizing which department needs more resources.
2. Understanding the evolution of diseases: data analysis on large logs of disease history will enable medical researchers to understand predictability of genetic disease according to the symptoms appearance.
3. Better decision making: by the analysis of surgical history of hundreds of patients there are a higher chances of finding correlations that can help in order to find the suitable treatment of other patients.

4.4 Trading

1. Changing traditional strategies: analysis of customer behavior provides valuable insight, enabling the sector to change its strategies according customer behavior and preferences. Analysis of customer feedback and knowledge enables the high level management to enhance their strategies.
2. Reselling results: Analysis to big data enables observing micro and macro economy, and selling the analysis result.

5   Big Data Challenges

5.1 Landscape Uncertainty

NOSQL frame work is different from conventional data management techniques in terms of data accessing, storage, processing and visualization. Each category in NOSQL have a dozens of models which have been developed by the development department of large scale organizations as per their commercial and noncommercial needs. Different models provide different performance characteristics.

In simple world, the different models and the status of the market has lead to an uncertainty in data base landscape. Making it difficult to choose a NoSql tool, as using the wrong technology can turn out to be very costly for the organization.

5.2 Big Data Talent Gap

Big data requires an interdisciplinary approach: statistics, hacking, machine learning etc. we are still at the early stage in evolution of big data. While many top organizations are spending millions trying to build a big data platform and tools. Despite the promotion of data science and big data there is a huge gap in skills required. As for acquiring skills one needs to practice knowledge and experience which can only be gained by practical implementation.

5.3 Big Data Complexity Factor

Some might consider big data as analysis of a large dataset and gaining information to improve decision making. In practical implementation many have faced many exceptions because of the degree of complexity. Taking stored data from enormous sources, moving them and loading them into big data platform is only a part of the challenge another challenge is faced during the extraction and transformation of unstructured and quasi structured data sources [3].

An additional challenge is the response time by processing the data through hundreds of pipelines having limited bandwidth cannot provide the desired performance.

5.4 Cost of Initialization

The world can see big data as the future to gain competitive advantage by gaining an insight of customers and behavior which directly impacts the business. Enterprises are trying to build customize big data platforms according to their future needs but the cost and the risk factor have caused a lot of delay [4].

5.5 Data Source Heterogeneity

Data from different sources after being copied to big data platform faces a challenge of inconsistency and invalidity of information. Inconsistency of data in conventional data storages can result in wrong information flow, leading to wrong analysis of result. With data being loaded from conventional data sources [5].

6 Conclusion

This paper reviewed the concept of big data, which has been taken this decade to whole new innovation level. Various characteristics of big data are volume, velocity, Veracity, value, Visualization and Variability. Showed availabilities and opportunities in various sectors and various challenges faced by big data.

References

1. Berman, J.J.: Principles of Big Data: Preparing, Sharing and Analyzing Complex Information, 1st edn. Morgan Kaufmann Publisher Inc., San Francisco (2013)
2. Tiwari, A.K., Chaudhary, H., Yadav, S.: A review on big data and its security. In: International Conference on Innovations in Information Embedded and Communication Systems, pp. 567–573 (2015)
3. Menon, S.P., Hegde, N.P.: A survey of tools and applications in Big Data. In: International Conference on Intelligent Systems and Control (JSC) (2015)

4. Gupta, P., Tyagi, N.: An approach towards big data - a review. In: International Conference on Computing, Communication and Automation, pp. 118–123 (2015)
5. George, K., Mathew, T.: Big database stores: a review on various big data datastores. In: International Conference on Green Computing and Internet of Things, pp. 567–573 (2015)
6. http://searchdatamanagement.techtarget.com/definition/bigdata-management

An Efficient Approach for Motion Detection in Video Surveillance and Enhance the Video Quality

Sharfuddin Waseem Mohammed[(✉)] and Sai Rama Krishna Indarapu

Department of Computer Science and Engineering, Kakatiya Institute
of Technology and Science, Warangal 506015, Telangana, India
waseem.cse@kitsw.ac.in, srk.kitswgl@gmail.com

Abstract. In recent studies video surveillance become an important task for identifying the motion detection (moving objects) to avoid the burglars in home security systems. Most of the video surveillance systems works on algorithms like background image subtraction, double background filter (DBF), optical flow method for motion detection where video is recorded by digital video recorder when an moving object is identified to save the memory, but in due process some frames are missed even moving objects are identified as they are treated as stable objects (without considering the minor movement in objects under threshold value), here we propose a method to integrate background image subtraction and double background filtering with morphological dilations to identify the moving objects and enhance the video quality by using the trained filters to improve the low quality frames.

Keywords: Background image subtraction · Double background filters (DBF) · Motion detection

1 Introduction

In recent studies of computer vision many algorithms has proposed for motion detection for various applications like video surveillance for home security systems [1], traffic monitoring, or sign language recognition [2], but still this algorithms need an robustness when applied to complex environment. Many techniques have been proposed [5–12] for motion detection among which the commonly used techniques are background subtraction, double background filtering [3], optical flow. Background subtraction method find the temporal difference between frames to frames in instance of time to identify the change in pixel from current frame to previous frame to identify the moving objects, but this methods exhibits a poor results when there is huge interference in background i.e. no still cameras. This method with statistical model is flexible and fast, but the background image and the camera are required to be still. Optical flow [4] is used to find the approximation of the local images motion and specifies how much each image pixel is moving form adjacent images. It achieved the motion detection even for changing background and camera in motion but requires a huge computational effort to compute the flow from frame to frame. Double background filters (DBF) [3]

© Springer Nature Singapore Pte Ltd. 2016
A. Unal et al. (Eds.): SmartCom 2016, CCIS 628, pp. 698–705, 2016.
DOI: 10.1007/978-981-10-3433-6_84

method is used to obtain a stable background image even there are variations in background image and obtain the moving objects from the interference background.

In this paper we propose a technique to integrate the background subtraction and double background filtering (DBF) with dilations, uses a trained filters to improve the quality of frames and motion area is detected.

The paper is organized as following: Sect. 2 describes the model of integration, Sect. 3 describes the background subtraction method, Sect. 4 describes the double background filtering with morphological dilations and frame enhancement technique, Sect. 5 describes the motion object area detection Sect. 6 experimental results and Sect. 7 concludes the paper with future scope.

2 Proposed Work and Model of Integration

Surveillance video is captured via a hardware ip based camera and the frame segmentation is applied to identify the sequence of frames to apply the following algorithm.

Step 1: Image acquisition and dividing the input video into frames
Step 2: Applying background subtraction method
Step 3: Accumulation of 10 frames to apply double background filtering
Step 4: Applying Double background filtering (DBF) method with morphological dilations and applying image enhancement technique
Step 5: Motion area detection
Step 6: Invoking Alarm when object motion is detected else repeat the steps from step number 2–6 until object motion is detected.

Algorithm first classify the input video surveillance into number of frames and background subtraction method is applied to identify the object motion from frame to frame, after identifying the existence of object in current frames those will be accumulated (i.e. 10 Frames) to be processed for applying double background filtering (DBF) method with morphological dilations to separate the motion object from the background interference, and motion area is detected and image or frame is enhanced using trained filters to repair low quality images and an alarm is triggered when an object motion is detected. Figure 1 shows the flow-chart of proposed model, where frames acquisition is done and frames background subtraction method is applied if frames with objects is identified then frames are accumulated else the process is repeated until 10 frames are collected.

Then Double background filtering is applied for motion detection if there is a motion in object then an alarm is raised else repeat the process to identify motion detection in video sequence.

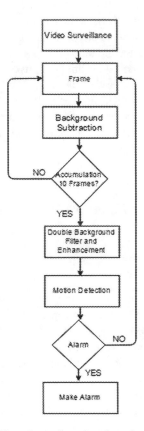

Fig. 1. Flowchart of motion detection method

3   Background Subtraction Method

Temporal difference detection or background subtraction works on the principle of frame difference which is used to identify the object motion from one frame with another when background is stable. Differencing between two consecutive images or frames is calculated, suppose I_m (x, y, t) is an image at 't' instance of time and I_n (x, y, t + 1) is an image at 't + 1' instance then provides a temporal difference of I_d.

$$I_d = I_n - I_m \tag{1}$$

For an image with slower frame sequence, calculation of the average running image R is computed as:

$$R_x(x, y, t) = (1 - W) \bullet I_m(x, y, t) + W \bullet I_n(x, y, t + 1) \tag{2}$$

Where W is the factor of degrading the old pixel.

As the computation continues, instead of using $I_m(x, y, t)$ pixels values, the function will replace it with $R[x, y]$ values to form a repetition equation and thus making the equation formed as:

$$R_x(x, y, t) = (1 - W) \bullet R_x(x, y, t) + W \bullet I_n(x, y, t + 1) \tag{3}$$

Here x and y denotes the location of the certain pixels. Thus every pixels belonging to the image are computed to give a resulting average running image R_x of the same size which is used as the background image. Here a threshold value T_d is computed to decide the temporal difference between selected frames.

$$T_d = 2.8 \times \text{mean}(R_x(x, y, t + 1)) \tag{4}$$

Where I_d lies between 0 and 255 for a gray scale image.

$$\begin{aligned} I_d &= 0 \text{ otherwise} \\ &255 \text{ if } (R_x(x, y, t)) > T_d \end{aligned} \tag{5}$$

The Temporal difference detection is a simple technique for detecting moving objects in a static environment and the adaptive threshold T_d can restrain the noise very well, but does not work properly for moving background.

4 Double Background Filtering with Morphological Dilations

In real environment due to noise like light and vibrations the interference information of the background still can be detected hence in this situations it is difficult to recognize real object motion to be differentiated from the background interference, here we apply the DBF method and separate the moving object from the background interference and apply the morphological dilations to improve the results. Double background principle [3] is based on long-term background and short-term background, in long-term background interference information which happened long time is saved and for short term most recent changes are saved but it has observe from practical results that for moving objects for some specific areas the motion cannot be detected perfectly hence an approach is made to separate/filter foreground image with background image and effectively identify the moving objects, here we follow a process in 3 different steps to filter foreground with background image.

Step 1: Frames are accumulated to stable the background interference i.e. first 5 frames are collected to find the frame difference

$$\begin{aligned} A^5(i, j) &= A^5(i, j) + 1 \text{ if difference} = 255 \\ A^5(i, j) &\text{ if difference} = 0 \end{aligned} \tag{6}$$

Step 2: Last three frames accumulated for moving object detection $A^3(i, j)$ be the accumulation matrix then

$$A^3(i,j) = A^3(i,j) + 1 \text{ if difference} = 255$$
$$A^3(i,j) \text{ if difference} = 0$$
(7)

Step 3: By combining the results of step 1 and step 2 and finding the difference between the frames by computing to an area of window of size M × M and identifying the pixel position from frame to frame flow. The algorithm to detect whether a pixel P(x, y) belongs to an object with salient motion

Suppose P(x, y) is detected in the object movement then

$$P(x,y) = 0 \text{ if } A^5 > 0 \text{ and } A^3 > 0$$
$$255 \text{ if } A^5 = 0 \text{ and } A^3 = 0$$
(8)

Two unused frames are used to separate foreground and background image. Above steps are repeated for the set of 10 frames and foreground and background image is filtered by repeating the steps 1 through 3. After applying filters to identify the motion objects in the still background, if the image background interference is dominating the foreground then we apply the morphological dilations to preserve the foreground image from background. The dilation techniques are defined in [14] to preserve the main shape while suppressing the noise morphological dilations and erosions are used to detect the object and erose the object, here a Structuring Element (S.E) of {111; 111; 111} is used to preserve the frame and enhance the motion object detection. Image enhancement can be done after applying morphological dilations to enhance the quality of image we uses a trained filter [15] to repair low quality image.

5 Moving Object Area Detection

The moving object area can be identified by the Rate Of Change (ROC) from the foreground motion information and background information. Here the accumulate flow of first five frame and last three frames decide the rate of change from the foreground and background image.

$$\text{Rate of change (ROC)} = \frac{\text{Accumulated foreground information}}{\text{Accumulated background information}}$$
(9)

We set an threshold value to decide the triggering of alarm we consider a Threshold of 0.3

i.e. if ROC > T Trigger Alarm
else ROC < = T No Alarm

6   Experiment Results

Experiment is conducted using a custom video recorded with ip based camera, results shows a detection of motion object in different scenarios following table describes the various images.

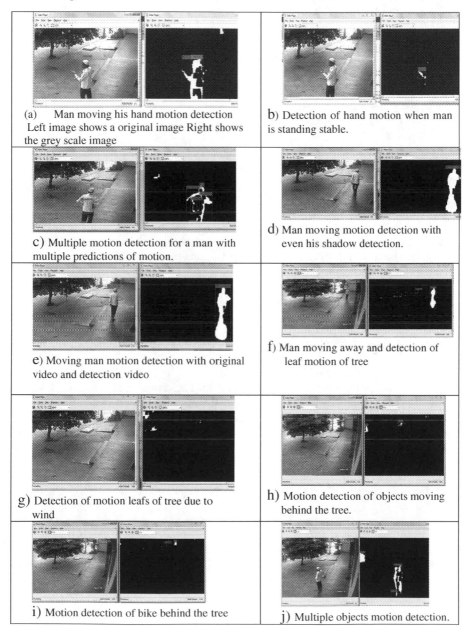

(a) Man moving his hand motion detection Left image shows a original image Right shows the grey scale image	b) Detection of hand motion when man is standing stable.
c) Multiple motion detection for a man with multiple predictions of motion.	d) Man moving motion detection with even his shadow detection.
e) Moving man motion detection with original video and detection video	f) Man moving away and detection of leaf motion of tree
g) Detection of motion leafs of tree due to wind	h) Motion detection of objects moving behind the tree.
i) Motion detection of bike behind the tree	j) Multiple objects motion detection.

7 Conclusion and Future Scope

The algorithm is implemented with MATLAB using a custom input video of size 640 × 480 pixels with sample rate of 30 FPS obtained from a surveillance night vision camera to identify the moving objects to alarm. Experiment shows a robust results when the methods are integrated to find the moving objects.

Most of the Digital Video Recorders (DVR) works on the principle of identifying the motion of objects and starts recording the sequence of frames, but it has observe that most frames are missed even there exist an object, hence an efficient algorithm is needed to record the frame sequence even there exist a miniscule change in environment.

References

1. Tian, Y.L., Hampapur, A.: Robust salient motion detection with complex background for real-time video surveillance. In: IEEE Computer Society Workshop on Motion and Video Computing, Breckenridge, Colorado, 5–6 January 2005
2. Bahlmann, C., Zhu, Y., Ramesh, Y., Pellkofer, M., Koehler, T.: A system for traffic sign detection, tracking, and recognition using color, shape, and motion information. In: Proceedings of IEEE Intelligent Vehicles Symposium, pp. 255–260 (2005)
3. Zheng, J., Li, B., Zhou, B., Li, W.: Fast motion detection based on accumulative optical flow and double background model. In: Hao, Y., Liu, J., Wang, Y.-P., Cheung, Y.-M., Yin, H., Jiao, L., Ma, J., Jiao, Y.-C. (eds.) CIS 2005. LNCS (LNAI), vol. 3802, pp. 291–296. Springer, Heidelberg (2005). doi:10.1007/11596981_43
4. Zhou, D.X., Zhang, H.: Modified GMM background modeling and optical flow for detection of moving objects. In: Proceedings of IEEE International Conference on Systems, Man and Cybernetics, vol. 3, pp. 2224–2229 (2005)
5. Shao, L., Wang, J., Kirenko, I., de Haan, G.: Quality adaptive trained filters for compression artifacts removal. In: Proceedings of the 33rd IEEE International Conference on Acoustics, Speech, and Signal Processing (ICASSP), Las Vegas, USA, pp. 897–900 (2008)
6. Guo, J., Rajan, D., Chng, E.S.: Motion detection with adaptive background and dynamic thresholds. In: Fifth International Conference on Information, Communications and Signal Processing, 6–9 December 2005, pp. 41–45 (2005)
7. Spagnolo, P., D'Orazio, T., Leo, M., Distante, A.: Advances in background updating and shadow removing for motion detection algorithms. In: Gagalowicz, A., Philips, W. (eds.) CAIP 2005. LNCS, vol. 3691, pp. 398–406. Springer, Heidelberg (2005). doi:10.1007/11556121_49
8. Elnagar, A., Basu, A.: Motion detection using background constraints. Pattern Recogn. 28 (10), 1537–1554 (1995)
9. Vazquez, J.F., Mazo, M., Lazaro, J.L., Luna, C.A., Urefla, J., Garcia, J.J., Guillan, E.: Adaptive threshold for motion detection in outdoor environment using computer vision. In: Proceedings of the IEEE International Symposium on Industrial Electronics, ISIE 2005, 20–23 June 2005, vol. 3, pp. 1233–1237 (2005)
10. Butler, D.E., Bove Jr., V.M., Sridharan, S.: Real-time adaptive foreground/background segmentation. Eurasip J. Appl. Sig. Proces. 2005(14), 2292–2304 (2005)

11. Choi, Y.S., Piao, Z.J., Kim, S.W., Kim, T.H., Park, C.B.: Salient motion information detection technique using weighted subtraction image and motion vector. In: Proceedings of 2006 International Conference on Hybrid Information Technology, vol. 1, pp. 263–269 (2006)
12. Wu, J.W., Trivedi, M.: Performance characterization for gaussian mixture model based motion detection algorithms. In: Proceedings of International Conference on Image Processing, vol. 1, pp. 1097–1100 (2005)
13. Hasanzadeh, P.R.R., Shahmirzaie, A., Rezaie, A.H.: Motion detection using differential histogram equalization. In: Proceedings of the Fifth IEEE International Symposium on Signal Processing and Information Technology, pp. 186–190 (2005)
14. Gonzalez, R.C., Woods, R.E.: Digital Image Processing, 2nd edn. Prentice-Hall, Upper Saddle River (2002). ISBN: 0130946508
15. Shao, L., Zhang, H., de Haan, G.: An overview and performance evaluation of classification-based least squares trained filters. In: IEEE Transactions on Image

Study of Electronic Stethoscope as Prospective Analysis Tool for Cardiac Sounds

Sibghatullah I. Khan$^{(\boxtimes)}$ and Vasif Ahmed

Department of Electronics and Telecommunication Engg,
Babasaheb Naik College of Engineering,
Karla Road, Pusad, Yavatmal 445215, MS, India
{khanofpusad, ahmedvasif}@gmail.com

Abstract. The work described in this paper intends to explore the possibility of using electronic stethoscope as potential analysis tool to aid automatic diagnosis of heart related problems/diseases. Heart sounds plays an important role in preliminary diagnosis of various cardiac disorders. It is pertinent to check the fidelity of electronic stethoscope for its usage as primary auscultation device in telemedicine applications. 3M Littmann 3200 electronic stethoscope was chosen for experimentation due to its popularity amongst medical practitioners. The features and operating parameters of the stethoscope are analyzed and frequency response in different operating modes is observed. The various aspects of stethoscope in phonocardiology are discussed with reference to future scope of implementation.

Keywords: Auscultation · Electronic stethoscope · Phonocardiology · Frequency response

1 Introduction

The Heart sounds are important class of human body sounds used as primary indicators of underlying diseases. Traditionally stethoscope is acknowledged as an important tool in diagnosing pathological characteristics of heart sound by expert physician. Nowadays with the advances in technology, the electronic stethoscope with capability of amplifying and band filtering the received sound are replacing the traditional stethoscopes to a great extent [1–5]. The progress in signal processing techniques in recent past has motivated many researchers to explore the possibility of development of automatic diagnosis system based on human body sounds. Some researchers have also proposed the usage of electronic stethoscope in detection of coronary artery diseases [6]. The integration of diagnosis framework to telemedicine platform will ultimately lead to sustainable telemedicine model for resource poor regions of the world especially countries like India where heart diseases are on the verge of becoming leading cause of death [7].

There are numerous methods available for acquisition of heart sounds. One of the simplest form is to integrate traditional stethoscope with microphone [8]. In this approach microphone is inserted in rubber tube of stethoscope near chest piece and electrical terminals of the microphone are connected to audio input interface of

© Springer Nature Singapore Pte Ltd. 2016
A. Unal et al. (Eds.): SmartCom 2016, CCIS 628, pp. 706–713, 2016.
DOI: 10.1007/978-981-10-3433-6_85

computer or mobile phone. This approach suffers from disadvantages like microphone not being compatible with acoustic body sounds frequency range and requirement of additional de-nosing circuitry. Additionally, ambient noise encountered and recording quality is affected by cross interference generated by computer or mobile phone. Other options include using dedicated sensors to be attached permanently to chest of the subject under expert guidance. This approach causes uneasiness for the subject/ patients.

Now-a-days commercialization of electronic stethoscope with various inbuilt features opens a wide opportunity for the researchers in the biomedical field. Littmann is most trusted brand in the stethoscope market since many years. 3M Littmann traditional models were the most popular amongst the doctors especially amongst the pulmonologists and cardiologists. So after surveying different available electronic stethoscope models in the market [1–5], 3M Littmann 3200 model was chosen for experimentation and feature verification due to its exquisite features.

One of the important criterion of selecting electronic stethoscope is its ability to reject the noise. Noise during auscultation mainly arises due to skin contact with that of chest piece. The other important criterion is its frequency response. The frequency response is the key property of any auscultation device as it decides the faithful range of operation for a particular frequency band. The study mainly aims to verify 3M Littmann 3200 characteristics for recording of heart sound and plotting its frequency spectrum and spectrogram for different modes of operation of the device (Fig. 1).

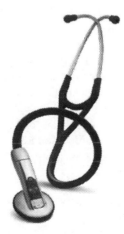

Fig. 1. 3M Littmann 3200 electronic stethoscope [1]

2 Features of Stethoscope Model

The design of the device is similar to the traditional stethoscope with difference only in the chest piece, where one sided diaphragm is placed with set of control buttons. The complete description and function details are specified in the user manual. So only some basic features and parameters of the device are discussed here.

According to manufacturer specification the stethoscope 3M Littmann 3200 provides amplification of signal up to 24 fold (each step of 10 dB). The frequency range is 20 to 2000 Hz. This band of frequency contains most of the information in respiration as well as cardiac sounds [9, 10]. Three modes of operation are provided by the manufacturer.

Bell mode: In this mode, the device amplifies the signal with frequency range 20–2000 Hz with emphasizing the band of 20–200 Hz. This mode resembles the bell mode of traditional stethoscope used for listening to low frequency sounds specially for abdomen and heart related sounds.

Diaphragm mode: In this mode, the entire frequency range of 20–2000 Hz is amplified with emphasizing the 100–500 Hz band. The mode is useful in listening to the respiration sounds (Lung sounds) as well as Cardiac sounds.

Extended mode: This mode is a unique feature of 3M Littmann 3200 model as it nearly combines the frequency response of Bell and Diaphragm mode. This mode amplifies frequency range of 20–2000 Hz with emphasis on 20–500 Hz band.

The connectivity options include Bluetooth 2.0 which is used to transmit and receive recorded sound between computer and stethoscope. 3M Littmann software StethAssist software is used to initiate and manage file transfer process. The sounds can be recorded on device itself with option of recording 12 tracks with 30 s duration each. The sound can also be recorded in real time with StethAssist software which facilitates to record sound up to the duration of 60 s. In both the cases the recorded sound can be exported as 16 bit PCM with 4000 Hz sampling frequency in .wav format. 3M Littmann 3200 also allows playing and saving recorded sounds in Bell, Diaphragm or Extended mode. Means sounds recorded in Bell mode can be played or saved in extended mode. This operation is nothing but superposition of different filters depending on the modes and is not recommended procedure for analysis. So the good practice is to use same mode for both recording and saving the sound.

The recordings can also be integrated with cloud server of 3M Littmann called TeleSteth for exchange and remote auscultation of human body sounds. The server is maintained by 3M Littmann. The recorded sounds can also be integrated with third party software for telemedicine applications.

3   Frequency Response of Stethoscope

The Frequency Response is an important Auscultation characteristics of 3M Littmann 3200 model. Researchers have conducted experiments to determine frequency response of the device.

Figure 2 shows the frequency response of the 3M Littmann 3200 model obtained by V.N Oliynik [11]. The detailed procedure for obtaining the response could be found in the paper [11]. The graph shows amplitude envelopes for frequency responses obtain under three modes. The overall error estimated is ± 3 dB. The plot clearly shows that extended mode provides widest bandwidth with 0–200 Hz portion of the spectrum being flat. It peaks at 550 Hz followed by a second peak at 780 Hz. The diaphragm

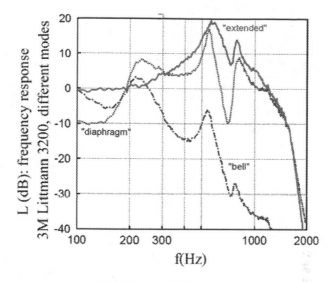

Fig. 2. Frequency response of 3M Littmann 3200 stethoscope for three modes of filtering

mode attenuates the below 200 Hz signal and peaks occur at 230 Hz. The second peak in diaphragm mode appears at 550 Hz. The Bell mode tries to emphasis frequency range between 200–300 Hz after which signal is attenuated by –15 dB.

4   Experimentation

The analysis of different filter (modes) for 3M Littmann 3200 electronic stethoscope for cardiac signals is presented here. Heart sounds were recorded on the PC via StethAssist software provided by the Littmann. Sounds were recorded with different modes and saved accordingly. Frequency spectrum of each case is been plotted and effect of change in the filter (mode) of stethoscope was observed.

Figure 3. shows cardiac sounds with clearly visible 'Lub' S1 and 'Dub' S2 sounds. The sound is recorded for a healthy 56 years old male subject (Fig. 4).

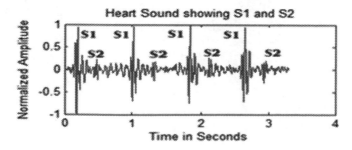

Fig. 3. Typical heart sound recorded using electronic stethoscope

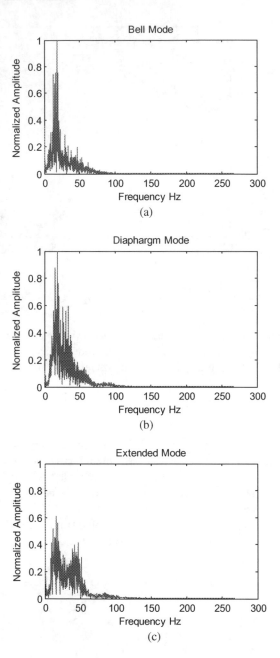

Fig. 4. (continued)

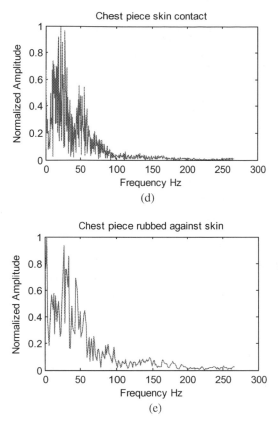

Fig. 4. Frequency spectrum of recorded sound using 3M Littmann 3200 electronic stethoscope of (a) Bell mode (b) Diaphragm mode (c) Extended mode (d) Chest piece hard contact with subjects skin (e) Chest piece rubbing against skin of subject.

5   Observations and Results

From the plots it is evident that the spectrum of heart sounds differ according to the mode used for recording and storing the sound. The energy calculated for different bands is tabulated in Table 1. From the table it is clear that the modes used during the recording and saving influences the energy in different predefined bands. As expected the Extended mode is showing maximum energy in the band significant to heart sounds compared to other two modes. The sound produced due to rubbing of chest piece and chest piece movement against skin contains maximum energy in the 20–100 Hz band. So it is important to note this unwanted sound during further analysis. This sound can be minimised by avoiding any hard movement of chest piece against the skin of the subject. In conducted experiment, chest piece was rubbed and contact to the skin was deliberately done in hard manner to evaluate the maximum effect. It can be concluded from plots and energy distribution table that it is convenient to use extended mode for recording of heart sounds.

Table 1. Energy vs. Modes

Mode	Energy in 20–100 Hz band		
	Regular Heart sound	Rubbing	Chest piece movement
Bell	1.93	3.11	9.29
Diaphargm	8.03	7.03	8.13
Extended	11.59	8.15	11.42

6   Conclusion

From the conducted investigation we can draw the conclusion that the 3M Littmann 3200 electronic stethoscope is capable of faithfully recording heart sounds which can further be conditioned for further analysis. The extended mode shows maximum energy content in the 10–100 Hz band which is an important range for frequencies in the heart sounds. The noise reduction capability of stethoscope plays an important role in compensating high frequency noise due to rubbing of chest piece to skin of the subject. So it is concluded that electronic stethoscope can be used as potential tool for the heart sound analysis and can be integrated with third party telemedicine application for automated diagnosis of heart diseases.

Acknowledgments. We express our sincere thanks to Dr. H.B.Nanvala, Principal Babasaheb Naik College of Engineering Pusad for providing necessary facilities for carrying out this work. We also acknowledge our deep gratitude to Dr. N. P. Jawarkar, Head, Department of Electronics and Telecommunication Engineering for his continuous inspiration and encouragement to embark on this project. We would also like to convey our thanks to Dr. Akil Memon (Renowned Cardiologist and Founder Director, lifeline hospital Pusad), Dr. Mohibul Haque (Director, Oasis Hospital, Nagpur), Dr. Naim Niayzi, Dr. Hasanulbanna, Dr. Anwar Siddiqui and Dr. Adnanulhaque Khan, Nagpur, for providing necessary guidance during recording auscultation of cardiac sounds.

References

1. 3M Littmann electronic stethoscope. Model 3200, User Manual, 3M (2011)
2. Thinklabs digital stethoscope. http://www.thinklabs.com/#!ds32-digital-stethoscope/cr76
3. HD medical group ViScope. http://hdmedicalgroup.com/our-products/viscope/
4. Cardionics   E   Scope.   http://www.allheart.com/cardionics-the-e-scope-ii-electronic-stethoscope/p/ca718712x/
5. Makarenkov, A.P., Makarenkova, A.A.: Studying the efficiency of electroacoustic transducers of electronic stethophonendoscopes. Acoust. Bul. (Akustychny Visnyk) **12**(1), 3–10 (2009)
6. Schmidt, S.E., Toft, E., Holst-Hansen, C., Struijk, J.J.: Noise and the detection of coronary artery disease with an electronic stethoscope. In: 2010 5th Cairo International Biomedical Engineering Conference (CIBEC), Cairo, pp. 53–56 (2010). doi:10.1109/CIBEC.2010.5716077

7. http://food.ndtv.com/health/world-heart-day-2015-heart-disease-in-india-is-a-growing-concern-ansari-1224160
8. Khan, S.I., Jawarkar, N.P., Ahmed, V.: Cell phone based remote early detection of respiratory disorders for rural children using modified stethoscope. In: 2012 International Conference on Communication Systems and Network Technologies (CSNT), Rajkot, pp. 936–940 (2012). doi:10.1109/CSNT.2012
9. Pasterkamp, H., Kraman, S.S., Wodicka, G.R.: Respiratory sounds. Advances beyond the stetoscope. J. Respir. Crit. Care Med. **156**, 974–987 (1997)
10. McKusick, V.A.: Cardiovascular Sound in Health and Disease. Williams and Wilkins, Baltimore (1958)
11. Oliynik, V.N.: Determining the amplitude-frequency response for electronic stethoscope 3M Littmann 3200. Acoust. Bul. (Akustychny Visnyk) **16**(3), 46–57, 2013–2014

Critical Review on Software Testing: Security Perspective

Mohd Waris Khan[1(✉)], Dhirendra Pandey[1], and Suhel Ahmad Khan[2]

[1] Department of Information Technology, BBAU, Lucknow, India
Wariskhan070@gmail.com, prof.dhiren@gmail.com
[2] Department of Computer Application, Integral University, Lucknow, India
ahmadsuhel28@gmail.com

Abstract. Software plays a crucial role in day to day life; hence its security and reliability cannot be neglected. Creating a secure software system is not just to secure sensitive and confidential information but it needed to establish a system which could stand true on the benchmark set for being a secure software system and further derive a roadmap to construct impregnable and efficient software. In order to fulfill this criterion, security testing is vital for the development of a secure software system as it pursue all the aspects of SDLC. Security should form an integral part of a SDLC, hence to maximize and maintain the defenses of a software system and to keep its development cost in limits, Security Testing Profile (STP) provides a reliable platform for testing software. STP is an uncharted territory and more progress can be made in this area, which may help in developing robust software systems.

Keywords: Security testing · Security factors · Security Testing Profile (STP)

1 Introduction

The purpose of security testing is to find out whether the system meets its specified security objectives, or security requirements. The various phases of security testing during the software lifecycle, starts from requirements elicitation and analysis, design phase, implementation and verification & validation. Figure 1 describes a technical view for security test plan specification. The test plan specifications of software security testing can be classified into four parts, which are as follows: Technical (C1), Strategic (C2), Environmental (C3) and Operational (C4). After classification of these aspects of security, the role of STP in this research paper has been observed and discussed. Furthermore, the importance of STP is defined and its future scope is explained. The test results obtained by these four parameters will provide the background for creating STP. Security Testing Profile will be a sum total of all test results based on the above four parameters.

In this study, we focus on security testing in software development, from a tester's perspective. The main objective is to provide an insight in the use of security testing from the starting point in the SDLC for the sole purpose of creation of secure and robust software. For that, in this paper, we discuss about the security testing profile which will help in the evaluation of software in terms of security. This introduces the

© Springer Nature Singapore Pte Ltd. 2016
A. Unal et al. (Eds.): SmartCom 2016, CCIS 628, pp. 714–723, 2016.
DOI: 10.1007/978-981-10-3433-6_86

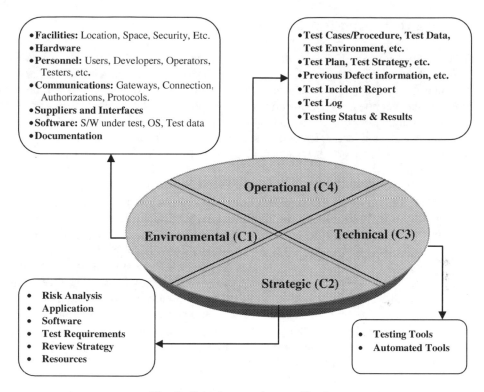

- **Facilities:** Location, Space, Security, Etc.
- **Hardware**
- **Personnel:** Users, Developers, Operators, Testers, etc.
- **Communications:** Gateways, Connection. Authorizations, Protocols.
- **Suppliers and Interfaces**
- **Software:** S/W under test, OS, Test data
- **Documentation**

- **Test Cases/Procedure, Test Data, Test Environment, etc.**
- **Test Plan, Test Strategy, etc.**
- **Previous Defect information, etc.**
- **Test Incident Report**
- **Test Log**
- **Testing Status & Results**

Operational (C4)

Environmental (C1)   Technical (C3)

Strategic (C2)

- Risk Analysis
- Application
- Software
- Test Requirements
- Review Strategy
- Resources

- Testing Tools
- Automated Tools

Fig. 1. Security test plan specification

basic terminology and concepts regarding security testing profile. We will also examine where and how the security testing profile is useful in software development process.

Additionally, in this article we also discuss how important is testing profiling from security point of view. Which brings us to the uses of security testing profile like it is vital for finding loopholes, for zeroing in on vulnerabilities, for identifying design insecurities, for identifying implementation and dependency in securities and for organization wide software security. For the purpose of reliability testing as well as security testing, profile based testing is a resourceful method. The development of operational profile and security intrusion profile of software are both resource consuming, this is why separate testing for both is required to validate the dependability of the software.

This paper has been divided into 7 sections, starting with an introduction in Sect. 1. Section 2, describes the background and related work presented by researchers. Section 3, defines the Classification of test plan specification. In Sect. 4, detailed description of Software Security Testing Profile is discussed. Section 5, describes the STP with respect to design perspective. Importance of Security Testing Profile is defined in Sect. 6 and conclusion of the paper is discussed in last section i.e., Sect. 7.

2 Background and Related Work

In 2015, the author S. Krishnaveni et al., paper entitled on "Analysis of Software Security Testing Technique in Cloud Computing" was presented, in which issues and challenges to cloud security testing were addressed [1]. Cloud computing is a new field and since there is no such clear methodology to follow in order to complete the cloud security testing, it makes cloud computing vulnerable to attacks and the bulk of information and confidential data is at risk until and proper methodology is developed. This paper focus on the C1 (environmental) and C2 (strategic) aspects as it targets both the environment where the application is set to use and the strategy related to the mitigation of problems and counter mechanism to face threats.

In 2014, the Author R. Kumar et al., have written the paper on "Software Security Testing: A Pertinent Framework", in this paper a mathematical formula is proposed for preparing test cases during any security development life cycle [2]. The paper presents a life cycle for software security and also enlightens the major methods, tools and technique of software security. It signifies the criteria of C4 (operational) specification.

In 2013, Suhel A. Khan et al., presented a paper entitled "Software Security Testing Process: Phased Approach" illustrated the importance of early identification of defects and its mitigation through the software security testing process [3]. It also emphasized on the early incorporation of security testing activities and prescribed the key activities of security testing that are interconnected with security development lifecycle. The paper signifies the various activities that can be classified under C3 and C4 specifications of security test plan.

In the year 2012, German authors Ina Schieferdecker et al., have written the paper on "Model-Based Security Testing" which intend to validate software requirements associated with security properties like confidentiality, integrity, authentication, authorization, availability and non-repudiation [4]. Model based security testing (MBST) is a somewhat new field and focus mainly on the C2 and C4 test plan specification. The paper signifies the requirement of an initial survey on Model based security testing. It is prepared by analyzing the related work and confers the model that can be used for model security testing by outlining the two main approaches namely – Risk-based security and Model-based fuzzing.

In 2011, a paper titled "An Overview of Penetration Testing" published in which the author Aileen G. Bacudio et al., have discussed the benefits, strategies and the methodologies of conducting penetration testing [5]. The methodology of penetration testing consists of three stages: test preparation, test and test analysis. The test stage deals with information gathering, vulnerability analysis and vulnerability exploit. Security is a major concern regarding information systems. This paper explains the need and ways to enhance the defense of software against getting penetrated by any malicious software or internet virus. Focusing on the C1 (Environmental) and C2 (strategic) specifications, the paper describes that because of growing connectivity of computers through the internet the massive rise in the sharing of information, the uncontrolled growth in the size and complexity of systems.

3 Classification of Test Plan Specification

These research papers give us a detail account on the progress, methods and use of various tools and related information regarding current trends in the field of software security testing. After reviewing these research papers, it can be concluded that a lot of research is being performed to enhance the quality of work and to achieve state-of-the-art software security and reliability parameters by the use of newer strategies and testing software systems in various test environments. The test plan specifications most targeted in the above research papers are C2 and C1 respectively as it is imperative to integrate security within the basic software design from the beginning of SDLC. Development of new testing tools i.e., C1 specification is another important issue that has been duly addressed in some papers, as also the development of operational quality of a software security and dependability has been given impetus classified under C4 test specifications (Table 1).

Table 1. Classification of test plan specification

Environmental specification (C1)	Test environment is a stable area for independent systems and integration testing by the test team [9] Test environment includes the physical characteristics of the facilities like hardware, communications and system software, mode of usage/interface and other software or supplies [10] Documentation the physical components required for test execution is also a part of environmental specification [16]
Strategic specifications (C2)	It is the heart of the test plan, contains a descriptive guide of testing procedures to be performed and explain issues that have major impact on the success of the test [11] It describes the overall approach and techniques involved in each phase during test It describes phase wise testing approach Outline the steps involved in overall testing process [12] Identification of all software features, combination of software features to be tested and the associated design specifications [9, 13] It includes test requirements like completeness, accuracy, stability etc. Includes review strategies - walkthroughs, inspection, desk checks etc. Completion criteria for overall test plan will be set in advance Preparation of a checklist at each phase to know whether the testing phase is complete or not [14]
Technical specifications (C3)	Selection of appropriate tools and automation [6, 8, 11]
Operational specifications (C4)	Inputs: Test case/procedures, Test data, Test environment [6, 7] Test Plan, Test Strategy Previous defect information etc. [10, 12] Outputs: Test Incident report, test log, testing status and results [13, 15]

By reviewing these papers, we get a better understanding of various conceivable vulnerabilities and potential security threats in a software system, and also we could study the various methodologies used by the researchers to encounter, endure, contain and fix those problems. The first and foremost research problem is to gather and understand security requirements and constraints. It has become a matter of utmost necessity to integrate security profile testing in the lifecycle of software. The aim is to embed security profile testing into the entire software development life cycle as to achieve the objective of 'defense in depth' concept which focus on integrating and implementing security testing profile to provide a security at different layers. We have presented the importance of the security testing profile wherein the purpose of identification, documentation and setting optimal parameters for a security test of a software system could be realized. A good documentation of security test helps to reduce the system vulnerabilities, security threats and testing vulnerabilities, as also it will help in patching up the security loopholes in a software system.

4   Software Security Testing Profile

Security testing profile is an approach of integrating security requirements, risk-analysis, design, implementation and testing into development life cycle stages or in other words, the structured process of identifying and documenting all optimal security testing is called security testing profile. Profiling of security testing and its use to design a software with minimum loopholes and design faults is guided by the operational profile of the program under testing to ensure that the most used operations receives the most testing. This way by a continuous or repetitive testing most of the nags, latent security breach areas, vulnerabilities to a certain environment and threats by malicious bugs can be detected and mitigated.

Security testing profile in an internet environment can help providing protection to an enormous amount of important and confidential information shared on the internet. It also provides an organization wide data protection and accurate identification of causes of the security leakage. Number of test in a given environment also affects the reliability of the software components. In order to assess the performance of software keeping the factor of reliability in mind, testing profile needs to be evaluated accurately.

The performance of a test during the process of executing a program with an intention of finding design errors in a given environment precisely will define the success of such test. The risk analysis on the basis of these tests will help in plugging the loopholes and developing a framework to fix the program errors and design faults. It goes without saying that you cannot build a secure application without performing sharp security testing on it. It has been defined that a program is correct if it needs its specification for all valid inputs. During testing phase, test cases are selected according to operational profile/testing profile and applied to the software under test. The various stages of the security testing life cycle are shown in the following Fig. 2.

STEPS	STAGES	DESCRIPTION

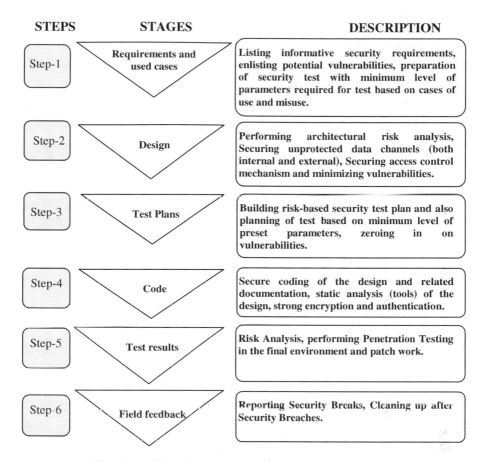

Step-1	Requirements and used cases	Listing informative security requirements, enlisting potential vulnerabilities, preparation of security test with minimum level of parameters required for test based on cases of use and misuse.
Step-2	Design	Performing architectural risk analysis, Securing unprotected data channels (both internal and external), Securing access control mechanism and minimizing vulnerabilities.
Step-3	Test Plans	Building risk-based security test plan and also planning of test based on minimum level of preset parameters, zeroing in on vulnerabilities.
Step-4	Code	Secure coding of the design and related documentation, static analysis (tools) of the design, strong encryption and authentication.
Step-5	Test results	Risk Analysis, performing Penetration Testing in the final environment and patch work.
Step-6	Field feedback	Reporting Security Breaks, Cleaning up after Security Breaches.

Fig. 2. Profiling of testing in security development life cycle

5   Software Testing Profile: A Design Security Perspective

Software security is to engineer software in such a way that the required application functions uninterrupted and is able to adequately neutralize all the security threats during malicious attacks. In general practice, security is left out in early stages of the software development life cycle (SDLC), rather a software engineering approach must have adequate security criteria from the beginning of SDLC. Inadequate security practice in the software development process can lead to the creation of insecure software. Integrating the security testing profile in the early stages of design and development, working on the behavioral aspect of the software with respect to security in case of malicious attacks and minimizing the potent vulnerabilities in the design phase will ultimately help us in realizing the goal of achieving reliable and secure software. The steps of secure testing profile specification are explained in the Fig. 3 which is as follows:

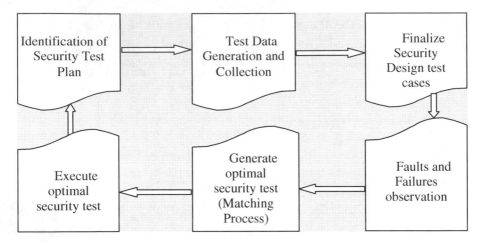

Fig. 3. Steps of secure testing profile specification

5.1   Identification of Security Test Plan

In this process problem areas should be identified and program targeted for its testing and mitigation will be prepared. The test plan should also be prepared keeping in mind the original objectives and prepare a risk based test plan should be prepared and implemented.

5.2   Test Data Generation and Collection

It is a crucial part of software testing which describes the process of creating a set of data for testing the reliability and adequacy of the new software application. The main aim of data collection is to reduce the time wasted by manually search for or creating test data. It also eliminated the risk of data breach and improves the quality of testing by early detection of defects and design faults in the original software application. This will also identify the vulnerabilities in the original software design, reduce the infrastructure cost, create missing data and generate large volumes of realistic data.

5.3   Finalize Security Design Test Cases

In this stage a comprehensive security test strategy for software security test cases is developed, focused on the security components of threats, exposures, risks to the assets and controls.

5.4   Fault and Failures Observation

The goal to observe faults and failures is to minimize the efforts of software vendors as well as security researchers so as to efficiently discover and evaluate security vulnerability. The benefit of this process is that it helps in localization of faults that lead to the categorization of individual software failures and distribution of different types of software faults.

5.5 Generate Optimal Security Test (Matching Process)

Software testing has been critical part of the entire software development lifecycle where success of software projects is heavily dependent. Therefore, there has been a widespread effort to improve SDLC practices especially during testing. In this process cases can be prioritized by considering various domains for which software is being developed and conduct optimal security test and validation of the final software that should match with the user's requirements and applicability. The actual goal of this task is to generate optimal security test plan which combine all sorts of security testing and validation processes in single compact form and execute them to produce a final improved, more user requirement specific and secure software system.

5.6 Execute Optimal Security Test

In this phase execution of all the prepared and approved test cases using recommended tools and techniques in the final stage is implemented. The final execution consists of the regression test for software security fixes, execution of new software security test and documentation of all software security defects of overall result.

6 Importance of Security Testing Profile (STP)

In order to estimate correct reliability of software, security testing profile needs to be evaluated accurately. A number of tests affect the reliability of software components with respect to security viewpoint such as accurate identification of test density over lifetime which is essential to estimate correct reliability of the software system. STP may provide the platform that how to select the minimum set of test case adequately, effective for revealing faults in a program. Security testing profile provides a platform for finding loopholes present in the system/software. It may also identify faults in the design phase which helps us zeroing in on vulnerabilities. By identifying dependency insecurities and failures, we could create a better action plan to deal with the problems regarding the implementation insecurities of the software in a given environment. Information security is a one of the major concerns as these days there is huge amount of transfer of information over the internet every second, most of which is unsecured or less secured which creates big proximity areas from where confidential and important information could be stolen. A small bug in software can create a breach in the system which could then be exploited by hackers to siphon off confidential information.

Most of the organizations take their own security systems and countermeasures to secure their important information and process confidential information using software systems via internet. But, it is seen that even after that organization wide security of information is hacked into and stolen. This leads to our original viewpoint that how much security testing profile is essential for developing any software from the beginning of its life cycle. Security testing profile should be embedded from the very start of the preparations and designing, development and releasing a software system so as to minimize the risks and/or eradicate any insecurities or potential vulnerabilities of software system. Figure 4 shows the integration of STP into each stages of SDLC.

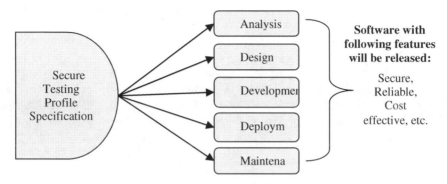

Fig. 4. Secure testing profile specification on SDLC

7   Conclusion

This paper outlines the basic problems and constraints that affect the security and reliability of software system. The purpose of this paper is to suggest a new way to prepare the security testing profile and to integrate it in the software development life cycle. Further the paper discusses research problems focused on security testing, understanding the causes of vulnerabilities which will enable us to target our testing on the root cause of those problems. The security requirements that developers have to follow should carefully be documented and future tests of software system shall be based on the data acquired from these documentations. Future work will concentrate on developing a framework for integrating security requirements for STP, its documentation and its implementation into the life cycle stages to achieve maximum security standards at all the layers of software development. A continuous preeminence on the improvement of the process and defect-reduction avoids the degeneration or process statement and it will further the process of improvement in productivity, reduced defect leakage and greater reliability and timeliness of a software system.

References

1. Krishnaveni, S., Prabakaran, Sivamohan, S.: Analysis of software security testing technique in cloud computing. Int. J. Mod. Trends Eng. Res. (IJMTER) 2(1), 417–424 (2015)
2. Kumar, R., Khan, S.A., Khan, R.A.: Software security testing: a pertinent framework. J. Global Res. Comput. Sci. (JGRCS) 5(3), 23–27 (2014)

3. Khan, S.A., Khan, R.A.: Software security testing process: phased approach. In: Agrawal, A., Tripathi, R.C., Do, E.Y.-L., Tiwari, M.D. (eds.) IITM 2013. CCIS, vol. 276, pp. 211–217. Springer, Heidelberg (2013). doi:10.1007/978-3-642-37463-0_19
4. Schieferdecker, I., Grossmann, J., Schneider, M.: Model-based security testing. In: Workshop on Model-Based Testing, EPTCS, vol. 80, pp. 1–12 (2012)
5. Bacudio, A.G., Yuan, X., Chu, B.-T.B., Jones, M.: An overview of penetration testing. Int. J. Netw. Secur. Appl. (IJNSA) **3**, 19–38 (2011)
6. Khan, S.A., Khan, R.A.: Software security testing process. In: Proceeding of the International Conference on Recent Trends in Computing and Communication Engineering (RTCCE), pp. 38–42 (2013)
7. Cao, P., Dong, Z., Liu, K., Cai, K.-Y.: Robust dynamic selection of tested modules in software testing for maximizing delivered reliability. (cs.SE), pp. 1–16 (2013)
8. Tian-yang, G., Yin-sheng, S., You-yuan, F.: Research on software security testing. Int. J. Comput. Electr. Autom. Control Inf. Eng. **4**, 1446–1450 (2010)
9. Mao, C.: Experiences in security testing for web-based applications. School of Software, Jiangxi University of Finance and Economics, 330013 China, ICIS 2009, 24–26 November, Seoul, Korea (2009)
10. Zhang, D., Nie, C., Xu, B.: A Markov decision approach to optimize testing profile in software testing. In: 9th International Conference for Young Scientists. IEEE, pp. 1205–1209 (2008)
11. Türpe, S.: Security testing: turning practice into theory. In: First ICST Workshop on Security Testing. IEEE Computer Society, pp. 295–302 (2008)
12. Ma, C., Zhao, J., Gu, G., Ma, X.: Research on software dependability testing profile in internet environment. IEEE Computer Society, pp. 206–209 (2008)
13. Flechais, I., Mascolo, C., Sasse, M.A.: Integrating security and usability into the requirement and design process. Int. J. Electron. Secur. Digit. Forensics **1**(1), 12–26 (2007)
14. Potter, B., McGraw, G.: Software security testing. IEEE Computer Society, IEEE Security & Privacy, pp. 32–36 (2004)
15. Gilliam, D.P., Wolfe, T.L., Sherif, J.S., Bishop, M.: Software security checklist for the software life cycle. In: Twelfth IEEE International Workshops, Enabling Technologies: Infrastructure for Collaborative Enterprises, WET ICE, pp. 243–248 (2003)
16. Wenliang, D., Mathur, A.P.: Testing for software vulnerability using environment perturbation. Qual. Reliab. Eng. Int. **18**(3), 261–272 (2002). Special Issue on Computer Security

Performance Analysis of Expander Graph Based Key Predistribution Scheme in WSN

Monjul Saikia$^{(\boxtimes)}$ and Md. A. Hussain

North Eastern Regional Institute of Science and Technology,
Nirjuli 791109, Arunachal Pradesh, India
monjuls@gmail.com, ah@nerist.ac.in

Abstract. Secret communication in Wireless Sensor Network is considered to be a challenging task due to high risk of node capture. Secret communication is only possible when communicating nodes share a common key for cryptographic purpose. Sensor nodes are often loaded with required secret key in its memory prior to deployment called key pre-distribution scheme (KPS). Various KPS have been proposed to provide secure communication and to minimize damage caused by intruder. In this paper, we will discuss properties of expander graph that are suitable in designing KPS and perform various experiments on KPS based on Ramanujan Expander graph for performance evaluation.

Keywords: Key Pre-distribution Scheme · Connectivity · Expander graph · Incidence graph · Resilience · Sensor network

1 Introduction

The main objective of a WSN is to collect information from a physical world in a collective way from environments which are infusible for human beings and wired communication is not possible as well. In view of security aspects of the sensor nodes it is very important to load all required security features [2] early before deployment in the target area. Propagation of message from some event of interest to the base station in the network has to travel via nearby sensor network in its communication range. To achieve desired security over sensitive information, it is essential to encrypt message prior to transmit between sensor nodes. Assigning cryptographic key for the sensor nodes is indeed necessary prior to deployment and therefore various scheme for the purpose have been proposed. Sensor nodes are not to be recycled; therefore it is to be inexpensive to reduce total cost of the network. Sensor nodes are battery operated and may be damaged as when it is running out of battery. Utilization of sensor networks is for monitoring dangerous target area or hostile environment, hence it is considered to be lack of prior knowledge of post-configuration considering location and condition. Sensor nodes are generally having limited memory location and limited bandwidth [2, 9]. They are vulnerable to physical capture or in other words, sensor nodes can easily be physically compromised by adversary. Moreover, after compromises, all credential information in the sensor node will be exposed to the adversary. Sensor nodes are capable of less computation power as most of the sensor nodes.

© Springer Nature Singapore Pte Ltd. 2016
A. Unal et al. (Eds.): SmartCom 2016, CCIS 628, pp. 724–732, 2016.
DOI: 10.1007/978-981-10-3433-6_87

Table 1. Edge table for $X^{5,17}$ Ramanujan graph

z	$\gamma_0(z)$	$\gamma_1(z)$	$\gamma_2(z)$	$\gamma_3(z)$	$\gamma_4(z)$	$\gamma_5(z)$
0	0	2	8	9	15	0
1	6	14	1	1	11	3
2	12	10	0	14	0	6
3	1	16	12	15	5	9
4	7	4	5	10	4	12
5	13	3	14	4	8	15
6	2	7	10	8	16	1
7	8	15	11	13	6	4
8	14	5	6	0	0	7
9	3	0	0	11	12	10
10	9	11	4	6	2	13
11	15	1	9	7	10	16
12	4	9	13	3	14	2
13	10	13	7	12	13	5
14	16	12	2	5	1	8
15	5	0	3	0	7	11
16	11	6	16	16	3	14
17	0	2	8	9	15	0

Table 2. Edge table for $X^{5,29}$ Ramanujan graph

z	$\gamma_0(z)$	$\gamma_1(z)$	$\gamma_2(z)$	$\gamma_3(z)$	$\gamma_4(z)$	$\gamma_5(z)$
0	0	2	8	21	27	0
1	7	26	1	1	19	25
2	14	18	4	12	0	21
3	21	28	19	4	25	17
4	28	24	3	2	26	13
5	6	25	18	9	24	9
6	13	23	21	13	7	5
7	20	6	14	19	10	1
8	27	9	23	0	14	26
9	5	13	5	20	8	22
10	12	7	26	22	28	18
11	19	27	24	0	13	14
12	26	12	2	14	12	10
13	4	11	6	16	9	6
14	11	8	12	7	0	2
15	18	0	22	17	21	27
16	25	20	13	23	18	23

(*continued*)

Table 2. (*continued*)

z	$\gamma_0(z)$	$\gamma_1(z)$	$\gamma_2(z)$	$\gamma_3(z)$	$\gamma_4(z)$	$\gamma_5(z)$
17	3	17	15	27	17	19
18	10	16	0	5	2	15
19	17	1	7	3	22	11
20	24	21	9	24	16	7
21	2	15	0	6	20	3
22	9	19	10	15	23	28
23	16	22	16	8	6	24
24	23	5	20	11	4	20
25	1	3	27	26	5	16
26	8	4	25	10	1	12
27	15	0	17	25	11	8
28	22	10	28	28	3	4
29	0	2	8	21	27	0

2 Expander Graph Based Key Pre-distribution Scheme

Various Key Predistribution Schemes have been proposed in past years. Among these an expander graph based KPS is widely used scheme. An expander graph is a sparse graph (graph with few edges) that has strong connectivity properties. Camtepe *et al.* uses *Ramanujan Expander graph* [3–5] for key pre-distribution scheme and discusses mapping of the expander graph property to key pre-distribution technique. As Ramanujan Expander graph has good expansion, hence use of these graph in KPS minimizes key-path length, maximize the key ring size, maximizing the pairwise key-share probability and resilience [11]. As in combinatorial design [12], Ramanujan Expander graph based KPS has some limitations in choosing [7, 12] number of nodes. A Ramanujan graph $X^{s,t}$ is a graph with number of nodes $n = t + 1$ and the degree of the graph k = s + 1, where both s and t are prime congruent to $1 \, mod(4)$. A Ramanujan graph can be constructed as follows:

Step 1: Generate a vector $a_j = \;<a_0, a_1, a_2, a_3>\;$ for $0 \le j \le s$ where:

(a) $a_0 \in \mathbb{N}$ is an odd number
(b) $a_1, a_2, a_3 \in \mathbb{Z}$ are even numbers
(c) $a_0^2 + a_1^2 + a_2^2 + a_3^2 = s$

Step 2: For $z = 0 \, to \, z = t + 1$, calculate $\gamma_j(z)$ with vector a_j for $0 \le j \le s$ as:

$$\gamma_j(z) = \frac{(a_0 + ia_1)z + (a_2 + ia_3)}{(-a_2 + ia_3 z + (a_0 - ia_1)} (mod)t \text{ for } z \in \mathbb{N}$$

For node $z = 0 \, to \, z = t + 1$, $\gamma_j(z)$ for $0 \le j \le s$ will be the neighbours.

2.1 An Experiment with $X^{5,17}$ Ramanujan Graph

Here is explanation of an example of $X^{5,17}$ Ramanujan graph, where $t+1=18$ vertices with degree $s+1=6$ including self loop and multiple edges. The $s+1=6$ vectors will be:

$$a_0 = <1,2,0,0> \quad a_1 = <1,0,2,0> \quad a_2 = <1,0,0,2>$$
$$a_3 = <1,0,0,-2> \quad a_4 = <1,0,-2,0> \quad a_5 = <1,-2,0,0>$$

For each node z where $0 \le z \le t+1=18$ the edge table for the Ramanujan graph is shown in Table 1.

Figure 1 shows key graph using $X^{5,17}$ Ramanujan graph after deletion of self-loops and multiple edges.

A physical sensor network modelled as a random graph [10] $G(V,E_R)$ with 18 nodes as shown in Fig. 2 and deployed the keys based on Ramanujan $X^{5,\ 17}$ expander graph $G(V,E_X)$. An intersection graph [6] $G(V,E_s) = G(V,E_R \cap E_X)$ with the Ramanujan graph shows the secure communication link between nodes as in Fig. 3.

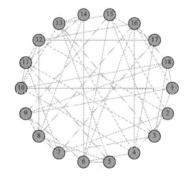

Fig. 1. Ramanujan Expander graph $X^{5,\ 17}$

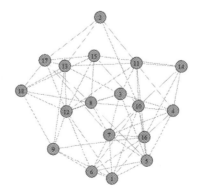

Fig. 2. A random graph $G(V,E_R)$, showing physical communication

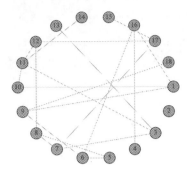

Fig. 3. Intersection Graph $G(V, E_s) = G(V, E_R \cap E_X)$

It is observed that almost all nodes (except node no. 2) can securely communicate with their neighbour node with an immediate pair wise key or via a key path establishment.

Network Scenario#1: it is assumed that every node in the expander graph is in communication range and

Network Scenario#2: communication can take place as in the random graph shown in Fig. 2.

2.2   Experiment with $X^{5,29}$ Ramanujan Graph

Here is explanation of an example of $X^{5,29}$ Ramanujan graph, where $t+1 = 30$ vertices with degree $s+1 = 6$ including self loop and multiple edges. (Table 2) The $s+1 = 6$ vectors will be:

$$a_0 = <1,2,0,0> \quad a_1 = <1,0,2,0> \quad a_2 = <1,0,0,2>$$
$$a_3 = <1,0,0,-2> \quad a_4 = <1,0,-2,0> \quad a_5 = <1,-2,0,0>$$

For each node z where $0 \le z \le 29$ the edge table for the Ramanujan graph is shown in Table 2.

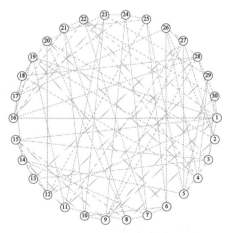

Fig. 4. Ramanujan Expander graph $X^{5, 29}$

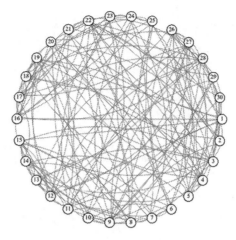

Fig. 5. A random graph $G(V, E_R)$, showing physical communication

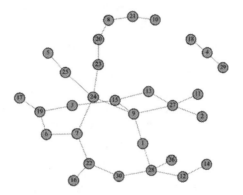

Fig. 6. Intersection Graph $G(V, E_s) = G(V, E_R \cap E_X)$

Figure 4 shows key graph using $X^{5,29}$ Ramanujan graph after deletion of self-loops and multiple edges. An intersection graph is shown in Fig. 6.

Network Scenario#*1:* it is assumed that every node in the expander graph is in communication range and

Network Scenario#*2:* communication can take place as in the random graph shown in Fig. 5.

3   Comparative Analysis

3.1   Connectivity Comparison of Ramanujan Graph Based KPS Vs Random KPS

Plot in Fig. 7 shows probability of having a key between any two randomly chosen nodes. Ramanujan KPS gives perfect resilience against an adversary but lower

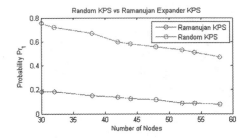

Fig. 7. Probability of Key share in Random KPS Vs Ramanujan KPS

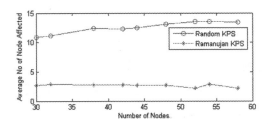

Fig. 8. Random KPS vs Ramanujan Graph based KPS resilience comparison

connectivity and expansion than Random KPSs, for the same network size and key storage. Since random graphs are known to be good expanders with high probability, this means that, contrary to intuition, a key graph based on an expander graph construction is likely to be a worse expander than a key graph generated by Eschenauer Gligor KPS scheme [1, 4].

3.2 Resilience Comparison of Ramanujan Graph Based KPS Vs Random KPS

Although random KPS gives high probability of connectivity but at the same time its resiliency seems to be lower than that of Ramanujan graph Based KPS. Figure 8 we shows average number of nodes affected in case of one node compromise in both the techniques.

Table 3. Number of path with different lengths

Path	Number of Nodes									
	18	30	32	38	42	44	48	52	54	58
1-hop	44	76	86	100	112	112	124	87	148	98
2-hop	84	237	243	297	362	317	451	336	549	397
3-hop	8	92	132	259	319	430	446	500	642	681
4-hop	0	1	4	10	27	44	60	320	39	410
5-hop	0	0	0	0	0	0	0	32	0	10

3.3   Hop Count in Ramanujan KPS

The Table 3 gives Number of path with different lengths denoted by 1-hop, 2-hop etc. If two sensor nodes does not share a common key, they need to establish a secure path called path key establishment. A key path with shorter length is preferable for good key pre-distribution scheme. Once path key discovery is successful, i.e. a sequence of secure links has been achieved between two sensor nodes, these nodes can establish their shared key by sending the shared key from one end to other. As each link is secure, the confidentiality of shared key between two nodes can be therefore guaranteed.

4   Conclusion

In this paper we have discussed the essential requirements such as key storage, connectivity and resilience for a good key pre-distribution scheme along with some important considerable requirements like good expansion in intersection graph. To maximise the total key-share between the pairs of nodes, it is desirable to consider the concept of edge expansion coefficient, Cheeger constant, global connectivity in the secure communication graph. Random KPS is considered to be suitable for good connectivity with smaller storage by randomly distributing keys form a large key pool. We have performed some experiments on Ramanujan expander graph based KPS and analyze the results in various deployment scenarios. It is seen that Ramanujan Expander graph based KPS helps in achieving a security for WSN to some extent by increasing secure connectivity with minimum hop count and by avoiding cut-edge and cut-point in the network and give us better resilience against node compromise as compared to Random KPS.

References

1. Eschenauer L, Gligor V.: A key-management scheme for distributed sensor networks. In: Proceedings of the Annual ACM Computer and Communications Security (CCS) (2002)
2. Chen, C.-Y., Chao, H.-C.: A survey of key distribution in wireless sensor networks. Secur. Commun. Netw. **7**, 2495–2508 (2014). doi:10.1002/sec.354
3. Hoory, S., Linial, N., Wigderson, A.: Expander graphs and their applications. Bull. Am. Math. Soc. **43**(4), 439–562 (2006)
4. Kendall, M., Martin, K.M.: On the role of expander graphs in key predistribution schemes for wireless sensor networks. In: Armknecht, F., Lucks, S. (eds.) WEWoRC 2011. LNCS, vol. 7242, pp. 62–82. Springer, Heidelberg (2012). doi:10.1007/978-3-642-34159-5_5
5. Godsil, C., Royle, G.: Incidence Graphs. Section 5.1 in Algebraic Graph Theory, pp. 78–79. Springer, New York (2001)
6. Chung, F.R.K.: Spectral Graph Theory. American Mathematical Society, California State University, Fresno (1994)
7. Çamtepe, S.A., Yener, B.: Combinatorial design of key distribution mechanisms for wireless sensor networks. IEEE/ACM Trans. Netw. **15**(2), 346–358 (2007)
8. Du, W., Deng, J,, Han, Y.S., Varshney, P.: A pairwise key pre-distriubtion scheme for wireless sensor networks. In: Proceedings of the Annual ACM Computer and Communications Security (CCS) (2003)

9. Blundo, C., Santis, A.D., Herzberg, A., Kutten, S., Vaccaro, U., Yung, M.: Perfectly-secure key distribution for dynamic conferences. In: Brickell, E.F. (ed.) Advances in Cryptology – CRYPTO 1992. LNCS, vol. 740. Springer, Heidelberg (1993)
10. Chan, H., Perrig, A., Song, D.: Random key predistribution schemes for sensor networks. In: Proceedings of IEEE Symposium on Security and Privacy (S&P) (2003)
11. Camtepe, S.A., Yener, B., Yung, M.: Expander graph based key distribution mechanisms in wireless sensor networks. In: ICC 2006, IEEE International Conference on Communcations, pp. 2262–2267 (2006)
12. Saikia, M. Acharjamayum, I., Hussain, Md.A.: A review on desirable measures for good key pre-distribution scheme in wireless sensor network. In: ICGCIoT-2015, pp. 129–134, 8–10 October 2015. doi:10.1109/ICGCIoT.2015.7380443

A Survey of Discriminating Distributed DoS Attacks from Flash Crowds

N. Srihari Rao[1], K. Chandra Sekharaiah[2(✉)], and A. Ananda Rao[3]

[1] CVR College of Engineering, Hyderabad, Telangana, India
raon2006@gmail.com
[2] School of Information Technology, JNTUH University,
Hyderabad, Telangana, India
chandrasekharaiahk@gmail.com
[3] JNTUA College of Engineering, JNTUA University,
Anantapur, Andhra Pradesh, India
akepogu@gmail.com

Abstract. The Internet is becoming part and parcel of everyone in everyday life. Almost all people are depending heavily on the Internet for all types of online activities. Hence, many Information Technology (IT) companies and organizations do business with people or enable businesses for people by running and/or supporting online web services continuously and try to attain or guarantee continuous service availability. From the old and recent bitter experiences of web servers with Distributed DoS (DDoS) attacks, one can realize that they become a serious threat to web site's availability. Along similar lines, flash crowds also prove to be damaging to web servers by losing business, if not properly discriminated from DDoS attacks and handled well. In this context, the task of differentiating the DDoS attacks from the flash crowds gets more significance and hence, we carried out an extensive survey over this. We analysed numerous existing approaches and compared important features used for discrimination.

Keywords: Web server · DDoS attacks · Flow · Distance metric · Flash crowds

1 Introduction

Denial-of-Service (DoS) attack can be defined as security violation caused to deny service to legitimate clients, while servicing components are maliciously misused by an attacker to allocate all resources to illegitimate traffic. The DDoS attack is the collective effort put by geographically or logically distributed machines in order to cause a much larger attack impact than a single DoS attack as shown in Fig. 1(b). DDoS in effect is equivalent to multiple DoS attacks on a single host or network. All the different DDoS attacks exploit the weaknesses present in the protocols existing at the corresponding layer and fulfil their goals.

A flash crowd (FC) or flash event (FE) is an unexpected surge in number of visitors to a particular website resulting in a sudden increase in server load as shown in Fig. 1(a).

© Springer Nature Singapore Pte Ltd. 2016
A. Unal et al. (Eds.): SmartCom 2016, CCIS 628, pp. 733–742, 2016.
DOI: 10.1007/978-981-10-3433-6_88

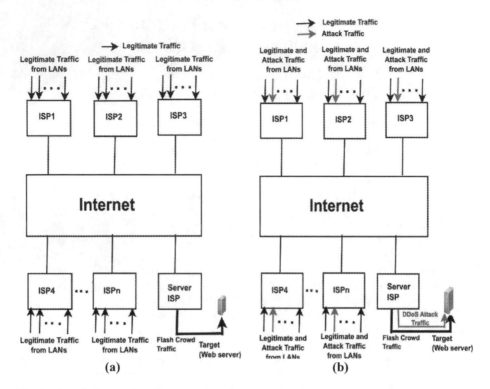

Fig. 1. (a) Flash crowd traffic towards web server (b) Flash crowd traffic and DDoS traffic towards web server.

It may impose a great amount of strain on the network paths reaching to a server resulting in a noticeable increase in loss of packets and network congestion. This unexpected surge in number of visitors may be due to the sudden increase in popularity of a web site due to an important event that has recently occurred. It may also be due to the immense announcement of latest web services introduced for public or non-commercial software download put on this website.

Discriminating flash crowds from DDoS attacks is very much significant, because protecting and running the web server constantly requires us to confirm the occurrence of DDoS attack or flash crowd. In case of the DDoS attack defense system needs to determine malicious IPs and filter that traffic. On the other hand, if it is a flash crowd, the defense system needs to handle this instead of filtering, by resource overprovisioning or via other approaches like Content Distribution Networks. Few researchers [5–7, 9, 12–14] conducted a good deal of research for this differentiation exploiting the properties mentioned in [1] and ended with sufficient results.

The sections of this paper are as follows. Section 2 presents a survey of approaches with their pros and cons. Section 3 compares nature of features with respect to DDoS attacks and flash crowds. Section 4 presents graphical analyses of existing approaches in qualitative terms. Section 5 contains conclusions and future directions.

2   Literature Survey

The survey conducted for discrimination of opposite traffic is presented here.

2.1   Using Important Characteristics

Some important characteristics are identified and recommended to be used to formulate strategies to help web servers quickly filter malicious requests. Jaeyeon Jung et al. [1] characterise opposite traffic using three major features, namely 1. Traffic patterns, 2. Client characteristics, and 3. File reference characteristics. These strategies neither require too many CPU cycles nor modify TCP/IP stack on web servers. It has the overall benefit of serving many legitimate requests under overloaded conditions. Some of these techniques are biased against clients in tiny clusters because it is more likely to reject requests of clients from these clusters.

2.2   Using Kill-Bots: A Kernel Extension

S. Kandula et al. [2] propose "Kill-Bots" that protects web servers against flash crowd attacks. It consists of two functions namely 1. Authentication, and 2. Admission Control. When the web server is overloaded, the authentication mechanism that consists of two stages is activated. Bloom filter drops requests from illegitimate IP addresses and allows normal users who cannot or do not will to solve graphical tests, despite the DDoS attack being on. It protects the authentication mechanism from being DDoS-attacked. It improves performance of the server in both the cases of DDoS attacks and flash crowds. It imposes a good amount of computation complexity on the defense system.

2.3   Using Decoy Hyperlinks

Dimtris Gavilis et al. [3, 4] accomplish distinguishing when there is a combined traffic, by embedding decoy hyperlinks in web pages. These hyperlinks are designed in such a way that these are invisible to human users, but an automated program treats a normal hyperlink and a decoy hyperlink equally. Therefore, it is possible to detect DDoS attacks by inspecting for zombies which follow these decoy hyperlinks. It is totally transparent to users. It succeeds by embedding few of deceiving hyperlinks in very few of web pages. It is more suitable for web sites that do not require authentication. It is possible for an attacker to mimic normal navigational patterns and use them later.

2.4   Using Analyses on Features of Source IP Distribution and Request Volume Escalation Process

Typical features used by Quyen Le et al. [5] for discrimination include 1. Source IP distribution of requests, and 2. Request volume escalation process. Discrimination based on source IP distribution is based on 1. Source probability, 2. Source distribution map, and 3. Source address aggregation. It is very difficult to manually mimic the normal or flash crowd source IP distribution pattern for any web server. In spoofed DDoS attack the attackers use randomized IP addresses to fool the system that the request traffic is from distributed source IP addresses. The traffic escalation can be inspected using digital signal processing by Discrete Wavelet Transform (DWT) or simple request volume histograms. The analysis methods used here for spoofed DDoS attacks are also applicable to other types of DDoS attacks. This method is proved to be efficient for real world applications. Other reliable metrics have to be considered for improving the system's promptness and reliability.

2.5   Using Information Theory [6]

Attack flows share the same attack pattern whereas flash crowd flows do not share this type of pattern in a short period of time. Once an attack alarm is raised, the Kullback-Leibler distance between every pair of suspicious flows is calculated and the accumulative distance is compared to a selected threshold for making a decision. It can be implemented easily and independently in a community network. It can detect the attack within a few seconds. It need not store past packages for analysis and costs only little router's computing power. The detection accuracy and confirmation time need to be optimized. This technique suffers if attackers can mimic normal traffic patterns.

2.6   Using Randomness Check

Huyndo Park et al. [7] propose *FE and DDoS Distinguisher (FDD)* to check randomness of the client distribution among clusters. Initially, a matrix is constructed that captures the cluster distribution of the incoming requests. Then XOR and AND operations are separately applied to the two matrices constructed at current and previous time intervals and stored for the next step. Rank is calculated for these three matrices and it serves as a feature for testing randomness of the element distribution in these matrices. FDD can infer a particular traffic through these ranks. It is a simple and effective mechanism. It has high discrimination accuracy and needs low memory usage. It is implementable on large speed networking devices. It throws no light on quantitative aspects of the accuracy measure.

2.7   By Modelling Human Behavior

G. Oikonomou, and J. Mirkovic [8] model human behaviour using 1. Request dynamics, 2. Request semantics, and 3. Ability to process visual cues. Bots with aggressiveness in one or more of the selected features are detected by inspecting interaction of clients with servers. Bots generate valid but unlikely, and low-probability sequences hence can be detected. Bots can automatically detect and request human invisible objects such as hyperlinks, action triggers etc., and hence be detected. All these defenses are transparent to humans and can be active to work for each service request. All these defenses can be combined for more protection. The attackers have to use more number of bots to succeed. This approach presents few false positive probabilities which results in small collateral damage. Its performance needs to be improved.

2.8 Using Information Distance

Shui Yu et al. [9] utilized three distance metrics namely the Jeffrey distance, the Sibson distance, and the Hellinger distance, for calculating flow similarity. This strategy is scalable and practical. Detection can be conducted with only two cooperative routers on the Internet. The attack packets could be filtered far away from the victim. This approach works against a variety of DDoS flooding attack tools and can detect even new types of attacks. The accuracy achieved is almost 65% in experiments with real data sets. It needs an improvement in the percentage of discrimination accuracy achieved.

2.9 Using Probability Metrics

Ke Li et al. [10] use the mixed probability metric of total variation and Bhattacharyya coefficient to identify traffic as belonging to normal flows, flash crowd flows, and DDoS flows. It reduces both false positive rates and false negative rates. It performs early detection. Few characteristics of IP packets and flows are considered for the DDoS attack detection and response. Detection accuracy still needs to be improved.

2.10 Using CALD: An Architectural Extension

CALD [11] protects web sites against multiple DDoS attacks that pretend to be flash crowds. The mess tests facilitate online detection. It consists of three functions namely (1) Abnormal traffic detection, (2) DDoS attack detection, and (3) Filter. The difference between observed behaviour and the output of the model where the output of the model represents normal system behaviour is used for detecting anomalies. Anomalous source IP addresses, which are found out by applying mess tests are provided to the filter component. It works for different application-layer DDoS attacks. It is simple. It gains high performance on the kernel web servers in spite of DDoS attacks because the protection modules are away from the web services. The updating and deployment of these modules is more convenient. Currently, it is sensitive to the slowly increasing DDoS attack.

2.11 Using Packet Arrival Patterns [12]

The packet transmission rates for the attack flows appear to be predictable which form a pattern in a short period of time, whereas human users unpredictably issue requests at any time. Using mathematical models and/or statistical analysis as in [12] DDoS attacks are detected. Its detection accuracy is good enough. It is useful for global DDoS detection and can be implemented in any network equipment and in any of the layers of TCP/IP protocol stack. The large number of observations of packet transmission rates can cause delay in detection. This technique needs to be improved for fastness and reduced complexity.

2.12   Using Flow Correlation Coefficient (FCC)

Shui Yu et al. [14] notice that the recent DDoS attack flows resemble more compared to the flash crowd flows. FCC is used here as an indicator of the similarity between a pair of flows. If a sudden traffic rise occurs to the server, the method has to identify the nature of traffic. At this instant of time, the routers in the network sample suspected flows by counting the number of packets per time interval. By using a suitable flow length, the FCC is calculated between each pair of suspected flows. The FCC value is compared with an appropriately chosen threshold value as an indication for DDoS attack. The defense diameter is extended far from the potential victim. It works for a variety of DDoS flooding attacks. It is free from unnecessary delays and can effectively detect DDoS attacks. Super botnet consists of live bots whose number is exactly equal or nearly equal to the number of simultaneous users of a flash crowd. This method fails, if a super botnet can be organized by an attacker to beat it. When this detection method is known to attackers they may try to invent new strategies to escape detection.

3   Behaviour of Features Used in Existing Approaches

For different existing approaches, nature of corresponding features with respect to DDoS attacks and flash crowds is summarized in Table 1 given below.

4   Graphical Analyses of Existing Approaches

Many of research works done earlier with respect to our survey have not quantified the results of measurements made. Hence, we are unable to compare quantities of importance such as detection accuracy, the false positive rate, response time etc. between these approaches. However, we are able to represent the qualities of these different approaches in terms of addressed features of DDoS/FC Detection and/or DDoS Flow Identification, and Mitigation/Prevention as indicated in Fig. 2. From the graph, we can understand that some methods which are able to detect are not used to identify, and mitigate or prevent. Hence methods which are presented to only detect can be further investigated to add mitigation or prevention capabilities.

Table 1. The list of features identified and utilized for discrimination.

Approach name	Feature(s) utilized for discrimination	Nature of feature in case of:	
		Clients of flash crowds	Zombies of DDoS attacks
1. Using important characteristics [1]	a. Traffic Volume	Increases due to increase in the number of clients	Increases due to increase in the number of clients or number of requests generated per client
	b. Rate of Incoming Traffic	Gradually increases over time before reaching the maximum	Suddenly increases to the maximum
	c. Rate of New Source IP Addresses	Rate constantly increases	Rate increases suddenly and largely at the start of the attack and remains low after the start of DDoS attack
	d. Number of clients and their distribution	Number of clients matches with the request rate. Client distribution across ISPs and networks follows population distribution	Number of clients may or may not match with the request rate. Generally, client distribution across ISPs and networks does not follow population distribution
	e. Cluster Overlap	Between clusters before and during flash crowd is significant	Between clusters before and during the DDoS attack is very small
	f. Per-client Request Rate	Lower during flash crowd than usual because the server usually gets slower during the flash crowd and the legitimate clients are responsive to the performance of a server	Stable during the DDoS attack and deviates from normal in cases of 1. Few clients emitting very high request rates, and 2. Large number of clients generating a low request rate
	g. Requested Files	Requested file distribution is Zipf-like	Requested file distribution is unlikely to be Zipf-like
2. Using Kill-Bots: a kernel extension [2]	a. Authentication using graphical tests	Pass the test except for search-bots or unwilling clients	Cannot pass the test
	b. Admission Control	These can get through this	Recognized zombie IPs cannot get through this
3. Using decoy hyperlinks [3, 4]	Decoy hyperlinks as traps	Decoy hyperlinks are not followed	Decoy hyperlinks are followed
4. Using analysis of two features [5]	a. Source IP distribution	Roughly distributed and difficult to mimic	Randomly distributed
	b. Request volume escalation process	Request volume rises gradually before flash event and falls gradually after the flash event	Request volume rises suddenly before the DDoS attack event and falls suddenly after the DDoS event
5. Using information theory [6]	Package distribution distance among the two suspicious flows	Distance is not less than the given threshold	Distance is less than the given threshold
6. Using randomness check [7]	Rank value of three computed matrices	Differ from DDoS and possess a pattern	Differ from Flash Crowds and possess a pattern
7. By modelling human behavior [8]	a. Chosen-parameters captured by request dynamics model	Non aggressive w.r.t. chosen parameters	Aggressive w.r.t. chosen parameters
	b. Normal users' request patterns that are common	Match	Do not match because bots generate unlikely and low-probability sequences

(continued)

Table 1. (*continued*)

Approach name	Feature(s) utilized for discrimination	Nature of feature in case of:	
		Clients of flash crowds	Zombies of DDoS attacks
	c. Human invisible objects for deception	Do not request these objects	Request these objects
8. Using information distance [9]	Distance metric	Large	Very small
9. Using probability metrics [10]	a. Total variation	Large	Very small
	b. Bhattacharyya Coefficient	Close to the zero	Close to one
10. Using CALD: an architectural extension [11]	a. Normal system behavior	Observed behaviour is close to normal	Observed behaviour is very much abnormal
	b. Mess tests	Normal source IPs	Abnormal source IPs
11. Using packet arrival patterns [12]	Packet transmission rates	Unpredictable	Predictable
12. Using Flow Correlation Coefficient (FCC) [14]	FCC between suspected flows	Negative for DDoS if the cumulative value lies less than the chosen threshold value	Positive for DDoS if the cumulative value lies more than the chosen threshold value

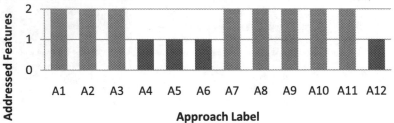

Addressed Features 1: DDoS/FC Detection Only
Addressed Features 2: DDoS/FC Detection + DDoS Flow Identification, and Mitigation/Prevention

A1: Using Important Characteristics

A2: Using Kill-Bots: A Kernel extension

A3: Using Decoy Hyperlinks

A4: Using Analysis of Two Features

A5: Using Information Theory

A6: Using Randomness Check

A7: By Modeling Human Behavior

A8: Using Information Distance

A9: Using Probability Metrics

A10: Using CALD: An Architectural Extension

A11: Using Packet Arrival Patterns

A12: Using Flow Correlation Coefficient(FCC)

Fig. 2. Qualitative aspects of approaches discussed in this work

5 Conclusions and Future Work

Differentiating DDoS attacks from the flash crowds is not trivial for an automated DDoS detection or defense system, because of the very near similarities between them. In this work, we presented an elaborate survey carried out for this purpose. Detailed taxonomy regarding flash events is presented in [15] and this helps researchers to effectively attempt finding more discriminative characteristics. From the literature, we predict that there are some unexplored areas which facilitate this discrimination. Hence we would like to proceed further in order to come up with some more informative and distinguishing characteristics in the near future to detect DDoS attacks as well as identify DDoS or flash crowd traffic flows.

References

1. Jung, J., Krishnamurthy, B., Rabinovich, M.: Flash crowds and denial of service attacks: characterization and implications for CDNs and web sites. In: Proceedings of the 11th International Conference on World Wide Web, New York, USA, pp. 293–304 (2002)
2. Kandula, S., Katabi, D., Jacob, M., Berger, A.: Botz-4-sale:surviving organized DDoS attacks that mimic flash crowds. In: Proceedings of the 2nd Symposium on Networked Systems Design & Implementation (NSDI), pp. 287–300 (2005)
3. Gavrilis, D., Dermatas, E.: Detection of Web Denial-of-Service Attacks using decoy hyperlinks. In: 5th International Symposium on Communication Systems, Networks and Digital Signal Processing (CSNDSP), Patras (2006)
4. Gavrilis, D., Chatzis, I., Dermatas, E.: Flash crowd detection using decoy hyperlinks. In: IEEE International Conference on Networking, Sensing and Control, pp. 466–470 (2007)
5. Le, Q., Zhanikeev, M., Tanaka, Y.: Methods of distinguishing flash crowds from spoofed DoS attacks. In: 3rd EuroNGI Conference on Next Generation Internet Networks, pp. 167–173 (2007)
6. Yu, S., Zhou, W., Doss, R.: Information theory based detection against network behavior mimicking DDoS attacks. IEEE Commun. Lett. **12**(4), 318–321 (2008)
7. Park, H., Li, P., Gao, D., Lee, H., Deng, R.H.: Distinguishing between FE and DDoS using randomness check. In: Wu, T.-C., Lei, C.-L., Rijmen, V., Lee, D.-T. (eds.) ISC 2008. LNCS, vol. 5222, pp. 131–145. Springer, Heidelberg (2008)
8. Oikonomou, G., Mirkovic, J.: Modeling human behavior for defense against flash-crowd attacks. In: Proceedings of IEEE International Conference on Communications (ICC 2009), pp. 1–6 (2009)
9. Yu, S., Thapngam, T., Liu, J., Wei, S., Zhou, W.: Discriminating DDoS flows from flash crowds using information distance. In: Proceedings of the 3rd IEEE International Conference on Network and System Security (NSS 2009), pp. 351–356 (2009)
10. Li, K., Zhou, W., Li, P., Hai, J., Liu, J.: Distinguishing DDoS attacks from flash crowds using probability metrics. In: Third International Conference on Network and System Security (NSS 2009), pp. 9–17 (2009)
11. Wen, S., Jia, W., Zhou, W., Zhou, W., Xu, C.: CALD: surviving various application-layer DDoS attacks that mimic flash crowd. In: 4th International Conference on Network and System Security (NSS), pp. 247–254 (2010)

12. Thapngam, T., Yu, S., Zhou,W., Beliakov, G.: Discriminating DDoS attack traffic from flash crowd through packet arrival patterns. In: IEEE Conference on Computer Communications Workshops, pp. 952–957 (2011)
13. Bhatia, S., Mohay, G., Tickle, A., Ahmed, E.: Parametric differences between a real-world distributed denial-of-service attack and a flash event. In: Proceedings of Sixth International Conference on Availability, Reliability and Security (ARES), pp. 210–217. IEEE (2011)
14. Yu, S., Zhou, W., Jia, W., Guo, S., Xiang, Y., Tang, F.: Discriminating DDoS attacks from flash crowds using flow correlation coefficient. IEEE Trans. Parallel Distrib. Syst. **23**(6), 1073–1080 (2012)
15. Pal, R., Kumar, S., Sharma, R.L.: A detailed classification of flash events: client, server and network characteristics. In: International Conference on Computer Science & Service System (CSSS), pp. 960–963 (2012)

High Speed Low Power Implementation of Combinational and Sequential Circuits Using Reversible Logic

Sanketa Keshkamat[(✉)] and S.T. Gandhe

Department of Electronics and Telecommunication,
Sandip Institute of Technology and Research Centre, Nashik, India
Sanketa.keshkamat@gmail.com, stgandhe@gmail.com

Abstract. In this paper a survey on design options is carried out. An investigation of comparative analysis of 1-bit full adder with various options on the basis of power dissipation, propagation delay, and area concerning to the of number of transistors used, Energy Delay Product (EDP) & Power Delay Product (PDP).

In present scenario, reversible logic based designing is attracting researchers because of its less power usage. Reversible logic is playing important role in low-power circuit scheme. The application areas of reversible logic is nanotechnology, CMOS(less power), cryptography, DSP, DNA & quantum computing, communication, computer graphics. To contract quantity price, the profundity of circuits & count of drivel outputs are the main aim of intending reversible logics gates. This work will give brief idea about building of full adder circuits using the basic reversible gates.

Keywords: Reversible logic · Power dissipation · Propagation delay · Energy delay product and power delay product

1 Introduction

VLSI Circuit design has gain interest in the past few decades and substantial growth is done in the development of this. As the Application Specific architectures & microprocessors comprises many components needed big rooms in the 70's, but the present scenario is that too many transistors are built up on about square millimeters. These are the results of the accomplishments made in the world of semiconductors based on Moore's law. Still, it's apparent that such extensive development will attain its boundaries in the future when the shrinking attains a level, whereas single transistor sizes are approaching the nuclear scale. Because of this, few researchers anticipate that from the 2020 about, germination of transistor density won't be potential anymore. Furthermore to meet the demands for extra computational power, alternatives are demanded that go outside the range of conventional technologies such as CMOS. Several design options are available in order to achieve the low power high speed VLSI circuits & the design target of any such circuit includes high speed, low power consumption, less area or a combination of any of the above & is a wide topic of research.

© Springer Nature Singapore Pte Ltd. 2016
A. Unal et al. (Eds.): SmartCom 2016, CCIS 628, pp. 743–751, 2016.
DOI: 10.1007/978-981-10-3433-6_89

The power dissipation & thereupon heat generation is a crucial problem for system architecture & energy dissipation is because of the un-ideal nature of transistors & materials.

The work is divided in two phases as survey of work done on the design options of a 1-bit Full Adder & implementation of the same by using reversible logic for efficient performance.

The first phase presents a detailed survey about the design options for performance efficiency of VLSI designs so as to build up in low power & high speed. The physical & geometrical parameters have been studied along with various logic techniques proposed till the date.

The phase two of the presented work consist of the analysis of few design options for the implementation of a 1-bit Full Adder & structured a design approach with reversible logic style in order to notice its power dissipation, speed as a function of propagation delay, power delay product, energy delay product & area as transistor count.

The information is never lost in Reversible circuits as they have one-to-one mapping among input & output vectors.

2   Design Consideration

PHASE I

2.1   Physical and Geometrical Parameters

a. Supply Voltage Scaling
   Scaling down supply voltage is a means to lessen the power utilization efficiently of digital circuitry as there is a relationship in among the dynamic power uptake & supply voltage. But simultaneously degrade the circuit delay & current level as they are having inverse relationship in between. For this effect the verge voltage in intense submicron processes is reduced for palliating issue.
b. Technology Scaling
   From 1947, the efforts are taken in continuous progress for transistor regarding its reliability, flexibility, cost effective & energy efficiency in final product. The continuous scaling down of the transistor size made is possible to functions into sub-micron & after that in Nano scale regime so as to acquire less area & high speed. The another challenge in MOSFET scaling is its interconnect technology for wiring of Nano scale transistor.
c. Power Consideration
   Designing Circuits that are directed towards low power consumption is a difficult task & it is related to not one thing but multiple aspects need to be considered. There are certain levels wherein there are no specific steps given to reduce the power consumption so statistical or probabilistic modeling or theoretical analysis are used to guess the power consumption of a given design. There are 3 major parts of power dissipation in complementary metal compound semiconductor (CMOS) circuits.

1. Switching Power: It is defined as Power used by the circuit capacitances while switching of transistors.
2. Short Circuit Power: It is defined as Power used due to the current flowing from supply Vdd to ground while switching of transistors.
3. Static Power: Due to leakage & static currents.

3 Logic Techniques in VLSI Circuits

PHASE II

This paper emphasizes the implementation of full adder circuits using reversible logic gates. Basic gates required for designing such circuits are *NOT* gate, Feynman gate, Fredkin gate & Toffoli gate. In low-power circuit design & quantum computing reversible logic is very significant.

The method accustomed style full adder are truth table-based reduction. one among the reduction approaches for reversible circuits depends on truth table descriptions of the perform to be synthesized. Here the given functions typically would like thereby to be reversible. This generates a reversible description of the given perform that later wards will be accustomed notice the required circuit. during this paper, some steps, i.e. the embedding additionally because the synthesis of functions has been given within the variety of truth tables that may be exemplarily reviewed.

3.1 Designing the Standard Cells

The standard cells used in this work to employ the basic reversible gates: Feynman, Toffoli, & Fredkin gates. By definition a reversible gate has identical variety of inputs & outputs, & due to the no fan-out restriction, routing between the cells is straightforward & inserting the cells directly side-by-side is feasible. this may not work for static CMOS, that have many-to-one gates & fan-out. Our commonplace cells can have the subsequent properties:

- All primitive reversible gates are either two- or three-input gates &, therefore, on every side there is up to six input/output pins (three dual-line pins).
- A Vdd & a Vss-rail are added on the top & bottom, respectively. These are important for polarization of the substrate & the well.
- Only two metal layers are used. as enough metal layers for routing between the cells will be leaved.

3.2 The Feynman Gate

Feynman gate are one of the simplest cell; it has a width of 10.5 μm, & uses 8 transistors (Fig. 1).

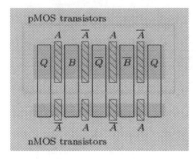

Fig. 1. Abstract layout of Feynman gate

3.3 The Fredkin Gate

The Fredkin gate appears more complicated than the Feynman gate function wise. It has one additional input (three in total) & updates two outputs. That the values & complemented values are often computed severally isn't a full surprise. The Fredkin gate is parity maintaining & the trick of using dual-line values is, thus, not essential, but we still have & compute to both complementary lines such that they can be used in the next gate (Fig. 2).

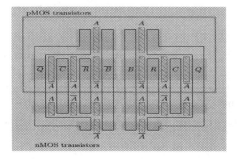

Fig. 2. Abstract layout of Fredkin gate

3.4 The Toffoli Gate

As compare to the Fredkin gate, the design of the Toffoli gate (Fig. 3) shows that this gate is more complicated than the Feynman gate. Twice, it contains two pass-gates in parallel & two pass-gates in serial (Table 1).

3.5 Adder and Counter Layout of Proposed System

We have developed the adder & counter layout using the MICROWIND tool. MICROWIND Tool is specifically developed by French University INSA (National institute of science application) keeping in mind ASIC/CMOS design training needs of

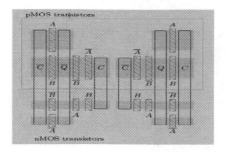

Fig. 3. Abstract layout of Toffoli gate

Table 1. Comparative analysis

Parameter	Feynman gate	Fredkin gate	Toffoli gate
Power dissipation	0 nW	0 nW	0 nW
Efficiency	HIGH	HIGH	HIGH
Quantum cost	ONE	FIVE	FIVE
No. of input-output gates	2 * 2	3 * 3	3 * 3

universities worldwide. In this tool we can see labeled nodes in simulation, which allows us the intuitive control of the simulation (Supply, clock, pulse, PWL, sinus, math) etc. Similarly we can hide particular node in simulation.

Also this tool allows generating the spice netlist of the layout.

Figures 4 and 5 depicts the proposed layout designed. The approach is direct design of sequential circuit with reversible gates.

4   Results

The Results are generated on MICROWIND simulation tool. We have designed the adder using the reversible logic. The results show (Fig. 6) that the adder uses less power than the conventional adders. For this reversible adder we required 3 Toffoli gates & 3 Feynman gates. The total quantum cost of adder is 18 only which is less as compared to the traditional adder. Proposed system design depicts that our direct styles save one .54%–49.09% price & fifty one .43%–81.82% garbage outputs than the substitute design approach advised earlier. Hence, our advised direct style technique beats the antecedently reportable replacement design approach (Table 2).

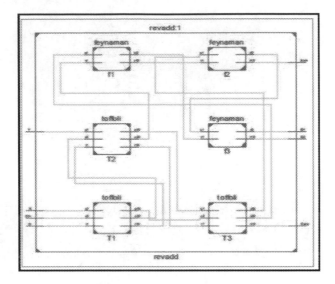

Fig. 4. Adder layout

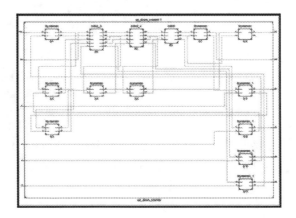

Fig. 5. Counter layout

In this project, we present a novel approach of direct design of counter (Fig. 7) with reversible gates using PSDRM expressions describing the state transitions and output functions of the circuit. Design examples show that our direct designs save 1.54%–49.09% quantum cost and 51.43%–81.82% garbage outputs than the replacement design approach suggested earlier. Thus, our proposed direct design method outperforms the previously reported replacement design approach.

1. XILINX waveform for full adder:-
2. XILINX waveform for counter

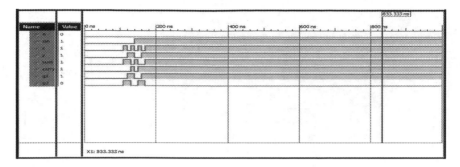

Fig. 6. XILINX waveform for full adder

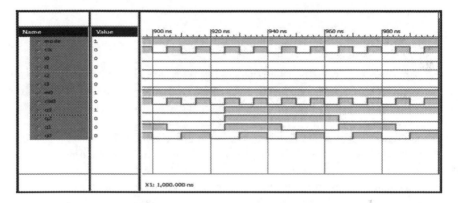

Fig. 7. XILINX waveform for counter

5 Comparative Analysis

Table 2. Comparison results

Parameters	Reversible gate	Garbage input	Constant input	Quantum cost
Mod 8 counter	8	4	1	19
Mod 8 counter[2]	18	4	1	24
adder	6	1	3	12

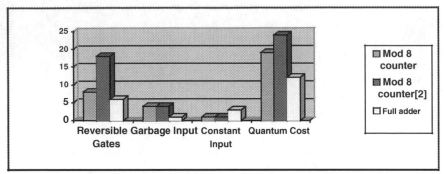

Chart 1: shows the graphical representation of table no.2

6 Conclusion

In this paper we present the archaic reversible gates which are studied in the literature & this paper provide a way to schemers in scheming more complicated computing circuits employing reversible gates. The performance analysis of the designed Adder & Counter layout is done using MICROWIND simulation tool. The results show that the projected Adder layout offers far better results than the normal layouts.

The application space of the reversible logic is beneficial in optical & quantum & deoxyribonucleic acid computing, low power CMOS, cryptography, ddigital signal process, communication, tricks. These gates may be applied in regular circuits realizing Boolean functions. Likewise it's doubtless to construct multiple-valued reversible gates sitting similar properties. The proposed nonparallel designs have the app Timer/ Counter, building reversible ALU, reversible processor etc. are the applications of the proposed designs in digital circuits. This paper depicts an crucial move in developing big & complex reversible sequential circuits.

References

1. Thapliyal, H., Ranganathan, N.: Reversible logic based concurrent error detection methodology for emerging nanocircuits. In: 2010 10th IEEE Conference on Nanotechnology (IEEE-NANO), pp. 217–222 (2010)
2. Bennett, C.H.: Logical reversibility of computation. IBM J. Res. Dev. **17**, 525–532 (1973)
3. Thapliyal, H., Ranganathan, N.: Design, synthesis and test of reversible circuits for emerging nanotechnologies. In: 2012 IEEE Computer Society Annual Symposium on VLSI (ISVLSI), pp. 5–6 (2012)
4. Vasudevan, D.P., Lala, P.K., Parkerson, J.P.: A novel scheme for on-line testable reversible logic circuit design. In: Proceedings of the 13th Asian Test Symposium, pp. 325–330, October 2004
5. Thapliyal, H., Vinod, A.P.: Designing efficient online testable reversible adders with new reversible gate. In: Proceedings of ISCAS 2007, New Orleans, USA, pp. 1085–1088, May 2007

6. Thapliyal, H., Ranganathan, N.: Concurrently testable FPGA design for molecular QCA using conservative reversible logic gate. In: Proceedings of ISCAS 2009, Taipei, pp. 1815–1818, May 2009
7. Toffoli, T.: Reversible computing, Tech memo MIT/LCS/TM-151. MIT Lab for Computer Science (1980)
8. Orlov, A.O., Amlani, I., Bernstein, G.H., Lent, C.S., Snider, G.L.: Realization of a functional cell for quantum-dot cellular automata. Science **277**, 928–930 (1997)
9. Patel, K.N., Hayes, J.P., Markov, I.L.: Error testing for reversible circuits. IEEE Trans. CAD **23**(8), 1220–1230 (2004)
10. Polian, I., Fiehn, T., Becker, B., Hayes, J.P.: A family of logical error models for reversible circuits. In: Proceedings of the 14th Asian Test Symposium, Kolkata, India, pp. 422–427 (2005)
11. Zhong, J., Muzio, J.C.: Analyzing error models for reversible logic circuits. In: IEEE Congress on Evolutionary Computation, Vancouver, BC, pp. 2422–2427 (2006)
12. Mitra, S.: Diversity techniques for concurrent error detection. Ph.D. thesis. Department of Electrical Engineering, Stanford University (2000)

Study the Impact of Carmichael Function on RSA

N. Ramanjaneya Reddy[1(✉)], Pakanati Chenna Reddy[2],
and Mokkala Padmavathamma[3]

[1] Vaagdevi Institute of Technology and Science, Proddatur, AP, India
ramanji.nalavala@gmail.com
[2] Jawaharlal Nehru Technological University, Anantapur, AP, India
pcreddyl@rediffmail.com
[3] Sri Venkateswara University, Tirupati, AP, India
mpadma@svuniversity.ac.in

Abstract. Achieving security is a key aspect for any computer system. Many modern technologies have been applied to achieve the required security. Cryptography provides a primary way to achieve best security. A recent trend shows that many of the cryptographic algorithms are modified with new functionalities to provide better security in all aspects. One major research branch of Cryptography is Public key cryptography. In this paper, one of the popular public key cryptography algorithms, RSA with arithmetic functions are reviewed and analyzed. This paper mainly focused on the use of Carmichael function instead of Euler totient function applied on RSA algorithm. Results have shown that use of Carmichael function results in smaller value for decryption key. This leads to reduced decryption time of RSA algorithm.

Keywords: Encryption · Decryption · Carmichael function · Euler totient function

1 Introduction

Encryption is a process which converts plain text into cipher text in such a way that it is very difficult for the intruder to decipher. In this paper one of the popular public key cryptography algorithm, RSA [1–3] is analyzed using different mathematical functions like Euler totient [4] and Carmichael function [5, 6]. The computational steps of RSA are as follows.

1.1 RSA Algorithm Steps

1. Let p and q be two random prime numbers having same bit length.
2. Calculate the value of $n = p*q$
3. Evaluate $\varphi(n) = (p–1)*(q–1)$, where φ is Euler's totient function.
4. Choose a contingent positive number e, such that gcd of $\varphi(n)$ and number e, should be equal to 1, where $e \in (1, \varphi(n))$

© Springer Nature Singapore Pte Ltd. 2016
A. Unal et al. (Eds.): SmartCom 2016, CCIS 628, pp. 752–756, 2016.
DOI: 10.1007/978-981-10-3433-6_90

5. Evaluate number $d = e^{-1} \bmod \varphi(n)$
6. Calculate cipher text using $c = m^e \pmod{n}$, public key (n, e)
7. Compute plain text using $m = c^d \pmod{n}$, private key d of (p, q).

1.2 Euler's Totient Function

The Euler Φ function measures the number of positive integers less than 'n' that are relatively prime to n. i.e., $\varphi(n) = n \prod_{p|n} (1 - \frac{1}{p})$. This function satisfies Euler theorem, for any integer n > 1. If gcd(a, n) = 1, then $a^{\Phi(n)} \equiv 1 \pmod{n}$. For p and q prime numbers $\varphi(n) = (p - 1)*(q - 1)$.

1.3 Carmichael's Function

Carmichael function [1] of a positive integer n, represented by $\lambda(n)$, which measures the smallest positive integer m such that $a^m \equiv 1 \pmod{m}$ for every integer a that is coprime to n. If p and q are prime numbers then the Carmichael function can be calculated as follows.

$$\lambda(n) = \operatorname{lcm} (p - 1,\ q - 1) \text{ or } (p - 1) * (q - 1)/\gcd((p - 1)(q - 1))$$

2 Analysis

Introduction of Carmichael's function in place of Euler's totient function in RSA can result in faster decryption and also it reduces computational steps for finding private key value using extended Euclidean algorithm.

For example:

Case1: when p and q are small numbers

1(a) Analysis of RSA with an Euler's totient function:

Let p = 19, q = 23; N = pq = 19*23 = 437; $\varphi(n)$ = (p−1)*(q−1) = 18*22 = 396 select e such that 1 < e < $\varphi(n)$, gcd(e, $\varphi(n)$) = 1; gcd(396,13) = 1; Cipher text c = m^e (mod n) = $123^{13} \bmod 437 = 386$. Determine d such that d = e^{-1} mod $\varphi(n)$ = 13^{-1} mod 437; Using extended Euclidean algorithm A1 = 396, A2 = 13 (Table 1).

Table 1. Calculating private key using Extended Euclidean algorithm

1	A	Q	S	T
0	396	–	1	0
1	13	30	0	1
2	6	2	1	−30
3	1	6	−2	61

Finally d = 61, Decryption = m = c^d (mod n) = 386^{61} mod 437 = 123.

1(b) Analysis of RSA with Carmichael function:

Let p = 19, q = 23, N = pq = 19*23 = 437, $\lambda(n)$ = lcm(p–1, q–1) or (p–1)(q–1)/ gcd(p–1, q–1) = (19–1)(23–1)/gcd(19–1, 23–1) = 18*22/gcd(18, 22) = 9.22 = 198. Select e such that 1 < e < $\lambda(n)$, gcd(e, $\lambda(n)$)) = 1; gcd(198, 13) = 1; e = 13. Cipher text c = m^e (mod n) = 123^{13} mod 437. = 386. Determine d such that d = e^{-1} mod $\lambda(n)$ = 13^{-1} mod 198. Using extended Euclidean algorithm A1 = 198, A2 = 13 (Table 2).

Table 2. Calculating private key using Extended Euclidean algorithm

	A	Q	S	T
0	198	–	1	0
1	13	15	0	1
2	3	4	1	–15
3	1	3	–4	61

Finally d = 61, Decryption = m = c^d (mod n) = 386^{61} mod 437 = 123. Discussion for case1: plain text = 123, cipher text = 386 (Table 3).

Table 3. Both private keys are same

P	Q	N	Phi(n)	E	d (private key)
19	23	437	396	13	61
19	23	437	**198** (lamda)	13	61 (both are same)

For small values of p and q there is no difference in private key values computed by both functions.

Case 2: When p and q are large prime numbers

2(a). Analysis of RSA with an Euler's totient function

P = 2357, q = 2551, N = pq = 2357 * 2551 = 6012707 $\varphi(n)$ = (p–1) (q–1) = 6007800, choose e value such that gcd(e, $\varphi(n)$) = 1 now choose e = 2674913, for this d(private key) = 4154777(large private key) (Fig. 1).

2(b). Analysis of RSA with Carmichael function

P = 2357, q = 2551, N = pq = 2357 * 2551 = 6012707 $\lambda(n)$ = lcm(p–1, q–1) = 3003900, e = 2674913 (same e value) d' (private key) = 1150877 (less private key) Here **d'** value is **less than d** value (d' < d) (Fig. 2).

Discussion for case2

In this case cipher text can be decrypted by two private keys. Private key computed by Carmichaels function is less than Euler totient function. Also the number of steps are reduced for finding private key by extended Euclidean algorithm when using Carmichaels function as compared with Euler totient function. Decryption is applied on cipher text by small values of private key value, which results in same plain text. Results can be verified from RSA calculator [7].

Case 1:   d and d' are different d' < d

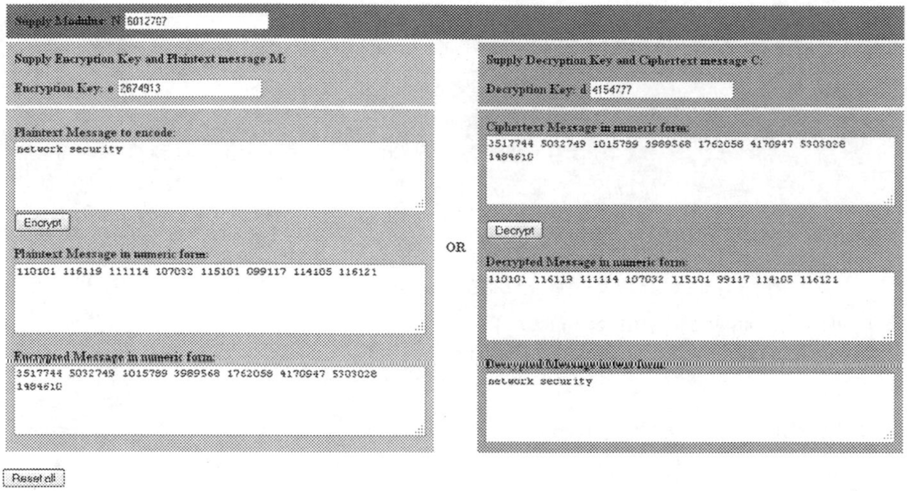

Fig. 1. Case 2(a): Encryption and Decryption using Euler totient function

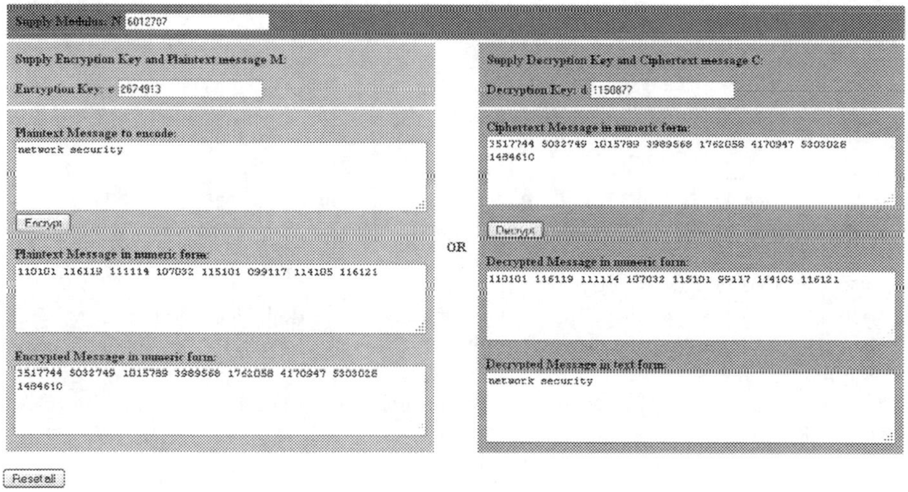

Fig. 2. Case 2(b): Encryption and Decryption using Carmichael function

Case 2: d and d' are different when e < lamda(n) result d' < d
Case 3: d and d' are different when e < lamda(n) result d' <=d
Case 4: d and d' are different when e > lamda(n) result d' < d
Case 5: d and d' are different when e > lamda(n) result d' < d

Case 1 in Table 4 is illustrated in previous page, and remaining cases in Table 4 are not illustrated for want of space.

Table 4. comparison of Euler totient function and Carmichael function for different p and q values

Case no	P	Q	N	Euler $\varphi(n)$	Carmichael $\lambda(n)$	e (choose)	d	d'
1	2357	2551	6012707	6007800	3003900	2674913	4154777	1150877
2	4483	4513	20231779	20222784	3370464	370457	12169961	2058569
3	4483	4513	20231779	20222784	3370464	3058571	765347	765347
4	4483	4513	20231779	20222784	3370464	4058569	19160569	2308249
5	4483	4513	20231779	20222784	3370464	3870569	16554137	3072281

d (private key computed by Euler function)
d' (private key computed by Carmichael function)

3   Conclusion

In all cases Carmichael function produces small or equal private key as compared with Euler totient function. Both d and d' can decrypt the same cipher text. Cipher text can be decrypted by small values of private key which can result in fast decryption and gets original plaintext. From above analysis, it is best to replace Euler totient function with Carmichael function.

References

1. Rivest, R., Shamir, A., Adleman, L.: A method for obtaining digital signatures and public-key cryptosystems. Commun. ACM **21**(2), 120–126 (1978)
2. Menezes, A.J., van Oorschot, P.C., Vanstone, S.A.: Hand Book of Applied Cryptography. CRC Press, Boca Raton (1997)
3. Mao, M.: Modern Cryptology, Theory and Practice. Prentice Hall, Upper Saddle River (2004)
4. Apostal, T.M.: Introduction to Analytic Number Theory. Springer International Students Edition, New York (1980)
5. Carmichael, D.R.: Note on a new number theory function. Bull. Am. Math. Soc. **XVI**, 232–238 (1910)
6. Yimin, G.: A note on the Carmichael function
7. www.cs.drexel.edu/~introcs/Fall/notes/10.1_Cryptography/RSA_Express_EncryptDecrypt.html

Detection of Epileptic Seizure Patient

K.V. Pardeshi[(✉)] and P.A. Dhulekar

ENTC Department, Sandip Institute of Technology
and Research Center, Nashik, India
komalpardeshi30@gmail.com, pravin.dhulekar@sitrc.org

Abstract. In many application areas like video scrutiny, biomedical scrutiny the human motion detection from videotape is the point of interest. This paper represents the progression in topic to epilepsy, in which human motion is most vital element of patient's clinical video. This paper illustrates the topical achievements in video processing, scrutiny along with identification of human motion in epilepsy designed for marker free system. Epilepsy is a disorder of CNS characterized by loss of cognizance with paroxysm. Seizure defines a sudden occurrence of disease. These seizures are attended through hysterical, frequently regular actions of body parts when seizure activity starts, brain areas amenable meant for unveiling with restraint of movement. The dynamics of these modulations is usually indefinite. In order to obtain adequate data for verdict and to plan remedial strategy human have to be monitored for long duration. The primary principle of the manuscript is to present a method by which clonic as well as tonic seizures can be detected using video processing. The proposed algorithm specifies optical flow for motion detection; global group transformation velocities for feature extraction with band pass temporal filtering to classify the incidence of tonic and clonic movement in video string. This paper shows a substantiation set of 10 prerecorded epileptic seizures, proposed system is extremely sensitive and precise in detecting recorded string containing tonic and clonic actions.

Keywords: Clonic · Epilepsy · Motion scrutiny · Neurological · Seizures · Tonic · Video processing · Video scrutiny

1 Introduction

Epilepsy is a common medical and social disorder or group of disorders with unique characteristics. Epilepsy is a chaos that can take place in all mammalian groups, possibly more repeatedly as brains have turn into more complexes. There are no national, geological or public class limitations. It occurs in both genders, at all age groups, mainly in babyhood, teenage years and gradually more in aged populations. Different types of seizures and epilepsy syndromes have been identified at a wide range. Patients are now treated with pharmacotherapy, rarely with neurosurgical techniques, as well as with psychological and social support. There are different types of seizures. These seizures are classified into two groups, partial and generalized.

© Springer Nature Singapore Pte Ltd. 2016
A. Unal et al. (Eds.): SmartCom 2016, CCIS 628, pp. 757–767, 2016.
DOI: 10.1007/978-981-10-3433-6_91

A. Partial seizures

Partial seizures are frequently very delicate or abnormal, and might ignored or be mystified with other events. They transpire in one small region of the brain and can rarely stretch to further regions. When they stretch, they can become a generalized seizure, most ordinarily a tonic clonic seizure. Partial seizure is observed in 60% of people and these are sometimes very unwilling to antiepileptic medication.

B. Generalized seizure

These transpire when seizure movement in the intact brain. At the beginning of the seizure, consciousness is lost. Generalized seizures are classified into two standard types tonic seizure and the clonic seizure. Patient initiates with an unexpected loss of consciousness and generally person will cry out. If person is standing, he/she will fall and their body stiffens for duration of 10 to 30 s followed by jerking of the muscles for the duration of 10 to 30 min (clonic). Sometimes a saliva or blood may accumulate in the person's mouth. The seizure activity generally happens for two minutes or less than two minutes. It is the duration of confusion, sleep with anxiety. The common symptoms are headaches and pain.

The existing methods to monitor or to treat epileptic seizure patient is an EEG can support in emplacement the focus of the epileptic seizure. One main drawback of existing system is there are no standard recordings. The recording tapes are handled by doctors to detect or examine the activities of patient during seizure. One major drawback of existing system is environment of patient, which causes tracking or detection problem. Primarily the proposed method is needed to epileptic seizure patient because patient feels well when they are hospitalized for 2/3 weeks, but in that duration movements of patient are restricted and patient monitoring will be done intelligently or automatically without any practitioner. Secondly as monitoring will be done without any involvement of practitioner the system will become cost.

2 Literature Survey

Syed, Imitiaz offered a data selection algorithm with encoding and data transmittal for a reduced power hardware implementation and it exhibits the tradeoffs between in accuracy and the general system power consumption [1]. Gitte Bager, adnan vilic, Thomas sams represented color marker system for tracking of epileptic seizure patient under video surveillance. The marker system overcomes the limitation of tracking system like occlusion, lightning issues, and fast movements. This system contains marker bands of twelve different colors; these are connected at each joint. The limitation of this method is that the movement is detected if and only if markers are visible [2]. Stiliyan kalitzn, ben vleder, George petkov proposed a method for detecting the clonic movements only. It uses a remote sensing device such as video camera [3]. Pediaitis, M. Gralczyl, V. Krisotakis, P vorgia describes the home monitoring system for detection of epilepsy patients activities [4]. Matthew Pediaditis, Norber leitgeb, Monolis Tsiknasia decribes recent topic in relation with epilepsy. It describes the scrutiny with detection of human motion in epilepsy with marker based and marker free system for the detection of epilepsy. The primary objective of this paper is to obtain the existing knowledge in the field of epilepsy diagnosis and management of the disease based on video scrutiny [5]. Primarily epileptic seizure detection specifies the analysis of EEG; in this the recorded tape of EEG is recorded for long duration and monitored in specialized hospitals. Some people are observed under constant observation with the help of trained operators and these system uses hardware like accelerometer and other motion sensor. The sensors are attached to body, which are not comfortable for patient. If these sensors are depends on wireless transmission, they must have to be monitored at a regular interval of time and in each phase family member or trained person is involved [6–8]. Thus the one possibility is to give appropriate information about the epileptic seizure patient using video string.

3   Proposed System

Figure 1 depicts block diagram of proposed system. Each block is described in detail as follows;

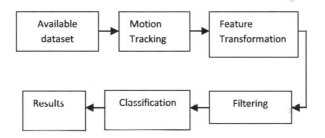

Fig. 1. Block diagram of proposed system

A. Motion Detection

Optical flow is substantially proven method for estimate restoration of suspicious activities as recorded in the form of optical images, main objective of this method is from the luminance changes restructure the vector field of velocities. These luminance changes might be generated from object as in recorded tape, by manipulating the velocity field as follows:

$$L(x, y, t) = \{Vx(x, y, t), Vy(x, y, t)\} \tag{1}$$

Where intensity field contained in recorded tape is given as $L(x, y, t)$ which shows x & y are 2D function (x, y) and t is time. The "Horn–Schunck" method is applied with one iteration with one frame delay. In this paper we have done several trials with the help of iteration and frame delay after processing these delay we have obtained some identical results.

B. Group Motion Parameters Reconstruction

We decrease the data by extracting rates of global motion parameters after reconstruction of velocity fields. Consequently, we commence intricate coordinates with velocities

$$W(z,t) = Vx(z,t) + iVy(z,t); z = x + iy; i = \sqrt{-1} \qquad (2)$$

Linear decomposition defines a group of nonhomogeneous linear transformation and it is given by,

$$w(z,t) = T(t) + R(t)z + S(t)z; z = x - iy \qquad (3)$$

Where, $T(t)$ is Translational rates, $R(t)$ is rotational &, and $S(t)$ is rate of shear. These quantities are individually defined for system, coordinated at centered in centre of images.

C. Feature Extraction

Gabor wavelet technique using principle component is used for extraction of features. It extracts some content of signal used for filtering which decreases the six degrees of autonomy. For this purpose proposed method uses a function of Gabor aperture which gives temporal resolution with spectral resolution.

D. Filtering and Detection

Normalized quantities are extracted from spectral weights; proposed system uses a spectral contrast technique, which is defined as,

$$C(n) \equiv \sum_{v} k(v).Q(v,n) \div \sum_{v} |k(v)|Q(v,n) \qquad (4)$$

Where, k(v) is function of spectral weight, it generally has positive & negative values in order to things to see definite spectral component on the backdrop of other. Equation (4) determines the relative difference between two values first value is 'a' which is positive & other is 'b' which is negative value, that means (a − b) divide by (a + b) and it obtains the values either (−1) or (+1). To decide the values of k(v) the more unique approach is used by postulating weights as,

$$
\begin{aligned}
k(v) &= 1; v \in (2,6) \\
&= -1; v \in (1,2) \, U \, (6,10) \\
&= 0; v \, not \in (1,10)
\end{aligned}
\qquad (5)
$$

Equation (5) shows if spectral contras are (−1) then seizure is not detected and if spectral contrast is (+1) the certain seizure is detected.

4   Results and Discussions

Figure 2 depicts the difference between motion detection using optical flow Horn-Shunk and Lucas Kanade method which concludes the Horn-shunk method gives promising results. Hence in proposed system uses optical flow Horn-shunk method.

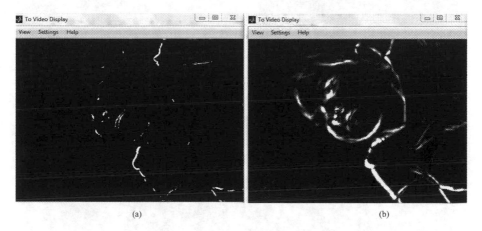

Fig. 2. Motion detection using optical flow (a) Lucas- Canade (b) Horn Shunk

Figure 3 describes the motion detection using Horn-Shunk from original video. Figure 3 containing 4 images original videos, motion vector, thresholded frame, detected motion using blob analysis respectively.

Figure 4 depicts input frame for feature extraction methods. Figure 5 illustrates the comparison between the different types of feature extraction methods. Out of these four methods PCA method is used. PCA gives accurate result by considering all the challenges like occlusion, execution rate, anthropometric variations etc. Figure 6 describes the classification using Adaboost classifier.

Figure 7(a) depicts the flow vectors from recorded video and Fig. (b) shows the principal component analysis of recorded video which shows the "dx" (red) & "dy" (green) components near to zero and the "dt" (Blue) have highest amplitude.

Figure 8(a) depicts the flow vectors from recorded video and Fig. (b) shows the principal component analysis of recorded video which shows the "dt" (Blue) component is almost zero in case of myclonic seizure, "dy" (green) component have highest amplitude and the "dx" (red) component is between dt and dy component.

Figure 9(a) depicts the flow vectors from recorded video and Fig. (b) shows the principal component analysis of recorded video which shows the "dt" (Blue) component is near to zero in case of tonic seizure, "dx" (Green) component have highest amplitude and the "dy" (red) component is between dx and dt component.

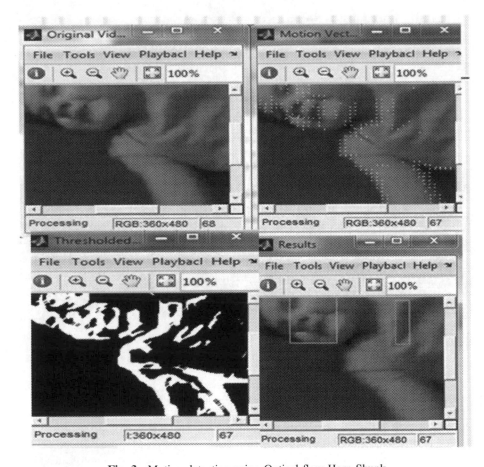

Fig. 3. Motion detection using Optical flow Horn Shunk

Figure 10(a) depicts the flow vectors from recorded video and Fig. (b) shows the principal component analysis of recorded video which shows the "dt" (Blue) component have highest amplitude in case of random activity, "dx" (red) component is near zero and the "dy" (green) component is between dx and dt component.

Table 1 shows the response type of each type of seizure.

Fig. 4. Input Frame

Fig. 5. Result of different Feature extraction methods for input Frame shown in Fig. 4

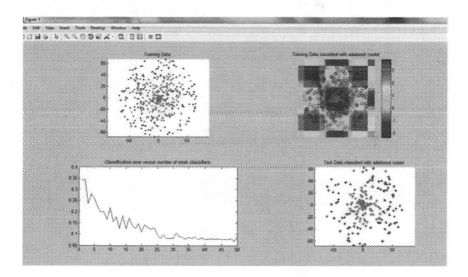

Fig. 6. Adaboost Classification for input frame shown in Fig. 4

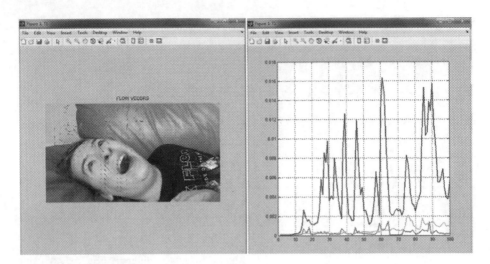

Fig. 7. (a) Flow vectors (b) Principal component analysis of Tonic clonic Seizure (Color figure online)

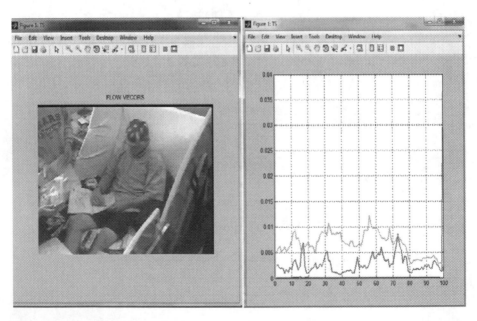

Fig. 8. (a) Flow vectors (b) Principal component analysis of Myclonic Seizure (Color figure online)

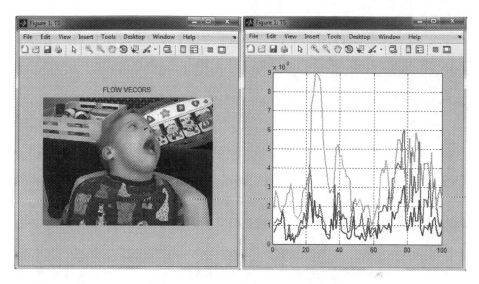

Fig. 9. (a) Flow vectors (b) Principal component analysis of Tonic Seizure (Color figure online)

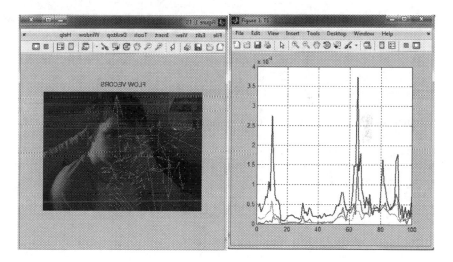

Fig. 10. (a) Flow vectors (b) Principal component analysis of Random activity (Color figure online)

Table 1. Response time

Sr. No.	Type of Epilepsy	No. of videos applied	Correct detected epilepsy	Response time (sec)
1	Tonic-Clonic	5	4	58
2	Tonic	7	5	30
3	Myclonic	10	8	14
4	Random activity	15	8	24

5 Conclusion

As review of the existing techniques shows the available solution are either costlier due to inclusion of ECG monitoring and supervision of medical practioning or the existing methods based on software tools are time consuming as they require more processing time while provides less accuracy. Our work will provide cheaper solution to above problems with less processing time and increased diagnosis accuracy. This work will be great help for the patients of clonic seizure and can be extended for all kinds of seizure. The proposed work can be enhancing for the real time application like human machine interaction, video surveillances.

References

1. Imtiaz, S.A.: Performance power consumption trade off in wearable Epilepsy monitoring system. J. Biomed. Health Inform. 839–847 (2015)
2. Bager, G., Vilic, K., Vilic, A., Alving, J., Wolf, P., Sams, T., Helge, B.D.: Video surveillance of Epilepsy patients using color image processing. In: 2014 36th Annual International Conference of the IEEE Engineering in Medicine and Biology Society (EMBC) (2014)
3. Kalitzin, S., Petkov, G., Velis, D., Vledder, B., Lopes da Silva, F.: Automatic segmentation of Episodes containing. IEEE Trans. Biomed. Eng. 59, 3379–3385 (2012)
4. Pediaditis, M., Tsiknakis, M., Kritsotakis, V., Voutoufianakis, S., Góralczyk, M., Vorgia, P.: EVideo analysis technologies for a smart home monitoring platform for epileptic patients: technological xploiting advanced and legal preconditions. In: International Conference on Telecommunications and Multimedia (TEMU) (2012)
5. Pediaditis, M., Tsiknakisa, M., Leitgebb, N.: Vision-based motion detection, analysis and recognition of epileptic seizures - a systematic review (2012). Elsevier
6. Ferrie, C.D., Panayiotopoulos, C.P.: Epileptic syndromes in childhood and adolescence
7. Schulc, E., Unterberger, I., Saboor, S., Hilbe, J., Ertl, M., Ammenwerth, E., Trinka, E., Them, C.: Measurement and quantification of generalized tonic–clonic seizures in epilepsy patients by means of accelerometry—an explorative study. Epilepsy Res. 95, 173–183 (2011)
8. Kramer, U., Kipervasser, S., Shlitner, A., Kuzniecky, R.: A novel portable seizure detection alarm system: preliminary results. J. Clin. Neurophysiol. 28, 36–38 (2011)
9. Becq, G., Bonnet, S., Minotti, L., Antonakios, M., Guillemaud, R., Kahane, P.: Classification of epileptic motor manifestations using inertial and magnetic sensors. Comput. Biol. Med. 41, 46–55 (2011)
10. Moeslund, T.B., Granum, E.: A survey of computer vision-based human motion capture. Comput. Vis. Image Underst. 81, 231–268 (2001)
11. Lu, H., Pan, Y., Mandal, B., Eng, H.L., Guan, C., Chan, D.W.: Quantifying limb movements in Epileptic seizures through color-based video analysis. IEEE Trans. Biomed. Eng. 60(2), 461–469 (2013). doi:10.1109/TBME.2012.2228649. Epub 21 November 2012
12. Cuppens, K., Vanrumste, B., Ceulemans, B., Lagae, L., Van Huffel, S.: Detection of Epileptic seizures using video data. In: Sixth International Conference on Intelligent Environments (IE). IEEE (2010)

13. Conradsen, I., Beniczky, S., Wolf, P., Terney, D., Sams, T., Sorensen, H.B.: Multi-modal intelligent seizure acquisition (MISA) system — a new approach towards seizure detection based on full body motion measures. Conf. Proc. IEEE Eng. Med. Biol. Soc. **2009**, 2591–2595 (2009). doi:10.1109/IEMBS.2009.5335334
14. Horn, B.K.P., Rhunck, B.G.: Determining Optical Flow Horn
15. Epilepsy Action. 1300 epilepsy (37 45 37)

Diagnosis of Diabetic Retinopathy Using Principal Component Analysis (PCA)

Amol P. Bhatkar[1]([✉]) and Govind Kharat[2]

[1] Anuradha Engineering College, Chikhli, India
apbhatkar@rediffmail.com
[2] Sharadchandra Pawar College of Engineering, Otur, India
gukharat@gmail.com

Abstract. Diabetic retinopathy is an eye disease due to diabetes, which is not detected in its early stage, may cause vision loss. The need of automated diagnosis methods of diabetic retinopathy increases day by day because of its severity. Authors proposed the design of diabetic retinopathy automated diagnosis system based on neural networks. Multi Layer Perceptron (MLP), Principal Component Analysis (PCA), Generalized Feed Forward (GFF) neural networks are employed to design automated classifier system in first experiment. In second experiment, the input dimensionality reduction method based MLP, GFF neural networks classifier systems are designed and compared the performances. In experiment 1, the average classification accuracy for MLP network is nearly 99.00% whereas GFF-NN has 92.00% on CV data. In experiment 2, using Principal Components (PCs), the average classification accuracy for MLP network is nearly 97.22% whereas GFF-NN has 84.37% on CV data. The N/P ratio for MLP and GFF networks is large in second experiment which is 0.273 and 0.219 respectively having less neural network's architecture complexity.

Keywords: Principal component analysis · Diabetic retinopathy · Neural network

1 Introduction

Diabetic Retinopathy (DR) is very serious health problem as it directly concern to vision loss [1]. There are more possibilities for progress of diabetic retinopathy if the patient is not treated for long period of time. In the first stages, the patients are not to be awaked of infection by such disease. Diabetic retinopathy becomes symptomatic in later stages [2]. The fundus retinal images are observed by ophthalmologist to find the DR symptoms. As the numbers of patients are too much more it requires more time for detection of DR in retinal images. An automated system can be helpful for early diagnosis of diabetic retinopathy [3, 4].

This paper compared different neural networks based classifier methods [5–8] by using different feature sets of the 130 retinal images of DIARETDB0 database to classify the normal and DR affected (Abnormal) images. The feature sets are composed of 64-point DCT, 64-point FFT and 64-point SVD features and statistical parameters as entropy, contrast, energy, mean, standard deviation, homogeneity, Euler number,

© Springer Nature Singapore Pte Ltd. 2016
A. Unal et al. (Eds.): SmartCom 2016, CCIS 628, pp. 768–778, 2016.
DOI: 10.1007/978-981-10-3433-6_92

average, and correlation. Table 1 show three cases are formed of extracted features of retinal images. These feature vectors are considered as input data sets for neural network training and cross validation.

In first experimentation three neural networks namely MLP, GFF and PCA neural networks are employed for all the cases. For every network with every case, various designing parameters are changed, modified and observed the performances. It is again observed that which features are best suitable as an input data to these neural networks. The best feature vector (case) is used for PCA analysis by XLSTAT 2008. The best results achieved principal components are again provide to the MLP and GFF NNs to check the performance of networks.

2 Related Work

The classifier systems identify the DR affected (abnormal) and provide to an ophthalmologist for taking decision for further action. It would minimize workload and time for ophthalmologists so that they can provide more attention on treatment other than detection of disease [9]. María García, et al. [10] proposed lesion based and image-based criteria. They achieved 95.9% mean sensitivity on MLP and mean positive predictive value of 85.7% on RBF NN. They also achieved 100% mean sensitivity and 87.5% specificity for MLP and RBF NN respectively on image-based criterion. G.G. Gardner, et al. [11] proposed MLP to detect the presence of red lesions in retinal images. They achieved 73.8% image-based accuracy. Hayashi, et al. [12] proposed CAD system which supports physician for detection of abnormalities present in fundus images of the retina. X. Zhang, et al. [13] proposed Support Vector Machine. True positive rate of 90.6% with 2 false positives per image is achieved by SVM. In this work cross validation is not mentioned. E. Grisan, et al. [14] presented image-based results on two databases. They obtained sensitivity and specificity, 75% and 99% respectively on 200 retinal images as well as 83% and 98% respectively on 60 images. A. Claudio et al. [15] proposed cascaded classifier system for online optic disc detection. The system extracted the Haar features from rectangular windows. Dr. Govind Kharat and Dr. Sanjay Dudul [16] were employed MLPNN and GFFNN to recognize six fundamental human emotions. DCT and Statistical Parameters based extracted features were used for emotion classifier system. Carla Agurto, et al. [17] proposed the system which automatically classifies subjects with hypertensive retinopathy using 74 retinal images. An area under the ROC curve (AUC) of 0.84 was achieved with sensitivity and specificity of 90% and 67%, respectively.

3 Designing of Classifier System

It is considered that Neural networks act as living animal's brain activities. The brain activities means to observe the surrounding, think on evidences, learn from the past experiences, memories the events, find analogy in the patterns and many more. So, for mass population classification, automated classification system based on pattern

Table 1. Formation of feature vectors (cases)

Sr. No.	Extracted features of retinal images
Case I	64-point DCT + 9 statistical parameters
Case II	64-point FFT + 9 statistical parameters
Case III	64-point SVD + 9 statistical parameters

recognition will be definitely more useful to analyze and solve the problem. The neural networks as already discussed having such capabilities.

So, the proposed work employed MLP, GFF and PCA neural networks to classify the retinal images into two classes as normal or abnormal (DR affected) images. The generalized classifier is as shown in above Fig. 1. As already discussed with Table 1, we formed three cases of retinal images features. Every case is formed by using 73 features of each of 130 images.

Therefore, for the training of the neural networks, these feature vectors might be bulky which creates the computational complexity. The complexity is in concern with the processing time requirement and performance of the neural network. Ultimately, network's better performance depends on the minimum number influencing features which are extracted from the retinal image databases. In general, principal components analysis (PCA) techniques are used to find best suitable features.

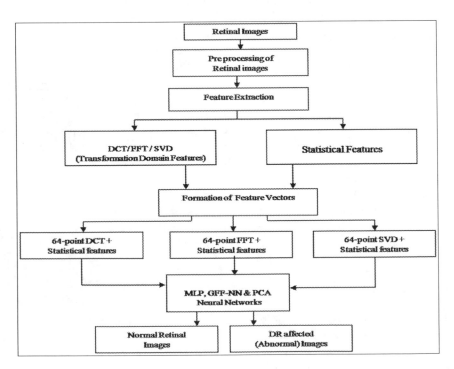

Fig. 1. MLP, GFF and PCA NNs based classifier system for diagnosis of diabetic retinopathy

4 Experimental Results

4.1 Experimentation - I

For the first experiment, we used all above mentioned cases separately to the PCA neural network. It is found PCANN with single hidden layer perform well. The number of principal components plays very important role in designing of PCA NN. Sangersfull learning rule is preferred for PCA because it naturally orders the PCA components by magnitude. TanhAxon, Sigmoid, Liner tanhAxon, Linear-sigmoid, Softmax transfer functions and different Step sizes are verified on training and testing datasets.

The learning rule used for correction term specification. Momentum, Conjugate-Gradient, Quick Propagation, Delta Bar Delta, Levenberg Maquardt learning rules are used to train the PCA NN. The numbers of processing elements (PEs) in hidden layer are changed from one to more and the final minimum MSE is monitored. Mean Square Error (MSE) and Classification Accuracy on training and CV datasets are compared with different issues like percentage of tagging, transfer functions, learning rules and variation in step sizes. Based on above discussion, Selection parameters for designing of PCA network classifier for case I, Case II and case III are as above shown in Table 2.

Above mentioned different selection parameters of PCA NN are set and train the network. Final minimum MSE is obtained on cross validation data when 05 PEs are used in the hidden layer as indicated in Fig. 2. Figure 3 shows the variations in average

Table 2. Selection parameters for PCA network for case I, Case II and case III

Selection parameters for designing of neural network	Case I	Case II	Case III
% of CV data tagging	10%	10%	10%
Input PEs.	73	73	73
Output PEs.	02	02	02
Exemplars (N)	117	117	117
Hidden layers (H.L.)	01	01	01
Principal components	14	14	14
Learning rule	SangersFull	SangersFull	SangersFull
H.L. 1, Number of PEs	20	05	12
H.L. 1, Transfer function	TanhAxon	TanhAxon	Linear TanhAxon
H.L. 1, Learning rule	Momentum	Delta Bar Delta	Momentum
H.L. 1, Step size	0.1	0.1	0.1
Unsupervised learning maximum epochs	1000	1000	1000
Supervised learning maximum epochs	5000	5000	5000
Total epochs	6000	6000	6000
Number of free parameter (P)	1522	382	914

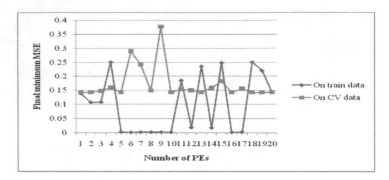

Fig. 2. Minimum MSE versus number of PEs

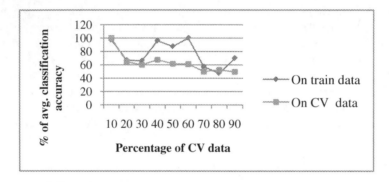

Fig. 3. Percentage average classification accuracy versus % of CV data

classification accuracy across percentage of tagging of cross validation dataset. Optimal results are obtained when 10% and 90% exemplars are used for training and CV datasets respectively.

Percentage of average classification accuracy (ACA) across different transfer functions as well as with different learning rules are shown in Figs. 4 and 5.

Tanh is found as best transfer function with Delta Bar Delta (DBD) learning rule. Figure 6 shows the variation of % of average classification accuracy (ACA) with different step sizes. 0.1 is the best step size.

The performance of a neural network is observed in term of classification error, Mean Square Error (MSE). Confusion matrix generated the matrix which shows actual true and false samples are diagnosis by neural network properly on training, cross validate data samples. In other words, this matrix estimates the number of misclassifications exactly. The confusion matrices generated on cross validate (CV) data samples for all three cases are summaries as below in Table 3.

It is clearly observed from above table that for the case II, classifier identified all 13 normal and abnormal CV data samples truly with 100% accuracy. The PCA network's sensitivity, specificity and overall accuracy for case II is 100%. The performance matrices generated by PCA network for these cases on CV data samples are as shown

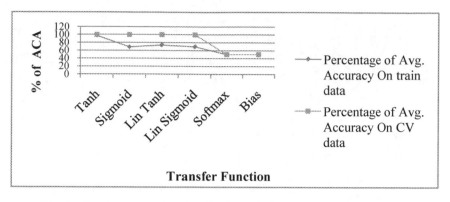

Fig. 4. Percentage average classification accuracy versus transfer functions

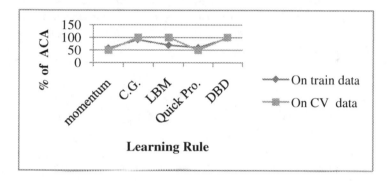

Fig. 5. Percentage average classification accuracy versus Learning rules

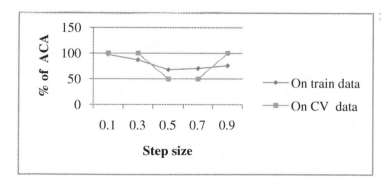

Fig. 6. Percentage average classification accuracy versus step sizes

in Table 4. Case II with 64-point FFT with statistical features is the best feature vector for PCA network which achieved 100% average classification accuracy on cross validation data. As well as from following Table 5, N/P ratio is highest for 64-point FFT feature vector, is an indication of simplicity of PCA design. For case II, the percentage

Table 3. Confusion matrices for all feature vectors

	Case I		Case II		Case III	
	o1 (Abnormal)	o2 (normal)	o1 (Abnormal)	o2 (normal)	o1 (Abnormal)	o2 (normal)
o1 (Abnormal)	10	1	12	0	11	1
o2 (normal)	0	2	0	1	0	1

Table 4. Performance matrices of PCA network for case I, case II and case III

Performance Parameters	Case I		Case II		Case III	
	o1	o2	o1	o2	o1	o2
MSE	0.1198	0.1162	0.0054	0.0053	0.0692	0.0672
NMSE	0.6749	0.6547	0.0761	0.0758	0.5317	0.5163
MAE	0.2567	0.2471	0.0569	0.0569	0.1323	0.1401
Min Abs Error	0.0152	0.0137	0.0039	0.0038	0.0217	0.0167
Max Abs Error	0.9164	0.9249	0.1666	0.1647	0.9047	0.8692
R	0.5748	0.5960	0.9690	0.9688	0.7551	0.7559
Percent correct	100	66.67	100	100	100	50

Table 5. Performance comparison of PCA network for different cases

	Final Min. MSE		% of ACA		Time elapsed (ms)	N/P Ratio
	Train	CV	Train	CV		
Case I	0.0012	0.149	100	83.33	0.084	0.076
Case II	0.0019	0.143	97.36	100	0.088	0.306
Case III	0.1940	0.143	83.33	75	0.085	0.128

classification accuracy is 97.36% and is 100% for training and CV data respectively. It means 64-point FFT based feature vector is most suitable for identification of diabetic retinopathy in retinal images using PCA NN.

As shown in Fig. 1, the classifiers are also designed with MLP and GFF neural networks. The procedure is same as discussed above for PCA neural network. The comparison of the performance of all employed neural networks based on percentage of average classification accuracy (ACA) is shown in following Table 6.

The comparison of all the three neural networks for the performance parameters like, Time elapsed per epoch per exemplar and N/P ratio is as shown in Table 7.

By comparing all the performance parameters discussed in above Tables 6 and 7, it is proposed that multi layer Perceptron (MLP) network with FFT based feature vector is best suited classifier for diagnosis of DR in retinal images.

Table 6. Percentage of average classification accuracy of MLP, GFF and PCA NNs on DCT, FFT and SVD feature vectors

Neural networks	% of Average classification accuracy (ACA)					
	64-DCT feature vector (Case-I)		64-FFT feature vector (Case-II)		64-SVD feature vector (Case-III)	
	Train	CV	Train	CV	Train	CV
MLP	100	100	100	100	99.48	91.66
GFF	100	95.45	100	100	98.97	95.83
PCA	100	83.33	97.36	100	83.33	75.00

Table 7. Other performance parameters comparisons for MLP, GFF, and PCA NNs

Neural networks	Time Elapsed/Epoch/exemplar (ms)			N/P ratio		
	Case I	Case II	Case III	Case I	Case II	Case III
MLP	0.070	0.001	0.063	0.1280	0.170	0.0809
GFF	0.070	0.095	0.091	0.5080	0.255	0.1024
PCA	0.084	0.088	0.086	0.0768	0.139	0.1280

4.2   Experimentation - II

Principal Component Analysis (PCA) is feature development method that uses an orthogonal transformation. The number of principal components is less than or equal to the number of original variables. In experimentation-I, every feature vector having 73 input features of 130 images. It requires the large amount of calculations as numbers of features are more. Less number of efficient input features is very important to reduce the calculations complexity of neural network. Reduction in the input dimensionality can be achieved by PCA of XLSTAT 2008. Figure 7 shows the architecture for PCA based classifier system with 64-point FFT input feature vector. XLSTAT offering the rules such as Pearson (n), Pearson (n-1) Covariance (n), Covariance (n-1), Spearman for principal component analysis for extracting principal components(PCs). To get an optimal network structure, these PCs are fed to the network as an input for training and tested the results.

The performance parameters, for example, for the MLP neural network for different rules of PCA are as follows as shown in Table 8.

From Table 8, it is observed that Pearson (n) rule of PCA tool provides highest result on training and CV datasets on MLP neural Network. Pearson (n) rule used 22 numbers of principal Components (PCs). Different performance parameters for MLP and GFF neural networks with PCA as input is shown as Table 9.

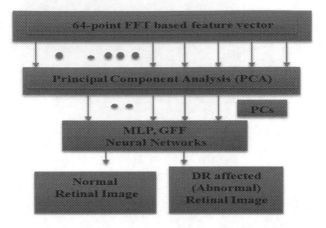

Fig. 7. Architecture for PCA based classifier system

Table 8. Performance parameters of MLP neural network with different PCA rules

PCA rules	Final minimum MSE		% of ACA	
	On train data	On CV data	On train data	On CV data
Pearson(n)	0.00042	0.13095	90.57	97.22
Pearson(n-1)	0.00361	0.19722	85.56	75.00
Covariance(n)	0.36766	0.46282	62.50	50.00
Covariance(n-1)	0.04673	0.06643	50.00	50.00
Spearman	0.00334	0.21984	98.00	83.33

Table 9. Different performance parameters for MLP and GFF neural networks

NNs	% of ACA		Sensitivity	Specificity	Accuracy	Time elapsed (ms)	N/P ratio
	Train	CV					
MLP	90.57	97.22	94.45	100	95.00	0.43	0.273
GFF	90.62	84.37	93.75	75.00	90.00	0.37	0.219

5   Conclusion

The evaluations of performance of different neural networks with and without PCA analysis are explored in this paper. The impact of less numbers of input features on the performance of automated diagnosis system was observed on MLP, GFF neural networks. The performance parameters of MLP network with 64-point FFT based feature vector with different PCA rules are shown in Tables 8 and 9. It is observed from Table 6 that PCA network has comparatively less % of average classification accuracy for all cases than MLP, GFF-NN whereas these networks carried 100%.

It is observed that N/P ratio is the highest for MLP and GFF-NN after PCA analysis. It indicated the simplicity of both MLP and GFF-NNs. The N/P ratio is 0.273 and 0.219 for respective networks. Time elapsed per epoch per exemplar for MLP and

GFF NNs is 0.043 ms and 0.037 ms respectively. In both experimentations, the % of average classification accuracy for MLP network on CV data is nearly 99.00% whereas GFF- NN has 92.00% accuracy. If we compared MLP and GG NNs with PCs feeding, it is easily observed that they achieved the compact formation of systems. From Table 9, it is concluded that the PCA based input dimensionality reduction method along with MLP is capable for the diagnosis of diabetic retinopathy in retinal images. The % of average classification accuracy of MLP classifier system is 90.57% and 97.22% on training and cross validation data respectively.

References

1. Niemeijer, M.: Retinopathy online challenge: automatic detection of microaneurysms in digital color fundus photographs. IEEE Trans. Med. Imaging **29**(1), 185–195 (2010)
2. Klein, D., Klein, B.E., Moss, S.E., et al.: The wisconsin epidemiologic study of diabetic retinopathy VII. Diabetic non proliferative retinal lesions. Br. J. Ophthalmol. **94**, 1389–1400 (1986)
3. Goldbaum, M., Moezzi, S., Taylor, A., Chatterjee, S., Boyd, J., Hunter, E., Jain, R.: Automated diagnosis and image understanding with object extraction, object classification, and differencing in retinal images. Br. J. Ophthalmol. **83**, 695–698 (1999)
4. Sinthanayothin, C., Boyce, J., Cook, H., Williamson, T.: Automated localisation of optic disc, fovea, and retinal blood vessels from digital colour fundus images. Br. J. Ophthalmol. **83**, 902–910 (1999)
5. Anil, K.: Jain Michigan State University, Jianchang Mao IBM Almaden Research Centre, Artificial neural networks: A tutorial (1996)
6. Rosenblatt, F.: Principles of Neurodynamics: Perceptrons and The Theory of Brain Mechanisms. Spartan Books, Washington, D.C. (1962)
7. Rumelhart, D.E., Geoffrey, E.H., Williams, R.J.: Learning internal representations by error propagation. In: Rumelhart, D.E., McClelland, J.L., the PDP research group (eds.) Parallel Distributed Processing: Explorations in the Microstructure of Cognition, vol. 1: Foundations. MIT Press (1986)
8. Cybenko, G.: Approximation by superpositions of a sigmoidal function. Math. Control Sig. Syst. **2**(4), 303–314 (1989)
9. Kumar, S.J.J., Madheswaran, M.: Extraction of blood vascular network for development of an automated diabetic retinopathy screening system. In: International Conference on Computer Technology and Development. IEEE (2009). 10.1109/Icctd.2009.212
10. García, M., Valverde, C.: Comparison of logistic regression and neural network classifiers in the detection of hard exudates in retinal images. In: 35th Annual International Conference of the IEEE EMBS Osaka, Japan, 3–7 July (2013)
11. Gardner, G.G., Keating, D., Williamson, T.H., Elliot, A.T.: Automatic detection of diabetic retinopathy using an artificial neural network: a screening tool. Br. J. Ophthalmol. **80**, 940–944 (1996)
12. Hayashi, J., Kunieda, T., et al.: A development of computer-aided diagnosis system using fundus images. In: Proceeding of the 7th International Conference on Virtual Systems and MultiMedia (VSMM 2001), pp. 429–438 (2001)
13. Zhang, X., Chutatape, O.: Top-down and bottom-up strategies in lesion detection of background diabetic retinopathy. In: Proceedings of IEEE Computer Society Conf. Computer Vision and Pattern Recognition, vol. 2, pp. 422–428 (2005)

14. Grisan, E., Rugger, A.: A hierarchical Bayesian classification for non-vascular lesions detection in fundus images. In: Proceeding of the IFMBE Conference on Biomedical Engineering, Prague (2005)
15. Perez, C.A., Schulz, D.A., Aravena, C.M.: A new method for online retinal optic-disc detection based on cascade classifiers. In: IEEE International Conference on Systems, Man, and Cybernetics (2013)
16. Kharat, G.U., Dudul, S.V.: Neural network classifier for human emotion recognition from facial expressions using discrete cosine transform. In: First International Conference on Emerging Trends in Engineering and Technolog, 978-0-7695-3267-7/08$25.00©. IEEE (2008). doi:10.1109/ICETET
17. Agurto, C., Joshi, V., et al.: Detection of hypertensive retinopathy using vessel measurementsand textural features, pp. 5406–5409, 978-1-4244-7929-0/14/$26.00. IEEE (2014)

Evaluation of Ultrasonic Transducer with Divergent Membrane Materials and Geometries

Rashmi Sharma[1(✉)], Rekha Agarwal[1], and Anil Arora[2]

[1] Amity School of Engineering and Technology, New Delhi, India
rashmiapj@gmail.com
[2] Thapar University, Patiala, Punjab, India

Abstract. Nowadays Capacitive Micromachined Ultrasonic Transducers (CMUTs) appeared as a preference over piezoelectric transducers in terms of bandwidth, fabrication of layer arrays, efficiency and sensitivity. This paper presents the CMUTs cavity filled with air with different membrane materials namely silicon, silicon nitride and polysilicon. The operation of the device is discussed in detail with various electromechanical parameters like pull in voltage, Eigen frequency and deflection of membrane with applied DC and AC bias along with comparison between square and circular geometries of CMUT. 3D analysis is carried out in COMSOL where Solid Mechanics, Electrostatics and Moving Mesh modules have been combined to model the dynamics of CMUT. Finally, the time evolution of the device is derived for several frequencies, from where the maximum frequency of operation is obtained and comparison is demonstrated to help the researchers.

Keywords: Ultrasonic transducers · Eigen frequency · Membrane materials · FEM · Electromechanical parameters · Pull in voltage

1 Introduction

Ultrasonic transducers convert electrical energy into ultrasound and vice versa. Piezoelectric and electrostatic (i.e. capacitive) transducers are two of the most common type of ultrasonic transducers. Piezoelectric transducers are the most widely used ultrasonic transducers to generate and detect ultrasound. The piezoelectric transducers generate sound waves by compressing and expanding the piezoelectric crystals in response to an electric signal [1]. On the other hand, capacitive transducers are comprised of a flexible membrane separated from a rigid plate by air. They generate ultrasonic waves by varying the applied electric field across the gap which subsequently induces a mechanical force causing the membrane to move. Both piezoelectric and capacitive transducers have successfully been used for generating and sensing ultrasonic waves [2]. However, the usefulness of piezoelectric transducers has been compromised by the complex fabrication required and a large acoustic mismatch between the piezoelectric crystals and the surrounding medium (i.e. air). In comparison, capacitive transducers have shown better impedance matching with the medium than

© Springer Nature Singapore Pte Ltd. 2016
A. Unal et al. (Eds.): SmartCom 2016, CCIS 628, pp. 779–787, 2016.
DOI: 10.1007/978-981-10-3433-6_93

the piezoelectric transducers [3]. The fundamental component of ultrasonic transducer i.e. CMUT is a capacitor formed with one fixed electrode which is the substrate of the device and second by a moving membrane which can oscillate. When an AC voltage is overlaid on the DC bias voltage, applied between the membrane and the substrate, electrostatic forces are induced which turn up into vibration of membrane and generation of ultrasound. Contrarily, if the biased electrode i.e. the membrane is subjected to an incident ultrasound wave, capacitance changes, due to oscillating membrane, which can be sensed. The advancement of micromachining technology permitted the fabrication of electrostatic ultrasonic transducers consisting of an array of membranes with the dimensions in the order of tens of microns for operation in the megahertz (MHz) range [4]. With this fabrication technology the electrode detachment can be made very thin, in the submicron range, empowering high electric fields inside the gap that result in high transduction efficiency and sensitivity. Integrated circuits (IC) fabrication methods are being used to fabricate CMUTs onto silicon wafers.

2   Theory of Operation

A schematic diagram of a capacitive micromachined ultrasonic transducer (CMUT) shown in Fig. 1(Left), can be viewed as a parallel plate capacitor where the top plate is moveable, and separated from the fixed bottom plate by an air gap. If the gap between two plates is small compared to the lateral dimension of the plates, the plates can be considered as the parallel plates [6]. When the top plate moves, the stiffness of the plate introduces a restoring spring force which opposes the electrostatic force. Therefore, a CMUT can be represented as an electro-mechanical system with one degree of freedom [6]. This electro-mechanical system consists of a spring k, a mass m and a parallel plate capacitor C, shown in Fig. 1(Right).

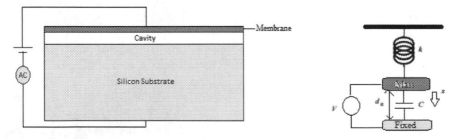

Fig. 1. Schematic view of capacitive micromachined ultrasonic transducer cell (*Left*) Electromechanical model of capacitive micromachined ultrasonic transducer (*Right*)

The total force acting on the plate under an applied bias can be written as [6]:

$$F_{Mass} = F_{Spring} + F_{Electrostatic} \tag{1}$$

where F_{Mass} represents the force due to the mass, F_{Spring} is the restoring spring force exerted by the elasticity of the plate and $F_{Electrostatic}$ is the electrostatic force between two parallel plates induced by the applied voltage. When a voltage is applied, the electrostatic force pulls the top plate toward the bottom plate, and causes the reduction of gap height. The capacitance between two plates may be expressed as:

$$C = \frac{\varepsilon A}{d_0 - x} \qquad (2)$$

The electrostatic force, generated by an applied DC bias, between two parallel plates, can be written as [6]

$$F_{Electrostatic} = \frac{d}{dx}\left(\frac{1}{2}CV^2\right) = \frac{\varepsilon A V^2}{2(d_0 - x)^2} \qquad (3)$$

where ε is the dielectric permittivity of the material between two plates, A is the plate area, V is the applied bias, d_0 is the initial gap height, and x is the initial plate displacement under a static bias. The mechanical spring also produces a restoring force that is proportional to the displacement of the plate and can be written using Hooke's law,

$$F_{Spring} = -kx \qquad (4)$$

Where k is the stiffness of the plate. For an applied voltage

$$V(t) = V_{DC} + V_{AC}\text{Sin}(wt) \qquad (5)$$

Substituting all the force expressions into Eq. 1, a time dependent behavior of the system can be found to be

$$m\frac{d^2x}{dt^2} - \frac{\varepsilon A V(t)^2}{2(d_0 - x)^2} + kx = 0 \qquad (6)$$

where V_{DC} is the DC voltage, V_{AC} is ac voltage, w is the operating frequency and m is the mass of the plate. Therefore, a CMUT can be modeled as a mass-spring-capacitor electromechanical system, where the CMUT membrane is the moveable plate and the substrate is the fixed bottom plate.

2.1 Pull in Voltage

For static operation, only DC bias is considered to be applied to the CMUT membrane. At equilibrium, the electrostatic force is balanced by the spring force and hence the condition for force balance becomes [6]

$$F_{Electrostatic} = -F_{Spring} \qquad (7)$$

$$\frac{\varepsilon A V_{DC}^2}{2(d_0 - x)^2} = kx \tag{8}$$

The condition for the stable state can be mathematically written as [7]

$$\frac{d(F_{Electrostatic} + F_{Spring})}{dx} < 0 \tag{9}$$

Making the calculation and solving for pull in gives

$$V_{Pullin} = \sqrt{\frac{8kd_0^3}{27\varepsilon A}} \tag{10}$$

2.2   Spring Softening Coefficient and Resonant Frequency

As V_{DC} is increased, the electrostatic force increases quadratically and pulls membrane closer to the substrate. As the membrane gets closer to the bottom electrode, the generated electrostatic force modifies the spring constant of the membrane. This effect can be interpreted as the spring softening effect [8]. The natural frequency expression of a simple mass-spring mechanical system and can be given by [9]

$$f_r = \frac{1}{2\pi}\sqrt{\frac{k}{m}} \tag{11}$$

Where f_r is the resonant frequency, m is the effective mass of the vibrating membrane with clamped edges and k is the spring stiffness of the membrane. The effective mass m can be calculated as [9]

$$m = \rho h A \left(\frac{2\sqrt{2}}{(\lambda_a)_{mn}}\right) \tag{12}$$

where $(\lambda_a)_{mn}$ is a constant corresponding to the shapes of different modes of membrane vibration. The value for $(\lambda_a)_{mn}$ would be changed for different modes of vibrations and hence the mode frequency.

$$f_r = \frac{1}{2\pi}\sqrt{\frac{1}{m}\left(\frac{16\pi E h^3}{3(1-V^2)R^2} - \frac{\varepsilon A V_{DC}^2}{d_0^3}\right)} \tag{13}$$

The resonant frequency is a function of membrane thickness, radius, membrane material, membrane mass, gap height and applied bias.

2.3 Dynamic Operation

For dynamic operation, an AC voltage signal is applied with the DC bias between the two electrodes. The ac voltage magnitude is typically much smaller than the DC bias which causes a small perturbation to the membrane. This perturbation of the membrane produces an ultrasound pressure wave. For an applied bias,

$$V(t) = V_{DC} + V_{AC}\text{Sin}(wt) \tag{14}$$

The force acting on the membrane is given by

$$F_{DC+AC} = \frac{\varepsilon A V^2}{2(d_0 - x)^2} = \frac{\varepsilon A (V_{DC} + V_{AC}\text{Sin}(wt))^2}{2(d_0 - x)^2} \tag{15}$$

3 Results and Discussions

The dimension of the CMUT cell used for implementation in COMSOL are listed in Table 1. Table 2 tabulates the material properties of different layers and these specifications were collected from the COMSOL inbuilt material library. The material properties required for the plates are used from the COMSOL inbuilt Material library enlisted in Table 2. A FEM of CMUT cell is constructed in COMSOL Multiphysics software where the three subdomains are coupled together namely the structural mechanics subdomain, electrostatics subdomain and the moving mesh subdomain. The MEMS devices measuring small dimensions usually involve complex interactions in coupled domains and FEM is commonly used to treat with nonlinear models. In this section FEM analysis is done in 3D for both geometries and compared for the different membrane materials.

Table 1. Parameters used for simulation

Description	Value (μm)
Radius of circular	56.4
Side of square	100
Gap thickness	1
Diaphragm thickness	0.5
Substrate thickness	2

From Fig. 2 deflection with applied DC bias for Square and Circular geometry are obtained with the three membrane materials. A constant pressure is applied on the membrane with the DC voltage being incremented until the membrane is about to contact the substrate, to obtain the parametric analysis in coupled fields. When this condition of precollapse is achieved the solution constrain to converge and results in termination of simulation. The final value of voltage before divergence of the solution is

Table 2. Material properties used for simulation

Material property	Silicon	Silicon Nitride	Polysilicon
Density (kg/m3)	2329	3100	2320
Young's modulus (Pa)	170e9	250e9	160e9
Poisson's ratio	0.28	0.23	0.22
Relative permittivity	11.7	9.7	4.5

the collapse or pull in voltage. Table 3 shows the pull in voltages for both geometries with the three materials which confers the minimum pull in voltage is given by Polysilicon material i.e. 41 V when used with circular geometry and the maximum pull in voltage is of Square geometry with Silicon Nitride as the membrane material which is 57 V. Figure 2 also demonstrate maximum deflection with applied DC bias is given by Polysilicon in the downward direction with increasing bias in Circular geometry and minimum deflection is given by Silicon Nitride material with Square geometry. The resonant frequency of the CMUT is a function of both geometry and the material properties. COMSOL Multiphysics is one of the best Finite Element Method (FEM) modeling software which can couple different physics phenomena was employed for this goal. To achieve this mechanics and electrostatics were coupled. Electromechanics interface of MEMS module of COMSOL was used to have the first eigenfrequency mode for both circular and square geometries. The Structural Mechanics, Electrostatics and Moving Mesh modules are precoupled and Electrostatics is assigned to all domains by default. The membrane was actuated by only AC voltage and DC was kept to be zero. Resonance frequencies for both the geometries with different materials is shown in Table 4. It is preferable for the CMUT to have high center frequency for getting better resolution, and broad bandwidth for detection of defects that are closer. At high frequencies there exist a drawback of attenuation of ultrasound with increasing frequencies. Maximum resonance frequency is shown by Silicon Nitride Material with Square geometry. The graph of frequency versus deflection for both the geometries are given in Fig. 3. Maximum deflection is shown by Polysilicon membrane with Square geometry and Silicon membrane with circular geometry.

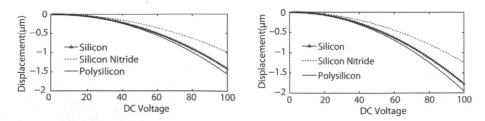

Fig. 2. Displacement with applied DC for Square Geometry (*Left*) Displacement with applied DC for Circular Geometry (*Right*)

The membrane is attracted towards the bulk by the electrostatic forces when the DC voltage is applied between the membrane and the substrate also stress is induced in the

Table 3. Pull in voltages with different membrane materials

Geometry	Silicon	Silicon Nitride	Polysilicon
Circular	43 V	51 V	41 V
Square	48 V	57 V	46 V

Table 4. Eigenfrequencies with different membrane materials

Geometry	Silicon	Silicon Nitride	Polysilicon
Circular	6.583362e5	6.81926e5	6.290296e5
Square	7.048537e5	7.641238e5	7.120000e5

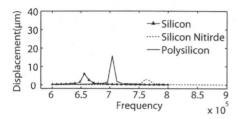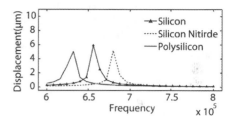

Fig. 3. Displacement with respect to frequency for Square Geometry (*Left*) Displacement with respect to frequency for Square Geometry (*Right*)

membrane which balances the attraction. Membrane starts vibrating when the DC bias is overlaid by the AC voltage and leads to generation of ultrasound waves. Figure 4 demonstrates the ultrasound generated with all membrane materials for both the geometries. AC bias is applied simultaneously with DC given by Eq. (5) and the membrane starts vibrating. To study the effects when the field variables change over time the Time dependent study is used in COMSOL. Figure 4 depicts the time varying deformation and motion of solids when subjected to transient loads, Solid mechanics is used to obtain this in COMSOL.

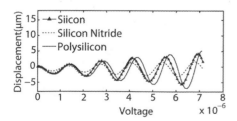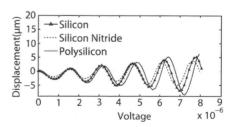

Fig. 4. Displacement with applied AC for Square Geometry (*Left*) Displacement with applied AC for Circular Geometry (*Right*)

4   Conclusion

In this paper, we presented a comprehensive comparison between a Square and Circular CMUT with three membrane materials. A COMSOL FEM analysis of a square and circular CMUT was performed. The validated boundary conditions were used in the construction of both square and circular CMUTs. We managed to obtain all the electric and structural characteristics of the device via simulation. This work provides researcher with complete comparison for deflection profile, resonant frequency, and generated ultrasound for both the geometries. This work can be further extended for the CMUT with rectangular and hexagonal geometries and can provide researchers with advance results for different materials used for membranes. The different existing materials having improved mechanical and electrical characteristics are also advised for the membranes. Now we are prepared to step forward and study the configuration of maximum efficiency by analyzing the acoustic power transferred to the surrounding medium and to optimize the geometry that provides the maximum efficiency.

References

1. Matzuwa., K.: Capacitive ultrasonic transducer. Phys. Soc. Jpn. **13**, 1533 (1958)
2. Kuhl, W., Schodder, G.R., Schodder, F.K.: Condenser transmitters and microphones with solid dielectric for airborne ultrasonics. Acoustica **4**, 520–532 (1954). 94
3. Haller, M.I., Khuri-Yakub, B.T.: A surface micromachined electrostatic ultrasonic air transducer. In: Ultrasonics Symposium IEEE, pp. 1241–1244 (1994)
4. Ergun, A.S., Yaralioglu, G.G., Khuri-Yakub, B.T.: Capacitive micromachined ultrasonic transducers: theory and technology. Areosp. Eng. **16**(2), 76–84 (2003)
5. Ergun, A.S., Yaralioglu, G.G., Oralkan, O.: MEMS/NEMS techniques and applications of capacitive micromachined ultrasonic transducers. In: Leondes, C.T. (ed.) MEMS/NEMS, pp. 553–615. Springer, New York (2006)
6. Ladabaum, I., Jin, X., Soh, H.T., Atalar, A., Khuri-Yakub, B.T.: Surface micromachined capacitive ultrasonic transducers. IEEE Trans. Ultrason. Ferroelectr. Freq. Control **45**(3), 678–690 (1998)
7. Bao, M.-H.: Micro Mechanical Transducers: Pressure Sensors, Accelerometers and Gyroscopes. Elsevier Science, Amsterdam (2000). 30 October 2000, Chap. 4, p. 148
8. Pacheco, S., Zurcher, P., Young, S., Weston, D., Dansker, W.: RF MEMS resonator for CMOS back end-of-line integration. In: 5th Topical Meeting on Silicon Monolithic Integrated Circuits in RF Systems, pp. 203–206 (2004)
9. Hsu, T.R.: MEMS and Microsystems- Design, Manufacture, and Nanoscale Engineering, 2nd edn. Wiley, Hoboken (2008)
10. Sharma, R., Agarwal, R., Arora, A.: Performance analysis of MEMS-based ultrasonic transducer with different membrane materials. Recent Trends Sens. Res. Technol. **1**(3), 1–8 (2014)
11. Caronti, A., Carotenuto, R., Pappalar, M.: Electromechical coupling factor of capacitive micromachined ultrasonic transducers. J. Acoust. Soc. Am. **113**(1), 279–288 (2003)
12. Wygant, I.O., Kupnik, M., Khuri-Yakub, B.T.: Analytically calculating membrane displacement and the equivalent circuit model of a circular CMUT cell. In: Proceedings of the IEEE Ultrasonics Symposium, pp. 2111–2114 (2008)

13. Oguz, H.K., Olcum, S., Senlik, M.N., Tas, V., Atalar, A., Köymen, H.: Nonlinear modeling of an immersed transmitting capacitive micromachined ultrasonic transducer for harmonic balance analysis. IEEE Trans. Ultrason. Ferroelectr. Freq. Control 57(2), 438–447 (2010)
14. Bayram, B., Oralkan, Ö., Ergun, A.S., Hæggström, E., Yaralioglu, G.G., Khuri-Yakub, B.T.: Capacitive micromachined ultrasonic transducer design for high power transmission. IEEE Trans. Ultrason. Ferroelectr. Freq. Control 52(2), 326–339 (2005)
15. Introduction to COMSOL Multiphysics Users Manual, October 2012

Identifying Prominent Individuals or Groups in Terrorist Network Using Social Network Analysis and Investigative Data Mining

Vinay Rishiwal$^{(\boxtimes)}$ and Gaurav Kumar

Department of CS and IT, M.J.P Rohilkhand University, Bareilly, UP, India
rishi4ul00@gmail.com,
midhagauravl@rediffmail.com

Abstract. This is a major concern for most of the countries all over the world to fight against terrorism. Post 9/11 attacks it became important for the legal enforcement agencies to intercept such attacks in advance, otherwise at least identify the key suspects and their associated network. Although the huge amount of information generated and lack of effective analysis approach and methods impede the effective analysis. It cannot be done on the basis of traditional approaches and defend criminal and terrorist activities. However a novice approach like Investigative Data Mining (IDM), a type of Data Mining may provide a well defined approach to tackle the uprising situation. In this paper, an effort is made to understand and illustrate how IDM works and show its importance in identifying key nodes in terrorist networks with social network Analysis.

Keywords: SNA · IDM · Centrality · Eigen centrality

1 Introduction

Most of the crimes performed by the individuals or groups are not performed in isolation – they generally operates in groups to perform illegal activities. Organized crimes such as terrorist attacks, drug trafficking armed robberies etc. are performed in groups [1]. The network of individuals (nodes) is connected with relationships (links).

Every individual in the network has a specified position and can be a leader or gateway in the network structure to transfer malicious goods or information flow. The networks may exist in the form of teams or groups in the form of covert networks [2].

These groups may have communication within them. Some individuals may be interacting as gatekeepers and some individuals may be interacting with each other as group leaders for information transfer or passage of malicious goods [3].

Due to enormous data generation the traditional approaches fails to properly analyze such networks.

To identify prominent individuals from huge data, use of recent concepts and tools must be incorporated. Investigative Data mining (IDM) and other advanced data analysis approaches can provide a solution for legal agencies to work against such networks actively.

© Springer Nature Singapore Pte Ltd. 2016
A. Unal et al. (Eds.): SmartCom 2016, CCIS 628, pp. 788–795, 2016.
DOI: 10.1007/978-981-10-3433-6_94

The paper is organized further in 4 sections with approach for basic discussion about the social network analysis, investigative data mining to identify such networks, a case study and final the conclusion and future work aspects.

2 Backdrop and Existing Concepts

As discussed, problem with the legal and investigative agencies regarding the prevention of future terrorist acts is that the huge amount of information required to be processed where as limiting resource are there for processing the information.

The other fact is that if or not data is relevant or not. One has to identify the interlinking of the data between the people places and events in collection rather individually so that it could be inter-related [4].

The objective is to identify the deductible patterns which are required finally by the investigative agencies. Thus some advanced approaches must be developed so that law agencies could be able to identify the malicious individuals or groups well in advance for proper action. There are various examples of identifying such links between individuals and groups (social networks, e.g., [5]) and other entities (modes of transport, accounts, fin. transactions, contact details, operating modus).

After 9/11 attack it is very much evident that such social network exist between malicious individuals [6].

There are various types of transactions which can be analyzed from the vast amount of the data related to the transactions which are taking place can be correlated with the terrorist attacks. Data is available for such type of transactions in relational databases where transactions like application for visa, driving license, work permit, automotive rentals, air tickets etc. but cannot be analyzed. Yet it is difficult but that can be started with the initial link and a graph can be constructed with the set of data associated.

In the graph nodes are representing observational (e.g. individuals or groups) units and links reflect connection which can be tightly connected or loosely connected depending upon the data or resource transfer between the nodes.

3 Investigative Data Mining

Traditional approach of associated data with statistical techniques and other old approaches of relational database queries are not sufficient to visualize the data effectively [7] rather one can use IDM as future trending approach for finding the deductible patterns in huge datasets.

The IDM can be defined as: "A method that can be used for identifying the pattern of association and determining and predicting the criminal behavior by analyzing the network graph in order to identify prominent nodes for purpose of destabilizing malicious network".

IDM provide the capability to map furtive nodes, and evaluate the interaction criteria for such nodes. This framework goal is to identify the pattern of individual interaction in the network and further understanding the nature of interaction between the nodes or individuals to predict the behavior.

3.1 Social Network Analysis

Social Network Analysis (SNA) provides a scientific and analytical approach for finding relationship between individuals and groups [8].

There are various mathematical formulae and algorithms for evaluation of important parameters between groups of individuals connected through such networks [9]. These parameters and algorithm are very much important to evaluate connectedness and centrality issues related to the analysis [10]. This can be used by the law and enforcement agencies, as in case of Saddam Husain [11, 12].

3.2 Network and Graph Concepts

A social network between individual can be defined as graph G with V as vertices and E as edges G = (V, E) as pair where V can be further considered as Individuals or actors and E represents the relationship between them [13].

The four important parameters defined by Baker and Faulkner are given as follows which are the important part of overall analysis [14].

The Adjacency matrix for the graph can be defined as

$$A_{ij} = \begin{cases} 1 \ if \ i \ and \ j \ are \ connected \\ 0 \ Otherwise \end{cases} \tag{1}$$

If $A_{ij} = A_{ji}$ then symmetric link is there.

Where i and j are nodes.

The main observation start with the centrality measures which can be defined on the basis of degree of a node which represents the number of nodes connected with an individual node. The high degree specifies that the node is representing some important person

The mathematical equation of degree Di of a node

$$D_i = \sum_{j=1}^{n} Aij \tag{2}$$

A node with high degree can be considered as a prominent person or individual in the network. Betweenness B_a calculates a value for a node a about the number of shortest paths passing through the given node (geodesics) for any two other nodes i, j.

$$B_a = \sum_{a}^{n} \sum_{j}^{n} g_{ij}(a) \tag{3}$$

B_a calculates the betweenness and $g_{ij}(a)$ specifies whether the shortest path between i and j pass through a or not.

The next parameter can be closeness C_a which is the sum of the length of geodesics between a particular node 'a' and all the other nodes in a network. It evaluates that how far away one node is from other nodes also called farness.

$$C_a = \sum_{i=1}^{n} l(i,a)$$ (4)

l (i,a) represents the shortest path between i and a.

Another important factor which can be analyzed is eigenvector centrality which does not provide importance to all the connections associated with the network. It can be defined for node i as

$$x_i = \frac{1}{\lambda} \sum_{j=1}^{n} A_{ij} X_j$$ (5)

Where λ is a constant. The eigenvector centrality provide that a node with high influence may be connected to less nodes which may be highly connected to other nodes which leads to the influence of an individual node on others.

3.3   Removal of Prominent Nodes to Crackdown the Network

The important objective is to crackdown such terror networks which can be achieved by identification and removal of such prominent nodes either by killing or by putting them in legal custody [15].

Network can be crackdown by identifying and evaluating key parameters discussed in the previous subsection with respect to the nodes. The nodes which have high values associated with the parameters can be targeted for removal from the network [16, 17].

4   Case Study for Implementation (Madrid Train Bombing)

To illustrate the above concepts practically, a data set by Jose A. Rodriguez of the University of Barcelona created a network of the individuals involved in the bombing of commuter trains in Madrid is taken for evaluation of various discussed parameters [18]. An adjacency matrix representing 70 individuals and their relationships considered with linkage values as 0 and none zero values depending upon the strength of the relationship.

UCINET software is considered to manipulate the data. Figure 1 show the Net-Draw [19] outcome showing the network of all 70 individuals in the network.

This shows the overall connectivity of the individuals and from the figure itself it can be deduced quite easily that which are the nodes those are working as key individuals or prominent personalities who are most connected ones and governs the overall network.

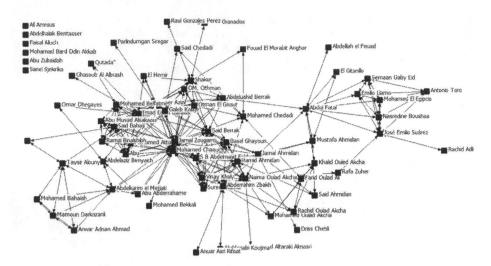

Fig. 1. Network representing suspected persons involved in Madrid train bombing for analysis

The network showed in Fig. 1 displays the connection of individuals. Few nodes shown in the network are highly connected where as few nodes may be isolated from the network.

Table 1 represents the adjacency matrix sample data from actual available data. The entire data used in the analysis is attached with the paper. The UCINET software [20] used for the analysis and excel exported data is taken to show sample data.

Table 1. Adjacency matrix data from the actual dataset

ID	1	2	3	4	5	6	7	8	9	10
Jamal Zougam	0	1	3	1	1	1	4	1	1	0
Mohamed Bekkali	1	0	1	0	0	0	0	0	0	0
Mohamed Chaoui	3	1	0	1	1	0	3	1	1	0
Vinay Kholy	1	0	1	0	1	0	0	0	0	0
Suresh Kumar	1	0	1	1	0	0	0	0	0	0
Mohamed Chedadi	1	0	0	0	0	0	0	0	0	0
Imad Eddin Barakat	4	0	3	0	0	0	0	1	0	1
Abdelaziz Benyaich	1	0	1	0	0	0	1	0	1	2

On the basis of centrality other measure the network can be represented in the following Fig. 2

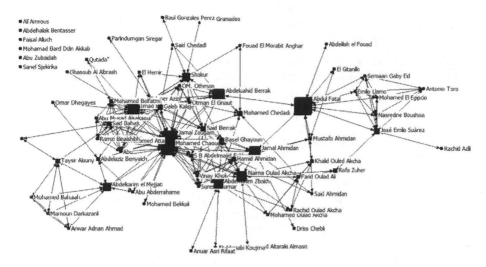

Fig. 2. Network representing highlighted nodes with high centrality

Table 2 represents the sample data of centrality measure values of the various associated nodes where Degree (D), 2 Step Betweenness (2S), Average Reciprocal Distance (ARD), Closeness (C), Eigenvector (EV), Betweenness (B) are calculated using UCINET tool.

Table 2. Different parameters of centrality

ID	D	2 s	ARD	C	EV	BW
Jamal Zougam	29	54	44.3	150	0.35	392
Mohamed Bekkali	2	29	26	211	0.05	0
Mohamed Chaoui	27	54	43.3	152	0.34	321
Vinay Kholy	10	41	32.7	182	0.15	0
Suresh Kumar	10	41	32.7	182	0.15	0
Mohamed Chedadi	7	39	30.8	187	0.07	61.3
Imad Eddin Barakat	22	43	39	168	0.26	268
Abdelaziz Benyaich	6	36	29.1	200	0.08	12.6
Abu Abderrahame	4	34	27.8	204	0.06	0
Omar Dhegayes	2	24	24.2	227	0.03	0
Amer Azizi	18	40	36.5	175	0.25	91.7
Abu Musad Alsakaoui	10	36	31.1	196	0.17	0

By analyzing the final information for the above specified parameters the major person involved in the attack Jamal Zougam was trapped by Investigative agencies with another important terrorist S B Abdelmajid Fakhet and Jamal Ahmidan but they committed suicide.

By analyzing such network one can have following facts about the social network of such malicious groups [21].

- Who are the prominent people in the network responsible for entire operation
- Quantitative analysis quickly identifies prominent individuals with proved facts
- The nodes which are highly connected.
- The terrorist whom should be removed to provide maximum damage to such network
- To find the maximum betweenness between the nodes

The above specified points are very useful for proper analysis of such network which is identified on the basis of social network analysis.

One can identify the prominent persons or groups for the cracking down the network structure by removing them which isolate the other nodes associated with the network [22].

Such type of study provides a scalable effort for the evaluation of parameters with large set of network data [23].

5   Conclusion and Future Directions

It is evident that traditional approach for analysis of data may not be that fruitful for investigative and legal agencies to counter the criminal and terrorist attacks. Hence the new techniques should incorporated to process the huge amount of data generated one cannot deduct the reliable outcome to counter such individuals which are part of terror or criminal network. In this paper IDM has provided a basic but promising approach for network mining on the basis of social interaction evidences.

Further we can have introduction of web mining (particularly web log mining) which could be associated with the individuals who may be prime suspect of the criminal or terrorist network and can be useful for destabilizing such networks. Other fuzzy approaches can also be evaluated for social network analysis in comparison to Investigative data mining.

References

1. McIlllwain, J.S.: Organized crime: a social network approach. Crime Law Soc. Change 32, 301–323 (1999)
2. Carley, K.M.: Estimating vulnerabilities in large covert networks. In: Proceedings from 9th ICCRTS Command and Control Research and Technology Symposium, 14–16 September, Copenhagen, Denmark (2004)
3. Jennifer, X., Chen, H.: Criminal network analysis and visualization: a data mining perspective. Commun. ACM (CACM) 48(6), 101–107 (2005)
4. Muir, H.: Email traffic patterns can reveal ringleaders, new scientist (2006). http://www.newscientist.com/news/news.jsp?id=ns99993550. Accessed 10 Feb
5. Pillar, P.R.: Counterterrorism after Al Qaeda. Wash. Quar. 27(3), 101–113 (2004)

6. Krebs, V.E.: Uncloaking terrorist networks, first Monday, vol. 7(4) (2002). http://Hfirstmonday.org/issues/issue4_11/fleck/index.html. Accessed 11 Feb 2006
7. Heuer, R.J.: Psychology of Intelligence Analysis. Center for the study of Intelligence, Central Intelligence Agency, Fairfax (2001)
8. Degenne, A., Forse, M.: Introducing: Social Networks. Sage Publications, London (1999)
9. Wasserman, S., Faust, K.: Social Network Analysis: Methods and Applications. Cambridge University Press, Cambridge (1994)
10. Stewart, T.: Six Degrees of Mohamed Atta (2002). http://Hmoney.cnn.com/magazines/business2
11. Sparrow, M.: The application of network analysis to criminal intelligence: an assessment of the prospects. Soc. Netw. **13**, 251–274 (1991)
12. Hougham, V.: Sociological skills used in the capture of Saddam Hussein (1991). http://www.asanet.org/footnotes/julyaugustO5/fn3.html. Accessed 10 Feb 2006
13. Newman, M.E.J.: The structure and function of complex networks. SIAM Rev. **45**, 167–256 (2003)
14. Baker, W.E., Faulkner, R.R.: The social organization of conspiracy: Illegal networks in the heavy electrical equipment industry. Am. Soc. Rev. **58**(12), 837–860 (1993)
15. Borgatti, S.P.: The key player problem. In: Proceedings from National Academy of Sciences Workshop on Terrorism, Washington DC (2002)
16. Xu, J.J., Chen, H.: CrimeNet explorer: a framework for criminal network knowledge discovery. ACM Trans. Inf. Syst. **23**(2), 201–226 (2005)
17. Freeman, L.C.: Centrality in social networks: Conceptual clarification. Soc. Netw. **1**, 215–239 (1979)
18. http://moreno.ss.uci.edu/data.html#
19. Netdraw software: http://www.analytictech.com/download_products.htm
20. UciNet Software: http://www.analytictech.com/download_products.htm
21. Robb, J.: Destabilizing terrorist networks (2004). http://globalguerrillas.typepad.com/globalguerrillas/2004/03/destabilizing_t.html. Accessed 02 Jan 2006
22. Hildorsson F.: scalable solutions for social network analysis, Master thesis, Uppsala University (2009)
23. Opsahl, T., Agneessens, F., Skvoretz, J.: Node centrality in weighted networks: Generalizing degree and shortest paths. Soc. Netw. **32**(3), 245–251 (2010)

Enigma of User Privacy in Android

Atul Kumar Dwivedi[1]([✉]), Kanaiya Kariya[2], and Pranav Botti[3]

[1] Chameli Devi School of Engineering, Indore, India
atul.dube.391@gmail.com
[2] Vishwakarma Institution of Information Technology, Pune, India
kanaiya.kariya@gmail.com
[3] Nalla Malla Reddy Engineering College, Hyderabad, India
Pranavbotti@gmail.com

Abstract. Android is an open source operating system with equal proportions of pros and cons. Android provides third party applications that include access to network communications, personal information, storage, location etc. The diverse range of applications available makes life easy, but comes with associated risks and potential threats to the user's privacy. Each time a user installs an application, they are presented with access permissions required to install the application. Users are generally not able to understand the aforementioned permissions due to highly technical jargon presented. In this paper we are focusing on designing an application having access to all the modules (resources) in the smart phone. This application will let the user to select the modules which user wants to be secured. Once this application is installed, user will select few modules to keep private, for example let us consider camera, gallery, etc. Once selection is done, this security application will be running always in the back-end to monitor the security for the modules selected. If Any other application tries to access the secured module, user will get the notification saying that active app is trying to access the camera and needs permission for its working. User can select whether or not to grant the access and also save the selected preference for future.

Keywords: Android · Information privacy · Security · Permission system

1 Introduction

Users are unaware of the security issues related with the application installation. They install the application, often ignoring the requests of the applications for permissions which may potentially put the users' privacy at risk. Once users ignore the risks and approve these requests, the application never seeks for these permissions until they are re installed [11]. Many applications seek unnecessary permissions and tend to misuse the users' data. No availability of choices for the user to select the permissions to be allowed to the application and the permissions to be blocked. Available solutions for the security do allow to change

© Springer Nature Singapore Pte Ltd. 2016
A. Unal et al. (Eds.): SmartCom 2016, CCIS 628, pp. 796–803, 2016.
DOI: 10.1007/978-981-10-3433-6_95

the permissions given to the application only after installation and does not feature the things to be blocked or allowed which does make the application stable [10]. Permission is a form of capability for an application to do its intended work without any constraints enforced on it. There are two types of permissions (1) Time of Use (2) Install time. Based on the time of approval of permission to their request they are categorized. If permissions are approved by user when the application executes a operation of using sensitive resources it is time of Use and if permissions are granted at the time of installation it is install-time. [14] For Android it is only install time i.e. either user has to agree to all the terms for installation or else have to deny the installation of application. There are four level permissions (i) Normal (ii) Dangerous (iii) Signature (iv) Signature or System.

Normal: Default value and low level risk to apps and users. System grants permissions to these without the explicit approval of users [9,12].

Dangerous: Higher-risk permission that requests permission to access the private data of user that can negatively impact user [9,12].

Signature: A permission that the system grants only if the requesting application is signed with the same certificate as the application that declared the permission [9,12].

Signature or System: A permission that the system grants only to applications that are in the Android system image or that are signed with the same certificate as the application that declared the permission [9,12].

Currently Android is the only application that allows flexible application communication and components can interact only if the caller app has permission specified on the Calley component. Android relies on developers to specify security policy, applications may introduce vulnerabilities for core system resources and hence has to prevented [13]. The solution can be redefining the norms of the application development and the application access restrictions through the Operating System. The solution contributes to the user accounts and user data privacy without being misused. The technical challenges involved in this project are understanding the application development in-depth, and working the communication between the application and the operating system. In proposed model we are going to develop an application so that user gets the notification while application is trying to access the private modules selected by user. Application gives the user the flexibility to choose the resources that are private for him to enforce the access restrictions on it. User selected resources are monitored in the application where any application requests or uses the access to the resource, the user will be notified of the resource access. Enhanced security to user and user data is the expected outcome of the project. The other possible solutions can be:

1: Application developers should provide more information to the user regarding the permissions needed and it should be in a language which user will be able to understand.
2: There should be third party agency to provide certificates to the applications which can be trusted.

2   Related Work

1: Security, integrity of system is up to the user to grant access permissions to the apps initially, before they are installed [1]. But in the real world the app descriptions for the request they make are unclear and doesn't show any transparency in how they deal with the private data of user [1].
2: The data stored in databases of app on same physical device in which the app is installed was not encrypted and any malicious person with physical access to the device can retrieve the data [2]. Apps do share the personal info of the user without prior mentioning in the privacy policy. Apps do behavioural tracking i.e. recording of each user activity along with time stamp. Many privacy policies do not cover about the third party advertisers they do have in connection with [3].
3: Misuse of the user private data by collecting the information not required by the app. A prototype is developed and tested on nexus one device with android OS version of 2.1 and the prototype is privacy setting manager which allows the user to control what kind of data is to be sent to the app which requests the permissions [4]. The prototype has successfully protect the data based on control settings of the users from the apps that have been tested on particular device from play store apps [1].
4: Android permissions screen which is shown at the time of installation lack adequate info and users struggle through to understand key terms and the implications associated with permissions requested [5].
5: A prototype is designed and implemented with the strategy of shadow data. When an app requests for user sensitive data then results of shadow i.e. either empty or false data is supplied to the app to protect user data and in a way that app doesn't recognize the trick [6].
6: Few of the top most sensitive and frequently used permissions are INTERNET, READ_PHONE_STATES, ACCESS_COARSE_LOCATION, CAMERA, GET_ACCOUNTS, SEND_SMS, READ_SMS, RECORD_AUDIO, [7].
7: There is also a proposed model where the applications are scanned before they are installed into the device and suspicious activity or code in the app if detected then it is quarantined and the application is installed in the packages of the anti-virus or anti-malware system and the suspicious activities of the application are monitored and restricted [8].

3   Background

3.1   Android

Shown in Fig. 1, smart phones retrieve apps from application markets and run them within a middle ware environment. Existing smart phone platforms rely on application markets and platform protection mechanisms for security. We now overview protections currently implemented in popular platforms [15].

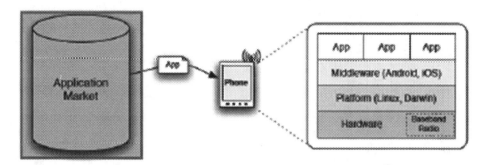

Fig. 1. Smartphone architecture

Android is an operating system designed for smart phones It is implemented in the kernel, and you can easily build RPC interfaces on top of it using the Android Interface Definition Language (AIDL) [9]. There exists hundreds and thousands of apps in the play store developed by many developers. Also apps from other sources can be installed on to the phone instead of Play Store, by configuring the mobile device [16].

3.2   Se-curable IPC Mechanism

Activity: An Activity is, generally, the code for a single, user focused task. Intents are used to specify as Activity, and this may be done ambiguously to allow the user to configure their preferred handler [17] (Fig. 2).

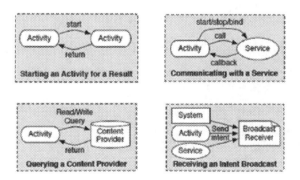

Fig. 2. Androids IPC mechanism

Broadcast: Broadcasts provide a way to send messages between applications, for example, alerting listeners to the passage of time, an incoming message, or other data. Broadcasts that are broad-casted by a intent or application are received by other modules of the application or other applications are received by BroadcastReceivers [18].

The key security features of android to achieve the objectives like protection of user data, protection of system resources including the network and provide application isolation are as follows: 1. Robust security at the OS level through the Linux kernel. 2. Mandatory application sandbox for all applications. 3. Secure inter process communication. 4. Application signing. 5. Application defined and user granted permissions [19].

4   Methodology

For conducting our experiments we have developed a standalone monitoring app, called AIPMA. We have developed a library centric application instead of kernel level or OS centric application as a prototype i.e., while it is easy to install on a user's off-the-shelf device, it is also capable of gathering all system events necessary for our analysis, without requiring the modification of either the Android platform or apps themselves. In the proposed model we have designed an Algorithm for developing an application. The algorithm is given below:

4.1   Algorithm AIPMA:

```
List resources available;
Resource Selection;
Store RList in Database;
Application run in background;
Trace resource status;
if request.access
boolean Result = DatabaseCheck(Resource);
if ResultAccessCheck();
boolean DatabaseCheck(Object Resource)
Check Resource in database list;
if(Resource.exists)
return true;
else
return false;
AccessCheck()
if resource.access()
Return Dialogbox(applicaion name accesing resource)
else
exit() ;
}
```

User needs to install the application on the device and select the resources that are private to him/her. For example Camera, Gallery, Contacts etc. When the user confirms the selections made, then the selected resources are written to a SQLite Database which resides on the device and doesn't need any outside communications. When any access requests to the particular resource is requested, then firstly the application checks if resource exists in its database. If the resources does exists in the database, then the user is prompted with a dialog box which specifies application name which is trying to access a resource and also the resource which is being accessed. User has two choice either to deny or to allow the request. If the user accepts the permission or allows it, then resource can be used by the application which has requested. If user opts for the choice of deny, then the permission to it is denied. It also features an option of remember the choice made so that frequent pop up messages doesn't annoy the user. This choice is once again written to the database and from next time if any applications requests for resource access, this feature will be checked in database. The GUI presented in the app will be hassle free for the user and will be user friendly. The app will be running in the background, monitoring the resources requests made to the operating system.

5 Implementation

We have included few of the common user private modules as resources in application as Camera, Contacts etc. selected from category of most users' considering them to be their private ones. They are made available in xml layout where user can choose which resources to be protected. The selected components are then stored to database where SQLITE database is used. The system calls are intercepted by the ptrace method in android. The status of the resource is monitored and if access requests are made to any application, it is checked to the database if resource is protected or not. If protected then a dialog box pops up notifying the user that particular application is trying to access the resource. The user has to select resources to allow or deny the application request and can save the choice for further use. The SQLite database stores the data selected from user into a database table which can be accessed via the DB browser for sqlite available for free download on web. We have used Android Studio for prototype building and targeted the OS version of 4.2.2.

6 Tests and Evaluation

When the prototype is deployed on Panasonic p81 mobile device with the android OS version 4.2.2, it worked fine the user interface needed to be adjusted as when designed it was targeted for a 4 in. screen where the testing mobile device had 5.5 in. Screen. But the transitions and working of the database and background running app were fine. It could write the data to database from user selection as expected. It could successfully monitor the single selected resource, and notify the user when in monitoring stage. The prototype could successfully notify the user about the resource access and worked as expected.

7   Conclusion

Low barriers of entry for applications in terms of security increases the security risk for end users. The permission requirements for an app are determined by the app developer and also third parties if app is included with third party modules. The end-user is presented with a list of required permissions, but may contain potentially dangerous permissions which user is unaware when they choose to install an app. The security integrity of this system relies on the end-user being aware of what these permissions actually mean. The reality is that most users will ignore or not understand these permissions and simply install an app. The analysis of popular apps shows there are a number of potential information privacy risks associated with specific permissions required by apps. However it is often unclear for end-user perspective as to what information is being accessed by an app and how this app is using information accessed from end-user's smart phone. In this paper we have developed an application called AIPMA to avoid access information and privacy issues in android system. Once this application is installed it will always work in back-end in the android system. After the installation of this application user gets the notification while an application is trying to access the private modules selected by user. If user want to give access of those modules then only the application can access those modules and if the user declines the access of those modules then that particular application can never access those modules.

In the end there arises a question, as the prototype uses the permission to access the resources to monitor, how can the prototype be trusted. Hence there should be privacy modules and security measures implemented at OS level.

References

1. Hanna, S., Song, D., Felt, A.P., Chin, E., Wagner, D.: Android permissions demystified. In: Proceedings of the 18th ACM Conference on Computer and Communications Security, pp. 627–638 (2011)
2. Kelley, P.G., Consolvo, S., Cranor, L.F., Jung, J., Sadeh, N., Wetherall, D.: A conundrum of permissions in- stalling applications on an android smartphone. In: Proceedings of the 16th International Conference on Financial Cryptography and Data Security, pp. 68–79 (2012)
3. Pacheco, C., Lahiri, S., Ernst, M., Ball, T.: Feedback-directed random test generation. In: Proceedings of the International Conference on Software Engineering (2007)
4. Vidas, T., Christin, N., Cranor, L.: Curbing android permission creep. In: W2SP (2011)
5. Enck, W., Octeau, D., McDaniel, P., Chaudhuri, S.: A study of Android application security. In: Proceedings of the 20th USENIX Security Symposium (2011)
6. Enck, W.: Defending users against smartphone apps: techniques and future directions. In: Jajodia, S., Mazumdar, C. (eds.) ICISS 2011. LNCS, vol. 7093, pp. 49–70. Springer Berlin Heidelberg, Berlin, Heidelberg (2011). doi:10.1007/978-3-642-25560-1_3

7. Felt, A.P., Hay, E., Egelman, S., Haneyy, A., Chin, E., Wagner, D.: Android permissions: user attention, comprehension, and behavior. In: Proceedings of the Eighth Symposium on Usable Privacy and Security, Article No. 3 (2012)
8. Bhonde, A., Chatterjee, M.: Security solution for Android application assessment. Int. J. Adv. Res. Comput. Commun. Eng. 3(9) (2014)
9. Tchakounte, F.: Permission-based malware detection mechanism on Android: analysis and perspectives. J. Comput. Sci. Softw. Appl. 1(2), 63–77 (2014)
10. Lane, M.: Does the Android permission system provide adequate information privacy protection for end- users of mobile apps? In: Proceedings of the 10th Australian Information Security Management Conference, Novotel Langley Hotel, Perth, Western Australia, 3rd–5th December (2012)
11. Barrera, D., Clark, J., McCarney, D., van Oorschot, P.C.: Understanding and improving app. installation security mechanisms through empirical analysis of Android. In: Proceedings of the Second ACM Workshop on Security and Privacy in Smartphones and Mobile Devices, pp. 81–92 (2012)
12. Mohini, T., Kumar, A.K., Nitesh, G.: Review on Android and smartphone security. Res. J. Comput. Inf. Technol. Sci. 1(6), 12–19 (2013). ISSN:2320–6527
13. Njie, C.M.L.: Technical Analysis of the Data Practices, Privacy Risks of 43 Popular Mobile Health, Fitness Applications Research Performed For: Privacy Rights Clearinghouse, Privacy Right clearing house (2013)
14. Zhou, Y., Zhang, X., Jiang, X., Freeh, V.W.: Taming information-stealing smartphone applications (on Android). In: McCune, J.M., Balacheff, B., Perrig, A., Sadeghi, A.-R., Sasse, A., Beres, Y. (eds.) Trust 2011. LNCS, vol. 6740, pp. 93–107. Springer Berlin Heidelberg, Berlin, Heidelberg (2011). doi:10.1007/978-3-642-21599-5_7
15. Lin, J., Liu, B., Sadeh, N., Hong, J.I.: Modeling users' mobile app. privacy preferences: restoring usability in a sea of permission settings. In: Symposium on Usable Privacy and Security (2014)
16. Hornyack, P., Han, S., Jung, J., Schechter, S., Wetherall, D.: These aren't the droids you're looking for: retrofitting Android to protect data from imperious applications. In: Proceedings of the 18th ACM Conference on Computer and Communications Security, pp. 639–652 (2011)
17. Bugiel, S., Davi, L., Dmitrienko, A., Fischer, T., Sadeghi, A.R.: XManDroid: a new Android evolution to mitigate privilege escalation attacks. Technical report TR-2011- 04, Technische Universitat Darmstadt, Center for Advanced Security Research Darmstadt, Darmstadt, Germany, April 2011
18. Bugiel, S., Davi, L., Dmitrienko, A., Heuser, S., Sadeghi, A.R., Shastry, B.: Practical and lightweight domain isolation on Android. In: Proceedings of the ACM Workshop on Security and Privacy in Mobile Devices (SPSM) (2011)
19. Burguera, I., Zurutuza, U., Nadjm-Tehrani, S.: Crowdroid: behavior-based malware detection system for Android. In: Proceedings of the ACM Workshop on Security and Privacy in Mobile Devices (SPSM) (2011)

Quality Evaluation of Apple Fruit for Automated Food Processing

Sindhi Komal[1(✉)], Jaymit Pandya[1], and Sudhir Vegad[2]

[1] G. H. Patel College of Engineering and Technology, Anand, India
sindhikomal@gmail.com, jaymitpandya@gcet.ac.in
[2] A. D. Patel Institute of Technology, Anand, India
svegad@gmail.com

Abstract. Quality inspection of fruits with help of computer vision or image processing is gaining much attention nowadays because of the costly and labor intensive techniques used earlier. It has been proven much useful to the agricultural sectors and other industries in the past. The present research work is based on the quality evaluation of apple fruit. Since less work is done for the quality evaluation of internal part of apple, i.e. slices, here the experiment will be done; first on the external surface and then on the slices. Here hue histogram intersection is used for external surface defect detection and for slices defect checking; features called Color Coherence Vector and Complete Local Binary Patterns are extracted from the slice images and they are given as input to Multi-Class Support Vector Machine classifier. Both linear and nonlinear SVMs were used and linear classification gave better results.

Keywords: Digital image processing · Quality evaluation · Apple disease · Feature extraction · Classification · Apple slice · Color Coherence Vector · Computer vision · Complete local binary patterns

1 Introduction

Tons of apples are produced every year and they are used for variety of applications like exporting them to other countries, production of fruit juices and jam, etc. The major concerns of these applications are quality and safety. This quality assurance or inspection has been done through a variety of methods in the past. The traditional techniques used are explained below. The former one is the normal checking of fruits performed by experts and the next one is a chemical molecular method based on chain reaction. But both of these are time consuming and require much capital. So there is an obvious need of an automated method that can overcome their limitations and that alternative is image processing. In this paper, we have basically focused on quality evaluation of apple fruit.

Much work has been done to perform this defect detection of apple fruit. Vijayrekha et al. [3] proposed a technique in which first defect segmentation was done with the help of multi-way PCA and the main method used was multivariate image analysis. Wang et al. [4] basically created a robot for the purpose of defect recognition. Here median filtering was used for preprocessing. A combination of color and shape features were

© Springer Nature Singapore Pte Ltd. 2016
A. Unal et al. (Eds.): SmartCom 2016, CCIS 628, pp. 804–812, 2016.
DOI: 10.1007/978-981-10-3433-6_96

extracted after that and fed into a classifier called Support Vector Machine. A digital parameterization method was proposed in [5] to measure size, shape and surface spottiness. Gopal and Subhasree in [6] performed the experiment on 187 images of apple fruits in which the first step included extraction of features called mean and Probability Density Function. To avoid mismatch by the above two, hue histogram intersection was calculated to determine more precise results. A fine approach for preprocessing was in used in [7] in which image was first converted into L*a*b color space and global threshold segmentation was performed; followed by extraction of various invariant features and finally neural network was trained to classify them. Referring to the most recent work performed in [8], different combinations of features namely Global Color Histogram, Color Coherence Vector, Local Binary Patterns, Complete Local Binary Patterns and Zernike Moments were given as an input to Multiclass Support Vector Machine classifier. Highest accuracy was obtained for the combination CCV + CLBP + ZM which was 95.9%.

All the above work is done on the quality evaluation of external surface which mainly targets the export application and as a result food processing applications like production of juice, jam, etc. are not focused much. So the internal part of apple i.e. slices is not checked for defects. For this reason, the present paper focuses on defect detection of apple externally as well as internally (i.e. slices).

2 Flow of the Proposed Work

As mentioned earlier, the present work is mainly divided into three parts. First the apple will be checked externally for defects, after that slicing will be done and these slices will be checked further for defects. The flow of external defect detection is as shown below:

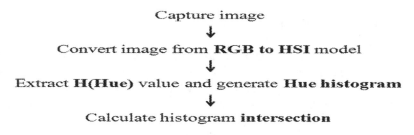

Fig. 1. Flow of external defect detection process

As shown in the Fig. 1, first the image is captured. Then it is converted from RGB to HSI model. After converting in to HSI model, Hue value was extracted. With these hue values hue histogram was generated. The final step is to calculate histogram intersection; which is the difference between the hue histograms of the query image and that of normal apple image which is not infected. The value of this histogram intersection ranges from 0 to 1; where 0 indicates totally dissimilar and 1 indicated totally similar images. On the basis of histogram intersection value, slicing is done. If the value is greater than a particular threshold, i.e., if the apple is damaged one, then two vertical slices will be made. Otherwise two vertical slices will be made for safer side because the apple which appears to be of good quality from outside may be infected from inside. Similarly, the flow of slices defect detection process is as follows:

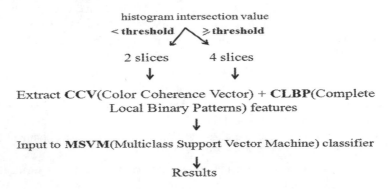

Fig. 2. Flow of slice defect detection process

Now for the defect detection in slices, a combination of color and texture features will be extracted from each slice image as shown in the Fig. 2. The color feature extracted will be Color Coherence Vector and the texture feature will be Complete Local Binary Patterns. A combination of these features will be given as an input to Multiclass Support Vector Machine classifier. On the basis of this, percentage of infected fruit will be calculated. The classifier will group the query images into various classes on the basis of amount of infected part and thus for a particular slice image, it will show the class to which the slice belongs to, as an output.

3 Dataset Preparation

For the purpose of dataset preparation, various types of apples having different defects have been collected and multiple views of a single apple are captured for performing external surface defect detection. So two datasets are prepared; external defect dataset and slices defects dataset. Some examples of defects included in the dataset are as shown below (Figs. 3 and 4):

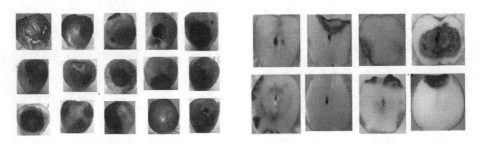

Fig. 3. Sample images from the defects taken   **Fig. 4.** Overview of slices dataset

4 External Defect Detection

Elaborating the steps shown in Fig. 1, the steps are explained as follows:

1. Conversion from RGB to HSI model.
   Generally RGB color space is used to sense the color information, but human beings do not perceive color in this manner. Hence HSI color space is used as it provides efficient segmentation also.
2. The H (Hue) value was extracted after converting into HSI model.
3. Generate Hue histogram for each query image.
4. Calculate histogram intersection of the query image with that of normal apple image. This is done with the help of following formula:

$$H(\text{Target}, \text{Query}) = \frac{\sum_{j=1}^{n} \min(H_r[j], H_g[j])}{\sum_{j=1}^{n} H_g[j]} \begin{cases} =1; \text{if totally similar} \\ =0; \text{if totally dissimilar} \end{cases} \quad (1)$$

Where Hr is the reference histogram and Hg is the test histogram. The value of histogram intersection is obtained 1 for totally similar images, (i.e. good quality apples) and it will be 0 for totally dissimilar images (i.e. totally defected ones). The different intersection values according to the amount of damage can be seen with the help of following figure (Fig. 5):

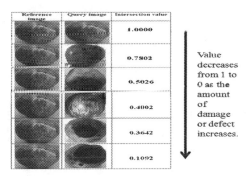

Fig. 5. Histogram intersection value increasing with varying amount of defects

As seen in the above table, every query image is compared to a reference image. As the amount of damage or defect in the apple increases, the intersection value decreases from 1 to 0.

Since we need to consider 3 views; the three views of the single apple can be red, yellow and bi colored as well. But if the image is yellow and not defected, then too it will show less intersection value because the reference image is red. Same will happen when the query image is red and non-defected but the reference image is yellow. So here the histogram intersection of query image is calculated with both red and yellow reference images and the maximum of both is taken as the final value. An example of that is as shown below (Fig. 6):

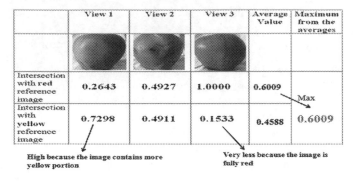

Fig. 6. Method of calculating final intersection value

As shown above, the averages of both reference images with the three views are calculated and finally both the averages are compared and the maximum of them is taken as the final intersection value.

Slicing after deciding threshold: On the basis of observation of values of the examples taken, it has been concluded that the samples of apples which are good in quality were having final hue intersection value greater than 0.75. So the concluded threshold value is 0.75. If the final hue intersection value is less than 0.75 then four slices will be done; otherwise two slices will be done for further checking.

5   Slices Defect Detection

Here first color and texture features are extracted from slices and then they are given as input to Multiclass Support Vector Machine classifier.

5.1   Feature Extraction from Slices

5.1.1   CCV (Color Coherence Vector)

Pass et al. [9] performed research on the use of color feature named Color Coherence Vector to distinguish images. Color coherence is basically the degree to which image pixels of same color are parts of huge continuous areas of similar color or not. If yes, then those pixels are considered to be coherent pixels. Otherwise, they are declared as incoherent. It works by finding connected components of same color in an image and checks if the pixel under consideration is a part of them or not. As an output, it gives two histograms; one for coherent pixels and another for incoherent ones.

5.1.2   CLBP (Complete Local Binary Patterns)

It is a texture based feature which gives a unique code for each pixel. It generally works by comparing the center pixel with its neighbouring pixels. To find the CLBP feature descriptor, it considers both the signs (S) and magnitude (M) of local differences as well as the original center gray level (C) value as shown by Guo et al. [10]. CLBP_S, CLBP_M and CLBP_C are the three features of the CLBP feature descriptor.

CLBP_S is similar to the actual LBP and used to encode the sign information of the local differences. CLBP_M is considered to encode the magnitude information of the local differences:

$$CLBP_{N,R} = \sum_{n=0}^{n-1} t(m_n, c)2^n, t(x,c) = \begin{cases} 1, & x \geq c \\ 0, & x < c \end{cases} \tag{2}$$

Where c is a threshold and considered as the mean value of the intensity of the image.

CLBP_C is considered to encode the actual center gray level information:

$$CLBP_{N,R} = t(g_{c,c_l}), t(x,c) = \begin{cases} 1, & x \geq c \\ 0, & x < c \end{cases} \tag{3}$$

where threshold c_l is taken as the average gray level of the input image. In the experiment, the value of 'R' and 'N' is considered as '1' and '8', respectively, to extract the CLBP feature descriptor.

A combination of both the above features is given as input to MSVM (Multi-class Support Vector Machine) classifier.

5.2 Training and Classification of Slice Images

5.2.1 Training

Here for classification, a machine learning approach also known as supervised classification is used which works by training a database and thereby finding classification function. The learning process included training the classifier by using sufficient samples which in turn gives an accurate value of classification function for a new entity. The classifier used here is SVM (Support Vector Machine). Both linear and nonlinear SVMs are used. The classifiers were trained on the following basis (Fig. 7):

Category	Percentage of damage	Examples
Class 1	<10%	
Class 2	10–50%	
Class 3	>50%	

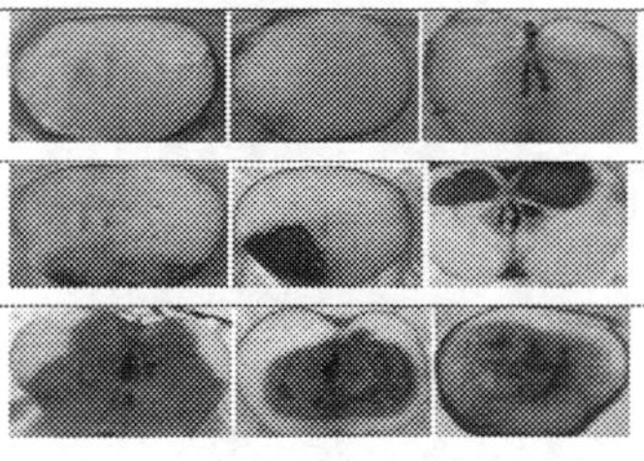

Fig. 7. Categories for slice images according to amount of damage

The above table indicates that the slice image having least amount of damage are grouped to class 1, the ones that are half damaged or less than that are grouped in class 2 and the remaining ones are placed in class 3.

5.2.2 Classification Results

Now when the testing images are given as an input to the classifier, the classifier extracts features from them and based on the previous feature vectors from the training database, it returns the category or class for each input slice image. The results obtained after using linear classifier are shown in following table (Table 1):

Table 1. Classification output for each image using linear classifier

The results were measured in terms of accuracy which is defined as

$$\text{Accuracy}\ (\%) = \frac{Total\ number\ of\ images\ correctly\ classified}{Total\ number\ of\ images\ used\ for\ testing} * 100 \qquad (4)$$

Here 300 slice images were used for training and 100 images were used for testing. Out of these 100, 39 images were from class 1, 31 images from class 2 and 30 images from class 3. The following table shows their results after giving them as input to each of the SVM classifier. The analysis for the linear classifier is shown below (Table 2):

Table 2. Result analysis of linear SVM

	No of input images	Number of correctly classified images
Class 1	39	32
Class 2	31	24
Class 3	30	24
Total	100	80

So here the accuracy will be 80%. Similarly, the accuracy for the nonlinear classifiers is also measured. The following table shows the results of both linear as well as nonlinear classifiers like Polynomial, Quadratic and RBF (Radial Basis Function) (Table 3):

Table 3. Accuracy of linear and nonlinear SVM functions

Sr. No	Kernel function	Accuracy (%)
1	Linear	80
2	Polynomial	60
3	Quadratic	55
4	RBF (Radial Basis Function)	30

Thus it is proved that linear SVM showed highest accuracy for the classification of slice images to their appropriate classes whereas nonlinear SVM is not a much suitable approach.

6 Conclusion

According to the above research performed, it can be concluded that hue histogram intersection is an efficient method to distinguish between defected and normal apples. Also, considering three views instead one provides more accurate results. Moreover, the combination of the features viz. Color Coherence Vector and Complete Local Binary Patterns can highly distinguish different types of slices from each other based on the amount of defect present in the particular slice. These features were given as an input to linear and nonlinear Support Vector Machine classifiers; among which the linear classifier showed the highest accuracy which is 80%. In future, the accuracy of the classification of slice images can be improved by using other classifiers. Also, the slices can be cut from various other angles and then the quality evaluation can be done on those images. Various other features can be extracted from slices and its results can be compared to the existing ones.

References

1. Dubey, S.R., Jhalal, A.: Adapted approach for fruit disease identification using images. Int. J. Comput. Vis. Image Process. (IJCVIP) **2**(3), 44–58 (2014)
2. Hartman, J.: Apple fruit diseases appearing at harvest. Plant Pathology Fact Sheet, College of Agriculture, University of Kentucky (2010)
3. Vijayarekha, K.: Multivariate image analysis for defect identification of apple fruit image. In: IEEE Conference on Industrial Electronics, Orlando, Florida, pp. 1499–1503 (2008)
4. Wang, J.-J., Zhao, D.-A., Ji, W.: Application of support vector machine to apple recognition using in apple harvesting robot. In: IEEE International Conference on Information and Automation, Zhuhai, Macau, pp. 1110–1115 (2009)
5. Radojević, R.L., Petrović, D.V.: Digital parameterization of apple fruit size, shape and surface spottiness. Afr. J. Agric. Res. **6**(13), 3131–3142 (2011)
6. Gopal, A., Subhasree, R., Srinivasan, V.K.: Classification of color objects like fruits using Probability Density Function (PDF). In: IEEE International Conference on Machine Vision and Image Processing, Taipei, pp. 1–4 (2012)

7. Ashok, V., Vinod, D.S.: Automatic quality evaluation of fruits using probabilistic neural network approach. In: IEEE International Conference on Contemporary Computing and Informatics, Mysore, India, pp. 308–311 (2014)
8. Dubey, S.R., Jhalal, A.: Apple disease classification using color, texture and shape features from images. Signal Image Video Process. **10**(5), 819–826 (2015). Springer
9. Pass, G., Zabih. R., Miller, J.: Comparing images using color coherence vectors. In: Proceedings of the Fourth ACM International Conference on Multimedia, New York, USA, pp. 65–73 (1997)
10. Guo, Z., Zhang, L., Zhang, D.: A completed modeling of local binary pattern operator for texture classification. IEEE Trans. Image Process. **19**(6), 1657–1663 (2010)

Protein Classification Using Hybrid Feature Selection Technique

Upendra Singh[✉] and Sudhakar Tripathi

Department of Computer Science and Engineering,
National Institute of Technology Patna, Patna, Bihar, India
dobestupendra@gmail.com, stripathi.cse@nitp.ac.in

Abstract. Protein function prediction is a challenging classification problem. A computational method is vital to perform the function prediction of Proteins. For this various Feature Selection techniques had proposed by eminent researcher. But several techniques are model based or for a specific type of problem. In this paper, we make a comparative analysis of different supervised machine learning methods for the prediction of functional classes of proteins using a set of physiochemical features. For an attribute or feature selection we have used a novel hybrid feature selection technique to overcome some of the limitations of existing technique and also present a comparative analysis of the classification of enzymes function or family using different computational intelligence techniques with proposed hybrid feature selection.

Keywords: Classification · Machine leaning · Data mining · Feature selection · Function prediction

1 Introduction

Protein function prediction is a very challenging task in Bioinformatics. The Functional knowledge of a protein is very crucial to design or evolve new approaches in the biological process. Protein Function Prediction methods are used to assign biological or biochemical roles of proteins. The Information required for prediction might be coming from nucleic acid sequence homology [1], protein domain structures, gene expression profiles and protein-protein interaction, etc. Protein function prediction involves mainly sequence similarity based approach, structure based approach or by using both sequence and structural properties. The protein function prediction based on experiment requires a large amount of experimental resources and human exertion to analyze a single protein. Computational techniques which are capable to explore the functional discovery of protein functions surprisingly reduce lab testing and also provide an efficient way of function prediction. In earlier times, approaches based on homology were used for the prediction of protein function, but these approaches were unable to perform with accuracy in case of a new protein was dissimilar to previous one. Hence, to address these types of classification problems several computational techniques have evolved during the past several years.

© Springer Nature Singapore Pte Ltd. 2016
A. Unal et al. (Eds.): SmartCom 2016, CCIS 628, pp. 813–821, 2016.
DOI: 10.1007/978-981-10-3433-6_97

The most popular computational methods for protein function prediction are based on amino acid sequences, since this information is available for the most of existing Proteins. It may not be always adequate for prediction. It also has a less percentage of accuracy. The assumption behind this approach is the different proteins or enzyme having similarity in sequences perform preserve the same functionality.

2   Related Work

There has been done an extensive research on Protein functional classification. In recent decades of research the prime focus was given to the functional class prediction based on either sequence derive features or structural features. Several classification techniques such as SVM, ANN, and Decision Tree have been used in earlier studies [1–5]. The SVM has shown significant performance as compared to other traditional machine learning techniques for example, neural networks (NNs) in various domains. However, the performance of SVM is quite similar to the black box model. They dont produce comprehensive models that involve to the predictions work. In recent decades of research, many studies have focused on Protein Structure prediction by the use of machine learning techniques like Neural network or Support Vector Machine have attained a worthy figure of accuracy [6–10]. Besides of this, how a learning was made and why a decision was being taken, does not reveals by these methods. It is very important to contain the ability to explain why and how a conclusion is made for the approval of the machine learning technology. Kumar et al. [11] have used the structural properties and sequence derive feature set to determine the enzyme functional class and subclass domain using support vector machine. They have used three tier model in which at the first level of model they have distinguished the queried protein in enzyme or non-enzyme. At the second level of their model they have performed or carried out the enzyme functional classification and at the third level they have performed the sub functional classification. Lou et al. [12] have used sequence based information to find the DNA-binding sites using support vector information. Dobson et al. [8] proposed a method by using EC number to assign the function with the help of the structure of protein. They have used one class against one class strategy using SVM for protein function prediction. He get the accuracy in the range of 35–60%. Paliwal et al. [7] have explored the physicochemical feature of the amino acids with PSSM containing information concerned with evolutionary activities to carry out feature extraction. These features are used for the prediction task of protein structural class with the help of an ensemble classifier over 4 different benchmarks. For the evaluation of classification performance they have used 10-fold cross validation method. Liu et al. [13] have proposed a method using random forest to determine the DNA binding proteins and amino acid sequences of protein for predicting DNA-binding residue prediction. The author claims that using a novel and hybrid approach of feature selection results better prediction performance.

3 Methodology

Various Classification techniques and Feature selection methods are used for Protein Function Prediction. This section contains a brief description of different classification techniques and feature selection methods below which are used here for functional classification of protein

- **SVM:** Traditionally SVM was used for binary classification. But in recent year of research work, it is widely used in multi class problems [14]. In SVM, we construct a set of hyper plane that separate the class members. In multi class classification where linear separation of data is not possible, SVM use Kernel function. In SVM mostly used kernels are Sigmoid, RBF, Polynomial, linear, etc. One against all and All vs All are mainly used approach in Multi Class Classification by SVM. The basic steps which involve by Support Vector Machine in solving a classification problem can be describe briefly as follows. Initially, with the help of a non-linear mapping function, it processes the transformation of the input space into a large dimensional feature space. After that, it constructs hyper plane which separate the data instances by maximum distance from the nearest training points set [15].
- **Random Forest:** This is an ensemble classifier [16–18] which creates no. of decision trees. These individual trees predict the output class for testing instance. Majority of predicted class by individual tree is taken into account for final prediction. Feature Selection Attributes :- p1, p2, p3., pn.
  Size of subset for feature selection = sqrt(n).
  No of tree generation = 100 (user specified).
- **Radial Basis Function Network:** Logistic regression applied to K-means clusters as basis functions. Radial basis function network uses k-means while implementing the input layer architecture. The hidden layer of network uses radial basis function.

$$f_i(x) = \sum_{i=1}^{n} W_i.j.r_i(x) \tag{1}$$

where f is the function corresponding to j^{th} output unit and r_i is the radial basis function.
- **Naive Bayes:** This is very basic approach for supervised classification problem. In Naive Bayes the conditional probability is calculated for each attribute. After that by product rule we calculate the joint conditional probability of attribute. The well-known Bays rule is used to derive conditional probability of Class variable which depicts the target class. Output class with highest probability.

$$P(C/A1, A2, ..., An) = (\sum_{i=1}^{n}(P(A_i)P(c)))P(C)/P(A1, A2, ..., An) \tag{2}$$

- **Feature Selection:** Feature selection refers to the attribute selection or attributes subset selection. The main purpose of feature selection technique is to remove the irrelevant and redundant features and also for dimension reduction [1].

There are the list of different feature selection algorithms provided in WEKA tool from which we have applied four feature selection methods for efficient feature selection.

– **CfsSubsetEval:** This feature selection technique select those features which have higher co-relation value with target class and preferably lower co-relation among them.

Pearson's correlation coefficient [13] is used while evaluating the relevance of attribute. Pearson's correlation coefficient is covariance of two variables divided by the product of their standard deviations.

$$\rho xy = cv(x, y)\sigma x\sigma y. \tag{3}$$

where cv is covariance and σ is the standard deviation of data.

– **InfoGainAttributeEval:** It is an attribute selection method inbuilt in WEKA tool. It calculate the significance of an attribute by measuring the information gain with respect to the class.

$$Information_Gain(Class, Attribute) = H(Class) - H(Class|Attribute)$$
$$Gain = H(y) - H(y/x) = H(x) - H(x/y) \tag{4}$$

where H denotes the entropy and entropy is the measure of impurity in dataset and is calculated as:

$$H(x) = -\sum_{i=1}^{n} p(x_i)log_2p(x_i) \tag{5}$$

– **FilteredSubsetEval:** This feature selection method provide a subset of features by applying an inbuilt arbitrary filter. Here filter that is used does not make change in order or no of attribute.

4   Implementation

Protein Functional classification involves different steps as data acquisition, data preprocessing, Feature Selection and Classification.

Data Acquisition: We have acquired the raw data from protein server RCSB. We have used twelve Physiochemical feature or attribute in this paper for making comparative analysis. These features are structure based attributes. The Features used in this paper are Angle Beta, Z-no., Resolution, Structure Molecular wt., Residue count, Average B Factor, Refinement resolution, Ligand mw, pH value, Percentage solvent content, Chain length and Molecular wt.

Dataset Description: Dataset contains following no of instances from different classes shown in Table 1.

Data Pre-processing: Since this is a multi class classification problem, we have consider sampling technique so that we can get sufficient no of training

Table 1. Dataset description

Enzyme class	Transferase	Oxidoreductase	Lyase	Ligase	Isomerase	Hydrolase
No. of instances	3711	1380	632	414	362	3363

and test instances from each class. After preprocessing the raw data we get a labeled refined dataset having different or unequal figure of instances from corresponding class. Hence, here we applied stratified sampling to get a balanced dataset sample.

We applied different feature selection algorithms after data preprocessing to find out the most relevant attribute for our target class prediction using WEKA.

Proposed Method for Feature Selection: In our proposed method of feature selection we have used frequency of occurrence of attributes in above used four feature selection methods. We have calculated the count of frequency of different attribute in all four applied feature selection methods as Molecular weight, Chain length, Structure Molecular weight, Ligand molecular weight with 4 frequency and Residue Count, Angle Beta, Percentage solvent content with 3 frequency. These sub set of 7 features selected using hybrid feature selection technique. We arrange the attribute in their descending order of count. If count is equal for two

Table 2. Feature selection applied

Feature selection techniques	Infogain AttributeEval	Classifier SubsetEval	Filtered SubsetEval	cfSubsetEval
Features	Molecular wt	Angle Beta	Angle Beta	Angle Beta
	chain length	Z-no		
	Residue count	Resolution	Residue count	Residue count
	Structure MW	Structure MW		
	Ligand mw	residue count	Ligand mw	Ligand mw
	Angle Beta	Average B Factor		
	pH value	Ligand mw	Chain length	Chain length
	Z-no	pH value		
	Percentage Solvent content	Percentage Solvent content	Molecular Weight	Molecular Weight
	Resolution	Chain length		
	Refinement resolution			
	Average B Factor			

Table 3. Result summary on imbalanced data without using feature selection

Classification technique	Accuracy (%)	Precision	Sensitivity	F-measure
Nave bays	33.13	0.44	0.331	0.344
RBF network	47.95	0.466	0.48	0.447
Random Forest	80.6125	0.806	0.806	0.801
SVM	60.21	0.58	0.60	0.59

or more attribute then arrange in order of having max information gain first and so on.

To get a relevant and significant subset of feature subset we use back elimination process on above ranked attribute. In back elimination process we remove the feature iteratively having lowest rank to get desired level of accuracy. Table 2 shows different feature selection applied here. For make a comparative analysis of Enzyme Classification we have used four classification techniques, SVM, RBFN, Random forest and Nave Bays. For simulation and analysis we have used data mining tools weka and Knime which are open source softwares. We have use 8-fold cross-validation method on weka tool to asses and test the model. Since we have enough no of data sample from each class after sampling of data for simulation, it decrease the possibility of biasing the result. We have iteratively check the result on K = 5 to 10 and get significant result over k = 8 in k-fold validation method.

5   Result and Analysis

For classification we consider two cases and compared their accuracy.

Case-1. Take all attribute and do classification without feature selection or data balancing.

Case-2. Apply various feature selection algorithm and decide the rank of attribute [19, 20] based on frequency or occurrences of attribute, we select first 7 attributes and classification algorithms applied on selected attributes with imbalanced dataset and random sampled dataset. We compute accuracy as well as other performance measures of two cases and analyses which scenario is more cost effective and will give best result. Table 3 shows the accuracy level of different classification techniques using the protein dataset without using any feature selection or any data balancing or sampling approach such as random sampling etc. Table 4 shows the classification accuracy of same classifiers by using hybrid feature selection with same imbalanced dataset and with random sampled dataset (Fig. 1).

Table 4. Result summary using hybrid feature selection and taking first 7 attributes. (RS = Random Sampling ID = Imbalance Dataset)

Classification	Accuracy (%)		Precision		Sensitivity		F-measure	
	RS	ID	RS	ID	RS	ID	RS	ID
Nave bays	35.35	35.02	0.446	0.45	0.353	0.35	0.359	0.367
RBF network	48.87	50.00	0.494	0.476	0.488	0.5	0.490	0.462
Random Forest	80.49	80.9775	0.802	0.808	0.804	0.81	0.801	0.806
SVM	63.21	62.90	0.667	0.60	0.632	0.629	0.646	0.618

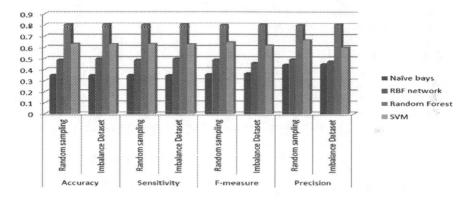

Fig. 1. Graphical representation of prediction

6   Conclusion and Future Work

In this paper we have used four different classification method and present a very brief description about the classification techniques used here and also about feature selection technique. The prediction result shows a significant increase in accuracy level by using hybrid feature selection. The above result analysis shows that Random Forest method has a better accuracy over other classification techniques using feature selection over imbalanced dataset. The present research work addresses the feature selection issue in context of Protein classification by using a novel hybrid approach of feature selection which improve the performance of classification model. Adjusting various parameters for training, further data refining and modeling of whole dataset and ensemble of SVM with RBF kernel AND Random Forest would result a comprehensive computational model for Protein Function Prediction using hybrid feature selection. Here we have used only twelve attribute for protein function prediction. Hence in future the classifier performance might be improved by using more relevant and appropriate attribute for protein function prediction.

References

1. Lee, B.J., Lee, H.G., Ryu, K.H.: Design of a novel protein feature, enzyme function classification. In: CIT Workshops 2008. IEEE 8th International Conference on Computer and Information Technology Workshops, pp. 450–455. IEEE (2008)
2. Yadav, A., Jayaraman, V.K.: Structure based function prediction of proteins using fragment library frequency vectors. Bioinformation **8**(19), 953–956 (2012)
3. Garg, A., Raghava, G.P.: A machine learning based method for the prediction of secretory proteins using amino acid composition, their order and similarity-search. Silico Biol. **8**(2), 129–140 (2008)
4. Mer, A.S., Andrade-Navarro, M.A.: A novel approach for protein subcellular location prediction using amino acid exposure. BMC Bioinform. **14**(1), 1 (2013)
5. Jensen, L.J., Skovgaard, M., Brunak, S.: Prediction of novel archaeal enzymes from sequence-derived features. Protein Sci. **11**(12), 2894–2898 (2002)
6. Capra, J.A., Laskowski, R.A., Thornton, J.M., Singh, M., Funkhouser, T.A.: Predicting protein ligand binding sites by combining evolutionary sequence conservation and 3d structure. PLoS Comput. Biol. **5**(12), e1000585 (2009)
7. Dehzangi, A., Paliwal, K., Sharma, A., Dehzangi, O., Sattar, A.: A combination of feature extraction methods with an ensemble of different classifiers for protein structural class prediction problem. IEEE/ACM Trans. Comput. Biol. Bioinform. **10**(3), 564–575 (2013)
8. Dobson, P.D., Doig, A.J.: Predicting enzyme class from protein structure without alignments. J. Mol. Biol. **345**(1), 187–199 (2005)
9. Wang, L., Yang, M.Q., Yang, J.Y.: Prediction of DNA-binding residues from protein sequence information using random forests. BMC Genomics **10**(1), 1 (2009)
10. Kumar, C., Choudhary, A.: A top-down approach to classify enzyme functional classes and sub-classes using random forest. EURASIP J. Bioinform. Syst. Biol. **2012**(1), 1 (2012)
11. Yadav, S.K., Bhola, A., Tiwari, A.K.: Classification of enzyme functional classes, subclasses using support vector machine. In: 2015 International Conference on Futuristic Trends on Computational Analysis and Knowledge Management (ABLAZE), pp. 411–417. IEEE (2015)
12. Lin, W.-Z., Fang, J.-A., Xiao, X., Chou, K.-C.: iDNA-Prot: identification of dna binding proteins using random forest with grey model. PLoS One **6**(9), e24756 (2011)
13. Wu, J., Liu, H., Duan, X., Ding, Y., Wu, H., Bai, Y., Sun, X.: Prediction of DNA-binding residues in proteins from amino acid sequences using a random forest model with a hybrid feature. Bioinformatics **25**(1), 30–35 (2009)
14. Samb, M.L., Camara, F., Ndiaye, S., Slimani, Y., Esseghir, M.A.: A novel RFE-SVM-based feature selection approach for classification. Int. J. Adv. Sci. Technol. **43**, 27–36 (2012)
15. Tiwari, A.K., Srivastava, R.: A survey of computational intelligence techniques in protein function prediction. Int. J. Proteomics (2014)
16. Gao, M., Skolnick, J.: DBD-hunter: a knowledge-based method for the prediction of DNA-protein interactions. Nucleic Acids Res. **36**(12), 3978–3992 (2008)
17. Frank, E., Hall, M., Trigg, L., Holmes, G., Witten, I.H.: Data mining in bioinformatics using weka. Bioinformatics **20**(15), 2479–2481 (2004)
18. Nagao, C., Nagano, N., Mizuguchi, K.: Prediction of detailed enzyme functions and identification of specificity determining residues by random forests. PloS one **9**(1), e84623 (2014)

19. Gulati, H.: Predictive analytics using data mining technique. In: 2015 2nd International Conference on Computing for Sustainable Global Development (INDIA-Com), pp. 713–716. IEEE (2015)
20. Kishore, R., Tripathi, S.: A comparative analysis of enzyme classification approaches using hybrid feature selection technique. In: International Conference on Circuit, Power and Computing Technologies (ICCPCT). IEEE (2016)

Facial Expression Recognition Invariant to Illumination Using ROI Based Local Binary Pattern

Zankhana H. Shah[1(✉)] and Vikram Kaushik[2]

[1] Information Technology Department, B V M Engineering College,
Vallabh Vidyanagar, Anand, Gujarat, India
zankhana.shah@bvmengineering.ac.in
[2] Manish Institute of Computer Studies, Visnagar, Gujarat, India
dr.vikramkaushik@gmail.com

Abstract. Facial expressions are the most effective way of communication between humans. Hence, recognition of facial expressions is an emerging research topic in the area of image processing and pattern recognition. The task of recognizing facial expressions is challenging because of variation in many parameters like illumination, pose, ethnicity etc. This article presents an effective approach for recognition of facial expressions with variation in illumination. ROI based Local Binary Pattern is used for extracting feature information and Neural Network as classifier. Japanese Female Facial Expressions (JAFFE) database is used for obtaining the results.

Keywords: Region of interest · Expression recognition · Feature extraction

1 Introduction

Face expressions are much powerful and effective way of exchanging information between people. Researchers says that communication through facial expressions is even more effective compared to speech. Several applications can be found for automatic facial expression recognition in the field of man-machine interaction such as behavioural analysis, emotional studies, 3D face animation, robotics, crowd surveillance etc. Because of extensive range of applications, facial expression recognition and related work has gained much notice of researchers since last decade.

Though much progress has been made [4–7, 20, 21], automatic facial expression recognition remains an attention-grabbing and demanding problem. Recognition of facial expressions with a high precision and recognition rate remains difficult due to the much range of facial expressions. Along with variety of expressions, many factors make this task complex such as variation in pose and illumination, presence of occlusion such as hair, spectacles etc. The variety of expressions can be available from the people of different culture. Ekman and Friesen [24] concluded from their research that the expressions "Happy, Anger, Sad, Disgust, Surprise and Fear" are seen and understood in same way among all human ethnicity. Figure 1 shows six universal expressions.

© Springer Nature Singapore Pte Ltd. 2016
A. Unal et al. (Eds.): SmartCom 2016, CCIS 628, pp. 822–830, 2016.
DOI: 10.1007/978-981-10-3433-6_98

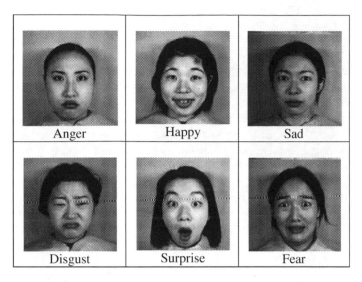

Fig. 1. Six universal expressions of JAFFE database [25]

Three fundamental subtasks associated to facial expression analysis and recognition is: face detection in an image, drawing out the characteristics of expressions, commonly known as features, and classification of the expression in different categories, such as smile, surprise etc. The factors like changes in pose and illumination, presence of occlusions like hair also affect the recognition system. Non-frontal faces and presence of hair and glasses make the feature extraction task more difficult, as some of facial features will become unavailable. Change in illumination also requires handling as that also makes some of the features non-visible or partly visible.

The work presented here focuses on illumination invariant facial expression recognition. The modified Local Binary Pattern technique is used for feature extraction purpose and neural network is used as a classifier. The method is tested on the database, namely JAFFE (Japanese Female Facial Expression) [25] which contain images of 10 Japanese females with 7 expressions, with different lighting conditions.

The rest of this paper is organized as follows. Section 2 describes the literature work related to facial expression recognition methodology. In Sect. 3, ROI based Local Binary Pattern has been described. Section 4 shows the analysis of results. In Sect. 5, conclusion is drawn.

2 Related Work

Facial expression recognition is a three step task namely faces detection, feature extraction and classification. Extracting an effective and relevant facial expression features from face images is a crucial action for effective and correct facial expression recognition. The two widespread approaches to extract expression features are: geometric feature-based approach and appearance-based approach [4]. The geometrical feature-based approaches depend on the geometric features, which are always present on the face and correspond to the shapes and locations of various facial parts such as eyebrows, eyes, nose, mouth etc. While the appearance-based approaches focus on the features which are prone to change/appear due to facial expressions such as wrinkles, bulges etc. The detailed description about various approaches used for face acquisition and feature extraction can be found in [1–3].

Most of the previous works [4–7, 10, 13, 14, 21–23] on facial expression recognition have focused on classifying six universal expressions, that are anger, disgust, fear, happy, sad and surprise. These categories had been proposed by Ekman [24].

Feature extraction methods based on geometric features take out features of face components, such as eyebrow, eyes, and a mouth and identify the expressions from variation in their usual shapes. However, determining the accurate location of relevant features becomes much complex due to variety of parameters such as variation in skin colour, variation in illumination conditions and pose variations. Pose and illumination variation are the most interesting parameters to be taken care of and can be found in [6, 7, 10–12, 16, 18, 19].

The process of feature extraction and selection is followed by classification of expressions into six universal categories. Many methods have been used for the said purpose which include neural network [14, 15], soft computing [8], k-means clustering [9], naive base classifier [20], support vector machines [12, 16, 18, 25] etc.

3   Proposed Method

The proposed technique uses Local Binary Pattern with a modification that it is applied on few selected area of input image. The method is enhanced from the famous LBP technique, where instead of finding LBP features of entire image, they are obtained for selected regions called ROI of the face. The region of interest, such as eye, eyebrow and mouth is obtained using canny edge detection method.

3.1   Local Binary Pattern

In the applications like video conferencing and visual surveillance, the input images may be available with different illumination conditions. The changes in illumination in input images make facial expression recognition task much more difficult. There are two approaches to deal with this problem. One, image pre-processing techniques can be applied before feature extraction process to compensate different illuminations [17]. Second, illumination invariant feature extraction technique can be used to compensate different illuminations. In this work, we have focused on second approach by using LBP features for expression identification in different illumination conditions. Experiments on images with different lighting conditions show that LBP features perform on all kinds of face images in very stable and strong manner.

The two important characteristics of LBP features are: one, they perform almost similar even in different illuminations and second, they are easy to be computed. The LBP operator labels the pixel of an image by taking a 3×3 neighbourhood of

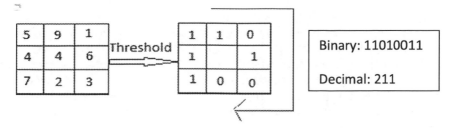

Fig. 2. The working of LBP operator

each pixel, thresholding with the centred value and using the result as a binary number (as shown in Fig. 2). The 256-bin histogram of the LBP codes found for a region, is used as a texture descriptor.

The computed binary numbers (generally known as LBP features or LBP codes) represents texture features such as curved edges, spots, line end, corner etc. (Figure 3).

Fig. 3. Texture primitive detected by LBP

After labelling an image as shown in Fig. 2, histogram of the labelled image F1(x, y) can be found using following equation·

$$Hi = \sum_{x,y} I(F1(x,y) = i)$$

Where i range from 0 to n−1 and n represents number of different labels obtained by applying the LBP operator.

This LBP histogram represents the information about various patterns in the face such as edges, spot and flat areas. Hence, this information can be used as features of the images.

3.2 ROI Based LBP

As per the discussion in previous section, LBP technique computes histogram of whole face image, which determine only the occurrences of the features. This information does not reveal the indication about their locations. To also consider shape information of faces, instead of entire face image, part of face can be used to extract LBP features. Entire face image can be divided into small parts, from each part; the LBP features can be extracted and finally all histograms, of different parts, can be concatenated into a single feature histogram. To improve performance of feature extraction stage, few parameters like LBP operator and number of sub regions can be varied and experimented.

Regions of Interest are those regions which contain most relevant information about expressions. The eyes, eyebrows and mouth regions are most affecting regions by facial expressions. For example, the length of mouth will be more with happy expression compared to normal length. Similarly, the width of open eyes would be more with surprise expression compared to neutral expression. The importance of these regions is used while obtaining LBP features. Hence, LBP features are obtained for these ROI. The classifier takes input as single feature vector, obtained by concatenating all sub regions' feature vectors.

Many approaches are available to extract ROI. In this paper, edge detection is used to determine ROI information. The idea behind edge detection is to considerably condense the amount of data in input image, while protecting the structural properties of image which may be important for further image processing.

The concept of detecting edges is materialized with the help of maximum and minimum threshold. Edges can be found by determining local maxima of the gradient of the input image having different intensity values. The derivative of a Gaussian filter is used to calculate gradient of an image. Following are the steps to detect edges:

Step 1: Noise removal is done using Gaussian filter such that input image will be smoothening. A Gaussian filter with $\sigma = 1.4$ is

$$B = \frac{1}{159} \begin{bmatrix} 2 & 4 & 5 & 4 & 2 \\ 4 & 9 & 12 & 9 & 4 \\ 5 & 12 & 15 & 12 & 5 \\ 4 & 9 & 12 & 9 & 4 \\ 2 & 4 & 5 & 4 & 2 \end{bmatrix}$$

Step 2: The edges are those where there is a drastic change in gray scale intensity value. The gradients of the image help in determining these areas. First the image will be smoothed by Gaussian filter and then, gradients at each pixel will be computed by applying Sobel-operator. The basis matrix for x and y directions are:

$$H_x = \begin{bmatrix} -1 & 0 & 1 \\ -2 & 0 & 2 \\ -1 & 0 & 1 \end{bmatrix}$$

$$H_y = \begin{bmatrix} 1 & 2 & 1 \\ 0 & 0 & 0 \\ -1 & -2 & -1 \end{bmatrix}$$

The magnitude of gradient is then calculated using following equation:

$$|G| = \sqrt{Gx^2 + Gy^2}$$

Here, Gx and Gy represents the gradient in x and y direction respectively.

After extracting the edges from input image, Region of Interest (ROI) has been extracted. As discussed earlier, the regions namely eyebrows, eye and mouth, which contributes most in expression images, are selected as ROI. This selection of ROI is done using iterative search algorithm. It iteratively searches for white pixels in the face region. The area, which contains maximum number of white pixels are estimated as ROI.

After extracting three Regions of Interest, LBP is applied on each individual region and histogram of LBP features is found. The LBP feature histogram of three ROI are taken together to make a single feature vector.

3.3   Classification

As discussed above, many classifiers are available and can be used for the classification purpose. That includes Euclidian distance, neural network, support vector machine, naive base classifier, k-means clustering etc. The work presented here uses pattern recognition neural network which classifies expressions into 6 universal categories. As for one sub-region, total number of bins of a LBP histogram is 256 and there are such 5 sub regions on which LBP is applied, input layer in this network contains 1280 neurons. The number of neurons at hidden layer varied from 35 to 40 to optimize the result. As per the number of universal expressions, which is 6, the output layer contains 6 neurons. The architecture of neural network is as shown below:

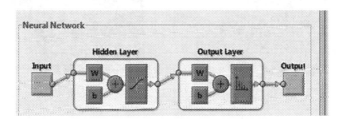

Fig. 4. Neural network architecture

4   Result Analysis

Japanese Female Facial Expression (JAFFE) database contain 210 images of six universal expressions and neutral expression with varying illumination conditions [25]. The ROI of all images and LBP features of those ROI are found using canny edge detection and LBP approach respectively and stored as a feature vector.

The sample result of two expressions with original input image and LBP features on five sub regions, namely, two eyebrows, two eyes and a mouth is shown below:

The LBP features of images are used to train neural network. From 210 images of JAFFE database, 70% images are used to train the neural network and remaining 15% images are used for testing purpose and 15% images are used for validation. The images of each expression are auto selected, i.e. neural network selects expression image. Following table shows the analysis of recognition rate of nine such cases.

Table 1. Sample results of feature extraction

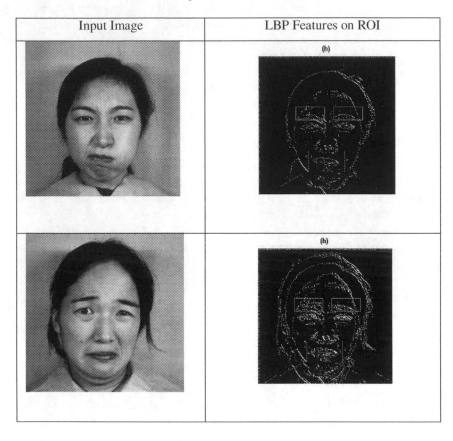

Table 2. Result analysis (images are auto selected)

	Type & Number of expressions							Recognition rate
	Angry	Disgust	Fear	Happy	Neutral	Sad	Surprise	
Case 1	5	5	2	2	6	7	4	96.9%
Case 2	2	3	0	8	7	5	7	93.8%
Case 3	2	5	4	4	2	7	8	71.9%
Case 4	3	6	4	6	5	4	4	100%
Case 5	6	3	3	5	5	5	5	84.4%
Case 6	7	3	7	2	4	3	6	96.9%
Case 7	6	3	1	1	6	7	7	96.9%
Case 8	3	4	7	5	3	6	4	90.6%
Case 9	1	5	4	4	6	4	8	93.3%

The Table 3 shows the result analysis of those cases where 15% images are used for testing and rest of images (85%) is given to train neural network. The total images of JAFFE database are 210. Here, the number of images of each expression is manually selected and given as input to neural network.

Table 3. Result Analysis (images are selected manually)

No of test images	Type of expressions							Recognition rate
	Angry	Disgust	Fear	Happy	Neutral	Sad	Surprise	
32	5	2	3	5	6	8	3	93.8%
32	3	3	5	8	4	6	3	84.4%
32	5	5	5	4	6	4	3	90.6%
32	7	6	3	4	4	6	2	96.9%
32	5	8	2	0	5	6	6	96.9%
32	5	6	4	4	5	4	4	90.6%
32	3	3	4	8	7	4	3	84.4%
32	7	5	5	4	3	5	3	93.8%
32	8	2	5	3	5	4	5	100%

5 Conclusions

A novel approach of enhanced LBP feature extraction technique is presented here. As LBP features are themselves illumination invariant, it is the best method to be used to compensate illumination changes. Applying LBP feature extraction technique on specific regions of faces increases the possibility of correct recognition as these specific regions, normally named as ROI, are those which are most affected due to expressions. Canny edge detection is used to take out ROI from an image which is further used for LBP feature extraction. Neural network is used as classifier where seven expressions including neutral are classified based upon the input features. JAFFE database is used for experimental purpose which includes 210 images of 10 females and 7 expressions. It can be concluded from result analysis that average recognition rate is above 92%.

References

1. Pantic, M., Rothkrantz, L.J.M.: Automatic analysis of facial expressions: the state of the art. IEEE Trans. Pattern Anal. Mach. Intell. **22**(12), 1424–1445 (2000)
2. Fasel, B., Luettin, J.: Automatic facial expression analysis: a survey. J. Pattern Recogn. Soc. **36**(1), 259–275 (2002)
3. Kaur, M., Vashisht, R.: Comparative study of facial expression recognition techniques. Int. J. Comput. Appl. **13**(1), 43–50 (2011)
4. Murthy, G.R.S., Jadon, R.S.: Effectiveness of eigenspaces for facial expressions recognition. Int. J. Comput. Theory Eng. **1**(5), 1793–8201 (2009)
5. Hosseini, I., Shams, N., Amini, P., Sadri, M.S., Rahmaty, M., Rahmaty, S.: Facial expression recognition using wavelet based salient points and subspace analysis methods. In: IEEE CCECE/CCGEl, May 2006

6. Kumano, S., Otsuka, K., Yamato, J., Maeda, E., Sato, Y.: Pose-invariant facial expression recognition using variable-intensity templates. In: Yagi, Y., Kang, S.B., Kweon, I.S., Zha, H. (eds.) ACCV 2007. LNCS, vol. 4843, pp. 324–334. Springer, Heidelberg (2007). doi:10.1007/978-3-540-76386-4_30
7. Zarwin, K.T., Chen, F., Izawa, J., Kotani, K.: Pose invariant robust facial expression analysis. In: IEEE 17th International Conference on Image Processing (2010)
8. Kim, D.-J., Lee, S.-W., Bien, Z.: Facial emotional expression recognition with soft computing techniques. In: 2005 IEEE International Conference on Fuzzy Systems (2005)
9. Ma, L., Xiao, Y., Khorasani, K., Ward, K.R.: A new facial expression recognition technique using 2D DCT and K-means algorithm. In: International Conference on Image Processing (2004)
10. Zheng, W., Tang, H., Lin, Z., Huang, T.S.: A novel approach to expression recognition from non-frontal face images. IEEE 12th International Conference on Computer Vision (ICCV) (2009)
11. Karande, K.J., Talbar, S.N.: Face recognition under variation of pose and illumination using independent component analysis. ICGST-GVIP **8**(IV) (2008). ISSN: 1687-398X
12. Hong, J.-W., Song, K.-T.: Facial expression recognition under illumination variation. IEEE (2007)
13. Pantic, M., Rothkrantz, L.J.M.: Facial action recognition for facial expression analysis from static face images. IEEE Trans. Syst. Man Cybern. **34**(3), 1449–1461 (2004)
14. Perveen, N., Gupta, S., Verma, K.: Facial expression classification using statistical, spatial features and neural network. Int. J. Adv. Eng. Technol. **4**(1), 424–435 (2012)
15. Sreevatsan, A.N., Sathish Kumar, K.G., Rakeshsharma, S., Roomi, Md.M.: Emotion recognition from facial expressions: a target oriented approach using neural network. In: Proceedings of 4th Indian Conference on Computer Vision, Graphics and Image Processing, ICVGIP, pp. 497–502, December 2004 (2004)
16. Shan, C., Gong, S., McOwan, P.: Facial expression recognition based on Local Binary Patterns: a comprehensive study. J. Image Vis. Comput. **27**, 803–816 (2008). Elsevier
17. Chen, W., Joo Er, M., Wu, M.: Illumination compensation and normalization for robust face recognition using discrete cosine transform in logarithm domain. IEEE Trans. Syst. Man Cybern. Part B Cybern. **36**(2), 458–466 (2006)
18. Shan, C., Gong, S., McOwan, P.: Robust facial expression recognition using local binary patterns. IEEE (2005)
19. Moore, S., Bowden, R.: Local binary patterns for multi-view facial expression recognition. J. Comput. Vis. Image Underst. **115**, 541–558 (2011). Elsevier
20. Lajevardi, S.M., Hussain, Z.: Feature extraction for facial expression recognition based on hybrid face regions. Adv. Electr. Comput. Eng. **9**(3), 63–67 (2009)
21. Zhang, L., Tjondronegoro, D.: Facial expression recognition using facial movement features. IEEE Trans. Affect. Comput. **2**(4), 219–229 (2011)
22. Zhang, Z., Lyons, M., Schuster, M., Akamatsu, S.: Comparison between geometry based and gabor wavelet based facial expression recognition using multi layer perceptron. In: 3rd IEEE International Conference on Automatic Face & Gesture Recognition, 14–16 April 1998
23. Ahonen, T., Hadid, A., Pietikainen, M.: Face description with local binary patters: application to face recognition. IEEE Trans. Pattern Anal. Mach. Intell. **28**(12), 2037–2041 (2006)
24. Ekman, P., Friesen, W.V.: Facial Action Coding System. Psychologist Press Inc., San Francisco (1978)
25. JAFFE database. http://www.kasrl.org/jaffe_info.html

Effect of Process, Voltage and Temperature Variation in DYNOC Approach for Domino Logic Circuits

Shani Jain, Vaibhav Neema, Praveen Singh[(✉)],
and Ambika Prasad Shah

E & TC Department, IET-DAVV, Indore 452017, India
jainshani02@gmail.com, vaibhav.neema@gmail.com,
psinghdavv@yahoo.com, ambika_shah@rediffmail.com

Abstract. In this modern era of technology control of leakage power consumption is a growing design challenge with scaling down in deep-submicron. This paper presents the DYNOC logic approach which has less leakage current with more stability with PVT parameters variation. Six PVT parameters of DYNOC circuit and conventional Domino logic circuit has been analyzed and compare using Tanner EDA tool at 70 nm technology node. Simulation results shows that the DYNOC logic approach has high voltage gain and gain margin with more temperature variation stability and also has improvement in leakage current reduction with variation in parameters like channel length, oxide thickness, threshold voltage size of PMOS to NMOS, supply voltage over Domino logic approach.

Keywords: DYNOC logic · Deep-submicron · Domino logic · Precharge · Evaluation

1 Introduction

With more progresses in semiconductor technology have leaded to features size reduction through the deep-submicron processes. As technology scaling down in nanometers, leakage power consumption inverse exponentially depends on supply voltage (V_{dd}) and threshold voltage (V_{th}) of a transistor [1]. With substantial growth in mobile device in last few years, minimization of leakage power dissipation is big challenge in high performance circuits to maximize the battery life of the device. The dynamic logic approach is accepted among all other approach due to high performance designs because of high speed over static CMOS circuits. Effect of PVT parameter variations increases with undesired manufacturing process, biasing connections and operating condition of the transistors [2]. In MOS circuits parameter scaling make change the operation of integrated circuits that's by it pose a risk to continue down scaling of the transistor size. Logic circuits disturbed by parameter variations in different ways. [3].

In the MOS device all physical parameter depends on channel length except source and drain junction depth. There are many parameters which is responsible to

© Springer Nature Singapore Pte Ltd. 2016
A. Unal et al. (Eds.): SmartCom 2016, CCIS 628, pp. 831–839, 2016.
DOI: 10.1007/978-981-10-3433-6_99

characterize the MOS device. These all parameters may be dependent to Each other. Some of them are Supply Voltage (V_{dd}), Threshold voltage (V_{th}), Oxide Thickness (t_{ox}), Channel Length (L), Channel Width (W) and Environmental Temperature (T) [8]. Reliability of a circuit is a key challenge in nanoscale technology. PVT variation increase as technology node decreases. Effect of PVT variation becomes more critical at 70 nm or less technology node.

This paper is presented in following manner. Section 2 present the related previous works, Sect. 3 present the working operation of dynamic logic circuits. Section 4 shows the simulation output of the circuits and Sect. 5 present conclusion of the paper work.

2   Previous Work

There are many techniques to understand the parameter variations at the transistor level approach to design with low leakage at deep-submicron MOS circuits. HKMG standard cells library with considering the effect of process variations [3]. INDEP approach depends on logic function calculation for input signal of the one more transistor between the pull-up block and pull-down block of the CMOS approach. Designing by INDEP approach has advantage, give a less leakage current and also offer good performance in terms of the parameter variations with minimum propagation delay [4].

To reduce leakage power consumption a Novel design method used when circuit is in off condition with the help of novel adaptive supply voltage generating technique for deep-submicron VLSI system. Using this sub threshold leakage current, gate tunneling current and one band to other band–tunneling current also controlled [5].

To control process and temperature variations, a lookup table method is used by generating adaptive minimum V_{dd} and optimal device body [6].

Leakage reduction technique LECTOR-B [7] is used to analyse the variability issue and also less effect on PVT parameter [8] variation.

DYNOC approach used for Domino approach circuits to reduces the leakage current and delay [9].

3   Dynamic Logic Circuits

To increase the performance of integrated circuits dynamic circuits have been used in place of static CMOS circuits. In this section the operating principle of standard domino logic approach and proposed DYNOC logic approach has been analyzed using buffer.

3.1   Domino Logic Approach

Symbolic representation of footed domino logic approach is shown in Fig. 1. The working process of domino logic circuit can be learned in the following manner. In dynamic approach output depends on clock value. This circuit operates in two modes, first is precharge mode, when clock at logic low value (clock = 0 V) and second is evaluation mode when clock at logic high value (clock = V_{dd}).

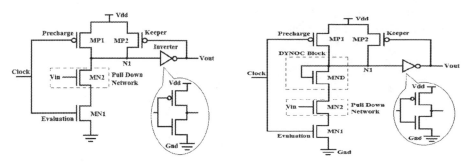

Fig. 1. Domino logic approach based buffer.   **Fig. 2.** DYNOC logic circuit based buffer.

When clock at logic low value, the domino circuit work is in precharge mode, in this mode, dynamic node N1 is charge to V_{dd} through MP1 transistor and at the same time output V_{out} of a circuit is low which turn on transistor MP2. Here MP2 transistor work as a keeper transistor.

When clock signal at logic high value, the circuit comes into the evaluation mode. In this mode with respect to input combination at pull-down block, dynamic node N1 is discharged to ground or remains high. In the evaluation mode output Vout can get maximum one transition from 0 to 1.

In the above circuit keeper transistor and inverter is used to prevent the cascading and charge sharing problem of dynamic circuit but by adding keeper transistor performance of a circuit also degrade. Small sized keeper transistor is used for high speed requirement on the other hand upsize keeper transistor used to improve the robustness of a circuit with high delay and more power dissipation.

3.2   DYNOC Logic Circuit

Figure 2 represents the DYNOC logic approach. In this circuit a DYNOC (**DY**namic **NO**de **C**ontrolled) transistor MND (NMOS) transistor is inserted between dynamic node N1 and pull down network in domino logic circuit to get the better performance of a circuit. The gate of MND transistor is connected to dynamic node N1. Body terminal of all PMOS transistor are connected to V_{dd} and body terminal of all NMOS transistors are connected to Gnd.

When clock signal at logic high value, then MP1 is turn on and DYNOC logic circuit comes in prechrage mode. When circuit works is in precharge mode, the dynamic node N1 is charged to V_{dd} by MP1 transistor which turn on MND transistor. At same time V_{out} of the circuit at logic low level which turn on the keeper transistor (MP2).

When clock signal at logic high value, the circuits enter comes into the evaluation mode. In evaluation mode, when $V_{in} = 1$ (high) then dynamic node N1 discharge through MND and MN1 and becomes 0 V and when input $V_{in} = 0$ (low) the dynamic node N1 is unaffected means charged to V_{dd}.

Figure 3 shows the voltage transfer characteristic of Domino logic circuit and DYNOC logic circuit based buffer with varying the input voltage from 0 V to V_{dd}. It can easily observe from the DC characteristics, DYNOC circuit has better noise margin as compare to Domino logic circuit.

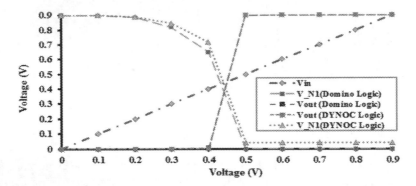

Fig. 3. DC characteristics of domino logic and DYNOC Logic based buffer.

4 Simulation Results

The simulation has been performed Using T-SPICE simulator at 70 nm technology node with supply voltage 0.9 V. Channel length and width are equal for all NMOS transistor which is same as technology node except DYNOC transistor is same and width double of technology node. Channel width of all PMOS is double of channel length except keeper transistor. Channel length of keeper transistor is five times and width is two times of technology node. 100 MHz clock frequency (f) and 27 °C have been selected for simulation.

4.1 Variation of Threshold Voltage

In the CMOS circuits threshold voltage is very important parameter for controlling the variability problem at the transistor level designing. If V_{th} change from their accepted value that also affect the value of sub- threshold leakage current.

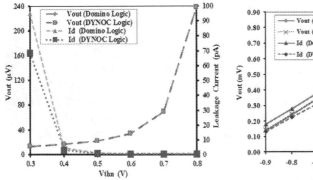

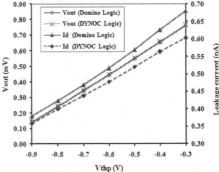

Fig. 4. Comparison of domino logic and DYNOC logic in terms of V_{thn} variation when $V_{in} = 0$

Fig. 5. Comparison of domino logic and DYNOC logic in terms of V_{thp} variation when $V_{in} = 0$

Figure 4 describes the output voltage and leakage current of domino logic circuit and DYNOC logic circuit with scaling in threshold voltage of NMOS transistors (V_{thn}) from 0.3 V to 0.8 V, when at input voltage at logic low level. Domino circuit has more leakage current as compare to DYNOC logic circuit with variation in threshold voltage. So DYNOC circuit has better performance over Domino logic circuit. Average improvement in leakage current is 35% for DYNOC logic circuits as compare to standard domino logic circuit.

Figure 5 also describe the output voltage and leakage current of a Domino logic circuit and DYNOC logic circuit with scaling in threshold voltage of PMOS transistors (V_{thp}) from −0.9 to −0.3 when input voltage at logic low level. Domino circuit has more leakage current as compare to DYNOC logic circuit with variation in threshold voltage so DYNOC circuit has better performance over Domino logic circuit. Average improvement in leakage current is 8% for DYNOC logic circuits as compare to standard domino logic circuit.

4.2   Variation of Channel Length

As channel length is the important parameter which affects the process variation of a circuits. Figure 6 describes variation in leakage current with variation in channel length (L) of MOS transistors. Domino circuit has more leakage current as compare to DYNOC logic circuit with ±10% variation of channel length means DYNOC circuit has better performance over domino logic circuit. Average improvement in leakage current is 20% for DYNOC logic circuits as compare to standard domino logic circuit.

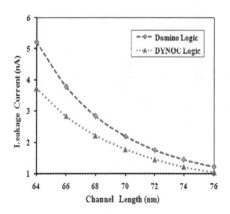 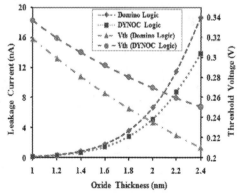

Fig. 6. Effect on leakage current in terms of channel length variation

Fig. 7. Effect on leakage current in terms of oxide thickness variation

4.3 Variation of Oxide Thickness

When vary the oxide thickness, it direct affects the gate capacitance per unit area and gate capacitance direct affect the value of threshold voltage. The size of T_{ox} is very important to get the desire value of leakage current and delay.

Figure 7 describes domino logic circuit and DYNOC logic circuit with scaling in oxide thickness from 1 nm to 2.4 nm. It is observed that threshold voltage of transistors decreases as oxide thickness increases and because of decrease in threshold voltage leakage current also increases. The rate of increase of leakage current for DYNOC logic circuit is less as compare to domino logic circuit. Domino circuit has more leakage current as compare to DYNOC logic circuit with variation in oxide thickness. Average improvement in leakage current is 20% for DYNOC logic circuits as compare to standard domino logic circuit.

4.4 Variation of Width Ratio

Width of a MOS transistors one of most important parameter for the designer to get the desired configuration of a circuit. Proper scaling of the transistor width moderates the variability issue in MOS circuits.

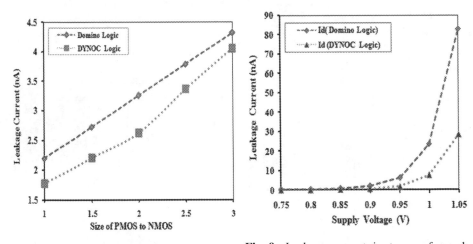

Fig. 8. Leakage current in terms of transistor size (Wp/Wn) variation.

Fig. 9. Leakage current in terms of supply voltage variation.

Figure 8 shows that DYNOC logic circuit has better performance over domino logic circuit with scaling in size of PMOS to NMOS ($W_p : W_n$) from 1 to 3. Domino circuit has more leakage current as compare to DYNOC logic circuit with variation in size. Average improvement in leakage current is 15% for DYNOC logic circuits as compare to standard domino logic circuit. At size $W_p : W_n = 2$, DYNOC circuit gives a best performance.

4.5   Variation of Supply Voltage

Supply reduction is also important method to decrease the total power dissipation of the ICs. Less value of V_{dd} decrease the Speed of a transistors and reduce the noise margins of a CMOS circuits. If noise margin is less than the probability of transient noise error in the output increases, so optimum value of V_{dd} is chosen where we need desire value of both leakage current and circuit speed.

Figure 9 shows the variation in leakage current with supply voltage variation. Simulation has been done for ±15% supply voltage variation. Domino circuit has more leakage current as compare to DYNOC logic circuit with variation in supply voltage. Average improvement in leakage current is 71% for DYNOC logic circuits as compare to standard domino logic circuit. It can also observe that as supply voltage increases rate of change in leakage current also increases.

4.6   Variation of Temperature

Environment temperature is a factor which also affects the performance of ICs. In MOS circuits where is many parameters which depends on temperature like mobility of carrier, threshold voltage, leakage current etc. So temperature plays a very important role in proper performance of a circuit.

Figure 10 describes Domino logic circuit and DYNOC logic circuit with scaling in environmental temperature from 0 °C to 120 °C. Domino circuit has more leakage current as compare to DYNOC logic circuit with variation in temperature. Average improvement in leakage current is 17% for DYNOC logic circuits as compare to standard domino logic circuit. In other words, DYNOC logic circuit is less sensitive to temperature as compare to Domino logic circuit. It can also observe that as temperature increases rate of change in leakage current also increases.

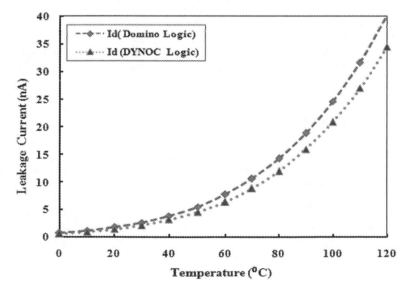

Fig. 10. Effect on leakage current in terms of temperature variation.

5   Conclusion

This paper shows comparative study of DYNOC logic approach with Domino logic approach in terms of PVT parameter variations. Based on the scaling of MOS parameters, optimum value is obtained to decrease the leakage current in dynamic logic circuits. We have observed mean improvement in leakage current with variation in PVT parameters, like 21.5% with V_{th}, 71% with V_{dd}, 20% with L, 20% with T_{ox}, 15% with width and 17% with temperature in DYNOC circuit and also more robust to temperature over Domino circuit.

In DYNOC logic circuit, Leakage current increases with increasing V_{th} of transistors and circuit has less leakage current. With scaling down in channel length, leakage current is increased and also the performance of DYNOC circuit is increased. With increasing the oxide thickness, rate of change of leakage current is also increased and thickness variation is less effective in DYNOC logic circuit. As increase the size of MOS transistors, leakage current is also increased, but for each size, DYNOC circuit have better performance. With increasing the supply voltage, rate of change of leakage current and performance of DYNOC circuit is also increased. With temperature variation from 0 °C to 120 °C, leakage current is increased for both the circuits, but DYNOC circuit is less sensitive over Domino circuit.

Acknowledgement. We are thankful to M.P. Council of Science & Technology, Bhopal, India, for finical support under R&D project scheme. No: 1950/CST/R&D/Phy & Engg Sc/2015: 27th Aug 2015.

References

1. Kang, S.M., Leblebic, Y.: CMOS Digital integrated circuits Analysis and Design. Tata McGraw Hill, New Delhi (2013)
2. Lanuzza, M., Frustaci, F., Perri, S., Corsonello, P.: Design of energy aware addercircuits considering random intra-die process variations. J. Low Power Electron. Appl. 1(1), 97–108 (2011)
3. Ghai, D., Mohanty, S.P., Kougianos, E., Patra, P.: A PVT aware accurate statistical logic library for high- k metal-gate nano-CMOS. In: IEEE International Symposium on Quality Electronic Design (ISQED), pp. 47–54 (2009)
4. Sharma, V.K., Pattanaik, M., Raj, B.: PVT variations aware low leakage INDEP approach for nanoscale CMOS circuit. Microelectron. Reliab. **54**, 90–99 (2014)
5. Kim, K.K., Kim, Y.B.: A novel adaptive design methodology for minimum leakage power considering PVT variations on nanoscale VLSI systems. IEEE Trans. VLSI Syst. **17**(4), 517–528 (2009)
6. Neema, V., Chouhan, S.S., Tokekar, S.: Novel circuit technique for reduction of leakage current in series/parallel PMOS/NMOS transistors stack. IETE J. Res. **56**(6), 350–354 (2010)
7. Shah, P., Neema, V., Daulatabad,S.: Effect of process, voltage and temperature (PVT) variations in LECTOR-B technique at 70 nm technology node. In: IEEE International Conference on Computer, Communication and Control, pp. 1–6, September 2015

8. Shah, A.P., Neema, V., Daulatabad, S.: PVT variations aware low leakage DOIND approach for nanoscale domino logic circuits. In: IEEE Power, Communication and Information Technology Conference, pp. 529–534, October 2015
9. Shah, A.P., Neema, V., Daulatabad, S., Singh, P.: DYNOC: an energy efficient novel approach for nanoscale domino logic circuits. In: 3rd International Conference on Microelectronics, Circuits & Systems, Micro 2016, 9–10 July 2016, pp. 42–47

Efficient Fuzzy Min-Max Neural Network for Pattern Classification

Milind Anand$^{(\boxtimes)}$, Ravi Kanth R, and Meera Dhabu

Visvesvaraya National Institute of Technology, Nagpur 440010, Maharashtra, India
milindjune1988@gmail.com , meeradhabu@cse.vnit.ac.in

Abstract. In this paper, an efficient fuzzy min-max neural network (EFMNN) method is proposed for classification to overcome the limitations of Simpson's method (FMMNN). Classifier is basically union of fuzzy set hyperboxes. Algorithm comprises of three steps i.e. Expansion, Overlap and Contraction. The first input pattern coming to the classifier is not given same min and max values so that more points are accommodated in the created hyperbox and overlap criteria is recognized easily. In the expansion process next highest membership value is used when maximum membership hyperbox is bounded by maximum size specified by user to expand. Spiliting of bigger hyperbox is done to minimize the loss in area in contraction process. Experiments are done on standard datasets to compare the results of original FMMNN and EFMNN. The results empirically validated the usefulness of the modification proposed.

Keywords: Neural network · Fuzzy sets · Membership · Hyperbox

1 Introduction

Pattern recognition [2] objective is to label the pattern(data) based on previous knowledge. It builds gists from noncognitive data, using tools from scientific, business, medical and mathematical areas, such as statistics, probability, algorithm design, signal processing and machine learning. Thus, it is of main ponderability to artificial intelligence and computer vision and has significance in many applications in varied field of science and engineering. Few prominent classifiers are decision tree, neural networks [4], naive bayes classifier, support vector machine. In late nineties a new branch of computer science i.e. soft computing is discovered, where two or more than two technologies is combined to build a hybrid technology. Fuzzy Min-Max Neural Network [1](FMMNN) architecture was designed by simpson's in 1991 and it is a very good example of soft computing [6] technology. Fuzzy systems and neural networks [4] are combined together to overcome the drawbacks of both the technology. There are severals advantages of FMMNN, which motivated to work in this area. The model made using FMMNN is adaptable for new incoming patterns which is seen in online scenarios. Also FMMNN works on single pass training principle.

© Springer Nature Singapore Pte Ltd. 2016
A. Unal et al. (Eds.): SmartCom 2016, CCIS 628, pp. 840–846, 2016.
DOI: 10.1007/978-981-10-3433-6_100

1.1   Fuzzy Min-Max Neural Network

The classification done using FMMNN is a three layer network. Input layer tells about dimensionality of input pattern. Hidden layer starts with empty node. Output layer contains no. of classes present. Nodes in input and output layer are fixed. Hyperbox [15] is a part of hypercube, which is n-unit dimensional cube. The min-max membership function [1] tells about the belongingness of an object into a hyperbox. Each hyperbox is defined by min and max value, which goes on changing while learning phase of neural network. This min max value uses the concept of fuzzy sets [16] and membership value of each hyperbox is calculated. The aggregation of fuzzy set values results in single fuzzy set class, which is ultimately resulting in union of hyperboxes. The membership of incoming patterns to the existing hyperboxes is calculated using hyperbox membership function. Input pattern is contained in hyperbox [15] for unit value of membership function. Sensitivity parameter(γ) present in the fuzzy membership function control how quick the membership value reduces as distance between input pattern and hyperbox increases. Figure 1 shows the hyperbox defined by its minimum and maximum value. Fuzzy min max neural network working structure is shown in Fig. 2.

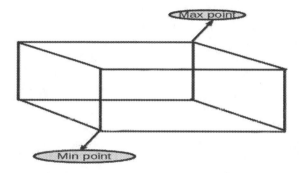

Fig. 1. Hyperbox and its min and max points

The membership function measures the degree to which the zth input pattern P_z falls outside of the hyperbox This condition always holds, $0 \leq s_r(P_z) \leq 1$.

Equation for the hyperbox membership function.

$$s_r(P_z) = \frac{1}{2t} \sum_{m=1}^{t} [max(0, 1 - max(0, \gamma min(1, p_{zm} - c_{rm})))$$

$$+ max(0, 1 - max(0, \gamma min(1, d_{rm} - p_{zm})))]$$

$\mathbf{P_z} = (\mathbf{p_{z1}}, \mathbf{p_{z2}}, \mathbf{p_{z3}}, ...\mathbf{p_{zt}})$ is the zth input pattern.
$\mathbf{D_r} = (\mathbf{d_{r1}}, \mathbf{d_{r2}}, \mathbf{d_{r3}}, ...\mathbf{d_{rt}})$ is the min point for S_r.
$\mathbf{C_r} = (\mathbf{c_{r1}}, \mathbf{c_{r2}}, \mathbf{c_{r3}}, ...\mathbf{c_{rt}})$ is the max point for S_r.

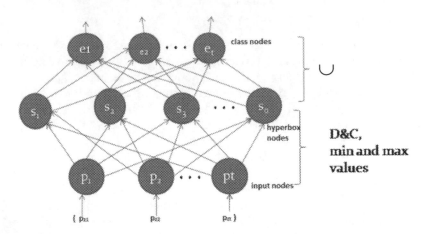

Fig. 2. Neural network structure

2   FMMNN Classification Algorithm

The whole idea of simpson was put into three step algorithm.

1. **Expansion:** Find the hyperbox who gives the maximum membership value is allowed for expansion. If there is no such hyperbox belongs to same class as input pattern, new hyperbox is created.
2. **Overlap Test:** Overlapping of hyperboxes from different class is determined.
3. **Contraction:** Overlapped area of different hyperbox classes is eliminated by minimally adjusting the hyperboxes.

Hyperbox Expansion. For the hyperbox S_r to expand to include X_z(input pattern), the following condition must be satisfied and those conditions are formulated below in mathematical Eqs. 1, 2 and 3.

$$t\theta \geq \sum_{m=1}^{t} \left(max\left(c_{rm}, x_{zm} \right) - min\left(d_{rm}, x_{zm} \right) \right) \tag{1}$$

If the Expansion criteria is met for Hyperbox S_r, then max point is:

$$c_{rm}^{new} = max\left(c_{rm}^{old}, x_{zm} \right) \quad \forall i\ 1, 2, ...t. \tag{2}$$

And the min point is adjusted as:

$$d_{rm}^{new} = min\left(d_{rm}^{old}, x_{zm} \right) \quad \forall i\ 1, 2, ...t. \tag{3}$$

All the conditions of overlapping and contraction step is well defined in simpson's paper on fuzzy min-max neural network for classifications [1].

3   Efficient Fuzzy Min-Max Neural Network for Pattern Classification

3.1   Proposed Approach

EFMNN does some modification in the algorithmic steps of FMMNN.

3.2   Hyperbox Creation

In the phase of learning itself hyperbox is created. EFMNN does some modification in the algorithm of FMMNN. For the new input pattern, if the minimum and maximum values are same for the hyperbox, the contraction condition is not recognized properly in the overlapping criteria. So new value is chosen as

$$d_{rm}^{new} = x_{zm} - 0.0001$$
$$c_{rm}^{new} = x_{zm} + 0.0001$$

Where epsilon is the parameter which plays a vital role in distinguishing dnew and cnew.

3.3   Hyperbox Expansion

The object belongs to the hyperbox having maximum membership. Then expansion criteria is checked and hyperbox is expanded if it full-fills the condition otherwise new hyperbox will be created. But FMMNN expansion criteria fails when maximum membership hyperbox is bounded by maximum size specified by user, to expand. Then a new hyperbox will be created for that class. This will increase the number of small hyperboxes and testing time of a pattern will also increase. So in EFMNN, hyperbox which gives next maximum membership and allowed for expansion is found. If such hyperbox is found, that hyperbox is expanded. Otherwise keep on checking for next maximum membership hyperbox in the same class. If such hyperbox is not available then create a new hyperbox for that class. The modification done in the creation and expansion step is depicted in Fig. 3.

3.4   Hyperbox Contraction

Contraction is done on minimal overlapping dimension to keep the hyperbox size maximum but it also results in loss of some area. So in EFMNN an idea is implemented in which bigger hyperboxes are spiltted so that there is no significant loss in area for that particular class. Also some overlapping cases was not handled in FMMNN. like $C_{em} - D_{rm} = C_{rm} - D_{em}$ in handled here.

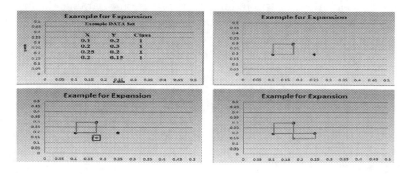

Fig. 3. Expansion steps comparision.

844   M. Anand et al.

Equations. If $\Delta > 0$, then the Δth dimensions of the two hyperboxes are adjusted.

Case1: $d_{r\Delta} < d_{e\Delta} < c_{r\Delta} < c_{e\Delta}$,

$$c_{r\Delta}^{new} = d_{e\Delta}^{new} = \frac{c_{r\Delta}^{old} + d_{e\Delta}^{old}}{2}$$

Case2: $d_{e\Delta} < d_{r\Delta} < c_{e\Delta} < c_{r\Delta}$,

$$c_{e\Delta}^{new} = d_{r\Delta}^{new} = \frac{c_{e\Delta}^{old} + d_{r\Delta}^{old}}{2}$$

Case3a: $d_{r\Delta} < d_{e\Delta} < c_{e\Delta} < c_{r\Delta}$ and $(c_{e\Delta} - d_{r\Delta}) <= (c_{r\Delta} - d_{e\Delta})$,

$$d_{r\Delta}^{new} = c_{e\Delta}^{old}$$

Create new hyperbox as $c_{r\Delta}^{new} = d_{e\Delta}^{old}$ and d_r

Case3b: $d_{r\Delta} < d_{e\Delta} < c_{e\Delta} < c_{r\Delta}$ and $(c_{e\Delta} - d_{r\Delta}) > (c_{r\Delta} - d_{e\Delta})$,

$$c_{r\Delta}^{new} = d_{e\Delta}^{old}$$

Create new hyperbox as $d_{r\Delta}^{new} = c_{e\Delta}^{old}$ and c_r

Case4a: $d_{e\Delta} < d_{r\Delta} < c_{r\Delta} < c_{e\Delta}$ and $(c_{e\Delta} - d_{r\Delta}) <= (c_{r\Delta} - d_{e\Delta})$,

$$c_{e\Delta}^{new} = d_{r\Delta}^{old}$$

Case4b: $d_{e\Delta} < d_{r\Delta} < c_{r\Delta} < c_{e\Delta}$ and $(c_{e\Delta} - d_{r\Delta}) > (c_{r\Delta} - d_{e\Delta})$,

$$d_{e\Delta}^{new} = c_{r\Delta}^{old}$$

4   Experimental Results

4.1   Input Data for Experiments

The code is written in matlab and tested on various datasets taken from UCI machine repository. Results are obtained by varying some parameters like hyperbox size, sensitivity parameter. There is a significant change in performance, Training time for change in parameter values. All the results are obtained from Ten-fold cross validation and tabulated in Table 1.

Table 1. Details of datasets

Sl No.	Datasets	No. of Instances	No. of Attributes	Classes
1	Ionosphere	351	34	2
2	Mushroom	8124	22	2
3	Image Segmentation	2310	19	7
4	WDBC	569	32	2
5	Iris	150	4	3

4.2   Classification Results

For different value of θ and γ, hyperbox count and performance measured is different. Results are good in case of EFMNN. For Script Classification and Ionosphere dataset better performance is achieved. For Iris and Wine dataset performance is comparable. Classification results in terms of performance and

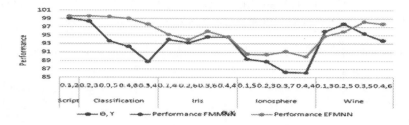

Fig. 4. Comparison of performance between FMMNN vs EFMNN.

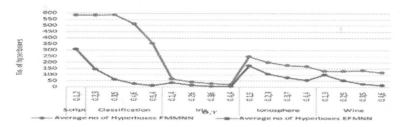

Fig. 5. Comparison of hyperbox count between FMMNN vs EFMNN.

Table 2. Performance FMMNN vs EFMNN

Dataset	Parameter		Performance		Avg no. Hyperbox count	
	θ	γ	FMMNN	EFMNN	FMMNN	EFMNN
Script classification	0.1	2	99.21	99.73	583.6	306
	0.2	3	98.41	99.73	582.6	145.1
	0.3	5	93.75	99.47	588.2	64.4
	0.4	6	92.35	99.03	512.2	27.1
Iris	0.1	4	94.0	95.33	65.6	37.4
	0.2	6	93	94.0	42.4	15.2
	0.3	6	94.66	96.0	32.4	8.4
	0.4	4	94.6	94.67	22.4	6.6
Ionosphere	0.1	5	89.44	90.55	247.4	175.3
	0.2	3	88.79	90.46	201.7	108.7
	0.3	7	86.29	91.20	178.2	77.8
	0.4	4	86.20	90.09	168.2	57.3
Wine	0.1	3	95.97	94.86	130.4	100.5
	0.2	5	97.78	96.04	131.1	53.2
	0.3	5	95.48	98.33	136.3	29.3
	0.4	6	93.81	97.78	117.9	16.5

hyperbox count is shown in Figs. 4 and 5. Also comparative results based on performance and hyperbox counts are shown in Table 2.

5   Conclusions

1. The modification made in expansion process of EFMNN gives percentage gain in the reduction of hyperboxes which varies from 48% to 98% for different datasets.
2. Less number hyperboxes results in less time for finding the belongingness for new input pattern.
3. The loss in the area is minimized by splitting of larger hyperboxes in contraction phase.

Acknowledgments. I would like to express my special thanks of gratitude to Dr. P.S.V.S Sai Prasad, who always motivated me in my research work.

References

1. Simpson, P.K.: Fuzzy min-max neural networks. I. Classification. IEEE Trans. Neural Netw. **3**(5), 776–786 (1992)
2. http://en.wikipedia.org/wiki/Pattern_Recognition
3. Simpson, P.K.: Fuzzy min-max neural networks. In: 1991 IEEE International Joint Conference on Neural Networks. IEEE (1991)
4. https://en.wikipedia.org/wiki/Artificial_Neural_Network
5. https://en.wikipedia.org/wiki/Backpropagation
6. https://en.wikipedia.org/wiki/Soft_Computing
7. https://en.wikipedia.org/wiki/Fuzzy_Logic
8. Gabrys, B., Bargiela, A.: General fuzzy min-max neural network for clustering and classification. IEEE Trans. Neural Netw. **11**(3), 769–783 (2000)
9. Simpson, P.K.: Fuzzy min-max neural networks-Part 2: clustering. IEEE Trans. Fuzzy Syst. **1**(1), 32 (1993)
10. Zhang, H., et al.: Data-core-based fuzzy minmax neural network for pattern classification. IEEE Trans. Neural Netw. **22**(12), 2339–2352 (2011)
11. Nandedkar, A.V., Biswas, P.K.: A fuzzy min-max neural network classifier with compensatory neuron architecture. IEEE Trans. Neural Netw. **18**(1), 42–54 (2007)
12. Quteishat, A., Lim, C.P., Tan, K.S.: A modified fuzzy min-max neural network with a genetic-algorithm-based rule extractor for pattern classification. IEEE Trans. Syst. Man Cybern. Part A: Syst. Hum. **40**(3), 641–650 (2010)
13. Mohammed, M.F., Lim, C.P.: An enhanced fuzzy minmax neural network for pattern classification. IEEE Trans. Neural Netw. Learn. Syst. **26**(3), 417–429 (2011)
14. Li, J., et al.: Brief introduction of back propagation (BP) neural network algorithm and its improvement. Advances in Computer Science and Information Engineering, pp. 553–558. Springer, Heidelberg (2012)
15. Alpern, B., Carter, L.: The hyperbox. In: Proceedings of the IEEE Conference on Visualization, Visualization 1991. IEEE (1991)
16. Zadeh, L.A.: Fuzzy sets. Inf. Control **8**(3), 338–353 (1965)

Vehicle Speed Control Using Zigbee and GPS

Pallavi Kochar[✉] and M. Supriya

Department of Computer Science and Engineering, Amrita School of Engineering,
Amrita Vishwa Vidyapeetham, Amrita University, Bengaluru, India
pallavi.kochar1@gmail.com, m_supriya@blr.amrita.edu

Abstract. With the current population and growing number of vehicles on road, speed control has become an important requirement due to the increased number of accidents reported in our day-to-day life. Measures like traffic management, improving quality of road infrastructure and safer vehicles can prevent the road accidents. Though there are many technologies available for speed management of a vehicle, practical implementation of each is to some extent is not up to satisfactory level. This paper discusses a speed monitoring and control system that can provide safer environment in critical zones like schools, colleges etc. The proposed method uses Zigbee and GPS for the speed control and which is also cost effective and can be fixed easily on vehicles.

Keywords: Speed control · Zigbee · GPS

1 Introduction

With the growing population and advancement in technologies, human life has become easier for an individual but the threat of life is at increasing pace because of the irresponsible uses of its application in day to day life. The growth of automobile industry has made the transportation more easy, comfortable and fastest to travel from one place to other. But this has increased the chances for threat to life on road. The major factor that contributes to this is the speed of a vehicle. Though a lot of safety related features are available in vehicles, they cannot assure 100% safety to the life of a person as well as the pedestrian. The development of embedded technology has addressed these issues by making the speed of an advantage and not the disadvantage of the vehicle. Some existing embedded technologies include Cruise control, Adaptive Cruise Control etc. Researchers are still working on an efficient algorithm which can alert the driver and direct him to drive in a safe speed limit. The speed control algorithm generally works on the principle of automatic speed control which works by adjusting the throttle plate for proper and required fuel flow or using servo motor controlled by Engine Control Unit (ECU). To make successful working of ECU, it is important to get proper input parameters. The literature review presented in the next section discusses the various speed monitoring and control systems proposed in the literature, and analyze the various input scenarios they are designed for along with their limitations.

© Springer Nature Singapore Pte Ltd. 2016
A. Unal et al. (Eds.): SmartCom 2016, CCIS 628, pp. 847–854, 2016.
DOI: 10.1007/978-981-10-3433-6_101

2   Literature Survey

Govindraju et al. [1] has designed a system that helps to avoid accidents and also alerts driver about speed limit for safe travelling. This has been achieved by combining the GPS with wireless system using ARM processor. The transmitter side uses the GPS and the RF signal is sent using frequency modulation. Since the frequency modulator is fixed at particular frequency, the frequency check happens automatically when the vehicle moves in critical zones and it transmits the signal to the receiver side. The receiver side also has an ARM processor to collect the data from GPS. It sends the data to the device driver which is designed to fit in vehicles dashboard and it automatically alerts the driver about the speed according to the time and zone.

An effective speed control system proposed in [2] deals with the objective to detect speed violation on road and influence the driver to obey the traffic rules. The system has alerting, recording and reporting system to monitor the violation of the traffic rules. Speed limits and traffic signs are pre-programmed in microcontroller and the message is transmitted with the help of Xbee module which serves as a transmitter module at predetermined lanes/area. The receiver module which is divided into two sub-modules is placed inside the vehicle. First sub module placed near rear view mirror consists of Zigbee, microcontroller and CAN bus. On receiving the wireless signal, the Zigbee microcontroller sends signal to this CAN controller which in turn communicates with another CAN controller placed near the dashboard, part of second sub module. CAN controller sends the restricted speed limit after comparing it with the current speed obtained from the speedometer. If the difference is more, driver gets continuous warnings on the dashboard, and if the driver does not act accordingly speed gets automatically controlled. However, the number of times driver has violated speed limit is recorded which is later sent to the nearest authority and penalty is imposed on the driver.

An attempt to control the speed of vehicle by third party with the help of GPS, GSM/GPRS technology is proposed in [3]. Here, the user can track the vehicle and get the up to date information with the use of GPS and GSM. The vehicle tracking device installed in the vehicle uses GPS to track the information with the help of software installed in windows phone or computer system. From the obtained details, owner/user can send speed limits to vehicle or can stop the vehicle as a measure to control the speed and avoid accidents.

A system designed in [4] uses RFID and M-RFID technology for recording the traffic violations and is able to control speed limit violation along with unauthorized overtaking. RFID tags used in this work stores the traffic sign information mainly "No overtaking Sign" and "Speed Limit Sign". As RFID reader reaches within few meter distance from the card, the information stored in the card is dispatched to the tag reader. Driver is informed at the beginning of the speed limit zone about the authorized speed, which is stored in the systems memory embedded into the vehicle. Whenever the driver violates the preset limit, he receives this warning and in case of the ignorance to the warning message, traffic violation is documented and recorded. The recorded violation is immediately sent to the central server placed at the traffic controller room via driver's cell phone which is equipped with RFID technology and he is charged for this offense. Thus this system gives proper control on driver's behavior.

Hirakata et al. [5] propose a novel solution for navigation of vehicle in parking using Zigbee networks. The proposed work forms a Zigbee network area with the Zigbee terminal equipped in the vehicle and in the parking lot. When the vehicle possessing the Zigbee module embedded in it comes at the parking entrance, it gets recognized by the coordinator module installed at the entrance which then adds the newly recognized Zigbee to the Zigbee network of the parking area. Once registered, it collects the information on the available vacant space every time period. Once the newly added vehicle receives the vacant space information, it sends an ACK message to reserve the same for the parking. The status about the parking and the direction to the vacant space is updated periodically.

3   Proposed Work

The literature survey presented in the previous section discusses some of the systems proposed for vehicle speed monitoring and control. However, the literature lacks in an efficient system that is cheaper in the implementation process. In our work, we have designed the hardware module for the work proposed in [1] using Zigbee. The speed limit control system proposed in [1] uses Zigbee as the communicating unit to transmit the message about speed control, for example, sending the speed limit for a particular lane. But in this proposed work, vehicles that are moving in all the lanes (both current and opposite) reduce the speed which is not necessary. This happens because, vehicles do not have an idea about the lane in which they move, so all the vehicles that receives the speed limit information tend to reduce the speed. Thus, to overcome this problem, GPS has been introduced in our work which is explained in detail here. The block diagram of our work is shown in Fig. 1.

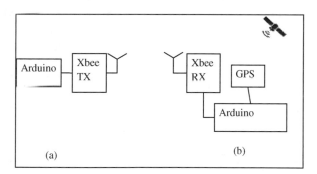

Fig. 1. Block diagram of proposed work. (a) Transmitter at speed control zone with controller. (b) Receiver in the vehicle with GPS.

Components used to implement this work are explained below:

(A) Zigbee: The Zigbee is one of the popular protocols to create radio sensor networks for varied reasons. In the situations where power availability is limited and has to conserve Wireless sensor networks are used. Many times, the communications that these networks send are small in nature. There are two basic varieties of Zigbee radio physical hardware, XBee Series1 hardware and XBee Series2 hardware. In this work we have used Xbee series1 hardware. The main purpose of using XBee in this work is to create V2I communication as it transmits the message which contains the relevant information about the speed limit of that road and coordinates with the transmitter's location to the XBee RX. Xbee reading range is approximately 1.2 km outdoor which is advantageous for this work. The XBee's has been configured using XCTU software.

(B) Arduino: To develop the complete control environment Arduino Mega board has been used for this work because of its ease of use.

(C) GPS: The Global Positioning System (GPS) [6] provides satellite tracking services that are useful in a wide range of commercial and personal applications. The GPS SKG13BL has been used in this work in order to provide the information of the vehicle's location.

This is used to inform the vehicle where exactly is the transmitter in order to avoid blind listening of it. Here, the GPS is also used to inform the vehicle that about the lane it is following and whether to reduce the speed or not. The algorithm for receiver side is explained as the flowchart below in Fig. 5.

4   Case Study and Results

The pictorial view of the real time implementation of XBee network and speed control using XBee and GPS is shown in Fig. 6. XBee transmitter has been implemented in a school zone which continuously transmits the packet containing speed limit at different locations of the school zone to the receiver and it also transmits the coordinate of transmitters location. Figure 3 describe the pictorial view of our proposed work and explains how it work. We have consider different scenarios for effective results. The numbers 1, 2, 3, 4, 5, and 6 represents lane number which we will be using to show their distance and position from school zone. As shown school zone is at lane 6, lane 5, 4, and 3 forms junction near school zone. Vehicles which are near to school zone will be moving in lanes 3, 4, 5, and 6. Vehicle moving in lane 1 and 2 can enter in any of 2, 3, 4, 5, and 6. The small dotted line represents the Xbee's interfacing with receiver. The small triangle represent XBee receiver and circle represents the XBee transmitter in school zone.

```
while(Serial1.available()          lcd.print(lat/100);
){if(gps.encode                    delay(1000);
(Serial1.read())){                 lcd.setCursor(0,1);
gps.get_position(&lat,&lon         lcd.print("lon:");
);                                 lcd.print(lon/100);
lcd.setCursor(0,0);                delay(1000);
lcd.print("lat:");                 lcd.clear();   }}
```

The code to read the coordinates from GPS receiver is given above. The GPS at receiver side stores the latitude and longitude and gives the updated value of "current" coordinate. For the speed limit area, the coordinates that are already known are transmitted to the receiver side. Now with these coordinates, the following cases are observed.

Scenario 1: When the vehicle is travelling in lane 1 and entering into the lane 2, if the current is in the range of transmitted location then a warning message "Near School Zone" is displayed, as shown in Fig. 2.

Fig. 2. Warning message for vehicle near the school zone but so near to lane 6.

Scenario 2: If the vehicle is moving near the school zone and current is in limit specified by the coordinate (3) and coordinate (7) which is already defined in code(refer Fig. 5), it will get a warning about the speed limit. (i.e.) Vehicles travelling in 3, 4, 5, and 6 are near to the school zone and they will get immediate warning message, "Speed limit is 30 km, Reduce the speed", as shown in Fig. 3.

Fig. 3. Warning message for vehicle near to the lane 6 i.e. in the lane 3, 4, 5.

Fig. 4. Warning message for the vehicles those have diverted from the school area.

Scenario 3: Vehicle moving near school zone but not entering into the school zone is considered as scenario 3. Since XBee is broadcasting the message, all the XBee RXs which are in its RF range will read the packet sent by TX. But they should not reduce the speed if they are not entering the school zone. This is done with the help of GPS introduced in the vehicle. Once it is near the zone, it will get warning as in scenario1. But due to the continuous coordinate matching, as discussed in scenario 2, if the *current* is not in the range of those coordinates that correspond to the school zone, the message "Out of Speed Limit zone" is displayed (refer Fig. 4).

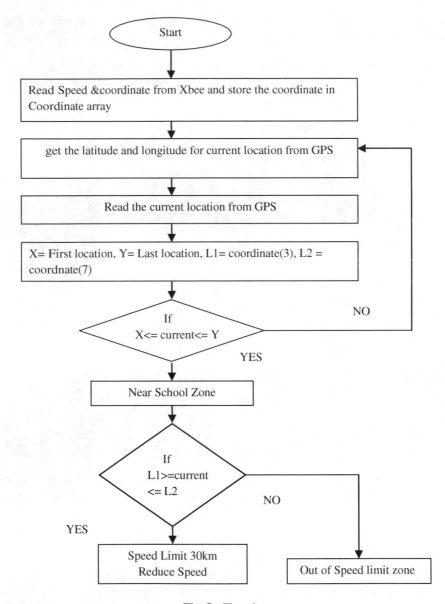

Fig. 5. Flowchart

5   Results and Discussion

The system designed in [1] alerts the driver with a warning message if the vehicle moves into the school zone. The entry of the vehicle in critical area is registered with the use of GPS. Here base station has to continuously transmit if the current location of the vehicle is matching with the transmitted location from the base station. But in our proposed work we have avoided this transmission by using Zigbee. The vehicle will only compare the current location with transmitted location when Zigbee receiver is receiving the packets from transmitter in the School zone. Many of the existing systems use RFID, Bluetooth, Wifi and low power RF transmitter and receiver to alert the vehicle about the speed limit zone. But the use of Zigbee is efficient because of its good range and low power energy consumption. Also, the use of GPS in our work is not necessary to be active continuously and is sufficient to be activated only if the Zigbee receives packet containing zone information (i.e.) location coordinate and speed limit. This makes our work efficient and better when compared with the literature discussed in this paper.

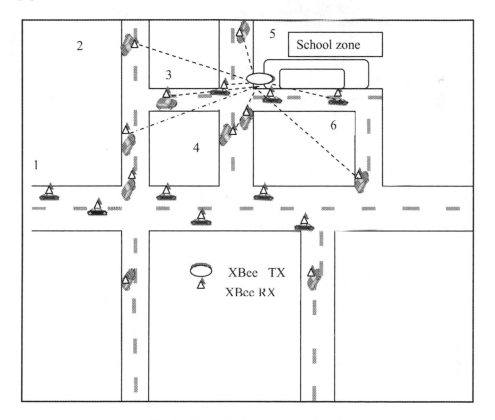

Fig. 6. Pictorial view of proposed work

6   Conclusion and Future Work

The aim of the proposed work was to insure maximum safety in school zone and colleges. This can be achieved only if one can deal with all the limitation arrives in its implementation and testing. Thus the system has been successfully designed and results have been displayed. The complete setup is formed as a prototype which is to be embedded into vehicle, as shown in Fig. 7. This work was to test whether the system removes all limitation proposed in the objective or introduced in other existing work. The results have been obtained by designing prototype in real time which has been shown in Fig. 4.

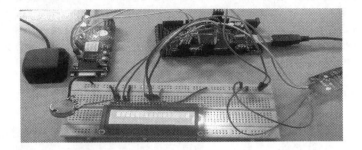

Fig. 7. Prototype of the proposed work, which is to be embedded in vehicle.

Even though we have tried to remove all the limitation the accuracy of the results depends on the GPS Rx. The more accurate data can be obtained using filters. XBee modules comparative studies for good range can bring more stability for the efficiency of the work.

References

1. Govindraju, K., Boopathi, S., Parvez, F., Thulasi Ram, S., Jagdeeshraja, M.: Embedded based vehicle speed control system using wireless technology. Int. J. Innov. Res. Electr. Electron. Instrum. Control Eng. **2**(8), 1841–1844 (2014)
2. Sarower, S.S., Shende, S.M.: Over speed violation management and control of speed of vehicle based on Zigbee. Int. J. Eng. Res. Gen. Sci. **3**(1), 1168–1173 (2015)
3. Devikiruba, B.: Vehicle speed control system using GSM/GPRS. Int. J. Comput. Sci. Inf. Technol. **4**(6), 983–987 (2013)
4. Nejati, O.: Smart recording of traffic violations via M-RFID. In: 7th International Conference on Wireless Communication, Networking and Mobile Computing, pp. 1–4. IEEE, Wuhan (2011)
5. Hirakata, Y., Nakamura, A., Ohno, K., Itami, M.: Navigation system using ZigBee wireless sensor network for parking. In: 12th International Conference on ITS Telecommunications, pp. 605–609. IEEE, Taipei (2012)
6. Pillai, P., Supriya, M.: Real time CO_2 monitoring and alert system based on wireless sensor networks. In: Berretti, S., Thampi, S.M., Dasgupta, S. (eds.) Intelligent Systems Technologies and Applications. AISC, vol. 385, pp. 91–103. Springer International Publishing, Cham (2016). doi:10.1007/978-3-319-23258-4_9

Clustering Based User Preference Resource Scheduling in Cloud Computing

Ramasamy Madhumathi[1(✉)], Radhakrishnan Rathinavel[2],
Sureshkumar Sadhasivam[1], and Reshma Sultana[1]

[1] Sri Ramakrishna Engineering College, Coimbatore 641022, India
rmadhumathisrec@gmail.com,
reshmasultana2016@gmail.com, sureshkumar@srec.ac.in
[2] Vidhya Mandhir Institute of Technology, Erode 638052, India
rlgs14466@gmail.com

Abstract. Many of the available researches have been concentrating on the profits maximization of cloud providers, while the actual necessities of cloud users have been ignored. Here, a Clustering based User preference (CUP) resource scheduling technique is proposed that can be used by a cloud provider for meeting the resource needs of a user in a better way. The novel CUP scheduling mechanism consists of four stages: resource matching, resource selection, clustering and resource scheduling. The user must be given a consideration if the same user puts forward multiple requirements. Updating of user demands and preferences are done at the resource scheduling stage. This method chooses the "best" VM which improves resourcefulness of CC and thereby minimizes the average response time of tasks. The results show that the CUP algorithm proposed efficiently satisfies the diverse requirements of the users and assists in the better resource utilization.

Keywords: Cloud computing (CC) · Resource scheduling (RS) · Clustering · Enhanced fuzzy C means · Clustering based user preference (CUP)

1 Introduction

CC concentrates on provisioning of on demand access to computing resources that are always-on like storage, platforms, and software applications [1, 2]. Many of the cloud computing systems that are operational today are proprietary, which depends upon the infrastructure and hidden from the research community, or else their design is not explicit in order to be instrumented and changed by system researchers [3]. For the case of IaaS, there are few popular open-source cloud systems, like Eucalyptus [3], Open Nebula [4], Nimbus [5], etc. Therefore, operators of the so-called IaaS clouds, such as Amazon EC2 [6], allow their customers to be able to allocate, access, and have a set of virtual machines that run within their data centers and use them only for the time period the machines were allocated.

Many of the already available researches concentrate on maximization of the profits of cloud providers, whereas attention to the real needs of cloud users has largely been

© Springer Nature Singapore Pte Ltd. 2016
A. Unal et al. (Eds.): SmartCom 2016, CCIS 628, pp. 855–863, 2016.
DOI: 10.1007/978-981-10-3433-6_102

neglected. The information regarding the real resource needs of a user is a serious affair in the case of cloud resource scheduling.

In this research work, the resource scheduling of the CC Environment in practical life is discussed. At first, the resource scheduling model is studied and the assumptions of the model are described. Then CUP resource scheduling mechanisms for various components are designed. The final stage introduced a BFS based resource scheduling algorithm depending on the demands of resource needs of users and its priority level.

2   Literature Review

The resource scheduling has been observed to be a difficult job in cloud particularly since it is the one that determines the utilization and time period it is being used [7]. Conventional static resource scheduling algorithms consists of Round-Robin Scheduling, Weighted Round-Robin Scheduling [8], Destination Hashing and Source Hashing Scheduling [9]. These algorithms applied different techniques to seek for physical nodes for satisfying the computing or storage demands of users, without any consideration over the resource utilization on an overall and service quality. A novel resource scheduling model called loyalty-based trust mechanism is developed which uses distributed computing system that is built over a hardware that is not robust [10]. This type of dynamic feedback mechanism assures the stability of the system and also the services reliability in an effective manner.

Li and Li presented the composition of various layers in the cloud like IaaS and SaaS and its joint optimization for efficient allocation of resource [11]. Continuous Double Auction (CDA) technique is used for maximizing cloud users' profit and enhances the market efficiency in the asymmetric scenario that is nearer to the real cloud market as per [12]. Optimal Cloud Resource Provisioning (OCRP) algorithm is introduced by the formulation of a random programming model. The demand and price uncertainty is taken into consideration in OCRP [13].

3   Proposed Resource Scheduling Model

In this section, a user preference based resource scheduling model is presented that comprises of two significant parts: user requirements model and cloud computing model. The assumptions used in this paper are defined as below:

- Every resource request that is submitted by a user is considered as a unit of integral importance in resource scheduling.
- $R = \{r_1, r_2, \ldots, r_n\}$ to represent all the available resource instances present in the cloud system.
- $U = \{u_1, u_2, \ldots, u_m\}$ to specify the set of active users present in the cloud system.
- $VM = \{vm_1, vm_2, \ldots, vm_o\}$ to indicate the set of VM existing in the cloud system.
- The Cloud Provider (CP) is capable of grouping together all of the resource requirements to have the expected 'time of utilization' that are same or similar.

- When smaller jobs wait for long time, a new concept Enhanced Fuzzy C Means (EFCM) is given, which clusters same kind of requirements.
- At any point of time, every user in 'U' might have only one single resource requirement being taken into consideration by the cloud system.

Resource model: A resource instance in a cloud is described by a pre-determined list of parameters like processing power, memory space, timeliness, reliability, security, and cost. The mapping of a resource instance $r \in R$ to a row vector is denoted by

$$\omega(r) = [w_1, \ldots .w_y] \tag{1}$$

Where every $w_k (1 \leq k \leq y)$ refers to a value of the respective resource feature. Here, refers to a value of the respective resource feature. Here, $\omega(r)$ is used for referring to the vector that is returned by the function ω, and $\omega(r, k)$ is used for referring to the kth element of $\omega(r)$. The vector $\omega(r)$ is called as the capability model of the resource r. The capacity model of every resource in R is expressed by:

$$W = \begin{bmatrix} \omega(r_1) \\ \omega(r_2) \\ \ldots \\ \omega(r_n) \end{bmatrix} = \begin{bmatrix} w_{11} w_{12} \ldots w_{1y} \\ w_{21} w_{22} \ldots w_{2y} \\ \ldots \\ w_{n1} w_{n2} \ldots w_{ny} \end{bmatrix} \tag{2}$$

User Preference based resource scheduling model: A user resource requirement submitted to a cloud comprises of two parts: resource demand and resource preference. Both parts can be gathered from the online form that is submitted by a user. A resource requirement submitted by a user u_i is expressed by (ud_i, rp_i), where $ud_i = [ud_{i1}, ud_{i2} \ldots ud_{ix}]$, $rp_i = [rp_{i1}, rp_{i2} \ldots rp_{ix}]$.

All the resource demands and preferences of the users are grouped separately into two matrices. In Eqs. (3) and (4) the same resource demands and preferences of users are grouped as matrix that is treated as clusters.

$$UD = \begin{bmatrix} ud_1 \\ ud_2 \\ \ldots \\ ud_m \end{bmatrix} = \begin{bmatrix} ud_{11} & ud_{12} & \cdots & ud_{1x} \\ ud_{21} & ud_{22} & \cdots & ud_{2x} \\ \ldots & \ldots & \ldots & \ldots \\ ud_{m1} & ud_{m2} & \cdots & ud_{mx} \end{bmatrix} \tag{3}$$

$$UP = \begin{bmatrix} up_1 \\ up_2 \\ \ldots \\ up_m \end{bmatrix} = \begin{bmatrix} up_{11} & up_{12} & \cdots & up_{1x} \\ up_{21} & up_{22} & \cdots & up_{2x} \\ \ldots & \ldots & \ldots & \ldots \\ up_{m1} & up_{m2} & \cdots & up_{mx} \end{bmatrix} \tag{4}$$

4   CUP Resource Scheduling Mechanism

Figure 1 shows the clustering based user preference resource scheduling framework. The CUP framework does the manipulation of the two models chiefly at four stages, by passing requirements (ud_i, up_i).

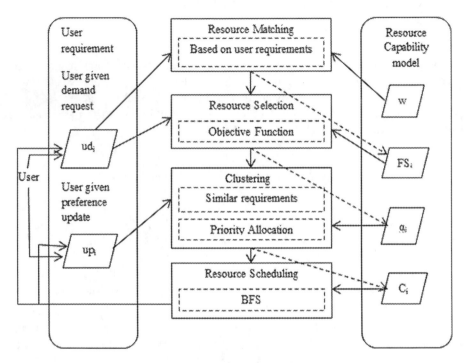

Fig. 1. CUP resource scheduling framework

Resource matching: At this stage, all of the resource instances available in the cloud are matched with ud_i, up_i and every instance with a similarity degree larger than a set threshold $r_{thershold}$ are gathered into a set FS_i^t. During this stage similarity is calculated between user's resource demand ud_i and a resource instance $r \in H$,

$$sim(ud_i, r) = \frac{\sum_{k=1}^{f} ud_{ik}\omega(r, k)}{\sqrt{\sum_{k=1}^{f} ud_{ik}^2 \sum_{k=1}^{f} \omega(r, k)^2}} \qquad (5)$$

Resource selection: At this stage, the resource instances in FS_i^t are scrutinized further, in which the one having the maximal utility to the user u_i is selected. A utility function is used for measuring the appropriateness [14].

Clustering: At this stage cloud users who have the same resource requirement specifications are clustered by making use of EFCM clustering technique. This minimizes
the resource allocation complexity. The work is then extended to grouping of similar
users on the basis of the resource demands and the priority value is allocated to user
who is inside the cluster on the basis of their resource requirements. Hence BFS is
employed in this research work for the purpose of resource allocation.

Resource allocation: In this stage, the resources that are grouped in the stage of
clustering are assigned to users. The user requirement that is updated will be utilized in
the next round for searching for a resource which might be even nearer to the real
resource need of the user. This resource scheduling is done as "Best Fit Strategy". For
every user, the cloud resource scheduling mechanism executes these four stages which
are mentioned above repeatedly for up to $\max_{fi}$ rounds. As a result, this process induces
a sequence of selected resources, one for every round.

Algorithm 1. Clustering User preference resource scheduling mechanism
Input: $UD_{m\times p}$, $UP_{m\times p}$, R, Matching threshold$r_{thershold}$
Output:HS $= \{HS_1, HS_2, \dots, HS_m\}$ is a set of global variablesHS$_i$ is the resource
scheduling history for userU_i
1: Procedure CU($UD_{m\times p}$,$UP_{m\times p}$, R, $r_{thershold}$, $\max_{fi}$)
2:$H \leftarrow R$
3: for$i = 1$ to m do
4: for$t = 1$ to $\max_{fi}$ do
5: $FS_i^t = Resource\ Matching\ (ud_i, H, r_{thershold})$
6: if$FS_i^t = \emptyset$ then
7: if $t = 0$ then HS$_i \leftarrow$ HS$_i + \varepsilon$
8: end if
9: break // No more refinement useα_i^{t-1} the last element of HS$_i$
10: else
11: $\alpha_i^t = Resource\ Selection\ (FS_i^t, ud_i, rp_i)$
12: $c_i = Clustering\ (\alpha_i^t, ud_i, rp_i)$
13: Best Fit Strategy (BFS)(ud_i, rp_i, c_i, VM)
14: end if
15: end for
16: $H \leftarrow H - lastof\,(HS_i)$
17: end for
18: end procedure

FCM [15] divides them into c fuzzy clusters, in which c limits to $1 < c < o$. The
centroids of the clusters are $= \{z_1, z_2, \dots, z_c\}$, here the centroid is treated as the number
of resource parameters that are of interest to users and the number of the times user has
requested the demands. The characters of μ are expressed in the following:

$$\mu_{il} \in [0, 1], 0 < \sum_{i=1}^{m} u_{il} < m \sum_{l=1}^{c} u_{il} = 1 \tag{6}$$

In FCM clustering technique, the sum of the membership degree must be 1, the results might be not good in case the sample data is not ideal. As in this research work cloud resource requirements demands of user is varied in a dynamic manner, hence weighted mean subtractive clustering is proposed to FCM. The potential value of user resource demands $UD_{m \times x}$, represented as Pot_i is calculated by Eq. (8).

$$Pot_i = \sum_{l=1}^{c} \exp\left(-\frac{||ud_i - z_l||^2}{\left(\frac{rad_a}{2}\right)^2} \right)$$

$$||ud_i - z_l||^2 = \sqrt{(ud_1 - z_1)^2 + \cdots + (ud_i - z_l)^2}$$

$$(7)$$

Where, rad_a refers to a positive constant that defines a neighborhood resource demands, $||ud_i - z_l||^2$ indicates the Euclidean distance. The potential of centroid of the clusters Z is represented as $PotVal(z_l)$. Subsequently, the potential of every user resource demands $UD_{m \times x}$ is revised as below:

$$Pot_i = Pot_i - PotVal(z_1)\exp\left(\frac{||ud_i - z_1||^2}{\left(\frac{rad_b}{2}\right)^2} \right) \tag{8}$$

Where,

$$PotVal(\bar{Z}_t) = \sum_{i=1}^{n} \exp\left(-\frac{||\bar{Z}_t - ud_i||^2}{\left(\frac{rad_b}{2}\right)^2} \right) - \sum_{q=1}^{s-1} \exp\left(-\frac{||\bar{Z}_t - \bar{Z}_q||^2}{\left(\frac{rad_b}{2}\right)^2} \right) \tag{9}$$

Step 1: Determine the EFCM parameters, rad_a, rad_b fuzzy exponent weight ew

Step 2: Calculate the potential Pot_i utilizing Eq. (8), set the number of cluster centers as $l = 1$

Step 3: Choose highest cluster centers represented as pz_l, the user resource demands surrounding pz_l, with radius smaller than r_a. Then, the weighted mean cluster center $\bar{Z}_l$ is computed as below:

$$\bar{Z}_t = \frac{\sum_{i=1}^{n(l)} PotVal\left(ud_{n(l)}^{(s)}\right) * ud_{n(l)}^{(s)}}{\sum_{i=1}^{n(l)} PotVal\left(ud_{n(l)}^{(s)}\right)} \tag{10}$$

Where, $n(l)$ refers to the number of resource demands that surrounds pz_l

Step 4: The potential of user resource demands is revised using Eq. 10

Step 5: Verify the termination constraints are accomplished. The maximum iteration is attained, the operation process stops. Else, turn to step 3

5 Simulation Experiment

An experimental environment is set up using CloudSim Simulation Toolkit [16].

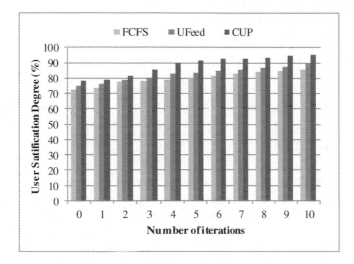

Fig. 2. User satisfaction degree as number of iterations

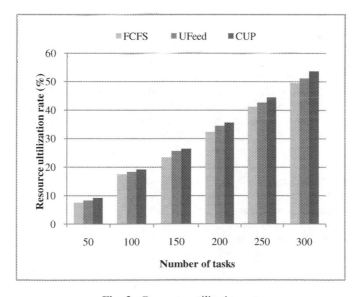

Fig. 3. Resource utilization rate

User satisfaction degree: The degree of user's satisfaction with a cloud resource can be generally defined as the quality of service that is rendered by the resource to the user. In Fig. 2, CUP can accomplish more than 80% of user satisfaction degree once just two iterations of EFCM algorithm are completed, and it attains close to 90% when the two iterations of EFCM goes up to 4. This is because of the EFCM algorithm, mechanism is implemented and user preference is allocated to every cluster on the basis of the resource requirements of users.

Resource utilization rate: Resource utilization rate can be defined as the ratio of the total number of assigned resources to the total number of resources available when CUP begins. It can be observed from Fig. 3 that the resource utilization rate of every method increases with the increase in the number of users from 50 to 300.

6 Conclusion

This paper introduces a cloud computing resource dynamic scheduling strategy which is based on CUP. The CUP framework helps in maximizing the user's degree of satisfaction in both the quality of services offered and monetary expenditure. A new resource scheduling scheme making use of Enhanced Fuzzy C means for formulating a computation model in order to group similar user resource requirements and resolve priority level allocation problem under the given cloud computing resources. In accordance with the degree of resource requirement and resource availability of current Virtual Machine, Best Fit Strategy is used for resource scheduling.

References

1. Ostermann, S., Iosup, A., Yigitbasi, N., Prodan, R., Fahringer, T., Epema, D.: A performance analysis of EC2 cloud computing services for scientific computing. In: Avresky, D.R., Diaz, M., Bode, A., Ciciani, B., Dekel, E. (eds.) CloudComp 2009. LNICST, vol. 34, pp. 115–131. Springer, Heidelberg (2010). doi:10.1007/978-3-642-12636-9_9
2. Armbrust, M., Fox, A., Griffith, R., Joseph, A.D., Katz, R., Konwinski, A., et al.: A view of cloud computing. Commun. ACM **53**(4), 50–58 (2010)
3. Nurmi, D., Wolski, R., Grzegorczyk, C., Obertelli, G., So-man, S., Youseff, L., Zagorodnov, D.: The Eucalyptus open-source cloud-computing system. In: IEEE International Symposium on Cluster Computing and the Grid (CCGrid 2009) (2009)
4. Open Nebular. http://www.opennebula.org
5. Nimbus. http://nimbusproject.org
6. Amazon Elastic Compute Cloud (Amazon EC2). Amazon Web Services LLC (2009)
7. Abu Sharkh, M., Jammal, M., Shami, M., Ouda, A.: Resource allocation in a network-based cloud computing environment: design challenges. IEEE Commun. Mag. **51**, 46–52 (2013)
8. Rasmussen, R.V., Trick, M.A.: Round robin scheduling - a survey. Eur. J. Oper. Res. **188**(3), 617–636 (2008)
9. Chen, B.X., Fu, X.F., Zhang, X.Y., Su, L., Wu, D.: Design and implementation of intranet security audit system based on load balancing. In: Proceedings of 2007 IEEE International Conference on Granular Computing, pp. 588–591 (2007)

10. Liu, Y., Yang, S., Lin, Q., Kim, G.B.: Loyalty-based resource allocation mechanism in cloud computing. In: Qian, Z., Cao, L., Su, W., Wang, T., Yang, H. (eds.) Recent Advances in Computer Science and Information Engineering. Lecture Notes in Electrical Engineering, vol. 125, pp. 233–238. Springer, Heidelberg (2012)
11. Li, C., Li, L.: Efficient resource allocation for optimizing objectives of cloud users, IaaS provider and SaaS provider in cloud environment. J. Supercomputing 65, 866–885 (2013)
12. Shi, X., Xu, K., Liu, J., Wang, Y.: Continuous double auction mechanism and bidding strategies in cloud computing markets. IEEE Trans. Cloud Comput. (2013)
13. Chaisiri, S., Lee, B.S.: Niyato, D: Optimization of resource provisioning cost in cloud computing. IEEE Trans. Serv. Comput. 5(2), 164–177 (2012)
14. Ding, D., Fan, X., Luo, S.: User-oriented cloud resource scheduling with feedback integration. J. Supercomputing 72, 1–22 (2015)
15. Wang, W., Zhang, Y., Li, Y., Zhang, X.: The global fuzzy c-means clustering algorithm. In: The Sixth World Congress on Intelligent Control and Automation, WCICA 2006, vol. 1, pp. 3604–3607 (2006)
16. Himani, A., Sidhu, H.S.: Comparative analysis of scheduling algorithms of Cloudsim in cloud computing. Int. J. Comput. Appl. 97(16), 29–33 (2014)

System Control Using Real Time Finger Tip Tracking and Contour Detection with Gesture Recognition

Arjunlal$^{(\boxtimes)}$ and Minu Lalitha Madhavu

Department of Computer Science and Engineering,
Sree Buddha College of Engineering, Alappuzha, India
arjunlal92@gmail.com, minulalitha@gmail.com

Abstract. Gestures are very important for the communication between humans. Nowadays new technologies of Human Computer Interaction (HCI) are being developed to convey commands from user's to computers. Among them, communication though hand gesture is a natural and instinctive way to interact with the computer. Over the years Vision based real time gesture recognition system has witnessed a large growth because of its different beneficial applications, such as sign language to virtual reality and its capability to interact with system efficiently through HCI. In HCI using hand gesture, the main elements are hand gesture recognition and its tracking. At first a brief history of hand gesture recognition is deliberated and the technical challenges during the recognition process also enumerated. The methodologies for hand gesture identification, such as glove-based, vision-based and depth-based, are compared briefly. Bare hand gesture recognition and tracking using CamShift can provide a better Human-Computer Interaction.

Keywords: Hand gesture · Human-Computer Interaction (HCI) · Viola and Jones algorithm · CamShift · Haar-like features · Convex hull

1 Introduction

Now a days computing devices become the part of human life. Human computer interaction (HCI) is the study of how user can interact with computer and the growths on successful interactions between computers and human users. Different methods are using for the reliable effects from user computer interaction. The word Gestures can define as meaningful body actions containing the actions and motions of head, fingers, hands etc. Communicating with computing devices using hand gesture is more natural and has least restriction for users in HCI. There is no need of any specially designed intermediate input devices for the interaction or communication between human and computer, when user's bare hand is used as direct input device of a computing system. Keyboard and mouse are the common devices which used to interact with the system. Instead of them user can use hand and finger gestures for the communication in natural way.

The recognition process of gestures can be generally categorized into two. First one is static hand gesture and second is dynamic hand gesture recognition [1]. Dynamic gestures are not constant and changes over a period of time but static gestures remains

© Springer Nature Singapore Pte Ltd. 2016
A. Unal et al. (Eds.): SmartCom 2016, CCIS 628, pp. 864–872, 2016.
DOI: 10.1007/978-981-10-3433-6_103

motionless and is commonly known as postures. Pre-defined postures are used as the reference for static hand gesture recognition method. In real time gesture recognition system, input to the system will change in every instance, so this real time recognition method mainly focused to dynamic gestures. In our smart growing technical world hand gesture recognition has its own significance in the field of computer vision, image processing (IP) and artificial intelligence (AI). Mainly using hand gesture recognition methods are based on glove, depth and vision.

While considering glove based approach, it is reasonably fast and easier to interact with the system because of the usage of specially designed sensing device termed data glove. Even if it has advantages it is quite difficult to wear or use an external device every time to control computing devices. In vision based technique, users don't want to use any special purposed devices. In this method camera is act as the input device. So vision based approach points to natural way of interaction between computer and user without using any additional expedients. The third one is depth based recognition technique which is more robust and reliable. Due to the presence of expensive technologies and methods such as 3D laser scanning and structure light, the wide range usage of depth based recognition is limited.

2 Related Works

2.1 About Hand Gesture

Hand gestures are meaningful body languages which interpreted using shapes and positions of palm and fingers. There are mainly two types of hand gestures. First one is dynamic and the next is static hand gestures. As mentioned in its name, static hand gestures state to still patterns of the hand and the dynamic hand gestures refers to moving actions of hand. There is the possibility to affect the gestures by the time, backgrounds and gestures definitions of different people. Hand gestures are defined in the paper is the grouping of all sort of movements produced by arms and other hand parts. It includes both static and dynamic gestures were the dynamic gesture derive the meaning from moving hands and static derive the meaning from motionless hand stills. When consider gesture and postures. While comparing posters and gestures, still shapes and state of the hands are used in posters and hand movements are used in gestures [2]. Here we can consider hand gestures as the collection of all kinds of movements and gestures which formed by hand parts. The main thing distinguish poster and gesture is that the poster points to the state or shape of the body or hand parts and instead of still shapes gestures emphasis on the movements of hand [2].

2.2 Hand Gesture Recognition Approach

The first step of dynamic hand gesture recognition approach is recognizing and distinguishing the hand region from input image. Several techniques are there for this purpose. Technology changes with time, then the gesture recognition approaches were also updated with these technologies. Hand gesture recognition methods are able to categorize into different classifications based on technology changes. Data glove based, Vision based and Depth-based approaches are the main hand gesture recognition methods.

Data glove based approaches: In Data glove based approach specially designed hardware device, Data glove [3], is used to identify hand positions, movements and finger patterns. A deice which is almost like as glove has to wear by the user and the Can collect the information from different hand and finger joints. Neural network is usually using to analyse the collected data. This method can provide accurate finger's position and coordinates of hand [4, 5]. In real time, glove method can identify and analyse a variety of gestures with high accuracy. The main gains of this approach are fast response, not as much of input data required and can bring the finger movement information directly. The main benefit of this scheme is great accurateness, high speed, fewer input data and can produce the selective information about the finger position and it's movement directly to the system. Even if this method has this much of advantage, it is not appropriate for natural human computer interaction and more expensive (Fig. 1).

Fig. 1. Data glove

Vision based approaches: User need not to use any additional hardware devices for HCI in Vision-based gesture recognition (VGR) method. Just a video capturing camera is required as input device and hand actions are directly act as input. VGR process has multiple stages in HCI. First phase is recognising and differentiating the hand portion from input frames. Second phase is continuous tracking of this differentiated hand portion throughout the time. Accuracy of this approach depends on the techniques that used to distinguish and track the hand.

Hand Segmentation: Skin color is used as the parameter to identify hand region from the captured input image. Color video camera generates RGB image frames. Hand segmentation directly depends to background variations. Detection of hand region using skin color in this varying background is little difficult and tough. While relating RGB with YCbCr, the YCbCr [6] color format is insensitive to deep color deviation. So RGB image from the camera need to convert to YCbCr to get better outcome.

     Due to the presence of background noise the binary image generated by performing threshold to converted YCbCr can not deliver accurate hand image. We can reduce the presence of these noise by using image morphology algorithm by performing image dilation and erosion [7, 8]. Average filleting [9] for background subtraction also helps to reduce unsolicited noise.

Depth-based gesture recognition: The technology using depth camera give a new set of paths for the data or information acquisition process of 3D geometrics [18]. Currently in depth camera technology, two main approaches are there. One is based on light coding and the second is based on time of flight (TOF) principle.

Depth image can reflect the 3D feather directly while compared with normal image. Hence the factors such as shadow of the object, illumination and color would not be affected to this depth image. By using various distance information of depth image, it is possible to separate the required part from the covered region. But it could not be done using the normal visible light [19]. Even if the depth based approach gives accurate result, it is too expensive compared to other approaches.

3   Real Time Hand Tracking and Finger Gesture Recognition

Viola and Jones algorithm is a good object detection algorithm in real-time environment. Harr-like feature [11] can deliver accurate result which is robust to different lighting conditions [10] and noise. The lighting variation and noise will effect entire pixel values of feature region. Here, A[x,y] is the actual image and AI[x,y] is the integral image at the location of pixel [x, y] that can be calculated by using following equation:

$$AI[x,y] = \sum_{x' \leq x, y' \leq y} AI[x', y'] \qquad (1)$$

In practical point of view, simple Haar-like feature can't recognise the object with greater accuracy. But it is not hard to find out a Haar-like feature-based classifier which has well accuracy than the random predicting. Different learning algorithms improve accuracy of tracking by combining these separately feeble classifiers [4]. The AdaBoost based learning algorithm is an example of the same. This algorithm initially allots an equal weight to each training trials. In the first step we start the selection of a Haar-like classifier. And get classification accuracy better than 50%. In the second step, classifier is merged to the linear combinations to improve accuracy and training sample weights are updated. The next classification stage is to reduce the error rate. By this process we can increase the total classification accuracy for object detection [16]. Till the overall accuracy meets the required level, new classifiers generated in different iterations will add to the linear combination. We will get a strong classifier, builds by the combination of selected required week classifiers, at the final stage.

Convex Hull is one of the best algorithms to identify or distinguish a region based on boundary points. Convex Hull algorithm can use to distinguish the hand region from the input image on the basis of skin color. Segmentation of hand is the first step in this approach. The skin color is characteristic sign of hands and it is unvarying to rotation and scale [8]. A counter is extracted after the segmentation of hand from the background. The co-ordinate details of hand edges contains in a counter vector. The processing on this counter vector gives the location of each finger tips. The input images after applying threshold and noise removal contains only two pixel values of 1 and 0. The convex hull algorithm takes the advantage of this and finds the boundary based on pixel value variation. In this approach, firstly calculate the maximum and minimum x and y coordinate values and joints them after iterations to get a polygon boundary of required pixel values. From this polygon it is possible to focus on the convex defects that is the defects between each arm of convex hull. Here for hand detection and recognition Haar like feature set algorithm and AdaBoost algorithm are adopted.

4   Finger Tip Tracking with CamShift and Contour Detection for System Control

In this paper, ambiguity during the hand portion identification process will reduce by using face masking. The informations regarding graphical positions of hand will get from the centre of hand. Be able to track distinguished hand region accurately and reliably using CamShift algorithm (Fig. 2).

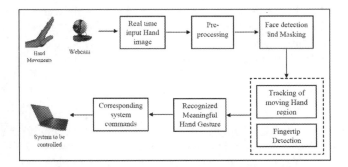

Fig. 2.   Flow of hand gesture to system control.

4.1   Face Detection and Masking

While considering the captured frame, there is a chance to occur face portion in the frame other than hand region. The skin colored face portion leads to ambiguity while identifying hand region. To remove this face region, we have to recognise the face using haar like features and then mask that identified portion from the boundary. After the masking process the frame may contains only hand regions as skin colored pixels. Face masking reduce the ambiguity and increase the accuracy.

4.2   Size and Center of the Hand

After separating hand portion from its background, center of the hand region can be calculate using the following equation:

$$\bar{x} = \frac{\sum_{\{i=0\}}^{k} x_i}{k}, \quad \bar{y} = \frac{\sum_{\{i=0\}}^{k} y_i}{k} \tag{2}$$

where xi and yi are the coordinates of the ith pixel of identified hand area, k is the number of pixels in the region. Then will get the hand size by draw a circle growing the radius from center of the region to the first black pixel value meets. Lack of proper image separation will lead the tracking algorithm to meet the boundary before the original background and size of the hand area becomes smaller than the original one.

4.3 Finding Finger Tip

With the help of convex hull algorithm, we can identify whether the finger is outside the palm circle or not. This algorithm can wont to resolve the issues of identifying the largest polygon which including all required pixels. We can identify or check fingertip points on the hand using this convex hull algorithm. It helps to recognise whether a finger is closed or not. To identify those conditions, multiply two times to the radius value of hand and check the gap between a pixel which is in convex polygon and the center. The hand is closed, if the distance is lesser than the radius of the hand.

4.4 Hand Tracking Based on the CamShift Algorithm

In real-time HCI using hand gesture recognition, hand position and gestures or posters changes quickly. To track this actions, desires a fast responding algorithm. For this purpose here we used CamShift [14]. This algorithm has some step by step procedure. The processing area of the object is detected by using distribution [13, 15] of hue. This distinguished window will help to find the center point. A new tracking window can obtain from frames using hand region based on color histogram. If the CamShift [17] is worked on background removed regions, then the accuracy of the search window will increase and also can overcome the performance problems in the noisy background. For increasing tracking accuracy, AND operation applied among the hand region and original image. The combination of background subtraction [12] and CamShift provide an accurate tracking method. This method is enough to track fast hand movements on real-time.

4.5 System Control Operations

Hand gestures can convert to mouse movements for better HCI system. Mouse Cursor movements depends on the x, y position of hand gestures with respect to the particular computer screen. As mentioned, by using Convex Hull algorithm we can find the size of the palm and centre of the hand. The x, y coordinates of this centre can be used for the position of mouse pointer. Centre of the gesture is used for the mouse movements. Likewise the actions of fingers, positions of figure tips and finger counts can convert to different mouse click operations. Index finger is used here to perform single click.

The actions of middle finger and index finger is analyzed and transform to double click. Right click is performed based on the action of small finger.

5   Experimental Results

The HCI system was tested using a 2.5 GHz intel core i5 processor, running in Manjaro Linux with 2 GB RAM. Image capturing is done using inbuilt 2 mega-pixel camera. The project was implemented in C++ programming language using OpenCV version 2.4.

We consider accuracy and time as the parameters for evaluating performance of the experiment. Three different testing environment were used for six different trials. Finger counting, mouse pointer movement and mouse click operations were tested in three different backgrounds. Time taken for each operations are shown below (time in seconds) (Tables 1, 2 and 3).

Table 1. Performance result: Background 1.

Operation	Trial 1	Trial 2	Trial 3	Trial 4
Finger counting [4 as count]	1.2	1.7	1.2	1.8
Mouse movement	0.8	1.0	0.5	0.5
Left click	1.5	1.8	1.5	2.1
Right click	2.0	1.7	2.1	1.8

Table 2. Performance result: Background 2.

Operation	Trial 1	Trial 2	Trial 3	Trial 4
Finger counting [4 as count]	1.1	1.0	0.9	1.3
Mouse movement	0.9	0.6	0.7	0.9
Left click	1.3	1.3	1.8	1.9
Right click	1.9	1.7	1.8	1.5

Table 3. Performance result: Background 3.

Operation	Trial 1	Trial 2	Trial 3	Trial 4
Finger counting [4 as count]	1.0	1.2	1.2	1.6
Mouse movement	1.2	0.8	1.1	0.9
Left click	1.5	1.6	1.9	1.9
Right click	1.8	2.2	2.0	1.7

Time taken to perform each operations changes with trials and backgrounds. The mouse movement task showed almost similar times with testers. The time taken for click operations showed as unstable. Even if the time is unstable, finally it produced accurate clicking process within the maximum limit of 1.7 s (Fig. 3).

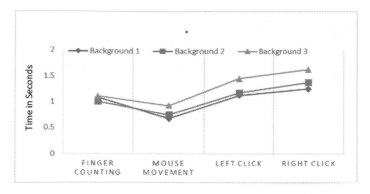

Fig. 3. Performance Result

6 Conclusion

Hand gesture recognition became one of the major and interesting interaction method with the advanced technology growth in the area of human-computer interaction (HCI). The proposed HCI method is cheap and reliable with different environmental conditions. In this system the user need not use any other external recognition device other than the computer's built-in camera. Bare hand communication for mouse operations provides a natural effect to the user. Because of the variety of skin colors and lighting, it is tough to acquire stable results. Most vision based methods have some sort of illumination issues. By analysing the result, can expect that the proposed system can work in almost all environments. In the future works existing system will be improved and additional features such as zooming, window switching etc. will be added to the existing system.

References

1. Weng, C., Li, Y., Zhang, M., Guo, K., Tang, X., Pan, Z.: Robust hand posture recognition integrating multi-cue hand tracking. In: Zhang, X., Zhong, S., Pan, Z., Wong, K., Yun, R. (eds.) Edutainment 2010. LNCS, vol. 6249, pp. 497–508. Springer, Heidelberg (2010). doi:10.1007/978-3-642-14533-9_51
2. Mitra, S., Acharya, T.: Gesture recognition: a survey. IEEE Trans. Syst. Man Cybern. Part C Appl. Rev. **37**, 311–324 (2007)
3. Sturman, D.J., Zeltzer, D.: A survey of glove-based input. IEEE Comput. Graph. Appl. **14**(1), 30–39 (1994)
4. Harshith, C., Shastry, K.R., Ravindran, M., Srikanth, M.V.V.N.S., Lakshmikhanth, N.: Survey on various gesture recognition techniques for interfacing machines based on ambient intelligence. (IJCSES) **1**(2) (2010)
5. Garg, P., Aggarwal, N., Sofat, S.: Vision based hand gesture recognition. World Acad. Sci. Eng. Technol. **49**, 972–977 (2009)
6. Park, H.: A Method for Controlling Mouse Movement using a Real-Time Camera

7. Hussain, I., Talukdar, A.K., Sarma, K.K.: Hand gesture recognition system with real-time palm tracking. In: Annual IEEE India Conference (2014)
8. Erdem, A., Yardimci, E., Atalay, Y., Cetin, V.: Computer vision based mouse. In: Proceedings of the IEEE International Conference Acoustics, Speech, and Signal Processing (ICASS) (2012)
9. Park, H.-S., Jo, K.-H.: Real-time hand gesture recognition for augmented screen using average background and CAMshift. In: 19th Korea - Japan Joint Workshop on Frontiers of Computer Vision (2013)
10. Mazumdar, D., Talukdar, A.K., Sarma, K.K.: Gloved and free hand tracking based hand gesture recognition. In: ICETACS 2013
11. Viola, P., Jones, M.: Rapid object detection using a boosted cascade of simple features. In: Proceedings of the CVPR 2001 (2001)
12. Zhang, C., Zhang, Z.: A survey of recent advances in face detection. Technical Report, MSR-TR-2010-66, June 2010
13. Ambika, L.A., Hidananda, H.C.: A comparative analysis of hand tracking algorithms for gesture recognition. Int. J. Eng. Res. Technol. (IJERT) 3(5), 1227–1231 (2014). ISSN: 2278-0181
14. Nadgeri, S.M., Sawarkar, S.D., Gawande, A.D.: Hand gesture recognition using CAM-SHIFT algorithm. Third International Conference on Emerging Trends in Engineering and Technology (2010)
15. Bradski, G.R.: Computer vision face tracking for use in a perceptual user interface. Microcomputer Research Lab, Santa Clara, CA, Intel Corporation (1998)
16. Bradski, G.R., Clara, S.: Computer vision face tracking for use in a perceptual user interface. Intel Technol. J. Q2 (1998)
17. Huang, S., Hong, J.: Moving object tracking system based on CAMshift and Kalman filter. In: 2011 International Conference on IEEE Consumer Electronics, Communications and Networks (CECNet) (2011)
18. Xiang, X.-Q., Pan, Z.-G., Tong, J.: Depth camera in computer vision and computer graphics: an overview. J. Front. Comput. Sci. Technol. 5(6), 481–492 (2011)
19. Zhu Y.-M., Yang Z.-B., Yuan B.: Vision based hand gesture recognition. In: Published by International Conference on Service Science (2013)

A Study on Classification Algorithms for Crime Records

K.B. Sundhara Kumar and N. Bhalaji$^{(\boxtimes)}$

SSN College of Engineering, Chennai, India
{sundharakumarkb, bhalajin}@ssn.edu.in

Abstract. Data mining has its popularity among crime data analysis significantly due to increasing crime rates across the globe. In this research, classification methods are applied for predicting the nature of a crime that is whether the crime is a violent crime or a non-violent crime. In this work, we present two classification algorithms – Gradient Boosting algorithm and Random Forest algorithm for predicting the crime as a violent or non-violent crime and analyze the accuracy, precision and recall values of these algorithms for the crime records. The dataset is taken from the Communities and Crime data from UCI repository for processing. Further, to improve the accuracy of the predicted results, we use Boruta algorithm which is primarily a wrapper-algorithm for all relevant feature selections. The study finds that Boruta algorithm performs better in feature selection than the Chi-Square feature selection algorithm.

Keywords: Classification · Crime data mining · Gradient boosting · Random forest · Chi-square test · Boruta

1 Introduction

The goal of any country is to provide security to its citizens. Reducing crime in the nation is one solution to overcome the security concerns in the country. In order to predict and prevent a crime, it is very critical to understand the underlying patterns of a crime. There has been a significant rise in crime pattern mining, predictive policing, hotspot analysis and spatial and temporal analysis of crime. However, due to inconsistency in the crime data which vary drastically with time, it is a herculean task to choose appropriate methods for mining the crime pattern. Machine learning and data mining are widely used techniques in crime pattern detection. These are very apt techniques that provide some fairly interesting results.

Though there are various widely used techniques, like K-Nearest Neighbor, Naïve Bayesian, decision trees, support vector machines, etc., with the crime data growing exponentially, these techniques doesn't prove to provide accurate results. With the organized crime involving various gangs are also increasing, in order to understand the organizational structure, the data is modeled as a graph. This can provide some interesting results and can be useful for gang network analysis.

In this work, crime dataset from the UCI machine learning repository – the communities and crime data is taken for analysis. Two new algorithms, Random Forest and

© Springer Nature Singapore Pte Ltd. 2016
A. Unal et al. (Eds.): SmartCom 2016, CCIS 628, pp. 873–880, 2016.
DOI: 10.1007/978-981-10-3433-6_104

Gradient Boosting Method are taken and the accuracy, precision and recall values of these algorithms are formulated. This work focuses on feature extraction using Boruta algorithm [1]. It is available as a package in R studio, an efficient tool for data mining. The random forest and GBM methods are performed using R to predict the status of the crime. The parameters such as precision, recall and accuracy are all calculated. R is a free software environment [9] for statistical computing. It is also used for predictive analytics.

The objective of this paper is to classify the crime status into one of the two classes - violent crime or non-violent crime based on the different parameters from the dataset. From the dataset using Boruta algorithm, the features are selected and the random forest and GBM methods are applied to the crime data for predicting the crime status (violent or non-violent crime). From these experimental analysis, parameters such as accuracy, precision and recall values are calculated based on the predicted crime status.

2   Related Work

Techniques such as Association mining, clustering, classification, prediction, machine learning are applied to predict crime status. This section elaborates on the closely related work to mining, machine learning, feature selection [10] and crime status prediction techniques.

Wortley and Mazerolle [2] explained the concept of crime pattern theory in a more suitable form that is straightforward. The authors suggested that there have to be simple rules and a procedure to join those rules in order to understand a complex pattern problem. Starting with individual offenders and moving on to a network of offenders, the authors suggested guiding rules for obtaining crime templates. They defined patterns as a recognizable inter-connectiveness of objects and concluded that crimes occur in patterns; the decision to commit crimes have patterns and the methods by which a crime is committed also occur in patterns.

Nath [3] presented the idea of applying clustering techniques to solve crimes faster by identifying crime patterns. The author suggested that k-means with some enhancements can be used to understand the crime patterns. The paper also had an implementation of semi-supervised learning along with the geo-spatial plot. The main contribution of this paper is applying data mining and machine learning techniques to the crime data and help police solve crime faster.

Buczak and Grifford [4] suggested that manually inspecting each and every crime is infeasible as the amount of data is too huge to be processed in a limited time frame. The research suggests the use of fuzzy association rule mining on crime dataset. The metrics and rules had helped them in identifying interesting and novel rules to extract the essence of crime patterns. The authors had also given a list of trends in crime analysis such as applying mining and machine learning, geo-spatial mechanisms, finding crime hot-spots, predicting gang criminal offenses, etc. The main contribution of the work by these authors lies in fuzzification of the data sets and the application of fuzzy apriori algorithm on the dataset to generate new rules. Some rare and interesting results were found on applying this algorithm. The work concludes on discovering certain crime patterns that are consistent across all regions and states.

The authors of [5] developed an incremental mining algorithm to discover the crime patterns through temporal association rules. Honk Kong district has been taken into consideration and the incremental algorithm called as ITAR has been developed by understanding the Modus Operandi of the criminals. The authors had applied an incremental algorithm as the size of the database keeps increasing dynamically with the happenings of a new crime. So, applying mining techniques on these, leads to an understanding of the crime patterns.

Friedman [6] explained the effect of randomization on gradient boost procedures. The sample size and distribution function taken are the most important characteristics that affect the performance of the problem. The gradient boosting technique constructs an additive regression model by fitting a function sequentially using least-square principles in each iteration. To incorporate randomness as a significant feature few minor modifications were made to the gradient boosting algorithm and henceforth called as stochastic gradient boosting. The performance metrics also depends on the error rate of the derived estimate. The author concluded that the accuracy of the procedure could be improved by increasing the randomness by taking few smaller samples in each iteration.

Flaxman [7] proposed a fully bayesian spatio-temporal model that incorporates Gaussian model to forecast the crime. The author used a relative risk service as the mean in a Poisson likelihood estimation. The crime data of Chicago city were used and grouped based on the type of crime, community area and week of the year. The author had chosen types of crime that are prone to happen frequently. Other than forecasting the crime, the model also is suitable for statistical inference like how the crime rates varied over a decade. The results of this model were compared with kernel intensity estimation approach which is the most widely used tool by the police department.

Somayeh Shojaee, Aida Mustapha, Fatimah Sidi, Marzanah A. Jabar [8] has done an extensive work in applying various classification algorithms for predicting the crime status using the crime and communities dataset from the UCI machine learning repository. They had used two different feature selection techniques - one is the manual technique that is the features are selected based on the human understanding of the domain. The second is a Chi-Square distribution which offers a feature selection package. They had applied the classification algorithms like Naive Bayesian, k-Nearest neighbor, Neural networks, Decision trees and support vector machines (SVM) and calculated the accuracy, precision, recall and area under the curve. Their worked comprised of pre-processing techniques and feature selection by the two methods as explained above. They had concluded that k-Nearest neighbor algorithm is an efficient algorithm to predict the crime status by way of visualizing the ROC curve.

In this study, we select two prospective algorithms namely Gradient Boosting and Random Forest algorithm, that were not discussed related to crime records. Also, we select a wrapper feature selection algorithm - Boruta algorithm another looming feature selection algorithm. The following section discusses these selected algorithms.

3   Analysis of Selected Algorithms

3.1   Boruta Feature Selection Algorithm

Boruta [1] is an all-relevant feature selection wrapper algorithm available as a package with R. It finds relevant features by comparing the importance of original attributes with the importance that is achieved at random, estimated using the permuted copies. It is available in the CRAN repository licensed by GPL. It has an important method called as attstats which show the summary of a Boruta run in an attribute-centered way. Boruta iteratively compares the importance of attributes by shuffling principle.

Those attributes which have more importance than the shadow attributes are labeled as confirmed and those attributes that are of low importance than the shadow attributes are labeled as rejected. Few attributes which have very close values to the shadow values are labeled as tentative. This happens iteratively till only the list of accepted attributes remain or it runs till a threshold value called as MaxRun is reached. Usually, MaxRun is set as 100. The object of Boruta class has various components like finalDecision that describes whether the attribute is confirmed, rejected or tentative, ImpHistory that projects the importance of attributes, timetaken – the time taken for a single run of the algorithm, etc.

3.2   Random Forest

The base of Random Forest is Classification and Regression Trees. Random Forest performs classification and regression based on a forest of trees that uses random inputs [11]. The main purpose of using a Random Forest algorithm is to improve the accuracy of prediction [12]. By growing an ensemble of trees drastic improvements in classification accuracy is found and then voting for the most popular class occurs. This procedure is referred as Random Forest procedure.

These forests use randomly selected inputs or combinations of split inputs at each node to grow the tree. It is found to be robust to outliers and noise. It is very simple to implement and can be easily parallelized. It also gives useful estimates of errors, strength, correlation and variable importance.

3.3   Gradient Boosting

Gradient boosting is a machine learning technique [13] that is also used for Classification and Regression. It produces an ensemble of prediction models. This algorithm works with a variety of loss functions. This algorithm builds additive tree-models in logistic regression. The size of the tree used in this method is a very significant factor. It inherits all the good features of the trees and improves on the weaker features such as the prediction performance.

This algorithm consists of two steps - a dictionary is constructed in the first step using the weak learners. The second step details about fitting a model [6]. This ensemble is grown in an adaptive fashion which is then averaged at the end.

4 Dataset Description

The Communities and Crime dataset [14] from UCI machine learning repository is considered for this study. The dataset comprises of 2215 instances with 147 attributes of which 125 attributes are predictive attributes, 4 attributes are non-predictive and 18 attributes are the goal attributes. This data set focuses on United States communities linked to the socio-economic status, Law enforcement Management administrative Statistics (LEMAS) and the crime statistics report of FBI [4]. The dataset was submitted to the UCI repository in July 2009. This work is only a study on the classification algorithms. We have used these algorithms for the crime records.

4.1 Data Preprocessing

The dataset contains lots of attributes with missing and inconsistent data. There are various methods for handling the missing values. Some of the widely used techniques are removing the missing values, manually entering the values, creating a prediction model which provides values to the missing data. In this work, we remove the attributes containing missing and inconsistent values. This is a very important step as completely removing an attribute may lead to a wrong result even if it contains lots of missing values. So when a particular attribute is completely removed, proper justification has to be maintained. This step is followed by a feature selection method which has two methods – one is the manual method of feature extraction and the other is using the Boruta wrapper algorithm.

4.2 Feature Selection

As mentioned above, the feature selection is done in two methods. The feature selection is mainly done in order to increase the performance and at the same time avoid overfitting of data. The two methods used are discussed below:

- Manual Method – In this method, based on the views from [4, 8] along with the human understanding of the scenario, we derived 38 attributes which gave better results while calculation of accuracy, precision and recall on applying random forest and gradient boosting ensemble methods.
- Boruta Algorithm – The Boruta wrapper runs till it reaches the maximum threshold and provides a result plot that suggests the important, tentative and rejected attributes. The green color represents the important attributes. Red color represents the rejected attributes and yellow suggests tentative attributes which may be considered as important.

The Boruta algorithm is run on the dataset with all the attributes and it yielded 55 attributes as important. With these 55 attributes, the accuracy precision and recall were calculated.

5   Results and Discussions

In this experiment, a comparison between the random forest and gradient boosting is performed over the crime dataset. The accuracy, precision and recall (in %) are calculated for the dataset using both these algorithms. Accuracy denotes the percentage of instances that are classified correctly. Precision shows what ratio of the data is classified correctly. Recall shows the percentage of information relevant to the class that is correctly classified.

The existing scheme in Table 1 denotes the results from the authors of [8]. That is we have assumed the existing scheme to be the best method from the discussions in [8]. As discussed above, they had used Chi-Square algorithm for feature selection and with that the accuracy, precision and recall were calculated. However, we have used the Boruta algorithm for feature selection.

A confusion matrix is built using both the algorithms. The confusion matrix consists of the following parameters: True positives (TP) - correctly identified instances, True Negatives (TN) - correctly rejected instances, False Positives (FP) - incorrectly identified instances and False Negatives (FN) - incorrectly rejected instances.

Table 1. Accuracy, Precision and Recall

Algorithm	Manual feature selection			Algorithmic feature selection		
	Accuracy	Precision	Recall	Accuracy	Precision	Recall
Existing scheme	87.51	86.90	87.50	88.00	87.30	88.00
Random forest	95.60	97.20	96.66	98.00	98.66	97.44
Gradient boost method	97.80	99.72	98.66	98.40	99.17	98.62

The accuracy, precision and recall parameters used in this work are calculated using the below given formulas

$$Accuracy = (TP + TN)/(P + N) * 100. \tag{1}$$

$$Precision = TP/(TP + FP) * 100. \tag{2}$$

$$Recall = TP/P * 100. \tag{3}$$

where

$$P = TP + FP(Total\ Positives). \tag{4}$$

and

$$N = TN + FN(\text{Total Negatives}). \tag{5}$$

The Table 1 shown above shows the comparison between the accuracy, precision and recall values for the crime and community dataset taken under consideration. The existing scheme mentioned in the above table is the k-Nearest Neighbor algorithm taken from the work by the authors of [8].

The Fig. 1 shown above describes the graphical comparison between the two algorithms and the existing scheme for both the manual feature selection and algorithmic approach. The goal attribute here is whether the crime is a violent crime or nonviolent crime. It is clear from Fig. 1 that our work outperforms the existing scheme by a great margin.

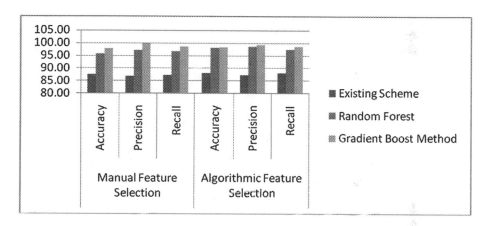

Fig. 1. Comparison of random forest and gradient boosting with the existing scheme

A classifier with high accuracy is termed as a good classifier. There is almost 8–10% increase in the accuracy percentage of our algorithms. Also using the Boruta feature selection method the number of attributes was also reduced significantly compared to chi-square method. Thus, with a limited number of parameters through the Boruta feature selection algorithm and with the random forest and gradient boosting algorithm, we have achieved higher accuracy and precision. Feature selection is proved to be one of the important aspects of data mining. It is very evident from the Table 1 that with the manual feature selection strategy we had 95.6% accuracy while the algorithmic approach to feature selection resulted in an accuracy of 98%.

6   Conclusion

The aim of this paper is to classify the crime as violent crime or non-violent crime. This work presents a detailed analysis of the two classification algorithms viz random forest and gradient boosting for predicting the crime status. The experimental results suggested that the two algorithms we have considered performed better than the k-Nearest Neighbor method which was proposed as one of the best classification methods. Also, this work suggested using the Boruta wrapper algorithm that can be used for feature selection. The results also indicated that using this feature selection algorithm is also better than choosing the attributes manually with less domain knowledge in this area.

Acknowledgments. We extend our heartfelt gratitude towards SSN institutions for providing us with the necessary infrastructure and funding in carrying out this project.

References

1. Kursa, M.B., Jankowski, A., Rudnicki, W.R.: Boruta–a system for feature selection. Fundamenta Informaticae **101**(4), 271–285 (2010)
2. Wortley, R., Mazerolle, L. (eds.): Environmental Criminology and Crime Analysis. Willan, London (2013)
3. Nath, S.V.: Crime pattern detection using data mining. In: IEEE/WIC/ACM International Conference on Web Intelligence and Intelligent Agent Technology Workshops, WI-IAT 2006 Workshops. IEEE (2006)
4. Buczak, A.L., Gifford, C.M.: Fuzzy association rule mining for community crime pattern discovery. In: ACM SIGKDD Workshop on Intelligence and Security Informatics. ACM (2010)
5. Ng, V., et al.: Incremental mining for temporal association rules for crime pattern discoveries. In: Proceedings of the Eighteenth Conference on Australasian Database, vol. 63. Australian Computer Society, Inc. (2007)
6. Friedman, J.H.: Stochastic gradient boosting. Comput. Stat. Data Anal. **38**(4), 367–378 (2002)
7. Flaxman, S.R.: A general approach to prediction and forecasting crime rates with Gaussian processes (2014)
8. Shojaee, S., et al.: A study on classification learning algorithms to predict crime status. Int. J. Digit. Content Technol. Appl. **7**(9), 361 (2013)
9. Ihaka, R., Gentleman, R.: R: a language for data analysis and graphics. J. Comput. Graph. Stat. **5**(3), 299–314 (1996)
10. Tsymbal, A., Puuronen, S., Patterson, D.W.: Ensemble feature selection with the simple Bayesian classification. Inf. Fusion **4**(2), 87–100 (2003)
11. Random Forest. https://cran.r-project.org/web/packages/randomForest/randomForest.pdf
12. Random Forest. http://perso.math.univ-toulouse.fr/motimo/files/2013/07/random-forest.pdf
13. Gradient Boosting. https://cran.r-project.org/web/packages/gbm/gbm.pdf
14. Crime dataset. http://archive.ics.uci.edu/ml/datasets/Communities+and+Crime

Efficient Remote User Authentication Technique for Internet Based Applications Using Keystroke Dynamics

Neha[✉] and Kakali Chatterjee

Department of Computer Science and Engineering,
National Institute of Technology Patna, Patna, Bihar, India
{neha.cse14,kakali}@nitp.ac.in

Abstract. Now-a day's remote users can get the benefit of different services from different servers using the internet. In such multi-server environment, one major security drawback is to identify the legitimate remote user of a web service on the internet. Traditional two factor authentication technique is vulnerable to, password guessing attack, stolen verifier attack, man-in-the-middle attack, etc. To eliminate this security problem, biometric authentication is essential. Keystroke dynamics, one of the behavioural biometric features can be used for remote user authentication. In this paper, a three factor based remote user authentication protocol has been proposed which uses keystroke dynamics as a third factor with two other previous factors. This authentication protocol will use machine learning techniques which results low false acceptance rate (FAR), false rejection rate (FRR) and low equal error rate (ERR).

Keywords: Authentication · Keystroke · Biometrics · E-commerce · Multi-server

1 Introduction

With the increase of on-line and network applications like: e-shopping, e-commerce, e-banking, and the trend of cashless transaction using debit, credit or smart cards, it has now become very essential to make the remote user authentication process very secure and full proof. This user authentication technique can be knowledge based which is already in use everywhere. It fully depends on the memory of the user. There are various vulnerabilities associated with this technique. Another type of remote user authentication techniques is object based. It is strictly based on possessing objects like: ID card, smart card, debit card which proves the authenticity of the user. Many papers on smart card based authentication has been proposed [1–3]. The major limitation of object based authentication is that, it does not have capacity to authenticate that exactly the same person is using the card to whom it was issued, or someone one else on behalf of him is using the card. Recently OTP based transactions are used to remove this drawback [4–6]. Hence we need some factor that is inside the user or

© Springer Nature Singapore Pte Ltd. 2016
A. Unal et al. (Eds.): SmartCom 2016, CCIS 628, pp. 881–888, 2016.
DOI: 10.1007/978-981-10-3433-6_105

that is owned by him only that means biometric features. The biometric can be categorized as: Physiological and Behavioural [7,8]. The physiological features are the physical characteristic of the human body that can prove his identity like: thumb impression, hand impression, iris or retinal scan, face, etc. [9,10]. The behavioural features are behavioural pattern or action unique enough to authenticate a person. [7] "An important issue while selecting authentication feature is user acceptance, ease of use, technology cost, ability for deployment, invasiveness of technology, maturity of the technology, and time it takes for the user to become habituated". Keystroke dynamics one of the behavioural biometric satisfies all these criteria. In this paper, we are proposing a keystroke dynamics based authentication technique that will consider the keystroke behaviour with the emotion of the users. Different threshold will be set for different emotions and based upon that the number of attempts to authenticate will be dynamically decided. Hence the proposed system will be smart and sensitive enough to understand the user mental state and give enough chance to a valid user for authentication. The organization of the paper is as follows: Related work is presented in Sects. 2 and 3 discuses Proposed Authentication Model, a Performance Analysis is done in Sect. 4; Sect. 5 presents Security analysis; and finally Sect. 6 concludes the paper.

2   Related Work

Keystroke Dynamics comes under the category of behavioural biometric technique. Lots of work in the area of keystroke has been done in the past few years [11–14]. It focuses primarily on calculating the time intervals between two key press and analyzing the behavioural parameters associated with it. Many features can be extracted from a keystroke dynamics which can help in uniquely identifying any user. In 2008 Rybnik et al. proposed a keystroke Dynamics based user identification [15]. It uses dwell time and flight time to identify or authenticate any user. Their work also specifies the various keystroke features that can be extracted and used for authentication but, it fails to provide sufficient measures for better outcome. In 2009 Giroux et al. proposed a keystroke time interval as a complementary measure for authentication [16]. A software was developed which accepted the entered passwords for eleven users who entered the password twenty times over a period of four sessions. Results show that this system could allow access to illegitimate user, thus increasing the value of FAR. But it did have low FRR value. In 2011 Syed et al. proposed the use of keystroke dynamics in user-name, password based systems [17]. It analyses the change in variance once the user becomes habituated in typing its credentials in case of a long and complex password. A time window is set for any user to get habituated to typing its password and this makes a decrease in the value of EER over the time. In [18] Modi et al. Surveyed the various keystroke techniques that have been proposed in the past. It highlights the various feature and feature selection algorithms for keystroke dynamics. In 2015 Lima et al. proposed a password authentication scheme using keystroke dynamics [19]. ANN is used as the modeling technique to identify any user. In 2013 Kolakowaska A. et al. proposed emotion detection using keyboard and mouse movement [20]. Features like dwell time, flight time and typing speed in case of keystroke dynamics and mouse acceleration, speed and clicking position is used. In 2011 Epp et al. proposed a scheme for identifying emotion of any user using keystroke [21]. User's typing rhythm and continuous user feedback regarding its emotion is captured to analyze any users typing trait under the influence of different emotion. In 2015 Koakowska A. proposes emotion detection using keystroke dynamics [22].

3   Proposed Authentication Model

3.1   Description

The terminology and features we will be using are discussed as follows:

- **Dwell time**: It is the key press duration. The time duration for which a user depresses a key while typing.
- **Flight time**: It is the time interval between releasing the key and pressing next key.
- **Query time**: Here query time is total time taken to answer the security question.
- **Key code**: Each key of the keyboard has some key code associated with it.
- **Digraph**: It is defined as the time interval between consecutive key press.
- **FAR (False Acceptance Rate)**: It shows the rate at which, the system will accept illegitimate user as a valid user. For a good authentication model the FAR should be low.
- **FRR (False Rejection Rate)**: It shows the rate at which legitimate user are rejected as invalid user. It must not be higher, because that will cause valid user to be rejected.
  ERR (Equal Error rate): it is a point where FAR and FRR are equal.
- **Mean**: It defined as the ratio of total number of observation and number of observations.
- **Variance**: The variance is a measure of the extent to which the individual observations vary with reference to the average of a given set of observations.
- **Standard Deviation**: It is the widely used measure of variation. It is also called root mean square deviation.

3.2   Working of Proposed Model

The proposed model works in three phases: Registration, Login and Authentication. Mainly here we are proposing a smart, intelligent system which analyses user's mental state(emotion) or behaviour. Based upon the user's mental state, the number of attempts for authentication will vary. The working of the model is as follows:

Registration Phase

- In this phase first the user will enter user details such as name, address, UID password, etc.
- The timing features: dwell time, flight time, typing speed, key code, digraph and statistical features of ID &password will be calculated, and stored in the database.
- Then corresponding to particular user six emotions: Angry, Sad, Happy, Busy, Tired, and Neutral will be taken and same fixed text or free text will be entered by the user under these emotions. The corresponding Emotion-Feature mapping is shown in Table 1 below.
- The various features like: dwell time, flight time, typing speed and query time in various emotions, will be calculated from the entered text and stored in the database, with user details. The standard deviation will be taken as threshold. In the Table 1 below, each feature's maximum and minimum value is calculated and SD (Standard deviation) of that will be taken. This SD will act as threshold. If the value of entered text in testing phase lies below SD then user accepted, if lies above SD then user rejected or re-authenticated. Dn represents dwell time values of n different emotions and Da, Ds, Dh, Db, Dt, Dn are standard deviation calculated or threshold value of each emotion. Similarly, Fn is flight time of n different emotions and Fa, Fs, Fh, Fb, Ft, Fn are standard deviation calculated or threshold value of each emotion. The Qn represents Query time of n emotions and Qa, Qs, Qh, Qb, Qt, Qn are standard deviation calculated or threshold value of each emotions. Similarly Tn represents typing speed for n different emotions and Ta, Ts, Th, Tb, Tt, Tn are standard deviation calculated or threshold value of each emotion.

Table 1. Emotion-Feature mapping

Emotions	Angry (min-max)	Sad (min-max)	Happy (min-max)	Busy (min-max)	Tired (min-max)	Neutral (min-max)
Dwell time (SD)	D1_D2 (Da)	D3_D4 (Ds)	D5_D6 (Dh)	D7_D8 (Db)	D9_D10 (Dt)	D11_D12 (Dn)
Flight time (SD)	F1_F2 (Fa)	F3_F4 (Fs)	F5_F6 (Fh)	F7_F8 (Fb)	F9_F10 (Ft)	F11_F12 (Fn)
Query time (SD)	Q1_Q2 (Qa)	Q3_Q4 (Qs)	Q5_Q6 (Qh)	Q7_Q8 (Qb)	Q9_Q10 (Qt)	Q11_Q12 (Qn)
Typing speed (SD)	T1_T2 (Ta)	T3_T4 (Ts)	T5_T6 (Th)	T7_T8 (Tb)	T9_T10 (Tt)	T11_T12 (Tn)

Login phase

- First the user will enter his UID, Password and answer the security question asked.
- Then the features dwell time, flight time, typing speed, key code, digraph will be calculated, from these data.
- The calculated feature's value will be sent to the comparator for authentication. Here machine learning technique will be used for comparison of data.

Authentication Phase

- In this phase, the comparator first takes the calculated feature value of the particular user from login phase. Then it will fetch the feature values of the particular user stored in the database. It means one to one matching will be done.
- Then the standard deviation between two feature sets will be calculated.
- Then, if the value lies between the threshold range of any emotions, then user will be granted access, otherwise not.
- In case of no, it will be checked, it is closest to which emotion using distance algorithm. And according to that user will be allowed for more login attempts as many times as criteria of that emotion.
- Then, if the user exhausts all his attempts his authentication will be rejected/ fails. With every failure data a record will be maintained in the database and will be used as training data in machine learning.

So this way, using our model valid user will be treated smartly by the system.

4 Performance Analysis

We have implemented the proposed authentication protocol using Java Web Application pages. During the user registration process all the parameters (flight time, dwell time etc.) are collected and data set is created by the system administrator. Both Training and Testing data set is created in SQL when a user registers and logs in to the Server. Training phase has done using Weka tool. Training and testing data are retrieved as a Csv file and converted to Arff file which is Weka compatible file format. In Weka, there are various machine learning algorithms, which show their performance with respect to the given dataset. The first one is a rule based algorithm called zero-R. For the given entries of Mapp table, it shows error of 39% which means a success rate of 61%. Zero basically checks the highest occurring value to true and the other to be false in case of binary classification. This serves as a initial measure for other classifiers. Using SMOreg, this is a binary classifier in Weka and uses Support Vectors for classification. Smoreg for Mapp table using poly kernel and Normalized poly kernel shows an error of 36% and 29% respectively, with a success rate of 64% and 71% respectively.

5 Security Analysis

This section includes brief security analysis which shows that the scheme resists the following attacks (Fig. 1):

- **Password guessing Attack**: Suppose the attackers gets the smart card and he attempts to login the server by guessing different words as password from a dictionary. As the authentication process also considers the key stroke parameters, the system will identify him as an illegal user. After limited attempts,

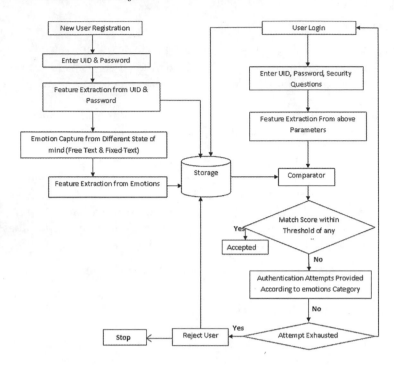

Fig. 1. Authentication model

it will lock the system for security. Sometimes a legitimate user may behave as an abnormal user during some particular emotional state and repeatedly enter wrong passwords for login process. This type of situation can also successfully handled by this scheme due to emotion recognition.

- **Impersonation Attack**: Suppose the attacker track the registration message contains user ID and Password of a user by setting fake server. Now the attacker inserts the correct password to the user terminal to get a valid login. It is impossible for the attacker impersonate as a valid user because during the login process from the user parameters some selected features will be extracted and send to the comparator for matching. Extracted features must satisfy a threshold value. It is impossible for an attacker to pass through such type of biometric authentication. So the proposed protocol resists impersonation attack.

- **Insider Attack**: In such attack, any insider gets the stored value of an ID and password of a user and later he uses this UID and password for login. Now, once he wants to get a valid login using this user credentials, the key stoke values do not match with the stored data. Hence he does not get a valid login and also his activity is recorded as a malicious activity in the activity log. Now, as an insider if he wants to change the keystroke values which is stored in the data set, then also he will unable to do it because the activity log shows him as an intruder. So, the proposed scheme can successfully resists insider attack.

- **Stolen-verifier Attack**: The server of proposed scheme doesn't only hold the password verification table, it also holds the key stroke features with emotional states. The authentication server authenticates the user from values, user provides to them and matching of the extracted features with stored values. Any type of intrusion which is recorded during login also recorded in the activity log. Hence the stolen-verifier attack is impossible to occur.
- **Man-in middle Attack**: This type of attack is very common in such networks. To resist this type attack, different key stroke parameters are used with UID and password. Emotional state changes this value, hence threshold will be set for different emotions and based upon that the number of attempts to authenticate will be dynamically decided. Hence the proposed system will smart and sensitive enough to understand this type of attack.

6   Conclusion

This paper proposed keystroke dynamics as a third factor of authentication while making the system intelligent enough to judge user's mental state, and based on that provides the varying number of attempts to authenticate themselves. The performance analysis also shows that the proposed scheme achieves low FAR and FRR values.

References

1. Song, R.: Advanced smart card based password authentication protocol. Comput. Stand. Interfaces **32**(5), 321–325 (2010)
2. Xu, J., Zhu, W.-T., Feng, D.-G.: An improved smart card based password Authentication scheme with provable security. Comput. Stand. Interfaces **31**(4), 723–728 (2009)
3. Lee, N.-Y., Chiu, Y.-C.: Improved remote authentication scheme with smart card. Comput. Stand. Interfaces **27**(2), 177–180 (2005)
4. Gong, L., Pan, J., Liu, B., Zhao, S.: A novel one-time password mutual authentication scheme on sharing renewed finite random sub-passwords. J. Comput. Syst. Sci. **79**(1), 122–130 (2013)
5. Huang, Y., Huang, Z., Zhao, H., Lai, X.: A new one-time password method. IERI Procedia **4**, 32–37 (2013)
6. Prakash, M.V., Infant, P.A., Jeya-Shobana, S.: Eliminating vulnerable attacks using one time password and passtext analytical study of blended schema. Univ. J. Comput. Sci. Eng. Technol. **1**(2), 133–140 (2010)
7. Kotani, K., Horii, K.: Evaluation on a keystroke authentication system by keying force incorporated with temporal characteristics of keystroke dynamics. Behav. Inf. Technol. **24**(4), 289–302 (2005)
8. Revett, K.: Introduction to behavioural biometrics. Behavioural Biometrics: A Remote Access Approach, pp. 1–29 (2010)
9. Choi, H., Choi, K., Kim, J.: Fingerprint matching incorporating ridge features with minutiae. IEEE Trans. Inf. Forensics Secur. **6**(2), 338–345 (2011)

10. Jain, A.K., Hong, L., Pankanti, S., Bolle, R.: An identity-authentication system using fingerprints. Proc. IEEE **85**(9), 1365–1388 (1997)
11. Das, R.K., Mukhopadhyay, S., Bhattacharya, P.: User authentication based on keystroke dynamics. IETE J. Res. **60**(3), 229–239 (2014)
12. Nahin, A.F.M., Haque, N., Alam, J.M., Mahmud, H., Hasan, K.: Identifying emotion by keystroke dynamics and text pattern analysis. Behav. Inf. Technol. **33**(9), 987–996 (2014)
13. Chandrasekar, V., Suresh Kumar, S., Maheswari, T.: Authentication based on keystroke dynamics using stochastic diffusion algorithm. Stoch. Anal. Appl. **34**(1), 155–164 (2016)
14. Karnan, M., Akila, M., Krishnaraj, N.: Biometric personal authentication using keystroke dynamics: a review. Appl. Soft Comput. **11**(2), 1565–1573 (2011)
15. Rybnik, M., Tabedzki, M., Saeed, K.: A keystroke dynamics based system for user identification. In: 7th Computer Information Systems and Industrial Management Applications, CISIM 2008. pp. 225–230. IEEE (2008)
16. Giroux, S., Wachowiak-Smolikova, R., Wachowiak, M.P.: Keystroke-based authentication by key press intervals as a complementary behavioral biometric. In: IEEE International Conference on Systems, Man and Cybernetics. SMC 2009, pp. 80–85. IEEE (2009)
17. Syed, Z., Banerjee, S., Cheng, Q., Cukic, B.: Effects of user habituation in keystroke dynamics on password security policy. In: 2011 IEEE 13th International Symposium on High-Assurance Systems Engineering (HASE), pp. 352–359. IEEE (2011)
18. Modi, M.T.J., Upadhaya, H.G.: Password less authentication using keystroke dynamics a survey. In: International Journal of Innovative Research in Computer and Communication Engineering, IJIRCCE, pp. 7060–7064 (2014)
19. Lima, J.M.N.D.: Password authentication using keystroke dynamics. In: International Conference on Communication, Information and Computing Technology, ICCICT, pp. 5316–5322 (2015)
20. Kolakowska, A.: A review of emotion recognition methods based on keystroke dynamics and mouse movements. In: 2013 The 6th International Conference on Human System Interaction (HSI), pp. 548–555. IEEE (2013)
21. Epp, C., Lippold, M., Mandryk, R.L.: Identifying emotional states using keystroke dynamics. In: Proceedings of the SIGCHI Conference on Human Factors in Computing Systems, pp. 715–724. ACM (2011)
22. Kolakowska, A.: Recognizing emotions on the basis of keystroke dynamics. In: 2015 8th International Conference on Human System Interactions (HSI), pp. 291–297. IEEE (2015)

Hardware Implementation of Obstacle Detection for Assisting Visually Impaired People in an Unfamiliar Environment by Using Raspberry Pi

Sanket Khade$^{(\boxtimes)}$ and Yogesh H. Dandawate

Department of E&TC,
Vishwakarma Institute of Information Technology, Pune, India
sanket.khade5@gmail.com, yhdandawate@gmail.com

Abstract. For assisting blind or visually impaired persons, many computer vision technology has been developed. Some camera based systems were developed to help those people in way finding, navigation and finding daily necessities. The motion of the observer causes all scene object stationary or non-stationary in motion. And hence it is very much important to detect moving object with the moving observer. In this context we have proposed a camera based prototype system for assisting blind person in detection of obstacles by using motion vectors. We have collected dataset of their indoor and outdoor environment and estimated the optical flow to perform object detection. Furthermore we have detected the objects in the region of interest without using costly Depth cameras and sensors. The hardware used in the proposed work is 'Raspberry Pi 2-B' and the algorithms used for object detection is performed using MATLAB (for simulation purpose) and Python language.

Keywords: Optical flow · Computer vision · Blind people · Object detection · Raspberry Pi

1 Introduction

The blind and visually impaired people face many challenges in their everyday life. In known environments the blind person depend on their sense of orientation and memories. But, daily routines like crossing streets, walking, searching, recognizing objects, places and people which becomes difficult or sometimes impossible without vision. Recent statistics from the World Health Organization estimate that in developing countries there are 285 million people worldwide who are visually impaired [10]. Thus there is no other options for the blind and visually impaired people to rely only on their canes [2], guide dogs, or an assistant for navigating in an unfamiliar environment [3, 12].

There are some vision based hardware systems available to assist them. They used stereo cameras [7], depth cameras [1], Microsoft Kinect [3], ARM processors and GPS [4]. But these are very much expensive and bulky. And hence common man cannot afford these costly hardware systems. In this paper we have introduced a new method

© Springer Nature Singapore Pte Ltd. 2016
A. Unal et al. (Eds.): SmartCom 2016, CCIS 628, pp. 889–895, 2016.
DOI: 10.1007/978-981-10-3433-6_106

which will help them to identify nearby obstacles without using costly cameras and processors. To address this issue we have used 'Raspberry Pi'. Raspberry Pi is like a mini computer which has its own RAM, expandable memory and many more. It is cheaper, easily available and less bulky as compared to other. In our case the observer i.e. the camera is not stationary. Observer is also moving along with the surrounding environment and hence the stationary objects seems to be moved. So it is very much important to detect moving object with the moving observer. Thus in computer vision and video processing motion detection and tracking is found to be challenging task [9]. And that is the reason why we have selected optical flow technique to detect the obstacles.

2 Literature Survey

Since the technology is new and application development and research era has just begun, the work carried out is limited. So before proceeding, a huge and detailed literature survey is necessary.

As far as hardware implementation is considered, researchers have used stereo cameras [7], depth cameras [1], Microsoft Kinect [3], ARM processors and GPS [4] to build their system. Bhambare, R.R., Koul, A. et al. used ARM 7 LPC2148, which works on traditional power supply of 12 V (made up step down transformer) which makes this system more bulky. GPS technology has been used to locate outdoor objects. For that continuous updating of surrounding environment & satellite communication is required, which makes system more complex in terms of coding as well as system design [2]. Chucai Yi, Roberto W. Flores et al. builds a system which uses number of cameras to locate query object by using SURF (Speeded up Robust Technique) descriptors and SIFT (Scale-Invariant Feature Transform) [3]. For that huge amount of dataset of a single object is required for feature extractions [6, 7]. A small change in environment will not give proper output since the system is trained only for limited area and objects. So we need to adopt a different techniques which will work in an unfamiliar environment and will not affect the change in the size and shape of the objects.

'Raspberry Pi' is tiny low powered computer having more RAM, expandable memory, Ethernet and USB connections and many more. We can say that it is a good substitute for costly processors and micro-controllers. We can adopt either background subtraction algorithm or optic flow technique which are most widely used in surveillance systems. If camera is stationary then background subtraction will be good choice. In our case camera i.e. observer is moving along with the surrounding environment and hence the stationary object seems to be moving. It is very much important to detect moving object with the moving observer. Optic flow technique is used to detect motion area in image sequences. It gives better performance under the moving camera, at the expense of computationally complex algorithms [8]. Optical flow presents an apparent change of a moving object's location or deformation between frames. Thus from this estimation and by using blob analysis we are able to figure out the obstacles in the frames [9].

3 Generation of Database and Some Challenges

Before starting the actual building of the algorithm we have to first generate our own database because readymade database is not available for us. We have visited nearby blind school named 'The Poona School and Home for the Blind Girls', Pune for this purpose. The database is taken by mounting the webcam on girls head and video is captured for a minute. We have taken near about 25 videos of indoor as well as outdoor.

By observing the database we should say that the algorithm should detect and track every single object in the scene. As shown in the figure there are many obstacles present in the scene, so detecting and tracking them was challenging task (Fig. 1(a)).

When we capture the video, it covers almost all the objects which are near as well as far from the observer. In short it covers the entire environment which is in line of sight of the camera. Now those object which are too far from an observer will be identified and informed as the obstacles which is of no use (Please refer Fig. 1(b)). For e.g. suppose you are an observer and wish to go to the second door, for that you need to cross the girls on your right hand side and then the girls present near the door. Further you can proceed further for the next door. Thus we need to frame the region near to blind person. If something comes in this region only then it can be notified as an obstacle (Fig. 1(c)).

(a)   (b)   (c)

Fig. 1. Illustration of presence of too many objects such as benches, students, table, teacher etc. as shown in (a), and (b) gives illustration of line of sight of a camera & respective ROI

4 Methodology and Software Implementation

Some assumption were made prior to start of the work. We have assumed that the illumination and brightness conditions are constant throughout. The input to the system will be a video of some predefined parameters as discussed below. In every digital video processing, the first step is to convert the given video into frames. And on every single frame we performed the below specified operations step by step. For detection of obstacle we have estimated the motion vectors. After that the segmentation is done in which we have performed tracking part with the help of background subtraction algorithm. Lastly we have detected the obstacles within ROI.

4.1 Optical Flow

Optical flow or optic flow is the pattern of apparent motion of objects, surfaces, and edges in a visual scene caused by the relative motion between an observer (an eye or a camera) and the scene. Moving images are often disturbed by noise depending on variety of Conditions. The detected noise can be framed either as additive white Gaussian noise, or due to some weak signals. And hence there is necessity to implement some smoothing operations which can handle different types of noise. So we have used 'Median Filter'. Median filters are widely used since they exhibits excellent performance as compared to that of linear filters.

4.2 Segmentation

The detection of objects can be successfully done by segmenting the image into no of blobs or regions. To accomplish this we may have to take help of some of segmentation techniques such as background subtraction, graph cuts and mean shift clustering. These segmented regions are then re-joined to represent an obstacle. In tracking part the data of each frame is read and the background is determined. The objects which are of no interest are eliminated by background subtraction. The gray to binary conversion can be done by using thresholding. And thus this threshold limit highlights the object of interest.

(1) Morphological Close

In order to extract the significant features from the image frames so as to represent and describe the object we need to use morphological operations. They are most commonly used in the image segmentation and pattern recognition. In our proposed framework we have used both morphological erosion and dilation to remove unwanted portion of floor, road and other unwanted objects. After the closing operation we get the result in which many small holes and separated pixels are combined into one big actual object of interest.

(2) Blob Analysis

To detect 2-dimensional object of any shape 'Blob Analysis' is used. The detection is achieved depending upon some spatial characteristics. Many application where we need to save computational time, blob analysis finds its use. Blob analysis eliminates the blob which are unwanted and preserves only those of necessary. This can be achieved by using spatial characteristics. The blobs which fulfils our System are many moving and stationary object within the region of interest. Other unwanted blobs are eliminated by setting some conditions on the features in the algorithm.

4.3 Region of Interest

Now this is the uniqueness of our proposed framework. One can use depth cameras or the sensors to know the nearby object but it will be costly and bulky system.

The blind person generally walk with their eyesight little bit downward toward floor. And by using this characteristic we have drawn the region of interest at the pixel level only. The following figure will illustrate the operation. We have found out the ROI by extracting the 4 co-ordinates points at pixel level as a rectangular blob.

Then we have used simple 'imcrop' function specifying the pixel value as shown in Fig. 2.

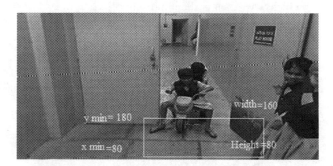

Fig. 2. Illustration of Region of Interest (ROI). They illustrate the value required for writing and simulating the 'imcrop' function.

5   System Design or Hardware Implementation

The system consists of a wearable camera (Logitech C290 having 5 MP resolution and 1920 × 1080 image resolution) which is mounted on the head. The overall processing is done in the Raspberry Pi-2, B model. It has 1 GB RAM, 4 USB ports, 900 MHz quad-core ARM Cortex-A7 CPU, Full HDMI port, Ethernet Port, camera interface, micro SD card slot and many more. We have used MATLAB 2012 for simulation purpose. The Operating System installed on raspberry pi is 'Raspbian' Software used for building algorithm on 'Raspberry Pi' is Open CV2.4.9 which uses Python as one of the programming language.

5.1   Some Hardware Issues

While designing the system, we encountered some hardware issues. We can't install MATLAB directly on Raspberry Pi. We need to install some 'Simulink Support Packages' for Raspberry Pi. We can program Raspberry Pi boards to run our algorithms using Simulink Support Package for Raspberry Pi Hardware. The support package generates code from our Simulink model in a click of a button that then runs on the Raspberry Pi board. These packages are available for MATLAB version which were released after 2015. In MATLAB we have used some computer vision function which supports only '.avi' video file format. If we want to make real time system then it must support every video file format. So we need to build our algorithm in Open CV by using Python language. Python supports every video file format and gives nearly same result as that of MATLAB.

The overall cost of system is near about $200. But it will get increased due to more external memory, RAM and camera resolution.

6 Result

The experimental results were shown in this section. The results were obtained on the standard database which was taken at the blind school. The processing time was taken at initialization and finalization of steps which covers pre-processing, filtering and estimation of motion vectors (Fig. 3). The processing time was near about

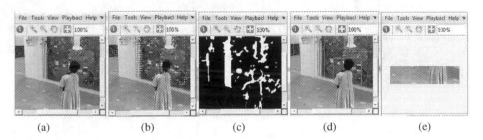

| (a) | (b) | (c) | (d) | (e) |

Fig. 3. Illustration of final results. (a) Shows the input video frame. After estimating motion vectors (b) we have done segmentation (c) and then blob analysis (d) to detect nearby obstacles which is shown by green squares. The last frame shows the final detected output (e)

7 Conclusion and Future Work

In this paper we have proposed a simple cost effective system to help visually challenged people. We have given a camera based technique that can detect and track obstacle effectively. In order to evaluate the performance of proposed algorithm we have used database generated at the blind school. Experimental results shows that, the proposed algorithm can effectively detect and track the nearby obstacles. Due to the use of 'Raspberry Pi' the system became more cost effective and less bulky. However this algorithm fails if illumination and brightness conditions are not proper.

In future we will try to classify each objects and obstacles under different categories such as chair, door, table etc., so that blind people will get actual information of the obstacles and they can move freely in any kind of environment.

Acknowledgement. We would like to thank Mrs S.A. Pujari, (Principal, the Poona School and Home for the Blind Girls; Kothrud, Pune) for giving us chance take database from their institute. We would also like to thank Prof. K.J. Raut and Riddhi Zaveri for giving us constant support and helping in documentation part respectively.

References

1. Wang, S., Pan, H., Zhang, C., Tian, Y.: RGB-D image-based detection of stairs, pedestrian crosswalks and traffic signs. J. Vis. Commun. Image Representation **25**(2), 263–272 (2014)
2. Bhambare, R.R., Koul, A., Bilal, S.M.: Smart Vision System for Blind
3. Bhowmick, A., Prakash, S., Bhagat, R., Prasad, V., Hazarika, Shyamanta, M.: *IntelliNavi*: navigation for blind based on kinect and machine learning. In: Murty, M.,Narasimha, He, X., Chillarige, R.R., Weng, P. (eds.) MIWAI 2014. LNCS (LNAI), vol. 8875, pp. 172–183. Springer International Publishing, Cham (2014). doi:10.1007/978-3-319-13365-2_16
4. Lee, K., Lee, C., Kim, S.-A., Kim, Y.-H.: Fast object detection based on color histograms and local binary patterns. In: Proceedings of TENCON 2012 - 2012 IEEE Region 10 Conference, 19–22 November 2012, vol. 1, no. 4 (2012)
5. Chen, Q., Song, Z., Feris, R., Datta, A., Cao, L., Huang, Z., Yan, S.: Efficient maximum appearance search for large-scale object detection. In: Proceedings of the IEEE Conference on Computer Vision and Pattern Recognition, pp. 3190–3197 (2013)
6. Wang, S., Tian, Y.: Camera-based signage detection and recognition for blind persons. In: Miesenberger, K., Karshmer, A., Penaz, P., Zagler, W. (eds.) ICCHP 2012. LNCS, vol. 7383, pp. 17–24. Springer, Heidelberg (2012). doi:10.1007/978-3-642-31534-3_3
7. Yi, C., et al.: Finding objects for assisting blind people. Netw. Model. Anal. Health Inf. Bioinform. **2**(2), 71–79 (2013)
8. Aslani, S., Mahdavi-Nasab, H.: Optical flow based moving object detection and tracking for traffic surveillance. Int. J. Elect. Electron. Commun. Energy Sci. Eng. **7**(9), 789–793 (2013)
9. Royden, C.S., Connors, E.M.: The detection of moving objects by moving observers. Vis. Res. **50**(11), 1014–1024 (2010)
10. Visually Impairment and Blindness: WHO Fact sheet–282 (2014). http://www.who.int/mediacentre/factsheets/fs282/en
11. Rajput, D., Ahmed, F., Ahmed H., Ahmed Shaikh, Z., Shamshad, A.: Smart obstacle detector for blind person. J. Biomed. Eng. Med. Imaging **1**(3), 31–40 (2014)
12. Thakoor, K.A., Marat, S., Nasiatka, P.J., McIntosh, B.P., Sahin, F.E., Tanguay, A.R., Weiland, J.D., Itti, L.: Attention biased speeded up robust features (AB-SURF): a neurally-inspired object recognition algorithm for a wearable aid for the visually-impaired. In: 2013 IEEE International Conference on Multimedia and Expo Workshops (ICMEW), pp. 1–6. IEEE (2013)
13. Jafri, R., Ali, S.A., Arabnia, H.R., Fatima, S.: Computer vision based object recognition for the visually impaired in an indoors environment: a survey. Vis. Comput. **30**(11), 1197–1222 (2014)

Layer Based Security in Internet of Things: Current Mechanisms, Prospective Attacks, and Future Orientation

Isha[1], Ashish Kr. Luhach[1(✉)], and Sumit Kumar[2]

[1] Lovely Professional University, Phagwara, Punjab, India
ashishluhach@acm.org
[2] Dronacharya College of Engineering, Gurgaon, Haryana, India

Abstract. Internet of things (IoT) has now become a fascinating system that improves information technology for its use in homes, cities and medical sectors. IoT works as an extension of internet to realize interconnections among every day object based on platform independent communication protocols. Object forming IoT must possess sensing, communication, and computation capabilities leading to a convenient as well as economical assistance for society. Interaction among heterogeneous objects enhances the security vulnerabilities in IoT. The current four layered communication stack of IoT supports protocols at each layer for enabling connectivity of heterogeneous objects. With security as a prime concern, communication in IoT need to maintained using a secure mechanism to protect the system from attacks. This paper analyzes various existing protocols at each layer with their inherent security mechanisms and exposing their vulnerabilities to different attacks. This paper will unlock new research areas for improving the inbuilt security mechanisms.

Keywords: Internet of Things · Perception layer security · Network layer security · Transport layer security · Application layer security · Attacks

1 Introduction

In this fast moving era of linked objects, information is exchanged among physical and virtual objects seamlessly making them as a part of IoT. IoT comprises of various sensing devices for information collection such as Radio frequency identification (RFID), sensors, or Global positing system (GPS) [1]. Once the data is collected, this raw data is converted to meaningful information that can be used for making decisions in real time. IoT is emerging as a intellectual technology that is being used in number of applications like health care, cities, industries, inventory etc., for making them more efficient and interactive [2].

Huge data is accumulated in IoT applications due to interconnection of different objects that calls for high end security [3]. IoT security revolves mainly around three aspects- network security, system security, and application security [4]. System security maintains security and privacy of objects as many of the connected objects often remains unattended, network security works on offering security while communication through wireless links, and application security is used to solve problems in

© Springer Nature Singapore Pte Ltd. 2016
A. Unal et al. (Eds.): SmartCom 2016, CCIS 628, pp. 896–903, 2016.
DOI: 10.1007/978-981-10-3433-6_107

applications like smart homes, cities, etc. With the increase in internet usage, each user wants to access any object of its choice that is connected to the network. This vast use of information and resources requires a special attention on security side of IoT. Institute of Electrical and Electronics Engineers (IEEE) and Internet engineering task force (IETF) have defined set of standardized communication as well as security protocols for IoT [5]. Each layer in IoT offers communication protocols with certain security mechanism available in each of them. The embedded security solutions at each layer have certain problems that may lead to various attacks.

Some security principles or guidelines must be satisfied to attain a secure and reliable communication support for users, objects, and software.

- Confidentiality: End to end communication must be made secure. Data collected by the sensor must be communicated to the receiver object in a secure way. But it cannot be assured that sensor will not reveal this information to other unauthorized objects [6]. Complete Data management and movement process should also be made secure [7].
- Integrity: While date transmission from one object to other, it should not be tampered by malicious devices. Main aim of imposing integrity is to have a check on privacy of the user by preventing the modification of data.
- Authentication: Authentication mechanism is used to initiate the communication among objects by mutually identifying each other [8]. Authentication mechanism lessens the probability of attacks in the network. The major challenge faced while authentication is due to identification process of diverse objects and newly connected objects [9].
- Availability: With number of objects connected to IoT, vision is to ensure availability. Availability is not only for the data, it can be in terms of services of objects, applications, and resources. Certain intrusion detection mechanism can be employed in order to detect the malicious or faultily behaved objects.
- Lightweight Solutions: Constrained objects forming IoT require light weight security solutions to be implemented. Lightweight solutions do not intend to be weak rather they entail less computational and power capabilities for their processing ought to be compatible with IoT. That is why lightweight solutions are apt for operation of IoT for their long life and secure implementation.

This research paper focus on security concerns in IoT at each layer of operation. In Sect. 2, in-built security mechanism and protocols at each layer are discussed. Section 3, presents the problems or challenges still faced by that make security mechanism vulnerable to attacks. In Sect. 4, certain solutions to existing challenges are given. Finally Sect. 4 concludes the work with future work scope to help the research move in positive direction.

2 Security in IoT at Architecture Layers

General architecture of internet cannot be directly applied to IoT, as IoT extends communication over object and human, objects with other objects [10]. IoT architecture comprise of 4 operating layer- perception, network, transport and application layer [11].

Security protocols used in internet architecture cannot be implemented in IoT due to constrained requirements like limited power in hardware based IoT nodes, or sensor nodes. Secure IoT architecture is constructed by applying security mechanism at each layer of IoT architecture. The overall construction of security in IoT covers security of the physically deployed nodes, information gathering security, information communication security, and information computation security present at perception, network, transport, and application layer respectively as shown in Fig. 1.

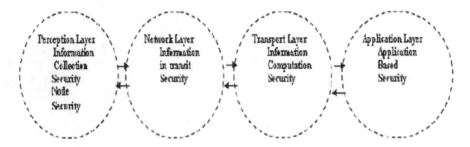

Fig. 1. Security construction criteria at each layer

2.1 Perception Layer Security

Perception layer employs IEEE 802.15.4 standard as it supports communication for low energy devices. IEEE 802.15.4 works on both Physical layer and MAC layer with 250 bits/s communication rate [12]. IEEE 802.15.4 standard offer security at the MAC layer that is important to support security mechanisms at upper layers of protocol stack. RF based transceiver of Texas employ single chip cc2420. Crossbow developed TelosB mote provides security using symmetric cryptography in IEEE 802.15.4 using Advanced Encryption Standard (AES) [15]. Various security modes of AES used by

Table 1. IEEE 802.15.4 security modes for AES

Security mode	Security provided
No security	Data is not encrypted
	Data authenticity is not validated
AES-CBC-MAC-32	Data is not encrypted
	Data authenticity using a 32 bit MIC
AES-CBC-MAC-64	Data is not encrypted
	Data authenticity using a 64 bit MIC
AES-CBC-MAC-128	Data is not encrypted
	Data authenticity using a 128 bit MIC
AES-CTR	Data is not encrypted
	Data authenticity is not validated
AES-CCM-64	Data is encrypted
	Data authenticity using a 64 bit MIC
AES-CCM-128	Data is encrypted
	Data authenticity using a 128 bit MIC

IEEE 802.15.4 at MAC layer are specified in Table 1. Different security modes of AES are categorized on the basis of their security assurances and extent of data integrated.

2.2 Network Layer Security

Transmitting IPv6 packets over heterogeneous networks requires a standard specification. Therefore, IPv6 low power wireless personal area network (6LoWPAN) is used with IEEE 802.15.4. 6LoWPAN enables end to end communication using IPv6 for constrained sensing objects to achieve low power communication. 6LoWPAN can also operate by using low energy of Bluetooth [16]. 6LoWPAN do not have its own security mechanism instead it takes advantage of AES mechanism used at MAC layer to overcome the vulnerabilities.

6LoWPAN uses routing protocol for low power and Lossy networks (RPL) to adapt to the needs of diverge applications used in IoT [17]. RPL adapts to the needs of a specific application. Application requirement are different for urban applications, home applications, or industry applications. RPL can opt one out of three modes of operations available [17].

- Unsecure Mode: RPL uses this mode by default for its operation. No security mechanism if imposed in this mode on control messages for routing.
- Preinstalled Mode: An already available symmetric key is used by a device to join the existing instance of RPL. Device can act as a router or host. Messages for controlled routing are offered integrity, confidentiality, and authentication in this mode.
- Authenticated Mode: This mode is employed for the devices acting as routers. Initially, device can work with aforementioned modes by using the available key but later on it can fetch a new key from key sharing authority for authorization and authentication seeking.

2.3 Transport Layer Security

IoT has constrained environment with applications running over User Datagram Protocol (UDP) at transport layer. To provide secure communication at this layer Datagram Transport Layer Protocol (DTLS) is preferred over Transport Layer Security (TLS). DTLS maintains a basic protocol known as Record layer, other different protocols on its top [18]. In IoT applications, security mechanism is decided depending on the communication features required and threats that it can overcome [19]. Certain security protections are provided using DTLS such as accessing network, secure communication setup, and key management and sharing. Network access is protected by letting only legitimate users to access the network. DTLS employs a authentication protocol that initializes handshake between new device and the existing device in network. If handshake is successful, two devices can start communicating with each other. DTLS relaying is used to forward the handshake messages to authorizer and device if they are multi hop apart [19]. Once the devices are authenticated, communication session is setup where messages are transmitted by encrypting them with unique and new generated session key. DTLS also provides the mechanism of secure key management and sharing among the devices.

2.4 Application Layer

Constrained application protocol is used at the application layer of operation for IoT. CoAP messages are secured by binding DTLS to each message generated at each layer. Therefore, CoAP makes use of DTLS for rendering security to messages at application layer [20]. Use of transport layer security mechanism DTLS at application layer reflects that no inbuilt security mechanism is available solely at application layer. DTLS process involves same steps with starting one as handshaking process, secure communication set up, and key management and sharing. This will add additional cost on constrained IoT devices for handshake and overhead for each message transmitted. CoAP can also employ its own security mechanism along with the predefined DTLS security. CoAP works on four security modes- NoSec, Raw PublicKey, PreSharedKey, and certificate mode. Therefore, both symmetric and asymmetric cryptographic mechanism can be used with CoAP. Current implementation of CoAP is employing AES or ECC for its operation [21].

3 Attacks in IoT at Architecture Layers

Each layer in IoT supports security mechanisms as mentioned above. Despite of aforementioned available security approaches each layer is susceptible to number of attacks. This section discloses attack vulnerability at each layer of IoT.

3.1 Perception Layer Based Attacks

Technologies such as RFID or sensor based nodes are available at perception layer that makes this layer vulnerable to following attacks:

- Capture Attack: Nodes in the network are directly captured by the attackers either physically or by modifying the software. Therefore, the nodes do not work as per their expected functionality.
- Atmosphere Attacks: Natural adversity like irregular wind or snow can destroy the nodes used for sensing and stop their usual functioning.
- Power Loss: As sensor devices are power operated that diminishes after some time. This power loss can affect the normal functionality and will create a situation of denial of service.

3.2 Network Layer Based Attacks

Network layer carries huge amount of data from multiple devices. Serious issues like congestion of network or integrity of data may arise at network layer. Existing attacks on network layer are:

- Denial of Service (DoS): Malicious devices can overload other devices or the server system by sending fake messages. This will ultimately chop off the services of legitimate devices to other devices which require their services.
- Privacy Disclosure: Data collected from different users is stored on cloud or other secondary medium of storage. People have varying access to this stored data that may cause unauthorized access to data and will escort the privacy leak of the users.

3.3 Transport Layer Based Attacks

Transport layer works for data collection using sensor nodes or RFIDs. Therefore, attacks may be injected at node level where intruder tries to deviate normal operation by replacing the original code. Existing attacks on perception layer are:

- Eavesdropping: Involvement of internet with wireless communication mode will make IoT devices vulnerable to eavesdropping attack. Therefore, other devices can continuously monitor data of compromise device and can also send fake messages to collect personal information of that device [20].
- Noisy Data: as data is transmitted wirelessly and if it is over large distance, it may lead to noisy addition in it. This will affect the originality of the message, as either message content will be lost, or damaged. False information or data misinterpretation can also be its severe result.
- Sniffing: Malicious devices are put closer to legitimate sensor devices by the attacker in order to fetch information of legitimate devices [21].

3.4 Application Layer Based Attacks

Attacker can launch bugs in the application program that can restrict the normal application function.

- Illegitimate Data Access: Applications in IoT involve diverse number of users. These users actively participate and may generate malicious information. Therefore, strong authentication mechanism is required that will maintain the security of network.
- Software Bugs: Different programmers write code that do not follow standard pattern. This leads to buffer overflow and hinder the services to the legitimate users. Malicious users take over this benefit to overrule the whole system.

Based on the aforementioned security mechanisms opted by enabling technologies at each layer, certain vulnerable attacks are identified on each layer and are summarized in Table 2.

Table 2. Existing layer wise security mechanism and their vulnerabilities

Layer	Technology used	Security mechanism	Attacks
Perception layer	RFID/Sensors	IEEE 802.15.4 Security using AES modes	Capture Attack, Atmosphere Attacks, Power Loss
Network layer	IPv6 Addressing, 6LoWPAN	Inbuilt RPL Security	DoS, Privacy Disclosure
Transport layer	UDP	DTLS	Eavesdropping, Noisy Data, Sniffing
Application layer	CoAP	Inbuilt DTLS, Cryptography solutions	Illegitimate Data Access, Software Bugs

4 Conclusion and Future Orientation

IoT is taking its place in homes, office, cities, agriculture, business and many more at a very fast pace. Huge numbers of devices connect to IoT through internet that also involves their personal information details as well. Therefore, to maintain the personal information and security of each and every user becomes responsibility of IoT to maintain the survival of this technology. This paper explores the security mechanisms that are employed at each of 4 layers of operation. Perception, network, transport layers have inbuilt security mechanisms, on the other hand application layer makes use of transport layer security. Hence, user defined solutions can be exercised at application layer based on the application required. These security mechanisms are still susceptible to attacks. This paper helps the novice to understand the security risks at each layer and these security mechanisms can be extended to overcome the risks. Moreover, application layer security can be improved by proposing a new mechanism solely for this layer.

References

1. Gubbi, J., Buyya, R., Marusic, S., Palaniswami, M.: Internet of Things (IoT): a vision, architectural elements, and future directions. Futur. Gener. Comput. Syst. **29**(7), 1645–1660 (2013)
2. Bélissent, J.: Getting clever about smart cities : new opportunities require new business models (2010)
3. Xiaohui, X.: Study on security problems and key technologies of the Internet of Things, pp. 407–410 (2013)
4. Ning, H., Member, S., Liu, H., Yang, L.T.: Aggregated-proof based hierarchical authentication scheme for the Internet of Things, 26(3) (2015)
5. Palattella, M.R., Accettura, N., Vilajosana, X., Watteyne, T., Grieco, L.A., Member S., Boggia, G., Dohler, M.: Standardized protocol stack for the Internet of (important) Things, pp. 1–18 (2012)

6. Farooq, M.U., Waseem, M.: A critical analysis on the security concerns of Internet of Things (IoT). Int. J. Comput. Appl. **111**(7), 1–6 (2015)
7. Roman, R., Najera, P., Lopez, J.: Securing the Internet of Things, pp. 51–58 (2011)
8. Singh, D.: Developing an architecture : scalability, mobility, control, and isolation on future internet services, pp. 1873–1877 (2013)
9. Roman, R., Zhou, J., Lopez, J.: On the features and challenges of security and privacy in distributed Internet of Things. Comput. Netw. **57**(10), 2266–2279 (2013)
10. Li, L.: Study on security architecture in the Internet of Things, pp. 374–377 (2012)
11. Wu, M., Lu, T., Ling, F., Du, H.: Research on the architecture of Internet of Things, pp. 484–487 (2010)
12. IEEE Standard Association: IEEE Standard for Local and metropolitan area networks–Part 15.4 : Low-Rate Wireless Personal Area Networks (LR-WPANs). IEEE Computer Society Sponsored by the LAN/MAN Standards Committee, September 2011
13. Selent, D.: Advanced encryption standard. Rivier Acad. J. **6**(2), 1–14 (2010)
14. Qiu, Y., Ma, M.: An authentication and key establishment scheme to enhance security for M2 M in 6LoWPANs, pp. 2671–2676 (2015)
15. Klein, B.A.: RPL : IPv6 routing protocol for low power and lossy networks, pp. 59–66, July 2011
16. Han, J., Ha, M., Kim, D.: Practical security analysis for the constrained node networks : focusing on the DTLS protocol, pp. 22–29 (2015)
17. Brachmann, M., Keoh, S.L., Morchon, O.G., Kumar, S.S.: End-to-end transport security in the IP-based Internet of Things (2012)
18. Capossele, A., Cervo, V., Cicco, G.D., Petrioli, C.: Security as a CoAP resource : an optimized DTLS implementation for the IoT, pp. 549–554 (2015)
19. Granjal, J., Monteiro, E., Silva, J.S.: Networking end-to-end transport-layer security for Internet-integrated sensing applications with mutual and delegated ECC public-key authentication, pp. 1–9 (2013)
20. Luhach, A.Kr., Dwivedi, S.Kr., Jha, C.Kr.: Applying SOA to an E-commerce system and designing a logical security framework for small and medium sized E-commerce based on SOA. In: 2014 IEEE International Conference on Computational Intelligence and Computing Research (ICCIC), pp. 1–6. IEEE (2014)
21. Luhach, A.Kr., Dwivedi, S.K., Jha, C.K.: Implementing the logical security framework for E-commerce based on service-oriented architecture. In: Satapathy, S.C., Joshi, A., Modi, N., Pathak, N. (eds.) Proceedings of International Conference on ICT for Sustainable Development. AISC, vol. 409, pp. 1–13. Springer, Singapore (2016). doi:10.1007/978-981-10-0135-2_1

An Effective Approach for Mining Weighted Sequential Patterns

Mukesh Patel[1](✉), Nilesh Modi[2], and Kalpdrum Passi[3]

[1] Sarvajanik College of Engineering and Technology, Surat, Gujarat, India
mukesh.patel@scet.ac.in
[2] Department of Computer Science and Applications,
Indus University, Ahmedabad, Gujarat, India
drnileshmodi@yahoo.com
[3] Department of Mathematics and Computer Science,
Laurentian University, Sudbury, Canada
kpassi@cs.laurentian.ca

Abstract. Sequential pattern mining is one of the most studied data mining problem and has wide range of application domains including weather prediction, network intrusion detection, web access analysis, customer purchase analysis, etc. The weighted sequential pattern mining is an approach to find only interesting sequential patterns by assigning weights to data elements present in the sequences. The time-interval weighted sequential pattern mining is another approach in which different weights are assigned to the time-interval values between the successive transactions. From customer purchase pattern analysis point of view, both item's importance as well as time-interval gap values is useful and more interesting patterns can be discovered by considering them while assigning weights to the sequences. This paper aims to propose a novel approach for finding weighted sequential patterns from customer retail database which incorporates both the item's importance and time-interval gap information so that the discovered sequential patterns will be more meaningful and effective for the end-user. The results infer a lot of computation cost can be saved by focusing on few interesting patterns.

Keywords: Sequential pattern mining · Time-interval · Weighted patterns

1 Introduction

The aim of sequential pattern mining is to discover interesting relationships between occurrences of sequential events is introduced in [1]. A typical example of a sequential pattern is a customer who buys a Desktop computer, returns to buy a printer within 2 months and then after 1 month to buy a scanner [1]. Sequential Pattern mining is one of the main and challenging research topics with broad applications such as web access pattern analysis, biological data analysis, customer purchase pattern analysis etc. In general, sequential pattern mining finds all frequent sequential patterns for a given sequence database. The key issue of mining sequential patterns is that a vast set of sequential patterns are generated and the computation time is too high. It would be

© Springer Nature Singapore Pte Ltd. 2016
A. Unal et al. (Eds.): SmartCom 2016, CCIS 628, pp. 904–915, 2016.
DOI: 10.1007/978-981-10-3433-6_108

better if the insignificant patterns could be removed first, resulting in fewer but important patterns after mining.

Majority of previous researches treated sequential patterns and items in a sequential pattern equally. These approaches generate large number of sequential patterns in a large database. But in real world, a user is more interested in only small subset of such patterns and also in real world every items have different significance. Based on this observation, few researchers had proposed weighted sequential pattern mining [14, 15] in which they treated each items differently by assigning weights to them. They have considered both the occurrence as well as item's importance to find more interesting and meaningful sequential patterns. While mining sequential patterns, not only the ordering of items but also their generation time and time-interval gap is also important. Focusing on time-interval, few researchers have proposed their work [5, 6], in which they considered time-interval between two successive items as constraint. An idea of weighted sequential pattern using time-interval weight is recently proposed in [11] which assign different weightage to the sequences in a sequence database by treating the time-intervals in the sequences differently. If the importance of individual items in the sequences and significance of different time-intervals will be assimilated and collective weight will be assigned to the sequences, more significant and useful sequential patterns can be discovered.

To elaborate the above idea, let us consider the following example. Suppose we have a sequence database gathered from a retail electronics store, let us say the following sequential patterns were found:

Customer A having bought a PC returns to buy a printer after 12 month and then buys a CD ROM after 6 month.
Customer B having bought a PC returns to buy a printer after 6 month and then buys a CD ROM after 3 month.
Customer C having bought a Digital Camera returns to buy a printer after 6 month and a flash drive after 3 month.
Customer D having bought a Digital Camera returns to buy a printer after 12 month and a flash drive after 6 month.

In the above set of patterns, the sequence by customer A and customer B consist of the same items and the orders of items are also same but the time-intervals span between the successive purchases of items is different. If the time-interval between two successive purchases are ignored then both patterns appears to be same. But if importance is given to the time interval between two successive purchases then both patterns are significantly different. In fact, the sequence by Customer B is more useful to us as it has shorter time-span. Now look at the sequences by customer C and customer D. They are just replica of previous two sequences w. r. t. the time-interval based sequential pattern mining. If importance is given to time-interval, the sequence by customer A and customer D have equal weight and are more significant than others as they have shorter time-interval in consecutive purchases. But if sequences are mined by assigning weights to individual items based on its contribution in profit generation, the sequences by customer A and customer B has same weight while customer C and customer D has same weight. Assuming the itemset containing {PC, Printer, CD-ROM} earns more profit than itemset {Digital Camera, printer, flash drive}, the sequences by customer A and B are more important. Now, if comparison made between all four sequences in earning more profit and within short span of time, the sequence by Customer B has highest significant value. Motivating by this example, we have proposed a novel approach for finding weighted sequential patterns which incorporates weights of individual items as well as time-interval weights and discover only few but more meaningful patterns close to real world situation. If we focus on few interesting patterns only, we may be able reduce the computation cost of processing insignificant sequences. This directly leads to improving efficiency of mining by focusing on the effectiveness of mining results.

This paper is organized as follows: Sect. 2 summarizes the related work. Problem definition with working example is described in Sect. 3. In Sect. 4, a novel approach for weighted sequential mining algorithm [WUTiSpam] is described. Results analysis and performance evaluation is described in Sect. 5 followed by conclusion and further research in Sect. 6.

2 Related Work

The concept of sequential Pattern mining was first proposed by Agrawal and Srikant in 1995 [1] in their study of mining customer purchase sequences. Several algorithms for mining sequential patterns have been proposed thereafter and most of them are for general sequential patterns mining [2–4, 7, 8, 12] which can only reveal which items are frequently purchased together and in what order they appear. Some popular algorithms amongst them are GSP [2], SPAM [3], SPADE [4], FreeSpan [7], PrefixSpan [8] etc. Amongst these, GSP [2] is an apriori-like approach for mining sequential patterns which generates all candidate sequences. To overcome this limitation, the database projection growth based approaches, FreeSpan [7] and PrefixSpan [8] were developed which are more efficient. The SPADE [4] is a vertical idlist data format based in which the frequent sequence enumeration was performed by a simple join on id-lists. The SPAM [3] utilizes depth first traversal of the search space combined with a vertical bitmap representation of each sequence.

For mining sequential pattern, not only order of items but their occurrence is also important. Some of the researchers had already considered the time-interval based sequential patterns which consider the time span between the successive purchases [5, 6, 9, 10]. Time-interval between successive transactions are already introduced in [2] as the gap constraint. Chen et al. [5] generalized the problem to discover time-interval sequential patterns mining which reveals the order of items as well as the time intervals between successive items. Chen and Huang extended the work and proposed fuzzy time-interval sequential patterns [6]. Yang [9] extended the single-time-interval approach of Chen et al. [5] to find multi-time-interval sequential patterns. This additional time information helps us to figure out long-term behaviour of the customers and we can plan the appropriate execution. In 2010, Cheng and Huang [10], applied the concept of fuzzy sets to solve the sharp boundary problem in multi-time-interval sequential patterns. Time-interval Sequential Pattern Mining is further extended by Chang [11] in 2011, by proposing the concept of weighted sequential patterns in a sequence database with a time-interval weight. He presented a new framework for finding weighted sequential (TiWS) patterns in a sequence database based on time-interval weight. In his proposed work, they first obtained the weight of each sequence in a sequence database from the time-interval between the items present in the particular sequence and then assigned the weights to the sequences and subsequently discovered TiWS patterns based on min-TiWS support. Weights are assigned to the sequences based on the assumption that a sequence with small time-interval is more valuable. He presented a PrefixSpan [8] based method called psTiWS [11] to mine the TiWS patterns.

To improve the usefulness of sequential pattern mining results in real world applications, weighted sequential pattern mining proposed in [13–15]. In [13] a method is proposed to predict the status of customer backing for the next day by considering time-weighted concept on association algorithm. Yun [14, 15] proposed a framework to push the weight constraints into the sequential pattern mining. They consider weight range to restrict weight values of items and prices of items in a normalized range. They proposed an algorithm for weighted sequential pattern mining (WSpan). So we need an algorithm which considers the significance of items as well as time-gap information for weight assignment in mining weighted sequential pattern mining.

3 Problem Definition

In general, sequential pattern mining is the mining of frequently occurring orderly subsequences. When it was first introduced by Agrawal and Srikant in 1995 [1] in their study of customer purchase sequences, they considered only data elements without their occurrence time. The time-interval based sequential pattern was proposed by Chen et al. [4, 5] as a constraint and then by Chang [11] for finding time-interval weighted sequential pattern mining. In 2006, Yun [14, 15] introduced the concept of Weighted Sequential pattern mining (WSpan) by pushing weight constraints to differentiate items' importance in addition to frequency threshold in discovering sequential patterns.

An itemset $I = \langle i_1, i_2,\ldots, i_n \rangle$ be a set of all items. A sequence is a collection of itemsets in specific order. A sequence $S = \langle s_1, s_2,\ldots, s_m \rangle$ is an ordered list of itemsets, where s_j $(1 \leq j \leq m)$ is an itemset, and its time stamp list $TI - \langle t_1, t_2,\ldots, t_n \rangle$ is an ordered list of corresponding time stamps of the itemsets, which stand for the time when they occur, where t_j $(1 \leq j \leq n)$ is the time stamp of s_j and $t_{j-1} \leq t_j$. A set of such sequences forms a sequence database SDB as $S = \langle S_1, S_2\ldots, S_n \rangle$. Length of the sequence is a total number of items in a sequence. A sequence $X = \langle x_1, x_2,\ldots, x_n \rangle$ is a subsequence of Y is $Y = \langle y_1, y_2,\ldots, y_m \rangle$ if $1 \leq k_1 < \ldots < k_n \leq m$ such that $x_1 \subseteq y_{k1}$, $x_2 \subseteq y_{k2},\ldots, x_n \subseteq y_{kn}$.

In practice, a sequence S can also be represented set of triplets as $S = ((i_1, p_1, t_1),$ $(i_1, p_2, t_2), (i_n, p_n, t_n))$,Where ij is an item, p_j is any non-negative value and tj stands for the time at which sj occurs, where $1 \leq j \leq n$; $t_{j-1} \leq t_j$ for $2 \leq j \leq n$. Consider sequence database shown in Table 1. If the items are sold together, the third component in the triplets shows the same values of time stamps. P(i) denotes the importance the importance of items. It can be items' price values or profits attached with them. Weighted utility (items' importance) of a sequential pattern can be calculated by summing the total values associated with the itemsets in the sequence divided by sequence length. The time intervals between the itemsets can be calculated based on the time stamps associated with the itemsets. The weights of different time-intervals are assigned by some weight assignment function which gives some higher value to smaller time-interval and lower value to larger time-interval.

Table 1. Sample time stamped sequence database

Sid	Sequence
10	<(a,200,1),(c,60,3),(b,100,14),(a,200,14),(d,40,26),(e,35,26)>
20	<(c,60,9),(b,100,12),(e,35,12),(d,40,20),(g,10,20)>
30	<(b,100,5),(a,200,13),(c,60,13),(d,40,16),(h,5,16),(f,25,25)>
40	<(a,200,2),(b,100,14),(c,60,14),(a,200,30),(e,35,30)>
50	<(a,200,3),(a,200,5),(b,100,5),(c,60,5),(d,40,6)>

The problem is to discover most significant weighted sequential patterns for a given minimum frequency threshold (Min_Sup) and minimum integrated weighted support representing time-interval and items' importance (minWUTiSupp) from a sequence database (SDB).

4   Weighted Sequential Pattern Mining Based on Items' Profit and Time-Interval Weight

In our approach, we propose frame work for weighted sequential patterns based on item's importance and time-interval weight. So we have considered both time-interval and items' sale price in the sequence database. For understanding the concept, let us consider an example retail database as shown in Table 1. It shows few instances of sequences. Each sequence has list of items with sale price and its corresponding time stamps. The items having same time stamp values indicate those items are belongs to same transactions of sales.

In traditional sequential pattern mining only frequency (or occurrence) of items are considered while counting the support of the items. It only considers whether an item is present or not in a transaction, it does not reveal the importance of item which is more important to user. The second component shows the items' sales price which may directly proportional to items' profit or importance. In our approach for finding weighted sequential pattern, first we assign weight to the sequences based on items' price. Because of big variation found in the actual prices of retail database, we have normalized the weights in some range using min-max normalization technique. Table 2 shows the items in descending order of their prices and its normalized weights. Here new_min and new_ max can be selected based on items' importance in real world. For the current example database we considered new_min = 0.1 and new_max = 0.9. The item 'a' is assigned maximum weights as it has highest sale price.

Like in WSpan [14], the weights of the sequences can be obtained by calculating the average value of weights of the items in the sequence. For example, if we take a sequence belongs to sid = 20 i.e. <a,(abc),d> , then weight of a sequence is calculated

Table 2. Items with price and normalized weight.

ItemID	a	b	c	d	e	f	g	h
Price	200	100	60	40	35	25	10	5
Weight	0.9	0.49	0.33	0.24	0.22	0.18	0.12	0.1

as $SWU_{id=50}$ = (0.9 + (0.9 + 0.49 + 0.33) + 0.24)/5 = 0.57. In similar way, weights for other sequential patterns are calculated as shown in Table 3. It shows that Sequence $S_{id=40}$ is most important as it has a highest weights amongst all and it has the items which more important.

Table 3. Sequence and weighted-utility

Sid	Sequence	SWU
10	<a,c,(ba),(de)>	0.51
20	<c,(be),(dg)>	0.28
30	<b,(ac),(dh),f>	0.37
40	<a,(bc),(ae)>	0.65
50	<a,(abc),d>	0.57

For discovering weighted sequential patterns based on time-interval weights, we have adopted a strategy similar to as proposed in [11]. From the Table 1, the time stamps of itemsets in the sequences are separated as shown Table 4.

Table 4. Separate time components

Sid	Sequence	Time stamp list
10	<a,c,(ba),(de)>	1,3,14,26
20	<c,(be),(dg)>	9,12,20
30	<b,(ac),(dh),f>	5,13,16,25
40	<a,(bc),(ae)>	2,14,30
50	<a,(abc),d>	3,5,6

These time stamps values are used to get the time-interval weight of each sequence. If a sequence consists of n itemsets, there exist n(n−1)/2 pairs of itemsets in the sequence, and the time-interval between the itemsets of each pair is defined as TI_{ij} = t_j−t_i where t_j and t_i are time-stamps of two itemsets in a sequence. These time-intervals between all pairs of itemsets have no limitation for the value. If the big variation found, these time–interval values are also needed to be normalized within some range. Also, we have to give importance to time-intervals which are small in size as compared to large intervals. We have to extract the maximum and minimum time interval component and we can adopt min-max normalization again to assign normalized weight. For current example we used new_max = 0.9 and new_min = 0.1.

To illustrate the computation of time-interval weight, take the sequence sid = 50, the sequence is <a,(abc),d> and it consists of three itemsets, (acf) and d and corresponding time-intervals are 3,5 and 6. All possible pair of itemsets, their corresponding time-intervals and itemset-lengths are shown in Table 5. The itemset-length (IL) between each pair of itemsets is calculated as $IL_{ij} = IL_i * IL_j$. For example, the itemset-length between itemset <a> and <abc> is $1 * 3 = 3$.

Table 5. Itemsets pairs with Time-interval

Itemset 1	Itemset 2	Time-interval	Itemset-length
a	abc	2	3
a	d	3	1
abc	d	1	3

To assign weights to different time-intervals, we have considered min-max normalization techniques. Here the smallest time-interval is to be assigned highest weight so the min-max technique is modified to return the same. For current example, we have normalized the time-interval values in the range from Ti = 1−30 to new range Ti = 0.9−0.1. Table 6 shows the all possible time-interval values (Ti) and its corresponding normalized weights (WTi).

Table 6. Time-intervals and its normalized weights

Ti	WTi	Ti	WTi	Ti	WTi	Ti	WTi	Ti	WTi	Ti	WTi
1	0.9	6	0.76	11	0.62	16	0.48	21	0.34	26	0.21
2	0.87	7	0.73	12	0.59	17	0.45	22	0.32	27	0.18
3	0.84	8	0.7	13	0.56	18	0.43	23	0.29	28	0.15
4	0.81	9	0.67	14	0.54	19	0.4	24	0.26	29	0.13
5	0.78	10	0.65	15	0.51	20	0.37	25	0.23	30	0.1

By using the normalized weights of the time interval values (WTi) as in Table 6, now we can calculate the total time-interval weight of a sequence (SWTi) as

$$SWTi(S) = \sum \{W(TI_{ij}) \times IL_{ij}\} / \sum IL_{ij}$$

For example, for the sequence Sid = 20,

$SWTi(S_{id=50})$

$$= (W(TI_{12}) * IL_{12} + W(TI_{13}) * IL_{13} + W(TI_{23}) * IL_{23}))/7$$
$$= (W(2) * 3 + W(3) * 1 + W(1) * 3)/7$$
$$= (0.87 * 3 + 0.84 * 1 + 0.9 * 3)/7$$
$$= (2.61 + 0.84 + 2.7)/7$$
$$= (6.15)/7 = 0.88$$

Similarly, the time-interval weights of other sequences present in the sequences database are as shown in Table 7. The sequences which contain the smaller time-interval gap will be assigned higher total time-interval weight (SWTi) and are more important for discovering frequent patterns.

Table 7. Sequence and Time-interval weight

Sid	Sequence	SWTi
10	<a,c,(ba),(de)>	0.51
20	<c,(be),(dg)>	0.54
30	<b,(ac),(dh),f>	0.55
40	<a,(bc),(ae)>	0.42
50	<a,(abc),d>	0.88

The Table 8 shows both weighted utility (SWU) and weighted time interval (SWTi) measures for all the sequences in given example sequence database. The example shows that the sequences of S_{id} = 10, 40 and 50 have higher SWU weights which can be used for mining the frequent sequence patterns and will be more interesting and useful from the sales manager's point of view as it includes the items of high cost and may be useful and can contribute more in revenue generation. Now, if we observe the time-interval weights of the sequences, the sequence $S_{id=50}$ is most promising and has a highest value, the sequence $S_{id=40}$ is least promising as it has lowest value amongst all sequences. If we only consider the profit-based approach with minSWU = 0.5, we may select the sequences Sid = 10, 40 and 50, and if we restrict to time-interval weight with minSWTi = 0.5, the sequences with Sid = 10, 20, 30 and 50 are all promising to us. As both the factors are important for supermarket manager for sales promotion and targeted marketing, so to discover weighted sequential patterns which reflects both, we can integrate both the measures by taking average of SWU and SWTi. Now we observe the average measure (SWUTi), we will able to filter those sequences which are most promising and interesting. In current example, the sequences $S_{id=10}$ and $S_{id=50}$ are satisfying the minSWUTiSupp = 0.5.

Table 8. Sequence Weighted-utility-time-interval

Sid	Sequence	SWU	SWTi	SWUTi
10	<a,c,(ba),(de)>	0.51	0.51	0.51
20	<c,(be),(dg)>	0.28	0.54	0.41
30	<b,(ac),(dh),f>	0.37	0.55	0.46
40	<a,(bc),(ae)>	0.56	0.42	0.44
50	<a,(abc),d>	0.57	0.88	0.73

Based on the illustrated example, we have proposed the WUTiSpan algorithm to discover weighted sequential patterns. The overall process is similar to psTiWS [11] method and PrefixSpan [08] based approach is used for finding the frequent sequences. In our approach, we scan the database initially to obtain the maximum and minimum time-interval values in the sequences as well as for finding minimum and maximum items' sale price. We then assign WUTi Support to the sequences by calculating SWU and SWTi using normalized weight values of the items' price and time-interval value. The sequences which satisfy the minWUTiSupp threshold are passed to the PrefixSpan for finding frequent subsequences. The detail procedure is presented in Fig. 1.

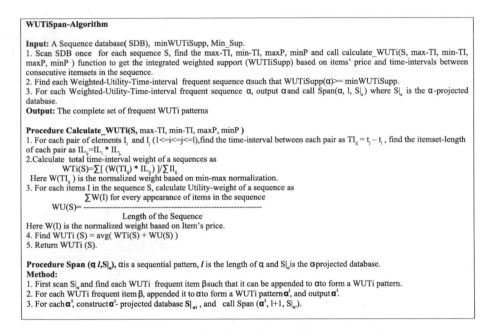

WUTiSpan-Algorithm

Input: A Sequence database(SDB), minWUTiSupp, Min_Sup.
1. Scan SDB once for each sequence S, find the max-TI, min-TI, maxP, minP and call calculate_WUTi(S, max-TI, min-TI, maxP, minP) function to get the integrated weighted support (WUTiSupp) based on items' price and time-intervals between consecutive itemsets in the sequence.
2. Find each Weighted-Utility-Time-interval frequent sequence α such that WUTiSupp(α)>= minWUTiSupp.
3. For each Weighted-Utility-Time-interval frequent sequence α, output α and call Span(α, l, S|$_\alpha$) where S|$_\alpha$ is the α-projected database.
Output: The complete set of frequent WUTi patterns

Procedure Calculate_WUTi(S, max-TI, min-TI, maxP, minP)
1. For each pair of elements I$_i$ and I$_j$ (1<=i<=j<=l),find the time-interval between each pair as TI$_{ij}$ = t$_j$ − t$_i$, find the itemset-length of each pair as IL$_{ij}$=IL$_{I_i}$ * IL$_{I_j}$.
2.Calculate total time-interval weight of a sequences as
   WTi(S)=$\sum$[(W(TI$_{ij}$) * IL$_{ij}$)]/$\sum$II$_{ij}$.
   Here W(TI$_{ij}$) is the normalized weight based on min-max normalization.
3. For each items I in the sequence S, calculate Utility-weight of a sequence as
                 $\sum$W(I) for every appearance of items in the sequence
   WU(S)= --
                           Length of the Sequence
Here W(I) is the normalized weight based on Item's price.
4. Find WUTi (S) = avg(WTi(S) + WU(S)).
5. Return WUTi (S).

Procedure Span (α l,S|$_\alpha$), α is a sequential pattern, l is the length of α and S|$_\alpha$ is the α projected database.
Method:
1. First scan S|$_\alpha$ and find each WUTi frequent item β such that it can be appended to α to form a WUTi pattern.
2. For each WUTi frequent item β, appended it to α to form a WUTi patternα', and outputα'.
3. For eachα', constructα'- projected database S|$_{\alpha'}$, and call Span (α', l+1, S|$_{\alpha'}$).

Fig. 1. WUTiSpan Algorithm for mining weighted sequential patterns

5   Result Analysis and Performance Study

We have performed comprehensive experimentation both on real and synthetic dataset to evaluate the efficacy and efficiency of the proposed algorithm. Our all algorithms are implement in JAVA and the experiments carried out on Windows platform on Intel® i5® 4 CPU 2.60 GHz with 4 GB RAM. We have generated synthetic dataset using java random function. It contains 1000 sequences with 10 distinct items and average sequence length is 20. The real datasets is about items purchased in Chinese grocery retail store. The datasets are preprocessed and 16,578 customer purchase sequences are extracted with 17,225 distinct items. The price values of all items are stored externally with average sequence length is 20. The datasets contains itemsets purchased by customer that includes items purchased; time stamp at which time specific item is purchased and sales price value of an item in the itemsets.

The WUTiSpan is the first weighted sequential pattern mining algorithm which incorporates both the weight of the items and weight of the time-intervals within a sequence. We inferred our experimental results on the performance of WUTiSpan in comparison with related algorithms like WU(based on Wspan [14]), WTi(based on psTiWS [11]) and simple prefixSpan [2] for finding sequential pattern mining. The main aim of this experiment is to demonstrate the efficacy of the approach in mining weighted sequential patterns. The proposed algorithm is efficient in terms of reducing the processing time for uninteresting sequences. We demonstrated that how only few quality or interesting frequent sequences are generated.

Figure 2 shows the no. of frequent subsequences generated from the synthetic dataset by three approaches WU, WTi and WUTi at minimum threshold = 0.5 and different minimum frequency thresholds. The graph clearly reveals that WUTiSpan

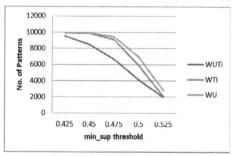
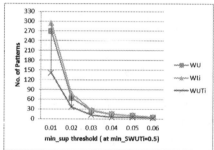

Fig. 2. No. of sequential pattern at min_threshold = 0.5 from synthetic dataset.

Fig. 3. No. of sequential pattern at min_ threshold = 0.5 from real dataset.

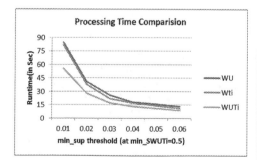
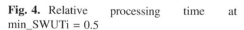
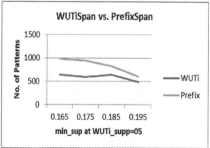

Fig. 4. Relative processing time at min_SWUTi = 0.5

Fig. 5. Relative processing time at min_SWUTi = 0.5

generates less number of subsequences compared to WU and WTi algorithms. When experimented on real dataset, WUTi outperforms the other two in terms of generating number of subsequences or patterns. We kept the minimum frequency threshold very low in order to generate frequent subsequences from very large dataset. Figure 3 reveals the performance of WUTiSpan on real dataset.

We have also quantified and analyzed the processing time for all the three approaches while generating number of patterns from real dataset. When the program runs for the different thresholds as in Fig. 3, we calibrated the corresponding execution time (in seconds) and illustrated in Fig. 4. Finally, we compared the WUTiSpan algorithm with simple PrefixSpan in terms of number of patterns generations. Figure 5 reveals that the performance of WUTiSpan is outperforming the PrefixSpan as maximum number of insignificant sequences is filtered in WUTiSpan approach before frequent pattern generation.

6 Conclusion and Future Research

We have presented a novel and effective approach of mining weighted sequential patterns is suggested in this paper. An algorithm WUTiSpan is developed to discover more significant sequential patterns. We applied the proposed algorithm in customer retails sequence database. The discovered patterns can be highly useful in marketing campaign, customer segmentation and timely promotion of the products. Some of the other areas like network intrusion detection, web log analysis, fraud detection in the telecommunication industry and financial data analysis. In future, we will perform more experiments with some other weight assignment techniques as well as for calculating the integrated supports of the sequences. We will consider some other factors to assign weights to the individual items like quantity, user's preferences based on market trends etc. We need to experiment on periodicity analysis, customer profile while mining weighted sequential patterns.

References

1. Agrawal, R., Srikant, R.: Mining sequential patterns. In: 1995 Proceedings of the Eleventh International Conference on Data Engineering, pp. 3–14. IEEE, March 1995
2. Srikant, R., Agrawal, R.: Mining sequential patterns: generalizations and performance improvements. In: Apers, P., Bouzeghoub, M., Gardarin, G. (eds.) EDBT 1996. LNCS, vol. 1057, pp. 1–17. Springer, Heidelberg (1996). doi:10.1007/BFb0014140
3. Ayres, J., Flannick, J., Gehrke, J., Yiu, T.: Sequential pattern mining using a bitmap representation. In: Proceedings of the Eighth ACM SIGKDD International Conference on Knowledge Discovery and Data Mining, pp. 429–435. ACM, July 202
4. Zaki, M.J.: SPADE: an efficient algorithm for mining frequent sequences. Mach. Learn. 42 (1–2), 31–60 (2001)
5. Chen, Y.L., Chiang, M.C., Ko, M.T.: Discovering time-interval sequential patterns in sequence databases. Expert Syst. Appl. 25(3), 343–354 (2003)

6. Chen, Y.L., Huang, T.K.: Discovering fuzzy time-interval sequential patterns in sequence databases. IEEE Trans. Syst. Man Cybern. Part B Cybern. **35**(5), 959–972 (2005)
7. Han, J., Pei, J., Mortazavi-Asl, B., Chen, Q., Dayal, U., Hsu, M.C.: FreeSpan: frequent pattern-projected sequential pattern mining. In: Proceedings of the Sixth ACM SIGKDD International Conference on Knowledge Discovery and Data Mining, pp. 355–359. ACM, August 2000
8. Han, J., Pei, J., Mortazavi-Asl, B., Pinto, H., Chen, Q., Dayal, U., Hsu, M.C.: PrefixSpan: mining sequential patterns efficiently by prefix-projected pattern growth. In: Proceedings of the 17th International Conference on Data Engineering, pp. 215–224, April 2001
9. Hu, Y.H., Huang, T.C.K., Yang, H.R., Chen, Y.L.: On mining multi-time-interval sequential patterns. Data Knowl. Eng. **68**(10), 1112–1127 (2009)
10. Huang, T.C.K.: Knowledge gathering of fuzzy multi-time-interval sequential patterns. Inf. Sci. **180**(17), 3316–3334 (2010)
11. Chang, J.H.: Mining weighted sequential patterns in a sequence database with a time-interval weight. Knowl. Based Syst. **24**(1), 1–9 (2011)
12. Garofalakis, M.N., Rastogi, R., Shim, K.: SPIRIT: sequential pattern mining with regular expression constraints. In: VLDB, vol. 99, pp. 7–10, September 1999
13. Lo, S.: Binary prediction based on weighted sequential mining method. In: Proceedings of the 2005 IEEE/WIC/ACM International Conference on Web Intelligence, pp. 755–761. IEEE Computer Society, September 2005
14. Yun, U., Leggett, J.J.: WSpan: Weighted Sequential pattern mining in large sequence databases. In: 2006 3rd International IEEE Conference Intelligent Systems, pp. 512–517. IEEE, September 2006
15. Yun, U.: A new framework for detecting weighted sequential patterns in large sequence databases. Knowl. Based Syst. **21**(2), 110–122 (2008)

Author Index